Biological Psychology

Visit the *Biological Psychology*, third edition Companion Website with Grade Tracker at **www.pearsoned.co.uk/toates** to find valuable student learning material including:

- Interactive exercises and animations
- Multiple choice questions with Grade Tracker function to test your learning and monitor your progress
- Explanation of the 'test your knowledge' answers found in the book
- Further details of key research in the area
- Links to relevant sites on the web
- Online glossary

3rd edition

Biological Psychology

Frederick Toates

The Open University

Prentice Hall
is an imprint of

PEARSON

Harlow, England • London • New York • Boston • San Francisco • Toronto • Sydney • Singapore • Hong Kong
Tokyo • Seoul • Taipei • New Delhi • Cape Town • Madrid • Mexico City • Amsterdam • Munich • Paris • Milan

Pearson Education Limited
Edinburgh Gate
Harlow
Essex CM20 2JE
England

and Associated Companies throughout the world

Visit us on the World Wide Web at:
www.pearsoned.co.uk

First published 2001
Second edition 2007
Third edition 2011

ISBN: 978-0-273-73499-4

British Library Cataloguing-in-Publication Data
A catalogue record for this book is available from the British Library

Library of Congress Cataloging-in-Publication Data
Toates, F. M. (Frederick M.)
   Biological psychology / Frederick Toates. -- 3rd ed.
       p. cm.
   ISBN 978-0-273-73499-4 (pbk.)
   1.   Psychobiology.   I. Title.
   QP306.T632 2011
   612.8--dc22

                                                      2010046059

10 9 8 7 6 5 4 3 2 1
15 14 13 12 11

Typeset in 9/12pt Stone Serif by 30
Printed and bound by Rotolito Lombarda, Italy

Brief contents

'Professor of Biological Psychology Frederick Toates from The Open University has done the field an enormous service in the Third Edition of Biological Psychology. Students worldwide will enjoy this text as it sets a new benchmark for a life science approach to brain and behaviour. The inclusion of evolutionary (both ultimate function and phylogeny), neurobiological and developmental perspectives on brain and behaviour make this textbook a first choice for the next generation of undergraduates studying biology and psychology.'

Dr William Brown, University of East London

'Biological Psychology is the only biological text that places the physiology and and neuroscience of behaviour firmly in the broader context of psychology. Toates cleverly weaves in perspectives from evolutionary psychology and uses current and relevant real-life examples to illuminate key points. This updated and improved 3rd edition should be at the top of any psychology student's book list.'

Dr Michelle Lee, Swansea University

'Toates' third edition is both readable and palatable. It arouses interest by focusing on the thought-provoking questions that arise within a study of biological psychology. The author's conversational style is helpful as he talks the reader through the more straightforward and also the more conceptually demanding sections. Although accessible, the text provides a thorough account of key areas. It answers questions and stimulates interest. This up-to-date third edition retains the excellent pedagogical features of the previous edition. This is an enormously useful textbook. The author understands the problems, questions and fascinations of biological psychology students. Toates is an excellent teacher and a real authority in this area. This textbook captures his knowledge and understanding, and his infectious love of the subject.'

Dr Graham Mitchell, University of Northampton

'If the processes of the mind and brain have baffled you, this book is the key to unlocking its mysteries. Toates introduces the main topics of neuroscience in a beautifully simple yet highly informative manner. Each topic is covered in a massively integrative way. This renders the text suitable for both students and lay readers, for both medics and psychologists, for both undergraduates and postgraduates. Chapters are hugely informative and achieve the perfect combination of presenting scientific findings and research with the author's personal experience and good humour. This text is engaging at all times, and I strongly recommend it in the study of biological psychology. No stone is left unturned in the quest for understanding the brain.'

Dr Anna Scarnà, Oxford Brookes University

Contents

Chapter 11 Learning and memory

Chapter 12 Emotion

Chapter 13 Stress and coping

Chapter 14 Pain

Chapter 15 Motivation

Chapter 22 When things go wrong

Biological Psychology

Supporting resources

Visit **www.pearsoned.co.uk/toates** to find valuable online resources

Companion Website for students

- Interactive exercises and animations
- Multiple choice questions with Grade Tracker function to test your learning and monitor your progress
- Explanation of the 'test your knowledge' answers found in the book
- Further details of key research in the area
- Links to relevant sites on the web
- Online glossary

For instructors

- Instructor's Manual featuring teaching ideas, answers to test yourself questions, essay and tutorials ideas and suggestions for discussion activities
- PowerPoint slides that can be downloaded and used for presentations
- Testbank of question material

Also: The Companion Website provides the following features:

- Search tool to help locate specific items of content
- E-mail results and profile tools to send results of quizzes to instructors
- Online help and support to assist with website usage and troubleshooting

For more information please contact your local Pearson Education sales representative or visit **www.pearsoned.co.uk/toates**

Preface

When I produced the first edition of this book, I asked myself, what is the justification for another book on biological psychology? I noted that there already existed some excellent, well-established and frequently updated texts. In the meantime, still more have appeared. However, the time since the 1st and 2nd editions has confirmed my belief in the book. Based upon enormous amounts of feedback, this rather different and, I trust, improved third edition has appeared. So what is it about my prototypical reader that has motivated the long hours of work?

The present book (as with editions 1 and 2) sets out to put the emphasis in a rather different place from that of other texts. The rationale behind it derives from several considerations. First, I believe that there is a need to present the biological material in a broader context of psychology. My guess is that you probably did not enter psychology to understand some of the favourite tools of the trade of biological psychology. These include the mechanism of the action potential of the giant axon of the squid and the nature of absorption of light by rhodopsin in the human retina. However, you are probably open to persuasion as to their relevance. Therefore, it seemed to be worth trying to show exactly why such topics are important in understanding broader issues of mind and behaviour. That is to say, material needs contextualization into a 'person-friendly' psychological picture. In so doing, I believe that, as a bonus, the subject demarcations between the biological and other perspectives, e.g. social, become less clear.

Psychology can sometimes seem more like a political election rally than a science. On one extreme wing, a type of 'nuts-and-bolts' physiological psychologist stands on a platform of reducing everything to neurons, while making disapproving noises towards such 'soft' approaches as social psychology. On the other extreme, social constructivists appear like a medieval French religious sect in the zeal with which they reject everything to do with the flesh, while placing their faith in higher things. This book is based upon a rejection of both extremes. It is based on the conviction that the fragmentation of psychology is to be regretted and that the future lies in reinforcing bridges rather than blowing them up.

In my opinion, an appreciation of biological psychology cannot be achieved simply by statements of the kind, 'This chapter is about learning and memory, which you study in courses on animal learning and human cognition'. Even if they have taken such courses, students will probably have forgotten what is meant by, for example, working memory or taste-aversion learning, by the time that they get to do a biology course. Therefore, before describing the biology of an aspect of behaviour, I briefly review the basic psychology.

I was tempted to call the book *Biological Psychology – a Social Sciences Introduction* but decided against this. It might suggest that there is something peculiarly social about the approach adopted, which would make it less applicable to the more biologically orientated student. This is not the case. In my view, the Janus-head nature of psychology, pointing in one direction to the social sciences and in the other to the traditional sciences of chemistry and biology, etc., should be seen as the subject's strength rather than as a weakness.

An author confronts a dilemma in writing of this kind. To what extent should the links between topics be emphasized, or should each be dealt with simply in its own right? For example, should the student be able to close the chapter on emotion when they move on to motivation, or should they be reminded constantly about the interactive nature of all things? The chapters are more self-contained than in the first and second editions. This allows teachers to 'cut and paste' chapters to some extent.

I believe that we can only know 'who we are' by understanding something of the principles of evolution and function. These topics are introduced at the outset and reference is made to them throughout. Students often find evolutionary ideas difficult to grasp and they confuse causal and functional levels of explanation.

However, I felt the need to confront these issues rather than avoid them. If they are not discussed, there is the risk that the student will apply their own homespun wisdom (not necessarily a bad thing) but without relating this to contemporary ideas. The book is based on the conviction that biological psychology should be presented in the context of whole functioning animals living in a 'normal' environment (whatever that might mean for either rat or human!).

I also felt the need to relate the biological material to a philosophical context. Again students will apply their own logic here but it needs at least to take cognizance of established thinking. For example, physiological accounts often leave students perplexed about issues of brain and mind, whereas a brief philosophical orientation can serve to clarify the issues and describe openly the gaps in our understanding.

In my long experience, a fundamental problem with biological psychology is that students are often totally overwhelmed by the mass of detail, isolated facts, technical terms and Latin and Greek words. Thereby, they fail to follow the story-line and details tend to get collected, if at all, by rote. I have therefore tried to impose strict limits on the amount of detail, while expanding the space devoted to explanation and integration. I use a number of analogies to aid understanding. This unashamedly top-down approach might offend some of my more purist, reductionist ('hard-nosed') colleagues, who exhibit an insatiable appetite to present Latin names and microscopic dimensions. However, the book is as much about the proverbial forest as the trees and leaves. It is not that details are unimportant; on the contrary. References are provided to allow the students to pursue these if they so wish. It is all a question of balance.

It seems to me that the difficulties that students encounter in studying biological psychology are a mixture of two kinds: (i) those inherent in the natural world and (ii) the human-made kind. I can do little about the first contribution to difficulty, since some biological processes (e.g. the action potential or aspects of evolution) seem to be inherently complex to understand. However, in my experience, the 'natural-made' factor is the smaller of the two. I feel that we often blame nature as a cover for our own self-made failure to explain clearly. I have several times heard students, after being told the essence of something, respond: 'Is that the point of it all? I suspected it might be something vaguely like that but after struggling so hard I thought that there had to be more to it than that!' This book is unashamedly an attempt to hold the student's hand and tread very gently as they meet the difficulties. It tries hard to avoid intellectual overkill.

Since psychology is about people, I have attempted to give a human dimension and story-line as much as possible. Each chapter starts with 'scene-setting questions', which relate to everyday human experience. It is not guaranteed that, after reading the chapter, you will have a convincing answer to these. For example, the mind–body problem might well remain a problem even after reading Chapter 21! However, I would be very disappointed if you were not able to make a better attempt at an answer than before reading it.

After years of teaching biological psychology in introductory courses, I have seen quite a range of conceptual misunderstandings. Also, in getting the response 'yes – I see', I have learned to distinguish the sentiment 'Please leave me alone', accompanied by a forced smile devoid of positive emotion, from genuine understanding. I hope that I have learned a thing or two about how students can go off the rails and alternative models of reality. In the present study, I have tried to exploit this experience by avoiding such confusion as much as is humanly possible.

Some students have a curiously ambivalent attitude towards the biological perspective. On the one hand, they seem unsure why they need to study a subject felt to be inaccessible to all but the scientifically gifted, more the domain of weird scientists in white coats, who like to inject rats with complex-sounding chemicals. On the other hand, there is a kind of distant admiration, a feeling that the secrets of life are most likely to be revealed by such things as PET scans and genetic analysis. If the present book serves to give some balance to such feelings it will have performed its role.

There are two types of boxed components throughout, marked 'Evolutionary psychology' and 'A personal angle'. The 'Evolutionary psychology' box points to the relevance of evolutionary psychology to the topic under discussion at that point. 'A personal angle' is designed on the basis that the student is probably especially interested in the lives of individual humans. These examples range from sombre case studies of patients with damaged brains to insights into the more memorable and eccentric events in the lives of scientists. The latter will give you (I hope) a moment of light relief and distraction in an otherwise demanding text. I believe that 'A personal angle' box can give you a tag for forming an association with a substantial amount of otherwise less-memorable material.

The book is accompanied by an Instructor's Manual (available on the website) designed to assist lecturers who have adopted it for their courses. The book has an associated website (**www.pearsoned.co.uk/toates**), designed to serve a number of purposes:

1 On the 'noticeboard' will be found (a) details of significant new research advances and pointers to where they relate to the content of the book, and (b) feedback information on the book, e.g. (i) how something might be better understood, (ii) new cross-references between material and (iii) notification of any errors, which, in spite of all attempts to eliminate them, have crept through.

2 Justifications of the answers to the 'Test your knowledge' questions found in the book.

3 Multiple-choice questions, with feedback.

There are a number of people whose influence and help I would like to acknowledge. The efforts of the Open University library staff are much appreciated. The enthusiasm and dedication of Pearson Education staff, Melanie Beard, Georgina Clark-Mazo, Mary Lince, Jodie Mardell, Maggie Wells. Janey Webb and Catherine Morrissey, amongst others, were invaluable, as was, in the Open University, Giles Clark's advice and Becky Efthimiou's help throughout. On the editorial side, I would like to acknowledge the contribution of Sue Gard, Annette Musker and Ros Woodward. In addition to the reviewers listed (page xx), one or more chapters or parts of chapters were read by the following:

Kent Berridge, University of Michigan

Angus Gellatly, Oxford Brookes University

John Podd, Massey University

Sinead Rhodes, University of Strathclyde

Edmund Sonuga-Barke, University of Southampton

Lance Workman, Bath Spa University

I am very grateful to them for their efforts to improve earlier drafts, which has made an immense difference. Of course, I do not hold them responsible for the final product.

My students have given me inspiration and useful feedback and have taught me how to teach. Finally, I would like to record my thanks to my wife, Olga Coschug-Toates, who encouraged the project, has been a source of strength and patience and has read and critically commented on each chapter. I would like to dedicate the book to her.

Should anyone have any comments, I would be delighted to hear from you, e.g. at F.Toates@Open.ac.uk

Frederick Toates
Milton Keynes, England
February 2010

Guided tour of the textbook and website

Learning outcomes give you a taste of what you'll be covering.

Scene-setting questions begin each chapter, encouraging you to engage with the main issues and concerns of the topic.

The access code packaged with this book allows you to explore the companion website at **www.pearsoned.co.uk/toates**. This contains a range of resources including questions, animations, interactions, further reflections on a topic and web links to help you consolidate and develop your understanding.

The new edition is richly illustrated with diagrams and photographs.

Evolutionary psychology boxes provide you with an insight into a psychological concept from an evolutionary perspective.

Personal angle boxes provide you with personal examples of patients' experiences and the lives of famous psychologists and others.

The web icon alerts you to particular resources on the accompanying website to complement your studies. You will find videos to accompany some of the scene-setting questions.

---

464 CHAPTER 17 SEXUAL BEHAVIOUR

Such imitation would allow a limited degree of cultural relativity based on learning. That is to say a fixed output from disgust detection coexists with some flexibility in terms what elicits such disgust (Rozin et al., 2000). There are certain cultural differences in triggers to disgust. For example, rigid caste systems prescribe certain unfortunates as untouchable. Within an industrial society, we could speculate that the body odours that trigger disgust in the 21st century might have been perceived as relatively benign to most of our ancestors! Also new diseases emerge (e.g. sexually transmitted ones) and do not always advertise themselves by unique external signs, thus allowing cultural transmission of information.

The functional explanation

In contrast to depression (Chapter 2), the functional advantage of a disgust system in terms of survival and thereby genetic perpetuation is surely beyond dispute. Disgust exemplifies where the functional explanation and evolutionary psychology can provide a unifying framework for understanding (Oaten et al., 2009). Disgust puts a distance (physical or psychological) between the person and the triggering event and it signals disapproval to others.

Evolutionary psychology

Broadening the basic processes

Rozin et al. (2000) argue that disgust emerged first as a defence against ingestion of harmful foods. They suggest that the facial gesture of disgust serves to minimize contact with the food and that nausea, the hallmark of disgust, is linked to ingested foods.

In triggering disgust, evolutionary logic suggests that an individual can err in one of two ways (Oaten et al., 2009):

1. False alarms. Disgust is triggered in the absence of an actual threat.
2. False safety. Disgust is not triggered in the presence of a threat.

Evolutionary logic suggests that the cost of getting it wrong in the first case is likely to be less than in the second (where it can prove fatal) and hence we might expect an excess of false alarms. This is suggested by the tendency to form irrational disgust reactions. For example, sadly, HIV/AIDS can trigger disgust and social distancing by others, out of proportion to the actual risk of contamination. This might be linked to the sexual connotation of the infection.

Whatever its evolutionary origins, it is clear that the triggers to disgust are now much broader than stimuli that can be defined simply by their physical properties. The role of cognition becomes evident. Consider disgust triggered by sexual stimuli. Women show increased sensitivity to such disgust, compared with men, as might be expected from functional considerations since the costs can be so much greater (Tybur et al., 2009).

Sexual disgust is only in part based upon physical triggers as in pathogen avoidance. Rather, sexual disgust can be triggered by unwanted and unattractive sexual advances and intrusions or sexual contact with a close relative. Such disgust would logically have served to avoid actions where the reproductive consequences might well have been costly in terms of fitness (Tybur et al., 2009). A degree of information extraction and contextualization of this information is exemplified by avoidance of sexual contact with a sibling (incest avoidance), where the sibling has no intrinsic disgust-triggering qualities.

Evolutionary psychology suggests some interesting developmental questions (Tybur et al., 2009). For example, assessments of a potential mating partner would present a challenge for fitness at a later age than does detection of pathogens. Therefore, one might expect the capacity for sexual disgust to mature somewhat later.

Consider the argument that moral disgust gained access to the brain processes that evolved to serve physical disgust (Rozin et al., 2000). This would exemplify what is termed a 'pre-adaptation' (sometimes described as an 'exaptation'): existing processes are recruited ('co-opted') to serve an additional function. The authors draw a comparison with the teeth and tongue, which facilitate spoken language but evolved originally in the service of feeding. On moral disgust, they state (p. 650): 'A mechanism for avoiding harm to the body became a mechanism for avoiding harm to the soul'.

Moral disgust is presumably a purely human attribute. Theories of moral reasoning have tradition-

---

THE COMPARATIVE APPROACH: PSYCHOLOGY AND ETHOLOGY 15

Section summary

1. Genes are a factor that helps to determine the structure of the body including the nervous system.
2. Behaviour cannot be 'all in the genes'.
3. Development refers to changes that are a function of age.

☞ **Test your knowledge**

1.5 Why would it be over-simple to claim that genes cause behaviour?.

Answer on page 19 ➡

The comparative approach: psychology and ethology

Animal models, evolution and comparative studies

The **comparative approach** consists of comparing different species to gain insight into how each adapts to its habitat and how this is reflected in differences in behaviour. The example of taste-aversion learning introduced this topic earlier.

In this book, the comparative approach is used mostly for trying to understand humans. Psychologists look at so-called simpler species to gain understanding of more complex species. The term **animal model** is used to refer to the simpler animal as a model that captures features of the more complex animal.

With some basic processes and components, the same solution employed by so-called simple animals is also seen in the more complex. Evolution is described as being 'conservative' (Epstein, 1982). For example, there are striking similarities in how neurons operate and communicate among species. By dissecting large neurons from such species as squid, the knowledge gained can be applied to other species, including humans. However, evolution could also be described as 'inventive' in finding new solutions. Thus, there are limitations on how far one can push the process of appealing to simpler animal models. Although the components have striking common features, their combination can take on properties that mean animal models have a limited value.

Certain species show exceptional abilities. A study of their brains in comparison to species not showing the exceptional ability can give insight into how this ability is linked to the brain. For example, some bird species show an incredible ability at hoarding food in a multitude of different locations and remembering where (Clayton and Dickinson, 1998). Other, closely related, birds do not have this ability. So, a comparison of their brains can guide us in searching for the brain regions that underlie the exceptional spatial and memory skills.

A personal angle

A lunch-break worth remembering by all

The psychology department at the University of California at Davis is associated with some rather peculiar cognitive skills but is also known for theft, cunning and deception. I hasten to add that I am not describing the academic staff but rather some winged visitors.

During their lunch-break, wife and husband team Nicola Clayton and Nathan Emory (both now at the University of Cambridge) observed the behaviour of Western scrub-jays, who were taking morsels of food left by students. The birds would bury some of the food for later consumption (termed caching). However, occasionally, other birds were witness to this and, after the competitor left the scene, the first bird would dig up the morsel and bury it in a different place. Controlled laboratory studies, done later at Cambridge, confirmed that this behaviour is characteristic of the species.

The study points to the value of looking at special abilities possessed by particular species. It also shows what can be gained by observing behaviour under natural conditions – well, maybe more precisely, 'semi-natural', in the case of a university campus. The research suggests sophisticated cognition that involves the anticipated likely moves of a competitor. It prompts the search for special underlying processes in the brains of such species.

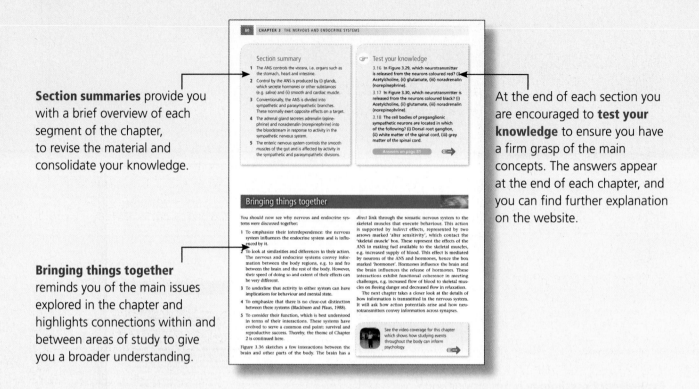

Section summaries provide you with a brief overview of each segment of the chapter, to revise the material and consolidate your knowledge.

At the end of each section you are encouraged to **test your knowledge** to ensure you have a firm grasp of the main concepts. The answers appear at the end of each chapter, and you can find further explanation on the website.

Bringing things together reminds you of the main issues explored in the chapter and highlights connections within and between areas of study to give you a broader understanding.

Each chapter has a summary giving you a comprehensive outline of the topics covered and the conclusions reached.

Explanations to the answers provided for **test your knowledge** questions can be found on the website.

An annotated list of useful books at the end of each chapter allows you to explore the topic further.

Colourful **interactions and animations** accompany several chapters. These offer a visual illustration of concepts to deepen your understanding. Details of these can be found at the end of each chapter.

Multiple choice questions can be found on the website to help you assess your progress and reinforce what you've learnt.

Watch **video clips** exploring topics covered and issues raised in the text.

Reviewers

The publishers would like to express their appreciation for the invaluable advice and encouragement they have received for this book from educators within Europe, Scandinavia and New Zealand:

Dr Matthew Bristow, Anglia Ruskin University

Dr Michelle Lee, Swansea University

Dr William Brown, University of East London

Dr Louisa Edwards, Loughborough University

Dr Christine Norman, Nottingham Trent University

Dr Rob Bell, Queen's University Belfast

Dr Claire Rostron, The Open University

Dr Clare Cunningham, University if Abertay Dundee

Dr Katherine Finlay, University of Buckingham

Dr Sue McHale, Sheffield Hallam University

Dr Eamon Fulcher, University of the West of England

Acknowledgements

We are grateful to the following for permission to reproduce copyright material:

Figures

Figure on page 2 from H. Damasio, T. Grabowski, R. Frank, A. M. Galaburda and A. R. Damasio (1994) The return of Phineas Gage: clues about the brain from a famous patient, *Science*, 264, 1102–1105. Dornsife Neuroscience Imaging Center and Brain and Creativity Institute, University of Southern California. Cover of *Science*, Vol. 264, No. 5162, 20 May 1994. Reprinted with permission from AAAS; Figure 1.2 from *Introducing health sciences: a case study approach, SDK125, Book 2*, The Open University, Fig. 4.1b; Figure 1.5 from *History of the Neurosciences*, 18(3), Fig. 1, p. 341 (Wilgus, B. and Wilgus, J. 2009), Collection of Jack and Beverly Wilgus; Figure 2.4 after *Introduction to Psychology*, Vol. 1, pub Lawrence Erlbaum Associates Ltd. in association with The Open University (Toates, F. M. 1990) pp. 191–249, Fig. 5.12, p. 209, edited by I. Roth © 1990 The Open University; Figure 2.7 from *Behaviour and Evolution, SD206: Biology, Brain and Behaviour, Book 1*, The Open University (Hall, M. and Halliday, T. eds 1998) Fig. 3.2, p. 53; Figures 3.2, 3.3 after *The Senses and Communication, Course SD206: Biology, Brain and Behaviour, Book 3*, The Open University Press (Halliday, T. ed. 1998); Figures 3.4, 7.1, 7.7, 8.13, 9.16 from *Psychology – An Integrated Approach*, edited by M. Eysenck, Pearson Education Ltd. (Toates, F. M. 1998) pp. 100–137, Sensory Systems; Figures 3.16a, 5.12, 10.9, 17.3 after *Human Physiology*, McGraw-Hill (Vander, A. J. *et al.* 1994), © 1994 reproduced with permission from The McGraw-Hill Companies, Inc; Figure 3.21 adapted from *Growing and Responding, Course SK220, Book 2*, edited by M. Stewart, The Open University (Toates, F. M. 1997) Fig. 3.1, p. 142; Figure 4.1 adapted from *Introducing health sciences: a case study approach, SDK125, Book 2*, The Open University, Fig 4.1b; Figures 5.13, 5.37 from *OU Course SD286*, The Open University, Module A, Fig. 22, p. 31; Figures 5.14, 5.32, 5.38 from *The Prefrontal Cortex – Anatomy, Physiology and Neuropsychology of the Frontal Lobe*, Lippincott Williams & Wilkins (Fuster, J. M. 1997) with permission from the author; Figure 5.30 from KALAT, *Biological Psychology, 6E* © 1998 Wadsworth, a part of Cengage Learning, Inc. Reproduced by permission. www.cengage.com/permissions; Figure 5.35 from *Principles of Neural Science*, 3rd ed., McGraw-Hill (Kandel, E. R. *et al.*, eds 1991) Fig. 65–1, p. 1010, Cellular mechanisms of learning and the biological basis of individuality by E. R. Kandel, © 1992 reproduced with permission from The McGraw-Hill Companies, Inc; Figure 5.36 from *Brain Size and Evolution of Mind*, American Museum of Natural History (Jerison, H. J. 1991) Fig. 15, p. 64, with permission from the author; Figure 5.39 reprinted from *Trends in Neurosciences*, 18, 9 (Povinelli, D. J. and Preuss, T. M. 1995), Theory of mind: evolutionary history of a cognitive specialization, Fig. 1, pp. 418–424, Copyright 1995, with permission from Elsevier; Figure 5.40 from Darwin and the ghost of Phineas Gage: Neuro-evolution and the social brain, *Cortex*, 45, pp. 1119–1125, Fig. 1, p. 1120 (Dunbar, R. I. M. 2009), Copyright Elsevier 2009; Figure 5.41 from The Hippocampal complex of food-storing birds, *Brain, Behaviour and Evolution*, 34, pp. 308–317, Fig. 4, p. 314 (Sherry, D. F. *et al.* 1989), reprinted by permission of S. Karger AG; Figure 5.46 reprinted from *Fundamental Neuroscience*, edited by M. J. Zigmond *et al.*, G. S. Aston-Jones *et al.*, Attention, pp. 1385–1409, Copyright 1999 with permission from Elsevier; Figure 5.47 from Orbitofrontal cortex and dynamic filtering of emotional stimuli, *Cognitive Affective and Behavioural Neuroscience*, 2, pp. 264–270, Fig. 2, p. 267 (Rule, R. R., Shimamura, A. P. and Knight, R. T. 2002), with permission from Psychonomic Society Publications; Figure 5.48 reprinted from *Journal of Psychiatric Research*, 43, 13, Kronenberg, G. *et al.*, Reduced amygdala volume in newly admitted psychiatric in-patients with unipolar major depression, pp. 1112–1117, Copyright 2009, with permission from

Elsevier; Figure 5.49 reprinted from *Biological Psychiatry*, 67, 2, Suslow, T. *et al.*, Automatic mood-congruent amygdala responses to masked facial expressions in major depression, pp. 155–160, Copyright 2010, with permission from Elsevier; Figures 5.53, 5.54 from *Physiology of Behaviour*, 6th ed., Allyn and Bacon (Carlson, N. R. 1998), © 1998 Pearson Education, Inc. Reproduced by permission of Pearson Education, Inc; Figure 6.1 from *The Evolution of Development*, Cambridge University Press (Bonner, J. T. 1958) Fig. 10, p. 44; Figures 6.7, 6.11, 6.12 after *Neural Activity and the Growth of the Brain*, Cambridge University Press (Purves, D. 1994); Figure 6.9 from Binocular interaction in striate cortex of kittens reared with an artificial squint, *Journal of Neurophysiology*, 28, pp. 1041–1059, Fig. 5, p. 1049 (Hubel, D. H. and Wiesel, T. N. 1965), Am Physiol Soc, used with permission; Figures 6.20, 6.21 from Increase in prefrontal cortical volume following cognitive behavioural therapy in patients with chronic fatigue syndrome, *Brain*, 131, 8, pp. 2172–2180 (de Lange, F. P. *et al.* 2008), by permission of Oxford University Press; Figure 7.2 from *Eye and Brain: The Psychology of Seeing*, 5th ed., Oxford University Press (Gregory, R. L. 1998), by permission of Oxford University Press; Figure 8.1 from Gazzaniga, Michael S., ed., *The Cognitive Neurosciences*, figure 23.1 from pages 365–382 © 1994 Massachusetts Institute of Technology, by permission of The MIT Press; Figure 8.6 from Visual pigments or rods and cones in a human retina, *Journal of Physiology*, 298, Fig. 2, p. 505 (Bowmaker, J. K. and Dartnall, H. J. A. 1980), with permission from John Wiley & Sons Ltd. and J. K. Bowmaker; Figure 8.7 from *Introduction to Psychology*, Vol. 2, edited by I. Roth, pub. Lawrence Erlbaum Associates Ltd. in association with The Open University (Greene, J. 1990) Fig. 10.5, p. 483 © 1990 The Open University; Figures 8.23, 9.21, 10.10, 10.11, 10.12, 11.11, 20.5 after *Neuroscience: Exploring the Brain*, Williams & Wilkins (Bear, M. F. *et al.* 1996), with permission from Lippincott Williams & Wilkins; Figures 8.24, 8.25, 8.26 reprinted from *Cognition*, Vol. 67, M. A. Goodale and G. K. Humphrey, The objects of action and perception, pp. 186, 198, 199, Copyright 1998, with permission from Elsevier; Figure 8.27a from *Sight Unseen: An Exploration of Conscious and Unconscious Vision*, Oxford University Press (Goodale, M. A. and Milner, D. A. 2003) Fig. 2.1, p. 17, by permission of Oxford University Press and the authors; Figure 8.27b reprinted by permission from Macmillan Publishers Ltd: A neurological dissociation between perceiving objects and grasping them, *Nature*, 349,

6305, 10 January, Fig. 1 (Goodale, M. A. *et al.* 1991), copyright 1991; Figure 8.28 from Mechanisms of contour perception in monkey visual cortex. I. Lines of pattern discontinuity, *Journal of Neuroscience*, 9, pp. 1731–1748, Fig. 3, p. 1735 (von der Heydt, R. and Peterhans, E. 1989), Copyright 1989 by Society for Neuroscience. Used with permission of Society for Neuroscience; permission conveyed through Copyright Clearance Center, Inc; Figure 8.29 from Visual properties of neurons in a polysensory area in superior temporal sulcus in the macaque, *Journal of Neurophysiology*, 46, pp. 369–384, Fig. 7, p. 379 (Bruce, C. *et al.* 1981), Am Physiol Soc, used with permission; Figure 8.30 reproduced with permission of Nature Publishing Group, from How the brain learns to see objects and faces in an impoverished context, *Nature*, 389, Fig. 1, p. 597 (Dolan, R. J. *et al.* 1997); permission conveyed through Copyright Clearance Center, Inc; Figures 8.31, 8.32, 8.33a, 8.33b, 8.34, 20.13 from Brain mechanisms associated with top-down processes in perception, *Philosophical Transactions of the Royal Society of London B, 352* (Frith, C. and Dolan, R. J. 1997), reprinted by permission of Professor Christopher D. Frith; Figure 9.2 from *Physiology of Behaviour*, 5th ed., Allyn and Bacon (Carlson, N. R. 1997) Fig. 7.5, p. 186, © 1997 Pearson Education, Inc. Reproduced by permission of Pearson Education, Inc; Figure 9.14 after Intensity of sensation, *Journal of Physiology* (London) 300, Fig. 9, p. 262 (Knibestol, M and Vallbo, A. B. 1980), Copyright © 1980 The Physiological Society. Reproduced with permission of Blackwell Publishing Ltd; Figure 9.15 from *The Skin Senses*, edited by D. R. Kenshalo, Charles C. Thomas (Weinstein, S. 1968) Fig. 10.5, p. 203, in Intensive and extensive aspects of tactile sensitivity as a function of body part, sex and laterality, Courtesy of Charles C. Thomas Publisher, Ltd., Springfield, Illinois; Figures 9.17, 9.19, 9.20, 11.23 from *Principles of Neural Science*, 3rd ed., McGraw-Hill (Kandel, E. R. *et al.* eds 1991) Touch by E. R. Kandel and T. M. Jessell, © 1992 reproduced with permission from The McGraw-Hill Companies, Inc; Figure 9.22 after *Development and Flexibility, course SD206: Biology, Brain and Behaviour*, The Open University (Whatson, T. and Sterling, V. 1998) Fig. 5.3, p. 146; Figure 9.26 from Odor/taste integration and the perception of flavour, *Experimental Brain Research*, 166, Fig. 1, p. 347 (Small, D. M. and Prescott, J. 2005), pub Springer, courtesy of Dana Small; Figure 10.3 adapted from *Eye and Brain: The Psychology of Seeing*, 5th ed., Oxford University Press (Gregory, R. L. 1997), by permission of Oxford University Press; Figure 10.5 from

The neural basis for learning of simple motor skills, *Science*, 242, pp. 728–735, Fig. 1, p. 729 (Lisberger, S. G. 1988). Reprinted with permission from AAAS; Figure 10.7 adapted from *Growing and Responding, course SK220, Book 2*, edited by M. Stewart, The Open University (Toates, F. M. 1997) Fig. 4.1, p. 113, in The control of movement; Figure 10.13 from *Textbook of Medical Physiology*, Elsevier, Inc. (Guyton, A. C. 1991) Fig. 54–8, p. 597, Copyright Elsevier; Figure 10.19 from *From Cells to Consciousness, course SD226, Book 6, Biological Psychology: Exploring the Brain*, The Open University (2004) Fig. 1.1, p. 6; Figure 10.20 from The cerebellum and the adaptive coordination of movement, *Annual Review of Neuroscience*, 15, pp. 403–422, Figs 5a, 5b and 5c, pp. 428, 429 and 431 (Thach, W. T., Goodkin, H. P. and Keating, J. G. 1992), Copyright 1992 by Annual Reviews, Inc. Reproduced with permission of Annual Reviews, Inc; permission conveyed through Copyright Clearance Center, Inc; Figure 11.5 reprinted from *Neurobiology of Learning and Memory*, 76, Woodruff-Pak, D. S. *et al.*, MRI-assessed volume of cerebellum correlates with associative learning, pp. 342–357, Copyright 2001, with permission from Elsevier; Figure 11.6 adapted from A neural substrate of prediction and reward, *Science*, 275, pp. 1593–1599 (Schultz, W., Dayan, P. and Montague, P. R. 1997). Reprinted with permission from AAAS; Figure 11.14 from The medial temporal lobe memory system, *Science*, 253, pp. 1380, Fig. 3 (Squire, L. R. and Zola-Morgan, S. 1991). Reprinted with permission from AAAS; Figure 11.15 from *Introduction to Psychology*, Vol. 2, edited by I. Roth, Lawrence Erlbaum Associates in association with The Open University (Cohen, G. 1990) pp. 570–621, Fig. 12.10, p. 596, in Memory © 1990 The Open University; Figure 11.18 from Frontal lobes and working memory: evidence from investigations of the effects of cortical excisions in nonhuman primates, *Handbook of Neuropsychology, Vol. 9*, edited by F. Boller and J. Grafman, pp. 59–82, Fig. 16, p. 73 (Petrides, M. 1994), with permission from Elsevier; Figure 11.19 from Classical conditioning and brain systems: The role of awareness, *Science*, 280, pp. 77–81, Fig. 3, p. 79 (Clark, R. E. and Squire, L. R. 1998). Reprinted with permission from AAAS; Figure 11.21 after Repeated confocal imaging of individual dendritic spines in the living hippocampal slice: evidence for changes in length and orientation associated with chemically induced LTP, *The Journal of Neuroscience*, 15, pp. 5560–5573, Fig. 10, p. 5570 (Hosokawa, T. *et al.* 1995), Copyright 1995 by Society for Neuroscience. Used with permission of

Society for Neuroscience; permission conveyed through Copyright Clearance Center, Inc; Figure 11.24 after Mind the gap, *Medical Research Council News*, No. 74, pp. 24–27, Fig. 2 (Collingridge, G. 1997), reprinted by permission of Medical Research Council; Figures 12.3, 12.4 from *From Cells to Consciousness, course SD226, Book 1, Biological Psychology: Exploring the Brain*, The Open University (Toates, F. M. 2004); Figure 12.5 adapted from Attachment and separation distress in the infant guinea pig, *Developmental Psychobiology*, 12, pp. 73–81, Fig. 2 (Pettijohn, T. F. 1979), reprinted by permission of John Wiley and Sons; Figures 12.9, 13.8 from *Neuroanatomy: Text and Atlas*, 2nd ed., McGraw-Hill (Martin, J. H. 1996), © 1996 reproduced with permission from The McGraw-Hill Companies, Inc; Figure 12.12 from *Neuroscience: Exploring the Brain*, 3rd ed., Williams & Wilkins (Bear, M. F., Connors, B. W. and Paradisio, M. A. 2006), with permission from Lippincott Williams & Wilkins; Figure 12.13 from *Understanding Emotions*, Blackwell Publishing Ltd. (Oatley, K. and Jenkins, J. M. 1996) Fig. 5.5, p. 146, Copyright © 1996 Blackwell Publishing Ltd. Reproduced with permission of Blackwell Publishing Ltd; Figure 12.14 from Amygdala acticity at encoding correlated with long-term, free recall of emotional information, *Proceedings of the National Academy of Sciences of the USA*, 93, pp. 8016–8021, Fig. 3 (Cahill, L. *et al.* 1996), Copyright (1996) National Academy of Sciences, USA; Figure 12.16 adapted from Analysis of aversive memories using the fear-potentiated startle paradigm, *Neuropsychology of Memory*, pp. 470–484, Fig. 41.3, p. 474 (Davis, M. 1992), with permission from The Guilford Press; Figure 13.5 from Vegetative and somatic components of tree shrews' behaviour, *Journal of the Autonomic Nervous System*, Suppl. pp. 657–670, Fig. 3, p. 665 (von Holst, D. 1986), Copyright 1986, with permission from Elsevier; Figure 13.9 adapted from The subretrofacial nucleus: its pivotal role in cardiovascular regulation, *News in Physiological Sciences*, 5, pp. 63–67, Fig. 3, p. 65 (Dampney, R. 1990), reprinted by permission of The American Physiological Society; Figures 14.1, 14.7, 14.8 from *The Human Condition, Course SK220, Book 4*, edited by F. M. Toates, The Open University (Toates, F. M. 1997); Figure 14.6 from Pain mechanisms: Labeled lines versus convergence in central processing, *Annual Review of Neuroscience*, 26, pp.1–30, Fig. 2, p. 11 (Craig, A. D. 2003), Copyright 1992 by Annual Reviews, Inc. Reproduced with permission of Annual Reviews, Inc; permission conveyed through Copyright Clearance Center, Inc; Figure 14.9 adapted from Perception of phantom limbs, *Brain*,

121,9, pp.1603–1630, p. 1612, Fig 4(B) (C) (Ramachandran, V. S. and Hirstein, W. 1998), by permission of Oxford University Press; Figure 14.12 from Empathy for pain involves the affective but not sensory components of pain, *Science*, 303, pp. 1157–1162, Fig. 4A, p. 1161 (Singer, T. *et al.* 2004). Reprinted with permission from AAAS; Figure 15.2 from Sensory pleasure, *Quarterly Review of Biology*, 54,1, pp.1–29, pub. University of Chicago Press (Cabanac, M. 1979), © 1979 by The University of Chicago. All rights reserved; Figure 15.3 reprinted from *Progress in Psychobiology and Physiological Psychology*, Vol. II, edited by J. M. Sprague and A. N. Epstein, H. J. Grill and K. C. Berridge, Taste reactivity as a measure of the neural plasticity of palatability, pp. 1–16, Copyright 1985, with permission from Elsevier and K. C. Berridge; Figure 15.4 from Relation of consummatory responses and preabsorptive insulin release to palatability and learned taste aversions, *Journal of Comparative and Physiological Psychology*, 95(3), pp. 363–382, Fig. 1, p. 366 (Berridge, K. C. *et al.* 1981), reprinted with permission; Figures 15.6, 18.2, 18.3, 18.6 after Neuropharmacological mechanisms of drug reward: beyond dopamine in the nucleus accumbens, *Critical Reviews in Neurobiology*, 12, pp. 37–67 (Bardo, M. T. 1998), reprinted by permission of Begell House, Inc; Figure 15.8 reprinted from *Cognitive Brain Research*, Vol. 25, Cohen, M. X. *et al.*, Individual differences in extraversion and dopamine genetics predict neural reward responses, pp. 851–861. Copyright 2005, with permission from Elsevier; Figure 15.13 from *Affective Neuroscience*, Oxford University Press (Panksepp, J. 1998) Fig. 13.4, p. 254, by permission of Oxford University Press; Figure 15.14 reprinted by permission of Elsevier from The biology of social attachments: Opiates alleviate separation distress, by J. Panksepp *et al.*, *Biological Psychiatry*, Vol. 13, pp. 607–13, Copyright 1978 by the Society of Biological Psychiatry; Figure 15.15 adapted from *Emotions: Interdisciplinary Perspectives*, Lawrence Erlbaum (Panksepp, J. 1996) Fig. 2.3, p. 50, Affective neuroscience: A paradigm to study the animate circuits for human emotions, in R. D. Kavanaugh *et al.* (eds), reproduced with permission of Taylor & Francis Group LLC – Books; permission conveyed through Copyright Clearance Center, Inc; Figure 15.16 from A single administration of testosterone induces cardiac accelerative responses to angry faces in healthy young women, *Behavioural Neuroscience*, 115, pp. 238–242, Fig. 1, p. 240 (van Honk, J. *et al.* 2001), pub APA, reprinted with permission; Figure 15.17 from Curiosity in

zoo behaviour, *Behaviour*, 26, pp. 151–188, Fig. 1 (Glickman, S. E. and Sroges, R. W. 1996), with permission from Koninklijke Brill NV; Figure 16.2 from *Animal Behaviour – A Systems Approach*, John Wiley & Sons (Toates, F. M. 1980), Copyright 1980. © John Wiley & Sons Limited. Reproduced with permission; Figure 16.3 from Role of a lipostatic mechanism in regulation by feeding of energy balance in rats, *Journal of Comparative and Physiological Psychology*, 84, pp. 1–23, Fig.1 (Le Magnen, J. *et al.* 1973), pub. APA, reprinted with permission; Figure 16.4 from *Physiology of Behaviour*, 1st ed., Allyn and Bacon (Carlson, N. R. 1977), © 1977. Reproduced by permission of Pearson Education, Inc; Figures 16.5, 16.6 adapted from *Human Physiology*, McGraw-Hill (Vander, A. J. *et al.* 1975), reproduced with permission from The McGraw-Hill Companies, Inc; Figure 16.10 reprinted from *Food Quality and Preference*, Vol. 19, 6, Yeomans, M. R., Chambers, L., Blumenthal, H. and Blake, A., The role of expectancy in sensory and hedonic evaluation: The case of smoked salmon ice-cream, pp. 565–573, Copyright 2008, with permission from Elsevier; Figure 16.11 from *Handbook of Physiology, Section 6, Alimentary Canal*, Vol. 1, The American Physiological Society (Le Magnen, J. 1967), used with permission; Figures 16.12, 16.15 after *Challenging Obesity*, edited by H. McLannahan and P. Clifton, Oxford University Press (Clifton, P. 2008) pp. 93–116, by permission of Oxford University Press; Figure 16.13 from Preclinical Study: Ghrelin administration into tegemental areas stimulates locomotor activity and increases extracellular concentration of dopamine in the nucleus accumbens, *Addiction Biology*, 12, pp. 6–16, Fig. 2, p. 10 (Jerlhag, E. *et al.* 2007), with permission from John Wiley and Sons; Figure 16.18 reprinted from *Physiology and Behaviour*, Vol. 62, 1, Yeomans, M. R. and Gray, R. W., Effects of naltrexone on food intake and changes in subjective appetite during eating: Evidence for opioid involvement in the appetizer effect, pp. 15–21, Copyright 1997, with permission from Elsevier; Figure 16.19 from Differences in salivation to repeated food cues in obese and non-obese women, *Psychological Review*, 58, pp. 160–64, Fig. 1, p. 161 (Epstein, L. H., Paluch, R. and Coleman, K. J. 1996), pub. APA, reprinted with permission; Figure 16.20 reprinted from *The Lancet*, Vol. 357, Wang, G.-J. *et al.*, Brain dopamine and obesity, Fig. 2, p. 356, Copyright 2001, with permission from Elsevier; Figure 16.26 with kind permission from Springer Science+Business Media: *Thirst: Physiological and Psychological Aspects*, Inhibitory controls of drinking:

satiation of thirst, 1991, pp. 313–334, Verbalis, J. G., Fig. 19.5, in D. J. Ramsey and D. Booth (eds); Figure 16.27 with kind permission from Springer Science+Business Media: *Handbook of Behavioural Neurobiology, Vol. 10, Neurobiology of Food and Fluid Intake*, Clinical aspects of body fluid homeostasis in humans, 1990, pp. 421–62, Verbalis, J. G., Fig. 8, in E. M. Stricker (ed.); Figure 17.4 adapted from Features of a hormone-driven defined neural circuit for a mammalian behaviour, *Annals of the New York Academy of Sciences*, 563, pp. 131–147 (Pfaff, D. W. 1989), reprinted by permission of New York Academy of Sciences and the author; Figure 17.6 from *Pleasures of the Brain*, edited by M. L. Kringelbach and K. C. Berridge, Oxford University Press (Georgiadis, J. R. and Kortekaas, R. 2010) pp. 178–201, The sweetest taboo: Functional neurobiology of human sexuality in relation to pleasure, by permission of Oxford University Press; Figure 17.7 after *The Human Condition, course SK220, Book 4*, edited by F. M. Toates, The Open University (Toates, F. M. 1997) Fig. 3.6, p. 53; Figure 17.8 (bottom) reprinted from *Fundamental Neuroscience*, edited by M. J. Zigmond *et al.*, M. J. Baum, Psychosexual development, pp. 1229–1244, Copyright 1999, with permission from Elsevier; Figures 18.4a, 18.4b from Role of dopamine in drug reinforcement and addiction in humans: results from imaging studies, *Behavioural Pharmacology*, 13, 5–6, pp. 355–366, Fig. 1, p. 356 (Volkow, N. D., Fowler, J. S. and Wang, G.-J. 2002), Wolters Kluwer Health; Figure 18.5 after Role of dopamine in drug reinforcement and addiction in humans: results from imaging studies, *Behavioural Pharmacology*, 13, pp. 355–366, Fig. 2, p. 357 (Volkow, N. D., Fowler, J. S. and Wang, G.-J. 2002), Wolters Kluwer Health; Figures 18.7, 18.8, 18.9 from Compulsive drug use linked to sensitized ventral striatal dopamine transmission, *Annals of Neurology*, Vol. 59, pp. 852–858 (Evans, A. H. *et al.* 2006), with permission from John Wiley and Sons; Figure 18.10 with kind permission from Springer Science+Business Media: *Psychopharmacology*, Chronic caffeine exposure potentiates nicotine self-administration in rats, Vol. 142, No. 4, 1998, p. 330, Shoaib, M., Swanner, L. S., Yasar, S. and Goldberg, S. R; Figure 18.13 from *Pleasures of the Brain*, edited by M. L. Kringelbach and K. C. Berridge, Oxford University Press (Leyton, M. 2010) pp. 222–243, The neurobiology of desire: Dopamine and the regulation of mood and motivational states in humans, © M. Leyton, by permission of Oxford University Press; Figure 18.14 from *Psychology – An Integrated Approach*, edited by M. Eysenck, Pearson

Education Ltd. (Toates, F. M. 1998) Fig. 2.25, p. 55, Biological bases of behaviour; Figure 19.1 adapted from *Control of Behaviour*, The Open University (Toates, F. M. 1992); Figure 19.2 from *Biological Clocks*, Hodder Education (Brady, J. 1979) Fig. 2.5, p. 10, © J. N. Brady, 1979. Reproduced by permission of Edward Arnold (Publishers) Limited; Figure 19.5 adapted from Dijk, D.-J., Schwartz, W. J. (ed.): *Sleep Science: Integrating Basic Research and Clinical Practice. Monogr Clin Neurosci.* Basel, Karger, 1997, vol. 15, pp. 10–33; Figure 19.6 from *Principles and Practice of Sleep Medicine*, edited by M. H. Kryger *et al.*, Carskadon, M. A. and Dement, W. C., Normal human sleep: and overview, p. 20, Copyright Elsevier 1994; Figure 19.7 from *Neuroscience*, 1st ed., Sinauer Associates (Purves, D. *et al.* 1997) Fig. 26.1, p. 498; Figure 19.8 from *The Dreaming Brain*, Basic Books (Hobson, J. A. 1986) p. 14, Copyright © 1989 by J. Allan Hobson, Md. Reprinted by permission of Basic Books, a member of the Perseus Books Group; Figure 19.9 adapted from *Physiology of Behaviour*, 5th ed., Allyn and Bacon (Carlson, N. R. 1994) p. 289, © 1997 Pearson Education, Inc. Reproduced by permission of Pearson Education, Inc; Figure 19.10 adapted from Modelling states of waking and sleeping, *Psychiatric Annals*, 1, pp. 137–143, Fig. 4, p. 141 (Sutton, J. P. *et al.* 1992), reprinted with permission from Slack Incorporated; Figure 19.11 from Ontogenesis of the states of sleep in rat, cat and guinea pig during the first postnatal month, *Developmental Psychobiology*, 2, pp. 216–239, Fig. 21, p. 236 (Jouvet-Mounier, D. *et al.* 1969), with permission from John Wiley and Sons; Figures 19.12, 19.13 from Overnight therapy? The role of sleep in emotional brain processing, *Psychological Bulletin*, 135, pp. 731–748 (Walker, M. P. and van der Helm, E. 2009), pub. APA, reprinted with permission; Figures 20.4, 20.6 reprinted from *Hormones and Behaviour*, Vol. 55, 4, Hummer, T. A. and McClintock, M. K., Putative human pheromone androstadienone attunes the mind specifically to emotional information, pp. 548–559, Copyright 2009, with permission from Elsevier; Figure 20.8 reprinted from *Trends in Cognitive Sciences*, Vol. 4, 6, Bush, G., Luu, P. and Posner, M. I., Cognitive and emotional influences in anterior cingulate cortex, p. 217, Copyright 2000, with permission from Elsevier; Figures 20.9, 20.19 from Specializations of the human brain, *Scientific American*, 241, No. 3, September, International Edition, pp. 158–168 (Geschwind, N. 1979), reproduced by permission of the illustrator, Carol Donner; Figure 20.10 reprinted from *Fundamental Neuroscience* edited by M. J. Zigmond *et al.*, Kosslyn,

S. M. *et al.*, Hemispheric specialization, pp. 1521–1542, Copyright 1999, with permission from Elsevier; Figure 20.11 from Anatomical study of cerebral asymmetry in the temporal lobe of human chimpanzees and rhesus monkeys, *Science*, pp. 387–389, Fig. 1, p. 388 (Yeni-Komshian, G. H. and Benson, D. A. 1976). Reprinted with permission from AAAS; Figure 20.12 reprinted from *Neuropsychologia*, 24, Robertson, L. C. and Delis, D. C., 'Part-whole' processing in unilateral brain-damaged patients: dysfunction of hierarchical organization, pp. 363–370, Copyright 1986, with permission from Elsevier; Figures 20.14, 20.15, 20.16 reprinted from *Brain and Cognition*, Vol. 55, 1, Bechara, A., The role of emotion in decision-making: Evidence from neurological patients with orbitofrontal damage, pp. 30–40, Copyright 2004, with permission from Elsevier; Figure 20.17 from Language and the brain, *Scientific American*, 226, No. 4, pp. 76–83, p. 78 (Geschwind, N. 1972), reprinted by permission of Donald Garber, Executor of the Estate of Bunji Tagawa; Figure 20.18 from Paul Broca's historic cases: high resolution MR imaging of the brains of Leborgne and Lelong, *Brain*, 130, 5, pp. 1432–1441, Fig. 3, p. 1436 (Dronkers, N. F. *et al.* 2007), by permission of Oxford University Press; Figure 20.20 reprinted by permission from Macmillan Publishers Ltd: Positron emission tomographic studies of the cortical anatomy of single-word processing, *Nature*, 331, Fig. 1, p. 586 (Petersen, S. E. *et al.* 1988), copyright 1988; Figure 20.21reprinted from *Cognition*, Vol. 92, 1–2, Boatman, D., Cortical bases of speech perception: evidence from functional lesion studies, pp. 47–65, Copyright 2004, with permission from Elsevier; Figure 20.22 from Organization of language cortex derived from investigations during neurosurgery, *Seminars in Neurosciences*, 2, pp. 297–305, Fig. 1 (Ojemann, G. A. 1990), Copyright Elsevier 1990; Figures 20.23, 20.24 from Language: tools and brain: the ontogeny and phylogeny of hierarchically organized sequential behaviour, *Behavioural and Brain Sciences*, 14, pp. 531–595 (Greenfield, P. M. 1991), © Cambridge University Press; Figure 21.1 from *Experimental and Theoretical Studies of Consciousness*, edited by G. R. Bock and J. Marsh, John Wiley & Sons Ltd. (Searle, J. R. 1993) Fig. 1, p. 66, from The problem of consciousness, Copyright 1993. © John Wiley & Sons Limited. Reproduced with permission; Figure 22.3 from Mapping adolescent brain change reveals dynamic wave of accelerated grey matter loss in very early-onset schizophrenia, *Proceedings of the National Academy of Sciences*, 98, pp. 11650–11655, Fig. 1a, p. 11651 (Thompson, P. *et al.* 2001), Copyright 2001 National Academy of Sciences, reprinted by permission of National Academy of Sciences and P. Thompson; Figure 22.4 reprinted by permission from Macmillan Publishers Ltd: A functional neuroanatomy of hallucinations in schizophrenia, *Nature*, 378, Fig. 2a, p. 178 (Silbersweig, D. A. *et al.* 1995), copyright 1995; Figures 22.5, 22.6 reprinted from *Brain Research Bulletin*, Vol. 25, 3, Geyer, M. A. *et al.*, Startle response models of sensorimotor gating and habituation deficits in schizophrenia, pp. 485–498, Copyright 1990, with permission from Elsevier.

Figures 1.1, 3.17, 4.15, 5.1b, 5.2, 5.3, 5.4, 5.5, 5.6, 5.7, 5.8, 5.10, 5.11, 5.16, 5.18, 5.20, 5.21, 5.22, 5.23, 5.24a, 5.24b, 5.25, 5.26, 5.27, 5.29, 5.31, 6.3, 6.4, 6.8, 8.3, 8.4a, 8.5, 8.17, 9.1, 9.5, 9.6, 9.10, 9.13, 9.23a, 9.24, 9.25, 10.6, 10.8, 10.17, 10.18, 12.8a, 12.8b, 13.2, 17.8 (top). Figures from *Human Anatomy 3rd ed.* by Frederic H. Martini, Michael J. Timmons and Michael P. McKinley. Copyright © 2000, 1997 by Frederic H. Martini, Inc. and Michael J. Timmons. Reprinted by permission of Pearson Education, Inc.

Figures 3.18, 3.19, 3.20, 3.27a, 3.29, 3.30, 3.33, 4.13, 5.15, 5.17, 5.19, 8.20, 9.8, 9.11, 10.4, 10.14 have been adapted and modified in some way from the original source. Figures from *Human Anatomy 3rd ed.* by Frederic H. Martini, Michael J. Timmons and Michael P. McKinley. Copyright © 2000, 1997 by Frederic H. Martini, Inc. and Michael J. Timmons. Reprinted by permission of Pearson Education, Inc.

Pearson Education Limited would like to credit the renowned medical illustrators Bill Ober, M.D. and Claire Garrison, R.N., and the biomedical photographer Ralph T. Hutchings for the illustrations developed and drawn for Martini: *Human Anatomy, 3rd edition*. Copyright © 2000, 1997 by Frederic H. Martini, Inc. and Michael J. Timmons.

Picture Credits

The publisher would like to thank the following for their kind permission to reproduce their photographs:
(Key: b-bottom; c-centre; l-left; r-right; t-top)

p. 4 © Bettmann / Corbis; p. 9 courtesy of Bundy Mackintosh: (r); p. 15 courtesy of Ian Cannell and Nicky Clayton; p. 21 Jealousy and Flirtation, King, Haynes (1831–1904) / Victoria & Albert Museum, London, UK /

The Bridgeman Art Library; p. 50 Empics; p. 83 © Gallo Images / Corbis; p. 92 US Library of Congress / Science Photo Library; p. 94 © Dennis Kunkel / Phototake, Inc; p. 106 © Victor Fraile / Reuters / Corbis; p. 112 © Copyright Ralph T. Hutchings/Visuals Unlimited (l, r); p. 138 courtesy of Professor M. Stewart; p. 144 Wellcome Department of Cognitive Neurology / Science Photo Library (t); CC Studio / Science Photo Library (b); p. 145 courtesy of Professor Shitij Kapur; p. 151 Getty Images / Iconica; p. 155 Alex Bartel / Science Photo Library; p. 177 © Martin Harvey / Corbis (l); © Ariel Skelley / Corbis (r); p. 178 Science Photo Library Ltd; p. 197 Slave Market with the Disappearing Bust of Voltaire, 1940 (oil on canvas), Dali, Salvador (1904–89) / Salvador Dali Museum, St. Petersburg, Florida, USA / © Salvador Dali, Fundació Gala-Salvador Dali, DACS, 2010 / The Bridgeman Art Library; p. 243 © Copyright G. W. Willis / Visuals Unlimited (t, b); p. 251 Getty Images / Altrendo; p. 253 © Winfried Wisniewski / zefa / Corbis; p. 270 Empics (t, b); p. 336 © David Parry / epa / Corbis; p. 341 Getty Images / Workbook Stock; p. 347 © Rod Williams / naturepl.com; p. 349 Gerry Ellis / Minden / FLPA; p. 364 Topham Picturepoint / TopFoto. co.uk; p. 379 Ian Hooton / Science Photo Library; p. 388 © Michael Keller / Corbis; p. 404 Getty Images / Photographer's Choice; p. 410 TopFoto / Rachel Epstein / Image Works; p. 431 © Ariel Skelley / Corbis; p. 441 image courtesy of The Advertising Archives; p. 468 image courtesy of The Advertising Archives; p. 470 Janine Wiedel Photolibrary / Alamy; p. 473 courtesy of Bruce Alexander; p. 483 Luca DiCecco / Alamy; p. 492 Topham Picturepoint / TopFoto.co.uk; p. 508 The Stuff that Dreams are Made Of, 1858 (oil on canvas), Fitzgerald, John Anster (1832–1906) / Private Collection / The Bridgeman Art Library; p. 515 Getty Images / The Image Bank; p. 522 Ethno Images, Inc. / Alamy; p. 533 Empics; p. 560 james andrew / Alamy; p. 564 © Bettmann / Corbis; p. 566 © Julian Calder / Corbis; p. 567 Alfred Pasieka / Science Photo Library. 580 courtesy of Jeffrey Schwartz.

In some instances we have been unable to trace the owners of copyright material, and we would appreciate any information that would enable us to do so.

Chapter 1
Introduction

Learning outcomes for Chapter 1

After studying this chapter, you should be able to:

1 Justify why psychologists need to understand some biology. In so doing, distinguish four types of explanation involved: causal, developmental/learning, evolutionary and functional.

2 Outline some general principles underlying the science of physiology and how it relates to psychology.

3 Describe some techniques used to link brain and behaviour: (i) experimental intervention, (ii) looking at the effects of damage to human brains and (iii) neuroimaging the activity of brains while people perform tasks. Outline some problems associated with these techniques.

4 Justify the statement that the 'link between biology and psychology is a *reciprocal* one', meaning that understanding is exchanged between the two disciplines. In so doing, describe some of the social implications involved in biological explanation.

5 Describe what is meant by the terms 'gene', 'development' and 'learning'.

6 Explain how investigators can gain insight into brain and behaviour by studying different species.

7 Speculate on the nature of the relationship between the brain and the conscious mind and, in so doing, explain what is meant by identity theory.

Scene-setting questions

1 Are we no more than our biology?
2 Does brain damage provide valid grounds to plead 'not guilty due to diminished responsibility'?
3 Are we free and responsible for our own actions?
4 Can something be 'all in the genes'? If so, are criminals 'born not made'?
5 Is the brain really a computer?
6 Can a person's problems be 'all in the mind'?
7 Can biological psychology help to explain social attachments?

Can biological psychology help to explain social attachments? Explore the video on the website accompanying this book at **www.pearsoned.co.uk/toates**

Why should a psychologist be interested in biology?

Background

Why should psychologists study biology? Humans are part of the biological world and you might already be convinced that biology can provide a secure base for psychology. Outside psychology, the public often seems to have little idea of what kind of subject psychology really is. Try asking your fellow students studying, say, French or chemistry what they think of it as a subject.

Psychologists are sometimes portrayed as people with fancy theories that are either banal or at odds with common sense. By contrast, at other times they are depicted as all-knowing and thereby somewhat sinister. Even Frankenstein-like imagery is sometimes associated with psychologists, on the assumption that they want to control the brains of others. Similarly, witness the comment familiar to any psychologist, 'Oh dear – you must have been reading my mind!' I hope to give a perspective that counters both of these extreme views.

To the public, biology has a certain unambiguous and accurate image as a true science and has produced spectacular insights into the living world. It might seem a safe anchor for psychology.

Others of you might not share such enthusiasm for biology. You might not be clear why, as psychology students, you are asked to study another discipline. After all, biologists are generally not required to study psychology. You might have tried to avoid biology, or even all science, in school or feel that science forms an inappropriate basis for trying to understand mental life. Perhaps you consider that the human mind has peculiarities that cannot be captured by a traditional science, such as the possession of feelings, conscious awareness and free will.

Such tension within psychology is healthy and indeed forms an integral part of the subject. I will show where biology is essential to understanding the human psychological condition but will do so with respect for the reservations that some justifiably hold. First, it is necessary to consider what the subject-matter of biology is, as far as it concerns psychology, and how explanations within psychology can be guided by biology.

Types of explanation

Biology is the science of living things, animals and plants, and how they function in the natural world. How do we link biology and psychology in such a way that an understanding of biology can help us explain behaviour and our mental life? In doing this, there are various types of explanation within biological psychology. We will focus on four of these (Tinbergen, 1963), as follows.

1. The causal explanation

The **causal explanation** concerns how things work in the 'here and now', i.e. the immediate *determinants* of behaviour. This type of explanation is the principal concern of biological psychologists, as they attempt to link events in the brain to behaviour and mental life. Consider two examples:

1 A person treads on a thorn (a cause) and immediately yells (an effect). Information of some sort is conveyed from the foot to the brain, where it triggers the reaction of yelling. Scientists know the pathways that information follows in the body, which link such causes (in this case, damage to the skin at the foot) and effects (producing the yell).

2 A particular event within our body, a low body temperature (a cause) triggers action as behaviour, seeking a warmer location (an effect). Scientists understand something of how the body detects its own temperature and causes action.

Thus, the causal explanation consists of looking at behaviour and seeing how it arises in relation to the current state of the body's biology and the environment.

We are concerned with how identifiable biological processes contribute to behaviour. In so doing, the **nervous system** forms our primary focus. The nervous system consists, in part, of the **brain** and the **spinal cord**. The latter runs through the backbone (Figure 1.1). As another biological consideration, **hormones** are

This is a reconstruction of a terrible accident suffered by Phineas Gage. An iron passed through his head, following the trajectory indicated. What can such damage reveal about how brains normally work?

Source: Damasio *et al.* (1994). From cover of *Science* Vol. 264, no.5162, 20 May 1994. Reprinted with permission from AAAS.

Figure 1.1 Brain and spinal cord.
Source: Martini *et al.* (2000, Fig. 13-1, p. 330). Copyright © 2000, 1997 by Frederic H. Martini, Inc. and Michael J. Timmons. Reprinted by permission of Pearson Education, Inc.

chemicals that are released into the bloodstream and that have effects at various sites in the body.

Particular hormones sensitize specific regions of the brain. This increases the probability that, in response to the presence of another animal, the brain will direct behaviour to, say, mating. In humans, such hormones sensitize our thoughts in the erotic direction. In this case, the biological psychologist investigates motivational processes that are organized in the brain (Mass *et al.*, 2009). These processes depend upon internal factors (e.g. hormones) and external factors (e.g. potential mate) and help to determine the direction that behaviour and cognition take. These processes are said to have a physical structure (or 'embodiment') within the brain. The role of biological psychologists is to obtain insight into these processes, e.g. to try to understand how the brain is influenced by such things as hormones and how this relates to mind and behaviour.

Of course, not all behaviour can be understood in terms of causes as simple as treading on a thorn, the action of hormones or a low body temperature. Much behaviour arises from more subtle and hidden determinants within the brain and we also need to ask about how such processes operate.

Apart from this principal concern, there are three other types of explanation, as follows.

2. The developmental/learning explanation

The second type of explanation is what can be called the **developmental/learning explanation**. The compound of two terms 'developmental' and 'learning' emphasizes their common features. This type of explanation concerns events that occur over a lifetime or at least a much longer time than the fraction of a second normally involved in the causal explanation. For example, on studying the learning of a skill, events over weeks or months might be considered. These would be in terms of *changes* that occur in the brain and the corresponding *changes* in the behaviour that the brain directs.

As a developmental/learning explanation, psychologists try to account for how a living being proceeds from the moment of fertilization to the adult form. They attempt to answer how brain and behaviour develop over this period and this involves a consideration of genetics. We inherit **genes** from our parents and genes play a role in determining the development of the structure of our bodies, including the nervous system. Through this structure, genes indirectly play a role in behaviour. This type of explanation is involved in discussions of **nature** (what we inherit) and **nurture** (what we experience throughout life), as determinants of behaviour.

3. The evolutionary explanation

The third and fourth types of explanation arise from the theory that, over millions of years, we have evolved from a simpler form. The **evolutionary explanation** is in terms of the evolutionary history of the animal, its brain and associated behaviour (Eastwick, 2009). Looking back over countless generations, Darwin's theory of **evolution** has something to say not only about how the physical structure of our bodies has arisen but also about behaviour. Darwin suggested that species in existence today have evolved from a simpler form, i.e. they have been successful in the competition for survival. The term **'phylogeny'** refers to the history of a species over evolutionary time. We can gain insight into behaviour by considering how it relates to this process of evolution. Psychologists ask, where did present forms of behaviour come from in terms of evolution? What was the nature of the brain and behaviour of our evolutionary ancestors and how did these relate to the kind of demands posed by their environment?

Darwin's theory of evolution, as expressed in his book *The Origin of Species*, was met with some disbelief and triggered some ridicule. What is so challenging about its assumptions?

Source: © Bettmann/CORBIS.

4. The functional explanation

Closely related to the evolutionary explanation is the fourth type of explanation: the **functional explanation**. It asks – what is the function of behaviour (Workman and Reader, 2008)? Certain behavioural strategies, as with physical characteristics, have been successful in the evolution of the members of a species and we see these today. We can ask *how* they emerged in evolution. The answer is that they reflect what was **adaptive** to the animals' ancestors (Tooby and Cosmides, 1990). By 'adaptive' is meant something that evolved because it helped the survival of the genes of the animal showing that characteristic. For example, an ability to react to danger by fleeing clearly serves a function that contributed to genetic survival.

Consider again treading on a thorn. Apart from yelling, we quickly and automatically lift our foot from the thorn. What function does this serve? It protects the foot. If we did not lift it, we would risk more damage and infection. This seems clear. An animal not reacting would be at a disadvantage in terms of survival and reproduction. What is the function of yelling? This is less obvious and often the functional explanation involves rich speculation. One possibility is that signalling pain alerts others of our distress. For instance, parents or mates might offer help.

Linking the four types of explanation

This section gives an example of behaviour and suggests how these four types of explanation can be applied to it and linked.

Suppose that your home is near to where some foxes live. You decide to leave out food for them and observe their behaviour. Each night, one particular fox comes to your house and takes the food that you offer. Then, one night you notice that it declines to eat what was previously a very acceptable cut of meat. The *causal* type of question would be, what are the events in the brain of the fox at this point in time that cause it to decline the meat? It could be that it is not hungry but is simply following a routine of patrolling its environment. It might have fed well just prior to visiting you and the brain is detecting adequate nutrients in the body. However, you notice that the fox gets some of the food on its whiskers and then tries to remove it by wiping its mouth on the ground. So, on this occasion, something about the particular food appears to cause the fox to decline it. You offer a slightly different food and it quickly eats this, so it clearly is hungry. Between visits, it seems that it has formed an aversion to the particular food offered first. This *causes* it to reject the food.

You might then pose questions of the *developmental/ learning* type (with the emphasis on learning). What has happened to the fox in the period since you last offered it food of this kind? Something has changed in its brain, so that the reaction to this food has changed. What could well be the explanation is that the fox ate some of this type of meat but it had gone bad ('off') and it gave the fox gastrointestinal upset. So, it has learned to avoid this type of meat; so-called **taste-aversion learning** (Garcia, 1989). The taste has become aversive to the fox.

You can then ask *evolutionary* questions of this behaviour – such as at what stage in the evolution of foxes did the capacity for this type of learning first appear? How widespread is it among similar species? The answer is that the capacity is very widespread and is said to be evolutionarily old. You might well have experienced this effect, since humans have the faculty to do so.

You can also ask the *functional* type of question. What is the advantage in showing this behaviour? How does it enable foxes to survive and reproduce? The answer is clear: foods that cause gastrointestinal upset are dangerous and could even prove lethal. By rapidly learning to avoid them, foxes, as with humans, tend to live to see another day.

By bringing the evolutionary and functional types of explanation together, we gain a very powerful tool for understanding. We can compare species and their lifestyle. For example, in species such as humans, rats and dogs, the taste and smell of food are particularly easily associated with gastrointestinal upset. In birds, the visual characteristics of foods are particularly well associated. Birds normally discriminate foods by visual cues.

Is there a species that does *not* exhibit taste-aversion learning? If so, what might this tell us about the species' evolution and lifestyle? Very conveniently, in 2003 one such species did emerge to claim this so-far unique distinction (Ratcliffe *et al.*, 2003). It was the common vampire bat (Latin name *Desmodus rotundus*), perhaps not one's first choice of species to cultivate as either research subject or house guest. What does this species characteristic say about the functional value of taste-aversion learning and how to survive without it? Vampire bats suck the blood of *living* animals and so are very unlikely ever to ingest a meal that has 'gone off'. Hence, they have little or no need for such a faculty. In their evolutionary specialization for blood-eating, they have lost the faculty of taste-aversion learning. Other bat species, which are related but which eat fruit and insects, show taste-aversion learning.

Chapter 1 will discuss further the four types of explanation and show where each has something to contribute. Much of this book is concerned with the immediate determinants of behaviour, the causal explanation. Biological psychologists are concerned with what causes behaviour in the here-and-now. This requires an understanding of the physiology of the body, the topic of the next section.

Section summary

1 Understanding behaviour can involve a parallel consideration of four types of explanation:

   (a) Here-and-now questions of what determines behaviour, a causal explanation.

   (b) Developmental/learning explanations. How events over periods within an individual lifetime affect behaviour, e.g. how the animal *changes* from a simple form to a more complex form.

   (c) The evolutionary history of the species.

   (d) The functional value of behaviour.

2 The theory of evolution states that the species in existence today have evolved from simpler forms.

3 An adaptive characteristic is one that evolved because it helped to promote the survival of the genes of the animal.

☞ Test your knowledge

1.1 'Coughing is (i) triggered by an irritant in the respiratory system and (ii) defends the lining of the system against damage'. This represents which of the types of explanation?

 Answer on page 19 WEB

The physiology of the body

Organs, systems and cells

The science of **physiology** is concerned with the structure and function of the body, i.e. how its organs, such as the heart and kidney, work. There are various ways of dividing the body for the purpose of explanation. One is in terms of *systems* defined by the role that they serve. Thus, the circulatory system is responsible for moving blood around the body and consists of the heart and blood vessels. As psychologists, the nervous system, serving communication and control, is our principal focus.

To explain how the body works, another way of dividing it is based on the fact that it is composed of billions of very small **cells**. Each organ (e.g. brain, heart or stomach) is made up of such cells. Cells are the fundamental building blocks of an organ and thereby the body (Figure 1.2). The interior of each cell has a liquid composition ('intracellular fluid') and the cell is to some extent 'self-contained'. The cell has a 'cell membrane' around itself and the chemical environment on the inside is different from that on the outside ('extracellular fluid'). However, like a person within society, the cell survives only by interaction with its immediate environment. Thus, nutrients are brought into the cell and waste materials are carried away from the cell by the blood. Cells contain a 'nucleus' (explained later).

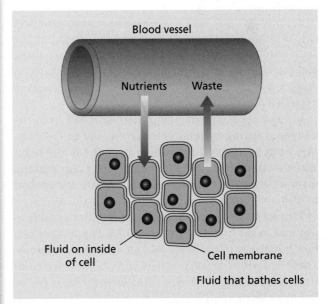

Figure 1.2 Some cells of the body, shown in association with a blood vessel (the latter is also composed of cells but for simplicity these are not indicated).

Source: Open University Course SDK125 Book 2 Figure 4.1b.

All cells, whether in the brain, kidney or wherever, have certain features in common, e.g. each cell is surrounded by a membrane. However, cells also differ, in their structure and function. As well as the general properties, cells are (again, rather like people) specialists, serving particular functions according to where they are located and to which organ they belong. For instance, red blood cells are specialists at carrying oxygen in the blood to be delivered to cells throughout the body. Nerve cells, termed **neurons**, are a type of cell that is specific to the nervous system and they are specialized at transmitting and processing information. Exemplifying communication, it was just noted that a thorn in the foot triggers a signal that is transmitted through the body to the brain. This involves transmission of information by neurons.

Physiology and behaviour

Biological psychologists try to link physiology to behaviour and cognition. This section describes some forms that the link takes.

General principles

In achieving survival and optimal conditions within the body, various forms of information are conveyed to the brain. Information concerns (1) internal events within the body and (2) events in the external world. For instance, a low or high body temperature is signalled to the brain. Information on the external world (e.g. presence of a source of warmth) is also signalled, e.g. through sensations of heat or cold arising at the skin. Based upon this information, decisions are made and priorities of behaviour are established. For example, detection of cold within the body will make the sight of a warm location attractive.

In organizing reproduction, internal signals from the body (e.g. arising from hormone levels) and external signals from prospective mates are integrated in the brain and decisions on courtship made. Decision-making involves establishing priorities, e.g. to mate rather than to feed.

Threats to the individual trigger emotions, such as fear and anger (van Honk *et al.*, 2010). The level of certain hormones in the body also affects these emotions. These emotions are associated with both behaviour, such as attacking or fleeing, and intrinsic changes to the body, such as an accelerated heart-rate. During, say, feeding, the sight of a predator might trigger fear and cause prioritization to be instantly switched to fleeing.

Homeostasis

The inside of the body has an 'optimal condition', where it functions best (Hogan, 1980). For example, a body temperature of around 37 °C is optimal. Body temperature is regulated within close limits, with the help of behaviour, such as moving to a warmer or cooler location or buying a cold drink. Similarly, there is an optimal level of body water content. Maintaining the condition of the internal 'environment' of the body is therefore crucial to survival. As part of this, each cell requires a supply of energy and nutrients, obtained from outside the body with the help of the behaviour of ingesting food.

When internal conditions deviate from their optimal values, action is usually triggered to restore normality, a process termed **homeostasis**. Homeostasis exemplifies the broadly used term **negative feedback**. Negative feedback is exhibited by the control of the temperature of a room with the help of a thermostat: when room temperature drops below that set at the thermostat, heating is switched on automatically. In other words, deviations from optimum tend to be *self-eliminating*, hence the adjective 'negative' before feedback. In Figure 1.3, the minus sign indicates negative feedback.

For body temperature, homeostasis involves intrinsic processes, such as shivering and sweating, but also behaviour, e.g. moving to Florida. According to what is the internal variable that deviates from optimum, we are *motivated* to seek sources of nutrients, water, heat or cold. The behavioural aspect of homeostasis will be a topic of the present book.

Given a basic introduction to physiology and behaviour, the following section will explore the application of this to the causal type of explanation.

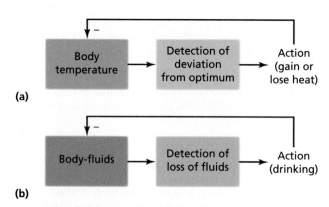

Figure 1.3 Homeostasis: (a) body temperature, (b) body fluids. The minus sign indicates that behaviour corrects the initial deviation that triggers behaviour, e.g. drinking corrects the loss of body fluids.

Some sources of understanding

The methods employed

The task

Biological psychology tries to understand what the brain does and how it does it. It is possible to identify different regions of the brain and to understand their contribution to behaviour and mind. For example, some regions ('sensory regions') are responsible for processing information arriving at the eyes and others process auditory information from the ears. Some regions are involved in detecting the temperature of the body or the level of body fluids. Parts of the brain described as 'emotional' are responsible for the organization of fear and anger, and trigger changes in heart-rate, blood flow to the muscles and the flow of food along the gut.

This section looks first at some of the techniques that are employed in establishing 'what causes what' and their implications.

Experimental intervention

The causes of behaviour arise inside and outside the animal. Scientists wish to make controlled manipulations of these external or internal factors under reproducible conditions and see what happens to behaviour. For example, a rat is injected with a drug and it starts to eat. What is the cause of this? Feeding would

normally be triggered by the sight of food or a fall in the level of energy available in the body, detected by the brain. So, the drug might stimulate the feeding control processes in the brain that normally detect a low energy level. Alternatively, the drug might alter how the rat's attention is directed, causing food to attract attention. Experimentation would be needed to distinguish such possibilities.

For an everyday human example, researchers seek drugs to reduce appetite (Clifton, 2008). Suppose a potential drug has been developed and reports suggest that humans lose weight while taking it. Researchers would need to know how it acts and on which brain regions. Does it target regions specifically concerned with appetite and suppress their activity, in effect fooling the body into not noticing that it is lowering its energy reserves? Alternatively, the drug might simply make people feel nauseous and suppress a range of different behaviours. Subjective reports from the participants, in terms of their feelings, need to be taken into account, as well as objective biological evidence. Herein, a particular role of the biological psychologist lies in trying to link different sources of evidence.

Causal questions are of the kind 'If X occurs, does Y follow?' They might be: 'Does a new drug reduce pain?', 'Does alcohol cause deterioration in driving skills?' or 'How does damage to a brain region disrupt emotional expression?' In some cases, one looks for a relationship in which cause and effect are close together in time, e.g. a drug reduces pain immediately. In other cases, manipulations relate to a developmental/learning explanation. A relationship might be observed only over days or weeks, e.g. a drug improves the speed of learning a maze. In either case, in order to assess whether an effect is there, investigators need an experimental condition (e.g. injected with the drug) and a control condition (e.g. injected with a neutral substance) and they compare the two. Only then can they assess whether a causal factor is at work.

We now come to an area of biological psychology that causes controversy in the broader society. For non-human species, particular bits of the brain can be deliberately damaged by targeted surgery and the effects observed. The investigation of brain damage usually involves a form of causal explanation, i.e. what determines behaviour? In each case, investigators need some form of control: how does the damaged brain compare with one that is not damaged?

Consider Figure 1.4. In part (a), an experimenter presents an event (a 'stimulus') to an animal that does not have brain damage and notes what happens. In part (b) the same event is presented to an animal with brain damage and any difference in reaction from (a) is observed. Comparing the reactions in the two cases,

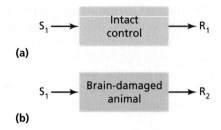

(a)

(b)

Figure 1.4 Testing for the effects of brain damage:
(a) intact control reacts to event S_1 with behaviour R_1;
(b) brain-damaged subject reacts to S_1 with behaviour R_2.

experimenters can try to understand the role of the damaged brain region. Of course, such experimentation raises profound ethical issues, of which psychology is aware.

Human brain damage

In understanding what regions of the human brain do, one source of insight is to look at damaged brains. Brain damage can arise in various ways. Sometimes the brain of a baby is traumatically damaged during birth. In other cases, damage, such as that from traffic accidents and gunshot wounds, happens later in life. Brain surgery on humans often involves removing parts of the brain that are diseased.

The comparison between intact and damaged brains can, at least in principle, be relatively straightforward. Scientists can look at the same human patient before and after surgery and compare behaviour. Of course, for there to have been surgery, there must have been some abnormality in the first place, so this creates problems of interpretation of the evidence. In other cases, rigorous control is impossible.

When the brain damage occurs as an accident of birth or later injury, what do investigators use as a control? They can compare with other matched humans not having brain damage or with any records and memories of the individual prior to the trauma, but this is far from ideal.

Subsequently, other individuals with similar brain damage to the front of the brain have been observed and the evidence tends to match that of Gage (Gazzaley and D'Esposito, 2007). To be precise, brain damage reveals the working of the remainder of the brain, i.e. how it functions without the damaged region. Psychologists need intelligent speculation to get from this to understanding the normal role of the damaged region.

A personal angle

Phineas Gage

Phineas Gage, who is perhaps the most famous case in the history of biological psychology, appears to have been born in 1823 in East Lebanon, New Hampshire. He was a shrewd and well-respected foreman of a gang of railroad workers, blasting rock for the construction of a line in Vermont.

In 1848, as a result of an explosion going wrong, a tamping iron, 3 cm in diameter, passed through his brain, causing extensive damage to the front part on the left and some damage to the right (Damasio, 1996; Macmillan, 1986). It landed some 30 m away. Amazingly, Gage survived the accident and showed relatively little intellectual or linguistic impairment. However, he became more egocentric, obstinate and capricious than before and adopted foul language. This suggests that parts of the brain concerned with emotional expression based on the here-and-now were previously restrained by the damaged regions. Damage lifted the restraint. His doctor wrote: 'The equilibrium or balance, so to speak, between his intellectual faculties and his animal propensities, seems to have been destroyed' (quoted by Macmillan, 1986).

Phineas Gage died in San Francisco in 1861 but his skull was removed from the rest of his body and, together with the tamping iron, put on exhibition in a museum in Massachusetts. Recently, a photo of him surfaced (Wilgus and Wilgus, 2009) (Figure 1.5).

Figure 1.5 Phineas Gage. The image has been laterally reversed to show the features correctly since daguerrotypes are mirror images.
Source: Wilgus and Wilgus, 2009, Figure 1, p. 341. Collection of Jack and Beverly Wilgus.

Such damage can be understood at a biological level and has clear consequences for behaviour. However, the cases call for caution in their interpretation. Accidents do not usually yield 'neat' damage, where investigators can specify exactly which brain region is affected. Neither, of course, do they occur under the control of the experimenter. Typically, they involve individual, often unique, cases. Researchers cannot be confident that they have eliminated all other factors that might have been involved. They do not have a control for Phineas Gage, to see the effect of the passage of time itself, etc. Nonetheless, the insight from such cases has been impressive and fits well into a broader picture. The biological psychologist can point to how the study of the structure and functioning of the brain provides insight into mind and behaviour.

As a second example, consider the patient known as D.B. D.B. had surgery to remove a tumour in a region of brain concerned with processing visual information (described later) and exhibited a phenomenon known as **blindsight** (Weiskrantz, 1976). We are fortunate in his case; D.B. was studied in the 1970s using the methods of biological psychology, in Oxford. Experimenters were able to target visual stimuli precisely; the stimuli were carefully positioned relative to D.B.'s eyes. In this way, D.B.'s reactions could be compared between two conditions: processing that made demands on the damaged part of his brain and other processing that involved only the intact part. That is, D.B. served as his own control. When processing was triggered in the intact regions, D.B. reported seeing things as normal.

In certain positions, the location of the stimuli was such that detecting their presence would apparently require visual processing in the damaged region. At these locations, D.B. denied seeing anything. However, other evidence pointed to a rather subtle conclusion. Without D.B. knowing it, he was extracting information from the visual stimuli that he denied seeing. If the experimenter asked D.B. to *guess* what he saw, D.B. did so better than chance – implying something like 'the stimulus that I simply cannot see is vertical this time'. D.B. knew something but didn't know that he knew it. Such patients are blind to the stimuli as far as conscious awareness is concerned, hence the term 'blindsight'.

Dissociation of this kind, between behaviour and conscious awareness, is important for understanding the role of the brain in consciousness. A brain abnormality has radically changed a psychological system in ways that can be specified. Disturbances (if any) that occur following damage can give important insights into how the brain normally works.

Human neuroimaging techniques

With the help of what are termed 'neuroimaging techniques', investigators can examine the activity of

When we say that a person can 'feel' the suffering of another, does this have any identifiable basis in the brain?
Source: PhotoDisc, Inc.

particular parts of the brain while human participants engage in a specific task. For example, asking a participant to concentrate on a visual display increases the electrical activity within brain regions known from other evidence to be involved in processing visual information.

These techniques have generated immense excitement in biological psychology, with much hope for further insights to come. They have yielded some profound understanding and are even shaping our ideas of what it is to be human. For example, consider an observer watching someone else in pain (the 'observed'). This can activate brain regions in the observer that are active when a person experiences pain directly from a noxious stimulus (Singer *et al.*, 2004). Thus, the notion of human empathy is given biological roots.

Consider also the following experiment. Without knowing what was going on behind the scenes, participants were asked to engage in a game of virtual

Does social exclusion have anything in common with 'real pain'?
Source: courtesy of Bundy Mackintosh.

ball-tossing, while activity of their brains was neuroimaged (Eisenberger *et al.*, 2003). They were then abruptly excluded from the game. Anyone like the present author, who is seriously 'athletically challenged', might have found exclusion to be a merciful escape but this was not so for these participants. Following exclusion, activation was seen in the same brain regions as are activated by physical pain. So, in some real biological sense, social rejection appears to hurt and has an identifiable basis in the brain, surely an important message for society at large.

Can the biological psychologist see what is going on in your mind? In some as-yet limited ways and with the help of neuroimaging, the answer is 'yes'. When a person thinks of a human face, a specific brain region is particularly active. The region that is strongly activated is different from that activated when thinking of, say, a house (O'Craven and Kanwisher, 2000). Neuroimaging of the brain region termed the hippocampus enables researchers to distinguish which of three target memories a participant is recalling in the conscious mind (Chadwick *et al.*, 2010). In future, there could be unpredicted developments of such 'objective mind-reading'.

Putting biological psychology into context

Biological psychology assumes a lawfulness of behaviour, i.e. that behaviour can be understood in terms of some identifiable principles and that the place to look for these is in biological processes. This section shows how this biological approach can be put into a broader context.

The social link

Understanding behaviour can require an input from both biological and social perspectives. Thus, biological factors influence social behaviour and, reciprocally, social behaviour influences biology.

For a non-human example, consider the courtship of a male dove. Observing the male's courtship display alters certain hormone levels of the female. The change in the female's hormonal levels then changes her behaviour. This, in turn, changes the behaviour of the male. Similarly, in **primate** (the group that includes gorillas, chimpanzees and humans) males, levels of the hormone testosterone affect mating and competition. In turn, the outcome of interaction with receptive females and competitive males can influence testosterone level (Rose *et al.*, 1975).

In one study on primates, the drug amphetamine appeared to have no reliable effect on behaviour (Cacioppo and Berntson, 1992). However, that was before the animals' places in the social hierarchy were taken into account. Amphetamine increased the dominance tendencies of primates high in the hierarchy. It increased the submissive tendencies of those low in the hierarchy. No matter how sophisticated the analysis of physiological events, it might have missed the link that became apparent from looking at social context.

In humans, pain is determined in ways that are clearly the business of the biological sciences. There are detectors of tissue damage at the skin and elsewhere, and they signal information to the brain, along pathways of neurons. However, pain can also be influenced by factors such as the nature of the interaction between therapist and patient and the confidence of the patient that this will bring relief (Wall, 1993). Here lies a meeting ground between biological and social approaches.

Human drug addiction depends not only on the chemical properties of drugs taken but also on social context (Alexander, 2008). A person's desire to take drugs arises from physiological factors (e.g. sensitivity of certain brain regions) and external factors (e.g. social context). Studying only one of these factors in isolation would miss the subtle nature of the determinants of addiction.

So, the most effective way of understanding behaviour can be to include a study of social interactions. For example, if we were not to consider these, we might be puzzled why hormone levels seem to be going up and down in a random way. Similarly, we might conclude that amphetamine has no reliable effect on dominance–submissive behaviour.

When correctly applied, a biological perspective can help to end fruitless and irrational debates of the kind: 'What is the most important factor determining behaviour? Is it biology or sociocultural context?' (Gilbert, 1998). Both need to be considered, together with their links.

The cognitive link

Within cognitive psychology, some influential theories of how the mind processes information are based on knowledge of the brain. For example, Rumelhart and Norman (1989, p. 17) suggest that it might: '. . . become a necessary exercise for those proposing particular memory representations to provide at least an argument to show that the brain could encode information in the way required by the theory'.

Similarly, suppose that psychologists generate a theory of how visual perception occurs. This needs to be compatible with biological understanding of the visual system (Zeki, 1993). A psychological theory that seems to require structures that do not exist in the real visual system, as described by physiologists, would be suspect. Several psychological theories might equally well account for the psychological data, so how does one choose between them? A theory might be favoured to the extent that it is compatible with biological understanding (Cacioppo and Berntson, 1992).

A concern in cognitive psychology is whether there are several systems of memory and, if so, how they differ (Schacter and Tulving, 1994a). Brain damage sometimes disrupts one class of memory while leaving another intact. This is evidence in favour of distinct classes of memory.

Evolutionary and functional explanations are also brought into the discussion of biology and cognition. For example, emotion has been considered in these terms. It used to be suggested that emotion is a hindrance rather than a help to sophisticated modern humans. The argument was that emotions might have served a useful function in our distant evolutionary past but we have now outlived this. Living in large urban centres, we have become creatures dependent on pure cool thought and rationality. Biological approaches have illustrated why such dichotomies between emotion and rationality are false. People with damage to brain regions involved in linking cognition and emotion have been found to make disastrous social decisions (Damasio, 1999). Rather, a contemporary position is that emotions are an integral part of our decision-making. We are somewhat protected from running serious risks because the mere prospect of doing so triggers negative emotion and this restrains us.

Having introduced the basics of the study of the immediate determinants of behaviour, the following section looks more closely at the way of thinking of biological psychologists.

Section summary

1 To infer a causal link, controlled experimentation is needed. Interventions into the biology of the body are made and the consequences observed.

2 Insight into behaviour can be obtained from studying individuals with brain damage.

3 Neuroimaging of human brains reveals which regions change their activity during specific tasks.

4 Understanding can be provided by considering biology in the context of social interaction.

5 For a suggested cognitive process to be viable, it needs to be compatible with biological understanding.

☞ Test your knowledge

1.3 What might it mean to say that the blindsight patient (D.B.) could 'act as his own control' in the study of vision and consciousness?

 Answer on page 19

The way of thinking of biological psychologists

The foundations

The biological psychologist tends to be a **determinist,** reflecting the belief that he or she can identify physical causes for behaviour. The faith of biological psychology is that events within the nervous system cause behaviour and the task is to identify and characterize these causes.

The biological psychologist has some justification for a faith in **determinism** (for every event there can, in principle, be identified a cause). For example, there is evidence for the effects of accidental brain damage. Also, under some conditions, the researcher can take an experimental subject, e.g. rat, and determine its immediate behaviour. The rat can be injected with, say, a thirst-inducing drug and a prediction made: the animal will drink or learn to navigate a maze to obtain water.

Insight can be gained at this level of analysis and some biological psychologists might see no limits on how far this approach can be taken. However, I shall suggest that biological factors need to be *interpreted* within a context of rather subtle psychological principles.

A two-way street

In two closely related respects, the link between biology (brain) and psychology (behaviour) is a 'two-way street' (Figure 1.6). The brain controls behaviour. In turn, behaviour (e.g. social contact) influences events within the brain (part (a)). Also, there is the relationship between biologists of the brain (e.g. neuroscientists) and psychologists (part (b)). Psychologists need to look to the biological level to seek brain mechanisms that explain mind and behaviour. However, researchers concerned with the brain can get insight into its working by looking to psychology. Knowing what the brain is doing at a psychological level can give vital insight into how it does it and the

Figure 1.6 Links between levels of (a) the phenomena of behaviour and brain and (b) the disciplines studying them. The psychological level is shown above the physiological, since, as we go up, we get to a larger scale.

kind of brain structures involved. Thus, there is a regular exchange of information between biology and psychology.

A good example to illustrate the interdependence of biology and psychology is the **immune system** (Michel and Moore, 1995). This system consists of specialized cells, and it comes to the rescue when the body is invaded by bacteria or a virus, or cells become cancerous. So, it is clearly the business of the biological sciences. However, in the latter part of the 20th century, psychologists gave scientific respectability to what had been believed by folk wisdom for centuries: mood states can affect the disease vulnerability of the body (Ader and Cohen, 1985). Stress can lower the activity of the cells of the immune system that are recruited to fight invasion. The basic science of immunology had to assimilate a fundamental change: psychological events affect the immune system.

Reductionism

The term **reductionism** refers to a process of trying to explain events at one level (e.g. mind and behaviour) by looking at a different level (e.g. the activity of the cells of the brain). Biological psychologists make use of this principle (Figure 1.6(b)). Indeed, the notion of *biological psychology* implies some kind of reduction to biology. For example, insight into the cause and possible cure of the movement and mood disorder Parkinson's disease has been obtained from reducing to the biological level. The disease is caused by the malfunction and death of certain neurons in a particular part of the brain. However, the disease cannot be understood *simply* in terms of the diseased cells. The whole brain needs to be considered in understanding why, for example, patients show a tremor of the hands and have difficulty in walking. The environment needs consideration in terms of the demands placed on the patient. So, we shall see where insight can be gained at a biological level but will need to put this information into a *psychological* context, as described in the next section.

Emergent properties

Properties are said to *emerge* at different levels, e.g. there are **emergent properties** at the psychological level. Phenomena (in terms of mind and behaviour) appear and these cannot be understood simply by considering the components of the brain in isolation. These psychological properties depend upon the parts that make up the brain but cannot be understood by *simply reducing* the explanation to their sum.

An **analogy** can illustrate what 'emergent property' means. An analogy is an attempt to explain something that we don't understand in terms of a suggested similarity with (*an analogy with*) something that we do. For example, consider two *gases*, oxygen and hydrogen, observed at room temperature. They each exhibit familiar general properties characteristic of gases and also some peculiar properties. When these two gases come together and combine, their combination gives us water. Water exhibits a new ('emergent') property that was not evident in a study of either gas on its own: it is *liquid*. It flows downhill, among other things.

We cannot take the property of oxygen, simply add it to that of hydrogen, and thereby hope to understand the properties of water. However, the property of the water, though said to be at a different level, i.e. at that of the combination, *depends upon* the properties of each gas. The peculiar properties of the component gases are necessary to give the combined effect. Take away the gases and the liquid vanishes. So, we need to understand the bits that make up the whole *and* how the bits act together.

If emergent properties are evident in something as simple as this, imagine how rich are the possibilities for unexpected psychological phenomena to emerge when billions of neurons combine in forming a brain. For example, biological psychologists assume that the conscious mind (discussed in a moment) emerges in this way from the properties of billions of neurons in combination, though none can explain how!

For another example, psychologists can now associate disorders such as schizophrenia with disturbances in identifiable brain regions and the chemicals located there. However, we should not try to reduce the study of schizophrenia to *simply* these regions and chemicals. Rather, we need to see how the psychological phenomena of schizophrenia, such as apathy and hallucinations, emerge from a whole brain that contains such local disturbances.

Why biological psychology is so important to us

Linking biology and psychology is not just words of lofty academic discussion. (Not that you would ever have suspected that!) Rather, it is of fundamental practical significance to how we lead our lives, organize society and make decisions about human welfare.

Mental illness

Imagine that a patient who is suffering depression goes to his or her doctor. The doctor prescribes the drug Prozac, which has known chemical effects on particular neurons in specific parts of the brain. After a few weeks, the patient, mercifully, returns much better and the Prozac is assumed to have taken its effect.

There are at least three levels of description here: (i) the biology of the drug's action, (ii) the patient's observable reactions in terms of body and behaviour and (iii) the patient's reported subjective conscious experience. The last of these is described in such terms as fears, feelings and hopes. It would be foolish to suggest that any one of the three is the most important. It would be equally foolish to try simply to substitute biological terms for the patient's subjective account. In trying to understand phenomena such as depression, no source of insight can be ignored or written out of the script.

Just imagine telling someone with depression, 'it is only your neurons that are not acting right, so there's nothing else wrong with you'. Only a poor therapist would understand merely the biological level without a corresponding familiarity with the way patients describe their feelings. The skill of biological psychology comes in relating these corresponding levels of discussion. That is to say, psychologists try to understand *how*, by their action on neurons in the brain, drugs change the patient's mental state. Some therapies favour use of biological means as in Prozac and others go for 'talking cures'. Some combine both, in which case we need insight into how these approaches might interact.

So, *in addition* to the psychological approach there is also a place for the biological approach in understanding behaviour (Bolton and Hill, 1996). The types of description are not in competition for explanation. Rather, as the analogy to gases and water illustrates, they refer to different aspects of the same system.

Social policy

Violence is a major social problem. Discussions of its causes can be informed by biological psychology. Psychologists have long held that aggression depends upon (i) such biological things as genes and levels of particular hormones and (ii) such 'non-biological' factors as peer pressure, role modelling of aggressive others, etc. The argument is often given as the need 'to understand aggression in terms of the *mix* between biological and social factors'. However, genes, hormones and social factors do not just mix as if they were parts of a fruit salad. Rather, there are complex rules of organization involved in linking them.

Aggression might be explained in part by an appeal to cognitive and social factors, in terms of self-esteem, expectation and frustration. The nature of such cognitive processing depends, among other things, on levels of particular hormones that affect activity of neurons in the brain (McAndrew, 2009). By their action on neurons, some hormones (e.g. testosterone) appear to tilt thinking and behaviour towards dominance seeking and conflict.

Personal responsibility

In law, there exists the notion of responsibility versus diminished responsibility. One way of pleading diminished responsibility is to suggest that the accused has a brain abnormality. In Britain, when capital punishment was used, such evidence could save the accused person's life. Evidence of abnormal brain activity could take the form of a brain tumour or an abnormal pattern of electrical activity. Pleas of diminished responsibility have been made on the basis of an abnormal level of one of the brain's natural chemical messengers (Fenwick, 1993).

What exactly is such a claim saying? It might be as follows. We are normally guided in our behaviour by conscious goals, for which we are responsible. We monitor our behaviour as we move towards these goals. However, there can be a malfunction as a result of, say, a tumour. A person might set socially inappropriate goals (MacKay, 1974) or act abnormally strongly on impulse and against the goal. A biological disturbance distorts the control of behaviour. Under these conditions, such people might be judged to be sick and their behaviour outside their control. Where behavioural malfunction, e.g. violence, occurs without evidence of biological abnormality, we might assume that the person is responsible for setting their own goals. The person might, to adopt a cliché, be said to be 'bad rather than mad'.

So, do we appeal to a biological level when things go wrong but are happy to accept that the normal principles of psychology (i.e. those of the 'person in the street') apply when everything works well? This is one possible approach (Bolton and Hill, 1996) and it more or less corresponds to law and folk psychology. However, this raises philosophical dilemmas and more questions than it answers. There is always the possibility that such an argument can be informed by further discoveries in biological psychology.

The following section will turn to the role of genes, development and learning.

Section summary

1 Biological psychology takes a deterministic approach, which assumes that behaviour is determined by events in the nervous system.

2 We shall seek insight by looking to biology but interpret what we find in psychological terms.

3 The expression 'emergent property' refers to new properties that emerge at increasing levels of complexity.

☞ Test your knowledge

1.4 Complete the following: 'In explaining consciousness, the _____ could be described as emergent property of _____'

Answer on page 19

Genes, development and learning

Genes

In bringing together the four types of explanation described earlier, genes play an important role. Genes form a component of the cells throughout our bodies, including neurons (Figure 1.7). Lay logic has something to say about the role of genes too: 'It's all in the genes' and 'Criminals are born that way, not made' are expressions occasionally heard. Such claims have a strong feel of determinism, suggesting that the gene sets a course of action and the individual is a slave to this. They reflect implicit theories about the role of genes and suggest that phenomena at a behavioural and psychological level can be *simply reduced* to a small part of the biology.

Biological psychology suggests the more modest claim that genes play *a role* in determining behaviour. However, they do this in conjunction with many other factors that interlock with them in complex ways. By understanding something about genes at a biological level, the psychologist can formulate more precise questions about the control of behaviour. Thus, we can rule out certain ideas, e.g. that genes can be either more or less important than the environment in determining behaviour.

Genes trigger the production of chemical structures called **proteins** that are constituents of cells.

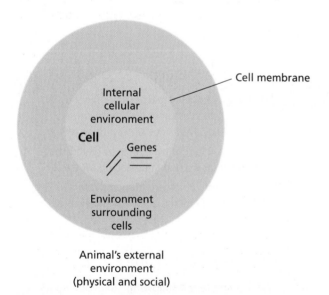

Figure 1.7 Genes within cells. Note the cellular environment surrounding the genes and the environment surrounding the cells and the whole animal. For simplicity just one cell is shown.

Figure 1.8 Behaviour is both caused by the nervous system and affects the nervous system. One site of this effect is where the genes affect nervous system structure.

These proteins form body structures and interact with their immediate environment in the cells of the body. Nervous systems, like other systems, are structures that are determined in part by genes. So, one link is (genes) → (nervous system) → (behaviour). However, life is more complex than this since behaviour tends to influence the structure of the developing body (Figure 1.8). Already, subtle complexity appears. This cautions against a simple causal link, such as 'it's all in the genes'. We will look to the biological properties of genes but will interpret them in the context of a psychological account.

Developmental/learning explanations

The process of change that starts at conception and continues until maturity is known as 'development', also termed **ontogeny**. This refers to the history of the development and growth of the individual and relates most obviously to the developmental/learning type of explanation.

The structure of the body changes as a result of the interdependence between genes and their environment. By 'environment' is meant both the internal environment of the body that surrounds the genes and the environment that surrounds the whole animal. Nervous systems grow and change as a result of protein synthesis. New connections between neurons are formed and some established connections get broken. As the nervous system changes, so behaviour changes. New possibilities for behaviour emerge, while some behaviour drops out of the animal's repertoire.

Within this type of explanation, learning represents a process of change but was traditionally discussed as something distinct from development. Alas, it is not easy to define the nature of this distinction, a topic discussed in Chapter 6. Hence, there is the caution of the compound term 'developmental/learning'.

The next section considers trying to understand the behaviour of one species by studying that of another.

Section summary

1 Genes are a factor that helps to determine the structure of the body including the nervous system.

2 Behaviour cannot be 'all in the genes'.

3 Development refers to changes that are a function of age.

 Test your knowledge

1.5 Why would it be over-simple to claim that genes *cause* behaviour?.

Answer on page 19

The comparative approach: psychology and ethology

Animal models, evolution and comparative studies

The **comparative approach** consists of comparing different species to gain insight into how each adapts to its habitat and how this is reflected in differences in behaviour. The example of taste-aversion learning introduced this topic earlier.

In this book, the comparative approach is used mostly for trying to understand humans. Psychologists look at so-called simpler species to gain understanding of more complex species. The term **animal model** is used to refer to the simpler animal as a model that captures features of the more complex animal.

With some basic processes and components, the same solution employed by so-called simple animals is also seen in the more complex. Evolution is described as being 'conservative' (Epstein, 1982). For example, there are striking similarities in how neurons operate and communicate among species. By dissecting large neurons from such species as squid, the knowledge gained can be applied to other species, including humans. However, evolution could also be described as 'inventive' in finding new solutions. Thus, there are limitations on how far one can push the process of appealing to simpler animal models. Although the components have striking common features, their combination can take on properties that mean animal models have a limited value.

Certain species show exceptional abilities. A study of their brains in comparison to species not showing the exceptional ability can give insight into how this ability is linked to the brain. For example, some bird species show an incredible ability at hoarding food in a multitude of different locations and remembering where (Clayton and Dickinson, 1998). Other, closely related, birds do not have this ability. So, a comparison of their brains can guide us in searching for the brain regions that underlie the exceptional spatial and memory skills.

A personal angle

A lunch-break worth remembering by all

The psychology department at the University of California at Davis is associated with some rather peculiar cognitive skills but is also known for theft, cunning and deception. I hasten to add that I am not describing the academic staff but rather some winged visitors.

During their lunch-break, wife and husband team Nicola Clayton and Nathan Emory (both now at the University of Cambridge) observed the behaviour of Western scrub-jays, who were taking morsels of food left by students. The birds would bury some of the food for later consumption (termed caching). However, occasionally, other birds were witness to this and, after the competitor left the

scene, the first bird would dig up the morsel and bury it in a different place. Controlled laboratory studies, done later at Cambridge, confirmed that this behaviour is characteristic of the species.

The study points to the value of looking at special abilities possessed by particular species. It also shows what can be gained by observing behaviour under natural conditions – well, maybe more precisely, 'semi-natural', in the case of a university campus. The research suggests sophisticated cognition that involves the anticipated likely moves of a competitor. It prompts the search for special underlying processes in the brains of such species.

This Western scrub-jay is recovering food it has buried. What special talent does it reveal?

Source: courtesy of Ian Cannell and Nicky Clayton.

Ethology and psychology

Ethology, a branch of zoology, involves a particular approach to the study of animal behaviour. Whereas psychologists have traditionally focused on a few species, mainly humans, rats and pigeons, ethologists have looked at a wider range. Ethologists place weight upon functional and evolutionary explanations. They have also emphasized looking at animals within their natural environment. The rationale is that, if we wish to understand how animals solve problems by their behaviour, it is necessary to consider them in relation to the environment in which they evolved.

The approach to doing research has been somewhat different between ethologists and psychologists. Traditionally, psychologists have looked at animals in a more restricted laboratory environment, such as a small cage or **Skinner box** (an apparatus in which an animal presses a lever or pecks a key and earns a reward, e.g. a pellet of food). Psychologists put their animals in a box and looked in at them, whereas ethologists put themselves in a box and looked out at the animals.

There is now a welcome breakdown in the divisional boundary between these two sciences. Psychologists are showing an increasing willingness to relate their findings to the species' natural environment (Bolles, 1970; Garcia, 1989). Indeed, a number of psychologists have become very fired by ideas of evolution, discussed in the next chapter.

We now pick up again the issue of brains and minds and it will be shown where evolutionary thinking is relevant.

Section summary

1 Ethologists study a range of species in their natural environments and thereby suggest how behaviour has served a function in evolution.

2 Psychologists have traditionally focused on a few species, mainly rats, pigeons and humans.

3 There is now a coming together of ethology and psychology.

☞ Test your knowledge

1.6 How can some components that are very similar across species yield brains with very different properties?

Answer on page 19

Linking brains and minds

Introduction

How do brain and mind relate? If only I knew! Biological psychology has much to contribute regarding how brains and minds *might* relate and even more on how they probably do not relate but there are no comprehensive explanations. It is sometimes said that 'the mind is what the brain does' or 'the mind is the brain in action'. How would we try to assess the value of these statements? We will consider an analogy that might help.

Is the brain a computer?

A popular and persuasive analogy to brain and mind is with modern computers, though there is debate on the extent to which even this analogy is appropriate (Dennett, 1993; Penrose, 1987). However, the brain does not need to be exactly like a computer for the analogy to be useful. Indeed, if two systems were identical, the word 'analogy' would be misleading. Where an analogy breaks down can be insightful, by highlighting badly understood or unique characteristics of the system under study.

The computer might provide a useful analogy in terms of the distinction between hardware, its physical structure, and software, the program that is run on it. As a first approximation, the hardware is analogous to the structure of the brain, as composed of neurons. The software is analogous to the mind and the cognitive operations that are performed by the brain, i.e. 'what the brain does'. The hardware and software each has its own principles and organization appropriate at each level. As part of the analogy, the hardware is also of interest in that it sets certain possibilities for the software operations and limits to what can be run.

Brains and computers each show phenomenal but different abilities. My simple computer humiliates me every time in terms of speed and the ability to spot spelling mistakes but, casting modesty aside, I believe that I am more original and creative. You might not find an analogy with a computer particularly flattering. Why not? There seems to be something essentially human that is missing from a computer. You might swear at your computer when it loses a file or crashes but surely you do not feel sympathy or guilt towards it afterwards (or do you?!). Computers seem cold and mechanical in a way that a person or a cat just isn't. So, let us try first a more homespun approach and this will lead us to a crucial aspect of mind – its consciousness.

The conscious mind

Introduction

Throughout history, philosophers have been concerned with the relationship between the mind and the physical body. These days, this concern is framed in terms of the *conscious* mind. Unconscious activity seems slightly similar to what computers do, but the peculiar property of consciousness is very problematic for attempts to explain the mind. For example, psychologists speculate about when consciousness first emerged in evolution – what sort of brain is necessary to support consciousness? Another question is, what functional advantage does consciousness confer?

Self-reflection

The issue can perhaps best be illustrated by your reflecting upon your own conscious mind and body. This might lead you to suggest two different types of phenomena. First, consider your conscious mind. I assume that you experience a private conscious world of thoughts that are peculiarly *yours*. This is only my assumption since I do not know for sure that you experience this, or anything else for that matter. However, it would seem a reasonable assumption, since I know that I experience it. I would be narcissistic and arrogant to think that only I do so.

Suppose that your conscious mind is now occupied with thoughts about the biological psychology of your brain and mind. The thoughts might be firmly focused on this topic or, of course, they might not be! However, you have the ability to switch these thoughts to something else, idiosyncratic and far removed from this topic. You might be wondering whether you will shortly go to make a coffee or not, or you might be thinking about some other subject known only to you. Go on – try switching your thoughts. This is a private world of your own and I have very little, if any, access to it except by means of what you might choose to tell me (though, as was noted, brain neuroimaging can give some insights). We might like to call it the 'software' but does this term really capture its essence? There is a raw subjective feel to this existence, that peculiar feel of *what it is like* to be you, a conscious human (Nagel, 1974).

Now consider a different set of phenomena, those associated with the objective description of your brain. This seems like hardware, comprising billions of neurons, i.e. structures, in turn made up from chemical components. Communication between neurons is by means of other specialized chemicals. Looking at the chemicals that make up the neurons and the messengers between them, investigators see nothing very special about their structure. These chemicals seem to have no properties that set them aside as peculiar to the world of biological psychology, let alone the mental world. In principle, any scientist with the right equipment can observe this world of physics and chemistry.

The fundamental question of 'mind–brain', or to be more precise 'conscious mind–brain', concerns the nature of the relationship between these two domains, the one private, with privileged access by you, and the other public, with privileged access by a scientist. There are various theories on this relationship, one of which is considered next.

Identity theory

These days, among neuroscientists and psychologists, the most popular model of the mind–brain relationship is a variety of **identity theory** (Gray, 1987b). Identity theory suggests that for every mental event there is a corresponding brain event. According to identity theory, a mental event cannot have an existence distinct from a corresponding brain event. The languages describing brain and mind are said to be two different ways of talking about the *same underlying reality*. For example, I might use the alternative levels of description that 'I feel depressed' or 'There are abnormal levels within a cocktail of different chemicals in part of my brain'. One uses mental language and the other brain language but, to an identity theorist, they refer to the same reality. The depression could not exist without the abnormal chemical states. The two descriptions are obviously appropriate for different contexts of discussion.

For an analogy, it is a bit like French and English. The language chosen is appropriate to the context. One could use English and refer to 'the table' or French and refer to '*la table*' but there is only the one table that is being described. Using this analogy, the puzzle comes in trying to establish the rules of translation between the two languages.

A final thought

These days, philosophers, psychologists and neuro-scientists (not to forget defence lawyers and priests) still passionately debate the nature of the relationship between brain and conscious mind. Although it is important to have some understanding of this, mercifully trying to solve it need not concern us too much. Rather, we need merely to keep it in focus and be aware of what we are claiming and the implications of muddled thinking. Remember the depressed patient at the doctor's surgery. According to the favoured contemporary model, the patient's problem is not '*all* in the mind' or '*all* in the body' but in both simultaneously.

Section summary

1 The relationship between mental and brain events is a hotly discussed issue.

2 A possible analogy for understanding brain and mind is that the brain is like a computer and the mind is like the software program.

3 The *conscious* aspect of mind creates particular problems in seeking an explanation.

4 A modern view tends to favour identity theory, i.e. that languages describing brain and mind are different ways of referring to the one underlying reality.

☞ Test your knowledge

1.7 According to identity theory, can something be 'all in the mind'?

Answer on page 19

Bringing things together

The present chapter emphasizes the value of applying different types of explanation to a given behaviour or mental event. Different insights can be mutually supportive. Subsequent chapters will build on the four types of explanation introduced here, i.e. causal, developmental/learning, evolutionary and functional, and will show their interdependence. Another message is the importance of taking the middle ground between the extremes of either regarding biology as the answer to everything or rejecting biological explanation. It will be argued that biology is of fundamental importance for understanding behaviour and mind. However, wholesale reduction of psychology to biology, in effect writing psychology out of the script, will not be attempted.

Everything in the introduction will be used in the subsequent chapters. However, it is worth particularly highlighting two topics:

1 The next chapter will return to the four different types of explanation introduced here. It is only by applying these to examples of behaviour that you can appreciate their full significance.

2 I hope that the difficult issue of the relationship between the conscious mind and the brain will have fired your curiosity, rather than intimidating you. All of us find it hard to get our minds (!) around this issue. It will be discussed in much greater detail in Chapter 21, 'Brains, minds and consciousness'. For the moment, try not to lose sleep over it.

 See the video coverage for this chapter which shows how behavioural scientists do research.

Summary of Chapter 1

1 There are different kinds of explanation: causal, developmental/learning, evolutionary and functional. Our principal concern is with the causal kind, which links events in the brain to behaviour and mind.

2 Physiology is concerned with how the body works in terms of its organs and cells among other things. Our main interest is with an organ, the brain, and a type of cell called a neuron.

3 Biological psychologists draw evidence from (i) experimental intervention, (ii) looking at the effects of damage to human brains and (iii) neuroimaging the activity of brains while people perform tasks.

4 The link between biology and psychology is a 'two-way street' with information and insight exchanged in each direction.

5 We develop and learn. Behaviour changes correspondingly.

6 Investigators can get insight by studying how different species adapt to their different environments.

7 An unsolved problem is how the brain and the conscious mind relate. The favoured explanation is identity theory.

Further reading

For general considerations of the links between biology and psychology, see Workman and Reader (2008). For the interdependence of the brain and its social environment: Blakemore and Frith (2005). For culture and evolution: Richerson (2006). For ethology: Dawkins (2007) and Eibl-Eibesfeldt (2007). For the mind and consciousness: Warren (2007) and Weaver (2010).

Answers

Explanations for answers to 'test your knowledge' questions can be found on the website www.pearsoned.co.uk/toates

1.1 (i) Causal; (ii) functional
1.2 Deviations from optimum in body fluid level triggers action (e.g. drinking) that tends to correct the deviation.

1.3 Visual stimuli could be located in parts of his visual world corresponding to damaged and intact parts of the brain and his conscious perception compared under these two conditions.
1.4 mind; brain
1.5 Genes code for proteins including those that form the nervous system. They are only one factor influencing the form that the nervous system will ultimately take. Therefore the link to behaviour is not direct.
1.6 Complex properties *emerge* as a result of the way that components are assembled.
1.7 No – anything in the mind is also simultaneously encoded in the body, to be precise the brain.

Visit www.pearsoned.co.uk/toates
for a range of resources to support study.
Test yourself with multiple choice questions and access a bank of over 100 videos that will bring the topics to life.

Chapter 2
Genes, environment and evolution

Learning outcomes for Chapter 2

After studying this chapter, you should be able to:

1 Understand how genes and environment influence behaviour and relate this to evolution.

2 Give an example of the principle that, in functional terms, any behaviour is associated with costs and benefits.

3 In causal terms, describe some processes that underlie behaviour (e.g. reflexes, rhythms and motivation). Relate these to their functional significance.

4 Outline the basic principles of genetics and define 'gene' and 'allele'. Describe the role of genes, both within an individual and between generations.

5 Explain the link between genes and behaviour.

6 Describe the dynamic interaction between genes and environment and the subtlety of this interdependence as far as behaviour is concerned. Explain why dichotomies of the kind 'which is most important – genes *or* environment?' are misleading.

7 Give the basics of evolutionary psychology in an informed and critical way. Explain why it stirs passion.

8 Using depression as an example, illustrate how the different types of explanation can be brought to a given phenomenon.

Scene-setting questions

1 Is nature basically selfish?
2 The popular image suggests that 'expectant fathers' pace up and down. What is the biological basis for this?
3 Why is there a liking for sweet tastes even in an epidemic of obesity?
4 Why do we reproduce sexually when the cost is so great and some species do not do so?
5 Why do we tend not to be sexually attracted to close relatives?
6 Can there really be a 'gene for' adultery or religious worship?
7 Why does natural selection not eliminate such apparently harmful features as depression?
8 What does the term biopsychosocial perspective mean in terms of understanding and treating mental distress?

What does the term biopsychosocial perspective mean in terms of understanding and treating mental distress? Explore the video on the website accompanying this book at **www. pearsoned.co.uk/toates**

Birmingham City University - High Demand
Collection and Reservations
Self Service Receipt for items borrowed

Title: Biopsychology
Item: 6135344903
Due: 12/Mar/2015 14:40

Title: Biological psychology
Item: 6135349344
Due: 12/Mar/2015 14:40

Total items: 2
12/03/2015 10:41

Please allow time to return your books to avoid
fines. Fines are charged on items returned late.

VAT No: 614117673

Jealousy appears to have existed at all times and places. Is this evidence for a specially evolved brain process that underlies the characteristic?

Source: Victoria & Albert Museum, London, UK/Bridgeman Art Library.

Introduction

Consider how you got to where you are today. Your parents' initial contribution was a single fertilized cell, which was the start of you. Each parent contributed genes to this cell. Those genes were the product of a process of evolution spanning back millions of years. Within the environment of early evolution, some ancestor genes were obviously successful in that you are here today. The nervous system that you possess and the behaviour that you show are the outcome of this evolutionary process.

So, genes, environment and evolution are closely related and can best be considered together. To do this, the chapter will call upon the four types of explanation introduced in the last chapter: causal, developmental/learning, evolutionary and functional. Brains and behaviour will, of course, never be far from the discussion. Genes and environment influence the form that brains take and, thereby, we can understand better how brains control behaviour.

Human evolution has not always been a smooth ride. Sexual reproduction brings many problems (e.g. jealousy, abandonment) and these also need to be understood in the context of genes, environment and evolution.

Figure 2.1 shows some means by which behaviour can contribute to passing on genes. Aggression, fear, feeding, drinking and temperature regulation maintain the integrity, stability and survival of the body, so that the animal (human or other) is around to pass on genes. Feeding, drinking and temperature regulation are associated with the homeostasis of the body (Chapter 1). Sexual behaviour contributes to the continuation of genes by means of reproduction. Offspring share genes with parents and so caring for young helps to ensure that the offspring reach maturity and are themselves able to breed, and so on. The diagram should not be interpreted as if the individual *wants* its genes to be passed on to future generations or consciously strives to do so. It is simply that the genes of an animal (human or other) can be passed on only if the animal engages in a range of such behaviours, each finely tuned to conditions inside and outside the body.

All members of a given species are genetically similar but are, of course, not identical. A 'lion is a lion' and has 'lion genes' but within the species there are genetic differences. That is to say, a particular gene comes in different varieties or 'variants' when comparing individuals. Some variants are more successful than others. Those variants of genes that coded for successful strategies were perpetuated and their products represent successful animals that are here today (e.g. you and me!). Those that coded for less successful strategies tended to find themselves more often in such places as predators' stomachs. In this way, there is *selection* for those variants of genes that code best for their own transmission. In other words, evolution is said to occur through the process termed **natural selection** (Darwin, 1874/1974).

The next section looks in more detail at the principles of evolution and natural selection.

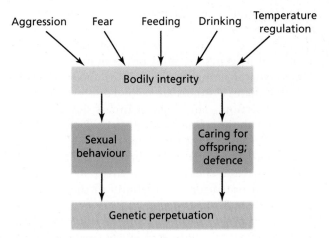

Figure 2.1 Means by which behaviour can increase the chances of genetic perpetuation.

Section summary

1 Some behaviours contribute to passing on genes by helping to maintain the stability and integrity of the body (e.g. temperature regulation), whereas sexual behaviour contributes through reproduction.

2 Evolution is based upon 'natural selection' for variants of genes that code best for their own perpetuation.

 Test your knowledge

2.1 **(i)** In Figure 2.1, which of the behaviours contributes directly to physiological homeostasis? **(ii)** What is the link between homeostasis and passing on genes?

Answer on page 48

Principles of evolution

This section further develops the basis of the evolutionary and functional types of explanation.

Functional explanation, fitness and natural selection

In the present context, 'function' is used (in the ethological sense) in terms of reproductive success. The term **fitness** refers to the potential of an animal to reproduce successfully. Fitness is a measure of the animal's ability to pass on its genes, in terms of the number of viable reproducing offspring that arise. Thus, types of behaviour that increase fitness are favoured in evolution by natural selection. (This sense of fitness should not be confused with the reference simply to bodily health.)

Closely related to the functional level of explanation is the notion of **adaptation** (Chapter 1). A physical feature or behaviour is *adapted to* an environment in that it has been tested for its suitability to that environment. Those individuals that provide the best fit survive and pass on genes. However, there are some complications to this account (Buss *et al.*, 1998; Gould and Vrba, 1982), as follows.

A trait ('characteristic') that evolved by means of natural selection might no longer serve a useful function

in the present environment. A good example of this is our excessive liking for sweet substances, which is associated with contemporary obesity (Power and Schulkin, 2009). It is assumed that, in an early environment, our ancestors were more physically active and an attraction to rare ripe fruits would have been of enormous adaptive value. They provide energy in an environment where the supply of food is uncertain. However, we now have a relatively inactive lifestyle and an abundance of refined sweet items alongside the supermarket checkout, and so the same characteristic leads us into dangerous temptation.

Also, something might now be observed to serve a useful function but it evolved in the service of some different function. Noses and ears did not evolve because of their advantage as mechanical supports to those who wear spectacles! A capacity to read and write is doubtless advantageous in our society and there are identifiable brain mechanisms that underlie it. However, seen in evolutionary time, a written language and reading emerged recently. Reading and writing attach themselves to brain mechanisms that evolved much earlier than the appearance of written language. The combination of reading/writing and its biological bases has not had time yet to be tested by natural selection.

Of course, we do not have access to the environment of an animal's ancestors. Life on Earth has been around for a very long time! However, psychologists have insight based on extrapolation from the present (Tooby and Cosmides, 1990). They can be certain that (except in, say, the depths of the ocean) the environment was illuminated in an approximately 24 hour cycle of light–dark. They know about the magnitude of gravity that birds had to overcome in flying and the saltiness of seawater. Our species was probably subject to parasites. Psychologists can try to interpret the pressures for survival of present species' ancestors in terms of what they know about constant features of the environment and then speculate about different and past environments.

What can we expect adaptation to achieve? Suppose that an animal detects a predator and, predictably, responds by fleeing rather than carrying on with what it was doing. It gets ambushed by an unseen fellow 'gang-member' predator and is then eaten by both predators. This might not seem beneficial to the fleeing animal's reproductive success! Natural selection cannot arrive at the perfect solution. It cannot account for *every* instance of behaviour but can merely favour certain ranges of options (Tooby and Cosmides, 1990). Of course, animals cannot inherit genes that tell them what to do under *every different circumstance encountered*. Rather, genes help to organize nervous systems that have certain general tendencies. Scientists assume that, in the ancestral history of the animal just described, a nervous system that played a role in the reaction of fleeing was of *overall advantage*, compared, say, with carrying on regardless. The strategy worked more often than it failed.

A principle of ethology (the study of the behaviour of animals under natural conditions) is that no behaviour can bring pure gain. There is a mixture of costs and benefits involved in anything that an animal does, as is argued next.

Costs and benefits

The principle can be illustrated as follows. When a jungle fowl is incubating eggs, it loses weight by staying on its nest and not eating (Hogan, 1980). How could this increase its fitness? Suppose that the mother leaves the eggs to obtain food. This increases the chances of the eggs cooling or being eaten by predators. Thus, in terms of the chances of passing on genes, there is a potential **cost** attached to leaving the eggs. There is also a potential **benefit** of doing so, i.e. to gain food and hence replenish reserves and strengthen the body. However, it appears that over evolutionary history, the cost of leaving the eggs has outweighed the benefit, and so there is a *net advantage* in staying. Investigators assume that the ancestors of jungle fowl were confronted with the problem of predation and cooling of eggs. Genes that coded for staying were placed at an advantage. However, rather as with fleeing and getting captured, evolution cannot guarantee that sitting on eggs will work in every instance. Both the sitting bird and its eggs might get eaten at the same time. It is merely that a strategy of staying has, over countless

This fowl lets its weight fall as it incubates eggs. What are the costs and benefits associated with this behaviour?

generations, been more successful than not, relative to the alternative of regularly leaving the nest. The example illustrates a number of issues associated with relating causation and function:

1 In terms of homeostasis, it is not to the female's *individual* bodily advantage to stay on the eggs. Individual survival of her body might be best served by leaving them, to obtain food. However, the chances of passing on her genes are increased by incubation. She might have several eggs, each containing copies of her genes.

2 We should not suppose that the jungle fowl has knowledge in terms of function, i.e. she has no conscious intention to pass on genes (or even unconscious intention!). She just acts in such a way that this is achieved. Among her ancestors, jungle fowl that behaved in this way have been successful and their descendants are around today. Their genes have been favoured by natural selection. A gene coding for 'not incubating' has tended to perish.

3 Related to 2, in asking *how* behaviour is organized, we should not confuse causal and functional explanations. Claims that the bird acts this way because she *needs* to reproduce are misleading and can lead to the implicit assumption that she has conscious intentions. Birds do not read Darwin!

On a causal level, in the brain there is an inhibitory link from incubation to feeding. Natural selection will favour such a mechanism for restraining feeding.

4 It is often argued that natural selection acts on *individuals* via their genes rather than species as a whole, i.e. it acts to the relative advantage or disadvantage of passing on the genes of individuals within a given population. In this sense, the whole process is sometimes described as 'selfish', as in the term **selfish gene** (Dawkins, 1976). However, although genes are not selected to act for the good of the species as a whole, genes that bias in favour of acting for the immediate social group could prove advantageous (Wilson and Csikszentmihalyi, 2007).

Having described principles of function and evolution, in the next section we focus on the processes that control behaviour, involving the causal and developmental/ learning types of explanation. In doing so, we look for links with functional and evolutionary considerations.

Section summary

1 Any behaviour has both costs and benefits.

2 Behaviour for which the benefits on average outweigh the costs is favoured. Genes that play a role in the production of behaviour with a net benefit are favoured by natural selection.

3 Natural selection acts in the interests of survival of the genes of individuals. Bodily survival is favoured since this serves the passing on of genes.

4 Animals (except, in some cases, humans) do not have conscious intentions to promote genetic survival.

 ## Test your knowledge

2.2 Complete the missing word in the following: 'Natural selection favours solutions where the _____ outweigh the costs'.

2.3 Which of the following human capacities is assumed to have evolved by being tested in natural selection? (i) Hearing, (ii) reading, (iii) writing.

 Answer on page 48

Processes controlling behaviour

Introduction

This section looks at some examples of the processes that underlie the control of behaviour. It shows how links can be made between (i) causal explanations and (ii) developmental/learning, evolutionary and functional explanations. The discussion exemplifies where understanding of brain mechanisms in causal terms can be enriched by a consideration of other types of explanation.

Reflexes

A **reflex** forms the basis of a relatively straightforward and automatic **reaction** (or 'response') that is triggered by a stimulus. Each reflex is found in all members of the species, unless there is malfunction, e.g. every dog salivates to meat in its mouth. We automatically move

a limb away from a damagingly hot object. We close our eyes when an object comes rapidly towards us. As a result of how the nervous system is constructed, reflexes 'just happen' when an appropriate stimulus is presented. We do not need to think about producing them. The genes of an animal help to determine a nervous system that is equipped with a number of fitness-enhancing reflexes.

From functional and evolutionary perspectives, reflexes provide ready-made 'built-in' answers to common problems that have presented themselves throughout the evolution of the species. They are an economical means of operating. For example, all animals have a reflex that reacts rapidly to damaging stimuli, such as sharp objects touching the skin. Humans cannot afford to engage sophisticated but very slow conscious processing with finding creative and original solutions to such a problem. This would not be cost-effective. By contrast, other problems cannot be solved on the basis of 'ready-made' solutions and they need to engage our conscious processing.

When comparing different animals within a species, reflexes are not entirely the same or triggered by exactly the same stimuli. Their form can vary to some limited extent. For example, all dogs have a reflex that triggers salivation to food in the mouth in much the same way. However, the range of stimuli that triggers salivation in an individual dog depends partly upon its learning experiences. Particular stimuli that have been associated with food (e.g. the sound of a can-opener) can act as a trigger for a particular dog. There is a fixed prescription, 'salivate to food', but there is flexibility for individual experience to determine the trigger stimuli.

The strength of the human withdrawal reflex can be modified to some extent by psychological processes, which exert a 'top-down' influence from the brain.

A personal angle

Darwin's 'experiment'

As an example of an automatic reflex, Charles Darwin (1872/1934) put his face against the glass in the London Zoo and tried to keep it there when a puff-adder struck out at him. He could not keep his head still, even though objectively he knew that he was not in danger. Rational insight and a conscious intention were no match for the reflex. No zoo would appreciate your doing the same experiment, so it is best to take Darwin on trust.

Actions

Whereas a reflex is triggered by external stimuli, an **action** is not so closely tied to stimuli. In humans, action that takes the form of **voluntary behaviour** is associated with having a conscious intention (Baars, 1997). Although no obvious external stimulus need be present, of course, action commonly follows changes in external events.

A reflex is relatively stereotyped, whereas voluntary behaviour is highly flexible and open-ended. Voluntary behaviour can be exploited in a multitude of ways according to individual experience. Our brains have evolved with a capacity for flexibility and learning by experience. The functional advantage of voluntary behaviour is our ability to exploit it even under novel circumstances and thereby to find a creative solution to a problem. Humans could not be equipped with a preformed system for reacting to every situation, as in a reflex.

Although a dichotomy 'reflexes versus voluntary' is sometimes described, behaviour normally depends upon both processes acting in combination. Furthermore, the same muscles that execute reflexes are controlled by the brain in performing voluntary behaviour. The differences between these controls match different functional considerations.

Complementary roles

Consider the response to tissue damage, e.g. a burn. There is (i) a reflex organized at the spinal cord, i.e. the limb is moved from the heat, and (ii) the conscious sensation of pain, which teaches us to be more careful in the future (Melzack and Wall, 1996).

Reflexes and voluntary behaviour serve different and complementary roles. For example, tissue damage that arises externally triggers an immediate reflexive reaction. Damage that arises internally triggers something rather different. Suppose that an animal damages its leg muscle. It behaves so as to favour the leg involved by, say, putting more weight on the intact ones. Alternatively, or in addition, the animal might be able to rest and thereby speed recovery. The example of tissue damage illustrates the functional value of joint control by (i) a reflex that is relatively simple and **hardwired** into the nervous system ('ready-made') and (ii) a more complex action system that is flexible and can find novel solutions.

Concerning withdrawal reflexes, all humans act in a similar way, since the pathway within the nervous system is the same for all. By contrast, the system involving the conscious sensation of pain has flexibility and enables creative solutions to be found. This route is relatively slow. For such situations as treading on sharp objects, information would reach conscious awareness only after any local reflex action had already been initiated.

Tissue damage might require widely different solutions depending upon circumstances, and it would be impossible to specify all of these in advance. Suppose that a local withdrawal reflex fails, e.g. a thorn gets stuck in a foot. Other solutions might then be possible, e.g. to extract the thorn with the teeth. Humans can recruit the help of others. We learn how to solve such problems and this requires the emotional state of 'pain' and actions that are followed by its reduction. Pain serves as the arbiter ('judge') of how effective an action is. If behaviour reduces pain, the animal is encouraged to repeat this, an example of a developmental/learning type of explanation. For example, imagine yourself trying to lower the intensity of a back pain. You adopt various positions, determined by pain and its reduction. You learn strategies for coping.

Effects of behaviour

As part of a developmental/learning explanation psychologists ask how the consequences of past behaviour have influenced present behaviour, e.g. through learning. The adaptive value of learning is that it gives flexibility to behaviour: an animal alters its behaviour according to its past experience. There can be various consequences of behaviour. One possibility is **reinforcement**: the situation where behaviour is *more likely* to be repeated in the future as a result of its consequences on past occasions (Skinner, 1966). This principle applies to a whole range of species.

In humans and based on subjective experience, behaviour is said to have **hedonic** consequences, i.e. it produces pleasure or pain (Cabanac, 1992). We could reasonably argue that at least some non-human species also experience this. Some behavioural choices seem to be made on the basis of trying to maximize their positive consequences and minimize their negative. So, how might such a subjective experience relate to the activity of the nervous system? If identity theory (Chapter 1) is correct, subjective pleasure and pain are features ('an alternative description') of the activity of certain brain regions.

The developmental/learning and functional types of explanation can be related. Thus, behaviours that are necessary for survival and passing on genes, such as feeding or mating, have consequences that encourage the animal to repeat them. An animal learns how to gain access to food and mates. If this were not so, the duration of advanced life on Earth would have been rather short! However, the earlier caution can usefully be repeated: in our present environment, not all immediate consequences described as positive serve fitness in any obvious way. Think again of the example of reinforcement associated with excessive sugar intake.

Considerable insight into one aspect of causation has been gained by studying motivation and homeostasis, described next.

Motivation

An internal process that gives direction and strength to behaviour is **motivation**. Motivation directs attention and behaviour to appropriate events in the environment and is at the basis of the selection of actions.

Link with homeostasis

Consider feeding, drinking and body temperature. In terms of the four types of explanation, by applying the principle of motivation, homeostasis and negative feedback (Chapter 1) we can gain understanding. For example, when body temperature rises, actions are motivated, such as switching on a fan or moving to the shade. These depend upon the automatic monitoring of body temperature and thereby the production of the appropriate motivation. Such behaviour is also termed **regulatory behaviour** (or 'homeostatic' behaviour) since it regulates the internal environment.

This kind of behaviour can be understood in terms of its different aspects, such as:

1 In causal terms, the activity of particular neurons controls this behaviour, which exhibits negative feedback.

2 In developmental/learning terms, the immediate consequences of behaviour strengthen the tendency to repeat the behaviour ('reinforcement').

3 In evolutionary terms, such behaviour can be seen across mammalian species.

4 In functional terms, behaviour puts the body in an optimal condition and thereby contributes to fitness.

In relating causal, functional, developmental/learning and evolutionary explanations, behaviour 'makes sense'. Reflecting this, a water-deprived rat can be trained to perform a task to earn water; it is *motivated* to do so. For example, it can be taught to run through a maze or to press a lever in a Skinner box for reward (Figure 2.2).

Link with sexual behaviour

Not all motivation and behaviour is regulatory. For example, homeostasis does not lie at the basis of sexual motivation and behaviour, though these also depend

Figure 2.2 Skinner box

on internal and external factors and exhibit a form of negative feedback. That is, after a while, sexual activity induces satiety, thereby lowering motivation and the tendency to engage in this activity. Sexual behaviour is not associated with the maintenance of optimal bodily conditions but, of course, it makes sense in terms of causation and function. This draws attention to different means by which behaviour contributes to fitness (Figure 2.1). On a causal level, such things as sex hormones and perception of a mate contribute to triggering sexual motivation and behaviour. Behaviour's immediate consequences are described as positively reinforcing (and in our case, pleasurable). That is, in terms of a developmental/learning explanation, the animal is encouraged to repeat the behaviour.

Understanding 'abnormal' behaviour

General principles

Behaviour sometimes seems self-defeating and contrary to the individual's best interests. In this sense, the behaviour is *abnormal*, though it might not be abnormal in the sense of being uncommon – try glancing at the behaviour exhibited in a pub, burger bar or supermarket. Behaviour fails to make sense functionally. However, this should not cause us to abandon the functional type of explanation for such cases; rather, we can use it for speculation. We can ask how the behaviour is produced by brain processes that were once functionally matched well to their environment and indeed might still be so with a change of environment.

For example, evolution has not tracked the rapid environmental change of large amounts of refined sugar appearing in our foods. This was a recent change in culture. Excessive intake of fats tells a similar story. Given very many years of exposure to this environment, psychologists of the future might find that people with only a weak liking for either sugar or hamburgers are favoured.

Consider the intravenous self-injection of psychoactive drugs by humans. Of course, intravenous injection was not around to influence our early evolution – syringes and refined forms of drug did not exist. Drug-taking exploits mechanisms (tapping into positive reinforcement and pleasure systems) that evolved in a very different context from the one in which contemporary drug-taking behaviour occurs (Nesse and Berridge, 1997).

A central 'faith' of biological psychology is that *any* behaviour is determined by external and internal factors acting in interaction with the nervous system. Although some behaviour is difficult to interpret, scientists still ask: 'What nervous system events trigger it and what (if anything) is achieved as its immediate consequence?' (Würbel *et al.*, 1998).

Stereotypies and self-destructive behaviour

As another example of abnormality, animals in zoos or intensive agriculture often perform apparently pointless behaviour, such as rituals of chewing or pacing, termed **stereotypy**, plural stereotypies (and, yes, just in case you are wondering, that is the correct spelling, rather than 'stereotypes') or self-mutilation. Such behaviour is abnormal in not fitting an adaptive interpretation but not in the sense of being 'different from the norm', since, under intensive housing, most animals might exhibit it (Mason, 1991). Some human behaviour seems irrational and compulsive in a similar way to that of domestic animals. Under stress, humans occasionally engage in self-mutilation, finger-chewing or hair-pulling. In severe mental retardation, there is an increased tendency to stereotypies (e.g. body-rocking) (Emerson and Howard, 1992).

The environment in which such behaviour of domestic animals is exhibited is very different from that in which the animals' ancestors evolved. Therefore, it would seem inappropriate to ask what advantage stereotypies have conferred in evolution. Evolution can only favour broad categories of behaviour as being those that *on average* were beneficial in the natural environment. It cannot account for behaviour shown in abnormal modern environments. Nonetheless, we might still ask a related question – how can processes that generate adaptive behaviour in a natural environment also generate aberrant behaviour in an abnormal environment? This is a similar question to that concerning human drug-taking.

In trying to understand the brain processes that trigger stereotypies, we can be guided by the observation that repetitive ('rhythmic') patterns are an important feature of some adaptive behaviour. Chewing, grooming and running exemplify this. As a cause of stereotypies, such a rhythm could become unmasked and uninhibited in an environment that offers no opportunity to exhibit flexible behaviour (Dantzer, 1986).

It remains an open question as to what is the immediate consequence of stereotypies. Stereotypies might provide, say, stimulation in a boring environment or lower the level of stress. However, it is possible that they have no beneficial consequence. It appears that there is a time-filling process where inactivity is not an option. In terms of a developmental/learning explanation, the fact that they increase in frequency over time suggests some kind of reinforcement process (Mason, 1991).

Whether describable in rational terms concerning immediate consequences (e.g. drinking following deprivation) or seemingly irrational (e.g. self-mutilation), behaviour reflects the activity of nervous system processes. So, how did we get the kind of nervous system the properties of which are described in this section? To start to answer this, the next section looks at the role of genes.

Section summary

1 Reflexes provide rapid solutions. For a given species, reflexes are relatively stereotyped.

2 Action, as exemplified by voluntary behaviour, exhibits flexibility and variability between individuals.

3 Behaviour is influenced by the consequences of past behaviour, e.g. via reinforcement.

4 Abnormal behaviour can sometimes make functional sense as a manifestation of processes that were adaptive under earlier conditions.

 ## Test your knowledge

2.4 Which of the following qualities are associated with reflexes? (i) High speed, (ii) hard-wired, (iii) common to members of a given species, (iv) relatively slow.

2.5 (i) What is the name given to repetitive and apparently pointless behaviour? (ii) Why would it probably be misleading to search for a functional advantage of exhibiting such behaviour?

Answer on page 48

Genes, replication and reproduction

This section describes the gene, both as the unit of inheritance of information from one generation to another and as a source of information that plays a role in determining the form of the body throughout life. The section links genes and evolution.

Body structure

How does body structure, including the nervous system, form? The body is constructed in large part from proteins (Chapter 1), which are found in thousands of varieties within humans. They are analogous to the bricks, wood and mortar of a building. However, in addition to fixed structure, certain proteins serve as messengers and affect reactions. Some are **enzymes,** which speed up or slow down chemical reactions. Of course, not all the body consists of proteins. In fact, most of it is water (Figure 1.2). However, proteins form a part of the structures that hold everything together.

Proteins are made from substances termed amino acids (Figure 2.3). A combination of different amino acids joining together in a particular form yields a particular protein. Genes are responsible for the construction of proteins. So, in coding for the construction of proteins from amino acids, genes have a role in the formation of structures. Putting together the right combination of amino acids to produce the right protein at the right place and time is crucial to biological success. Who 'says' what is right? In effect, natural selection does and the 'right combination' means a viable one by the criterion of fitness.

The cells of the body, whether neurons or not, have features in common. Each has a **nucleus.** The nucleus contains the genetic material of the cell. The collection of all the genes within an individual constitutes its **genotype.** Each cell contains an identical set of such genes. The genotype represents a source of information, which, together with the environment, determines the current form of an organism. Genotype is determined at fertilization by the combination of genes that are contributed by the parents and it remains constant throughout life.

In terms of both physiology and behaviour, the form that appears as a result of the genotype interacting with the environment is termed the **phenotype**. Your phenotype is 'the you' sitting reading this book right now. Features of the phenotype change as a result of growth and experience. The genotype represents a source of information, a kind of potential for development into a number of different phenotypes. The end product depends also upon the environment experienced along the way.

In development, the genes that you inherited interact with their immediate environment in the body and, if all goes well, you end up with a correctly functioning nervous system. This interaction of genes and their environment is a complex dynamic process. The mature nervous system does not exist in a miniature form at the start of life just waiting to expand. This and the next sections start to unravel this interaction.

Genes and evolution

The theory of evolution states that, over millions of years, complex species evolved from simpler ('ancestor') animals as a result of natural selection. How does this happen? First consider that, for a given species, the potential number of offspring that can be produced is usually greater than the number that can survive. The limitation on survival is due to such things as predation and competition for resources, such as food and shelter. As a result of their genes, among other things, some individuals will be better equipped than others in this struggle.

How is it that, within a species, individuals differ genetically? In coming together at fertilization, new *combinations* of different variants of genes are produced and then, in effect, tested in the environment. Some combinations are more successful than others (they are '*selected for*') and some will be unsuccessful. A successful combination will, by definition, tend to reproduce at a relatively high rate. It will increase in numbers in the population. Less successful combinations will decline in numbers or even become extinct. That is, *evolution* will occur. For example, a combination might code for extra height so that taller trees can be exploited for food or a nervous system having a faster than normal capacity to learn. This particular offspring will have an advantage over others.

Also, occasionally, in producing either an egg or a sperm, a **mutation** occurs: the genes contributed to reproduction by one partner are changed slightly with respect to the parent genes. The altered phenotype

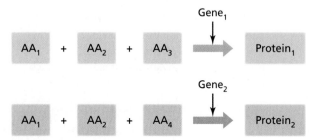

Figure 2.3 Two proteins formed from two different combinations of amino acids under the control of two genes. AA = amino acid. These show just a small sample of the many amino acids and combinations that are possible.

that results from this change in genotype is termed a 'mutant'. Most mutant phenotypes are either of no increased benefit relative to the previous form or are less viable. However, suppose that a mutant version of a gene carries information that improves the offspring's chances relative to the previous form. This particular offspring will have an advantage over others, who do not share the mutation. The mutant form will tend to be copied in future generations and increase in frequency. The argument is that, over long time periods, the processes of (i) combination and (ii) mutation have contributed to the evolution of forms from the simple to the complex.

Now we need to look more closely at the gene.

Replication and reproduction

Consider the two roles that are served by genes:

1 We first come into being via genes inherited from our parents and we transmit genes to the next generation.

2 Within the individual, genes are responsible for protein synthesis.

This section looks at these interdependent processes. The biological inheritance of information by offspring from their parents is by means of genes that are located within sperm cells in the male and egg cells in the female. These two types of cell, which come together at fertilization, are collectively termed **gametes**.

Within each cell, whether gamete or not, genes are located in structures called **chromosomes**. These are shown as paired coloured lines in Figure 2.4. With the exception of gametes, the nucleus of a human cell contains 46 chromosomes. These 46 chromosomes come in two sets of pairs, i.e. 23 pairs. For simplification, only three such pairs are shown in each of the non-gamete cells of Figure 2.4. As represented in Figure 2.4, within each such cell, 22 pairs are termed matching or homologous chromosomes, meaning that the genetic material held by one chromosome of a pair corresponds to that held by the other (the 23rd combination will be described later).

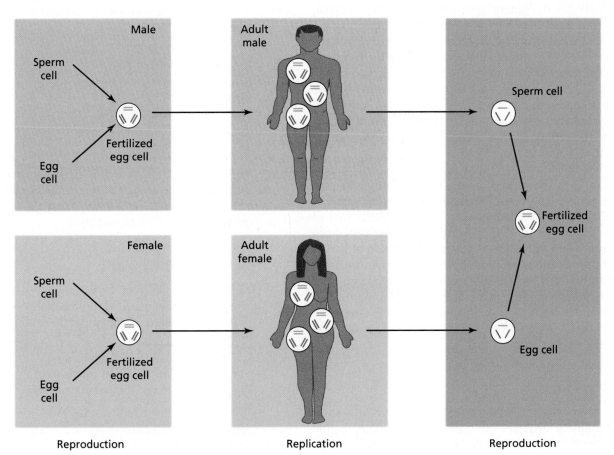

Figure 2.4 Replication and reproduction. Replication of the fertilized egg cell gives the adult human male and female. Reproduction is a coming together of gametes, a sperm cell and an egg cell. For simplification, each cell is shown with only 3 of the 23 chromosomes, or pairs of chromosomes.

Source: after Toates (1990, Fig. 5.12, p. 209).

In the process of forming gametes in the body, a division of chromosomes occurs such that each gamete contains only 23 *unmatched* chromosomes, shown in Figure 2.4 as three unpaired chromosomes. Note that the division of chromosomes is not random. One of each pair is represented within each gamete.

At fertilization, two sets of 23 chromosomes, one from the mother and one from the father, join, to give 46 chromosomes, a process termed **reproduction**. The coming together of individual chromosomes at reproduction is not haphazard (Figure 2.4). Rather, each one finds its match, such that chromosome number 1 from the mother finds number 1 from the father, etc. In other words, chromosomes are divided at the formation of the gametes but then, at reproduction, they form new combinations with those from another individual.

Consider that an egg has been fertilized to produce a cell with 46 chromosomes, termed a 'zygote'. That we are now somewhat larger is due to the process termed **replication**. The initial cell, the zygote, divides into two and each then grows. These two then divide to give four cells and so on, until we are fully developed. Each time a cell divides, the genetic material in its nucleus is copied, so that both cells have the same genetic information as in the cell from which they were formed. With the exception of gametes (and some other cells that need not concern us), no matter what the role served by the cell is, it will contain a full copy of the original genetic material held in 23 pairs of chromosomes. In contrast to reproduction, replication is intrinsic to a given animal and the genetic material of each cell is an exact replica of that of the cell that divided.

Reproduction is a process involving two individuals, whereby a sperm and an egg come together to produce a new individual. Therefore, the genetic material of the new cell is *not an exact replica* of either that of the mother or the father. Bringing together cells from mother and father yields a *novel combination* of genes. Of course, the novelty is somewhat relative since the offspring often bear a close resemblance to one or other parent and yet they are not identical. Following the formation of the novel combination of genes in a new cell and then a long process of replication, we get the 'you or me' of the present.

Role of genes

From conception onwards, genes interact with their immediate physical environment in playing a role in development (Champagne and Mashoodh, 2009). At first this is the environment of the zygote in the womb. Subsequently, development is determined by the multicellular new organism interacting with its environment in the womb. After birth, the whole growing animal interacts with both the physical and social environments. Together with the environment, genes influence body structure and function, e.g. height, hair colour and the structure of the nervous system.

We now look more closely at the process of inheritance.

Section summary

1 Natural selection plays a role in the evolution of complex life forms from simpler animals.

2 Sexual reproduction means that new combinations of genes arise.

3 New genetic material is tested in the environment.

4 Some combinations of genes are advantageous relative to others and will tend to increase in frequency in future generations. They will be 'selected for'.

5 In producing either a sperm or egg cell, mutations sometimes occur.

6 Genes are located in the nucleus of cells, including neurons.

7 Chromosomes in the nucleus are the physical base of genes.

8 The synthesis of protein structures is triggered by genes.

9 At fertilization, genes from the mother and father come together to give, in humans, a new cell containing 23 pairs of chromosomes.

 ## Test your knowledge

2.6 In humans, which of the following contain 23 pairs of matched chromosomes? (i) Zygote, (ii) sperm cell, (iii) unfertilized egg cell.

2.7 In humans, which of the following contain 23 unmatched chromosomes? (i) Zygote, (ii) sperm cell, (iii) unfertilized egg cell.

Answer on page 48

The process of inheritance

Introduction

Offspring acquire genes from their parents. We now need to look more closely at this and we will see some important implications for psychology. As will be discussed later, the pattern of inheritance of certain characteristics such as eye and hair colour in humans as well as some disorders (including some behavioural ones) can be followed from generation to generation and a picture of inheritance obtained.

Basics of genetics

Although investigators speak of *a* gene as the unit of inheritance of a characteristic (e.g. eye colour), genes exist in pairs, mainly located on paired chromosomes (Figure 2.5). As you saw, one of each pair of chromosomes (and its associated genes) is derived from the father and one from the mother. To be exact, a gene *pair* plays a role in determining a trait such as eye colour.

A gene for a characteristic such as eye colour is located at a specific region of a chromosome termed the locus (plural, loci) for that gene. The locus of a given gene exists in the same place for the two halves of a pair of chromosomes (Figure 2.5). At fertilization, the individual receives one of each of the pair of chromosomes from each parent (Figure 2.4). In the simplest examples, for a given phenotypic characteristic, there is just one pair of genes that need to be considered in its determination.

With caution, we may speak of a gene 'for' some phenotypic characteristic such as eye colour, meaning that (i) a particular gene at a particular locus on the chromosome is responsible and (ii) this gene would normally exist twice, once on each chromosome. However, a gene 'for' a characteristic, at a particular locus, does not necessarily come in one standard form. Rather, there can be different variants of a particular gene at a given locus (Figure 2.6).

Each variant of a given gene is termed an **allele** of that gene. For example, a gene that determines eye colour can be identified at a particular locus but different alleles of the gene exist. What colour the eye actually becomes (e.g. blue or grey) depends on the alleles. In Figure 2.6(a), $Gene_1$ comes in the form of two identical alleles, a_1. However, for $Gene_2$, two different alleles, a_2 and a_2', can exist at the two halves of the gene pair. Now imagine gametes from a given individual, as shown in Figure 2.6(b). Note that there are different alleles present in the two gametes.

Figures 2.4 and 2.5 can help to answer a very basic question. Surely few questions, whether described as 'evolutionary and functional' or not, could be more basic than this one – why bother with sex? Sexual reproduction is costly. Wouldn't it be simpler, even if (one imagines!) less pleasurable, to reproduce by replication? Well, it is doubtless too far down the evolutionary route of sexual reproduction to imagine us now switching to asexual reproduction. But how was it that evolution went down the sexual route at a very early stage? Sexual reproduction might be more fun but we also need to explain its appearance in functional and evolutionary terms. In principle, we might have evolved to reproduce simply by a process of replication. Some organisms do just this. Think what is avoided by reproducing without the help of sexual behaviour: problems of frustration, broken hearts, betrayal, jealousy, sexually transmitted diseases and injury suffered during fights over mates, etc. The list is a long and tragic one indeed.

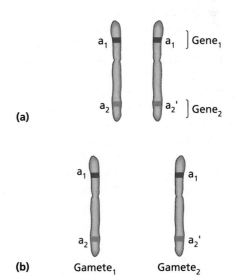

(a)

(b)   Gamete$_1$ Gamete$_2$

Figure 2.6 Schematic sketch of genes and alleles. (a) For Gene$_1$ the same allele a$_1$ occurs twice, whereas for Gene$_2$ different alleles, a$_2$ and a$_2$' exist. (b) Two gametes from the same individual shown to contain two different alleles of Gene$_2$.

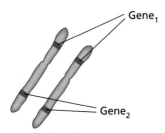

Figure 2.5 Two gene pairs each occupying corresponding places on paired chromosomes.

Sexual reproduction offers a rich possibility for testing different solutions since different alleles from male and female are brought together to yield *novel combinations*. Also, the alleles provided by each sex show a rich variety. Consider just the alleles that make up Gene$_2$ in Figure 2.6. As shown in part (b), the allele that occupies this location can, in one gamete, take this form of a$_2$ and, in another gamete from the same individual, some other form, a$_2$'. By producing more than one form of allele, sexual reproduction in effect enables you to play safe ('hedge your bets'). Even if a$_2$ is not particularly successful when in combination with genetic material from the opposite sex, the slightly different a$_2$' might prove more successful.

Suppose that the environment changes. Given the enormous range of outcomes regarding alleles coming together at reproduction, it is possible that one of the combinations is put at an advantage in a new environment. To take the simplest example, suppose that suddenly, for a strange reason, blue eyes might become particularly favoured over all others in the new environment. We might speculate that opposite sex partners start to find them irresistible. The alleles coding for this colour would correspondingly be favoured relative to alleles coding for a different colour.

The advantage of testing novel combinations of alleles appears to provide a functional explanation for the universality of the avoidance of inbreeding, including a taboo against incest in human societies (Thornhill, 1991). Incestuous reproduction involves bringing genetically similar material together. This reduces the chances of novel combinations of alleles appearing. It also increases the chances of certain genetically determined disorders being transmitted (Bateson, 1979), discussed shortly.

The biological basis of heredity

A complex molecule termed 'deoxyribonucleic acid' (DNA) constitutes the base of genetic information. Different genes correspond to different segments of the DNA molecule (Figure 2.7). A single molecule of DNA contains thousands of genes. A molecule of DNA plus supporting protein constitutes a chromosome.

In cell division, DNA replicates itself. A sperm or egg cell contains a copy of the DNA of the cell that gave rise to the new one. In such copying, occasionally the copied form of DNA is slightly different from the form giving rise to it, i.e. a mutation occurs.

How does DNA contribute to different characteristics? DNA codes for the synthesis of proteins. Proteins that form the basis of the cells of the nervous system are constructed at a time and in a form determined by particular genes at particular loci. Those that form other cells are constructed in a similar way. The genetic material is the same for each cell within a given individual. However, within a particular cell only a small subset of the genes is actually expressed in the form of protein synthesis. Thereby, the cell becomes, say, a part of the nervous system or a part of a kidney, as the case may be.

Sex-linked characteristics

So far, the chapter has described paired chromosomes and their alleles coming together at fertilization, without specifying which parent contributes which chromosome and thereby which allele. That is to say, it described inheritance of genes on the basis of a male and a female contributing with equal probability to any effect. Now we need to turn to a complication. It involves the 23rd of these chromosome pairs and means that, for some phenomena, we can no longer disregard the sex of the parent contributing the particular chromosome and alleles.

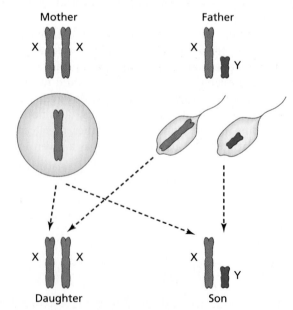

Figure 2.8 Inheritance of sex chromosomes.
Source: Plomin *et al.* (1997, Fig. 3.2, p. 20).

Figure 2.7 A section of a DNA molecule corresponding to three genes. Each triggers the construction of a particular protein. Not all the DNA molecule acts in this way.
Source: Hall and Halliday (1998, Fig. 3.2, p. 53).

Considering humans, 2 of the 46 chromosomes are termed **sex chromosomes** because they are different between males and females. Also described as the '23rd pair' of chromosomes, females possess two X chromosomes and males one X chromosome and one Y chromosome. In spite of this difference from the other 22, the sex chromosomes appear in the gametes by a process of cell division just like the other 22 (Figure 2.8). Note that a daughter inherits two X chromosomes, one from each parent, whereas a son inherits an X chromosome from the mother and a Y chromosome from the father. In other words, the sex of children is determined by which chromosome they inherit from the father.

In the next section, we consider the role of genes in behaviour, as mediated by the nervous system.

Section summary

1 Most genes come in pairs, one of each pair being found on each chromosome.

2 The site at which a gene is located is described as its locus.

3 A given gene can come in different forms termed alleles.

4 The biological basis of genes is deoxyribonucleic acid (DNA).

5 Some alleles are sex linked, associated with either the X or Y chromosome.

☞ Test your knowledge

2.8 Complete the following: 'On a section of a DNA molecule a particular gene codes for a particular ____'

2.9 Who inherits two X chromosomes?

2.10 Who inherits one X and one Y chromosome?

 Answer on page 48   WEB

Genes, brains and behaviour

By their effect on the synthesis of proteins, certain genes play a role in the construction of the nervous system. In turn, nervous systems underlie behaviour, so there is a sequence of links (gene) → (nervous system) →

(behaviour). This section considers the role of genes in constructing nervous systems and looks at how certain disorders of the brain can be linked to particular genes. In fact, since certain disorders give a particularly clear insight into the role of genes, we start with a consideration of them and then go on to consider some more complex gene effects.

Inherited disorders

Some human disorders have behavioural manifestations and their chromosomal and genetic basis can be understood in terms of the principles just developed.

Phenylketonuria (PKU)

Phenylalanine is an 'essential amino acid', from which certain vital proteins are constructed. It is found in many foods. It is an essential component of our diet; otherwise these proteins cannot be constructed. In the 1930s, an abnormally large amount of phenylalanine was observed in the urine of some people with severe learning difficulties (Plomin *et al.*, 1997). Mental retardation associated with this condition is termed **phenylketonuria (PKU)**. It appears that a failure to utilize phenylalanine results in its build-up in the body and causes damage to the brain.

The parents of PKU patients do not usually suffer from the condition, which might suggest that it arises from environmental factors. However, the pattern of inheritance reveals a genetic basis (Figure 2.9). PKU can be traced to the influence of a particular allele (*p*). Note the possible combinations of alleles that can result in the offspring. On average, only 25% of the phenotypes develop PKU, i.e. those having the combination *pp*.

PKU can be described as a 'genetic condition', since the basic abnormality is 'solely due to a gene mutation'

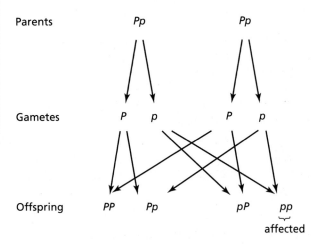

Figure 2.9 Pattern of inheritance of phenylketonuria (PKU). *Source:* Plomin *et al.* (1997, Fig. 2.5, p. 9).

in a single gene (Plomin and Rutter, 1998, p. 1224). Although scientists do not need to look to the environment to understand how PKU arises, nonetheless the environment is important in coping with it. PKU can be managed successfully by environmental intervention, a qualification that needs to be made to any straightforward genetic determinism. The patient needs to avoid excessive phenylalanine in the diet.

Huntington's disease (HD)

Huntington's disease (or 'Huntington's chorea') also has a straightforward genetic basis. It is characterized by involuntary movements of the body, personality changes and forgetfulness (Plomin *et al.*, 1997). Normally it strikes in middle age, after the person might well have become a mother or father. Figure 2.10 shows its pattern of inheritance. Note that the combination *Hh* yields an affected individual but not the combination *hh*. Allele *H* is the problem and it dominates the influence of *h*.

HD is a good point at which to take stock of where we are with regard to genetic determination. Investigators can associate the disease or its absence with the forms that certain alleles take. According to their form, these alleles code for neural structures that either do, or do not, manifest HD. The difference between individuals with or without the disorder can be traced to differences in the alleles at a particular locus. However, of course, the ultimate expression or not of the HD characteristics depends also upon all the other genes that code for normal neurons and other cells that underlie movement control.

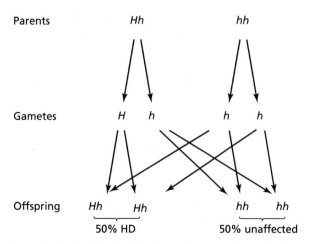

Figure 2.10 The inheritance of Huntington's disease (HD).
Source: Plomin *et al.* (1997, Fig. 2.4, p. 8).

A personal angle

A rational explanation

Huntington's disease (HD) is named after George Huntington, who, in 1872, described the feature that it runs in families, its adult onset and the gradual deterioration of the sufferer. The grandfather of Huntington had recognized some characteristics of HD in Long Island, United States, in 1797. George Huntington recorded a boyhood experience of being out riding with his father in 1860 (Vessie, 1932, p. 564):

> Driving with my father through a wooded road leading from East Hampton to Amagansett, we suddenly came upon two women, mother and daughter, both tall, thin, almost cadaverous, both twisting, bowing, grimacing. I stood in wonderment, almost in fear. What could it mean? My father paused to speak with them and we passed on.

Almost all sufferers from HD living on the United States East coast were descended from a small family group who emigrated to Boston Bay from Bures, Suffolk, in England in 1630.

In the 17th century, the abnormal movements of HD were commonly said to be triggered by demonic possession. Sufferers were lucky to escape execution by hanging for witchcraft, this usually being used against women. Clearly, the combination of a known genetic pedigree and a consequent dysfunction of parts of the brain is a radically different view. It gives a more accurate and humane account.

Down's syndrome

Down's syndrome consists of, among other things, short stature, a small round head and learning difficulties but often also an especially pleasant personality. Down's syndrome is caused by a chromosomal abnormality. Rather than inheriting two copies of one particular chromosome, the child inherits three copies. As a manifestation of the chromosomal abnormality, there are abnormalities in certain brain regions (Kleschevnikov *et al.*, 2004).

Complex characteristics

Introduction

Recall the discussion of phenylketonuria and Huntington's disease, which are (a) in terms of their genetic basis, all-or-nothing phenomena and (b) linked to the effects of single genes. A person either suffers from phenylketonuria or HD or does not. In this regard, the population can be classified into two groups and family pedigrees can be worked out, both for individuals and most probable outcomes for populations. However, not all genetic influences are single-gene effects acting in this all-or-nothing way. The present section addresses these cases.

Characteristics such as height, weight and general cognitive ability have *quantitative dimensions* that we all exhibit to some degree. One cannot, of course, identify 'affected individuals' and compare them with normal individuals. People can be attributed a number and, if a variable such as height is plotted, it forms a bell-shaped distribution. In a similar way, cognitive abilities, as measured by, say, an IQ test, are something that we all possess to varying degrees and can be plotted on a graph (Plomin *et al.*, 1997).

Does this difference between, say, phenylketonuria and cognitive ability mean that genetic differences between individuals do not contribute towards differences in quantitative dimensions? No. The evidence suggests a role of a genetic factor here also. The genetic influence on a quantitative dimension such as general intelligence is mediated not by one but by numerous genes. In this way, a number of discrete components can, for a whole population, give rise to a smoothly varying effect.

Complex gene effects and behaviour

Although genetic determinants play a role in a number of psychiatric conditions (e.g. depression), genes represent only one contribution (Plomin and Rutter, 1998). Variables in the environment interact with genetic variables as determinants (described by the developmental/learning type of explanation). In these cases, a particular combination of genes is more correctly seen as contributing a *certain probability* that a condition will appear, e.g. varying from highly likely, through some risk, to not very likely. In other words, genes give a 'probabilistic bias' towards a condition appearing (more complex than a simple 0% versus 100%). Thus, combinations of genes can give a bias so that the probability of a disorder appearing varies almost smoothly, in a similar way to that in which it varies as a function of the environment. A number of genes might contribute towards, say, chronic anxiety and their influence acts in combination

with that of a smoothly varying environmental factor such as its stressfulness. The label 'genetic condition' would be inappropriate here but we should not ignore the genes' contribution.

For another example of this, the gene called *ApoE* is relevant to Alzheimer's disease (Plomin and Rutter, 1998), a form of cognitive decline (dementia). An allele of this gene, termed *ApoE4*, is found at a higher frequency in sufferers than in controls. Through the allele, one can identify people at increased risk of developing the disorder. This is a probabilistic, not deterministic, prediction; many people possessing the allele reach 80 years or more without developing Alzheimer's. The genetic relationship is found in some countries but not others. The allele might exert an effect such that the brain is more vulnerable to certain types of trauma under specific conditions.

There are still more possibilities of gene–environment interaction. A gene might bias a person to seek a certain environment and that environment might then exert a particular effect. For example, a gene might bias towards seeking novel, high-risk environments, which could then affect vulnerability to, say, drug-taking. Again, this illustrates why simple dichotomies – 'is it genes or environment?' – are misleading, a topic addressed in more detail in the next section.

Section summary

1 Certain conditions, e.g. Huntington's disease, are associated with a particular allele.

2 Characteristics that vary on a quantitative dimension are determined in part by multiple genes.

 ## Test your knowledge

2.11 Complete the missing word here: 'Huntington's disease is associated with the combination *Hh* rather than *hh*. The letters *H* and *h* refer to different ___'.

2.12 Complete the two missing words in the following: 'The ___ called *ApoE* is relevant to Alzheimer's disease. An ___ of this gene, *ApoE4*, is found at a high frequency in sufferers'.

Answer on page 48   WEB

Genes, learning and the environment

Introduction

Language can invite misunderstanding of genes and environment. Alas, discussions are commonly premised on misleading questions of the kind: 'Is it genes *or* environment?' or 'Is aggression *all* in the genes?' Of course, in reality, without genes, we would have no body. Similarly, without an environment, we could not exist. The nervous system depends upon genes and environment, and behaviour depends upon the nervous system in interaction with an environment (Figure 2.11). By feedback, the environment, in a broad sense, acts at each level in the production of behaviour. For example, the environment affects events in the body. In turn, this affects the environment within cells such that the timing of when genes produce proteins, a process termed 'gene expression', is affected (Champagne and Mashoodh, 2009).

Neither one nor other is the most important

The question 'What is the most important – genes or environment?' is meaningless. It is like asking, 'What is the most important determinant of the area of a rectangle, its height *or* length?' Without either a height or a length, a rectangle cannot exist. Another analogy is baking a cake. Without ingredients or cooking, there can be no cake. Such analogies are an important first advance over naive polarizations between genes *or* environment.

It can sometimes be logical to ask whether *differences* between individuals are due to *differences* in genes or *differences* in environment. To pursue the analogy, if two rectangles are different in area, this might be due to differences in height or length, or both. The degree to which differences in a characteristic are due to genetic differences is called the **heritability** of that characteristic. By definition, the heritability within a population of genetically identical individuals would be zero.

Instinct and innateness

Before scientists had such a good understanding, behaviour was sometimes divided into one of two exclusive categories. Some was said to be 'instinctive' or 'innate' (i.e. genetically determined), whereas other behaviour was called learned (i.e. environmentally determined). Outside behavioural science, people still dichotomize in this way and it is not difficult to see why.

Watching a bird constructing a nest characteristic of its species in its first breeding season, might lead us to suggest that this behaviour is innate. The bird seems not to have gone through a trial-and-error process; neither is it imitating another bird. Conversely, an animal showing clever circus tricks would seem to be revealing learning, rather than any 'circus-trick' instinct.

However, no behaviour is purely innate. From conception onwards, an animal reacts to events in its environment and thereby surely learns something relevant to each behaviour. The skills of a bird in constructing a nest doubtless owe much to earlier experiences with manipulating objects. Perceptual systems have a developmental history. Reciprocally, an animal exhibiting learning is employing nervous system structures that are partly determined genetically.

When we look closely at 'innate', it is not clear what exactly it means (Elman *et al.*, 1996). The term is used in a number of different ways and this adds confusion (discussed by Griffiths, 1997), which has led to calls for the term to be abandoned. Behaviour might be innate by one criterion but not by another.

Figure 2.11 Genes and environment interacting in determining behaviour.

If all members of a species exhibit a characteristic, does this mean that it is innate? The universal presence of something does not necessarily point in any simple way to its origins. Looking back to those grand and green days when virtually everyone in the industrialized world showed skill at riding a bicycle, it would have been absurd to describe this skill as 'innate'. Apart from genetic similarity, another factor that gives constancy between individuals within a species is constant features of their environment (Hofer, 1988). During development, the infant mammal interacts with the mother's uterus and breast and the nature of this interaction might be very similar when comparing different individuals.

Most of the inhabitants of the United Kingdom speak English but that specific language could hardly be encoded genetically. The same population if raised from birth in France would presumably speak French.

Innate is sometimes used in the sense of being relatively insensitive to variations in the environment during development, given the presence of such basic necessities as heat, oxygen and energy (see Griffiths, 1997). However, a form of behaviour might normally be seen by all members of a species, have a clear functional explanation and yet be very sensitive to changes in the environment during development (e.g. as revealed by experimental manipulation). For example, performance of sexual behaviour by adult rhesus monkeys counts as innate by the criteria of being seen by all normal members of the species and having a functional explanation. However, it depends upon a social environment during development and early social deprivation severely disrupts later mating. Since some authors jump indiscriminately between these different meanings of innate, the word needs using with qualification if it is not to be abandoned.

Species-typical behaviour

The problems associated with the use of 'innate' might be avoided by employing instead the terms **species-typical behaviour (STB)** or 'species-specific behaviour' (Bolles, 1970). This means that the behaviour is exhibited by most, if not all, members of a species, given (i) normal development and environment and (ii) the later presence of certain trigger stimuli. The existence of STB might be as closely associated with the identity of a species as are species-typical anatomical forms such as horns or antlers. It is probably best to consider a given behaviour to be on a continuum of more or less species-typical rather than either species-typical or not.

Strain differences

General

A **strain** is a subdivision within a species. It refers to members of a species who are similar to each other genetically but different from others of the same species, e.g. a high-anxiety strain of rat as opposed to a stable strain. Crossbreeding between strains (e.g. high-anxiety and stables) results in viable offspring (i.e. offspring that can, in turn, reproduce).

By selectively breeding within a strain, one can strengthen a selected characteristic, something known to breeders of dogs and horses for a long time. For example, Tryon (1940) measured the ability of rats to learn a maze. Starting with a group of founding rats, Tryon bred within the brightest subgroup and within the dullest subgroup. Within the offspring of each subgroup, he then inbred among only the brightest and the dullest, respectively. Thereby, he produced two strains, known as 'maze-bright' and 'maze-dull'. The result was a divergence of the two groups' scores on the maze task until there was little overlap.

Genes and environment – a caution

Consider two strains of mice housed under identical conditions in terms of space, diet and lighting, etc. (Southwick, 1968). Strain 1 has a high level of aggression, whereas strain 2 has a low level. Since the environment is said to be constant, it would seem to follow inevitably that differences in behaviour are due to genetically determined differences in the two strains. So far, so good, but now be very careful! The developmental/learning type of explanation calls for extreme vigilance.

To investigate, crossbreeding was done between strains. When a strain 1 female was mated with a strain 2 male, the male offspring had a high score for aggression. When a strain 2 female was mated with a strain 1 male, the male offspring had a low score. This suggests an effect linked to sex chromosomes, in which the male offspring acquire an allele for aggression from the mother. However, this does not exhaust the possibilities.

So, researchers tried cross-fostering, e.g. the product of a strain 1/strain 1 mating was raised by a strain 2 mother. The aggression score of the offspring followed that of the foster-mother rather than the biological mother. This suggests that something about the *social* environment of the young rather than their genotype determines the tendency to aggression. So, is it a genetic or environmental difference? The subtlety of genes and environment comes into focus here and precision of logic is crucial.

Suppose we accept that *certain differences* in genes between strains are apparently responsible for differences in aggression. To solve the puzzle, we need to probe further than this and to ask, whose genes are involved? Are the genes exerting their effect at the level of the mother's behaviour or that of the infant? Are they controlling aggression directly or via something else that in turn influences aggression?

Suppose that the nature of the maternal behaviour shown towards a pup has an influence on the subsequent aggressiveness of the pup. Figure 2.12 suggests that there might be a difference in degree of proximity between mother and offspring but countless other differences could be suggested. Suppose too that genetic differences between strains underlie differences in maternal behaviour. This is still a genetically mediated difference but one for which the gene influencing *maternal* behaviour, not aggression as such, is responsible. Thus, the genetic difference between strains as revealed

in the behaviour of the offspring does not reside in the offspring but rather in the mother. That is to say, what is a genetic difference at the level of the mother is an environmental difference at the level of the pup, since the mother is part of the pup's environment. The experimenter might be able to control the lighting and the cage size, etc. but this does not control the social behaviour of the mother.

This example has a message for the study of humans. Sometimes people explain differences between children not by genetic differences but by differences in environment, e.g. parenting styles. However, these styles might themselves be in part genetically determined (Plomin *et al.*, 1997).

The next section looks at an argument on genes and evolution that is powerfully influencing our view of ourselves as humans.

Strain 1

Strain 2

Figure 2.12 Two strains housed under identical conditions.

Section summary

1 It is misleading to ask, 'What is most important, genes or environment?'

2 It can sometimes be valid to ask whether a given difference between individuals is due to genetic or environmental differences.

3 Heritability is a measure of the degree to which differences between individuals are determined by genetic differences.

4 We need to avoid describing behaviour as either innate or learned.

5 Genetic differences at the level of one individual can constitute environmental differences for another.

☞ Test your knowledge

2.13 Imagine observing a society as it becomes more egalitarian and people are treated more equally. What happens to the heritability of characteristics over this period? (i) It increases, (ii) it decreases.

Answer on page 48   WEB

Evolutionary psychology

General principles

A development of evolutionary thought has assumed great importance in suggesting explanations of human mind and behaviour. It is termed **evolutionary psychology (EP)** and its followers search for integrative principles linking evolution and psychology, in terms mainly of function (Barkow *et al.*, 1992). Evolutionary psychologists argue that, in order to understand mind and behaviour, we need to look way back to consider the environment in which we evolved and the nature of the demands that it imposed on our early ancestors (Workman and Reader, 2008).

EP employs the metaphor of **design**. For instance, a bird's wing looks *as if* a designer planned it with flight in mind. Similarly, it is as if our brains were *designed* so that behaviour fitted our early evolutionary environment. The environment in which we evolved was, of course, very different from that of modern London or Oslo. Our hunter-gatherer ancestors lived very different lives in that early environment, compared with ourselves. Yet we are still adapted for life in this older environment and our nervous systems were, in effect, 'designed' for solving the problems of life there. EP argues that it would be absurd to try to explain the workings of a car or a radio, or a heart or lung, without knowing what it was designed to do. By analogy, they argue that psychology also needs an evolutionary 'design' perspective. In this way, EP claims to have a unifying theoretical approach for all psychologists, including those concerned with causation and the brain.

Viewed in these terms, we can make sense of features of behaviour that otherwise might appear bizarre, e.g. our contemporary love of sweet foods even in the midst of an epidemic of diabetes, obesity and dental decay. Our behaviour reflects what was 'designed' for a life where there was not an abundance of sugars. For another example discussed by evolutionary psychology, why do symmetrical faces tend to be more attractive than asymmetrical ones (Perrett *et al.*, 1999)? One possible answer is that the symmetrical face is indicative of a younger age and a healthier developmental history. Thus, being attracted to such a stimulus would increase the chances of successful mating and is a factor that would be favoured by natural selection.

EP assumes that many features of human social life (e.g. worship), which might have been thought to be explained purely by cultural influences, are really to be explained at least in part in evolutionary terms (Workman and Reader, 2008). This is sometimes expressed uncritically by those who either promote or condemn a simple EP, as 'a gene for adultery' or 'a gene for religion' (note the singular 'a'). However, EP does not rest or fall on an assumption of single-gene effects. A combination of genes might give a bias towards, say, religious worship, since, by so doing, this combination has been placed at an advantage. Indeed, religion might still confer some adaptive advantages: as the cliché would have it 'families who pray together stay together'.

An immediate and well-worn qualification needs repeating: worship cannot literally be 'in the genes'. However, given certain genes, together with their social and learning contexts, worship might tend to emerge. By the same token, neither, for example, could physical height be determined simply by genes. Genes are a factor but for height to emerge also requires an appropriate environmental input, e.g. adequate food.

Such discussion has some important social messages. One of the reasons why EP is controversial is that it might at first seem to lend itself to rigid determinism. If something is 'in the genes', there appears to be little we can do about it. However, even if certain genes do exert a tendency in favour of, say, adultery, they represent only one contributory factor. The 'favoured' outcome is not necessarily inevitable.

The aspect of EP that has most fired the popular imagination and controversy is what it says about differences between the sexes (Workman and Reader, 2008). One point needs to be emphasized here. Though evolutionary theory might give insights into how behaviour has emerged in evolution, it cannot prescribe what humans *should* do morally. Such an unwarranted extrapolation is termed the 'naturalistic fallacy', and is a reason that doubtless turns some against evolutionary approaches.

Sex differences

Why do males appear to make more use of prostitutes and pornography and show a wish for greater indiscriminate promiscuity than do females? One might suppose that this reflects cultural norms and prohibitions ingrained in our institutions, i.e. 'social role theory' (see Archer, 1996). Change society, give enough time, and behaviour might change correspondingly. On the contrary, EP would suggest that such differences between the sexes reflect evolutionary history and different strategies of mating.

The optimal strategy for a human male (as with many species) to pass on his genes is different from that of a female. An instant and relatively indiscriminate sexual motivation and arousal, accompanied by promiscuity, might be to the advantage of the male since it maximizes his reproductive chances. There is relatively little to lose. The emphasis is on 'relatively' since, as always, there is not zero cost. For example, diseases can be caught and, since mating tends to focus the mind, genetic perpetuation might be rudely halted by an approaching tiger or jealous partner. However, for the female there is relatively much to lose. Some female inhibition and reserve ('coyness') might be to her genetic advantage, since in this way she can patiently wait to select the optimal male with whom to tie up her reproductive capacity for nine months or so and provide support.

Of course, few if any males visit prostitutes with the intention of passing on genes but no one is supposing that conscious intentions have had much to do with the evolution of sexuality. It is simply claimed that genes tend to code for those strategies that *in general* have served their own 'selfish' interests. In evolutionary history, a combination of genes that tended to promote male promiscuity via sexual motivational processes has been successful. Not all males are promiscuous. EP does not suggest that they should be, just as it does not suggest that all females should show coyness and fidelity. Genes give rise to tendencies not instructions carved in stone. It is simply that one can see a biological rationale in there being a difference between the sexes in this direction.

There is a point here many people misunderstand. Throughout evolution, rather than favouring desire for obtaining children as such, natural selection favoured sexual motivation. Of course, in the absence of a reliable technology of contraception, sexual motivation tends rather frequently to lead to children! This is not to deny that these days some people do desire to produce children as such but sexual desire was doubtless the driver in evolution. A casual glance at society today might suggest that this particular driver has lost none of its momentum over the course of human evolution.

While not denying the possibility that genetic differences might exert different degrees of tendency, explanations need to be framed in the broad gene–environment context discussed earlier. Biology is revealed within a cultural matrix (Barkow *et al.*, 1992).

Jealousy

EP makes testable predictions concerning sexual jealousy. What is the cost to an individual's chances of passing on his or her genes if the partner exhibits infidelity? The cost to a male partner could be large since it might be that his female partner produces offspring bearing another male's genes. Hence, the male partner misses his own opportunity of genetic transmission. The male partner could even unwittingly help with bringing up someone else's offspring. Thus, male sexual jealousy might involve a strong imperative against the sexual infidelity of his mate.

In terms of the female's genetic perpetuation, the cost of a partner's infidelity might seem to be much less. The female can at least be sure that the offspring she

---

A personal angle

Some early intellectual roots of evolutionary psychology?

As a teenager growing up in Rockville, Maryland, Leda Cosmides (personal communication), a founder of evolutionary psychology, read – and reread – *Walden Two*, a utopian novel by B.F. Skinner. She writes:

> Skinner, the most radical of the behavourists, claimed that by delivering rewards on just the right schedule, he could 'engineer' people to do anything, e.g. mothers who were indifferent to whether they raised their own child or someone else's. I was skeptical – isn't there such a thing as human nature?

In your opinion, who was right?

---

produces are in part genetically hers. A male can recover his sexual potency relatively quickly, and with it, his capacity to contribute genes to reproduction with the female partner. However, there is a threat to the partner from other females, which comes from the risk of being abandoned. The danger of this might be signalled by the male showing an abnormally large *emotional* interest in the well-being of another female, i.e. warmth and empathy. If that were to happen, the female might be put at a disadvantage in raising offspring. Therefore, one might expect some asymmetry in the trigger stimuli to jealousy, with males triggered more strongly by sexual infidelity and females by 'emotional infidelity'.

Working in the USA, Buss *et al.* (1992) invited people to imagine various scenarios and estimate the magnitude of the negative feelings that were evoked. These scenarios were of your mate (i) having sexual intercourse with another or (ii) forming a deep emotional attachment to another. Eighty-five per cent of the women found the second to arouse more negative emotions, whereas 60% of the males found the first to do so. EP predicts a difference in this direction. A similar effect was found in the Netherlands, a country with a tradition of egalitarianism and more progressive culture.

Some argue that, rather than reflecting evolved differences, such differences are due to different perceptions of the respective roles of men and women in our culture. For example, society suggests that in women, sexual infidelity is not likely to occur without emotional infidelity – the so-called 'double shot'. By contrast, male *sexual* infidelity can be dismissed as being without emotional attachment (DeSteno and Salovey, 1996; Harris and

Christenfeld, 1996). However, although not denying a cultural/cognitive factor, the EP researchers suggested that these different perceptions of sex roles are themselves to be understood in biological terms and directly capture the biological difference (Buss *et al.*, 1996). Cultural transmission of information might be expected to reflect and reinforce genetically determined differences.

Critiques of evolutionary psychology

Critiques of EP take many forms. Indeed, there now seems to be a small publishing industry dedicated to the polarities of claim and counter-claim. Few would argue against the notion that looking at evolution is essential for understanding current behaviour. The disputes mainly concern a particular interpretation of EP. This is sometimes termed the 'Santa Barbara school', named after the University of California location of its principal disciples (Tooby and Cosmides, 1990).

One point of criticism is that this school of evolutionary psychologists put their faith in what they term **modules**, special-purpose processors, each of which is dedicated to solving a particular problem. For example, the human brain would be described as being made up from such modules as a jealousy module, dedicated to detecting and acting upon threats as in sexual infidelity. Another such module is described as a cheating detection module. EP suggests that our mind is equipped with dedicated processes that alert us when someone is trying to cheat us, as in an unfair exchange of goods. Modules are something like cognitive equivalents of reflexes – fast, automatic and dedicated, with each solving just a single problem.

Tooby and Cosmides use the analogy of a Swiss army knife, a tool equipped with a number of components such as a knife and a can-opener, each serving just one particular function. You would have some difficulty in trying to use the can-opener to pull a cork from a wine bottle.

Critics of EP argue along two lines. First, they deny that we are quite as modularized ('compartmentalized') as EP suggests. Second, they suggest that, although some modularization of the brain does occur, EP has misunderstood its determinants. EP is said to put too much weight upon genetic factors and insufficient upon development. In fact, we turn out as we do as a result of the subtle dance between genes and environment. As noted earlier, a skill at riding a bicycle does not arise from *genes* producing a particular 'cycling module' – as one critic memorably expressed it, there were surely rather few bicycles around in our early evolution for this skill to be genetically encoded as a module! In reality, it emerges as the result of a combination of genes encoding for a brain with a *broad* capacity for controlling balance and early learning of the *particular* motor skills

involved in balancing a bicycle. The behaviour becomes automatic ('modularized') with practice.

EP and the critiques of it are a particularly good demonstration of the need to bring together different types of explanation. EP is based firmly in the tradition of functional and evolutionary explanation. However, its conclusions need to match an understanding of the possibilities arising from the brain and its development.

Later chapters will explore the relevance of EP to such topics as emotion, feeding and sexual motivation. We now turn to a case study that will serve to bring together the different types of explanation.

Section summary

1   Evolutionary psychology (EP) suggests that many features of human social life that might be seen as purely socially constructed have, in reality, a biological basis in genes.

2   EP makes some predictions regarding such things as differences in behaviour between the sexes (e.g. in triggers to jealousy).

3   EP uses the metaphor of design. It is as if the brain were designed for certain functional roles by employing dedicated modules.

4   Critics of EP suggest that it underestimates the flexibility of behaviour and the extent to which the environment is involved in forming modules.

☞ Test your knowledge

2.14 Suppose someone were to argue that the use of contraceptives is evidence against evolutionary psychology. What would a follower of EP most likely say in reply?

 Answer on page 48   WEB

Depression: a case study

Now it is time for an example that can bring some of the parts of the chapter together. Depression serves this role well.

The nature of depression and its causes

Most people feel sadness at times but psychologists would not call this 'depression'. Depression is a serious disorder, characterized by a long-term feeling of negative **affect** ('negative hedonic feelings'), powerless-ness, lack of motivation and an inability to influence events (Beck, 1967). The mental state is one of despair and fear, etc. Possible behavioural symptoms include early morning waking and withdrawal from social contact. Memory recall tends to be biased towards negative events. These disturbed mental and behavioural states are associated with abnormalities in brain function.

Depression covers a number of different disorders and the present section can take only a simplified view. In some cases, depression appears to be a consequence of developmental/learning events, e.g. successive failures or repeated marital breakdowns. This is sometimes termed 'reactive depression' and it can be understood in terms of external factors. However, such external events are experienced and interpreted by the nervous system and so we should not see their role as disconnected from the biology of the brain.

In other cases, there might be no obvious change in the external world associated with the onset of depression and one supposes that some internal change (e.g. abnormal hormonal level acting on the brain) is the trigger. However, such internal changes affect the patient's interpretation of events in the world, to see things more negatively. Either way, it is safest to assume that depression depends upon the interdependence between (i) activity in basic brain regions that underlie emotions common to all people (Panksepp, 1994) and (ii) the events within an individual lifetime and the way in which they are interpreted.

Depression is a good example of where a **biopsychosocial perspective** (Engel, 1977) can provide a valuable framework for understanding. Although depression is felt at an individual level (the 'psychological aspect'), its triggers are often classed as biological or social. Interventions to treat depression can be grouped under one of the three components of the term 'biopsychosocial': bio, psycho or social.

Depression is characterized by so-called 'rumination', repeatedly chewing over specific events (Andrews and Thomson, 2009). Such rumination is difficult, if not impossible, to suppress. It often relates to particular events that came before the episode of depression and which appear to be the triggers to the episode.

Genes and environment

Depression tends to run in families (McGuffin and Katz, 1993). This might reflect a social (developmental/learning) influence. Parents prone to depression might be remote in their interaction with offspring. This could affect the developing nervous system and hence the child might learn depressed ways of reacting. Also, differences between individuals in their tendency to depression

might be due to genetic differences. Depression could result from a combination of a direct genetic contribution and exposure to a depressed social context, which itself might be partly genetically determined.

How could genes give a direct tendency towards depression? It is still uncertain exactly how this happens but we can speculate. Our mental states depend upon the structure and activity of the brain. Evidence shows abnormalities in the blood flow to a region of the brain in depressed individuals (Drevets *et al.*, 1997). In their case, this region might be smaller than that of controls with fewer incoming connections from neurons. Since neurons, like other cells, arise in part from the action of genes, particular forms of genes possessed by depressed people might bias towards abnormality within this region. In other words, genes are responsible for the synthesis of proteins (Figures 2.3 and 2.11) and nervous systems are constructed in part from proteins.

The fact that there is a tendency for depression to run in families is suggestive of a genetic factor but is not sufficient to prove this. One way of investigating is to compare identical twins (who are genetically identical) and fraternal twins (who are not genetically identical), though even this is problematic.

Investigators believe that there is a genetic contribution but estimates vary as to its size, depending in part upon the type of depression (McGuffin and Katz, 1993). Even though there might be a strong genetic contribution to depression, this does not mean that depression is 'written in the genes' as a predetermined property of the brain. Rather, a gene (or genes) could exert a tendency towards depression but this might only be revealed in combination with (i) such developmental factors as the mother's exposure to stress or alcohol or (ii) later stressful life events. Even the emergence of an adult brain that is prone to depression does not mean that the disorder is inevitable. The environment might give a tendency towards mental health. By analogy, knowing that a piece of glass is brittle does not necessarily mean that it will break. Rather it means that, given an external 'stressor', the brittle glass has a higher probability of breaking.

It might be that the genes coding for a *tendency* to depression also manifest in an aspect of brain and behaviour that can be measured. This aspect might be detectable in people not currently suffering from depression but who have suffered in the past or are likely to suffer in the future. Such a marker is sometimes termed an **endophenotype**. One possibility under investigation is a relative lack of responsiveness to hedonic stimuli (McCabe *et al.*, 2009). Using neuroimaging, McCabe *et al.* showed that people who have recovered from depression show a relatively low reaction of brain regions normally triggered by reward (in this experiment, chocolate). By contrast, they showed enhanced activity in brain regions encoding disgust, when presented with a trigger stimulus.

Function

Would we expect to make sense of depression from a functional perspective? Using evolutionary psychology, theorists like to speculate. Arguing by analogy, it would be absurd to ask, what is the evolutionary advantage of having a broken leg? However, we might reasonably discuss the evolutionary costs and benefits of constructing bones from material that is able to break. Similarly, we could ask about the advantage of having a nervous system constructed in a way that brings particular benefits but does so with an inevitable associated risk of depression.

Is depression an example of dysregulation?

Depression is normally considered to be a mental illness or disorder. Indeed, it can (i) be seriously disabling, (ii) cause much psychological pain and (iii) be frequently treated with medicines. If it is a case of pathology, then EP would, of course, not describe the underlying process as an 'adaptation'. Similarly, we would not use 'adaptation' to describe the processes underlying, say, cancer or diabetes. However, investigators do consider the evolutionary 'design' of the body that means that inevitable trade-offs leave us vulnerable to such disorders (Nesse, 2009).

A number of investigators have suggested that depression is an example of 'dysregulation'. This is where a brain process that is itself an adaptation (e.g. giving a capacity for sadness) can none-the-less play a role in performance that is non-adaptive (e.g. major depression) (Nettle, 2004). To understand depression in such terms, it is easy to appreciate the value of negative ('aversive') emotion in our evolution (Nesse, 2009). A starting point is to consider first that positive emotions play a role in forward engagement with the world, e.g. exploring the environment, approaching tasty food, courting partners and consolidating social bonds. They underlie the motivation that keeps us going when we are making progress towards goals (Carver and Scheier, 1990).

Symmetry suggests the 'design requirement' of a reciprocal emotion, characterized as negative, which is triggered when things are not going 'according to plan'. A condition called 'mild depression' or 'sadness' appears to arise when something socially valued is lost, social goals are thwarted, an individual perceives social exclusion or social rank is lost (Allen and Badcock, 2003). Such emotion could play a functional role in causing individuals to abandon pointless goals and pursue other goals when the opportunity arises or, as Nesse (2009, p. 23) suggests: 'in situations when all possible actions will bring costs greater than benefits, the best thing to do is … nothing'.

Such mild depression causes a focus of attention upon social threats and a hypersensitivity to them (Allen and Badcock, 2003). Information processing is biased to construe events in terms of threats to the social standing of the self. By comparison, the design consideration underlying other negative emotions seems self-evident. Pain caused by damage to the body is an obvious example and it motivates people to try to eliminate or, at least, reduce the triggers that are causing the pain (Chapter 14). Nesse (2009, p. 23) argues that where individuals cannot relinquish pursuit of a goal, then what is ordinary sadness can 'escalate into pathological depression'.

Depression might be the inevitable consequence of excessive stretching of an adaptive system of negative emotion to beyond its adaptive range. By analogy, other systems that are of undoubted adaptive value can get 'out-of-kilter' and have harmful consequences. An example is the immune system, which normally protects the body against invasion by bacteria and viruses, as well as cancerous cells. None the less, the same system that organizes this reaction to invaders sometimes over-reacts. It treats even perfectly healthy body tissue as if it is the enemy and launches an attack on it. Chronic and debilitating pain is a similar example. Such excesses seem to be the price that is occasionally paid (part of the trade-off) for possessing systems of such sensitivity.

So, depression might appear to be a pathological extreme in the performance of a system of negative emotions that in milder doses has served a vital function. The question raised is – at what intensity, does a useful function turn into pathology, where it impairs fitness? Alternatively, could even full depression be an adaptation?

Could full depression be an adaptation?

EP encourages us to think 'outside the box'. It has led several authors to the counter-intuitive suggestion that, not just sadness, but full depression might be an adaptation (Andrews and Thomson, 2009; Price *et al.*, 1994). What functional role might it have played? Several possibilities have been suggested and these might also, less controversially, apply to sadness at a level below full depression:

1 Depression might have served to signal appeasement in social conflicts and thereby to have deflected hostility and aggression (Gilbert and Allan, 1998).

2 Related to (1), depression might have elicited sympathy and thereby assistance from kin, as a 'cry for help' (Watson and Andrews, 2002). There is a characteristic facial expression associated with depression (Allen and Badcock, 2003), which could help to trigger an empathetic ('mirroring') emotion in others.

3 By lowering motivation, depression could have encouraged withdrawal from high-risk activities (e.g. aggression, competition for resources, mating) and thereby served conservation of energy at a time when it was beneficial to do so (Allen and Badcock, 2003). Some non-human species, e.g. tree shrews, show a similar reaction in the face of defeat (Gilbert and Allan, 1998; see present text, Chapter 13). (It is worth noting here that something like depression seems to be the emotional reaction by which infections persuade animals to remain immobile, which surely aids their recovery; Hart, 1988.)

4 Finally, it might have facilitated adaptive cognitive processing that served to solve those social dilemmas that appear to be the fundamental trigger to depression, something termed the 'social navigation hypothesis' (Andrews and Thomson, 2009; Watson and Andrews, 2002). As part of this process, depression directs attention to social threats and sensitizes their effects (Allen and Badcock, 2003).

Clearly, these four are not mutually exclusive and interactions between them are evident. Concerning (4), persistent rumination might have served to deliver solutions to social dilemmas (Andrews and Thomson, 2009). Given limited conscious processing resources, depression exerts a powerful bias on cognition, such that rumination on the source of the depression engages these resources. Rumination is persistent, difficult to suppress and relatively immune from distraction. Factors 1–3 might have facilitated such rumination on social dilemmas. The negative emotional state gives a bias against activities (e.g. sexual behaviour) that might have competed with the rumination processing.

Social dilemmas appear to be at the core of human life (Andrews and Thomson, 2009). On the one hand, there are rather obvious benefits to fitness in living in social groups, e.g. mutual hunting and defence, sharing of food and child-rearing duties. On the other hand, at times, there can be fitness benefits to pursuing one's own selfish agenda even at the expense of others (e.g. cheating on food distribution, abandoning a mate for a more desirable one, sexual infidelity). Such multiple and conflicting goals seem to characterize the social dilemmas that are said to be the triggers to depression.

Andrews and Thomson suggest (p. 643) that: 'depression evolved by natural selection, probably because depression helped people analyse and solve the problems about which they were ruminating'. Part of the evidence that they cite in support of their argument is that depression shows a number of coordinated features which act together towards the same end point. We have considered just two of these: increased rumination and withdrawal from activities. However, Andrews and Thomson suggest that there are others, such as regulated changes in the chemical environment of particular regions of the brain that are involved in producing the depression reaction. This makes it more likely that these regions can sustain their high activity over long periods of time. This combination of coordinated changes suggests a function rather than chance. If this logic is correct, then those variations in genes that contribute to depression might be seen as having conferred an advantage in evolution rather than being abnormalities (Nesse, 2009).

Andrews and Thomson use an analogy to make their point: fever. Fever is sometimes treated as if it is a disease in its own right and people feel that they should act so as to counter it. However, fever is indicative of an infection and it helps the body to fight the infection. To try to get rid of the fever might well prove counterproductive. It would be better to try to fight the *cause* of the fever: the infection.

To suggest that depression is an adaptation that arose in our early evolution does not necessarily imply that it is still advantageous in the 21st century. However, it might still serve some useful function. Of course, the only reliable way that investigators can test its possible functional value is to consider the evidence around us today and to speculate from this.

Some evidence points to social dilemmas being more readily solved in a depressed state (Andrews and Thomson, 2009). Of course, now some people seek escape from the pain of depression by means of alcohol, drugs or suicide, rather than finding more viable solutions to social dilemmas. However, this does not deny a functional role for depression in our early evolution or even that it brings advantages these days. By way of comparison, some people in chronic physical pain tragically seek an outlet in these same ways but this does not deny the evolutionary significance of physical pain as a means of defence against damage to the body (Chapter 14). Even in recent times, there is evidence of people born with insensitivity to pain and who do not survive for long.

Evolutionary psychology encourages speculation that depression is much more common in modern industrial societies than among our hunter-gatherer ancestors. Of course, we can only speculate since we have no reliable information (Nesse, 2009). However, it is easy to identify factors that seem to be particularly present as triggers in today's world. These include lack of physical exercise, alienation from the social group, unemployment, pressures through the media to have a perfect body and material possessions, associated with a failure to thrive in a highly competitive environment. Also, in a society in which many are alienated from kin, any potential adaptive value of depression in terms of soliciting help might now be lost (Allen and Badcock, 2003).

Critiques of depression as an adaptation

While acknowledging that the system underlying negative emotion is an adaptation, Nettle (2004) presented a case that major depression itself is not. Some of the aspects to his argument are summarized next.

Watson and Andrews (2002) suggested that the very wide prevalence of depression and its cross-cultural universality point to its being an adaptation. Nettle disputes this. As an example of where something is widely prevalent but is clearly not an adaptation, he gives maternal death at childbirth. Tragically, this is very widespread across cultures and surely was much more so prior to sophisticated surgical assistance. It appears to arise as a result of evolutionary dynamics. The newborn infant is vulnerable and has a long period of development before the vulnerability declines. It appears advantageous that as much of this development as possible takes place in the shelter of the womb.

Alas, developing brains mean big brains and thereby big heads. This creates a problem for infant and mother at childbirth, and there is an upper limit on brain size.

The fact that genes that contribute to depression can be identified does not make it an adaptation. Rather, depression could be an example of a so-called 'maladaptive by-product' of something that is an adaptation, i.e. a capacity to show sadness.

Watson and Andrews note that physical pain has been fruitfully investigated from a functional perspective and suggest that this can be extended to depression. Nettle objects on the grounds that all humans (with the very rare exception) have the capacity to experience physical pain. He argues that (p. 93): 'there is no evidence that all individuals have the capacity to become clinically depressed'. Although social stresses are considered a prime trigger to depression, most people who experience such stresses do not become depressed. Rather, they experience 'normal' levels of sadness.

If depression is an adaptation, its appearance should be appropriate to the triggering circumstances. Much evidence points to social dilemmas as being a trigger. However, since depression tends to recur, it is difficult to disentangle cause and effect (Nettle, 2004). Some social dilemmas might well be the result of depression. Nettle notes that, by far, the greatest risk factor for an episode of depression is having had an earlier episode. This is true in the case of postnatal depression in women, where subsequent episodes of depression are not necessarily associated with birth. There appears to be sensitization of brain processes, such that subsequent episodes are only weakly, if at all, related to life events.

An additional factor is that, whereas sadness might trigger sympathy and help, protracted and major depression appears to lead to 'compassion fatigue' on the part of kin (Allen and Badcock, 2003).

Assessment of the arguments

No conclusive answer can be given to the question of adaptation. On balance the evidence seems to favour the view that major depression represents dysregulation of a process of sadness that undoubtedly serves an adaptive function. Some benefits of depression as articulated by the advocates that it is an adaptation might be achievable with subclinical sadness (Nettle, 2004). Maybe pain provides a useful comparison, as something representing an adaptation most of the time but which can occasionally tilt into dysregulation. Evolution cannot guarantee the perfect solution.

Whatever the truth, I hope that you agree that EP presents some challenging ideas and helps us to ask insightful questions.

Treatments

Treatments for depression include cognitive therapy (targeting how the patient views events in the world) and drugs. A biological psychologist would assume that, when a cognitive therapy works, in some way it changes the brain's operating characteristics. Drugs act on the neurons of the brain and thereby change their information processing, reflected in cognitive and mood changes.

Triggers to depression are often social in nature (Allen and Badcock, 2003). Examples include marital problems, such as divorce, and these are perhaps best addressed at the social level (Andrews and Thomson, 2009), as in marital reconciliation. Taking an evolutionary perspective might prove relevant to treating depression (Andrews and Thomson, 2009). Since the triggers so often involve social dilemmas and the ruminative content concerns these dilemmas, this suggests that the best treatment would come in trying to resolve social dilemmas. From this perspective, faulty cognition and attempts to correct it would be seen as of secondary value, except where the therapy provides insight into action to resolve social dilemmas. Trying to interrupt the pattern of rumination might even be counterproductive. By comparison, good medical practice looks beyond pain and fever to search for their causes as targets of intervention (Nesse, 2009). However, not all doctors have time, expertise or the remit to try to alter a person's social context.

An example of an unambiguous biological cause of depression is the excessive secretion of certain hormones associated with Cushing's disease (Conrad, 2008). This arises from a tumour and so such depression clearly needs to be addressed at the level of a biological intervention (in this case, surgery). In the more usual cases of depression, treatments by means of drugs clearly also represent a biological intervention, no matter what the cause of the depression.

There is much interest at the moment in the therapeutic possibilities of electrical stimulation of particular regions of the brain through surgically implanted electrodes. Applied to depression, the rationale is that the brain of a depressed person is in a different state of activity from that of a non-depressed. If successful, such simulation would move the pattern of activity of the brain of the depressed individual to nearer that of the non-depressed (Kringelbach *et al.*, 2007).

Section summary

1 Depression is a mental and behavioural state of powerlessness and low affect.

2 It is logical to seek a disturbed biological basis in the brain underlying this disorder, whatever its cause.

3 There appears to be a genetic contribution to depression.

4 Evolutionary psychology poses interesting challenges regarding depression.

5 Depression could be a contemporary exaggerated expression of a behavioural tendency that was adaptive in small doses earlier in evolution.

☞ Test your knowledge

2.15 What would it mean to suggest that depression is an 'adaptation'?

Answer on page 48   WEB

Bringing things together

Having its focus on functional and evolutionary types of explanation, this chapter has shown how the four types of biological explanation, including causal and developmental/learning (Chapter 1), are interrelated. It showed where we can gain a fuller picture of any one type, with at least some knowledge of the others.

From now on, the main focus of the book is the nervous system and behaviour. However, it can be useful, for example, when trying to understand how the brain controls behaviour to be able to ask well-informed questions on functional aspects. Similarly, asking about the function that behaviour has served in evolution (what it has been 'designed' to do) can sometimes usefully inform causal explanations (Barkow *et al.*, 1992).

Researchers have gained much insight into the brain mechanisms of, for example, memory by asking a simple functional question: What was it 'designed' to achieve? In our early evolutionary environment, what sort of information was it important for humans to remember? In the spirit of EP, it appears that there are different types of memory, each adapted to solving a particular type of problem.

Similarly, one can make better sense of the brain's role in sexual choice by considering the functional value of particular choices of partner in terms of reproductive advantage. We can better understand the dynamics of a colony of wild animals in terms of care for offspring and apparent altruism to kin, etc., if we can see a rationale for this in terms of the evolution of their ancestors. We can be informed of what kinds of process might be expected to underlie causation involving social dynamics.

The issues raised in this chapter will be with us throughout the book. You should try to get into the habit of thinking in terms of the four types of explanation when you encounter instances of behaviour in the subsequent chapters. Sometimes the relevance of the particular type of functional and evolutionary explanation summarized by the term 'evolutionary psychology' will be made explicit.

 See the video coverage for this chapter and experience how psychologists use different kinds of explanation.

Summary of Chapter 2

1 The activities in which an animal engages, such as feeding, sex and aggression, have a role in passing on its genes.

2 Any behaviour has both benefits and costs. Natural selection favours strategies for which, on average, benefits outweigh costs.

3 The understanding of processes, such as reflexes, at a causal level can both help, and be helped by, an understanding of them in functional and evolutionary terms.

4 In sexual reproduction, different combinations of genetic material are formed and then tested in the environment.

5 A molecule of DNA forms the base for genetic information.

6 Genes code for the construction of proteins that form, among other things, the nervous system. Hence, as part of complex loops of influence, there is a sequence of effects: (gene) → (nervous system) → (behaviour).

7 Genes and environment act together as determinants of behaviour.

8 Evolutionary psychology suggests the controversial idea that the brain is composed of genetically determined modules, each adapted to serve just one function.

9 Depression is a good example to illustrate where causal, developmental/learning, evolutionary and functional explanations can be brought together.

Further reading

For genes and behaviour, see Flint *et al.* (2010). For an excellent balanced approach to evolutionary psychology, see Workman and Reader (2008). For an argument for evolutionary psychology, see Buss (2008), and for a challenging critique, see Buller (2005).

Answers

Explanations for answers to 'test your knowledge' questions can be found on the website www.pearsoned.co.uk/toates

2.1 (i) Feeding, drinking and temperature regulation. (ii) Homeostasis protects the integrity and efficiency of the body so that an animal survives to mate and be in a healthy reproductive condition, as well as (in some species) caring for offspring.

2.2 Benefits

2.3 (i) Hearing

2.4 (i) High speed, (ii) hard-wired, (iii) common to members of a given species

2.5 (i) Stereotypy. (ii) It might only appear under abnormal conditions, e.g. captivity, not experienced in the natural environment, where evolution took place.

2.6 (i) Zygote

2.7 (ii) Sperm cell, (iii) unfertilized egg cell

2.8 Protein

2.9 A daughter

2.10 A son

2.11 Alleles

2.12 Gene, allele

2.13 (i) It increases

2.14 That evolution uses sexual desire as its means of genetic perpetuation, rather than using a desire to produce children as such.

2.15 That depression has been tested in early evolution and humans showing this were placed at an advantage. Thereby the genes responsible were passed on to future generations.

Visit www.pearsoned.co.uk/toates
for a range of resources to support study.
Test yourself with multiple choice questions and access a bank of over 100 videos that will bring the topics to life.

Chapter 3
The nervous and endocrine systems

Learning outcomes for Chapter 3

After studying this chapter, you should be able to:

1 Distinguish between the nervous system and endocrine system, while illustrating how behaviour depends upon their close integration.

2 Describe some of the ways in which the nervous system can be divided and classified for the purposes of explanation. Give a rationale for classification and, on the basis of it, exemplify how information is transmitted within the nervous system.

3 Explain how information is communicated at synapses, distinguishing excitation and inhibition. Compare and contrast neurotransmission and neuromodulation.

4 Compare and contrast the transmission of information *within* a neuron and *between* neurons.

5 Describe how the properties of synapses can change with development/learning and explain the significance of this for psychology.

6 Distinguish between (i) neurotransmitters and neuromodulators and (ii) hormones. Compare and contrast communication mediated by (i) and (ii).

7 Explain the origin of the term 'autonomic nervous system' and describe the ways in which its divisions can be classified.

Scene-setting questions

1 How and why does fear make the heart beat faster?
2 Why do we have so little conscious control over the inside of our bodies? For example, why can't we stop ourselves blushing?
3 How can mood affect the gut as in a 'tummy upset' following trauma?
4 Do expressions such as 'gut feelings' and 'matters of the heart' have any meaning in terms of biology? Is there feedback from periphery to brain?
5 How might hormones affect mood?
6 Can hormones affect the structure of the cells of the brain? ◀WEB▶

Can hormones affect the structure of the cells of the brain? Explore the video on the website accompanying this book at **www.pearsoned. co.uk/toates**

How does our survival depend upon coordinated action between nervous systems and hormones?

Source: Empics.

Introduction

Threats come in many forms, from floods to wild animals. There are some common features of our reaction to them. Imagine that you suddenly confront a threat such as a large angry bear in a forest. Not a pleasant prospect but one that serves to focus the mind of student, author and bear alike. You react by running, to get back to your tourist bus before the bear gets there (recalling that bears too can run). Your heart beats furiously. This indicates that, as well as organizing running, the brain automatically accelerates the heartbeat. Energetic behaviour requires a large supply of fuel to the muscles, particularly those of the legs, and the blood delivers it. This scenario exemplifies *coordination* between physiology (changes in blood supply) and behaviour (running). Nervous and hormonal ('endocrine') systems are involved in producing such coordination. The system involving hormones is the **endocrine system.**

By contrast, imagine yourself now relaxing on a sofa after a meal, with thoughts far from angry bears. Your body is at rest and your brain has automatically lowered your heart-rate. There is now an automatic diversion of relatively large amounts of blood to the gut to facilitate digestion and relatively little blood is flowing to the muscles of the legs. Again, there is coordination between behaviour and physiology in the interests of efficiency and thereby survival.

These two examples introduce the organizing theme of the present chapter: adaptation involves coordinated action that is exerted simultaneously within the body's internal and external environments. How do we investigate such coordination?

As a convenience for explanation, the body is divided into systems. Chapters 1 and 2 introduced two of these: the nervous system and the endocrine system. The present chapter examines coordinated action: the nervous and endocrine systems in interaction. These systems detect events at one location in the body, communicate information throughout the body and trigger action at another location.

Hormones are chemicals that are secreted from **glands** (although there are also glands that do not secrete hormones, e.g. the salivary glands). The nervous system affects the release of hormones. On perceiving danger, for example, the nervous system would trigger release of hormones that facilitate an increase in the supply of fuel to the muscles. In turn, hormones affect the activity of the nervous system.

The action of the brain on the heart was just described as 'automatic'. By contrast, other features of the scenarios would be described as 'voluntary'. It might not feel as if you have much voluntary control or free-will when you confront an angry bear. However, at least in principle, you could have stood your ground and asserted your right to walk in the forest. Resting after a meal illustrates voluntary behaviour – you might have chosen to go for a walk.

So, a fundamental distinction is between 'automatic' and 'voluntary'. In the examples just given, the brain's action on instigating behaviour in the outside world is voluntary, whereas its action on the inside environment is automatic. However, it is not only action on the internal environment that is automatic. Consider the example of the reflex that protects you from tissue damage (Chapter 2). It 'just happens' automatically as a result of the stimulus, the construction of the nervous system and the activation of the muscles. As also observed in Chapter 2, such distinctions are not absolute. Although there are some rather clear instances of voluntary and automatic, some behaviour exhibits bits of each. (If there were not such complication, it would surely not be psychology!)

We will look first at the nervous system, then the endocrine system and finally their interaction.

Section summary

1 The nervous and endocrine systems are involved in coordinating action between the internal and external environments.

2 These systems serve an adaptive function, as do their interactions.

Test your knowledge

3.1 Within which of the following systems is communication mediated by chemicals being transported in the bloodstream? (i) Nervous, (ii) endocrine, (iii) both (i) and (ii).

Answer on page 81

What nervous systems do

Whether exhibiting reflexes, feeding, fighting or fleeing, or whatever, the nervous system controls behaviour. Similarly, our internal feelings, such as fear, depression or joy, depend upon the nervous system. So, understanding the system and the cells that form it is fundamental. We will start with a description of the nervous system, then give some relatively simple examples to illustrate what neurons do. We then look at action exerted on the external environment, and at coordination between internal and external events. Finally, we consider emotions.

Basic division of the nervous system

The nervous system (Figure 3.1(a)) is made up of billions of neurons, which have different shapes and sizes. (The terms 'neural' and 'neuronal' are adjectives to refer to neurons, e.g. 'neural pathways'.) There are other cells located alongside neurons, discussed later. The nervous system comprises brain, spinal cord and neurons located throughout the 'periphery' of the body.

The neurons in the brain and the spinal cord make up the **central nervous system (CNS)**. The spinal cord is a column of neurons located within the backbone (Figure 3.1(a)). The CNS is sheltered from traumatic damage by bony structures: the skull for the brain and the backbone for the spinal cord. All of the nervous system that is not in the brain or spinal cord is called the **peripheral nervous system**.

How a reflex works

A simple reflex can illustrate how collections of neurons work. These same principles can then be adapted to be applicable more broadly.

You might feel that Figure 3.2 has an ancient appearance but please be patient: the logic underlying the age of the figure will be revealed shortly. The diagram shows two neurons marked in blue. Suppose that the 'Neuron ending' comes into contact with a noxious stimulus, e.g. heat or a sharp object. This excites activity in the neuron indicated with the ending. Activity follows the ascending arrow and a message is sent to the spinal cord. In response, a message comes back from the spinal cord in the neuron indicated by the descending arrow, to the muscle of the leg. The leg moves away from the noxious object, i.e. a reflex action. Now let us see in detail how this happens.

Figure 3.1(b) shows some of the neurons of the spinal cord and periphery. (In reality, few neurons look anything like the 'typical' cells shown in Figure 1.2.) These are some of the neurons involved in the reflex of withdrawing the foot from a noxious object. Neuron 1 corresponds to the neuron with its ending indicated in Figure 3.2. The tip of neuron 1 is at the foot and this neuron extends to the spinal cord. Neuron 4 conveys the signal from the spinal cord in Figure 3.2.

Consider the sequence of neurons represented by the arrows ($1 \rightarrow 2 \rightarrow 3 \rightarrow 4$) in Figure 3.1(b). Through such neurons, signals from the foot instigated by real or impending tissue damage (the noxious stimulus) communicate with the muscle of the leg to trigger a movement of the foot away from this stimulus.

The noxious stimulus very rapidly triggers electrical activity in neuron 1, which was previously inactive. This takes the form of a series of electrical pulses, termed **action potentials**. Activity in neuron 1 triggers action potentials in neuron 2. In turn, neuron 2 triggers activity in neuron 3, which triggers neuron 4. Action potentials in neuron 4 trigger muscle cells controlling the foot (muscles are made up of many such cells). So, the foot is moved from the noxious stimulus. Figure 3.1(b) is a simplification; in reality, there are many such parallel pathways of neurons acting simultaneously.

The sequence of events in neurons 1–4 and the muscle constitutes the basis of a reflex. Figure 3.1(c) shows a trace of action potentials and four such traces are included in Figure 3.1(b). This defensive action against damage to the body is local, organized at the spinal cord and termed a **spinal reflex.**

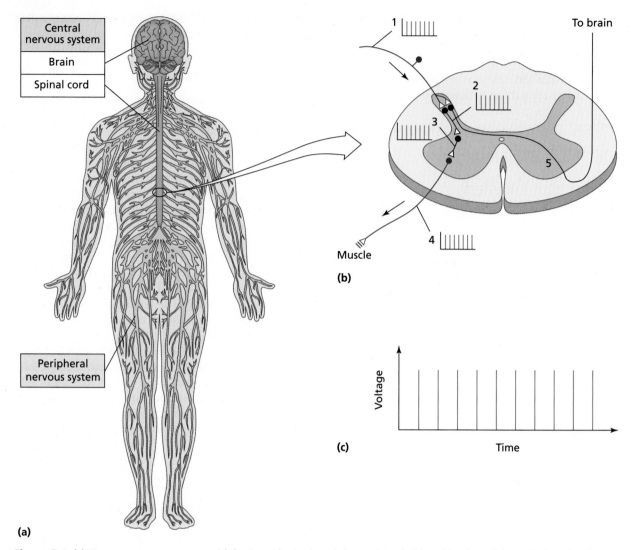

Figure 3.1 (a) Human nervous system, with brain and spinal cord shown in red. (b) A thin slice of the spinal cord with some of the neurons located there. (c) Graph showing action potentials.

Figure 3.2 Two of the neurons that underlie a simple reflex. *Source:* after Halliday (1998, Fig. 5.22).

Reflexes, the spinal cord and the brain

Neuron 1 of Figure 3.1(b) is a member of a class of neurons termed **sensory neurons**, neurons that detect information on events in the external world or inside the body and transmit it to the CNS. The neuron's tip constitutes a **receptor**, not to be confused with a receptor molecule (described shortly). In the present example, it is sensitive to tissue damage, suffered either directly at the tip itself or in the near vicinity.

The reaction to the stimulus of Figures 3.1 and 3.2 has two aspects, both triggered by a type of neuron that is sensitive to tissue damage, termed a **nociceptive neuron** (neuron 1 in Figure 3.1(b)). The expression 'nociceptive' refers to tissue damage and pain, and it derives from the same root as the word 'noxious'. First, the reflexive aspect consists of quickly moving the foot.

Second, nociceptive information reaches the brain, mediated by neuron 1 and then neuron 5, which carries the information up the spinal cord. This triggers pain. A nociceptive neuron would not be receptive to other stimuli such as harmless touch.

Sometimes investigators speak in abstract terms of 'information' conveyed along neurons and, at other times, in the physical terms of 'action potentials'. These are two different languages for describing the same reality: the brain is 'informed of a stimulus' or 'action potentials arrive at the brain'. By analogy, the sound of your doorbell conveys information on someone's presence. Alternatively, you might speak in terms of electric currents and sound waves.

Neurons communicate information, process it and trigger action. Information (e.g. heat at the foot, sounds and lights) is communicated to the brain, where decisions are made. In the brain, the physical embodiment of our mental life – perception, emotion, memory, decision-making, etc. – consists of the activity of neurons. For example, pain plays a part in labelling flames in memory as dangerous, to be avoided.

As part of the spinal reflex (Figures 3.1 and 3.2), information travelling from tissue damage to the muscle does not go via the brain. Therefore, the distance that information needs to travel to trigger a response is relatively short. Removal of the foot from the noxious stimulus is correspondingly rapid. The reflexive response is well under way by the time you experience the pain. At your 'leisure', you can then think about your mistake in getting too near to the flame and experience the pain as a reminder.

The scenario illustrates how mind and behaviour relate to the underlying neural components. For example, how information arises from tissue damage and the speed with which it is conducted to the brain can be understood in terms of the properties of neurons. This can then be related to pain.

Coding of information

Information is coded in neurons by how *frequently* action potentials occur (other codes also exist but are beyond our scope). Some neurons produce action potentials spontaneously and so a signal is carried by increases or decreases in frequency relative to the spontaneous rate. Other neurons are inactive until triggered into activity. For an example of how frequency conveys information, a sharp object that penetrates the skin would trigger action potentials at a higher frequency than one making only superficial impact. In Figure 3.1(b), a higher frequency of action potentials in neuron 4 would produce a stronger reaction by the muscle.

A personal angle

René Descartes

Consider Figure 3.3: an example of behaviour described by René Descartes, who was working in the 16th–17th centuries and concerned with explaining what causes behaviour. It must be one of the most reproduced figures in all behavioural science. Now you can see the idea behind the historical flavour of Figure 3.2: to facilitate comparison. Descartes observed automatons in the gardens of St Germain-en-Laye, near Paris. These hydraulically activated statues of monsters were triggered into activity by a visitor stepping on a pedal. Descartes reasoned that all non-human behaviour (and much human behaviour) was like this: an automatic response to a stimulus.

Descartes wondered how heat triggers the reaction ('reflex') of limb withdrawal and the perception of pain. In those days, no one knew about neurons and he speculated in terms of wires, pulleys and valves in the body. Descartes suggested that information had to get to the brain to trigger action (Figure 3.3). Action can indeed be initiated by this route and the sensation of pain does involve transmission to the brain. However, the fast reaction of moving the foot from the noxious stimulus is the outcome of an automatic reflex organized by a collection of neurons at the leg and spinal cord (Figures 3.1 and 3.2).

Incidentally, it is not surprising that we can improve on Descartes, who was working with little to guide him.

Figure 3.3 Descartes' model of action. The foot touches a hot object, a message is sent to the brain and the person quickly withdraws the foot.
Source: after Halliday (1998, Fig. 5.21).

Figure 3.4(a) represents a different sensory system: that detecting cold. It introduces some more terminology. Two components of neurons 1 and 2 are the **axon** and the **cell body**. Their role will be described in more detail shortly. For the moment, consider just two of their properties.

1 The axon is the long extension component of the neuron and along which action potentials are conducted. (This component is also shown in Figure 3.1 serving this same role of communication.)
2 The cell body is the site where the genetic material of the cell is located. Note the different location of the cell body in neurons 1 and 2, relative to the axon. (You can also see the comparable cell bodies in Figure 3.1(b).)

Imagine that you put your hand in a glass of cold water (Figure 3.4). A series of action potentials is triggered by cold at the tip of a type of sensory neuron sensitive to cold. In Figure 3.4(b), trace (i) represents the response to a moderate cold, whereas trace (ii) is when the temperature at the skin is further decreased. Decreasing temperature is coded by an increase in *frequency* of action potentials. A further decrease in temperature might be coded by an even higher frequency (trace iii).

Suppose cold (Figure 3.4) has initiated action potentials in neuron 1. Action potentials arise at the tip of the axon and are transmitted along its length by the following means. Action potentials at the tip influence the neighbouring region so that this region then shows an action potential. The action potential then invades the next bit of axon and so on. The effect is that the action potential moves along the axon.

In a given neuron, each action potential travels at the same speed. Also, one action potential is exactly like another in shape and duration. Information is coded not by the form or speed of the action potential but by how many of them occur in a period of time. Information is carried to the brain by means of (a) *which* neurons are active and (b) the frequency of action potentials that they exhibit.

At the brain, the arrival of action potentials in a neural pathway is interpreted in terms of the events that would normally trigger that pathway. Information arriving in the pathway mediated by neurons 1 and 5 in Figure 3.1(b) would be interpreted as pain. That arriving in the pathway of which neurons 1 and 2 in Figure 3.4(a) form part would be interpreted as cold. If you accidentally put pressure on your eye, you tend to 'see' visual objects even though they are not present physically. The mechanical disturbance triggers action potentials in neurons that normally convey visual information and this is interpreted as visual events.

(a)   **(b)**

Figure 3.4 (a) Information on cold temperature is conveyed from periphery to the brain via neurons 1 and then 2. (b) The reaction of neuron 1.
Source: after Toates (1998c).

Communication between neurons

Neurons almost make direct contact with their neighbouring cells: another neuron or a muscle cell (Figures 3.1(b) and 3.4(a)). The region where one neuron almost touches another cell is known as a **synapse** (Figure 3.5). This synapse represents any one of the links between cells of Figure 3.1 and 3.4. Details of communication involving synapses will be developed later. For the moment, we consider only one type of synapse, where activity in one neuron induces activity in another cell. The synapse consists of part of each cell and the small gap between them.

Communication at the point of contact between neurons is by means of a chemical termed a 'chemical messenger', 'transmitter' or **neurotransmitter**. In Figure 3.5, in response to activity, neurotransmitter is released at the terminal of what is termed the **presynaptic neuron**. This neurotransmitter influences the activity of the **postsynaptic neuron**. How does this occur?

Embedded at the surface of the postsynaptic neuron, there are molecules termed **receptors** (not to be confused with the earlier use of this term). They are receptors specifically for the neurotransmitter released at the adjacent neuron. The occupation of these receptors by neurotransmitter influences the electrical activity of the second neuron, so that, in the examples described so far, an action potential in one neuron will tend to trigger a further action potential in the next cell. Although this shows a general principle, you might like to consider the presynaptic neuron to be neuron 1 of Figure 3.4(a) and the postsynaptic to be neuron 2. The same sequence applies to the connections between neurons in Figure 3.1(b). A similar process applies to the link between neuron 4 and the muscle cell, where the latter is termed the postsynaptic cell.

The brain and action

Action within the external world

Apart from reflexes, movement can, of course, be commanded by a voluntary decision made in the brain (Figure 3.6). Imagine that a person suddenly points his or her finger at an object. A decision to move the finger is made in the brain and information conveyed down the spinal cord. The first neuron in the sequence (neuron 1 of Figure 3.6) transmits action potentials to the synapse between neurons 1 and 2. Action potentials are then instigated in neuron 2 and information transmitted to muscle cells, where mechanical ('motor') action by a finger is triggered. Neurons of the kind shown as neuron 2, termed **motor neurons**, carry information to muscles. The term 'motor system' refers to the motor neuron and the control exerted via it.

Most neurons are neither sensory nor motor. Rather, they are located somewhere between the input and output sides, wholly within the brain or spinal cord. They are called **interneurons**. Neurons 2, 3 and 5 in Figure 3.1(b) are interneurons.

We now look at the role of neurons in triggering coordinated action inside the body and outside.

Coordinated action inside and outside

Whether as part of voluntary behaviour or as a reflex, action that has an effect on the outside environment involves the **somatic nervous system**. This system employs **skeletal muscles**, e.g. see Figure 3.6. The term 'skeletal' draws attention to links with the skeleton; most skeletal muscles are attached to the skeleton via tendons.

Figure 3.5 A synapse.

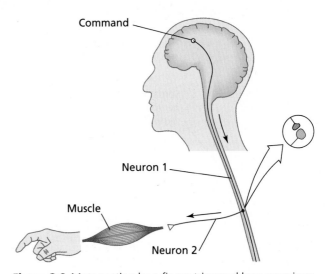

Figure 3.6 Motor action by a finger triggered by a conscious decision in the brain. (In the bubble, the synapse between neurons 1 and 2 is shown enlarged.)

A division within the nervous system is between the somatic nervous system and the **autonomic nervous system** (described in detail later). The autonomic nervous system (ANS) is automatic ('involuntary') and triggers action on the internal environment, partly through a class of muscle termed **smooth muscle**.

Figure 3.7 shows the distinction between controls exerted by the somatic and autonomic nervous systems. Figure 3.8 shows a simplified version of a small part of each system. A neurotransmitter links activity in neuron 2 and the skeletal muscle that controls the position of the leg. Neurotransmitter is also employed at the junction of neuron 5 and the muscle that controls the beating of the heart.

The somatic nervous system and the ANS normally work in a coordinated way in controlling action. Consider again meeting a bear. The brain rapidly translates this into the emotion of fear, makes a decision – 'run!' – and triggers action. In Figure 3.8, the brain sends a command down the spinal cord (neurons 1 and 2) to the muscles that control the legs. This is within the somatic nervous system. Simultaneously, the brain, acting through the ANS, accelerates the heart (neurons 3, 4 and 5) and triggers other internal changes to support the energized behaviour. Digestion is inhibited as the blood is needed elsewhere (Lisander, 1979).

In general, heart-rate is not under voluntary control, though there are techniques for gaining some voluntary control over it. Many situations cause the heart to accelerate, e.g. the anxiety of a nightmare or night terror (Kellerman, 1987). However, there are more subtle stimuli. It is not just threats to physical integrity, real or in dreams, that excite the heart. Challenges that require action do so, e.g. mathematical puzzles (Gianaros and Sheu, 2009). For someone trying to give up drugs, seeing cues to drug-taking can activate the heart (Weinstein *et al.*, 1997).

One change in the physiology of your body can sometimes be more obvious to others than to you: the changes in blood flow described as a blush (Darwin, 1872/1934). This is not under voluntary control and trying to resist it seems only to make it worse. If you are like me, you will cringe as you recall incidents that demonstrated how little voluntary control you have over this. That's enough!

Deep within the brain – thoughts and moods

Connections between neurons at synapses, mediated by neurotransmitters, are fundamental to the control of behaviour and mental processes. There are billions of synapses in the nervous system, most being in the brain. (The term 'neurochemistry' describes the study of the effects of chemicals on nervous systems.) As an example of information processing, the emotions, e.g. fear, depression and elation, depend on the activity of many neurons in the brain and the properties of the synapses that link them (Panksepp, 1994). Think what the image of the bear would do to your neurons that underlie fear.

Researchers manipulate neural events to see what happens to behaviour and mental states, e.g. to excite neurons in particular brain regions. It is possible to

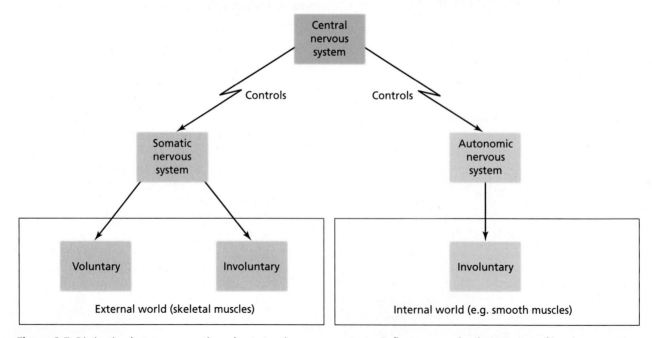

Figure 3.7 Distinction between somatic and autonomic nervous systems. Reflexes are under the category of involuntary action on external world.

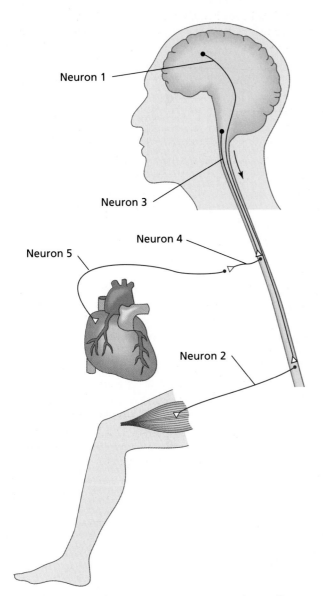

Figure 3.8 Part of the somatic nervous system (controlling a skeletal muscle in a leg) and part of the ANS (influencing muscle of the heart).

change the activity of groups of neurons by drugs that target particular classes of synapse, a science termed **psychopharmacology**. That drugs, both legal and illegal, can alter mood indicates the interdependence between mental states and physical events, e.g. levels of chemicals in the body. For instance, a drug, e.g. Prozac, can boost activity at a type of synapse, change the activity of many related neurons and thereby affect mood. The rationale of much of the pharmaceutical and psychiatric professions is to enable us to change our neurochemistry, whereas the rationale behind much police and customs activity is to stop us from doing so.

The next section looks in more detail at chemical events at synapses.

Section summary

1 The nervous system contains billions of neurons, most being in the brain.

2 The nervous system is divided into the central nervous system (the brain and spinal cord; abbreviated as CNS) and the peripheral nervous system.

3 Information is transmitted in neurons as action potentials.

4 Systems of neurons in the spinal cord trigger local actions, termed spinal reflexes.

5 The region of communication between a neuron and another cell (neuron or muscle cell) is a synapse.

6 Neurotransmitter is released from one neuron (presynaptic neuron) and occupies receptors at a second cell (e.g. a postsynaptic neuron).

7 Neurons that are neither sensory nor motor but that convey information between other neurons are termed interneurons.

8 In the cases described so far, on occupying receptors, neurotransmitter excites the postsynaptic cell.

9 Both voluntary behaviour and some reflexes are produced via skeletal muscles.

10 The autonomic nervous system (ANS) controls the internal environment of the body.

11 The ANS employs smooth muscle.

12 The synapses of the brain are a target for drug interventions.

☞ Test your knowledge

3.2 As described so far, information is transmitted between cells by means of what?

3.3 See Figure 3.4. (i) Neurotransmitter is stored and released where? (ii) It attaches to receptors where?

3.4 As described so far, neurotransmitter conveys information between which of the following? (i) Neuron to neuron, (ii) neuron to skeletal muscle, (iii) neuron to smooth muscle, (iv) muscle to neuron.

Answers on page 81

Neurochemical actions at synapses

This section looks at how neurochemicals act at synapses in the nervous system and the information processing that this permits.

Classical neurotransmission

Excitation and inhibition

Figure 3.9 shows a 'system' of four neurons. Neurons 1, 2 and 3 form synapses with ('synapse on') neuron 4. Neurons 1 and 3 form 'excitatory synapses', i.e. they release neurotransmitter that occupies receptors at neuron 4 and thereby excite it. Activity in either neuron 1 or 3, or both, triggers activity in 4. This is the type of synapse described so far.

In Figure 3.9(a), there is no activity in any neuron. In part (b), neuron 1 is active, which excites neuron 4, indicated by action potentials in 4. In part (c), both neurons 1 and 3 are active. Note that the *frequency* of action potentials in 4 increases in (c) relative to (b); that is to say, more action potentials occur in a unit of time. Neuron 4 is increasingly excited on going from (a) to (b) and to (c).

Rather than excitation, activity of a different type of neuron can *inhibit* the activity of another, a process mediated by a different combination of neurotransmitter and receptor. A neuron exerting such an effect is known as an **inhibitory neuron**. In Figure 3.9, whereas activity in neurons 1 and 3 tends to cause action potentials in neuron 4 (excitation), activity in neuron 2 suppresses them, i.e. lowers their frequency (termed 'inhibition'). Compare part (d) with (b).

Inhibition is fundamental to the control of behaviour and cognition, as some examples will illustrate. Figure 3.10 shows part of an example introduced earlier. Tissue damage triggers the withdrawal of a limb from an object and associated pain. Within pathways from the brain, inhibition can be applied to the activity of neurons in this system, represented by neuron 6. When inhibition is exerted, it is less likely that the reflex will be shown or that pain will be experienced. From a functional perspective, it might occasionally be an advantage *not* to respond to tissue damage. For example, animals in fight or flight show inhibition on this tendency (Rodgers and Randall, 1987). Attention to a wound mediated via pain would detract from fight or flight. Soldiers injured in battle have reported that they did not feel pain until they got away from the battlefield (Melzack and Wall, 1996).

The neurotransmitter action that you have met so far, whether excitation or inhibition, was the first to be discovered and is sometimes termed 'classical

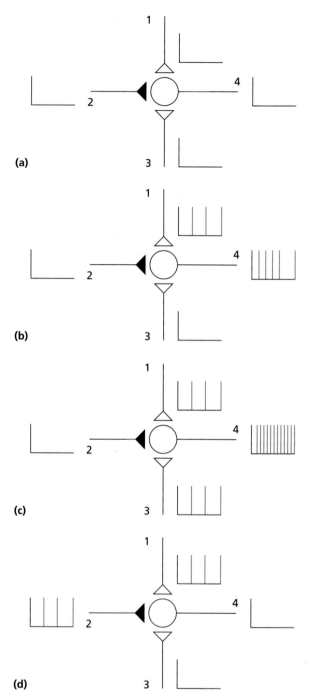

Figure 3.9 Activity in neurons: (a) no activity, (b) activity in neuron 1 excites 4, (c) activity in 1 and 3 add their effects in exciting 4, (d) the effect of 1 in exciting 4 is opposed by activity in the inhibitory neuron 2. △ = excitation, ▲ = inhibition.

neurotransmission'. Blackburn and Pfaus (1988) use the expression 'detonating' to describe it (Figure 3.11). For as long as it releases neurotransmitter, one neuron produces a sharply defined action on one or more receiving cells, e.g. another neuron or a muscle. The second cell

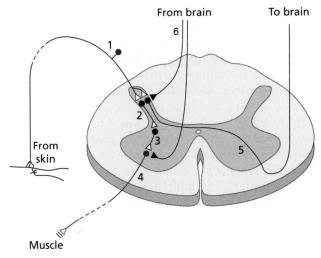

Figure 3.10 Inhibition. (As with the others, this figure is a simplification. In reality paths of neurons rather than single neurons would be involved in such processes.)

is a very small distance from the first. Following release of neurotransmitter from the presynaptic neuron, there is a very slight delay (0.5 ms) as the neurotransmitter crosses the gap, attaches to receptors on the

postsynaptic membrane and exerts an effect. This is termed the **synaptic delay**.

The effect of a classical neurotransmitter can sometimes be localized to one target neuron (one-to-one neuron–neuron links of the kind shown are not the most common but introduce the subject clearly).

Consider that, in Figure 3.12(a), synapse A is excitatory and synapse B is inhibitory. Typically, excitatory and inhibitory neurons employ different neurotransmitters. For example, the excitatory neurotransmitter, represented by a triangular shape, might be glutamate and the inhibitory neurotransmitter, represented by a rectangular shape, might be GABA (γ-aminobutyric acid). The shape of each neurotransmitter is drawn to correspond to its specific receptor at the surface of neuron C, analogous to a lock and key.

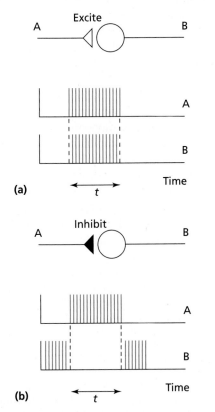

Figure 3.11 Two different types of connection between two neurons mediated by a classical neurotransmitter: (a) excitatory connection (a burst of activity in neuron A triggers B) and (b) inhibitory connection (neuron B is spontaneously active but is inhibited by activity in A).

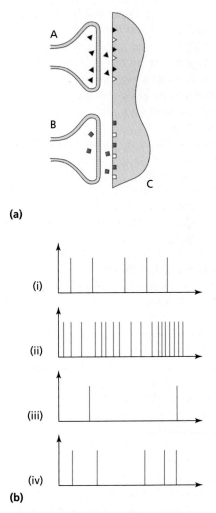

Figure 3.12 Two synapses, one excitatory (A) and one inhibitory (B), and the effects of activity in the presynaptic neurons A and B. (a) Synapses and (b) response of postsynaptic neuron C: (i) background activity; (ii) neuron A active (excitation); (iii) neuron B active (inhibition) and (iv) both A and B active (cancellation of effects).

We shall meet various types of neurochemical. They are classified according to their chemical structure and function. Adrenalin and noradrenalin (known, respectively, as 'epinephrine' and 'norepinephrine' in the American literature), serotonin (also termed 5-HT) and dopamine are members of the class termed **monoamines**. A subgroup of monoamines, consisting of dopamine, adrenalin and noradrenalin, is termed **catecholamines**.

A personal angle

Arvid Carlsson

In 1958, the Swedish scientist Arvid Carlsson, at the Universities of Lund and Göteborg, made the discovery that dopamine acts as a neurochemical in the brain (Carlsson, 2002). Carlsson also described the particular location of neurons that release it in the brain. The discovery has had a monumental impact in biological psychology, since, as you will see in subsequent chapters, dopamine plays a fundamental role in motivation and the control of movement. Also, abnormalities in the action of dopamine lie at the basis of many disorders, e.g. Parkinson's disease and schizophrenia. Correspondingly, some drug treatments work by targeting and altering dopamine activity in the brain.

In 1960, just a few years after Carlsson's discovery, the idea was met with almost universal scepticism at a distinguished conference in London where he spoke (Vane, 1960; Iversen and Iversen, 2007). The world was not yet ready for the idea that neurons in the brain communicate by means of chemicals. Rather, neurons were thought to communicate electrically by direct physical connection (Chapter 4). However, in 1960–1961, other scientists were able to show gross reductions in the amount of dopamine in the brains of patients suffering from Parkinson's disease and also a temporary improvement in their condition by injection of L-dopa, which is involved in the synthesis of dopamine. In 2000, Carlsson was awarded the Nobel Prize.

Linking nervous system and function

How did synapses evolve? Let us speculate. Take, for example, the system that reacts to a nociceptive stimulus (Figure 3.10). Speed often confers an important advantage. However, between sensory detection and the muscle, there are four neurons and four synapses, with an inevitable slight delay at each synapse (Guyton, 1991). Therefore, at first glance, it might seem more logical for evolution to have provided simply a bundle of single neurons that extend the distance from the site of detection of the stimulus to the muscle.

The adaptive advantage of flexibility offers one answer to why the more complex and very slightly slower system has evolved. As was just noted, there is not invariably a straightforward and predictable connection between stimulus and response (cf. Floeter, 1999a). There is also some processing of information as it passes along the route, e.g. inhibition can be exerted on the signal. That is to say, the magnitude of the withdrawal reaction can be modulated according to circumstances. Such processing requires synapses.

Neuromodulators

Apart from classical neurotransmission, there is **neuromodulation** in the CNS (Dismukes, 1979). A given substance might serve as a **neuromodulator** in one context but as a classical neurotransmitter in another. Like neurotransmitters, neuromodulators are released from a neuron and influence other neurons at receptors. However, compared with the small distances travelled by neurotransmitters, neuromodulators can diffuse relatively large distances within the CNS from the site of release to that of action.

On occupying the receptor, neuromodulators do not have a direct excitatory or inhibitory action. Unlike the sharp detonating action of neurotransmitters (Figure 3.11), neuromodulators have a smooth modulation role (i.e. ranging from amplification to attenuation of strength of a signal). They are something like the volume control on a radio set, which makes the signal stronger or weaker but does not change its content.

In some cases, acting via receptors at presynaptic neurons, a neuromodulator can amplify the release of classical neurotransmitter (Figure 3.13). In parts (a) and (b), the frequency of action potentials in neuron 1 is the same. However, the amount of neurotransmitter that is released is different. Correspondingly, the postsynaptic neuron in part (b) is more strongly affected than in part (a) as a result of neuromodulation.

Alternatively, acting via receptors at the postsynaptic membrane, a neuromodulator can make the neuron occupied more sensitive to classical neurotransmitters. Other neuromodulators inhibit release of transmitter or make a neuron less sensitive to neurotransmitter.

So far the chapter has considered the structure of connections between neurons as static. We now need to consider how connections between neurons can change over time.

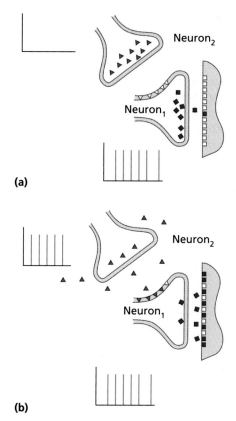

(a)

(b)

Figure 3.13 Classical neurotransmission and neuromodulation at a presynaptic site. Presynaptic neuron$_1$ is active and neuromodulator (from neuron$_2$) is either (a) unavailable or (b) available. Note increased release of neurotransmitter and occupation of receptors in (b), which increases the effect on the postsynaptic neuron. Note also the diffusion of neuromodulator around the site of release.

Section summary

1 Comparing different synapses, a neurotransmitter has either an excitatory or an inhibitory effect, depending upon the combination of transmitter and receptors.

2 At an inhibitory synapse, activity in one neuron lowers the activity in another neuron.

3 The classical ('ballistic') action of a neurotransmitter produces a localized effect in a specified period of time.

4 The effects of classical neurotransmitters can be modulated. Neuromodulators are released from one neuron and, for example, make other neurons more or less sensitive in terms of generating action potentials.

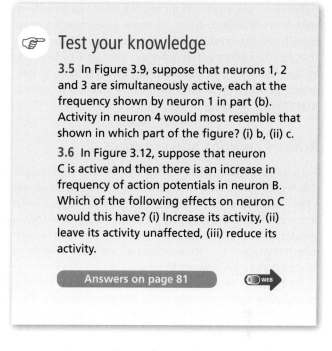

☞ **Test your knowledge**

3.5 In Figure 3.9, suppose that neurons 1, 2 and 3 are simultaneously active, each at the frequency shown by neuron 1 in part (b). Activity in neuron 4 would most resemble that shown in which part of the figure? (i) b, (ii) c.

3.6 In Figure 3.12, suppose that neuron C is active and then there is an increase in frequency of action potentials in neuron B. Which of the following effects on neuron C would this have? (i) Increase its activity, (ii) leave its activity unaffected, (iii) reduce its activity.

Answers on page 81   ⬤WEB ➡

Neurons: development and learning

Introduction

Over the years, we grow and develop. Certain aspects of our behaviour change but some behaviour stays roughly the same. For example, we learn new skills but reflexes remain much the same. Reflecting this, nervous systems show some changes and some constancy.

Some connections between neurons at synapses seem to be fixed and clearly identifiable from animal to animal, e.g. the connections underlying the reflex of Figure 3.1. Such systems are sometimes described as 'hard-wired', meaning that there is normally relatively little flexibility in their formation. The response of the system to its input is largely defined in advance. However, the term 'hard-wired' should not detract from the idea that adult nervous systems are the product of development. A developmental history underlies the formation of even straightforward sequences of neurons common to all members of a species. So, the developmental/learning explanation comes in here. Nothing can be absolutely predetermined; neural circuits do not exist preformed in the genes.

Over a lifetime or periods within it, there are also changes in the structure and properties of the nervous system. Synaptic connections change and these underlie development and learning. Thus, the neural systems in which such changes occur are termed **soft-wired**. In other words, parts of nervous systems exhibit **plasticity**.

Behaviour can show plasticity, which corresponds to that of its biological bases. In some cases, the apparent rigidity of the adult can be the outcome of processes that had flexibility when younger; alas some of us are at an age where we can almost notice any last signs of soft-wiring giving way to hard-wiring (try starting to learn a new foreign language at age 50).

Role of neurons and synapses

Functioning synapses, i.e. ones across which messages are regularly transmitted, can exert a self-reinforcing effect such that the connection gets stronger. With activity in the presynaptic neuron, there develops a greater effect on the postsynaptic neuron. Conversely, 'silent' synapses (i.e. those across which there is little or no traffic) can become ineffective.

In Figure 3.14(a), the presynaptic neuron at the top is regularly active, indicated by action potentials. That at the bottom is permanently inactive. In part (b), after

a period of time and as a result of activity in the pre-synaptic neuron, the top synapse gets strengthened by means of increasing levels of neurotransmitter and receptors. The lower one becomes non-functional, indicated by loss of transmitter and receptors. Such changes in structure at the synapse involve changes in the formation of proteins at the presynaptic and postsynaptic sides (building in the top synapse and breaking down in the lower one).

For example, visual stimulation from a rich environment can activate and strengthen synapses in the visual system, with implications for perception. Conversely, if an eye is damaged or if it is covered for a period of time, the synapses in the pathway normally deriving information from that eye can weaken.

Figure 3.14 Changes in efficacy of synaptic transmission: (a) initial situation, showing two synapses, the upper regularly active and the lower permanently inactive; and (b) later situation: the upper is strengthened but the lower becomes ineffective.

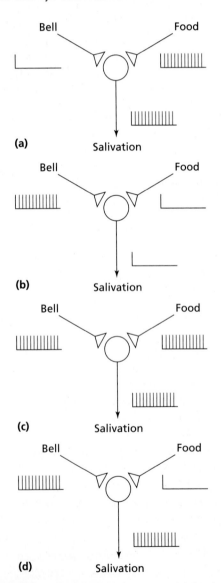

Figure 3.15 Simplified model of learning: (a) food triggers salivation, (b) bell does not trigger salivation, (c) bell and food are paired and (d) bell triggers salivation.

Learning represents plasticity in that the reaction changes with experience, e.g. Pavlov's study on salivation. All dogs tend to salivate to food in the mouth, owing to connections between neurons that are common to them. Dogs do not normally salivate to ringing bells. In Pavlov's experiment, a bell was paired with food a number of times. After this, the dog salivated when the bell was presented on its own.

How might this be explained in neural terms? As a first approximation, one possibility is as follows. Imagine that food in the mouth activates a neuron and triggers salivation (Figure 3.15(a)). Suppose that the bell activates another neuron but normally does not trigger salivation (Figure 3.15(b)). In the procedure of conditioning, bell and food are paired. There might be a link formed by the parallel activation of the two neurons (Figure 3.15(c)) such that later the bell on its own is able to trigger salivation (Figure 3.15(d)).

We described reinforcement earlier, as in a rat learning a task for food, an example of a developmental/ learning explanation. The embodiment of this in the nervous system is assumed to be changes at certain synapses, e.g. those mediating links between the perception of the lever and the act of pressing it.

The discussion now considers in more detail (a) how neurons are organized in forming a nervous system that contributes to coherent action and (b) the terminology used for describing the nervous system.

Section summary

1 Some combinations of neurons are hard-wired and others soft-wired.

2 Development and learning consist, among other things, of strengthening some synapses and weakening others.

 ## Test your knowledge

3.7 In Figure 3.15 the synapse between neurons marked 'bell' and 'salivation' is: (i) excitatory or (ii) inhibitory?

3.8 In Figure 3.15, following conditioning, the neuron marked 'bell' would tend to store and release (i) more or (ii) less neurotransmitter, compared with prior to conditioning?

Answers on page 81   WEB

Terminology and organization of the nervous system

This section takes a closer look at the nervous system in its details and its overall construction; it considers how it is organized and classified.

Spinal cord organization

It is necessary to get some anatomical orientation and we can start with the spinal cord. Figure 3.16(a) shows a short segment of spinal cord and the protection that the bone of the vertebra offers to the neurons located therein. The term **dorsal** means towards the back, so the imaginary person represented in Figure 3.16(a) is facing out of the page. In humans, **ventral** means towards the belly, the front. Note the left–right symmetry. In sensory and motor terms, nerves to the person's left (the right-hand side of the page) relate to the left side of their body and nerves to the person's right relate to the right side.

In the peripheral nervous system, a group of the cell bodies of neurons is termed a **ganglion** (plural, ganglia). In Figure 3.16(a), exemplifying this, a particular bulged area, termed the **dorsal root ganglion (DRG)**, is indicated to each side. It contains the cell bodies of sensory neurons, two of which are illustrated in Figure 3.16(b).

The ventral root is made up of the axons of motor neurons, two of which are shown in Figure 3.16(b). They convey information from the spinal cord to skeletal muscles. The cell bodies of motor neurons are located within the spinal cord and so the ventral root has no bulge comparable to the dorsal root ganglion (part (a)). The dorsal root and the ventral root converge to form a **spinal nerve** (Figure 3.16(a)).

The spinal cord and the associated spinal nerves are organized on a segmental basis (Figures 3.16 and 3.17). Each segment of spinal cord is associated with a particular spinal nerve. Figure 3.17 shows the spinal nerves and the corresponding segmentation of the vertebrae (backbone). The sensory surface of the body can be represented as a series of **dermatomes** (Figure 3.18). Each is associated with a particular spinal nerve such that sensory information arising from within this dermatome travels to the spinal cord in the associated spinal nerve. For example, tissue damage arising at a toe would correspond to dermatome L5 and would be conveyed by axons that form part of nerve L5 (Figure 3.18).

The spinal cord comprises 'grey matter' and 'white matter' (Figure 3.16). Strictly speaking, white matter is pink rather than white (it is 'whitish' relative to the grey matter). The difference between these two regions arises from differences in their cellular constituents. Thus, the grey matter contains a relatively high density of cell bodies of neurons (e.g. those of the interneurons and motor neuron in Figure 3.16(b)).

The white matter consists of the axons of neurons the cell bodies of which are located elsewhere and associated cells described later. In Figure 3.16(b), for much of its length the axon of neuron 6 descends within the white matter of the spinal cord.

Neurons, nerves and tracts

Figure 3.16(b) shows part of the central and peripheral nervous systems. Neurons 2, 3 and 6 are located wholly within the CNS. Neurons 1 and 4 are partly in the CNS and partly in the peripheral nervous system. Figure 3.16(b) also shows a bundle of axons of sensory and motor neurons. The light blue axons represent axons of neurons that detect events at the periphery (e.g. one neuron detects tissue damage and another detects cold) and the dark blue represent those that trigger action (e.g. muscular action). A bundle of axons in the peripheral nervous system is termed a **nerve**, the axons being physically located alongside each other and extending over the same distance (Figure 3.16(b)). By analogy, they are something like a bundle of wires in a cable.

An individual axon within any nerve can be classified according to its role: it *either* conveys information to the CNS (light blue) *or* from it (dark blue). Most nerves are composed of a mixture of both. The 'light blue' axons convey to the spinal cord information on events at a particular region of the body, in this case the foot. Each axon usually carries one specific type of information on, e.g., tissue damage, cold or harmless touch, at a particular region of the skin of a toe.

In the CNS, as in the periphery, a number of axons serving a common function would normally run in parallel transmitting information along the same route. Thus, alongside the axon of neuron 1 there would be others also carrying nociceptive information. In the CNS, a group of axons is termed a **tract** or pathway. A tract in the CNS is comparable to a nerve in the peripheral nervous system.

(a)

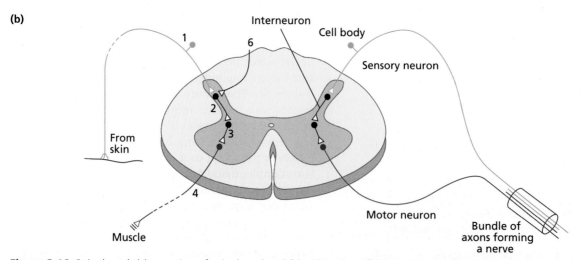

(b)

Figure 3.16 Spinal cord: (a) a section of spinal cord and (b) a thin slice of this section showing sensory, motor and interneurons. The bundle of axons corresponds to one of the nerves shown in blue in Figure 3.1(a).

Source of part (a): after Vander *et al.* (1994) *Human Physiology*, Fig. 8.35, p. 215, reproduced with permission of The McGraw Hill Companies, Inc.

Neuron types

Neurons can be characterized by their structure or role. We shall look first at structure and then at role.

Structure

So far, neurons have been shown in a greatly simplified form. Some are shown more realistically in Figure 3.19, indicating that they come in different shapes and sizes.

In each case, the neuron has a cell body, often termed a 'soma'. Among other things, the cell body contains the nucleus, which houses the genetic material. Some neurons have what are known as 'processes'. You have met already a type of process, a long structure termed an 'axon' or a 'nerve fibre' (e.g. Figure 3.16(b)). Another type of process is termed a 'dendrite' (Figure 3.19(a), (b), (d) and (e)).

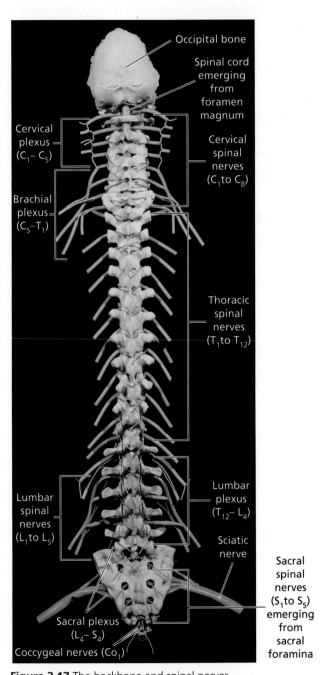

Figure 3.17 The backbone and spinal nerves.

Source: Martini *et al.* (2000, Fig. 14-3, p. 355). Copyright © 2000, 1997 by Frederic H. Martini, Inc. and Michael J. Timmons. Reprinted by permission of Pearson Education, Inc.

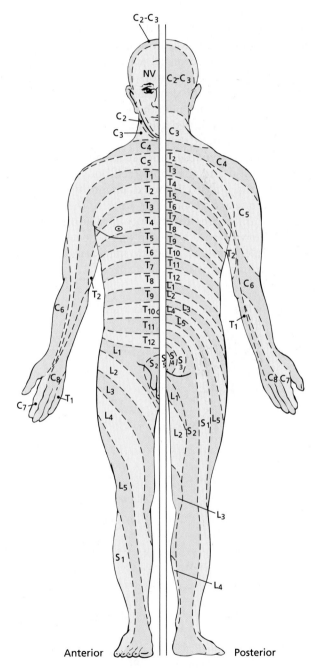

Figure 3.18 Dermatomes.

Source: adapted from Martini *et al.* (2000, Fig. 14-8, p. 360). Copyright © 2000, 1997 by Frederic H. Martini, Inc. and Michael J. Timmons. Reprinted by permission of Pearson Education, Inc.

Neurons 2, 3 and 4 in Figure 3.16(b) are examples of the kind shown in Figure 3.19(a). In Figure 3.19(b), the cell body is out to one side of the axon. The sensory neurons of Figure 3.16(b) (e.g. neuron 1) are of this kind. Figure 3.19(c) represents a small neuron, without a process. It conveys information only a very small distance. This should be contrasted with the large distances that information is transmitted in neurons of the kind shown in Figure 3.19(a), (b) and (d).

Let us focus upon the type shown in Figure 3.19(a). The cell body is located at one end and the axon carries action potentials away from it. Figure 3.19(d) shows the same neuron (neuron 1), with some of its synaptic connections included. Neuron 1 can be influenced by synaptic contact at the dendrites (neurons 2, 3 and 4), the cell body (neuron 5) and the axon (neuron 6).

Synapses are classified according to where they are located. For example, that between neurons 5 and 1 is an axo-somatic synapse, since it is between the axon of one neuron and the soma (cell body) of another. That between 6 and 1 is an axo-axonic synapse since it is from one axon to another. In turn, the activity of neuron 1 influences the activity of neuron 7. Figure 3.19(e) shows part of a neuron and a development of the dendrite known as 'dendritic spines', the site where synaptic connections are often made.

Most of the neurons that we discuss transmit information by action potentials, i.e. brief pulses of electricity. However, some transmit by means of smooth changes in voltage. For neural communication over anything but very short distances, action potentials are involved. The neuron of Figure 3.19(c) would communicate by smooth changes.

The speed at which neurons transmit action potentials varies between around 0.2 to 100 metres/second ($m\ s^{-1}$). If the diameter of the axon is large, the speed is higher. When they are transmitting action potentials, neurons are said to be showing 'activity'.

The role of neurons can be related to a classification based on their different types, as follows.

Afferent neurons

The term **afferent neuron** describes sensory neurons, though it is also applied more broadly. Thus, every sensory neuron is an 'afferent neuron' but 'afferent neuron' refers not only to a sensory neuron. As the general definition, given a location within the nervous system, 'afferent' refers to a neuron conducting information *to* this location. For example, 'afferents' to a brain region conduct information to the region. Since the spinal cord is the frame of reference for Figure 3.16(b), afferents are sensory neurons that carry information to it (e.g. neuron 1).

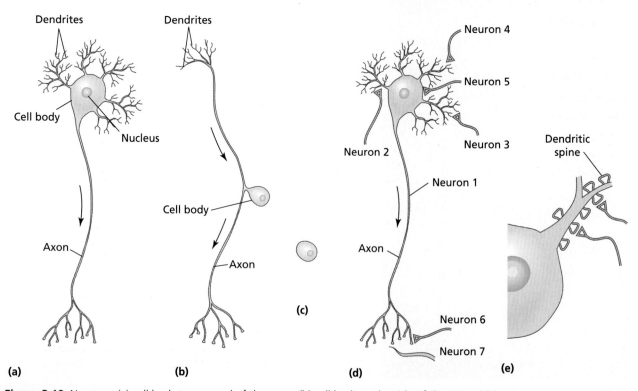

Figure 3.19 Neurons: (a) cell body to one end of the axon, (b) cell body to the side of the axon, (c) having no processes, (d) inputs and output represented and (e) with dendritic spines shown.

Source of (a) (b) and (d): adapted from Martini *et al.* (2000, Fig. 13-10, p. 340). Copyright © 2000, 1997 by Frederic H. Martini, Inc. and Michael J. Timmons. Reprinted by permission of Pearson Education, Inc.

Efferent neurons

A class of neurons, motor neurons, conveys information from the CNS to the periphery, where they trigger action through what are termed **effectors**. These are the muscles and glands that exert the *final effect* within an action. Another name for motor neurons is **efferent neurons**. As with 'afferent', this term can also be used more widely. Efferent neurons carry information away from a structure that forms a frame of reference; in the present case, the spinal cord, e.g. neuron 4 of Figure 3.16(b).

Motor neurons are said to 'innervate' a muscle, which means that they supply the neural input to it. What triggers activity in a motor neuron? There are basically two types of trigger (Figure 3.16(b)). The motor neuron can be activated either as part of a local reflex (neurons 1, 2, 3 and 4) or as part of a descending pathway from the brain (neurons 6, 2, 3 and 4). It is through such a descending pathway that voluntary commands to move are put into effect.

An increase in the strength of activation of a muscle is achieved partly by increasing the frequency of action potentials within motor neurons. Imagine that you consciously exert increasing force at a leg muscle to overcome some obstacle. The physical basis of this is an increasing frequency of action potentials in neurons that descend from the brain (e.g. neuron 6 in Figure 3.16). In turn, this triggers increased activation of the motor neurons that extend to the muscles doing the work.

The cranial nerves

The spinal cord mediates information transmission between the brain and regions of body below the neck (Figure 3.16). However, as you might have guessed, communication between the brain and other regions of the head is not via this route (Figure 3.20). Rather, information travels via a series of special nerves, termed **cranial nerves**, e.g. the optic nerve transmits visual information from the eyes to the brain. In the opposite direction, neurons within cranial nerves also transmit information from the brain to regions of the head, e.g. motor neurons activate the eye muscles. Some information is conveyed between the brain and the body below the neck via cranial nerves, discussed later.

The cranial nerves complete the introduction to the nervous system. The discussion now turns to chemical transmission by hormones, in the context of interactions with the nervous system.

Olfactory nerve (I)
Olfactory tract
Optic nerve (II)
Infundibulum
Oculomotor nerve (III)
Trochlear nerve (IV)
Trigeminal nerve (V)
Abducens nerve (VI)
Facial nerve (VII)
Vestibulocochlear nerve (VIII)
Glossopharyngeal nerve (IX)
Vagus nerve (X)
Hypoglossal nerve (XII)
Accessory nerve (XI)

Spinal cord

Figure 3.20 The cranial nerves, shown cut away at the point of entry to the brain.

Source: adapted from Martini *et al.* (2000, Fig. 15-21(b), p. 405). Copyright © 2000, 1997 by Frederic H. Martini, Inc. and Michael J. Timmons. Reprinted by permission of Pearson Education, Inc.

Section summary

1 A nerve is a bundle of axons in the peripheral nervous system.

2 Sensory (or afferent) neurons carry information to the CNS.

3 Each sensory neuron is specialized to convey information on a particular sensory quality (e.g. cold temperature).

4 Motor neurons (also termed 'efferent neurons') carry information from the CNS to activate muscles.

5 A ganglion (plural, ganglia) is a group of cell bodies of neurons in the peripheral nervous system.

6 Above the neck, cranial nerves communicate information between the CNS and the regions of the head.

Test your knowledge

3.9 In Figure 3.19(d), relative to neuron 1 which of the following is postsynaptic? (i) 2, (ii) 3, (iii) 7.

3.10 In Figure 3.19(d), which of the synapses shown are axodendritic? (i) 6 → 1, (ii) 4 → 1, (iii) 5 → 1.

3.11 In Figure 3.19(d), which synapse is axosomatic? (i) 5 → 1, (ii) 4 → 1, (iii) 1 → 7

3.12 Which part of the neurons of Figure 3.19 would be housed within a dorsal root ganglion? (i) Axon shown in (a), (ii) cell body shown in (b), (iii) cell body shown in (d).

Answers on page 81 WEB

Hormones – the endocrine system

Introduction

The term 'endocrine system' describes the hormones, the cells and glands that secrete them and the effects that hormones exert (Becker *et al.*, 1992). In some cases, a collection of neurons (not called a gland) secrete a hormone, a **neurohormone,** into a blood vessel. Hormones come in various types and examples of the more 'conventional' hormones are described first. More 'unconventional' hormones, which were relatively recently discovered, follow rather different principles of organization and are described later. They have been selected to illustrate different features of the collaboration between nervous and endocrine systems.

Chemically, a hormone and its receptors can sometimes be identical to a neurotransmitter and its receptors. Similar to the action of a neurotransmitter, when a hormone occupies a receptor, the target cell is affected.

Classical hormones

Hormones that were discovered relatively early are termed here 'classical hormones'. They fit a well-understood pattern of action. Figure 3.21 shows some of the glands in the body that secrete hormones. This section gives some examples of classical hormones and illustrates their function.

Insulin

The pancreas secretes insulin, which influences a large number of the cells. It is released into the general circulation and distributed widely. Cells use a sugar, glucose, as fuel for their energy requirements and take this up from the blood. Insulin promotes glucose uptake. Neurons are an exception since their glucose uptake is not insulin-dependent.

If the glucose level in the blood increases, a control system detects this and triggers the release of insulin, so that cells take up glucose (Figure 3.22(a)). Conversely, when levels of blood glucose are low, the secretion of insulin is reduced and insulin-dependent cells are

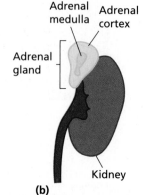

Figure 3.21 Hormones: (a) location of some of the glands that secrete them and (b) kidney showing adrenal gland and its divisions.

Source: adapted from Toates (1997a, Figure 3.1, p. 142).

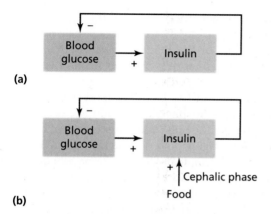

(a)

(b)

Figure 3.22 The insulin–glucose system: (a) control of insulin by blood glucose level and (b) addition of cephalic control. + = raises, − = lowers.

unable to take it up. This has an important functional significance. Cells of the brain rely upon glucose as their fuel, whereas other cells can exploit alternative substances for energy. This means that, at times of low availability of blood glucose, any glucose is targeted for privileged use by the brain.

Consider an artificial situation of the injection of glucose into the blood, such that glucose levels in the blood rise sharply. After a delay, secretion of insulin increases, which increases the movement of glucose into cells. This shows that the insulin control system is sensitive to blood glucose. So, where is the interest of psychologists in insulin?

Consider more natural circumstances; a rise in blood glucose level would be due to food arriving from the gut. This is preceded by the sight and smell of food and its ingestion. The nervous system detects these stimuli and neural signals trigger insulin secretion, termed the **cephalic phase** of insulin release (Langhans and Scharrer, 1992) (Figure 3.22(b)). Thus, an increase in secretion of insulin normally occurs before the glucose even gets to the blood (Figure 3.23). The insulin response *anticipates* the arrival of glucose.

Thus, shortly after encountering food, cellular uptake of glucose from the blood and the **metabolism** of glucose (its chemical conversion and use as a fuel by the cell) can proceed, since replenishment of the blood glucose is on the way. This illustrates how the nervous system (detection of food) and the endocrine system (release and action of insulin) act in a coordinated way to facilitate regulation of a vital parameter of the body.

Arginine vasopressin

Arginine vasopressin (AVP) serves regulation of body fluids and illustrates neuroendocrine control, involving neurons that secrete hormones (Verney, 1947). (AVP is sometimes termed anti-diuretic hormone or ADH.) AVP

is a hormone synthesized in neurons located in particular **nuclei** (singular, **nucleus**) of the brain. In this sense, a nucleus is a collection of cell bodies of neurons in the CNS, not to be confused with the earlier meaning, as part of a neuron. A particular nucleus can provide a landmark when describing bits of the brain.

AVP is synthesized in the cell bodies of neurons and transported along their axons to the terminals at the pituitary gland, where it is stored. In Figure 3.24, neuron 2 represents one such neuron. When the body is deficient in water, neurons (e.g. neuron 1) detect this and excite AVP-containing neurons. Activation of AVP-containing neurons causes them to release AVP into the blood. AVP is transported to the kidney where it slows the production of urine. Conversely, excess water in the body inhibits the secretion of AVP and the kidney excretes large amounts of urine.

(a)

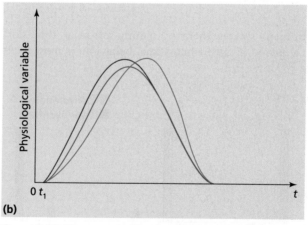

(b)

Figure 3.23 The control of insulin secretion. Absorption of glucose, insulin concentration in the blood and uptake of glucose by cells: (a) response in the absence of a cephalic phase and (b) response with cephalic phase functioning.

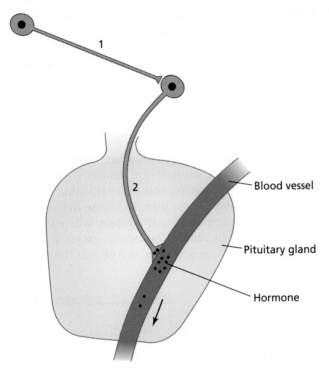

Figure 3.24 The control of AVP at the pituitary gland.

The AVP–kidney system cannot gain water. In dehydration, it can only inhibit water loss, which is, of course, better than doing nothing. Water can only be gained by drinking and the AVP–kidney system acts alongside the behavioural system of thirst and drinking to regulate the level of body water (Figure 3.25). The AVP–kidney system involves both the nervous and endocrine systems. The example again illustrates how the nervous system (detection of fluid level) and the endocrine system (action of AVP) act together to preserve homeostasis.

Oestrogen

In many species, there is a mating season or 'time-slot', i.e. period of time when sexual behaviour is most likely to occur (Beach, 1947). Hormones termed **oestrogens** show cycles of activity within the female's body. A biological basis of the mating season is that oestrogens sensitize sexual motivation. This makes the female sexually responsive and fertile in a part of the cycle. At a causal level, this can be understood as a changed reaction to the male, depending upon the cyclic action of hormones on the brain and other organs of the body.

Consider Figure 3.26. The female rat's reflex reaction to the touch of a male depends upon whether a particular set of neurons in her brain has been sensitized by oestrogens. In a causal sense, the hormone does not *trigger* mating, since the touch does that, but the hormone makes a mating response to touch more likely to occur. At a fertile point in her cycle, sensitization is evident. At infertile times, the hormones do not exert this effect and she is unresponsive to the advances of the male. Part (a) shows the situation when hormones have sensitized her. She reacts to touch by assuming the mating posture, termed **lordosis**. Such behaviour also makes functional sense: by biasing towards sexual behaviour at a time when the female is fertile, the chances of reproduction are maximized.

Testosterone

The hormone **testosterone** is secreted within the body of both sexes, though it is sometimes termed a 'male sex hormone'. In the male, it is secreted from the testes. In females, the adrenal gland is its principal source. Testosterone's secretion is controlled by other hormones which are secreted into the bloodstream at the pituitary gland at the base of the brain and then travel to the glands that secrete testosterone (Figure 3.21). Neural events within the brain determine the secretion of the 'trigger hormones', in a way somewhat similar to that for AVP.

Figure 3.26 Rat mating: (a) the posture, showing the female lordosis response and (b) female sexual motivation, and therefore behaviour, depend upon both the trigger of the male and the effects of hormones on her nervous system.

Figure 3.25 Regulation of body water level by control exerted over drinking and urine production.

After its release, testosterone moves throughout the body to target organs. These include certain nuclei in the brain, where it has effects upon particular groups of neurons (McEwen *et al.*, 1986). There is a reciprocal relationship between the level of hormone and psychological factors. In the direction (hormone) → (nervous system) → (behaviour), testosterone increases tendencies to sexual and aggressive behaviour. In the direction (behaviour) → (nervous system) → (hormone), defeat of male primates leads to a fall in production of testosterone (Rose *et al.*, 1975). The fall has an effect on behaviour, steering it away from challenging the dominance of other animals. There is functional significance to this: defeat might be a time to readjust strategy away from confrontation and offence. Testosterone exemplifies the need to take into account the interaction of nervous and endocrine systems as well as social interactions.

We now look at a type of hormone that does not fall into this classical pattern.

An 'unconventional' system

General

Investigators identify two clearly defined actions: classical neurotransmitters and classical hormones. However, they now see them not as two exclusive classes. Rather, they are two cases on a spectrum of effects. There are shades of grey: a range of systems that have features of each, described with expressions such as **neurohormone** (Deutch and Roth, 1999). (Neither do neuromodulators, described earlier, fit into an entirely neat category.) Life might appear more and more to be a 'mess', as compared with the neat and simple elegance of the classical picture (Dismukes, 1979). You might feel that psychology students of the 1950s and earlier were lucky.

As a generic definition, a hormone is carried in the blood from where it is released to where it produces action. However, there are differences in how far different hormones are distributed. Some neurohormones are not circulated in the whole bloodstream to influence distant targets. Instead, they are released from neurons into one particular vessel and transported a short distance within it to influence a local target.

Local hormones (corticotropin releasing factor)

Figure 3.27 illustrates a 'local hormone'. Neurons, with cell bodies in the brain region termed the hypothalamus (coloured green) and median eminence (coloured purple), release local hormones at their terminals in the pituitary gland. These local hormones then trigger the release of 'classical hormones' from endocrine cells in the pituitary gland, into the circulation ('hypophyseal veins'). One local hormone is corticotropin releasing

hormone (CRH), or 'corticotropin releasing factor' (CRF) (Akil *et al.*, 1999; Rivier, 1991).

CRF is synthesized, stored and released by neurons with cell bodies in the hypothalamus. Other neurons

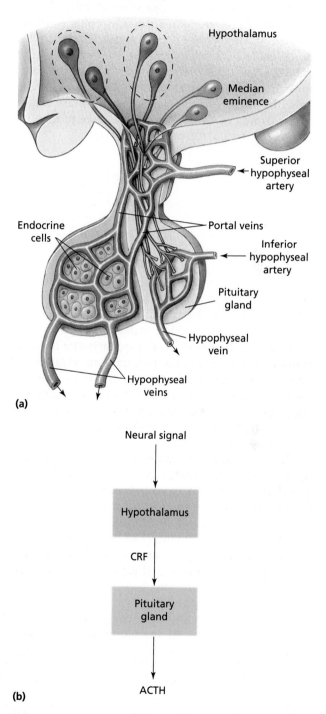

(a)

(b)

Figure 3.27 The pituitary gland. (a) Links to the brain region termed hypothalamus and blood flow to and from pituitary gland. (b) Hormonal sequence.

Source of (a): adapted from Martini *et al.* (2000, Fig. 19-6, p. 505). Copyright © 2000, 1997 by Frederic H. Martini, Inc. and Michael J. Timmons. Reprinted by permission of Pearson Education, Inc.

within the brain, which encode fear, excite the CRF-containing neurons to release CRF. CRF is released into a small local blood vessel. Then it is transported the very short distance to CRF receptors in the pituitary gland. Their occupation by CRF stimulates the secretion of another hormone, adrenocorticotrophic hormone (ACTH). ACTH acts as a conventional ('classical') hormone, i.e. it is distributed in the whole bloodstream and its distant target is the adrenal gland. At the cortex (meaning outer layer) of the adrenal gland ('adrenal cortex'), ACTH triggers the release of a class of hormones termed corticosteroids. These serve to mobilize the body for action, e.g. in recruiting fuels.

Classification and comparison

Neurotransmitters and hormones have an important feature in common: they communicate information from a cell that releases them to a cell *that has receptors for them*. A difference between neurotransmitters and hormones lies in the distance between the releasing cell and the cell with receptors: very small for neurotransmitters and relatively large for hormones.

Whether a substance is neurotransmitter or hormone depends not on its chemical make-up but on its mode of release and transport. A substance acts as a hormone where it is (a) released at a distance from its target and (b) carried to the target by the blood. It acts as a (classical) neurotransmitter where (i) it is released by a neuron and occupies receptors at an immediately adjacent cell, e.g. neuron or muscle cell and (ii) has a sharply defined onset and end of its action.

There are possibly some substances that serve uniquely as neurotransmitters and others that act only as hormones. However, in several cases the same chemical substance can serve as either neurotransmitter or hormone. Adrenalin and noradrenalin (epinephrine and norepinephrine), for instance, can be classified as either neurotransmitters or hormones, depending upon where they are released and exert their effect. Evolutionary processes utilized some 'raw materials' (e.g. noradrenalin) in serving different roles.

There are receptors at the muscles of the heart, which adrenalin, circulating in the bloodstream, occupies. When they are occupied, the activity of heart muscle is accelerated (Dampney, 1994), a hormonal action. However, within the CNS, there are also receptors for adrenalin. These are at the membrane of neurons. Typically, adrenalin that is released from an immediately adjacent neuron attaches itself to such receptors. Acting in this mode, adrenalin is a neurotransmitter (Figure 3.28). In some cases, a particular hormone and a chemically identical neurotransmitter attach to the same set of receptors.

Why has nature evolved two means of communication: action potentials (with associated neurotransmitters) and hormones? They serve different but complementary roles. A hormone usually serves the general and broad transmission of information to sites in different locations throughout the body. By contrast, a neurotransmitter can be more specific and localized: for instance, one neuron might transmit information only to a second neuron or to a muscle fibre.

For information transmission over relatively long distances, neurons have a clear advantage over hormones: speed. Time is involved in a hormone being released, circulating in the blood and finally influencing a distant location. Thus, neurons can transfer specific information at a relatively high speed.

Hormones are more suitable for certain roles. Although a hormone is slower, it can transmit information to a large number of different distant sites all influenced in the same way. Hormonal action is typically broader than that of a classical neurotransmitter, affecting wide areas of influence and being more diffuse in time. (By analogy, a television programme can be broadcast from one location to many homes, whereas a telephone is suitable for one-to-one messages.) Insulin exemplifies such 'broadcast' action. The same message, 'take up glucose', is appropriate for a very large number

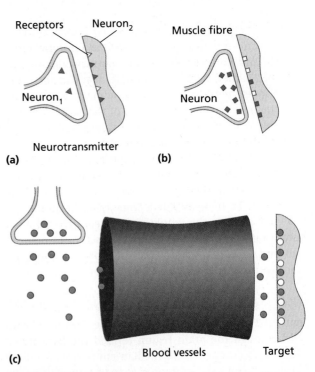

Figure 3.28 Classification of (classical) neurotransmitters and hormones: (a) a neurotransmitter, released from a neuron and influencing another neuron, (b) a neurotransmitter, released from one neuron and influencing a muscle and (c) a hormone.

of cells that are influenced by the single hormonal command. Only a hormone is able to broadcast this information throughout the body. It is impossible to imagine a network of neurons transmitting information to every cell outside the nervous system.

Occupation of a receptor by a hormone can have either a sharp and acute effect or a more long-term effect that is mediated via action at the gene of the target cell (Deutch and Roth, 1999; McEwen *et al.*, 1986).

Knowledge of nervous and endocrine systems is essential in trying to understand the autonomic nervous system, the topic of the next section.

Section summary

1 The endocrine system consists of the sites of secretion of hormones, the hormones and their targets.

2 A hormone is released at one location and carried by the blood to cause action at another location.

3 A hormone's effect is generally more wide-ranging and diffuse than that of a classical neurotransmitter.

4 A classical hormone is (i) secreted into the blood at one site and (ii) circulated broadly by the blood, and (iii) exerts actions at more distant sites.

5 Examples of classical hormones include (i) insulin acting on cells taking up glucose, (ii) arginine vasopressin's acting at the kidney and (iii) testosterone.

6 A given substance might act as either neurotransmitter or hormone. The difference lies in the mode of release of the substance and how it gets to its target.

7 Conventional ('classical') hormones are an effective way of influencing multiple targets in different places at the same time.

8 Corticotropin releasing factor (CRF) is an atypical ('local') hormone. It is released from neurons in the brain and carried, in a local blood vessel, the very short distance to its receptors in the pituitary gland.

9 Neuronal communication is faster than hormonal communication.

 Test your knowledge

3.13 Which of the following is involved in the homeostatic regulation of body-fluids? (i) Insulin, (ii) testosterone, (iii) AVP.

3.14 What might be meant by the claim that the difference between neurotransmitters and hormones lies not in the substance but in its mode of delivery?

3.15 Which of the following has the shortest distance from site of release to site of action? (i) AVP, (ii) CRF, (iii) insulin.

Answers on page 81

The autonomic nervous system

Introduction

Adaptation requires *coordination* between action on the external world and activity of the internal environment. This section focuses upon such coordination in the internal environment.

Activity in the autonomic nervous system (ANS) determines such things as the production of saliva in the mouth and the state of the **viscera** (the internal organs) of the body, e.g. the beating of the heart, digestive activity by the stomach and intestine and adjustments of blood flow as in blushing. The ANS is also involved in energy exchanges between stores. Autonomic effects are mediated by special types of muscle and gland. The muscles that control internal actions are different anatomically from skeletal muscles. As noted earlier, many of these are smooth muscles. An exception is the muscle that controls the contractions of the heart: 'cardiac muscle'.

Whether we are asleep or awake, the ANS controls our internal environment, making adjustments to maintain optimal conditions. Examples of the activity of the ANS include (i) by its control of the stomach's churning action, digestion is facilitated and (ii) by its control over blood flows, food in the gut normally triggers a diversion of blood to the gut in the interests of digestion. Under ANS control, such activities normally proceed at an unconscious, involuntary level, serving the body's 'housekeeping functions'. The ANS is sometimes termed the 'involuntary nervous system'. It is perhaps good that housekeeping is organized unconsciously (cf. Powley, 1999). Consider some of the disastrous actions that we inflict on our external environments through conscious choices and the triggering of the somatic nervous system. In all probability, we would do an even worse job at trying consciously to organize the internal environment!

The ANS also controls the activity of certain glands that secrete hormones (e.g. some adrenal hormones, described earlier) and other substances. For instance, an elevation in body temperature triggers parts of the ANS to promote the secretion of sweat from glands on the body surface. Sweating cools the body.

Definitions

What is autonomic?

The ANS derives its name from the fact that it can operate with some *autonomy* ('automatically') from the rest of the nervous system. Its activity does not require conscious intervention. Thus, the functions that the ANS controls are clearly to be distinguished from those triggered by the skeletal muscles on the external environment.

Neurons that innervate the effectors of the body (muscles and glands) can be unambiguously identified as those of *either* the somatic nervous system *or* the autonomic nervous system. For example, a motor neuron controlling a skeletal muscle is part of the somatic nervous system and one innervating the heart is part of the ANS.

How autonomous?

Under various conditions, the ANS operates autonomously. However, conscious strategies can also influence its activity. As we have seen, parts of the nervous system outside the ANS normally exert an influence over it, so that the autonomic changes are functionally appropriate to behaviour (Hess, 1981). The bear incident illustrates this.

For another example, the blood flow to the genitals is under autonomic control. However, it can be affected by conscious mental strategies involving imaginary sexual themes, as some people probably discover for themselves without a textbook of biological psychology. Conversely, indicating the limitations of conscious control, the ANS sometimes 'goes its own way' in the face of conscious commands. For example, in their courting days, over-anxious men have found that they could not will the blood to flow to where they would most like it to flow.

Autonomic changes appear in anticipation of associated behaviour (Hilton, 1979). For example, the CNS perceives a threat and selects a defensive behavioural strategy. This then excites the ANS (Lisander, 1979) and the ANS causes the heart to beat faster. This can be seen even in the absence of overt reactions as when we seethe with anger, the behavioural expression of which remains inhibited in spite of triggering autonomic effects on the heart and other organs.

Humans can sometimes learn some control over the body functions that are part of the ANS, e.g. to reduce heart-rate (Lal *et al.*, 1998). This again underlines the fact that the ANS can only be understood in the context of its interaction with parts of the CNS concerned with conscious awareness and voluntary decision-making.

Divisions of the ANS

The ANS can be classified into two branches (sometimes termed 'systems' or 'divisions'): the **sympathetic branch** and **parasympathetic branch**. Figure 3.29 illustrates the sympathetic division. The roots of the term 'sympathetic' lie in the observation of its role in harmonization (coherence) between organs (Powley, 1999). Figure 3.30 shows the parasympathetic division (meaning 'lying alongside the sympathetic').

Note the organs innervated and, on comparing divisions, the different locations at which neurons of the ANS leave the CNS for the periphery. Sometimes the expression 'sympathetic neuron' or 'parasympathetic neuron' is used. This refers to a neuron that forms part of one or other of these divisions.

The two branches normally exert opposite effects as a 'push–pull' control. For example, activity in the sympathetic branch increases the vigour of the heart's pumping, whereas parasympathetic activity inhibits it. (Figure 3.12 showed the action of inhibition and a similar principle applies here.) There is normally some activity in both branches, so 'activation' or 'producing action' means increasing activity in one branch and decreasing it in the other (Polosa *et al.*, 1979). Under some conditions, one or other ANS branch dominates. This means that we can refer to 'sympathetic activation' or 'parasympathetic activation'.

Generally, the sympathetic branch is activated when the animal is engaging in (or about to engage in) active behaviour mediated via the somatic nervous system. This is particularly evident at times of fight or flight, e.g. the heart is stimulated to beat faster. Under sympathetic control, mobilization of energy reserves from stores is instigated, so fuel is available for the muscles. Adrenalin (epinephrine) and noradrenalin (norepinephrine) secreted from the adrenal glands exert this effect. Sometimes the term 'autonomic activation' is employed with no specification as to branch. This would mean sympathetic activation.

The parasympathetic branch is activated and the sympathetic relatively inactivated at times of relaxation, e.g. heart-rate is slowed. At rest, as a result of the autonomic state, blood is diverted from the skeletal muscles to the gut to assist digestion. In terms of function, at rest, blood does not need to be circulated so rapidly. However, there can be situations of emergency in which the parasympathetic branch is activated. These depend upon the species and situation. Parasympathetic activation tends to occur at times when there is no active behavioural strategy that can be switched in (Vingerhoets, 1985). For example, in rabbits, detection of a predator can be associated with immobility and a slowing of heart-rate (Jordan, 1990).

Within the ANS, there are two ways in which control is exerted over the internal environment, described next.

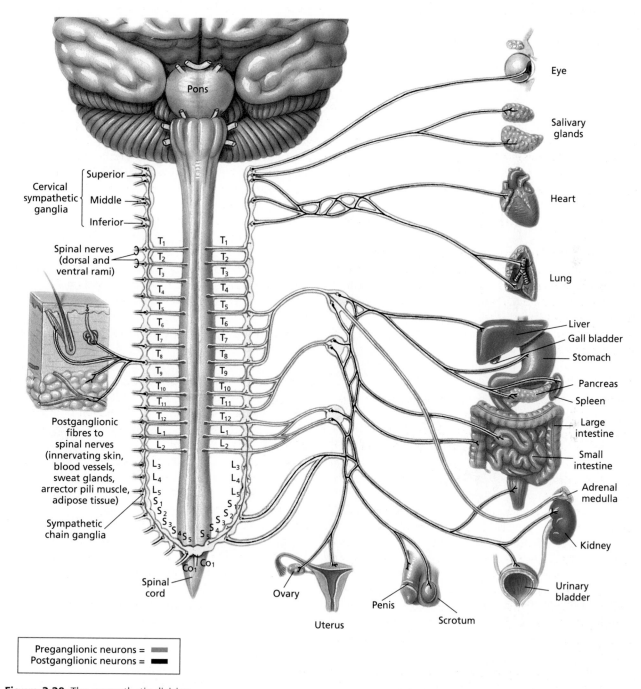

Figure 3.29 The sympathetic division.

Source: adapted from Martini *et al.* (2000, Fig. 17-5, p. 449). Copyright © 2000, 1997 by Frederic H. Martini, Inc. and Michael J. Timmons. Reprinted by permission of Pearson Education, Inc.

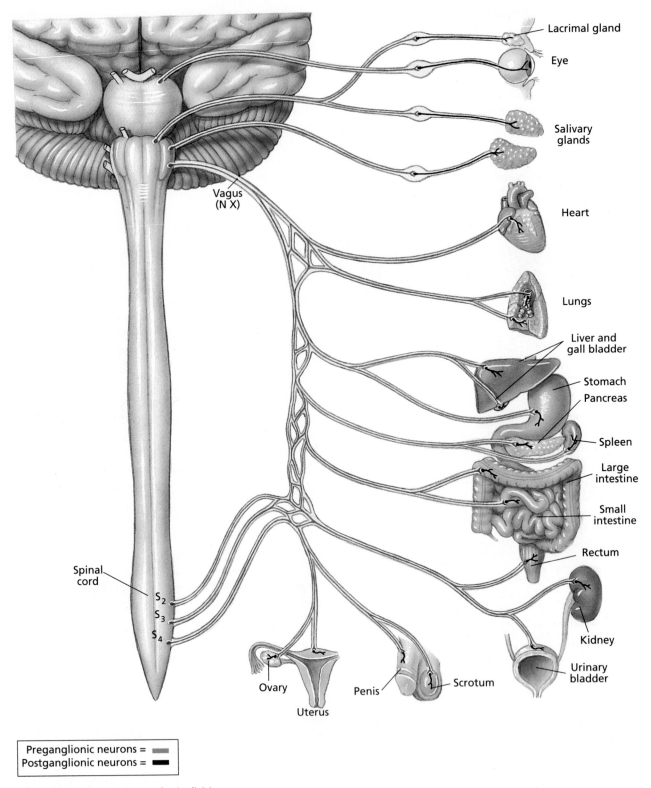

Preganglionic neurons = ▬▬
Postganglionic neurons = ▬▬

Figure 3.30 The parasympathetic division.

Source: adapted from Martini *et al.* (2000, Fig. 17-9, p. 454). Copyright © 2000, 1997 by Frederic H. Martini, Inc. and Michael J. Timmons. Reprinted by permission of Pearson Education, Inc.

The effectors of the system

Muscles

Throughout the body there are smooth muscles, the activity of which is determined by the ANS, e.g. in the wall of vessels of the circulation (Figure 3.31) (Loewy, 1990). The diameter of blood vessels depends in part upon the contraction of this smooth muscle. Contraction is determined by neural activity of the neurons of the ANS that innervate the muscle. Transmitter is released from autonomic neurons, attaches to smooth muscles and these change their contraction, comparable to motor neurons and skeletal muscles.

The activity of cardiac muscle that causes the heart to beat can be modulated by the ANS. It is either excited or inhibited, thereby either increasing or decreasing the vigour of the heart's activity and blood flow from the heart.

Secretions

Figure 3.21 showed the adrenal gland. Although there are two glands, the term 'gland' is commonly used. At this gland, activity within neurons of the ANS causes the hormones adrenalin and noradrenalin (epinephrine and norepinephrine) to be released into the bloodstream. These hormones are then transported around the body and influence multiple distant sites, e.g. the heart.

In emotional excitation, there is acceleration of the heart's activity mediated via two routes in parallel: (i) neurons acting directly on heart muscle and (ii) neurons that trigger adrenal hormones that in turn act on heart muscle. The adaptive function of this link between nervous and endocrine systems is clear. It helps to prepare the body for fight or flight, e.g. in accelerating heart-rate and mobilizing fuels for use by the muscles.

Figure 3.29 shows one aspect of how the adrenal gland operates. Sympathetic neurons terminate at a part of the gland: the adrenal medulla. The adrenal medulla comprises cells, which secrete their product, the hormones adrenalin and noradrenalin, into the bloodstream when the sympathetic neurons are activated. At times of emergency and exertion of effort, adrenalin

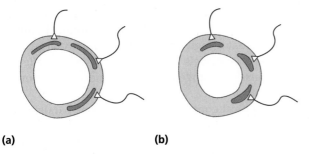

(a)   (b)

Figure 3.31 Smooth muscle in the wall of a blood vessel: (a) relaxed and (b) contracted.

A personal angle

The kind of dream that we would all welcome

Artificial stimulation of the vagus nerve (which innervates the heart) slows the heartbeat and this is chemically mediated, as part of the parasympathetic division. In 1921, Otto Loewi working at the University of Graz in Austria had a famous dream (Kuffler and Nicholls, 1976). Loewi dreamed that a chemical released from the neuron endings mediated the effect. So, if Loewi were to bathe the heart of a frog, some of the chemical would be released into the bathing solution. Suppose that this solution were then applied to the heart of another frog. The chemical might cause a reduction in beat of the second heart. Loewi woke up and wrote down the idea for the experiment. Alas, the next morning, he was unable to read what he had written. Fortunately, the following night, he awoke with the same idea and this time did the experiment. The result of Loewi's experiment was as he dreamed it.

The chemical involved is acetylcholine, and Loewi's demonstration was highly influential. It is interesting that the role of acetylcholine, a substance having a profound effect on dreaming, should itself have been discovered by means of a dream (Perry *et al.*, 1999). The moral of the story is to keep a pencil and paper by your bed and write clearly.

and noradrenalin are released in large amounts. These effects help the body to cope. For example, metabolic fuel is mobilized from the liver and distributed along with oxygen at a high rate.

Cell bodies and axons

Figure 3.32 compares and contrasts the anatomy of part of the ANS and the somatic nervous system. In each case, neurons span the distance between the spinal cord and the effector organ. However, a difference is also represented. In the somatic nervous system, single effector (i.e. motor) neurons, with cell bodies in the spinal cord, link the CNS and the skeletal muscles. In the ANS, combinations of two neurons span the distance from the CNS to the effector organ.

An **autonomic ganglion** (plural, autonomic ganglia) houses the collection of cell bodies of the second neurons, physically located together. The axons of

Figure 3.32 Part of the somatic and autonomic nervous systems compared. In reality, a ganglion contains many such cell bodies.

autonomic neurons are described as either 'preganglionic axon' or 'postganglionic axon'.

Try comparing Figures 3.29 and 3.30, looking at the location of ganglia, i.e. where preganglionic neurons contact postganglionic neurons. The site of the ganglia is different in the two branches of the ANS. Most of the sympathetic ganglia are located close to the spinal cord. In the parasympathetic branch, the ganglia are all in the periphery, at, or close to, the organ that the fibre innervates. For example, the cell body of the representative neuron that innervates the heart is located at the heart itself.

Figure 3.33 shows part of a chain of sympathetic ganglia and can be compared with Figure 3.29. A series of sympathetic ganglia lie close to the spinal cord and constitute the 'sympathetic trunk'. In Figure 3.33, it can be seen that sympathetic fibres leave the spinal cord as part of the ventral root.

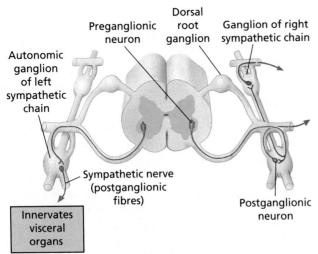

Figure 3.33 The sympathetic chain.

Source: adapted from Martini *et al.* (2000, Fig. 17-4(a), p. 447). Copyright © 2000, 1997 by Frederic H. Martini, Inc. and Michael J. Timmons. Reprinted by permission of Pearson Education, Inc.

Sensory feedback

Feedback is involved in the ANS. The CNS influences the ANS effectors but it is also informed of their state. The nerves within which autonomic effector neurons are located also contain sensory axons which carry information back to the CNS. As with other sensory neurons, their cell bodies are located in the dorsal root ganglia (Figure 3.33) and cranial nerve ganglia. Such information is used in feedback control, e.g. over heart-rate (Dampney, 1994).

The vagus nerve (Figure 3.30) is made up of both efferent and afferent neurons. The latter convey information to the CNS concerning such things as events within the liver and stomach. For example, the availability of fuel to the liver is signalled to the brain and plays a role in the control of feeding.

Local control and global coordination

The ANS shows both local control and global coordination.

Local control

Local control is based in part upon local feedback of information. For example, heart-rate and the strength of heartbeats can be adjusted as local actions involving only part of the ANS. Typically, this occurs in response to detection of events at the heart and blood vessels (e.g. blood pressure) by sensory neurons with tips located there. This information is fed back to the CNS and local corrective action instigated. Similarly, salivation can be triggered by substances in the mouth and might involve only a small part of the ANS.

Global coordination

Above local control, there is global coordination of the ANS, controlled by **command neurons** in the brain. This ensures that autonomic activity matches the functional demands of the whole body. For example, acting globally in an emergency, the sympathetic branch can be excited and the parasympathetic branch inhibited. Comparable to control of the somatic motor output, such control is sometimes termed **hierarchical control**, meaning that a high level in the hierarchy determines events at lower levels. Anticipatory changes in the ANS in response to changes in posture and goals exemplify such control.

Hierarchical control over the ANS has parallels with government administration, where action can depend upon both central decisions and local factors responding to local conditions. Local decisions can be modulated or overridden in the interests of national coherence.

In attack or escape, a global signal is sent from the brain to accelerate the heart-rate and alter the diameter of blood vessels, among other things. As another aspect of the global command, blood is diverted away from the gut and to the skeletal muscles.

The chemistry of the ANS

Figure 3.34 shows the 'classical pattern' of chemical neurotransmission. Preganglionic neurons in both sympathetic and parasympathetic systems employ acetylcholine. Postganglionic neurons of the sympathetic system usually employ noradrenalin. However, the sympathetic neurons that innervate the sweat glands employ acetylcholine. Also, more than one neurotransmitter can be employed by a given neuron (Loewy, 1990). Postganglionic neurons of the parasympathetic system employ acetylcholine.

How do the two branches of the ANS normally exert opposite effects? This is achieved in part by different neurotransmitters being released by the end neurons within the branches (Figure 3.34). When noradrenalin attaches to receptors at the cardiac muscle, the muscle is activated more strongly. Within the parasympathetic system, when acetylcholine binds to receptors at the cardiac muscle, the heart's activity is reduced, i.e. inhibited (as in Loewi's dream-inspired experiment).

The enteric nervous system

Introduction

The ANS has sympathetic and parasympathetic divisions. In Figures 3.29 and 3.30, neurons belong to one or other division. The effectors of the ANS normally involve two such neurons between CNS and a muscle or gland (Figure 3.32). However, a complication appears when we go beyond these figures, in a direction away from the CNS. At some organs, e.g. the gut, between these two neurons and the smooth muscles, there are specialized networks of neurons that organize the activity of the muscles (Wood, 1979).

The movement of ingested material through the stomach and along the intestine, i.e. the alimentary tract, occurs because of contraction and relaxation of its walls. This is caused by changing contraction within the muscles of the walls. Also, digestive fluids are secreted from the walls. There are various determinants of the neural activity of the gut and thereby its muscular and hormonal actions. For example, events intrinsic to the gut itself determine activity within local neural networks in the gut. The network of local neurons at the wall of the gut is known as the **enteric nervous system (ENS)**.

Hierarchical control

Local circuits of neurons within the gut wall generate the rhythms that propel food along the gut. Because of this network of neurons, the ENS is often treated as a division of the ANS. However, the sympathetic and parasympathetic systems also exert control over the activity of this network. Thus, within the ANS but outside the ENS, neural activity influences the activity of the ENS (Figure 3.35). This speeds up or slows down the rhythms.

The role of the sympathetic, parasympathetic and enteric nervous systems in determining gut contraction illustrates hierarchical control. Some control is exerted by local factors (e.g. the rhythms are produced within the ENS and depend upon gut contents). However, a layer of control arises in the brain and its action is mediated via the sympathetic and parasympathetic systems. This allows the activity of the ENS to be excited or inhibited according to the broader context. For example, in an emergency, digestion can be slowed and blood diverted away from the gut.

Surely, most of us have had experiences demonstrating that factors outside the ENS can exert some control over it. At times of high emotion, we experience disturbances in our gut. This implies a route of information from CNS to ANS and so to ENS.

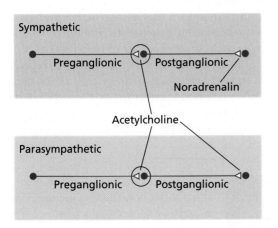

Figure 3.34 The neurotransmitters of the autonomic nervous system.

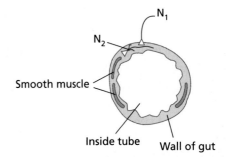

Figure 3.35 The enteric nervous system. There is an input from neurons of the ANS. N_1 = a neuron within ANS but outside ENS. N_2 = a neuron within the ENS.

Section summary

1 The ANS controls the viscera, i.e. organs such as the stomach, heart and intestine.

2 Control by the ANS is produced by (i) glands, which secrete hormones or other substances (e.g. saliva) and (ii) smooth and cardiac muscle.

3 Conventionally, the ANS is divided into sympathetic and parasympathetic branches. These normally exert opposite effects on a target.

4 The adrenal gland secretes adrenalin (epinephrine) and noradrenalin (norepinephrine) into the bloodstream in response to activity in the sympathetic nervous system.

5 The enteric nervous system controls the smooth muscles of the gut and is affected by activity in the sympathetic and parasympathetic divisions.

Test your knowledge

3.16 In Figure 3.29, which neurotransmitter is released from the neurons coloured red? (i) Acetylcholine, (ii) glutamate, (iii) noradrenalin (norepinephrine).

3.17 In Figure 3.30, which neurotransmitter is released from the neurons coloured black? (i) Acetylcholine, (ii) glutamate, (iii) noradrenalin (norepinephrine).

3.18 The cell bodies of preganglionic sympathetic neurons are located in which of the following? (i) Dorsal root ganglion, (ii) white matter of the spinal cord, (iii) grey matter of the spinal cord.

> Answers on page 81

Bringing things together

You should now see why nervous and endocrine systems were discussed together:

1 To emphasize their interdependence: the nervous system influences the endocrine system and is influenced by it.

2 To look at similarities and differences in their action. The nervous and endocrine systems convey information between the body regions, e.g. to and fro between the brain and the rest of the body. However, their speed of doing so and extent of their effects can be very different.

3 To underline that activity in either system can have implications for behaviour and mental state.

4 To emphasize that there is no clear-cut distinction between these systems (Blackburn and Pfaus, 1988).

5 To consider their function, which is best understood in terms of their interactions. These systems have evolved to serve a common end point: survival and reproductive success. Thereby, the theme of Chapter 2 is continued here.

Figure 3.36 sketches a few interactions between the brain and other parts of the body. The brain has a *direct* link through the somatic nervous system to the skeletal muscles that execute behaviour. This action is supported by *indirect* effects, represented by two arrows marked 'alter sensitivity', which contact the 'skeletal muscle' box. These represent the effects of the ANS in making fuel available to the skeletal muscles, e.g. increased supply of blood. This effect is mediated by neurons of the ANS and hormones, hence the box marked 'hormones'. Hormones influence the brain and the brain influences the release of hormones. These interactions exhibit functional coherence in meeting challenges, e.g. increased flow of blood to skeletal muscles on fleeing danger and decreased flow in relaxation.

The next chapter takes a closer look at the details of how information is transmitted in the nervous system. It will ask how action potentials arise and how neurotransmitters convey information across synapses.

 See the video coverage for this chapter which shows how studying events throughout the body can inform psychology.

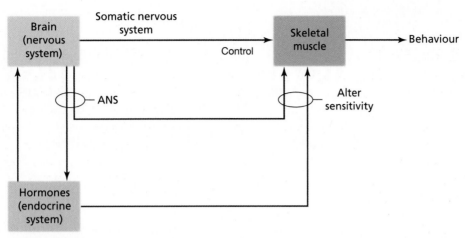

Figure 3.36 Some interactions between the nervous and endocrine systems.

Summary of Chapter 3

1 The nervous system, which contains neurons, and the endocrine system, which involves hormones, coordinate emotions, physiology and behaviour.

2 Nervous systems communicate information and process it. Information is transmitted to the central nervous system (CNS) and action triggered there.

3 Synapses are where one neuron influences another. They can be either excitatory or inhibitory.

4 The strength of connections between neurons at synapses can change, corresponding to development/learning.

5 Hormones are secreted into a blood vessel, transported in the blood to other sites where they occupy receptors, and thereby trigger action.

6 By means of muscles and hormones, the autonomic nervous system controls the body's internal environment.

Further reading

For neuroscience, see Bear *et al.* (2006) or Squire *et al.* (2008). For hormones, see Pfaff *et al.*, (2004). For a perspective that echoes the four types of explanation, see Adkins-Regan (2004).

Answers

Explanations for answers to 'test your knowledge' questions can be found on the website www.pearsoned.co.uk/toates

3.1 (ii) Endocrine
3.2 Neurotransmitter
3.3 (i) The terminal of neuron 1 (in the spinal cord); (ii) the cell body of neuron 2.
3.4 (i) Neuron to neuron, (ii) neuron to skeletal muscle, (iii) neuron to smooth muscle
3.5 (i) b
3.6 (iii) Reduce its activity
3.7 (i) Excitatory

3.8 (i) More
3.9 (iii) 7
3.10 (ii) 4 → 1
3.11 (i) 5 → 1
3.12 (ii) Cell body shown in (b)
3.13 (iii) AVP
3.14 A given substance can serve as neurotransmitter or hormone so the difference is not in the chemical form. A neurotransmitter is delivered to the receptors across the small gap within the synapse, whereas a hormone is delivered via the blood.
3.15 (ii) CRF
3.16 (i) Acetylcholine
3.17 (i) Acetylcholine
3.18 (iii) Grey matter of spinal cord

Visit www.pearsoned.co.uk/toates
for a range of resources to support study.
Test yourself with multiple choice questions and access a bank of over 100 videos that will bring the topics to life.

Chapter 4
How the cells of the nervous system work

Learning outcomes for Chapter 4

After studying this chapter, you should be able to:

1 Describe the general properties of cells, while highlighting the particular properties of neurons.

2 Summarize how ions move across the cell membrane of neurons.

3 Explain how action potentials arise and are transmitted. Link this to how information is encoded by the nervous system.

4 Describe the properties of glial cells and link this to their role.

5 Explain how different types of synapse are classified and the properties associated with this classification.

6 Describe the kinds of intervention that alter the working of synapses and how this occurs.

Scene-setting questions

1 Why is grey matter associated with the intellect?
2 How can degenerative diseases of the nervous system impair cognitive and motor function?
3 How do psychoactive drugs such as cocaine work?
4 How can a chemical such as Prozac alter mood?
5 Why do drugs have side-effects?
6 How might studying squid help to understand the basis of neural communication in humans?

How might studying squid help to understand the basis of neural communication in humans? Explore the video on the website accompanying this book at **www.pearsoned.co.uk/toates**

The speed of reaction can be vital to survival. What does a study of the cells of the nervous system tell us about how this is attained?

Source: © Gallo Images/Corbis.

Introduction

Chapter 3 described communication by neurons, in the context of the nervous and endocrine systems. Now we look at the cells of the nervous system in their own right and how they function as individual units. Such cells are mainly, but not exclusively, neurons. A principal concern will be how action potentials arise and travel in neurons. Another is how neurons process information and communicate information across synapses. We shall ask how the properties of individual neurons and synapses contribute to the properties of the nervous system and thereby behaviour. How do the parts of the cells of the nervous system (with a focus on neurons) help to explain how the cells work? How does similar insight help to explain how synapses work? Building on this, we consider how it is possible to manipulate events at neurons and synapses to change their performance and how this might affect nervous system properties, mood and behaviour.

The individual cell forms a fundamental building block of the body (Chapter 1). Neurons share some properties with most other cells. For example, each neuron has a nucleus, a membrane that surrounds the cell and an internal fluid environment. Each cell is bathed by the external fluid environment that surrounds cells' membranes (this has a different composition from the internal fluid).

First, the chapter considers some general properties of cells and then looks at specific properties of neurons. An understanding of general properties is necessary to explain how action potentials arise and are transmitted. We then look at communication between neurons at synapses.

The neuron as a typical cell

Structure

Figure 4.1 (developed from Figure 1.2, p. 5) shows a number of cells, the blood and interstitial fluid. The term **extracellular fluid** describes all the fluid that is not in the cells. It is made up of the interstitial fluid and the plasma, the fluid part of the blood. The interstitial fluid bathes the cells and is in close contact with the blood. By means of the interstitial fluid and the blood, energy and nutrients are brought to the cell and waste

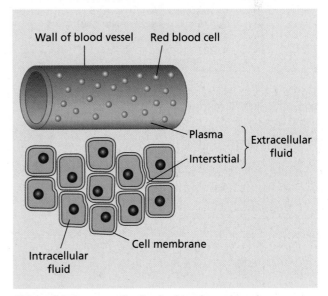

Figure 4.1 A group of cells, the blood supply and surrounding fluid.

Source: Adapted from Toates (2007, Fig. 4.1b, p. 33).

products are carried away. The fluid that is on the inside of the cell is termed **intracellular fluid** and has a different chemical composition from the extracellular fluid on the outside. The extracellular and intracellular fluids consist of water and a number of other substances.

The cell is surrounded by a cell membrane, which forms a barrier between the inside of the cell and the interstitial fluid surrounding the cell. The membrane is not equally permeable (meaning 'allows substances to pass through') to all the substances in the interstitial fluid, being permeable by various degrees to some but impermeable to others.

Figure 4.2 shows the difference in chemical composition between extracellular and intracellular fluids. For example, the concentrations of sodium (symbol Na^+) and potassium (symbol K^+) are different on either side of the cell membrane. This difference is crucial for the neuron to serve its role in communication, i.e. to produce action potentials.

Electrical events

Ions and voltages

In Figure 4.2, the symbols for sodium (Na) and potassium (K) have an associated plus sign. What does this signify? Each minute particle ('atom') of sodium and potassium has a 'charge' (a positive or 'plus' charge) of

Figure 4.2 Concentration differences between extracellular and intracellular fluid (concentration in arbitrary units).

electricity associated with it. Electrical charge will be familiar to you in terms of hair standing on end and sparking when you comb it or in static electricity associated with television sets, car doors, etc. That is, electrical charge produces action. Figure 4.3 illustrates charge and the action that this triggers: suspended spheres that carry electric charges. Charges of the same sign repel, so in part (b) the spheres are repelled from each other. Charges of opposite sign attract and so in part (c), the spheres are drawn together.

To say that Na^+ and K^+ have an electric charge means that each atom, termed an **ion**, is electrically active. Na^+ and K^+ are active in a way described by their plus sign and are termed 'positive ions'. There are also negative ions in the fluid inside and outside the cell, indicated by a minus sign. For example, Figure 4.2 shows one of these, chloride, represented as Cl^-. The minus sign indicates that a negative ion is electrically active in a way opposite to that of Na^+ and K^+. If you dissolve table salt, sodium chloride (chemical symbol NaCl), in water, each very tiny particle (termed 'molecule') of NaCl will split into two parts: the ions Na^+ and Cl^-. A type of large ion trapped on the inside of the cell and with a negative charge is indicated as A^- (Figure 4.2).

When ions are in solution, they tend to move around according to the electrical forces that act on them (Figure 4.2). In turn, ions contribute to the electrical forces that exert effects on all ions. Whether an ion is positive or negative influences its tendency to move. Imagine a region of solution where suddenly there arises a surplus of negative ions relative to positive ions and another region of excess positive ions (Figure 4.4(a)). So-called 'like ions' repel whereas so-called 'unlike ions' attract (Figure 4.3(b) and (c)). So, in Figure 4.4(a) positive ions are attracted to the negative region while negative ions are attracted to the positive region. The effect of attraction and repulsion is that, if there are no other, counteracting, factors operating to move them, electrical charges become evenly distributed within a solution (Figure 4.4(b)).

Intracellular fluid
K+ 150
Na+ 15
Cl− 10
A− 385

Extracellular fluid
K+ 5
Na+ 150
Cl− 110

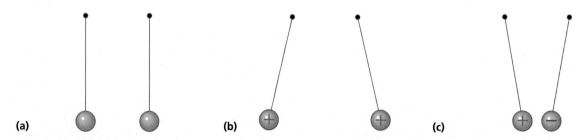

(a) **(b)** **(c)**

Figure 4.3 Hanging spheres: (a) no charge, (b) charges of same sign and (c) charges of opposite sign.

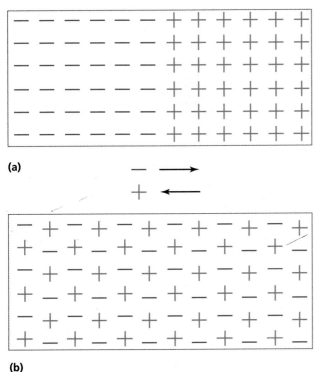

(a)

(b)

Figure 4.4 Ions in solution: (a) initially and (b) after distribution.

Figure 4.5 Comparison between (a) a cell and (b) a battery.

The membrane potential

Figure 4.4(a) shows an imbalance of ions, more of one sort than another in a location. If you had a measuring instrument you would be able to detect an electrical voltage between the two ends. A voltage tends to move ions. Where an imbalance of ions exists, so does a voltage. In part (b), a voltage no longer exists and there is no net movement of ions.

Biology is no exception to this principle: there is an unequal distribution of positive and negative ions comparing one side of a cell's membrane to the other side. Thus, a cell is like a miniature battery (Figure 4.5(a)). (Don't worry about how nature got constructed this way. For your sake, and mine, please just take it on trust!) That is, there exists a small electrical voltage across the cell's membrane or, as it is sometimes called, a **membrane potential**. In other words, there is an electrical 'polarity' across the cell; it is 'polarized'. This voltage is normally of magnitude –60 mV to –70 mV (mV = millivolt or one-thousandth of a volt). Remember: where a voltage exists, there exists also a force tending to move ions. In the case of the cell, the voltage tends to cause a movement of ions across its membrane. By analogy, a battery causes an electric current to flow between its terminals if a wire is placed there (Figure 4.5(b)).

Electrically, the interior of a cell is negative with respect to the outside. What does this mean? 'Positive' and 'negative' specify the polarity. As a result of the membrane potential (voltage), positive ions such as sodium and potassium will *tend to* move from the outside of the cell to the inside and negative ions will *tend to* move out (Figure 4.5(a)).

Note the qualifying expression 'tend to'. Sodium and potassium move across the membrane to the extent that: (a) there is *not* a stronger force (something other than voltage) tending to pull them in the opposite direction and (b) the membrane is permeable to them. Another force, which also acts on these ions, is described next.

The concentration gradient

As just implied by the qualification 'tend to', the voltage is not the only force present across the membrane. Considering Na+ and K+, there exist chemical **concentration gradients**, which also tend to move them. The term 'gradient' usually refers to a slope, as in the gradient of a hill being 1 in 5. Gradients tend to cause things to move down them from a high point to a low point, as in when you cycle with no effort down the gradient of a hill. The force moving you is greater for a 1 in 5 gradient than for a 1 in 10. By analogy, a concentration gradient refers to a tendency to cause movement that arises from different concentrations of a substance.

To understand this, think of two rooms that are segregated by a barrier in the form of a membrane. They are isolated from the outside world and there are no air currents blowing through either room. One room contains pure air but the other room has a high concentration of cigarette smoke uniformly distributed throughout. Imagine now that the membrane is suddenly made slightly permeable. There exists a 'concentration gradient for smoke', which refers to the difference in concentrations of smoke in the two regions. In response to the smoke concentration gradient, smoke will move from a high concentration area to a low concentration area. Given time, smoke will distribute itself evenly between the two rooms.

That smoke tends to become evenly distributed depends upon the random activity shown by its molecules. For substances in air or liquid, where a difference exists between two regions, the difference tends to disappear, i.e. the substance becomes evenly distributed. A similar principle is at work in the distribution of dust. Any mud dropped from shoes will tend to become dust. This dust will then tend to distribute itself evenly over surfaces such as a table-top.

In Figure 4.2, the concentration gradient for sodium (150 versus 15) acts from the outside of the cell to the inside. That for potassium acts in the opposite direction (150 versus 5). In response to the Na^+ concentration gradient, Na^+ will tend to move into the cell. K^+ will tend to move out, down the K^+ concentration gradient. Note that concentration gradient is always specific to a given substance, e.g. a concentration gradient for sodium.

The net force

Voltages and concentration gradients

The *net* force tending to move an ion across a membrane depends upon both (i) the voltage and (ii) the concentration gradient for that ion. Figure 4.6(a) shows the voltage and concentration gradients that arise from the distribution of ions on the two sides of a cell membrane. Typically, cell membranes permit a slight flow of K^+ and Na^+; they exhibit some permeability to these ions. Normally, the permeability to K^+ is greater than that to Na^+. In response to the forces shown in Figure 4.6(a), Na^+ tends to move into the cell, since the voltage and the concentration gradient for Na^+ act in this direction. However, the membrane normally has a relatively low permeability to Na^+, so only a slight inwards movement occurs.

The concentration gradient for K^+ will tend to move K^+ out of the cell. However, the voltage will tend to move it in. In practice, the strength of the voltage is less than that of the K^+ concentration gradient. Therefore, as a result of the forces shown in Figure 4.6(a), there is a slow net movement of K^+ out of the cell.

Pumps

Suppose that the forces described so far (Figure 4.6(a)) were the only ones to be operating. What would be their effect? K^+ would be depleted from the cell and Na^+ would accumulate on the inside. So, how are the stable concentrations (Figure 4.2) maintained in the face of these forces that are tending constantly to break them down?

An additional process is involved, a so-called pumping mechanism, a **sodium–potassium pump** (Figure 4.6(b)). Across the membrane, the pump expels Na^+ from the cell and pulls in K^+. Over time, this pump will counter the tendencies to break down the segregation of ions. The differences in ion concentration between inside and outside (Figure 4.2) are normally well maintained. The pump helps to keep the segregation of different types of ion and the imbalance in charge across the membrane, i.e. an excess of negative charge on the inside. The term 'pump' is only a useful metaphor and should not suggest literally a mechanical pump. In reality, it is a chemical reaction requiring energy. Enormous amounts of energy are devoted to maintaining the difference in ion concentration by pumping.

So far, what has been described is applicable to cells in general. However, neurons and muscle cells show certain peculiar properties and these form the topic of the next section.

Figure 4.6 Ion movements across a cell membrane: (a) in response to voltage and concentration gradients and (b) representation that includes the role of pumps.

The neuron: an excitable cell

In the baseline electrical state of the cell, a stable voltage of between –60 and –70 mV is maintained, a so-called **resting potential**. However, as you have seen, neurons are 'dynamic'. Having understood the basis of the stable ('resting') condition of the neuron, you are now in a position to understand how the action potential arises.

Basis of the action potential

Action potentials are electrical impulses, which arise in a neuron and convey information by their transmission along an axon. That is, neurons and muscle cells have the property of *excitability*. To understand this, view it in the context of the 'resting potential' (Figure 4.7). Note the action potentials, one of which is enlarged. In the enlarged diagram, note the membrane potential from time zero through time 1 to time 2. This represents the resting potential and is –70 mV, the inside of the cell being 70 mV negative with respect to the outside. To remind you: the existence of a membrane potential depends upon the relative numbers of positive and negative ions on the two sides.

At time 2, a change starts: a move to a less negative voltage. At time 4, there is a rapid move of the voltage across the membrane from a negative value, through

zero to a positive value (at 6) and then a rapid return to the original negative value. This is the *action potential*; a feature of neurons and muscle cells. How is it triggered?

Triggering an action potential

The membrane of a cell was described as having a certain *permeability* to the movement of ions across it, to be 'semi permeable'. The excitability peculiar to neurons and muscle cells depends upon the fact that the permeability of the membrane to K^+ and Na^+ is variable.

You have met two ways in which an action potential can be initiated: (a) at the tip of a sensory neuron as a result of stimulation (e.g. Chapter 3, Figure 3.1(b), p. 52) and (b) as a result of synaptic input to a neuron (e.g. Chapter 3, Figure 3.9, p. 58). We shall describe each of these in more detail.

Consider a sensory neuron that is sensitive to a tactile stimulus at the skin. It requires such stimulation before it will generate action potentials, i.e. it is not spontaneously active (Chapter 3). Suppose that a tactile stimulus is applied to the skin and pressure increased until it is sufficient to generate an action potential at the tip of the neuron.

Consider again the action potential shown enlarged in Figure 4.7 and this time how the sequence of electrical changes that occurs is explained. Suppose a tactile

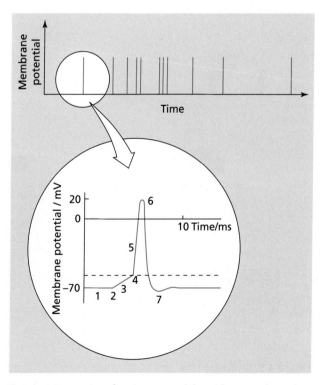

Figure 4.7 A series of action potentials, with one enlarged. (Note the different baselines in the two traces.)

(a)   **(b)**

Figure 4.8 Tip of a sensory neuron: (a) resting condition with sodium channels almost closed (indicated by almost closed doors) and (b) deformation at tip as a result of tactile stimulus (arrow), triggering local sodium channels to open.

stimulus starts to be applied at time 2. By deforming the membrane, the stimulus increases the membrane's permeability to Na^+ at the neuron's tip (Figure 4.8). Both the voltage and the Na^+ concentration gradient tend to move Na^+ into the neuron. Therefore, when the permeability to Na^+ is increased by the tactile stimulus, Na^+ moves into the neuron at a higher rate than normal. It moves in along sodium channels in the membrane. These are normally almost closed but are opened by the deformation of the membrane.

Movement of positive ions (Na^+) into the neuron shifts the membrane potential in a positive direction, away from the negative resting potential, i.e. the stages marked 2, 3 and 4 in Figure 4.7. Since this is a move towards zero, away from the polarized value, it is known as **depolarization**.

At stage 4, a sudden change occurs, the voltage reaches the **threshold** and the action potential is triggered. This is an explosive depolarizing move of membrane potential, i.e. stages 4 and 5, through zero and then briefly to a positive polarity (at 6). Over the period 4–6, incoming Na^+ makes the inside more positive, which increases Na^+ permeability, which brings in still more Na^+, and so on ..., i.e. there is an explosive ('vicious circle' or 'positive feedback') effect.

The sequence 1–6 might be better appreciated with an analogy (Figure 4.9). The ship is in equilibrium (part (a)) until something disturbs it (part (b)). A small disturbance triggers a corrective force. However, if the disturbance is large enough (part (c), compare with point 4 in Figure 4.7), the ship will suddenly topple over.

The move of membrane potential in a positive direction ceases at stage 6 (Figure 4.7). What causes this? It is a property of the sodium channels in the membrane. Their opening is the basis of the movement of Na^+ into the cell and thereby the move in a positive direction. At stage 6, the channels slam shut, which prevents further Na^+ from moving into the cell and the movement of membrane potential in a positive direction ceases.

The voltage now moves in a negative direction, i.e. stages 6–7 in Figure 4.7. What causes this? The opening of K^+ channels, which occurs just after the opening of Na^+ channels. K^+ moves out of the neuron at a relatively high rate as a result of its concentration gradient. The movement of positive ions out of the cell changes the voltage in a negative direction (6–7).

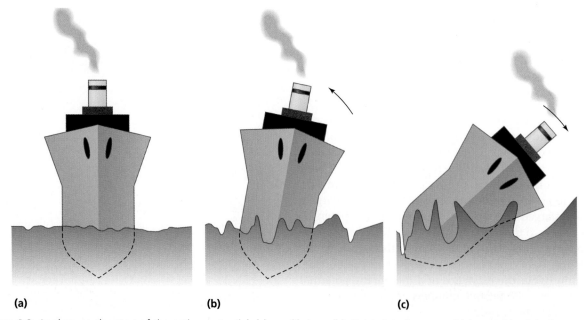

(a)   **(b)**   **(c)**

Figure 4.9 Analogy to the start of the action potential: (a) equilibrium, (b) slight disturbance and (c) unstable disturbance.

Movement of action potentials

So much for the generation of an action potential at one location, but how does it move along an axon? An action potential at one location of axon influences neighbouring locations. This influence opens Na^+ channels and changes membrane potential to a less negative value, and thereby tends to create a new action potential in the neighbouring location. This new action potential appears just as the instigating action potential is dying out. In effect, the action potential moves along the axon. This property enables action potentials to communicate information.

In Figure 4.10, tactile stimulation at the tip of the sensory neuron triggers an action potential at time t_0. The action potential then travels smoothly from the tip. However, it can be easier to think in terms of chunks of axon. So, consider that an action potential at the tip then tends to create an action potential at a region marked A, just away from the tip, at a brief instant later,

t_1. In turn, when the action potential gets to A, it then tends to create a new one a moment later (t_2) at B. This means that, by the time the action potential at A has finished, there is a new one at B, and so on along the axon. At time t_3, it has almost reached the end of the axon in the CNS.

When the action potential gets to the end of the axon, it terminates. However, as discussed earlier, information can be carried further by means of a synapse.

The frequency of action potentials

Information is carried by the frequency with which action potentials occur, so what determines frequency? We are, in effect, asking, after undergoing one action potential, how soon can a region of axon exhibit another one? The sooner it can recover and generate another action potential, the higher will be the frequency.

Figure 4.11 shows a 'snapshot' of an action potential travelling from left to right. At the time shown,

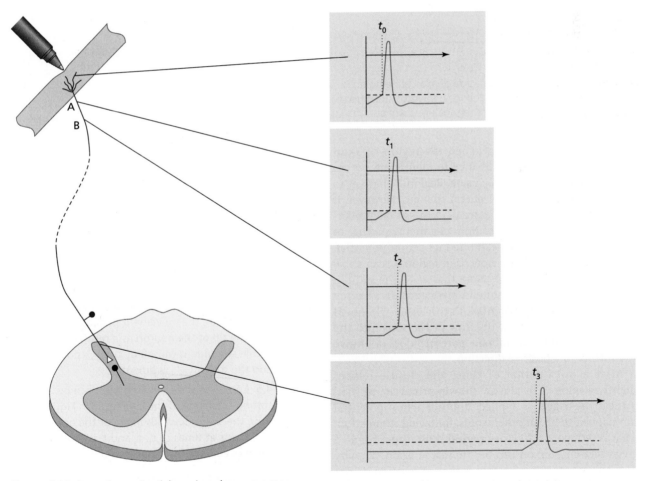

Figure 4.10 An action potential moving along an axon.

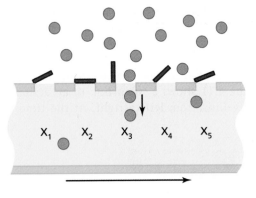

(b)

Figure 4.11 A 'snapshot' of a region of axon undergoing an action potential: (a) voltage change (i.e. disturbance from resting voltage) and (b) events at the sodium channels.

the action potential has reached the region of axon labelled X_3. Note the disturbance to membrane potential at location X_3 and to each side. Region X_4 has yet to undergo the sequence of electrical changes. However, it is already showing the influence of events at neighbouring region X_3, in that the sodium channel is starting to open. Region X_2 has just exhibited an action potential. So, what sets the limit on how soon region X_2 can show a second action potential? Note that at X_2 the sodium channel is shut, i.e. the state immediately after having undergone an action potential. Such closure was noted earlier as the reason that the flow of Na^+ ions into the axon ceases and the membrane potential does not move any further in a positive direction.

After a brief period of time, the closure relaxes slightly. Region X_1 is already showing recovery, so that, if the right trigger is applied, another action potential can happen there. In other words, following stimulation, what is termed a **refractory period** must elapse before a given section of axon can be stimulated again. So, why does the action potential that is now at location X_3 not trigger another at X_1? The action potential at X_3 is too far 'down the track' to influence events at X_1 sufficient to form another action potential (note there is only a slight

disturbance of voltage at X_1). This explains why action potentials do not 'travel backwards'. It explains why, once one action potential is initiated, an indefinite series of them do not move chaotically along the axon in both directions. However, if the original tactile stimulus is still present, this will tend to instigate further action potentials, which again move from left to right.

Frequency of action potentials can be high or low. Frequency normally depends upon the intensity of the stimulus. With more intense stimuli, one action potential follows very rapidly after another. Figure 4.12 shows the effect of increasing the intensity of stimulation, e.g. increasing the deformation of the tip of a sensory neuron. At first, frequency goes up with increasing stimulation but then (part (c)) a saturation point is reached where frequency can increase no more. The refractory period sets this upper limit on frequency.

Section summary

1   The movement of sodium and potassium ions across the membrane of a neuron forms the basis of an action potential.

2   An action potential generated at one location tends to invade a neighbouring region of neuron when this region is in a state to support an action potential.

3   An action potential normally moves along an axon in only one direction.

 ## Test your knowledge

4.3 In Figure 4.7, at which of the following times is the membrane potential at its resting potential? (i) 1, (ii) 5, (iii) 6.

4.4 Complete the following sentence: 'In Figure 4.8(b), the movement of sodium ions into the tip of the neuron as a result of the tactile stimulus, is caused by the ___ potential and the sodium ___ gradient'.

4.5 Complete the following sentence by stating the name of the chemical: 'In Figure 4.10, the sharp upwards move of the graph that starts at times t_0, t_1, t_2 and t_3 is caused by the movement of ___ ions into the neuron'.

Answers on page 104

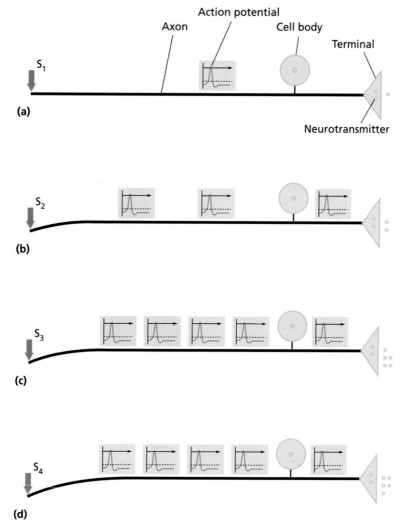

Figure 4.12 Different frequencies of action potentials in an axon as a function of increasing intensity of stimulation (S): (a) S_1, (b) S_2, (c) S_3 and (d) S_4.

Glial cells

Neurons are closely associated with another type of cell termed **glial cells** (or 'glia cells' or just 'glia'). There are many more glial cells than neurons in the nervous system. In the CNS, a type of glial cell is described as 'oligodendrocytes', whereas in the peripheral nervous system glial cells are termed 'Schwann cells'.

Traditionally glial cells were thought to play 'only' a supporting role in the maintenance of the nervous system, e.g. they help to regulate its chemical composition. However, recent evidence suggests that they do much more than this. They seem to play a role in the development of the nervous system, e.g. in the sculpting of new synapses. Also, they appear to listen to the activity of their associated neurons and influence the signalling properties of these neurons. Glial cells 'speak' to each other within networks of glial cells by means of chemical communication.

Figure 4.13 shows one role of glial cells: a neuron together with a part of some specialized glial cells that form an insulating coating termed **myelin**. Many axons are coated with myelin and are termed 'myelinated axons'. Sheaths of myelin cover the axon, the gaps between them being known as **nodes of Ranvier**. At nodes of Ranvier, ions can cross the membrane and it is here that action potentials occur. Action potentials travel along myelinated axons at high speed relative to an unmyelinated axon of the same diameter. Myelin increases this speed. The speed of some reactions, e.g. in escaping from a predator, can be crucial to survival.

A personal angle

Einstein's brain

An extraordinary story surrounds the brain of Albert Einstein, taken from his body following an autopsy in 1955. The pathologist Thomas Harvey took the brain home with him and preserved it for 40 years. He would occasionally take a small slice of brain and give it to people who wanted it for research. All wished to find something abnormal in its tissues that might reflect Einstein's genius. Researchers found no abnormality in the form or number of neurons. However, an abnormal number of glial cells were found in regions associated with 'advanced' cognition. Of course, we cannot say that this proves a relationship between an aspect of brain and associated intellect but has fuelled fruitful speculation.

Can the study of the brains of people with exceptional abilities reveal anything interesting?

Source: US Library of Congress/Science Photo Library.

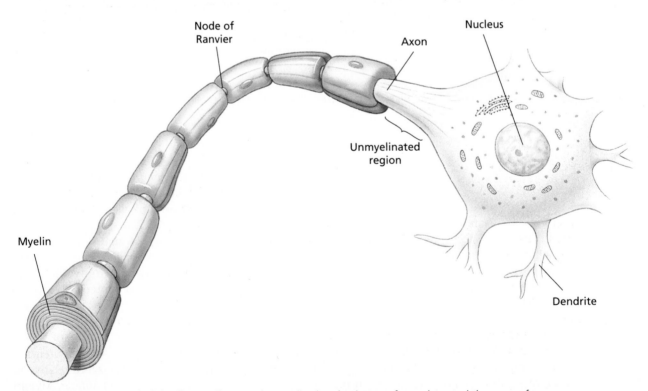

Figure 4.13 A number of glial cells contribute to the myelin sheaths that are formed around the axon of a neuron.

Source: adapted from Martini *et al.* (2000, Fig. 13-8, p. 337). Copyright © 2000, 1997 by Frederic H. Martini, Inc. and Michael J. Timmons. Reprinted by permission of Pearson Education, Inc.

Myelin has a whitish appearance. Hence, where there is a high concentration of myelin, neural tissue appears 'whitish' or 'pinkish' (Figure 4.10). In the white matter of the spinal cord, a large number of myelin-coated axons convey information up and down. In the brain and spinal cord, grey matter consists of a high density of cell bodies. This is where information processing rather than 'simply' transmission occurs. Hence, in the popular imagination, there is an association of grey matter with cognition and the intellect.

How does myelin increase the speed of an action potential? An axon that is without myelin is known as 'unmyelinated' (Figure 4.14(a)). Note the drop in strength of the influence of the action potential (disturbance from resting potential) to each side of the region directly experiencing the action potential. Now compare this with the less steep drop in Figure 4.14(b).

An action potential at one node of Ranvier creates a change in membrane potential in the axon at the next node such that a new action potential occurs there. The influence of an action potential at one region of a myelinated axon spreads a relatively large distance compared with the same axon but without myelin. Hence, there is the capacity for the action potential, in effect, to jump far ahead (to the next node of Ranvier) in a myelinated axon.

A consideration of myelination explains the destructive effect of degenerative diseases that destroy myelin. The action potential either cannot travel or is greatly reduced in speed. When the myelin that surrounds motor neurons is lost, there is disruption to motor performance. Loss of myelin within the CNS can affect cognition.

The following section looks at how synapses function and thereby at communication *between* neurons.

Figure 4.14 Myelination: (a) unmyelinated axon and (b) myelinated axon.

Section summary

1 Apart from neurons, nervous systems also contain glial cells.

2 Glial cells provide support for neurons and facilitate processing within circuits of neurons.

3 One type of glial cell provides a myelin coating to axons.

4 Gaps between myelin coating are known as nodes of Ranvier.

5 In a myelinated axon, action potentials in effect jump from one node of Ranvier to another.

6 Myelination of an axon speeds up the transmission of an action potential.

☞ Test your knowledge

4.6 In Figure 4.13, action potentials jump along the axon between nodes of Ranvier in which direction? (i) Right to left, (ii) left to right.

Answer on page 104   ◖▬▷ WEB

The synapse and neurotransmitters

Introduction

In Chapter 3, you met chemical synapses. (There are also synapses that do not use chemical transmitter, discussed later.) Figure 4.15 shows a detailed view of a chemical synapse. Note the axon terminal, presynaptic membrane, postsynaptic membrane and the gap between membranes, termed the **synaptic cleft**. Myelin sheath surrounds the axon. You have also met a special chemical synapse, the point of communication between a neuron and a muscle: a **neuromuscular junction**. This follows the same principles of organization as the synapse between neurons (Figure 4.15).

As you have seen, neurotransmitter is stored at the terminal of a neuron and released by the arrival of an action potential. A number of transmitter molecules are stored in packages, termed 'synaptic vesicles'. See Figures 4.15 and 4.16. (However, for some purposes, it is convenient to represent free molecules of transmitter, without vesicles.) On arriving at the terminal, the action potential triggers the movement of calcium ions into the neuron, which, in turn, triggers the vesicles to fuse with the presynaptic membrane and release their contents into the synaptic cleft.

On release from neuron$_1$, transmitter rapidly moves across the gap between the two neurons and attaches to receptors on neuron$_2$ (Figure 4.16). There is a slight delay (the 'synaptic delay'), of about 0.5 milliseconds (ms), between the arrival of the action potential at the terminal of neuron$_1$ and the start of electrical events in neuron$_2$. On attaching to neuron$_2$, the neurotransmitter changes the membrane potential at the local site of attachment. This change will typically make an action potential in neuron$_2$ more likely to occur (i.e. excitation) or less likely (i.e. inhibition), described shortly.

Neurotransmitter is commonly synthesized or partially synthesized in the neuron's cell body. It is slowly transported to the terminal and stored there until release. In some cases, synthesis occurs at the terminal.

Figure 4.12 showed the effect of increasing the frequency of action potentials in a neuron. As frequency increases, so does the amount of neurotransmitter released. Correspondingly, the effect on the postsynaptic cell increases with the amount of neurotransmitter

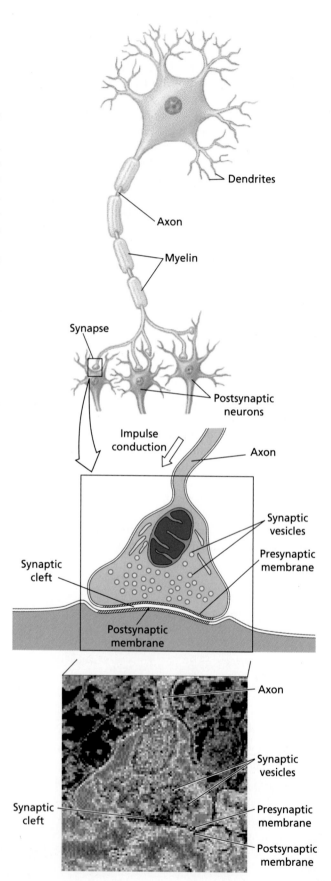

Figure 4.15 The chemical synapse.

Source: Martini *et al.* (2000, Fig. 13-12, p. 343) Copyright © 2000, 1997 by Frederic H. Martini, Inc. and Michael J. Timmons. Reprinted by permission of Pearson Education, Inc.; *photo*: © Dennis Kunkel/ Phototake, Inc.

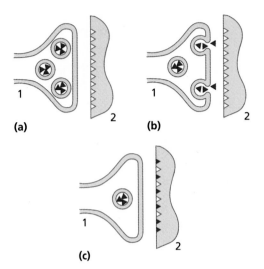

Figure 4.16 Neuron terminal showing neurotransmitter in vesicles: (a) unstimulated, (b) arrival of action potential and fusion of vesicles with presynaptic membrane and (c) reformation of membrane and occupation of receptors with transmitter.

attaching itself to receptors. For an example, you can imagine the postsynaptic cell to be a muscle cell, forming part of a skeletal muscle. The neuron would be a motor neuron triggering increasing degrees of force in the muscle as a result of increasing commands to do so.

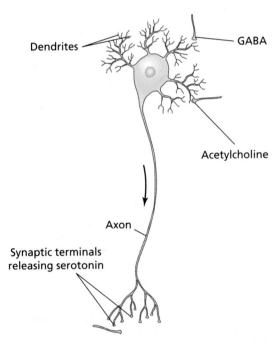

Figure 4.17 Serotonergic neuron with receptors for GABA and acetylcholine.

Dale's principle and beyond

The principle

A neuron is characterized by the neurotransmitter that it *synthesizes, stores and releases*, e.g. one that synthesizes, stores and releases serotonin is called 'serotonergic'. Note the ending '-ergic', which makes the adjective that characterizes each neurotransmitter and associated synapses. For example, at a cholinergic synapse, acetylcholine is released and occupies acetylcholine receptors on the membrane of the second neuron.

This classical picture, enshrined as **Dale's principle**, states that a given neuron synthesizes, stores and releases only one neurotransmitter. Hence, a term such as 'serotonergic' would uniquely label such a neuron. A neuron is labelled by this criterion, rather than by the neurotransmitter(s) for which it has receptors. For example, Figure 4.17 shows a serotonergic neuron, with receptors for GABA and acetylcholine. Although it has multiple types of receptor, it is characterized as serotonergic.

Beyond the classical picture

Dale's principle is now known to be only partly true (Dismukes, 1979). Although some neurons conform to it and can be uniquely described by a single neurotransmitter (Figure 4.17), others release more than one. A given neuron can contain different substances (termed 'colocalization') and can release them simultaneously or at different times according to its pattern of activity (Figure 4.18(a) and (b)). The associated postsynaptic sites can have multiple types of receptors. As an example, postganglionic neurons of the parasympathetic system (Chapter 3) secrete both acetylcholine and 'vasoactive intestinal polypeptide' (Powley, 1999). This combination is involved in the swelling of blood vessels at the genitals in sexual excitement. Figure 4.18(c) shows another mode of operation: the same neuron releases different neurotransmitters from different sites.

The effect of synaptic inputs

Types of neuron

Neurons come in different shapes and sizes (Figure 3.19, p. 66). The location at which an action potential arises depends upon the type of neuron. It can normally be triggered in at least two ways. The present chapter described earlier its initiation at the terminal of a sensory neuron. Another way that it can be triggered is at the 'axon hillock' of an interneuron or motor neuron (Figure 4.19) by activity at synapses, the topic of this section.

As a simplification, the chapter described just a few presynaptic inputs to a postsynaptic neuron (e.g. Figure

Figure 4.18 Colocalization: (a) co-release, (b) separate release as a function of the frequency of action potentials and (c) different transmitters stored and released at different locations in the presynaptic neuron.

4.19). Occasionally, such simple connections are found. However, more commonly, certainly in humans, very many synapses, up to 100 000, are formed on a single postsynaptic neuron. Typically, many synapses are made on a neuron's dendrites. For simplicity, I shall describe just a few synapses formed on a neuron. The principles can be scaled up for the more realistic situation.

For the neuron of Figure 4.19, if depolarization reaches threshold, action potentials are initiated at the axon hillock and then travel along the axon. What determines depolarization at the axon hillock? It is the effect of activity in neurons (1 and 2) that form excitatory synapses with neuron 3.

Postsynaptic potentials

The arrival of an action potential at an axon terminal normally contributes only a small change in voltage, termed a **postsynaptic potential** (PSP) at the local postsynaptic membrane. See top trace in Figure 4.19 for this event at synapse 1. What is termed an 'excitatory postsynaptic potential' (EPSP) is, as shown, a brief move in a positive direction, i.e. a local reduction of the negative voltage (depolarization). Local depolarization at the

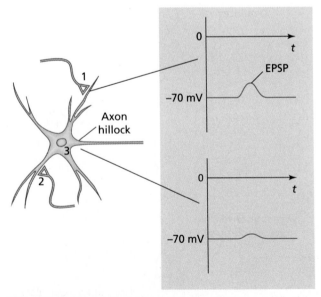

Figure 4.19 Neuron 3 showing location of the axon hillock, an excitatory postsynaptic potential (EPSP) at synapse 1 and its effect at the axon hillock.

postsynaptic site extends away from this site, including to the axon hillock. However, as shown, between the site of the EPSP (location 1) and the axon hillock, there is a decrement in the strength of the change in voltage.

Suppose that two EPSPs occur in succession at synapse 1. Depending upon their timing, they can add their effects. In Figure 4.20(b), the effect of the first action potential has not decayed to zero at the time that the second occurs and there is an addition of their effects, termed **temporal summation**. In distinction to events at a single synapse, the addition of EPSPs at different synapses is termed **spatial summation**.

Depending upon the nature of transmitter and receptor, there can be either an excitatory postsynaptic potential (EPSP) or an inhibitory postsynaptic potential (IPSP) (Figure 4.21). In other words, the arrival of an action potential at an inhibitory synapse causes an increase in negative voltage, termed **hyperpolarization**.

Inputs, whether excitatory or inhibitory, are *integrated* at the axon hillock. If the membrane potential reaches the threshold, an action potential is triggered (Figure 4.7). Figure 4.22 represents another example of this: the neuron requires an excitatory input to trigger an action potential. The positive move of voltage needs to reach threshold at the axon hillock for an action potential to arise. Each postsynaptic potential extends a distance from the site where the postsynaptic receptors are located. Therefore, each contributes to just a very small voltage change at the axon hillock. The *net* summation ('integration') of inputs, excitatory and inhibitory, determines whether a neuron generates an action potential (Figure 4.22 shows just a sample of inputs). Hyperpolarization caused by the inhibitory input acts in the opposite direction to the depolarizing effect of the excitatory inputs.

A large number of incoming action potentials at excitatory synapses triggers a high frequency of action potentials in the postsynaptic neuron. Conversely, activity at inhibitory synapses reduces the frequency of action potentials arising. This represents information processing, i.e. weighing up the relative strengths of excitation and inhibition.

Avoiding cross-talk

Considering the synapse, the receptor is like a lock and the neurotransmitter is like a key that fits just this one lock. This is termed the **lock and key principle**. It enables specificity of neurotransmission between presynaptic and postsynaptic neurons. Figure 4.23 represents specificity of neurotransmitter and receptor between neuron 1 and neuron 2 and also between neuron 3 and neuron 4.

Figure 4.20 The effect at the axon hillock of two excitatory postsynaptic potentials at times T_1 and T_2: (a) apart in time, so that summation does not occur and (b) closer in time, so that summation occurs.

Figure 4.21 Excitatory (EPSP) and inhibitory postsynaptic potentials (IPSP).

(a)

(b)

(c)

Figure 4.22 (a) Neuron 3 with two excitatory inputs (E; 1 and 2) and one inhibitory input (I; 4). (b) Effects of action potentials arriving in sequence at each of the three inputs, as measured at the axon hillock. (c) Integration of effects at the axon hillock when they occur simultaneously.

Suppose that a different neurotransmitter or hormone were to drift into the synapse that neuron 1 makes with neuron 2. As shown, the neurotransmitter normally communicating from 3 to 4 might. This shape does not fit the receptors at neuron 2, which means that the 'foreign' neurotransmitter cannot influence the synapse between 1 and 2. This allows different synapses to be close together and yet little cross-talk occurs.

Removal of neurotransmitter from the synapse

Neurotransmitter is released, crosses the synaptic cleft, attaches to receptors and, depending upon the synapse, either excites or inhibits the postsynaptic cell. Figure 3.11 (p. 59) showed that the effect on the postsynaptic

Figure 4.23 Avoidance of cross-talk.

cell can reflect very closely the duration of activity in the presynaptic cell. For example, when a burst of action potentials ceases, the release of neurotransmitter and its postsynaptic effect also cease. Why does neurotransmitter not remain attached to the receptors and continue either to excite or to inhibit, even though no more is being released?

There are processes at the synapse that remove neurotransmitter immediately after it has contacted the receptors. For a substance to qualify as a neurotransmitter, not only must it be synthesized, stored and released from a neuron and there must be receptors at a postsynaptic site, but also a process of inactivation must be present.

To understand inactivation, raise your arm in the air. Hold it there for a moment and then decide to lower it. Almost immediately, contraction is relaxed in the muscle and the arm comes down. The contraction was maintained by occupation of receptors at the muscle by neurotransmitter. When the motor neurons cease activity, as a result of inactivation the effect of neurotransmitter also stops. The automatic removal of neurotransmitter means that the postsynaptic cell, whether neuron or muscle, can closely follow signals in the presynaptic neuron.

How then is a sustained activity in the postsynaptic cell maintained? For example, a muscle can be held in a contracted position over time (e.g. raising your arm for minutes). There must be some occupation of the receptors at the muscle throughout. It happens by means of sustained activity in the motor neurons that innervate the muscle. Sustained activity in the postsynaptic cell (muscle cell, in this case) implies sustained activity in the presynaptic cell to produce neurotransmitter. This replaces the neurotransmitter that is removed from the synapse (Figure 4.24).

Figure 4.24 Balance of factors at the neuromuscular junction during a sustained effort. The rate of release of transmitter (1) equals rate of removal (2).

There are two different processes of removal, depending upon the type of synapse. At some synapses, a chemical (an enzyme) that is present at the synapse literally breaks down the neurotransmitter (Figure 4.24). For constant activity at the postsynaptic cell, the rate of release and breakdown arrive at equilibrium. Breakdown is also shown in Figure 4.25(a). Another process is that neurotransmitter is taken back into the presynaptic neuron from which it was released, termed **reuptake**. Figure 4.25(b) shows such a two-way traffic of neurotransmitter across the cell membrane of the first neuron. Neurotransmitter is recycled.

Metabolites

When neurotransmitter is broken down into components (Figures 4.24 and 4.25(a)), the breakdown products are termed its **metabolites**. Metabolites provide useful information to the investigator, since they

will probably appear in the urine and can be measured. Knowing these metabolites, investigators have an idea of the neurotransmitter that gave rise to them. For example, suppose that a neurotransmitter (e.g. acetylcholine) has been activated unusually strongly. This should be reflected in increased levels of secretion of its metabolites in the urine, which points to the neural activation giving rise to them.

Studying brain function in this way can be compared to trying to understand the events in a house by monitoring the contents of its rubbish bin. In each case, the method lacks precision. However, as any detective knows, though less reliable than hidden cameras, very useful insight can be gained from examining rubbish bins.

Second messengers

So far, the chapter has portrayed the classical picture in which a neurotransmitter occupies receptors on a postsynaptic cell and thereby immediately influences the cell, to excite or inhibit. However, more complex effects also occur. To form a starting-point, Figure 4.26(a) shows the classical situation already described. When neurotransmitter occupies receptors, ion channels open and ions move through the channel. This has the immediate effect of either depolarizing or hyperpolarizing the cell, according to the nature of the ion channels that are affected. For example, opening sodium channels causes an inflow of Na^+, which depolarizes the cell.

Figure 4.26(b) shows a different effect, involving what is termed a **second messenger**. On occupying receptors, neurotransmitter does not change ion channels but causes the release of a further substance, the second messenger, within the cell. (In these terms, the neurotransmitter is a 'first messenger'.) The second messenger can have one of several effects depending upon the cell. As one such, it can open ion channels. In other cases, it targets the genetic material of the cell, influencing the activity of particular genes.

Electrical synapses

It is worth comparing the chemical synapse with a type of synapse that does not employ neurotransmitter, the **electrical synapse** (Figure 4.27). Note in part (b) that there is no synaptic gap: one neuron contacts directly another. Electrical events in neuron$_1$ trigger electrical events in neuron$_2$.

Figure 4.25 How transmitter is removed from the synaptic cleft: (a) enzymatic breakdown and (b) reuptake.

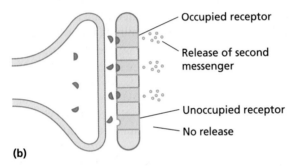

Figure 4.26 (a) Classical neurotransmission and (b) a second messenger system.

Figure 4.27 Synapses: (a) chemical and (b) electrical.

Section summary

1 A neuron forming a chemical synapse can be characterized by the neurotransmitter that it synthesizes, stores and releases at a synapse.

2 A given neuron can have receptors for several types of neurotransmitter.

3 Shortly after attaching, neurotransmitter is normally dislodged from the receptors and removed from the synapse (by enzymatic destruction or reuptake).

4 The breakdown products of a neurotransmitter are termed its metabolites.

5 Second messengers are released within certain neurons in response to neurotransmitter.

6 At electrical synapses, there is direct electrical communication from one neuron to another.

☞ Test your knowledge

4.7 In Figure 4.20(a), what description is given to the membrane potential at time 20 ms?

4.8 In Figure 4.20(b), the membrane potential at time T_2 would be described as which of the following? (i) Hyperpolarized, (ii) depolarized, (iii) positive.

4.9 What is the missing word in the following sentence? 'In Figure 4.25(a), the green rectangle and square represent ___ of the transmitter'.

Answers on page 104

Alterations in synaptic strength

Introduction

Maintaining the strength of transmission at synapses (e.g. dopaminergic and serotonergic) within a certain range is vital to behaviour, physical and mental health. For example, normal synaptic activity at neuromuscular junctions is crucial for exerting control in the somatic and autonomic nervous systems. However, the strength of synaptic connections can vary, as a function of (i) physical interventions made in the interest of research or therapy, (ii) drugs such as nicotine, (iii) disease or (iv) genetic differences between individuals. There can be over-activity or under-activity in a particular neurotransmitter. This section will describe some implications of this for behaviour.

Consider the sequence involving neurotransmitter: (1) release, (2) movement across the synaptic cleft, (3) attachment to receptors and (4) removal from the synapse. A change in any of 1–4 changes the strength of synaptic connection, i.e. for a given presynaptic activity, the postsynaptic activity will be different. 'Change' can mean, for example, those over time in a given individual as a result of a manipulation such as medication or genetically determined differences between individuals.

Naturally occurring changes

This section will consider 'natural' differences in synaptic efficacy to be those that do not arise as a result of deliberate artificial manipulations. For example, depression is associated with abnormalities in serotonergic, noradrenergic and dopaminergic synapses. There might be differences between individuals as a result of, say, genetics, which could contribute to depression (Chapter 2). It is possible that genes and/or environment play a role in producing synapses that are different, in terms of, say, the amount of transmitter stored or number of receptors.

How can disease alter the strength of synaptic connections? A possible source of malfunction is the loss of receptors at the postsynaptic membrane. In addition, consider events prior to neurotransmitter being released at the terminal of a neuron. Neurotransmitter is synthesized from precursor substances in the cell body and terminal. Inadequate amounts might be synthesized.

Artificially changing synapses

Drugs (e.g. alcohol) have effects on mood because they exert action at particular classes of synapse. Drugs are commonly used as research tools by psychologists interested in probing their effects on the nervous system.

Agonists and antagonists

Certain unnatural substances that are different from the natural neurotransmitter nonetheless occupy its receptors after being introduced into the body. On occupying receptors, substances can have various effects. Such substances can be exploited as therapy and research tools. For example, the effect of the natural neurotransmitter on the postsynaptic cell can be mimicked by drugs called **agonists**. If the natural neurotransmitter excites the postsynaptic cell, by definition so does its agonist. If the natural substance inhibits, so does its agonist. Therapeutically, an agonist might be employed where there is a deficiency of natural neurotransmitter.

Conversely, a drug might occupy receptors but not exert any effect on the second cell (i.e. it is inert), thereby blocking the natural neurotransmitter's action. A substance having this property is termed an **antagonist**. An antagonist might be used in a therapy to lower the effect of a natural neurotransmitter.

For an excitatory synapse, Figure 4.28 shows the effects of agonists and antagonists, sometimes known as 'direct agonists' and 'direct antagonists' because of their site of action at receptors.

A natural neurochemical can interact with more than one subtype of receptor (Figure 4.29(a)). In this case, there are distinct D1 and D2 subtypes of dopamine (DA) receptor. Different subtypes are sometimes found in different brain regions. Figure 4.29(b) represents agonists or antagonists that target a specific subtype of receptor. For example, the D1 type of agonist fits the D1 receptor subtype but not the D2 subtype. Note their unique configuration but the generic ('all-purpose') configuration of the natural neurotransmitter.

Other substances are termed 'indirect' agonists and antagonists. The term 'indirect' contrasts with the direct substance in the sites at which they act. For example, an indirect agonist might trigger the release of neurotransmitter from a presynaptic neuron even in the absence of action potentials. An indirect antagonist might block its release.

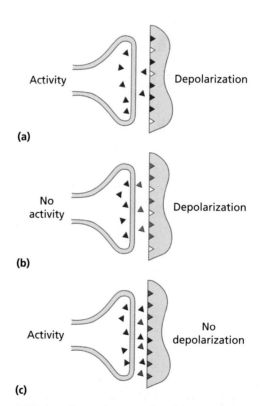

Figure 4.28 Agonists and antagonists: (a) normal situation, (b) addition of agonist and (c) addition of antagonist.

Drugs can also affect synaptic efficacy by changing the rate of removal of neurotransmitter from the synaptic cleft. Neurotransmitter is removed in one of two ways (Figure 4.25). Some drugs block reuptake (Figure 4.25(b)) and this increases the amount of neurotransmitter at the synaptic cleft and hence increases that at the receptors (Figure 4.30). For example, cocaine blocks the reuptake of dopamine.

Elevating dopamine levels by cocaine is experienced as 'euphoric', a 'high'. However, it comes at a price, both literally and metaphorically. The high has a limited duration, set by the length of time that elevated dopamine levels are available and before dopamine drifts from the synapse. The effect is powerful and dramatic. Since dopamine is not being recycled by reuptake into the presynaptic neuron, the 'high' is followed by dopamine depletion and hence under-activity at the synapse. This triggers negative emotion and translates into a craving for more cocaine. In time, dopamine will be replenished at the presynaptic neuron.

Artificially altering synaptic function can trigger homeostatic-like changes at the synapse. For example, if a synapse is repeatedly over-excited there can be a compensatory loss of receptors at the postsynaptic membrane, termed **down-regulation**. Conversely, loss of transmitter can trigger a proliferation of receptors termed **up-regulation**.

(a)

(b)

Figure 4.30 The action of a drug on blocking reuptake: (a) without drug and (b) in the presence of drug.

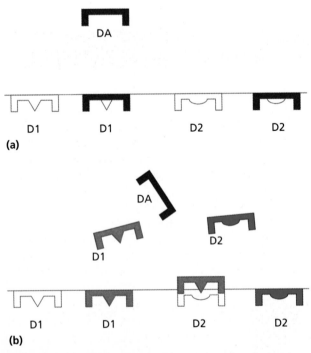

(a)

(b)

Figure 4.29 Dopamine exemplifying a neurochemical and subtypes of receptor: (a) natural situation and (b) addition of artificial chemicals that target only a subtype of receptor (either D1 or D2).

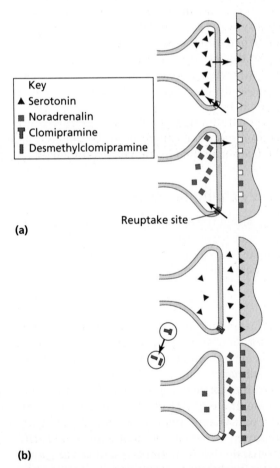

(a)

(b)

Figure 4.31 A drug that targets a natural neurotransmitter and the side effect of a metabolite on noradrenergic synapses: (a) without and (b) with the drug present.

Antidepressant medication

Mood-altering drugs, legal and illegal, act in several ways, one of which was shown in Figure 4.30. A number of legal antidepressants change the reuptake of neurotransmitters, though less dramatically than cocaine. A drug, fluoxetine (Prozac), used to treat obsessive-compulsive disorder (e.g. compulsive checking or intrusive thoughts), inhibits the reuptake of serotonin. It is termed a **reuptake inhibitor**. Its reputation has now spread far. Some argue that happiness is everyone's birthright and, if we cannot achieve this by natural means, we should artificially elevate serotonin levels with Prozac. Other antidepressants reduce levels of the enzyme that breaks down a particular neurotransmitter, which increases levels of neurotransmitter at the postsynaptic membrane.

In time, drugs are broken down into their metabolites. In some cases, these metabolites influence neurons at receptors, having undesirable effects. Effects that are unintended are termed 'side effects'. For example, the drug clomipramine blocks serotonin reuptake and provides therapy for obsessive-compulsive disorder and depression. Logically, the efficacy might be attributed to its targeting of serotonin. However, clomipramine does not remain chemically unaltered in the body. It is metabolized and a metabolite is desmethylclomipramine, which blocks noradrenergic reuptake (Figure 4.31). This has side effects, among others, of blocking orgasm.

Section summary

1 A direct agonist occupies postsynaptic receptors and mimics the natural neurotransmitter.

2 A direct antagonist occupies postsynaptic receptors and blocks the effect of the natural neurotransmitter.

3 Some drugs block reuptake and thereby elevate levels of natural neurotransmitter available at the synapse.

☞ Test your knowledge

4.10 What effect does a direct agonist have on the membrane potential of a postsynaptic neuron at (i) an excitatory synapse and (ii) an inhibitory synapse?

4.11 Which of the following occupy dopamine D1 receptors? (i) Natural dopamine, (ii) a D1 agonist, (iii) a D1 antagonist, (iv) a D2 agonist.

Answers on page 104

Bringing things together

This chapter has described how information is transmitted and processed. Knowledge at the level of individual neurons and synapses (the 'cellular level') needs to be interpreted in the context of the function of the whole nervous system, the topic of the next chapter. However, sometimes psychologists can understand rather straightforwardly how actions at the level of the neuron and synapse affect behaviour and mental states. For example, side effects of medication are an important issue; a drug might be prescribed to target a certain part of the CNS but its metabolites have effects elsewhere, to induce sleepiness.

One sometimes sees an expression such as 'the dopaminergic hypothesis of depression' or 'the serotonergic hypothesis of obsessive compulsive disorder', implying that an abnormality in a particular neurotransmitter forms the basis of the disorder. In order to make sense of such ideas, you need to know about the classification of neurons, their release of neurotransmitter and removal of neurotransmitter from the synaptic cleft.

Chapters 1–4 have covered a large territory and different levels, ranging from evolutionary processes, nervous systems, neurotransmitters and ions. The scale has got smaller with each chapter. You might be wondering – now where? Do we consider the properties of subatomic particles and the world of quantum physics? You will probably be relieved to know that the answer is 'no'. The next chapter looks at whole brains. Knowledge of how hormones, neurons and neurotransmitters work is invaluable in understanding how whole brains work.

See the video coverage for this chapter for how a study of the cells of the nervous system can help us to understand behaviour.

Summary of Chapter 4

1 As a result of the distribution of ions, there is a small voltage across the membrane of cells, including neurons.

2 In neurons, a rapid change in the voltage (membrane potential) constitutes an action potential, this being their means of communication.

3 Apart from neurons, another type of cell found in the nervous system is the glial cell.

4 Signals are integrated at postsynaptic cells, by means of the effects that neurotransmitters have on these cells.

5 Both natural events and artificial manipulations can change the activity at synapses.

Further reading

For neurons and synapses, Bear *et al.* (2006) and Squire *et al.* (2008). For glial cells, see Fields (2004).

Answers

Explanations for answers to 'test your knowledge' questions can be found on the website www.pearsoned.co.uk/toates

4.1 There are several possibilities here but they will be something along the lines of 'Neurons are a particular type of cell, which are found in the nervous system and which communicate at synapses'.

4.2 Concentration gradient tending to move them into the cell; membrane potential tending to move them out of the cell.

4.3 (i) 1
4.4 Membrane; concentration
4.5 Sodium
4.6 (i) Right to left
4.7 Resting potential
4.8 (ii) Depolarized
4.9 Metabolites
4.10 (i) Excitation (depolarization); (ii) inhibition (hyperpolarization)
4.11 (i) Natural dopamine, (ii) a D1 agonist, (iii) a D1 antagonist

Visit www.pearsoned.co.uk/toates
for a range of resources to support study.
Test yourself with multiple choice questions and access a bank of over 100 videos that will bring the topics to life.

 Interactions and animations relating to topics discussed in this chapter can be found on the website at www.pearsoned.co.uk/toates. These include:

Interaction: Labelling the main components of a typical brain neuron
Animation: Exocytosis, neurotransmitter release and breakdown

Chapter 5
The brain: basics of structure and role

Learning outcomes for Chapter 5

After studying this chapter, you should be able to:

1 Understand the conventions for describing regions, locations and orientations within the brain and explain the meaning of such terms as ipsilateral, contralateral, gyrus and sulcus.

2 Describe the principal routes by which information is transmitted to the brain and motor information is conveyed from the brain to the periphery.

3 Give an account of the role of the brain in regulating the body's internal environment and in mediating links between the body and its external environment. Describe the special features of how the brain regulates its own environment.

4 Give an example of a link between brain structure and cognition.

5 Argue the case that our understanding of how nervous systems work can be aided by taking a comparative and evolutionary perspective.

6 Outline a number of the techniques employed to study the brain and relate this to the ways in which they can aid our understanding of how brains work.

Scene-setting questions

1 Why has the human brain a wrinkled appearance, rather like a walnut?

2 How do we know what different bits of the brain do?

3 Where is the brain's famous grey matter to be found?

4 What is a stroke?

5 What is it about the human brain that makes us special?

6 How can neuroimaging help to treat disorders?

How can neuroimaging help to treat disorders? Explore the video on the website accompanying this book at **www.pearsoned.co.uk/toates**

The brain has the task of interpreting various sources of sensory information to obtain perceptions and emotions, while controlling behaviour. How is all of this integration achieved?

Source: © VICTOR FRAILE/Reuters/Corbis.

Introduction

The brain is composed of billions of neurons and supporting cells. Earlier chapters described the processing that systems of neurons in the brain perform and information that goes to the brain (e.g. visual) and from it (e.g. controlling muscles). The present chapter focuses on the structures of the brain and introduces the relationship between each structure and its role. This chapter gives a framework in which you can locate the more detailed discussion on the brain, which will be presented in later chapters.

A prerequisite for understanding the brain is to build a description of its anatomy. This enables us to locate regions and to identify connections between them. The chapter should allow you to gain familiarity with some of the brain's principal landmarks. To simplify, the focus is mainly on humans. A mental map of the human brain can be useful in finding your way around other brains, e.g. that of the rat.

Understanding the brain is helped by knowledge of its component cells, the neurons. Researchers have identified some of the types of neuron found in different regions and the neurotransmitters that they employ. For example, researchers identify neuron terminals in one region as predominantly releasing, say, dopamine and trace where the associated cell bodies and axons are located. In this way a picture of interconnections between brain regions can be constructed.

There are various sources for information on the human brain (discussed later in this chapter). One source is to study the behavioural deficiencies of patients with damage to the brain, e.g. accidents and disease. In therapy and in experiments on both humans and non-humans, manipulations of the brain (e.g. injection of neurotransmitter agonists and antagonists) are made and effects on behaviour noted. Cautious extrapolation from the more common non-human studies can yield insight into the human brain. A technique of growing importance is to form neuroimages of the human brain, so as to reveal its workings.

In order to understand the brain, you need to learn the names of some regions and also navigational terms that provide a kind of route-map for finding your way. These are conventions agreed by all investigators. The next section turns to this subject.

Section summary

1 Understanding the brain requires an unambiguous description of its anatomy.

2 Identification of the brain's neurons, their location and the neurotransmitters that they employ is crucial for understanding the role of different brain regions.

☞ Test your knowledge

5.1 In terms of cell bodies, axons and neurochemical, what is meant by saying that a tract of dopaminergic neurons projects from brain region A to brain region B?

Answer on page 149

Describing the brain and finding your way around it

Directions

Figure 5.1 shows how to orient with respect to the brain and, more generally, the whole body. For brain and spinal cord, the expression 'anterior' (also termed 'rostral') means towards the 'nose-end'. The expression 'posterior' (or 'caudal') means towards the 'tail-end'. The meaning of the term 'ventral' (Chapter 3) is relative to context. In the case of animals which normally stand horizontal (e.g. rat or goat), it means towards the lower

(a)

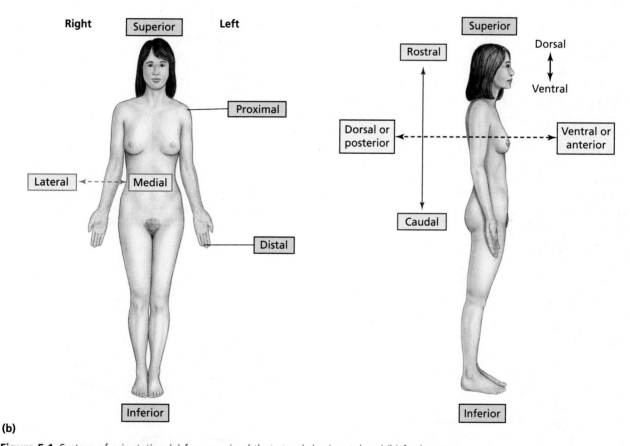

(b)

Figure 5.1 System of orientation (a) for an animal that stands horizontal and (b) for humans.

Source of (b): Martini *et al.* (2000, Fig. 1-10, p. 16). Copyright © 2000, 1997 by Frederic H. Martini, Inc. and Michael J. Timmons. Reprinted by permission of Pearson Education, Inc.

part of the body. So, a ventral brain region is one that is in a relatively low part of the brain. Similarly, a ventral region of the rat's spinal cord is on the side of the bottom of the body.

Because of the vertical posture of humans, the term 'ventral' needs some qualification (Figure 5.1(b)). In humans, it refers to relatively low parts of the brain. When used to describe the spinal cord, it refers to parts near to the front of the body. A similar qualification is needed for 'dorsal' (Chapter 3), which refers to the upper parts of the brain and body of the rat and the upper parts of the human brain. For the human spinal cord, it refers to the part towards the back.

The terms 'medial' and 'lateral' are unambiguous, regardless of species. With reference to the midline shown, medial refers to the centre of the body and lateral means 'away from the centre'. There are further terms in common use: 'superior' means in the direction towards the top of the brain and 'inferior' in the direction towards the bottom of the brain. Use of these terms is relative. Thus, the description 'superior' does not mean that the region is necessarily at the top of the brain, rather it is in that direction relative to a specific frame of reference. A given brain region might be divided into superior and inferior regions. A 'superior view' of the brain is one from above and an 'inferior view' is one from below.

Building on the term 'lateral', **ipsilateral** refers to the same side of the brain and **contralateral** to the opposite side. For example, if a neuron that originates in the left half of the brain projects to another region of the left half, it is an ipsilateral connection. If it crosses over and projects to the right half, it forms a contralateral projection.

Figure 5.2 shows planes of reference, which you can imagine to be taking slices through the brain. The 'sagittal plane' either divides the brain down the middle or is parallel to such a line. A midsagittal section is one made through the centre-line. The 'horizontal plane' represents a real or imaginary cut made at the horizontal. The 'coronal plane' (or 'frontal plane') is at right angles to the sagittal plane.

Some landmarks

Figure 5.3 shows a gross division of the human brain into some of its structures. Of course, further sub-categorization of these is possible. Note the 'telencephalon'

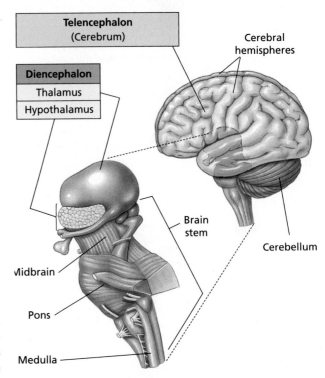

Figure 5.3 The human brain, showing its outer appearance and, relatively enlarged, some of its structures.

Source: Martini *et al.* (2000, Fig. 15-1, p. 379). Copyright © 2000, 1997 by Frederic H. Martini, Inc. and Michael J. Timmons. Reprinted by permission of Pearson Education, Inc.

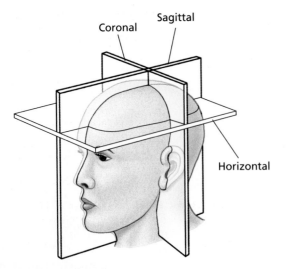

Figure 5.2 Planes slicing the brain.

Source: Martini *et al.* (2000, Fig. 15-13, p. 395 inset). Copyright © 2000, 1997 by Frederic H. Martini, Inc. and Michael J. Timmons. Reprinted by permission of Pearson Education, Inc.

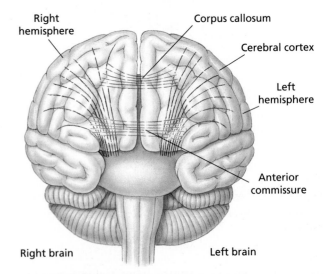

Figure 5.4 Anterior view of the brain.

Source: Martini *et al.* (2000, Fig. 15-10b, p. 391). Copyright © 2000, 1997 by Frederic H. Martini, Inc. and Michael J. Timmons. Reprinted by permission of Pearson Education, Inc.

(also known as the 'cerebrum'), 'diencephalon' and 'midbrain' (also termed the mesencephalon). The cerebellum, pons and medulla, together constitute the 'hindbrain'. The telencephalon and diencephalon together constitute the 'forebrain'. The medulla is the region of brain that links to the spinal cord. The term 'brain stem' refers to the combination of midbrain, pons and medulla.

A brain can be divided into two, almost identical halves, along its midline. Figure 5.4 illustrates the outward aspect of the brain's near-perfect symmetry across its centre (midsagittal) plane. Note that, by convention, the terms left and right are with respect to the perspective of the individual represented. As a telencephalic structure, the outer layer of the brain is termed **cerebral cortex**. It is made up of folds and ridges.

Figure 5.5 shows, among other things, two paired structures of the midbrain (appearing as bumps on the dorsal surface): the 'superior colliculus' (concerned with vision) and the 'inferior colliculus' (concerned with hearing). These structures, of plural name 'colliculi', exemplify the meaning of the terms 'superior' and 'inferior'. Two paired structures termed the 'lateral geniculate nucleus' and 'medial geniculate nucleus' illustrate the meaning of medial and lateral. To remind you, the term 'nucleus' (plural: nuclei) refers to a collection of cell bodies in the CNS, analogous to a ganglion in the peripheral nervous system (Chapter 3). By convention, the single term 'nucleus' is sometimes used as a generic for paired nuclei, comparable to the use of 'gland' (Chapter 3).

Understanding the structure of the adult brain can be aided by an appreciation of how it grew into its adult form. It also enables the logic behind anatomical description to be better understood (Rosenzweig *et al.*, 1996). For example, not only is the part of the brain nearest the front termed the forebrain but so is that nearest the back (Figure 5.3). Why is this description used?

(a)

(b)

Figure 5.5 The brain stem and diencephalon in (a) lateral and (b) posterior views (note cerebellum is removed).

Source: Martini *et al.* (2000, Fig. 15-16(a) and (c), p. 400). Copyright © 2000, 1997 by Frederic H. Martini, Inc. and Michael J. Timmons. Reprinted by permission of Pearson Education, Inc.

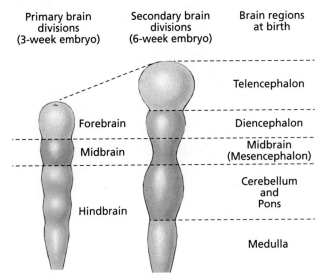

Figure 5.6 Human brain development.

Source: Martini *et al.* (2000, Table 15-1, p. 379). Copyright © 2000, 1997 by Frederic H. Martini, Inc. and Michael J. Timmons. Reprinted by permission of Pearson Education, Inc.

With increasing age up until maturity, bodies develop more and more complexity, derived from an earlier and simpler form. A human brain early in development is shown in Figure 5.6 (left) and a slightly more developed one to the right. The basics of the three divisions of Figure 5.3 are evident: forebrain, midbrain and hindbrain, defined by the location of swellings. To the right, the particularly extensive development of the forebrain is seen and, by now, its two subdivisions are also evident. Still further development ends with the adult structure. From these early forms, you can see why, in the adult, even the part of the brain nearest the back is termed 'forebrain'.

The diencephalic structure termed the 'thalamus' consists of a left and right thalamus (Figure 5.5(b)). (Again, the singular is used though a structure is subdivided into halves.) This left–right pairing is typical of most brain structures. Located immediately under the thalamus is another paired diencephalic structure, termed the 'hypothalamus' (hypo means lower/less than) (Figures 5.3 and 5.7).

The two halves of the brain are known as 'cerebral hemispheres' (Figure 5.4), which gives a classification into left and right half brains. A large bundle of fibres, termed the 'corpus callosum', links the left and right hemispheres (Figure 5.4). It is made up of axons of

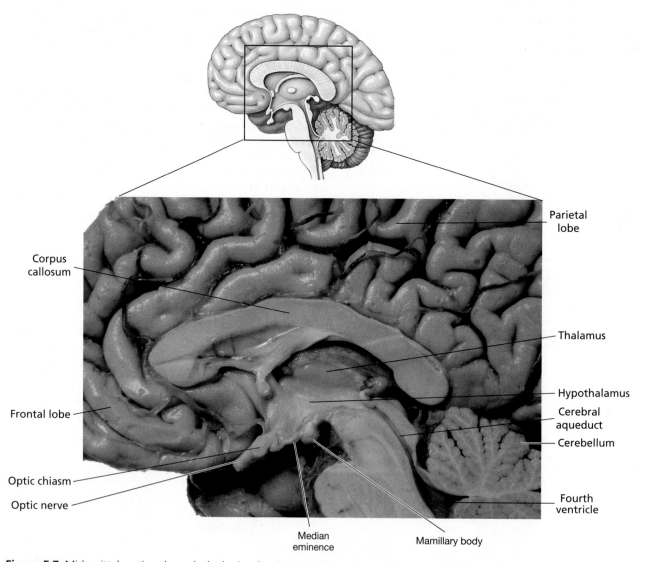

Figure 5.7 Midsagittal section through the brain, drawing attention to hypothalamus and thalamus. (Here, as elsewhere, the relevance of some labels will become apparent only later.)

Source: Martini *et al.* (2000, Fig. 15-11(a) and (b), p. 392). Copyright © 2000, 1997 by Frederic H. Martini, Inc. and Michael J. Timmons. Reprinted by permission of Pearson Education, Inc.

neurons that communicate information between one half of the brain and the other. A midsagittal view of the right half of the brain is shown in Figure 5.7. This reveals a section through the corpus callosum. A frontal section of the brain can also show the corpus callosum (Figure 5.8). Another means of communication, for anterior parts of the cortex, is a small bundle of axons termed the 'anterior commissure' (Figures 5.4 and 5.8). In Figure 5.8, note regions of grey matter (high concentration of cell bodies) in the outer part of the brain and white matter (high concentration of myelin) at the inner part (cf. Chapter 3 and the spinal cord).

The exterior surface of the brain has a wrinkled appearance rather like a walnut (Figures 5.4, 5.7 and 5.8). This arises because the cerebral cortex is folded. The word 'cortex' is Latin for bark, as in the outer layer of a tree, comparable to the cortex being the outer layer of the brain. Folding allows a large amount of the tissue that constitutes the outer layer to be packed into the space of the skull. The folds ('grooves' or 'furrows', depending upon which word conveys the best image) provide important landmarks (Figure 5.9). A generic term for these folds is 'sulcus' (plural, sulci).

(Confusingly, a distinction is sometimes made between types of fold, in which a small one is termed a sulcus and a larger one a fissure.) The structure between two sulci is termed a 'gyrus' (pl. gyri). The positions of the principal sulci on the cortex are not arbitrary but show a regular pattern from person to person and provide landmarks for locating particular cortical regions.

Based upon their outer appearance, the cerebral hemispheres are divided into lobes. Figure 5.9(b) shows these four lobes: the frontal, temporal, occipital and parietal lobes. Cortex is classified by the lobe within which it is located, e.g. occipital cortex. The lateral sulcus (sometimes termed the Sylvian fissure) provides a boundary between the frontal and temporal lobes. The central sulcus (central fissure) forms the boundary between the frontal lobe and the parietal lobe. Two landmark gyri are indicated in Figure 5.9(b), one to each side of the central sulcus: the precentral gyrus and the postcentral gyrus.

A more detailed classification of the cortex is in terms of numbered areas, named 'Brodmann's areas', after the person who first plotted them (Figure 5.10). Brodmann's areas give a system for finding a location within a lobe.

Figure 5.8 A frontal section of the brain.

Source: Martini *et al.* (2000, Fig. 15-15(a), p. 398). Copyright © 2000, 1997 by Frederic H. Martini, Inc. and Michael J. Timmons. Reprinted by permission of Pearson Education, Inc.

Figure 5.9 The brain highlighting some sulci and gyri: (a) superior view, (b) lateral view.
Source: Martini *et al.* (2000, Fig. 15-8(a), p. 388 and Fig. 15-9(a), p. 389). © Ralph T. Hutchings/Visuals Unlimited

Figure 5.10 Lateral view of the left cerebral cortex showing some of Brodmann's areas. (In a full account, the entire cortex is numbered in this system.)

Source: Martini *et al.* (2000, Fig. 16-7(c), p. 435). Copyright © 2000, 1997 by Frederic H. Martini, Inc. and Michael J. Timmons. Reprinted by permission of Pearson Education, Inc.

There are other systems of description also employed. For example, posterior temporal cortex refers to that part of the temporal cortex near the back of the brain. Inferior temporal cortex refers to that forming the lower part of the lobe. The compound 'posterior inferior' means towards the back and low.

Figure 5.11 shows a midsagittal section through the brain. Some familiar regions are apparent from this perspective and also a new one, the cingulate gyrus. The cortex that comprises the cingulate gyrus is termed 'cingulate cortex'.

Figure 5.11 Midsagittal section through the brain.
Source: Martini *et al.* (2000, Fig. 15-13, p. 395). Copyright © 2000, 1997 by Frederic H. Martini, Inc. and Michael J. Timmons. Reprinted by permission of Pearson Education, Inc.

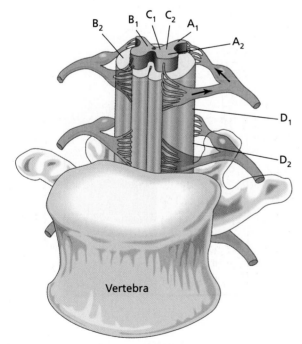

Figure 5.12 Segment of spinal cord.
Source: Vander *et al.* (1994) *Human Physiology*, Fig. 8-35, p. 215, reproduced with permission of The McGraw-Hill Companies, Inc.

Section summary

1 Terms such as dorsal and lateral provide a means of finding our way around the CNS.

2 The brain can be divided into forebrain, midbrain and hindbrain.

3 The cerebral cortex forms the outer layer of the forebrain.

☞ Test your knowledge

5.2 Complete the following: 'Axons that make up the corpus callosum would be said to project _____' (i) ipsilaterally; (ii) contralaterally.

5.3 Which is more caudal, (i) the superior colliculus or (ii) the inferior colliculus?

5.4 Figure 5.12 shows a segment of spinal cord.

(a) With reference to each set of paired letters (e.g. A_1, A_2), indicate the following:

    (i) Which is the most ventral? A_1 or A_2

    (ii) Which is the most dorsal? A_1 or A_2

    (iii) Which is the most lateral? C_1 or C_2

    (iv) Which is the most medial? C_1 or C_2

    (v) Which is the most caudal? D_1 or D_2

    (vi) Which is the most rostral? D_1 or D_2

(b) Which is (i) white matter (A_2 or B_2) and which is (ii) grey matter (A_2 or B_2)?

Answers on page 149   WEB

Relating structure to role: sensory and motor systems

Introduction

The brain makes decisions on what behaviour to perform. Making decisions is based upon events in the external world (e.g. presence of danger, food or a mate) and internal world (e.g. levels of nutrients, water or hormone). This section and the following two relate this information processing to some of the brain regions where it is performed. In this section, we start by considering some routes by which information gets to the brain, and how it is initially processed. We then consider how information leaves the brain and is used in motor control.

This section gives an embodiment to the brain processes involved in Chapter 3, where sensory inputs and motor outputs were discussed.

Sensory information

Introduction

In order to discuss the initial stages of processing by the brain, some of its landmarks are introduced in the context of what they do. That is, cortical areas are discussed in terms of the information that they process. Sensory information from the external environment is conveyed

to the brain either via the spinal cord or via cranial nerves (Chapter 3).

Cortex – defined by role

For some of the cortex, it is possible to associate a region with a particular role in processing sensory information (Figure 5.13). Visual information, derived from the eyes and transmitted via the optic nerve (Chapter 3, Figure

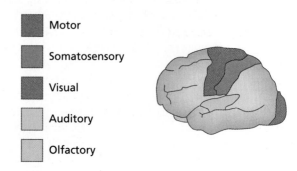

Motor

Somatosensory

Visual

Auditory

Olfactory

Figure 5.13 The cortex described by its role in information processing.
Source: OU course SD286 (Module A, Fig. 22, p. 31).

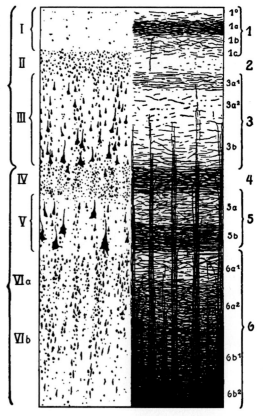

Figure 5.14 Section through cerebral cortex showing layered organization.
Source: Fuster (1997, Fig. 2.2, p. 12).

3.20, p. 67), arrives at the **visual cortex**, located in the occipital lobe (area 17 in Figure 5.10). Here, further analysis of visual information occurs. The visual cortex is also termed the striate cortex, because, on close inspection, striation (a striped appearance) of this region is evident. Similarly, auditory information, derived from the ears, arrives at the **auditory cortex**, a region of the temporal lobe. It is then processed further to extract meaning.

Information on touch arrives at the **somatosensory cortex** (soma: body, i.e. sensations from the body), a region of the parietal lobe. It is then further analyzed to extract information on the touch stimulus. More will be said later about the large areas that are not involved in the early stages of sensory processing (pink colour).

Short tracts (Chapter 3), consisting of bundles of axons of neurons, convey information from one cortical area to neighbouring areas, whereas longer tracts convey information between distant cortical areas.

Within a given area of cortex, information is communicated between superficial and deeper regions. Figure 5.14 shows a typical section of cerebral cortex. The cortex is organized in six distinct layers of cell type (Northcutt and Kaas, 1995). Different layers are associated with different functions. For example, in parts of the cortex concerned with sensory processing, sensory information projected from the thalamus tends to arrive in layer 4. Information is communicated between layers.

The access of sensory information to the cortex is to some extent controlled by other brain mechanisms, the topic of the next section.

Controlling input to the cortex

Figure 5.3 shows some regions that are involved in the transfer of sensory information: (1) the hindbrain regions termed the medulla and pons, (2) the midbrain and (3) the thalamus. Running through the medulla and pons is a network of neurons termed the 'reticular formation' (Figure 5.15) (Moruzzi and Magoun, 1949). The name derives from the Latin word 'reticulum', which means network.

Part of the reticular formation contributes to a system termed the **ascending reticular activating system**, or just 'reticular activating system' (RAS) (Moruzzi and Magoun, 1949). See Figure 5.16. Sensory inputs trigger the RAS and, in turn, the RAS makes projections to the cortex and other higher levels.

Particular neurons carry information on specific sensory events such as visual events. Other specific neurons

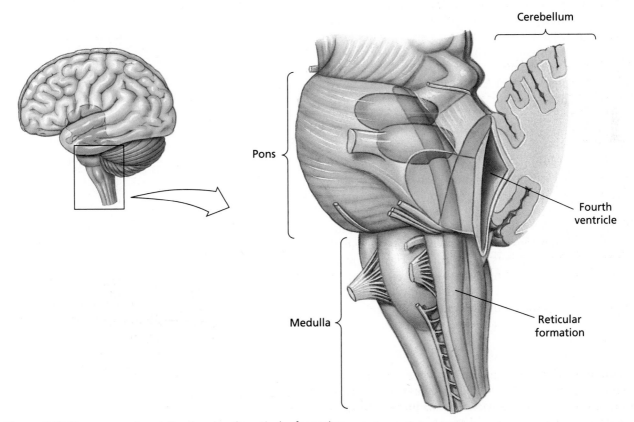

Figure 5.15 The pons and medulla, showing the reticular formation.
Source: after Martini *et al.* (2000, Fig. 15-18, p. 402). Copyright © 2000, 1997 by Frederic H. Martini, Inc. and Michael J. Timmons. Reprinted by permission of Pearson Education, Inc.

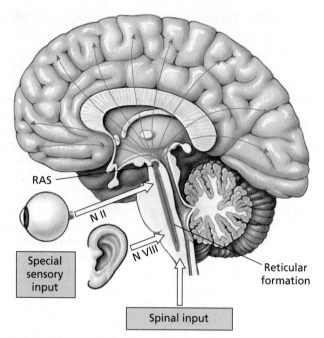

Figure 5.16 The reticular activating system.

Source: Martini *et al.* (2000, Fig. 16-9, p. 437). Copyright © 2000, 1997 by Frederic H. Martini, Inc. and Michael J. Timmons. Reprinted by permission of Pearson Education, Inc.

as red and white. Within the spinal cord, the second ('white') neuron crosses from one side to the other and ascends to the brain in the cord's 'white matter', as part of a tract. The white matter is made up largely of axons of neurons that carry information up and down the spinal cord and the cells that provide support to these neurons (contributing to myelin). Information from the right side of the body (to the left of Figure 5.17) arrives in the left half of the brain. In addition to the route shown in Figure 5.17, the white neuron would send a branch (sometimes termed a 'collateral') to the reticular formation. This would excite neurons in the reticular formation. The link via the reticular formation probably plays a role in the arousing and emotional aspects of pain. Pain can, of course, very effectively prevent sleep, as you might have experienced.

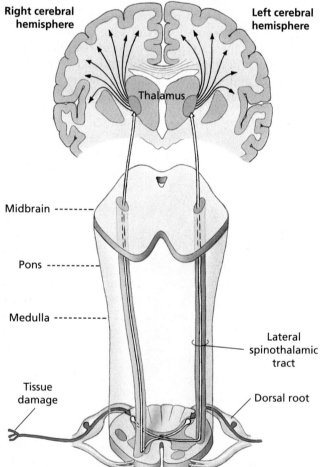

Figure 5.17 The transfer of nociceptive information (meaning, 'relating to tissue damage') to the brain.

Source: after Martini *et al.* (2000, Fig. 16-2(b), p. 426). Copyright © 2000, 1997 by Frederic H. Martini, Inc. and Michael J. Timmons. Reprinted by permission of Pearson Education, Inc.

convey information on other specific events, e.g. auditory events. Such specific neurons send branches to the reticular formation, where their effects converge. Neurons from the spinal cord also provide an input. Thus, the output of the RAS is non-specific to any given sensory channel.

The role of the reticular formation is, in association with other brain regions, a general one of modulating ('tuning') sensory processing and thereby exerting a control over waking, alertness and sleep. Output neurons from the reticular formation change the operating characteristics of neurons throughout large regions of the brain. They trigger states of high or low 'arousal'.

The RAS provides a non-specific gate for sensory information. We now look at some specific routes by which sensory information gets to the cortex. The first route of information processing discussed concerns information that is conveyed via the spinal cord. Vision is then employed to illustrate how information can be detected and transmitted to the brain via a cranial nerve.

Some specific spinal links to the brain

Earlier, the topic of information on tissue damage being transmitted to the brain was introduced (Chapter 3, Figure 3.1(b), p. 52). Figure 5.17 shows the equivalent of neurons 1 and 5 of Figure 3.1(b), indicated respectively

In a number of sensory systems, the thalamus forms a relay station within the specific pathway. Figure 5.17 shows this for nociceptive information. At the thalamus, synapses are formed between neurons in the sensory pathway. Nociceptive information arrives at a particular nucleus of the thalamus. A set of neurons (indicated by black) conveys this information from the thalamus to the cortex. This route is specific to nociceptive information.

Similarly, for harmless (non-nociceptive) tactile information, there is a projection from the periphery to the thalamus and then to the somatosensory cortex (Figure 5.18). In anatomical terms, this region of cortex is the postcentral gyrus (Figure 5.9(b)). As you can see in Figure 5.18, information crosses from one side to the other but in this case it occurs at a higher level than in Figure 5.17, at the medulla. So again, information from the right side of the body arrives at the left side of the cortex and vice versa.

As represented in Figure 5.18, there is a relationship between particular areas of somatosensory cortex and the role of neurons located there: a given region of cortex is consistently associated with a given region of the sensory surface of the body. Tactile stimulation in a particular body region triggers neural activity in a particular cortical region. The body can be mapped across the surface of the somatosensory cortex according to the association between brain region and body region, and the result, a bizarre-looking person, is known as the **sensory homunculus**.

For their size, some body regions (e.g. fingers) are associated with relatively large areas of cortex (Figure 5.18). Other body regions (e.g. the back) are associated with relatively small areas. The relative sizes within the homunculus correspond to the sensitivity of resolution at the corresponding skin areas. For example, the fingers have a fine resolution, which enables them to discriminate detail, and a large cortical representation. The back has a lower resolution and correspondingly smaller cortical representation. The lips are associated with a relatively large area of cortex. You might like to speculate on the functional significance of this!

A specific cranial nerve link

Vision is an example of information that gets to the brain via a cranial nerve. Later chapters will look at other examples of how information gets to the brain via cranial nerves (e.g. auditory information). Figure 5.19 shows the eye: the cornea and lens bend light to form an inverted image of the world on the retinal surface.

At the retina, there is a layer consisting of a mosaic of millions of cells, which are sensitive to light (Figure 5.20).

These are **receptor cells** (also termed just 'receptors') and they absorb light. Absorption changes their electrochemical state ('membrane potential'); thereby, in 'receiving' light, they register its presence. Although these cells change state, action potentials are not instigated in them. Rather, smooth changes in voltage are seen.

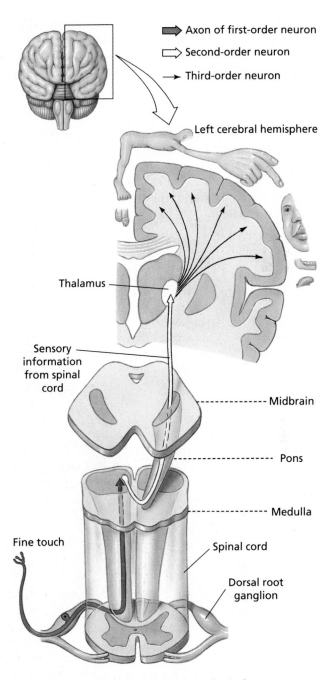

Figure 5.18 The route from periphery to brain for non-nociceptive tactile information.

Source: Martini *et al.* (2000, Fig. 16-2a, p. 426). Copyright © 2000, 1997 by Frederic H. Martini, Inc. and Michael J. Timmons. Reprinted by permission of Pearson Education, Inc.

When receptors absorb light, the change causes information to be passed on to other neurons with which they form synapses. That is to say, a change in electrical activity at the receptors triggers a change in activity at the associated bipolar cells. Still no action potentials occur. In turn, the bipolar cells trigger further electrical events: the excitation or inhibition of action potentials in ganglion cells with which they form synapses. Information is transmitted to the brain in the form of a pattern of action potentials in the axons of ganglion cells. The optic nerve, one of the cranial nerves (Figures 5.19, 5.20 and 5.21), is the bundle of millions of axons of ganglion cells. The bundle is termed the 'optic tract' after entering the brain.

There is something rather odd in the way that the eye is constructed and you might be able to spot it in Figure 5.20. It appears to be inside out: light passes through various cell layers before it reaches the receptors, at the back of retina. However, these layers are almost completely transparent.

Information is conveyed to the brain in the optic nerve (the 'optic tract' describes this pathway within the brain) and arrives at the lateral geniculate nucleus (LGN), a nucleus of the thalamus. The LGN then performs the next stage of information transmission (Figure 5.21). Apparently, to early anatomists, the LGN looked something like a knee, the Latin name of which is *genu*. As Kalat (1998) suggests, if you use a rich imagination, you might be able to see a knee there! (Try looking especially at Figure 5.5.)

Looking at the level of neurons, at the LGN, ganglion cells form synapses with other neurons (termed LGN cells). LGN cells carry the message further, their axons terminating in the visual cortex (Figure 5.21).

So much for information getting to the brain; the chapter now turns to how processed information leaves the brain to trigger motor action.

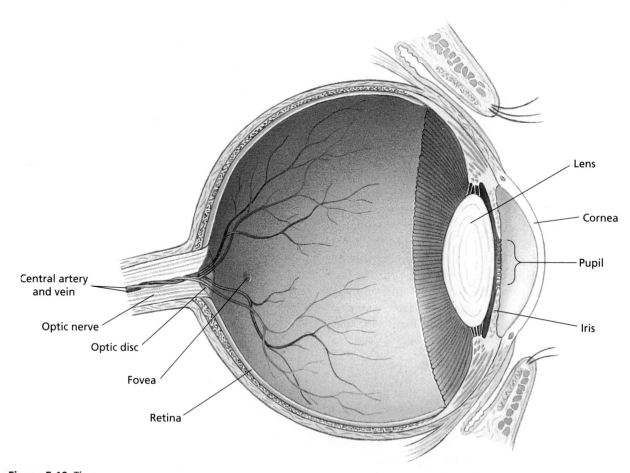

Figure 5.19 The eye.

Source: after Martini *et al.* (2000, Fig. 18-20(a), p. 486). Copyright © 2000, 1997 by Frederic H. Martini, Inc. and Michael J. Timmons. Reprinted by permission of Pearson Education, Inc.

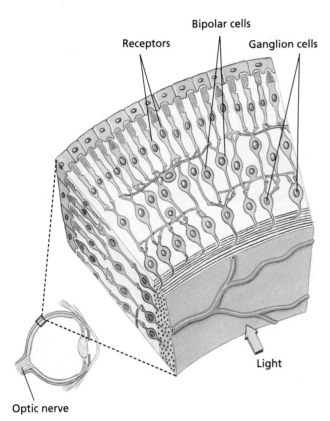

Receptors   Bipolar cells   Ganglion cells

Optic nerve   Light

Figure 5.20 A part of the retina shown in cross-section.
Source: Martini *et al.* (2000, Fig. 18-22(a), p. 490). Copyright ©
2000, 1997 by Frederic H. Martini, Inc. and Michael J. Timmons.
Reprinted by permission of Pearson Education, Inc.

Motor control

Chapter 3 described the control that the brain exerts
over motor neurons and thereby over skeletal muscles.
There are many brain regions concerned with orches-
trating this control. The present section considers some
of these.

Motor cortex

Figure 5.9(b) showed the brain region termed, anatomically, the precentral gyrus. In terms of its role, this
region is described as 'motor cortex'. Via sensory pathways, it is informed of such things as the current state
of the body and, based on this, has a role in the generation of motor action. Information on touch is extracted
at the somatosensory cortex (postcentral gyrus) and
is communicated the short distance to the precentral
gyrus, where it contributes to motor control. Imagine
the dexterity of some manual actions such as reading
Braille, which are based upon tactile information.

There is a **motor homunculus** associated with the
motor cortex, which is similar to the sensory homunculus associated with the somatosensory cortex (Figure

5.22) (Penfield and Rasmussen, 1968). The motor
homunculus identifies regions of motor cortex that
exert control over those areas of the body that are
represented in the homunculus. As with the sensory
homunculus, some regions of the body have a relatively
large amount of associated cortex. Regions with a large
representation have a fine resolution of motor ability
(e.g. fingers).

Some neurons with cell bodies at the motor cortex
have axons that extend down the spinal cord to contact motor neurons (or neurons in close proximity to

A personal angle

A rarely acknowledged Swedish polymath

It might seem improbable but historical evidence
shows that the role of the cerebral cortex was first
correctly described, not by an established medical researcher or neuroscientist, but rather by a part-time
amateur scientist and full-time mystic, Emanuel Swedenborg (Gross, 2009; Ramstrom, 1910). Swedenborg
(1688–1772) was a polymath who contributed original ideas to physics, astronomy and engineering. Some
contemporaries thought that he was mad.

Swedenborg correctly concluded that the cortex has
anatomically distinct sensory and motor functions. He
also described the basic principles of the functional organization of the motor cortex in the form now summarized by the motor homunculus (Figure 5.22) and articulated the role of subcortical brain regions in the more
automatic aspects of motor control (Ramstrom, 1910).

As far as is known, the Swedish mystic based his insights mainly upon meticulous scrutiny of other investigators' reports of human brain damage and its consequences. A century was to elapse and then electrical
stimulation of the motor cortex and the observation of
motor reactions confirmed Swedenborg's assertions.
Some 111 years after his death, a review of Swedenborg's book in the journal *Brain* recognized (Rabagliati,
1883, p.407): 'The general correspondence of these
statements with the positions of the most modern science cannot fail to strike the reader'.

The moral of the story is to be patient. Recognition
does not always come within one's own lifetime!

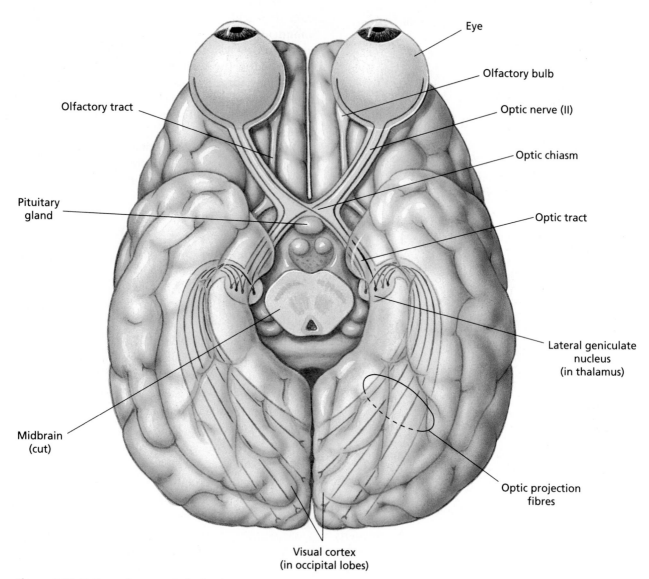

Figure 5.21 Pathway from eye to brain.

Source: Martini *et al.* (2000, Fig. 15-23, p. 407). Copyright © 2000, 1997 by Frederic H. Martini, Inc. and Michael J. Timmons. Reprinted by permission of Pearson Education, Inc.

motor neurons) (Chapter 3). You can see this in Figure 5.22. Other neurons (not shown) extend only so far as intermediate brain regions, which, in turn, perform further computation of motor commands, and then they project axons down to synapse with motor neurons, or further intermediate neurons.

Basal ganglia

The 'basal ganglia' are a collection of brain structures near to, and in close communication with, the cortex.

Among other things, they process information on movement control. Figure 5.23 shows part of the basal ganglia, drawing attention to their proximity to the thalamus and cortex.

The cerebellum

Along with the motor cortex, basal ganglia and some other regions, the cerebellum (Figures 5.3, 5.9(b) and 5.11) plays a role in computation of the commands sent to cause motor action. In humans, the cerebellum

Motor homunculus on primary motor cortex of left cerebral hemisphere

To skeletal muscles

To skeletal muscles

Motor nuclei of cranial nerves

Motor nuclei of cranial nerves

Midbrain

Medulla

Cross-over

To skeletal muscles

Spinal cord

Figure 5.22 Motor homunculus.

Source: Martini *et al.* (2000, Fig. 16-4(a), p. 429). Copyright © 2000, 1997 by Frederic H. Martini, Inc. and Michael J. Timmons. Reprinted by permission of Pearson Education, Inc.

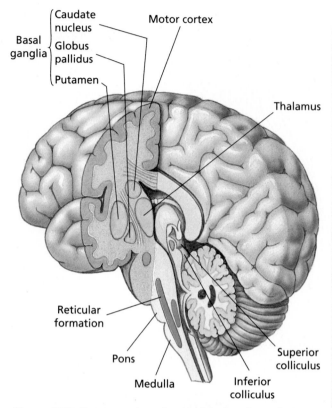

Figure 5.23 Cut-away view of part of the basal ganglia in relation to the thalamus and cortex.

Source: Martini *et al.* (2000, Fig. 16-5, p. 430). Copyright © 2000, 1997 by Frederic H. Martini, Inc. and Michael J. Timmons. Reprinted by permission of Pearson Education, Inc.

Section summary

1 Sensory information reaches the brain via the spinal cord and cranial nerves.

2 Sensory cortex processes sensory information (e.g. visual or somatosensory).

3 The reticular activating system gates access of sensory information to the cortex.

4 The sensory homunculus represents how different regions of the body are represented in the somatosensory cortex.

5 At the retina, there is a mosaic of light-sensitive receptor cells.

6 Visual information is converted into electrical signals at the retina.

7 Different regions of motor cortex have a role in the motor control exerted over different regions of the body. The motor homunculus represents this responsibility.

8 The basal ganglia and cerebellum play a role in motor control.

Test your knowledge

5.5 What constitute (i) the afferent and (ii) the efferent sides of the lateral geniculate nucleus?

5.6 The cell bodies of motor neurons serving the lower parts of the body are located where? (i) Ventral horn of the spinal cord, (ii) dorsal horn of the spinal cord, (iii) white matter of spinal cord, (iv) medial geniculate nucleus.

Answers on page 149

contains the largest number of neurons of any brain region (Courchesne and Allen, 1997). Traditionally, it was described as playing a role in the organization of balance and locomotion, which it does indeed do. However, the cerebellum is now associated with a broader role, being concerned with sensory, motor and cognitive aspects of the organization of action, including such things as language production. Specifically, Courchesne and Allen (p. 2) propose that its role is: '*to predict internal conditions needed* for a particular mental or motor operation and *to set those conditions* in preparation for the operation at hand'.

The cerebellum has a large ratio (approximately 40:1) of afferent axons (bringing information to it) to efferent axons (carrying information from it). This gives pointers to its function: to integrate information. Thus the cerebellum integrates information from the external environment and from internal decision-making. It then acts to predict the future. That is, it appears to process and integrate sensory information within the context of the use of the information in motor action (Gao *et al.*, 1996).

Emotion, regulation and motivation

Introduction

The last section introduced the nervous system's input and output of information. The present section and the following one concern the processing of information between input and output. The present section focuses upon how the brain makes certain decisions based upon both the external environment and the internal physiology of the body, as characterized by the terms 'emotion' and 'motivation'.

Emotion: cognition and action

Within the telencephalon beneath the cortex, other structures lie. Figure 5.24 highlights several: the amygdala, hippocampus (and the associated fornix) and mammillary bodies. Each of these is a paired structure, one half in each hemisphere.

Note the amygdala, just below the cortex of the temporal lobe. Amygdala means 'almond' and the structure got its name from its resemblance to an almond. There are neural connections between temporal cortex and amygdala. The cortex performs cognitive processing concerning the world and conveys this information to the amygdala, where some emotional rating is attached to the information (Le Doux, 1989). The amygdala then passes this information to other brain regions, where further emotional processing occurs and emotion is translated into action by somatic and autonomic nervous systems. In addition to relatively highly processed information from the cortex, the amygdala receives, more directly from the sensory channels, raw information on threats (e.g. loud noises). Short-cutting the cortex, this provides an early-warning system to instigate such things as freezing. Short routes from sensory channels to the amygdala can be identified neurally.

The hippocampus is concerned with memory formation among other things. Hippocampus means 'sea-horse' and to early investigators the shape of the structure bore a resemblance to this animal. It receives information on the world derived from sensory processing and appears to compare this with expectations. In this way, the hippocampus derives a measure of how well programmes of action are running (Gray, 1987a). Disparity between expectation and reality can serve as a trigger to emotion, e.g. in the frustration of when reality is less good than what is expected.

I am indebted to Kalat (1998) for pointing out that the term 'fornix', which means arc or arch, derives from an arch in ancient Rome. This was a meeting place for prostitutes (the link is with the term 'fornicate'). The fornix serves as an output pathway to link the hippocampus to the mammillary body, among other places.

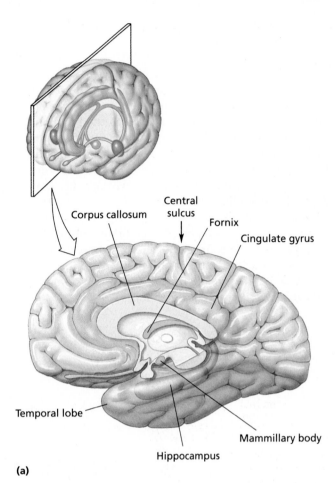

(a)

(b)

Figure 5.24 Some structures concerned with emotion.

Source: Martini *et al.* (2000, Fig. 15-12(a) and (b)), p. 394). Copyright © 2000, 1997 by Frederic H. Martini, Inc. and Michael J. Timmons. Reprinted by permission of Pearson Education, Inc.

Internal and external environments

Introduction

In making behavioural decisions characterized as emotional and motivational, the brain takes into account (a) its own immediate environment, (b) the environment of other parts of the body as relayed to the brain and (c) the external environment, e.g. availability of food.

The brain not only has a role in regulation throughout the rest of the body but it also has some responsibility for regulation of its own local environment. The brain, like the rest of the body, exists within a fluid environment and the neurons require a source of energy. This section describes some brain regions that are implicated in a complex 'juggling act' of regulation. First we look at the nutrient and fluid environment of the brain. We then relate this to general physiological and behavioural aspects of regulation.

The brain's environment

The brain contains a rich supply of blood vessels. Among other things, these bring nutrients, water, oxygen and hormones to it. Arteries carry fresh blood to the brain (Figure 5.25). Note the paired 'internal carotid artery' that supplies the anterior part of the brain with blood and the arteries that derive from this, e.g. the anterior cerebral artery. Veins carry away the waste products of metabolism. A principal fuel for the CNS is glucose. Since neither glucose nor oxygen can be stored in significant amounts, a moment-by-moment unfailing blood supply is crucial.

The blood supply to different brain regions is of interest to psychologists, allowing links to be identified between structure and function. Suppose that an artery were to be blocked at, say, location X in Figure 5.25. This would result in a failure of blood supply. Thereby, it would deny oxygen and glucose to a region

Figure 5.25 A view of the brain from underneath, showing arteries.

Source: Martini *et al.* (2000, Fig. 22-15(a), p. 578). Copyright © 2000, 1997 by Frederic H. Martini, Inc. and Michael J. Timmons. Reprinted by permission of Pearson Education, Inc.

of the temporal lobe, causing death of neurons located there and the probable loss of some behavioural function. Modern techniques, discussed shortly, allow sites of such disruption to be identified.

The flow of blood to different regions is not constant but varies with their activity (Smith and Fetz, 1987). Variations in blood flow follow within a few seconds of changes in energy demands as a result of the changing activity of neurons. A change in blood flow is mediated by change in the diameter of blood vessels: high neural activity at a region promotes local dilation and thereby a relatively high blood supply. This is a local homeostatic process comparable to whole-body homeostasis (Chapter 2). The blood flow to a region is termed **regional cerebral blood flow (rCBF)**. A person can be asked to engage in a task (e.g. reading) and changes in rCBF monitored. Changes implicate a brain area as being involved in performing the task.

Two special features of the fluid environment of the brain are as follows. As the imaginary view of Figure 5.26 shows, the brain contains large spaces, termed **ventricles**, which are filled with fluid. This fluid is a filtration from the fluid component of the blood (i.e. minus such things as the red blood cells) and is known as **cerebrospinal fluid (CSF)**. This same fluid also fills the central canal that runs throughout the spinal cord. The cerebral aqueduct is a channel between the third and fourth ventricles. The CSF serves to cushion the brain against shocks. In some pathological conditions, the ventricles become enlarged. This can be due to a build-up of CSF pressure following hydraulic malfunction, which can damage surrounding neural tissue. In other cases, the ventricles enlarge as a result of filling the space that remains from the loss of surrounding neural tissue in degenerative disease.

The ventricles provide a rationale for some terminology of structures. The term 'peri' means 'surrounding' and so a periventricular structure is that surrounding a ventricle. More specifically, a midbrain structure called the 'periaqueductal grey matter', often simply termed 'periaqueductal grey' (PAG), surrounds the cerebral aqueduct. So, the PAG refers to grey matter surrounding the aqueduct (Figure 5.27).

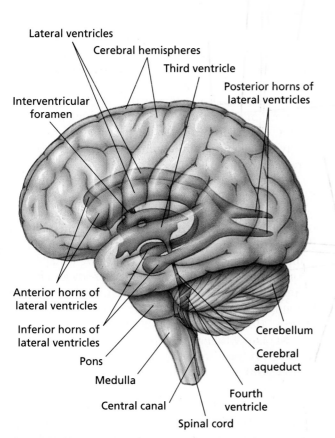

Figure 5.26 X-ray view of the brain that shows the ventricles.
Source: Martini *et al.* (2000, Fig. 15-2, p. 381). Copyright © 2000, 1997 by Frederic H. Martini, Inc. and Michael J. Timmons. Reprinted by permission of Pearson Education, Inc.

Figure 5.27 Section through the midbrain, showing PAG.
Source: Martini *et al.* (2000, Fig. 15-17(a), p. 401). Copyright © 2000, 1997 by Frederic H. Martini, Inc. and Michael J. Timmons. Reprinted by permission of Pearson Education, Inc.

In relation to the blood, the role of the brain represents a delicate compromise. The brain needs fluid and energy/nutrients from the blood. Indeed, relative to its weight, the brain is extremely energy-demanding (Aiello and Wheeler, 1995). Also, the chemical composition of the blood represents sources of information to be monitored, such as hormones and nutrients. This information is used in the control of behaviour. Detecting certain information on toxins can trigger vomiting and steer the animal to their future avoidance. However, in other respects, most neurons represent a delicate and sheltered environment. They are relatively protected against the toxins and swings in ion concentration that arise elsewhere and can be tolerated by the rest of the body. How is this conflict of interests resolved?

The ventricles are large spaces of fluid within the brain. A similar quality of fluid is also found in spaces between cells. Figure 4.1 showed a principle applicable to most cells of the body: cells are situated in such a way that the spaces between them and the boundary with the capillary allow ready exchange of chemicals between plasma and interstitial fluid. However, this openness in general does not apply to the brain, where the pattern of cells forming the boundary of a capillary is tighter. This contributes to a selective barrier, termed

the **blood–brain barrier**, between the brain's neurons and blood vessels. Figure 5.28(a) shows a simplified representation of this; note the tight junction between cells that form the wall of the blood vessel. The barrier protects the brain from potentially damaging contents of the blood. However, there are two ways in which the barrier can be crossed, each of which reflects adaptive considerations.

First, throughout the brain, there is a special mechanism that facilitates the transport of vital substances, such as glucose, into the neuron (Figure 5.28(a)). Second, in places, the barrier is relaxed allowing the fluid of the blood to gain access to special neurons in certain key regions (Figure 5.28(b)). These are the neurons that are specialized to detect such things as ion concentration and toxins, information that is utilized by the brain to perform adaptive responses. Regions of brain consisting of neurons of this type are given the collective name of **circumventricular organs**.

Linking behaviour to internal and external environments

For the moment, we shall focus on two structures closely implicated in regulation. They *look in two directions*, their role being to integrate information on the internal and external world. Figures 5.3, 5.7, 5.11 and 5.24 showed one of these structures, the hypothalamus. Figure 5.29 shows a structure of the medulla termed the solitary nucleus, also known as the 'nucleus of the solitary tract' and, for those who prefer the more classical term, the 'nucleus of tractus solitarius' (NTS). Nuclei of the hypothalamus and the solitary nucleus act together in regulation.

Afferent neurons that detect various physiological events of the body project to the NTS. Figure 5.29 shows one example: processing information on substances at the tongue. Taste information arrives as messages at the NTS carried by part of the vagus nerve and another cranial nerve, the glossopharyngeal nerve (Chapter 3). Information on events deep within the body also arrives there. For example, at the liver, nutrients derived from the gut are detected by afferent neurons of the ANS (Novin, 1993). This information is conveyed to the NTS by axons that make up part of the vagus nerve (Chapter 3). Neurons with their cell bodies at the NTS project information to other brain regions, where it is further processed (e.g. thalamus and hypothalamus). This concerns particular events within the body. For taste, gustatory cortex continues the processing.

Nutrient-related projections *from* the hypothalamus affect both physiology and behaviour. In Figure 5.30, note the signals from the hypothalamus to the prefrontal cortex, which play a role in behavioural

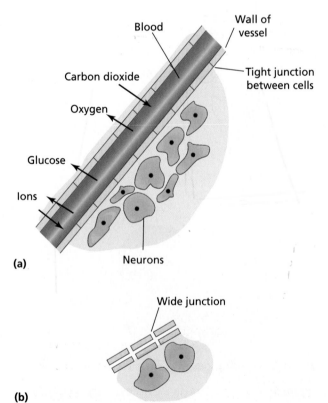

Figure 5.28 Blood–brain barrier: (a) links between neurons and blood across barrier and (b) relaxed barrier.

decision-making (see later). Information at the prefrontal cortex can then direct behaviour towards, say, food-seeking. Other projections from the hypothalamus appear to modulate information on taste that is available at the NTS. Such modulation presumably adjusts the signal so that its role fits the nutrient needs of the animal. For instance, at times of nutrient depletion, the animal approaches food and ingests it (Berridge, 1995).

Descending projections from the hypothalamus, via the NTS, adjust physiology in a way that fits nutrient needs. For example, according to internal nutrient availability (Chapter 3), adjustments are made to the secretion of the hormone insulin (Woods and Stricker,

1999). Efferent neurons of the vagus nerve are involved in such action. Efferent neurons of the glossopharyngeal nerve control the muscles of the throat involved in ingestion.

Regulation of the nutrient environment is only one role of the hypothalamus. Other nuclei have roles in other behaviour. For example, the hypothalamus and NTS are also involved in the circulatory and respiratory systems, conveying information for both psychological decisions and physiological adjustments. The next section looks at some other nuclei of the hypothalamus.

Hypothalamic nuclei – broader aspects

Throughout the book, nuclei of the hypothalamus will be discussed in the context of their role in behaviour. Figure 5.31 shows some of these. It also shows the pituitary gland (Chapter 3), with which the hypothalamus is closely connected.

The term 'preoptic area' arises from the proximity of this region to the optic pathway (Figure 5.21). The term 'para' means alongside and so a paraventricular structure lies alongside a ventricle. The 'paraventricular nucleus' of the hypothalamus lies alongside the third ventricle. The suprachiasmatic nucleus derives its name from the fact that it is just above the optic chiasm.

Figure 5.29 A focus upon the solitary nucleus.

Source: Martini *et al.* (2000, Fig. 18-8, p. 472). Copyright © 2000, 1997 by Frederic H. Martini, Inc. and Michael J. Timmons. Reprinted by permission of Pearson Education, Inc.

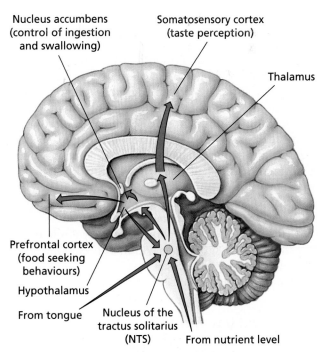

Figure 5.30 The hypothalamus as a link between nutrient state, food and behaviour.

Source: derived from Kalat (1998, Fig. 10.17, p. 288) and Carlson (1988, Fig. 7.30, p. 218). From KALAT. *Biological Psychology,* 6E © 1998 Wadsworth, a part of Cengage Learning, Inc. Reproduced by permission. www.cengage.com/permissions.

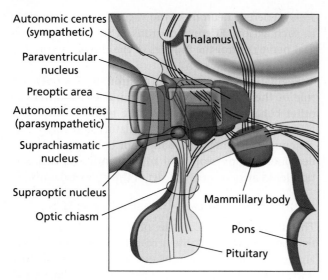

Figure 5.31 Hypothalamus.

Source: Martini *et al.* (2000, Fig. 15-15(b), p. 398). Copyright © 2000, 1997 by Frederic H. Martini, Inc. and Michael J. Timmons. Reprinted by permission of Pearson Education, Inc.

As just exemplified by nutrient regulation, the hypothalamus plays a pivotal role in mediating between internal and external environments. Each one, among several of its nuclei, plays a distinctive role in organizing a particular behaviour. In so doing, they are informed of internal conditions, such as level of a particular hormone. Neurons in some nuclei are informed about the body's fluid level. When this falls, these neurons appear to be activated and to inform parts of the brain concerned with decision-making, so the animal is motivated to seek water. As an integrated part of homeostasis, they also play a role in triggering the secretion of arginine vasopressin at the pituitary gland (Chapter 3).

Other nuclei are concerned with the regulation of body temperature. The electrical activity of specific neurons in the hypothalamus depends upon local temperature. Thus, when body temperature is not at its optimal value, neurons detect this and action, both physiological (e.g. sweating) and behavioural (e.g. moving to another environment), is triggered.

Other nuclei of the hypothalamus play a role in the organization of sexual behaviour. For example, they contain neurons that are sensitive to the hormone testosterone taken up from the blood (Chapter 3).

Sleep, waking and alertness

At times, the animal needs to engage actively with the environment, as in seeking food or a mate. At other times, it needs to withdraw and conserve resources, as in sleep. You have already met a region of the brain stem, the role of which is triggering variation between sleep, waking and alertness: the reticular formation (Figures 5.15 and 5.16). Axons from here project to the cortex and other regions, where they synapse upon local neurons, i.e. the reticular activating system (RAS). Ascending pathways project information in a caudal → rostral direction. Activity by the RAS neurons changes the activity of the cortex between states corresponding to sleep, drowsiness and arousal (i.e. a state of being awake and alert). Breaking the connections between the RAS and the cortex causes a coma.

The activity of such ascending pathways has a broad influence over neurons in the forebrain. Large numbers of target neurons can all be influenced simultaneously by an ascending pathway. These pathways can be characterized by the neurochemical that they employ, and are cholinergic (i.e. employing acetylcholine), noradrenergic or serotonergic. The RAS and other brain regions, in interaction, control cycles of sleep and waking. The brain contains an intrinsic clock mechanism. An area that, in part, embodies this is the 'suprachiasmatic nucleus' of the hypothalamus (Figure 5.31).

Section summary

1 The amygdala has a role in linking sensory input, cognition and emotion.

2 The blood–brain barrier protects the brain's neurons.

3 The hypothalamus and solitary nucleus have roles in linking the physiology of the body to behaviour. Both behavioural and physiological action depends upon monitoring internal and external events.

4 Different hypothalamic nuclei have different roles in motivation and behaviour, e.g. hypothalamic neurons are sensitive to nutrient level or testosterone, etc.

5 The reticular activating system participates in the regulation of states of waking, alertness and sleep.

☞ Test your knowledge

5.7 With regard to Figure 5.27, complete the two expressions in the following: 'The cerebral aqueduct contains ___ whereas the grey matter consists largely of ___ '.

Answer on page 149

Integration, reasoning, planning and anticipation

So far, the chapter has described areas of cortex devoted to sensory and motor processing. However, if you look back at Figure 5.13, you will see that a large part of the cortex of the human brain (coloured pink) serves neither a sensory nor a motor role. These areas serve the role of *integration*, described in this section.

Association areas?

A term sometimes given to areas of cortex that are not concerned directly with sensory or motor processing is 'association cortex' (J.H. Martin, 1996). This implies that they associate ('integrate') information processed in other areas, e.g. to link visual and olfactory (smell) information in perceiving a rose or to link sensory and motor information in the control of action.

Certain areas of association cortex continue the processing of one sensory input, e.g. vision (Preuss and Kaas, 1999). For example, such an area of processing for visual information, termed the 'prestriate cortex', is immediately anterior to the primary visual cortex. Further areas of visual processing are found in the temporal lobes. Considering such areas, some authors reserve the term association cortex only for areas where there is evidence that information from more than one sensory area is being associated (Fuster, 1997), e.g. portions of the frontal cortex, discussed next.

Prefrontal cortex

An important structure involved in planning is the anterior part of the cortex of the frontal lobes (i.e. excluding regions directly concerned with motor control such as the motor cortex). It is termed **prefrontal cortex (PFC)**. Figure 5.32 shows three subdivisions of the prefrontal cortex. You should see the logic for the name of one division: 'dorsolateral'. It refers to the dorsal side considering the dimension of dorsal–ventral and the lateral side in the dimension of lateral–medial.

Although the prefrontal cortex can be subdivided into such sub-regions each serving a somewhat different role, the over-arching role of the whole structure can be summarized as (Gazzaley and D'Esposito, 2007, p.188): '... the executive control of mental processes ...'.

These processes, over which control is exerted, are located elsewhere in the brain. So, unlike sensory and motor cortex, the prefrontal cortex has neither a

Figure 5.32 Views of the brain that highlight the prefrontal cortex, as defined by the regions with (Brodmann) numbers attached. Three broad divisions of prefrontal cortex are shown. Note that area 24 constitutes the anterior cingulate cortex ('cingulate'). The remaining numbers on the 'medial/cingulate' cortex refer to 'medial prefrontal cortex'. The term 'orbital' is often used to refer to the 'orbitofrontal cortex'.
Source: Fuster (1997, Fig. 6.5, p. 173).

specifically sensory nor motor function. Rather, its role is one of *coordination*. Such coordination is between (i) the control involved in acting in the external world, (ii) perceptual and cognitive processes and (iii) activity of the autonomic nervous system. Indicative of this role in coordination, the PFC is massively interconnected with other brain regions. Coordination by the PFC involves exerting an influence over a number of processes that are described later in the book:

1 *Organization of motor control.* Pursuing a particular goal requires inhibition on tendencies to pursue other goals, e.g. ignoring potentially strong triggers to action, as in resisting temptation.

2 *Attention.* Whatever a person is doing, even remaining motionless while planning action, attention might need to be focused on a single task, while diverting attention from competitive candidates that might otherwise seize attention.

3 *Memory and reasoning.* Particular memories need to be revived so as to be used in the control of cognition and behaviour. Sometimes behaviour cannot be guided by physically present stimuli but requires a memory of past events or prediction based upon possible future scenarios. Other memories that are irrelevant to the task need to remain dormant.

4 *Emotion*. There might need to be amplification or suppression of emotion in the interests of achieving a current goal. Emotions might need to be rapidly adjusted with changing circumstances.

When humans are engaged in planning, blood flow to the frontal lobes increases. At such times, the neurons of the region are particularly active and require a large supply of glucose and oxygen.

One source of insight into what the PFC does derives from the problems that people encounter following disruption to it. Given the PFC's role in executive control, it will probably not surprise you to know that a variety of different disturbances to cognition and behaviour can follow such disruption. These include inappropriate social behaviour and a difficulty with keeping an item of information in mind (Gazzaley and D'Esposito, 2007). The exact nature will depend upon the site of disruption, its cause and its rate of onset, e.g. from sudden breaking of a blood vessel or slowly growing tumour. Phineas Gage (Chapter 1) is an example of such behaviour change following damage to the PFC.

As a rather broad term, the expression **frontal lobe syndrome** is given to people showing effects of PFC damage. Such patients are often unable to perform forward planning and are described as living in the 'here-and-now' (Luria, 1973). Luria's patients were controlled predominantly by stimuli that are physically present and have difficulty in extrapolating to imagined situations.

A personal angle

A patient of Luria

A patient, with damage to the prefrontal cortex, was asked to light a candle and carry it to another place. After lighting the candle, he tried to smoke it like a cigarette. One imagines that there was a strong pre-existing association between the acts of lighting and smoking an object, an association that remained intact after the damage. Damage lifted the inhibition on 'smoking' the object that would normally have been activated in this context.

Section summary

1 The term 'association' is used with regard to regions of cortex not concerned directly with either sensory or motor processing, e.g. the prefrontal cortex.

2 The prefrontal cortex serves the role of coordination of activity in other brain regions.

☞ Test your knowledge

5.8 A high blood flow to the PFC is suggestive of what at (i) neuronal and (ii) cognitive levels?.

Answer on page 149

Comparative and evolutionary perspectives

Introduction

Comparing nervous systems between different species and relating these to evolution and lifestyle can be an important means of understanding how nervous systems work. Some species are studied as a matter of convenience and convention, e.g. the rat. Rats are relatively cheap and simple to breed, and are unlikely to become an endangered species. In addition, strains can be 'standardized' across laboratories. Other species are brilliant with a particular skill, e.g. the hawk and its use of vision. Examining how the nervous system of such species is different from species that are less developed at the particular skill can give insight. Some closely related species have found rather different solutions to a given problem, which makes it revealing to study divergence in brain structure underlying behavioural differences.

Evolutionary considerations

Understanding of the brain can be assisted by considering the evolutionary type of explanation (Chapter 1). One issue that this brings to mind is the nature of the best metaphor to describe evolution and the link with natural selection, to which the chapter now turns.

Engineering or tinkering?

Evolution is more like an amateur tinkerer than a professional engineer. The tinkerer does not know what is going to emerge but tries various possibilities, working with whatever materials are to hand.

Evolutionary psychology

Evolution as design

Evolution is sometimes compared to an engineer in producing a design (recall the design metaphor of evolutionary psychology (Chapter 2)). However, this analogy can be misleading (Jacob, 1977). Unlike evolution, an engineer has an idea in mind of a product and sets out to achieve it. Also an engineer can start from nothing, largely unconstrained by existing designs. Evolution has no design in mind (as far as we know!) and never sets out from nothing. Rather, evolution builds on what is there already.

The products of evolution are not necessarily optimal: they simply do the job sufficiently well. They might have design flaws when viewed from an engineering perspective. For example, Jacob suggests (1977, p. 1166) that attaching an evolutionary new cerebral cortex to the rest of the evolutionary older brain is an example of tinkering: 'It is something like adding a jet engine to an old horse cart. It is not surprising, in either case, that accidents, difficulties and conflicts can occur.'

Homology and analogy

In comparing characteristics of different species (e.g. the eye and vision), biologists employ the terms **homology** and **analogy** (Preuss and Kaas, 1999). Each term refers to a similarity in a characteristic but they distinguish between evolutionary origins. If something is 'homologous' between two species, it refers to a common evolutionary origin. Both species have a common precursor at an earlier stage of evolution. In the cultural domain, a similar logic applies to human languages where, say, similarities between Romanian and Italian can be traced to common roots in Latin.

In comparing two species, if a characteristic is 'analogous', this refers to its independent emergence in evolution. Common evolutionary pressures gave rise to the same characteristic. For example, insect vision and vision in humans have some common features but these cannot be traced in evolution to a common ancestor. This is comparable to the independent appearance of an idea, e.g. a new theory in science, at two different and unconnected places.

Vertebrates and invertebrates

Comparison

Animal species can be divided into **vertebrates** and **invertebrates**. Mammals (e.g. humans), birds, reptiles, amphibia and fish are vertebrates, defined as having a backbone. Our principal interest in this distinction is that a section of the nervous system, the spinal cord, is housed within the backbone (Chapter 3, Figure 3.16, p. 64). Invertebrates, which include beetles, flies, worms, snails and slugs, lack a backbone.

Much understanding of the action potential (Chapter 4) was derived from recordings made from so-called giant axons (the diameter is giant relative to vertebrate axons) of the squid. The fundamental principles of how neurons work and communicate at synapses appear to be very similar, comparing vertebrates and invertebrates (Jerison, 1976). However, even by exploiting similar components, *assemblies* of these components can, of course, yield very different results when comparing species.

Because of the relative simplicity of their nervous systems, invertebrates permit us to understand how particular behaviours are organized. In some cases, the precise 'wiring diagram' of neural connections underlying behaviour can be mapped (Kandel, 1976). The neurons of such invertebrates as snails and leeches are often relatively large, few in number and able to be identified. This facilitates electrical recording (see later) from individual neurons within the sequence (sensory) → (intermediate processing) → (motor output). Particular individual neurons can be relatively easily identified and are similar from one animal to another. By contrast, in vertebrate species, individual neurons can only rarely be identified and compared between animals.

There are also some important differences between invertebrates and vertebrates. For example, invertebrates have not 'invented' myelination (Chapter 4) as a means to speed up conduction of action potentials. Rather, speed is achieved by the large diameter of their axons.

Aplysia – an invertebrate example

Figure 5.33(a) shows an invertebrate, *Aplysia californica*, a member of a zoological group termed molluscs (by convention, the names of species are written in italics) (Kandel, 1976). It might not possess much beauty but has proved invaluable in understanding links between nervous systems and behaviour. Rather than having a brain as such in which information processing occurs and motor control is initiated, *Aplysia* has a series of ganglia, each containing about 2000 neurons. Projections from neurons link ganglia to each other and link ganglia to sense organs and effectors. For example, the eyes and tentacles are innervated by the cerebral ganglia.

In response to tactile stimulation, *Aplysia* can withdraw their gill (respiratory organ) and siphon (a 'spout' through which it expels waste) (Figure 5.34). This occurs in response to even mild stimuli.

Aplysia has relatively few neurons, which are large and individually identifiable. Figure 5.35 shows a simplified version of the system responsible for the withdrawal reflex. (In reality, there would be a number of parallel pathways of this kind.) The tip of a sensory neuron is embedded in the skin of the siphon. Tactile stimulation of the siphon excites this neuron. The sensory neuron makes synaptic connections with both the motor neuron that triggers the reaction in the gill and an interneuron. In turn, the interneuron also excites the motor neuron. By both routes, activity in the sensory neuron evokes a muscular response by the gill, i.e. withdrawal.

(a)

(b)

Figure 5.34 The reflex underlying defensive-withdrawal of the siphon and gill: (a) relaxed state and (b) following application of a jet of water, withdrawn state.
Source: Kandel (1976, Fig. 9-2, p. 351).

(a)

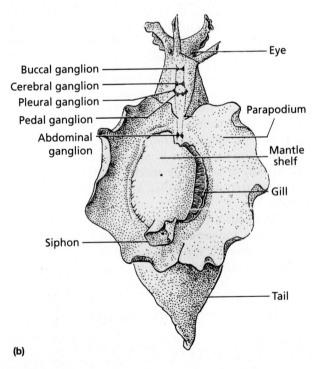

(b)

Figure 5.33 *Aplysia*: (a) side view and (b) dorsal view.
Source: Kandel (1976, Fig. 4-4, p. 76).

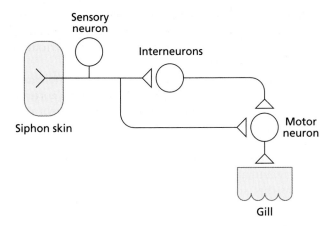

Figure 5.35 Simplified diagram of some neurons and their connections.

Source: Kandel (1991) *Principles of Neural Science*, 3rd edition, Fig. 65-1, p. 1010, reprinted by permission of The McGraw-Hill Companies, Inc.

Comparing vertebrate species

The study termed 'comparative psychology' compares the behaviour of different species and tries to link this to differences in their brains. Considering vertebrates, this section will compare brains between species, to see what insight can be gained.

Conservation and diversity

A comparison of the brains of different vertebrate species led to the principle of the *conservation of organization*, which states (Stebbins, 1969, p. 124):

> Whenever a complex, organized structure or a complex integrated biosynthetic pathway has become an essential adaptive unit of a successful group of organisms, the essential features of this unit are conserved in all of the evolutionary descendants of the group concerned.

The implication is that most principles of brain organization are general rather than species-specific (Jerison, 1976). The same brain structures are to be found comparing various vertebrate species. Thus, psychologists can speak of a brain region, say, the amygdala and assume that, comparing rather widely across species, it reveals certain features in common.

Of course, the amygdala of a rat is not identical to that of a human, nor is its role. Rather, there are merely some common principles of organization. This illustrates the analogy that evolution can appear as a tinkerer or tuner, making slight changes to basic structures. For another example, fish, snakes and mammals all have a cerebellum, used for motor control. However, there are differences in the degree of specialization of such a structure. Certain species are adapted to show more flexible and nuanced locomotion, reflected in greater development of the cerebellum.

Although, on wide inter-species comparison, similar structures with similar areas of responsibility are found, the degree of responsibility associated with a structure can vary. For example, vision is organized in both cortical and brain stem regions. However, in fish, amphibians and reptiles a brain stem structure (comparable to the superior colliculus of the human, discussed earlier) has a greater role than in humans. In humans, the visual cortex has a relatively large responsibility for vision.

Brain size

Humans have an outstanding intellect and sometimes describe themselves as 'big-brained'. However, all is relative and the 1.3 kg human brain is modest by comparison with the toothed sperm whale of brain size 5–8 kg and the Indian elephant which has a 5 kg brain (Harvey and Krebs, 1990).

Figure 5.36 compares various types of animal in terms of brain size and body size. As a general principle, brain size increases with body weight. However, the brains of primates are large relative to body weight (Northcutt and Kaas, 1995). This is especially true of humans. The term **encephalization** refers to the degree to which brain size exceeds what might be expected on the basis of body weight (Harvey and Krebs, 1990). Humans are said to be strongly encephalized. Brain size depends on the factors determining the rate of development of neurons early in life and the length of time over which development occurs (Finlay and Darlington, 1995) (discussed in the following chapter).

Figure 5.36 Brain size as a function of body size.
A amphibians, B birds, F bony fish, h humans, M mammals, R reptiles.

Source: Jerison (1991a, Fig. 15, p. 64).

For body weight, reptiles tend to have smaller brains than mammals. What might we expect to be the relationship between brain size and body size? Presumably in some respects a larger body requires more processing of information (e.g. the somatosensory surface is greater and muscles have more fibres requiring control). In other respects, the processing demands might be independent of body size. For example, we might expect that the need to detect odours and thereby the amount of brain devoted to olfactory processing would not vary with body size (Jerison, 1976). Somewhat surprisingly, olfactory bulb volume increases with body size. Some parts of the brain increase in proportion to brain mass (Jerison, 1991a). The hippocampus and cerebellum show this relationship.

Localization of function

The **principle of localization** is that discrete parts of the nervous system are concerned with discrete roles. We saw earlier that, *within* humans, differences in amount of brain tissue underlying control of something reflects differences in information processing, e.g. large amounts of somatosensory and motor cortex are devoted to the fingers and are associated with high resolution. Can the principle of localization be extended to comparisons *between* species?

Based upon a comparison between species, the 'principle of proper mass' (Jerison, 1976, p. 24) states that: 'The mass of neural tissue controlling a particular activity is appropriate to the amount of information processing involved in performing the activity.'

Metaphorically speaking, the importance that a species attaches to an activity and the information processing involved in performing it tend to be reflected in the amount of neural tissue dedicated to its control. Thus, for example, a species that makes extensive use of vision, involving fine-grained discrimination, tends to have a relatively large visual cortex and superior colliculus. If this species makes little use of sound it tends to have a relatively small auditory cortex and inferior colliculus.

In the following sections, some examples of this principle are considered.

The cortex

Among vertebrates, a difference between mammals and the rest (e.g. reptiles and birds) is the extent of the six-layered mammalian cortex (Figure 5.14), sometimes termed neocortex ('new cortex', in evolutionary time) (Preuss and Kaas, 1999). The cortex of reptiles and birds is normally classified as three-layered. The cortex of mammals is enlarged as a percentage of brain mass compared with other vertebrates. In turn, within mammals, a feature of primates is the disproportionately large

cortex, the size of which is increased by folding (Jerison, 1991b). A relatively large cortex is generally associated with the capacity to show flexibility in behaviour, a hallmark of primates.

Is the cortex of mammals analogous or homologous to that of other vertebrates? Is the mammalian cortex a completely new 'invention'? It is generally thought that the mammalian cortex derives from that of a non-mammalian precursor and that there exists homology (Preuss and Kaas, 1999). Figure 5.37 shows the cerebral cortex of some mammals. Note differences in size of the cortical regions that are concerned with particular sensory, e.g. visual and auditory cortex, and motor functions. As a difference between humans and other species, relatively little of the human cortex is either sensory or motor cortex. This remaining amount (represented in pink) is sometimes termed 'association cortex'.

Figure 5.38 also shows the brains of some mammalian species (Fuster, 1997). Two things are evident. First, the degree of folding is greatest in humans. Second, as a percentage of the cortex, the prefrontal region reaches a maximum in humans. The PFC, especially the dorsolateral PFC, appears to be involved in the primate specialization of advanced cognition involving extrapolation beyond current sensory input. Compared with non-primates, primates such as monkeys are good at performing special tasks that are guided by memory (Goldman-Rakic, 1987). For example, in one experimental design, one of two food wells is shown to be baited with food and then covered. After a delay, the monkey is given a choice of wells. The solution cannot be solved

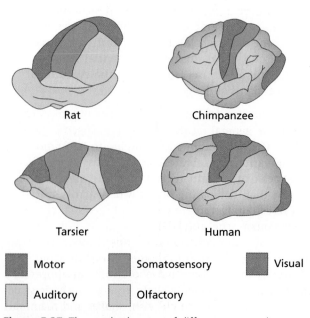

Figure 5.37 The cerebral cortex of different mammals.
Source: OU course SD286 (Module A, Fig. 22, p. 31).

on the basis of current sensory input but requires a memory of a single event from the past (observing the baiting). Of course, the human skill at bridging such time delays hardly needs mention.

In certain primates (most obviously humans), the enlarged PFC might form a basis of a sophisticated extrapolation beyond sensory data: the utilization of a **theory of mind** of the self and others (Frith, 1996). That is, humans employ theories of the intentions of others, e.g. that they are using honesty or deceit.

Povinelli and Preuss (1995) ask whether humans are unique in employing a theory of mind. If so, the capacity emerged in evolution at a stage after our line diverged (Figure 5.39). Another possibility is that this capacity has an earlier origin and is shared with gorillas and chimpanzees. Some evidence is suggestive that these primates exploit a theory on the intentions of others.

Figure 5.38 The brain of several mammalian species showing the prefrontal cortex (blue).
Source: Fuster (1997, Fig. 2.1, p. 10).

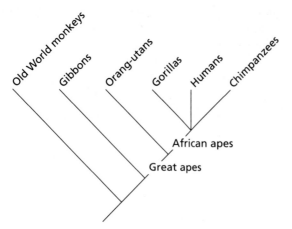

Figure 5.39 Evolutionary tree of primates. Note a common ancestor of gorillas, humans and chimps in African apes and a divergence of orangutans before this stage.

Source: Povinelli and Preuss (1995, Fig. 1, p. 419).

The hippocampus

As Sherry (1992, p. 521) notes: 'Animals that make unusual demands on memory have unusual memories'. In turn, a useful working assumption is that an unusual species-typical memory is associated with an unusual biological basis in the brain. For example, some species of bird cache food in a large number of sites and have an exceptional capacity to remember where these are, so that they can later retrieve the food (Sherry, 1992). In a single day, the black-capped chickadee (*Parus atricapillus*) is able to contribute food to several hundred caches and retain a memory of their location for weeks. Having depleted a cache, the bird refrains from revisiting it.

The hippocampus of such a caching species is over double the size of that of an otherwise similar but non-caching species. Caching is disrupted by hippocampal damage. Evidence points to the hippocampus being associated with, among other things, spatial memory formation (O'Keefe and Nadel, 1978). This suggests that differences in the hippocampus of caching species can be associated with differences in their memory capacity.

Figure 5.41 shows the relationship between volume of the telencephalon and the volume of the hippocampus for several 'families' (in zoological terms, closely related species) of bird (Sherry *et al.*, 1989). Three families of caching birds and ten families of non-caching birds are shown. In each case, hippocampal size increases with size of telencephalon but the disproportionately increased size of hippocampus in the caching families relative to non-caching is clear. Differences in migratory or social behaviour between species cannot account for differences in hippocampal size.

Evolutionary psychology

Social cognition

Dunbar (2009) speculates that the evolutionary pressure for increased cortical volume in primates came from the need to negotiate their social worlds successfully. He finds a correlation between the size of cortex and the size of the group in which primates normally live (Figure 5.40). Humans normally have about 150 contacts in their social worlds. As Figure 5.38 shows, the most drastic enlargement in humans is in the prefrontal cortex, which is closely involved in complex emotional reactions, social assessments and decision-making.

Figure 5.40 Relationship between the size of social group and the neocortex ratio. The latter is calculated as the volume of neocortex divided by the volume of the remainder of the brain. Three types of symbols refer to three different genera (groups of species).

Source: Dunbar (2009, Fig 1, p. 1120).

The olfactory bulb

For their size of brain, primates (especially humans) have a relatively small olfactory bulb (Jerison, 1991a). See Figure 5.21. This suggests that, compared with, say, wolves, primates have made relatively little use of fine-grained olfactory discrimination in their evolution. Comparing bird species, there are enormous differences in the size of olfactory bulb (Healy and Guilford, 1990). Olfaction might, to some extent, act as a substitute for vision in species that are active in poor illumination. Nocturnal birds might be expected to exhibit an enhanced olfactory capacity as compared with diurnal

Figure 5.41 Relationship between hippocampal and telencephalic volumes for caching (filled triangles) and non-caching (open triangles) families.
Source: Sherry *et al.* (1989, Fig. 4, p. 314).

('day-active') birds. Birds with high olfactory capacity might be expected to have relatively large olfactory bulbs. Olfactory bulb increases with brain size but an independent effect of activity is found, with a larger olfactory bulb in nocturnal species.

Section summary

1   Evolution can be likened to a tinkerer rather than a design engineer.

2   Similar characteristics can reflect either homology or analogy.

3   Certain invertebrates have relatively few, large and identifiable neurons.

4   In vertebrates, to some extent the size of a region of brain devoted to a form of processing reflects the amount of information handled.

Test your knowledge

5.9   Which of the following is a feature of the vertebrate but not invertebrate nervous system? (i) Axon, (ii) synapse, (iii) interneuron, (iv) node of Ranvier.

5.10   Supply the missing words in the following: 'Rather than being an ___, as in the design metaphor of evolutionary psychology, a comparison between species suggests that a better metaphor would be that evolution is a ___'.

 Answers on page 149   WEB

Techniques for studying the brain

This section looks at some of the techniques that are employed to gain understanding of how brains work. It considers both the activity of living brains and postmortem analysis.

Defining neural connections

So far the chapter has discussed, on one level, individual neurons and, on the other, gross anatomy of the brain as revealed in its structures. It described neural pathways running from one structure to another, e.g. pathways from the lateral geniculate nucleus to the visual cortex. How have scientists been able to establish the route that such neural pathways take? This section introduces some of the techniques.

Tracing pathways

Imagine a particular nucleus in the brain (e.g. lateral geniculate nucleus) and the cell bodies of the neurons that are located there. To which locations do the axons of these ('efferent') neurons project? A technique for establishing this in non-humans is termed 'anterograde labelling'. Special chemicals are injected into the nucleus. These are taken up by the cell body and its associated dendrites. They are then slowly transported along the axon towards its terminal. The term 'anterograde' is because of this forward movement, i.e. in the same direction as the movement of action potentials in the axon (Figure 5.42(a)). The location of the chemical can be measured and hence the course of the trajectory established.

With reference to a nucleus, afferent neurons are defined as those that bring information to it. To establish the source of these, 'retrograde labelling' is employed. Chemicals are injected that are taken up by axon terminals. They are then transported away from the terminal along the length of the axon towards the cell body (Figure 5.42(b)). The term 'retrograde' relates to the direction of chemical migration being backwards relative to the movement of the action potential.

Since these techniques involve killing the animal and analyzing its brain tissue (see next section), they are obviously inappropriate for use with living humans.

Histology

Insight is provided by techniques that look at samples of brain ('tissue') taken from either deceased humans or, say, rats killed in the laboratory. The term 'tissue' refers to collections of cells that make up a particular structure, e.g. kidney tissue is that which forms a kidney,

(a)

(b)

Figure 5.42 Labelling: (a) anterograde and (b) retrograde.

consisting of millions of component cells. Of course, the tissue of most interest to us is neural tissue.

The science of 'histology' investigates tissue by preparing samples of it in a way that opens it to analysis. To study brain tissue, it is necessary to look at it under

a microscope. Thin slices of tissue are cut shortly after death and preserved by chemical means so that they do not decay; they are then hardened so that their structure is fixed. Slices are mounted on microscope slides, a procedure that facilitates their microscopic analysis.

Simply looking at slices of neural tissue under a light microscope reveals only a limited amount of information. Neurons are usually too small to be distinguished. Further histological techniques are employed to make the details of the sample more visible. One technique is **staining**, in which a chemical is applied which reacts with neurons in various ways. The chemical makes these neurons more visible by picking out and highlighting parts of them. A particular stain can have a special affinity for a part of a cell such as its membrane. The technique of forming a **Golgi stain** reveals the whole cell (Figure 5.43). The technique termed **Nissl stain** reveals the cell body. In some cases, a particular stain will target only neurons characterized by a certain type of neurotransmitter. A pathway made up of such neurons would then stand out against a background of neuron types that remained unstained. Some stains target myelin so that bundles of myelinated axons can be distinguished against a background of unmyelinated neurons.

For reasons not entirely clear, some stains target only a small fraction of all the neurons in a region but those neurons are stained throughout. Thus, in tissue containing large numbers of apparently identical neurons, only a small fraction becomes evident. This phenomenon can be exploited, since it enables just the trajectory of a few neurons to become visible against their background.

Electron microscopy

Although a certain amount of detail can be gained by such techniques as staining and the use of a high-powered light microscope, the resolution is limited. To obtain a magnification large enough to see more fine details, the technique of **electron microscopy** is employed. A slice of tissue is prepared on a slide and then a beam of electrons is projected at it. A film

(a) **(b)**

Figure 5.43 Golgi stain: (a) cell showing processes and (b) enlarged process showing spines.
Source: courtesy of Professor M. Stewart.

sensitive to their presence is placed on the other side of the tissue. Electrons in the beam tend to pass through the tissue. The degree to which they appear at the film and expose it depends on the physical properties of the material they are passing through. For example, the membrane of a neuron would stand out as different from the material on the inside and outside.

Measuring electrical activity

There are techniques for observing the electrical activity of the CNS, peripheral nervous system and muscles. These are sometimes described as 'non-invasive', where the technique does not involve breaking the skin (e.g. a surface electrode) or 'invasive' where the skin is broken (e.g. in implanting an electrode).

Electroencephalography

Electrodes (objects that detect electrical voltages), when attached to the scalp, detect electrical activity in the underlying brain region and recordings are made of these signals (Andreassi, 2007). This study of the brain's activity is called **electroencephalography (EEG)**, the record being an electroencephalogram (also abbreviated EEG) (Figure 5.44).

The location of the electrode is necessarily some distance from the neurons that contribute to the signal. There is, of course, biological tissue (e.g. bone and skin of the scalp) between the electrode and the neurons. Voltage changes produced by individual neurons are too small to be detected. Rather, such electrodes give a picture of the brain's 'overall' electrical activity in the region near to the electrode, i.e. the combined activity of millions of neurons. The activity of the brain's outer layer, the cerebral cortex, is particularly evident in such a record. Many of the brain's neurons are synchronized in their activity and thus add their electrical effects, thereby contributing to a larger signal detectable by EEG. Using this technique, signals characteristic of sleep or arousal are measured.

There are numerous applications of EEG (Andreassi, 2007). For example, patterns characteristic of epilepsy (Hommet *et al.*, 2005) or the development of other abnormalities, e.g. a brain tumour, can be detected. The EEG can register *coherent* patterns of voltage change when the signals from two or more electrodes are compared. Suppose that electrodes at locations A and B show similar ('coherent') patterns of activity. This suggests anatomical, or at least functional, links between A and B. Asymmetries in patterns of activity between the hemispheres can be detected as can changes in activity as a function of experience, e.g. in the course of acquiring a skill.

Since it can detect only the averaged activity of the more superficial regions, the EEG cannot reveal what is

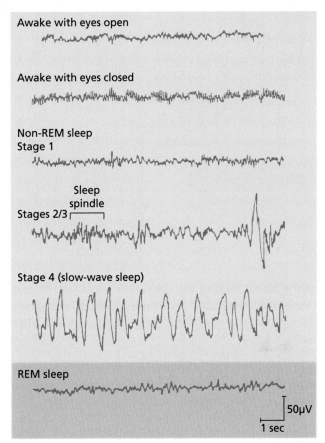

Figure 5.44 Electroencephalograms indicate different phases of sleep, e.g. that during which rapid eye movement (REM) is shown.

happening in deeper brain regions. Implanted electrodes can do this for non-humans. Of course, it is not usually possible scientifically or ethically to perform similar studies on humans.

Evoked potentials

A stimulus triggers a change in electrical activity in the brain and this change is termed an 'evoked potential' or, as it is also called, **event-related potential (ERP)** (Andreassi, 2007). Using electroencephalography, the ERP is recorded by surface electrodes at the scalp. An 'idealized' example is shown in Figure 5.45. Note the background activity (termed 'noise') that exists before the stimulus is applied and after the stimulus is over. The signal that the stimulus triggers is clear against this background.

In reality, on a single observation, the difference between what is evoked (event-related) and what is background is not immediately obvious. However, by repeatedly presenting the same stimulus, and analyzing the electrical signal, a clearer picture of the consequence of the stimulus emerges.

The average electrical activity is taken over a number of trials. Averaging tends to cancel out the ups and downs

Figure 5.45 An 'idealized' signal against background.

of the noise, leaving the consistent event-related part clearly evident. Figure 5.46 shows such recordings. In the first (top trace) it is unclear what signal exists since there is a relatively high electrical activity even before presentation of the stimulus. As each successive recording contributes to an average (going from top to bottom), so an unambiguous signal progressively emerges from the background. For example, at time 550 ms, voltage X in trace 1, being negative, tends to cancel voltage Y in trace 3 and contributes to an average signal at this time that is near to zero in trace 5 (32nd recording).

Event-related potentials contribute to our understanding of a number of psychological phenomena (Andreassi, 2007). For example, if a person's attention is drawn to a stimulus, the change in potential that it evokes is typically increased. A potential can be detected even in the absence of an external triggering event but at the time when an event is expected to occur, a so-called 'endogenous potential'.

Figure 5.47 shows the result for evoked potentials exhibited by patients with damage to the orbitofrontal cortex (OFC), a region of prefrontal cortex (Figure 5.38), and controls (Rule *et al.*, 2002). The stimuli were described as 'emotionally arousing': an abrupt sound or an electric shock to the hand. The term P300 describes a particular change of the potential that usually, as here, occurs at around 300 ms after the onset of the stimulus. Note the larger change of potential in brain-damaged people. Rule *et al.* suggested that an intact OFC would play a role in emotional regulation by restraining the effect of the stimuli employed here. Damage lifts this inhibition.

Muscle activity

Chapters 3 and 4 described the contraction of muscle as a result of activity in motor neurons. Behavioural scientists need to be able to record the activity of muscles. Sometimes this is carried out by electrodes with their tips inside a muscle. At other times, rather like the EEG, it is done at a distance from the muscle, e.g. on the skin and picking up the activity of a muscle immediately below the skin. The technique is termed 'electromyography', the recording being an **electromyogram (EMG)** (Andreassi, 2007).

The electromyogram can give an objective measure of a facial reaction indicative of emotion that might not be obvious from looking at the face itself. For example, researchers into disgust ask the question, is there a similarity in the facial expressions of disgust at physical stimuli and moral transgressions? Chapman *et al.*

Figure 5.46 Event-related potentials in response to a stimulus at time 0. Response is averaged over 32 trials, 5 of these being shown from 1st (top) to the 32nd (bottom).
Source: Aston-Jones *et al.* (1999, Fig. 54.2, p. 1388).

Figure 5.47 Averaged evoked potentials in response to auditory and somatosensory (in this case electric shock to the hand) stimuli. Arrows indicate time of onset of stimulus.
Source: Rule *et al.* (2002, Fig. 2, p. 267).

(2009) recorded the electrical activity of the muscles that control the movements of the face. They found a similar reaction of the facial muscles to (i) a disgusting taste, (ii) a non-taste-related physical stimulus (picture of a wound) and (iii) a moral transgression (an unfair financial transaction). Subjectively expressed disgust correlated with both the specific muscular reaction and the tendency to reject an unfair offer. Next time that someone describes an injustice as leaving a 'bad taste in the mouth', you might think that this is more than just a colourful metaphor.

Neuroimaging

Recent years have seen a revolution in our ability to form images of the brain, a process termed **neuroimaging**. Neuroimaging comes in two broad classes: **structural neuroimaging** (or anatomical neuroimaging) and **functional neuroimaging** (Papanicolaou, 1998). Structural neuroimaging looks at the anatomy of the brain in terms of sizes and locations of different regions, etc. It helps to identify structural abnormalities in the form of, for example, diseased tissue. These might then be related to behavioural manifestations. Functional neuroimaging looks at the brain in action, i.e. which parts of the brain are relatively active or inactive at given times. Abnormality can be identified in terms of unusual patterns of under-activity or over-activity in a brain region. For example, a case of epilepsy might be characterized by transient over-activity in regions of the frontal lobe, seen at particular times (Papanicolaou, 1998).

This section looks at three techniques of neuroimaging.

Computerized tomography

A form of structural neuroimaging is that of **computerized tomography** (CT) scanning, the image being termed a computerized axial tomogram (CAT) (Smith and Fetz, 1987). The term 'tomography' refers to the three-dimensional nature of the scan, 'topographic' being two-dimensional.

In CAT, a source of X-rays is projected at the brain and an X-ray image is formed at the detectors. The X-rays interact differently with different types of tissue within the brain, hence an image of the X-rays leaving the brain conveys a picture of what has been encountered en route. The X-ray source is rotated around the brain in increments, each time a different 'shot' being made. A computer assimilates the information obtained from each view and provides a comprehensive picture of the brain. Abnormalities in the brain, such as an abnormal size of ventricles, can then be revealed.

Magnetic resonance imaging

The technique of **magnetic resonance imaging (MRI)** is a way of revealing details of the brain (Andreassi, 2007). It exploits the fact that the substances that make up the body have intrinsic magnetic properties (are 'magnetically responsive') and react when an artificial magnetic field is applied to them, rather as a compass needle reacts to a magnet (Doran and Gadian, 1992). For example, water, a major component of the body, is made up of hydrogen and oxygen and the hydrogen atoms exhibit such a magnetic property. First, I shall describe the use of MRI to form images of the *structure* of the components of the brain.

MRI involves placing a person's head in an apparatus that generates a magnetic field. The interaction between molecules of the brain and the applied magnetic field is monitored in the form of an image of the brain. The apparatus makes small incremental movements such that a series of scans of the brain is made and a series of images obtained, each at a different orientation. According to the nature of the different tissues, their interaction with the magnetic field will differ and hence the part of the image corresponding to each tissue encountered will differ. By crude analogy, compass needles of different compositions would react differently to a given magnetic field applied. Thereby, MRI is able to detect different tissues on the basis of the kind of molecules from which they are made. MRI does not require that anything be injected into the person, and hence it is described as 'non-invasive'.

Researchers who wish to study possible structural differences in the brains of people with psychological disturbances, as compared to controls, can exploit MRI. They ask the question whether the brain difference is a cause of the disorder, or a consequence or possibly a bit of each. Figure 5.48 shows the result of such a study into major depression (Kronenberg *et al.*, 2009). The focus of interest here is the amygdala, a region known to be involved in emotion, e.g. is it changed in size in depression? Figure 5.48(a) shows an MRI image. A population of people with depression was sampled and compared with controls. The trend is for the group of patients to have a lower amygdala volume. This is not a universal finding and so further research is clearly required to indicate the conditions under which a reduction in size occurs.

So much for the static structures of the brain: a variation of MRI, termed **functional magnetic resonance imaging (fMRI)**, looks at what the brain is doing. The neurons of the brain require a supply of oxygen in the blood in order to function. As the neurons in a particular region of the brain become more active, so more blood carrying more oxygen is diverted to that region. The techniques of fMRI (as well as PET, described shortly) measure the blood flow to different brain regions, termed regional cerebral blood flow (rCBF). fMRI is based on a property of the cells of the blood ('red cells') that convey oxygen around the body. These cells contain a small metallic component, which exhibits magnetic properties that can be measured. Suppose that neurons in a part of the brain are particularly active: for example, when a person addicted to heroin is suddenly shown an image of a needle containing heroin. Regions of the brain concerned with emotion and motivation will be strongly excited. Increased

activity by these neurons leads automatically to dilation of blood vessels supplying the regions and thereby an increased flow of blood to the active regions. fMRI is able to detect such changes in blood flow and form an image that shows the levels of activity in different brain regions across the whole brain.

This technique offers high spatial and temporal resolution (better than PET) in detecting activity by different regions of the brain (Andreassi, 2007). Relatively active and inactive sites in the brain can be identified and linked to psychological functions.

An example of where results from fMRI imaging provide input to psychological thinking again concerns depression and the amygdala (Suslow *et al.*, 2010). People with depression and controls were shown very brief images of faces with either sad or happy facial expressions. The images were so rapidly presented that they did not reach conscious awareness. However, the neuroimaging revealed that they had effects on the activity of the amygdala. One particular region of the right amygdala (its lateral and basal nuclei) showed distinctive responses according to stimulus and group membership of participant. It was particularly activated by sad images in depressed people and happy images in controls (Figure 5.49). This provides an important input to psychological theories on the causation of depression. It suggests that even before conscious awareness arises, negative stimuli are already attributed extra weight by people with depression. This could well contribute to consciously experienced emotion.

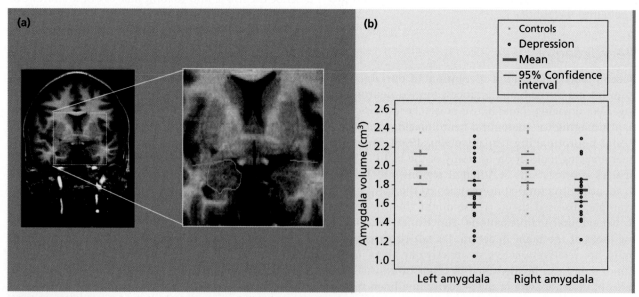

Figure 5.48 (a) MRI image of the brain, part of which is enlarged to the right. Note the grey matter and white matter. The dark butterfly shape is a ventricle. The green outline delineates the amygdala. (b) Amygdala volumes in people with depression compared with controls.

Source: Kronenberg *et al.* (2009, Fig. 1, p. 1113), courtesy of L. Tebartz van Elst, Section for Experimental Neuropsychiatry, University Clinic Freiburg.

Figure 5.49 fMRI investigation of depression. Left: coronal view of brain, indicating focus of activity in part of the right amygdala. Right: contrast values of reactions in patients and controls.
Source: Suslow *et al.* (2010, Fig. 1, p. 157).

Positron emission tomography

The technique of **positron emission tomography (PET)** reveals differences between brain regions in their blood flow, metabolism of fuels (discussed earlier) or presence of substances, such as a particular neurotransmitter. Differences can be seen both (i) within an individual but between brain regions and times and (ii) between different individuals.

Part of the logic of PET is similar to that just described for fMRI. Blood flow varies with activity of local neurons, which is a possible measure of the magnitude of local information processing (Smith and Fetz, 1987). As the frequency of action potentials in a brain region increases, so the need for oxygen and glucose in that region increases. PET consists of putting a radioactively labelled substance, a tracer, into a person, either by inhaling or injecting (Myers *et al.*, 1992). The procedure is described as 'minimally invasive' (Andreassi, 2007). The relative density of that tracer throughout the brain regions is then measured by the neuroimaging apparatus, which constructs an image of the brain showing different densities. In one variety of PET, by inhaling radioactively labelled oxygen, the blood flow to different brain regions (rCBF) can be measured.

The brain uses specific chemical fuels for metabolism. That is, each of its neurons has energy needs involved in transmitting information. Only a few types of fuel are able to be used by neurons, a principal one being glucose. A variety of PET exploits the properties of an artificial substance similar to glucose, 2-deoxyglucose (2-DG). This enters neurons as glucose does but, rather than serving as fuel, accumulates there. Brain regions in which neurons are most active, i.e. the highest frequency of action potentials, accumulate most 2-DG.

One variety of PET consists of first injecting some radioactive material (e.g. 2-DG) into the blood. The scanning apparatus detects the levels of injected radioactivity that arise from 2-DG accumulated in the different regions of brain. The level of radioactivity is detected and brain regions can be scaled according to activity level. Such a PET scan is shown in Figure 5.50, for regions of cortex as the person performs linguistic tasks. Different levels of activity are indicated by different colours alongside the representation of the brain. Whether oxygen or 2-DG, the radioactively labelled substance eventually leaves the neurons and is harmlessly lost from the body.

What kind of information can be revealed by a PET scan? There are various applications. For intact brains, researchers have had success in identifying what region does what. For example, a person can be asked to perform a response, e.g. clenching a fist. Regions of brain concerned with motor control of the hands will then be particularly strongly activated. Sensory stimuli in a particular modality can be presented and regions of brain associated with their processing identified. Regions of brain that are diseased can be identified by their activity level being different from normal. Recovery of function can be monitored in terms of increased activity.

PET scanning offers good 'spatial resolution', i.e. ability to discriminate between neighbouring brain regions, one of which might be active and the other inactive. Different activity levels in regions of brain about 3–5 mm apart can be discriminated. However, a problem with PET scanning is that of its low 'temporal resolution', i.e. the technique cannot detect rapid fluctuations in the activity in a region of brain. Changes in action potential frequencies in a region are not reflected

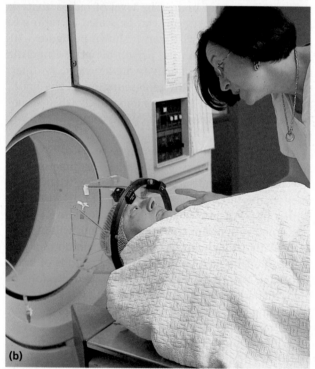

Figure 5.50 (a) Coloured positron emission tomography (PET) scan of areas of the brain involved in two different tasks: hearing (top) and a semantic task (bottom). (b) A nurse talking to a patient about to undergo a PET scan of the brain.

Source: (a) Wellcome Department of Cognitive Neurology/Science Photo Library. (b) CC Studio/Science Photo Library.

instantaneously in changes in the supply of metabolic fuels to that region. Following a sudden change in neural activity in a region, it might take some 45–60 seconds before this is reflected in the neuroimage that is being formed.

Chemicals that are employed by neurons to synthesize neurotransmitters ('precursors') are normally taken up by neurons and utilized. Labelled varieties of these precursors can be injected and their uptake monitored (Myers *et al.*, 1992). Their subsequent activity, in the form of release of the labelled neurotransmitter, can be tracked (Papanicolaou, 1998). If a type of neuron (e.g. dopaminergic) in a region is diseased, the uptake of labelled precursors and their activation as part of neural activity might show as abnormally low.

A further variation of PET scanning allows an estimate to be made of sites in the brain where receptors to a particular type of neurotransmitter are occupied and the extent of their occupation. For example, Figure 5.51(a) shows a representative neuron that releases dopamine. When the neuron is active there is a high rate of release of dopamine and a high occupation of receptors by dopamine. Now imagine a large number of such synapses all situated in a particular part of the brain. If there is high activity at this population of synapses, there will be a high occupation of dopamine receptors within this region of the brain.

So, how could investigators get a measure of receptor occupation at different brain regions? The trick is to inject a substance that competes with the natural substance for occupation of receptors. This injected substance is radioactive and so it sends a signal of its presence. Figure 5.51(b) shows the situation of low and high activity of dopaminergic neurons when there is competition for occupation of dopamine receptors. Low dopaminergic activity means less competition and a high occupation by the radioactive marker, with a subsequent strong signal from the radioactive marker in this region. As dopaminergic activity increases, so there is more competition for occupation and the density of the marker will be less and the signal correspondingly lower. An example of a radioactive marker is ^{11}C-Raclopride, which attaches to dopamine D2 receptors.

Researchers into the use of drugs in clinical practice wish to know where in the brain particular agonists and antagonists occupy receptors. Suppose that an agonist or antagonist to dopamine is injected: it too will compete with dopamine for receptors. If, in addition, a marker is injected, there will be a three-way competition. Assume that the natural release of dopamine is constant at a low level. Consider the situation shown to the left of Figure 5.52. Some ^{11}C-Raclopride is injected

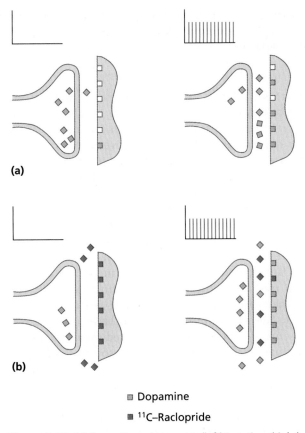

(a)

(b)

▢ Dopamine

◼ ¹¹C–Raclopride

Figure 5.51 (a) Dopaminergic neuron (left) inactive, (right) active (b) after injection of a substance that competes for occupation of the receptors (left) dopaminergic neuron inactive, (right) active.

and occupies receptors to dopamine, indicated by areas of red and yellow. Next, when haloperidol is injected, this occupies dopamine D2 receptors and is in competition with ¹¹C-Raclopride (right of figure). Note that occupation of receptors by ¹¹C-Raclopride falls.

Microdialysis

A fraction of any neurochemicals released by the activity of neurons moves into the extracellular fluid surrounding their terminals. Investigators wish to know what is happening within this chemical environment of animals' brains as they behave.

Using a technique termed 'microdialysis', a probe is inserted into the brain and fixed to the skull (Figure 5.53). Fluid is passed into and out of the probe, and that leaving is analyzed chemically for its content. Chemicals present in the extracellular environment of the brain are able to pass into the tip of the probe and mix with the fluid that is passing. Their presence can later be detected.

Therefore, this technique can provide insight into the timing of neuronal events defined by particular neurotransmitters at particular sites. For example, researchers are interested in which neurochemicals are activated when an animal injects itself with a psychoactive drug through an implanted tube.

¹¹C-Raclopride PET scan

Coregistered MRI scan

¹¹C-Raclopride PET scan

Before treatment

Haloperidol 2 mg/d (74% Occ.)

Figure 5.52 Use of ¹¹C-Raclopride in a PET scan. Left: before haloperidol administered, showing in red and yellow, regions of high occupation, implying a high density of occupation of dopamine D2 receptors. Right: after haloperidol administration, showing lower density of occupation (regions now represented by light blue colour). Centre is an MRI scan of the same brain to act as a source of reference for the structures of the brain.

Source: By courtesy of Professor Shitij Kapur.

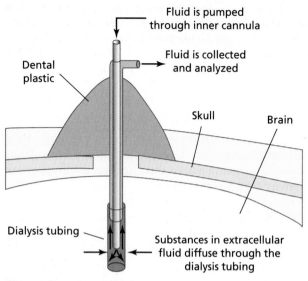

Figure 5.53 Microdialysis.

Source: Carlson (1998, Fig. 5.27, p. 138). Reprinted by permission of Pearson Education, Inc.

Brain damage

Introduction

The observation of behaviour following brain damage provides insight into how the brain works. Brain damage can arise in several ways:

1 A result of gunshotwounds, traffic accidents, missiles in war and suicide attempts as in poisoning with gas.

2 A result of 'natural pathology' of the brain. Examples include a tumour and the disruption of neural activity associated with a **stroke**. A stroke can be caused by blocking an artery in the brain (Figure 5.25) or rupture of a blood vessel (Gardner, 1982).

3 Therapeutic interventions into the brain of humans in the form of surgery, e.g. cutting the corpus callosum to prevent disruption in one hemisphere influencing the other. The surgery in response to, say, a tumour can cause changes in brain function.

4 In the case of non-humans, experimental damage made to a specific region of the brain in order to study the effect on behaviour.

We normally assume that, if a type of behaviour is lost following damage to a brain region, then that region normally exerted a role in the control of the behaviour (Gardner, 1982). Understanding the effects of damage is rarely straightforward and needs subtle interpretation. The brain is an integrated system and a disturbance at one location will have influences elsewhere. Brain tissue other than the intended target might get damaged. Similarly, axons passing through the area might be damaged and there could be a disruption of their influence

in regions some distance away. Other brain regions might be able to compensate and thereby mask the effect of damage.

Pathology, accidents and surgery

Regrettable as they are, strokes, tumours, wars, crime and accidents have produced a rich insight into how the brain functions. A complication for the investigator is that normally damage is to several regions and is associated with general trauma. It is difficult to establish exactly where the damage is. However, development of techniques such as MRI is giving an increasing possibility of establishing localization.

The loss of function following brain damage in, say, a stroke is sometimes revealing in that relatively clear fracture lines of behavioural disruption appear (Damasio and Damasio, 1983). Thus, a patient might lose the ability to read and write while preserving speech intact. In other cases, reading is lost but writing remains intact. The writing of only certain classes of word, e.g. nonsense syllables, can be disrupted (Shallice, 1981). Examination of the brain regions associated with such specific losses can give insight regarding the normal flow of information and how this is disrupted.

Experimental lesions

In non-humans, damage can be made to the brain in order to investigate its effect. Specific parts of the brain, e.g. a particular nucleus, can be targeted. This damage is termed a **lesion** and the procedure is called lesioning (though 'lesion' can also refer to natural damage such as that caused by a blood clot). Surgical removal of part of the brain is a form of lesioning but here the more specific term **ablation** is also employed. A somewhat counter-intuitive terminology is used to describe such a subject: for example, an animal with the hippocampus removed is termed a 'hippocampal'. The means used to lesion the brain depend upon the intended target. Being on the outside of the brain, specific locations on the dorsal surface of the cerebral cortex can be identified and targeted with surgical knife cuts. Of course, deeper regions of brain require some form of penetration from the surface.

Under anaesthetic, an animal's head can be held in a fixed position in what is termed a 'stereotaxic apparatus' and 'stereotaxic surgery' performed. See Figure 5.54. A stereotaxic atlas is a three-dimensional map of the brain, which enables the exact coordinates to be located. With the help of a stereotaxic atlas, an electrode can be inserted into the brain until the tip is where the lesion is to be. By passing a particular electrical current through the tip, a region of brain can be selectively lesioned. Following the experiment, the animal is killed and its brain examined histologically to make sure that the lesion was at the intended site.

Figure 5.54 Stereotaxic apparatus.
Source: Carlson (1998). Reprinted by permission of Pearson Education, Inc.

For an example of the difficulty of interpretation, suppose that a lesion is followed by excessive drinking. This suggests that regions of brain concerned with inhibition of drinking have been damaged. However, the effect might also be due to disturbance to urine production (as you saw in Chapter 3, hormones secreted at the brain play a role in urine production). In this case, excessive drinking is secondary to water loss. Further experimentation is required to tease apart these possibilities.

Another way of lesioning a brain region is to employ toxic chemicals that specifically target and damage cell bodies, sparing axons in the vicinity. This protects axons that are passing through the region. Using toxic chemicals, one particular class of neuron, as characterized by its neurotransmitter, can be damaged. Thus, a toxin that selectively targets, say, dopaminergic neurons might be injected. This can either be applied generally or specific brain regions can be targeted.

Brain stimulation

Specific brain regions can be stimulated by chemical or electrical means. By the same stereotaxic surgery as just described, an electrode can be inserted and fixed in place. Wires can be joined to the electrode that is attached to the animal's skull and electric currents delivered to selected brain regions. The electrode and the magnitude of the current are such that neurons are stimulated. In the scientist's 'ideal case', stimulation of a site triggers behaviour whereas lesioning the same site disrupts it.

Modern technology permits the outer regions of the human brain to be stimulated by means of a powerful magnetic field applied just to a local region of the brain. This is known as **transcranial magnetic stimulation**

(TMS) (Figure 5.55). Depending upon the frequency of the magnetic field that is applied, the underlying neurons can either be excited or inhibited relative to their spontaneous level of activity. The technique therefore permits researchers to investigate the effects of overactivity or under-activity of a particular brain region in terms of the participant's psychological state and behaviour. For example, at a certain frequency of stimulation and targeted at specific regions of the brain (areas of the frontal lobe), speech will be disrupted leaving other faculties relatively intact. This enables a mapping between brain structure and the function that it serves.

Recording through implanted electrodes

In living animals (including humans), experimenters sometimes need to know what particular neurons are doing under particular conditions. Recordings can be made from a group of a few neurons or even from individual neurons while a non-human animal is stimulated with, say, light or while it explores its environment. An electrode with a very fine tip, capable of recording from single neurons, is termed a **microelectrode**. The technique of making recordings of this kind is termed 'single-unit recording' (Carlson, 1994).

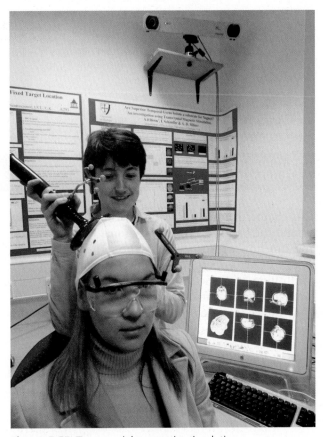

Figure 5.55 Transcranial magnetic stimulation.
Source: Science Photo Library Ltd: UNIVERSITY OF DURHAM/SIMON FRASER

The electrode is chronically implanted in the brain, i.e. fixed to the animal's skull and inserted until the tip is in the region of interest. Wires are attached to the electrode and these are connected to an apparatus for recording electrical activity. A cat, for example, is anaesthetized and its head held in a stereotaxic apparatus. The experimenter then stimulates the retina with light and the activity of, say, a retinal ganglion cell is monitored on a screen.

Another type of investigation is where an animal is free to move within a cage and correlations are observed between behaviour and electrical activity in particular neurons. For example, by this means, O'Keefe and Dostrovsky (1971) identified 'place cells', neurons that fire when an animal is in a particular place in its environment.

Section summary

1 Techniques are available for tracing neural pathways in the brain.

2 Electron microscopy enables details of cellular form and connections within the nervous system to be revealed.

3 Electroencephalography (EEG) is a technique for recording the gross electrical activity of the brain with surface electrodes.

4 Neuroimaging techniques consist of structural (MRI) and functional types (fMRI and PET).

5 Functional neuroimaging enables the activity of different brain regions to be monitored.

6 A valuable source of insight is brain damage, though results need to be handled with caution.

 ## Test your knowledge

5.11 Suppose that a chemical is injected into the lateral geniculate nucleus of a living animal. (i) Suppose also that it is taken up by the cell body of neurons located there. By means of anterograde labelling, where might it be expected ultimately to appear? (ii) Suppose also that it is taken up by axon terminals. By means of retrograde labelling, where might it appear?

5.12 Complete the following sentence: 'Under conditions of artificial injection, brain regions that are particularly active tend to accumulate relatively large amounts of _____'. (i) Glucose, (ii) 2-deoxyglucose (2-DG).

Answers on page 149

Bringing things together

This chapter has shown how to start to find your way around the brain and to identify some key landmarks. You can now appreciate better how the brain serves its role in perception, motivation and emotion and in controlling both the somatic and autonomic outputs introduced in Chapter 3.

As the chapter has shown, ways of gaining insight include a detailed description of brains, looking at differences between brains in different species (comparative psychology) and manipulating the brain by lesioning and stimulation. Knowledge of neurons and their associated neurochemicals (Chapter 4) is valuable in plotting pathways and understanding what they do.

Sometimes simpler systems, e.g. invertebrates, provide 'animal models' of more complex systems.

More recently developed techniques such as PET and fMRI have radically improved our ability to observe the working brain.

 See the video coverage for this chapter to understand how studying the brain enriches psychology.

Summary of Chapter 5

1 An understanding of the nervous system requires universally agreed conventions of orientation within it and anatomical description of its parts.

2 Information is brought to sensory processing regions of the brain via identifiable pathways. Distinct regions of the brain organize motor control and execute movement via identifiable motor pathways to muscles.

3 In exerting control on the external environment, the brain processes and utilizes emotional and motivational information. The brain regulates the internal environment of the body and there is special regulation over the brain's own environment.

4 Based on extensive processing of information done beyond the dedicated sensory regions, the brain forms predictions of the future. A brain region having a role in the associated control of behaviour is the prefrontal cortex.

5 Insight into how nervous systems work can be gained by comparing different species, in terms of their brains and their solutions to the control of behaviour.

6 Techniques used in the study of the brain include tracing pathways, microscopic examination of brain regions, brain neuroimaging, electrical recording of brain activity and studying the consequences of brain damage.

Further reading

For all of the material in this chapter, see Gazzaniga *et al.* (2008) and Nolte (2008). For brain anatomy, see J.H. Martin (1996) or Martini *et al.* (2008). For a comparative perspective on the brain, see Butler and Hodos (2005) and on the basal ganglia, see Reiner *et al.* (1998). For the frontal lobes, see Miller and Cummings (2007). For techniques, see Carlson (2009). For neuroimaging, see Bremner (2005).

Answers

Explanations for answers to 'test your knowledge' questions can be found on the website www.pearsoned.co.uk/toates

5.1 Cell bodies of the dopaminergic neurons are located in region A, while a bundle of their axons (forming a tract) extend to region B, where dopamine is released.

5.2 (ii) Contralaterally

5.3 (ii) The inferior colliculus

5.4 (a) (i) A_2, (ii) A_1, (iii) C_2, (iv) C_1, (v) D_2, (vi) D_1 (b) (i) B_2, (ii) A_2

5.5 (i) The axons of ganglion cells that form the optic nerve; (ii) the axons of LGN cells ('optic projection fibres') that convey the message to the visual cortex.

5.6 (i) Ventral horn of the spinal cord

5.7 Cerebrospinal fluid; cell bodies of neurons

5.8 (i) High frequency of action potentials in neurons located there; (ii) planning and/or executing action.

5.9 (iv) Node of Ranvier

5.10 Engineer; tinkerer

5.11 (i) Their axon terminals in the visual cortex. (ii) At the cell bodies in ganglion cells in the retina.

5.12 (ii) 2-Deoxyglucose (2-DG)

Visit www.pearsoned.co.uk/toates
for a range of resources to support study.
Test yourself with multiple choice questions and access a bank of over 100 videos that will bring the topics to life.

Chapter 6
Development and plasticity

Learning outcomes for Chapter 6

After studying this chapter, you should be able to:

1 Describe what the term 'environment' can mean and link the terms 'environment', 'cell', 'genotype' and 'phenotype'.

2 Outline some conceptual traps in studying development. Explain how they can be avoided by careful analysis and use of language.

3 Describe the changes in the structure of cells and their connections, which constitutes neural development.

4 Explain the role of hormones in development. Thereby, distinguish 'organizational effects' and 'activational effects'.

5 Show how cognitive and social development can be linked to biological development.

6 Give examples of the types of influence that can disturb normal development and how their effects can be characterized in biological and psychological terms.

7 Illustrate how a comparison between species can help understanding of the principles of development.

8 Describe plasticity in adults with examples.

Scene-setting questions

1 How did you develop from a single fertilized cell to the person you are today?
2 Are genes a 'blueprint', a plan for a future construction?
3 Are discussions of the role of 'genes versus environment' useful or misleading?
4 What makes us male or female?
5 Can a bad upbringing damage the brain?
6 Is the adult brain fixed or flexible?
7 Is exercise good for your brain?

Is exercise good for your brain? Explore the video on the website accompanying this book at www.pearsoned.co.uk/toates

How does the social context affect the developing brain of an infant, involving its cognitive and emotional aspects?

Source: Getty Images/Iconica.

Introduction

At fertilization, life begins as a single cell, a fertilized egg (a 'zygote') and thereby the genotype is formed (Chapter 2). In humans, starting from this single cell, there *develops* a body having a nervous system that ultimately contains some 100 billion neurons and probably even more glial cells. This chapter is about how nervous systems and behaviour develop from fertilization.

In mammals, development, growth and change of the **embryo** (also termed 'fetus'), starts in the uterus and continues after birth. Development depends upon genes and environment. The term 'environment' means several things: (i) the chemical environment that surrounds the genes within each cell, (ii) the fluid environment surrounding the cells and (iii) the environment within the uterus or, in birds, the egg. Later there are the external physical and social environments.

For a given species, some features of the early environment are similar (Chapter 2). For mammals, there is a similar origin in a uterus. Subsequently, feeding is via the mother's breast and the environment has some common social dimensions. Comparable to the influence of genetic similarity of individuals, environmental consistencies tend to give some common directions to early development (Hofer, 1988). Environments are similar but, of course, not identical. Identical twins illustrate the interactive nature of development: they are genetically, but not phenotypically, identical. They commonly exhibit differences in, for instance, size at birth, suggesting a different availability of nutrients prior to birth.

Because development of the nervous system and behaviour are inextricably linked, understanding either needs consideration of both. Looking at changes in the nervous system during development provides insight into changes in behaviour. Different brain regions develop at different rates, corresponding to changing functional demands. Hence, the behavioural controls that are available and the possibilities for behaviour also change (Diamond, 1996; Prechtl, 1982).

Some biological measures (e.g. electrical activity of the brain) made at around the time of birth, or earlier, have predictive value concerning features appearing later (e.g. hearing defects) and can suggest therapies. Psychological indices, e.g. mental retardation, are important in diagnosis of developmental disorders, to be considered alongside biological indices such as abnormal levels of hormones. Disturbances to a baby's development, as a result of biological or chemical disruption (e.g. the mother drinking alcohol), are manifest in later disruptions of behaviour.

In rats, an enriched environment tends to enrich connectivity between neurons in the developing brain (Petrosini *et al.*, 2009; Rosenzweig *et al.*, 1996). If this principle applies to humans, its social implications are potentially enormous. For the developing child, inadequate social conditions, such as parental neglect, are manifest in abnormal development in certain brain regions (Teicher *et al.*, 2004).

The term 'plasticity' (Chapter 3) refers to the capacity to exhibit change. In other words, given a particular genotype, it represents the capacity for *variation* in the phenotypic characteristics that can emerge dependent upon different environments.

Those processes that exhibit plasticity during development are also sometimes capable of limited plasticity in the adult. For example, they can compensate to some extent for disturbances, such as neural damage, a property termed **malleability** (Cairns, 1979). This is relevant to therapies for overcoming the effects of neural damage. Conversely, knowing when underlying processes have become inflexible is relevant to the stubborn refusal of adult behaviour to show plasticity under some circumstances.

Early in the study of development, it is useful to clarify some conceptual issues that lie behind our understanding of it, the topic of the next section.

Conceptual issues in development

This section looks at some issues in development, considering some pitfalls and how to avoid them. For example, confusion surrounds the interdependence between gene, developing biological structure and environment. Analogies are useful in getting a grasp of this issue.

Analogies

Analogies can capture important similarities with psychobiological processes. However, any analogy will also differ from real psychobiological development. Analogies can be misleading in subtle ways but recognition of where the analogy fails can also be an important guide.

One analogy is that development is like a ball rolling down grooves on a hill (Waddington, 1936, 1975) (Figure 6.1). At the top (fertilization), there are more possibilities for the ball's trajectory than when it is nearer the bottom (adulthood). As it descends, the future direction becomes more constrained. By analogy, development becomes less open-ended as it progresses. However, the analogy fails to capture the dynamic interaction involved in development – the ball changes the grooves!

Another analogy is that genetics is like an architect's plan for a construction, whereas development is like the work of the builder (Rosenzweig *et al.*, 1996). Neither the architect's plan nor the genotype can contain enough information to specify every local 'decision' in construction. Such plans would be impossibly complex and hopelessly inefficient (ask any builder). So, the builder's implementation of the plan is achieved by taking local circumstances and materials into account. Given two identical plans, differences in construction are inevitable. Through biological evolution or architectural practice, plans ('genotypes') that are proven to work will survive.

So far, so good, but the analogy has a serious weakness: an architect's plan ('blueprint') describes what the building will *finally* look like. By contrast, in spite of the common use of the term 'blueprint' in biology, the genotype does not specify an end point (Gottlieb, 1998). Genes cannot provide a reference against which 'correct' or 'wrong' development is compared. There is not enough capacity in the genes to encode for all the details of an adult. The gene exerts effects on the course of development but the environment does the rest. Thus, we need caution even in an expression such as 'a gene for blue eyes'. Such a gene is different from one 'for' brown eyes but the gene acting in isolation does not create the blue eyes.

Learning and development

How do we distinguish development and learning? Should we even try? Is learning a subdivision of development? I am sorry that you have just had three rhetorical questions. I would love to give clarification but I cannot put my hand on my heart and come up with it.

There are cases that psychologists would unambiguously call 'learning', e.g. an adult learning a foreign language. Although there are other situations, which psychologists would usually call 'developmental' but not 'learning', they

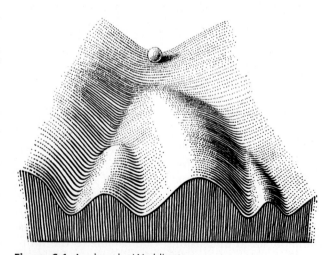

Figure 6.1 Analogy by Waddington.
Source: Bonner (1958, *The Evolution of Development*, Cambridge University Press, Fig. 10, p. 44).

can never assert that no learning is involved. For a young animal, change usually involves both development and learning, as traditionally understood.

The term 'learning' normally refers to change that is peculiar to a particular individual within a particular environment. For example, young children in France learn French and those in Britain learn English. These different changes in behaviour are not to be explained in terms of initial differences within the brains of the two sets of children. Rather, they reflect different linguistic environments.

As an attempt at definition, 'development' describes a sequence of general changes that are more dependent simply upon time since fertilization than of specific experiences peculiar to an individual. Changes that occur in the nervous system corresponding to development are sometimes described as **maturation**, e.g. formation of a myelin coating around axons. Development proceeds in a way that is less subject to differences of personal experience. However, development does not proceed independently of the environment, since an animal can only exist provided that it is within a certain range of environments. It is possible to define certain species-typical routes of development that are apparent within a range of different environments. For instance, developmental changes occur in the brain mechanisms underlying language. Provided that there is exposure to a language, some of these are similar whether it is, say, French or English to which the child is being exposed.

In some important respects, development is a process that cannot be reversed. We can hardly take a mature rat and reconstruct the infant form! By contrast, learning can, in at least some respects, be 'reversed'. We can first teach a dog that food is to the left and no food to the right. We can then teach it that food is to the right. However, the distinction between learning and development is becoming more blurred all the time.

Right from time zero

From the start, there are subtle conceptual traps for investigators. For example, consider that more dominant mothers tend to give birth to sons rather than daughters. How could the status of the mother influence the sex of the child, since surely the male contribution of an X or Y chromosome determines this (Chapter 2)? The male indeed determines the sex but the hormonal condition of the female might determine whether sperm carrying an X or Y chromosome can more easily penetrate the egg cell and fertilize it (Grant, 1994a,b).

Consideration of the determinants of sex raises the possibility that the uterine environment surrounding a male might on average be different from that of a female.

A personal angle

Henry VIII of England

Henry VIII was angered by his wives' failure to produce a son, blaming them. Suppose that Henry had today's textbooks of biology and psychology to consult. He would have discovered that the sex of the child is determined by the father, which presumably would not have pleased him. However, Henry might have found a 'get-out' in the suggestion that mothers can bias which type of sperm is most likely to fertilize. A psychologically dominant mother will tend to favour sperm containing a Y chromosome. So, from the perspective of inheritance (though not from that of marital harmony), Henry might have been advised to select his wives on the basis of dominance.

The dynamics of development

The developing nervous system influences behaviour and is influenced by behaviour, while the animal *influences* and is *influenced by* each environment that it encounters. Following birth or, for birds, hatching, there is an abrupt change of environment. This section looks at this interactive nature of biological and psychological development.

The embryo

Investigators need to be attentive to what can reach the developing embryo from the outside world. Elements of the environment, e.g. the sound of television, penetrate even to the human foetus. That really is something to worry about.

Does an embryo already *behave*? There is evidence for coordinated responses. The interactive nature of development can be summarized as (genetic activity) ↔ (body structure) ↔ (behaviour), meaning that each is affected by the other (Gottlieb, 1998). Thus, behaviour of the embryo has implications for the structuring of the body including the nervous system and its links to the muscular system.

Later stages

Development is influenced dynamically at different levels (Figure 6.2). Interactions occur between cells. Cells change shape and function. A combination of cells contributes to the physical form of the animal, which exists within an external environment. Gene activity ('gene expression') forms the nervous system, the basis of behaviour (Champagne and Mashoodh, 2009).

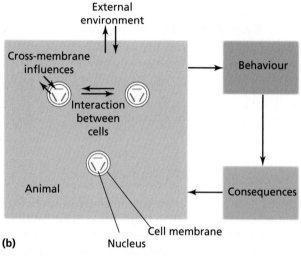

Figure 6.2 Determinants of development. (a) Modified from a model of Gottlieb (1997, Fig. 5.4). The downward pointing arrow from 'neural activity' to 'genetic activity', represents an aspect of the observation that events within the body can affect gene expression (Champagne and Mashoodh, 2009). (b) A cell interacts with its extracellular environment and thereby with other cells. The nucleus containing the genes influences, and is influenced by, the cell's intracellular environment. The whole animal interacts with its external world by behavioural and non-behavioural routes. The consequences of behaviour alter such things as the hormonal environment of the body which can have multiple effects, e.g. on gene expression.

Consideration of the physical environment shows the interactive nature of development. For example, there is fine-tuning of connections within the visual system that occurs following exposure of the eyes to visual stimulation (Blakemore, 1973). Considering the social environment, behaviour has consequences for the individual and for others.

It is often assumed that there exist *distinct* inputs to development. In rejecting any such clear dichotomies, Michel and Moore (1995, p. 76) assert: 'It is not necessary – in fact, it may not be possible – to begin a psychobiological analysis by separating biological from psychological components'. Why?

As Michel and Moore (1995, p. 101) express it: 'The organism and its environment are in a reciprocal relationship. The environment shapes the organism and its behaviour, while simultaneously, the organism and its behaviour are shaping the environment'. For example, in understanding the development of a newborn mammal, the mother cannot be described as an independent entity since her reactions are affected by the offspring's behaviour (Stern, 1997). Reciprocally, developing biological structure is inevitably influenced by the social environment (Gottlieb, 1997).

A human baby typically elicits such emotional reactions as smiling, while the mother's reaction of smiling or rejection affects the baby's emotional reactivity. Comparing depressed and non-depressed mothers, differences are also seen in their babies, mediated in part via differences in social interaction. These might have lasting effects on the infant's emotional development (Dawson, 1994).

Consideration of interactions poses problems for analysis of the role of genes and environment (Michel and Moore, 1995). For instance, siblings might be said to inhabit the same environment and this might be so in terms of such things as food intake and room temperature. However, genetic differences might manifest in, say, different personalities, such that siblings are treated differently by parents and hence their social environments are not equal (Plomin, 1989). This section shows the need to advance beyond simple analogies of genes and environment, these being like, for example, two sides of a rectangle (Chapter 2). Although such an analogy can improve upon certain fallacious assumptions, it does not capture the *dynamics of interaction*.

Determinants and developmental time

Development does not proceed as if driven by an inner clock regardless of the environment. In using the concept of age, is it time from fertilization or, when it concerns events following birth, postnatal age that should be considered (Schulte, 1974)? For some aspects, time from fertilization can provide a more reliable predictor of development than postnatal age, irrespective of whether the latter part of the time was spent *in utero* or not.

What measure can be used for when the nervous system has reached maturity? One possibility is myelination. Some neurons are surrounded by myelin, which facilitates the passage of action potentials (Chapter 4). Different parts of the nervous system acquire myelin at different times (Bronson, 1982). The timing of acquisition reflects the functional significance of the emerging neuronal systems. In humans, some myelination of sensory and motor pathways is evident at five or six months before birth. Subcortical regions start myelination next, with cortical regions myelinating last. Some myelination of pathways to and from the cerebellum still occurs up to three years of age, mirroring increasingly refined motor control.

Myelin can be necessary for the functioning of a structure. For example, the capacity of the corpus callosum (Chapter 5) to convey rapidly information from one hemisphere to the other depends upon myelination of its axons (Salamy, 1978). However, we cannot assume that myelination proceeds regardless of information processing within the neurons concerned. The degree of myelination depends to some extent upon the activity of the neurons around which it forms its sheath.

Another index of development is the electrical activity of a region of the brain (Chapter 5). If two animals are of the same chronological age but have differing degrees of myelination and electrical activity, this could alert us to possible developmental differences between them.

Functional considerations

Of course, to pass on genes, an animal has to survive during development and move to sexual maturity. Genes are selected because of the success of their contribution to development and beyond (Gottlieb, 1973). Some adaptations serve the here-and-now by their consequences at the current developmental stage. So, during development, behaviour both serves present needs and is a preparation for maturity.

Developing animals find themselves in very different environments from adults (e.g. uterus, egg) and need adaptations to cope with them. For example, by suckling, mammals gain nutrients but the processes that underlie it are different from those of adult feeding (A.N. Epstein, 1990). Suckling is not something that gets successively refined until the adult feeding pattern emerges. It is more like the first stage of a multistage space vehicle: necessary for survival and movement early on but which can be jettisoned when a later stage takes over.

Twin studies

Twins can provide a natural and well-controlled experiment. They attract attention from researchers, who try to tease apart the contribution of genes and environment. This section considers some of the issues that this raises.

Types of twin

Twins are one of two kinds: **monozygotic twins (MZs)** (or 'identical twins') and **dizygotic twins (DZs)** (or 'fraternal twins'). MZs derive from a single zygote

and are genetically identical. Therefore, any differences between them in, say, cognitive ability can be attributed to 'environmental differences' (considering environment in a broad sense). Each member of a pair of DZs derives from a separate zygote and so they are not genetically identical.

The extent to which twins correlate in something, e.g. height or IQ, is known as their **concordance**. Thus, if genetic differences play a role in determining differences in behaviour, a higher concordance of MZs on a number of dimensions would be predicted. The concordance of MZs is commonly found to be higher than that of DZs (Phelps *et al.*, 1997) and this is usually attributed to the influence of identical genes.

Twins that are reared apart are sometimes said to share no common environment. However, this ignores the womb and the fact that it must offer some common features as an environment (Phelps *et al.*, 1997). Conversely, it might be assumed that twins, whether MZ or DZ, share an identical environment in the womb and differences in environment start from birth. Take the case of MZ twins. Since they are genetically identical, differences can be attributed to differences in environment. If the environment of the womb is identical, then any difference in environments would start only after birth. However, it is difficult to imagine that the environment of the womb for the twins is absolutely identical, even though it is doubtless very similar. For example, one twin might be located in the womb more comfortably than the other.

Identical twins are identical genetically but what other factor is very similar when they are compared? How might we try to separate the influences of these factors?

Source: Alex Bartel/Science Photo Library.

Section summary

1 Analogies can capture certain features of development.

2 The terms 'plan' or 'blueprint' imply a representation of an end point, which is not how genes operate.

3 Genes interact with the cellular environment that surrounds them, while the whole animal interacts with the external environment.

4 Developing biological structure, including the nervous system influences, and is influenced by, the environment. The infant's biological form and behaviour affect the social environment.

5 Stages of myelination give some indication of development.

6 Some specific adaptations serve the here-and-now only during development.

7 A comparison of monozygotic and dizygotic twins provides insight into development.

☞ Test your knowledge

6.2 In Figure 6.1 and by analogy, the nervous system being relatively 'hard-wired' would be associated with which part of the slope? (i) The top, (ii) the bottom.

6.3 Complete the following sentence: 'The process of ___ associated with the development of functioning neural connections via axons gives rise to an increased speed of conduction of action potentials'.

6.4 Complete the following sentence: 'Monozygotic twins derive from a single ___ and have identical___ but different ___ .'

Answers on page 183   WEB

The basic biology of nervous system development

Introduction

The nervous system does not exist in a miniature form in the zygote. In development, neurons appear, grow and sometimes establish functionally appropriate connections with other cells (Grobstein, 1988). Sometimes all or part of them dies. So, how do developing neurons know where to go, what to extend and what form to take? For example, a frog darts its tongue out at a bug and has a good chance of hitting it. Such sensory-motor coordination implies that, during development, appropriate functioning connections between *particular* cells are formed: sensory neurons, interneurons, motor neurons and muscles.

Gross structural changes

The human zygote, the first cell, is about the size of the full-stop ('period') that terminates this sentence. Within 12 hours of fertilization, this cell divides (Chapter 2) into two cells. In turn, these also divide to give four cells and so on, such that the number of cells within the embryo rapidly increases. Figures 6.3 and 6.4 show part of nervous system development (Martini *et al.*, 2000).

The pattern of cell division is not even and the unevenness contributes to the formation of distinct structures. Figure 6.3 (at 21 days) shows the formation of neural folds and the neural groove. By 22–23 days, the neural folds come together to form the 'neural tube'. The neural tube is made up of 'stem cells', those that will form neurons and glial cells. The length of the tube defines the axis rostral–caudal of the developing CNS, e.g. the caudal 50% or so becomes the spinal cord and the remainder defines the brain. The cavity of the tube is destined to define the fluid-filled spaces of the CNS (Chapter 5): the cerebral ventricles and the central canal of the spinal cord and interconnections. The neural crest contains the cells destined to form the peripheral nervous system (Figure 6.3).

Figure 6.4 shows the development of the brain and cranial nerves from age 23 days. By 23 days, what will become the divisions of the brain emerge, e.g. the swelling that will become the forebrain. Behind it, two swellings are destined to become the midbrain and hindbrain. At a late stage of development, distinct and characteristic gyri and sulci are also evident.

Analyses suggest some increase in number of neurons at least up to the age of six years (Shankle *et al.*, 1998). The increase in weight of the brain seems to be due to an increase in the number of glial cells and neurons, as well as a growth of existing neurons.

The volume of the human cerebral cortex at birth is about one-third that of the adult (Huttenlocher, 1994).

The main period of growth is in the first year. Synaptic density reaches its peak at around three years, at a level 50% higher than that at birth and puberty (Bruer, 1998). However, fine structural changes continue until adulthood, corresponding to the appearance of new cognitive capacities. The number of neurons in the cerebral cortex appears to double between the ages of 15 months and

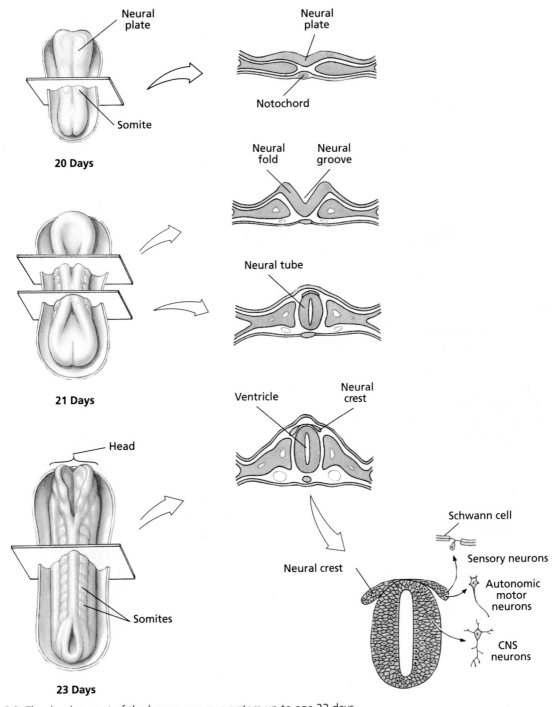

Figure 6.3 The development of the human nervous system up to age 23 days.

Source: Martini *et al.* (2000, p. 338). Copyright © 2000, 1997 by Frederic H. Martini, Inc. and Michael J. Timmons. Reprinted by permission of Pearson Education, Inc.

6 years (Shankle *et al.*, 1998). Development is not a one-way process of growth and increasing complexity. It is also associated with a loss of some neurons and neuronal connections (Edelman, 1987).

To understand the changes in gross structure (Figures 6.3 and 6.4), you need familiarity with the underlying changes that occur at the cellular level, the next topic.

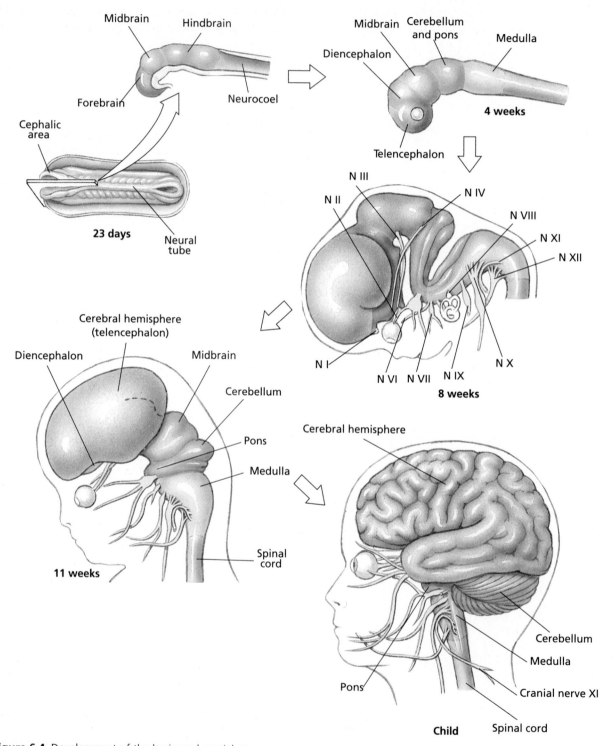

Figure 6.4 Development of the brain and cranial nerves.
Source: Martini *et al.* (2000, pp. 416–417). Copyright © 2000, 1997 by Frederic H. Martini, Inc. and Michael J. Timmons. Reprinted by permission of Pearson Education, Inc.

Changes at a cellular level

Considering development at the level of changes within, and between, neurons, theorists identify *stages* (Rosenzweig *et al.*, 1996). In humans, most changes occur prior to birth. There is some overlap and simultaneity between stages of development. Therefore, we might consider them as different processes of change rather than clear-cut events in a predetermined time-sequence. When things go wrong in these stages, adult behavioural pathology can result (Nowakowski and Hayes, 1999).

Figure 6.5 shows a summary of these stages, which are as follows:

1 *Neurogenesis*. This consists of repeated cell division (Chapter 2) among the cells of the neural tube, so as to form new cells (Figure 6.5(a)–(c)).

2 *Migration*. There is a movement of neurons from their place of origin to another location, where the final anatomical location of neurons starts to be established (Figure 6.5(d), (e)).

3 *Differentiation*. Distinct types of neuron are formed from a standard precursor neuron (stages 2 and 3 can overlap). Neurons start to produce extensions, termed neurites, which will form axons and dendrites (Figure 6.5(f), (g)).

4 *Synaptogenesis*. Accompanying the growth of axons and dendrites, synaptic connections between neurons form (Figure 6.5(h)).

5 *Selective death of neurons*. Neurons that fail to establish functioning synapses (stage 4) tend to die (Figure 6.5(i)). Contact alone may not be sufficient for survival, as represented here by the yellow cell.

6 *Synaptic reorganization*. Some synaptic connections are strengthened and others weakened (compare Figure 6.5(i) and (j)). If the outcome is weakening as a result of a failure to establish a functioning link, it might lead to cell death (compare Figure 6.5(h) and (i)).

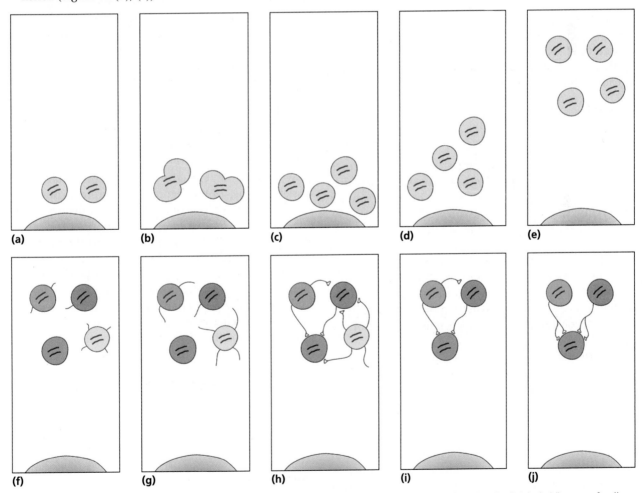

Figure 6.5 Development: (a) cells initially located by the ventricle, (b) cells starting to divide, (c) cells divided, (d) start of cell migration, (e) migration complete, (f) start of differentiation, (g) continuation of differentiation, (h) synapses formed, (i) death of some cells and (j) synaptic restructuring.

As noted earlier, in humans, the number of neurons that will finally be present has not been reached at birth. Thus, at a time that some brain regions are still at stage 1, others have reached stage 6.

We shall now look at these stages in more detail.

Neurogenesis

The process termed **neurogenesis** (stage 1; Figure 6.5(a)–(c)) constitutes the formation of neurons from general ('precursor') cells. The diagram can represent only a very small part of this sequence of cells dividing and then these newly formed cells in turn dividing, and so on. When the process of repeated cell division ceases, this initial stage of early development has reached a stable point. This point in time represents the birth date of neurons. The neurons so formed then tend to migrate from the location associated with their birth.

Cell migration

How do cells migrate from their location of birth to another location, where they will perform their role in the functioning nervous system (stage 2; Figure 6.5(d), (e))? There exist chemicals that attract particular cells and guiding factors that influence the direction taken by them. For example, in some cases 'radial glial cells' already exist and these guide growing neurons (Rakic, 1971). These radial glial cells act something like the wires that gardeners use to grow peas and other vegetables.

Differentiation

Different cells acquire different shapes and structures and serve different functions, a process termed **differentiation** (stage 3). This occurs because, among other things, genes exert different effects at different times. The initial trigger to this is termed **gene expression**. That is, various genes are switched on, meaning that they start to trigger the manufacture of proteins. Proteins form a physical base of the developing structure of neurons. For example, in a particular neuron at developmental age t_1, switching on $gene_1$ results in the production of $protein_1$, which might be part of the physical base of a dendrite.

In vertebrates, development of a particular neuron is generally determined by a *combination* of intrinsic factors and a range of possible immediate environments (e.g. hormones surrounding the cell or events at neighbouring neurons) (Gottlieb, 1997).

Various factors determine the environment of a neuron. In the development of mammals, one general factor is the current nutrient status of the mother. A deficiency of an essential component needed to make a protein will interfere with the ability of genes to express

themselves in protein construction. An excess of a toxic element such as alcohol might similarly have a disruptive effect.

A 'specific factor' is one that applies particularly to the neuron(s) under consideration. For example, the timing of gene expression can be determined by chemical influences from neighbouring cells. An influence of one group of cells on events within a neighbouring cell is termed **induction** (Purves and Lichtman, 1985). For example, in some neurons of the ANS, the neurotransmitter that a neuron synthesizes (e.g. acetylcholine) is determined only after it establishes contact with smooth muscle (Harris and Hartenstein, 1999). One consequence of induction is that, if a neuron gets damaged, others might be able to respond to the message and, to some extent, compensate for the role of the missing one, a phenomenon termed 'regulation'.

Neurons grow. They come to assume complex shapes and form connections with other cells. Axons and dendrites grow out from the cell body (Brown *et al.*, 2001). Consider some related questions. What determines the 'tree-like' shape that mature neurons commonly take, with branches: axons and dendrites? What determines the connections made between neurons? Interactions between what are initially relatively distant cells (e.g. two neurons) determine the direction that growing extensions take, their form and their connections. How do cells that are physically separated manage to interact with each other in such a way as to determine their form and interconnections?

Central to such interactions is a feature of the growing neuron termed a **growth cone** (Raper and Tessier-Lavigne, 1999) (Figure 6.6). A growth cone is the swollen ending of an extending axon or dendrite, with fine extensions termed 'filopodia'. Consider the case of an axon. Filopodia attach themselves to their environment and then grow out, something like ivy growing over a building. In doing so, they pull the axon behind them. They are attracted towards chemical cues in their environment, termed **chemoattraction**. These cues are signals from other cells, some of which, the attractors, form targets for the axon with its growth cone serving

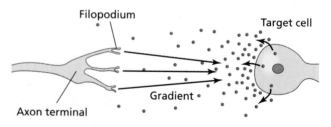

Figure 6.6 Growth cone.

as path-finder. As the growing axon gets nearer the target, the concentration of chemoattractive substance increases. The growth cone seems to ascend a gradient of chemical concentration (rather like a male moth ascending a gradient of chemicals released into the air by a female or like a heat-seeking missile maximizing infrared stimulation) (Whatson and Sterling, 1998).

Often the growing axon extends relatively large distances for which the chemical signals emitted by target cells might initially be too weak to direct it. How does it 'know' where to go? Again, interactions with other cells play a role. Along the trajectory of many axons, a series of 'guidepost cells' are found, like beacons crossing the countryside in former centuries. These are cells that space out the distance between the start and end of the trajectory. The growing axon is attracted to first the nearest and then the next guidepost cell until it nears its target. In many cases, several cues such as guideposts and chemoattraction by the final target act together to determine the trajectory.

Yet another guidance system is provided by 'pioneer axons' (Raper and Tessier-Lavigne, 1999), which start the journey first. Other developing axons then follow the trajectory set by the pioneers. This guiding process is termed 'fasciculation', meaning that functionally related axons that will come to form a neural pathway tend literally to stick together (Bear *et al.*, 1996). There are molecules termed 'cell-adhesion molecules' on the surface of growing axons and these bind axons together.

Cell life and death

During development, many neurons die (Edelman, 1987). This varies from 20% to 80%, depending on the region of nervous system. Some compare this to evolution by natural selection (Chapter 2), with the fittest neurons and connections surviving and the less fit dying. For neurons, fitness is determined by their success at establishing contact with other cells and passing information (Figure 3.14 on p. 62). An abundance of cells accompanied by selective cell death represents competition, between one cell and its neighbour, for an influence over targets. Something about making contact helps to protect neurons from destruction. What is it about the target cell that decides its new-found neighbour's life or death?

Physical contact itself might be enough to secure the fate of some neurons. A life-giving chemical, termed a **neurotrophic factor** (or 'chemotrophic factor'), is secreted by target cells and taken into cells with which they make contact (Purves, 1994). In some neuron–target interactions, a specific neurotrophic factor termed **nerve growth factor (NGF)** has been identified (Purves, 1994).

Among other places, it acts within the sympathetic branch of the ANS (Chapter 3). NGF produced in target cells in smooth muscle is taken up by axons that innervate them and is transported to the cell body. It exerts survival-promoting effects on the presynaptic neuron.

In the absence of a neurotrophic signal, **programmed cell death (PCD)**, also termed 'apoptosis', can occur (Oppenheim, 1999). The death of cells has functional significance for the establishment of an effective nervous system. In many cases PCD is the result of the expression of 'suicide genes' that initiate the cell's own self-destruction. It appears that they trigger the clearance of what amounts to the refuse of a non-functional cell and thereby allow recycling of its useful chemical constituents.

Damage to an afferent input during development is usually associated with atrophy of its target region in the brain (Purves, 1994). Development of sensory areas of the brain requires a minimal level of appropriate input.

Establishing physical contact can be a necessary, but not sufficient, condition for the continued existence of the extensions of a neuron. A synapse might need to be operative, in conveying messages, for a survival-enhancing effect of contact to be felt (Figure 6.5(h), (i)).

Synaptic restructuring

As just noted, when a growing axon meets its target cell, it stops extending. Synaptic contact is made and this contact tends to consolidate the link in the form of structuring the synapse (Lichtman *et al.*, 1999). Rather as whole neurons live or die according to their experience during development, so synapses are strengthened or eliminated as a result of their connections and functioning in terms of transmitting messages. Transmitting messages tends to strengthen, as a self-reinforcing effect.

Seen in a broader context of influences, the life or death of a synapse and thereby part or whole of a neuron can depend upon interactions between the animal and its external environment (Rosenzweig *et al.*, 1996) (Figure 6.2). Suppose that the survival of a particular neuron depends upon it forming part of a functioning neural circuit. Whether a circuit functions or not can depend upon the motor output and behavioural consequences. That is, behaviour causes changing sensory stimulation, which provides an input to developmental processes. The fate of the individual neuron is locked into its role as part of the whole system (Grobstein, 1988).

We now consider some cases of the development of neurons in the context of the neural systems of which they form a part and the behaviour with which they are associated.

Section summary

1 Viewed at a cellular level, there are six stages to development:

(a) Neurogenesis: repeated cell division, the formation of neurons from general precursor cells.

(b) Migration: the movement of neurons from their place of origin to their destination.

(c) Differentiation: distinct types of neuron are formed from a standard precursor neuron.

(d) Synaptogenesis: the formation of synaptic connections between neurons.

(e) Selective death of neurons.

(f) Synaptic reorganization: changes in the strength of synaptic connections.

2 The development of neurons is a function of intrinsic factors as well as their immediate environment.

3 Induction refers to the effect on one neuron of events in neighbouring neurons.

4 Growth cones have a role in 'navigating' the course of a growing axon.

5 Target cells attract axons.

6 Neuronal survival can depend upon a neurotrophic factor secreted by target cells, e.g. nerve growth factor.

 ## Test your knowledge

6.5 Which two of the following suggest the strengthening of a synapse by the establishment of a functional connection? (i) An increase in number of postsynaptic receptors, (ii) a decrease in number of postsynaptic receptors, (iii) an increase in number of presynaptic vesicles, (iv) a decrease in number of presynaptic vesicles.

6.6 Which of the following classes of neuron is most likely to be attracted to a smooth muscle cell? (i) Dopaminergic, (ii) serotonergic, (iii) cholinergic.

Answers on page 183

Development of neurons, neural systems and behaviour

Introduction

In development, how do the changing properties of neurons and their interconnections give rise to changes in behaviour and cognition? How does feedback from behaviour and the environment act upon neural structures? This section addresses these issues.

According to contemporary understanding, developmental changes in behaviour and cognition are *bound to be* associated with changes in the brain. Non-invasive technologies (Chapter 5) for studying the brain permit a picture of the changing activity of its regions (Fischer and Rose, 1994). Psychologists can try to relate this to both changing neural interconnections and to cognitive and behavioural changes. In some cases, changes in gross electrical activity in regions of cortex can be related to changes in synaptic growth and pruning and to cognitive development.

When does development cease? Is it when the animal is mature, as suggested by the analogy of a ball rolling down a hill and arriving at the ground? This is one definition. However, adult nervous systems are not static and some of the same kinds of reorganization of neural connections that occur during development are also seen in the adult (Purves, 1994). When a change occurs in an adult, e.g. damage to an axon, some compensatory reactions are seen (Whatson and Sterling, 1998). The analogy with building would suggest that, even after the house is complete, some repairs and extensions might occur, using similar principles to those used in its initial construction. Learning is an example of plasticity ('malleability') that is retained in adulthood. So, this section considers a continuity of principles that give plasticity to developing systems and, in a more limited way, to adult systems.

Neuron–neuron connections

General

When new demands are placed upon an adult, neural plasticity can sometimes be seen. For example, the female mammal is posed new problems when she suckles young for the first time. In rat mothers, neurons within regions of the somatosensory cortex are triggered via sensory input derived from tactile stimulation at the nipples. The cortical area concerned increases in size when suckling begins (Xerri *et al.*, 1994).

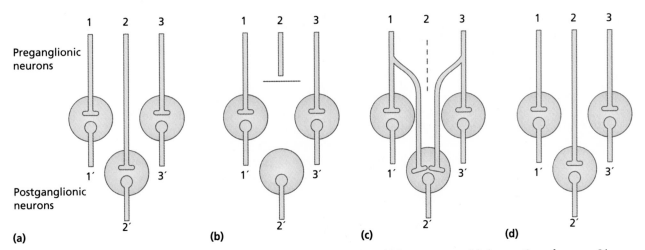

Figure 6.7 Growth of axon branches and synapses following denervation: (a) intact system, (b) denervation of neuron 2′, (c) sprouting of axon terminals from 1 and 3, and (d) reinnervation from axon 2.

Source: after Purves (1994, p. 59).

There can be competition between axons to innervate a target neuron. Figure 6.7 shows an example of this in a mature system (Purves, 1994). In (a), three axons (1, 2 and 3) innervate three target neurons (1′, 2′ and 3′). In (b), axon 2 is cut such that the innervation of neuron 2′ is lost. In response (part (c)), sprouting occurs, triggered by chemical factors released from neuron 2′. That is to say, loss of innervation of neuron 2′ (termed **denervation**) provokes the formation of new axon branches from neurons 1 and 3. The control of 2′ by 1 and 3 is not necessarily permanent. If 2 re-grows, it can reinnervate 2′ and displace the innervation by axons 1 and 3 (part (d)).

An example of competition for control of a target is provided by vision, discussed next.

The visual system

In the developing human visual system, the connections that form between neurons depend upon activity within the system, which is initially triggered by light (Blakemore, 1973; Hubel and Wiesel, 1965). So, what developmental processes bring this system into being? Before answering, let us digress briefly to consider the properties of the adult visual system, which we seek to explain.

Figure 6.8 should remind you of the neural connections from retinal ganglion cells (forming the optic nerve), to the lateral geniculate nucleus and then to the visual cortex. Note the cross-over of some axons of retinal ganglion cells at the optic chiasm. Thereby, each hemisphere derives inputs from each eye. Electrical recordings can be made from cortical neurons while each eye is stimulated with light. The cortical neuron can then be categorized according to the strength of input to it. This ranges from evenly binocular, i.e. being driven with equal weighting by either the ipsilateral eye (that on same side as the brain region) or contralateral eye (that on opposite side to the brain region), to heavily monocular, i.e. being driven predominantly by input coming from either ipsilateral or contralateral eye.

Figure 6.9 shows the inputs to a sample of neurons in the visual cortex and compares normal development (part (a)) with when a squint has been produced in one eye (part (b)). In part (a), most neurons are binocularly driven (groups 3 and 4). Some (group 1) are driven only by the contralateral eye and others (group 2) are mainly contralaterally driven. Some (group 7) are driven only by the ipsilateral eye. In part (b), relatively few neurons are driven equally by both eyes. A large number are influenced by only one eye.

For a cortical neuron to be captured by an input from both eyes, it seems that corresponding regions of the retina need to provide input to it. As you view the present *word* in the text, its image falls on each retina. Neurons from this same region project to cortical neurons and activate them. Hence, firing of cortical neurons represents an integration of the detail of information within *word* in the two eyes. If the eyes are unable to perform this integration because a squint disrupts eye movements, then one dominant connection will tend to capture all the input to the cortical neuron.

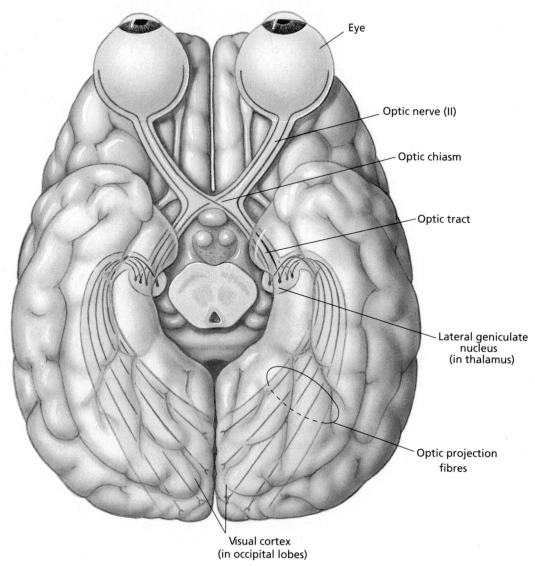

Figure 6.8 Visual pathways.

Source: Martini *et al.* (2000, Fig.15-23, p. 407). Copyright © 2000, 1997 by Frederic H. Martini, Inc. and Michael J. Timmons. Reprinted by permission of Pearson Education, Inc.

Neuron–muscle connections

Introduction

There is plasticity in the developing neuron–muscle connections and also some plasticity in these connections in adults. Adult muscles develop with exercise, whereby the size of existing muscle cells increases and new cells are formed. Their innervation derives from sprouting of neighbouring axon branches (Figure 6.10).

Spontaneous movement

A necessary condition for movement is the establishment of functional synapses between motor neurons and muscles. As evidence for the early appearance of such links, every mother knows that the foetus is not passive but shows considerable motor activity. During **gestation** (the period from fertilization to birth or hatching), the embryos of all species that have been studied exhibit movement at some stage (Hamburger, 1963). For example, prior to hatching, chicks show responsiveness to sensory stimulation, coordinated activity and some spontaneity (Provine, 1988). Early spontaneous movements appear to be random but then coordination is imposed on this. Given the array of spontaneous movements, Robinson and Smotherman (1988) suggest a selection process by which certain are chosen, comparable to the developmental selection of neurons and synapses (discussed earlier).

The triggers to survival

Consider the axon of a cholinergic neuron that establishes contact with a muscle cell (Whatson and Sterling, 1998). Following contact, there is an increase in density of cholinergic receptors at the postsynaptic membrane and heightened electrical activity within the muscle cell. At the presynaptic membrane there is an accumulation of vesicles. The presence of a functional connection between neuron and muscle then triggers differentiation of the muscle cell. The link is consolidated by chemical messages passing in both directions between the functionally joined cells.

Figure 6.11 shows the effects on dendrites of loss of innervation to a target cell. Note their retraction when contact is lost and their regeneration once innervation of the smooth muscle is regained.

Figure 6.9 Histograms showing the responses of neurons in the visual cortex of adult cats: (a) normal and (b) after a squint has been produced.

Source: Hubel and Wiesel (1965), *Journal of Neurophysiology*, Fig. 5, p. 1049 Am Physiol Soc, used with permission.

Figure 6.10 Sprouting of axon branches to innervate newly formed muscle fibres: (a) original system, (b) development of new muscle fibre and (c) extension of axon branch to innervate new fibre.

Figure 6.11 Effects on a neuron's dendrites of the loss of innervation of a target by a neuron's axon: (a) normal, (b) immediately after loss, (c) two weeks after loss and (d) after regeneration of the axon and restoration of innervation.
Source: after Purves (1994, p. 62).

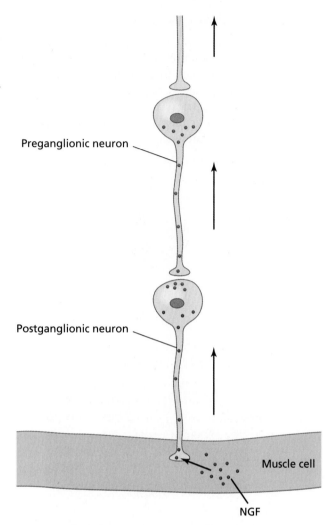

Figure 6.12 Feedback effects triggered by a target.
Source: after Purves (1994, p. 66).

What is the feedback signal that promotes neural connections? Nerve growth factor (NGF) plays a role in the development of the growing nervous system by promoting survival of neurons (Purves, 1994). Figure 6.12 shows a suggestion regarding axons in the sympathetic branch of the ANS (Purves, 1994). The target tissue, smooth muscle, produces NGF, which is taken up by receptors on the postganglionic neuron. NGF promotes the survival of this axon. NGF is also transported to the cell body, where it has several effects. It promotes the survival of dendrites (Figure 6.11). In the presence of NGF, the postganglionic neuron produces a chemical which, in turn, promotes the connection between the preganglionic and postganglionic neurons.

The following section looks at hormones, considering links with developing neural structures.

Section summary

1 Changes in neurons and their interconnections can be associated with changes in nervous systems and then to changes in cognition and behaviour.

2 Similar principles to those underlying early development also apply (in a more limited way) to plasticity in adults.

3 In adults, as in developing systems, structural and functional connections tend to exert a self-reinforcing effect.

4 In the absence of such connections, links tend to get weakened.

5 There are regulatory processes such that, when an input is missing, other sources of input can increase their effects and tend to take over.

 Test your knowledge

6.7 In Figure 6.8, the neurons represented by green in the half of the brain to the left of the figure receive which kind of input from the eye? (i) Ipsilateral, (ii) contralateral.

6.8 In Figure 6.12, along which type of neuronal structure does NGF travel in getting to the cell body?

 Answers on page 183   WEB ➡

Hormones and development

Introduction

As described earlier, hormones are chemicals secreted into a blood vessel and transported in the blood to another location, where they occupy receptors and produce action. This description was of a so-called **activational effect**. However, in addition, there is the 'organizational' role of these same hormones in development.

Organizational and activational effects

Hormonal effects are divided into **organizational effects** and activational effects (see Fitch and Denenberg, 1998). An organizational effect is a permanent, or semi-permanent, change in the *structure* of part of the nervous system that occurs (most often) during development as a result of hormones.

Figure 3.28 (p. 72) showed occupation of receptors by hormone at the surface of a cell. Another mode of action is for the hormone to penetrate the cell and affect the cell's nucleus. Occupation of receptors at the nucleus by hormone affects gene expression and thereby protein synthesis and the formation of new structures, e.g. sprouting of dendrites. Such structural changes (exemplifying organizational effects) were thought to be possible only during a **sensitive period** (sometimes termed a 'critical period') within early development. An example of an organizational effect is the role of sex hormones in the early development of the nervous system, exerting a bias towards one type of adult sexual behaviour or another.

By contrast, an activational effect of a hormone was traditionally thought not to involve structural changes (Fitch and Denenberg, 1998). It would commonly be seen in an adult animal and involve transient changes in the property of neurons. For example, by occupying receptors at a neuron, a hormone might make it easier to generate action potentials. Activational effects either occur for only so long as the hormone is present at the neuron or last for only a short time following removal of the hormone. The *structure* of neurons would be unaffected by whether their receptors are occupied by hormone, even though their functioning is changed.

To some extent, the original distinction still holds: some irreversible structural effects on the developing nervous system contrast with reversible effects in the adult. However, the distinction is not as clear-cut as it once appeared (Fitch and Denenberg, 1998). In some cases, hormones can induce structural changes also in adult nervous systems. For example, maintenance of the structure of the adult hippocampus relies upon the continued presence of hormones.

There is plasticity of some neural systems throughout life and these are said to be 'permanently transient'. This can depend upon the presence of hormones. For example, natural fluctuations in sex hormones in female rats are associated with changing *structures* within the hypothalamus and thereby changes in sexual behaviour (Fitch and Denenberg, 1998). In women, changes in some neural connections follow changes in hormone levels during the menstrual cycle (Stahl, 1997). Thus, a hormonal effect lies somewhere on a continuum (that qualification seems to tell the story of psychology!) rather than being within one of two distinct categories of organizational or activational.

The development of the brain depends on the presence of circulating hormones (Gould *et al.*, 1991). For example, the hippocampus contains receptors for hormones of gonadal origin (the **gonads** are the male testes and female ovaries) and hormones secreted from the adrenal gland among others. Changes in their levels can affect the development of the hippocampus and thereby affect later learning. For example, an animal deficient in hormone might have fewer dendritic spines and less chance for plasticity of connections.

Sexual development

Introduction

The term **sexual development** refers to the development of sex organs and neural systems underlying sexual attraction and behaviour, as well as secondary sexual characteristics such as, in humans, breaking of the male voice.

Our biological sex is determined by chromosomes (Chapter 2). The cells of a normal male have an X and a Y chromosome. Those of the female have two X chromosomes. This is fixed at fertilization and remains the same throughout life. In the period shortly following fertilization, the structures that will later come to underlie the reproductive system (e.g. testes, ovaries, brain mechanisms) have the potential to develop into a male or female form. Comparing genetic males and females at a very early stage, termed the 'sexually indifferent stage' (Reinisch and Sanders, 1992), these structures are identical. Initially, the term 'gonad' refers to an organ that can become either testis or ovary. The gonad, as with the rest of the reproductive structures, is initially *undifferentiated*. The structures later become differentiated.

Differentiation

The term **sexual differentiation** (Phoenix *et al.*, 1959) refers to forming *either* a typical female *or* a typical male reproductive system (e.g. genitals and brain mechanisms of motivation) from an undifferentiated precursor structure. Sexual development has some striking similarities across species of mammal (Morris *et al.*, 2004). This means that researchers can gain insight into humans by studying rats. However, extrapolation must be done with caution, since, of course, humans have a unique sexual self-identity and culture. What triggers differentiation?

In early development, a gene on the Y chromosome in males will normally induce the gonads to become testes. They release a class of hormone termed **androgen**, which (acting with other factors) causes the reproductive system to take the male form. Testosterone is a principal androgen. In the absence of the Y chromosome and thereby the absence of secretions of androgens at typical male levels, the gonads normally become ovaries and the reproductive system takes the female form (Reinisch and Sanders, 1992).

Before birth and shortly afterwards as part of differentiation, hormones play a role in establishing the structure of the CNS processes that later underlie sexual behaviour (Fitch and Denenberg, 1998). With a focus on rats, researchers have established a principal site of action of testosterone at a nucleus of the preoptic area of the hypothalamus (POA) (Morris *et al.*, 2004). See Chapter 5, Figure 5.31, p. 128. (The term 'nucleus' refers here to a collection of cell bodies forming a structure.) This nucleus is termed the **sexually dimorphic nucleus (SDN)**, meaning that it has two ('di') different *morphologies* or structures, comparing male and female rats. So, the structure is abbreviated as SDN-POA. It is several times larger in males than females. Such differential development of the male nervous system is a feature of what is termed **masculinization** and involves the action of testosterone. In females, natural cell death occurs in this nucleus, a process that is inhibited by the local hormonal environment in males.

In some species, androgens cross the cell membrane of neurons in regions such as the SDN-POA and attach to receptors in the cell's nucleus (sorry – but note the abrupt switch in meaning of the term 'nucleus'). These neurons later form part of the motivational processes underlying sexual behaviour. However, in other species (e.g. rats), androgens are converted chemically to oestradiol (yes – it is as if nature set out to confuse us), which then occupies receptors (Fitch and Denenberg, 1998). This conversion is termed **aromatization**. See Figure 6.13. Androgens or their aromatized product alter the expression of genes within the cell. This causes, for example, cells to survive when they would otherwise die, to extend dendrites or to form synapses. In females, oestrogens play a role in differentiation.

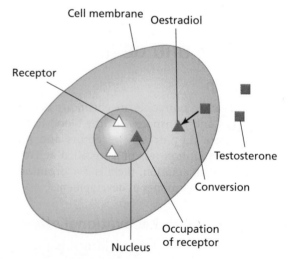

Figure 6.13 Entry of an androgen (testosterone) to the inside of a neuron of the male rat. In this case, it is then converted to oestradiol. Oestradiol occupies receptors at the nucleus, which then triggers the action of masculinization of the neuronal systems so affected.

As determinants of adult sexual preference and behaviour, the social context (e.g. maternal behaviour) plays a role in interaction with these early hormonal influences. For example, in humans, there can be different reactions towards the growing child depending upon whether it possesses male or female genitalia (Reinisch and Sanders, 1992).

In rats, the nervous systems of both sexes possess the basic processes (neural circuits) that underlie the later performance of male sexual roles (e.g. mounting and thrusting) and female sexual roles (e.g. assuming an arched receptive posture). Depending upon the early hormonal environment, one or both of such behaviour types, masculine and feminine, can be observed later in either sex. That is, the neural circuits can be more or less strengthened or weakened and thereby more or less reactive to a given stimulus depending upon the early hormonal environment.

Presumably, the basis of such sexual differentiation is that certain synapses between neurons can be strengthened or weakened, hence making more or less effective connections within the circuit (Figure 6.14). The neural circuit of which 1 →1' forms a part might underlie mounting, whereas that involving 3→3' might underlie a receptive posture.

A nervous system with a strong potential to trigger typical male behaviour is termed 'masculinized'. One with a strong potential to trigger female behaviour is termed 'feminized', a process known as **feminization** (Reinisch and Sanders, 1992). In males, testosterone secreted by the testes has a masculinizing and defeminizing effect on such CNS structures. In rats, brain structures are given a bias towards playing a role in typical male mating and away from the typical female pattern (Figure 6.15(a)).

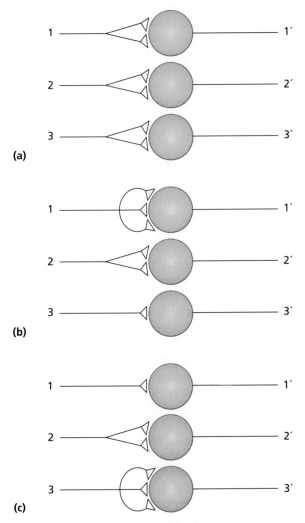

(a)

(b)

(c)

Figure 6.14 Some simple neuronal connections. (a) Initial, undifferentiated form, showing excitatory (neurons 1 → 1', 2 → 2' and 3 → 3') synapses. (b) Form changed by hormone exposure. Note strengthening of 1 → 1' and weakening of 3 → 3'. 2 → 2' remains unchanged. (c) Different change induced by a different hormonal environment. Note converse effect from (b): strengthening of 3 → 3' and weakening of 1 → 1'.

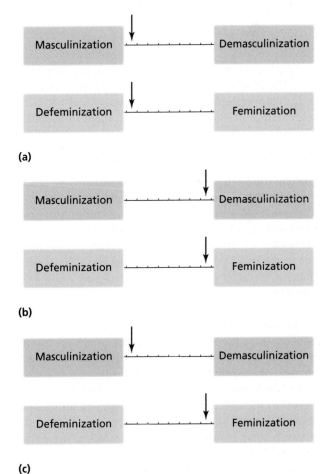

(a)

(b)

(c)

Figure 6.15 Sexual differentiation: (a) masculinization and defeminization, (b) demasculinization and feminization and (c) masculinization but no defeminization.

An absence of testosterone results in *demasculinization* and *feminization* and so the normal process that underlies female sexual behaviour emerges (Figure 6.15(b)). Normal females (and males denied access at this early developmental stage to testicular hormones) show a bias towards female behaviour and away from male behaviour. Female rats exposed early in life to androgens tend to show more male-typical behaviour and less female-typical behaviour when adult (Beach, 1975; Phoenix *et al.*, 1959). Under some conditions, an animal might be masculinized but not defeminized, thus having a strong potential to exhibit both forms of behaviour, e.g. mounting and adopting the receptive position (Tobet and Fox, 1992) (Figure 6.15(c)).

These organizational effects of hormones occur only at a particular stage of development (i.e. before and just after birth). Hence, psychologists would refer to a 'sensitive period' ('window of opportunity') during which they occur. Hormones that appear following sexual maturity normally act upon these organized structures to activate them in a way that contributes to sexual behaviour (McCarthy and Albrecht, 1996).

Human sexual development

Can the general principles just described also be applied to humans, or does social context play the dominant role? The actions, (1) masculinization and defeminization or (2) feminization and demasculinization, might occur somewhat as in other species. Clearly, there are normally two different sequences (genes) → (hormones) → (genitalia), which distinguish males and females. In the human brain, there is some difference between males and females, particularly in the preoptic area, analogous to sexual dimorphism in other species (Tobet and Fox, 1992).

However, it would be wrong to see genes and environment as two *independent* categories. Thus, the possession of different genitalia can then trigger different reactions, expectations and self-images. It is possible that some gender differences in sex role, etc. arise from assuming gender identities (Morris *et al.*, 2004).

After having exerted developmental effects, sex hormones remain relatively inactive until puberty. At puberty there is a further input from gonadal hormone to sexual development. For example, in girls the breasts enlarge, whereas in boys, the voice breaks. Reinisch and Sanders (1992) refer to a 'multiplier effect' in the determination of human sex differences, meaning as follows. At fertilization, the only difference between sexes is in chromosomes. In males, there then occurs differentiation of the testes, with production of testosterone. Comparing males and females, this creates different hormonal environments for the developing foetus. These are associated with differences in development of sexual characteristics and CNS processes.

Following birth, the social context interacts with the developing child to produce sex differences. Boys will typically be treated differently from girls. One supposes that humans alone possess the notion of **gender identity**. Normally, at an age of between 2 and 4 years, a child acquires the concept 'I am a girl' or 'I am a boy' (Bancroft, 1989, p. 159). Events in the world, reactions and inner feelings are subsequently interpreted in terms of the concept. Hormonal and social influences play roles in forming this concept but psychologists imagine that, once acquired, it biases the interpretation that is placed upon experiences and knowledge related to sexuality. These different treatments and expectations will be encoded in the growing child's brain.

At puberty, the adult level of hormones is secreted and this promotes the development of sexual characteristics which serve to enlarge differences between the sexes. On the basis of their physique, muscle mass and secondary sexual characteristics, etc., boys will again typically be treated differently from girls (Mazur and Booth, 1998).

Unusual hormonal conditions

There can be unusual hormonal effects in humans ('natural experiments') and important insight can be obtained by studying such individuals. For example, before birth some girls are exposed to high levels of testosterone produced by the adrenal gland, termed **congenital adrenal hyperplasia (CAH)** (Berenbaum, 1999). Girls with CAH show some masculinization of the genitals and a tendency to engage in male-typical play. On becoming adult, most girls with CAH are heterosexual but a larger percentage is homosexual as compared with controls. There is a shift towards male-typical occupations. Could this be because of parental treatment, the girls' own learned self-image or a hormonal masculinization of the brain? We don't know, but Berenbaum argues for early masculinization of the brain.

Some genetic males (i.e. with XY chromosomes) produce normal levels of testosterone but have a dysfunction in the gene coding for the androgen receptor, termed a **complete androgen insensitivity syndrome (CAIS)** (Hines *et al.*, 2003). Hence, androgens cannot exert their effect. At birth, CAIS individuals appear to be girls and are unambiguously treated as this. As adults they have female bodily characteristics and assume a female gender identity, with a sexual orientation comparable to that of control women. Thus, hormonal environment overrides what might otherwise be expected to occur based on chromosomal sex.

Section summary

1 Certain hormones have organizational and activational effects.

2 The distinction between early organizational and later activational roles is relative rather than absolute.

3 During the sensitive period, hormones exert an organizational effect on sexual organs and neural structures. In the adult, hormones exert an activational effect on these structures.

4 Androgens play a role in masculinization and defeminization.

5 Oestrogens secreted by the ovaries play a role in feminization.

6 There are some peculiarly human features of development that apply to sexuality, such as conscious awareness of gender identity.

Test your knowledge

6.9 Complete the following sentence: 'In order for a hormone to be able to target receptors at the cell nucleus, it must be able to cross the cell ____'.

6.10 Which of the following effects are organizational and which activational? (i) A hormone induces the growth of new dendrites, (ii) for so long as the hormone is present at receptors on the neurons' surface, there is a facilitation of the generation of action potentials.

Answers on page 183 WEB

The brain: cognitive and social development

This section relates changes in brain processes to changes in cognition and behaviour. It also considers briefly social development. It starts with a focus on development of the cortex seen in the context of other brain structures.

Cortical and subcortical structures

The normal timescale of development

In human newborns, the regions that are most active metabolically and, by implication most developed, are the primary sensory-motor cortex, thalamus, brain stem and cerebellum (Chugani, 1994). These structures are described as 'phylogenetically old', meaning that, relative to, say, the prefrontal cortex (Chapter 5) they emerged at an early stage of evolution. The behavioural repertoire of newborn humans is controlled predominantly by subcortical structures, including those underlying reflexes (e.g. the grasp response) organized at a brain stem level. The pattern of activity across brain regions of newborns is sometimes seen in older children who have suffered brain damage. In the latter case, an abnormal persistence of so-called primitive reflexes is also observed. This points to a failure of cortical mechanisms to exert control over subcortical processes (Chugani, 1994).

In the first year, cortical development is indicated by the increasing formation of synaptic links, the appearance of more adult EEG patterns and an increase in cortical glucose metabolism (Schulte, 1974). Functional development, in terms of visuo-spatial integration with the motor system, corresponds to anatomical development. Chugani (1994, p. 159) remarks that: 'the ontogeny of glucose metabolic patterns proceeds in phylogenetic order, with functional maturation of older anatomical structures preceding that of newer areas'. The last area to show maturation is the frontal cortex, corresponding to the acquisition of so-called higher cognitive abilities, discussed next. The cortex has greater plasticity than subcortical structures and is more strongly sensitive to experience (Elman *et al.*, 1996).

The plasticity of cortical connections is central to ideas about development, e.g. the role of genes and environment (Elman *et al.*, 1996). Distinct cortical regions normally emerge, each dedicated to processing only visual, auditory or somatosensory information (Chapter 5). When a sensory input is abnormal, neurons can be taken over by other sensory inputs, so that boundaries between cortical areas show plasticity. For example, regions that process the spoken word in people with hearing can be 'captured' by the visual system, so as to process visuo-manual information associated with sign language in deaf children. In other words, cortical boundaries depend in part upon sensory inputs.

We now look at a specific example of cortical development in the context of the input from subcortical structures.

Vision: an example of cortical and subcortical interactions

Starting at a very early age, the human infant has a tendency to look at faces. The adaptive value is clear: faces signal vital information. In the beginning, the process appears to be organized at a subcortical level. Features bearing even some crude resemblance to those of a face trigger attention (Elman *et al.*, 1996). Of course, in the real world the initial trigger would be an actual human face. Using subcortical processes as a base, this focus of attention upon certain features possessed by a face leads to a build-up of more refined cortically based representations of the unique features of a human face.

There has been a tendency to explain this behaviour as *either* learnt *or* innate (see critique by Elman *et al.*, 1996). Thus, it represents respectively the outcome of either a history of reinforcement from staring at an arbitrary object or the product of an innate face recognition process. The existence of the disorder **prosopagnosia**, a defect primarily in face recognition in brain-damaged adults, has been used as evidence for an innate face recognition module.

An alternative explanation takes a middle course between the extremes. Face recognition becomes 'modularized', i.e. brain circuits become specialized for this as the child gains experience with faces. As Elman *et al.* (1996, p. 116) express it: 'Some minimal face-specific predispositions give development a kick start in this domain'. This kind of analysis does more than simply assert that both genes and environment are involved. Rather, it shows the nature of their interdependence.

Evolutionary psychology

Localization of function

In the spirit of evolutionary psychology, it is sometimes argued that the localization of function, i.e. area x has responsibility for processing information X, is evidence for the innate genetic specification of brain structure. To use a favoured expression, 'innate systems have inherited their own dedicated neural architecture' (see Elman *et al.*, 1996, p. 378 for critique).

As Elman *et al.* somewhat ironically point out, with the advent of PET scans investigators are finding an ever-increasing number of such apparently dedicated systems. For instance, in chess-masters, specific regions of the brain are active at particular points in the game. Yet surely no one would suggest that dedicated chess-playing modules are genetically specified!

We now turn to the development of one particular cortical region.

The role of representations

Introduction

An aspect of development consists in acquiring the ability to utilize *representations* of events (Piaget, 1954) (Chapter 5). Prior to this, the animal is dependent upon the stimuli themselves to trigger behaviour. For representations to control behaviour, they need to be held 'on-line' in the absence of the corresponding sensory stimulation. For example, when an object goes out of sight, continued pursuit of it depends upon a particular sort of memory, a representation, of the missing object.

There are several tasks which require (a) representations of events, (b) a focus of attention on a particular representation and (c) the suppression of any tendency to respond to other features. The fact that, in children, mature performance on these tasks appears at roughly the same age, suggests maturation of a common underlying process (Diamond *et al.*, 1994a, b). For example, in the **object permanence task**, a child observes an object being hidden behind a screen. Early in development the child acts as if such objects that have gone out of sight cease to exist. At a later stage, the child acts on the basis that they still exist (Piaget, 1954). If the object is to be retrieved, the child needs to act on the basis (a 'representation') of its existence and to inhibit any rival tendencies. This skill is acquired at a stage of development.

Brain regions

Development of the prefrontal cortex is closely implicated in the object permanence task (Fischer and Rose, 1994). EEG activity (Chapter 5) at the prefrontal cortex appears to be an index of the memory being utilized in behaviour; when children succeed in retrieving the object, activation is seen. Those who fail the task do not show activation. Also, on successful performance, an integration of activity between the prefrontal and occipital cortices is seen, suggestive that the solution involves simultaneous utilization of sensory information (e.g. the cover and the hand) and representations (of the hidden object). A rapid growth of synapses in the prefrontal cortex corresponds to acquisition of this capacity and the appearance of the associated EEG pattern.

The **A-not-B test** is a measure of one feature of cognitive development and can be related to brain development (Diamond, 1996). A human infant is seated before a table which contains two identical wells. The experimenter places a favourite toy in one well, either to the left or right, while the child observes this. The wells are then covered. A delay is imposed (e.g. 0–10 seconds) and then the child permitted to reach. If the child reaches to the correct target, the hidden toy is revealed. After the child has succeeded at the task a few times, the well in which the toy is hidden is reversed. Following reversal, children tend to make the mistake of persisting with the original choice rather than reversing. Increasing the length of the delay makes the task more difficult. With increasing age, children get more proficient: a longer delay is needed in order to induce them to make the error of repeating what they did on earlier trials.

A failure to perform this task correctly is seen by human infants of age 7.5–9 months, infant macaque monkeys of age 1.5–2.5 months and adult macaques who have suffered bilateral removal of the dorsolateral prefrontal cortex (Diamond *et al.*, 1994a,b). After suffering prefrontal brain damage, adult humans also experience difficulty. How do we explain this? Reaching to A earns a reward, and, with repeated experiences, there is a strengthening of this tendency. Following a move of the bait to well B, success requires inhibition of the tendency to reach to A. Diamond (1996, p. 1485) suggests that:

> it is when we must act in a different way than our first inclination and when at least some of the information needed for action must be held in mind that dorsolateral prefrontal cortex is most clearly required.

The ability of adult monkeys to perform tasks that involve representations depends upon dopaminergic projections to the prefrontal cortex. Development of the ability corresponds to increases in levels of dopamine in the prefrontal cortex. In humans, it appears that this structure is not fully mature until the age of 10 years.

We now consider development of a social representation.

Social development and autism

A key notion in social development is that children normally acquire a 'theory of mind' (ToM) of the other (Baron-Cohen, 1999), i.e. the understanding that others have *intentions* (Chapter 5). Successful social interactions depend upon making decisions based upon this assumption, for example, *I think* that *Mary thinks* that the apple is in the box and therefore *I think* she will look there to find it. Some argue that there is a dedicated **theory of mind mechanism (ToMM)**, which extracts information on the intentions and desires of others (Leslie, 1999).

The condition termed **autism** represents a different course of social development. There are deficiencies in social communication and behaviour and in use of the imagination in solving social problems. That is, it represents a deficiency in ToM. There is a deficiency specifically of a type of social cognition, in the absence of a more general cognitive deficit. It appears that the ToMM is compromised.

Evidence points to a genetic component in autism. So, which brain regions are different comparing people with autism and controls? Various structural neuroimaging studies have found that very young children with autism have larger brains than controls but the evidence is conflicting on whether this difference is maintained into adulthood (Hyde *et al.*, 2010). This draws attention to differences in brain development and trying to link gross brain structure to the cellular level. In people with autism, differences have emerged in certain brain regions thought to be involved in social cognition, e.g. anterior cingulate cortex. Theorists suggest that social cognition recruits representations of the self in modelling the minds of others. An important basis for the encoding of 'self representation' is the ventromedial region of the prefrontal cortex (VM PFC) (Lombardo *et al.*, 2010). Participants were observed using fMRI while 'self-metalizing' and under-activity was found in the VM PFC and regions of cingulate cortex of people with autism. In autism, increased cortical thickness was shown (relative to controls) in the visual and auditory cortex. This might be mapped to enhanced perceptual abilities shown by children with autism (Hyde *et al.*, 2010).

Section summary

1. In human newborns, phylogenetically older brain regions tend to be the most active.

2. Phylogenetically older brain regions control stimulus-driven behaviours.

3. With development, metabolic activity increases in phylogenetically newer regions that underlie cognition.

4. Development involves acquiring both cognitive and social skills.

☞ Test your knowledge

6.11 Which term accurately completes the following: 'The ___ of dopaminergic neurons are located in the prefrontal cortex'. (i) Cell bodies, (ii) axon terminals.

Answer on page 183

Atypical development and health issues

This section considers some factors that can disrupt normal development. Studying atypical development provides useful insight into typical development (Munakata *et al.*, 2004).

Nutrition

The developing brain is very vulnerable to disruption from malnutrition (Kar *et al.*, 2008). In humans, a positive relationship exists between (1) malnutrition during gestation and up to age 2 years and (2) a lowering of scores in measures of cognitive performance (Rizzo *et al.*, 1997). However, it is difficult to distinguish changes due to malnutrition from other factors, such as stresses suffered by the parents and disrupted child-rearing. What would appear to distinguish some of these effects is the following observation. At the foetal stage and after birth, children of diabetic mothers, where there is a disturbance of nutrient regulation, exhibit delayed development.

Occasionally the tragedy of war provides insight, e.g. the famine (*Hongerwinter*) of the Dutch in 1944–1945 (Stein *et al.*, 1972). Birth cohorts that had been exposed to famine were compared with control birth cohorts. Groups were selected based upon interviews when men were drafted at age 18 into military service. Children in the famine group were born with relatively low weights. However, they did not show a higher frequency of mental retardation compared with the control group, indicating the resilience of the brain. Stein *et al.* point out that the study concerned mothers who had been adequately fed prior to the famine period. It also concerned a relatively short period of time. We should therefore not generalize to conditions of chronic famine. Also other tests might have detected effects. Subsequent research looking at the same population found an increased incidence of schizophrenia when adult (Brown *et al.*, 2000).

Environmental deprivation and enrichment effects

Does the physical environment in which a rat develops have effects on its brain (Bennett, 1976)? Rats were assigned randomly to one of three conditions, standard, impoverished and enriched, at weaning (about 25 days postnatal). Objects located in the enriched environment were changed daily.

Those raised in enriched conditions had higher levels of acetylcholinesterase (AChE) in their brains. This is an enzyme that breaks down ACh (Chapter 4). They also had higher weights of cerebral cortex, especially the occipital cortex (Bennett, 1976; Greenough, 1976). Other brain regions showed little difference between groups. Rearing in an enriched environment is associated with a greater extent of dendritic branching. However, enriched conditions do not inevitably lead to 'more' in every measure of brain structure. Under some conditions, an increase in dendritic branching is associated with a reduction in the density of dendritic spines (Kolb *et al.*, 1998), a reminder that development can be associated with pruning as well as growing.

Changes in the cerebral cortex are assumed to constitute the principal physical basis of changes in cognition. In general, rodents raised under enriched conditions do better in solving complex maze tasks than do other groups, apparently through a better ability to utilize cues outside the maze (Greenough, 1976).

It is tempting to extrapolate from this to human educational and cultural practices but caution is in order (Bruer, 1998). Traditionally, the rodent experiments involved extremes and we cannot, in any simple way, extrapolate to differences in, say, areas of a town and conclude that the poor are analogous to impoverished rats. It might be that a wide range of human environments provides adequate sensory stimulation.

Evidence on humans comes from studying the brains of children exposed to neglect, or to physical or sexual abuse. Using PET, a study was made of socially deprived children raised in Romanian orphanages. It found decreased metabolic activity in frontal and temporal cortex, as well as cognitive deficits, e.g. attention and impulse control (Chugani *et al.*, 2001).

In another study and using MRI, it was found that children exposed to neglect or abuse had a reduced size of corpus callosum, as compared with controls (Teicher *et al.*, 2004). This structure is vulnerable since its maturation, as measured by myelination of the axons that form it, is complete only in young adulthood. So, social context appears to play a role in the development of this pathway that links the two hemispheres. Of course, as the authors note, this observation on its own raises issues of lack of experimental control. Could a difference in the behaviour of such children present a cue to trigger abuse? Could there be an inherited tendency to a small brain region and this is also associated with abusive parents? Studies on rhesus monkeys under controlled conditions found a similar effect of an impoverished environment on the corpus callosum.

Social and tactile stimuli

For social species, optimal development depends upon steering a course between the stressful situations of either sensory isolation or overcrowding (Greenough, 1976). Separation of an infant from its caregiver has a detrimental effect on development (Schanberg and Field, 1987). For non-human primates, Harlow and Harlow (1962) showed that deprivation of contact from a caregiver was associated with retarded growth and indices of stress, e.g. increased tendency to show stereotypies (Chapter 2).

In rats, an influence of maternal behaviour on pups was described in Chapter 2: strain differences in levels of aggression. A similar observation is that licking and grooming of rat pups by their mothers influences the development of the hormonal control involving CRF and ACTH (Chapter 3) (Liu *et al.*, 1997; Meaney *et al.*, 1996).

Figure 6.16 shows an extension of the hormonal system introduced in Figure 3.27(b) (p. 71). CRF is synthesized within a nucleus of the hypothalamus (PVN) and is activated at times of stress. CRF triggers the release of ACTH, which in turn triggers the release of hormones of a class termed 'corticosteroids' from the adrenal gland. The hippocampus (among other structures) contains receptors for corticosteroids. Thereby, corticosteroids inhibit CRF release.

There is developmental plasticity here: the sensitivity of the pup's system is established early and depends upon maternal attention. Differences in mothers' behaviour are reflected in differences in the hormonal system of the pups. The biological basis is differences in the density of corticosteroid receptors in the hippocampus. Corticosteroids in excess are toxic to neural tissue, so possibly differences in their level have life-long implications for human health (Sapolsky, 1997).

Rat pups subject to stroking tend to exhibit less anxiety when adult. They also have a higher gain of weight and better performance on learning tasks (Schanberg and Field, 1987). Thus, it appears that the development of emotional circuitry in the brain can be influenced by early tactile stimulation. The therapy of tactile stimulation can compensate for some of the damaging effects of brain lesions, as indexed by the loss of cortical neurons (Kolb *et al.*, 1998). Some early studies pointed to enhanced development of human infants subject to supplementary tactile stimulation.

Play and its absence

In most species that exhibit play, there is a characteristic development, with the frequency of play increasing to a maximum in the juvenile phase and then declining (Panksepp, 1998). In rats and some other species, deprivation of the opportunity for social play in the period following weaning and up to sexual maturity has detrimental effects on development (Vanderschuren *et al.*, 1997). The deprivation effect can be ameliorated by allowing brief periods of daily play.

Play consists of features of adult social, sexual and aggressive behaviour. Early deprivation does not affect the capacity to exhibit these behaviours when adult but disturbs their control by the normal contexts in which they occur. For instance, deprived animals take much longer than controls to assume a submissive posture when subject to attack by a dominant rat.

Seen in a developmental context, social play seems to facilitate adult social interactions and the formation of social hierarchies. It might also help to acquire the skills of interpreting social signals and facilitate links between species-typical actions (e.g. fighting, submitting) and the motivational control ('contextual') signals that time their expression.

Phenylketonuria revisited

Diamond (1996) investigated the ability of children with phenylketonuria (PKU) (Chapter 2), who are believed to have a deficit specific to dopamine (DA). PKU is a genetically determined disorder, in which

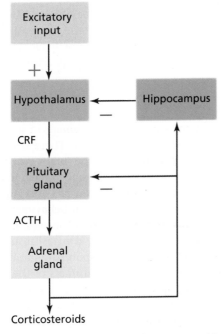

Figure 6.16 The hormonal control of corticosteroid secretion.

children are unable to convert one amino acid, phenyl-alanine (Phe), into another, tyrosine (Tyr). The blood level of Phe rises to a dangerous level and that of Tyr falls. Low levels of plasma Tyr result in low levels of Tyr in the CNS. DA neurons that project to the prefrontal cortex (discussed in the last section) are particularly sensitive to this.

Children for whom the condition has been diagnosed early and who have received continuous treatment are described as 'early continuous treatment-PKU' (ECT-PKU) individuals. Despite the treatment, they appear to have disruption of DA transmission. They show a range of cognitive impairments, in attention, persistence and problem-solving tasks that involve holding information in memory until a goal is reached and resisting the 'pull' of a familiar stimulus, such as the A-not-B task.

Diamond (1996) notes similarities with adults having damage to the dorsolateral prefrontal cortex, who also have difficulty in utilizing knowledge in controlling behaviour and overriding a prepotent response (Luria and Homskaya, 1964). An example of this is the **Wisconsin card-sorting test** (Figure 6.17). To solve it, participants need to sort cards according to a criterion of either colour or form. The criterion changes at the request of the experimenter. Participants are able to articulate verbally the correct criterion and have the intention to act according to it but get stuck in reacting according to the strongest stimulus–response link.

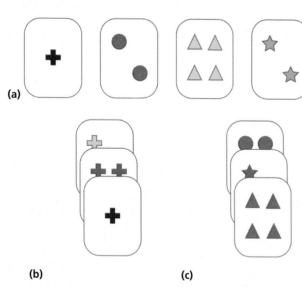

Figure 6.17 The Wisconsin card-sorting test: (a) cards, (b) sorted by shape criterion and (c) by colour criterion.

Section summary

1   Environmental complexity influences brain development of rats.

2   Social isolation can retard growth.

3   In rats, maternal behaviour influences the development of the infant's hormonal control system involving CRF and ACTH.

4   In humans, phenylketonuria (PKU) is associated with a disruption of the development of the prefrontal cortex.

☞ Test your knowledge

6.12 In Figure 6.16, how could a high density of corticosteroid receptors in the brain be associated with a low blood level of corticosteroids?

Answer on page 183   WEB

Ethology and a comparative perspective

Insights into development can be obtained by comparing species in terms of lifestyle and the problems that they have faced in evolution. Knowledge at this level can then be related to differences in development.

Brain development

Figure 6.18 compares brain development in some species (Dickerson, 1981; Dobbing, 1976). There is a phase of acceleration in growth, termed the 'brain growth spurt'. This occurs at different times relative to birth in different species. Note the contrast between rats and guinea pigs, which correlates with differences in behaviour following birth. The guinea pig is a **precocial** species, being born relatively competent. The rat by contrast is an **altricial** species, being born dependent upon parental help. So, it can be misleading to compare animals of the same age but in different species. For example, a drug given to the mother just before birth might be harmless for the young guinea pig since brain development is already in an advanced stage. It could prove harmful for the developing human and disastrous for a rat.

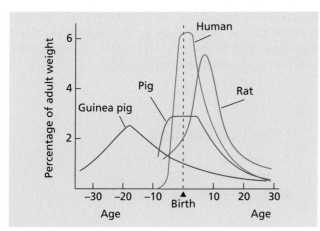

Figure 6.18 Comparison of species in brain development. The timescale is in units of months for humans, days for the guinea pig and rat and weeks for the pig. Vertical axis is percentage increase in brain mass.

Source: Dobbing (1976, Fig. 2, p. 140).

The length of development

Humans take an enormous time to reach maturity (on a less serious note, you might like to nominate some favourites to illustrate this). By contrast, as Elman *et al.* (1996) note, some species are literally up and running almost immediately after birth. In humans, for both offspring and parents, there are enormous costs attached to this length of development, in terms of vulnerability and effort expended in rearing. So what is its 'evolutionary logic'? Development depends upon interactions, both physical and social, and these take time. The period might be needed to permit sufficient opportunity for interactions between young and the environment.

For example, complex social cognition would need to be assimilated before decisions on, say, mate choice are made (again, call on personal anecdotes to illustrate).

Time might be the price of building complexity from a limited store of genetic information.

Open and closed programmes

Introduction

Consider the notion of a **closed programme** and an **open programme**. In some species, development results in an animal that reacts in a certain situation in a rather fixed species-typical way. Using a computer metaphor, this reveals a closed programme (Mayr, 1974).

Cuckoos lay eggs in the nests of other species. The unwitting foster parents of a variety of different species raise the young adoptees. However, no matter who the foster parent is, the young cuckoo grows up to mate with other cuckoos. Again the specification is closed, i.e. it is open to little or no differential influence by the very different species that raise the young bird.

In some cases, a programme is closed by early experience. The environment can have a feature to which the programme becomes rigidly committed (Elman *et al.*, 1996). (This emphasizes the danger of gene versus environment dichotomy.) Classical ethology made famous one example, **imprinting** (Lorenz, 1981). A newly hatched chick of some species, e.g. the greylag goose, follows the first moving object that it sees. The programme is left open, to be closed by the characteristic of this object.

The terms 'closed' and 'open' should perhaps be seen not to define two absolutely distinct categories but rather two ranges on a continuum of gene–animal–environment interdependence.

Functional considerations

From a functional perspective, what determined whether evolution provided closed or open programmes? Animals

Different species show different lengths of time before they can get up and move as well as achieve a level of independence. What kind of functional considerations underlie these differences?

Source: © Martin Harvey/CORBIS (left); © Ariel Skelley/CORBIS (right).

having a short lifespan, especially invertebrates, have little opportunity to learn by experience and tend to rely on closed programmes. In such animals, mating sometimes occurs only once and it is important to 'get the act together' on this occasion. In effect, instructions on what to do are inflexibly encoded on the basis of stimulus information.

An advantage of a closed programme is as an isolating mechanism, a way of eliminating mating with non-conspecifics. At best, such mating would waste time and, at worst, tie-up the reproductive process with a non-viable offspring. Mayr (1974, p. 657) summarizes it as: 'Selection should favour the evolution of a closed programme when there is a reliable relationship between a stimulus and only one correct response'.

For animals of a longer lifespan, there is often more opportunity to learn and more reliance on open programmes. An open programme is used where crucial information can be assimilated only on the basis of individual experience. Consider, for example, where an animal lives in a colony but specific parent–offspring interaction is needed (e.g. feeding the young). The programme can be closed only by the experience of the individual with its parent (Mayr, 1974). However, mate selection is still often relatively closed.

Section summary

1 Species differ in the dimension of precocial–altricial.

2 Programmes can be closed or open.

Test your knowledge

6.13 Which of the following would be described as the most precocial? (i) Pig, (ii) rat.

Answer on page 183   WEB

A personal angle

Imprinting on Konrad Lorenz

Normally, the stimulus on which a bird imprints would be a parent but it can be another species or even Konrad Lorenz. The programme is closed by the first exposure, such that the chick will later seek the imprinted stimulus as parent, companion or mate. The programme cannot then be reversed. In one case, as a result of their early exposure to him, chicks followed Lorenz as their object of choice (Figure 6.19).

Figure 6.19 The Nobel Prize-winning Austrian zoologist Konrad Lorenz (1903–1989) being followed by a group of ducklings.
Source: Science Photo Library.

Change and plasticity in adults

Introduction

Earlier sections described changes in the brain during development. This section considers plasticity in adults: which of the changes in Figure 6.5 also occur in the brains of adults? A caution is needed. Growth of new synapses in response to increased functional demands would surely fit the category of plasticity. However, not all changes in the adult brain would be described as 'plasticity'. The death of neurons shown in Figure 6.5(h) and (i) was described as being of functional significance in the developing brain. The neuron lost was not serving a functional role and was eliminated. By contrast, any large-scale indiscriminate loss of neurons in an aging brain and associated loss of function would not be serving a functional end. It would not be described as 'plasticity'.

The notion that the cortex of the adult brain exhibits plasticity is an old one, going back to the foundations of neuroscience in the 19th century and the Spanish researcher, Santiago Ramón y Cajal (DeFelipe, 2006). Cajal proposed the 'gymnastic hypothesis': links between neurons would change and multiply as a function of mental exercise (Mora *et al.*, 2007). The young were seen as having the greatest ability to exhibit such gymnastics, an ability that declines over years.

Recent evidence also points to changes in connections between neurons as the physical correlate of psychological changes, e.g. in stimulation from the environment and learning etc. That is to say, some of the changes in Figure 6.5 also occur in adults: sprouting of dendrites and axons, particular cells die and new synapses are formed, while other synapses are lost. However, for a long time it was believed dogmatically that no new neurons are formed in the adult brain (see Gross, 2000). This assumption is false. First, we look broadly at plasticity in the adult brain. Then we consider specifically evidence for the formation of new neurons ('neurogenesis') in the adult brain and its significance.

Some examples of plasticity

Spatial cognition and brain plasticity

A study concerned the spatial abilities and brains of London taxi-drivers (Maguire *et al.*, 2000). They have to pass a formidable test on their knowledge of London streets and how best to get from A to B. From evidence on non-human species, the hippocampus has been implicated in spatial skills (Chapter 5). Could London taxi-drivers have developed particular biologically identifiable changes in the hippocampus, corresponding to the functional demands of their task? Using MRI, Maguire *et al.* found enlargement of the posterior hippocampus in taxi-drivers compared with controls.

This change might not represent plasticity but, rather, individuals with such enlargement and thereby good cognitive skills are attracted to taxi-driving. Maguire *et al.* suggest that this is not the case, since the magnitude of enlargement correlated with the length of time spent driving a taxi.

Plasticity and ageing

With age, there is a decline in the size of the human brain, which starts in the third decade (Colcombe *et al.*, 2006). It is most evident in particular regions: the temporal, parietal and frontal lobes. The decline in structure parallels a decline in cognitive ability. With an ageing population, this has profound health implications. So, what can be done?

Reasoning and problem-solving exercises and playing video games improve cognitive performance of older people (Lustig *et al.*, 2009). Neuroimaging techniques identify areas of change in structure and function associated with skill acquisition. This gives some idea where plasticity is exhibited in the adult brain. An increase in the size of a brain region and/or its increased activity suggests increased use of that region in the acquisition of a new skill. A lack of decrease relative to a control group would also draw investigators' attention. Lowering of activity in a region as a skill is acquired suggests a shift of responsibility away from the region, as when skills become more automatic and some 'higher'

cognitive processing is thereby made free for other activities (Lustig *et al.*, 2009). Researchers then speculate on the nature of the changes at the level of neurons and other brain structures.

Aerobic exercise has a beneficial effect on both cognition and brain structure (Colcombe *et al.*, 2006). Work on non-humans shows that the effects of long-term exercise are mediated via increases in the levels of (i) neurotrophic factors in the brain, (ii) density of blood capillaries and (iii) the extent of dendritic connections between neurons, as well as the formation of new neurons in the hippocampus.

Colcombe *et al.* compared groups of participants aged 60–79 years: 'experimentals', who engaged in aerobic exercise for 6 months, and 'controls', who engaged in (non-aerobic) stretching exercises. The experimentals showed an increase in grey matter over the exercise period, most evidently in the frontal and temporal lobes. The frontal lobe is involved in executive functions (e.g. decision-making) and these normally show an age-related decline. In the experimentals, increases in volume were also seen in some white matter regions, e.g. the corpus callosum.

High levels of aerobic fitness help to preserve the integrity of the hippocampus (as measured by its volume) and the ability to acquire cognitive skills (Erickson *et al.*, 2009). Increased blood flow to the hippocampus appears to mediate at least some of the effects of aerobic fitness. The elevated blood flow might permit cells to survive and facilitate plasticity. Plasticity of the brain of 60-year-olds has been shown as they acquire a new skill: juggling (Boyke *et al.*, 2008). Increases in grey matter were evident in brain regions that would rather clearly be associated with the skill, e.g. the visual cortex (Figure 5.21). When practicing at the task stopped, the changes were reversed.

Pain

Repetitive stimulation with a pain-inducing stimulus leads to an expansion of grey matter in brain regions underlying pain processing, e.g. parts of the somatosensory cortex (Teutsch *et al.*, 2008) (Chapter 5). Cessation of stimulation is followed by a return to normal levels of grey matter. By contrast, chronic pain appears to cause a reduction in size of a number of brain regions functionally related to pain processing (May, 2008; Rodriguez-Raecke *et al.*, 2009). Some are involved in counteracting pain (Chapter 14), which might have clinical implications. Whether the changes represent death of neurons, shrinkage of neuron size or reduced connections within the cortex remains open to investigation. Where surgical intervention was able to cure the pain, there was a return of the size of the brain regions to normal (Rodriguez-Raecke *et al.*, 2009).

Cognitive behaviour therapy

People with chronic fatigue syndrome (CFS) show reductions in grey matter volume (GMV) in regions of the prefrontal cortex, detected by MRI (de Lange *et al.*, 2008). Could the reduced brain volume be a predisposing risk for the disorder or be a consequence of it? One way of addressing this is to see whether the reductions can be reversed with therapeutic interventions, such as cognitive behaviour therapy (CBT). CBT consisted of guiding the patient in a gradual increase in activity, while challenging unhelpful cognitions.

Figure 6.20 shows the baseline conditions, where a lower GMV is evident in CFS. Also evident in both CFS (triangles) and controls (squares) is the decline in GMV with age. Health, physical activity and cognitive speed were improved by CBT. Figure 6.21 shows the change in GMV after CBT, as well as a break-down as a function of age. The change in GMV as a result of CBT is evident in younger rather than older patients.

It is interesting to compare the decline in volume of regions of prefrontal cortex with CFS and traumatic damage to these regions. The effect of the latter is often one of apathy. This has similarities to the problems faced in CFS and it might be more than coincidental that the success of CBT correlated with the recovery of grey matter volume (de Lange *et al.*, 2008).

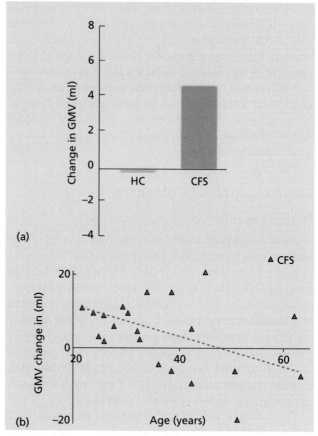

(a)

(b)

Figure 6.21 Change in GMV. (a) CFS patients compared with healthy controls (HC). (b) Change in GMV as a function of the age.

Source: de Lange *et al.* (2008, Fig. 2, p. 2176).

(a)

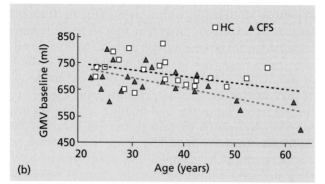

(b)

Figure 6.20 Grey matter volume (GMV) of people with CFS, compared to healthy controls (HC) at the start of the experiment (before CBT). (a) Comparison of the two samples; (b) GMV as a function of age.

Source: de Lange *et al.* (2008, Fig. 1, p. 2175).

Stroke

A trigger for reorganization within the adult brain is loss of tissue as in stroke. A stroke occurs when neurons in part of the brain are denied their supply of blood, as in blockage of a blood vessel or rupture of its wall. Neuronal death follows. When the stroke is in motor regions, there will be disruption to movement, e.g. of an arm. However, there is usually at least some recovery from stroke and lost abilities return albeit not to their former extent. Consider where neurons in the motor cortex of the brain are lost (Dancause *et al.*, 2005). The functional connections that other neurons make to the motor neurons are also lost, which can be the trigger for sprouting until other target neurons are found.

So, for some time there has been an acceptance of the existence of plasticity in the adult brain, in the form of changed connections between an existing population of neurons. This leads to the controversial issue of whether an additional contribution to brain plasticity arises from the birth of new neurons (Gross, 2000), described next.

The issue of neurogenesis

Background

Old dogmas die hard and this was the case with the dogma that there is no neurogenesis in the adult brain. It is not hard to appreciate reasons for the dogma. Early neuroanatomists had reasoned (Gross, 2009, p. 327): 'Because the elaborate architecture of the brain remained constant in appearance, the idea that neurons were continually added to it was, understandably, inconceivable'.

A personal angle

A prophet before his time

In the 1960s, Joseph Altman employed what is termed a 'cell birth marker', a substance known as ^{3}H-thymidine (Altman, 1962). This was injected into the brains of adult rats and it labelled cells at the time of their division (Figure 6.5(b)). Altman then followed the fate of the 'daughter cells' that also carry the label (Figure 6.5(c)–(e)). Cells carrying the label were subsequently found in various brain regions (e.g. cortex), implying that their birth was in the adult animal. Despite publication in the prestigious journal *Science*, researchers ignored or dismissed the result (Gross, 2009). Why? The techniques available did not permit the newborn cells to be unambiguously classified as neurons. Researchers puzzled – how could the adult brain repeat the developmental feat of migration of cells from their site of origin to their final location, as in Figure 6.5(c)–(e) (see Nottebohm, 2002). Altman was relatively unknown and the result did not fit the dogma of the times (Gross, 2009). Now such cells have been shown to have the form and characteristics of neurons and Altman takes his well-deserved place in the scientific literature.

Following Altman's study, a number of pieces of evidence emerged pointing to the existence of adult neurogenesis (Gross, 2000).

Song learning in birds

Nottebohm (2002) studied song learning in birds, identifying its neural basis. Two nuclei (collections of neurons) attracted interest, since they showed enormous fluctuations in size over time, e.g. with season and following injection of testosterone. At first, Nottebohm felt that the increase in size of a nucleus following administration of testosterone might be due to just increased growth of dendrites or to the formation of new synapses, as in Figure 6.5(h). Later he asked whether the production of new neurons also contributes to the enlargement. A labelling technique revealed the addition of thousands of new neurons daily and these neurons were assimilated into functioning circuits.

Nottebohm also studied a species of bird, the Black-capped chickadee, which stores ('caches') hundreds of items of food in different locations, an awe-inspiring feat of spatial cognition. This behaviour occurs as the days shorten and the temperature falls, a time at which incorporation of new neurons into the hippocampus is at its maximum. The new neurons only survive for a few weeks, which coincides with the length of time between caching an item of food and its retrieval.

Rodents

Refined techniques confirm the existence of neurogenesis in the adult rat hippocampus (Nilsson *et al.*, 1999) and in the olfactory bulb (discussed by Gross, 2009). Furthermore, the rate of neurogenesis in the hippocampus increases as the environment is made more complex and, in parallel with this, learning ability also increases. This suggests that adult neurogenesis is not simply some functionless vestige, a 'left-over' from early evolution or development. An enlarged hippocampus could have functional significance in facilitating the animal's coping with environmental complexity (Gross, 2000).

In mice, increased locomotor activity is associated with increased sprouting of new blood vessels and thereby increased blood flow to regions of the hippocampus where neurogenesis occurs (Pereira *et al.*, 2007). Regional cerebral blood volume correlates with neurogenesis.

Primates

In adult macaque monkeys, newborn cells appear to migrate from their birth-place near to the lateral ventricle, through white matter to various regions of the cortex (Gould *et al.*, 1999). The regions, such as temporal cortex, have a role in learning and memory. In humans, neurogenesis occurs within regions of the hippocampus (Eriksson *et al.*, 1998). Aerobic exercise increases the sprouting of new blood vessels in these regions, a possible measure of neurogenesis (Pereira *et al.*, 2007).

Broad reflections

Could adult neurogenesis have evolved as a means of repair of the brain, e.g. to counter natural 'wear-and-tear'? Nottebohm rejects this suggestion on the grounds that it appears to be selective to particular brain regions, which are not obviously the most vulnerable to damage.

Rather, he suggests (p. 746) that: 'it evolved to keep circuits functionally young, able to master skills in the way that young brains do …'.

In an argument compatible with this, others (Balu and Lucki, 2009; Gross, 2000) suggest that adult neurogenesis might be important for learning (Chapter 11), drawing upon several sources of evidence:

1 The phenomenon is most evident in brain structures most closely involved with learning and memory, e.g. the hippocampus.

2 Factors that decrease neurogenesis, such as stress, also impair learning on tasks that involve the hippocampus.

3 Presenting learning tasks that involve the hippocampus improves the survival of newborn neurons.

4 Factors that increase neurogenesis in the hippocampus (e.g. increasing environmental complexity) enhance learning.

5 Neurons formed when the animal is adult appear to be more plastic than older neurons, which could make them particularly suitable as a basis of learning. For example, they show a high capacity to sprout extensions.

There could be important health implications of adult neurogenesis. There are indications that the efficacy of anti-depressive interventions (e.g. medication, physical exercise) could lie, in part, in increasing neurogenesis in the hippocampus (Balu and Lucki, 2009).

Section summary

1 Some of the changes that characterize early development can occur to a limited extent in adults.

2 Adult experience influences plasticity of neural connections and in some cases neurogenesis.

Test your knowledge

6.14 At a cellular level what could contribute to an enlarged hippocampus as a result of experience?

Answer on page 183

Bringing things together

The development of behaviour reflects developing neural processes and, in turn, development of neural processes depends on behaviour. In turn, the environment is influenced by the behaviour of the developing animal.

Given the complexity of interactions that determine development, you might wonder whether the role of any factor can ever be understood. Rather than despair, complexity can be the stimulus for experimentation and theory. For example, a role of a hormone can be established but to do so can involve considering both the nervous system and the dynamics of interaction between two animals. Given such tortuously complex dynamic interactions underlying development, you might also have cause to wonder how a viable animal ever emerges. Even more so, how is sufficient consistency of form among conspecifics maintained that they are able to recognize each other as potential sexual partners and produce offspring? Awe seems an appropriate reaction, as is, in more down-to-earth terms, a consideration of the stabilizing effects of environmental consistencies.

Moving on from development to consider adult systems, the kinds of change in the nervous system that

underlie development (e.g. synaptic restructuring) can also be seen in some cases in adult nervous systems.

We asked, how do we distinguish between development and learning? With newer findings, the distinction becomes even more blurred (Elman *et al.*, 1996). The plasticity of the adult nervous system contributes to the blur since we can no longer assume an absolute distinction between early (development) and later changes (learning). The old distinctions between experience-independent (development or maturation) and experience-dependent (learning) are now suspect. Elman *et al.* suggest that we might risk calling the early series of changes consisting of cell division, migration, etc., 'maturation' as distinct from learning. Life seemed simpler before but there is no going back now, so we have to live with complexity and try to better understand it.

See the video coverage for this chapter to appreciate where a study of brain development informs the psychology of development.

Summary of Chapter 6

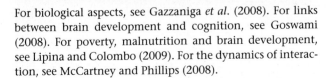

1 Development depends upon several layers of interacting factors.

2 Development of the nervous system consists of the net production of an increasing number of cells, accompanied by an increasing degree of complexity of these cells and their interconnections.

3 The changes in connections between cells associated with development have some similarities with more limited changes ('plasticity') in the adult system. In each case, changes depend upon what role the system of connected cells plays.

4 Hormones exert both organizational effects and activational effects on the nervous system and thereby behaviour. Sex hormones exemplify these roles.

5 The emergence of cognitive and social skills is associated with identifiable features of the development of the nervous system.

6 Atypical development can be contrasted with typical development and links made between developmental outcome, genes and environment.

7 Differences in functional demands posed on different species can be linked to differences in the development of their nervous systems.

8 Limited plasticity is evident in adult brains.

Further reading

For biological aspects, see Gazzaniga *et al.* (2008). For links between brain development and cognition, see Goswami (2008). For poverty, malnutrition and brain development, see Lipina and Colombo (2009). For the dynamics of interaction, see McCartney and Phillips (2008).

Answers

Explanations for answers to 'test your knowledge' questions can be found on the website www.pearsoned.co.uk/toates

6.1   (ii) Phenotype
6.2   (ii) The bottom
6.3   Myelination
6.4   Zygote (or fertilized egg cell); genotypes; phenotypes
6.5   (i) An increase in the number of postsynaptic receptors; (iii) an increase in the number of presynaptic vesicles

6.6   (iii) Cholinergic
6.7   (ii) Contralateral
6.8   Axon
6.9   Membrane
6.10 (i) Organizational; (ii) activational
6.11 (ii) Axon terminals
6.12 The larger the number of receptors, the higher the inhibitory feedback and the lower the excitatory input to the adrenal gland.
6.13 (i) Pig
6.14 (i) Formation (or enlargement) of new synapses or dendrites; (ii) neurogenesis.

Visit www.pearsoned.co.uk/toates
for a range of resources to support study.
Test yourself with multiple choice questions and
access a bank of over 100 videos that will bring the
topics to life.

Chapter 7
Sensory systems:
general principles

Learning outcomes for Chapter 7

After studying this chapter, you should be able to:

1 Appreciate how perception involves not just the detection of sensory events but also their interpretation.

2 Explain how both bottom-up and top-down processes are involved in perception of the world. In so doing, explain what is meant by the 'homunculus fallacy'.

3 Compare and contrast some sensory systems.

Scene-setting questions

1 Why do we see flashes of light when we receive a blow to an eye?
2 Do we see what we expect to see?
3 Why does the idea of a 'little person in the head' generate controversy?
4 Why do swimming pools feel less cold after a while?
5 Why can't everyone hear the 'Mosquito' ring tone?

Why can't everyone hear the 'Mosquito' ring tone? Explore the video on the website accompanying this book at www.pearsoned. co.uk/toates

Objectively speaking, this is a hollow mask but it does not look hollow, no matter which perspective on it you take. What else determines our perception, apart from raw sensory input?

Source: Richard Gregory and Priscilla Heard.

Introduction

How do we perceive the world so that we can behave in relation to it? Perception depends upon activity at various levels of the nervous system. At one level, a **sensory system**, which involves the eyes, ears, nose, skin or tongue, is responsible for (i) detecting the presence of physical events (e.g. the ears detect certain changes in air pressure), (ii) conveying information about them to the brain and (iii) processing some information as

it is conducted towards the brain. Information from the external environment contributes to the sensory qualities of visual, auditory, smell, tactile and taste sensations. These involve the **exteroceptive** senses, which provide information about *exterior* events, i.e. outside the body. A specialized system for nociceptive stimuli was introduced (Chapter 3).

Survival and reproduction require the detection of events in the environment and, if appropriate, reacting to them. The ability to detect events depends upon the properties of sense organs. Animals have evolved in specialized environmental ('ecological') niches in which particular information is vital to survival. For example, hawks rely on fine resolution of visual detail and detection of movement. They have evolved a different visual system from rats, which have a less sophisticated visual system and rely more on smell and touch. Humans are used to seeing the world through human eyes but it is useful to be reminded that different species vary widely in their sensory capacities.

In addition to sensory detection, *interpretation* of what is detected also occurs. As a convenience, psychologists distinguish between 'sensory systems', which *detect* events, and 'perceptual systems', which *interpret* detected information (Eysenck, 1998). For example, the visual system detects the presence of light at the retina, while perceptual systems interpret this as a particular moving object.

Perception seems so natural and without effort that we have difficulty appreciating how subtle it is. It seems direct; there is a world out there and we perceive it with the help of eyes and ears, etc. In fact, the study of perception is full of traps and contradictions. The words that roll off our tongues effortlessly, such as 'event', 'stimulus' and 'information', seem unproblematic and are often the best that psychology can offer. However, problems arise when we consider them more closely, as will be described in the next section.

Section summary

1 Sensory systems, which involve eyes, ears, nose, skin and tongue, detect physical events in the world, convey information about them to the brain and do some processing of information *en route*.

2 Perceptual systems interpret detected events.

 Test your knowledge

7.1 In the case of sound, distinguish between sensory and perceptual systems.

> Answer on page 195

Sensory systems and perception

Linking the physical world and sensory detection

Let us consider hearing. The physical stimulus that we perceive as sound consists of changes in air pressure (Figure 7.1(a)). The tuning fork is hit and it starts to vibrate. The vibration produces waves of compression (relatively high pressure) and rarefaction (low pressure) in the air, which we perceive as sound. Figure 7.1(b) shows a graph of these changes in pressure, which takes the form of a sinewave. The **wavelength** is the distance between any two corresponding points on the cycle, for example between two successive peaks. Suppose that the wave completes 50 cycles in one second (termed 50 hertz or 50 Hz for short). This is its frequency. Amplitude is the height of the waves of compression and rarefaction.

Figure 7.1(c) shows a different tuning fork, which vibrates at a different frequency, say, 100 Hz. See Figure 7.1(d). In this case, the amplitude is the same as in (b). If this tuning fork is struck harder; there is an increase in amplitude but the frequency remains the same (e). The ear converts such changes in pressure in the air to changes in the electrical activity of neurons.

A sound is produced in a listener's auditory system by the arrival of pressure waves at the ear, a psychological phenomenon. However, 'sound' is also used to describe the pressure waves themselves, a physical phenomenon, as in to *detect a sound*. This is more convenient than the expression to 'detect pressure waves in a medium'.

Consider the term 'event'. Things happen in the outside world and there is our conscious perception of these events. Based upon consensus between observers and occasional objective measurement, the external events and our perception normally correlate. For example, a physical object (e.g. a tall person) is simultaneously associated with a conscious perception of tallness by more than one person. If necessary, perception can be confirmed with a tape measure.

Vision, as with other perceptual systems, works according to a principle described by Martin (1991, p. 330): 'Perception therefore can be shown to be an accurate *organization* of the essential properties of an object that allows us to *manipulate* the object successfully'.

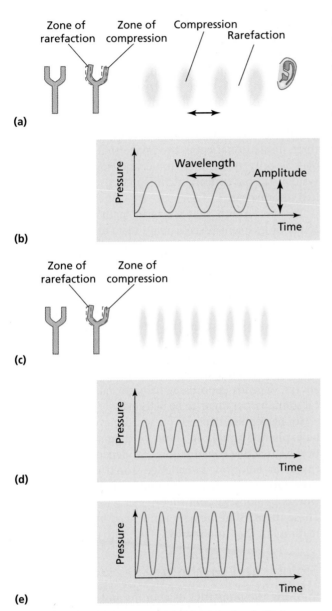

Figure 7.1 The production of sound: (a) tuning fork after being tapped (after Vander *et al.*, 1994), (b) changes in air pressure, (c) a different tuning fork, (d) changes in air pressure following tapping of fork shown in part (c) and (e) increased amplitude after a harder strike of the fork.

Source: after Toates (1998c).

The factors in perception

The expressions **data-driven** and **concept-driven** refer to two aspects of perception. Clearly, perception depends upon the raw data at the sense organs (e.g. the image at the retina), the data-driven aspect. This is

sometimes termed the **bottom-up** aspect. Perception also depends upon concepts (e.g. memories, expectations), the concept-driven aspect, sometimes termed the **top-down** aspect (Berthoz, 1996). In such terms, perception depends upon an interaction between bottom-up (data-driven) and top-down (concept-driven) processes. Techniques such as PET and fMRI scanning (Chapter 5) now enable insight into the brain mechanisms that underlie the top-down factor. The processing of neural signals set up by sensory events is modulated (enhanced or suppressed in strength) by top-down factors, such as selective attention (Gazzaley and D'Esposito, 2007).

Psychology abounds with ambiguous figures, such as those that can be perceived as either two faces or a vase (Figure 7.2). Normally, perception alternates between the two. The data remain constant but different perceptions occur. We might logically speculate that the top-down processing changes and thereby the perception changes.

If you have not seen Figure 7.3 before, it will probably look like meaningless blobs. If you turn to Figure 7.5 (on p. 190) you will see the solution suggested. Now turn back to Figure 7.3 and a form should be apparent. Figure 7.3 has not changed between first and second viewings but your perception has. The same information is driving perception but the top-down contribution appears to have changed.

The sensory systems of smell, taste and touch seem to have a simpler job to do than vision or hearing. Suppose that an animal tastes something that is intrinsically repulsive, such as a poisonous plant. It immediately expels the plant from its mouth. In a straightforward way, the taste is the stimulus for the reflex of expelling the substance. The information conveyed is a constant

Figure 7.2 Face–vase illusion.
Source: Gregory (1998, Figure 1.4c, p. 11).

Figure 7.3 Black blobs against a white background.
Source: Carraher and Thurston (1966, Fig. 10, p. 18)

(or 'invariant') property of the world: the plant is repulsive, associated in functional terms with being dangerous.

Suppose that a **pheromone** (an airborne chemical that plays a role in communication between animals of the same species) wafts from one animal to the nose of another. The pheromone has a certain chemical form and stimulates receptors in the nose. Whether the receiving animal responds or not can depend upon its own internal state, e.g. whether it is sexually receptive. However, the information that is conveyed can be understood simply in terms of the chemical that is detected. The information leaving the sender is intrinsically *invariant* and the receiver does not need an interpretation in order to extract **invariance**.

Consider, by contrast, a sensory system which needs to *extract* what is invariant from a varying signal (Zeki, 1993). Vision illustrates this. To a prey animal, a hawk is still a hawk, whether it is near or far, viewed stationary, flying across the sky or towards the prey. Yet under these different circumstances the information detected by the eyes is very different. There is a small image when the hawk is far and a large image when it is near, and the image can be moving or stationary. What is invariant, the perception of the hawk, depends upon processing of the image by the eyes and brain. Invariance is extracted from the visual information. Even if the hawk suddenly disappears from view, e.g. when in a cloud, a prey animal needs to base behaviour on the 'perception' that the hawk is still in pursuit. An understanding of how such invariance is achieved requires that both sensory systems and perception are considered.

Try doing a drawing in only two dimensions of a three-dimensional object, e.g. a cube. Even as bad an artist as I am can make such a two-dimensional representation look three-dimensional. Yet in reality it is only a collection of lines drawn in two dimensions. Perception corresponds to an active process of interpretation based in part upon the drawing. Even for a three-dimensional cube, the image that it forms at our eyes is only two-dimensional and so the perceptual system still has to form a construction based upon limited information.

The perception that we term 'pain' depends upon actual or incipient tissue damage (data-driven) and sometimes reflects it rather directly. However, a person might experience pain 'in a limb' that does not exist any more or has never existed. In such cases, pain seems to be at least in part a top-down construct (which does not make it any less painful). Conversely, there can be tissue damage with little pain (Melzack and Wall, 1996). Thus the chapter will speak of a *nociceptive neuron* detecting *tissue damage* rather than, as do some authors, a *pain receptor* detecting *pain*. Pain is a psychological experience that normally, but not always, depends upon tissue damage. Pain is not a physical stimulus 'out there' to be detected.

So, perception depends on sensory events but cannot be explained simply in terms of them. Rather, perception is an active construction that depends also on such things as emotion, knowledge stored in memory and expectations. In effect, all humans make sense of their worlds by constructing theories of what is happening. These theories are heavily influenced by sensory information but that information is put into context.

Biology and psychology

Knowing the properties of neurons and systems of neurons helps us to understand how events are detected and information conveyed to the brain. It is with the early stages of sensory detection that psychologists have the most detailed insight from biology. This reflects the fact that sensory systems are more accessible to investigation than the processes of interpretation that lie deeper in the brain.

The flow of information between biology and psychology is a two-way street (Chapter 1). A study of biology can suggest how sensory and perceptual systems are constructed and operate. However, the psychology of perception can suggest what sort of processes to look for at a biological level (Zeki, 1993). If we can identify some characteristics of a sensory and perceptual process, i.e. what it is actually doing, this can help to identify

Figure 7.4 The Muller–Lyer illusion.

underlying biological structures. For example, in Figure 7.4 most people see the bottom line as longer than the top. This is an **illusion** since the lines are physically identical. So, given this property of the perceptual system, researchers know that, underlying perception, there is processing by the brain that involves distortion.

Feedback

Sensory detection and perception involve feedback, which highlights the impossibility of drawing neat boundaries between them. Top-down information can modulate bottom-up signals in the sensory pathways conveying information to the brain. For example, deciding what to do (to flee or to fight) modulates the transmission of nociceptive information to the brain.

For another example, information arrives at the eyes, some processing is done on it and modified information is then conveyed to the cortex (Chapter 5, Figure 5.21, p. 120). Information regarding the outside world is interpreted. These later stages of visual processing feed back to modulate what is sent along the pathway from the eyes to the brain, a concept-driven, top-down aspect. Based upon the interpretation, the brain might command movements of the eyes and a scanning of the object. This brings additional information to the brain. Thus, eye movements change the flow of information. Similarly, a dog might detect a few molecules of an odour and the perception can trigger sniffing to maximize the flow of air to the receptors in its nose that are involved in smell.

The homunculus fallacy

It is difficult to explain what the brain does when a person smells a rose or admires a painting. Therefore, psychologists need all the help that they can get and tend, rightly, to devise analogies to help. However, there is one mode of 'explanation' that is to be avoided and it is useful to give an early warning of it.

Skinner (1984) used the following example to illustrate the dangers. A person's finger is pricked and messages are sent along a nerve to the brain. Shortly afterwards, the person moves the finger away from the offending object. So much is uncontroversial. However, in one educational film the brain events were shown in terms of a little person lying asleep inside the real person's brain. The messages in the nerve wake up the little person who then proceeds to pull a lever, which activates muscles and the arm of the real person responds. Of course, if we want to pursue the 'explanation', we would presumably need to put a still smaller person in the head of the little person and yet another person inside this head, and so on indefinitely (Gregory, 1997). Clearly, we need to stop thinking along these lines. This way of thinking is termed the **homunculus fallacy** (the fallacy of the little person in the head).

Although you might find this example amusing, there are more subtle variations on it. Thus, some people imagine that the visual system recreates in the brain the image that falls on the retina. They imagine that in the brain there is some kind of inner screen onto which is projected, via the retina, an image. For example, a Rembrandt painting would appear there when we stand and admire one. There is no such inner screen; the Rembrandt is represented by a series of action potentials in neurons, none of which looks anything like the painting.

What might make the homunculus fallacy tempting is that the representation of the body in the somatosensory and motor cortices preserves something of the form of the body, e.g. 'sensory homunculus' (Chapter 5). Also, the mapping of the retina onto the brain preserves the positional relationship at the retina but this lends no support to the idea of an homunculus. There is no reason to suppose that the chemicals of the brain turn yellow-gold when we view a Van Gogh sunflower!

A number of principles of sensory processing apply to each sensory system and the next section looks at these.

Section summary

1 Sensory systems are sensitive to physical events (e.g. changes in air pressure).

2 Perception depends upon the combined effect of data-driven (bottom-up) and concept-driven (top-down) factors.

3 Some perceptual systems (e.g. vision) extract what is invariant from a signal that is often varying greatly.

4 The term 'homunculus fallacy' refers to the idea of a little person in the head who interprets sensory events.

Test your knowledge

7.2 Two sounds, one of 50 Hz and another of 100 Hz, could be said with certainty to differ in which of the following? (i) Frequency, (ii) wavelength, (iii) amplitude.

7.3 Fill in the missing words in the following: 'Whereas a hormone is released into a ___ vessel and serves communication within one animal, a pheromone is released into ___ and serves as a communication ___ animals'.

Answers on page 195

Figure 7.5 Dalmatian in snow.
Source: Carraher and Thurston (1966, Fig. 10, p. 18)

General principles

Transduction

The neurons of our brain are not *directly* sensitive to the presence of such physical events as lights, odours and pressure waves in the air. Therefore, the first stage of processing is common to all sensory systems. It is a *translation* from physical events (e.g. a chemical on the tongue, damage at the skin) to an electrical signal, a change in membrane potential of specialized neurons at the periphery. This process is termed **transduction**. The book has described the transduction between a noxious stimulus and depolarization of a neuron. For other examples, there is transduction between (i) light at the retina and electrical signals, leading to action potentials,

and (ii) pressure waves in the air at the ear and action potentials. Of course, the sensory receptors of the eye and ear are not in immediate contact with the external environment but are within the organ.

Each sensory system is responsible for detecting a particular class of physical events. Within each system, the initial stage of detection, from physical stimulus to change in membrane potential, is done by **sensory receptors**. Figure 7.6 compares sensory receptors in nociception and vision. In part (a), the single nociceptive neuron spans the distance from periphery to CNS. This neuron can therefore be termed a sensory receptor, though some would call just its tip the sensory receptor since it is here that the transduction occurs. In part (b), there are two further neurons between the sensory receptors that detect light at the retina and the CNS.

Afferent neurons convey information on sensory events to the CNS, either directly to the brain, as in the cranial nerves, or to the spinal cord and then to the brain (Chapter 3). Each sensory system has general and specific features. As a general property, each translates physical events into an electrical signal that the nervous system can use. However, each receptor is specialized to detect only one type of physical event. A given sensory receptor usually responds only within a particular range of stimulation, e.g. in the olfactory system, to a few types of chemical.

In some sensory receptors, the change in membrane potential, if sufficient, gives rise immediately to an action potential. For example, a nociceptive neuron performs transduction between tissue damage and action potentials, which are transmitted along the axon to the CNS (Figure 7.6(a)). In other cases, a neuron serves as sensory detector (i.e. certain electrical changes occur in it) but action potentials appear only in neurons that

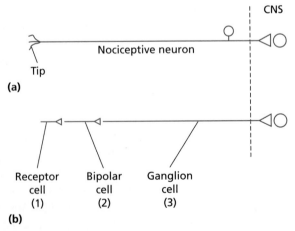

Figure 7.6 Sensory neurons involved in (a) nociception and (b) vision.

are situated later in the sequence. For example, in Figure 7.6(b), electrical changes are instigated in neuron 1 by light, which triggers changes in membrane potential in neuron 2 but it is only at neuron 3, the ganglion cell, where action potentials first appear. In each system, the language in which information is sent to the brain is that of the *frequency of action potentials in neurons*, termed 'neural encoding'.

The fundamental difference between sensory channels is in terms of (i) the particular neurons that carry the information and (ii) the parts of the brain to which these neurons project. This is termed the **labelled-line principle**.

Consider some examples. Activity within particular neurons of the tactile system is interpreted as touch to a particular part of the body. Hearing and vision are based on the auditory nerve and optic nerve, respectively. The difference between hearing and vision is not based on the means by which information is carried, since it is by action potentials in each case. The retina is sensitive to light and not to sound. We see lights because neurons of the optic nerve are activated and we hear sounds because neurons of the auditory nerve are active. However, if mechanical pressure is applied to the eye, owing to triggering action potentials we can sometimes see flashes that appear to be light. Objectively there is no light there but activity in this input channel is interpreted as light.

The information carried by action potentials

In a sensory system, specific physical events in the world trigger action potentials within particular neurons. Hence, the action potentials represent the triggering events. Such events can be characterized by, among other qualities, their duration and intensity. Pressure waves in the air are also associated with such qualities as pitch. How are these qualities encoded, given that the nervous system has only a series of action potentials available?

There are two means of conveying information about different qualities: (i) which neurons are active and (ii) the pattern of action potentials within each neuron. As just noted, differences *between* sensory systems, say, auditory and visual, correspond to different nerves. Similarly *within* a given sensory system, differences are also conveyed by different neurons. Sugar tastes sweet and a lemon tastes bitter because different neurons tend to be triggered by those two chemical qualities. Different neurons within the auditory nerve are triggered by different frequencies of sounds.

Information can be carried by the *population* of neurons that is activated, termed **population coding**. For example, pressing a fine-pointed object gently on the skin triggers few sensory receptors with a low frequency of action potentials. As the same object is pressed more strongly, it triggers both increased frequency of action potentials in these neurons and triggers neurons that were previously inactive.

Within a given neuron, the *pattern* of action potentials generated by an event conveys information on that event. Normally information is carried by the frequency of action potentials, known as **frequency coding**. For example, the frequency of action potentials can code for intensity. (You might recall the example of temperature shown in Figure 3.4, p. 54.) See Figure 7.7(a) and (b). As the intensity of the physical stimulus increases, so does the frequency of action potentials.

Figure 7.7(c) represents a receptor having the property of **adaptation**. The activity generated in the sensory neuron is high when the stimulus is first applied but decreases over the period of application. By contrast, the type of neuron that has the response represented in Figures 7.7(a) and (b) exhibits no adaptation: for as long as the stimulus is applied, the neuron reacts in the same way.

Figure 7.8 shows the response of a neuron as a function of stimulus intensity. Suppose that this represents pressure applied to the skin. As action potential frequency goes up, so our conscious perception of pressure might increase in parallel. Note the **threshold** of intensity (A), which needs to be exceeded before there is any response by the neuron. Also the response does not increase indefinitely with increases in intensity. A saturation point is reached, at which the neuron produces action potentials at its maximum rate.

As just discussed, one code that can be employed in a sensory pathway is that increases in intensity of stimulation are encoded by increases in the frequency of action potentials. However, this is not the only code. In some cases, increasing intensity is associated with a decrease in action potential frequency. As another type of encoding, in the auditory system and for certain sound frequencies, the pattern of action potentials varies in synchrony with the pressure waves in the air (Rose *et al.*, 1971) (Figure 7.9).

The duration of a stimulus can be encoded by the duration over which action potentials occur (Figure 7.7(a) and (b)). Another form of coding is shown in Figure 7.10: the neuron is active even when no physical stimulus is applied to the sensory channel, termed 'spontaneous activity'. When the stimulus is applied, there is an increase in action potential frequency. There is then some reduction in frequency, i.e. adaptation. When the stimulus is terminated there is a suppression of activity to below the background level.

(a)

(b)

(c)

Figure 7.7 Frequency coding: (a) weak stimulus, (b) strong stimulus and (c) adaptation.

Source: Toates (1998c, Fig. 4.1, p. 102).

Figure 7.8 Relationship between intensity of a stimulus and response of a sensory neuron.

Receptive fields

Let us reconsider nociceptive neurons. Comparing Figure 7.11(a) and (b), the extent of branching of the tip is different. Correspondingly, the tip in part (a) reacts to tissue damage over a wider area than that in part (b). The area over which the neuron detects tissue damage is termed its **receptive field**. More generally, 'receptive field' of a neuron refers to the sensory area within which a stimulus is able to change the activity of the neuron (Hubel and Wiesel, 1959).

Sensory thresholds

For each sensory system, there is a minimum level of stimulation that can be detected: the **sensory threshold**. A very faint sound or light or a chemical in a very low concentration in the air might not be detected. So, there is an 'absolute threshold'. There is also a 'relative threshold'. For example, you might be able to detect the change in illumination caused by one candle lit in a dark room but could you tell the difference in intensity between 99 and 100 candles? Part of the limitation on what can be detected is set at the level of sensory transduction. For example, in Figure 7.8 no increase in response occurs until point A has been reached. The stimulus needs to be larger than A to be detected.

Constancy and change

What conveys particularly important information is change, in both space and time. For example, imagine that a charging elephant is closing in on you. What

Figure 7.9 Encoding by means of pattern. Relatively low (a) and high (b) frequencies and the associated pattern of action potentials.

Figure 7.10 Coding set against a spontaneous background level of activity: (a) stimulus and (b) response.

matters most in avoiding the beast is the accurate detection of the contour between its dark skin and the lightness of the sky. The exact shade of grey throughout the elephant is of less importance. Visual systems are especially tuned to detect contrast between regions.

Figure 7.11 Nociceptive neurons: (a) large and (b) small receptive fields.

Tactile systems are also tuned to detect contours, the edges of objects. For example, consider how we manage not to fall out of bed. Information on the bed's edge carries special importance to our tactile systems. In the time dimension, the importance of change is exemplified in the information carried by a sudden onset of sound as opposed to a steady background noise level. Change might be caused by the arrival of predator or prey. As a general feature, sensory systems are especially tuned to change, showing some adaptation at other times (though pain is an exception here). For example, when you first get into a swimming pool, it often feels very cold. After some exposure it feels much less cold. This is partly because neurons sensitive to low temperatures adapt over time. Figure 7.7(c) represents adaptation at the level of a sensory receptor, which is the basis of the psychological effect.

This completes discussion of general principles; the next two chapters consider individual systems.

Section summary

1 Detection is done by sensory receptors, which translate physical events into an electrical signal in the nervous system, termed sensory transduction.

2 Information about different qualities is carried by (a) which neurons are active and (b) the pattern of action potentials over time within a given neuron.

3 The receptive field of a neuron is the area of sensory surface which when stimulated influences the activity of the neuron.

4 Sensory systems are particularly sensitive to *changes* in stimulation in the dimensions of space and time.

☞ ## Test your knowledge

7.4 In Figure 7.6, which part of the CNS is represented in (i) part (a) and (ii) part (b)?

Answer on page 195

Bringing things together

The chapter was organized around the theme of generality (what sensory systems have in common) and specificity (what is the distinct feature of each system). Any sensory system faces the general problem of achieving transduction between physical events in the world and electrical changes in neurons. In some cases, e.g. nociception, a physical event translates into action potentials at the sensory receptor (Figure 7.6(a)). In vision, action potentials first appear two neurons removed from the sensory receptors (Figure 7.6(b)). Either way, each system 'speaks' to the brain in the language of action potentials in particular neurons. Specificity is apparent in that different sensory systems are sensitive to different features of the physical world involving different means of transduction.

Some sensory stimuli, such as a pheromone, intrinsically convey information about the world that can be used in the production of adaptive behaviour. In other cases, as in examples of vision, complex processes of interpretation, top-down modulation and extraction of invariance from varying stimulus information are needed before adaptive behaviour is instigated.

 See the video coverage for this chapter and how perception can be linked to sensory organs.

Summary of Chapter 7

1 Sensory systems detect information and project it to the brain, where it is interpreted.

2 Perception of the world is sometimes direct but more generally it depends upon putting sensory information into a context of memories, emotions and expectations.

3 Neurons convey information to the brain, encoded in terms of which neurons are active and their level of activity.

Further reading

See Smith (2009) and section on 'sensation and perception' in Gazzaniga (2009).

Visit www.pearsoned.co.uk/toates WEB
for a range of resources to support study.
Test yourself with multiple choice questions and access a bank of over 100 videos that will bring the topics to life.

Answers

Explanations for answers to 'test your knowledge' questions can be found on the website www.pearsoned.co.uk/toates

7.1 A sensory system detects the existence of certain pressure waves in the air and a perceptual system gives this meaning in terms of a sound.

7.2 (i) Frequency and (ii) wavelength

7.3 Blood; the air; between

7.4 (i) The spinal cord if the tip is below the neck and the brain if the tip is above the neck; (ii) the brain.

Chapter 8
Vision

Learning outcomes for Chapter 8

After studying this chapter, you should be able to:

1 Justify the claim that visual perception depends upon bottom-up and top-down contributions.

2 Explain how, in order to understand visual perception, knowledge of the properties of the cells of the retina and their interconnections is needed.

3 Describe information transmission in the visual system from eye to brain. Explain how the receptive field properties of some of the cells encountered along the way arise.

4 Explain what is meant by the terms 'stream' and 'parallel processing'. Link this to the structure of the visual system.

5 Explain what is meant by 'functional specialization' within the system underlying visual perception.

6 Describe how neuroimaging has increased understanding of the top-down factor in visual perception.

Scene-setting questions

1 After looking at a photographic flash, you then look at a light wall. Why do you see a dark form of the flash floating in space? Why does it fade?

2 When you stare intently at a distant star it sometimes disappears. Why?

3 How do we see colours?

4 What underlies the attraction that human infants show towards faces?

5 Do we tend to see what we expect to see?

6 How does visual development relate to the role served by vision?

How does visual development relate to the role served by vision? Explore the video on the website accompanying this book at www.pearsoned.co.uk/toates

What determines how this ambiguous picture is perceived consciously?

Source: © Salvador Dali, Fundació Gala-Salvador Dali, DACS 2010/ The Bridgeman Art Library

Introduction

Look around you at a world of visual objects, such as tables, chairs and books. You have a conscious **perception** of them. When you close your eyes you can still conjure up images of such objects. Think of your action in the world. Sometimes your full conscious awareness is brought to bear on a problem involving vision, as in trying to thread a needle or ride a bicycle along an icy road. At other times, through vision you can interact unconsciously with the world. For example, you walk along a crowded pavement, avoiding collisions, even though your conscious mind is 'elsewhere'. How is this integration between perception and action achieved?

Visual perception involves active processes, which depend upon bottom-up factors (signals arising from light falling on the eye) and top-down factors (e.g. memories and expectations) (Humphreys *et al.*, 1997). This chapter looks at both sets of processes and considers how visual perception depends upon their cooperation. A set of cells at the back of the eye converts light energy into electrical signals. This provides the bottom-up factor common to all visual perception and action. Cells in the eye also do some processing of information as well as transmitting it towards the brain.

Figure 8.1 exemplifies some processing that the CNS does on raw sensory input (von der Heydt, 1995). It distinguishes between what is detected by the early stages of the visual system and perception of the world (Leopold *et al.*, 2003). In the case of the Kanizsa triangle of Figure 8.1(a), people perceive a white triangle but it is illusory. If you examine the physical stimulus, you will see that there are no full sides to the triangle.

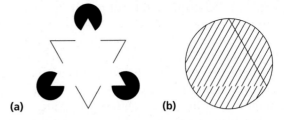

Figure 8.1 Reality and illusion: (a) Kanizsa triangle and (b) part real, part hidden and part illusory triangle.
Source: von der Heydt (1995, Fig. 23.1, p. 366).

Rather, any sides 'seen' are extrapolations by the brain. In part (b), is there a triangle of equal sides? The side to the right is clear. The base is not physically present but nonetheless it is perceived to be there. Conversely, the side to the left is physically present but is not generally perceived as part of a triangle. This illustrates that perception is much more than seeing exactly what stimulates the eye. It is also dependent upon context and involves extrapolation beyond the physical image.

Considering the bottom-up aspect, what is the nature of the stimulus, light? Light is difficult for most of us to understand. However, some familiarity with sound can help since light has features in common with it. Chapter 7 related pressure waves in the air to the perception of sound. Light and sound are characterized by wavelength and frequency. (However, whereas sound needs a medium through which to pass, e.g. air, light can pass through a vacuum.) Corresponding to variations in wavelength of light (physical stimulus) is the spectrum of colours that we perceive (the psychological dimension). For example, we usually describe light having a wavelength of 690 nanometres (nm) as red. Strictly speaking, red is a psychological quality, albeit one usually associated with a particular physical stimulus.

Figure 8.2 shows the visible spectrum, revealed by passing white light through a prism. You can see the component wavelengths of white light, corresponding to the colours of the spectrum.

The light emitted by, or reflected from, an object in part determines perception. By exploiting this input and stored information, the visual system extracts what

Figure 8.2 The visible spectrum.

is invariant about the world. For example, the hair of a blond person tends to look light under various conditions of illumination, from sunlight to moonlight. However, blondness is not intrinsic to the intensity of the light that is reflected from the hair and arrives in the eyes; blond people do not send off high levels of illumination in any absolute sense. More light is reflected from a person with black hair viewed in sunlight than a blond person in moonlight. What characterizes the blond person is that, *relative to a surround* (e.g. standing next to a dark-haired person), the blond hair tends to reflect more light. What is *invariant* is the hair's property of high 'reflectance' (i.e. it reflects a high percentage of light falling on it). Similarly, a robin's breast tends to look red because it reflects a large proportion of light of a particular wavelength, relative to other objects simultaneously present (e.g. its wings) (Zeki, 1993).

We consider first processes within the eye, the bottom-up contribution.

Section summary

1 Visual perception depends on bottom-up and top-down factors.

2 Light is characterized by wavelength, which is associated with the psychological phenomenon of colour.

3 The visual system extracts invariance by setting information in the image into context.

☞ Test your knowledge

8.1 Complete the following: 'Expressed in *physical* terms, Figure 8.2 reveals a range of different visible ___ and corresponding ___'.

Answer on page 223   WEB ▶

Within the eye

Detection of light in an image occurs at the layer of light-sensitive cells that form part of the **retina** of the eye (Figure 8.3). Also, some processing of information is performed by the cells of the retina. This section considers the properties of the eye as a whole and the cells that form the retina. It relates this to perception.

The eye's optics

Figure 8.3 shows the eye. The optics form an image of the outside world at the retina, i.e. the cornea and lens normally bring light to a focus there. The image on the retina is upside down and reversed left to right with respect to the external world (Gregory, 1997). The fact that the 'world' is upside down on the retina has no particular significance for vision, since the image has always been upside down. There is no homunculus looking at it. The important point is that there exists *consistency* between a particular pattern of image and the signals produced in particular neurons.

The eye is sometimes compared to a camera. Like a camera, there is an apparatus for forming an image and photosensitive material (sensory receptors). However, the analogy breaks down if it is suggested that perception is like forming a photograph. Visual perception is an active construction based only in part upon information at the retina.

As shown in Figure 8.4, by means of contraction of the ciliary muscle, the lens adjusts its curvature in order for objects to remain in focus on the retina as their distance from the eyes changes (Mellerio, 1966). This is known as **accommodation** and is under the control of the autonomic nervous system and smooth muscle (Chapter 3).

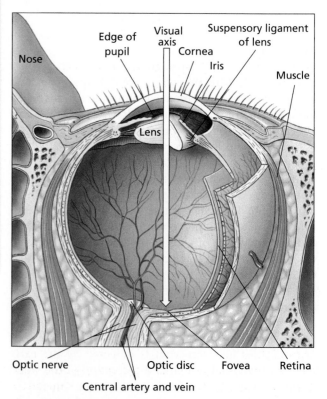

Figure 8.3 The eye.

Source: Martini *et al.* (2000, Fig.18-20e, p. 487). Copyright © 2000, 1997 by Frederic H. Martini, Inc. and Michael J. Timmons. Reprinted by permission of Pearson Education, Inc.

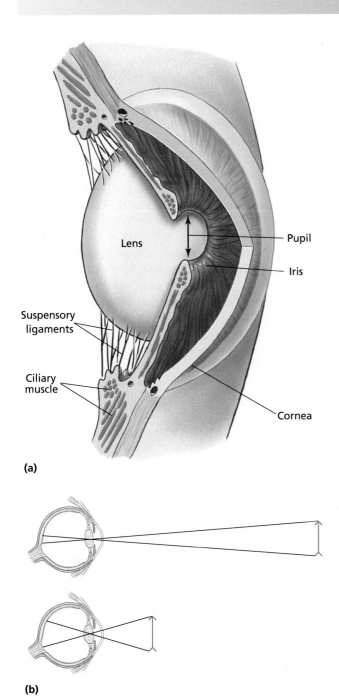

(a)

(b)

Figure 8.4 Accommodation: (a) lens and ciliary muscle and (b) accommodation for (above) far object and (below) near object.
Source: part (a) adapted from Martini *et al.* (2000, Fig. 18-21, p. 488). Copyright © 2000, 1997 by Frederic H. Martini, Inc. and Michael J. Timmons. Reprinted by permission of Pearson Education, Inc.

Eye movements

The objects of attention move relative to our eyes. Also, even when viewing detail in a static world, the object of attention can vary. In Figure 8.3, note a small depression at the centre of the retina, termed the **fovea**. The fovea is the optimal location on the retina for resolving

A personal angle

George Stratton

George Stratton of the University of California wore an optical instrument to 'invert' the images on his retina (Stratton, 1897). For the first time in his life (probably in anyone's life), the image became objectively the 'right' way up relative to the external world. When Stratton was not wearing this apparatus, he was blindfolded. He was interested in how the visual system adapted, if at all, to the new conditions. He walked around for eight days wearing the apparatus. At first Stratton experienced a complete inversion of the external world. He reported (p. 344): 'Almost all movements performed under the direct guidance of sight were laborious and embarrassed'.

A role of memory and integration between sensory channels was evident, as well as some conflict between bottom-up and top-down contributions to perception (p. 345):

As regards the parts of the body, their pre-experimental representation often invaded the region directly in sight. Arms and legs in full view were given a double position. Beside the position and relation in which they were actually seen, there was always in the mental background, in intimate connection with muscular and tactual sensations, the older representation of these parts.

Towards the end of the period, Stratton experienced some adaptation to the new condition. Movements came to be made with respect to the new perceived position of objects and without a conscious readjustment. The nervous system can show some adaptation to even a complete inversion of the visual image.

fine details within the image. These fine details are the object of attention. When the image of the detail does not coincide with the fovea, movements are made to bring fovea and object of attention into alignment. Such movement can be of the head or whole body or of the eyes relative to the head.

The eyes are rotated in their sockets by oculomotor muscles (examples of skeletal muscle) attached to the eyeballs. The oculomotor nerve (a cranial nerve) contains neurons that activate these muscles. Some eye movements are smooth, as when we track a smoothly moving target. Others are sudden and jerky, known as saccadic eye movements. Saccadic eye movements can be involuntary ('automatic'), to follow the sudden movement of the object of attention, corresponding to a move of the image from one retinal location to another. Saccadic movements can also be voluntary, as when we decide to move attention suddenly from one location to another.

Properties of receptors

Sensory detection

Figure 8.5 shows a simplified cross-section through a small segment of the retina. The eye's sensory receptors, **rods** and **cones**, form a layer within the retina. The chemicals contained within them (e.g. rhodopsin in rods) absorb light and, in doing so, the receptors change their electrical state (voltage). This is sensory detection.

The change in electrical activity that occurs at a sensory receptor when light is absorbed is not an action potential but a less abrupt change. On absorbing light, the rods and cones then pass on a message, via synapses, to other neurons, the bipolar cells (Figure 8.5). In turn, bipolars pass the information to ganglion cells, and so on.

For the moment, let us focus on rods. Rods come in just one variety and Figure 8.6 shows an absorption curve of the chemical contained within them (Bowmaker and Dartnell, 1980). Rods exhibit maximum absorption ('sensitivity') to light of a wavelength of 498 nm, with the sensitivity to each side being less. As far as the contribution to vision made by rods is concerned, sensitivity to light of different wavelengths corresponds to the curve of absorption by the chemical contained within them.

Cones come in three forms corresponding to three different chemicals contained within them (Martin, 1998). The absorption characteristics of the three kinds of cone are shown in Figure 8.6, the significance of this for colour vision being explored later. The three types are termed 'long-wavelength' (L), 'medium-wavelength' (M) and 'short-wavelength' cones (S), indicating the wavelength of light to which they are most sensitive (Martin, 1998). These are abbreviated as L, M and S cones. Sensitivity to wavelength varies with each type of cone. Thus, the L cone is most sensitive to light of wavelength 564 nm, corresponding to yellow, but exhibits some sensitivity to wavelengths to each side of this. Light of wavelength corresponding to red is detected by L cones. A wavelength of 534 nm is perceived as green, the result of its absorption by both L and M cones. Light of short wavelength is perceived as blue.

Adaptation

When receptors absorb large amounts of light they show adaptation, i.e. their sensitivity is lowered (Gregory, 1997). The chemical within them is said to be 'bleached'. When the light is switched off, sensitivity slowly increases, termed 'dark adaptation'. You can demonstrate this by going from a light room into relative darkness. At first you see rather little but then gradually you perceive more of your surroundings. Some fraudulent Victorian spiritualists exploited this to make ghostly images appear after a while in the seance room.

If you look at a bright object briefly, you tend to see a bright **after-image** of it, a positive after-image. This is due to activity in the nerve carrying information to the

Figure 8.5 Cross-section through part of the retina.

Source: Martini *et al.* (2000, Fig. 18-22a, p. 490). Copyright © 2000, 1997 by Frederic H. Martini, Inc. and Michael J. Timmons. Reprinted by permission of Pearson Education, Inc.

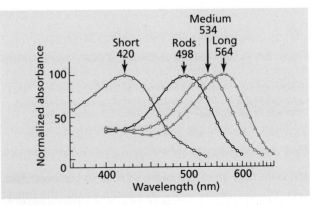

Figure 8.6 Absorption characteristics of rods and three types of cone.

Source: Bowmaker and Dartnall (1980, Fig. 2, p. 505).

brain outlasting the light stimulus. If you then divert your gaze to a light wall, a dark (negative) after-image of the object will appear on the wall. This is partly because the bright object has adapted the receptors in an area of retina; they are fatigued (Gregory, 1997). Neighbouring receptors are relatively non-fatigued and so yield a stronger signal. The fatigued area is interpreted as a dark object. In time, the after-image disappears, corresponding to when adaptation is equal across the receptors.

Between receptors and ganglion cells

In Figure 8.5, note the layers of cells (bipolar, amacrine and horizontal cells) that lie between receptors and ganglion cells. We shall focus on the sequence: receptor → bipolar cell → ganglion cell. The bipolar cells and other intermediate cells contribute to information processing by virtue of the connections that they form among themselves, with receptors and with ganglion cells. We shall consider the product of this processing in so far as it is reflected in the properties of ganglion cells.

Ganglion cells

The receptive field of a given neuron in a sensory system is defined in terms of the specific stimulus qualities that influence the neuron's activity. The present section introduces receptive fields in the visual system, defined in terms of the image at the retina. It asks, what features of the image falling on which part of the retina change the activity of the neuron under consideration? The connections within the retina are such that information on contours within the image is particularly emphasized.

Investigating the receptive field

To investigate the receptive fields of ganglion cells in the visual system, a cat was anaesthetized and its head held in a fixed position (Kuffler, 1953). Typically, ganglion cells exhibit some activity even when the animal is in complete darkness, an activity termed the 'spontaneous background activity' (Figure 8.7). A small spot of white light was projected onto a screen in front of the cat. An electrode was inserted into the optic nerve to detect the electrical activity within the axon of a single ganglion cell.

The retina is explored with the spot of light and the activity of the ganglion cell observed. Note the electrical activity shown on the screen of the oscilloscope, the recording apparatus. Since the head is held in a fixed location, there is a one-to-one correspondence between the screen and the retina, so the investigator can map between them.

First, the spot is in location 1 on the screen (Figure 8.8(a)). Suppose that there is no change in frequency of

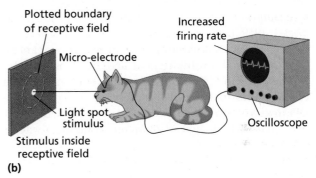

Figure 8.7 Investigating the receptive field. Spot (a) outside the receptive field of the cell and so activity is the same as the spontaneous background activity and (b) inside receptive field. (Note: in reality the size of receptive field is small compared with the size of screen.)

Source: Greene (1990, Fig. 10.5, p. 483).

firing from when the eye is in darkness. By definition, location 1 is outside the receptive field of the ganglion cell, i.e. stimulation at this site does not affect the neuron relative to its activity in darkness. Therefore, a zero (0) is indicated on the figure. Similarly, light falling at location 2 has no effect and a 0 is placed there. At location 3, the cell *reduces* its rate of firing relative to darkness. Light falling here is within the receptive field, since it influences firing. Since the cell fires less frequently, the light is within the *inhibitory* region of the receptive field and a minus sign is placed at 3. Similarly

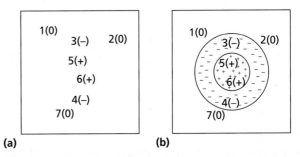

Figure 8.8 Results obtained from stimulating retina: (a) some points and (b) complete pattern of points joined together.

a minus sign is placed at 4. When light is projected to 5, the cell *increases* its rate of firing compared with darkness and a plus is placed at 5. The same is found at 6; 7 is outside the receptive field since light projected at 7 has no effect.

Suppose that we explore the entire retina, while recording from the same ganglion cell. Typically, we find the effect shown in Figure 8.8(b). If we join together all the pluses and then all the minuses, we obtain the shape shown. This defines the receptive field of the ganglion cell, consisting of an excitatory centre (termed ON region) and an inhibitory surround (termed OFF region), an example of **centre–surround** organization (Hubel and Wiesel, 1959; Livingstone and Hubel, 1988).

The example illustrates that information can be conveyed by the inhibition of activity as well as by excitation. Inhibition to below the spontaneous rate conveys information on the presence of light in the OFF region. Thus, a single cell can signal two different events, which appears to be an economical way of operating.

ON centre cells

What is the optimal stimulus to trigger activity in the ganglion cell that has the receptive field shown in Figure 8.8? It is a spot of light that fills the excitatory centre but does not invade the inhibitory surround (Figure 8.9(a)). Note the excitation when the light is switched on.

What is the optimal stimulus to *inhibit* activity in the cell? Now it is an annulus of light that fills the surround region but does not invade the centre (Figure 8.9(b)). Typically, the cell shows a burst of activity when light in the surround region is turned *off* (Figure 8.9(b)).

Suppose a light stimulus covers the centre and surround. Light in one region has a cancelling effect relative to light in the other region. Its precise effect depends upon the relative contribution of the two regions of receptive field. Typically, they might be of equal weight and so there would be no response from the ganglion cell when light falls onto both regions (Figure 8.9(c)).

Let us consider just a single ganglion cell. What light stimulus could correspond to Figure 8.9(a)? The light from a small star at night might just fill the ON region with no light falling in the OFF region. A bright sky would produce light falling on the entire receptive field and might not trigger any change in activity in the ganglion cell (part (c)).

OFF centre cells

There are ganglion cells that have the opposite characteristic to Figure 8.9: light falling on the centre region inhibits the cell whereas light on the outer area excites it (Figure 8.10). What kind of stimulus triggers such activity? I am grateful to an Open University student of mine, Jackie, for suggesting a memorable example: a polar bear's black nose surrounded by pristine white fur. As it approaches, at some distance the black of the nose will just correspond to the centre region of the receptive field.

Lateral inhibition

The receptive field organization of the ganglion cells that has just been described is defined by *location* on the retina, irrespective of the wavelength of light. Different types of cone (L, M and S cones) within one area of receptive field excite the cell and a similar variety of cones in the other area exert an opposite effect

Figure 8.9 Responses of a ganglion cell: (a) light spot in centre region of receptive field, (b) light annulus in outer region and (c) illumination of the entire receptive field.

Figure 8.10 An OFF centre/ON surround characteristic of a ganglion cell's receptive field.

(Livingstone and Hubel, 1988; Martin, 1998). In Figures 8.9 and 8.10, *any* visible wavelength of light falling within the ON area of the receptive field tends to excite the ganglion and light in the OFF area tends to inhibit it.

Let us look at this in terms of the neural input to the ganglion cell. One set of neural inputs to the ganglion cell tends to excite it, corresponding to the ON area. Another set tends to inhibit it, corresponding to the OFF. This is termed **lateral inhibition**. It depends on information being communicated from receptors via bipolar, horizontal and amacrine cells (Figure 8.5).

Because of this type of organization, such ganglion cells are unable to signal information on wavelength. They simply signal light–dark contrast between the sub-regions of receptive field. Based upon this property, it is possible to speculate on the neural connections that other cells make with a ganglion cell (Figure 8.11(a)). For a ganglion cell with an excitatory centre and inhibitory surround receptive field, all receptors within the inner area (e.g. R_1 and R_2) make (through other cells) excitatory connections to the ganglion, whereas all those in the outer area (e.g. R_3 and R_4) make (through other cells) inhibitory connections. These other cells are the bipolar, amacrine and horizontal cells (Figure 8.5). However, not all ganglion cells are of this type, and a type that signals differences in wavelength is discussed later.

There is overlap of receptive fields at the retina (Figure 8.11(b)). A given ganglion cell does not have exclusive 'territorial rights' over a population of receptors. Rather, a receptor can contribute an input to many different ganglion cells. Receptor R_1 is within the ON area of the receptive field of ganglion cell G_1 but in the OFF area of that of G_2.

Detecting detail and broad features

Sometimes an animal needs to resolve fine detail, e.g. a flying hawk distinguishing the movements of a mouse in a cornfield. At other times, a more global analysis is needed, e.g. a mouse detecting a slight change in overall intensity of illumination over a large area of the visual field that could be the shadow of a predator. Differences in these abilities vary across the retina, depending upon the region on which the image falls.

Cellular basis

In humans, there are about 106 million receptors for 1 million ganglion cells. Hence, there is **convergence** of the outputs from receptors onto ganglion cells. A single ganglion cell derives its input from more than one receptor (Figure 8.5 shows some convergence). The extent of the convergence varies over the retina. At the fovea (Figure 8.3), there is a dense packing of cones and little convergence. By contrast, in the periphery, very many rods all feed their inputs into a single ganglion cell, i.e. a high convergence (Figure 8.12).

The kind of visual processing that regions of the retina perform is a function of the variation in

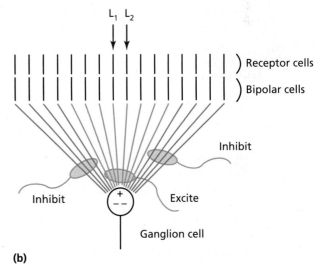

Figure 8.12 Different degrees of convergence. (a) Extreme foveal situation of no convergence, i.e. a one-to-one link between receptors and ganglions via bipolars. The eye can resolve the difference even between light L_1 and light L_2, since different one-to-one links are made. (b) Some convergence. Eight receptors all feed via bipolars to excite one ganglion cell and eight inhibit it. Contrast the surface area of excitation between (a) and (b).

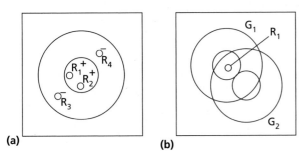

Figure 8.11 Receptive field properties. (a) Receptors within the centre region excite a ganglion cell. Receptors in the outer area inhibit it. (b) Overlapping receptive fields.

convergence. Where there is little convergence, i.e. at, or near, the fovea, the ability to resolve fine detail is high, described as high **acuity**. Receptive fields are very small.

Away from the fovea, there is a large convergence of inputs to ganglion cells and receptive fields are large. A large population of cells supplies excitatory inputs, corresponding to the ON region of receptive field, whereas another large population supplies inhibitory inputs, corresponding to the OFF region. In contrast to the fovea, the ability to resolve detail is less good since there is a pooling of output from receptors. However, as a result of pooling, the ability to detect the presence or absence of weak lights is relatively good, i.e. **sensitivity** is high.

An analogy

By analogy, suppose that we need to measure the rainfall at a series of streets of terraced houses. We inspect the flow of water down the drainpipes. Suppose that all the houses in a street have one communal drainpipe. Monitoring flow within it would give a measure of even light rain falling anywhere in the street since the roofs are *pooling* what falls on all of them. However, we would not be able to resolve the detail of where in the street the rain was falling.

Suppose instead that each house has its own drainpipe. It might be difficult to detect the presence of a light rain since rather little flow would be generated from what is caught by a single roof. If, however, it was pouring down at number 12 but dry at number 22 we would be aware of this from monitoring individual drainpipes. So, two different sorts of information are derived from the communal and the individual drainpipes.

By analogy with the drainpipes, the eye has the benefit of both systems. When you resolve fine detail, as in threading a needle, by means of eye movements the image is brought to the fovea. When you want to detect the presence of a weak light stimulating a relatively large area of retina, the eyes move to bring the image away from the fovea. You can experiment with this. Find a faint distant star and stare in an attentive way at it. You might find that it then disappears. Staring corresponds to bringing its image to a focus at the fovea. The fovea is an area where the cells show little convergence of their outputs and therefore it is not associated with the capacity to integrate weak light over a relatively large area. This is the capacity needed to detect a weak light. Look to one side of the star, and it should reappear. This corresponds to the image falling on a rod-rich area, with considerable convergence of output and thereby a high capacity to detect weak lights.

Colour

Introduction

So far, we have mainly considered the detection of light–dark. How do we perceive colour? Imagine an eye that has rods but no cones. Could it extract information on the wavelength of light? Rods are *differentially* sensitive to wavelength (Figure 8.6), which might suggest that they are able to do this. However, it is not possible for rods to exploit this differential sensitivity to extract information on wavelength, for the following reason.

A light of 498 nm is the optimal to stimulate rods (Figure 8.6). See Figure 8.13. Suppose that a light of this wavelength (indicated as X) and intensity 100 units falls on the rods. It generates action potentials at a frequency of 100 per second in the associated ganglion cell. Now keeping light intensity at 100 units, suppose that the wavelength is changed to Y, to which the rods are less

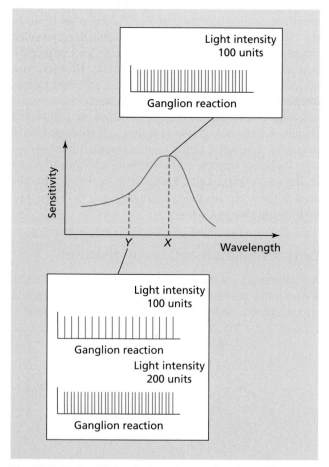

Figure 8.13 Sensitivity of a population of rods to different wavelengths and response of associated ganglion cell.
Source: after Toates (1998c, Fig. 4.21, p. 116).

sensitive. The action potential frequency falls to, say, 50 per second. Can the frequency of action potentials in the ganglion cell thereby give a measure of wavelength? This might work provided that the light intensity always stays the same. But, of course, the world is not made up of lights having constant intensity. The rods and thereby the ganglion could not distinguish between a light of 100 units intensity at wavelength X and one of 200 units intensity at wavelength Y (Figure 8.13). Of course, we are able to make such distinctions. Blue looks blue whether it is an intense blue light or a faint one. So how is this achieved?

Role of cones

By employing more than one type of cone, the visual system *in effect* compares the responses of one cone with that of another (Figure 8.6). Suppose that a light of wavelength 420 nm falls on the retina. The S cone will always be more strongly stimulated than the M or L, irrespective of intensity. Figure 8.14(a) demonstrates this. Contrast this with light of a wavelength of 534 nm (part (b)). The M cones are most activated, the L cones less so and the S cones the least. At 564 nm (part (c)), the L cones are most stimulated, the M cones less so and the S cones not at all. As shown, these ratios of responses will remain the same even if the intensity is halved to 50 units. That is to say, it is the *ratio* of responses between the component cones that determines colour.

You can understand a colour illusion (Figure 8.15) in terms of the properties of cones. Brightly illuminate the page, stare at the cross for 1–2 minutes and finally transfer your gaze to the white area. You should see colours appear for a while. They should be rather different from the cross at which you stared. This is an illusion since the paper is white. How is it explained?

When light first falls on them, a population of cones tends to give a strong response. However, by exposure to light, they soon adapt or 'fatigue'. Other cones, which are relatively non-stimulated, will not fatigue. While you stare at the green area, this will fatigue M cones within an area of retina but L cones within this same area will be relatively non-fatigued, since they absorb little of the light at this wavelength. When you divert your gaze to the plain white area, the light that is stimulating the 'green-fatigued' area of retina is white. White light is made up of all the colours of the spectrum, including green and red (Figure 8.2). So the red component of the white light will stimulate preferentially a population of L cones, which are not fatigued, and therefore they give a strong response. The M component

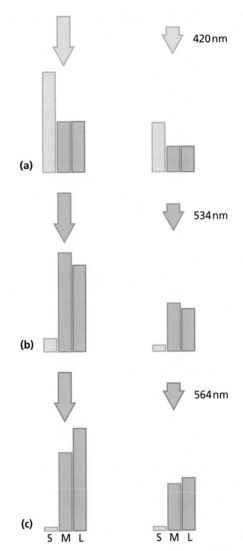

Figure 8.14 Relative sensitivities of the three types of cones to three different wavelengths of light at two different intensities (left 100 units and right 50 units): (a) wavelength 420 nm, (b) 534 nm and (c) 564 nm.

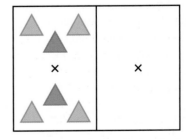

Figure 8.15 Coloured object for producing illusion.

stimulates a fatigued population of M cones, which respond weakly. It is therefore as if the eye is being stimulated with red light and that is what you perceive. Within a short time, the red cones are as fatigued as the green and so the perception is of white.

One possible mode of connections to a ganglion cell is that the output from, say, M cones within an area excites the cell whereas the output from L cones inhibits it (an M⁺L⁻ area) (Livingstone and Hubel, 1988). Thus, an increase in firing above the spontaneous level indicates medium-wavelength light and suppression to below this indicates long-wavelength light. This is termed **opponent-process coding** (Martin, 1998). A different receptive field property could consist of L cones exciting and M cones inhibiting, i.e. L⁺M⁻ (Figure 8.16(a)). Still other ganglion cells have receptive fields based on area rather than wavelength (Figure 8.16(b)).

We now consider the transmission of information to the brain.

 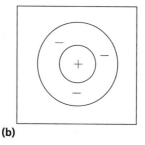

(a)   (b)

Figure 8.16 Opponent processing in inputs to a ganglion cell: (a) based on wavelength and (b) based on space at the retina.

Section summary

1 Oculomotor muscles rotate the eyes in their sockets to maintain the point of interest in the image in alignment with the fovea.

2 The retinal sensory receptors are rods and three types of cone. These absorb light and thereby change their electrical state.

3 Some retinal ganglion cells have a concentric (centre–surround) receptive field consisting of ON and OFF areas.

4 Light falling on the ON area excites the ganglion cell relative to its spontaneous firing rate whereas light falling in the OFF area inhibits it.

5 The three types of cone have different sensitivities to the wavelength of light.

6 Acuity is high at and near the fovea.

7 On going away from the fovea, sensitivity to weak lights increases.

8 In opponent-process coding for colour, light that is absorbed by cones of one type excites a ganglion cell, whereas that absorbed by cones of a different kind inhibits it.

☞ Test your knowledge

8.2 Which of the following types of cone have any sensitivity to light of a wavelength 580 nm? (i) Short, (ii) medium, (iii) long.

8.3 In Figure 8.9(a), which of the following would tend to increase the frequency of action potentials in the period marked 'light'? (i) Increasing the intensity of light, (ii) enlarging the size of the spot of light, (iii) decreasing the size of the spot of light.

8.4 In Figure 8.13, suppose that the rods are stimulated with light of wavelength Y and the response of the ganglion cell is 10 action potentials per second. What would be the expected response for a shift of wavelength to X, while holding intensity constant?

8.5 In Figure 8.16(a), suppose that just the central region of the receptive field (corresponding to the inner circle of part (b)) is illuminated with light of wavelength 620 nm. Which of the following would increase the activity of the ganglion cell? (i) Increasing the intensity of the light, (ii) keeping intensity constant but increasing the size of area within the receptive field stimulated, (iii) shifting the wavelength to 520 nm.

Answers on page 223

Basics of visual pathways

Introduction

The message from sensory receptors to bipolar cells conveys information about light absorbed by the receptors. Via synapses, bipolar cells relay information to ganglion cells (Figure 8.5). Ganglion cells then convey information to the brain as a pattern of action potentials in their axons. The first part of the bundle of axons of the ganglion cells constitutes the optic nerve, one of the cranial nerves. After entering the brain, the same bundle is termed the 'optic tract' (Figure 8.17).

As part of the 'classical' route, Figure 8.17 shows a destination of ganglion cells: a nucleus of the thalamus, the lateral geniculate nucleus (LGN). LGN neurons project to the visual cortex, where they form synapses with cortical neurons.

As part of different routes, other ganglion cells project to other destinations, e.g. the superior colliculus. This pathway, a **subcortical pathway**, also plays a role in perception.

The world viewed by the eyes is termed 'the visual field' (see top overlapping colours in Figure 8.17). Consider the visual field to the right of the midline of each eye. Light arising from the right half of the visual field arrives at the left half of each retina. Light from the left visual field arrives at the right half of each retina. Neural pathways project from the left half of each eye to the left half of the brain. Pathways from the right side of each eye project to the right side of the brain. Half the pathway from each eye crosses over to the other side, at the optic chiasm. Because of the cross-over of pathways, information arriving at each eye from a given object can be compared. The fact that the eyes have a slightly different perspective contributes to the perception of depth.

In stating that information is *conveyed* from the retina to the brain, an important qualification is needed. Information in the visual image is not converted one-to-one into an electrical signal that conveys exactly the same information. As just described, some information processing occurs. How this is done can be understood in terms of the connections between the neurons within the visual pathways. In the course of conveying information, some information potentially available in the image is *discarded* or given relatively little weight (e.g. on uniform illumination) and other information is *accentuated* (e.g. on changes in intensity or wavelength). The brain receives information already predigested as far as its importance is concerned.

Now for more details.

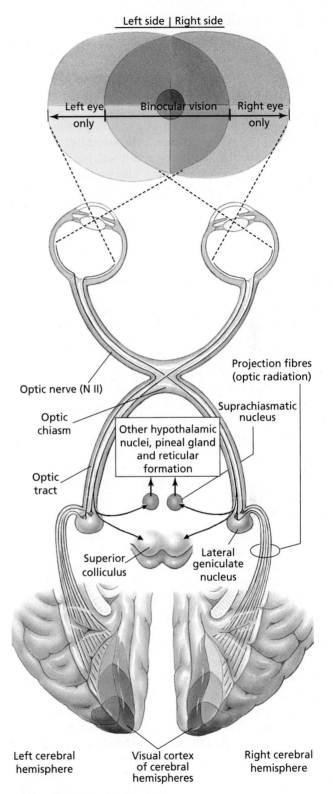

Figure 8.17 The visual system.
Source: Martini *et al.* (2000, Fig. 18-25, p. 492). Copyright © 2000, 1997 by Frederic H. Martini, Inc. and Michael J. Timmons. Reprinted by permission of Pearson Education, Inc.

Lateral geniculate nucleus

Ganglion cells have a concentric (centre–surround) receptive field. Ganglion cells synapse with LGN cells. Each LGN cell also has a concentric (centre–surround) receptive field property that is very similar to that of its associated ganglion cell. Suppose that a particular ganglion cell is a specialist at extracting information on colour. Because of its input, the associated LGN cell will also have this sensitivity and it will transmit information on colour to the cortex. Like ganglion cells, the receptive field of an LGN cell is in one or other eye but not both, i.e. LGN cells are monocular. LGN cells project their axons to the primary visual cortex.

The cortex

The role of different areas

The classical account (to which complications need to be added) is that LGN cells transmit visual information, which terminates at part of the visual cortex. This is termed the **primary visual cortex**, also known as the 'striate cortex', 'V1' and 'area 17' and occupies part of the occipital lobe (Figure 8.17). Neighbouring areas that are also concerned with visual processing are termed 'prestriate cortex' (Zeki, 1993).

Neurons within the primary visual cortex process information to extract features of the visual world and also project information to the prestriate cortex. In some primate species, over 50% of the whole cortex is engaged in processing visual information.

Simple cortical cells

When the response properties of neurons in the visual cortex are examined, an orderly relationship between retina and cortex appears. Adjacent regions of retina are associated with adjacent neurons in the visual cortex, termed a **topographical map** (Zeki, 1993). Damage to a region of visual cortex is associated with loss of vision in a particular area of visual field, termed a 'scotoma'.

The receptive fields of cortical cells are typically different from those of ganglion and LGN cells. Remember – the receptive field of a cell anywhere in the visual system is defined by what stimulus of light *at the retina* alters the cell's activity. Rather than being concentric, a cortical cell typically has a slit-shaped receptive field and is termed a 'simple cortical cell' (Hubel and Wiesel, 1959) (Figure 8.18). It shows little or no response to a spot of light (though some cells with concentric receptive fields are also found here; von der Heydt, 1995). A given cortical cell can often be driven from light in the retina of either eye, i.e. they are binocular.

How do scientists explain the form of this receptive field? Part of the explanation is as follows (Hubel and

Figure 8.18 The properties of a simple cortical cell: (a) receptive field, made up of excitatory inner slit and inhibitory surround, (b) receptive fields of a series of ganglion cells that provide the excitatory input to the cortical cell and (c) optimal stimulus to trigger the cortical cell.

Wiesel, 1959). Imagine a series of ganglion cells, G_1, G_2, ... Their receptive fields, made up from an ON centre and an OFF surround, form a straight line on the retina (Figure 8.18(b)). Each ganglion cell projects to a corresponding LGN cell, $G_1 \rightarrow LGN_1$, $G_2 \rightarrow LGN_2$, ... This *series* of LGN cells projects to excite a *single* cortical cell.

What is the optimal stimulus to trigger activity in this cortical cell? Activity in all the LGN cells that project to it. Such activity will derive from activity in all the ganglion cells that project to the LGN cells. What light stimulus will maximize the activity in these ganglion cells? A slit of light having a particular location and orientation (Figure 8.18(c)).

The sequence, receptor → bipolar → ganglion → LGN → simple cortical cell is an example of hierarchical processing. Each stage extracts a new or refined feature and the sequence continues even beyond simple cells.

A personal angle

A chance discovery

In 1981, David Hubel, Roger Sperry and Torsten Wiesel were awarded the Nobel Prize. Hubel (1982) explained how he and Wiesel discovered simple cortical cells. They had presented concentric stimuli to the retina but without much reaction from cortical cells. Then, by accident, the edge of the slide on which the test stimuli were presented cast a shadow in the form of a straight line on the screen. Hubel reported (p. 517) that 'the cell went off like a machine gun'. Never underestimate the role of chance in scientific discovery.

However, hierarchical processing is only one mode of cortical processing: there is extensive ('top-down') feedback of information throughout the visual pathways and this also contributes to cortical processing (Ferster, 2004).

Some simple cortical cells respond to a bar of light at a particular orientation and location on the retina but are particularly sensitive to change in the stimulus. A slit of light appearing and then rapidly extinguishing is a powerful trigger to them.

Complex cortical cells

Suppose that a series of simple cells, all with receptive fields of the same orientation but different locations (L_1, L_2, ...) on the retina, excite another cortical cell, termed a complex cell (Figure 8.19). A slit of light at any of the locations is sufficient to excite the complex cell. Firing of this cell encodes the feature that there is a slit of light of a given orientation (in this case, vertical) somewhere within a region of retina. This appears to be the start of extracting a feature of invariance from the image. A zebra is still the same zebra even if it moves.

Concerning simple cells that are sensitive to a dynamic stimulus (rapid on–off), one could imagine a series of them all projecting to a complex cell. The optimal stimulus to trigger such a cell could be a line of light rapidly moving through the receptive field. In this way the basics of a movement detection system can be seen.

Grandmother cells?

Such hierarchical information processing raises an interesting problem (Bowers, 2009). Consider the sequence, retinal receptors, to bipolar cells, ganglion cells, then LGN cells, to cells in the primary visual cortex and then to other regions of cortex. More and more features are 'extracted' from the information available at the image.

How we perceive, say, a yellow Volkswagen is still something of a mystery. Do we have a specific 'yellow Volkswagen' neuron at a late stage of processing in the cortex? The theory that we have a specific neuron for the perception of each object is summed up in the expression **grandmother cell**. Thus, following this line of theorizing, we would have a neuron specific to a particular grandmother (see Barlow, 1995).

It seems implausible that we have a single neuron (or even a dedicated number of neurons) for each perception. Remove this single neuron and we would fail to identify our grandmother! Only a slight accident or a lowered blood supply to the brain region might kill the neuron and then we would have a selective blindness for one grandmother (Zeki, 1993). The notion of grandmother cells is usually rejected as being naive, but scientists have difficulties in explaining the later stages of perception.

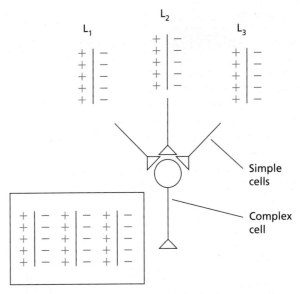

Figure 8.19 A complex cell with inputs from a series of simple cells.

Communication between the two hemispheres

General

Among other routes, the hemispheres communicate visual information between themselves by means of the axons that form the corpus callosum. Thus, certain information processed in one hemisphere can be made available to the opposite hemisphere: in the later stages of processing, cells are found with receptive fields sensitive to information processed in either hemisphere (Bullier, 2004). The visual system provides a good means for investigating inter-hemispheric communication.

Figure 8.20 shows how some responsibilities are divided between hemispheres, e.g. language is mainly processed in the left. This hemisphere controls the activity of the right hand. The left hand is controlled from the right hemisphere.

In Figure 8.20, information from the right half of the visual field (indicated by the right hand with a pencil) is transformed from light to electrical activity in the left half of each retina (indicated blue) and then arrives in the left hemisphere (via pathways represented as blue). Information from the left visual field impinges on the right half of each retina (red), is transmitted via pathways (represented as red) and arrives at the right hemisphere.

Split brains

Sometimes the corpus callosum (Figure 8.20) is surgically cut to stop epilepsy that arises from abnormal electrical activity in one hemisphere influencing the other (Sperry, 1974). Patients receiving this operation

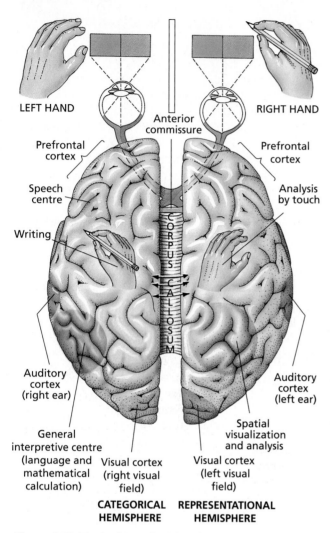

LEFT HAND

Anterior commissure

RIGHT HAND

Prefrontal cortex

Prefrontal cortex

Speech centre

Analysis by touch

Writing

C O R P U S   C A L L O S U M

Auditory cortex (right ear)

Auditory cortex (left ear)

General interpretive centre (language and mathematical calculation)

Visual cortex (right visual field)

Visual cortex (left visual field)

Spatial visualization and analysis

CATEGORICAL HEMISPHERE

REPRESENTATIONAL HEMISPHERE

Figure 8.20 The brain emphasizing the corpus callosum.
Source: adapted from Martini *et al.* (2000, Fig. 16-8, p. 436). Copyright © 2000, 1997 by Frederic H. Martini, Inc. and Michael J. Timmons. Reprinted by permission of Pearson Education, Inc.

are termed **split-brain** patients. Using such patients and tests in which images are very briefly flashed onto a screen, it is possible to send information to just one hemisphere, a 'divided visual-field presentation' (Figure 8.21). First, follow the sequence of Figure 8.20 shown as the 'red route'. Then you will appreciate that, when presented in the left visual field of Figure 8.21, the information 'nut' is available only to the right hemisphere. It is found that such patients can select the nut with the left hand but can neither select the correct object with the right hand nor verbalize 'nut'.

If the right hand touches the objects or they are projected to the right visual field, the patient can verbally name them (follow the blue route of Figure 8.20). Each hemisphere can function on its own but the person cannot perform tasks that require inter-hemispheric communication.

Figure 8.21 Projecting information to just one hemisphere.
Source: based on Sperry (1970), in Popper and Eccles (1977, Fig. E5-3).

Since the left hemisphere controls speech and therefore is responsible for reports of conscious experience, is it the case that only the left hemisphere is conscious? Although the right hemisphere can perform certain tasks, since these cannot be articulated verbally is the right hemisphere unconscious? Such questions pose enormous challenges.

We now look at processing that takes place beyond the primary visual cortex but in order to do so we need to look in a little more detail at the route from eye to brain.

Section summary

1 The classical sequence of information transfer is receptors → bipolar cells → ganglion cells → LGN cells → visual cortex.

2 Another route ('subcortical') is via the superior colliculus.

3 LGN cells have concentric receptive fields corresponding to the associated ganglion cells.

4 Simple cortical cells have slit-shaped receptive fields.

5 There is some hemispheric specialization.

6 The corpus callosum communicates visual information from one hemisphere to another.

Test your knowledge

8.6 Consider the simple cortical cell, the receptive field of which is shown in Figure 8.18 and the light stimulus shown. Which of the following would be expected to decrease the frequency of action potentials shown by the cell? (i) Rotating the light stimulus to an orientation of 45° to that shown, (ii) rotating the light stimulus to an orientation of 90° to that shown, (iii) keeping the position the same but increasing the intensity of light.

8.7 Figures 8.17 and 8.20 show cross-over of axons at the optic chiasm. These axons are part of which kind of cell?

8.8 Complete the following: 'When a person looks straight ahead, information from the left visual field arrives at the ___ half of each eye and is transmitted to the ___ hemisphere'.

Answers on page 223

Functional specialization: perception and action

Introduction

Anyone's intuitive guess as to how the link between perception and action is organized might be as in Figure 8.22(a), i.e. a single 'general purpose' sensory-perceptual system (Goodale and Milner, 2004). Sensory systems detect events in the world. These events are then perceived by the brain, at which point they enter conscious awareness. On the basis of conscious perceptions, we then organize motor action.

In reality, perception and action are linked rather as in Figure 8.22(b). Within the visual system, there is **parallel processing**. That is to say, there exists a *division of labour* between conscious perception of the world and rapid action on the world, i.e. **functional specialization** (Norman, 2002; Zeki, 1993). This distinction between perception and action can be better understood by first considering a related functional distinction, to which we now turn.

The initial stages of specialization

Qualities such as wavelength and movement are, to some extent, processed separately. This division of labour starts at the retina. Work on non-human primates reveals that different types of ganglion cell correspond to the start of separate systems ('channels') of processing (Bocanegra and Zeelenberg, 2009; De Valois and De Valois, 1980). We shall deal with the two best-known systems, though more exist (Kaplan, 2004). At the start of the two channels are two types of cell: magnocellular (abbreviated as magno or M) ganglion cells and parvocellular (parvo or P) ganglion cells.

The magno ganglion cells are especially sensitive to fast-moving stimuli and to differences in illumination in the image. They provide an input to the brain from which movement is calculated but are relatively insensitive to differences in wavelength. Their receptive fields are distributed over the retina.

The parvo ganglion cells are sensitive to stationary images and to colour, in that they tend to be strongly triggered by, say, contrast between red and green in the image (Zeki, 1993). Their receptive fields are found particularly at the fovea.

The functional segregation is emphasized at the LGN where the inputs from magno and parvo cells are anatomically segregated (Merigan and Maunsell, 1993) (Figure 8.23). Thus, a magno ganglion cell synapses onto an LGN cell, so the LGN cell has 'magno' properties similar to the magno ganglion cell. A parvo ganglion cell synapses onto a different LGN cell, so that this LGN cell has similar properties to the parvo

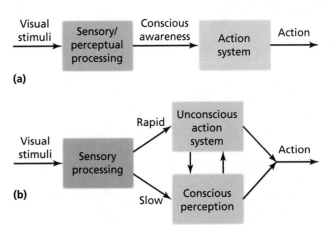

Figure 8.22 Perception and action: (a) intuitive view and (b) model of how perception and action really relate. There is a rapid unconscious route to action as well as a slow conscious route. There are interactions between these routes.

ganglion cell. Hence the information sent to the cortex remains functionally segregated, constituting what is termed a **magno system** and a **parvo system.**

The magno system is particularly tuned for changes in the image. Images that are visible with the help of only this system disappear within a few seconds if fixated (Livingstone and Hubel, 1988). Thus, it is tuned for the detection of moving objects. The parvo system is specialized for analysis of detail, which can take time and exploits differences in wavelength. The magno system appears to be evolutionarily older, with the parvo system being a more recent acquisition (Livingstone and Hubel, 1995).

In functional terms, the older system provides the trigger for rapid reactions to significant and dynamic, even life-threatening, events. The newer system provides the input to a slower but more fine-grained conscious resolution of detail. These two somewhat distinct sources of information feed into two corresponding streams within the brain, as described next.

Basics of the brain's streams

Figure 8.17 showed pathways of ganglion cells to the superior colliculus and some visual processing is carried out by such subcortical pathways. In Figure 8.24, note the subcortical route from the retina, via the superior colliculus and a region of the thalamus, the pulvinar, to the posterior parietal cortex. So, one division of processing is *between* cortical and subcortical processing. However, as Figure 8.24 shows, there also exists streaming *within* the cortex, and this is our primary concern here. These divisions exemplify parallel processing.

Basics of cortical streaming

Note that, beyond the visual cortex, further processing occurs at the prestriate area. Then visual information divides into the two streams for even more specialized processing (Figure 8.24). Within the cortex, there is a division of responsibility between two streams: the **ventral stream** and the **dorsal stream** (Norman, 2002; Ungerleider and Mishkin, 1982). There is still controversy on how the roles of these two streams should be characterized (Glover, 2004). However, particularly for humans, a general consensus is as follows.

The ventral stream is involved in high-level visual cognition, the handling of *knowledge* about the world. The dorsal stream constitutes a rather direct link between certain visual stimuli and the control of *action* (Goodale and Humphrey, 1998).

The ventral stream

See Figure 8.24. The ventral stream consists of the sequence, primary visual cortex → prestriate area → inferotemporal cortex. Within this stream, the inferior

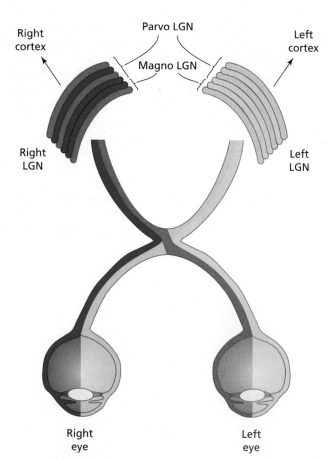

Figure 8.23 The LGN showing segregation of parvo and magno systems.

Source: after Bear *et al.* (1996).

Figure 8.24 The streams of visual processing, showing subcortical route via the superior colliculus (SC) and cortical streams termed ventral and dorsal streams. LGN = lateral geniculate nucleus; pulv = pulvinar, a region of the thalamus.

Source: based on Goodale and Humphrey (1998, Fig. 1).

temporal cortex is the last stage in processing of purely visual information (Gross *et al.*, 1993). Parts of this route encode and process information on the size, shape, colour and texture of a visual object (Merigan and Maunsell, 1993).

The ventral stream is responsible for conscious perception and interpretation of the world involving fine-grained discrimination, comparison with memories and allocation of meaning. It underlies the formation of 'models' of the world and the ability to use visual memory to link otherwise unconnected events. This stream is associated with the ability to articulate verbally 'what is it', such as the shape and colour of something and the meaning attached to it.

The ventral stream is especially sensitive to events at the fovea, where resolution of detail is high (Baizer *et al.*, 1991). The ventral stream is dominated by the parvo system but with a considerable magno contribution (Kaplan, 2004; Merigan and Maunsell, 1993). It is somewhat slower than the dorsal stream (Boussaoud *et al.*, 1996). Under some conditions, the ventral stream can play a role in controlling action but its activity is not directly linked to action. There are no specified links between this stream and motor output. Rather the ventral stream has links to areas of brain underlying memory, semantics and planning (Goodale and Humphrey, 1998).

The dorsal stream

The dorsal stream consists of the sequence, primary visual cortex → prestriate area → posterior parietal cortex (PC) (Reid, 1999) (Figure 8.24). It performs *visuomotor transformations* to allow adaptive behaviour, e.g. reaching to grasp an object. The dorsal stream is responsible for extracting information on the size and location of the object so that an appropriate motor response can be organized. The dorsal stream is dominated by information derived from the magno system (with a small parvo contribution) and has a relatively high sensitivity to information deriving from peripheral regions of the retina (Kaplan, 2004; Merigan and Maunsell, 1993).

Cooperation between streams and rationale for their existence

A 'perception' versus 'action' dichotomy captures part of the truth but a strict dichotomy would be over-simple. Perception and action have a seamless flow and coordination, so there seems to be a close interaction between streams (Figure 8.22). Indeed, there is anatomical cross-connections and corresponding functional cross-referencing of information between streams (Merigan and Maunsell, 1993).

Imagine that, through experience, objects become familiar and we acquire responses that are performed in association with them. The ventral stream acting together with the prefrontal cortex constructs plans and sets goals regarding these objects, e.g. pick a fruit (Goodale and Milner, 2004). Then, given the appropriate stimuli arising from these objects, the dorsal stream triggers action in relation to them. For example, the ventral stream and its associated processing might compute that a fruit, with a certain colour, significance and nutritional value, is hanging on a branch and desirable, whereas the dorsal stream would compute and organize the hand movements for reaching it.

Some division of labour between streams makes good sense from a perspective of 'design' and evolution. Consider the processing involved in perception of an object, e.g. identification, attachment of meaning of exactly what it is, etc. This is very different from the calculations involved in direct interaction with the object, e.g. how to position the fingers in picking it up. If there were no such division of labour and everything went through a single channel, we might well be seriously slowed in our interactions with the world.

Evidence from illusions

It is possible to dissociate the two visual streams. In Figure 8.25(a), the inner circle, to the left, surrounded by small circles looks larger to most people than the circle to the right, surrounded by large circles. In fact, they are the same size. Conversely, in part (b) the two inner circles look the same size, even though that to the right is physically larger. Participants were asked to

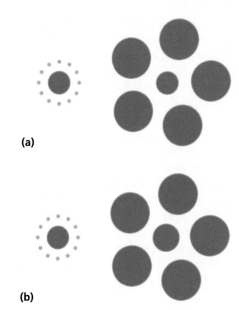

(a)

(b)

Figure 8.25 The Ebbinghaus illusion: (a) inner circles are the same size; (b) inner circles are of different sizes.
Source: Goodale and Humphrey (1998, Fig. 4, p. 198).

Figure 8.26 A three-dimensional version of the Ebbinghaus illusion, showing diodes emitting infrared light attached to thumb, finger and wrist. These allowed the trajectory of the response to be computed.

Source: Goodale and Humphrey (1998, Fig.5, p.199).

judge the size of such circles and the result was as just described. So, you can fool the perceptual part of the brain but can you fool the brain/hand?

To test this, a three-dimensional version of the illusion was constructed (Aglioti *et al.*, 1995) (Figure 8.26). Participants were asked to pick up the inner disc and the aperture of their grasp was recorded as the fingers prepared to take hold of it. The size of grasp was determined almost entirely by the actual size of the disc rather than its perceived size.

So, here is a functional dissociation between streams. Brain damage too can produce a dissociation, described next.

Lesions within the streams

Under some conditions, lesions to two different regions of the brain produce what is termed a **double dissociation**. That is, a lesion to a region y disrupts feature Y of behaviour but not feature X, whereas lesion to region x disrupts feature X but not Y. A double dissociation is a valuable finding, since it reveals a specific behavioural deficit linked to restricted damage to a particular brain region. By contrast, if a lesion knocked out all processing, this might tell us rather little.

A double dissociation arises when the effect of a lesion to the dorsal stream is compared with that of one made to the ventral stream (Goodale and Humphrey, 1998; Mishkin *et al.*, 1983; Pohl, 1973). A lesion to the ventral stream disrupts perception but not action, whereas a lesion to the dorsal stream disrupts action but not perception.

Damage to the dorsal stream

People with **optic ataxia** have damage typically to the superior region of the posterior parietal cortex, part of the dorsal stream. They have difficulty in making directed reaching movements and in adjusting the orientation and magnitude of their hand's grasp in a way that would facilitate holding the target object (discussed by Goodale and Humphrey, 1998; Goodale and Milner, 2004). However, they are able to give a verbal description of its orientation. Their problem is not one of vision per se: they can recognize people and can read. Neither is it a problem of motor control as such: they can point to parts of their body with eyes closed. It is specifically a problem of *visuomotor* translation.

Damage to the ventral stream

The term **visual agnosia** refers to an inability to recognize objects by the use of vision. It takes more than one form, a good example being the case of Dee Fletcher (see opposite).

Section summary

1   There is not just a single system underlying perception and visually guided action.

2   Within the cortex there is parallel processing in the form of the ventral stream, involved mainly with perception, and the dorsal stream, involved mainly with action.

3   Certain visual illusions and brain damage can dissociate the streams.

Test your knowledge

8.9 Consider the 3-D version of the Ebbinghaus illusion (Figure 8.26) and relate this to Figure 8.25. (a) In part (a), reaching to the left disc, would the size of grasp be (i) smaller? (ii) bigger or (iii) the same as reaching to the right? (b) In part (b), reaching to the left disc, would the size of grasp be (i) smaller, (ii) bigger or (iii) the same as reaching to the right?

Answer on page 223

A personal angle

Dee Fletcher

In 1988 and aged 34, Dee Fletcher, a Scottish woman living in Italy and working as a translator, suffered accidental carbon monoxide poisoning. This appears to have damaged regions of occipital cortex at the start of the ventral stream, while sparing the primary visual cortex and the dorsal stream (Goodale and Humphrey, 1998; Goodale *et al.*, 1991). Dee cannot recognize relatives visually but can do so based on their voices. She is deficient at identifying geometric shapes by vision but can do so by feel when placed in her hand. Dee has been studied extensively at the University of St. Andrews in Scotland.

Dee is impressive in her ability to perform action directed to the same shapes that cause her trouble in their perception. For example, she is able to reach out and post a card through a slot in a way that is appropriate to the slot's orientation but without being able to verbally describe this orientation (Figure 8.27). Whereas Dee can very accurately direct motor actions towards a target, she is unable to do this towards an imaginary target displaced from the actual one. Dee is 'stimulus-bound', acting in relation to certain physically present stimuli in the visual world.

Dee can discriminate colours and on the basis of this is able to recognize one of St. Andrews' better-known psychology professors, who is famous for his multi-tinted hair. Thus, comparing Dee and an optic ataxia patient (earlier) reveals a double dissociation between brain damage and deficit.

Figure 8.27 Visual abilities of Dee. (a) Grasping. Note that Dee can organize appropriate grasp of pencil, while being able only to guess whether it is horizontal or vertical. (b) (Left) matching and (right) posting tasks. Dee's results at matching and posting tasks, as compared with those of a control. White arrow head indicates orientation of slot for results shown.

Source: (a) Goodale and Milner (2004, Figure 2.1, p.17); (b) Reprinted by permission from Macmillan Publishers Ltd: A neurological dissociation between perceiving objects and grasping them, *Nature*, 349, 6305, 10 January, Fig. 1 (Goodale, M. A. *et al.* 1991), copyright 1991.

Functional specialization within perception

Introduction

So, there is functional specialization *between* perception and action. This section will show where functional specialization also occurs *within* perception. Beyond the primary visual cortex and largely within the ventral stream, distinct cortical regions analyse particular qualities of the visual image, such as form, colour or motion. It represents a daunting achievement that, at some level, this all appears to be integrated to give a unified perception.

In spite of changing retinal information that a given object provides, the brain performs processing that yields a perception of its invariance, or, as it is often called, its **constancy**. For example, if an object is rotated, the image changes but the brain's processing yields the perception that shape has remained the same, termed 'shape constancy'. In showing constancy, the brain's role is as a *categorizer* (Zeki, 1993). The brain does not remember the details of the varying information sent from an object as changes occur in its distance, orientation or wavelength. It perceives unchanging features attributed to the object.

How can particular parts of the visual system be identified with particular functional roles? A major source of understanding derives from brain-damaged patients who can exhibit selective deficits.

Analysis and identification of shapes

Filling in details

As an example of feature extraction, Figure 8.1 demonstrated illusory contours. In the ventral stream, cells have been identified in the prestriate area (but not V1) which encode illusory contours (Gross *et al.*, 1993) (Figure 8.28). In part (a) the cell responds to a real contour (light bar) when in an orientation near to vertical but not when it is near to horizontal. Part (b) shows that the cell responds also to an *illusory* contour at the same orientation. The cell has extracted a feature from the information provided by the white stripes.

It appears that, at area TE (a region of the inferior temporal cortex), information comes together into an integrated representation of the object, involving comparison with memory (Gross *et al.*, 1993). Processing in this area encodes invariance, in that the object is interpreted as the same irrespective of where in the visual field it is located. As the sequence of processing along the ventral stream progresses, neurons become less sensitive to simple features (e.g. a straight line) at specific locations and more sensitive to complex features regardless of location. Neurons here are relatively insensitive to image size and orientation on the retina.

The anterior regions of the temporal lobe encode 'prototypes' of visual objects, against which actual visual objects can be compared (Weiskrantz and Saunders, 1984). Memory storage is in a form that is independent of a number of features of the image such as its size at the retina. This means that it is not necessary to compute each new variation of an object, such as a new size or orientation, and assess it as a quite separate entity. It can be allocated to a category.

Size constancy

In estimating object size, the brain integrates information on distance and image size, termed **size constancy**. If the image size doubles but its distance halves, the brain computes that the object has stayed the same size. Figure 8.4(b) shows how the image size gets bigger as the object gets nearer.

Information processing at the level of the inferior temporal cortex involves calculating invariance, e.g. size constancy (Farah *et al.*, 1999). The processing performed there provides representations of objects *as they are in the world*, rather than as their image is on the retina.

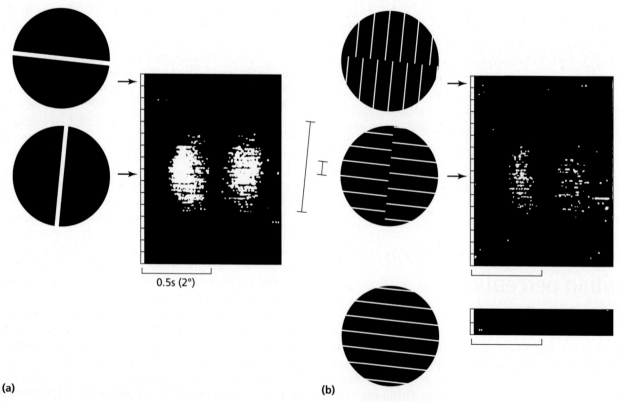

0.5s (2°)

(a)   (b)

Figure 8.28 Response of a cell in prestriate area to (a) real and (b) illusory contours. Figure at bottom part of (b) shows that there is no response to control condition of stripes in the absence of illusory contour.
Source: von der Heydt and Peterhans (1989).

For example, a monkey with an intact inferior temporal cortex can learn to discriminate two objects based upon their absolute size even though they are at different distances. This involves not responding on the basis of image size at the retina alone. Monkeys with inferior temporal cortex lesions have difficulty with this task and are more strongly driven by retinal image size.

Face perception

Some information processed in the ventral stream at area TE projects to a neighbouring area of cortex termed the 'superior temporal polysensory area' (STP) (Farah *et al.*, 1999). Figure 8.29 shows the response of a neuron in the STP area. The preference for facial features is clear. Is this the much discussed grandmother cell (see earlier)? The neurons found so far are not specific for particular faces. They respond to monkey and human faces, as well as showing some sensitivity to other features (Gross *et al.*, 1993).

Types of agnosia

As noted earlier, a disruption of visual object recognition is termed visual agnosia. It is particularly seen when damage is to inferior temporal (IT) regions of cortex in both hemispheres or in just the right (Farah *et al.*, 1999; Pallis, 1955). It takes various forms.

In some cases, agnosia takes a specific form. For example, in prosopagnosia, humans have difficulty in recognizing faces (Farah *et al.*, 1999; Rubens and Benson, 1971). They typically have suffered brain damage in the areas of the temporal lobe that are activated during face recognition (as measured by electrical recording). Some can recognize faces in a general sense and might be able to identify their gender and expression but be unable to identify specific faces (Tranel *et al.*, 1988), even that of their partner. This suggests that attribution of specific identity is a further stage of processing beyond the identification of a general facial form.

Analysis of movement

Parts of the ventral stream that are driven mainly by the magno system extract information on movement. In rare cases, damage to a region of the stream leaves an individual with the inability to detect movement (Zihl *et al.*, 1983). Pouring tea appears as a series of frozen frames. An oncoming car would be perceived at a distance and then again when it is near, as if it is based on two frames cut from a film.

Analysis of colour

An object tends to look much the same colour in spite of differences in the balance of wavelengths of light

A personal angle

Seeing but not recognizing

A 47-year-old male physician with a history of heavy alcohol intake and damage to the occipital lobe of the left hemisphere was studied by Rubens and Benson (1971) in Boston. He was unable to recognize people or identify common objects. However, the problem was not perceptual as such. Even though unable to identify what objects were, he was able (unlike Dee Fletcher) to copy diagrams of them. The problem was described as 'associative visual agnosia', a failure to contextualize perceptions in terms of meaning. Rubens and Benson raise the issue of why the intact right hemisphere was unable to perform the recognition task.

that is projected at it and therefore differences in what is reflected, termed 'colour constancy' (Spillmann, 2009). For example, viewed under normal conditions, an orange looks basically of orange colour in a range of wavelengths of illumination. Some neurons in the ventral stream extract invariance in the form of colour constancy. What is invariant is the nature of the surface in terms of its physical properties, i.e. its tendency to absorb some wavelengths more than others.

The signal produced in ganglion cells corresponding to a coloured object is not sufficient to explain how the object looks the same colour in various wavelengths of illumination, i.e. colour constancy. Colour is not an intrinsic quality of an object that gets impressed upon the brain (Zeki, 1993). Rather, it is a quality computed in the brain, based upon information on wavelength of light reflected from an object placed in context. One source of information is to compare neighbouring areas. Suppose that two objects are placed side by side. In the long wavelength region, one reflects a relatively high intensity and another reflects a relatively low intensity. The brain appears to allocate the colour red to the first object and blue to the second.

That brain damage can make a person blind for just one quality is evidence for functional specialization. Blindness just for colour is termed 'achromatopsia'. Colour perception involves the primary visual cortex (which appears to analyze wavelengths) and other cortical regions that are specific for processing colour (which appear to attribute colour to an object, by placing wavelength information in context). Loss of either area means loss of colour perception.

Figure 8.29 Response of STP neuron.

Source: Bruce et al. (1981 *Journal of Neurophysiology*, Fig. 7, p. 379 Am. Physiol Soc, used with permission).

Madame R.

In 1888, Dr L. Verrey, in Neuchâtel, Switzerland, described Madame R., 60 years of age, who experienced loss of colour sensation in the right part of the visual field (Verrey, 1888). Everything, including coloured objects, appeared in shades of grey. Verrey noted that earlier cases of such loss were accompanied by loss of other faculties such as reading. However, Madame R. seemed to represent a pure case of loss of colour sensation with other abilities remaining functional, albeit with slight impairment. This suggested that activity within a specific brain region is a necessary condition for colour analysis. Verrey noted that this was a notion that several authors had resisted. It continued to be resisted even after Verrey provided his evidence (Zeki, 1993).

At autopsy, Verrey noted that Madame R. had a discrete lesion in the left occipital lobe outside the primary visual cortex. Madame R. is a good example of insight gained from the misfortune of brain damage and that evidence not fitting the current fashion still needs to be given serious consideration.

The next section considers in more detail the interactions of bottom-up and top-down contribution to perception.

Section summary

1 Different regions of the visual system are responsible for processing different features of visual perception.

2 Within the cortex, it is particularly regions of the ventral stream that can be associated with such processing as extracting invariance.

3 Constancy refers to a stable perception of an object in the face of different images that it projects to the retina.

Test your knowledge

8.10 Complete the following: 'As a person moves from 50 metres distance to 100 metres, the image of them on the retina ___ but they appear to remain ___ size'.

8.11 Consider the ganglion cell, the receptive field of which is shown in Figure 8.16(a). Suppose that it is located near to the fovea. This ganglion cell most likely forms a part of which system? (i) Magno, (ii) parvo.

Answers on page 223   WEB

Linking brain activity and conscious perception

Introduction

Positron emission tomography (PET), functional magnetic resonance imaging (fMRI) and recording activity from particular neurons (Chapter 5) provide insight into such issues as how bottom-up and top-down factors operate and their link with consciousness (Frith and Dolan, 1997). This section describes their application to this issue.

Impoverished images

An example of the role of prior knowledge in perception was provided by the Dalmatian dog (Chapter 7, Figures 7.3 and 7.4). Figure 7.3 is an 'impoverished image', which at first is impossible to decipher. However, after the experience of Figure 7.4, it is difficult not to see a Dalmatian dog.

Objects

Faces

Pre-learning

Figure 8.30 Impoverished stimuli to vision.
Source: Dolan *et al.* (1997, Fig. 1, p. 597).

Similarly, when you first examine the images of Figure 8.30, they will probably look meaningless. However, try looking at Figure 8.31. When looking again at Figure 8.30 the images should make sense (Dolan *et al.*, 1997). It is possible to measure the activity of the brain when viewing each image of Figure 8.30, before and after exposure to Figure 8.31. The researchers suggest that parts of the brain that are concerned only with processing the visual input should be the same in both cases, since the image is the same (though top-down processing might affect even the input side). The assumption is that any changes in brain activity between first and second exposures represent the perception of the image, involving meaning and a top-down factor.

Comparing first and second exposures, parts of the brain termed the 'primary visual areas' (primary visual cortex) showed no change in activity, suggesting that their activity is involved in extracting features of the image per se.

Increases in activity were noted in two areas when the image was viewed a second time. One of these is the medial parietal cortex (Figure 8.32). Other brain regions in which increases in activity between first and second viewing occurred depended upon what was viewed (Figure 8.33). When it was a human face, the right inferior temporal cortex increased in activity (part (a)). When it was an object, the left inferior temporal cortex increased in activity (part (b)).

So changes in brain activity mirror changes in perception. How can we explain what is happening? Frith and Dolan (1997) suggest that processing of the full figure could leave permanent traces, a representation,

e.g. as modified synaptic connections. Thus, when the impoverished version is again presented, elements of this representation are triggered. Since the neural activity triggered now by the impoverished figure is similar to that triggered by the full figure, so too is the corresponding perception similar.

Global and local features

In Figure 8.34, what do you see? Presumably, a large letter S comprising a number of small letter Ls. Participants were given a number of different stimuli of the kind shown and asked to report the letter but instructed to respond either at a global level (group 1), i.e. S in Figure 8.34, or at a local level (group 2), i.e. L in the same figure (Fink *et al.*, 1996).

When participants were attending at a global level, increased activity at the right lingual gyrus (a region of prestriate cortex, the so-called visual association area) was observed. When they were responding at a local level, activity increased at the left inferior occipital lobe.

Figure 8.32 Averaged MRI scan of the brain of volunteers as seen in a horizontal slice when an impoverished image (face or object) was viewed for a second time. The black area represents activation in the medial parietal cortex (participant's front at top and left at left).
Source: Frith and Dolan (1997, Fig. 2, p. 1222).

Learning   Post-learning

Figure 8.31 A richer version of the image.
Source: Frith and Dolan (1997, Fig. 2).

In order to respond correctly according to instructions, presumably a brain region outside those concerned directly with visual processing must prime the areas responsible for interpretation of the image. The results of this experiment fit studies of patients with brain damage.

Right-sided damage tends to disrupt global processing and left-sided damage tends to disrupt local processing.

Ambiguous figures

Figure 7.2 (p. 187) showed the famous face–vase picture, an ambiguous figure, produced by the Danish psychologist Edgar Rubin. Your perception of it will probably alternate between two possible solutions. For a while perception will be as a vase and then it will switch to two faces. The raw sensory input ('bottom-up contribution') as detected on the retina is the same but it seems that the top-down contribution changes. The conscious mind cannot tolerate ambiguity and makes sense of the world by fixing on one interpretation, only for that to be displaced by the alternative, and so on.

Different parts of the ventral stream are particularly active when viewing a face as compared with an inanimate object such as a vase (Andrews *et al.*, 2002). (The fusiform face area (FFA) is activated when faces are perceived, while the lateral occipital area is activated by objects such as a vase.) Using fMRI, differential activation in the two regions was seen corresponding to the conscious perception, i.e. activation switched between regions in correlation with switches in conscious perception.

The question 'what do you see?' can be asked by presenting different images to the two eyes and creating **binocular rivalry**. The brain does not form a single perception that represents a compromise of the two possible perceptions. Rather, as in ambiguous figures, there is an alternation between the images in the two eyes. It is also possible to ask non-human primates what they see (Blake and Logothetis, 2002). In their case, researchers infer that something like conscious perception alternates between interpretations, much as in humans. For example, an upwards moving image could be presented to the left eye and a downwards moving image to the right eye. As an objective index, eye movements can be monitored and they exhibit a similar pattern to when humans are exposed to such stimuli. Corresponding movements in the two eyes indicate that a unified perception of movement upwards alternates with one of downwards.

(a)

(b)

Figure 8.33 Activity of the inferior temporal cortex: (a) when a face is viewed and (b) when an object is viewed.

Source: Frith and Dolan (1997, Fig. 3, p. 1223).

Figure 8.34 Visual stimulus.

Source: Frith and Dolan (1997, Fig. 4, p. 1224).

Another index is, in effect, to ask the monkey what it sees *subjectively*. It is seated in front of a screen and presented with two levers. Suppose that an unambiguous single image of a cowboy on the screen is rewarded with fruit juice if the monkey moves the left lever. An unambiguous single image of the sun is rewarded with a movement of the right lever. When binocular rivalry is introduced by presenting both images together, the animal alternates between levers in a way assumed to reflect changing subjective perception.

It is now possible to monitor the changes that occur in the brain corresponding to the change in interpretation of the figure. Researchers can ask, which neurons change their activity in synchrony with changes in perception? In a region of the medial temporal cortex, a percentage of neurons changed their firing in synchrony with perception. The remainder changed with changes in visual stimulation but not with perception. As the probing went further into the stages of processing, i.e. further into the inferior temporal cortex (away from primary visual cortex), cell activity more strongly reflected perception. That is, a larger percentage of neurons changed activity with the perception.

How do you know that the monkey is 'telling the truth'? What is to stop it from just reacting randomly and thereby getting reward? Surely, only the monkey knows what it perceives, but does it? Researchers introduce 'catch trials' in between trials of exposure to binocular rivalry (Leopold *et al.*, 2003). In the catch trials, single images are presented and the monkey is checked to make sure that it is still responding appropriately in terms of image-lever association.

Section summary

1 Researchers can measure changes in activity of the brain when a person looks at an object, before and after the acquisition of a concept concerning its meaning.

2 It is possible to distinguish changes in brain activity that correspond to either local or global viewing.

3 In parts of the visual system, changes in neural activity correlate with changes in conscious perception.

 ## Test your knowledge

8.12 Write a short statement concerning an ambiguous figure (e.g. Figure 7.2), in which you use the terms retina, perception, visual cortex, image, neuroimaging and brain activity.

Answer on page 223

Bringing things together

Some key overall themes of the chapter are as follows:

1 Visual perception is determined by interactions between bottom-up and top-down factors.

2 The visual system extracts invariance ('constancy') from the varying image produced by a given object.

3 There is functional specialization in the visual system including (a) parallel processing underlying perception and action and (b) separate brain regions are responsible for the components of visual perception, such as colour and shape.

Excitation and inhibition are fundamental features of how nervous systems work. Considerable weight has

been placed on these processes in the present chapter, where they underlie the antagonist properties of the sub-regions of the receptive field of some neurons. This chapter has briefly considered the phenomenon of consciousness, e.g. in contrasting the actions of the ventral stream and the dorsal stream.

 See the video coverage for this chapter where a study of the eye helps the understanding of the psychology of vision.

Summary of Chapter 8

1 Visual perception is an active process. That is, information contained in light falling on the eye is placed into context, including that of expectations and meanings.

2 At the retina, light energy is converted to electrical signals, i.e. it is the site of detection. Cells in the retina also process information before transmitting it towards the brain.

3 The classical visual pathway projects information from the retina, via the lateral geniculate nucleus, to the visual cortex. Features are analyzed at each stage. Beyond the primary visual cortex, information is contextualized in terms of memory and meaning.

4 Brain structures that have a primary responsibility for action can be distinguished from those underlying perception.

5 There exists functional specialization in the system underlying visual perception. For example, a particular brain region might process only one quality, such as shape, movement or colour.

6 Neuroimaging reveals the role of bottom-up and top-down factors in visual perception.

Further reading

For a very accessible text (now in its 5th edition), see Gregory (1997) and, particularly for illusions, Gregory (2009). For a very readable account of the streams of visual processing, see Goodale and Milner (2004). For neuroscience, see Milner and Goodale (2006) and the section entitled 'Sensation and perception' in Gazzaniga (2009).

Answers

Explanations for answers to 'test your knowledge' questions can be found on the website www.pearsoned.co.uk/toates

8.1 Frequencies; wavelengths (obviously in either order)
8.2 (ii) Medium, (iii) long
8.3 (i) Increasing the intensity of light
8.4 20 action potentials per second.
8.5 (i) Increasing the intensity of the light, (ii) keeping intensity constant but increasing the size of area within the receptive field stimulated.

8.6 (i) Rotating the light stimulus to an orientation of 45° to that shown, (ii) rotating the light stimulus to an orientation of 90° to that shown
8.7 Retinal ganglion cells
8.8 Right; right
8.9 (a) (iii) The same as reaching to the right; (b) (i) smaller.
8.10 Halves; the same
8.11 (ii) Parvo
8.12 The figure casts an *image* on the *retina*. Conscious *perception* alternates between two interpretations of this: two faces and a vase. *Neuroimaging* might be expected to reveal different patterns of *brain activity* beyond the *visual cortex* corresponding to the two different perceptions.

Visit www.pearsoned.co.uk/toates
for a range of resources to support study.
Test yourself with multiple choice questions and access a bank of over 100 videos that will bring the topics to life.

 Interactions and animations relating to topics discussed in this chapter can be found on the website at www.pearsoned.co.uk/toates. These include:

Animation: The eye and the retina
Interaction: The structure of the human eye
Interaction: The primary visual pathways from retina to visual cortex
Animation: The visual pathways from retina to visual cortex
Interaction: The dorsal and ventral visual pathways

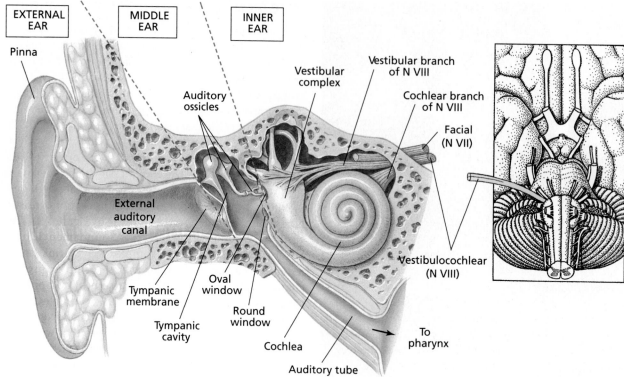

Figure 9.1 The ear.

Source: Martini *et al.* (2000, Fig.18-9, p. 473). Copyright © 2000, 1997 by Frederic H. Martini, Inc. and Michael J. Timmons. Reprinted by permission of Pearson Education, Inc.

investigate how changes in pressure within a fluid can cause changes in the activity of neurons.

The inner ear

Continuing the sequence of transmission, Figure 9.2 is a simplification of part of the auditory system. It shows transduction between oscillations of the tympanic membrane and vibrations of the basilar membrane, which is in the cochlea (von Békésy, 1960). Pressure waves at a particular *frequency* in the cochlea cause the basilar membrane to move back and forth at a *particular* location. The location depends on the frequency of the oscillations, a relationship termed a **place code**.

As Figure 9.3 shows, when the frequency of sound arriving at the ear is high, displacements in the basilar membrane occur near to the end at which it is secured, i.e. by the oval window (von Békésy, 1960). When the sound is of lower frequency, vibrations cause movements at points away from the oval window. In other words, there is transduction of the kind that frequencies of air pressure are represented by locations on the basilar membrane. The amplitude of changes in air pressure is represented by the amplitude of displacements of the basilar membrane. Suppose that there is more than one frequency of sound arriving at the ear. There are a corresponding number of sites of displacement on the basilar membrane (Figure 9.4).

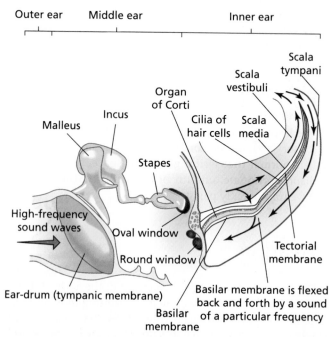

Figure 9.2 Transduction between oscillations of the tympanic membrane and displacement of the basilar membrane.

Source: Carlson (1994, Fig. 7.5, p.186). Reprinted by permission of Pearson Education, Inc.

Figure 9.3 Frequency of sound as a function of the location on the basilar membrane that is most responsive to that frequency.

Figure 9.4 Points of displacement of the basilar membrane caused by tones of frequency (a) F_1, (b) F_2 and (c) F_1 and F_2 simultaneously.

Associated with the basilar membrane are sensory receptors, fine cells termed **hair cells**. They form synaptic connections with neurons that project to the brain as part of the auditory nerve, a cranial nerve (Helfert *et al.*, 1991) (Figure 9.5). When hair cells are mechanically stimulated during displacement of the basilar membrane, electrical changes occur in them and thereby action potentials are triggered in the associated neurons. Action potentials are transmitted along the neurons forming the auditory nerve and arrive at the brain stem. Different neurons code for different sound frequencies. For example, frequency F_1 activates maximally one neuron and a lower frequency (F_2) maximally activates another neuron, the neurons corresponding to positions of membrane shown in Figure 9.4. As an additional means of coding, at very low frequencies, activity in certain neurons is in synchrony with the oscillations of air pressure (Chapter 7, Figure 7.9, p. 193).

Let's summarize the sequence of transduction from air pressure to mechanical changes and then to electrical activity. Via membranes and bones, transduction occurs between changes in air pressure at different *frequencies* and different *locations* of maximum vibration at the basilar membrane. There is then transduction between distortions of the membrane and activity within different *neurons*.

What is the evolutionary significance of such a seemingly cumbersome design? Couldn't nature have found a simpler way of achieving transduction between changes in air pressure and action potentials? At low frequencies, the cyclic pattern of action potential activity (i.e. burst–silence–burst …) in a number of neurons carrying information from the ear does indeed follow cyclic changes in air pressure (Chapter 7, Figure 7.9, p. 193). Why not code all frequencies in this way and cut out the complexity of place coding at the basilar membrane?

Playing designer can be a revealing exercise and it is interesting to see whether one can come up with better solutions. However, evolution can only act on what is already there. There is a limit to the rate at which neurons can produce action potentials, as set by the refractory period (Chapter 4). It is beyond the capacity of neurons to generate action potentials at a frequency of 20 000 per second in response to a 20 000 Hz frequency of sound. Even if evolution had 'invented' neurons with such a frequency range, there is still the problem of how to code for both frequency and amplitude of a given oscillation in the air. A second coding system would be necessary. Tinkering with one part of a system has knock-on consequences for other parts. Providing an efficient means of transduction between frequency and neural activity is the evolutionary rationale for place coding, which is perhaps not so cumbersome after all!

Neural mechanisms

The classical route of afferent projections

Figure 9.6 shows the classical sequence of neurally encoded information in the auditory system. Neurons convey information in the auditory nerve to the cochlear nucleus, where a synapse occurs (Helfert *et al.*, 1991). Information then ascends through various brain regions, e.g. inferior colliculus, medial geniculate nucleus of the thalamus, to the auditory cortex.

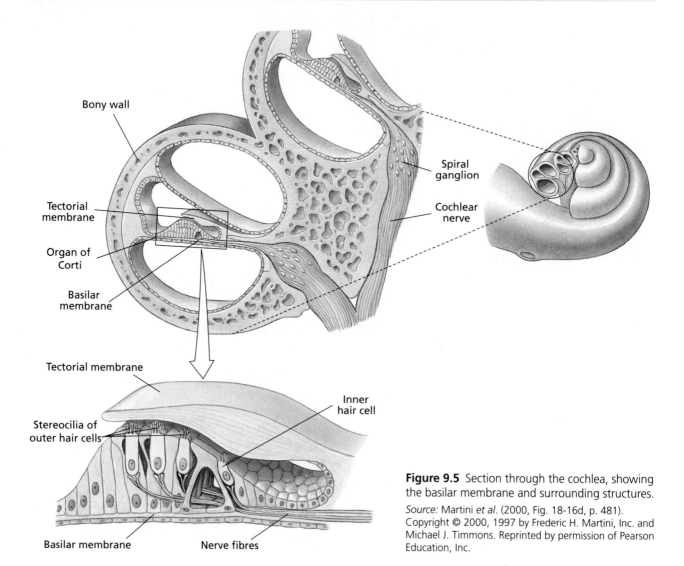

Figure 9.5 Section through the cochlea, showing the basilar membrane and surrounding structures.

Source: Martini *et al.* (2000, Fig. 18-16d, p. 481). Copyright © 2000, 1997 by Frederic H. Martini, Inc. and Michael J. Timmons. Reprinted by permission of Pearson Education, Inc.

There is a series of neurons and synapses between the afferent input, the thalamus and then to the auditory cortex. Some information remains on the same side and, as in Figure 9.6, other information crosses over. By means of partial cross-over, information derived from each ear can be compared and thereby information on the location of the sound source identified (described shortly). Neurons in the auditory system can be classified according to whether they are driven by the contralateral ear, ipsilateral ear or both (analogous to vision). Above the level of cochlear nucleus, neurons are often influenced by both, with a tendency for contralateral control to be stronger (Brown, 1999).

Tonotopic representation

As noted, at the basilar membrane, frequency is represented by location of disturbance on the membrane. A similar style of coding is preserved at the auditory cortex: particular neurons respond to particular sound frequencies, corresponding to particular basilar membrane locations. This is termed **tonotopic representation** (from the Greek 'tonos', meaning tone and 'topos', meaning place) or a 'place code' (Aitkin *et al.*, 1984). As with other sensory systems, there is some plasticity in cortical representation: frequencies that acquire particular relevance in the life of an animal can gain increased cortical representation (Weinberger, 1993).

Loudness

Intensity (amplitude) of pressure waves is coded in at least two ways (Green and Wier, 1984): the rate at which action potentials occur in a particular neuron and different thresholds of activation of neurons. Thus, at a given region (x) of the basilar membrane, there appears to be a population of sensory neurons all sensitive to frequency F_x but some are only triggered by high-intensity sounds corresponding to large displacements of the membrane.

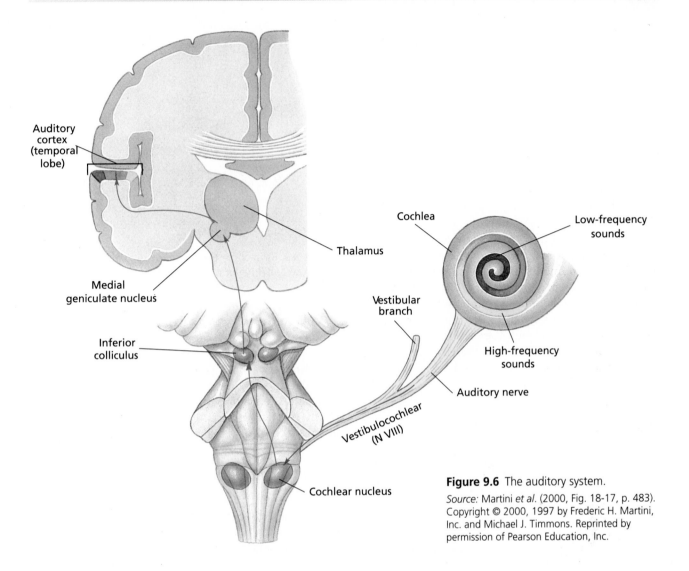

Figure 9.6 The auditory system.

Source: Martini *et al.* (2000, Fig. 18-17, p. 483). Copyright © 2000, 1997 by Frederic H. Martini, Inc. and Michael J. Timmons. Reprinted by permission of Pearson Education, Inc.

Biaural processing

The auditory system is able to discriminate the location of the source of sounds, whether to left or right. This is, of course, vital to survival. A sound that is to one side of the body will arrive at one ear slightly sooner than the other. Action potentials are initiated in the ear to this side slightly sooner than in the other ear (Hudspeth and Konishi, 2000; von Békésy, 1960). Neurons carrying information from each ear project to other neurons in a brain stem region (termed the superior olivary complex) that perform **feature detection** on incoming information (Tsuchitani and Johnson, 1991). For example, the brain exploits differences in the arrival times of action potentials to determine the direction of a sound's source.

The system can also exploit differences in intensity between the ears to extract a signal on location. If a source of sound is to the left, not only will the left ear receive stimulation slightly sooner than the right ear but stimulation will also be more intense. The right ear is said to be in a *sonic shadow* cast by the head. As an example of feature detection, certain neurons in the brain are sensitive to differences in intensity, being fed by information from each ear.

Different routes taken by auditory information

The route from the ears through the thalamus to the auditory cortex (Figure 9.6) is sometimes termed the

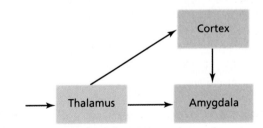

Figure 9.7 Routes of auditory information.
Source: based on Le Doux (1994).

'classical route'. However, in addition, there is a route from the thalamus to the amygdala (Figure 9.7). The amygdala is an important site of emotional processing and, compared with the classical route, the auditory system has a 'short-cut' pathway for access to it (Le Doux, 1994).

Descending pathways

Through descending pathways, feedback ('top-down') control is exerted at all levels in the auditory system (Spangler and Warr, 1991). There is feedback from the auditory cortex to the medial geniculate nucleus and inferior colliculus, by which the cortex modulates ascending information. Also, neural pathways that start in the brain stem project to the periphery of the auditory system, modulating detection sensitivity and thereby the afferent signal (Warr *et al.*, 1986). Muscles adjust the sensitivity of mechanical transduction (Figure 9.8). By the efferent signal to the muscles, sensitivity can be adjusted to ambient noise levels (decreasing sensitivity in a loud environment), thereby increasing the range of resolution of the system (von Békésy, 1960).

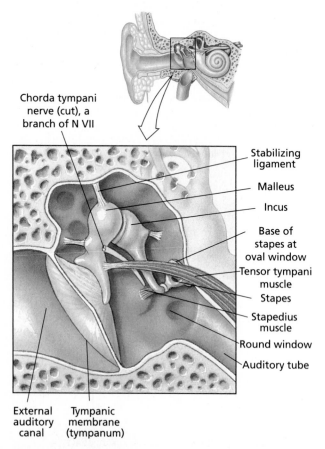

Chorda tympani nerve (cut), a branch of N VII

Stabilizing ligament

Malleus

Incus

Base of stapes at oval window

Tensor tympani muscle

Stapes

Stapedius muscle

Round window

Auditory tube

External auditory canal

Tympanic membrane (tympanum)

Figure 9.8 Site of feedback control.

Source: based on Martini *et al.* (2000, Fig. 18-10b, p. 474). Copyright © 2000, 1997 by Frederic H. Martini, Inc. and Michael J. Timmons. Reprinted by permission of Pearson Education, Inc.

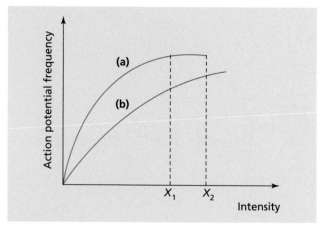

Figure 9.9 Relation between intensity and afferent signal (a) before and (b) after modulation.

What is the role of this feedback? One role is as follows. Suppose that in Figure 9.9 the system normally (curve (a)) saturates at intensity X_1. It cannot resolve the difference between X_1 and X_2. However, with modulation to a decreased sensitivity (curve (b)), both intensities are represented on the ascending portion of the graph and so can be discriminated. (Look at the change in vertical axis as you move from X_1 to X_2.)

Developmental factors

The developing foetus exists within a world that involves auditory stimulation (Fifer and Moon, 1988). In humans, the mother's voice reaches the foetus. After 24 weeks of gestation, pure tones of external origin cause heart-rate changes. The foetus is also exposed to sounds of internal origin such as the maternal heartbeat and movements within the gastrointestinal tract. It is possible, if not probable, that the sounds impinging on the foetus play a role in the development of the auditory system.

Exposure to sounds within the uterus also appears to play an important role in emotional development. The infant is exposed to an association between particular voice features (frequency, intonation) and the chemical and somatosensory environment within the uterus. Newborn humans can discriminate their own mother's voice and show a preference for it (DeCasper and Fifer, 1980). Sounds experienced *in utero* have later emotional and motivational significance, e.g. playing a recording of the heartbeat has a calming effect (Fifer and Moon, 1988).

Section summary

1 The ears transduce between changes in pressure in the air and action potentials.

2 Different frequencies of sound cause different locations on the basilar membrane to vibrate, i.e. a place code. Different neurons, corresponding to the different locations, are activated.

3 Beyond the thalamus, auditory information takes different routes within the brain.

4 At the auditory cortex, neurons at different locations respond to different sound frequencies.

Test your knowledge

9.1 What would be the effect of damage to a particular narrow region of the basilar membrane?

9.2 In Figure 9.6, the area of auditory cortex coloured dark pink is responsible for encoding which frequency of sounds? (i) High, (ii) medium, (iii) low.

Answers on page 249

The vestibular system

The **vestibular system** provides information on the position of the head, which is used in coordinating action (Goldberg and Fernández, 1984). A system detects disturbances to the body's equilibrium (Figure 9.10) and triggers compensatory action. The **vestibular apparatus** of the inner ear detects changes in the position of the head and transmits information to the brain along a cranial nerve, the vestibulocochlear nerve (Chapter 3).

The vestibular apparatus comprises fluid-filled chambers: the semicircular canals (or 'ducts'), the utricle and the saccule, coloured blue in Figure 9.10(b). Because of the physical principle of inertia, when the head moves, the fluid tends to follow slightly behind the movement of the chambers. Thus, there is relative movement between the chambers and their fluid contents. This relative movement is detected by hair cells (similar to those in the auditory system) that are situated in the chambers. Electrical activity in neurons of the vestibulocochlear nerve is altered, which constitutes signals to the brain that encode the movement.

Suppose that the head moves in a particular direction. This movement causes a population of hair cells to bend in a given way, which excites action potentials (Figure 9.10(d)). When the head moves in the opposite direction, there is inhibition of action potentials in this population of neurons (Goldberg and Fernández, 1984).

Another population of hair cells has a different direction of sensitivity, for example, this might be the opposite of the first population or at right angles to it. Thereby, the brain is informed of the movement of the head. The information is sent to the cerebellum, among other places, where it plays a role in maintaining stability. Via nuclei in the brain stem, signals are also sent to the sympathetic branch of the ANS such that heart-rate increases (Yates and Stocker, 1998). This might be understood in functional terms as a preparation for action at a time of disturbance.

In humans, evidence is also emerging to indicate a role for receptors of gravitational forces in such unlikely places as the kidney and veins of the limbs (Yates and Stocker, 1998). Such information is conveyed to the brain via the spinal cord and vagus nerve (Chapter 3).

Section summary

1 The vestibular apparatus of the inner ear detects changes in position of the head and transmits information to the brain along the vestibulocochlear nerve.

2 Following a disturbance to equilibrium, postural reflexes act to restore it.

Test your knowledge

9.3 Complete the following: 'In the vestibular system, there is a transduction from a ___ distortion to an electrical signal in neurons. The latter takes the form of the ___ of action potentials'.

Answer on page 249

The somatosensory system

Introduction

The **somatosensory system** detects events arising from various regions of the body. Rather than involving a localized organ, as in vision or hearing, this sensory system is distributed throughout the body. As part of it, **discriminative touch** involves the recognition of the location, shape, size and texture of mechanical objects that contact the skin (Kandel and Jessell, 1991). Touch involves bottom-up and top-down factors (Hsiao *et al.*, 1996). Consider reading Braille. Sensory information is detected and interpreted by means of comparison against representations in memory.

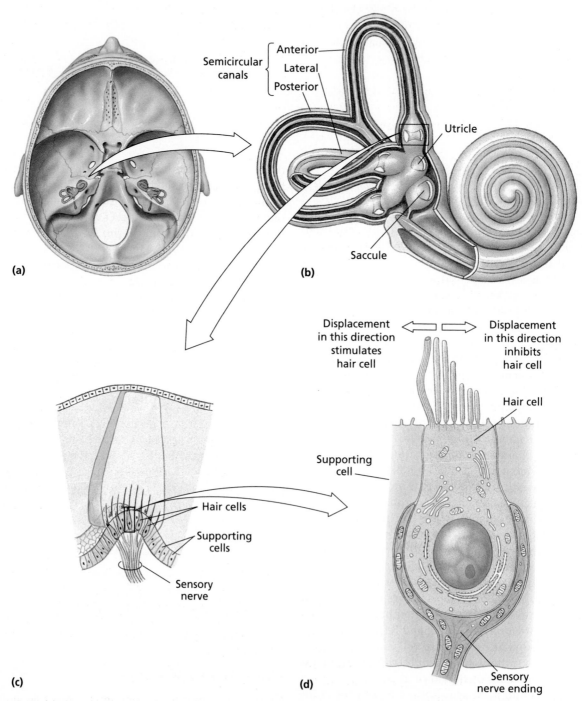

Figure 9.10 (a) The ear indicating the vestibular apparatus and (b)–(d) the vestibular apparatus in closer detail.

Source: Martini *et al.* (2000, Fig. 18-12, p. 476). Copyright © 2000, 1997 by Frederic H. Martini, Inc. and Michael J. Timmons. Reprinted by permission of Pearson Education, Inc.

Tactile stimuli are important to survival. For example, the manipulation of objects, as in lifting food to the mouth or grasping a branch, depends upon an ability to resolve fine detail with paws or fingers. On a gross scale, a tactile stimulus might represent an event that requires defensive action. From a developmental perspective, the tactile sense is also of obvious importance; infants learn from self-generated movements, resultant contact with objects and the tactile consequences of manipulation. In each case, the first stage of extracting tactile information consists of the activation of specialized receptors at the skin by objects. Each receptor has a receptive field at the skin.

Chapter 3 described neurons specialized for discriminative touch, tissue damage or temperature. Their cell bodies are in the dorsal root ganglia and such neurons are termed 'dorsal root ganglion cells' or 'DRG cells'. (Other comparable neurons project information from above the neck as part of a cranial nerve.) Each class of DRG cell detects information, which is transmitted to distinct brain regions for further processing (e.g. via further projection cells to distinct regions of cortex). This provides **modality segregation**, e.g. between touch and temperature (Mountcastle, 1984). The present section focuses upon just one of these qualities, discriminative touch involving harmless stimuli.

We tend to take the somatic sensory system for granted, perhaps since much of its work is done at an unconscious level. It is relatively easy for us to simulate blindness or deafness and thereby gain some understanding of what it is like to be without vision or hearing. To be defective in somatic sensory input is difficult to imagine. The very rare individual suffers this misfortune (Cole, 1991).

Chapter 5 described the system involved in processing tactile information, i.e. the somatosensory cortex and the mapping of the body, which constitutes the sensory homunculus (Figure 5.18, p. 117). Within the system of detecting innocuous touch, different regions of the body are represented in different regions of somatosensory cortex (Mountcastle, 1984).

How is the homunculus defined? Tactile stimulation of particular skin areas triggers activity in a cortical cell located at the point indicated by the homunculus. In humans, electrical stimulation of cortical neurons within the somatosensory area evokes the conscious sensation of tactile stimulation at the region of skin corresponding to the particular point of the homunculus (Penfield and Rasmussen, 1968). Damage to particular regions of somatosensory cortex disrupts somatosensation at particular points on the opposite side of the body as defined by the homunculus.

The next section looks in more detail at the neurons that form the first stage of processing in this system.

Sensory neurons

Neuron types

Around the body, just beneath the skin surface, there are the tips of sensory neurons that detect different qualities of tactile stimulation, collectively termed **somatosensory neurons** (Darian-Smith, 1984) (Figure 9.11). Some tips consist simply of bare neuron endings (as in nociceptive neurons), whereas others are associated with either small capsules, termed 'Merkel's discs' or a single capsule, termed a 'Pacinian corpuscle'. The hair follicle receptor consists of a neuron ending wrapped around the root of a hair and it detects deflection of the hair. Figure 9.11(f) shows a small section of skin and the location of some receptors. Merkel's discs detect superficial touch whereas the Pacinian corpuscle detects deeper distortion of the skin.

Whether there is a bare neuron ending or an associated capsule, mechanical deformation, as in touch, causes depolarization (Chapter 4) at the tip. If this is strong enough, action potentials are instigated.

Action potentials travel from the tip along the axon to the CNS. For example, in Figure 9.11(c), displacements of the hair trigger action potentials in the associated neuron. You can test the presence of such neurons in your own body; try gently brushing the tips of hairs on, say, your arm and a sensation will be triggered.

Receptive fields

Figure 9.12 shows the receptive fields of some sensory neurons. The receptive field is the area of sensory surface, which, when it is stimulated, affects the activity of the neuron. As a similarity with retinal ganglion cells, somatosensory neurons have receptive fields that vary in size between large and small (Greenspan and Bolanowski, 1996) (Chapter 7, Figure 7.11, p. 193). The smaller receptive fields (e.g. at the fingertips) are associated with processing of information that shows greater tactile acuity, analogous to foveal vision. The arm is associated with larger receptive fields, analogous to vision away from the fovea. Differences in tactile acuity correspond to differences in the relative proportions of somatosensory cortex devoted to analyzing information from these body regions (Chapter 5, Figure 5.18, p. 117). A small size of receptive field corresponds to a relatively large area of representation at the sensory homunculus. The size of a receptive field of a somatosensory neuron is determined by the extent of the branching of its tip. See Figure 9.13.

Detection of information

Some somatosensory neurons show a rapid adaptation to tactile stimulation (Chapter 7, Figure 7.7(c), p. 192) and others show little adaptation (Darian-Smith, 1984).

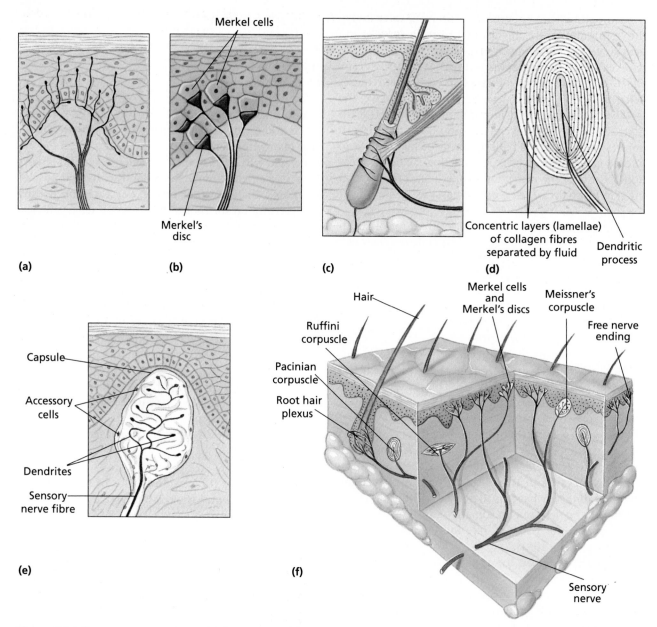

Figure 9.11 Somatosensory neurons: (a) free nerve endings, (b) Merkel's disc, (c) free nerve ending associated with the root of a hair, (d) Pacinian corpuscle, (e) Meissner's corpuscle and (f) skin showing various receptors.

Source: after Martini *et al.* (2000, Fig. 18-3, p. 467). Copyright © 2000, 1997 by Frederic H. Martini, Inc. and Michael J. Timmons. Reprinted by permission of Pearson Education, Inc.

The former type signals only the onset of a stimulus, which often carries most information. They extract what is changing in the tactile stimulus. For example, in a manual skill of picking up an object, it is obviously important that the dynamics of any slip provide information to the nervous system.

Under constant conditions, we cease to be consciously aware of much of the tactile stimulation of the body, such as the pressure of the top of a sock or that of our 'rear portions' against the chair. This is presumably due to both sensory processes and processes

of attention. Usually, *changes* in stimulation are most important. From a functional perspective, the constant pressure of the substrate as, for example, you lie on the ground does not need to command attention but any

Figure 9.12 Receptive fields of some sensory neurons.

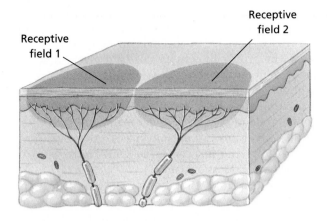

Figure 9.13 Receptive fields of two sensory neurons.
Source: Martini *et al.* (2000, Fig. 18-1b, p. 464). Copyright © 2000, 1997 by Frederic H. Martini, Inc. and Michael J. Timmons. Reprinted by permission of Pearson Education, Inc.

changes, as in the ground shaking, are important. In general, tactile stimuli excite different types of sensory neuron simultaneously. Texture is a feature extracted by processing information provided by such patterns of stimulation (Martin and Jessell, 1991).

Nociceptive neurons that detect real or threatened tissue damage adapt rather little. In evolutionary terms, the information that they signal cannot be ignored. Alas, so often we must have wished that evolution had selected some other option.

Somatosensory pathways

Introduction

Figure 5.18 (p. 117) introduced a route taken by harmless information from the periphery to the somatosensory cortex. The ascending neuron projects as part of a tract to nuclei of the medulla, where a synapse occurs. Other neurons then carry the message further by ascending to a nucleus of the thalamus (Kandel and Jessell, 1991). Note the cross-over of information from one side of the body to the opposite side of the brain.

The nucleus (the ventral posterolateral nucleus or VP nucleus) of the thalamus is comparable to that of the lateral geniculate nucleus in the visual pathway. The neurons with cell bodies in the thalamus, the third in the sequence, then project axons to the primary somatosensory cortex (Jones and Friedman, 1982).

Recording electrical activity

By placing the tips of fine electrodes within sensory neurons that convey information from the skin to the spinal cord, researchers monitor electrical activity (Vallbo, 1995). Through electrodes, the neuron can be stimulated electrically and the response recorded. Electrical activity of the neuron in response to mechanical stimuli at the skin can also be measured.

Researchers investigate the relationship between: (a) the tactile stimulus at the skin, (b) action potentials in a sensory neuron and (c) verbal reports of what people feel. See Figure 9.14. (Also, neurons can be stimulated artificially by the electrode and subjective reports noted.) The activity of the neuron increases with pressure (indentation), though the rate of increase declines (i.e. the slope gets shallower). However, this declining rate of increase is not reflected in the psychological perception of intensity. Some neurons are sensitive only to *changes* in tactile stimulation. Others are active for as long as the deformation at the skin lasts.

There are neurons that, when electrically stimulated, trigger sensations of painless mechanical touch, rather than, say, pain or temperature. Alongside such neurons others convey information on temperature and tissue damage. If the intensity of applied stimulation is increased, people do sometimes report pain. This suggests that adjacent neurons that normally carry information on tissue damage are simultaneously excited.

Figure 9.14 Responses to pressure (indentation) at three locations (1, 2 and 3): (a) subjective estimation of pressure and (b) response of sensory neuron.
Source: after Knibestol and Vallbo (1980, Fig. 9, p. 262).

Spatial acuity

People can also detect details in the stimulus, termed 'spatial acuity', analogous to visual acuity. The ability varies with different regions of skin. One measure is the ability to discriminate between one and two points of pressure (Figure 9.15). Two points close together are applied to the skin and the person reports that there is only one point. They are gradually separated and there is a distance at which the person reports that there are two points. This defines the **two-point threshold** at that location, a measure of spatial acuity (Weinstein, 1968). The two-point threshold varies across the surface of the body; the back has low acuity (large threshold) and the fingers high acuity (low threshold) (Figure 9.15). With a friend, you can try the experiment.

How does the difference in threshold arise? One factor is shown in Figure 9.16. In part (a), because of the physical segregation of their receptive fields, the profile of activity in the sensory neurons is different when comparing the effects of one and two stimuli. This is a region of high acuity, e.g. the fingertips. By contrast, in part (b), because of the overlap of their receptive fields, the profile in activity does not give a different signal comparing one and two points of stimulation. Although differences in receptive field size are a factor in determining differences in tactile acuity, there is not a one-to-one relationship (Greenspan and Bolanowski, 1996). Further processing is involved in the somatosensory pathway and this can mean some convergence of information and loss of acuity.

The connections that neurons make within the somatosensory pathway are an important factor in information processing (Kandel and Jessell, 1991). As information ascends from the receptor level to the cortex, there are varying degrees of convergence. For example, there is relatively little convergence of information arising from the fingertips of a primate and hence high resolution. This is comparable to the low convergence and high resolution of light at the fovea.

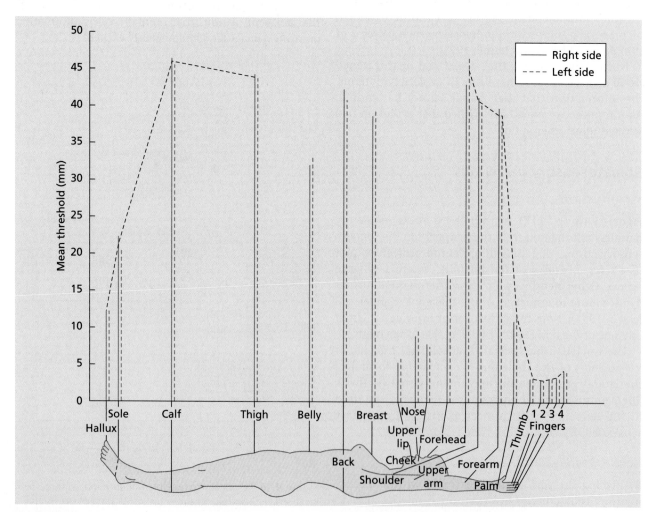

Figure 9.15 Variation in two-point threshold over the body surface. Increasing values represent increasing distances between points before two points can be discriminated.

Source: Weinstein (1968) in *The Skin Senses*, edited by D.R. Kenshalo, Fig. 10.5, p. 203. Courtesy of Charles C. Thomas Publisher, Ltd, Springfield, Illinois.

Processing within the somatosensory pathway

The receptive field of dorsal root ganglion (DRG) neurons is made up simply of an excitatory region (comparable to retinal receptors), defined by their tips. However, as information ascends in the somatosensory pathways, further processing based upon that detected by DRG neurons occurs. The activity of neurons in the medulla depends upon activity in DRG neurons. Medulla neurons have receptive field properties that are more complex than DRG neurons, comparable to that of ganglion cells in the visual system (Kandel and Jessell, 1991). Within the somatosensory pathway, there is lateral inhibition, comparable to that of the visual system. How does this arise?

Figure 9.17(a) shows three neurons, A, B and C, with cell bodies in the medulla and three representative sensory neurons (a, b and c), which excite A, B and C respectively. As always, the receptive field is defined in terms of the sensory surface, in this case the skin, even though the neuron in question is far removed from this surface. The receptive field of a neuron in the medulla, such as A, B or C, is made up of an excitatory (ON) region and an inhibitory (OFF) region.

Consider B. The excitatory area of its receptive field is made up of the terminals of neurons such as b (at the skin) and the inhibitory region is made up of the terminals of neurons such as a and c (at the skin). Activity in a and c inhibits B, acting via inhibitory connections (deriving from A and C) shown. Figure 9.17(b) shows the response to tactile stimulation in each region. Note the background 'spontaneous' level of activity of the medulla neuron (B) when there is no tactile stimulation. When a neuron such as b is active, B is excited. There are inhibitory connections

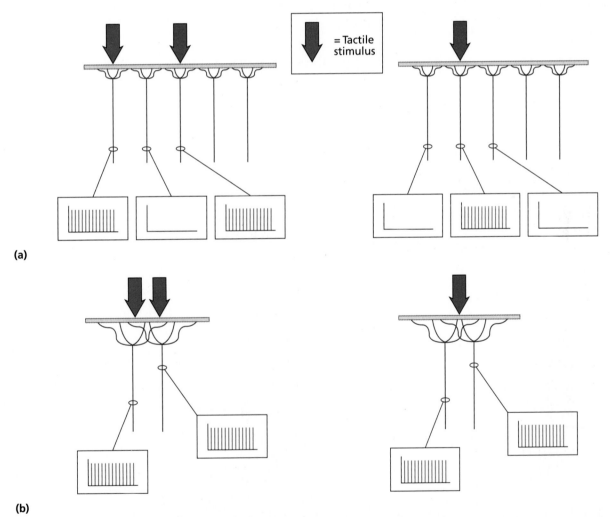

(a)

(b)

Figure 9.16 Differences in size and overlap of neuron branches. (a) Small non-overlapping branches. Distinct pattern of neural activity comparing two stimuli (left) and one stimulus (right). (b) Large overlapping branches. Two stimuli trigger activity that is indistinguishable from one stimulus.

Source: Toates (1998c, Fig. 4.32, p. 128).

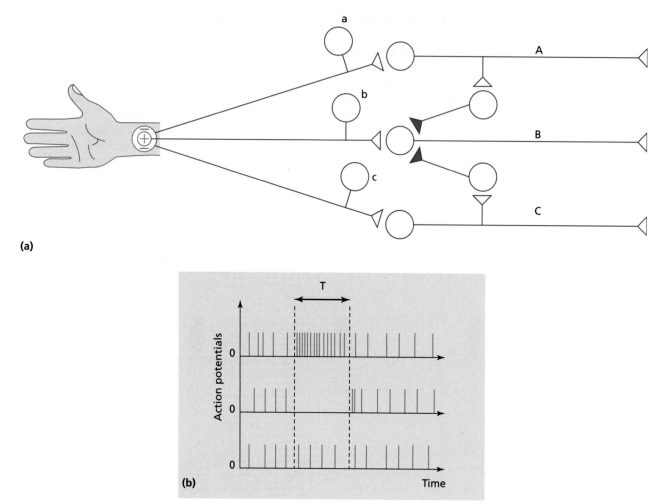

(a)

Figure 9.17 Receptive field properties: (a) neural connections and (b) response of neuron B. Upper trace: B is excited by activity in b (period T); middle trace: excitation of a and c; lower trace: a, b and c are simultaneously activated.

Source: after Kandel and Jessell (1991) *Principles of Neural Science*, 3rd edition, p. 375. Reprinted with permission of The McGraw-Hill Companies, Inc.

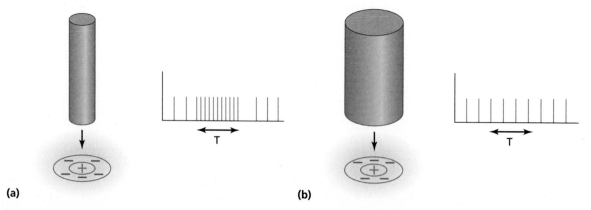

Figure 9.18 Two mechanical stimuli: (a) one that fills the excitatory region of receptive field and (b) one that covers both excitatory and inhibitory areas. Also shown is the excitation of a neuron such as B of Fig. 9.17 during application of the stimulus for time T.

from A to B and from C to B. Thus, excitation of a and/or c tends (via A and/or C) to inhibit B.

What is the optimal stimulus to maximize activity in neuron B? A tactile stimulus that fills the centre region but does not invade the inhibitory surround (Figure 9.18). This is analogous to an ON centre/OFF surround ganglion cell in the visual system. Also by analogy with vision, at the skin there can be overlap of tactile receptive fields of medulla neurons, analogous to that of retinal ganglion cells.

Note that feature detection requires a process of inhibition. On their own, sensory neurons cannot discriminate between small and large tactile stimuli. Only when processing neurons are connected together, as in Figure 9.17(a), is feature detection possible.

The axons of the medulla neurons project to the thalamus where further information processing occurs. Thalamic neurons then project this information to the cortex.

Cortical processing

At a gross level, the sensory homunculus shows the relationship between the body surface and its representation at the somatosensory cortex. It is now time to look at a detailed part of this representation. The evidence derives mainly from non-human primates.

Exactly how the somatosensory cortex should be classified varies to some extent with species (Kaas, 1996). Figure 9.19 shows three divisions: the primary somatosensory cortex (SI), the secondary somatosensory cortex (SII) and the posterior parietal lobe (Kandel and Jessell, 1991). The numbered divisions are based on Brodmann's classification (Chapter 5). The major input from the thalamus is to area SI, neurons from the thalamus arriving mainly in two of its subdivisions: areas 3a and 3b (Randolph and Semmes, 1974). Area 3a derives its input mainly from sensory neurons embedded in skeletal muscles (Burton and Sinclair, 1996).

In what sense is SI primary and SII secondary (Hsiao *et al.*, 1996; Burton and Sinclair, 1996)? Clearly pointing to a 'secondary' role, neurons in SII derive a principal input from SI, i.e. *hierarchical processing*. Another criterion is the nature of the receptive field properties of neurons located in each region. Neurons in SII respond to more complex features than those in SI and are less specific to a given sensory region. They might be triggered by stimulation anywhere on an arm and its hand or even bilaterally driven by either hand. Some neurons respond only to particular shapes. Also, SII neurons are more sensitive to attention than are SI neurons, suggesting a top-down contribution. SII appears to be a site at which sensory information is compared with stored memories of the tactile features of objects.

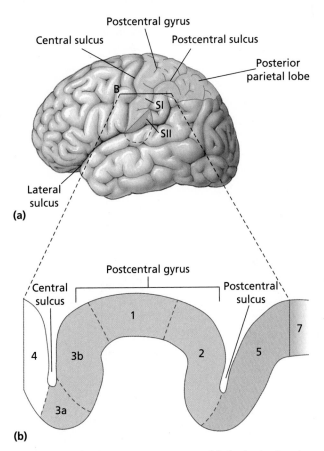

Figure 9.19 The somatosensory cortex: (a) the brain showing this region in relation to other parts and (b) enlargement of a section through it.

Source: Kandel and Jessell (1991) *Principles of Neural Science*, 3rd edition, p. 368. Reprinted with permission of The McGraw-Hill Companies, Inc.

Figure 9.20 shows in more detail the type of information processing associated with a part of region SI, in this case concerned with three fingers. In addition to the different properties of neurons within the different regions of Figure 9.19(b) (1, 2, 3a, etc.), neurons form distinct columns in the dimension running through successive layers from the surface inwards (i.e. layers i, ii, iii, etc.). In this dimension, neurons from the thalamus arrive at layer iv. Those in layers i and ii project to other cortical regions both within the somatosensory area (regions SI and SII) and outside. Projections from layers ii and iii to the posterior parietal cortex take part in the integration of tactile information with other sensory modalities. Some projections remain on the same side of the brain ('ipsilateral') and others cross to the other side ('contralateral').

Note also in area 3b the distinction in location between neurons that process rapidly adapting (RA) and slowly adapting (SA) information. These derive inputs from receptors at the skin having rapid and slowly

Figure 9.20 (a) and (b) Information processing in the primary somatosensory cortex.

Source: Kandel and Jessell (1991) *Principles of Neural Science*, 3rd edition, p. 378 reprinted with permission of The McGraw-Hill Companies, Inc.

adapting characteristics respectively. One assumes that information computed on the basis of these inputs has different destinations beyond the somatosensory cortex. In terms of its role, one stream computes information on the dynamics of a situation in terms of action and the other more in terms of its static features.

Top-down modulation

So far we have spoken of the flow of information from periphery to CNS. However, there is also top-down modulation of information in these pathways. The activity in cortical areas SI and SII is a function of the focus of attention. When the task required tactile discrimination, there was higher activity recorded from neurons in these areas (Hsiao *et al.*, 1993). As a control, the task was set to require visual discrimination. Descending pathways modulate ('top-down') the activity of the sensory pathway, amplifying some signals and inhibiting others, e.g. by means of projections from cortical layer vi (Figure 9.20) to the thalamus (Deschenes *et al.*, 1998).

Development and plasticity

In mice, there is a topographic relationship between whiskers on the face ('vibrissae') and neurons in the somatosensory cortex (Van der Loos and Woolsey, 1973; Woolsey and Wann, 1976). That is to say, a map of which neurons are activated by tactile stimulation of which vibrissae shows topographic form (Figure 9.21). Each vibrissa is associated with a group of neurons in the cortex termed a 'whisker barrel'.

Damage to the sensory neuron associated with a given vibrissa (e.g. by removing the vibrissa) early in life disrupts the development of cortical neurons in the associated whisker barrel, in spite of there being three or more synapses between the primary sensory receptor and the cortical neuron (Figure 9.22). Thus, cortical development requires an intact input from the periphery.

In the absence of its normal input, neighbouring vibrissae can take over control of cortical cells, analogous to the take-over of cortical neurons by one eye (Chapter 6).

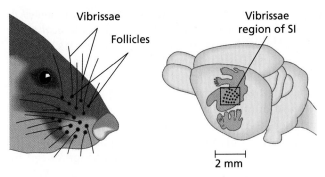

Figure 9.21 Relationship between vibrissae and neurons.
Source: Bear *et al.* (1996, p. 334).

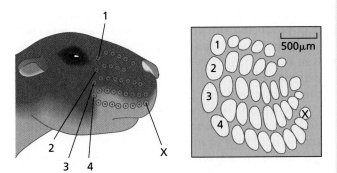

Figure 9.22 Damage to neurons (X) would result from damage to vibrissa X.
Source: after Whatson and Sterling (1998, Fig. 5.3, p. 146).

In rodents and primates, receptive fields vary as a function of peripheral damage (Merzenich *et al.*, 1983; Wall and Egger, 1971). Suppose that a skin region ('a') is associated with activation of a group of cortical cells (A). Furthermore, suppose that input from area 'a' ceases to arrive at the cortex as a result of localized damage in the sensory pathway. Neurons signalling information in neighbouring regions ('b' and 'c') can take over control of cortical cells A. In other words, cortical receptive fields exhibit plasticity.

One factor that appears to contribute to this plasticity is that there exist all along connections from b and c, through intermediate neurons, to A. However, they are normally masked by the dominant a → A links and hence functionally ineffective. After the damage that prevents the expression of a → A links, (b,c) → A links become unmasked and hence functionally effective. This appears to trigger further changes in connectivity based upon such things as levels of cortical activity arising from tactile stimulation at b and c.

Even under natural (i.e. undamaged) conditions, the receptive fields of neurons in the somatosensory cortex are not always static. For example, as a monkey becomes

proficient in using particular fingers to perform a novel motor skill, the cortical receptive fields corresponding to these fingers increase in size and complexity (Merzenich *et al.*, 1996). Presumably this is part of the basis of increasingly fine-grained sensory-motor connections. In humans, the fingers of musicians that have the most skilled activity (e.g. left-hand fingers of violinists) appear to acquire an enlarged cortical representation (Elbert *et al.*, 1995).

Section summary

1 Somatosensory neurons detect tactile stimulation.

2 Differences in the size of the receptive fields of somatosensory neurons at different areas of the skin relate to differences in the ability to resolve fine detail.

3 Within the medulla, there are neurons with receptive field properties consisting of ON and OFF regions at the skin.

4 Cortical processing extracts complex features from the sensory input.

5 There is some plasticity in the relationship between regions of skin and activation of neurons in the somatosensory cortex.

☞ Test your knowledge

9.4 Complete the following: 'The receptive field of a neuron in the medulla that is sensitive to touch has both excitatory and inhibitory regions, whereas the receptive field of a DRG neuron is purely ___'.

9.5 In Figure 9.17, artificial electrical stimulation of which of the following neurons would be expected to reduce the activity of neuron B to below its spontaneous firing rate? (i) a, (ii) b, (iii) the two neurons with terminals coloured blue.

9.6 Figure 9.18 shows the receptive field of a neuron in the medulla. What kind of mechanical object would be the optimal stimulus to reduce the neuron's activity to below the spontaneous background rate and where would the object need to be applied?

Answers on page 249   WEB

Chemical senses – taste and smell

Introduction

This section looks at two sensory systems that are sensitive to chemicals: taste and smell. In each, the detection of specific chemicals by **chemoreceptors** activates sensory neurons (McBurney, 1984). In evolutionary terms, the chemical senses are the oldest sensory systems, having a history of the order of 500 million years (Scott, 1990). Correspondingly, they mediate functions that are fundamental to existence, e.g. feeding and reproduction.

Taste and smell serve different, but related, functions. Both convey information to the CNS on chemicals present at the sensory detectors: the tongue and nose. However, its significance in terms of the animal's relation to the world is different between the two systems. Smell provides information on events and physical objects located some distance away, such as the pheromones (airborne chemicals used in communication between animals of the same species, as in mating) emitted by another animal. Of course, for taste to provide information, the object that is the source of it must already be in the mouth. For most of us, attention is drawn to the failure of chemical senses only when we experience a cold.

In both olfaction and taste, there is a distinction between the detection of chemical qualities and their motivational significance. Whereas certain tastes and odours will always evoke rejection and avoidance, others can evoke pleasantness/approach or unpleasantness/avoidance depending upon internal state.

We will deal first with taste and then with smell, noting similarities and differences.

Taste

Introduction

Taste signals information that is rarely neutral emotionally and motivationally (Scott, 1990). In addition to the prior analysis, done by touch, vision and smell to bring the substance to the mouth, taste analyses its appropriateness for ingestion or expulsion. An animal can be motivationally indifferent to much visual and auditory or even olfactory stimulation but this can hardly be so for taste.

Four primary ('basic') tastes were traditionally described: sweet, salty, sour and bitter (Coren *et al.*, 1994). Researchers now identify a fifth: *umami*, the word deriving from Japanese (Krebs, 2009; Kurihara and Kashiwayanagi, 2000). It is particularly associated with Asian cuisine. Primary tastes refer to *psychological* perceptions corresponding to different *physical* stimuli, i.e. broad classes of chemical molecules. Umami was included as a primary taste, since there are specific substances that preferentially trigger it and they are associated with activity in particular afferent neurons. Monosodium glutamate (a flavour-enhancing chemical used in Asian cooking) is a powerful trigger, whereas other substances fail to trigger such neurons.

A sensation of sweetness is generally produced by sugars and signals the availability of nutrients that can be ingested and used as energy. Saltiness signals a substance such as sodium chloride, common table-salt. Salt is needed in the diet since its components, sodium and chloride, are essential for the functioning of the body (e.g. producing the action potential). Sourness commonly indicates that a potential food has decayed and is to be avoided. In evolutionary history, a bitter taste is commonly indicative of poisonous plants and is, of course, to be avoided.

Sourness and bitterness are normally associated with rejection and avoidance, irrespective of circumstances and internal state of the body. However, in other cases, the reaction to a given substance depends upon physiological state. One distinguishes between the successive processes of (1) sensory detection of a chemical quality and (2) assessing its motivational significance. For example, the reaction to the perception of sweetness and saltiness depends to some extent upon the physiological state of the body.

Suppose we detect concentrated sodium chloride at the tongue. At a later stage of processing in the nervous system, this would normally trigger either acceptance or rejection as a function of the body's salt depletion or repletion. Even in sodium balance most mammals tend to ingest diets containing some sodium (Scott, 1990), ingestion being amplified in salt deficiency. In our evolution, especially at times of salt deficiency, it would be adaptive to ingest salt. Sodium concentrations that are avoided in sodium balance are ingested in deficiency.

Sensory detection

On the surface of the tongue is a mosaic of small organs, known as 'taste buds', each made up of receptors for chemicals (Norgren, 1984) (Figure 9.23). Taste buds are also in regions of the mouth other than the tongue. The tips of sensory neurons make contact with these receptors. When specific chemicals are detected by the receptors of the taste buds, action potentials arise in the associated sensory neurons.

At one time it was believed that each specific taste cell and associated neuron would respond only to a specific chemical quality such as a sugar: a quality-specific private line to the brain. Indeed, depending upon the species, there are a number of neurons showing this property and hence providing **labelled-line coding** for such qualities as sweetness and salt (McCaughey and Scott, 1998).

However, it is probably more common that the taste receptors of each taste bud and the associated neuron respond to some extent to a range of chemical qualities. Different taste buds respond *differently* to them. Thus, the information carried in a given neuron cannot discriminate between a low concentration of a chemical to which it is highly sensitive and a high concentration of a chemical to which it is less sensitive. The fact that tastes can be resolved implies a comparison between signals carried by different neurons, so-called **across-fibre pattern coding** (Norgren, 1984). This comparison is done in the brain where there is an integration of information.

This is analogous to colour vision where a particular cone (e.g. an M cone) responds preferentially to one wavelength but is sensitive to some extent to other wavelengths (e.g. long wavelengths) (McCaughey and Scott,

1998). The further processing that is done to information from sensory neurons to extract taste information is something like opponent-process coding for colour.

It appears that, as a result of top-down modulation, there is some plasticity in terms of which neurons code for which sensory quality. In sodium deprivation, neurons in the sensory pathway that normally code for sugars (see next section) become responsive to sodium (Jacobs *et al.*, 1988). This appears to be a means by which the hedonic quality of sugars can be temporally borrowed by the sodium ingestion system and contribute to increased sodium intake.

From tongue to brain

Figure 9.24 was introduced in Chapter 5 and it now points to some additional details: the receptors on the tongue in relation to the pathway of taste information carried by neurons to the gustatory cortex, in primates (Norgren, 1984). Sensory neurons travel as part of a cranial nerve (three of these are involved,

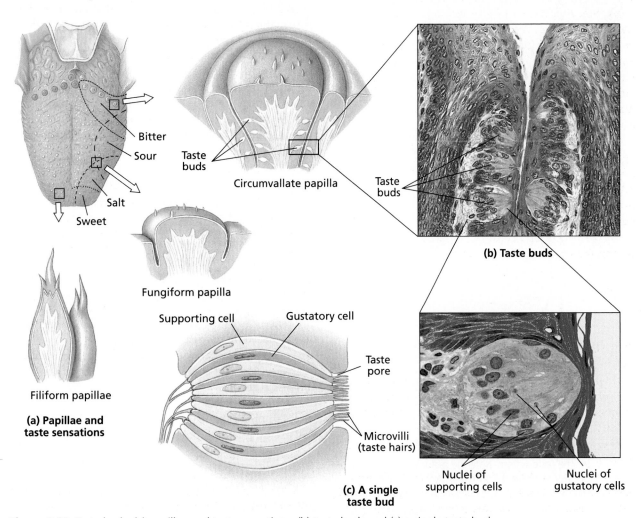

Figure 9.23 Taste buds: (a) papillae and taste sensations, (b) taste buds and (c) a single taste bud.

Source: Martini *et al.* (2000, Fig. 18-7, p. 471) Copyright © 2000, 1997 by Frederic H. Martini, Inc. and Michael J. Timmons. Reprinted by permission of Pearson Education, Inc.; (b) and (c) Copyright G.W. Willis/Visuals Unlimited.

facial, glossopharyngeal and vagus, as shown) to the nucleus of the solitary tract (NTS) in the medulla, where they terminate. Synaptic connection is made with further neurons that carry the information to a region of thalamus. These second-order neurons (with cell bodies in the NTS) exhibit plasticity in terms of the chemical quality needed to trigger them. This involves top-down modulation based upon need states.

Neurons project from the thalamus to the gustatory cortex. In addition to the pathway shown, other routes project to other brain regions such as the amygdala and

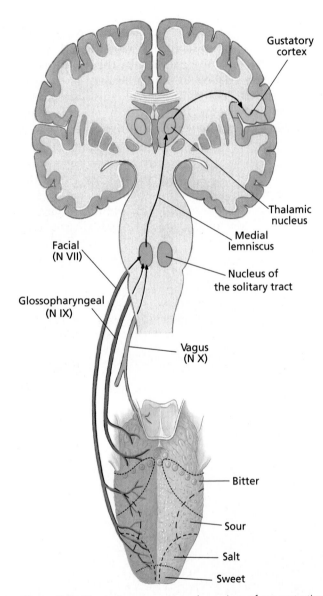

Figure 9.24 The taste system. Note the regions of concentration of the four ('classical') types of taste receptors. The diagram is drawn asymmetrically merely as a convenience for explanation.

Source: Martini *et al.* (2000, Fig. 18-8, p. 472). Copyright © 2000, 1997 by Frederic H. Martini, Inc. and Michael J. Timmons. Reprinted by permission of Pearson Education, Inc.

prefrontal cortex (de Araujo *et al.*, 2003). Throughout the routes of cortical processing, neurons can be identified that have 'preferred' tastes as trigger stimuli, such as umami.

Note a similarity with visual, auditory and somatosensory information, each of which also projects to its own region of thalamus. The similarity continues in that after the thalamus further neurons convey taste information to specific regions of cortex, which are specialized for processing it.

Much analysis of taste, in terms of appropriateness for ingestion, is performed at the brain stem (Grill and Kaplan, 1990). This process is sometimes termed a 'hedonic monitor'. Although the basic analysis of the chemical properties is done at this level, other brain regions also play a part in the decision to ingest or not, possibly by modulating the activity of the brain stem. Thus, tastes are put into a context of associations. For example, substances can increase in acceptance as a result of familiarity or become the targets of rejection as a result of nausea following their earlier ingestion. Much of this analysis appears to be performed at levels higher than the brain stem (Scott, 1990).

There are extensive feedback loops from cortex to lower structures in the taste pathway, by which ascending information can be modulated (Norgren, 1984). For example, the change in response of primary sensory neurons according to internal state (e.g. sodium balance) is due to a neural modulation mediated from higher levels of processing.

Smell

Introduction

The chemicals that trigger smell (olfaction) are described as 'volatile'. In a hungry person with a favourable history of associations, the smell of a favourite dish evokes approach but, following an association of the smell with subsequent gastric upset, it might evoke avoidance. The difference lies in the context into which sensory detection is placed by further processing.

We are all familiar with daily discriminations on the basis of vision and sound. Olfaction can be more subtle and less accessible to conscious awareness. The capacity of mothers to detect the odours of their babies and for babies to prefer the maternal odour (Weller, 1998) might well exert a role in human communication and bonding.

Sensory detection

Sensory detection of volatile chemicals by the nose has some similarities to the detection of chemicals by the tongue. The nose contains specific receptors that are sensitive to particular chemicals. In humans there are some 50 million such olfactory receptors, located as shown in Figure 9.25.

By sniffing, we increase the flow of air into the nose and increase the contact of volatile chemicals with olfactory receptors. Olfactory receptors are parts of neurons that perform transduction of chemical information and also, in the form of action potentials, convey information away from the site of detection and towards the brain. However, whereas there are a few basic types of taste qualities and receptors, it appears that olfactory stimuli and receptors cannot be categorized into a few classes (Bartoshuk and Beauchamp, 1994). Rather, there seem to be hundreds of different types of receptor, each specialized for a particular olfactory quality.

According to the **lock and key principle**, a volatile chemical triggering a receptor is analogous to a neurotransmitter attaching to a receptor at a synapse (Chapter 4). In each case, there is chemical specificity. Similarly, inserting the 'key' in the 'lock' (i) triggers further events within the cell and (ii) is normally short-lived as there are processes that remove the 'key' shortly after its attachment (Coren et al., 1994).

There are many odours that we identify as belonging to specific objects in our environment (e.g. frying eggs, vegetable vindaloo), each made up of many different chemicals. This implies that the outputs of numerous olfactory receptor types are combined to form our psychological perception of an odour. In other words, olfaction is a *synthetic* sense, one that puts together components of information to yield a combined perception (Carlson, 1994). In this sense, it is like vision. However, suppose three smells of familiar objects are present simultaneously, as in smoking a cigarette, while a curry is being served in the presence of someone wearing a strong perfume. We can still resolve the familiar components, so in this regard olfaction is *analytic*, something like hearing.

From nose to brain

The axons of olfactory receptors form synapses at the brain's olfactory bulb (Dodd and Castellucci, 1991) (Figure 9.25). Further neurons then convey olfactory information (as the olfactory tract) from the olfactory bulb to other brain regions, e.g. the olfactory cortex, amygdala and hypothalamus. Neurons are not organized in a topographic way at the olfactory bulb, so information on the site of the neuron originating the odour is lost.

Olfaction is the only system with a direct link to the cortex, bypassing the thalamus. Links to the amygdala provide rapid computation of the emotional significance of an odour and links to the hypothalamus have

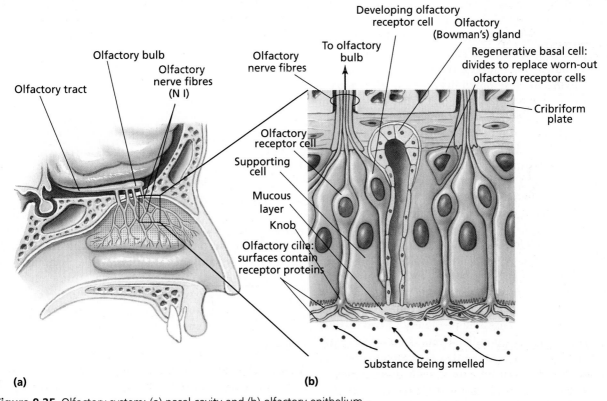

(a)   **(b)**

Figure 9.25 Olfactory system: (a) nasal cavity and (b) olfactory epithelium.

Source: Martini *et al.* (2000, Fig. 18-6, p. 470). Copyright © 2000, 1997 by Frederic H. Martini, Inc. and Michael J. Timmons. Reprinted by permission of Pearson Education, Inc.

motivational significance, as in mating. Some information ultimately reaches the orbitofrontal cortex, where processing is thought to be associated with conscious awareness (Dodd and Castellucci, 1991). In the latter regard, olfaction is similar to other sensory systems. There are also fibres which carry information 'top-down' to make synapses in the olfactory bulb.

Pheromones

In a number of species, there is a distinct olfactory system, in addition to that just described: the **vomeronasal system** (Bartoshuk and Beauchamp, 1994; Stevenson, 2010). Its detectors are also in the nasal cavity. This system specializes in the detection of pheromones. As an example, in secreting pheromones certain species advertise sexual arousal. By this means, a male can discriminate between potentially sexually receptive and unreceptive females. Distinct vomeronasal sensory neurons form synapses in the olfactory bulb. From the olfactory bulb, information is conveyed to brain regions concerned with, for example, reproduction, e.g. nuclei of the hypothalamus (Brennan and Keverne, 2004).

Evidence suggests that humans are sensitive to pheromones, a process that operates below conscious awareness (Monti-Bloch et al., 1994). However, some doubt that it is the vomeronasal system that mediates this functional role in humans (Brennan and Keverne, 2004). Thus, the conventional olfactory system could be responsible for pheromone detection in humans. The attraction of perfumes suggests that these may simulate pheromones that play a part in human sexual attraction. A role for pheromones in humans was suggested by the observation that women living in close proximity to each other have a tendency to synchronize their menstrual cycles (Stern and McClintock, 1998). Similarly, group-living female rats tend to show a synchrony of oestrous cycles (McClintock, 1984), which is mediated by pheromones.

Stern and McClintock demonstrated experimentally that there are shifts of the menstrual cycle in response to pheromones produced by women. Secretions taken from under the arms of donors were applied just above the upper lip of recipient women, which shifted their cycle. The control condition was alcohol, the chemical base for the samples in the experimental conditions. This again suggests that there might be natural synchronization. The direction of the shift, whether to bring the cycle forward or move it back, was such as to synchronize it with that of the emitter. This raises the possibility of two distinct pheromones having opposite effects. Women were not able to report the presence of the pheromone as distinct from the chemical base, indicating an unconscious effect.

What could be the functional significance of synchronization in group-living females, in terms of the advantage to the individual in timing mating? Could

synchronized mating coordinate group activities such as hunting and caring for offspring? This has enormous implications for anthropological and feminist discourse and the opportunities for speculation are vast.

Weller (1998) speculates that there might be significant emotional reactions due to pheromonal communication between two people. This could play a role in differences in social reactivity or as one factor among others in the phenomenon of emotional contagion, by which one person's mood influences another (Pause et al., 2009). It suggests that parapsychologists need to be vigilant about another possible route of communication of information in experiments on 'extra-sensory' perception.

Odour, emotion and mood

Odours are sometimes thought to have a more direct link to mood and emotion than do other sensory qualities. Compared with visual and auditory events, descriptions of odours have a more direct emotional label and thereby possibly a more personal 'meaning' (Ehrlichman and Bastone, 1992).

It might be that odours have more direct access to emotional processing, though cognitive factors (e.g. knowledge of what is the physical object giving rise to the odour) also play a role in labelling an odour. It is commonly said that odours have a peculiar ability to evoke emotion-laden memories from childhood. However, psychology lacks controlled studies showing that such odour-triggered memories are more potent than, say, visually cued memories. Since the trigger cues for any such odour → memory → emotion link would necessarily be personal and idiosyncratic, perhaps it is impossible to do formal research in this area.

In humans, anecdotal reports suggest that odour can influence mood, contributing to well-being (G.N. Martin, 1996) and some experimental evidence points in the same direction (Lehrner *et al.*, 2005). If psychological benefits derive from exposure to volatile chemicals, this is valuable no matter what the mechanism. However, it is not always certain that the route of such effects is via the olfactory system. Chemicals could be absorbed into the bloodstream via the lungs or through the skin in the case of massage oils and thereby influence the nervous system (Ehrlichman and Bastone, 1992).

From a functional perspective, it might make sense for unpleasant odours to trigger negative mood. Odours such as those deriving from rotting food are a sign of danger. Negative mood could motivate moving from the location.

Disorders of olfaction

With advancing years, humans become less sensitive to odours and elderly people commonly complain that foods lack taste (Smith and Duncan, 1992).

Analogous to other sensory systems, disorders of olfaction arise at various levels (Welge-Lussen, 2009). There can be a failure of volatile chemicals to gain access to the olfactory receptors by a blockage of the passageway. Failures can arise in the transmission of information to the brain or in the processing of olfactory information by the brain. A significant percentage of patients with loss of smell ('anosmia') have suffered head injury. This can involve severing neurons within the olfactory nerve. Alzheimer's patients are commonly deficient in smell, which can probably be related to the degeneration of neural tissue in the brain that is the hallmark of this disease.

A phantosmia or olfactory hallucination (OH) consists of the perception of an odour that is not physically present (Greenberg, 1992). An OH can take the form of a familiar smell or something novel to the person's experience. Sometimes the OH assumes a specific form of the kind 'roses presented on a fortieth birthday'. Such hallucinations have hedonic properties of liking or disgust and a frame of reference in space, e.g. to the left or right. Sometimes hallucinations have an 'as if' quality to them: people feel that there are features in common with, say, the smell of cigar smoke but they know that no such odour is present. In other individuals, the sensation has the vividness of a real odour.

OHs are associated with a number of conditions, one being epilepsy (Elliott *et al.*, 2009). This consists of sudden electrical activity, associated with such areas as the hippocampus and amygdala, with alteration of

Figure 9.26 Diagram showing regions of activation of selected brain regions by either olfactory or gustatory (taste) stimuli.
Source: Small and Prescott (2005, Fig. 1, p. 347). Courtesy of Dana Small.

consciousness. This identifies very broadly some processing of smell information with these regions.

Following brain lesions, as in accidents, OHs are sometimes experienced. Greenberg suggests that some of these represent release phenomena, i.e. they are released under the conditions of reduced afferent input.

Interaction of taste and smell

Taste and smell usually cooperate in analyzing substances for ingestion (Small and Prescott, 2005). For example, the psychological perception described as the **flavour** of food depends on their interaction. In addition, tactile stimulation of the mouth plays a role in flavour (Scott, 1990). When a cold impairs smell, food does not taste normal. Some common foods, e.g. garlic, coffee and chocolate, are difficult to identify when smell is impaired (Coren *et al.*, 1994). Disorders of smell are commonly described in terms of failures of taste (Smith and Duncan, 1992). When a substance such as a solution of sucrose is being tasted, there is an enhancement of sweetness by the simultaneous olfactory stimulation by food odours such as vanilla.

An odour can enhance a taste or even trigger a taste sensation in the absence of a taste stimulus. This effect requires *congruency* of the components, that is to say, odours and tastes that have a history of being paired reinforce or substitute their effects. This suggests a process of learning by association. Thus, you would not expect a strawberry odour to enhance or trigger the taste sensation of a fried egg.

What is the neural basis of this interaction? Neuroimaging studies reveal networks of brain regions, which are stimulated by either taste or odour (Figure 9.26). From this, it seems reasonable to speculate that these regions are responsible for the integration of taste and olfactory information. Indeed, in some cases, activation is increased by simultaneous stimulation of both modalities. The orbitofrontal cortex (OFC) participates in such networks. In non-human primates, recordings from single neurons in the OFC reveal triggering by taste or smell stimuli, or both, pointing to a convergence of inputs.

Section summary

1 Taste and smell are initiated by the detection of specific chemicals by chemoreceptors.

2 Taste buds at the tongue detect chemicals.

3 Five primary tastes, sweet, salty, sour, bitter and umami, are psychological perceptions corresponding to broad classes of molecule at the tongue.

4 Olfactory receptors in the nose are sensitive to volatile chemicals.

5 The vomeronasal system is specialized for the detection of pheromones.

☞ Test your knowledge

9.7 What are some similarities and differences between taste and olfaction?

9.8 Complete the following: 'A pheromone is a substance that is ___ by one individual and that is ___ by another individual'.

Answers on page 249

Bringing things together

The chapter has spanned the sensory systems of hearing, the vestibular sense, touch, taste and smell. In each case, a specialized detector captures a range within a particular physical quality. It is possible to see some features in common between certain of the sensory systems and some differences. In each case, we can see that the sensory systems are particularly sensitive to information that plays a role in survival and reproduction. In each case, an initial stage of detection of the physical event is followed by further processing in which more complex features are extracted and the sensory event is placed in context.

The tactile sense, hearing and the vestibular sense involve cells that respond to mechanical distortion.

There is some similarity in the type of cell that is found in the hearing system and the vestibular system. Taste and smell both respond to chemicals by a process of recognition of the form that the chemical takes.

> See the video coverage for this chapter and observe how psychologists can gain insight by studying the properties of the ear. WEB

Summary of Chapter 9

1 The auditory system analyses sounds in terms of their frequency and intensity.

2 The vestibular system is sensitive to movements of the head and can trigger corrective action.

3 The somatosensory system detects tactile stimuli and involves specialized detectors at the skin that are sensitive to various kinds of mechanical distortion.

4 The senses of taste and smell are triggered by particular chemicals that attach to specific receptors.

Further reading

For all of the neuroscience in this chapter, see Nolte (2008). For details of hearing, see Brown (1999). For the somatic sensory system, see Hendry *et al.* (1999). For taste and olfaction, see Rouby *et al.* (2005).

Answers

Explanations for answers to 'test your knowledge' questions can be found on the website www.pearsoned.co.uk/toates

9.1 Loss of sensation at a particular range of frequencies.
9.2 (ii) Medium
9.3 Mechanical; frequency
9.4 Excitatory
9.5 (i) a; (iii) the two neurons with terminals coloured blue

9.6 A tube, the size and location of which coincides with the inhibitory surround.
9.7 *Similarities.* Both detect chemicals with the help of chemoreceptors. Reaction to the chemical (e.g. acceptance or rejection) can depend upon internal factors, such as memories of past associations, hunger. *Differences.* Taste relates to objects in the mouth, whereas smell relates to distant objects. Taste receptors fall into a few classes, whereas very many types of olfactory detectors. Taste information is conveyed via the thalamus, whereas olfactory information has direct line to cortex.
9.8 Secreted (or released); detected (or sensed)

> **Visit www.pearsoned.co.uk/toates** WEB
> for a range of resources to support study.
> Test yourself with multiple choice questions and access a bank of over 100 videos that will bring the topics to life.

Chapter 10
The control of movement

Learning outcomes for Chapter 10

After studying this chapter, you should be able to:

1 Describe the problems that the movement control system confronts and the basic 'design' principles that enable their solution.

2 Distinguish between feedback and feedforward, while explaining why both processes are needed. Distinguish between automatic and controlled processing.

3 Explain what is involved in detecting change while maintaining stability.

4 Describe the basic principles of neuromuscular control and relate these to the properties of motor neurons and skeletal muscles.

5 Describe what is meant by the term 'stretch reflex' and how it maintains stability in the face of a disturbance.

6 Identify some of the principal brain regions involved in motor control and outline their roles. Link this account to a consideration of when motor control goes wrong and explain why Parkinson's disease is of particular interest to psychologists.

7 Distinguish the routes by which motor information descends from the brain to the periphery and compare their properties.

8 Understand the significance of performing mental simulations of actions and link this to the possible role of mirror neurons.

9 Outline what is meant by development of the nervous system, in the context of movement control.

Scene-setting questions

1 'That was a knee-jerk response!' is a term of mild abuse. What is this response and how is it produced?

2 'Sorry – I wasn't thinking – I went on autopilot.' Does this statement have any basis in biological psychology?

3 What goes wrong in Parkinson's disease?

4 Can you improve skills at, say, the piano or football by practising in your imagination?

5 What is the link between perception and the control of movement?

What is the link between perception and the control of movement? Explore the video on the website accompanying this book at www.pearsoned.co.uk/toates

When do we need to pay full conscious attention to a single task and when can we trust the brain's automatic processes?
Source: Getty Images/Altrendo.

Introduction

First, imagine that you are simply standing still and waiting somewhere. You remain upright in spite of gusts of winds blowing against you and people bumping into you. Though we usually take such ability for granted, it represents an astonishing achievement by the nervous and muscular systems; a shop-window dummy left balancing there would quickly fall to the ground. We manage the task without conscious attention being paid to it.

Now imagine that you start to move forward. Again, without thinking, you swing your legs back and forth, while moving the arms in synchrony. The control of movement is a crucial role of the nervous system but, in moving, you also need to maintain the body's stability, in this case, in an upright position. So, to trigger *change* against a background of *stability* is a task that evolution has solved.

Look at the effortless way in which you can negotiate and manipulate your environment, lifting objects and placing them in different locations, swinging a tennis racket or doing fine-grained and attention-demanding tasks such as sewing. In each case, there is coordination of muscles by the nervous system in order to achieve a goal, sometimes termed a **set-point**. So much of behaviour appears to be spontaneous, as in the tasks just described or when you decide to get out of bed for no obvious external trigger. These exemplify what is termed an **action** (Jahanshahi *et al.*, 1995) (Chapter 2).

Now contrast this with the automatic response of moving the foot quickly from a hot object. Some behaviour is triggered by external events and this, by contrast, is described as a 'reaction'.

Figure 10.1 summarizes the essence of the chapter. First note the 'Stimulus' that acts on the 'Neuromuscular system' to trigger 'Behaviour'. This is the part described

by the term 'reaction' and is exemplified by that shown to a noxious stimulus.

Now let's turn to the 'action' part of behaviour, where a role is played by the internal factor of a decision to act. In deciding, we establish goals; hence the arrow marked 'Goals'. The goal set can be as simple as standing upright without falling over or as complex as hitting a winning tennis stroke. Whatever the goal, the problem that it sets for the control of movement is to try to align the actual state of affairs with the goal. In other words, the system has the task of minimizing any disparity between the way things are and the way that the goal, in effect, says that they should be. In the case of standing upright, we simply need to maintain the goal of the *status quo* whereas movement is called for in other cases.

In Figure 10.1, 'Sensory/perceptual systems' detect 'External stimuli', which gives the 'Perception of world'. 'Sensory/perceptual systems' utilize information such as vision, and a comparison is made with the goal. The task of movement control is to try to minimize any difference that this 'Comparison' detects between the goal and how the world actually is. Exactly how this is achieved forms a theme of the present chapter. 'Behaviour' changes the 'External stimuli', as in hitting the ball with the racket.

Our 'Sensory/perceptual systems' are informed not only of the external world but also of events within the body. Quite unconsciously, we monitor the activity of our skeletal muscles. The CNS is constantly informed of their contraction, represented as 'State of muscles'. The term **proprioception** refers to the special sensory system that monitors muscles and feeds information on this to the CNS. Try closing your eyes and touching the tip of your nose with your finger. Although you do not have vision as a guide, you can still do it. Proprioception informs you of the state of the muscles and can be exploited as a guide.

Performing tasks, even of standing upright, requires signals from sensors of the state of your body, such as those of proprioception and those making up the

Figure 10.1 Neuromuscular control.

vestibular apparatus (Chapter 9). If you accidentally tilt from the vertical, these sensors detect this and instigate corrective action. Such tasks involve coordination over the activity of numerous skeletal muscles.

Imagine yourself performing some skilled action for the first time, such as tennis. Your behaviour is controlled consciously by the disparity between the way that things are and how you would like them to be. Wimbledon tennis champions all started out this way but the acquisition of skill has given them some additional processes to exploit. These will be discussed shortly.

Note one other feature of Figure 10.1. The 'Command to action' is also shown going to our 'Sensory/perceptual systems'. The brain compares what has been commanded with the effect this has on the world, through 'External stimuli'. Future modification can be made to this command, based on outcomes.

The next section looks at the issue of how we adjust behaviour so that the actual state is as closely aligned as possible to the goals that we set.

Section summary

1 The brain sets goals and, by its control of behaviour, attempts to match these.

2 Maintaining stability is a goal set by the brain.

3 Actions are organized against a background of maintaining some stability.

4 A system of proprioception detects the activity of skeletal muscles.

5 Proprioception as well as vestibular signals are involved in maintaining stability in the face of disturbances.

6 Particular stimuli trigger some behaviour, as a reaction rather than an action.

 ## Test your knowledge

10.1 Complete the following: 'Neural signals within the ____ system, involving hair cells, detect unintended movement of the head and trigger corrective action'.

10.2 Complete the following: 'A system of proprioception detects the state of ____ muscles and feeds this information to the ____.'

Answers on page 280

Basics of control

This section looks at some of the principles that underlie the control of movement. Later sections consider the details of how the nervous system achieves these tasks.

Types of control

Negative feedback

Exploiting negative feedback (Chapter 2), deviations of a body parameter from its normal ('optimal') level triggers action to restore normality. For example, when body temperature falls, shivering is triggered and this generates heat, which tends to raise body temperature back to normal. This same principle is employed in the control of movement. In terms of Figure 10.1, when the sense organs indicate that something is not aligned with a goal, action is taken to restore alignment.

In order to raise money for charities, village fetes sometimes offer various games that challenge contestants' visual and motor skills. One consists of having to pass a loop of metal wire along a bending metal wire but without the loop touching the inner wire. If contact is made, an electric bell rings and this is scored as a miss. Skill comes in not letting the loop come too close to the inner wire. If you find the loop getting near the wire, you take corrective action to move it away. Any deviation from the desired position is the trigger for action, i.e. negative feedback. To the novice, such a task is done with conscious awareness focused on it. You could verbally articulate what you were trying to achieve. However, the body also exploits negative feedback in quite unconscious ways, as follows.

It was noted that, when there is a disturbance to the body, corrective action occurs, such that you do not fall over. Sensors detect the disturbance and trigger a change to the signal sent to the skeletal muscles. This then restores stability, without there necessarily being conscious intervention. You just consciously set the goal to stand upright and the rest is done unconsciously.

When we try to perform a new action, we tend to be clumsy and make mistakes. Regular practice usually improves performance, termed 'motor learning' (Willingham, 1998). The system learns by mistakes; what is achieved is compared with the goal. Error tends to cause (i) immediate action such as to eliminate error and (ii) learning to adjust future action.

Feedforward

Negative feedback is not the only process involved in the control of movement and an additional process is termed **feedforward**. To understand this, consider some of the problems with relying only upon negative feedback, especially where speed is important.

For error to trigger action, an error must first occur and be detected, information on it must be fed back and only then action triggered. This takes time. When things change rapidly, negative feedback might not be able to trigger action quickly enough. The solution is feedforward, which operates within a framework of negative feedback and makes up for the latter's shortcomings.

In a simple unlearned form, feedforward is illustrated when we raise an arm out to one side of the body. At *the same time*, we automatically tilt the body slightly in the opposite direction to counter the disturbance to equilibrium that would *otherwise* occur. Tilt is not a response to a disturbance to equilibrium but is caused by putting into effect the intention to raise the arm. By reacting even before a disturbance to equilibrium occurs, it is said to avoid ('pre-empt') any disturbance.

Feedforward controls can also be learned based upon past experiences, using negative feedback. In such cases, feedforward control is something like a calculated guess as to what action is needed. To clarify this with a simple example, let us return to body temperature. Suppose that your body temperature drops as a result of an unexpected exposure to a cold environment. In response to cooling, the body triggers heating action such as shivering. This brings temperature back to normal. However, you can do better than this. Suppose that you hear from the weather forecast that the temperature has dropped sharply. You might wrap up warmly on leaving home. This is not in response to body cooling but a calculated guess that you will be cold unless you take this action. It thereby prevents chilling, a form of feedforward.

To return to movement control, suppose movements have been repeatedly performed under the guidance of negative feedback to bring something into alignment. The brain acquires memories of the movements and the

circumstances under which they were triggered. It can then instigate action slightly sooner than would be triggered on the basis of negative feedback. Action is based on a calculation of the *possibility* of future error, i.e. feedforward (Ito, 1984). Feedforward is also illustrated in the following example.

Consider a predator chasing prey. The predator exploits information on the distance between itself and the prey in order to try to close the gap. If the prey changes direction suddenly, the predator takes corrective action. This exemplifies negative feedback. However, the predator also exploits feedforward. When the moves of the prey can be predicted, the predator's behaviour is directed to where the prey will most likely be in future (Rosenblueth *et al.*, 1968). See Figure 10.2. This is why prey such as antelope suddenly change direction when they are being chased – they reduce the opportunity for predators to predict their position.

The difference between the novice tennis player and the Wimbledon champion is that the former is relying heavily on negative feedback, whereas the latter has an array of feedforward possibilities. Hence, the champion anticipates the moves of the ball and acts so fast that the behaviour could not be guided moment-by-moment simply by negative feedback. If, however, an error appears because of a failing by feedforward, then future behaviour is adjusted accordingly. Actions and feedback on their consequences are memorized and used to adjust behaviour in the future, so goals can be achieved more effectively.

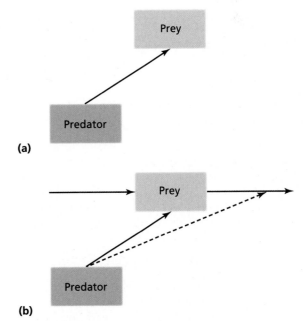

(a)

(b)

Figure 10.2 Trajectory of a predator based upon (a) a stationary prey and negative feedback and (b) moving prey and negative feedback alone (solid) compared with system that has, in addition, feedforward (dotted).

What kind of control system underlies a task of this kind?

Source: © Winfried Wisniewski/Corbis.

Controlled and automatic processing

Basics

Imagine you are walking across an icy bridge. You pick your steps very carefully, consciously focusing attention on the single task of moving but without slipping. You do not converse with anyone, since this would divert your attention from the task at hand. You hold on to a railing and monitor the effects of your feet, alert to any slight slippage. You are relying on moment-by-moment feedback.

Now imagine yourself in summer, walking over the same bridge. You are in conversation with a friend and give hardly a thought to the action of walking. In the first case, you brought full conscious awareness to the problem and this illustrates **controlled processing** (Schneider and Shiffrin, 1977). In the second case, the task was done without bringing conscious awareness to it and it would be said to involve **automatic processing**. Your conscious awareness was engaged elsewhere, with the conversation.

New tasks start out generally in the mode of controlled processing and with a weight on negative feedback. When people first start to learn to ride a bicycle, they are conscious of every move. When they become skilled at it, control shifts to a more automatic mode. If, however, the bicycle starts to skid on ice, they quickly bring full conscious awareness to the task. Learning a new skill and devoting conscious effort to it often involves silent speech-based instructions to ourselves (Seitz and Roland, 1992).

Although controlled and automatic represent two distinct modes, in practice most, if not all, tasks will be done by exploiting a combination of both. Even doing something in the conscious controlled mode will make considerable use of some automatic processes.

Behaviour that requires conscious decision-making is described as **voluntary action**. It is said to have a purpose or goal, which we can consciously reflect upon and articulate. By contrast, other aspects of behaviour are described as 'automatic reactions' or **involuntary reactions**.

With extensive repetition, voluntary ('controlled') behaviour moves to become automatic, and takes on certain new properties (Thach, 1998). Suppose that, over repeated experiences, controlled behaviour is performed by repetition of a given sequence of component acts A_1, A_2, A_3..., etc. With the move to automatic control, triggering of A_1 tends to trigger A_2, which then triggers A_3 and so on. Once such learned (feedforward) sequences are able to be run off automatically, they offer speed but also allow a sparing of conscious brain processes for other tasks.

Role of the CNS

The nervous system is organized at different levels of control. Some reflexes have a degree of autonomy from the brain and are organized at the spinal cord (Chapter

A personal angle

Ian Waterman

At age 19, Ian Waterman, an apprentice living in Southampton, England, contracted a very rare disease. He suffered inflammation specific to sensory neurons, leaving motor neurons unaffected. Large-diameter myelinated neurons that mediate touch and proprioception were particularly affected. A physician, Jonathan Cole, produced an account of Ian's life, *Pride and a Daily Marathon* (Cole, 1991).

Ian's movements and life were devastated by the disorder, indicating the importance of feedback from the body. He was in limbo. Since feedback from the mouth as from elsewhere was lacking, speech was very difficult. Ian could feel pain since the small-diameter axons that convey information on tissue damage were unaffected. When not looking at them, Ian's limbs would sometimes move on their own, indicative of the importance of feedback in maintaining stability. Amazingly, Ian learned to exploit visual feedback in regaining mobility. Recalibration of motor commands was a difficult trial-and-error process, involving full conscious control in place of unconscious proprioceptive feedback. Even a moment's loss of vision was disruptive and there was no spare cognitive capacity to permit daydreaming during walking. Ian could exploit his intact sense of temperature even without the use of vision, e.g. when in bed he knew that he had moved a leg on detecting a cooler place.

3). However, the brain still exerts some influence over reflexes, adjusting their parameters according to circumstances, thereby making them stronger or weaker.

To function optimally, speed is often essential. Conscious reactions based upon feedback are relatively slow and processing can become overloaded with information. The solution is to delegate some limited control to other levels, such as reflexes and brain processes that operate on automatic ('autopilot') control. However, conscious processes still monitor their success or failure. How the parts of the system and levels interact in producing adaptive behaviour is the central problem to be addressed in this chapter.

Skill learning

There is a distinction between learning skills (e.g. to ride a bicycle) and learning knowledge (e.g. that Chisinau is the capital of Moldova). Different brain regions are activated during learning of these different tasks. By positron emission tomography (PET) (Chapter 5), Seitz and Roland (1992) measured blood flow in the brain during skill learning, involving finger movements of the right hand similar to typing. There was activation in motor regions of the left motor cortex and the right cerebellum. Areas involved in acquiring a memory for facts and locations, e.g. the hippocampus, were not activated.

Differences in brain processes correspond to the dimension controlled–automatic (Jenkins *et al.*, 1994; Raichle *et al.*, 1994). When a task becomes automatic, there appears to be some short-circuiting of the higher-level goal-directed and cognitive processes. Jenkins *et al.* measured regional cerebral blood flow (rCBF) (Chapter 5) by PET scanning as people became skilled at a motor task. The cerebellum (Chapter 5) was strongly activated during learning of a new task but less so when skill was acquired. As a person becomes skilled at a finger movement (e.g. 'touch the thumb twice with index finger'), activation of speech areas of the cortex declines (Seitz and Roland, 1992). This corresponds to a reduction in the use of silent 'inner speech' by people to solve the problem. The nervous system stores programmes for well-practised responses that can sometimes be executed even if feedback from the muscles is disrupted due to disease (Marsden *et al.*, 1984).

This section has emphasized joint control by negative feedback and feedforward. The following section gives some instances of how stability is maintained in a changing world with the help of such control.

Section summary

1 Negative feedback control, based upon disparity, is at the core of movement control.

2 Action depends upon negative feedback, e.g. via the eyes and from within the muscles.

3 Feedforward control involves taking action in anticipation of events likely to occur.

4 Negative feedback control acts in combination with feedforward control, the latter bringing the advantage of speed.

5 Behaviour can be classified into categories such as voluntary movements and reflexes.

6 Most behaviour is a compound of voluntary and involuntary/reflex components.

7 Voluntary behaviour is directed towards a goal of which we are consciously aware.

8 A distinction is between the controlled mode (i.e. conscious and with focused attention) and the automatic mode (unconscious and without focused attention).

9 A criterion of skill acquisition is when a task is performed automatically.

 ## Test your knowledge

10.3 Complete the missing words in the following: 'Acting in response to a deviation from a goal is described as ___ control, whereas ('anticipatory') acting so as to prevent a deviation is termed ___ control'.

10.4 Complete the missing word in the sentence. 'Behaviour that starts out being 'controlled' can with extensive repetition become ___'.

Answers on page 280

How stability is maintained

Introduction

We are *active* in the world and this changes our relation to the external world. Thus, the brain confronts a fundamental design problem. Suppose that the eyes detect an image moving across the retina. This could be because something has moved in the external world relative to our eyes. Alternatively, it could be that the world has stayed still but the eyes have moved. A move of the body or just the eyes relative to a stationary world can cause a similar change in input to the exteroceptive ('arising in the outside world') senses as when the world changes (Gregory, 1997). In either case, there will be a movement of the image across the retina. Clearly, distinguishing the two is vital, so how is it achieved?

Similarly, a problem arises from interpreting a changing signal from the vestibular apparatus. This indicates that the vestibular apparatus (and presumably the whole head!) has moved somewhere in space, but what caused this? Did something in the world move us, as in an earthquake, or did the head move as a result of our voluntary action in a stable world?

This section gives some examples to illustrate how such problems are solved.

Eye movements

Consider the difference between Figures 10.3(a) and (b). In (a), the eye remains stationary and the object moves, whereas in (b) the external world is stationary and the eye moves (image of a stable world moves across the retina). We perceive correctly in (a) movement of the object and in (b) a stationary world, in spite of the fact that the image moves across the retina in both cases. In (b) information on the image movement and the eye movement cancel each other out, so that no movement is perceived. This indicates that perception is based upon both exteroceptive information and eye movements.

How do eye movements provide information for perception? Figure 10.4 shows two possibilities: the **inflow theory** and **outflow theory** (von Holst and Mittlestaedt, 1950). In each case, exteroceptive and intrinsic information is compared. Also, there is the same source of exteroceptive information, derived from image movement at the retina, conveyed via the optic nerve. However, the intrinsic source is different between (a) and (b). According to the inflow theory (a), the brain bases its calculation on *feedback* from the muscles. There are receptors located within eye muscles and these are said to provide the intrinsic information. By contrast, the outflow theory (b) suggests that information is

Figure 10.3 Movement: (a) stationary eye and changing world (object moves from left to right) and (b) stable external world but changing eye position (eye moves direction of pointing from square to round object).

Source: adapted from Gregory (1997, Fig. 6.1, p. 100).

based on the command to move (see also Figure 10.1). The latter is a variety of feedforward. In effect, the nervous system indicates that it has made a command to move the eyes and it anticipates that this will cause the muscles to move the eye.

An experiment can tease the theories apart. An after-image (Chapter 8) is fixed on the retina of the person in a dark room. The eye is then gently poked. The 'object' that the after-image represents does not appear to move. This favours outflow theory, since there is no command to the eye muscles and no change in exteroceptive input. Presumably there is an inflow from the muscles as a result of a poke-induced 'passive' change, which, if inflow theory were correct, should trigger perception of movement (Gregory, 1997).

Eye muscles can be paralyzed by curare, which blocks the junction between the motor neurons and the muscle, so commands cannot trigger contraction by the muscle. When the person attempts to move the eyes (i.e. makes commands), the world appears to spin around (Gallistel, 1980), which again supports outflow theory.

So, something to do with the command to action is involved in the perception of stability and movement (MacKay, 1966). Possible sources of information range from the initiation of the command to move the eyes to the activity of motor neurons. Such ideas are summed up in terms of a so-called 'efference copy' or **corollary**

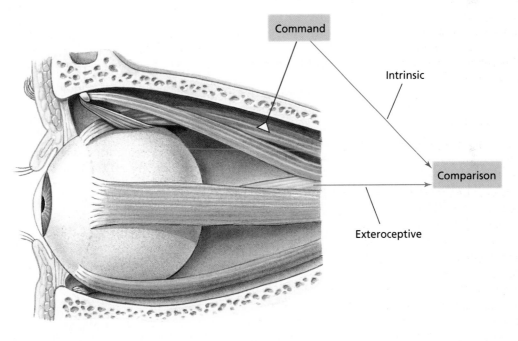

Figure 10.4 Two theories: (a) inflow and (b) outflow.

Source: adapted from Martini *et al.* (2000, Fig.10-5b, p. 268). Copyright © 2000, 1997 by Frederic H. Martini, Inc. and Michael J. Timmons. Reprinted by permission of Pearson Education, Inc.

discharge (von Holst and Mittelstaedt, 1950), i.e. a copy of the ('efferent') signal to the muscles is exploited for perception. In fact, information at an early stage in the production of movement appears to be used. Neurons within the parietal cortex encode locations of objects in visual space (Duhamel *et al.*, 1992). Prior to an eye movement, the anticipated new location of existing stimuli is calculated, i.e. an 'expectation' (Gallistel, 1980), and compared with their actual location after the movement. If the new situation corresponds to that calculated, perception is of a stable world.

A personal angle

The importance of getting data

The Austrian philosopher and physicist Ernst Mach (1838–1916) emphasized the importance of empirical data, sense impressions being crucial. His name is given to the speed of sound, Mach 1. Mach's ideas influenced the physicist Albert Einstein and the psychologist Burrhus F. Skinner. Mach was true to his principles and did an experiment on himself by bunging up his eyes with putty so that they could not move (Gregory, 1997). When he tried to move his eyes, the world appeared to spin around, demonstrating an intrinsic factor in perception and pointing to outflow theory. Wisely, Gregory advises students to take Mach on his word rather than trying to repeat the experiment!

The vestibulo-ocular reflex

Suppose that we are focused on something but voluntarily move our heads. Without any compensatory eye movements, the image would move across the retina, which would spoil any effort to focus on a particular object. Nodding your head in agreement with someone would take your attention away from their eyes – not an adaptive strategy in a close encounter. However, in reality, the head movement triggers compensatory movement of the eyes, so that the image tends to be stabilized on the retina, the **vestibulo-ocular reflex** (Ito, 1984). See Figure 10.5.

Movement of the head is detected by means of sensory input from the vestibular apparatus and its semicircular canals (Chapter 9). This triggers motor output to the eye muscles, so as to maintain stability of the eyes' direction of pointing. The parameters of this reflex can change over time, e.g. muscles become less effective with age. Unless checked, this would diminish the efficacy of the reflex. In fact, if the image fails to stabilize, other parameters are modified to compensate, i.e. motor learning. The neural link from semicircular canals to eye muscles through the brain stem is modified, by the action of what is termed a 'sidepath'. See Figure 10.5.

Maintaining postural stability

In order to stand upright without falling, the body's centre of gravity needs to be within the area of the base of support at the feet. Outside this, we are doomed to crash. Two types of disturbance might cause the centre of gravity to move beyond the safe zone: (1) an unexpected disturbance from outside, e.g. a very strong gust of wind, and (2) an expected change from inside, self-generated movements, e.g. voluntarily extending a limb.

Unexpected disturbances elicit corrective action by negative feedback, whereas, as we just noted, predicted changes by deliberate action instigate compensation as feedforward. If you are standing in a train that starts unexpectedly to move forward, this tends to cause you to sway backwards. However, this deviation initiates postural reflexes tending to bring the body's centre of gravity forward and restore the vertical posture. Postural reflexes are automatic, have a quick reaction time and are organized subcortically. There are several processes involved in detection of deviation from upright, including vision, information from muscles in the legs and signals from the vestibular system.

Factors termed 'cognitive' or 'higher' can influence postural reflexes by modulating neural signals at brain stem and spinal levels (Rothwell, 1994). For example, an expectation of an external disturbance can influence the magnitude of the corrective response. Learning is reflected in a modification of these reflexes with experience. Negative feedback and feedforward collaborate in achieving (1) control of movement and (2) stability of both body and perception. Negative feedback triggers corrective action in response to unexpected externally imposed disturbances. The disturbance to the body is the cue to action. Where movement is voluntarily triggered, rapid feedforward is recruited in parallel.

Whether by reflexes or voluntary behaviour, by feedback or feedforward, action is produced by motor neurons and skeletal muscles. This is the topic of the next section.

Figure 10.5 The vestibulo-ocular reflex (VOR).
Source: From Lisberger (1988, Fig. 1, p. 729). Reprinted with permission from AAAS.

Muscles and motor neurons

Section summary

1 Movement of the body produces changes in exteroceptive input. The perception of a stable world derives from comparing commands to movement and exteroceptive consequences.

2 The vestibulo-ocular reflex helps to stabilize the image on the retina.

3 Potential unwanted disturbances associated with voluntary movements can be anticipated. To pre-empt them, feedforward systems make postural adjustments.

 ## Test your knowledge

10.5 A boxer (i) 'throws' a 'long punch' and (ii) later receives an unexpected heavy punch to the upper body. What is the type of process responsible for stabilizing the body in these two conditions?

Answer on page 280   WEB

Introduction

Movement occurs by adjusting the degree of shortening of skeletal muscles (Chapter 3). Increased activity of the motor neurons that innervate the muscle causes shortening, termed 'contraction', which increases the force that the muscle exerts. In vertebrates, motor neurons only excite skeletal muscles, there being no inhibitory motor neurons. However, motor neurons are subject to both excitation and inhibition.

Skeletal muscle

A muscle attaches to the skeleton by tendons. Figure 10.6 shows a simplified section through a muscle. The muscle is composed of **muscle fibres** (the constituent cells) and blood vessels. In some cases, the muscle is a distance from the part of the body that it moves and the tendon is long, e.g. muscles that move the fingers are in the forearm.

Action potentials in motor neurons trigger action potentials in muscle fibres. As more muscle fibres are triggered into activity, the force generated by contraction increases. We look next at neurons within the spinal cord that determine the activity of motor neurons.

Figure 10.6 Skeletal muscle.

Source: Martini *et al.* (2000, Fig. 9-1, p. 242). Copyright © 2000, 1997 by Frederic H. Martini, Inc. and Michael J. Timmons. Reprinted by permission of Pearson Education, Inc.

Spinal cord organization

Figure 10.7 shows slices of spinal cord at three levels and some typical neural connections found there. Consider two motor neurons, A and B, and the location of their cell bodies in the ventral horn of the spinal cord (grey matter of the cord towards the front of the body) at slice 2. These two motor neurons, along with many others in parallel, innervate skeletal muscles.

As represented in Figure 10.7, there are various inputs that activate motor neurons: (a) sensory neurons also at level 2 in the spinal cord, (b) other levels in the cord, above (e.g. neuron D, the cell body of which is at level 1) and below (e.g. neuron C, the cell body of which is at level 3) and (c) the brain (via neurons that descend in the cord, indicated here as 'From brain'). The sensory input to motor neuron A arrives first at a short interneuron, which, in turn, makes contact with A. Typically, such interneurons are controlled both locally as part of a reflex and from the brain. A sensory neuron to motor neuron B synapses directly with it. A collateral of this neuron projects upwards, carrying sensory information to the brain. The input from the brain makes direct synaptic contact with motor neuron A but influences B through the short interneuron.

Neurons descending from the brain perform various functions. Some release classical neurotransmitter and excite motor neurons. Others release a different neurotransmitter and inhibit the same motor neurons. Through such neurons, commands to action by the brain are put into effect. Imagine that the neuron 'From brain' that synapses on the interneuron is of this kind.

Other neurons from the brain release neuromodulators (Chapter 4) that affect the reactivity of the stimulus–response connections organized at a spinal level. Imagine that the neuron 'From brain' forming a link with neuron A is of this kind. The sensory neuron's effect on the muscle depends on the activity in this descending pathway. A motor neuron's activity is determined by the net effect of excitatory and inhibitory inputs from brain, other spinal levels and sensory neurons. Thus, the control of movement depends upon inhibition of motor neurons as much as their excitation.

Motor neurons and myelin

Axons of motor neurons are myelinated (Chapter 4), which increases the speed of transmission of action potentials. High speed is important since it permits information to be conveyed rapidly from CNS to muscle. If a disease destroys myelin, speed is slowed and hence there is disruption of movement.

Motor units

The synapse between a motor neuron and a muscle fibre is termed a 'neuromuscular junction' (Chapter 4). At a muscle, typically the axon of a motor neuron branches (Figure 10.8). Each axon branch forms a synapse with a single muscle fibre and a given fibre is innervated by only one motor neuron. A motor neuron and the muscle fibres that it innervates make up a **motor unit**. Activity in a given motor neuron triggers activity in all the muscle fibres that make up the motor unit.

Motor units vary in size, with one motor neuron innervating few or many muscle fibres. Where high resolution is present, e.g. at the fingers, a given motor neuron innervates relatively few fibres. Coarse-grained control is associated with larger motor units.

Strength of contraction can be increased in two ways or by a combination of both: (a) increasing the frequency of action potentials in those motor neurons that are already active or (b) increasing the number of motor neurons and thereby motor units that are simultaneously activated, termed 'recruitment'. Increased

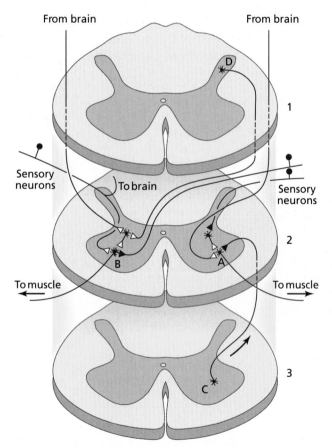

Figure 10.7 Sections of spinal cord at three levels. (Left–right asymmetry is for convenience of explanation only.)
Source: modified from Toates (1997b, Fig. 4.1, p. 113).

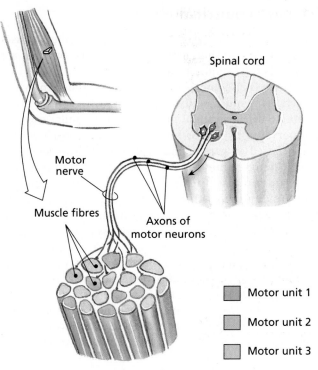

Figure 10.8 Motor units.

Source: Martini *et al.* (2000, Fig. 9-13, p. 252). Copyright © 2000, 1997 by Frederic H. Martini, Inc. and Michael J. Timmons. Reprinted by permission of Pearson Education, Inc.

excitation of motor neurons implies increased input to them, e.g. from a pathway arising in the brain.

The neuromuscular junction

The neurotransmitter employed at the neuromuscular junction of skeletal muscle is acetylcholine (ACh). Neuromuscular function requires that neurotransmitter is eliminated from the synaptic gap immediately after it attaches to receptors (Chapter 4). Acetylcholine is broken down rapidly by an enzyme, acetylcholinesterase (AChE), manufactured by the cholinergic (motor) neuron. Thereby, rapid changes in motor neuron activity can trigger correspondingly rapid changes in muscular contraction. If there is disruption of the breakdown of ACh, as in some pathological conditions, muscular control is correspondingly disrupted.

So far we have looked at how signals in motor neurons trigger contraction in muscle fibres. We now consider how whole muscles (composed of such fibres) act in moving a limb.

The arrangement of muscles

Figure 10.9 shows the muscles that control the position of the forearm and represents a general principle. The forearm's position depends upon equilibrium between the contraction of two opposing muscles: the biceps and triceps (part (a)). If the contraction of a muscle changes, the bone, and thereby the limb with which it is linked through a tendon, moves to a new equilibrium.

Figure 10.9(b) shows the result of increased contraction of the biceps muscle: raising the forearm. A movement in which the angle is decreased (in this case, from θ_1 to θ_2) is termed **flexion**. The term **extension** refers to a movement that increases the angle. Contraction of the triceps causes extension of the forearm, an increase in angle to θ_3 (Figure 10.9(c)).

A pair of muscles that produces opposite mechanical effects, as in Figure 10.9, constitutes a pair of **antagonist muscles**. Antagonistic control represents a general feature of how skeletal muscles produce action. It compares with antagonistically acting chemicals in the case of smooth muscle (Powley, 1999; Chapter 3).

This section has described the flow of information in one direction: the activation of muscles by motor neurons. The next section looks at this in connection with information transmission in the opposite direction, from muscles to the CNS.

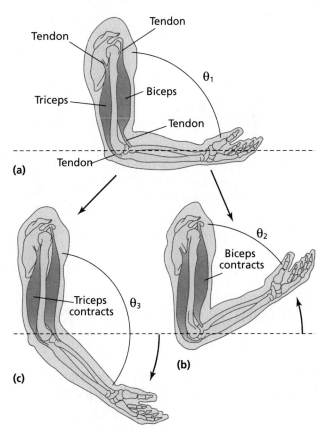

Figure 10.9 Muscles that control the forearm: (a) start, (b) flexion and (c) extension.

Source: adapted from Vander *et al.* (1994) *Human Physiology*, Fig. 1-33, p. 332, reprinted by permission of The McGraw-Hill Companies, Inc.

Section summary

1 Activity of motor neurons in the spinal cord is determined by local sensory inputs, inputs from other levels of the cord and from the brain.

2 Various inputs either excite or inhibit motor neurons.

3 Skeletal muscle is made up of muscle fibres.

4 Activity in motor neurons triggers activity in muscle fibres.

5 Action potentials within muscle fibres trigger contraction of the muscle.

6 A motor unit consists of a motor neuron and the muscle fibres that it innervates.

 ## Test your knowledge

10.6 In vertebrates, motor neurons have which of the following effects on skeletal muscle? (i) Excitation, (ii) inhibition, (iii) either excitation or inhibition.

10.7 In Figure 10.7, how would you characterize neuron C? (i) Sensory, (ii) motor, (iii) interneuron.

10.8 Suppose that contraction of a skeletal muscle is artificially induced by a pulse of activity in its associated motor neurons. Injection of which of the following would be expected to increase the size/duration of contraction? (i) An acetylcholine antagonist, (ii) a chemical that destroys acetylcholinesterase.

Answers on page 280

The control of skeletal muscle

Introduction

This section looks at the nervous system control of the activity of skeletal muscles, involving feedback from muscles to the CNS. Action potentials in sensory neurons detect the state of the muscle and this constitutes one factor that determines the activity of motor neurons, i.e. proprioception (Gordon and Ghez, 1991). To understand how this information is extracted, it is necessary to look more closely at the construction of muscle.

Types of muscle fibre

Most muscle fibres exert force and are termed **extrafusal muscle fibres**. Their activity is controlled by what are termed **alpha motor neurons**.

There is also another type of muscle fibre, known as **intrafusal muscle fibres** (Figure 10.10). These intermingle with extrafusal fibres and, in a similar way, are innervated by motor neurons. These motor neurons are classed as 'gamma motor neurons'. However, intrafusal muscle fibres serve a different function from the extrafusal muscle fibres. Rather than exerting force in moving limbs, they detect overall muscle stretch. Activity by gamma motor neurons simply adjusts their contraction to match that of their associated extrafusal muscle fibres.

The terminal of the axon of a sensory neuron is wrapped around an intrafusal muscle fibre and it signals the degree of stretch of the fibre (see Figures 10.10 and 10.11). The combination of muscle fibre, motor neuron and sensory neuron is termed a **muscle spindle** and the ending of the sensory neuron is a **stretch receptor**. As

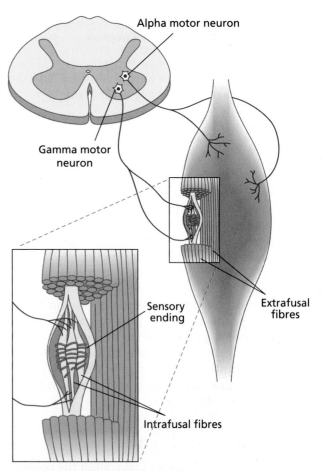

Figure 10.10 Muscle showing different types of fibre.
Source: Bear et al. (1996, Fig. 3.18, p. 367).

part of a feedback system, such sensory neurons form synapses upon the motor neurons that innervate the muscles with which they are associated (Figure 10.11). You will see shortly how a negative feedback loop involving proprioceptive information maintains the stability of the system.

Stability in the face of disturbance

Reflexes can compensate for disturbances. Whether disturbances are to equilibrium or to the body tissue arising from damaging stimuli, there are similar principles of organization, as this section will show.

Disturbances to equilibrium

Negative feedback compensates for an unexpected disturbance to equilibrium. Consider a stable situation, e.g. carrying a weight or just standing upright. Forces exerted by muscles overcome external forces that would otherwise make us collapse. Contraction of the muscles is set by the activity of motor neurons. Suppose that the muscles are disturbed by an unexpected external force, termed a 'passive change'. This distinguishes it from an active change, caused by a change in activity of motor neurons.

Figure 10.11 shows the neural system underlying the **stretch reflex**. For example, imagine that this shows

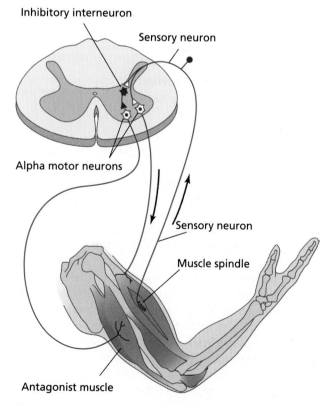

Figure 10.11 Feedback control of skeletal muscle.
Source: Bear *et al.* (1996, Fig. 13.22, p. 370).

your arm and you are carrying a weight, e.g. a shopping bag that is half full. Then the weight of the bag is suddenly and unexpectedly increased. Without your knowing, someone might have slipped a very heavy weight into the bag, which disturbs the muscles controlling the position of the arm. They will no longer be contracted appropriately for the half-empty bag, as set by motor neuron activity.

The increased weight causes a slight lowering of the arm, which stretches the flexor muscle (biceps muscle). Information on the new level of stretch is instantly detected by sensory neurons with endings embedded in the muscle and is fed to the spinal cord. With increased stretch, the frequency of action potentials in the sensory neurons increases, which has two effects: (i) it triggers increased activity in the alpha motor neurons innervating the biceps muscle. It causes increased contraction which, to a considerable extent, counters the disturbance. (ii) Because of the inhibitory interneuron, the sensory signal causes reduced activity in the alpha motor neurons innervating the triceps (antagonist) muscle. These effects act in the same direction (Gordon and Ghez, 1991), i.e. the principle of **reciprocal inhibition** (Floeter, 1999b). This is the stretch reflex (Ito, 1984). As a result of changes in neural activity to both muscles, a corrective response occurs. This partly returns the arm to its previous position. It occurs rapidly, without conscious intervention (Gordon, 1991).

The speed of the local reflex is an important contribution to maintaining stability. However, the afferent information is also projected to the brain and correction of the remaining error depends upon an increased centrally organized motor response (Evarts, 1984).

The knee-jerk response also demonstrates how negative feedback maintains stability (Figure 10.12). The muscle is stretched by the doctor tapping the knee with a hammer. The stretch triggers a compensatory increase in contraction of the extensor muscle, which causes the leg to jerk into the air. Although this is an artificial situation, it illustrates that a disturbance is resisted. By maintaining different values of contraction in the flexor and extensor muscles, the leg can be held in different positions, each defended against disturbances.

The reaction to a noxious stimulus

A spinal reflex protects against sudden tissue damage at a limb caused by an external stimulus (Chapter 3). In Figure 10.13, the position of the arm is the net result of contraction of flexor and extensor muscles. Suppose that a noxious stimulus, e.g. a pin, touches the bottom of the hand. In nociceptive neurons, this instigates action potentials, which are transmitted to the spinal cord, to excitatory synapses with interneurons.

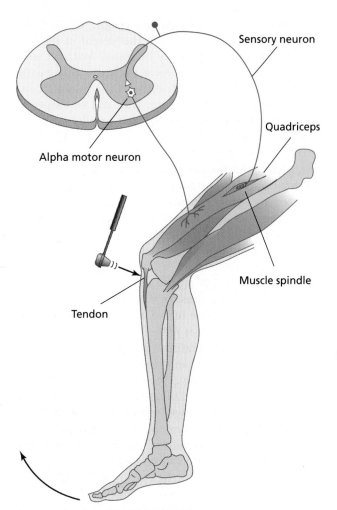

Figure 10.12 The knee-jerk response.
Source: Bear *et al.* (1996, Fig. 13.17, p. 366).

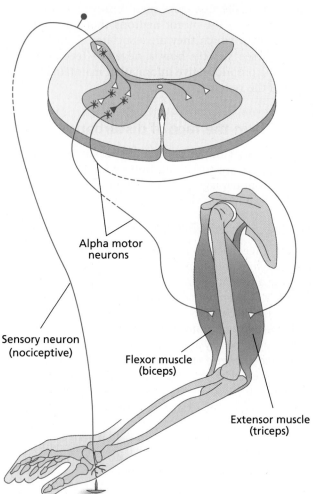

Figure 10.13 The nociceptive reflex.
Source: Guyton (1991, Fig. 54-8, p. 597).

In turn, interneurons form excitatory synapses on alpha motor neurons that activate the extrafusal fibres of the flexor (biceps) muscle. The flexor muscle contracts and thereby the arm is raised. In parallel, inhibition is exerted on the motor neuron that controls the extensor muscle (Gordon, 1991).

Interactions within the spinal cord

Events at one level of spinal cord are influenced by events at other levels. For example, treading on a noxious object and quickly withdrawing the foot could potentially disturb bodily equilibrium. In practice, we usually maintain equilibrium. How? Performance of the reflex triggers postural adjustments to maintain stability. Apart from synaptic contact within a layer of spinal cord, branches of the sensory neuron that detects the noxious stimulus extend to other spinal levels to influence other muscles (Figure 10.7). Their reaction causes the distribution of weight to change, to compensate for the defensive reaction.

Local autonomy

Figures 10.11–10.13 illustrate how reflexes are organized locally by the spinal cord (e.g. slice 2 in Figure 10.7). The sensory-motor sequence does not involve information transmitted via the brain. The delay between external stimulus and muscular response is so short that the reaction cannot be caused by a message travelling up to the brain and back down the spinal cord. In resisting disturbances, speed can be crucially important. If information had to travel up to the brain and down again before correction could be instigated, extra time would be involved. Fast reaction times can allow a stable position to be maintained, and make the difference between superficial and serious damage.

Local organization can achieve much. However, it does not have complete autonomy from controls at other levels. Other regions of the spinal cord as well as the brain are able to exert some control over the kinds of reflex just described (Figure 10.7).

Modulation by the brain

The strength of reflexes is modulated by the brain as a function of experience, e.g. learning when it is optimal to exhibit a reflex in full or inhibit it (Everts *et al.*, 1984). Also, emotion can modulate the magnitude of reflexes. This is exemplified by the knee-jerk reflex and the startle reflex, which is triggered by an unexpected stimulus (Lang *et al.*, 1990).

Voluntary behaviour

As effective as local negative feedback is, we do not remain like statues in a fixed position all day, responding only to disturbances. Rather we are the agents of change. Goals can be altered and we can consciously instigate movement. Voluntary behaviour takes many forms, such as walking or combing hair. This section considers just one form of voluntary behaviour, to illustrate how the brain, spinal cord and motor neurons cooperate.

Rhythms

Imagine you are walking or jogging. Behaviour is characterized by rhythms of muscular activity in the legs and arms, which run their course automatically. How does the CNS organize this? A type of motor programme, termed a **central pattern generator (CPG)**, which generates oscillations, is organized at the brain stem and spinal cord (Gallistel, 1980).

We consciously initiate and terminate commands that recruit control by CPGs but, once switched in, CPGs operate automatically. Automaticity spares our brain for activities such as conversation. When we are in, say, a 'walking mode', a frequency of local oscillation is selected top-down by the brain acting on spinal circuits (Lacquaniti *et al.*, 1999). Synchronized oscillations of activity are produced in motor neurons that innervate the muscles of the legs, arms and shoulders, etc. Excitation of some motor neurons is accompanied by inhibition of others. The CPG that produces alternating excitation and inhibition is intrinsic to the spinal cord. However, the pattern of motor activity can be influenced by feedback from the muscles. Adjustments can be made through local reflexes, for example, in response to changes in the muscles or a sudden change in the texture of the ground under the feet.

It is now time to investigate how and where commands to action arise and thereby to look at a range of voluntary behaviours.

Section summary

1 Proprioceptive information on contraction is fed back to the CNS.

2 Muscle is composed of extrafusal fibre (by which force is exerted) and intrafusal fibre (by which proprioceptive feedback is generated).

3 Feedback on the stretch of intrafusal muscle fibres influences activity in associated motor neurons.

4 External disturbances cause a change in tension in intrafusal muscle fibres and trigger a counter reaction.

5 By organizing reflexes locally, delays are minimized.

6 Oscillations that control limbs are programmed automatically (e.g. in the spinal cord) but switched on and off voluntarily by the brain.

 ## Test your knowledge

10.9 Complete the following: 'In Figure 10.11, artificial stretch of the biceps muscle triggers ___ activity in the sensory neuron, ___ activity in the alpha motor neuron innervating the biceps and ___ activity in that innervating the triceps muscle'.

10.10 Complete the following: 'In Figure 10.13, the effect of increased activity in the sensory neuron is one of ___ activity in the inhibitory interneuron and thereby ___ activity in the motor neuron that innervates the extensor muscle'.

Answers on page 280

The control of movement by the brain

Introduction

The control of movement depends upon interaction between various regions of the brain. Output signals are produced and are either conducted in cranial nerves (Chapter 3) or descend in the spinal cord. These output signals finally activate skeletal muscles (Figure 10.14).

Figure 10.15 summarizes some brain regions and pathways involved in movement that is executed via the spinal cord. Note direct pathways from the motor cortex to spinal cord neurons and also the pathways that descend to the spinal cord via synapses in the brain stem (not shown in Figure 10.14). The cerebellum receives sensory information and information on motor commands.

The higher areas represent decision-making and strategy, etc. At the bottom of the hierarchy is the process of *execution*, embodied within motor neurons with cell bodies in the spinal cord. At each lower level, the options become less open-ended and more constrained, based upon locally available information (Redgrave *et al.*, 1999).

In a hierarchy, commands are issued at a high level without specifying how they are to be implemented by lower levels (Gallistel, 1980; Toates, 1998a). By analogy, military decisions can be made by the UN Security Council (e.g. initiate peace-keeping operation) without reference to the specifics of how each foot-soldier will execute them (e.g. protect a particular village). Although the flow of commands is from top to bottom, there is also a flow of information in the opposite direction (Prescott *et al.*, 1999). Feedback is sent on the state of each level, i.e. what has actually been achieved. The lower spinal cord level is informed of the state of muscles, detailed information that is not normally available to the higher levels of conscious decision-making (von Holst and Mittelstaedt, 1950). It would be inefficient for attention to be drawn to information that can be best utilized simply at a low level (by analogy, the Security Council does not need precise details of events at each street in each village).

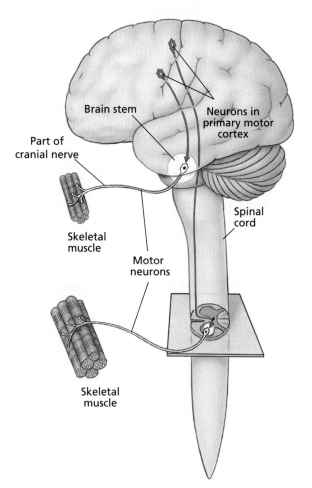

Figure 10.14 Motor control.

Source: adapted from Martini *et al.* (2000, Fig. 16-3(a) p. 428). Copyright © 2000, 1997 by Frederic H. Martini, Inc. and Michael J. Timmons. Reprinted by permission of Pearson Education, Inc.

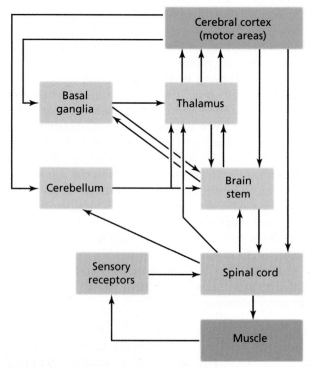

Figure 10.15 Motor control. Breaking a link at a box indicates a synaptic link within the box.

The cortex

Introduction

In Figure 10.15, the box marked 'Cerebral cortex (motor areas)' can be divided into several areas. The highest level of control (in the 'hierarchy') is one of deciding *strategy* and is embodied within regions of the cerebral cortex outside the primary motor cortex. The next layer down is concerned with *tactics* and is embodied within the primary motor cortex, subcortical brain regions and cerebellum.

Figure 10.16 shows the location of the primary motor cortex (M1) on the precentral gyrus (Chapter 5). Other cortical areas, the premotor area (PMA) and the supplementary motor area (SMA), are also involved in movement control and project to the primary motor cortex (Tanji and Kurata, 1985). The SMA also projects to the brain stem.

As a first approximation, the premotor area underlies strategy: *planning* of movement and selection of possible programmes for action, which is then translated into tactics, or *implemented*, by the primary motor cortex (Wise, 1984). The premotor area derives inputs from other regions of cortex, concerned with extracting perceptual information, e.g. occipital, temporal and parietal (Willingham, 1998). Thus, planning is based in part upon current information on the body and the external world, i.e. sensory-motor integration. The posterior parietal cortex computes features of objects that serve as the targets for action (Chapter 8).

We will look in more detail at the role of some cortical regions.

Primary motor cortex

The motor homunculus (Chapter 5, Figure 5.22, p. 121) indicates the responsibility that parts of primary motor cortex (M1) have for control over regions of the body. The expression 'control over regions of the body' does not mean that a region of M1 has *exclusive* control, since other brain regions are also implicated. However, investigators are able to associate specific bits of the body with specific cortical areas.

The primary motor cortex encodes a movement in space by a part of the body, as indicated by the motor homunculus (Carpenter *et al.*, 1999). Suppose that neurons in an area of M1 labelled 'finger' are active. This excites activity in pathways that descend to motor neurons in the spinal cord that control the finger (Evarts *et al.*, 1984). When this region of cortex is stimulated by an electrode, there is a response by a finger on the opposite side of the body to the side stimulated. Tumours at a particular location on the homunculus affect motor control at the part of the body indicated. A stroke (Chapter 5) affecting the motor cortex results in loss of

Figure 10.16 Some cortical regions involved in movement control. M1 = primary motor cortex, PFC = prefrontal cortex, PMA = premotor area, S1 = somatosensory cortex, SMA = supplementary motor area.

motor function in a region defined by the homunculus. The relationship between cortical motor areas and muscles has some plasticity, reflecting experience of using muscles (Schieber, 1999).

Prefrontal cortex (PFC)

Planning action and then producing it can depend upon memories of stimuli no longer present and exploiting imagined scenarios (Goldman-Rakic, 1995). The prefrontal cortex (PFC) has a responsibility for self-instigated voluntary ('willed') actions that are not triggered by stimuli. The PFC plays a role where there is a need to overcome habitual behaviour. This involves, in parallel, a suppression of the triggers to habitual behaviour and a favouring of the strength of appropriate cognition and 'non-habitual' stimuli. In some tasks, the PFC is strongly activated during learning but not once the task has become automatic (Raichle *et al.*, 1994).

Following damage to the PFC, a person is more 'stimulus-bound', i.e. vulnerable to stimuli capturing behaviour. For example, in a doctor's consulting room, a PFC patient might reach out to a familiar object and grab it even though this would otherwise have been considered 'inappropriate behaviour', termed **utilization behaviour** (Lhermitte, 1983).

Supplementary motor area (SMA)

Similarly, activation of the SMA is at its maximum at the start of training and decreases with skill acquisition (Jenkins *et al.*, 1994; Seitz and Roland, 1992). Associated with a voluntary movement there is a wave of electrical activity recorded at the motor cortex, termed a 'motor potential'. This is observed at about 55 ms before the muscular activity starts. At about 800 ms before the muscular activity starts, a change in electrical activity occurs at the SMA. This is termed a **readiness potential** and appears to be a correlate of preparing for action.

Somatosensory cortex

Just across the central sulcus from the primary motor cortex is the somatosensory cortex, concerned with processing tactile information (Figure 10.16). In an evolutionary context, the proximity of these regions would appear to be no coincidence. Feedback via the tactile sense is crucial for the production of movement. There are specific projections from regions of somatosensory cortex to the corresponding regions of primary motor cortex (e.g. from that concerned with processing tactile information from the thumb to the region controlling the thumb).

The cortex collaborates with the basal ganglia and cerebellum, to which the discussion now turns.

The basal ganglia

Structure and connections

A group of subcortical nuclei, termed the **basal ganglia**, are involved in the control of movement (Holmes, 1939; Marsden, 1987). They are situated to each side of the brain's midline and include, among others, the caudate nucleus, putamen and globus pallidus (Figure 10.17). A collective term for the caudate nucleus and putamen is the striatum. Researchers know of the basal ganglia's (BG's) involvement in movement, since:

- through the thalamus, the BG outputs convey information to areas of cortex concerned with motor control;
- neurons of the BG are active at times correlated with movement;
- damage to the BG is associated with disturbances to movement (Mink, 1999).

Major sources of input to the BG are the cortex and brain stem (Figure 10.15) (Prescott *et al.*, 1999). Inputs from the cortex project specifically to the striatum (Graybiel *et al.*, 1994). Neural activity in the striatum is modulated by dopaminergic projections that arise from a midbrain region termed the substantia nigra, meaning 'black substance' (Figure 10.18). The rich input to the BG from the prefrontal cortex suggests an important role for this link in planning action (Berns and Sejnowski, 1998).

A major output from the BG projects, via the thalamus, to areas of cortex concerned with both the preparation, e.g. the supplementary motor (SMA), and execution of motor action (Marsden, 1987). See Figure 10.15. Some information projects from the BG to areas of the brain stem concerned with motor control.

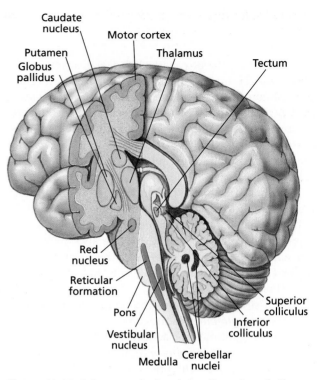

Figure 10.17 A focus on the basal ganglia and cerebellum.
Source: Martini *et al.* (2000, Fig. 16-5, p. 430). Copyright © 2000, 1997 by Frederic H. Martini, Inc. and Michael J. Timmons. Reprinted by permission of Pearson Education, Inc.

Within the BG, there are pathways exerting both excitatory and inhibitory links. If there is disease within excitatory or inhibitory links, the parameters are distorted and movement control is disrupted.

The role of the basal ganglia

What do the BG do? There are several theories (Prescott *et al.*, 1999) and what follows tries to capture a common feature of them.

Based on prediction of the next move, the BG appear to be able to select motor programmes and hold them slightly 'off-line' in the SMA in readiness for the appropriate signal to place them 'on-line' at the primary motor cortex and trigger action (Robbins and Everitt, 1992). The BG compute 'get-ready' information based upon scene-setting cues that are not themselves direct triggers to action but which specify conditions under which direct stimuli can trigger 'now go' (Schultz *et al.*, 1995). A runner awaiting the starting pistol might epitomize this situation. Some BG neurons are under the control of motivational signals, e.g. hunger, which signal the appropriateness of 'go' towards food-related stimuli.

Evidence suggests a role for the BG in producing automatic sequences of actions, where one component can be reliably selected on the basis of the preceding component (Jeannerod, 1997; Marsden, 1984). Once a sequence has been initiated, the BG could be responsible for triggering the remainder. Sequences arise from learning, e.g. a well-practised skill.

Parkinson's disease

Disruption of dopamine (DA) in the BG can profoundly disturb movement (Berns and Sejnowski, 1998). The basis of Parkinson's disease (PD) is degeneration of DA neurons with cell bodies in the substantia nigra (Figure 10.18).

In turn, there is a disturbance to the signals that the BG transmits to the supplementary motor area (SMA), such that the SMA is unduly inhibited (Jahanshahi and Frith, 1998). In PD, there is either an inability to initiate movement ('akinesia') or slowness in initiation ('hypokinesia') (Marsden, 1987). There is also 'bradykinesia', slowness in performing movement. Jahanshahi and Frith (1998, p. 502) characterize PD as difficulty in translating the 'will

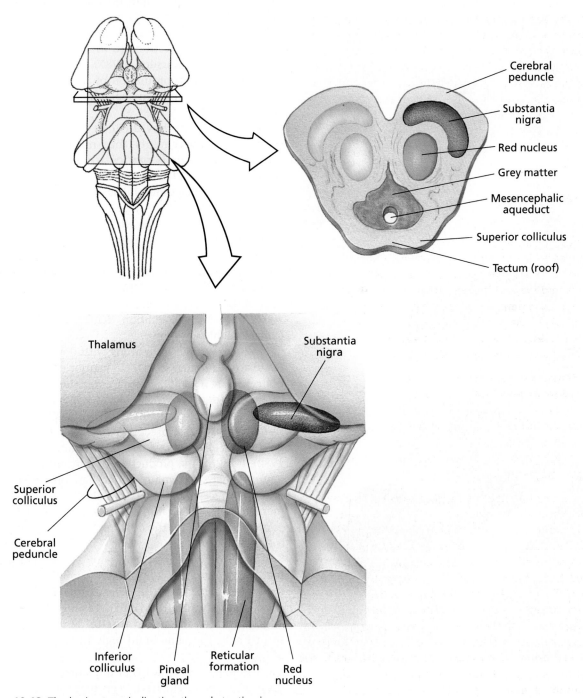

Figure 10.18 The brain stem, indicating the substantia nigra.

Source: Martini *et al.* (2000, Fig. 15-7a, p. 401). Copyright © 2000, 1997 by Frederic H. Martini, Inc. and Michael J. Timmons. Reprinted by permission of Pearson Education, Inc.

to action' into 'action': PD patients 'know what they want to do but cannot do it'.

For voluntary behaviour, the PD patient needs a large amount of concentration and will-power in overcoming muscular rigidity. Thus, patients have a disability in instigating action, e.g. putting into action an internally and spontaneously generated wish to get up (Jahanshahi *et al.*, 1995).

What happens to the control system for movement in Parkinson's disease?

Source: Empics.

The difficulty in 'self-instigating' behaviour contrasts with greater ease in responding to strong external cues (Jahanshahi and Frith, 1998); PD patients 'react better than they act'. For example, an otherwise immobile patient might be able to get up and leave if the word 'fire' is shouted. Auditory cues in the form of a rhythm can also help. Similarly, PD patients can sometimes walk more easily if visual cues with which they can pace their steps are given, e.g. stripes on the ground (Rothwell, 1994, p. 493).

Disorders of balance in PD appear to be due to deficiencies in BG projections to brain stem nuclei that control posture (Marsden, 1987). This could explain difficulties in the coordination of anticipatory postural corrections that accompany voluntary movement (Sanes and Evarts, 1985).

The PD patient has difficulty in executing the sequence of movements that normally constitute a motor plan. This is particularly so when the task requires coordination and combining component movements, either simultaneously or sequentially, into compound movements (Marsden, 1987).

Apart from difficulties with movement, PD is also associated with cognitive disruptions (e.g. to memory) and mood disturbances. This points to a possible role of the basal ganglia in processing cognitive and emotional information in addition their contribution to motor control (Lewis and Barker, 2010; Wijeyekoon and Barker, 2009). Instead, or in addition, damage outside the basal ganglia might be responsible.

It is not possible to treat PD with dopamine as such (Coté and Crutcher, 1991). DA cannot cross the blood–brain barrier (Chapter 5) and enter the brain. Certain treatments depend on the fact that neurotransmitters are synthesized within neurons from 'precursor substances'. L-Dopa, a precursor to DA in the synthetic pathway, is able to cross the blood–brain barrier (Sacks, 1982). It boosts the production of transmitter in the DA neurons that still remain, which has some therapeutic effect. DA receptor agonists can also be used as a treatment for PD, for example pramipexole, which has a particular affinity for the dopamine D_3 subtype of receptor (Stocchi, 1998).

It used to be the case that, where drugs had proven inadequate, surgical lesions were sometimes made to the globus pallidus (McIntyre *et al.*, 2004). These days, **deep brain stimulation (DBS)** (Tanei *et al.*, 2009) has largely replaced the use of surgical lesions. Somewhat surprisingly, the same brain region that was the target of lesions now forms the target of high-frequency electrical stimulation by means of implanted electrodes. An intuitive guess might have been that such stimulation would make matters worse. A brain region very near to the globus pallidus, termed the 'subthalamic nucleus', also forms a target.

So, how can stimulation and lesioning have similar effects? Discussion of neurons and the fine-grained dynamics of their action potentials gets highly technical and is probably beyond the understanding of both student and present author alike. Mercifully, it also gets beyond the brief of a psychology textbook. Suffice it to note some speculation by researchers (Modolo and Beuter, 2009). As one hypothesis, they ask whether DBS acts as something like a 'functional lesion' (i.e. similar to a surgical lesion). At the frequencies employed, DBS might disrupt the ability of the stimulated neurons to generate action potentials.

How is DBS carried out? An electrode with its tip in the target region is stimulated by a special battery. The electrode is surgically inserted into the brain and a wire from it is passed under the skin to a battery, which is also located under the skin, usually in the region of the collar-bone. The battery acts somewhat analogously to the pacemaker that people employ to stimulate the heart. Unlike lesions, the treatment can be terminated when desired. Using a hand-held magnet the patient can turn stimulation on and off according to their needs and adjustments can be made by a doctor without opening up the patient.

Other forms of treatment include using cell transplants to try to boost the declining numbers of dopaminergic neurons that project from the substantia nigra to the striatum, termed 'cell replacement therapy' (Wijeyekoon and Barker, 2009).

Treatments for Parkinson's disease exemplify where unusual psychological phenomena can be better understood by linking them to their biological bases. For example, the *expectation* that a treatment will bring benefits is a factor in the benefits that occur. This is an example of what is termed a **placebo effect**. The effect is observed under several circumstances:

1 Receiving an injection that has no active ingredient (in reality, saline) (de la Fuente-Fernández *et al.*, 2002).

2 Telling the patient that the deep brain stimulation apparatus has been switched on when in fact it has not.

3 Patients receiving an operation on the brain involving stereotactic implantation of dopaminergic neurons transplanted from embryos show an improvement relative to a sham operation. However, patients who *believed* that they received the transplant showed greater improvement than those who believed they were in the sham group, irrespective of which actual group they formed a part (McRae *et al.*, 2010).

The placebo effect can prove somewhat elusive and enigmatic but it should not be ignored. In the case of Parkinson's disease its biological bases appear to depend upon interactions between dopaminergic pathways. In Figure 10.19, note the pathway that projects from the substantia nigra to the striatum. This pathway is damaged in PD. Note also the dopaminergic pathway that projects from the ventral tegmental area to the nucleus accumbens. This pathway underlies motivation, reward seeking and goal-direction and it is central to understanding addiction. It remains intact in Parkinson's disease. It appears that the mere expectation of reward (in this case, relief of Parkinson's symptoms) can excite activity in the intact pathway and, in some way, excitation spills over to influence the part of the striatum that has lost its normal input in PD (Lidstone *et al.*, 2005). Another psychologically interesting phenomenon also arises from treating PD and appears to be similarly explicable in terms of interactions between intact and compromised DA pathways, as follows.

In some cases, treatment of PD patients with dopamine agonists results in an increased tendency to what are termed 'impulse control disorders' (ICD), which take the form of, amongst other things, excessive gambling, shopping or hypersexuality (Lim *et al.*, 2008). Use of L-dopa on its own rarely leads to ICD but it could exacerbate the tendency of DA agonists to do so. In

(a)

(b)

Figure 10.19 Dopaminergic pathways in the brain: (a) from substantia nigra to striatum and (b) from ventral tegmental area to nucleus accumbens.

Source: Toates (2004b, Fig. 1.1, p. 6).

some cases, patients find the ICD more intolerable than movement disorders and opt for a lowering of drugs that target dopamine. It appears that treating the compromised DA pathway boosts activity in the ventral tegmental area–nucleus accumbens (VTA-N.acc.) pathway to above normal.

Another phenomenon that sometimes arises from using dopaminergic drugs is termed 'punding' (Lim et al., 2008). It consists of what appear to be pointless, stereotyped and repetitive activities such as excessive cleaning, singing or dismantling and reassembling bits of technical equipment. Of course, the appropriateness of the terms 'excessive' and 'pointless' here might, to some, be open to debate. Punding is felt as disruptive (e.g. in disturbance of sleep) both to the patient and to the family. The patient can become distressed if prevented from engaging in punding. The study of punding draws attention to the links between motivation and movement control and the role of dopamine in both.

A personal angle

A determined collector and designer

Technical advances provide new opportunities for the expression of punding (Fasano et al., 2006). This is exemplified by a 52-year-old man studied in Rome, who had been affected by PD since the age of 44. As a child, he had shown a strong fondness for collecting things. With treatment to boost dopaminergic neurotransmission, he exhibited an unusual engagement with designing computer games, spending as much as 15 hours per day on this task. This was at the expense of sleep, family and even taking medications if this detracted seriously from the game. This was not a case of obsessive-compulsive disorder (Chapter 22) since he was not trying to avoid something terrible happening. Behaviour was apparently motivated by 'fascination', though he would get nervous when required to interrupt the activity to discuss his medical condition.

Huntington's disease

Another disorder of the basal ganglia, Huntington's disease (Chapter 2), consists of excessive movements. It is caused by degeneration of cholinergic and GABA-ergic neurons within the striatum (Kropotov and Etlinger, 1999; Reiner et al., 1998). Such neurons would normally exert inhibition on inappropriate candidates for behavioural expression.

The cerebellum

Connections to the cerebellum

The cerebellum is informed of intended actions and feedback from behaviour. It is provided with information from the motor cortex and information on posture and movement (Ghez, 1991a,b), e.g. proprioceptive, visual and vestibular information (only some of this is shown in Figure 10.15). Cerebellum outputs project (a) via the thalamus to the cortex (e.g. primary motor cortex) and (b) to the spinal cord, superior colliculus, vestibular nucleus and the red nucleus (Holmes, 1939; Thach et al., 1992). See Figure 10.15 for some of these links. In (i) receiving information on action from the cortex, (ii) computing information and (iii) projecting information back to the cortex, the cerebellum and basal ganglia have common features as modulators of motor action (Figure 10.15).

Defining the role of the cerebellum

The cerebellum (Figures 10.15 and 10.17) appears not to have an executive role, sometimes being termed a 'silent area'. Its electrical stimulation causes neither sensation nor, usually, a motor response. The control exerted by the cerebellum is unlike that of the cortex, in that one side of the motor cortex controls the body on the opposite side, whereas one side of the cerebellum has a role in the control of muscles on the same side.

The role of the cerebellum in handling feedback is seen over long periods of time, e.g. modifications as skills are acquired, and also on a moment-by-moment basis in the control of ongoing behaviour. In the course of movement, the cerebellum can revise the programme in the light of feedback.

The cerebellum is involved in the smooth performance of behaviour, i.e. controlling the *form* of movement, once started (Ito, 1984). Its role is to coordinate movements to form coherent patterns, such that goals are met optimally (Bastian et al., 1999). It compares the actual state of the body and muscles with the goals set and progress towards meeting them. We noted earlier the vestibulo-ocular reflex, which is an example of this role.

The cerebellum acts at an unconscious level in predicting outcomes and adjusting internal conditions to be appropriate (Chapter 5; Courchesne and Allen, 1997). It appears to be an intermediate step between the goals set by the cortex and their implementation in motor output (Marr, 1969). Its outputs, to motor regions of cortex and brain stem nuclei, indicate its function in coordinating component responses of parts of the body into coherent strategies of whole-body action (Thach et al., 1992). Postural corrective reflexes appear to be modulated so that they occur in a way that is appropriate to the goal.

Thus, reflexes that maintain standing can be switched in when the goal is to stand but not at other times.

Participants were set a pursuit task, to maintain alignment between the tip of a stylus held in their hand and a moving target (Grafton *et al.*, 1994). Success consisted of learning to predict the trajectory of the moving target and to maintain the hand in the right position. With a PET scan, Grafton *et al.* looked at regional cerebral blood flow and found an increase in the cerebellum. Rate of improvement correlated positively with increases in local blood flow.

A move to automaticity

The cerebellum appears to link negative feedback and feedforward (Ito, 1984). With experience of a task, it allows the weight of control to shift from negative feedback to feedforward. At the start of learning, it monitors performance in negative feedback mode, guided moment-by-moment by consequences. As a task becomes skilled, a store of possible solutions is acquired. Given an intention to act in a situation, the links (motor cortex) → (cerebellum) → (motor cortex) are activated and appropriate motor reactions instigated. If the consequences reveal a failure to meet the goal, the content of the memory store can be modified. Where a sequence of responses (R_1, R_2, R_3...) is involved, the cerebellum has a role in learning it, so that each component is produced automatically in response to the previous component (e.g. R_3 triggered by the production of R_2) (Thach, 1998). This is a role also attributed to the basal ganglia, suggesting close cooperation between these structures.

Some reactions are extremely rapid, e.g. a Wimbledon tennis champion making a move. The speed is formidable, with little opportunity for moment-by-moment revision. Such 'ballistic' moves need to be computed in advance and triggered automatically as feedforward but within a context of feedback-guidance (Bastian *et al.*, 1999).

Damage to the cerebellum

Patients with damage to the cerebellum have difficulty in modifying behaviour with experience and executing smooth and accurate actions, known as 'ataxia' (Holmes, 1939). They often show an awkward walk. Unlike Parkinson's patients, they are not deficient in initiating movement.

In an experiment investigating the role of the cerebellum in motor learning, participants wore prism spectacles, which shifted their visual world through an angle of 15 degrees to the right. See Figure 10.20. The task was to hit a dartboard with a dart. The participant had to aim the dart not at the location where the dartboard appeared to be but slightly to the side, to compensate for the shift. Controls with an intact cerebellum showed an initial error, which was corrected

(a)

(b)

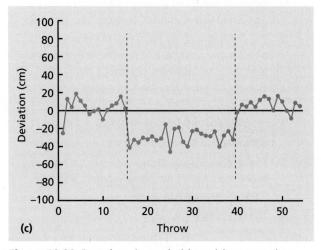

(c)

Figure 10.20 Dart-throwing task: (a) participant wearing spectacles, (b) result for control and (c) result for patient with damage to cerebellum. Dotted lines indicate start and end of period of wearing spectacles.

Source: Thach *et al.* (1992, Figs 5a, 5b and 5c, pp. 428, 429 and 431).

over trials until normal performance was attained (Figure 10.20(b)). Removal of the spectacles was followed by an error in the opposite direction. As shown in (c), participants with a damaged cerebellum had no such correction (Thach *et al.*, 1992).

The brain stem

Some organization of posture and movement occurs in the brain stem. In certain cases, the same nuclei have a role in activation within the sympathetic branch of the ANS (Chapter 3; Yates and Stocker, 1998). Thus, a sudden movement, as in energetically getting up, can trigger increased sympathetic activity. Exercise is associated with parallel activation of somatic and autonomic nervous systems.

Some species-typical motor patterns, e.g. licking and swallowing, are organized in nuclei of the brain stem (Berntson and Micco, 1976). Influences outside the brain stem, e.g. the hypothalamus, modulate these systems, making them more or less likely to gain expression in behaviour. Different combinations of species-typical motor patterns can be assembled according to central motivation (Spruijt *et al.*, 1992). For example, an aggressive motivation will play a role in assembling attack-related patterns.

The next section considers the transmission of information from brain to motor neurons.

Test your knowledge

10.11 Complete the missing words in the following: 'The primary motor cortex lies just ___ to the central sulcus, whereas the somatosensory cortex lies just ___ to it'.

10.12 Complete the following: 'Parkinson's disease is associated with disruption to __ neurotransmission'.

Answers on page 280   WEB

From brain to motor neurons

Introduction

This section describes how information is communicated from the brain to motor neurons.

Motor neurons have cell bodies in the brain stem or spinal cord (Figure 10.14). The axons of motor neurons with cell bodies in the brain stem form part of the cranial nerves. They innervate the muscles of the head. Motor neurons with cell bodies in the ventral horn of the spinal cord innervate the muscles of the remainder of the body (see also Figure 10.7). In Figure 10.14, note also the neurons in primary motor cortex, which innervate the motor neurons.

This section concerns the routes of information transmission (from brain to motor neuron) that occur via the spinal cord. One of these is shown in Figure 10.14 and the section also considers another route by which motor neurons in the spinal cord are activated. It looks at how voluntary behaviour is produced via these routes.

Neurons descend from the brain and make synaptic contact either with motor neurons (Figure 10.14) or with short interneurons, which, in turn, synapse on motor neurons (Figure 10.7). In addition, tendencies to respond that arise as a result of local factors can be inhibited by activity in descending pathways.

The corticospinal tract

One route is termed the **corticospinal tract** (or pathway), which you first met in Chapter 5. This is the pathway shown in Figure 5.22 (p. 121) and again as the spinal pathway of Figure 10.14. The cell bodies of the neurons that form this tract are located mostly in the primary motor cortex and the axons cover the

Section summary

1 Different regions of primary motor cortex are associated with control of different body regions.

2 The prefrontal cortex has a role in the instigation of voluntary action and in resisting inappropriate tendencies to respond triggered by stimuli.

3 The basal ganglia play a role in coordination of movement.

4 Degeneration of DA neurons in the substantia nigra leads to Parkinson's disease.

5 The cerebellum adjusts movement in the light of experience, both moment-by-moment and over repeated experiences.

6 The cerebellum links negative feedback and feedforward.

distance to specific locations in the spinal cord (motor neurons or local interneurons that contact motor neurons). This system of neurons is sometimes termed the **pyramidal system** and the pathway of axons is called the **pyramidal tract**. Within the medulla, the corticospinal tract can appear to be pyramid shaped, from which the name derives (by coincidence the cell bodies of these neurons are also somewhat pyramid-shaped). As you can see in Figure 5.22, there is a cross-over of axons from one side of the CNS to the other, just below the medulla ('decussation'). Thus, the motor cortex of one half of the brain is responsible for the control of muscles on the other side of the body.

The corticospinal tract permits manual dexterity. It is mainly associated with the control of fine-grained processes, e.g. movement of the fingers in manipulating objects. A number of factors contribute to this. The pathway from brain to muscle is relatively direct and the cortex mediates a 'high-magnification' resolution of motor information in the following way. Regions of motor cortex at the start of this route have relatively large areas of motor homunculus (Figure 5.22) associated with them. The axons are myelinated and some have a relatively large diameter, which contributes to a high speed of transmission of action potentials (Chapter 4). Each axon innervates relatively few muscle fibres.

Very high resolution of motor movements is obtained, particularly within certain parts of this system, e.g. some finger controls in primates can have a one-to-one exclusive relationship between an individual neuron of the tract and an individual motor neuron.

A non-corticospinal tract

Other descending tracts, sometimes collectively termed **non-corticospinal tracts**, start in the brain stem. They do not occupy the pyramid-shaped region of the medulla and hence are sometimes termed **extrapyramidal pathways**. Exemplifying this is the rubrospinal tract. It starts in the red nucleus of the midbrain (Figure 10.18) and terminates on interneurons in the spinal cord, which then synapse on motor neurons. This tract exerts more coarse-grained control than the corticospinal tract, e.g. over whole limbs. Inputs to the red nucleus are derived from the motor cortex and the cerebellum. Maintenance of posture, balance and movement is the responsibility of the non-corticospinal pathways.

A given neuron of this pathway can have axon branches that link to motor neurons at different sites in the body, which forms a basis for motor coordination. Thus, different parts of the body (e.g. arms and legs) are coordinated in maintaining stability and controlling movement.

Herein, there lies a contrast between the corticospinal and non-corticospinal pathways. The corticospinal pathway controls individual muscles that produce action in relative isolation, e.g. fine control over a finger. Non-corticospinal pathways are responsible for coordination of action involving several groups of muscles, e.g. in maintaining balance of the whole body. However, there is not an absolute distinction between the roles of the two pathways. Rather, the contrast represents two points on a continuum. Smooth and accurate movement can depend upon interactions between the pathways. There is some ability for compensation: if one pathway is damaged, the other can assume additional responsibility.

From an evolutionary perspective, it is interesting to consider a difference in weight attributed to the tracts. In humans, a greater degree of control resides with the corticospinal tract than with the rubrospinal tract.

Section summary

1 Information is transmitted from the brain down the spinal cord in corticospinal and non-corticospinal tracts.

2 The corticospinal tract starts at the cortex and is responsible for fine-grained motor actions.

3 Non-corticospinal tracts start below the level of the cortex and are responsible for more coarse-grained movements and maintaining stability.

Test your knowledge

10.13 Complete the following: 'Neurons of the corticospinal tract mediating ___-grained control by the fingers are associated with relatively ___ areas of the motor cortex, as indicated by the motor homunculus'.

10.14 Complete the following: 'Motor units associated with postural control by the non-corticospinal tracts are relatively ___ , whereas those of the corticospinal tract associated with control of the fingers are relatively ___'.

Answers on page 280

Motor imagery

Introduction

Cognition and motor action are interdependent (Jeannerod, 1997), e.g. in humans, motor systems have a close connection to the imagination. We can perform **motor imagery** in the absence of physical movement. Even those of us lacking any musical talent can enjoy the imagery of conducting Beethoven's 5th, in the role of an actor rather than a spectator.

Musical or sporting skill can sometimes be improved by observing the moves of an accomplished person and imagining yourself to be performing them (Jeannerod, 1997). Evidence suggests that such simulations can sometimes be beneficial and reorganization of the neural circuits underlying the planning of motor action takes place. You might then do some fine-tuning of the skill even in a crowded bus or in bed! Musicians and sportspeople often practise in this way (Feltz and Landers, 1983; Stephan *et al.*, 1995).

The time needed to simulate an action in imagination (e.g. write a signature) is similar to the time that the action would take in reality (Decety and Michel, 1989; Decety *et al.*, 1989). The length of a mental simulation reflects such factors as the size of any weight carried in performing the task and the task's complexity. For example, in reality, walking on very narrow beams takes longer than on wide beams, as is also true for its mental simulation. In people with Parkinson's disease, as the actual motor reaction is slowed, so is the simulated action. Where the disease affects only one side of the body there is also a slowing of imagined movements involving that side.

Biological bases

Imagination

Does conscious simulation of action exploit similar processes to those employed in performing the behaviour? Some computation of the exact motor response is performed by brain stem and spinal cord mechanisms, to which it appears we have no conscious access. Therefore, it would seem that, in our imagination, 'target' the high-level commands to the motor system (Jeannerod, 1997).

When a person simulates action mentally, increased electrical activity occurs in the skeletal muscles that would be involved if the action were really being executed (Jacobsen, 1931; Shaw, 1940). In some cases, this reflects the magnitude of the imagined task, e.g. increasing muscular activity accompanying increased imagined exertion of force. Such results suggest that imagining an action involves excitation of a motor programme, which is not executed because of inhibition (Decety *et al.*, 1990). The inhibition sometimes fails to oppose the excitation completely and some increase in motor neuron activity occurs.

Cerebral blood flow shows that performance of a skilled movement is accompanied by activation of the primary motor cortex, supplementary motor area and basal ganglia. Mental simulation of movement also involves the activation of a similar population of regions (Dominey *et al.*, 1995). The cerebellum is especially activated in an imagined motor task, e.g. tennis (Decety *et al.*, 1990).

Mental imagery can give insight into the determinants of ANS activation (Chapter 3). Performing physical exercise increases heart-rate and respiration, as does imagining it (Decety *et al.*, 1991, 1993), but the latter is probably not sufficient to provide an excuse for staying in bed and avoiding the gym. People whose limbs are paralyzed also show an increase in autonomic measures when they attempt a motor response (Gandevia *et al.*, 1993).

Instruction, imitation and mirror neurons

Certain neurons in area F5 of the premotor cortex and the parietal cortex of monkeys are active when the monkey performs a particular motor action or watches another animal (monkey or human) doing the same (Di Pellegrino *et al.*, 1992). Such neurons are termed **mirror neurons**, since their activity 'reflects' the performance of the other individual (Rizzolatti and Craighero, 2004). So, one trigger for mirror neuron activity is the visual presentation of an interaction between an object and another individual's effector, e.g. hand or mouth. For example, observing the grasping of a piece of food is a trigger to certain mirror neurons. The sight of either the object alone or another individual miming the action is insufficient to trigger them. Suppose that the monkey observes a noisy action such as tearing and mirror neuron activity is monitored (Kohler *et al.*, 2002). Subsequently, presenting the sound alone triggers a number of the same mirror neurons.

The activity of mirror neurons correlates with what the particular action *achieves* (its goal), e.g. picking up or tearing an object, rather than the exact muscle group or movement involved (Rizzolatti and Arbib, 1998). For a human or a monkey, the observation of another individual picking up, say, an apple triggers motor plans appropriate to this same action in the brain of the observer (Iacoboni, 2008). Hence, mirror neurons encode not only the triggers to action but a means of understanding the equivalent actions when performed by others.

What could be the functional value of mirror neurons? They could play a part in the perception of action and

A personal angle

An observation that simply did not fit

As is often the case in science, the discovery of mirror neurons owed much to chance (Iacoboni, 2008). Its exact nature is shrouded in mystery but the story is roughly as follows. Around 1988, a team in the laboratory of Giacomo Rizzolatti, in Parma, Italy, was performing electrical recordings of neurons in regions of the monkey brain concerned with motor control. Vittorio Gallese was moving around in the vicinity of a macaque monkey that had implanted electrodes, when suddenly he heard a sound from the apparatus that was recording activity in the electrodes. It appeared that, when Gallese had made a reaching movement, this excited the neurons, which were in the premotor cortex.

The result made no sense to the researchers and they found it hard to believe. The orthodox view confirmed countless times was, quite reasonably, that motor regions of the brain are concerned with organizing motor output and sensory regions are concerned with analysing sensory input! Yet here, in the absence of the monkey showing any movement, was activity in neurons in the area of brain concerned with planning movement. The neurons responded to the movements of another individual.

The discovery of mirror neurons undermined the assumption of a neat distinction between sensory, perception and motor regions and functions (Rizzolatti and Sinigaglia, 2008). Recognition of actions appears to be based in what were traditionally seen as motor regions.

facilitate motor learning. Establishing representations of actions based on observation, and doing so in a motor region of the brain, could facilitate the performance of the action when later initiated spontaneously. For a social species, they could facilitate coordination of activity.

In humans, for example, passively observing the action of another is associated with a desynchronization of electrical activity in the motor cortex, as is active performance of the behaviour (Rizzolatti and Craighero, 2004). This points to further possible links between biological and social psychologies. If you find yourself mirroring the gestures of another, a phenomenon known as the 'chameleon effect' (Leslie *et al.*, 2004),

you might like to reflect on the possible contribution of mirror neurons.

Mirror neurons in macaque monkeys are not activated by pantomime (Iacoboni, 2008). That is to say, performing the action of, say, grasping but in the absence of an object to grasp does not trigger them. Such monkeys do not perform pantomime but, of course, humans do and mirror neurons of humans are excited by pantomime actions.

The fact that a mirror neuron is activated by viewing the action of another individual means only that there is a tendency for this to trigger the action in the observer. Life would become impossible if we were invariably to mimic the actions of others! Clearly, the mirror neuron system lies within networks of modulation. In some cases of damage to the prefrontal cortex, it appears that restraint is lifted and patients tend to mimic actions that they otherwise would not (Rizzolatti and Sinigaglia, 2008).

Considering development, mirror neurons might explain the fact that human infants of 2–3 weeks perform imitation, in the apparent absence of any history of parental reinforcement for doing so (Meltzoff and Moore, 1977).

Jeannerod (1997) speculates about interaction between teacher and pupil, in which a manual skill is demonstrated. He suggests that, in the pupil, there is activation of motor regions involved in planning which has similarities to the pattern that occurs prior to performance (Stephan *et al.*, 1995). Reciprocally, when the teacher watches the pupil, there is a similar pattern of activation as that shown by the teacher performing the action.

A personal angle

A behaviourist's amazement

B.F. Skinner was a keen observer of his children's behaviour, as well as a famous advocate of the power of learning based upon reinforcement. He recorded (Skinner, 1979, p. 287):

One day when I had opened the window of the baby-tender and was talking to Debbie, I wrinkled my nose. To my amazement she immediately wrinkled hers. At the time I was not convinced that there was any innate tendency to imitate, but it seemed impossible that she could have learned that the muscles she moved produced an expression on her face like the one she had seen on mine.

Section summary

1 Mental simulation (imagination) of an action has features in common with performance, e.g. there is a correlation in the length of time taken to perform them.

2 The term 'mirror neuron' refers to a type of neuron that is active in performing behaviour or observing another performing it.

 Test your knowledge

10.15 A mirror neuron is a member of which of the following classes of neuron? (i) Sensory, (ii) motor, (iii) interneuron.

 Answer on page 280   WEB

Development of motor systems

The newborn or 'new-hatched' are not simply a bundle of uncoordinated reflexes, since even the embryo shows a degree of coordination, which increases after birth or hatching (Gottlieb, 1973; Prechtl, 1981). During development, the acquisition of increasing sensory-motor ability opens up new possibilities for exploiting the environment (Benson, 1990). Increasing skill is related to developmental changes in the nervous system. For example, development of descending mechanisms of control gives an increasing capacity for coordination over reflexes in serving goals.

The age of appearance of motor controls indicates the development of the neural systems underlying them (Chapter 6; Michel and Moore, 1995). For example, the capacity of human infants to show precision grasping is indicative of the maturation of neurons that link the motor cortex to spinal interneurons and motor neurons controlling the hand. Maturation of glial cells and the associated myelination of motor pathways is another factor that contributes to development of motor abilities.

Traditionally, researchers suggested that development consists of increasing cortical inhibition exerted on reflexes, associated with the portrait of the newborn as being essentially subcortically controlled (see Michel and Moore, 1995, for discussion). This is indeed part of the story. Primitive automatic reflexes are brought under increasing degrees of control by the later maturing cortical structures characterized as 'higher-order' and 'voluntary'. Thus, the disappearance of reflexes indicates maturation of the cortical regions that exert top-down inhibition. For example, the disappearance of the palmar grasp reflex is associated with the maturation of the supplementary motor area of the cortex (Michel and Moore, 1995). Later brain pathology is associated with the reappearance of previously suppressed reflexes.

A more general principle is that, with development, reflexes become incorporated into higher levels of control, i.e. goal-directed behaviour is constructed in part from reflexes (Michel and Moore, 1995). As well as inhibition, there is also some increase in top-down excitatory control of reflexes (Chapter 6; Schulte, 1974) or their replacement by the top-down control (McDonnell and Corkum, 1991). There is a changing *balance* between factors, giving rise to new patterns of control (Teitelbaum, 1977).

Section summary

1 Development consists, in part, of the acquisition of top-down control over reflexes.

 Test your knowledge

10.16 In addition to neurons, maturation of what other type of cell contributes to the development of motor skills?

Answer on page 280   WEB

Bringing things together

You have seen how the brain exploits different means to control movement. Negative feedback is fundamental; the brain exploits differences between the way that the world is and the way that it should be according to goals. Any difference instigates behaviour that tends to correct the difference. This is supplemented by another process: feedforward. So, animals have the benefits of negative feedback but can avoid its disadvantage of slowness. Feedforward control provides a facility for anticipating potential disparity with what is intended and triggering action so as to pre-empt this disparity. Feedforward brings increased speed of responding.

Some control of behaviour requires conscious awareness, e.g. learning new skills or in resisting habitual behaviour. However, when behaviour becomes predictable, it can be performed more automatically. The shift from full conscious control to an automatic mode can be identified with a changing responsibility of different brain regions.

The nervous system sometimes places weight upon physically present stimuli and preceding responses. Thereby, it produces sequences of behaviour in an automatic mode. This is appropriate in situations of high predictability where circumstances are invariant across trials. Where circumstances are novel or changing, automatic processes cannot perform the task and conscious control of action involving negative feedback is dedicated to the task. Even under these conditions, behaviour still relies upon some automatic implementation of sequences organized at lower levels in the hierarchy.

A consideration of the limited capacity of conscious processes and the need for speed explains why there is a delegation of some responsibility for predictable movements to brain stem and spinal mechanisms. In the cases of (a) defence against tissue damage, (b) control of posture and (c) production of oscillatory movements underlying locomotion considerable organization is at the spinal cord but with modulatory input from the brain.

See the video coverage for this chapter to get a feel for how psychologists study the control of movement by the brain.

Summary of Chapter 10

1 The nervous system sets goals and produces movements to meet them, against a background of maintaining stability.

2 Both negative feedback and feedforward are used in movement control.

3 In perceiving the world, the nervous system uses information on external events and movement of the body.

4 Neural influences at different levels of the CNS affect the activity of motor neurons, which, in turn, triggers contraction in skeletal muscles.

5 The state of skeletal muscles is monitored by specialized detectors and this information is used in maintaining stability and controlling movement.

6 Movement control depends upon an interaction between regions of cortex, basal ganglia, cerebellum and brain stem.

7 Different tracts convey information between the brain and motor neurons.

8 Even in the absence of overt behaviour, potential movements can be represented ('imagined') by the activity of specialized groups of neurons.

9 Mirror neurons encode the actions of others.

10 Development involves the acquisition of increasingly refined possibilities for motor control.

Further reading

For a text with links to learning, see Schmidt and Lee (2005). For all the neuroscience in this chapter, see Nolte (2008) and Gazzaniga *et al.* (2008). The role of the spinal cord in movement control is described by Pierrot-Deseilligny and Burke (2005). Parkinson's disease is described in Lozano and Kalia (2005), Hanin *et al.* (2005) and Bjorklund and Cenci-Nilsson (2010).

Answers

Explanations for answers to 'test your knowledge' questions can be found on the website www.pearsoned.co.uk/toates

10.1   Vestibular
10.2   Skeletal muscles; central nervous system
10.3   Negative feedback; feedforward
10.4   Automatic
10.5   (i) Feedforward; (ii) negative feedback
10.6   (i) Excitation
10.7   (iii) Interneuron
10.8   (ii) A chemical that destroys acetylcholinesterase
10.9   Increased; increased; decreased
10.10 Increased; decreased
10.11 Anterior; posterior
10.12 Dopaminergic
10.13 Fine; large
10.14 Large; small
10.15 (iii) Interneuron
10.16 Glial cells

Visit www.pearsoned.co.uk/toates
for a range of resources to support study.
Test yourself with multiple choice questions and access a bank of over 100 videos that will bring the topics to life.

Interactions and animations relating to topics discussed in this chapter can be found on the website at www.pearsoned.co.uk/toates. These include:

Animation: The role of the muscle spindles in muscle function
Interaction: The monosynaptic stretch reflex
Interaction: The motor areas of the cerebral cortex

of numerous breakfasts eaten over the years. Memory permits a form of 'time-travel': by recalling events, we recreate something of the situation in which the memory was acquired. We can relive the emotion associated with the event, surely a part of the essence of possessing consciousness. Other memories relate to more publicly available information such as the name of a capital city.

5 When memories are of emotionally potent events, they tend to be particularly durable and well recalled.

6 With disease, different memories are not equally vulnerable to disruption. There can be a failure to update memories in the light of new episodes of experience, while long-established memories are intact. The memory for words, grammar and skills can sometimes be retained in the face of severe loss elsewhere.

This chapter concerns the biological foundations of learning and memory. These foundations embody change as a result of experience and are a type of plasticity. Learning refers to the behaviour through which an animal either (i) changes subsequent behaviour or (ii) at least, acquires the *potential* for future change. Learning is the means by which certain *changes* in the brain (memories) are produced.

Memory refers to (i) the internal change that underlies learning (i.e. what is stored) and (ii) the process of recall of learning and its expression in behaviour. The internal change in the brain outlasts the remembered event to which it relates, sometimes for decades.

Learning and memory exploit adaptive processes. Therefore, psychologists would not cite just any change in behaviour (e.g. one arising from brain damage) as an instance of learning and memory.

The task of a biological psychology of learning and memory is to try to link three different levels of their description:

1 The psychology of these phenomena.

2 The brain regions that are involved.

3 Their cellular basis in terms of neurons and the connections between them.

Learning and memory are necessarily intertwined. However, researchers have tended to emphasize one or other and use one theoretical framework to organize their research. Therefore, while acknowledging the artificiality of any neat distinction between learning and memory, the following sections are organized as, first, learning and then, memory.

Section summary

1 Learning refers to a behavioural experience, which is associated with change and which exploits adaptive processes.

2 Memory is the process that encodes the learning experience.

3 Different types of learning and memory exhibit different properties.

4 There are differences in the vulnerability of different types of memory to disruption.

5 The physical basis of memory is a change in the brain.

☞ Test your knowledge

11.1 Complete the following: 'Learning and memory exemplify the property of p___y of brain and behaviour'.

Answer on page 310

The learning tradition

Traditionally, biological psychologists have studied some so-called models or paradigms of learning: habituation, classical conditioning, instrumental conditioning and taste-aversion conditioning. Mazes and Skinner boxes, and various developments of them, are used for the study of learning. As subjects, non-human species have been the favourite choice. This section looks at this psychological approach and its link with biology.

Habituation

Basics

A simple kind of learning can be demonstrated, as follows (Groves and Thompson, 1970; Sharpless and Jasper, 1956). An experimenter repeatedly presents a stimulus (e.g. a tone) that triggers a response but does not pair this stimulus with anything. If the stimulus has no significant consequence, a decrease in the magnitude of the response commonly occurs. If this behavioural change can be attributed to *central* changes among neurons, it is termed **habituation**. (You doubtless have shown habituation to a ticking clock.)

An example is provided by the marine snail *Aplysia* (Chapter 5). When the gill and siphon are stimulated by a jet of water, the animal withdraws its gill (Kandel, 1991). If the stimulus is repeatedly applied, a reduction in the magnitude of the reflex occurs (Figure 11.1). For another example, in dogs, at first a tone might evoke the response of orientation towards its source. Habituation would be evidenced by a decline in the magnitude of this response.

The mechanism

In principle, such decreases could be due to sensory adaptation (Chapter 7) or muscle fatigue. However, suppose that they can be shown to be due to changes at neither sensory nor motor ends but that they arise from ('central') changes at the intervening neurons. In this case, the phenomenon constitutes habituation. So, the criterion of habituation involves the combination of behaviour and the underlying neural mechanism.

Habituation is a relatively simple example of learning. The animal is exposed to a situation and changes behaviour as a result. The underlying changes in the nervous system (described later) constitute a basic form of plasticity: memory.

Function

From a functional perspective, how do investigators explain habituation? If a stimulus is presented repeatedly with no significant consequence, it appears *on average* to be adaptive to respond less strongly to it. For example, by withdrawing the gill, *Aplysia* uses energy. Not responding is an economy. However, life is a trade-off and, on a given occasion, it might prove beneficial to respond. The ripple that normally signals 'nothing of significance' might, on one occasion, be caused by a predator with a taste for biting off gills. The nervous

system can do no better than to generate behaviour that has *on average* been adaptive in the animal's evolutionary history.

Habituation is shown where the experimenter simply presents a stimulus repeatedly and does not explicitly associate events. Hence, it is termed 'non-associative'. By contrast, conditioning exemplifies **associative learning**, which involves the experimenter arranging a relationship (termed a **contingency**) between two events. This is discussed in the next sections.

Classical conditioning

One form of associative learning is **classical conditioning** ('Pavlovian conditioning') (Pavlov, 1935/1955). The foundation of its scientific study is Pavlov's observation that dropping meat-juice into the mouth of a hungry dog elicits the secretion of saliva in the mouth and digestive juices in the stomach.

Some terms and examples

Consider Figure 11.2. The process linking meat in the mouth and salivation is an **unconditional reflex**, common to all dogs. Salivation is termed an **unconditional response (UCR)** and food an **unconditional stimulus (UCS)**. The significance of the term 'unconditional' will become apparent in a moment (the expression 'conditioned' is sometimes seen where 'conditional' is used here).

Pavlov presented a **neutral stimulus (NS)**, such as a bell, just before food. At the start, the bell is 'neutral' in that it has no prior connection with food and no capacity to elicit salivation. After a few pairings of bell and food, even the bell on its own triggers salivation. The bell has

Figure 11.1 Habituation in *Aplysia*. Amplitude of the response (extent of withdrawal) is shown against time.
Source: Kandel (1976, Fig. 12-1, B-2, p. 543).

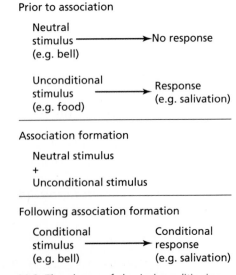

Figure 11.2 The phases of classical conditioning

become a **conditional stimulus (CS)** and salivation in response to it is the **conditional response (CR)**. The term 'conditional' means that the capacity of the bell to trigger salivation is *conditional upon* pairing with food. It has no unconditional capacity to elicit salivation. By contrast, the food has an unconditional capacity. (The term 'conditional stimulus' is sometimes used to refer to the neutral stimulus prior to, and after, conditioning.)

This is a relatively simple case but it illustrates well the notion of *change* as the basis of learning. The amount of saliva triggered by the bell increases with the number of times the bell is presented together with food. This change in saliva secretion is a measure of learning. Corresponding to this, a memory is formed within the brain.

For another example, consider the closure of the eyelid that occurs as a defensive reaction, triggered by such unconditional stimuli as a puff of air to the eye. It is termed the 'eye-blink reflex'. If a neutral stimulus (e.g. tone) is paired with the unconditional stimulus, the neutral stimulus becomes transformed into a conditional stimulus that has the capacity to trigger eyelid closure. That is, as a result of classical conditioning, there emerges the 'conditional eye-blink reflex'. The eye-blink reflex has been well studied and it serves to identify some of the biological bases of learning and memory (Woodruff-Pak, 1999). When comparing mammalian species, the brain structures underlying the conditional eye-blink reflex exhibit close similarities and the neural circuit has been identified.

Figure 11.3 compares two different forms of classical conditioning, delay conditioning and trace conditioning, which have yielded much insight into the biological bases of learning and memory (described later). In delay conditioning, there is no gap between when the CS (typically a tone) ends and the UCS (typically a puff of air to the eye) starts. In trace conditioning, there is a gap between the end of the CS and the onset of UCS. Trace conditioning is so-called because any association formed between the CS and UCS must depend upon a trace of the CS in memory, since at the time of the UCS the CS has ceased. Whereas delay conditioning occurs even where there is damage to the hippocampus, trace conditioning occurs only when this structure is intact (Clark and Squire, 1998), described later.

Function

Classical conditioning confers an adaptive advantage: by reacting to the CS, the animal is ready for the arrival of the UCS. For example, by salivating to cues predictive of food, the dog's body is prepared for the arrival of food. For another example, male fish of the species Blue gouramis (*Trichogaster trichopterus*) were exposed to a rival male, the appearance of which was either signalled by a red light (CS) or unsignalled (Hollis, 1997). Those males that had a warning of the arrival of the other fish were in a position of attack readiness and at an advantage in competition for territory.

What is learned?

What *exactly* is learned when an animal is exposed to a pairing of a neutral stimulus and an unconditional stimulus? Given that the food triggers salivation as an automatic reflex, does the bell come simply to trigger a reflex of salivation? Under some circumstances, animals simply form a straightforward and automatic link ('reflex-substitution') like that shown in Figure 11.4, i.e. between a stimulus and a response (O'Keefe and Nadel, 1978; White, 1989). This is described as a stimulus–response association (S-R learning).

Alternatively, or in addition to such learning, the animal might learn something about the situation ('knowledge'), which it can exploit in different ways. For instance, suppose that, following conditioning in one room, the dog finds itself in a different room. Would it come running at the sound of the bell? Anyone who has kept a dog will doubtless opt for this possibility since the sound of a can-opener can be a highly effective CS for locomotion. In this case, psychologists say that the animal has formed an association between two events: stimulus$_1$ (tone) predicts stimulus$_2$ (food). This is termed a **stimulus–stimulus association**, and it can be used flexibly in behaviour. Similarly, consider a hungry rat placed in a cage, where food pellets occasionally drop into a tray. A second or two before each pellet falls, a tone is sounded. After a few such exposures to the tone followed by food, on hearing the tone the animal goes

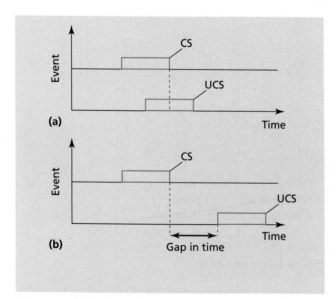

Figure 11.3 Two forms of classical conditioning: (a) delay and (b) trace.

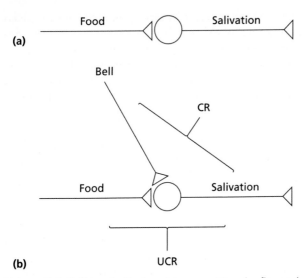

(a)

(b)

Figure 11.4 Reflex substitution: (a) unconditional reflex and (b) following conditioning, in which the bell acquires some of the capacity of the food.

immediately to the tray. The rat has formed a predictive association: stimulus$_1$ (tone) → stimulus$_2$ (food). If, subsequently, the tone is sounded repeatedly but without the delivery of food, the rat will stop going over to the tray in response to the tone. The tone is no longer a reliable predictor of food.

Biological basis

This section looks at examples that illustrate both the stimulus–response type and the stimulus–stimulus type of learning. In studying eyelid closure in rabbits, a tone

(CS) is paired with an air-puff (UCS), while brain events are observed (Krupa *et al.*, 1993; Thompson, 1990). Neurons were found in the cerebellum, which, prior to conditioning, responded to neither tone nor puff. Following conditioning, they responded to the tone. In regions of the cortex (outer layer) of the cerebellum, electrical activity followed the CS, came just before the CR and mirrored the magnitude of the CR. Lesions of these areas abolished the CR but left the UCR intact. Such conditioning does not require an intact hippocampus and would seem to be simple stimulus–response learning.

For humans, eye-blink conditioning is relatively easy to perform and can serve as a useful diagnostic tool for detecting abnormalities. For example, humans with damage to the hippocampus can learn a conditional eyelid response but cannot remember the learning experience (Thompson, 1990). Patients suffering from damage to the cerebellum are impaired in their ability to be conditioned to produce an eyelid response. For unilateral damage, the impairment is specific to the eye that is ipsilateral to ('same side as') the damaged cerebellum (Woodruff-Pak *et al.*, 2001).

In humans, there is some loss of the neural tissue of the cerebellum with age. The loss appears to be suffered by one class of neuron, termed the 'Purkinje cell', which is vulnerable to toxins such as alcohol. A positive correlation was found between the size of the cerebellum and strength of conditioning attained after 90 pairings of tone and air-puff (Woodruff-Pak *et al.*, 2001). Strength of conditioning was measured in terms of the percentage of times a CR was exhibited following presentation of the CS. See Figure 11.5.

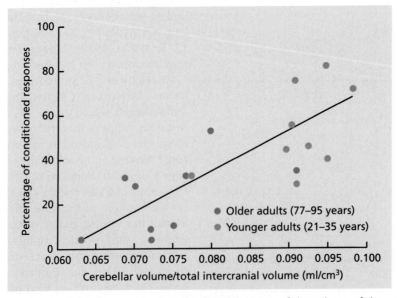

Figure 11.5 The strength of the conditional response of eye-blink as a function of the volume of the cerebellum for adults of various ages. Volume of cerebellum was measured by MRI.

Source: Woodruff-Pak *et al.* (2001, Fig. 4, p. 353).

Figure 11.6 Activity of dopaminergic neurons in response to (a) reward R (juice), (b) CS (tone) and reward and (c) CS and omission of juice at time normally occurring (indicated by arrow).

Source: adapted from Schultz *et al.* (1997, pp.1593–99). Reprinted with permission from AAAS.

Consider now the formation of a predictive association stimulus₁ → stimulus₂. Researchers have exposed animals to two events, stimulus₁ (tone) followed immediately by stimulus₂ (reward), and investigated the role of dopamine in forming the prediction stimulus₁ → stimulus₂ (Schultz *et al.*, 1997). When a hungry monkey received unexpectedly a small amount of fruit juice in the mouth, there was activation of dopaminergic neurons (Figure 11.6(a)). An aversive stimulus, such as a puff of air to the hand, did not cause activation. In other words, dopamine seems to be encoding the presentation of reward.

Subsequently, a number of times, the tone was sounded before the fruit juice was given (Figure 11.6(b)). There was now activation of dopamine by the tone but (perhaps surprisingly) not by the juice. The juice is *predicted* on the basis of the tone and it would seem that a predicted event no longer activates dopamine. In a final phase, after having learned tone → juice, the tone was presented but the juice omitted (Figure 11.6(c)). There was now a suppression of activity in dopaminergic neurons.

It is interesting to speculate on what might be happening. The unpredicted food in Figure 11.6(a) triggers dopaminergic activity, which appears to be involved in finding a predictor. The brain arrives at the only reliable predictor in this situation: the tone. Synaptic reorganization is assumed to occur, encoding the tone as a predictor. The food is now predicted on the basis of the tone and the food no longer triggers dopamine. Consider now when food fails to arrive (part c). Suppression of dopaminergic activity could be the trigger to weaken the predictive power of the tone (further synaptic reorganization), since it is no longer a reliable predictor of food.

Schultz and colleagues use the expression that dopamine is involved in the 'reward prediction error'. In (a) reward is unpredicted (an 'error' in prediction) and dopamine is excited (things better than expected). In (b) reward is predicted (no prediction error; things are as expected) and reward does not trigger dopamine, whereas in (c) reward is predicted but fails to occur (a prediction error; things worse than expected; a suppression of dopamine).

Instrumental conditioning

Basics

The other class of associative learning is **instrumental conditioning** (Mackintosh, 1974). The animal is 'instrumental' in what happens, e.g. in correctly negotiating a maze. The experimenter arranges a contingency between behaviour and a consequence, e.g. getting food. Sometimes the type of instrumental conditioning that is studied in the Skinner box is termed '**operant conditioning**' (Skinner, 1966).

The essence of instrumental conditioning is **reinforcement** (Skinner, 1966) (Chapter 2). Suppose that, on a number of occasions, a hungry rat is placed in the start-box of a T-maze (Figure 11.7) and has a choice of turning left or right. To the left, it finds food (reward) but to the right there is an empty food-well. At first, the rat takes the right and left turns roughly 50:50. With experience,

Figure 11.7 T-maze.

it takes only the left. Food acts as a reinforcer for the left turn and 'reinforcement' refers to a *procedure* by which behaviour is changed (Skinner, 1966).

In the laboratory, a situation ('contingency') is arranged such that getting food is *conditional upon* performing a particular behaviour, a left turn. Such contingencies also arise naturally in nature. More specifically, the term **positive reinforcement** is the procedure of *gaining* something contingent upon behaviour, where the behaviour is observed to increase in frequency. For example, food positively reinforces the lever-pressing behaviour of a hungry animal.

Biological bases

Animals form expectations of 'what leads to what' in the Skinner box, i.e. lever-press → food. However, rather as described for classical conditioning, animals can also form relatively automatic 'stimulus–response' type habits in this situation. With extensive experience in a Skinner box, the value of reward ('expectation') plays a declining role in guiding the behaviour (Dickinson and Balleine, 1992). Corresponding to the shift to habit, rats show increased control by a region of the striatum (a structure within the basal ganglia) (Yin *et al.*, 2004).

Humans also experience something like this; we start out a bit of behaviour in full conscious awareness of 'what leads to what' but then, with repeated experience, increasing weight is given to an automatic habit. When habitual, the behaviour becomes triggered by the appropriate stimulus and the role of the goal is relatively weakened. For example, a motorist might set out from London intending to go to Birmingham. Less than half way there, the motorist 'gets captured' by the familiar stimuli and turns off at Milton Keynes, since this is the habitual turn. The goal (cognition of Birmingham) is masked by the habit.

In humans, at the start of an instrumental task regions of prefrontal cortex are activated, and they appear to encode the goal of the action ('expectation') and be responsible for guiding the action. Over time, this representation seems to remain intact. However, with extensive experience, fMRI reveals increasing activation of parts of the basal ganglia (i.e. putamen and globus pallidus), shown in Figure 10.17 (Tricomi *et al.*, 2009). This appears to represent the increasing strength of the habit-based control relative to the goal-directed control. A number of disorders, such as obsessive-compulsive disorder, appear to involve an increasing weight of habitual control, so greater understanding of the underlying processes is important.

A special form of associative learning is described next.

Taste-consequence learning

Basics

Animals can also learn links between external events and consequences *inside the body*. Preferences can be acquired by learning. These are based upon favourable consequences of ingestion of food of a particular taste, e.g. to favour a food associated with correction of vitamin deficiency (Rozin and Schulkin, 1990). However, aversions are the most famous examples of taste-consequence learning.

Suppose an animal ingests a food and later experiences gastrointestinal upset. Conditioning is easier if the taste is novel or relatively so. Typically, the animal is reluctant in future to ingest food with this flavour, termed 'taste-aversion learning' or the 'Garcia effect' (Garcia, 1989) (Chapter 1). Normally events that are associated by conditioning cannot be very far apart. For example, for salivary conditioning, the food must arrive within a second or so of the bell for a link to be formed. By contrast, taste-aversion learning is characterized by a delay of several hours that can elapse between tasting and gastrointestinal upset. For some species, e.g. rats, it is an effect largely specific to taste; it is more difficult to associate a visual or auditory stimulus with gastrointestinal upset.

A personal angle

For psychologists, where does the blame lie?

Martin Seligman (co-founder of 'positive psychology') reported what has become a famous experience, consisting of eating filet mignon with sauce Béarnaise and feeling ill some six hours later (Seligman and Hager, 1972). The illness was caused not by the meal but by some other stomach upset. Nonetheless, Seligman developed an aversion to sauce Béarnaise, reporting that it was transformed in taste from being his favourite sauce to 'awful' (one imagines that it was not a daily regular meal). The Cambridge psychologist Anthony Dickinson has documented a similar experience (Dickinson and Balleine, 1992). Not to be outdone, I developed an aversion to (relatively novel) hummus after eating it and being ill shortly afterwards. It turned out that the illness had nothing to do with the hummus but that knowledge did nothing to restore its attraction, which took 10 years.

In humans, taste-aversion learning shows where an evolutionarily old process can be more powerful than rationality (Garcia, 1989). Suppose that a person develops a taste-aversion to a food. However, they get to know that there was no connection between the food and illness. They often still avoid this food.

Biological bases

Following taste aversion conditioning, the taste serves as a conditional stimulus (CS) and animals act towards it as if it tastes bad (Yamamoto, 2007). Brain structures implicated in conditioned taste aversion can be compared with those involved with processing intrinsically aversive tastes. Following conditioning, reactions within the gustatory cortex shift in such a way that the reaction to the CS resembles that to an intrinsically bad taste. Some other structures are activated by the CS to aversion but not to an intrinsically aversive taste and these include nuclei of the amygdala. Its basolateral nucleus (BLA) appears to control the shift to aversion in the reaction to the CS. A descending pathway projects from the amygdala to nuclei in brain stem. This link modulates the relative sensitivity of neurons conveying information on specific tastes, such as to increase the chances of detection of the offending one.

Neurons within the BLA have been identified which, following conditioning on just one trial, are activated by both the CS and the UCS, hence representing the convergence of these inputs (Barot *et al.*, 2008). Backward presentation of CS and UCS, with the CS coming after rather than before the UCS (Figure 11.8), does not produce conditioning. In this study, neither did it produce evidence of neurons with a convergent input. Also, for conditioning to occur the CS needs to be novel. A familiar CS forms a much weaker conditional aversion and indeed convergence onto BLA neurons was not shown for familiar CSs followed by the UCS. It appears that a novel taste sensitizes a set of BLA neurons in such a way that, if an aversive UCS follows, the convergence of these inputs is consolidated. If the order of CS and UCS is reversed, such sensitization to the UCS input cannot occur.

We now consider a case of learning that does not involve relatively simple associative processes of the kind described so far.

Forming cognitive maps

Basics

In their brains, animals construct cognitive representations of the environment, termed cognitive maps (Tolman, 1932). Consider the 'Morris water maze' shown in Figure 11.9 (Morris, 1981). A tank is filled

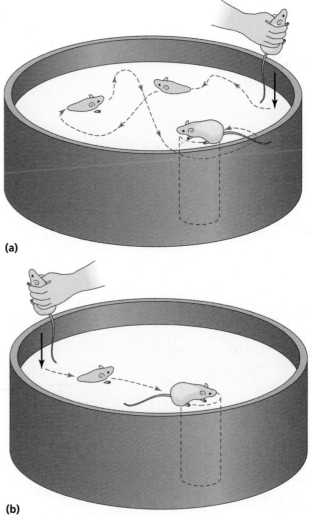

(a)

(b)

Figure 11.9 The Morris water maze apparatus: (a) first trial and (b) later trial.

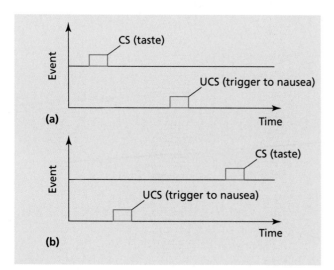

Figure 11.8 Classical conditioning: (a) forward and (b) backward.

with water and a submerged platform placed in it. Though rats have poor vision, milk is added to make sure that they cannot see the platform. A rat is then placed into the water and the trajectory of its swimming recorded (Figure 11.9(a)). Ultimately, it reaches the platform and climbs out of the water. It is then put back in at a different location and the trajectory observed. After a number of trials, the rat starts to swim directly towards the platform, regardless of where the rat is placed (Figures 11.9(b) and 11.10). If the platform is removed, the rat swims back and forth in the area where the platform used to be (Figure 11.10(b)).

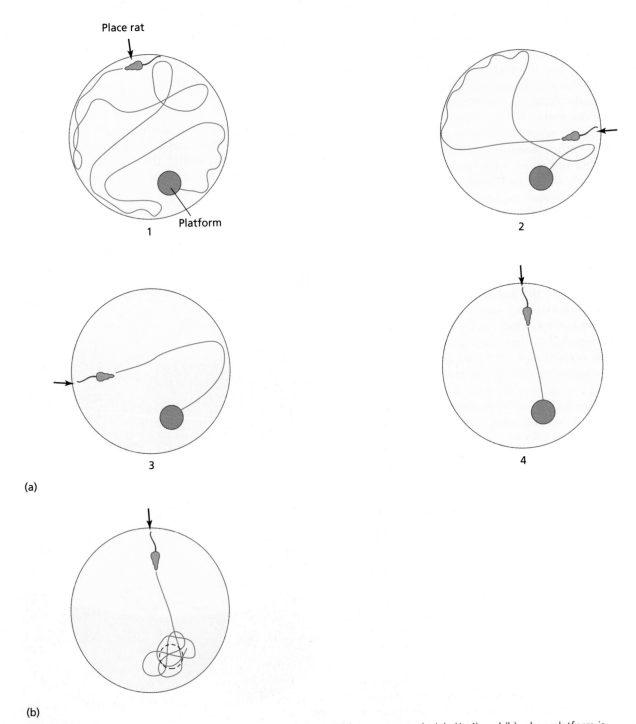

Figure 11.10 Behaviour in the Morris maze: trajectory followed (a) over repeated trials (1–4) and (b) when platform is removed.

The response is different according to where the rat is put into the water. It seems to involve knowledge about the environment, which can be utilized flexibly, i.e. a 'cognitive map'.

Biological relevance

The task cannot be solved on the basis of learning stimulus–response links. Rather, it involves the use of cognitive skills: the rat needs to extrapolate to where the platform is located. The cognitive processes necessary for solving the problem are vulnerable and performance declines with damage to the hippocampus (e.g. lesioning) or neural loss with ageing (Rendeiro *et al.*, 2009; Takatsu *et al.*, 2009). Giving dietary supplements can help to protect against the decline in cognitive ability with ageing.

The radial maze and foraging

Insight into different types of learning and memory and their biological bases has been obtained from studying foraging tasks in various species. Some general principles emerge, and can be illuminated by tasks set to laboratory rats.

The win–shift task

Figure 11.11 shows an Olton eight-arm maze (Olton *et al.*, 1979). Each arm contains a hidden morsel of food. The rat is placed in the centre and, when all eight doors are lifted, it has a choice of arm. Having depleted an arm of food, the optimal strategy is not to revisit that arm but to visit the others (see Figure 11.12). This involves recalling the arms already visited. The rat needs to visit each of the eight arms once only, to obtain a small reward at each goal, termed **win–shift**. Win–shift

Figure 11.11 The radial maze.
Source: Bear et al. (1996, Fig. 19.12, p. 537).

means that, having 'won' one reward, the animal has to shift to a different arm to win another. Rats become very good at performing this task.

The task requires the brain to *inhibit* the tendency arising from learning based on reinforcement. Reinforcement would *strengthen* a tendency to repeat the response to a particular arm at which reward had just been found. Having been reinforced at arm 1, the rat has to enter a different arm next time. The reinforcement of visiting arm 1 can only impede a solution and its effect must be resisted. Success at avoiding sites that

Taking food at a particular site can deplete it. What factors determine when to leave the site and when to come back?

Source: PhotoDisc, Inc.

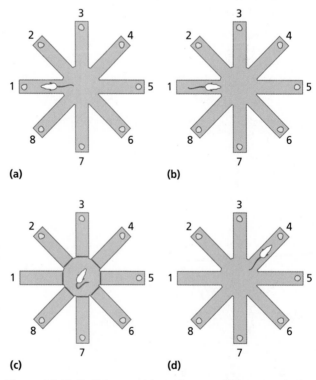

Figure 11.12 Radial maze: (a) rat about to deplete arm 1 of food, (b) return to centre, (c) doors descend so rat is held in centre for a few seconds, to put a load on memory, and (d) an unvisited arm (e.g. 4) forms the goal.

have been depleted seems to require representations of events, i.e. depleted sites and prospective sites of food.

The task seems to involve a combined capacity to use (1) spatial cues in a cognitive map and (2) a representation of the current state of each arm (i.e. as 'food' or 'depleted'). Weight appears to be given to each *particular instance* of recent experience, an 'episode' in resisting the reinforcement process (though a simpler process might also be involved; see Griffiths *et al.*, 1999). In these terms, the memory of the event that just happened, the rat's removal of a pellet, needs to be used in deciding whether to revisit an arm. Neither current sensory stimuli nor a weighted average of experience can solve the task. Rats with damage to the hippocampus (termed 'hippocampals') tend to repeat visits to arms that they have just depleted. They seem to be deficient at exploiting spatial cues outside the maze to establish where they are in space and, within this framework, to represent the state of the arm as 'food' or 'depleted' (Jarrard, 1993).

The win–stay task

The same radial maze can also be used to study a different schedule of reward, termed **win–stay** (Figure 11.13). In getting reward at one arm and when the experimenter signals that it has been re-loaded with food, the rat needs to return immediately to this same arm. The arm in which reward is located (in this case, arm 1)

is always indicated by a light and the task is solved by 'staying with the light'.

Solution of the win–stay task seems to be based upon food strengthening a habit ('reinforcement'), i.e. a simple S–R learned association between a light at an arm and an approach response (Petri and Mishkin, 1994). Any win–shift tendency would disrupt this task since the light is 'telling' the rat to repeat what it has just done. Normally rats find it easier to learn a win–shift task than a win–stay (Packard *et al.*, 1989). It could be relevant that, in the rat's natural environment, having depleted one location, it would appear to be natural to switch to elsewhere.

A double dissociation

By selective lesions, Packard *et al.* (1989) performed a double dissociation of these two foraging tasks. When animals were trained on a win–shift task, fornix lesions disrupted behaviour (the fornix is a brain region linking the hippocampus to the control of behaviour). Lesions to the fornix disrupt utilization of the hippocampus. The hippocampus is thought to mediate the use of a cognitive map. Lesions of the caudate nucleus, a region of the basal ganglia (Chapter 10), had no effect.

For the win–stay task, animals with lesions to the caudate nucleus were disrupted. This structure exerts an influence near to the motor output side and appears to be involved in S–R learning. By contrast to win–shift, the performance of animals with lesions to the fornix was *improved* relative to controls. By disrupting the expression of the hippocampus in behaviour, the tendency of the animal to show win–shift is disrupted and thereby the win–stay response is favoured.

The following section looks at memory.

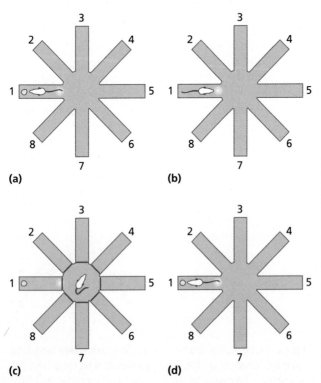

Figure 11.13 Win–stay task.

Section summary

1 A decline in response to a stimulus that has no significant consequence might be characterized as habituation (a case of non-associative learning). To meet this criterion, a change must occur between sensory and motor ends.

2 It can be adaptive to reduce the magnitude of response to such a stimulus.

3 In classical conditioning, a contingency is present between a neutral stimulus and an unconditional stimulus (UCS). The neutral stimulus becomes a conditional stimulus (CS) which evokes a conditional response (CR).

⇨

4 In instrumental conditioning, there is a contingency between behaviour and a consequence. If the consequence is one of reinforcement, the behaviour leading to it is more likely to occur in the future.

5 In its various forms, associative learning reflects the adaptive value of being able to form predictions.

6 In taste-aversion conditioning, an animal learns to avoid a food that has been followed by gastrointestinal upset.

7 Animals form cognitive maps of their environment and this can be tested in the Morris water maze.

8 The radial maze is used to observe foraging behaviour. A win-shift strategy is disrupted by damage to the hippocampus.

Test your knowledge

11.2 Which of the following is (i) an associative and (ii) a non-associative form of learning? Habituation, classical conditioning, instrumental conditioning.

11.3 What is the neutral stimulus and conditional stimulus in (i) Pavlov's classical conditioning of salivation and (ii) taste-aversion conditioning?

11.4 In a win–stay task in the radial maze, what is the optimal solution to maximize food intake?

11.5 In a win–shift task in the radial maze, what is the optimal solution to maximize food intake?

Answers on page 310

The memory tradition

Introduction

Whenever learning occurs, by definition a memory is formed. Researchers try to categorize memory into different classes (Squire, 1994). Multiple types of memory mean that it is not enough simply to state, for example, that 'memory is impaired'. Rather, we need to specify which class of memory is impaired (Tulving, 1995). Also a claim might need qualification of the kind that either acquisition or retrieval of information is impaired but not both.

In classifying memory, there is not absolute agreement on the criteria and various classifications exist side-by-side (Foster and Jelicic, 1999). What follows must therefore be a broad-brushstroke approach.

Types of memory

Declarative/explicit – non-declarative/implicit

With reference particularly to humans, a way of dividing memory is into declarative memory and non-declarative memory (Squire, 1994) (Figure 11.14). A **declarative memory** is for a fact or an event in the world, e.g. Paris is the capital of France. We have conscious access to it, and having retrieved it into consciousness, can choose whether to express it in behaviour (Schacter and Tulving, 1994b). The term 'declarative' means that humans can verbally declare its content. Declarative memory corresponds to the most common lay use of 'memory' and 'to remember' (Squire, 1994). Declarative memories can be acquired rapidly, e.g. in a single exposure (Moscovitch, 1994) and used in an indefinite series of different and novel situations (Eichenbaum, 1994).

Is there a non-human model of declarative memory? Of course, rats cannot literally *declare* anything but they can be set tasks that require forms of memory that appear similar to human equivalents. The radial maze tests the ability to learn and recall a particular instance of experience and to use it in the control of behaviour.

Another term that means much the same as declarative memory is **explicit memory**. We can be verbally explicit about the content. Since the ability to verbalize recall is the criterion for 'explicit', strictly speaking, it is applicable only to humans (Eichenbaum, 1994).

In contrast to declarative/explicit memory is **non-declarative memory** or **implicit memory** (Claparède, 1911; Squire, 1994). It cannot be expressed or 'declared' verbally. Being able to ride a bicycle exemplifies non-declarative memory. The distinction is between knowing 'what' (e.g. the explicit memory that Paris is the French capital) and knowing 'how' (e.g. the implicit memory of how to use chopsticks).

Skills and habits involve non-declarative memory. Non-declarative memory is also termed **procedural memory** and is automatic and unconscious (Eichenbaum, 1994; Schacter and Tulving, 1994b). Conscious awareness has, at best, a vague and fuzzy insight into such memory. Its contents cannot be described as true or false but only as more or less adaptive in a given situation. Procedural memories are usually acquired slowly and incrementally (see O'Keefe and Nadel, 1978).

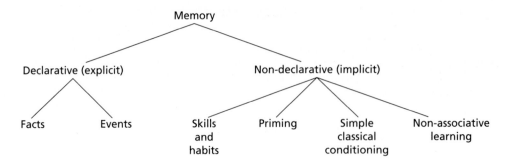

Figure 11.14 Classification of memory.

Source: From Squire and Zola-Morgan (1991, Fig. 3). Reprinted with permission from AAAS.

It is doubtful whether there are tasks that involve purely either explicit/declarative or implicit/procedural memory (Eichenbaum, 1994). All tasks probably require something of each. The question is perhaps best framed as some tasks being more or less dependent upon one or other system.

Semantic and episodic memories

For humans, a distinction within declarative memory is between **semantic memory** and **episodic memory** (Tulving, 1972). Semantic memory refers to that for facts. Episodic memory refers to a particular episode of *personal experience*. Griffiths *et al.* (1999, p.74) offer a memorable example:

> Remembering getting soaked in the London rain last Tuesday is an example of episodic memory, but knowing that it often rains in England is an example of semantic memory because it need not be acquired as a result of a personal experience of getting wet.

A personal angle

N.N.

A male patient, N.N., studied by Endel Tulving in Toronto had suffered head injury in a traffic accident (Tulving, 1985b). N.N.'s linguistic skills and general knowledge were intact. N.N. could draw a picture of the Statue of Liberty and could even define rather well the meaning of 'consciousness'. He had knowledge about his past, e.g. names of his schools, but the memory was devoid of personal events ('episodes') of experience. As Tulving describes it, N.N.'s life has an 'impersonal experiential quality'. This shows where damage can disrupt one form of memory while leaving another intact.

Occasionally, brain damage can disrupt episodic memory, while leaving semantic memory intact (Nielsen, 1958; Tulving, 1999).

Episodic memory has a tag of 'what', 'where' and 'when' for single instances. There is evidence that the bird species the scrub jay (*Aphelocoma coerulescens*) (Chapter 1) can exploit such memory in utilizing what it has cached (Clayton and Dickinson, 1998). The bird seems to know about each item of food and where it has been hidden.

Memory as a function of time

Memory classification presented so far is based on what is learned and how it is learned. Another classification is based on time, the *temporal* dimension, though it broadens to a wider consideration than this. With reference to declarative memory and based mainly upon humans, different temporal stages of memory are identified, varying from only about 0.5 s to a lifetime (Baddeley, 1997).

Figure 11.15 shows a classical representation of the temporal stages involved in learning visual or auditory information. The first stage is termed 'sensory registration' and is specific to a sensory system. It has been studied in the visual system (termed 'iconic memory') and auditory system (termed 'echoic memory'). There is a process of recoding that translates between sensory registration and the next stage, termed **short-term memory** (**STM**). STM has a limited capacity and information tends to decay from it unless it is actively rehearsed, e.g. reciting a telephone number. The traditional view is that, following a brief holding in STM, information is normally either lost or is transferred to **long-term memory** (**LTM**). The capacity of LTM seems virtually limitless and its durability potentially a lifetime.

Information is said to be either lost from STM or subject to **consolidation**. Memories that are consolidated are stored in the relatively durable form of LTM, as opposed to the more fragile STM. The durable physical embodiment of memory is termed an **engram**. Memory consolidation is surrounded by controversy and there

Figure 11.15 A classical representation of the temporal stages of memory.
Source: Cohen (1990, Fig. 12.10, p. 596).

could well be several different processes contributing to it (Meeter and Murre, 2004). An attempt at a broad consensus is presented here.

The short-term versus long-term distinction is relative rather than absolute. At a given point in time, a memory might be in part in each location. Some memories linger for much longer than a few seconds before being lost, e.g. what you ate for breakfast this morning. However, some kind of distinction, albeit ill-defined, between a more fragile 'provisional' memory and a more durable one still holds.

Working memory

The classification shown in Figure 11.15 has proven its value. However, limitations became apparent and a new model emerged, based on the concept of **working memory** (Baddeley and Hitch, 1974) (Figure 11.16). This borrowed important features of the STM/LTM distinction but incorporated additional features. A memory is said to be 'working' when it is active and involved in information processing. Working memory underpins cognition and conscious thought. In the spirit of the STM part of the old model, subsets of working memory hold information while it is transferred into LTM. Indeed, to capture this feature of memory and for historical continuity, the expression 'STM' is still used in the literature, alongside working memory.

Working memory does more than just hold memories while they are transferred into a more permanent form. Another of its roles can be illustrated as follows. Can you recall the looks of US President Obama? On the occasion(s) when you first saw him, his image was held in STM/working memory and was then assimilated into a durable form. Imagine now his features and

even try to draw a sketch of him. You were probably not thinking of him prior to reaching this paragraph. If so, his memory was secure in your brain but was inactive. Now it is active and is *working* as in being used to draw a sketch. It has re-entered working memory and presumably will exit in a paragraph or two (or maybe not!).

So, as a part of working memory, this temporary store of active information can perform additional tasks, such as reasoning and comprehension. Rather than being simply a passive store, information is held in working memory while it is *actively* manipulated (see Petrides, 1994). Baddeley (1994, p. 351) defines working memory as: 'the system for the temporary maintenance and manipulation of information, necessary for the performance of such complex cognitive activities as comprehension, learning and reasoning'.

A **central executive** is said to supervise the subsystems of working memory and is associated with holding information in conscious awareness. Within working memory, an articulatory control process recycles

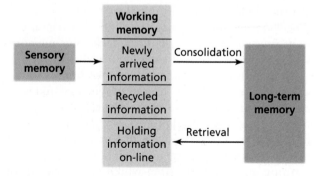

Figure 11.16 A representation of working memory and its links.

speech-based information as inner speech. Visual information can enter working memory either directly via visual perception of the external world or by the internal production of a visual image. Such an image can be manipulated, e.g. rotated. Try it now with President Obama. Skills such as negotiating an environment involve manipulating a visual image (Baddeley, 1997).

A personal angle

This moment in time

Working memory is something like the file that is open now on my computer, labelled 'Chapter 11'. It is 'active' and now receiving new information but, in the same file ('memory space'), established 'long-term' memories (i.e. yesterday's contribution to the writing) have also been retrieved and are accessible. Since the file is open, the information is able to be used, e.g. in interaction with the printer. In a moment, the file will be closed and have only the same status as the other files on the hard disk.

It is now time to look at the brain and the physical basis of memory.

Memory and the brain

Introduction

Detailed investigation of the brain gives insight into memory. For example, PET scans reveal which brain regions are most active under particular conditions of posing a recall task to memory. Measuring the effects of experimental lesions in non-humans and accidental brain damage in humans also provides understanding.

A source of insight into *systems* of memory is when damage to the brain disrupts one kind of memory, while leaving another intact (Schacter and Tulving, 1994a,b). Damage sometimes impairs declarative memory but not procedural memory. Damage to a different region disrupts procedural memory but not declarative memory. This is termed a double dissociation (Chapter 8).

Both cortical and subcortical structures are involved in learning and memory. Regions of temporal and parietal cortex are assumed to be the cortical sites at which memories are stored (Figure 11.17). The role of the hippocampus appears to be a dual one: to act as (i) a temporary store of information held immediately after learning and (ii) a site from which consolidation of memory by the cortex is controlled (Meeter and Murre,

2004). The hippocampus is thought to be a fast-learning system whereas the cortex is slower. Hippocampal damage disrupts more recently acquired memories, while leaving older ones intact. This suggests that, with time, the cortex is able to consolidate memories but, until this is achieved, the hippocampus is needed either to store them or to gain access to them.

The role of the prefrontal cortex is thought to be that of controlling memory, i.e. retrieving memory and holding it in a 'working' state so it can be used. The amygdala plays a role in enhancing consolidation, described in the next chapter.

This section looks at types of memory from the perspective of these brain regions and different kinds of learning and memory tasks.

Memory storage – cortical regions

In human patients undergoing brain surgery, local electrical stimulation of a part of the temporal cortex tends to evoke a particular memory, suggestive of localization (Penfield and Rasmussen, 1968). Experiments on non-human primates show that regions of cortex concerned with modality-specific processing (e.g. vision) and other regions concerned with multimodal processing (e.g. vision and tactile) are involved in memory (Petrides, 1994). For example, inferotemporal cortex is involved in later stages of visual processing (Chapter 8) and visual memory. Its damage can disrupt visually based memory, leaving memories based on other modalities intact.

Figure 11.17 Role of some brain regions.

As an aspect of working memory, Baddeley and Hitch's (1974) model involves the retrieval of visual memories. By this means, mental images can be manipulated. When humans are asked to *visualize* themselves negotiating an environment, there is an increase in blood flow to the occipital cortex (Roland and Friberg, 1985). Of course, this region is otherwise activated by visual stimulation from the external world (Chapter 8). Patients who have lost colour vision through damage to the occipital lobes also lose the capacity to think with coloured images (see Baddeley, 1997). They can sometimes draw a picture of an object from memory but be unable to say what colour the object should be.

A personal angle

Gottlieb L.

In 1888, the case of an 80-year-old German salesman, Gottlieb L. (G.L.), was reported (article reprinted as Lissauer, 1988). During a trip to Krotoschin, G.L. had been blown against a fence in a wind and banged his head. He reported difficulties seeing but had normal visual acuity. He was able to draw objects by copying them.

G.L.'s problem was specific to associating the meaning of objects with their visual stimulus. For example, he described an apple as a portrait of a woman. Whereas G.L. could not recognize a whistle by sight, he was able to name it by its sound. Thus, the problem was not a general failure of semantic memory. G.L. retained his business sense and had insight into his condition. Autopsy revealed G.L. to have suffered damage to the occipital and parietal cortex of the left hemisphere (Shallice and Jackson, 1988).

When he was only 27 years old, Heinrich Lissauer reported the case of G.L. at a conference in Breslau. Sadly, Lissauer, who was also noted for other medical achievements, died three years later.

In other cases, brain-damaged patients are unable to access semantic memory by touch but can do so by vision.

Executive functions

As part of the executive function of working memory, the ventrolateral and dorsolateral parts of the prefrontal cortex (PFC) have a role in the utilization of memory to control cognition and action (Gazzaley and D'Esposito, 2007; Geschwind and Iacoboni, 2007). To do so, they draw on ('reinstate') memories that are stored in more posterior cortical regions (Figure 11.18). This involves maintaining the activity of a memory, i.e. holding it 'on-line' so that its content can be utilized. In humans, based on intentions, the PFC helps to guide memory searches, direct thought processes, plan action and select and implement encoding, processes that are open to conscious introspection (Moscovitch, 1994). Figure 11.18 illustrates the interaction between the PFC and more posterior cortical regions (parietal and temporal) in performing tasks involving working memory (Petrides, 1994). Damage to the regions of PFC indicated is associated with disruption to working memory and planning (Miller, 2007).

Suppose that you are asked – where were you on Christmas day ten years ago and what did you do? An answer is unlikely to 'jump out at you' automatically. Rather, a lengthy retrieval process involving various strategies is likely. The role of the PFC is, in Moscovitch's terms, one of 'working-with-memory', corresponding to the role of the central executive. Although humans with damage to PFC can assimilate new information, they are deficient in organizing its recall (Milner, 1964, 1971). They have conscious insight into their deficiency, scoring low on measures of their confidence that they can recall information. The PFC has a role in discriminating true from false memories and its damage can result in 'confabulation' ('false memory', claiming as true experience something that did not occur) (Schacter, 1997).

Humans with damage to PFC experience difficulty in inhibiting inappropriate information, termed 'utilization behaviour' (Chapters 5 and 10; Lhermitte, 1983). They show interference from previously activated memories. In the laboratory, this consists of intrusions from a memory test conducted a few minutes earlier. At a biological level, this appears to reflect a failure of what

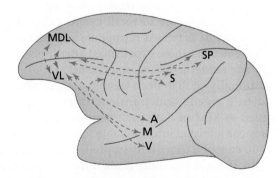

Figure 11.18 Interaction between prefrontal and posterior cortical regions and between prefrontal regions.
S, somatosensory; SP, visuo-spatial; A, auditory; M, multimodal; V, object vision; VL, ventrolateral PFC; MDL, mid-dorsal lateral PFC.
Source: Petrides (1994, Fig. 16, p. 73).

would normally be a PFC inhibition on processing carried out by more posterior cortical regions. For example, to remember where and when a memory was acquired might require extensive inhibition of 'false leads'.

Non-human primates with damage to the PFC are impaired in tasks that require observation of an event, its holding in working memory and its use in action slightly later (Petrides, 1994). Typically, a response to obtain reward is first cued, the cue extinguished, a delay imposed and only then is the choice of response able to be made. Damage to other cortical areas does not have such an effect.

Dopamine has a role in such tasks. Disruption of dopaminergic neurotransmission at the PFC has a disruptive effect on their performance (Chapter 6). However, a number of tasks that require working memory (e.g. recognition of an object, understanding speech) remain relatively unimpaired following damage to the PFC. Memory can be triggered in an automatic way, driven by stimuli that match the memory. This suggests that PFC damage does not disrupt the store of memory (e.g. the sensory attributes of a memory) and points to this region's involvement in management of memory, i.e. activating a memory even in the absence of appropriate sensory input and holding it 'on-line'.

Very valuable evidence on the brain and memory has been derived from studying when memory 'goes wrong', as in accidents and the unintended consequence of surgical interventions. The rest of the section turns to this topic.

Amnesia

General principles

The term **amnesia** means 'the pathological inability to learn new information or to retrieve information that has already been acquired' (Purves *et al.*, 1997, p. 549). Amnesia is sometimes due to trauma, as in brain injury (Milner, 1966). A failure to recall events experienced before the trauma is termed **retrograde amnesia** and a failure to remember those experienced after it is termed **anterograde amnesia** (Butters and Cermak, 1986).

Traditionally, it has been assumed that memory is held in a fragile and transient form as activity (expressed as STM or a division of working memory) until it is consolidated into a durable form, LTM (Lewis, 1979). If consolidation is disrupted, then memory is lost. In these terms, retrograde amnesia might be explained as trauma disrupting consolidation of memories formed prior to the trauma.

Retrograde amnesia often displays a temporal gradient: the memory for events nearest the time of trauma is most disrupted, with that for earlier events less so. The traditional interpretation of retrograde amnesia is that

there has been insufficient time for events just prior to the trauma to become consolidated. However, there are problems with this (Lewis, 1979)

1 Some patients show retrograde amnesia for events extending over years. Can consolidation really take that long?

2 Amnesia often displays shrinkage. Memories that were apparently lost immediately after trauma appear later, indicating that they were present all along. This suggests a failure of **retrieval** rather than consolidation.

3 Within the zone of retrograde amnesia there are often islands of retained memory.

In the phenomenon termed 'transient global amnesia', a wide variety of precipitating circumstances (e.g. mild head trauma, emotional stress) trigger an episode of anterograde amnesia (Agosti *et al.*, 2008; Venneri *et al.*, 1998). The amnesia usually lifts within 24 hours. The biological basis of the phenomenon remains unclear and reports vary as to whether there are alterations in blood flow to the brain and identifiable abnormal activity at particular brain regions. There could be subtle changes in the flow of information within the brain triggered by trauma that are undetectable by techniques such as imaging.

A personal angle

Princess Diana's bodyguard

Traumatic events are sometimes of legal and political significance, apart from their medical importance. In the car accident in Paris that killed Princess Diana in 1997, there was only one survivor, her bodyguard Trevor Rees-Jones. After his recovery, police were keen to interview him, to establish the circumstances of the accident, e.g. was a second car involved? However, he was unable to recollect the events immediately before the accident. Some memory returned slowly in the subsequent months.

Batchelor *et al.* (2008) investigated retrograde amnesia in stroke patients (stroke is the rupture or blocking of a blood vessel). When the stroke was on just one side of the brain a mild degree of retrograde amnesia was found. For there to be amnesia it was necessary that the damage affected the hippocampus. Damage to the right side more than to the left disturbed the recall of autobiographical incidents.

One type of profound amnesia for which the biological basis is clear is described next.

The human amnesic syndrome

In humans, damage specifically to the medial temporal lobe involving the hippocampus on both sides of the brain leads to the **amnesic syndrome**, consisting of an apparent failure to assimilate new episodic and semantic information (Milner, 1966). It might be more accurate to consider several amnesic syndromes subsumed under this heading. However, there is difficulty deciding how to formalize such classification. It could be in terms of (i) cause, e.g. from an infection that damages neural tissue, (ii) the site of brain damage (e.g. specific region of temporal lobes) or (iii) the nature of the memory loss.

A personal angle

The hidden pin

In 1911, the Swiss psychologist Edouard Claparède reported an observation on an amnesic patient, a 47-year-old woman in the refuge at Bel-Air. She had been ill since 1900 and appeared unable to update her memory. She didn't know where she was or how old she was. She asked the nurse who had cared for her for 6 months, '*à qui ai-je l'honneur de parler?*' (to whom do I have the honour to speak?). However, she could name without error the capital cities of Europe and could negotiate her way around the refuge. Claparède was in the habit of shaking hands with the patients on doing his rounds. On one occasion, in 1906, he held a pin in his hand so as to prick the hand of this patient. The incident appeared to be forgotten shortly afterwards. However, the following day and in response to Claparède's outstretched hand, the patient declined to advance hers and jerked it away. She had learned an association between the psychologist and trauma. In terms of memory, she had formed an implicit memory of the traumatic event. The result of Claparède might be put down to a single uncontrolled observation, but subsequent research has confirmed its broad applicability.

Usually, beyond this anecdote, little acknowledgement is given in the English-speaking world to Claparède's early profound insights into memory and its classification.

Claparède (1911) demonstrated a dissociation: by the index of behaviour, the patient appeared to remember but was unable to recall consciously the episode that triggered the change in behaviour. The emotional intensity of the experience might be implicated in its retention (Markowitsch, 1995), suggesting involvement of an intact amygdala (Chapter 12).

Patients such as H.M. (see overleaf) exemplify the amnesic syndrome. Baddeley (1997) cites H.M. as possibly providing the strongest evidence for a distinction between STM and LTM. Each seems to be functioning but there is a failure either of *certain* contents of STM to enter LTM or of *certain* contents of LTM to become accessible to conscious recall (Lewis, 1979).

A form of memory that is retained in the amnesic syndrome is revealed in the 'word-completion test' (Warrington and Weiskrantz, 1970). A person is presented with a word, e.g. ASSASSIN, and asked to recall it. Typically, people with amnesia cannot consciously recall it. However, suppose that they are asked to complete a word cued by A--A--IN. They show a higher probability of responding ASSASSIN as a result of prior presentation of ASSASSIN. Behaviour has been influenced by the prior presentation even though they cannot consciously recall the earlier event. The prior experience produces priming at later recall, a form of non-declarative memory (Figure 11.14). Amnesic patients can acquire motor skills (procedural learning) though they are not conscious of doing so and cannot articulate the learning experience (Weiskrantz and Warrington, 1979). H.M. exemplifies this.

Are there common features of the tasks at which amnesic humans are unimpaired (Weiskrantz, 1982)? In each task, the appropriate response, the index of memory, can be produced without placing the explicit question 'Do you remember this?' They can be solved by a straightforward mapping from sensory input to recalled memory and triggering by a cue, e.g. A--A--IN tends to trigger the memory ASSASSIN as a result of earlier presentation of ASSASSIN. Similarly, people with amnesia reveal intact memory in, say, reverse-mirror drawing, cued by the sight of the apparatus.

People with amnesia can show good recall of some episodic and semantic information that was encoded before the onset of the disorder. Information assimilated prior to the disorder might have benefited from repeated reactivation and forms part of a more automatic retrieval (Johnson and Chalfonte, 1994).

Insight into brain mechanisms of memory has come from the study of classical conditioning of the eye blink reflex (see earlier in this chapter) in people with amnesia (Clark and Squire, 1998). They were compared with controls in both delay and trace conditioning and it exemplifies where understanding can be gained by a parallel consideration of learning and memory. When exposed to the delay situation (Figure 11.3(a)), people with amnesia exhibit intact conditioning. Clark and Squire characterize such a conditioned eye-blink reflex as having (p. 77): 'the automatic, reflexive features that are characteristic of non-declarative memory'.

A personal angle

H.M.

H.M. was born in Manchester, Connecticut, in 1926 (Milner, 1966; Scoville and Milner, 1957). H.M. fell off his bicycle when he was aged 9, injuring his head. Epileptic attacks began when he was 10 and they were assumed to be connected with the accident. As an adult, he received surgery to treat the epilepsy after it had become an intractable problem. Tissue from the medial temporal lobe (including hippocampus) on both sides of H.M.'s brain was removed. The lesion included the amygdala (Squire, 2009).

Following the operation, H.M. was able to recall vividly information acquired in early life, e.g. a holiday in Florida. His personality appeared largely unchanged and there was no general intellectual impairment. H.M. was very good at recognizing faces of people famous in his childhood. This indicated that the regions removed from H.M.'s brain were not the permanent sites of such memory storage (Squire, 2009).

However, he could recall little of the 12 years prior to the operation. For example, he did not remember the death of a favourite uncle three years before.

H.M. experienced an unchanging anterograde amnesia for episodic and semantic information (Corkin, 2002). For example, he was unable to remember the faces of people he met after the operation. A psychologist might spend the morning testing him but in the afternoon H.M. would act as if the psychologist were a stranger. People who had come to H.M.'s house regularly for 6 years were not recognized. Reading and rereading the same magazine created no impression of familiarity. The failure to update such memories is a hallmark of the amnesic syndrome (Baddeley, 1997).

H.M. had a capacity for working memory, since he was able to carry on a normal conversation and could understand jokes. This required some minimal level of retention of what had just been heard and said. On being asked to recall the number 584, H.M. was able to do so even 15 minutes later, apparently by means of constant verbal rehearsal. However, after the task was over, the number and H.M.'s strategy in remembering it were lost to his memory.

Motor skills (procedural memories) were well maintained, e.g. how to mow a lawn. He showed improvement on the performance of learning new skills such as reverse mirror-drawing in which he had to acquire new eye–hand coordination (Corkin, 1968; Milner, 1966). H.M.'s ability to learn new skills is typical of the amnesic syndrome. However, such patients have no consciously accessible memory of acquiring the skill. H.M. had insight into his problem and, in response to a question he could not answer, was inclined to respond that he has 'trouble with his memory'. An MRI scan of H.M.'s brain was performed in 1992 and 1993 and details of the extent of the damage analyzed (Corkin *et al.*, 1997).

H.M. enabled a landmark in the study of cognition to be achieved. Prior to studies with him, it was believed, in the words of Squire (2009, p.6) that memory was 'integrated with intellectual and perceptual functions'. H.M. showed that disruptions to memory can occur without disruption to general cognition, attention or perception. Along with the patient studied by Edouard Claparède, H.M. provided an early clue that there is more than one kind of memory (Squire, 2009).

H.M. died on December 2nd, 2008, aged 82 years. He would seem to be the most closely studied individual in the history of biological psychology and neuroscience. H.M. had insights into his memory deficit and expressed pleasure that knowledge gained from the study of him might help others.

By contrast, trace conditioning (Figure 11.3(b)) presents serious problems for people with amnesia. The researchers looked into whether participants had acquired consciously accessible knowledge about the contingency to which they had been exposed. If so, they might articulate this as 'Each time there was a tone, this was followed by a puff of air'. The reasoning was that, unlike delay conditioning, trace conditioning might require such conscious insight.

Figure 11.19 shows the result. Both groups acquired delay conditioning. Among controls, only those who became aware of the contingency showed trace conditioning. Among people with amnesia, none of them became aware of the contingency and none showed trace conditioning.

So, why does trace conditioning require an intact hippocampus? It precludes formation of an automatic reflex. Clark and Squire suggest that it requires the

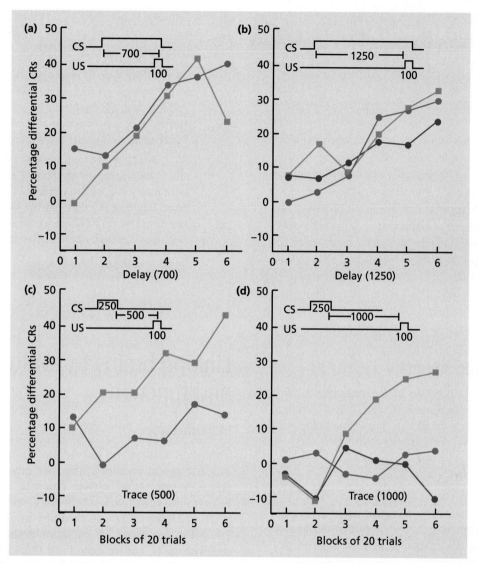

Figure 11.19 The magnitude of the conditional response over the course of the blocks of trials. (a) and (b) Delay conditioning with different delays between conditional stimulus (CS) onset and unconditional stimulus (US) onset. (c) and (d) Trace conditioning with different delays between CS offset and US onset. red circles, unaware controls; green squares, aware controls; blue circles, people with amnesia.

Source: From Clark and Squire (1998, *Science*, vol. 280, Fig. 3, p. 79). Reprinted with permission from AAAS.

formation of conscious knowledge. As is also shown in other experiments, the hippocampus is implicated in this ability. It appears to work in collaboration with the cortex and cerebellum.

Korsakoff's syndrome

People with **Korsakoff's syndrome** exhibit profound deficiencies of memory. It is a form of amnesia that is similar to, but distinct from, the classical form just described and has a distinct cause. This syndrome is normally due to

a thiamine (vitamin B1) deficiency, as a consequence of excessive alcohol intake. There are global signs of loss of brain tissue, this particularly being the case for the frontal lobe (Oscar-Berman *et al.*, 2004) and hippocampus (Sullivan and Marsh, 2003). Deficits of executive function are evident, i.e. working with memory, as in the Wisconsin card-sorting task (Chapter 6).

The next section considers types of memory and in the context of evolutionary and functional explanations (Chapter 2).

A personal angle

A Russian writer

In 1889, writing in a French journal, Sergei Korsakoff (1854–1900) discussed amnesia, which led to his name being given to the syndrome (Korsakoff, 1889). The paper concerned a patient, a 37-year-old Russian writer. When visiting Siberia, the writer did not get paralytically drunk but imbibed very large amounts of alcohol each day. Korsakoff noted the patient's inability to remember the events that occurred immediately prior to the consultation, such as the meal that he had recently eaten. However, some older memories were well retained.

  ### Test your knowledge

11.6 Which type of memory is revealed in the following? (i) How to balance on a rocking boat, (ii) that the biggest city in the Netherlands is Amsterdam, (iii) what you had for breakfast on a visit to Amsterdam.

11.7 Which type of amnesia is revealed in the following lapses of memory associated with injury in a traffic accident? (i) A failure to recall whether the lights at the junction were red or green, (ii) a failure to remember the first questioning by police after the accident.

Answers on page 310   WEB

Section summary

1 Memory is classified into (a) declarative ('explicit') memory (associated with conscious recollection) and (b) non-declarative ('implicit') memory (which cannot be consciously recalled).

2 A category of non-declarative memory is that underlying habits and skills, termed procedural memory.

3 Within declarative memory, a distinction is between semantic memory (for facts) and episodic memory (for episodes of personal experience).

4 Working memory is a multi-aspect store of information in which information is held while it is actively manipulated.

5 Amnesia refers to a pathological failure of memory.

6 Regions of temporal and parietal cortex are involved in memory storage.

7 Prefrontal cortex appears to be part of the embodiment of the central executive, which is involved in 'working with memory', as in directing searches.

8 In the amnesic syndrome, there is damage to the medial temporal lobe. People (e.g. H.M.) fail to update their memory with declarative information. Their procedural memory is intact.

Linking brains to evolution and function

Introduction

In both evolution and development, different systems of learning and memory appear to emerge at different stages. When a new system emerges, it increases the behavioural possibilities. Tulving (1985a, p. 387) suggests an analogy: 'we can think of an airplane with an autopilot as a more advanced or higher system than one without it, but we would not think of the autopilot alone as a higher system than the airplane'.

Tulving argues that the earliest system of learning and memory to appear in evolution and development is the procedural. Semantic memory emerges from this and brings the novel feature of being able to represent events that are not physically present. In turn, episodic memory emerges from semantic memory and allows representation of unique instances of individual experience. Tulving suggests that (p. 387): 'each higher system depends on, and is supported by, the lower system or systems, but it possesses unique capabilities not possessed by the lower systems'. In this interpretation, the lowest system, procedural, can exist without the other two and semantic memory can exist without episodic memory.

It is a general rule that, in evolutionary terms, new processes are relatively vulnerable to disruption, as compared with old processes (Ribot, 1885). Memory in general follows this principle. However, there can be disruption to implicit memory, leaving explicit intact. We have seen instances of this in the present chapter and Chapter 8 described such a case.

Evolutionary psychology

Different specialized adaptations

From a functional perspective, different forms of memory would be expected to reflect the different demands of the environments in which they evolved (Sherry and Schacter, 1987). In the terms of evolutionary psychology (Chapter 2), different systems of learning and memory appear to have evolved to serve different specialized functions and to reflect different 'design criteria' (Klein *et al.*, 2002a). Thus, understanding can best be gained, not by considering the tasks that learning and memory *can* perform, but what they were 'designed' to perform.

Sherry and Schacter suggest that memory systems reveal 'functional incompatibility'. This means that 'an adaptation that serves one function cannot, because of its specialized nature, effectively serve other functions' (p. 439). A single general 'all-purpose' system could not meet these demands.

The distinction does not necessarily mean that different systems are located in entirely different anatomical sites. Sherry and Schacter give taste-aversion learning as an example of a specialized learning and memory system.

Song learning

Sherry and Schacter (1987) identify song learning in birds as a special class of learning and memory. Its features include (a) neural systems that are dedicated to the task (identifiable brain nuclei), (b) a time-frame in early life during which learning can occur, (c) a considerable time between when a song is learned by the young bird and its performance when adult and (d) specificity in exactly what is learned. Birds learn songs specific to their species, often with a local dialect. This suggests a template for song recognition, with a capacity for fine-tuning by local experience. Such specificity serves to attract conspecific mates and warn potential rivals.

In canaries, two brain nuclei control singing. There is a positive correlation between their size and the size of the song repertoire. Both nuclei show variation in size over the year, correlated with the time when songs are performed. Increases in volume are due to a proliferation of neurons and glial cells (Chapters 4 and 6).

Food caching

Some species of bird cache food (earlier in this chapter and in Chapters 1 and 5) (Sherry and Schacter, 1987). The bird has a specialized memory system that enables it to remember the locations. Food is typically retrieved several days after caching. Following this, the bird does not revisit the site. This seems to involve episodic memory, similar to that involved in solving the radial maze task. The (transient) memory involved in caching food is fundamentally different from that involved in song learning (durable). Lesions to the hippocampus disrupt the ability to locate cached food.

Declarative and non-declarative learning and memory in primates

To illustrate functional specialization of learning and memory by primates, including humans, Sherry and Schacter contrast forms of declarative and non-declarative memory. They consider the evolution of, on the one hand, a declarative system that enables one-trial learning of specific episodes and, on the other, a non-declarative incremental learning system underlying habits and skills. Think about how the skill of riding a bicycle is achieved. The memory underlying it is not acquired on a single trial. Rather, sensory-motor links that were successful in maintaining stability tended to be strengthened and assimilated into a bank of solutions, i.e. by feedback some links are encouraged and others discouraged.

In contrast to skill learning, Sherry and Schacter suggest that episodic memory has evolved to assimilate unique information peculiar to an instance, i.e. to emphasize *variance* between episodes.

Sherry and Schacter propose a functional criterion for deciding how many different memory systems there are, which can be used alongside other criteria, such as susceptibility to brain damage. A 'conservative perspective' is that (p. 449): 'distinct memory systems evolve only when there is functional incompatibility between the properties of an existing system and the demands posed by a novel environmental problem'.

Having looked at the more gross brain structures and functional considerations, the next section looks at the cellular basis of learning and memory in terms of changes at the level of individual neurons, which encodes memory.

Section summary

1 Functional incompatibility is assumed to have led to the evolution of distinct memory systems.

2 In evolution, procedural memory appears to be the oldest type of memory.

3 Semantic memory seems to be evolutionarily more recent than procedural memory. In turn, episodic memory appears to emerge from semantic memory.

4 Functionally, there seems to be incompatibility between the properties of declarative and non-declarative memories in terms of what they are 'designed' to perform.

☞ Test your knowledge

11.8 In terms of both evolution and development, which is thought to be the earliest memory system to appear?

Answers on page 310   ◖WEB➡

Cellular mechanisms

The basic idea

As a possible starting point, consider again brain regions. Different regions play roles in different types of learning and memory and we described connections between regions, e.g. linking prefrontal cortex and more posterior regions of cortex. If we are able to associate memory with particular brain regions, in principle it is possible to associate it with the properties of some of the connections between neurons that are located in these regions.

Another possible starting point is with the psychology of learning and memory. Recall that some memories, such as those underlying motor skills, are formed gradually. Others are formed in a single exposure, such as those relating to a traumatic incident. Consider also the staggering differences in the rate of apparent loss of memory. Some memories are very fragile, being lost in seconds if they are not rehearsed. Others are durable over a lifetime. As physical bases, what kind of changes in neurons and their interactions might give rise to these different properties of memory?

The extremes of fragility and durability of memory have led researchers to suggest that memories are encoded in at least two different forms, which provides the organizing theme of this section:

1 Patterns of activity in networks of neurons.

2 The strength of connections between neurons.

These are not necessarily entirely distinct forms of storage; the same networks that are active as a temporary store might have their connections strengthened as the more permanent store.

Consider first a procedural memory. Learning a skill appears to correspond to a gradual change in the strength of connection between particular neurons. For example, learning to use chopsticks corresponds to strengthening of successful connections, i.e. those directing the bean-curd to the mouth, and weakening of connections that lead it to falling into your lap. However, there are also instances of where memory seems first to be encoded in a form other than as a change in strength of connections between neurons, as follows.

Consider a declarative memory, e.g. that formed by hearing a person's name for the first time. This is encoded immediately in short-term memory and in a form that can easily be lost. With repetition of exposure to the name or rehearsal, it comes to be relatively stable in long-term memory. An assumption is that such short-term and fragile memories are first encoded as patterns of activity within populations of neurons, most likely in the hippocampus or cortex. The hippocampus appears to be involved in maintaining the activity of a temporary store and consolidating it in the cortex (Meeter and Murre, 2004). Consolidation of memory with time and repetition is believed to correspond to a transfer of memory from this fragile form to a more durable form. Durable long-term memories are thought to be encoded in changes in the *structure* of connections between neurons in the cortex.

We will now look in more detail at these ways of holding information.

Changes in activity

By means of a change in frequency of action potentials, how might a circuit of neurons encode a memory? See Figure 11.20. A stimulus (A) sets up a cycle ('reverberation') of activity in a circuit of neurons 1–3 (pattern A). Stimulus B sets up a reverberation in a different circuit (B) and stimulus C activates circuit C. There is consistent mapping between different stimuli and different patterns of neural activity. This is a necessary condition in order to consider neural activity to embody memory.

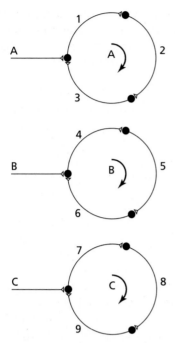

Figure 11.20 Neurons forming the physical basis of memory.

Another necessary condition is that activity can be triggered, even in the absence of the stimulus that is encoded by, for example, associated stimuli or an attempt to recall a specific memory.

It is generally assumed that particular sets of neurons are active at the time a memory is formed and the same set is activated when the memory is later revived (Mishkin, 1982). For example, neural systems within the inferior temporal cortex are known to be activated by visual patterns (Chapter 8) and are believed to play a role in encoding visual memories of the same patterns (Mishkin, 1982).

The assumption is that memory is translated from the more transient and fragile form of patterns of activity to the more durable form of structural changes in connections between neurons, the topic of the next section.

Structural changes

Structural changes might either immediately encode a memory, as in certain forms of procedural learning of a skill, or occur only as a result of activity in patterns of neurons that form a temporary store. The latter corresponds to consolidation.

The Hebb synapse

Hebb (1949) proposed that memory consolidation consists of structural change at one or more synapses (Chapter 3). A synapse exhibiting such a change is termed a 'Hebb synapse'. Differences of opinion concern

whether changes at synapses encoding a memory are local to a part of the brain or distributed widely.

What happens at the synapse as it changes strength with learning? For classical conditioning of salivation, Figure 3.15 (p. 62) suggested that, accompanying the exposure to the paired bell and food, there is increased *efficacy* at certain synapses. Transformation of the neutral stimulus into the conditional stimulus is based on such a change.

Presumably, there are chemical changes such as increased synthesis of neurotransmitter at the terminal of the presynaptic neuron or growth of new receptors at the postsynaptic membrane, or both. At this scale, researchers perform detailed biochemical analysis of the events that accompany learning and memory formation.

Changes at synapses, such as growth of dendritic spines (Chapter 4), accompany learning (Hosokawa *et al.*, 1995) (Figure 11.21). These changes might be the same as occur during early development (Chapter 6). What would distinguish one set of such changes as a possible basis of memory is a correlation of physical change with the learning experience and meeting a number of other conditions, described shortly.

Consider the case where memory is first encoded by patterns of activity. This is fragile and transient. How might it become consolidated into durable structural changes? One proposal is that those synaptic links that are activated in the dynamic phase become strengthened by use.

Consolidation – static or dynamic?

Traditionally, it was believed that, after consolidation, the memory is fixed more-or-less permanently in the form of new connections between neurons. However, this is at odds with the observation that memory can

(a)   (b)

Figure 11.21 Suggested changes at a synapse involving a dendritic spine and which accompany learning: (a) prior to and (b) after learning.

Source: based on Hosokawa *et al.* (1995, Fig. 10, p. 5570).

exhibit a reconstructive and dynamic feature (Nader, 2003). For example, people distort ('confabulate') memory and recalling a story is known to introduce creative shifts of the narrative.

Biologically orientated research has found a possible basis for this effect (Lewis, 1979). Even apparently well-consolidated memories can be disrupted at a time when they are reactivated. Electric shock to the brain can disrupt an old memory if given when this memory is in an active state. Of course, we do not normally go around getting electric shocks to our brain, leading to distortions of memory. However, more subtle triggers to disruption might normally be present. Indeed, there might even be a lifelong process of reconsolidation of memory; memory is reconsolidated after each activation (Nader, 2003). So, in this view, what was considered to be a stable lifelong feature of our cognition is really a constantly dynamic process.

Could this be exploited to get rid of those memories that people would prefer to be without, e.g. intrusive obsessive thoughts? Just reactivate the unwanted memory and then try to trigger the biological equivalent of pressing a computer's delete button, such as giving an electric shock to the brain. Theorists are working on such ideas (Nader, 2003).

The next section gives examples of structural change that underlies memory.

Plasticity in *Aplysia*

Cellular basis of habituation

In the marine snail *Aplysia californica*, if a tactile stimulus is repeated with no harmful consequence, habituation occurs, as shown in Figure 11.1 (repeated as the first part of Figure 11.22). What is the cellular change that forms the basis of this simple form of learning (Kandel, 1991)? See Figure 11.23. Note the pathway

linking the siphon skin, sensory neuron with its tip at skin, interneuron and motor neuron to the gill. A tactile stimulus excites the sensory neuron that has its tip at the siphon skin, which in turn excites the interneuron, and so on.

Action potentials, arising at the sensory neuron, travel the length of this neuron and release transmitter from the terminal. As habituation proceeds, so there is a decline in the amount of transmitter that is released. This draws attention to changes at the terminal. The basis of the change in transmitter release appears to be a change in properties of calcium channels in the membrane. When an action potential arrives at the terminal, it causes calcium to enter the neuron and trigger the release of transmitter (Chapter 4). If the calcium channels partly close, this lowers the amount of transmitter that is released. So, the durable embodiment of this memory lies in the closure of calcium channels.

Such changes can last for minutes, a form of STM, or even several weeks, a type of LTM. They underlie habituation in a number of species. The changes concern synapses involved in a motor response; they are not dedicated only to memory storage.

Cellular basis of sensitization

Another behavioural phenomenon illustrating plasticity is sensitization (Kandel, 1976). Suppose that a noxious stimulus is applied to *Aplysia*. After this, the animal tends to respond more strongly even to harmless stimuli. Sensitization makes adaptive sense; a context of noxious stimulation is probably a dangerous one, in which it could be of value to be prepared to react

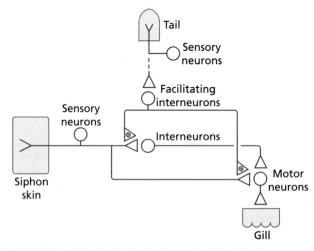

Figure 11.23 Suggested neural system underlying habituation and sensitization, showing representative neurons.

Source: Kandel and Jessell (1991) *Principles of Neuroscience*, 3rd edition, Fig. 65.3, p. 1013, reprinted by permission of The McGraw-Hill Companies, Inc.

Figure 11.22 Habituation and dishabituation in *Aplysia*. On one occasion, between the 18th and 21st presentation of the harmless test stimulus, another stimulus (a strong tactile stimulus to the neck) was given.

Source: Kandel (1976, Fig. 12-1, B-2, p. 543).

strongly in a defensive mode. A particular manifestation of sensitization is **dishabituation**: an increase in strength of a response that had previously been habituated (Figure 11.22).

Figure 11.23 shows the neural connections that appear to underlie both habituation and sensitization. The latter involves 'facilitating interneurons'. Note the axo-axonal synapses (Chapter 4) that the facilitating interneuron makes on the terminals of the sensory neuron that is part of the link from siphon skin to motor neuron. Suppose that a single noxious stimulus is applied to, say, the tail of *Aplysia*. This triggers action potentials in the sensory neuron with its tip at the tail, which triggers activity in the facilitating interneuron. Action potentials arriving at the terminals of the facilitating interneuron sensitize the synapses that the sensory neuron from the siphon skin forms with the motor neuron and interneuron. At some synapses, the chemical released by the facilitating interneuron is serotonin. It facilitates the entry of calcium into the neuron terminal at the arrival of an action potential and makes synapses more sensitive. These are the opposite effects to those that form the basis of habituation. (These links do not permit a stimulus at the tail to trigger a motor response by the gill.) Following sensitization, when the sensory neuron at the siphon skin is triggered, more neurotransmitter is released from its terminals. This is the basis of the increased response indicative of sensitization.

After discovering neural connections in *Aplysia*, researchers might be able to extend the approach to vertebrates. However, caution is in order. *Aplysia* has a relatively simple nervous system with some large and clearly identified neurons. There is controversy as to whether principles developed from *Aplysia* can be generalized to vertebrates, the topic of the next section.

Protein synthesis

Introduction

Even using a vertebrate, it is possible to investigate whether changes in structure occur at the time a memory is formed. First, a brief digression sets the research into its theoretical context, for which an analogy helps (Rose, 1992).

Imagine that the structure of the body is like a house designed by an eccentric architect. Every few minutes the builder takes out a brick from the house and breaks it up. The builder then puts in a new brick in place of the old one. The house retains its original shape, even though the actual ingredients are constantly changing. Over time, the rate at which bricks are removed and added is equal, so there is no net brick addition. The architect then decides to add a porch. During its construction, there is a net addition of bricks to the house.

By analogy, the body is constructed of proteins, which are constantly being broken down and replaced. However, a given body still looks like the same you or me of last week. The overall form remains the same but the precise components change. The assumption is that memory involves the formation of some new synapses or reinforcement of existing ones. Since these are constructed from proteins, it might be possible to detect increased protein synthesis in brain regions following learning.

Bricks are made of component substances and so are proteins. Synthesis of proteins requires a supply of simpler substances normally obtained in the diet. If one of these is labelled radioactively and injected, it will also tend to be incorporated into proteins. If a brain region is showing a high rate of protein synthesis, it should later show a relatively high content of radioactively labelled material. This seemingly needle-in-haystack search is the theoretical rationale behind Rose's studies, described next.

Passive avoidance learning

To study changes in the brain, it would be good to find a memory that is formed in a short time, ideally, in a single experience. There are examples of such memories. One is imprinting (Chapter 6). A better example for establishing the cellular basis of memory is one-trial **passive avoidance** learning in chicks (young domestic chickens). Passive avoidance involves learning *not* to do something that is followed by noxious consequences. Exposure to the situation is very rapid and the formation of memory can be studied in the period immediately following the experience. Passive avoidance will be employed here to illustrate more general principles (Rose, 1992).

Chicks tend to peck at small objects but, if the experience is noxious, they tend to avoid the object in the future. Chicks are offered a small white bead that is attached to the end of a wire. For one group ('experimentals'), the bead is coated with a noxious (bitter) tasting substance, methylanthranilate. For the controls, it is simply coated with water. On tasting the substance, the experimentals shake their heads and wipe their bills. The bead appears to taste disgusting. The controls show no such reaction.

The index of learning is that experimentals tend to avoid the bead in the future, whereas controls have no hesitation in pecking it. Where is the change in physical structure, the memory, corresponding to such learning? Just after the training trial, chicks can be injected with a radioactive substance, e.g. fucose, a sugar, that is used in the synthesis of the structure of neurons. Suppose that memory is stored as a change in this structure. More radioactive sugar would be incorporated into the brain of the chick that learns than into that of the control. Later, the quantity of radioactive substance in the brains of the two groups is compared. Experimentals have a higher level than controls.

How can one be sure that the change following learning is the physical embodiment of memory? The chick learns and the change occurs, but this might just be correlation. What are the criteria of memory?

Criteria of memory

Rose (1992) proposed criteria that need to be met for a change to qualify as the embodiment of memory; five of these are as follows:

1 There must be a physical change at a location in the brain. This will probably be an increase in synaptic structure but in principle it might be a loss of some synapses.

2 Other factors that accompany learning (e.g. arousal or stress) must be ruled out as causes of the change in structure.

3 If structural changes are prevented from happening, memory should not be formed. Injection of chemicals that inhibit protein synthesis should prevent learning.

4 A lesion to the site of memory should disrupt its expression in behaviour. (This raises the issue of whether a particular memory is localized to one site or distributed over many regions.)

5 The neurons at the site of proposed memory formation should show altered electrical characteristics.

Criteria (1)–(5) above were met in the case of the learning of passive avoidance. Thus, the proposal that changes forming the physical base of memory occur in particular brain areas was supported. More specifically, there is a growth in the number of dendritic spines (Chapter 4) in certain areas, suggesting the formation of new synaptic connections.

Long-term potentiation

Bliss and Lømo (1973) discovered a phenomenon termed **long-term potentiation** (LTP), exhibited at excitatory synapses in mammals. Suppose that a *presynaptic* neuron is active at a high frequency but for only a short time. For certain neurons, Bliss and Lømo found that this exposure caused a change in the reactivity of the *postsynaptic* neuron that lasted for hours or even days. In other words, presynaptic activity caused a 'long-term potentiation' of the ability of the postsynaptic neuron to be excited. Use of a synapse strengthened its efficacy, something anticipated by Hebb (see earlier). Could this be the long-sought-after basis of plasticity in the mammalian nervous system? What was responsible for the change at the synapse underlying this effect?

The neurotransmitter glutamate acts at several receptor types on postsynaptic membranes. Two of these are particularly important in LTP: the AMPA and the NMDA receptors (Martin *et al.*, 2000) (Figure 11.24). One theory is that AMPA receptors 'hide' inside the neuron (Figure 11.24(a)). Occupation of NMDA receptors triggers the movement of AMPA receptors to the surface (Figure 11.24(b)). When they are at the surface, the receptivity of the postsynaptic membrane to glutamate is increased and this is the basis of LTP. There is evidence for the presence of AMPA receptors below the surface of the postsynaptic membrane.

At one level of analysis, LTP might be the biological basis of long-term memory (Collingridge, 1997). This would suggest that in some cases LTP can remain for a lifetime. A given memory would probably be encoded by LTP at a number of synapses distributed throughout the brain. Forgetting might consist of a loss of such potentiation.

Figure 11.24 Long-term potentiation: (a) before activity in presynaptic neuron, (b) activity in presynaptic neuron and (c) after LTP. *Source:* after Collingridge (1997, Fig. 2).

Section summary

1 Memory appears to be encoded by changes in activity and structure of neurons.

2 Hebb proposed that the durable physical basis of memory is a change in structure at certain synapses.

3 Corresponding to habituation in *Aplysia*, calcium channels at the presynaptic membrane close and the amount of transmitter released from the sensory neuron decreases. Sensitization corresponds to opening calcium channels at the presynaptic membrane.

4 During passive avoidance learning in chicks, increased levels of protein synthesis occur.

5 Activity in a presynaptic neuron can cause long-term potentiation in the postsynaptic neuron.

☞ Test your knowledge

11.9 In Figure 11.23, suppose that sensitization is caused by a noxious stimulus to the tail. A given tactile stimulus is applied to the siphon skin before and after the noxious stimulus. In response to the tactile stimulus, in which of the following neurons would increased activity be seen after the noxious stimulus had been applied? (i) The sensory neuron with tip at the siphon skin, (ii) the interneuron, (iii) the motor neuron.

11.10 In Figure 11.24, long-term potentiation could be blocked by injection of which of the following at the time of activity in the presynaptic neuron? (i) A glutamate antagonist, (ii) a specific AMPA antagonist, (iii) a specific NMDA antagonist.

Answers on page 310

Bringing things together

The chapter has described the type of plasticity of the nervous system and behaviour that is termed 'learning and memory'. Several distinct systems of learning and memory exist that serve different roles and reflect different evolutionary pressures.

The adaptive value of non-associative and associative learning is clear. Thus, habituation is a means of conserving energy and Pavlovian conditioning gives the advantage of anticipation. Instrumental conditioning permits an animal to exploit the environment to gain food, water and a mate, etc.

The chapter illustrated the value of considering brain mechanisms and evolutionary/functional types of explanation in parallel. In terms of evolutionary psychology, some distinct systems of learning and memory emerge in evolution since they serve different functional considerations. The problem that procedural memory solves (e.g. gradual accumulation of a motor skill over repeated exposure) is very different from that solved with the help of an episodic memory (e.g. where a particular item of food was stored on a particular occasion). A memory system serving the one could not serve also the other.

 See the video coverage for this chapter and witness some of the most famous studies in the history of psychology.

Summary of Chapter 11

1 Learning refers to a behavioural experience and memory refers to a type of change that occurs as a result of the experience and that encodes information about it.

2 Some simple forms of learning (e.g. habituation) are non-associative, whereas associative learning is exemplified by classical and instrumental conditioning.

3 Different types of memory are characterized by differences in the type of information that is encoded and differences in their durability and vulnerability to disruption.

4 Various brain regions are involved in learning and memory. Different regions are associated with different types of memory and different roles in processing memory, e.g. site of short-term or long-term storage.

5 Seen in evolutionary terms, some differences in types of memory can be linked to the incompatibility in what is required to solve different problems that confront an animal.

6 At a cellular level, it is believed that memory is stored as patterns of activity within sets of neurons and as changes in strength of synaptic connection between neurons.

Further reading

For a more detailed account and one which takes an integrated perspective on learning and memory, see Anderson (2000). For memory as a whole, including biological aspects, see Dudai (2002). For the neuroscience of memory, see Gazzaniga *et al.* (2008). On biology and the classification of memory, see Foster and Jelicic (1999). For different levels of instrumental learning, see Balleine and Dickinson (1998). For working memory, linking the psychology and biology, see Andrade (2002). For episodic memory, see Griffiths *et al.* (1999). For a good review with some emphasis on the role of the hippocampus, see Eichenbaum and Cohen (2001).

11.1   Plasticity
11.2   (i) Classical conditioning, instrumental conditioning (ii) habituation
11.3   (i) neutral stimulus, bell before conditioning; conditional stimulus, bell after conditioning; (ii) neutral stimulus, taste prior to conditioning; conditional stimulus, taste after conditioning.
11.4   Repeat visits to the arm cued by light
11.5   Visit each arm only once
11.6   (i) Procedural, (ii) semantic, (iii) episodic
11.7   (i) Retrograde, (ii) anterograde
11.8   Procedural
11.9   (ii) The interneuron, (iii) the motor neuron
11.10 (i) A glutamate antagonist, (iii) a specific NMDA antagonist

Answers

Explanations for answers to 'test your knowledge' questions can be found on the website www.pearsoned.co.uk/toates

Visit www.pearsoned.co.uk/toates
for a range of resources to support study.
Test yourself with multiple choice questions and access a bank of over 100 videos that will bring the topics to life.

 Interactions and animations relating to topics discussed in this chapter can be found on the website at www.pearsoned.co.uk/toates. These include:

Interaction: Terminology used in classical conditioning
Interaction: The main components of the synaptic junction

Chapter 12
Emotion

Learning outcomes for Chapter 12

After studying this chapter, you should be able to:

1 State what is meant by the term 'emotion' and describe the coordinated role that emotions play in behaviour, physiology, cognition and affective experience.

2 Explain how emotions arise, describe their properties and link this to developmental/learning, functional and evolutionary explanations. Outline the principles of affective neuroscience.

3 Give an account of some representative emotions, highlighting how they meet the criteria of 'emotion'.

4 Present an account of the theory that emotions are triggered by peripheral feedback.

5 Describe some brain regions that form the basis of emotions, while identifying the evidence on which this description is based.

6 Give an account of some neurochemicals involved in emotion and link this to the understanding of interventions to alter emotion.

7 Describe the effects of some specific emotions on cognition, memory and reflexes.

Scene-setting questions

1 In coping with life, do emotions help or hinder?
2 Is there conflict between emotions and rationality?
3 What is the relationship between 'gut-feelings', physiology and behaviour?
4 Why do we blush?
5 Why is it difficult to conquer 'irrational' fears?
6 How well can introspection give insight into the causes of emotion?
7 Why are emotionally coloured memories sometimes particularly durable?
8 Are emotional expressions universal?

Are emotional expressions universal? Explore the video on the website accompanying this book at **www.pearsoned.co.uk/toates**

The facial expression suggests a positive emotion. How does the brain produce emotion? How can we interpret signs of it in others?

Source: PhotoDisc, Inc.

Introduction

Reflect on some experiences that you would describe as 'emotional', characterized as joy, fear, sadness, anger, frustration, etc. What characterizes them as emotions? For example, think of the frustration of turning up on a promising date, only to find that the prospective partner has pulled out. What did it *feel* like? Think of a fearful situation, when your heart pounded strongly and your gut was disturbed and compare that with the experience of anger. Now think of an embarrassing situation when blood rushed to the skin of your face. On a more positive note, can you recall shivers and goose-bumps on hearing a favourite piece of music or on seeing a loved one?

When did someone last identify your emotion by the expression on your face? Can you guess that someone has a problem from their facial expression?

There might be emotionally powerful events that are well etched into your memory – 'I will always remember where I was and how I felt then'. Were you ever in fear and interpreted a harmless situation as a threat? On an automatic level, you might have 'jumped out of your skin' in response to a sudden harmless touch by someone. You have doubtless heard of unfortunate people caught up in a conflict and traumatized for long periods afterwards, with flashbacks to the traumatic events.

Such reflection can identify some features of emotion that are also confirmed by a more scientific study and which form the organizing theme of Chapter 12, as follows.

1 An emotion plays a role in controlling behaviour. For example, fear can lead us to try to escape from a situation, anger to assert our rights. Emotions favour

some actions and counter others (e.g. fear inhibits feeding) (Oatley and Jenkins, 1996). In joy, we are likely to reach out to others. You have some freedom in what you do in response to an emotion. In a state of strong fear, you might run, hide or call the police but you are not likely to start cooking. From an evolutionary perspective, we can see emotions' advantage to fitness – for example, by fleeing in response to danger, we tend to survive.

2 The strength of reflexes can be altered by an emotion, e.g. being in fear and 'jumping out of our skin' in response to even a harmless sudden stimulus.

3 By means of the autonomic nervous system, emotions play a role in controlling the activity of the body's physiology. The body's reactions, e.g. those of the circulation and gut, are different in fear from those in joy. Emotions *coordinate* behaviour and physiology (e.g. in fear, running is associated with heart-rate acceleration) (Hess, 1981).

4 Each emotion involves a subjective conscious experience ('experiential factor'). There is a characteristic feeling of being afraid and this is very different from that of joy or embarrassment. Emotions are characterized by pleasure and pain, termed 'affect' (Chapter 2). We want to repeat those situations associated with positive affect, whereas we try to avoid those of negative affect.

5 Emotions influence the brain's information processing (Windmann and Krüger, 1998), e.g. how the brain interprets information and its focus of attention. They play a role in memory. Events associated with strong emotions are likely to be stored well in memory and often surface regularly.

6 An emotion can trigger a few stereotyped muscular patterns, for example, those controlling the human face, thereby revealing emotion (Ekman, 1992).

Figure 12.1 summarizes the role of emotion. Different stimuli, S_1, S_2, S_3..., trigger a particular emotion. In turn, the emotion organizes a number of functionally coherent effects: on behaviour, physiology ('autonomic'), sensory processing, enhancing memory for the events, reflexes and affective states ('subjective').

Looking broadly across species, in a particular emotional state, animals have a *tendency* to behave in certain ways, e.g. in fear, to freeze or flee. According to the

Figure 12.1 Any of a number of stimuli, S_1, S_2,..., trigger an emotion, which has the coordinated effects shown.

emotion, there is a set of highly probable outputs of somatic and autonomic nervous systems (Hess, 1981).

Anger or fear (e.g. running from a charging bull) activates the sympathetic branch of the autonomic nervous system (ANS) (Chapter 3). The terms 'emotion' and 'emotional arousal' are often used synonymously with 'sympathetic activation'. However, there can be situations termed 'emotional' in which the parasympathetic branch is activated (Vingerhoets, 1985). The latter occur where the animal remains immobile, e.g. faced by a predator or in submitting to a dominant animal. In a rather different state, relaxation is associated with reduced sympathetic and increased parasympathetic activity. The heart beats less energetically and blood is conveyed to the gut to facilitate digestion and absorption.

The effects of emotion on cognition are manifest in changes in perception and memory. The subjective aspect of emotions cannot be measured directly, though facial reactions are strongly indicative of it. By definition, only the person experiencing emotion can give a verbal report of a subjective state. However, we make guesses of subjective state based upon empathy with fellow humans and might extrapolate that the cry of an animal in pain is an effective communication of subjective state.

The sections that follow will describe and link the aspects to emotion: (i) behavioural, (ii) physiological, (iii) cognitive and (iv) subjective/affective.

Section summary

1 Emotion has functionally coherent effects on behaviour, physiology, cognition and subjective affect.

2 Emotions play a role in favouring certain courses of action.

3 Particular emotions trigger some stereotyped reactions, e.g. human facial reactions.

4 Emotion and emotional arousal usually mean activation of the sympathetic system.

 ## Test your knowledge

12.1 Complete the following: 'Embarrassment is associated with the ___ of blood vessels just under the skin. The smooth muscles that line the walls of the blood vessels are under the control of the ___ nervous system'.

 Answers on page 339   WEB

The nature and function of emotion

This section considers what emotions are, their triggers and expression. It shows how a parallel consideration of causation, development/learning, evolution and function can increase understanding of emotion.

Linking causation, function and evolution

Emotions have an influence on a range of processes, from voluntary behaviour to reflexes. This section considers some points on this range and the associated functional significance.

A limited flexibility under pressure

Imagine you confront the same bear in the forest, as in Chapter 3. From the perspective of survival, the bear needs to command your undivided attention, to be at the 'spotlight of conscious awareness' (Baars, 1997). Other potential demands that are less urgent (e.g. seeking food) can be put off until later. You have never seen a bear before. So what do you do? Do you search your memory for a rational solution, trying to remember earlier encounters with large objects and carefully weighing up the possibilities for action? Most probably not, since time is too pressing.

The emotion of fear automatically gives priority to certain options and acts against others (Tooby and Cosmides, 1990). For example, you might instantly flee or freeze. The nervous system appears to be programmed to react with fear to any large moving object (cf. Damasio, 1996). Our ancestors were confronted by large menacing animals and this suggests an evolutionary history for the reaction.

Suppose that you decide to run to a tree. Skeletal muscles need energy and oxygen. Fear triggers sympathetic activation, which increases the muscles' blood supply. Note the functional significance: fear exerts compatible influences over behaviour and physiology. Given time and a safe distance, declarative memories of past fear-related situations might be revived and brought to conscious awareness, with possible solutions suggested.

There are two cautions that need to be made here. The first is that our evolutionary heritage cannot tell us exactly what to do in a situation. It can only favour some options over others. The second is that a favoured option might turn out to be a mistake – after all, bears can run fast and climb trees! Emotions create tendencies to do what, on average, succeeded in our evolutionary past.

Tightly organized muscular reactions

An emotion creates a strong tendency to behave in limited ways but with some flexibility in what is actually done. However, it also triggers some relatively fixed and inflexible reactions. This principle applies to a few specialized cases in numerous species: emotions exert control over rather stereotyped patterns of neuromuscular activity. Psychologists assume that, where showing specific reactions has been successful in evolution, the underlying controls will be hard-wired in the CNS. This is an economic way of solving a problem.

We noted earlier the case of the human facial muscles and their control by emotion. For another example, Darwin (1872/1934) observed the principle of 'antithesis': a dog's posture in one emotion (e.g. anger) can be the opposite of that in an opposed emotion (e.g. joy) (Figure 12.2). This is an effective and unambiguous

Figure 12.2 Two opposite emotions and associated reactions: (a) hostility and (b) as Darwin described it, 'a humble and affectionate frame of mind'.

Source: Darwin (1872/1934, Figs. 1 and 2, pp. 1 and 15).

means of communication between dogs – and incidentally from dog to human! A similar principle of hard-wiring is illustrated by the calls made by a number of species. These are stereotyped and enable emotional states to be discriminated, e.g. for social species, the distress call at separation is distinct from the call of comfort at reunion with a parent (Kalin *et al.*, 1995; Panksepp *et al.*, 1978).

Learning, memory and individual experience

Although emotions create some tendencies that are universals, we should not ignore the role of *individual* learning in the production of emotions and their expression. There are universal emotions but learning adjusts both what triggers them and their precise form of expression. For example, being in a place associated with trauma in the past (e.g. the earlier experience of seeing a bear in the forest) can trigger fear (Gray, 1987a). Emotions enhance the formation of memories for the emotion-producing event (Bower, 1992; Herz, 1997). If the representation is tagged as emotional, merely seeing, or thinking about, the forest can affect future decision-making, e.g. it would be advantageous to show caution in the forest or stay away. We might develop a fear of forests. Unfortunately, such a process can lead to irrational fears.

Affective neuroscience

Introduction

The expression **affective neuroscience** refers to a school of neuroscience that forms a focus for the study of emotion. It is associated with Panksepp (1998), who claims that there are systems of emotion and affect that have important common characteristics across mammalian species. Some of these are shared with non-mammals, e.g. birds. Affective neuroscience has also become a banner and rallying call to psychologists (a) to put emotions at 'centre-stage', (b) to see an evolutionary continuity of affect/emotion and (c) to give the study of subjective events a place in psychology. It is a call for *affective* neuroscience to take its place alongside *cognitive* neuroscience (Davidson *et al.*, 2002).

Of course, human and non-human species exhibit such outward manifestations of emotion as attack and escape, accompanied by autonomic changes. However, Panksepp goes further than this and urges a leap across species boundaries in assuming that non-human animals have emotional and affective *experiences* similar to ours. Panksepp (1994, p. 37) suggests that emotions shared by all mammals are: 'anger–rage, anxiety–fear, joy–play–happiness, sorrow–distress, and curiosity'. Anger–rage is suggested by attacking and biting, whereas fear is suggested by freezing and fleeing. Alarm calls of an isolated animal are indicative of sorrow–distress.

Panksepp writes (1994, p. 29):

From the moment of birth, brain emotional systems allow humans to begin operating in the world as spontaneously active organisms with a variety of ingrained values and goals that mould and become moulded by experience.

Neural bases

Panksepp postulates that the basic neural systems that underlie emotions have the following characteristics:

1 They are very similar in structure and function across vertebrate species. They were laid down in subcortical structures early in mammalian evolution and have changed relatively little.

2 They are largely specified by genetic information and are therefore very similar among members of a given species.

3 When different species are compared, it is evident that a given emotion is associated with similar, if not identical, physiological (e.g. hormonal) changes.

4 Different species possess some very different brain structures outside the regions specifically concerned with emotion (e.g. newly evolved cortical structures). There are also vastly different bodies and ecological niches. This means different triggers to emotion and different modes of emotional expression.

5 The potential for affective experience is established by basic brain regions, though how that potential is channelled depends on individual experience.

Some evidence derives from electrical stimulation of subcortical regions of non-humans. Interpretations are reinforced by the effects of chemical manipulations, which excite or inhibit emotional expression. Homologous structures exist in humans and it seems reasonable that they serve a similar function. Damage to some brain regions leaves the capacity to perceive a stimulus intact but disrupts the capacity to attach emotional significance to it (Le Doux, 1998), hence producing an (albeit tentative and grey) line of fracture between emotion and cognition. Conversely, emotion appears to survive lesions to other regions (e.g. newly evolved regions of cortex), which disrupt cognition (Le Doux, 1998).

Panksepp (1994, p. 45) suggests the following criteria for defining neural systems of emotion:

1 The underlying circuits respond unconditionally to stimuli arising from major life-challenging circumstances. For example, we do not need to learn to fear certain events. The system is formed so as to react to life-threatening triggers.

2 The circuits organize those forms of behaviour (and concurrent autonomic-hormonal changes) that have proved adaptive in the face of such life-challenging circumstances during the evolutionary history of the species.

3 Emotive circuits change the sensitivities of sensory systems relevant for the behaviour sequences that have been aroused.

4 Neural activity of emotive systems outlasts the triggering circumstances. Suppose that a trigger to fear (e.g. predator) appears and then goes out of sight. The fear does not fall immediately but persists.

5 Emotive circuits can come under the conditional control of emotionally neutral environmental stimuli. Neutral stimuli paired with unconditional triggers become conditional triggers to emotion.

6 Emotive circuits have reciprocal interactions with brain mechanisms that elaborate higher decision-making processes and consciousness.

Panksepp suggests that raw affective experience is critically dependent on the activity of a collection of distributed brain systems. Of course, the cognitive side of emotion can be very different comparing, say, humans and mice. Language presumably gives us a much wider experience of emotion, e.g. based upon mental reflection. However, at base when comparing mammalian species, Panksepp suggests that we can identify common features of brain mechanisms and their expression. Although there are differences among species in emotional expression, there are also some striking similarities in function, which also encourages a search for similar underlying processes (Le Doux, 1998). For example, although a deer might run, a fish swim and a bird fly from danger, at a level of function each different motor response serves the same end of distancing from danger (Plutchik, 1980). Similarly, the adaptive advantage of freezing with fear would seem to pose similar design considerations across species.

Subjective experience

Identifying the properties of conscious states can help the search for underlying neural systems (Panksepp, 1994). For example, emotions, as subjectively felt, commonly linger for a long time after the triggering event has terminated and, presumably, there is neural activity that lasts the same time.

In treating and studying schizophrenic and cancer patients, Heath (1986) obtained correlations between stimulated electrical activity in brain regions (septum and regions of the amygdala) and the patient's report of pleasure. Correlated changes in electrical activity and subjective report followed a manipulation such as the administration of drugs. The pain of cancer was reduced by stimulating the so-called pleasure regions of the brain (Chapter 15). Other brain regions, including parts of the amygdala, are associated with negative affect when stimulated.

A subjectively described emotion that causes distress in modern society is anxiety, an ill-defined free-floating fear of events that might happen (Ramos and Mormède, 1998). Sometimes it takes the form of existential angst (fear of existence and a perceived meaningless life) and we only have insight from verbal reports of sufferers. However, by adopting a comparative perspective, there are a number of animal models that might represent features of human anxiety. For example, an anxiety-evoking situation for rats is the elevated maze (a maze located some distance off the ground). A rat is placed on an elevated plus-maze, having two open and two closed arms, and its reluctance to go out onto the open arms is a measure of anxiety.

Biological determination or cultural relativity?

Evolution and Darwin

Darwin (1872/1934) emphasized the role of emotions in evolution. He believed that emotions continue to be useful in humans (p. 171): 'Expression in itself, or the language of the emotions, is certainly of importance for the welfare of mankind'. However, Darwin's reader is left to speculate whether some human emotion is still useful, or is it so in a different way from the advantage it served in earlier evolution. Adaptive value might have changed in the course of evolution, a form of 'inertia'. An example is that of baring the teeth by angry humans (see Griffiths, 1997). Darwin speculated that originally this was a preliminary to attack, for which the teeth were employed. Now it forms part of the facial signal of anger.

Public display of emotion is sometimes said to be irrational and people are urged not to be emotional. This assumes conflict between emotions and rational cognition. On occasion we react in response to *gut*-feelings (note the expression) and later regret it. However, the fact that we sometimes get it wrong does not argue against a value of emotions. Emotion and cognition normally operate as an integrated whole, with emotion exerting an influence on decision-making. In this way, some appropriate consideration is usually made of the likely affective consequences of an action (Damasio, 1996).

Darwin classified the expressions of emotion in various species including humans. He also made cross-cultural comparisons to explore whether emotions are universal or culturally relative, finding that widely different cultures show much the same emotions. For example, the triggers to, say, disgust cause similar facial reactions across cultures. These are also observed in blind people, who have not had the opportunity to learn by imitation.

Social constructivism

Are human emotions biologically determined universals, as Darwin believed, or culturally relative constructions? Focusing on the diversity of emotional expression in different cultures, rather than its consistency, **social constructivism** suggests that emotions are culturally relative. For example, they might be reactions that are imitations of culture-specific role models. Particular emotions might be reinforced by a particular society. This is sometimes couched as being in opposition to biological determination. In a given situation, some cultures would find emotional reactivity appropriate whereas others would discourage it. For example, within Europe, continentals commonly find amusement at the apparent coolness of the English (Darwin, 1872/1934, p. 134). Is it then unrealistic to seek universal biological underpinnings?

In confronting what is often presented as a neat dichotomy between biology and culture, caution is needed. Inevitably, biology and culture each have a role to play in emotional development. So, any dichotomy of biology versus culture is surely false. A further complication is that similarities in behaviour within a species can owe as much to universal features of environments as to similar genetic contributions.

A point concerns the aspect of emotion that is being compared. Is it emotional expression or the cognitive triggers of emotion? There appear to be just a few emotions that are common across cultures and even species but, within certain limits, different culture-specific stimuli trigger them (Panksepp, 1998). Griffiths (1997, p. 55) noted that studies by Ekman: 'show that people in all cultures respond in a similar way to things that frighten them. They do not show that people in all cultures respond in a similar way to the same things'.

On a spectrum of universality versus relativity, the safest location is somewhere between the extremes. Let's assume a few universal brain structures that organize a small number of basic emotions located under the broad headings of positive/approach and negative/withdrawal (Panksepp, 1994). These structures show evolutionary continuities across species and similarities between individuals. There appear to be some universal triggers of emotion (e.g. fear to large moving animals or falling), panic and depression to the loss of a loved one. They are manifest in behaviour early in development, such as anger and frustration at being thwarted in reaching for an object (see Griffiths, 1997).

There are also culture-specific aspects to triggers. The way in which emotions are triggered and expressed can differ to some extent between cultures and individuals, as a function of imitation and reinforcement, etc. (Cacioppo *et al.*, 1992). Humans learn the cultural norms of emotional expression. Presumably, there is a two-way flow of information, from the brain mechanism underlying emotion to its culturally coloured expression and also from the culture-specific environment to the basic emotion.

Cultural relativity can be applied to the public expression of universal emotions, something Ekman (1984) terms **display rules**. Thus, people from Japan exhibit similar reactions to those of Americans when they are alone but suppress emotional expression in the presence of an experimenter. Voluntary controls that enable expression to be suppressed would seem a likely candidate for cultural relativity and individual differences (Cacioppo *et al.*, 1992).

The development of emotion in non-human animals is also dependent to some extent on the environment (Griffiths, 1997). Monkeys that have been socially deprived exhibit fear but the reaction is less easily interpreted by other monkeys than is the fear reaction of an animal that experienced a normal social development (Miller *et al.*, 1967). In dogs, normal development of the experience of pain and avoidance of damaging stimuli depends upon social factors (Melzack and Scott, 1957).

Stimuli and their appraisal

Some triggers to emotion can be understood in terms of their *intrinsic physical properties*, e.g. a loud explosion. Contrast this with the fear that you would feel if you calculated your income and outgoings, finding that your accounts did not balance. Such emotion is triggered only after sophisticated *cognitive processing* of external events.

Scientific evidence confirms that emotions are triggered by both raw sensory features and the interpretation placed upon sensory events (Lazarus, 1984). Some emotions are primitive, rapid responses to situations and can bypass cognition (Zajonc, 1980). For example, by their intrinsic quality, certain odours elicit positive and negative emotions (Alaoui-Ismaïli *et al.*, 1997). In many species, only basic processing is needed for the fear that is triggered by snakes (Le Doux, 1989).

The term 'cognition' can be used to refer to the 'high-level', longer and slower route by which emotion is produced. There is an interpretation (which might, or might not, correspond to reality) before emotion is experienced. An important aspect of therapy for such disorders as anxiety (Salkovskis, 1985) and coronary heart disease (Allan and Scheidt, 1996a) is getting patients to *interpret* emotionally sensitive events in less threatening ways.

In humans, the triggers for emotion appear to vary on a continuum from (i) stimuli as such that act directly and automatically to (ii) cognitive interpretations of stimuli, involving goals and the perception of the intentions of others, etc. (Johnson and Multhaup, 1992; Stein and Jewett, 1986). Evolutionary considerations suggest the retention of a quick and effective emotional system.

Unconscious determinants

Reflecting a rapid route to emotion, there can be triggers that do not reach conscious awareness. See Figure 12.3 (Winkielman *et al.*, 2005). Participants were set the task of deciding the gender of a person presented in an image for 400 ms ('gender identification'). They were then asked to pour, consume and assess a drink. Prior to the gender identification task, they were presented with subliminal images (i.e. images that failed to reach conscious awareness). The images ('subliminal emotion') were of happy, neutral or angry faces and were presented for 16 ms. The subliminal images affected the amount of drink poured and consumed (Figure 12.4).

Claparède's patient, Madame X (Chapter 11), illustrated a similar point. She showed fear in her behaviour but could not consciously recall the episode that triggered the fear (the hidden pin in the hand).

Consciousness seems so immediate and pressing and indeed we often have conscious insight into the determinants of our emotion. However, we sometimes assume that it provides a privileged and infallible route, but this may not always be so (Bauer and Verfaellie, 1992).

Social interaction

Emotion plays a central role in social interactions between animals both during development and when adult. Consider an infant rat that gets isolated. Its vocalizations indicate negative emotion (Panksepp, 1994). They alert the mother to the pup's state and location and they facilitate retrieval.

The sound and facial expression of a human baby crying indicate negative emotion. The baby persists until a caregiver takes corrective action, e.g. feeding or bringing a source of warmth. For the very young baby, one does not need to postulate awareness of intentions or goals; emotions organize reactions automatically. In mothers, the recorded sound of a baby's cry triggers activation in brain regions concerned with emotional processing (Lorberbaum *et al.*, 2002). This is associated with subjective emotions of sadness, anxiety and an urge to help. On the more positive side, an infant's smile can evoke emotions of approach.

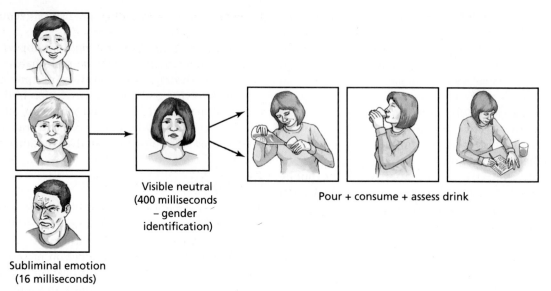

Figure 12.3 Experimental design employed by Winkielman *et al.* (2005).
Source: Toates (2004, Fig. 1.2, page 5).

In their social interaction, there appear to be mutual reward and positive reinforcement between child and caregiver (Tronick, 1989). Emotional expression forms an important part of the behavioural interaction. From this beginning, the child's capacity to exert social control emerges (Chorpita and Barlow, 1998). Such infant emotions, together with the action they help to trigger and their consequences, develop into voluntary action.

Emotions play a role in interactions between adult social animals, as in triggering vocal signals and in interpreting them. In some species, e.g. squirrel monkeys (Ploog, 1986), vocalizations are specific to different emotions. In humans, vocalization has, of course, obtained some autonomy from emotions, though it can still sometimes be a good index of them.

In humans, emotions are associated with characteristic facial reactions as part of a 'package'. Meeting a new person (or even a new dog!), whom we perceive to be of good intention, is accompanied by positive emotion, involving approach, eye contact and smiling. The same solution can be employed on numerous occasions. We decipher signals emitted by others. Seeing that another has an expression of disapproval does not tell us exactly what to expect but it reduces the possibilities.

Emotions have a privileged route to the motor control programmes that underlie facial expression and are central to social interaction (Ekman *et al.*, 1983). They are not the only route: we have some voluntary conscious control over our expressions. However, this is limited. It is difficult to fake facial expressions by will-power, something politicians and bad actors need to learn (Damasio, 1996).

We now look at a few examples of particular emotions, illustrating in more detail some of the points made so far.

Figure 12.4 Results obtained by Winkielman *et al.* (2005).
Source: Toates (2004, Fig. 1.3, page 5).

Some emotions and their triggers

This section looks at some emotions: fear, the anger associated with frustration, shame/embarrassment, trust and social attachment.

Fear

A range of events triggers fear, some of them evident on first exposure and others reflecting learned experience. This section considers a part of this range.

A special adaptation

Certain stimuli trigger intense fear in humans, a notable example being snakes (Öhman and Mineka, 2003).

A number of species, including other primates, also show fear of snakes and it appears to reflect an ancient evolutionary adaptation. Not only do most humans show strong fear, but we form aversive conditional associations with snakes more rapidly than with control stimuli.

Le Doux (1989) considers the reaction to the image of a snake at the eyes. An immediate automatic response is withdrawal of one's body from a snake on the path just under the feet. In a quite different context, your cognitions (p. 272): 'determine that a snake is a vertebrate, that it is biologically closer to an alligator than to a cow . . . '. The reasoning is done at a safe distance, say in a zoo. It involves semantic associations and consciousness and does not necessarily lead to any emotion or behaviour.

Consider the two following claims:

1 If the fear of snakes is evolutionarily old, it might not require conscious awareness for its expression.

2 Unconscious emotional organization is usually assumed to be mediated by subcortical mechanisms (Öhman and Mineka, 2003).

To illuminate these claims, the technique of backward masking was employed. A brief visual 'test' stimulus of a snake image (duration 30 ms) was presented, followed

Evolutionary psychology

A fear module

Öhman and Mineka (2001, 2003) propose a fear module that is specially tuned to the most common dangers that were present throughout mammalian evolution. Thus, we tend to fear snakes and spiders far more than guns and cars. This is in spite of the fact that the latter present a vastly greater threat in industrialized societies.

Öhman and Mineka suggest that the module is fast and automatic and it has dedicated neural processes as its basis, centred on the amygdala. The module is encapsulated ('self-contained') in that it is influenced little, if at all, by advanced human conscious cognition. For example, people suffering from phobias usually acknowledge that their fears are irrational and excessive but such conscious insight does little to calm them (Mineka and Öhman, 2002). (Of course, certain TV naturalists make their living by handling deadly snakes. Such people are either fear-deficient or able to exert considerable inhibition on any fear module.) It is not merely snakes that are able to trigger the module. In primates including humans, threatening faces also have easy access to it.

immediately by a masking stimulus. The masking stimulus is known to disrupt cortical processing of the test stimulus. Participants could not consciously perceive the test stimulus. Nonetheless, those of them who expressed a fear of snakes showed an enhanced skin conductance response (a measure of autonomic activity) to the unconsciously processed snake images.

Unconditional and conditional stimuli

A number of stimuli elicit fear on first presentation. For example, a rat does not have to learn how to freeze based upon trauma (Bolles, 1970). On first confrontation with a predator (e.g. a cat) and where escape is impossible, rats freeze, a species-specific defence reaction (SSDR).

Neutral stimuli paired with unconditional emotional stimuli acquire a conditional capacity to evoke emotion. For example, exposure of rats to the hair from a cat immediately reduces play, as they assume a fearful posture (Panksepp, 1998). Subsequently, rats show fear in the cage (a conditional fear) even though all signs of cat have been eliminated. This biases behaviour towards vigilance and caution, and away from play.

For another example, pairing a bell with a shock (UCS) gives the bell a fear-evoking property as a CS. Such fear conditioning is possible across various animal groups, including snails, birds, lizards, fish, rabbits, rats, monkeys and humans (Le Doux, 1994). This strongly points to its adaptive advantage. In rats, a cue paired with shock disrupts the appetitive behaviour of lever-pressing for food reward, termed a **conditioned emotional response** procedure.

A personal angle

Little Albert

In 1919 in Baltimore, USA, one of psychology's most famous figures, the 11-month-old child 'Little Albert', was subject to fear conditioning by the founder of behaviourism, John Watson (see D. Cohen, 1979). Little Albert was presented with his pet rat (a neutral stimulus) and, at the same time, Watson struck a piece of metal with a hammer just behind Albert's head (unconditional stimulus). Albert later showed fear of the rat (conditional response). History does not know what happened to Little Albert subsequently but we do know the fate of Watson. He was involved in a scandal and forced to leave academia.

Subsequent research has shown that classical conditioning of fear is not quite the simple process envisaged by Watson. Some 'neutral stimuli' are easier to turn into CSs than are others (Öhman, 1986). Little Albert's rat could well have already been a candidate that is strongly biased towards fear-triggering. It is easier to condition elevated levels of anxiety to snake-related 'neutral stimuli', such as pictures of snakes, than to flower-related neutral stimuli (Öhman and Mineka, 2003).

Frustration

Frustration describes the particular quality of the emotion of anger that is triggered when an actual state of the world is less good than an expected and desired state. This is an example of where an emotion can only be understood in terms of a sensory event in context, i.e. reality compared against the expectation. The anger associated with frustration is not a peculiarly human emotion. Rats show such a negative emotion. One way to induce it is to train a rat to earn pellets in a Skinner box and then put it on extinction conditions (omit the pellets). The emotion causes the release of 'stress hormones' and an increased tendency to escape or aggression, depending upon the environment (Gray, 1987a).

Embarrassment, guilt and shame

Embarrassment, guilt and shame can be placed under the heading of 'moral emotions' (Adolphs, 2003). In evolution and development, they emerge later than such 'basic' emotions as fear and anger. This exemplifies

A personal angle

A behaviourist's shame

Even the greatest and apparently most self-confident can suffer from a level of moral emotion that seems malfunctional. Consider B.F. Skinner's reaction of shame (embarrassment?) after speaking to the Royal Society in London at the height of his fame. Skinner feared that he had not acted correctly (e.g. to drink only one offering of sherry!) and had occasionally said the wrong thing (any readers who suffer similarly might take comfort in recognizing the company in which they find themselves). Skinner (1983) wrote:

> For months I felt a twinge of shame upon hearing any reference to London, seeing anything I had bought in London, seeing an English movie, hearing an English accent, or even seeing people sitting around a large table.

that the sequence of events appearing within individual development (ontogeny) is often similar to its appearance in evolution (phylogeny). Such 'newly-emerging' emotions are inherently social in nature and thought to serve social cohesion.

So-called 'violations of social conventions', e.g. belching, trigger an emotion of embarrassment that is distinct from shame, fear and guilt (Keltner and Buswell, 1997). People perceive that they have little control over such a situation, which arises by accident rather than intention, are uncertain how to act and report feeling (p. 254) 'funny, awkward, foolish, nervous, surprised, and self-conscious'. Embarrassment is accompanied by smiles, laughter, disturbances to speech, shifting eye positions, a 'rigid slouched posture', aversion and a so-called 'silly smile'. Blushing consists of a reddening of the face, neck, ears and the upper regions of the chest. It is caused by enlargement of surface capillaries.

Is the autonomic adjustment that is associated with embarrassment characteristic of just this emotion? Blood flow to the cheek increased more when people were placed in an embarrassing situation than one associated with fear. Embarrassment is associated with a reduction in heart-rate, suggestive of a move towards parasympathetic and away from sympathetic activation.

Darwin (1872/1934) referred to blushing as (p. 153) 'the most human of all expressions', suggesting something uniquely human. However, Keltner and Buswell (1997) see human embarrassment as part of an evolutionary continuity, which is related to social appeasement in non-humans. An embarrassed human, e.g. assuming a hunched posture, has similarities to other species in appeasement. A dominant conspecific showing threat is the trigger for a subordinate's appeasement and a threat to social identity triggers embarrassment. In group-living species, appeasement sends signals to a conspecific that might serve to restore social stability. The evolutionary roots could lie in embarrassment being a gesture of submission that restores social stability by evoking sympathy in others or at least deflects hostility.

Trust

An emotion of trust facilitates successful human social relations. It involves tilting the approach/avoidance reactions to another human in the direction of approach (Kosfeld et al. 2005). Kosfeld et al. found that the application of the neurohormone oxytocin via a nasal spray to people during a business negotiation increased the amount of trust that they showed. In a number of species, oxytocin is a neurohormone involved in forming bonds. The effect obtained by Kosfeld et al., was specifically a social one; oxytocin neither increased a general

tendency to risk-taking nor did it enhance mood. Within bounds, trust is, of course, a good thing but you might prefer to be a little cautious of someone who tries to waft synthetic oxytocin in your direction.

Attachment and social distress

An index of a negative emotion, 'distress', is given by **distress vocalization (DV)**: the crying that the young of all mammalian species (and some non-mammalian) exhibit following enforced separation from a caregiver (Herman and Panksepp, 1978). Figure 12.5 shows the distress vocalizations of guinea pigs as a function of age and different contexts. The close proximity of a caregiver suppresses DVs. This is usually most effectively the mother but in some species the father is particularly good in this role.

The term **opioid** refers to a particular natural neurochemical employed by the CNS. On the basis of their chemical form and function, opioids are part of a group of neurochemicals termed **neuropeptides**. Opioids play a role in reducing social distress and social contact triggers their release. The related term **opiate** refers to the drug class represented by heroin, which has opioid agonist properties.

In humans, breaking bonds, as in separation, divorce and bereavement, might have features in common with separation distress in non-humans (Panksepp, 1986). Studying non-humans offers possible insight into such human conditions as the depression that can follow separation (Panksepp et al., 1988).

Figure 12.5 Distress vocalizations of guinea pigs.
Source: Adapted from Pettijohn, T.F. (1979) Fig. 2, in Panksepp (1998a), Fig. 14.3, p.266.

Evolutionary psychology

Grief: more questions than answers

Grief is surely the most extreme negative emotion triggered by the breaking of a social bond. Similar arguments on function apply to grief as to depression (Nesse, 2005). Is the pain of grief adaptive, having beneficial consequences, such as triggering reorganization of goals and eliciting sympathy and help from others? This raises the issue of whether grief represents a specific adaptation or arises as part of a more general adaptation for sadness. Is it a gross exaggeration of a general reaction that, at lower intensity, has helped to preserve bonds? Is a negative reaction the inevitable design feature of the system of positive emotion and motivation that keeps bonds intact?

Again evolutionary psychology suggests novel ideas. Short of full grief, a negative emotion triggered by the awareness that someone is missing would doubtless trigger a search for them. Even full grief triggered by the loss of kin could prompt efforts to try to prevent loss of any other kin by monitoring them and warning of dangers. Public expressions of grief as in funeral ceremonies can help to build solidarity and to establish reputations in a community. The fact that expressions of grief show such enormous cultural variation does not point to grief being a social construction (Nesse, 2005). There is a deep-seated core of universal emotion onto which cultural variations form a layer.

A personal angle

A psychobiologist's awful insight

A major contributor to the neuropsychology of emotion is Jaak Panksepp, who was based at Bowling Green State University and is now at Washington State University. A pioneer of affective neuroscience, he has amassed a wealth of objective biobehavioural data on how various negative and positive emotional feelings are organized, including how separation distress is related to pain. However, hardly in his worst nightmare could he have imagined just how vivid would be his subjective insight. His experience demonstrates how emotion can dominate the control of behaviour and cognition.

Let me quote Jaak's own words, which describe the efforts of his friends to persuade him to continue writing his classic text, *Affective Neuroscience* (Panksepp, 1998, p. x):

. . . during the middle of the present efforts, I underwent the most painful time of my life: My precious daughter, Tiina Alexandra, died along with three friends, on a dismal Good Friday evening in 1991 when a drunken driver, evading arrest, careened into their car. After that event, my spirit was demoralized, and I could not face the labours of this book for several years. Through the magic of friends and modern psychiatric drugs, my spirits were partially restored.

In the sphere of emotions, life and science can meet in a most poignant way. Jaak's experience demonstrates vividly that brain systems that serve adaptive functions can be the source of sustained emotional distress. However, even out of the extremes of tragedy can come good: human empathy is such that Jaak was led to establish a Memorial Foundation for Lost Children. This demonstrates the motivational role of emotion.

So far, we have focused on triggers to emotion from outside the body. The following section looks at internal factors – the role of feedback from the periphery in central emotion.

Section summary

1 There are some potent triggers to fear, e.g. snakes in the case of humans. Such observations lead to the notion of an adapted 'fear-module'.

2 Frustration is induced when a desired and expected state fails to occur.

3 Violations of social conventions trigger embarrassment. It is associated with parasympathetic activation.

4 Oxytocin enhances trust.

5 Breaking a social bond triggers distress across a range of mammalian species and it has an identifiable neurochemical basis.

Test your knowledge

12.3 In terms of classical conditioning and Little Albert, how would the rat be described (i) prior to Albert meeting Watson, (ii) after the experience with Watson?

12.4 With regard to Figure 12.5, what would be the expected effect on DVs of injecting an opiate drug, for the groups (i) alone in a strange place and (ii) with mum at home?

Answers on page 339

Feedback from the periphery

Introduction

Was it ever suggested to you to 'wear a happy smile'? The implication is that 'putting on' an emotional expression might influence the central emotion. We need to consider the role of feedback from the periphery in influencing emotion, as in the case of wearing a smile.

During the history of psychology, argument has raged over the importance of peripheral sensations. Some notable investigators proposed that emotion, as an activity of the CNS, depends upon feedback from the periphery (Damasio, 1996; James, 1890/1950; Schachter and Singer, 1962). This section describes the discussion. The American philosopher William James is regarded as *the* pre-eminent pioneer of psychology. Therefore, his theory is worth discussing, even though few now believe it in quite such a strong form as was advanced by him.

The James–Lange theory

William James and the Danish physician Carl Lange separately suggested that emotion arises as indicated by Figure 12.6(a). James noted that common sense suggests that we see a bear, feel fear and then run. By contrast, he suggested the time sequence that (1) we see the bear, (2) react with the somatic and autonomic nervous systems and (3) feedback from these peripheral reactions determines the emotion as felt subjectively.

However, Cannon (1927) argued that the visceral (meaning 'of the organs of the body') changes are too slow to form the basis of emotional experience. If the James–Lange theory were right, subjective emotion would be eliminated by cutting the connection between the periphery and the CNS, yet signs of emotion are not lost (Cannon, 1927).

Suppose that, in response to an emotional event, a person does not react with the somatic nervous system. Only the ANS is strongly activated. Is there sufficient differentiation of autonomic reactions to account for the rich diversity of emotions? There is some differentiation (Ekman *et al.*, 1983). Anger tends to be associated with a stronger reaction by noradrenalin (norepinephrine) and fear by adrenalin (epinephrine) (Henry, 1986). In actors, there is a greater increase in blood pressure and heart-rate in inducing anger than fear. However, peripheral differentiation is probably inadequate to account for the rich variety of emotions.

Cognitive–physiological theory

Basics of the theory

Figure 12.6(b) shows a development of the James–Lange theory. Feedback from the periphery acts in combination with cognition in determining emotion. One prominent theory along these lines emphasizes visceral input, as follows.

Although Schachter and Singer (1962) gave an important role to feedback from the viscera, in their theory, feedback does not determine the *type* of emotion. The type, whether it is joy, fear or anger, is determined by a cognitive interpretation. See Figure 12.6(b). According to this theory, cognition on its own is not able to determine emotion. Rather, the combination of cognition and visceral response determines it. Without cognition,

(a)

(b)

Figure 12.6 Theories of emotion involving feedback:
(a) James–Lange theory and (b) Schachter–Singer theory.

visceral arousal is diffuse and undifferentiated but, given cognition, the individual can interpret it. The brain searches for meaning and labels visceral arousal in terms of cognitions.

Schachter (1975, p. 531) gives the example:

> Imagine a man walking alone down a dark alley when a figure with a gun suddenly appears. The perception–cognition 'figure with a gun' in some fashion initiates a state of physiological arousal, this state of arousal is interpreted in terms of knowledge about dark alleys and guns, and the state of arousal is labelled 'fear'.

If experienced as part of sexual arousal, the same visceral arousal might be labelled 'joy', 'lust' or 'love'.

Evidence

Is visceral arousal sufficient to produce emotion or is cognition also needed (Schachter, 1975)? Researchers injected people with adrenalin and then asked them to introspect. In most cases, the reply was not indicative of emotion. People tended to respond with 'I feel *as if* I were afraid' or 'I feel *as if* I were happy'. Schachter suggests that they are responding 'cold', on the basis of memories of emotion, but are not experiencing full emotion. In one version of the experiment, participants were given a cognition, e.g. before the injection they were spoken to about deceased relatives. In this condition, in some cases an enhanced 'hot' emotional reaction was obtained.

In another study, three groups of people were used: (i) adrenalin injected, (ii) control injected and (iii) injected with a blocker of sympathetic nervous system activity (Schachter, 1975). In a situation of humour, differences were in the predicted direction: the adrenalin-injected people laughed the most and those injected with the sympathetic blocking agent laughed the least (though criticism can be levelled at such studies; Reisenzein, 1983).

For humans and non-humans, emotional reactivity can survive breaking links from the sympathetic nervous system to the CNS. However, Schachter (1975) suggests that, in such cases, the emotion and its expression were well established, i.e. acquired before breaking the links. He appeals to a study made on patients with breaks to the spinal cord at different levels (paraplegic and quadriplegic patients). Patients were divided into five groups defined by the site of the lesion. The higher the lesion, the less the flow of neurally carried information to and from the viscera, though if the vagus nerve (Chapter 3) is intact, some information can still be transmitted via it. Feedback from facial expression and from crying is also intact. In addition, there are chemical means (e.g. hormonal) by which peripheral events might influence the CNS.

Schachter argues that, if his formulation is correct, one should see decreasing emotionality as the height of the lesion increases. Emotional reactivity was rated, based upon asking patients about the intensity of emotional experience after injury compared with before. Schachter plotted the data and the prediction was confirmed: the higher the lesion, the lower the emotional reactivity. Reports of the patient's internal state suggest that they feel 'as if' emotionally aroused but their reaction is 'cold'.

Reisenzein (1983) urged caution; patients with spinal cord injuries undergo a variety of changes. They have various sources of information available, including factual knowledge of the damage, apart from that mediated via feedback from the periphery. Memory is deceptive and the passage of time necessarily complicates reports from patients made before (intact state) and after (injured state). In patients with injuries to the spinal cord, Chwalisz *et al.* (1988) reported intense emotional arousal even where there was little feedback from the periphery.

A problem with the formulations of James–Lange and Schachter–Singer is that, before the peripheral emotional reaction can occur, there must be central processing of the significance of the stimulus as a trigger for behaviour and autonomic effects (Le Doux, 1998). At some level, the brain must calculate that a bear is threatening in order to instigate running. It is hard to see that this could be done in an 'emotionless' way.

Contemporary perspectives

General

Contemporary evidence suggests that peripheral signals do play a role in emotion. Feedback from the periphery can amplify central emotion (Chwalisz *et al.*, 1988; Haller *et al.*, 1998; Reisenzein, 1983). Discoveries suggest a range of possibilities for feedback from the periphery to the CNS but still CNS processing is necessary to trigger the peripheral reactions.

Various hormones are released by stress-evoking situations (Chapter 3), some peculiar to the nature of the situation (Panksepp, 1998). Some influence the CNS, though their time course of action suggests emotional biasing over hours rather than a reaction in a fraction of a second. The arousal of physical exercise can enhance emotions, the quality depending upon context and expectation, etc. (Steptoe, 1993). Events in the immune system can influence emotion (Chapter 13). The reaction to an infection can lead to a depressed mood. This suggests that negatively coloured cognitions are sensitized.

Recent research has located regions of the brain that are specifically activated by feedback signals from the body via the spinal cord and the vagus nerve (Craig, 2004; Critchley *et al.*, 2004). Regions of the insula cortex (also termed 'interoceptive cortex' and described shortly) among others exhibit sensitivity to interoceptive signals (Craig, 2009). This information could mediate the influence of the body on day-by-day affective changes. There are indications that people of high emotional sensitivity are particularly tuned to such feedback and have relatively large areas of cortex devoted to interoceptive processing.

Beta-blockers

A reduction in peripheral autonomic activity can be induced with, presumably, a reduction in feedback, by adrenergic blockers (the sympathetic branch employs adrenalin (epinephrine) between neurons and smooth muscles) (Reisenzein, 1983). **Beta-blockers**, employed by actors and musicians to reduce excessive cardiac activity, are in this class. Their action is primarily at cardiac muscle. They reduce peripheral activity but there are mixed reactions as far as anxiety is concerned. Where the principal problem is peripheral arousal (e.g. a perceived heart-rate that is a cause of concern), they are of value but this does not show that the effect is mediated via feedback within the ANS. Where central anxiety without specific reference to peripheral indices is the problem, there is little evidence of efficacy.

Somatic nervous system

What applies to the ANS seems also to apply to the somatic nervous system. For example, feedback from the muscles that determine the expression of the face has some influence on experienced emotion (Chwalisz *et al.*, 1988) and autonomic reactions (Ekman *et al.*, 1983). This is indicated in Figure 12.6(b) by the link 'somatic nervous system' → 'interpretation'. Suppose people are asked to put on particular reactions by the facial muscles, which correspond to particular emotional expressions. However, no emotion is suggested in the request. This has emotion-specific effects on the ANS. Under normal conditions, the facial expression itself would depend upon central emotion, so there appears to be a reciprocal interaction. However, the moral appears to be that it is worth 'putting on' a happy face.

Somatic markers

Damasio (1996) proposes an interactionist view of emotion. Feedback from autonomic and somatic nervous systems and hormonal feedback form an intrinsic part of our emotional profile. The brain cannot usefully be viewed in isolation from the remainder of the body. Emotion and emotional memory have a reference in terms of associated bodily sensations, termed the **somatic-marker hypothesis**. Thus, a memory of fear has a reference in gut feelings. This can literally derive from the viscera, the activation of which would form a loop with the memory currently activated. However, with experience, it might derive from what is termed an **as if loop** of information. This is activity that is intrinsic to the CNS and is based upon a memory of how 'gut feelings feel' (it is 'as if' the body is reacting).

Valins (1970) described an 'as if' effect. He showed pictures of naked females to males and deceived them by presenting recordings of heartbeats, which the males were told were their own. Valins had control over the recorded heartbeat. Men tended to rate slides as more attractive if they were accompanied by higher heart-rates. One interpretation is that participants had a lifetime of experiencing their own heartbeat mediated over conventional neural channels. The augmented feedback was interpreted in this context. In Damasio's (1996) terms, it would seem that Valins tapped into an 'as if loop', a CNS emotional circuit, that can operate with some independence from normal triggers and simulate peripheral arousal.

The following section looks at brain regions involved in emotion.

Section summary

1 Feedback from autonomic and somatic nervous systems plays a role in emotion.

2 The somatic-marker hypothesis suggests that memories of feedback can form 'as if' versions of emotional arousal.

☞ Test your knowledge

12.5 What is the significance of the blood–brain barrier (Chapter 5) for feedback theories of emotion?

Answers on page 339   ◖ WEB ➤

Role of brain regions

Introduction

This section assumes that emotion depends upon a number of brain regions acting in interaction. Within this interacting network, different regions have different roles. Figure 12.7 shows emotion as an intermediate factor linking, as inputs, cognition and raw stimuli and, as outputs, behavioural and autonomic reactions. Note the role of feedback from the periphery in emotion.

The limbic system

Introduction

Traditionally, an important focus for investigating emotion has been the so-called **limbic system** (MacLean, 1958), made up of a number of brain structures, with extensive connections to brain regions outside the system (Figure 12.7). Information on exteroceptive events (e.g. visual and auditory), as well as interoceptive events (e.g. certain hormone levels), forms inputs to the limbic system. Also, highly processed information

Figure 12.7 Summary of the control of emotion and its role.

('cognition') is conveyed there. In turn, the limbic system influences cognition, behaviour and the general physiology of the body.

The 'limbic system theory of emotion' proposed that the neural basis of emotion is the interaction between the brain structures that form this system. What has counted as a part of the limbic system has changed somewhat over the years (Oatley and Jenkins, 1996) but has included the septum, cingulate gyrus ('cingulate cortex'), hippocampus and amygdala. Indeed, so flexible has the limbic system proven to be that some researchers want the term banned from psychology but it refuses to go. See Figure 12.8. These days, parts of the prefrontal cortex (orbitofrontal cortex) are included in the limbic system, because of their intimate connections with 'established' limbic regions and their role in emotion.

Experimental evidence

Klüver and Bucy (1939) removed large parts of the temporal lobes, including the amygdala, in monkeys. The subjects became calm and ceased to show normally aggressive and fearful reactions. What became known as the **Klüver–Bucy syndrome** consists of a separation between the sensory processing of stimuli and the attribution of emotional and affective value to them (Le Doux, 1992). Sensory processing remains intact but such attribution is disrupted. Similar (but milder) changes occur when a lesion of just the amygdala is made.

Applied to humans, the role of these structures in the production of emotion can be contrasted with that of the cortex in cognitive processing. Electrical stimulation of the limbic system of conscious patients triggers emotion (Ervin and Martin, 1986), whereas stimulation of most of the cortex does not trigger reports of emotion or signs of autonomic activation (Le Doux, 1991).

Ploog (1986) stimulated different parts of the limbic system of squirrel monkeys and obtained different vocal reactions (e.g. growling, shrieking). These correspond, Ploog argued, to the elicitation of different emotions

Figure 12.8 Traditional notion of the limbic system.

Source: Martini *et al.* (2000, Fig. 15-12, p. 394). Copyright © 2000, 1997 by Frederic H. Martini, Inc. and Michael J. Timmons. Reprinted by permission of Pearson Education, Inc.

rather than simply the tapping of different motor outputs. Autonomic and somatic responses were elicited at the same time.

A contemporary perspective

The limbic system theory has value in drawing attention to the physical basis for emotions. However, trying to define limbic, as opposed to non-limbic, structures is problematic (Le Doux, 1991). Some authors include certain cortical structures, though they play a role in more than just emotional processing. A clear distinction between limbic (emotional) and cortical (cognitive) processing now appears an over-simplification (Le Doux, 1991). Emotional expression survives cortical removal. However, under more normal conditions the cortex appears to be involved in the fine-tuning of emotional experience and labelling, as implied by the input from cognitive processing in Figure 12.7. The hippocampus is an area originally assigned to the limbic system, though its role in emotion remains controversial (Gray, 1987a; Le Doux, 1991).

A safe statement regarding the limbic system theory would be along the following lines (cf. Le Doux, 1991). The structures of the system play a role in emotion. However, they do so in interaction with structures outside the system. Furthermore, some structures of the system play roles in processing other than emotional.

The safety of the statement needs to be seen in context – a similar claim might be made for many links between brain and mind/behaviour!

A part of the limbic system, the amygdala, forms the topic of the next section.

The amygdala

Introduction – linking psychology and structure

Electrical stimulation of the amygdala (Figure 12.9) in humans is associated with subjective reports of negative or positive emotion, depending upon which nuclei are stimulated (Aggleton and Mishkin, 1986). Aggleton and Mishkin (p. 281) described the amygdala as 'the sensory gateway to the emotions', noting that emotions commonly depend upon a compound of different sources of sensory information. Information processed by certain other brain regions (e.g. temporal cortex) comes together in the amygdala, where emotional significance is added.

In one study on humans, certain fear-related visual stimuli were presented and immediately followed by a masking stimulus. The target stimuli were not perceived consciously. Nonetheless, they were found to trigger activity in the right amygdala (Morris *et al.*, 1998), pointing to an unconscious trigger.

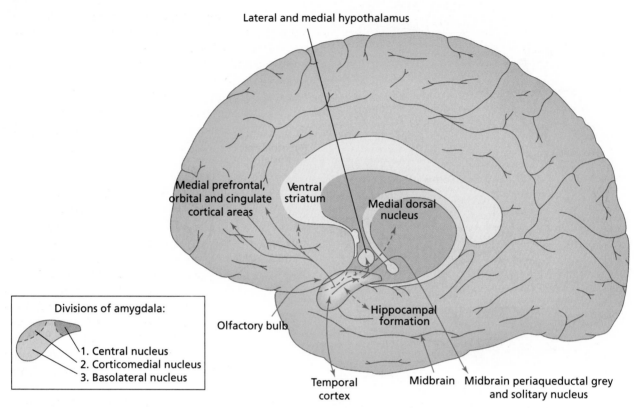

Lateral and medial hypothalamus

Medial prefrontal, orbital and cingulate cortical areas

Ventral striatum

Medial dorsal nucleus

Hippocampal formation

Olfactory bulb

Divisions of amygdala:
1. Central nucleus
2. Corticomedial nucleus
3. Basolateral nucleus

Temporal cortex

Midbrain

Midbrain periaqueductal grey and solitary nucleus

Figure 12.9 The amygdala in relation to other brain regions. Inset: the nuclei of the amygdala.

Source: Martin, J.H. (1996) *Neuroanatomy: Text and Atlas*, 2nd edition, Fig. 15.6, p. 458. Reprinted with permission of The McGraw-Hill Companies, Inc.

Inputs to the amygdala and extracting information

Inputs to the amygdala arise from various cortical and subcortical sources. Olfactory information has a more direct input than do other sensory channels (Aggleton and Mishkin, 1986). Note the input from the olfactory bulb in Figure 12.9. Olfactory input (e.g. a pheromone) carries information by virtue of its raw sensory properties, whereas the emotional significance of a visual stimulus might only be established after elaborate processing.

The emotion most consistently associated with the amygdala is fear and the structure is particularly sensitive to visual information on threat (Phan *et al.*, 2002). It appears to be activated preferentially by external stimuli rather than recalled information. Threatening faces are a powerful trigger. People with damage to the amygdala on both sides show abnormally high levels of trust when confronted with images of people judged by controls to be untrustworthy and unapproachable (Adolphs *et al.*, 1998). This could reflect a deficiency in extracting fear-related information. The amygdala is also activated by facial expressions of positive emotion (Hennenlotter *et al.*, 2005). Recent findings raise another possible interpretation: people with damage to the amygdala fail to attend to the facial features that are normally the cues to fear (Adolphs, 2009). So, the amygdala could direct attention to salient sensory features.

There are alternative routes by which some sensory systems project information to the amygdala. Different pathways are concerned with (i) extracting crude features of sensory input rapidly and triggering action (the so-called 'quick and dirty' route) and (ii) slower and more refined analysis (the 'slow and clean' route). Thus, sensory information (e.g. from ears and eyes) after reaching the thalamus takes one of two routes (or both simultaneously): the classical route to the cortex and a more direct route to the amygdala (Figure 12.10). A crude analysis, rapid emotional arousal and triggering of certain reactions, occurs through the direct route (Carlsson *et al.*, 2004; Le Doux, 1989) (Figure 12.10(a)). The speed advantage of the route from thalamus to amygdala is partly because only one synapse is involved, whereas the route through the cortex (Figure 12.10(b)) has several.

Some inputs derive from modality-specific cortical regions (e.g. visual and auditory) (Aggleton and Mishkin, 1986), thereby the amygdala gives an emotional aspect to particular sensory-related events. In addition, there are inputs from regions of cortex that are

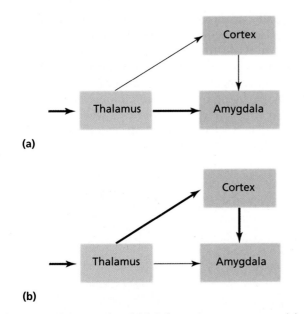

(a)

(b)

Figure 12.10 Routes by which information gets to amygdala: (a) with emphasis upon a direct route from the thalamus and (b) with emphasis upon a route via thalamus and cortex.

not modality-specific, e.g. prefrontal cortex. This link is believed to mediate the relationship between advanced stages of cognitive processing and emotion, either to amplify or inhibit emotion according to the nature of the cognition (Carlsson *et al.*, 2004; Drevets, 2001).

The amygdala also receives inputs from the hippocampus, which is involved in cognitive processing. Context is important in emotion and, via signals from the hippocampus, the amygdala is able to take this into account (Rosen and Schulkin, 1998). Thus, the roar of a lion might be emotionally neutral or pleasant when it is heard from the safety of a safari park bus. However, the same sound would most likely assume a different colouring when walking alone through a forest.

Thus, emotions can be triggered by different simultaneous levels of input to the amygdala. A rapid arousal of emotion might set the scene for interpreting the input via the cortex, which arrives slightly later. There is scope for conflict. Owing to the direct link to the amygdala, some basic stimulus features (e.g. a phobic object) might tend to trigger negative emotion, whereas more refined processing of the same object (e.g. based upon knowledge gained in therapy) would tend to inhibit it. A possible interpretation of, say, cognitive therapy is that this corresponds to strengthening the contribution of the indirect route (Le Doux, 1998).

The amygdala also receives information on internal physiology, e.g. via the brain stem, which, in turn is informed by hormones, and the vagus nerve (Chapter 3) concerning the viscera of the body. Artificial electrical stimulation of the vagus nerve affects the firing of

neurons in the amygdala. Under natural conditions, this route could mediate a role of emotional arousal generated by feedback from the viscera.

Integration of information involves not only extensive input to the amygdala but also connections between these sources of information. Anatomical evidence reveals networks of intrinsic connections within the amygdala. Links from the basolateral nucleus to the central nucleus are shown in Figure 12.9.

Outputs from the amygdala

The amygdala has a role in attributing *emotional significance* to events and, in so doing, interacts with other brain regions involved with emotional processing, e.g. cortex, hypothalamus and brain stem (Aggleton and Mishkin, 1986). Figure 12.11 shows a summary of some outputs of the amygdala, these being involved in behavioural, autonomic and conscious ('experiential') aspects of emotion. Emotion has a role in cognition, and pathways from amygdala to the cortex and hippocampus suggest that this role is mediated in part by the amygdala (Le Doux, 1989). For example, memories are better consolidated if they are of emotionally coloured information (described shortly).

Some outputs from the amygdala project to subcortical sites, e.g. hypothalamus, periaqueductal grey and solitary nucleus, which are also concerned with producing emotion and the behavioural and bodily reactions to it, e.g. elevated heart-rate (Aggleton and Mishkin, 1986).

Effects of damage to the amygdala and connected regions

In monkeys, bilateral amygdalectomy (removal of amygdala on both sides) leaves the animal emotionally relatively unresponsive to stimuli that would normally be arousing (Aggleton and Mishkin, 1986). For example, there is loss of the fear normally shown to loud sounds, snakes and capture by humans.

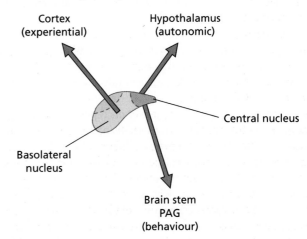

Figure 12.11 Some major outputs of the amygdala.

Suppose that connections are broken between a modality-specific region of cortex (e.g. visual cortex) and the amygdala. We might expect that emotional reactivity to information specific to the modality would be impaired, relative to that shown to information derived from other modalities.

A personal angle

A drab visual world

In Florida, Bauer (1982) describes a man who could no longer be emotionally aroused by visual stimuli. In 1979, the former city-planner aged 39, suffered a head injury in a motorcycle accident. His visual world became drab and dull. He stopped hiking since nature appeared 'all the same' and he was no longer attracted by the sight of the opposite sex. However, the disruption was modality-specific; he could experience normal emotional arousal to stimulation via other sensory modalities. Music gave him an uplift. Bauer tested the patient's autonomic reactivity to visual images. A diminished reactivity to visual stimuli was seen, compared with intact controls. The disturbance appeared to be caused by bilateral lesions to the pathway linking visual processing areas of the cortex to the limbic system, e.g. the amygdala. It could not be explained by a disturbance to vision as such.

In humans, extensive damage to both amygdala (e.g. as a result of viral encephalitis) can result in general emotional flatness. H.M. (Chapter 11) received bilateral amygdalectomy (among large amounts of other tissue being removed). Investigators reported emotional flatness. On the rare occasions that he exhibited anger or irritability, it was short-lived.

We need to consider closely the cause of amygdala damage. Damage caused by sudden trauma might give less scope for subsequent adaptation and relearning than that caused by a slow degenerative disease (Siebert *et al.*, 2003). For patients with degenerative disease affecting the amygdala, Siebert *et al.* reported some disruption in interpreting the emotional expressions of other people but not a dramatic loss of the ability. The patients might have acquired alternative strategies and pathways not involving the amygdala.

A double dissociation was reported by Bechara *et al.* (1995). A person, suffering from bilateral damage to the amygdala, failed to show conditional fear to a stimulus paired with a loud sound. However, the person was able to recall consciously the experience of conditioning. Conversely, a person with damage to the hippocampus failed to recall the same conditioning experience but exhibited a conditional autonomic response (a skin conductance change) to the cue paired with the loud sound. Although failing to form a conditional association, the person with amygdala damage showed an autonomic response to the loud sound itself. This points to the role of regions outside the amygdala.

A personal angle

The hidden pin revisited

Chapter 11 described Claparède holding a pin in his hand as he shook a patient's hand. The patient formed an implicit memory (revealed by a reluctance to approach Claparède) but not an explicit memory of the incident. Investigators do not know what neural damage the patient had suffered but, based on her behaviour, Le Doux (1998) speculated that although the temporal lobe was damaged, her amygdala functioned normally. Thus, she clearly processed emotional information (suggesting an intact amygdala) but her processing of episodic memory (Chapter 11) was disrupted, suggesting damage to the hippocampus.

The cortex

Different parts of the cortex play different roles in emotion. This section considers some sources of evidence concerning cortical regions and their contribution to emotion.

Inference from hemispheric disruption

Concerning the production of emotion, depression of activity in one hemisphere can be produced by injecting the anaesthetic amytal into one of the internal carotid arteries (the Wada test). When activity in the left hemisphere is lowered, depressed emotion/affect follows, whereas when activity in the right hemisphere is lowered, euphoria tends to follow (Sackheim *et al.*, 1982; Terzian, 1964). Of course, this test does not enable researchers to locate which part of the hemisphere is responsible and the cortical contribution is somewhat speculative. Pointing in the same direction as the results of the Wada test, damage to the left hemisphere tends to cause depression (Robinson and Price, 1982). Patients with right hemispheric lesions appear to be relatively indifferent to misfortune or euphoric in mood

(Davidson, 1984; Tucker *et al.*, 1990). The tendency to depression did not correlate with impairment (e.g. to speech) following stroke, suggesting a direct effect on emotional processing.

In a task of recognizing emotions in faces and spoken expressions, patients with damage to the right hemisphere (RH) were more impaired than those with damage to the left (Kucharska-Pietura *et al.*, 2003). Although the site of brain damage varied considerably within the groups, nonetheless the effect of hemisphere fitted other data. The deficit was greater for RH damage than left for both positive and negative emotions.

Prefrontal cortex

The prefrontal cortex integrates information on (i) the current situation, (ii) emotionally coloured memories of past instances and (iii) anticipated emotional consequences of current actions. It exploits somatic-marker signalling (or 'biasing'; see earlier) and holding the contributory bits of information in (conscious) working memory while decisions on behaviour are made (Damasio, 1996).

Phineas Gage (Chapter 1) suffered damage to the prefrontal region, specifically its orbitofrontal region (OFC), as a result of an explosion causing an iron bar to pass through it (Rule *et al.*, 2002). Gage became irresponsible and subject to emotional outbursts. Damasio (1986) speculates that Gage was defective in the ability to utilize emotional information concerning the probable consequences of his actions, e.g. offence caused by swearing. Normally the OFC would exert 'top-down' coordinated control over emotions. This involves favouring *task-relevant* emotional information and inhibiting the effect of any simultaneously present task-irrelevant signals to emotion (Rankin, 2007). When the OFC is damaged, subcortical brain regions are lifted from this inhibitory influence (Phillips *et al.*, 2003; Rule *et al.*, 2002).

Some emotions elicit approach (e.g. moving towards another person) and others avoidance (e.g. moving away from a person). Looking at activity in anterior regions of the cortex, approach is associated with activation of the left, whereas avoidance is associated with activation of the right (Carver and Harmon-Jones, 2009; Geschwind and Iacoboni, 2007). For most emotions, this maps on to approach being felt as positive (though anger also elicits approach) and avoidance as negative. Among the stroke patients of Robinson and Price (1982), the nearer the site of damage in the left hemisphere was to the front of the brain, the greater was the likelihood of depression.

Under-activity of the left prefrontal cortex (PFC) is associated with depression and withdrawal (Davidson, 2003). Anticipation that goal-directed action will bring reward is organized within the left PFC. Depression is associated with a failure of anticipation to control cognition and behaviour (Davidson *et al.*, 2002). The right PFC is more active in negative moods and withdrawal (Heller, 1990).

The insula and anterior cingulate cortex

The insula (Figure 12.12) is involved in, among other things, the perception of bodily states ('feeling states') and their contribution to emotion. The insula and the 'affective division' of the anterior cingulate cortex (ACC) act in unison and are activated in a range of emotional situations (Craig, 2009). For example, the ACC is involved in sadness (Phan *et al.*, 2002). The insula are involved in such direct emotions as disgust and nausea, as well as complex cognitively mediated emotions, such as guilt (Phillips *et al.*, 2003). They have a role in recognizing emotions in others, possibly reflecting somatic markers (Adolphs *et al.*, 2000).

Regions of the insula are activated when experiencing an emotion, such as joy, and seeing this emotion exhibited in another's face (Hennenlotter *et al.*, 2005), as is also true of disgust (Wicker *et al.*, 2003). The insula is a region of cortex having links to (i) cortical regions containing mirror neurons and (ii) other brain regions involved with emotion, such as the amygdala (Carr *et al.*, 2003). Looking at emotional faces is associated with activation in the mirroring system, the insula and the amygdala. Imitating the facial expression of the emotion causes stronger activation than observation (Carr *et al.*, 2003).

Motor-associated areas

Observing an emotion exhibited by another individual tends to trigger a degree of the same emotion in the observer (Gallese, 2006). Individuals differ in

Figure 12.12 The insula
Source: Bear et al. (2006, p. 209).

the strength of this effect, which is generally known as 'empathy' (Carr *et al.*, 2003). Humans tend to show facial expressions of emotion that match those of the person that they are observing (Hennenlotter *et al.*, 2005). The reaction by the muscles of the face is seen even when the duration of exposure to images of angry or happy faces is so rapid as to be below the threshold of conscious detection (Dimberg *et al.*, 2000). Regions of cortex that are involved in motor planning, e.g. premotor area and supplementary motor area (Chapter 10), are involved here, as are mirror neurons.

A personal angle

Insight from a neurological patient

Patients who are about to receive surgery for neurological conditions provide valuable insight. One such was a 19-year-old woman, treated for epileptic seizures in the Hôpital Neurologique, Lyon, France (Krolak-Salmon *et al.*, 2006). To define the brain structure responsible for triggering the seizures, she was implanted with several electrodes, including one near to the region of the supplementary motor area in the left brain (Figure 10.16, p. 267). Stimulation at this site triggered a smile, laughter and a report of joy as in 'seeing a Laurel and Hardy film'. On recording activity at this site while viewing a range of emotional faces, the one displaying happiness triggered the greatest effect. So, this fitted the interpretation that there is overlap in brain regions concerned with interpreting and producing emotion.

Leslie *et al.* (2004) distinguish (i) passively viewing emotionally expressive faces and (ii) actively mimicking such expressions. Passive viewing excites premotor regions of the right hemisphere (RH) more than the left (LH), which fits with observations that the RH is more involved than the LH in extracting emotional information. Thereby, the RH could play a greater role than the left in empathy, triggered even unconsciously at times. However, active facial mimicking (e.g. upon instruction) is associated with near equal activation of premotor areas of the hemispheres. Part of the activation of the LH (corresponding to Broca's area) might represent the biological basis of the *conscious intention* to mimic the emotional expression (Leslie *et al.*, 2004). Such goal-direction and choice is part of our psychological make-up. Of course, depending upon the context and timing, we do not invariably mimic the emotional

expressions of others, though there is a tendency to do so. Indeed, we might consciously resist, as when we wish to distance ourselves from what is judged to be an inappropriate emotional expression, such as laughter in a solemn context.

Regions involved with sensory processing

Emotionally loaded visual imagery more strongly activates the visual cortex and other visual processing areas, when compared with equally complex neutral scenes (Phan *et al.*, 2002). This is evidence of back-projection of information from brain regions that extract emotional significance, e.g. the amygdala, to the visual processing regions.

In humans, for the perception of emotion (e.g. emotional reactions of others), the right hemisphere seems to have an advantage over the left (Tucker and Frederick, 1989). Emotional tone is more easily detected when sounds arrive at the left ear, which projects mainly to the right hemisphere (Chapter 9). Similarly, the right hemisphere has an advantage for visual emotional information. Information from the left side of the visual field is projected to the right hemisphere (Chapter 8). Look at the nose in Figure 12.13 and describe the emotion shown. To most right-handed people (b) appears happier than (a), though they are mirror images.

Judgements of emotional value tend to be more positive when information is projected to the left hemisphere than to the right (Heller, 1990). Patients with right hemispheric damage (e.g. temporal and parietal lobes) have difficulty understanding emotional expression in others, e.g. facial reactions and speech intonation (Heilman and Bowers, 1990).

How can we share the emotion that another is *feeling*? Adolphs *et al.* (2000) found that, when presented with faces showing emotion, detection of that emotion involved processing by regions of somatosensory cortex. People with damage to the somatosensory cortex in the right hemisphere were particularly disrupted at this task. That is, an apparently visual task depended upon cortex normally attributed a role in detection of touch stimuli and sensations arising within the body. Adolphs *et al.* argue that the result fits the idea of somatic markers: to understand someone else's emotion, we need to experience ('simulate') something of the same bodily changes as occur in that emotion.

The hypothalamus

The hypothalamus is involved in the production of a range of emotions, such as anger and fear. Some evidence on its role comes from electrical stimulation of the different nuclei from which it is composed.

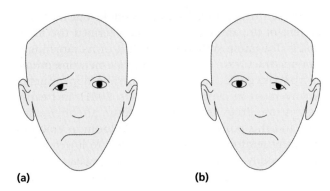

(a)   **(b)**

Figure 12.13 Two faces.
Source: Oatley and Jenkins (1996, Fig. 5.5, p.146).

Hess (1981) implanted electrodes in cats and stimulated regions of the hypothalamus. In certain areas, stimulation had two functionally related effects: (1) triggering defence and attack and (2) apparent excitation of the sympathetic system in the form of an accelerated heart-rate. By contrast, stimulation of a different hypothalamic region triggered behavioural calming and slowing of the heart. Electrical stimulation of distinct hypothalamic regions of the cat suggests two distinct types of aggression: affective ('rage') aggression, involving the medial hypothalamus, and ('non-emotional') predatory aggression, involving the lateral hypothalamus (A. Siegel, 2005). Based on studies involving electrical stimulation of the hypothalamus, rage appears to be an aversive state that the animal strives to reduce. By contrast, activity in the 'predatory region' is not aversive (Chapter 15).

Some evidence from human patients lends support to the involvement of the hypothalamus in emotion. In one patient, a tumour of the hypothalamus was associated with rage (Reeves and Plum, 1969) (if you want the specific region, it was the ventromedial part). Surgical lesions of parts of the hypothalamus have been reported to have a calming effect (Sano *et al.*, 1970).

The midbrain periaqueductal grey

Emotions were described earlier as exerting a 'tendency towards a class of behaviour'. This is a first stage of emotional processing. However, ultimately behaviour needs to be decisive, e.g. to flee or freeze, but not to be jammed in some middle position. Therefore, contributions to behaviour and ANS activity (summarized by the lower downwards-pointing arrows in Figure 12.7) must be translated into a single action, with all other options inhibited. Evidence in rats suggests that the midbrain 'periaqueductal grey' (PAG) (Chapter 5) represents a neural basis for both emotion and the organization of decisive action based upon it.

Inputs to PAG

Inputs to the PAG derive from various levels. In Figures 12.9 and 12.11, note the signals from the amygdala to the PAG. Other projections to the PAG arise from the prefrontal cortex and the medial hypothalamus (Bandler and Shipley, 1994; A. Siegel, 2005). Discrete inputs from the cortex appear to target discrete PAG columns and thereby affect particular sets of functionally related actions. Speculatively, this might be the site at which two sets of information come together: (i) initial processing of emotional significance and (ii) the sensory features of the situation in terms of the selection of action (Dampney, 1994). Another source of input to the PAG is the superior colliculus (Chapter 5; Redgrave and Dean, 1991). This structure performs primitive feature analysis of visual stimuli (e.g. a large moving object overhead) and sends a signal to PAG for triggering rapid action. More refined analysis depends upon other sources of input.

Action controlled by the PAG

Electrical stimulation of particular neurons in the PAG triggers specific courses of action (Bandler and Shipley, 1994). Neurons of the PAG are organized into functionally specific columns, e.g. one plays a role in the organization of freezing and another in active defence. Neurons within a specific column play roles in several functionally related outputs (Dampney, 1994).

Stimulation within certain columns of the PAG elicits passivity and lowered heart-rate. This reaction characterizes the defeat pattern of rats, a *passive strategy*. Neurons within other columns exert effects on the functionally related outputs of active defence (fighting) and acceleration of heart-rate through outputs to the ANS (Dampney, 1994). There is increased blood flow to the limbs and decreased flow to the viscera. Confrontation and flight represent *active strategies* for dealing with threat.

Vocalization depends on PAG neurons. In cats (de Lanerolle and Lang, 1988) and primates (Larson *et al.*, 1988), specific PAG sites are associated with specific calls indicative of emotion and intention. For example, there are calls of defeat, submission or attack and calls indicating friendly intention.

Certain PAG neurons project to the medulla where they synapse on neurons that form projections to the preganglionic neurons controlling the activity of the heart (Chapter 3; Dampney, 1994). This is the route by which emotions mediate their effects on heart-rate.

The next section considers some of the neurochemistry associated with emotion.

Section summary

1 The limbic system is made up from a number of brain regions involved in emotion, e.g. cingulate cortex and amygdala. The evidence suggests that emotion arises from a network of such interacting brain regions.

2 The amygdala attributes emotional significance to stimuli.

3 There is hemispheric asymmetry in emotional processing.

4 Depression of, or damage to, the left hemisphere is associated with negative mood.

5 Stimulation of regions of the hypothalamus elicits emotional expression in behaviour and autonomic reactions.

6 At the midbrain periaqueductal grey, in addition to a contribution to emotion, a *particular* course of behaviour is computed.

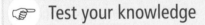 Test your knowledge

12.6 Of the two routes shown in bold in Figure 12.10, which, part (a) or part (b), corresponds to that described as 'quick and dirty'?

Answer on page 339

Neurochemicals

We considered briefly the role of opioids in emotion. This section looks at some other neurochemicals. Space precludes a detailed discussion of this subject and so we shall be selective. Neurochemicals have both general and specific effects in emotion and its expression. For example, the neurochemical acetylcholine appears to have a specific role in the hypothalamic region involved in rage (A. Siegel, 2005).

Neurochemicals involved in ascending pathways

Ascending pathways employing dopamine, noradrenalin and serotonin innervate structures of the limbic system (A. Siegel, 2005). Evidence on their role is derived from detailed study of neuroanatomy and the effects of therapeutic drugs. For example, one ascending system of dopaminergic neurons is termed the meso-*limbic* dopamine system on account of its targeting of limbic structures. That dopaminergic neurons project to the amygdala, suggested a possible dopaminergic involvement in depression (Drevets, 2001). In treating depression, drugs that target serotonin are often effective and this points to a role of serotonin in emotion. Boosting serotonin transmission tends to lower aggression, possibly acting on sites in the amygdala (A. Siegel, 2005), which could implicate a role for serotonin in rage.

Amino acids

Excitatory and inhibitory amino acids act as neurotransmitters in brain regions underlying emotion (Glue *et al.*, 1993). Glutamate is excitatory and gamma-aminobutyric acid (GABA) inhibitory. Among other things, these substances mediate, respectively, anxiety and its inhibition. A reduced sensitivity of GABA receptors appears to be part of the basis of what Glue *et al.* (p. 60) term 'overarousal, vigilance and fearful anticipation'. Depression is associated with a lower than normal level of GABA in the cerebrospinal fluid (Chapter 5) and plasma (Sutanto and de Kloet, 1993).

Some drugs that are used to improve mood block excitatory amino acid transmission (Glue *et al.*, 1993). However, glutamate has receptors throughout the brain in regions having various cognitive and motor functions (Panksepp, 1998). Only if a receptor subtype specifically involved in fear could be identified, is there hope for developing a therapy.

So-called 'benzodiazepine receptors' are found throughout the brain's fear circuits (Panksepp, 1998). Unusually, a receptor type is named after the drug that targets the receptor and is used in treatment of a disorder. The drug classes termed benzodiazepines and barbiturates bind to sites at the subtype $GABA_A$ receptor, enhance GABA function and thereby tend to reduce anxiety (Glue *et al.*, 1993). Prolonged stress can reduce the number of benzodiazepine receptors, an effect mediated via corticosteroids. Ethanol also has effects on enhancing GABAergic transmission, revealed in a temporary lowering of anxiety. Highly anxious people have reduced sensitivity to barbiturates.

Anti-anxiety drugs, **anxiolytics**, such as the types of benzodiazepine termed chlordiazepoxide and diazepam ('Valium'), have an established role in human psychopharmacology. Animal models of their action are available. For example, they help rats to overcome their fear of moving along the open arms of an elevated maze, whereas **anxiogenics** (drugs that increase anxiety) increase their reluctance to do so (Ramos and Mormède, 1998). Antidepressants are without effect on this task. Another test of drugs thought to target anxiety is the social interaction test. Anxiety counters a rat's tendency to interact socially with conspecifics, and alcohol, an anxiolytic, inhibits the effect of anxiety and increases social interaction.

Distress, as measured by distress vocalizations (DVs), is increased by glutamate agonists, which suggests a role for glutamate in the distress system (Panksepp, 1998). Diazepam decreases DVs in rat pups and anxiety in humans (Insel *et al.*, 1988). Insel *et al.* suggest that a system has evolved to serve distress-calling early in development. They raise the possibility that the action of such anti-anxiety agents as diazepam in adults is mediated by 'a residue of these developmental effects'.

Section summary

1 Various neurochemicals have specific or general effects on emotion.

2 Excitatory and inhibitory amino acids are involved in brain regions underlying anxiety.

 Test your knowledge

12.7 What sets a limit to the therapeutic use of agonists and antagonists to some of the best known neurochemicals involved in emotion? What might be the relevance of receptor subtypes to this?

 Answer on page 339   WEB

Some other effects of emotions

As Figure 12.1 showed, emotion has several roles. This section considers effects on cognition, learning and memory. A further topic is its effect on certain reflexes that are not actually triggered by emotion as such but their strength is altered by emotion.

Effects on cognition

On experiencing an emotion, thoughts and memories that are functionally related to it can sometimes be more easily retrieved and accessed than incompatible ones (Bargh and Tota, 1988). In an emotional state, ready access to memories congruent with that state might prove relevant for adaptive action and thinking out new strategies of coping (Tooby and Cosmides, 1990). Attention can be selectively drawn to compatible features of the environment. For example, anxiety biases attention processes towards the perception of threat (Rosen and Schulkin, 1998).

Stimulating brain regions such as the amygdala in chronically ill patients (see earlier) triggers (i) mood changes, (ii) a tendency to mood-specific behaviour and (iii) memories congruent with the mood (Heath, 1986).

What appears to be a normally adaptive process can also play a role in serious pathology. Depressed individuals have ready access to depressive thoughts (Bargh and Tota, 1988; Tucker *et al.*, 1990). The rumination (mental 'chewing-over') of negative and often guilt-related thoughts by depressed patients appears to be facilitated by over-activity of the amygdala (Drevets, 2001). The perceptual systems of people with phobias 'favour' detection of the object of their fear (Öhman, 2005).

Effects on forming memory

Introduction

Emotionally coloured experiences are often particularly well remembered. Emotion can strengthen memory consolidation (Chapter 11) (Herz, 1997). The persistent arousal following emotional experience and associated hormonal changes appear to be involved (Bower, 1992). Emotional arousal allocates priority to processing the emotion-evoking event and triggers its recycling in working memory.

Mechanisms

Cahill *et al.* (1996) employed positron emission tomography (PET; Chapter 5) to investigate the role of the amygdala in emotionally coloured memory. Participants (right-handed, males) were given two PET scans, while watching (i) neutral material and (ii) material that was emotionally negative. It was predicted that (a) emotionally loaded material would be better recalled and (b) there would be increased activity of the amygdala associated with this.

Participants were injected with *F*-fluoro-2-deoxy-glucose (FDG) to determine metabolic rate. The highest concentration of FDG gathers in regions that are the most active metabolically. Figure 12.14 shows scatterplots for the number of films recalled and the glucose metabolism of the right amygdala for (a) emotional and (b) neutral material. There is a significant positive correlation between the metabolic activity and the conscious recall of emotional material, but no correlation for neutral material.

(a)

(b)

Figure 12.14 Scatter plot for number of films recalled and metabolic activity of the right amygdala: (a) emotional film session and (b) neutral film session.
Source: Cahill *et al.* (1996, Fig. 3).

Specifically the basolateral amygdala is involved in this aspect of memory (McGaugh, 2004). It appears that, by means of its neural projections to other brain regions (e.g. cortex), the amygdala enhances consolidation there.

Consider Figure 12.15. In emotion, the hormones adrenalin and corticosteroids are secreted in increased amounts and they trigger a series of events that affect the establishment of memory (McGaugh, 1992). For example, there is improved retention of memory when injections of these hormones are made following training. Adrenalin seems to act via a circuitous route in activating peripheral adrenergic receptors on the vagus nerve (Chapter 3, Figure 3.30, p. 76). Acting via the nucleus of the solitary tract (NTS) (Chapter 5, Figure 5.30, p. 127), activation of the vagus nerve then influences the amygdala. This triggers the release of noradrenalin in the brain, which activates the projections involved in enhancing memory formation.

In addition, corticosteroids readily enter the brain and are thought to attach to receptors at the basolateral amygdala, where they exert the effect of enhancing memory (McGaugh, 2004).

A personal angle

Joseph Le Doux and snakes

The neuroscientist Joseph Le Doux relays an anecdote from his childhood in Eunice, Louisiana, when he was on a fishing trip (Le Doux, 1992, p. 269):

Suddenly, I noticed that the bank of the stream below was covered with more snakes than I ever care to see again. Had I not seen those snakes, my memory of that experience would surely be much less vivid than it is. I am unable to recall the more mundane events occurring before or after encountering the snakes, but I remember the image of the snakes slithering in the mud and the appearance of the surrounding countryside as if this experience had just happened yesterday. The arousal of emotion, fear in this case, presumably made me remember for more than 30 years the details of this excursion with such clarity.

Dr Le Doux describes his 'immense fear of snakes' (Le Doux, 1998, p. 179) and this reaction forms an important part of his scientific argument on emotion.

We usually form rather durable memories of traumatic incidents that we experience or learn about, such as the London bombings in 2005. What is the mechanism underlying this?
Source: © David Parry/epa/Corbis.

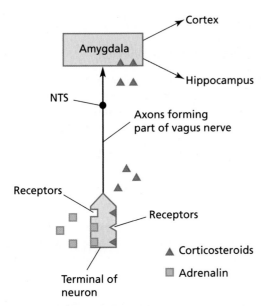

Figure 12.15 Effects on memory consolidation

The human startle reflex

It is almost certain that you have felt the **startle reflex** in action, a response to a sudden unexpected stimulus. Suppose that you are watching a horror movie and someone touches your back as they walk past. You are likely to flinch or jump. Fear accentuates your reaction, compared with when, say, watching a comedy. In humans, the startle reflex consists, in addition, in a blink of the eyes (Ehrlichman *et al.*, 1997; Lang *et al.*, 1990).

A conditional stimulus (CS) that has earlier been paired with an aversive unconditional stimulus (UCS) can affect the startle reflex. Rats are first exposed to a light (CS) paired with shock (UCS), which establishes conditional fear to the light (Davis, 1992). They are then subjected to a tone. The tone triggers the startle reflex. Startle can be measured in the presence or absence of the light. In spite of its pairing with shock, they do not react with startle to the light itself, showing that the light is not able to trigger this reflex. However, if light and tone are presented together, the light *amplifies* the reaction to the tone. This shows the influence of fear conditioned to the light.

Emotion triggered in various ways affects the strength of the startle reflex. In humans, amplification of the startle reflex can be used as an index of negative affect, e.g. during withdrawal from addictive drugs (Mutschler and Miczek, 1998). For another example, unpleasant odours increase it and pleasant odours decrease it (Ehrlichman *et al.*, 1997). Lang *et al.* (1990) investigated the relationship between this reflex and central emotion. They suggested that, if a reflex is incompatible

with an emotion, the magnitude of the reflex would be reduced. For example, the startle reflex would be weaker in a positive emotion than in a neutral emotion.

Slides of different affective value were employed. Affective value was determined by asking students to give a rating to each slide. Ratings were on a two-dimensional scale of valence (quality of emotion) and arousal (intensity of emotion). Typically, 'positive valence' would be an attractive image of a person, whereas 'negative valence' would be a bloody wound. A typical 'neutral valence' might be a mushroom. For different slides, there was a correspondence between (a) the person's ranking of their emotional valence and (b) the effect that viewing the slide had in modulating the reflex. Slides of negative valence enhance the magnitude of the reflex and positive ones lower it.

Davis (1992) proposed a model of the startle reflex (Figure 12.16). There is a direct stimulus–response (sound–muscles) link mediated via the brain stem. The strength of this link is modulated top-down by emotion. Within the lateral and basolateral nuclei of the amygdala, an association is formed between light and shock. This gives information on the light access to the central nucleus of the amygdala from which neurons extend to the brain stem structures that underlie the startle reflex (cf. Adamec, 1997). The signal from the amygdala modulates the strength of the reflex.

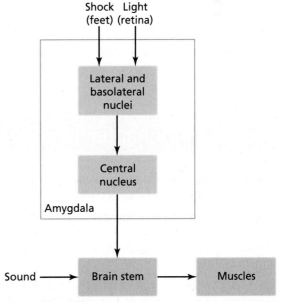

Figure 12.16 A representation of the role of conditioned fear in potentiating the startle reflex.

Source: adapted from Davis (1992, Fig. 41.3, p. 474).

Section summary

1   Emotion tends to trigger access to memories that are compatible with the emotion.

2   As embodied in the amygdala, emotion enhances the consolidation of memories.

3   Emotion alters the strength of the startle reflex.

 Test your knowledge

12.8 Complete the following with respect to Figure 12.16: 'Whereas the input marked "Sound" t____ the startle reflex, that derived from the amygdala m____ its strength'.

Answer on page 339

Bringing things together

Figure 12.1 summarizes much of the evidence presented in the chapter. Various inputs have the common property of triggering a particular emotion, which then has functionally coherent effects on behaviour, physiology, cognition (e.g. learning/memory) and subjective feelings. Its effects on behaviour consist of giving priority to certain actions (e.g. fear prioritizes escape), causing fixed patterns of reaction (e.g. alarm calls, characteristic facial expressions) and influencing the startle reaction.

In the spirit of affective neuroscience, the chapter proposes that a rapport between neuroscience and the investigation of subjective states is not only possible but indeed necessary.

Certain brain regions appear to have more to do with cognition (e.g. posterior regions of cortex) and others (e.g. hypothalamus) more to do with emotion. However, anything but basic stereotyped emotional expression depends on both. Psychologists cannot draw a neat boundary between cognition and emotion. The amygdala has a role in attributing emotional significance to stimuli and thoughts. Some stimuli both of internal and external origin target the amygdala directly whereas others first involve complex processing. Thoughts presumably arise in the cortex and are attributed with emotional value by the amygdala. Clearly, for this to happen there has to be a thought and there has to be a cortex. So, in this process (amongst others), the cortex is involved in emotional processing.

 See the video coverage for this chapter to understand both the adaptive role of emotions and how they can go wrong.

Summary of Chapter 12

1   Emotions exert a coordinated influence on behaviour, physiology, cognition and subjective experience.

2   Some basic emotions are common across mammalian species. The triggers to these emotions and the form of their expression vary between species and between human cultures.

3   The biological psychology of human emotion can be exemplified by the study of fear, frustration, embarrassment, trust and social attachment.

4   Feedback from the periphery, e.g. skeletal muscle and autonomic effects, plays some role in the production of emotion by the CNS.

5   Various interacting brain regions form the neural basis of emotion. These include the amygdala, hypothalamus and periaqueductal grey.

6   Different neurochemicals play general or specific roles in the production of emotions.

7   Emotion exerts a role in cognition, learning and memory, as well as in modifying the strength of certain reflexes.

Further reading

For general accounts by eminent researchers in the area, see Le Doux (1998) and Panksepp (1998). For a handbook of affective science, see Davidson *et al.* (2009). For the perspective of a leading researcher in which links are made with motivation, see Rolls (2005). For general accounts of emotion, see Lewis *et al.* (2008) and Oatley *et al.* (2006). For the detailed neuroscience of emotion, see Gazzaniga *et al.* (2008).

Answers

Explanations for answers to 'test your knowledge' questions can be found on the website www.pearsoned.co.uk/toates

12.1 Dilation; autonomic
12.2 Unconditional; conditional; unconditional
12.3 (i) Neutral stimulus; (ii) conditional stimulus
12.4 (i) It would reduce the level; (ii) no effect.

12.5 To influence emotional processing by the brain, the substance must either be able to cross the blood–brain barrier in some way or be able to trigger peripheral neurons that project to the brain (e.g. as part of the vagus nerve).
12.6 (a)
12.7 Such neurotransmitters are employed widely in the nervous system, including regions not concerned with emotion. If subtypes of receptor could be identified playing a specific role in emotion, drugs that target just them could offer promise.
12.8 Triggers; modulates

Visit www.pearsoned.co.uk/toates
for a range of resources to support study.
Test yourself with multiple choice questions and access a bank of over 100 videos that will bring the topics to life.

Interactions and animations relating to topics discussed in this chapter can be found on the website at www.pearsoned.co.uk/toates. These include:

Animation: The James–Lange theory
Interaction: Some of the main brain areas involved in emotion
Interaction: The low and high roads to the amygdala
Animation: The effects of benzodiazepines on punished responding

Chapter 13
Stress and coping

Learning outcomes for Chapter 13

After studying this chapter, you should be able to:

1 State what is meant by 'stress', while linking this to physiology, psychology and homeostasis.

2 Identify the criteria that point to the existence of stress. Relate these to measures of stress.

3 Describe features of the two principal neurohormonal systems that are stretched excessively under stress. Explain why they have a defining role in stress.

4 Explain why stress cannot simply be defined in terms of the potential stressors present in a situation. Outline the role of contextual factors such as coping.

5 Describe some of the basic features of the immune system and how the system can be affected by stress. Suggest how stress might have a part in exacerbating disorders that involve suppression of the immune system.

6 Identify some of the principal brain regions that are implicated in 'stress'. Relate their role under stress-free conditions to their performance in stress.

7 Show where understanding stress can help to explain the bases of a number of disorders: depression, coronary heart disease, post-traumatic stress disorder, irritable bowel syndrome and ulcers.

8 Outline how understanding the psychobiology of stress can give pointers as to reducing stress and can thereby make a positive contribution to health.

Scene-setting questions

1 Can someone actually enjoy stress?
2 Is stress invariably harmful to health?
3 Are stress-related diseases 'psychosomatic'?
4 How can the gut be sensitive to stress?
5 Can you die from a 'broken heart'?
6 Can science show how to live with stress or how to beat it?
7 Can self-harm serve as a coping strategy in response to insufferable stress?

 Can self-harm serve as a coping strategy in response to insufferable stress? Explore the video on the website accompanying this book at **www.pearsoned.co.uk/toates**

Stress in such an extreme situation is triggered by the failure to resolve a pressing problem over a period of time. How good is this as a general criterion of stress?
Source: Getty Images/Workbook Stock.

Introduction

Many of us know **stress** through personal experience. Think of some situations that you would describe as stressful. (An unexplained water leak in our house first springs to my mind. It feels that I am eminently qualified to write this chapter.) People report such things as isolation, being under siege, anticipation of exams, chronic ill-health, loss or breakdown of a close relationship and unemployment as being stressful. Is there a common feature that characterizes these situations?

They all engage our attention, pose demands for action and change, are largely uncontrollable and, in most cases, arrive against our wishes. They tend to leave us feeling helpless and a failure and they occur over periods of weeks or months. We cannot *cope*, sometimes expressed as not having a **coping strategy** or 'coping resources'. Stimuli that cause stress are termed **stressors.** In non-humans, these are often such things as prolonged exposure to noise or social conflict.

Stressors tend to add their effects. You hear comments such as, 'I might just have coped with the divorce *on its own* but not with that and the unemployment'. So, we are looking for neuropsychological processes that tend to cumulate negative effects.

In everyday use, stress mostly refers to psychologically disturbing events or events with psychological associations, involving long-term overload (Ursin and Olff, 1993). A challenge is to try to define common biological and psychological features of stressful situations.

Most would argue that stress is always negative and predisposes to illness but some suggest that mild stress can be exhilarating and only severe stress is bad. The workaholic entrepreneur is driven by the 'adrenalin rush' of stress. Such people may indeed be stimulating their adrenalin secretion but it is likely that they have considerable control over the situations in which they *willingly* engage. They are not stressed in the sense of being helpless and chronically beset by circumstances not of their choosing. Hormonal reactions do not always tell the whole story: as will be described shortly, they need to be seen in context.

To understand stress, let us consider homeostasis. The body is constructed so as to keep certain important parameters within close limits. When they shift from these, action is taken to bring them back. If something such as body temperature were to shift far from its norm, death would follow. A similar notion can be applied to stress. We try to protect our 'psychological homeostasis' by taking various actions, such as avoiding psychological overload, seeking comfort from others, finding prediction and control in our lives and avoiding conflict, etc. Stress represents a chronic disturbance to such *psychological* homeostasis. Disturbances to physiology, such as high blood pressure and adrenalin levels, are associated with this (Gianaros and Sheu, 2009).

Although we normally think of stressors as being psychological, two things need to be emphasized: (i) through the CNS, psychological stressors exert wide-ranging effects on the physiology of the body and (ii) some of these same effects on the body can be triggered by physiological stressors, i.e. deviations from physiological homeostasis, as in loss of blood (Selye, 1973). See Figure 13.1.

The term 'stress' can be used to cover the response to both psychological and physiological triggers (Ursin and Olff, 1993) and it thereby points to common reactions in the body. Physiological and behavioural mechanisms that are adaptive within a range (Chapter 12) can be stretched beyond this. Over a prolonged period, such

Figure 13.1 Stress, as determined by physiological and psychological stressors.

stretching is associated with psychological and physiological disruption described as 'stress' (Archer, 1979).

Of course, evolution did not produce systems that are intrinsically geared to produce pathology. Rather, stress is the pathological stretching of behavioural systems to beyond their adaptive range. For example, an elevated heart-rate and blood pressure can be adaptive in the short term in facing natural threats, such as bears. They can become seriously maladaptive if they are chronically activated day-after-day with little escape from the triggers to stress.

Awareness of stress is an important health issue. Stress can sometimes be better managed. We can direct attention to psychological states that are opposite to stress, as aspects of physical and psychological health.

Section summary

1 A long-term disturbance to psychological homeostasis is described as 'stress'.

2 Stress is associated with changes in the physiology of the body.

3 Physiological stressors, such as loss of blood, trigger some of these same changes.

Test your knowledge

13.1 Complete the following: 'Stress can be described as a chronic ___ to psychological homeostasis'.

Answer on page 362

Characterizing stress

This section considers starting points for understanding stress.

Signs of stress: arousal

Confronted with a stressor, an animal shows EEG **arousal**, also termed 'activation' (Chapter 5; Ursin and Olff, 1993). Protracted arousal gives a possible indication of stress. Although there can be arousal without stress there cannot be stress without arousal (Pfaff *et al.*, 2007).

In stress, animals take both behavioural and physiological (e.g. autonomic) action. The sympathetic nervous system is usually excited and thereby adrenalin

(epinephrine) and noradrenalin (norepinephrine) are released into the bloodstream in increased amounts. Hormones termed corticosteroids (Chapter 6) are usually secreted at a high rate and they mobilize metabolic resources in the body. The set of reactions is termed the 'emergency reaction'. Long-term excitation of these hormonal systems gives an indication of stress.

Types of stressor

External stimuli

Consider an animal that is exposed to 'potential stressors', e.g. (i) confrontation with predators, (ii) dealing with dominants of the group or (iii) competing for food and reacting to rivals in overcrowded conditions. As a reaction, heart-rate accelerates. The animal might have a coping strategy available that reliably corrects the situation, such as to avoid, make an appeasement gesture or flee. Suppose it suffers no ill effects; after each contact, heart-rate rapidly returns to normal. Lengthy confrontation is avoided and the notion of stress would seem inappropriate. This is coping, by the criteria of the success of behaviour and the relatively light demands on the corticosteroid system and the autonomic nervous system (ANS).

The chapter concerns where a coping strategy is unavailable, the challenge cannot be countered and the animal is stressed. For example, it might take evasive action with autonomic activation but repeatedly fails to get away from a dominant animal.

Typically, secretion of corticosteroids and sympathetic activation with heart-rate acceleration would occur over long periods (von Holst, 1986). The persistence of arousal and failure to resolve the situation are associated with a range of characteristic pathology, such as ulcers and blocking of arteries. The coexistence of behavioural and physiological indices encourages use of the term 'stress'.

Cognitive processes

Some potential stressors, e.g. loud sounds, can be defined in terms of their physical properties. However, many situations that cause stress are not so easily defined (Ursin and Olff, 1993). Rather, what evokes stress is an event placed in the *context of earlier experiences*.

Corticosteroid secretion is sensitive to situations placed in context. For example, novelty can trigger it. Novelty is not some intrinsic property of an environment. Rather, the environment is novel in the context of previously experienced environments. Similarly, loss of control in a previously instrumental situation (i.e. extinction in a Skinner box) triggers release of corticosteroids. Earning a reward smaller than expectation is another trigger that can only be understood in terms of what was expected (Chorpita and Barlow, 1998), i.e. frustration is a trigger. This implies comparison of expected and actual events and a triggering by the difference.

In humans, loss of something such as a job is a stressor but this is not a physical stimulus comparable to a loud noise. We might stress ourselves through endless problem-solving, as in trying to balance dubious financial accounts, or by engaging in 'inner dialogues' on personal failure (Burell, 1996). In this case, stressors are characterized by such features as 'informational discrepancy', e.g. reality differs from expectations (Ursin and Olff, 1993), or there is an inability to solve a problem (Gianaros and Sheu, 2009). Attempts to cope with cognitive challenges are associated with sympathetic activation (Steptoe, 1993). In trying to define stress, a measure in such a case might be a verbal report, e.g. 'I feel that I cannot cope any longer'.

In social species, isolation from conspecifics causes stress, the 'isolation syndrome' (Chapter 12; Greenough, 1976). Evidence of stress is provided by a comparison with the unstressed behaviour and the hormonal profile of a stable socially housed animal.

Physiological stimuli

Physiological disturbances, e.g. blood loss or stretch of the bladder (Selye, 1973), trigger activation and corticosteroid release. The mobilization of resources in this 'general emergency reaction' supports any specific action also triggered. For example, a physiological challenge such as loss of blood triggers specific behavioural homeostatic actions such as seeking water and salt to correct the disturbance (Chapter 16).

Behavioural indices

Confronted with a stressor we might flee or fight, and activate the sympathetic system, and these actions might or might not be successful. Another strategy is passivity, with parasympathetic activation and inhibition of the sympathetic system (Fowles, 1982). Confronted with a dominant animal, a subordinate sometimes reacts in this way. Typically, when an active strategy fails, an animal switches to the passive mode. According to the definition suggested here, a failure of strategy over long periods constitutes stress.

Four criteria of stress

Four criteria characterize stress and can be applied across species, as follows (Toates, 1995)

1 Over time, action occurs in response to a situation but it fails to correct this situation.

2 There is excessive and protracted activity in neurohormonal systems. Typically, this would be the sympathetic branch and the system that secretes corticosteroids from the adrenal gland (Selye, 1973; von Holst, 1986) or both.

3 There is vulnerability to certain pathology (e.g. gastric ulceration, hypertension, depression and disorders associated with suppression of the immune system) (Moberg, 1985).

4 There is a tendency to show apparently pointless behaviours such as stereotypies or inflicting self-harm (Mason, 1991).

In our case, to lower stress we might target voluntary behaviour. There could be some choice, e.g. we might readjust priorities and work less. We might be able to change how we interpret and react to events. Interventions might target the physiology of the body, e.g. drugs to lower the vigour of the heart's pumping.

The following section looks at the two neurohormonal systems that are involved in stress.

Section summary

1 External stimuli, defined as stressors, trigger behavioural and physiological activation.

2 The stress-evoking capacity of external events can often be understood only by taking account of their context and interpretation.

3 Humans can stress themselves by cognitive triggers such as protracted and unsuccessful problem-solving.

4 A capacity for coping reduces the impact of potential stressors.

5 An animal is stressed when coping resources are inadequate for the task.

6 Other criteria of stress are increases in (a) activity by neurohormonal systems, (b) the tendency to certain pathology and (c) the tendency to perform stereotypies.

7 Stress can be associated with (a) active strategies and sympathetic domination or (b) passive strategies with a bias towards parasympathetic activity.

☞ Test your knowledge

13.2 Apart from catecholamines, increased release of what other class of substance occurs in stress?

Answer on page 362

Two neurohormonal systems

Introduction

The perspective introduced here corresponds to the 'classical stress story' (Pfaff *et al.*, 2007). The focus is on two neurohormonal systems (Chapters 3 and 6): (i) the sympathetic branch of the ANS and (ii) the sequence CRF → ACTH → corticosteroids. Prolonged activation of these two systems can be used as one index of stress and it plays a role in disorders characterized as 'stress-related'.

The autonomic nervous system

Stress is associated with altered activity throughout the ANS, affecting its various outputs, such as the stomach and intestine. A principal concern is with parts that affect the circulatory system. We address this first.

Sympathetic branch

Emergencies activate the sympathetic branch of the ANS (SNS), especially when action appears possible. SNS activation triggers changes in the body, e.g. increased heart-rate. Also, a number of blood vessels are constricted but those in active skeletal muscles are dilated, facilitating blood flow.

SNS activation releases catecholamines: (i) noradrenalin from sympathetic neurons and (ii) adrenalin (A) and noradrenalin (NA) from the adrenal gland. In humans, most noradrenalin in the blood originates from the terminals of neurons of the SNS, some at the inner region of the adrenal gland, the **adrenal medulla**. Plasma adrenalin originates in the adrenal medulla (Musselman *et al.*, 1998).

Within the circulatory system, adrenalin and noradrenalin occupy two types of receptor: alpha adrenergic and beta adrenergic. For example, when these catecholamines occupy beta receptors at cardiac muscle, the frequency of the heartbeat is increased. The therapeutic drug class termed 'beta blockers' acts at this site (Scheidt, 1996). Cardiac muscle is excited by (1) direct sympathetic input via neurons and (2) noradrenalin and adrenalin from the bloodstream (Dampney, 1994). In response to sympathetic activation, blood flow through the heart can increase by a factor of 5. Occupation of catecholamine receptors on the smooth muscles that govern the diameter of blood vessels adjusts blood flow such that working skeletal muscle receives adequate blood (Vander *et al.*, 1994).

Parasympathetic branch

Parasympathetic activity is seen in day-to-day maintenance, e.g. promoting digestion, involving restraint on the heart. However, increased activation can occur in emergencies when no active strategy is perceived as possible (Bohus and Koolhaas, 1993).

The hypothalamic pituitary adrenocortical system

Introduction

Corticosteroids are secreted from the outer layer of the adrenal gland, the **adrenal cortex** (Figure 13.2). There are different corticosteroids having similar properties. In rats, the principal one is corticosterone (Bohus and de Kloet, 1981). In humans, it is cortisol (Baxter and Rousseau, 1979). Corticosteroids act throughout the

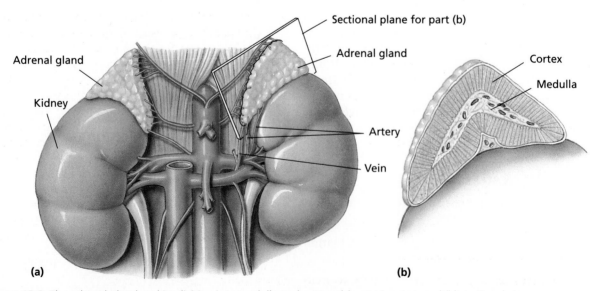

Figure 13.2 The adrenal gland and its division into medulla and cortex: (a) anterior view and (b) sectional view.

Source: Martini *et al.* (2000, Fig. 19-10, p. 510). Copyright © 2000, 1997 by Frederic H. Martini, Inc. and Michael J. Timmons. Reprinted by permission of Pearson Education, Inc.

body, e.g. at times of threat to mobilize energy and, at the brain, to alter arousal and cognitive and emotional processing (Erikson *et al.*, 2003). In primates, receptors for corticosteroids are found in the hippocampus, amygdala and regions of prefrontal cortex.

Consider Figure 13.3. At the first stage of the system, neurons with cell bodies at the paraventricular nucleus of the hypothalamus (PVN) (Chapter 5, Figure 5.31, p. 128) secrete corticotropin releasing factor (CRF), sometimes termed 'corticotropin releasing hormone' (Dunn and Berridge, 1990). At the pituitary, occupation of receptors by CRF releases adrenocorticotrophic hormone (ACTH). The sequence of hormones, CRF → ACTH → corticosteroids, is called the **pituitary adrenocortical system** (or pituitary adrenocortical axis). Since activity in the hypothalamus is the trigger for CRF secretion, this sometimes gives the axis the title 'hypothalamic pituitary adrenocortical system'. Mercifully, this is commonly abbreviated to 'HPA system' or 'HPA axis'.

Corticosteroids inhibit their own secretion (Figure 13.3). If such negative feedback is functioning optimally, when a stressor is terminated there is a prompt shut-down of the HPA axis and corticosteroid level quickly falls (Cullinan *et al.*, 1995). Malfunction can arise from inadequate negative feedback, in which case hormonal activation can long outlive the stressor. For example, excessive levels of corticosteroids can be toxic to neural tissue, e.g. in the hippocampus (Bremner, 1999). This can have negative effects on memory (Kim and Diamond, 2002).

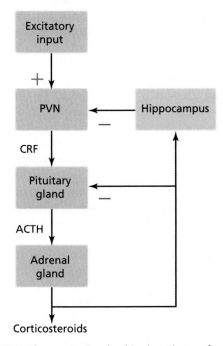

Figure 13.3 The system involved in the release of corticosteroids and their feedback effect.

Triggers

Acting via CNS processing, what triggers the set of hypothalamic neurons to release CRF? The HPA system is sensitive to (i) events in the internal environment (e.g. blood loss) and (ii) analysis by other parts of the brain that a challenge is arising in the external environment (Chorpita and Barlow, 1998). Psychological stimuli to stress are characterized by the common property of *uncertainty, challenge or threat and the possible need to take action.*

A long-term elevation of corticosteroid levels points to stress, since (i) this occurs at times of threat or challenge, (ii) it is associated with failure to resolve the problem and (iii) it has pathological consequences. However, brief activation of the HPA system does not indicate a stressor (Willner, 1993). Brief activation is a response to uncertainty (e.g. novelty, aversive stimulus) or arousal, whereas chronic activation reflects an inability to resolve uncertainty. From a functional perspective, triggering of corticosteroids by novelty makes adaptive sense since this represents a situation in which an animal might be called upon to fight, flee or freeze.

Where a well-tried strategy is available, there is little excitation of the HPA axis, even though a potential stressor is present. For example, if a tone is presented just before shock, the tone comes to evoke HPA activation. However, suppose that the animal successfully learns to perform an avoidance response by reacting quickly to the tone. Over this period, there is a gradual diminution in HPA activation until it returns to near baseline (Coover *et al.*, 1973).

Activation of the two systems

Successful action

To return to our favourite example (well, my favourite, at least), suppose that we meet a bear and run. The threat triggers SNS activation, which, among other things increases heart-rate. It also triggers HPA activation, which increases the supply of glucose to the blood. Both effects aid survival. Increased secretion of adrenalin and corticosteroid makes fuels such as glucose available from reserves. Fats are mobilized and their concentration in the blood increases (Guyton, 1991). Fats are metabolized (i.e. chemically converted to provide the fuel for action) as part of the physical exertion in running.

Assuming that one escapes, activity in the two neurohormonal systems might normally return to near baseline. If this happens the system is working optimally, i.e. the challenge promotes behavioural and neurohormonal actions that serve to resolve the challenge.

Stress and some consequences

Stress occurs when neurohormonal systems are excited in a way that is unjustified by the associated behaviour.

A classic example consists of exciting these systems while in a sedentary situation, e.g. internal turmoil caused by anger directed at the boss but where neither fighting nor fleeing is advised.

Why is stress damaging to health? Among other reasons, fatty substances termed lipids are brought into the bloodstream in large amounts. If they are not metabolized, they tend to gather on the walls of arteries. This is termed **atherosclerosis** (or arteriosclerosis) (Scheidt, 1996). A long-term elevation of lipid levels, associated with them not being metabolized (e.g. during stressful inactivity), risks the health of the circulation.

A similar argument can be applied to the HPA system. Activation of this system followed by a quick return to a basal level characterizes an efficient response (Dienstbier, 1989). Excessive levels of corticosteroids over a protracted period are damaging, e.g. to the immune and nervous systems (Seeman and Robbins, 1994). If corticosteroid level declines only slowly, this indicates a continued excitation of the HPA system, an inefficient function. Ageing can be associated with excessive boosting of the HPA system with an associated weakening of negative feedback.

We now look at some of the situations that trigger stress.

Section summary

1 Stress is associated with an identifiable pattern of physiological changes.

2 Stressors commonly cause activation of the sympathetic system and a lowering of activity within the parasympathetic system.

3 Stress is sometimes associated with activation of the parasympathetic system.

4 Stressors trigger the hypothalamic pituitary adrenocortical system.

5 A healthy profile consists of a rapid activation of sympathetic and HPA systems and then a quick return to baseline.

6 One risk associated with stress is the deposition of lipids on the walls of the arteries.

☞ Test your knowledge

13.3 With respect to Figure 13.3, what would be the effect of injecting (i) a CRF antagonist, (ii) corticosteroids?

Answer on page 362   WEB

Stressors, contexts and reactions

Introduction

Whether a potential stressor becomes an actual stressor can depend on context, e.g. (i) the capacity to predict when the stressor will occur, (ii) opportunities for action and (iii) what the animal does in response to the potential stressor and the outcome. Other factors include the history of the animal. Exposure to a stressor can change the animal, so that the future reaction to stressors is different. This section also considers that, confronted with a stressor, there can be more than one strategy.

Predictability and controllability

The consequences of exposure to a stressor vary with **controllability**. If an animal can exert control to terminate a stressor, indices of stress are lower, as compared with a passive ('yoked') control exposed to the same stressor (Weiss, 1972). Chronic lack of control is a developmental precursor of adult anxiety and depression (Chorpita and Barlow, 1998).

Weiss (1971) subjected yoked pairs of rats to electric shock to the tail. Both received identical shocks but, whereas one could exert control, the other ('control rat') could not. The active rat could terminate shock *for both rats* by turning a wheel, a coping strategy. The passive (control) rat also had access to a wheel but its actions were ineffective as far as the shock was concerned. Active rats showed greater weight gains and less gastric ulceration than did yoked controls. This experiment has proved to be a model of wide application, pointing to the importance of control. In humans, the impact of potential stressors is ameliorated by gaining control (Allan and Scheidt, 1996b). For example, a high pressure of work becomes less stressful if the person has capacity to make decisions on how the work is done.

Even in the absence of control, an animal that has some **predictability** of potential stressors shows fewer signs of stress compared with one without predictability, as indexed by gastric ulceration (Weiss, 1971). For example, predictability can be obtained where a warning sound occurs before shock.

Exposure to inescapable shock can lead to **learned helplessness**: an animal appears to learn that it has no agency and gives up. Following this, if a contingency of escape or avoidance is introduced, the animal fails to take appropriate action (Seligman, 1975). Learned helplessness is not 'non-behaving'. Rather, it exemplifies emotional-biasing of behaviour towards passivity, mediated via active inhibition of skeletal muscles. Experience with inescapable shock increases a rat's tendency to freeze in other situations, e.g. after shock in a novel environment. Passivity in the face of uncertain threat has some of the hallmarks of anxiety. This offers possible links with theorists who see anxiety as a precursor to depression (Chorpita and Barlow, 1998).

Sensitization

Exposure to a stressor can sensitize the nervous system such that the future behavioural and hormonal reaction to a stressor is increased (Sorg and Kalivas, 1995). Sensitization can be very long-lasting, even for a lifetime. In rats, exposure to an inescapable stressor can trigger a long-term increase in the tendency to immobility, a reduction in social interaction and increased HPA response to novelty (van Dijken *et al.*, 1993).

Developmental and age factors

Suppose that infant rats are briefly handled by the experimenter, involving separation from the mother. This intervention has a protective ('inoculating') effect regarding the impact of subsequent stressors. As an adult, the rat has a more healthy profile of HPA activity and an increased tendency to explore a novel environment (Castanon and Mormède, 1994). A capacity for control in the face of stressors when young gives rise to adult resilience, 'toughening-up' (Dienstbier, 1989), indexed by a greater density of corticosteroid receptors and lower levels of corticosteroids. Conversely, extended periods of separation from the mother have a detrimental effect upon later functioning of the HPA system.

Ageing is normally associated with some loss of corticosteroid receptors in the brain, reduced negative feedback and increasing levels of corticosteroids (Anisman *et al.*, 1998).

Active and passive strategies

Introduction

Related to the strategy that an animal adopts on confrontation with a stressor, Henry (1982) described two types of stress, which differ in the hormonal axis that is most activated:

1 The sympathetic system is associated with the behaviour of fight and flight and is activated when the power to gain access to such things as food or a mate is challenged: '. . . and the subject perceives that an adequate response is feasible'.

2 The HPA axis is strongly activated by: 'adverse conditions, such as immobilization, in which the animal is helpless'.

For various species (e.g. mice, rats and possibly humans), individuals have a bias towards either an active or a passive reaction (Castanon and Mormède, 1994), each with its characteristic hormonal profile. Genetic differences are associated with different biases. This difference in strategy suggests the application of the term 'personality' also to non-humans. However, the two behavioural options are not entirely distinct hormonally. Thus, a strategy of fight or flight with sympathetic activation also involves HPA activation. Henry suggests that there is an adaptive advantage in having the facility to inhibit behavioural tendencies to fight or flee. If an animal is confronted by regular challenges for which neither option is viable, there could be advantages in staying still.

An animal can be biased towards one strategy but have the facility for showing the other, albeit at a higher threshold. For instance, it might learn that one strategy has failed and then switch to the other. However, in stress either strategy can 'get stuck' outside its adaptive range. This leads to the notion of different kinds of stress, arising from a failure of one strategy or the other.

The next two sections review some classical studies of reaction to stressors in different species, looking for general principles.

Tree shrews

Von Holst (1986) placed a tree shrew (*Tupaia belangeri*; Figure 13.4) into a cage where a resident conspecific was already housed. A fight followed, the outcome of which established a victor (i.e. dominant) and a defeated animal ('vanquished'). According to their behaviour, the 'vanquished' group could be further divided into 'subdominants' and 'submissives'. Subdominants took active steps to avoid dominants. Submissives, by contrast, were passive and unresponsive, sitting in the corner in a way characterized as 'apathetic' or 'depressive'. In response to the threats of the dominant, they neither fled nor attempted to defend themselves.

Figure 13.4 Tree shrew.
Source: © Rod Williams/naturepl.com

Subdominants and submissives gradually lost weight. After 10 days of the encounter, testosterone concentration fell by 30% in subdominants and 60% in submissives. After 20 days, blood testosterone level doubled in dominants.

Corticosteroid concentration was elevated for the first three days in all animals, though more so in submissives than in dominants or subdominants. Following the establishment of a dominance relationship, this fell to its initial value in both dominants and subdominants. In the submissives, by contrast, corticosteroid levels were elevated dramatically (by 300%) and remained so throughout.

Von Holst looked at the level of tyrosine hydroxylase, a chemical in the synthetic pathway for catecholamines, in the adrenal glands. Following the encounter, this was not significantly changed in dominants and decreased by about 30% in submissives. It increased by more than 100% in subdominants, suggestive of sympathetic activation. The fact that their adrenal noradrenalin content increases by about 30% also points to this.

Figure 13.5 compares heart-rates for representative dominants and subdominants. In both cases, there is a sharp elevation on first meeting. In dominants, this soon returns to normal, whereas that of the subdominants remains elevated throughout. Note the near disappearance of the normal day–night rhythm in the magnitude of heart-rate in subdominants.

Dominants seemed to suffer no ill effects from the confrontation. Weight and testosterone levels were well maintained. Their heart-rate was restrained, in spite of the fact that they were required to exert authority in the occasional fight. According to the criteria proposed here, dominants were not stressed. They had a coping strategy. By contrast, both subgroups of vanquished animals were stressed. They lost weight and showed lowered reproductive capacity. Neither strategy, active or passive, seemed to work. The elevated heart-rate of subdominants would have been appropriate for a short-term fight or flight strategy with a high energy requirement. However, over long periods such elevation indicates that the underlying problem has not been

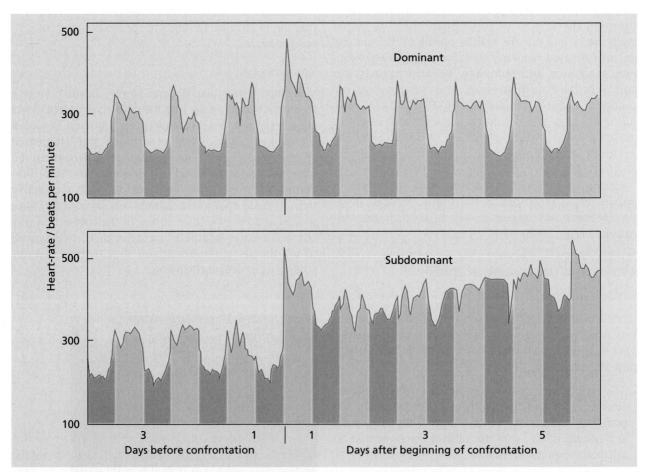

Figure 13.5 Heart-rate of dominant and subdominant tree shrews, before and after their encounter: dark purple, day; light purple, night.

Source: von Holst (1986, Fig. 3, p. 665).

solved. The physiological profile is inappropriate to behaviour. By the criterion of chronic elevated corticosteroids, submissives were also stressed. Such elevation is appropriate for increased activity. However, their behaviour was that of passivity, a situation in which elevated HPA activity would seem inappropriate.

Primates

Sapolsky (1990a,b) studied wild olive baboons (*Papio anubis*) living in social troops of 50–200 animals, in East Africa (Figure 13.6). Sapolsky (1990a, p. 863) notes that olive baboons have little threat from predators which 'leaves them hours each day to devote to generating social stressors for each other'. Thus, they might provide a model of some stresses of humans in affluent societies. Baboon society is hierarchical with dominants gaining most desirable resources, e.g. food and resting sites. Fights over dominance are frequent and often with serious injury. Riddled with cunning and deception, the worst aspects of baboon society appear to be as Machiavellian as those of humans.

In a stable hierarchy, low-ranking baboon males have a higher basal level of cortisol than do high-ranking males. However, in response to a challenge, dominant males show a sharper rise in cortisol secretion than do lower ranks. Sapolsky associates the high basal levels of cortisol of low-ranking baboons with events in their lives that trigger the HPA axis, e.g. disruption of ongoing activities, lack of predictability and control, frustration and being the innocent victim of displaced aggression. When there is instability in a hierarchy, e.g. a baboon equivalent of an impending *coup d'etat*, dominant males exhibit chronic elevated cortisol.

In 1984, East Africa experienced a drought and the time that needed to be spent in foraging increased considerably. This was associated with less aggression: as Sapolsky terms it (p. 865) the drought was 'a hidden blessing for subordinate individuals'.

Figure 13.6 Olive baboons.
Source: Gerry Ellis/Minden/FLPA

Sapolsky (1990a, p. 874) speculates: 'If one were giving stress management courses to baboons . . . ', and his advice is little different from that applicable to humans. Emphasis would be on acquiring predictability and control, forming reliable alliances, gaining skill at assessing social situations and finding suitable outlets for frustration. Success involves picking few fights and winning these.

The chapter now turns to the role of the immune system in stress.

Section summary

1 The impact of a stressor can be reduced by predictability and control.

2 In a situation of inescapable shock, learned helplessness can develop.

3 Exposure to a stressor can sensitize subsequent reactions to stressors.

4 There can be a bias towards either active or passive coping strategies.

5 Failure of either active or passive strategies corresponds to stress.

☞ Test your knowledge

13.4 Which neurohormonal system is particularly triggered at times when a threat is presented and *active* steps are taken to counter it?

 Answer on page 362

Stress and the immune system

Introduction

The *immune system* deals with threats to the body that are within its boundaries (Evans *et al.*, 1997). Such threats are described by the term **pathogen**. These are harmful bacteria and viruses, which can enter the body through, for example, cuts to the skin or food eaten or during sexual contact. The immune system is our defence against these invaders and against cancerous cells. Stress has effects upon the immune system. Reciprocally, events within the immune system affect the brain processes associated with stress. This section considers these interacting factors.

The interaction between psychological states, as embodied in the nervous system, and the endocrine and immune systems is summarized in such terms as 'psychoneuroimmunology' or 'psychoendoimmunology' (Ader and Cohen, 1985). If this book had been written in the 1970s or 1980s, it is very unlikely it would have had any mention of the immune system. It is relatively recently that the interactions between (i) the nervous and endocrine systems and (ii) the immune system have been formally recognized. Links from psychological states to immune activity provide a framework for understanding how stress can increase proneness to infection (Cohen, 1996).

Some details of the immune system

Consider the cells (Chapter 1) that make up the immune system: many millions of them, termed white cells or **leucocytes**. They are stored at certain 'depots' in the body, such as the spleen, from which, they are supplied to the body fluids. Leucocytes are carried in the body fluids (e.g. blood) to all parts of the body. They patrol, being, metaphorically speaking, on the look-out for invasion. Detection of pathogens activates the immune system. Immune cells launch an attack, which, if successful, destroys the invader. Our principal concern is with one class of leucocyte, known as the **lymphocyte**. When the body is invaded by bacteria or viruses, lymphocytes multiply ('proliferate') and go on the offensive (Evans *et al.*, 1997). In launching an attack, chemicals termed **cytokines** are released from cells of the immune system.

Interactions between immune and nervous systems

The immune system influences the brain and the endocrine system and also it is influenced by them. This section looks at each of these directions of influence.

The effects of the immune system

The immune activation in response to infection has consequences for nervous and endocrine systems. For example, cells of the immune system release hormones that affect the CNS. Cytokines, released as part of the immune response, influence the activity of the nervous system (Viamontes, 2009). Thereby, the CNS is informed of the activity of the immune system. The cytokine interleukin-1 (IL-1), which is released from activated immune cells, plays an important role here. Cytokines injected into the cerebrospinal fluid (Chapter 5) have a potent effect on behaviour, which leads to the suggestion that, under natural conditions,

central cytokines influence behaviour (Chapter 12). Injection of IL-1 produces a 'sickness reaction' of fever, withdrawal from social contact and reduction of exploration, etc. (Larson, 2002).

Information on immune cell activity from the periphery to the brain is conveyed in part by means of neural links (Viamontes, 2009). A major part of the effect of IL-1 on the brain is mediated via the vagus nerve (Figure 3.30, p. 76). Neurons within this nerve are triggered by IL-1 detected at their tips and they convey this information to the brain.

Interleukin-1 (IL-1) causes the release of CRF from the hypothalamus (Sapolsky *et al.*, 1987), suggesting the appropriateness of the term 'stressor'. In turn, the CRF excites ACTH and corticosteroid release.

Following infection by a virus, the body is not in a condition to be active and typically the animal curls up in a lethargic ball until recovery (Hart, 1988). This exemplifies coordination between behaviour and physiology. In humans, activation of the immune system can contribute towards a depressed mood (Viamontes, 2009).

That the brain is sensitive to these signals has led to the notion that the immune system can be considered to be an internal sensory organ, i.e. one responsible for detecting bacteria and viruses, etc. Maier and Watkins (1998) suggest that we underestimate the importance of the immune system for psychological state. Day-to-day fluctuations in mood might depend at least in part upon changes within the immune system.

Effects on the immune system

The nervous system affects the activity of the immune system, this being mediated directly and through the endocrine system. At times the nervous system excites the immune system and at other times inhibition is exerted (O'Leary, 1990). Cells of the immune system have receptors for substances on their walls, which, in the nervous and endocrine systems, constitute neurotransmitters and hormones. In this way, the nervous and endocrine systems can influence the activity of the immune system.

Sympathetic neurons innervate the organs that constitute part of the immune system (Ballieux and Heijnen, 1987), organs that would normally be packed with leucocytes. The leucocytes contain receptors for the transmitter released by these neurons, suggesting that nervous system activity can excite or inhibit the release of leucocytes into the body fluids. Activation of the immune system appears to be specifically by the sympathetic branch.

Stress can inhibit, or 'down-regulate', the activity of the immune system (Evans *et al.*, 1997). For example, the human immune response is down-regulated by such chronic stressors as divorce, bereavement, sleep deprivation and war (Maier *et al.*, 1994). Down-regulation means a less effective defence against challenges.

Rats that have been exposed to stressors have a decreased activity of immune cells. Placing a rat in a situation of helplessness has a detrimental effect upon the immune system and the ability to reject a tumour (Laudenslager *et al.*, 1983). To have some coping capacity, e.g. the capacity to terminate shock by lever-pressing, is of benefit. It is not easy to generalize from this to humans.

Cohen (1996) asked volunteers to fill in stress- and life-events questionnaires and then exposed them to the common cold virus by nasal drops. They were then quarantined. Blood samples were taken to assess infection. Would stress increase the risk of an upper respiratory illness? There was a significant effect in this direction. Even where people did not subjectively feel that they were stressed, life-events normally termed 'stressful' were associated with increased susceptibility to illness.

Some cells of the immune system, a type of lymphocyte termed 'natural killer' (NK) cells, target cancerous cells and destroy them. However, the relationship between stress and the onset and development of cancer in humans is, at the time of writing, still controversial. The link between depression and health as mediated by the immune system is also not entirely clear (Stein *et al.*, 1991). There are indications that cervical cancer is more likely in women who report hopelessness and that cancer patients with social support are better able to survive (Edelman and Kidman, 1997). Optimism appears to speed wound-healing after surgery, an effect that is mediated, it would appear, in part via an enhanced immune activity (Kiecolt-Glaser *et al.*, 1998).

The *acute* application of some stressors, i.e. a change over minutes rather than hours or days (e.g. a public speaking task), can trigger *up*-regulation (Evans *et al.*, 1997). The acute phase of up-regulation might be due to sympathetic activity.

Stressors can exert effects through routes other than those nervous and endocrine system processes described so far. For example, divorce or bereavement might mean less sleep and exercise and an increase in alcohol and cigarette consumption, with independent effects on disease. Also by changes in physiology (e.g. blood flow), stressors might influence disease through routes other than the immune system (Maier *et al.*, 1994). Some stressors lower the production of saliva, probably with a reduction in protection of the oral cavity (Evans *et al.*, 1997). In stress, people might be more inclined to seek the company of others, with increased risk of such things as the common cold and influenza.

Function

Consider first that events in the immune system affect the nervous system. Suppose that an animal is suffering an infection. It could be in its interests to rest and sleep, to allow recovery to occur (Hart, 1988). Therefore, it could be advantageous for chemical messengers that are secreted by activated cells of the immune system to steer behaviour in this direction.

Why should the nervous and endocrine systems influence the immune system? Why does stress tend to lower the activity of the system? It might prove crucial to distinguish two phases of stress: (i) an acute phase, during which the immune system seems to be excited, and (ii) a chronic phase, during which it seems to be inhibited (Maier and Watkins, 1998). A time of sympathetic activation might well correspond to fight or flight, when presumably there is a risk of injury and infection (O'Leary, 1990) and to boost immune activity could make adaptive sense. On the other hand, suppression of immune function during chronic stress might be a means of restraining the activity of the (already excited) system at a time when infection might be less likely.

At first sight, it might seem logical to play safe; surely the bigger the immune response, the better. However, there are costs attached to immune activity, e.g. an energy cost (Sapolsky, 1992). Also, an activated immune system can launch an attack against parts of the 'self' (Råberg *et al.*, 1998), the so-called autoimmune disorders. So, under some conditions, there could be an adaptive advantage in restraining the immune system.

A caution

Psychoneuroimmunology (PNI) gives a scientific basis to folk wisdom on the capacity of the 'mind to affect the body' (Evans *et al.*, 1997). PNI evokes reactions ranging from scepticism to unqualified acceptance. To sceptics, the effects seem fragile and offer little clinical hope. To some of those into 'alternative approaches', it is attractive to attribute ills to a psychological construct, stress. However, we must avoid exaggerated claims of the kind that psychological factors are all-important and the causation of, say, cancer lies 'all in the mind'.

A critical approach recognizes interacting factors in disease onset and development. The psychological effect is only one factor among many that influence the immune system and might thereby influence disease. We need more cautious claims of the kind that, under some conditions, certain stressors can affect parts of the immune system and probably disease onset and development.

Having looked at the more peripheral parts of the picture we now look at the brain mechanisms that underlie stress.

Section summary

1 The immune system protects the body against 'invaders' that penetrate its boundary, e.g. viruses and bacteria, as well as cancer.

2 There are reciprocal links between nervous, endocrine and immune systems.

3 The immune system affects the nervous system and thereby influences behaviour.

4 The nervous system can both excite and inhibit the activity of the immune system.

5 Chronic stress, a state of the CNS, can inhibit the activity of the immune system.

6 Some effects of stress on the immune system appear to be mediated by corticosteroids.

☞ Test your knowledge

13.5 By what criterion could we class a cytokine as a hormone?

Answer on page 362

Brain mechanisms

Introduction

We now consider those brain processes that are the neuropsychological embodiment of stress. There are some closely related leads in this investigation (Figure 13.7):

1 In stress, the neural mechanisms underlying such emotions as fear or anger (Chapter 12) are activated over long periods of time (Rosen and Schulkin, 1998).

2 The two hormonal systems described earlier (the sympathetic and HPA systems) are triggered by activity in particular parts of the brain. Therefore, psychologists can look at release of these hormones and trace the causal links back into the brain.

We shall now examine these sources of insight.

Initial triggers to emotion and stress

The amygdala is a site where emotional significance is attached to events. Some stimuli, such as loud sounds, evoke emotion simply by virtue of their sensory properties (Chapter 12). This draws attention to neurons within sensory pathways having collaterals that project to brain regions (e.g. amygdala) underlying stress. By contrast, other triggers such as frustration cannot be defined by sensory events per se but only by the comparison of sensory events with memories. Such 'cognitive input' suggests the involvement of the hippocampus and cortical processing (Glue *et al.*, 1993). Certain products of the immune system affect regions of brain underlying stress, as represented by 'physiological' in Figure 13.7.

Corticotropin releasing factor

Introduction

A neurochemical of the brain that plays a central role in emotional processing is corticotropin releasing factor (CRF) (Dunn and Berridge, 1990; Pfaff *et al.*, 2007). CRF was described earlier as a hormone, part of the HPA axis (Figure 13.3). At the pituitary gland, it plays this *peripheral* role (peripheral, that is, relative to regions deep in the brain). However, CRF also acts as a neurotransmitter or neuromodulator deep in the CNS, a *central* role. Stressors trigger coordinated CRF activity in both central and peripheral roles (Pfaff *et al.*, 2007). First, we look at the controls of CRF secretion when it acts as a hormone and we then consider its role as a neurotransmitter.

Hormonal role

CRF-containing neurons with cell bodies in the hypothalamus form the start of the HPA axis (Figure 13.3). These neurons receive inputs from various regions, e.g. other hypothalamic regions, brain stem, hippocampus and the central nucleus of the amygdala (Chapter 12; Amaral and Sinnamon, 1977). These neurons therefore form a common focus for various sources of information, conveying, in functional terms, 'challenge and the need to take action'.

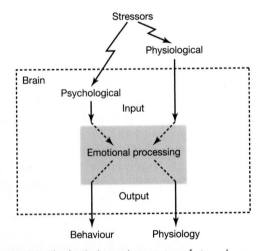

Figure 13.7 The brain is put into states of stress by means of stressors and their interpretation (the 'input'). In turn, the brain provides signals to the neurohormonal systems of stress (the 'output').

Neurotransmitter roles

Now we need to change hats, or, to be precise, roles of CRF and switch attention to a different role of the same substance.

CRF-containing neurons convey emotion-related information between various parts of the brain. Cell bodies of CRF-containing neurons are found in the amygdala (Bohus and Koolhaas, 1993). CRF's wide representation throughout the limbic system and in structures concerned with autonomic control suggests a coordinated role in autonomic and behavioural outputs, which is stretched excessively in stress.

Intracerebral CRF injection leads to EEG arousal and to an increase in the acoustic startle response (Chapter 12), an index of stress and anxiety (Dunn and Berridge, 1990). In exciting the locus coeruleus, CRF activates noradrenergic transmission over large areas of brain, discussed next.

Noradrenergic systems and the locus coeruleus

In reaction to stressors, noradrenalin (NA) acts peripherally as both neurotransmitter and hormone (Chapters 3 and 12). It is broadcast widely, attaches to a broad distribution of receptors and thereby influences diverse organs (e.g. cardiac muscle and smooth muscle in blood vessel walls). The same chemical is used in the CNS, where it is also widely distributed and serves a

Figure 13.8 The human locus coeruleus and projections. Descending projections influence the ANS.

Source: Martin, J.H. (1996). *Neuroanatomy: Text and Atlas*, 2nd edition, Figure 3.17 p. 87. Reprinted with permission of The McGraw-Hill Companies, Inc.

neuromodulatory role at diverse targets (Zigmond *et al.*, 1995). The functional coherence of noradrenalin's dual role in periphery and CNS points to interesting evolutionary roots. That is to say, in both cases stressors trigger its release.

Activity within noradrenergic neurons that project from the locus coeruleus appears to be an important feature of stress, associated with both behavioural and sympathetic activity (Dampney, 1994; Pfaff *et al.*, 2007). See Figure 13.8.

Figure 13.9 Some connections with an integrative nucleus in the medulla. LHA, lateral hypothalamic area; NTS, nucleus of the solitary tract; PAG, periaqueductal grey; PVN, paraventricular nucleus of hypothalamus.

Source: adapted from Dampney (1990, Fig. 3, p. 65).

Triggers to the sympathetic system

Moving to the output side of the brain, a nucleus that integrates information ('integrative nucleus') and controls sympathetic activity is located in the medulla (Figure 13.9; Dampney, 1994). Neurons project from here to sympathetic preganglionic neurons with cell bodies in the spinal cord and controlling the circulatory system (in Figure 13.8, note the link to the spinal cord). Figure 13.9 shows inputs to the 'integrative nucleus' from the lateral hypothalamus, nucleus of the solitary tract, paraventricular nucleus of the hypothalamus and the periaqueductal grey (Chapter 5). These brain regions are involved in recruiting defensive behaviours in response to threats. Considering adaptive functioning, the link with the sympathetic system points to coherence between behaviour (fight and flight) and physiology. In stress, these systems show elevated activity over long periods of time.

Following sections look at disorders associated with stress and, in so doing, further insight into the brain mechanisms that have been discussed in this section can be gained.

Section summary

1   Looking at the basic brain mechanisms of emotion and their protracted activation gives a lead to understanding stress.

2   In actions within the CNS and in triggering the HPA axis, corticotropin releasing factor (CRF) appears to play functionally coherent roles in its behavioural, autonomic and hormonal effects.

3   In stress, noradrenalin activation occurs in the periphery and CNS, indicating functional coherence.

4   Central noradrenergic systems trigger behavioural and autonomic activation.

5   The locus coeruleus and NA neurons that project from it have a pivotal role in activation at times of stress.

Test your knowledge

13.6 CRF acts as (i) a hormone, (ii) a neurotransmitter or (iii) both. Justify your answer.

Answer on page 362

Depression

Stress and depression can usefully be studied together, since stress is a risk factor for depression (Bremner, 1999). This section looks at areas of overlap in the two conditions.

The HPA axis

Increased HPA axis activity appears to be a major causal factor in depression (Bao *et al.*, 2008). Depression is associated with enlargement of the adrenal gland and elevated levels of cortisol in the blood (Holsboer and Barden, 1996). What triggers this activation? The drive from CRF-containing neurons at the start of the HPA axis is increased (Keller *et al.*, 2006). Increased drive might arise from the increased activity of noradrenergic neurons of the locus coeruleus that is observed in depression (Ur *et al.*, 1992).

An important factor in depression appears to be weakened negative feedback of corticosteroids in the brain. By reducing this inhibitory effect, the excitatory link is less opposed and thereby this contributes to HPA excitation (Holsboer and Barden, 1996). See Figure 13.3. Major depression is associated with some loss of tissue at the hippocampus, which could be the product of the toxicity of excessive corticosteroid levels (Bremner, 1999). This appears to be reflected in some deterioration of cognitive capacity, e.g. working memory (Hinkelmann *et al.*, 2009). A range of antidepressants tend to lower activity in the HPA axis (Mitchell, 1998) and an interesting idea is that antidepressants exert some effect by increasing corticosteroid feedback on the HPA axis (Barden *et al.*, 1995). Increasing age appears to lower the efficacy of corticosteroid feedback at the hippocampus (Seeman and Robbins, 1994) and might be a contributory factor to depression. Cushing's disease, which involves excessive secretion of corticosteroids, is commonly followed by depression (Holsboer and Barden, 1996).

The CNS affects the HPA axis and, reciprocally, the HPA axis (e.g. elevated corticosteroids) affects the CNS. Disturbances within these interactions appear to be fundamental to depression. By their actions at the brain, corticosteroids appear to bias towards negative emotion (Schulkin, 1994), vigilance and avoidance of conflict (van Honk *et al.*, 1998). Of course, in small doses and over a limited time period such changes could be adaptive.

Breier *et al.* (1988) found a tendency for people who had experienced separation from a parent in childhood to be predisposed to develop psychopathology when adult. Their cortisol levels were higher than controls.

In depression, there is increased blood flow to the amygdala and medial orbitofrontal cortex, both regions having a high density of corticosteroid receptors

(Erikson *et al.*, 2003). Thereby, elevated levels of corticosteroids appear to contribute to the negative bias to cognition in depression.

Role of CRF

The activity of CRF in the brains of people suffering depression is elevated (Bao *et al.*, 2008; Mitchell, 1998), i.e. there is a higher release level. This plays a role in increased activity in brain areas concerned with processing negative emotion, e.g. regions of the amygdala. In depression, increased activity of the locus coeruleus and the associated NA systems appears to be due to increased CRF-mediated input to the locus coeruleus. It might constitute an important biological basis of depression (Curtis and Valentino, 1994; Ur *et al.*, 1992). A number of effective treatments for depression lower CRF levels (Bao et al., 2008; Markou *et al.*, 1998), e.g. some antidepressant drugs oppose the excitatory effects of CRF in the locus coeruleus (Curtis and Valentino, 1994). New CRF antagonists are being sought as treatments (Keller *et al.*, 2006). Increased CRF activity in the brain is observed during withdrawal from drugs, pointing to common features between this state and depression (Markou *et al.*, 1998). Suicide victims show down-regulation (Chapter 4) of CRF receptors in their frontal cortex, suggestive of hyper-secretion of CRF (Markou *et al.*, 1998).

Section summary

1. In depression there is activation of the HPA axis.

2. Elevated corticosteroids appear to give a negative bias to mood.

3. Injection of CRF into the brain triggers features of depression and there is evidence of CRF activation in depression.

4. On balance, evidence suggests noradrenergic activation in depression.

☞ Test your knowledge

13.7 Complete the following: 'A decrease in corticosteroid feedback action in the brain causes ___ activity in the HPA system'.

13.8 In what way could the material in this section make any sense in terms of the functional type of explanation?

Answers on page 362

Stress and the cardiovascular system

Background

Associations between mental state and the heart have been observed for some 4500 years (Williams, 1989) and stress is central to the relationship.

What is termed **coronary heart disease (CHD)** is a disorder of the vessels that supply blood to the heart, in almost all cases consisting of atherosclerosis within the coronary arteries (Scheidt, 1996). CHD is the biggest killer in Western countries. This section explores the link between stress, personality and the health of the circulatory system.

Type A and Type B personalities

Early research identified **Type A behaviour**, particularly associated with CHD, the person who exhibits it being termed a 'Type A' (Friedman and Rosenman, 1959). Type A behaviour consists of being under excessive time-pressure, aggressively competitive, over-ambitious and easily aroused to hostility by situations judged as trivial by non-Type As. Billings *et al.* (1996) observe that CHD patients appear to be (p. 244): 'especially prone to the cultural emphasis on individualism and accomplishment, characteristics that promote isolation rather than interpersonal connection'.

The SNS is hyper-reactive in Type As, with the parasympathetic under-active (Friedman, 1996). There is high secretion of corticosteroids and (usually, though not always) a high blood level of cholesterol and a tendency to heart attacks (Williams, 1989). The cause of the problem appears to lie in a chronic tilting of the sympathetic–parasympathetic balance towards the sympathetic (Roberts, 1996). So what tilts the balance? Friedman (1996) incriminates covert features of the Type A personality, consisting of insecurity and a low value of self-esteem. The perfectionist goals of self-esteem through achievement are never reached.

Type B behaviour is the opposite of the Type A, i.e. relaxed and without hostility and competitiveness (Friedman, 1996). The 'Type B' has a relatively high level of self-esteem and feelings of security and can tolerate the mistakes of others. Type Bs do not exhibit the neurohormonal abnormalities of Type As. Blood cholesterol is relatively low.

Although we are all probably familiar with some 'textbook' Type As and Type Bs, it is wrong to think in terms of an absolute bimodal distinction. Rather, a person might lie somewhere between the two or show a mixture of the two according to context.

A personal angle

The role of hostility

B.G., a businessman, aged 44, enjoyed getting his own way (Williams, 1989). B.G. would threaten others into surrender. (You might know a 'B.G.' or two!) One day, B.G. was driving his car when another motorist had the audacity to overtake. Normally, B.G. would 'pay the bastard back', by accelerating and emitting a warning blast on the horn. However, this time, just as B.G. was getting into attack mode, he had an experience as 'though a red-hot poker was being driven into the centre of his chest'. B.G. had his first heart attack.

The electrical activity of the heart, recorded by an electrocardiogram, was normal. B.G.'s pain went away and he was free of symptoms for several days. Alas, on the day scheduled for discharge from hospital, as a blood sample was being taken, B.G. switched into the anger mode. Whereupon, 'the red-hot poker hit his chest again'. The electrocardiogram indicated that the blood supply to B.G.'s heart was inadequate. Arteriosclerosis had almost completely blocked one of the arteries. Surgeons removed a vein from B.G.'s leg and transplanted it to the heart.

Williams employed therapy to target B.G.'s hostility and lack of trust. B.G. lived in a world populated by people whose incompetence demanded eternal vigilance. Williams prescribed behaviour modification in the hope that B.G. could alter his behaviour and cognitions. B.G. is not an isolated case. A positive correlation is found between hostility score and magnitude of arteriosclerosis of the coronary arteries.

Rather than personality, could some other factor correlate with Type A behaviour and contribute to the effects on the coronary condition (Steptoe, 1993)? For example, Type As probably smoke or drink more alcohol than Type Bs. However, personality is an independent factor that contributes in interaction with other factors such as smoking (Williams, 1989). There is disagreement as to whether all the characteristics of the Type A are equally toxic, with some theorists placing a particular blame on hostility.

B.G. illustrates two aspects of coronary heart disease: (i) the chronic background state of hostility and atherosclerosis that sets the scene and (ii) that in some cases, but not all, an emotional incident is the immediate trigger to a heart attack (Allan and Scheidt, 1996b).

There is a clear link between low socio-economic status (SES) and poor health (Gallo and Matthews, 2003). Numerous factors mediate this link but one is central to the present chapter: low SES is associated with a high frequency of negative cognitive and emotional reactions and low coping resources. The link appears to be mediated in part by the SNS and HPA systems.

Negative emotion does not necessarily have to be expressed in overt behaviour to influence the ANS. By the use of the imagination and sub-vocal speech, people mentally re-run, and ruminate on, perceived injustices and personal insults (Allan and Scheidt, 1996b). Therapy for cardiac health counters covert 'behaviour': it monitors the 'inner dialogue' for the appearance of hostile thoughts and challenges them (Burell, 1996).

By neuroimaging, researchers can look in the brain for the basis of the exaggerated response to threat that forms a contribution to CHD (the link between a challenge and the trigger to the peripheral reaction). Regions known to be involved in emotion are implicated, i.e. high activity by the amygdala, anterior cingulate cortex and insula correlates with strong peripheral reactions as measured by increased blood pressure (Gianaros and Sheu, 2009).

Section summary

1 Among the factors that determine coronary health is personality.

2 A distinction is drawn between Type A and Type B behaviours, corresponding to Type A and Type B people.

3 Early studies found Type As to be more prone to coronary disease.

4 In Type As, there is excessive reactivity by the SNS.

 ### Test your knowledge

13.9 You are devising a drug to assist Type As with lowering the effects of their overreactivity on the circulatory system but not setting out to target the CNS. Your first thought would probably be antagonists to which kind of hormones/neurochemicals?

Answer on page 362

Post-traumatic stress disorder

The phenomenon

The condition termed **post-traumatic stress disorder (PTSD)** seriously disrupts many lives, e.g. war veterans (Richardson *et al.*, 2010). It follows trauma in which there is actual or threatened death or serious injury to the sufferer or another person. Some core symptoms of PTSD are regular activation of memories relating to the incident, nightmares and high SNS arousal (Davis *et al.*, 1997). In addition to core symptoms, depression, aggression, irritability and impulsiveness are common. PTSD is associated with a heightened magnitude of the startle response (Orr *et al.*, 1995) and increased heart-rate acceleration to sounds (Pallmeyer *et al.*, 1986).

Only a fraction of people exposed to trauma develop the disorder, which raises issues concerning the characteristics of sufferers (Yehuda *et al.*, 1995). Over one-third of the US soldiers who served in Vietnam have experienced PTSD (Davis *et al.*, 1997).

Biological bases

Pitman *et al.* (1993) refer to 'emotive biasing' in PTSD and suggest that its embodiment could be sensitization of links from the basal amygdala to the ventromedial hypothalamus, a form of long-term potentiation (Chapter 11; Adamec, 1997). Artificial stimulation of the amygdala is associated with 'memory flashback', suggesting that it triggers a search for emotionally tagged material that is brought into conscious awareness (Charney *et al.*, 1995). A range of stimuli might come to activate the amygdala and thereby retrieve traumatic memories (Le Doux, 1998). There is evidence suggesting damage to hippocampal tissue, in the cases of combat-related and childhood-abuse related PTSD. This is manifest as some loss of volume of this structure, particularly in certain subregions of the hippocampus (e.g. the dentate) that would normally exhibit neurogenesis (Wang *et al.*, 2010). This structure contains a high density of corticosteroid receptors and could be particularly vulnerable to an elevation in corticosteroid level. Given the role of the hippocampus in memory, early harm to this structure could have enormous implications for the recall of childhood memories (or a failure to do so).

One's intuitive guess would be that the HPA axis would also be chronically activated in this condition. Since the hippocampus is damaged and excessive corticosteroid levels are toxic to this structure, elevated levels of corticosteroids would be expected to accompany PTSD. However, there is some controversy on whether this is the case (Bremner, 1999; Yehuda *et al.*, 1995).

A personal angle

The tragedy of war

Pitman *et al.* (1993, p. 145) report:

A highly decorated war veteran patient of ours led a life tortured by fear and anger since his return from Vietnam more than 20 years ago. He was unable to close his eyes in the shower because of the dread that someone would grab him. He had impulses to shoot, stab, or strangle everyone he encountered. He panicked at the ring of a doorbell. Being kept waiting in line would send him into a rage. He washed his hands compulsively, and repetitively checked the stove and locks on the doors.

The patient illustrates three features of PTSD: (1) the coexistence of heightened fear and anger, (2) a range of situations in which over-reactivity is shown and (3) an association with other disorders, e.g. obsessive–compulsive disorder.

Section summary

1 Trauma, where there is actual or threatened death or serious injury, can trigger post-traumatic stress disorder (PTSD).

2 The hallmarks of PTSD are regular activation of traumatic memories, nightmares and SNS activation. Depression, aggressivity, irritability and impulsivity are often also shown.

 ## Test your knowledge

13.10 In PTSD, evidence points to a toxic effect of corticosteroids on the hippocampus. Not everyone subject to trauma suffers from PTSD, so is there any other possible explanation for why sufferers from PTSD might have a lower than normal volume of hippocampus?

Answer on page 362

Influence of stress on the gut

Introduction

Common sayings point to a belief that there exist causal links between mental states and gastrointestinal function. A link between stress and gastrointestinal disorders is indicated by (i) 'nervous irritation' and (ii) peptic ulceration, in the stomach and part of the small intestine, the duodenum (Levenstein, 1998). This section looks at these two examples of brain → gut links.

Irritable bowel syndrome

A disorder of the gut is the **irritable bowel syndrome (IBS)** (Stam *et al.*, 1997). It involves abdominal distension and pain, with abnormal patterns of defecation. Stressful events commonly precede an episode of IBS. IBS is associated with psychiatric illnesses, e.g. anxiety, depression and PTSD. Targeting depression or anxiety often alleviates it (Meyer and Gebhart, 1994).

The enteric nervous system (ENS) stimulates coordinated patterns of gastrointestinal activity (termed 'motility') involving waves of contraction (Chapter 3). The ANS modulates activity within the ENS. In IBS, it appears that activity is abnormal as a result of increased sensitivity somewhere within these networks of neurons (Stam *et al.*, 1997). Transit of material through the small intestine is slowed but large intestine transit is accelerated (Williams *et al.*, 1988). IBS patients show a higher than normal sensitivity to gut distension. There could be abnormal modulation of the link between the sensory detection of material in the gut and motor action by the smooth muscles. The modulatory signal would be sensitive to stress.

Figure 13.10 summarizes signals involved in gut motility and sensation. Disturbances within any of these could underlie IBS. Note the route from the external world to the CNS, then through the ANS to the enteric nervous system (ENS) and hence to smooth muscles of the gut wall. Abnormal activity in this pathway is assumed to underlie the stress-mediated contribution to IBS. Activity by CRF in the brain is implicated in this and CRF antagonists offer promise of help (Taché and Brunnhuber, 2008). Sensory neurons in the gut wall feed back through the pathway ENS → ANS → CNS (Zhou *et al.*, 2010). Abnormal sensitivity of this route or abnormal gut contents could set up disturbances in the feedback pathway, which might in turn influence motor outflow to the gut (Meyer and Gebhart, 1994).

IBS should not be seen simply as a brain-driven ('psychological') disorder. Such factors as a gut infection can also trigger it (Stam *et al.*, 1997). It is an interaction of local and central factors. Thus, an infection is more likely to trigger IBS in patients having prior stressful experiences.

Ulcers

Animal models show that **ulcers** can be triggered by several stressors. In baboons, gastric ulceration is highest in subordinates, who are subject to most social stress (Uno *et al.*, 1989). Increased risk of ulceration in people under stress (e.g. economic collapse) implicates psychosomatic disorders (Levenstein, 1998). As noted earlier, animals exposed to an uncontrollable aversive situation tend to develop gastric ulcers ('peptic ulcers'). Amelioration of the impact of stressors can be obtained by allowing the animal some facility for control (Weiss *et al.*, 1976).

There are neural and hormonal links between CNS and stomach (e.g. the vagus nerve), which could mediate causal links between psychological states and stomach pathology. However, a sensational discovery by the Australian doctor, B.J. Marshall, moved attention away from psychological factors: a microorganism, the bacterium *Helicobacter pylori*, is involved in peptic ulcers (Marshall, 1995). Targeting this with antibiotics led to a cure in many cases, which caused some to dismiss psychosomatic causes. In 1998, Levenstein wrote (p. 538):

> When *H. pylori* burst on the scene a few years ago, it revolutionised views on the aetiology and treatment of peptic ulcer. Psychosocial factors were quietly but firmly escorted off the stage, and gastroenterologists in particular banished psychological considerations with something approaching relief.

However, the world does not divide into neat physical versus psychological categories. Most people have the microorganism in their stomachs but do not develop peptic ulcers (Weiner, 1996). Some are not infected but still develop them. Antibiotic medication is not effective for all patients. Recognition of the role of a microorganism does not lower the importance of stress. There is the

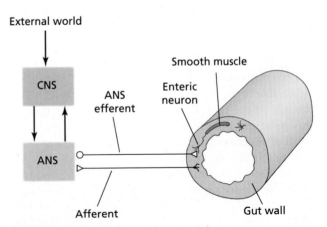

Figure 13.10 Some flows of information underlying gut motility.
Source: based on McKee and Quigley (1993).

possibility of interaction between them. For example, stress can probably increase the vulnerability of the stomach wall to bacterial infection (Overmier and Murison, 1997). The immune system normally mounts an attack against bacteria but might be compromised in stress.

Section summary

1 The enteric nervous system organizes contractions of the gut. The irritable bowel syndrome (IBS) is a disturbance to this.

2 Stress, the effects of which are mediated via the CNS and ANS, is a causal factor implicated in IBS.

3 Peptic ulcers can be caused jointly by psychological factors and bacterial infection.

 ## Test your knowledge

13.11 What type of muscle is involved in the irritable bowel syndrome? It is innervated by neurons of which system?

Answer on page 362   WEB

Positive action for health

A better understanding of stress can not only alert us to avoid stressful situations but also to try to maximize situations that are low on stress or can counter stress. It is unfortunate that, in the history of psychology, most emphasis has been on negative emotions. However, there is a growing recognition of the role of positive emotions (Burgdorf and Panksepp, 2006; Ganzel et al., 2010), as reflected in the term 'positive psychology'. We can promote good health and happiness rather than simply the reduction of negative indices. Optimism can be good for health, with the possibility that part of the effect is mediated via the immune system (Taylor et al., 2000). Optimistic expectancies and positive affect are associated with elevated reaction by the immune system (Segerstrom and Sephton, 2010). This can give a rationale for cognitive interventions designed to cultivate optimism. fMRI studies of the brain reveal that so-called 'resilient' individuals show relatively low levels of carry-over of negative emotion after brief exposure to aversive images (Waugh et al., 2008). Their closer study might be useful in devising cognitive interventions that can exploit positive emotions to overcome the effects

of negative emotions. The presence of positive affect is associated with recovery of blood pressure to normal levels after a stress challenge (Steptoe et al., 2009).

Social contact

Introduction

Concerning the role of maladaptive social reactions in coronary disease, action can be taken to undermine toxic Type A effects (Williams, 1989). Since learning seems to be involved in the acquisition of a hostile way of reacting, relearning might help to change behaviour and cognitions. Psychologists emphasize that, for healthy development, it is important for a child to be able to trust another human.

For several disorders, people who are socially isolated run a greater risk than those who are happily socially integrated (Allan and Scheidt, 1996b; Grant et al., 2009). A caring social relationship seems to offer defence against stress. The presence of a friendly other person can moderate the effect of a stressor, as indexed by heart-rate or the rise in fatty acid levels in the blood (Bovard, 1985; Steptoe, 1993) or length of recovery following surgery (Kiecolt-Glaser et al., 1998).

Support groups for patients with coronary heart disease attempt to counter isolation and alienation and boost self-esteem (Billings et al., 1996). The term **belonging** refers to a particular lifestyle, social context and way of reacting. The individual forms part of a harmonious network, with meaning and purpose, and has a capacity for prediction, control and coping. Goals are acceptable and attainable within a social network and the person values friendship above the acquisition of material resources (Allan and Scheidt, 1996b).

Comparing cultures

Japanese culture emphasizes good interpersonal skills, social interaction and trusting interdependence, stability, cohesion and achievement by the common group more than do Western cultures. Japanese show lower hostility scores than Americans. By contrast, Marmot and Syme (1976, p. 246) suggest that people in American and Northern European cultures:

display almost opposite characteristics to the protective features described, i.e. lack of stability, accent on the individual rather than the group, and a high likelihood of an individual finding himself in a situation for which his world-view has left him unprepared.

The United States has one of the highest rates of heart attacks in the developed world (Marmot and Syme, 1976). By contrast, the Japanese have one of the lowest. Comparing Japanese living in Japan and

California, the Californians have a much higher rate than those in Japan. Again, diet and smoking apparently can account for only part of the effect. Thus, comparing Japanese males eating a similar diet in Japan or California, the Californians had higher levels of blood cholesterol.

Explaining the effects

What could link social factors and the circulatory system? The effect appears to be mediated by what are termed 'lipoproteins'. Lipids (fats) such as cholesterol are found in the bloodstream in two forms, high-density lipoproteins (HDL) and low-density lipoproteins (LDL) (Scheidt, 1996). The ratio LDL/HDL gives an index of the risk of atherosclerosis, a high ratio being associated with a high risk (Roberts, 1996). As this ratio decreases, there is a decrease in the frequency of heart attacks. Could psychological factors be one determinant of this ratio? Looking at a group of 17-year-old Israelis, the ratio was higher in the non-religious than in the religious (Friedlander *et al.*, 1987). This could reflect differences in belonging and social cohesion.

What influences differences in circulatory systems between individuals? In early childhood, the Type B, in contrast to the Type A, was typically exposed to affection and admiration (Friedman, 1996). There might also be a role for genetic differences. How can positive social bonds with other humans influence the system? Psychobiological theories (Bovard, 1985) relate to the idea that humans have evolved as part of a social matrix. Presumably, brain processes of motivation and emotion (Panksepp, 1982) play a role in seeking and maintaining social bonds and have links to the ANS.

Trusting social contact moderates SNS activity (Bovard, 1985) and buffers against the stressors that will almost invariably arise (Ganzel *et al.*, 2010).

Meditation

Meditation, when a person sits relaxed, with closed eyes, and performs a repeated simple mental activity, triggers the 'relaxation response' that counters trends towards SNS domination and hyper-arousal (Bracke and Thoresen, 1996). Simultaneously, the parasympathetic contribution is strengthened (Sakakibara *et al.*, 1994). Group meetings for coronary heart disease patients involve meditation on feeling states and use of self-control in such forms as guided imagery (Billings *et al.*, 1996).

Section summary

1 Belonging (e.g. having a social bond) seems to benefit coronary health.

2 The effect of positive social contact seems to be mediated via the CNS restraining the SNS.

☞ ## Test your knowledge

13.12 Therapeutic interventions such as meditation tilt the ANS which way?

Answer on page 362

Bringing things together

A protracted disturbance to psychological homeostasis, associated with unsuccessful attempts to counter this, constitute stress. Neurohormonal systems that are triggered by stressors serve a useful function when activated *under appropriate conditions*. For example, when confronted with a bear and having a capacity to escape, accelerated heart-rate and a high rate of secretion of cortisol are appropriate. Such reactions are not to our advantage when we are stuck for hours in a traffic-jam or endlessly chewing-over our rejection for promotion. These days, at least among readers of the present text, stress hormones are more likely to be triggered by traffic jams than bears.

Psychological states such as depression and anxiety have a basis in the brain, which has effects outside the nervous system, e.g. in the accumulation of deposits on blood vessels or forming lesions in the walls of the stomach. Such phenomena illustrate the shortcomings of logic based upon 'either/or', e.g. a disorder is either somatic or psychological. For example, gastric ulceration appears to reflect interaction between bacterial infection and CNS-mediated events. Similarly, cardiovascular disease is the result of interactions between (i) such things as diet and smoking and (ii) psychological states, not to forget the possible role of genetic differences underlying nervous system differences.

Figure 13.11 develops a diagram shown in Chapter 3 (Figure 3.36, p. 81) and will help to consolidate your understanding. Included now is the immune system.

Note the ANS links to endocrine and immune systems and the influence of the immune system on the brain.

Figure 13.11 Nervous, endocrine and immune systems.

Summary of Chapter 13

1 The term 'stress' describes a long-term disturbance to psychological homeostasis.

2 Stress is associated with unsuccessful attempts to cope, excessive activity within certain neurohormonal systems and proneness to several disorders.

3 The sympathetic branch of the ANS and the pituitary adrenocortical system, involving corticosteroids, form a principal focus for understanding stress.

4 The level of stress depends on context, e.g. (i) the capacity to predict when a stressor will occur, (ii) opportunities for action and (iii) what is done in response to the potential stressor and the outcome of this action.

5 Stress reactions within the CNS can have effects on the immune system. Reciprocally, activity in the immune system has effects on the CNS and thereby stress-related behaviour.

6 Identifiable brain regions form the neural basis of stress and convey information to the neurohormonal systems that are activated under stress.

7 Stress increases the tendency to suffer from depression.

8 Stress has important implications for the health of the circulatory system.

9 Post-traumatic stress disorder (PTSD) follows trauma in which there is actual or threatened death or serious injury to the sufferer or another person

10 Stress can manifest as pathology of the stomach and intestine.

11 Interventions designed to lower the harmful effects of stress are based on lowering negative emotion and excessive sympathetic activity.

 See the video coverage for this chapter and experience something of the good and bad aspects of emotions.

Further reading

For classical writing, see Selye (1973). Sapolsky (2004) is also something of a classic, now in its 3rd edition. An account written by an eminent researcher is McEwen (2004). For theoretical and historical aspects, see Cooper and Dewe (2004). The link between stress and poverty is explored by Sapolsky (2005). For a (somewhat heavy-going) account, see Toates (1995). For applied ethology and stress, see Moberg and Mench (2000). For stress and the immune system, see Evans *et al.* (2000) and Clow and Hucklebridge (2002). For an integrative psychobiological account, see Ganzel *et al.* (2010). For positive emotions and health, see Post (2007).

Answers

Explanations for answers to 'test your knowledge' questions can be found on the website www.pearsoned.co.uk/toates

13.1 Disturbance (or, say, 'challenge')

13.2 Corticosteroids

13.3 (i) Lowered levels of ACTH and corticosteroids, increased levels of CRF; (ii) lowered levels of CRF and ACTH and a lowered rate of release of corticosteroids.

13.4 That involving the sympathetic nervous system.

13.5 It conveys information in the bloodstream to a location where it influences neural processing.

13.6 Both. As a hormone in the link to ACTH secretion; as a neurotransmitter in communication within the CNS.

13.7 Increased

13.8 That prolonged depression could reflect an exaggeration of a strategy that is adaptive in the short term, e.g. increased vigilance and temporary withdrawal from confrontation.

13.9 Adrenalin and noradrenalin

13.10 There could be a genetic/developmental influence leading to (1) lower than normal hippocampal volume and (2) increased tendency to PTSD.

13.11 Smooth, enteric nervous system

13.12 To activate the parasympathetic and inhibit the sympathetic nervous system.

Visit www.pearsoned.co.uk/toates
for a range of resources to support study.
Test yourself with multiple choice questions and access a bank of over 100 videos that will bring the topics to life.

Chapter 14
Pain

Learning outcomes for Chapter 14

After studying this chapter, you should be able to:

1 Describe what is meant by nociception and anti-nociception, while linking this to subjective pain.

2 Apply a functional explanation to nociception and anti-nociception. Give examples of pain that cannot be explained in adaptive terms and speculate why not.

3 Describe the route that nociceptive information takes from periphery to brain, while relating this to the observation that there is not a one-to-one link between the magnitude of the noxious stimulus and the intensity of pain.

4 Outline the principles of the gate theory of pain and what it can explain.

5 Identify the principal brain regions involved in pain and describe the link between them and the associated ascending and descending neural pathways.

6 Describe some forms of analgesia and the sites in the nociceptive system with which they are associated. Link analgesia to an understanding of the bases of pain.

7 State what is meant by the terms 'referred pain' and 'phantom pain' and explain how knowledge of the basics of pain allows us to understand them better.

8 Justify the claim that cognitive factors, such as expectations, play a part in pain. Link the role of cognitive factors to the biological bases of pain.

Scene-setting questions

1 How can something so debilitating as pain be said to be adaptive?

2 Why do we rub sore eyes?

3 Can you really suffer the pain of a broken heart?

4 What is it like to experience a phantom limb?

5 What is a placebo? Does it suggest 'mind over matter'?

6 Can you 'feel' the pain being suffered by another person?

7 What is the link between attention and pain?

What is the link between attention and pain? Explore the video on the website accompanying this book at **www.pearsoned.co.uk/toates**

 WEB

Under which circumstances can a person suffer injury but feel little pain?

Source: Topham Picturepoint/TopFoto.co.uk

Introduction

What is pain? It must be the exceedingly rare individual who cannot recall some experience of pain. Subjectively, pain is an unpleasant feeling that is usually caused by damage to the body and from which we try to escape. Pain, as from a toothache or a gut infection, takes command of attention (Eccleston and Crombez, 1999). We might be indifferent to certain stimuli but those triggering pain are different: pain poses overwhelming demands and moves us into action. People speak of the pain of rejection in love, something that also will not let go, and the pain of seeing someone else in distress. Are these just examples of the use of a colourful metaphor, or can we feel real pain from a broken heart or empathy?

People behave in ways characterized as pain-related and offer verbal reports on their inner experience. They describe their pain in terms of intensity, say, mild or excruciating, and can usually locate its source. Sometimes it is also possible to describe the pain's quality, e.g. gnawing, grinding, sharp, dull or stabbing. This suggests different stimuli as the cause of the problem.

Pain has a quality of intense *negative affect*, meaning that it feels bad. Do non-human animals suffer a similar affective experience? Of course, we do not know what subjective states they experience, if any. However, most of us would probably accept that they can suffer in this way. Their behaviour (e.g. writhing, squealing or jumping) suggests it. It forms a clear pattern associated with tissue damage and threat of such damage.

The term **nociception** refers to the detection of tissue damage or threatened damage. A **nociceptive system** is one that responds to tissue damage or potential damage (Melzack and Wall, 2008). The nociceptive system triggers action in an attempt to minimize the offending stimulation. Looking at the nervous system, there are close similarities in the nociceptive systems of humans and such species as rats. Therefore, the present chapter assumes that we and non-humans (or, at least, the more complex ones such as rats) share similar aversive experiences.

There is also a system of **anti-nociception**, which reduces nociceptive input to brain regions that underlie pain. For example, suppose that someone is engaged in competitive sport (e.g. the boxing champion Sonny Liston, who reputedly carried on fighting once even with a broken jaw) or escape from a battlefield. Activity of the anti-nociceptive system means that they are less likely even to notice wounds that they suffered (Melzack and Wall, 2008).

The medical profession and the lay public try to alleviate pain, a process termed **analgesia**. Substances that alleviate pain are known as **analgesics**. Analgesia can correspond to either a direct reduction of activity in the nociceptive system or an increase in activity of the anti-nociceptive system, which in turn blocks nociceptive activity.

The next section takes a functional perspective on nociception and anti-nociception.

Section summary

1 In response to tissue damage, a nociceptive system produces pain and triggers behaviour of a kind that tends to minimize this pain.

2 There exists also an anti-nociceptive system, which counters pain and the tendency to show pain-related behaviour.

☞ Test your knowledge

14.1 Agonists and antagonists acting where would be suggested as analgesics?

Answer on page 382   WEB ▶

Adaptive value of pain

Introduction

The adaptive value of a nociceptive system and pain is that this permits flexible solutions to the problem of tissue damage and the threat of it. For example, we can move our bodies around until we happen upon a position that minimizes pain or we can remove a thorn from the foot. We can recruit social help: caregivers can help to remove thorns, empathize with us and bring comfort. Suppose that an animal injures a limb. If pain then triggers rest, this increases the recovery chances. Surely, most of us have taken to bed in pain, e.g. a severe headache or general discomfort caused by influenza. Rest improves our chances of recovery.

Pain-related behaviour has a layer of cultural relativity in its expression. Different cultures show different pain-related strategies of reacting, e.g. stoicism or expression of distress (Craig, 1995). In some cultures, rituals that seem to be excruciatingly painful to outsiders are engaged in voluntarily in religious causes.

There are some very rare humans who are born with an inability to experience pain in response to tissue damage. Studying them can give useful insight into the adaptive value of pain.

A personal angle

F.C.

F.C., a Canadian university student, did not exhibit the reactions to tissue damage that are normal and necessary for self-preservation and she suffered serious damage to her body (Baxter and Olszewski, 1960; McMurray, 1950). For example, she repeatedly bit the tip of her tongue. She burned herself by kneeling on a radiator, oblivious to tissue damage. F.C. did not turn over in bed and did not move her weight around while standing. These reactions would have helped to protect from damage to joints and skin, etc. Neither did F.C. show the autonomic reaction of increased heart-rate in response to what would normally be painful stimuli. The study of F.C. confirms the importance of pain in protecting against tissue damage by not only *reacting* to such damage but also by *pre-empting* it. F.C. died in 1955, aged 29. At autopsy, she was found to possess the sensory neurons that detect tissue damage and her brain appeared normal. This was of course before the days of neuroimaging. It is highly likely that abnormalities in information processing and activation of key brain regions in F.C. would be identified these days.

Why has an anti-nociceptive system evolved? A possibility is as follows (Bolles and Fanselow, 1980). Pain triggers adaptive behaviour such as licking wounds and resting until recovery. However, this has a net adaptive value only when there is no greater immediate threat. At times, fighting or fleeing might have to take precedence and would require resisting the tendency to engage in pain-related behaviour. Thus, it might have proven useful to inhibit the activity of the nociceptive system, e.g. when fleeing injured from a predator. In humans, anecdotal evidence suggests that even serious injury incurred, for instance, on a battlefield is sometimes only associated with pain when the victim is away from danger (Bromm, 1995).

Why so intense and pervasive?

An attention-grabbing system means that cognitive and behavioural resources are directed to reducing the input from tissue damage. Why though, from a functional viewpoint, does intense pain create *so strong* a negative emotion, which has consequences that are often debilitating? It is perhaps possible to see an adaptive significance of the intensity of pain, as follows.

Pain commands our attention but also *forces* us to take particular adaptive actions, such as staying still or favouring a damaged ankle by not putting too much pressure on it. From the viewpoint of evolution, it could even be argued, 'no pain, then no pleasure'. Pleasure encourages us to engage in activities such as eating, pursuing a mate or exploring a new environment. However, to follow the guide of pleasure would not always be to our benefit. Pain counters the lure of pleasure, as in getting up too soon from the sick bed.

The use of 'cold cognition' or even 'slightly warm cognition' would be unable to counter the pull of pleasurable activities. Without persuasion by pain, humans might not be able to make rational choices to protect the body (cf. Ainslie, 1975). Even when we could understand the source of our pain, cold reasoning might have little effect. It would be no match for the temptation to 'get up and go' in the present. For some people, the pain of a headache from the occasional hangover is even *too little* to deter over-drinking except for a short period. It would surely be to our detriment to take a 'morning-after superdrug' to eliminate such headaches since the pain is 'motivating us not to do something'.

Some pains have adaptive value and need to be intense, e.g. those of a sprained ankle or a hangover headache. By keeping weight off the ankle, we speed its recovery. However, you might wonder how, say, the pain of childbirth or the severe and chronic pain of cancer could possibly reflect an adaptive process. A possible explanation has two parts, described next.

Although of general adaptive value, of course, we normally attempt to minimize pain. In so doing, we often pay lip-service to its value; the next-day hangover can be treated with aspirin and the good resolution not to drink to excess again.

Evolutionary psychology

What is adaptive?

For pain to be adaptive overall does not require every instance to be precisely appropriate in intensity. Indeed, evolution could only have provided solutions that *on average* worked to our ancestors' advantage (Sufka and Turner, 2005). As a general solution, we are equipped to feel pain in response to damage in most parts of our body. Given this basic 'design', inevitably there will be situations in which pains arise that are not obviously to our advantage. Chronic pain appears to represent a stretching of otherwise adaptive systems to outside their adaptive range.

The second aspect is that many of the chronic pains, such as those associated with cancer, appear most commonly in later years. At this stage, humans are past the age at which reproduction could normally have taken place in early evolution. Indeed, in our evolutionary history few might even have reached this age. Hence, such pains would not necessarily have been experienced sufficiently often to have been a disadvantage.

We now turn to considering the nervous system processes that embody the nociceptive and anti-nociceptive systems.

Section summary

1 Pain has adaptive value in allowing flexible solutions to protect against tissue damage.

2 At times it could be adaptive not to react to tissue damage and this provides the likely reason for the evolution of an anti-nociceptive system.

3 Chronic pain appears to be an exaggerated activation of otherwise adaptive processes.

Test your knowledge

14.2 Rats exhibit the response of freezing in certain situations of fear. What could be the relevance of the anti-nociception system to such freezing and its functional significance?

Answer on page 382

Tissue damage and the sensory input side

Introduction

This section describes the properties of the specialized neurons that detect tissue damage and convey information on this to the CNS. It asks how the signal that they produce contributes to pain. A later section describes what happens to this information when it reaches the brain. The chapter will discuss the limitations of trying to understand pain simply in terms of the input side.

Initial stage of a nociceptive pathway

Neurons that are activated by tissue damage are termed 'nociceptive neurons' (Chapter 3). In Figure 14.1, note the representative nociceptive neuron, by which information is transmitted from the periphery to the dorsal horn of the spinal cord. Tissue damage has a particular ability to trigger activity in these neurons, though some other stimuli have a limited capacity to do so.

At the tip of the axon of the nociceptive neuron, there is a free nerve ending sensitive to tissue damage. The tips of nociceptive neurons are termed **nociceptors** (detectors of 'noxious' stimulation). The branching of the tip defines the neuron's receptive field. Nociceptive neurons come in different forms corresponding to different types of stimuli that best activate them, e.g. 'sharp' or 'burning'. Nociceptive neurons have a high threshold: only strong stimulation will significantly excite them. In Figure 14.1, note also the other type of neuron, the large-diameter neuron. This type is sensitive to harmless touch but it also plays a role in pain, as discussed later.

The neurons in the spinal cord with which nociceptive neurons form synapses are termed **T cells** (Figure 14.1), meaning transmission cells (as distinct from immunological T cells). Nociceptive neurons release neurotransmitter that activates T cells. It appears that nociception employs more than one type of neurotransmitter, the principal ones being glutamate and substance P (Jessell and Kelly, 1991). T cells convey nociceptive information to the brain, e.g. in the **spinothalamic tract (STT)** (Figure 14.1).

The STT is not the only ascending pathway involved in pain but it can be used to exemplify the principles. Electrical stimulation of the STT results in the conscious sensation of pain. Surgical lesions of the tract can reduce pain but this is not always so.

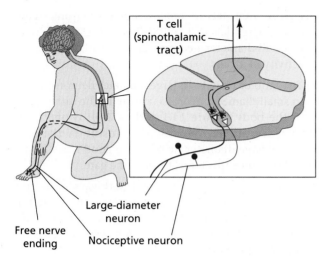

Figure 14.1 Sketch of body and part of the nervous system showing section of spinal cord. Also shown are a nociceptive neuron and a large-diameter neuron, sensitive to harmless touch.

Source: Toates (1997c, Fig. 4.2, p. 70).

Tissue damage, either to the tip itself or in its immediate vicinity, is normally the necessary stimulus to excite nociceptive neurons. When a neighbouring cell is damaged, chemicals are released and come into contact with nociceptors. This increases the chances that action potentials will arise. The high threshold of nociceptive neurons is due to the fact that their axons are of small diameter and are often termed 'small-diameter fibres'.

Since nociceptive neurons are particularly sensitive to noxious information, they are often termed 'pain receptors'. However, to be precise, they detect tissue damage rather than pain. Pain is not like light, a physical quality able to be detected. It is a complex sensation and emotion organized by the brain, and tissue damage does not invariably trigger pain. So the terms 'nociceptor' and 'nociceptive neuron' are preferred.

In Figure 14.1, imagine a region of body surface and the tips of nociceptive neurons located there. Typically, as shown, there are also other neurons with tips in the same area and with axons projecting to the spinal cord in parallel with those of nociceptive neurons. These axons are of larger diameter, have a lower threshold of activation and are often termed 'large-diameter neurons'. They can be triggered by nociceptive stimulation but even harmless stimuli, such as gentle touch, are sufficient. Both types of neuron make synapses in the dorsal horn of the spinal cord, though at slightly different locations (Figure 14.1). Thereby, they trigger activity in other neurons which then convey messages up the spinal cord to the brain. However, information derived from both types of neuron is also processed locally at the spinal cord location shown and this forms a focus in trying to understand pain.

No simple through-line

At one time it was thought that a simple one-to-one 'through-line' links activity in nociceptive neurons and the intensity of pain. Thus, patients who reported pain where no tissue damage (no 'organic disorder') could be identified were highly problematic. They might be referred to psychiatrists and/or labelled as malingerers (Melzack, 1993). Their pain, if it existed at all, was thought to have a quality different from 'real pain' and to be the business of the social, rather than biological, sciences. We now know that there is no *simple* through-line; the magnitude of pain sometimes does not reflect tissue damage. This provides one rationale for the study of the *psychology* of pain.

Suppose, for the sake of argument, that there were a direct link. Presumably, a surgical lesion at some point in the pathway would cure pain. By comparison, a lesion anywhere in the optic nerve would destroy vision. Indeed, surgery for chronic pain was once guided by making lesions in the so-called pain pathway. Again pointing to the true complexity, in many cases pain unfortunately returned after surgery (Melzack, 1993).

Today theorists and clinicians appreciate the complexity of pain. There can be intense pain with little evidence of tissue damage. Even after removing the initial trigger to pain, e.g. a tumour, the pain sometimes persists (Keefe *et al.*, 2005). There can be a relief of pain as a result simply of taking medicine of completely arbitrary content provided that the patient has a belief in its efficacy. So, we have a complex system with interacting factors, only one of which is the nociceptive sensory input. The biopsychosocial model of pain (Campbell and Edwards, 2009) has now largely replaced the older biomedical ('disease') model, which saw pain as a simple reflection of tissue damage. Of course, tissue damage often plays a crucial role but it is not a necessary or even sufficient condition for pain. Rather, social and cognitive factors can also play a significant role.

The next section looks at an influential theory of pain, which attempts to account for a range of phenomena partly in terms of events at the input side.

Section summary

1 Nociceptive neurons have small-diameter axons and a relatively high threshold of stimulation. They detect tissue damage by means of free-nerve endings at their tips.

2 Neurons with larger diameter axons are sensitive to non-noxious stimuli, i.e. have a lower threshold.

3 Both types of neuron form synapses in the dorsal horn of the spinal cord, where information processing occurs.

4 Pain commonly, but *not always*, corresponds to tissue damage and activity in nociceptive neurons.

☞ Test your knowledge

14.3 Consider a site in the spinal cord where a set of nociceptive neurons form synapses. What would be the expected effect of injecting a glutamate agonist into this region?

Answer on page 382   WEB

The gate theory

Basics of theory

In 1965, a new theory of pain, termed the **gate theory** appeared (Melzack and Wall, 1965). Its authors acknowledged that the details might be wrong but they were convinced that the important principles would stand the test of time. Gate theory offered explanations for a number of phenomena, such as (i) why pain does not bear a simple relationship to tissue damage and (ii) how the CNS could produce an anti-nociceptive effect. The theory proposed two processes of anti-nociception, both of which involve the site in the spinal cord where nociceptive neurons form synapses. First, there is the role of activity in large-diameter neurons (Figure 14.1). Second, there are pathways of neurons that descend from the brain. The ideas are summarized in Figure 14.2 and the assumptions of gate theory are as follows:

1 The capacity of nociceptive neurons to excite T cells (Figure 14.1) is not constant. There is, metaphorically speaking, a gate which determines this capacity (Figure 14.2(a) and (b)). When the gate is open,

action potentials in small-diameter neurons trigger action potentials in T cells. When it is closed, activity in small-diameter neurons fails to instigate as much activity in T cells.

2 The ratio of activity in large-diameter neurons to that in small-diameter neurons, arising in the same region of the body (Figure 14.1 and 14.2(c)) is one factor that determines opening and closing of the gate. Active large-diameter neurons are good news for the sufferer since this tends to close the gate.

3 Activity in descending neural pathways also tends to close the gate (Figure 14.2(c)). Note the inhibitory synapse from neuron (1) onto the nociceptive neuron and the inhibitory link through what is termed a 'small neuron' (S).

4 Cognitive processes organized in the brain influence gating, by their input to descending pathways described in (3).

(a)

(b)

(c)

Figure 14.2 Gate theory expressed (a–b) by the analogy of a real gate: (a) closed, (b) open and (c) a more realistic representation, showing neurons. Open triangles, excitation; closed triangles, inhibition. S = small (local) neuron within spinal cord. 1 = neuron descending from brain.

Consider the local region of spinal cord where nociceptive and other neurons from a particular small region of the body make synapses (Figures 14.1 and 14.2(c)). Small neurons (S) within this local region exert an influence in controlling the opening and closing of the gate (Figure 14.2(c)). Activity in S inhibits the nociceptive pathway ('closes the gate'). So, the more the activity in S, the greater is the inhibition on the nociceptive pathway. What determines activity of neuron S? It is excited by activity in either large-diameter neurons or descending pathways from the brain, or both. This is represented by the two open triangles adjacent to S in Figure 14.2(c). Note also neuron 1 which represents another route of descending inhibition on the nociceptive pathway.

Concerning the neurochemistry of anti-nociception, a principal focus in gate theory is opioids (Chapter 12). Opioids are a class of natural anti-nociceptive (analgesic) substances, e.g. the natural enkephalins.

Figure 14.3 shows some of the synaptic processes that appear to be implicated in gating. An opioid termed enkephalin appears to be the chemical released by neurons of type S. The precise form of inhibition exerted by such neurons is uncertain. However, there are opioid receptors at the terminals of nociceptive neurons and at the T cells (Benedetti and Amanzio, 1997). By occupying receptors at the terminal of nociceptive neurons, enkephalin seems to reduce the amount of excitatory neurochemical that is released. By occupying sites at the T cell, enkephalin opposes the excitation of this cell. Figure 14.3 also shows an inhibitory link from the brain synapsing directly onto the nociceptive neuron. Elsewhere, there are also opioid receptors in the brain at regions where descending inhibitory pathways arise (Harris, 1996). Acting on neurons in the brain, opioids excite these descending pathways.

Functional significance

From a functional perspective, what advantage is there for the nervous system to be constructed in the manner suggested by gate theory? Why do large-diameter neurons inhibit the effect of activity in nociceptive neurons and thereby give anti-nociception? A possibility is as follows. The reduction of pain would encourage animals to lick their wounds (a reinforcement process), which would cleanse the wounds. Why is there descending inhibition? The possible logic was advanced earlier, i.e. an anti-nociceptive system is activated when the animal is engaging in such defensive behaviour as fighting or fleeing.

Opening the gate

As well as processes that close the gate, other processes appear to open it (Benedetti and Amanzio, 1997). The neurochemical cholecystokinin (CCK) 'opens the gate'. CCK is found at spinal sites (Figure 14.4) and in various brain regions. Like opioid receptors, CCK receptors are both pre- and postsynaptic. In causing an increase in pain, termed **hyperalgesia**, the sites of action of CCK might act in a functionally related way and be symmetrical with the role of opioids in analgesia. Analgesia induced by opioids is inhibited by CCK and enhanced by CCK antagonists. Opening the gate would appear to be a means of accentuating the role of the nociceptive system, e.g. when attention to wounds is especially important.

The value of the gate theory

A gate that is influenced in part by psychological ('cognitive') factors is of great significance for an integrative biological psychology. The theory provided a broad framework for considering how interventions to control pain might work (described later).

Figure 14.3 Representation of the possible mode of action of enkephalin released from neuron S and that of another (unspecific) inhibitory neurochemical, labelled simply as 'inhibitory neurochemical'.

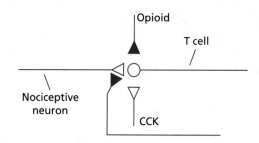

Figure 14.4 Gate showing inhibition and excitation.

Next we need to look at some brain processes involved in pain and thereby give further embodiment to the theory.

Section summary

1 Gate theory suggests that the relationship between activity in nociceptive neurons and T cells, depends, metaphorically, upon a gate.

2 Activity in (a) large-diameter afferent neurons and (b) descending pathways closes the gate.

3 In neural terms, the gate is provided in part by the activity of short interneurons at the spinal cord.

4 Evidence points to opioids playing the crucial role in closing the gate.

5 There are neural processes (employing CCK) that open the gate.

 ## Test your knowledge

14.4 In Figure 14.2(c), activity in which of the ascending and descending neurons would minimize activity in the T cell?

14.5 In Figure 14.3, injection of an antagonist to which of the following would tend to increase activity in the T cell? (i) The inhibitory neurochemical, (ii) enkephalin, (iii) the excitatory neurochemical.

 Answers on page 382

Brain processes

Introduction

Figure 14.5 summarizes both what has been described so far and the contents of the present section. In the spinal cord, sensory information ('Nociceptive input') ascends to the brain, conveying information on tissue damage. Information also descends in the spinal cord and it influences the ascending information. At the brain, pain arises from the activity in circuits of interacting brain regions, which are triggered by, among other things, the

sensory input. This central 'computation' of pain then plays a role in pain-related behaviours such as yelling or resting. It also plays a role in ANS reactions such as sweating and heart-rate acceleration.

Terminations of ascending pathways

Figure 14.6 shows ascending nociceptive information arriving at various sites in the brain, via the spinothalamic tract. Synapses are formed in the midbrain, including the periaqueductal grey (labelled 'Homeostatic regions'), as well as with nuclei in the thalamus (MDvc and VMpo). This ascending information will have been already modulated at sites in the spinal cord, as described by gate theory.

The pain neuromatrix

Processing in the brain underlies (1) the affective quality of pain, i.e. its emotional value, and (2) the discriminative quality, e.g. where in the body the pain appears to be located.

Ascending information arrives at various identifiable brain regions that form part of the biological bases of pain, e.g. two nuclei of the thalamus (Figure 14.6). Further neurons then convey information from there to other regions, such as the anterior cingulate cortex (ACC) and the 'interoceptive cortex' ('insula cortex'). The collection of interacting brain regions that forms the biological basis of pain is termed the **pain neuromatrix**. It is assumed that chronic pain arises in part from increased sensitivity of interactions ('enhanced synaptic efficacy') between these brain regions (Moseley, 2003). Once sensitized, various inputs, e.g. cognitive, are sufficient to trigger reverberation between the parts.

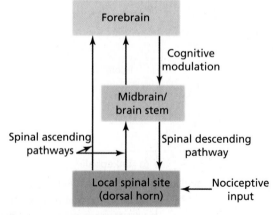

Figure 14.5 Different levels of the nervous system involved in pain.

In humans, some neurons of the primary and secondary somatosensory cortex, among other cortical regions, respond specifically to nociceptive stimuli, mainly on the contralateral side of the body (Area 3a in Figure 14.6). There is some topographic organization of neurons sensitive to nociceptive stimuli, comparable to that of neurons responsive to harmless somatosensory stimuli. This suggests that such neurons extract sensory and discriminative aspects of nociceptive stimuli (Kenshalo and Douglass, 1995; Rainville *et al.*, 1997).

The anterior cingulate cortex (ACC) and insula cortex appear to be closely involved in the affective aspect of pain (Oshiro *et al.*, 2009). In humans, positron emission tomography (PET) reveals an increase in regional cerebral blood flow in the ACC produced by nociceptive stimuli, whereas harmless stimuli do not have this effect. Nociceptive input to the ACC on one side of the brain tends to activate the ACC on both sides. This points to the role of the ACC in affective rather than sensory discriminative processing. For patients with chronic pain, surgical lesions of the ACC reduce the emotional ('affective') but not sensory aspects of pain. Patients having such lesions sometimes report that, although they still feel pain, it bothers them less (Rainville *et al.*, 1997).

Rainville *et al.* (1997) investigated the effect of hypnosis on pain and blood flow to selected brain regions. Hypnotic suggestion was given that the patient would experience either increased or decreased strength of pain, while the actual nociceptive stimulus was held constant. Such suggestion changed pain's actual affective rating and blood flow to the ACC but not to the somatosensory cortex. A positive correlation emerged between the unpleasantness rating and activation of the ACC, as indexed by blood flow. Only the ACC showed changes consistent with different affective values, which Rainville *et al.* interpreted to mean that it is involved in affective rating. Anatomical connections between ACC and somatosensory cortex suggest that there is integration of these regions in determining the normal experience of pain.

The pain of social rejection is also associated with activation of the ACC (Chapter 1; Eisenberger *et al.*, 2003). This cause is termed a 'psychogenic trigger', meaning that it lies in psychological processing as distinct from tissue damage. Yet this result gives psychogenically triggered pain a sound biological basis in the brain that is very similar to the basis of that triggered by a noxious stimulus.

There is a strong co-occurrence of pain and depression (Robinson *et al.*, 2009). That pain should lead to depression makes intuitive sense, whereas to understand that depression can sensitize pain requires insight from neuroscience. There is considerable overlap in the profile of regions of brain, neurotransmitters and hormones involved in pain and depression. Thereby, depression can sensitize the pain neuromatrix.

Descending pathways

Electrical and chemical stimulation of descending pathways from brain to spinal cord can reduce pain. Areas of the midbrain, e.g. the periaqueductal grey (PAG) (Fields and Basbaum, 1994), are a source of the descending signals. There is a cortical input to the PAG, e.g. from the ACC, by which cognitive information appears to modulate the activity of the PAG (Figure 14.5). The PAG projects to other axons in the midbrain, which in turn project downwards to the spinal cord and to the region of the terminals of nociceptive neurons in the dorsal horn (Mason, 1999).

We now consider analgesia.

Figure 14.6 Neural processes involved in pain. MDvc and VMpo are two nuclei of the thalamus.
Source: Craig (2003, Figure 2, page 11).

Answer on page 382

Analgesia

This section gives examples of where an understanding of biological processes is relevant to analgesia.

The role of large-diameter neurons

According to gate theory, gentle stimulation of low-threshold large-diameter neurons tends to close the gate. Most people know that rubbing a painful site tends to reduce pain (e.g. the sore eyes of hayfever sufferers), at least in the short term. Rubbing stimulates the large-diameter neurons, the tips of which are at the site of irritation alongside the nociceptors. Various therapeutic techniques, e.g. electrical stimulation, involve, in effect, massaging the skin. The technique termed **transcutaneous electrical nerve stimulation (TENS)** (Meissner, 2009) involves applying weak electrical stimulation at the skin corresponding to an affected area. This is of sufficient intensity to generate activity in large-diameter neurons but not sufficient to trigger (high-threshold) nociceptive neurons.

Acupuncture

Gate theory might help us to understand the traditional Chinese technique of acupuncture: it is possible that its pain-relieving effects correspond to closing the gate (Filshie and Morrison, 1988). Acupuncture is often, but not always, effective in treating pain. It appears to cause the release of opioids, involving the PAG (Murotani *et al.*, 2010). Such factors as expectation (described shortly) can play an important role in its efficacy (Liu, 2009).

Analgesic chemicals

Introduction

Analgesics can act either peripherally or centrally and can be swallowed, injected or applied locally to the skin. Antagonists to neurotransmitters involved in pain might seem an obvious candidate for analgesia. If there were a neurotransmitter employed only in the nociceptive system, then we might have optimism for the development of a safe and targeted antagonist (Jessell and Kelly, 1991). Alas, nature is not usually so kind. Neurotransmitters tend to be multi-purpose, acting at different sites in the CNS and serving different roles. Any neurotransmitter involved in pain will probably also form part of non-pain-related systems. Targeting this transmitter in sufficient strength to reduce pain might create new problems at other parts of the CNS. For example, glutamate is employed in the nociceptive system but also more widely in the CNS.

Aspirin

Prostaglandins and other substances are released from damaged cells. They sensitize any nociceptors that are in the vicinity of the damage. This increases the chances that tissue damage will initiate action potentials. Aspirin is a peripherally acting analgesic that blocks the synthesis of prostaglandins. Thereby, aspirin lowers the frequency with which action potentials are generated (compare Figures 14.7(a) and (b)).

Lignocaine

The passage of action potentials depends on the movement of sodium into the neuron. Lignocaine blocks sodium channels in the membrane of neurons of all kinds. In Figure 14.7(c), suppose that an injection of lignocaine is given at a location between 2 and 3. If, within a length of axon, sodium channels are blocked, the action potential is unable to pass the affected region and comes to an end on reaching it. Lignocaine does not discriminate in favour of neurons carrying nociceptive information. If you have been injected with it at the dentist, you will know that you tend to feel numb in the mouth as a result of blocking sensory information. You have difficulty initiating movements at the mouth as a result of blocking motor neurons.

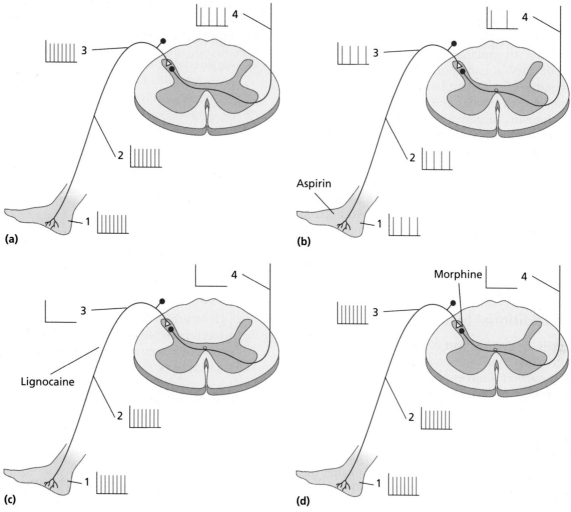

Figure 14.7 Action potentials arising at the tip of a nociceptive neuron (1) and monitored at two points along the axon (2 and 3) and in the T cell (4): (a) control, (b) with aspirin, (c) with lignocaine, injected between locations 2 and 3, and (d) with opiates. *Source:* after Toates (1997c, Fig. 4.6, p. 77).

Centrally acting drugs

A class of analgesics, termed opiates, e.g. heroin and morphine, act upon the CNS (Figure 14.7(d)). Years before the role of natural endogenous opioids (e.g. enkephalin) was established, it was of course known that opiate drugs have analgesic qualities. There are opioid receptors at the terminal of nociceptive neurons and at T cells (Figures 14.3 and 14.4). These are occupied by, say, morphine. This lowers the chances that action potentials arriving at the terminal are able to release sufficient neurotransmitter to stimulate activity in T cells. In addition, opioid receptors in the brain are occupied and this activates descending inhibitory pathways. Both sites of action have a mutually reinforcing action in triggering analgesic effects, 'closing the gate'.

Melzack (1988) reported that many people are denied narcotic (opiate) treatment for pain, since it is feared that they might become addicted. He argues that the risk is minimal and the reason for misunderstanding is simple: an unwarranted generalization from addicts to the person suffering from pain. Melzack suggests that morphine could alleviate the pain of cancer in between 80% and 90% of patients.

Comparing addicts and people in pain, the motivation of why people seek narcotics is quite different. Psychologically healthy people without a history of drug abuse do not usually become addicts on exposure to narcotics. One study looked at 11 882 patients, without a history of drug abuse. Of these, only four later showed abuse and for only one was abuse described as 'major' (Melzack, 1988). The Yom Kippur war resulted in thousands of Israeli casualties and these were treated with morphine but not one case of addiction was reported. An explanatory factor might well be an absence of classical conditioning: the environment of the hospital is very different from home or work.

Rather as with opiates and opioids, for some time anecdotal reports suggested a role for cannabis in pain relief. Only later was it realized that the body produces its own cannabis-like substances ('cannabinoids'), which have a role in anti-nociception. There are receptors for cannabinoids at various sites within the CNS (Rahn and Hohmann, 2009). Evidence points to a combined action of opioids and cannabinoids in anti-nociception. More recently, synthetic versions of cannabis have been tested and shown to have potent analgesic effects. The potential for pain therapy, for example, combined opiate–cannabinoid treatment, is under investigation.

Use of additional feedback

Feedback is an intrinsic part of the nociceptive system, e.g. pain causes a person to take action to try to lower pain. If the action is successful, it is likely to be repeated when in pain in the future. Note that the only measure normally involved is the perceived unpleasantness of the pain and its reduction. Investigators speculate: could there be some additional form of feedback that might improve things? For example, could patients monitor some biological correlate of pain and learn to alter this, thereby reducing their pain? Attempts have been made to monitor a correlate of pain, such as EEG activity, and reward patients if they are able to lower this. This amounts to instrumental conditioning with a lowering of pain as reinforcement (Flor *et al.*, 2002).

Although still at the experimental stage, neuroimaging of activity in the pain neuromatrix offers the possibility of using feedback to control pain. By fMRI neuroimaging, deCharms *et al.* (2005) gave participants feedback on the activity within the rostral ACC, while asking them to lower this level. Success was reported. As the authors noted (p. 18630):

> pain patients already have continuously available sensory feedback of their own pain level, they already have a strong motivation to learn to control their pain, and they typically have tried and practiced many strategies to alleviate their pain over many years.

There appears to be something special about adding the neuroimage of a key part of the pain neuromatrix to the feedback. Its visual aspect could prove to be of crucial significance.

Section summary

1 Aspirin lowers the frequency with which action potentials arise in nociceptive neurons and thereby has an analgesic effect.

2 Lignocaine blocks sodium channels in neurons including those in nociceptive neurons.

3 Opiates act on the CNS. They (a) block the capacity of nociceptive-neurons to trigger T cell activity and (b) activate a descending inhibitory pathway.

☞ Test your knowledge

14.7 Complete the following: 'The threshold of activation of nociceptive neurons is relatively ___ , whereas that of large-diameter neurons is relatively ___ '.

14.8 Which of the following has a broad effect on neurons, whether involved in nociception or not? (i) aspirin, (ii) lignocaine, or (iii) opiates.

Answers on page 382 WEB

Some unusual types of pain

This section considers some examples of phenomena that might be termed anomalous by the criterion of not fitting common-sense understanding. They start to make sense in light of understanding the neural systems that form the biological basis of pain.

Neuropathic pain

The term **neuropathic pain** describes pain that arises intrinsically as a result of damage to, or malfunction within, the nervous system (Seifert and Maihöfner, 2009). Neuropathic pain becomes chronic as a result of, for example, increases in activity within the pain neuromatrix or an expansion of the neuromatrix to take over other brain regions. The phenomenon of **wind-up** describes increased sensitivity of synapses in the nociceptive pathway (e.g. in the spinal cord), something like long-term potentiation (Sufka and Turner, 2005). Thereby, activity in the nociceptive pathway could be self-reinforcing, resulting in increased activity in the pain neuromatrix.

Referred pain

Suppose that there is tissue damage at a localized site. At times, pain is felt to be associated not with this site but with (i.e. 'referred to') some other site (Vahle-Hinz et al., 1995). There exist some striking examples of such **referred pain**. Pain arising from tissue damage at the heart can be experienced at the left shoulder and arm. A kidney stone can trigger pain that is referred to the genitals. The pattern of referral is not haphazard but can be understood in terms of the developmental origin of the neurons involved (Chapter 6). For example, nociceptive neurons with their tips at an internal organ (e.g. the heart) can trigger the same T cells as those with their tips at the skin (e.g. left shoulder and arm) (Figure 14.8) (Pomeranz et al., 1968). Note that neurons from both an internal organ and a region of skin make synaptic contact on the T cell in the spinal cord.

Why should tissue damage at, say, the heart, be perceived as arising at the skin? Why are pains having their origin at the skin not referred to the heart? The answer might lie in our relative familiarity with experiencing pain. Presumably, most of us know pain arising from tissue damage or threatened damage at our skin (e.g. banging a toe against a door) and such pain usually makes sense. For tactile stimulation, there is a relationship between the body region stimulated and the area of somatosensory cortex activated, i.e. the sensory homunculus (Chapter 5). Possibly, when nociceptive messages from the heart arrive at such brain regions, we interpret them in terms of the more familiar stimuli.

Functional chronic pain symptoms

Functional chronic pain symptoms are those in which (Harris et al., 2009, p. 3146): 'patients paradoxically report frequent pain symptoms in the absence of anatomic injury or objective pathological findings'. An example is fibromyalgia, which affects up to 4% of the population, and is associated with pains in the muscles and tendons throughout the body. Evidence points to activation of the pain neuromatrix (Derbyshire et al., 2009). Glutamate is involved in transmission within the pain neuromatrix and it is activated in fibromyalgia, as indexed by its cerebrospinal levels (Peres et al., 2004). The level of glutamate in parts of the insula is higher in fibromyalgia patients than controls, while successful treatment with acupuncture is associated with reduced levels (Harris et al., 2008, 2009). Ketamine blocks the NMDA receptor to glutamate and reduces fibromyalgia pain levels (Graven-Nielsen et al., 2000). The suggestion of changes in pain level (up or down) (e.g. by hypnosis) is associated with corresponding changes in patients' subjective pain and activation within the pain neuromatrix, as measured by fMRI (Derbyshire et al., 2009).

Phantom pain

Introduction

People with a part of the body (e.g. a limb) amputated often still feel pain, apparently 'in' the missing part, termed **phantom pain** (Melzack, 1993). Melzack (1989, p. 2) describes reports from amputees, for example: 'I continue to feel my leg as vividly as I felt my real leg and I often feel a burning pain in my foot'. It is not just limbs that are felt as phantoms; following their surgical removal, the rectum, breasts, bladder and penis can all be experienced much as before. Even after seven years following amputation, some 60% of people suffer phantom pain related to a lost limb. Phantom pains can be similar to pains that were felt much earlier, i.e. when the missing part was still present. This suggests that specific memories play a role. However, such memories are not always essential. For example, people born without a limb can still suffer phantom sensations 'in' the missing limb.

Amputees use such expressions as sweaty, cold or itchy to describe the phantom limb. The feeling of the presence of a missing limb can be so real that amputees have difficulty, e.g., in not getting out of bed 'onto' the missing limb. Points of reference that helped to define the limb when it was intact, e.g. the tightness of a ring on a finger or the pain of a sore on the foot, can persist in vivid detail.

In three situations, phantom pain can be experienced apparently in the absence of corresponding sensory input to the brain (Melzack, 1989): (i) after amputation, (ii) when a body region remains but its sensory input to the spinal cord has been lost or (iii) where a break in the spinal cord occurs. In (iii), the feeling corresponds to a body region below the break. For paraplegics, where a total section of the spinal cord has been suffered, there

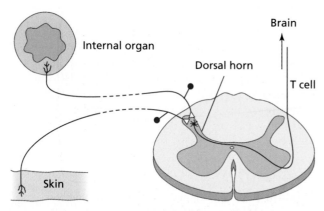

Figure 14.8 A possible neural basis of referred pain.
Source: after Toates (1997c, Fig. 4.5, p. 75).

can still be the experience of severe pain relating to a location below the break. This is referred to body sites for which, it appears, no neural communication with the brain is possible.

Explaining phantom pain

Theorists now view the brain as an active processor of sensory information, rather than a passive receiver. Melzack (1989) made the following points:

1 Patterns of activity in neural networks in the brain encode both nociceptive and harmless events in the world. Such patterns would normally be triggered by sensory inputs but do not always depend on them.

2 The sensation of a phantom body part feels like a real part. This suggests that brain processes activated are those that would, under normal circumstances, be triggered by afferent information arising from the lost part.

3 During the phantom experience, certain brain processes are active autonomously and 'revive' experiences associated with the part before there was a break in its connection with the brain.

How is the effect in people like Tom explained? Plasticity of neural connections is central to this (Ramachandran and Blakeslee, 1998). Consider the sensory homunculus in Figure 5.18 (p. 117) and look at the area of cortex devoted to analysing sensations from the fingers. This is surrounded by areas which analyse sensations from (on the one side) the face and (on the other)

the arm. When the region of cortex devoted to analysing the hand is lacking its normal input, neighbouring neurons (normally triggered by the face and arm) take over control. How does this occur? Neurons appear to sprout links and invade the hand area of cortex (Figure 14.10). Another process appears to be that the links (arm → finger area and face → finger area) are there all the time but are inhibited. Removing the normal sensory input from the fingers unmasks the links. Stimulation of either face or arm evokes the sensations of (i) the appropriate touch and (ii) touch on the phantom hand (by exciting neurons in the hand area of cortex). Tom only has to move his upper arm or face to trigger sensations in the phantom hand. Such cortical reorganization only occurs in those patients in whom amputation is associated with phantom limb pain (Flor and Diers, 2009).

Basic insights derived from treatment

To treat phantom limb pain, Ramachandran devised a simple piece of apparatus that was intended to fool the brain into perceiving movement in the non-existent arm. Figure 14.11 shows the situation for a patient who

Figure 14.9 A map of Tom's phantom hand. Numbers correspond to the number of the digit associated with each region.

Source: Ramachandran and Hirstein, (1998, Fig. 4(B), (C), p. 1612).

has lost part of the right arm. A box contains a mirror at the midline. There are holes on one side for the patient to insert the stump (to the right) and the intact arm (to the left). The patient sees his/her intact left arm as normal and, on looking in the mirror, the image of this left arm, which appears to be a now intact right arm. On giving commands to both arms to move in synchrony, this is exactly what appears to happen. When the patient's right arm was previously felt to be frozen, it now feels as unfrozen. Visual feedback now matches the commands sent out to move the phantom right arm and thereby unfreezes it.

Regular practice with this apparatus is sometimes effective in eliminating the pain of the phantom limb. Why should pain abate as a result of seeing an intact limb? It appears to be due in part to reorganization (back to nearer normal) of the abnormal connections (Flor *et al.*, 2006). However, reorganization takes time and yet some reduction in pain can be immediate. Harris (1999) suggests that an important component of phantom limb pain arises from incongruity between (i) the commands to move the limb and (ii) the lack of appropriate tactile, proprioceptive and visual feedback that the limb has actually moved. The mirror apparatus lowers the incongruity. Ramachandran and Altschuler (2009) suggest that the false visual perception that the arm is intact enables the brain to interpret the pain message as spurious and thereby reject it. The visual sense appears to dominate.

In one study, patterns of stimulation were triggered at the stump and patients given the task of discriminating them (Flor *et al.*, 2001). Over days, patients got better

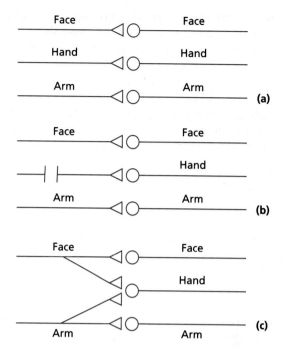

Figure 14.10 Possible plasticity of neural connections underlying phantom effects: (a) before injury showing specificity of connections from the periphery to sensory perception systems of brain; (b) breaking of input from hand; (c) loss of input from hand and sprouting of new links from neurons detecting touch at face and arm. Touch at face or arm could trigger phantom sensation of hand.

at this discrimination. In parallel, the pain reduced and there was reorganization of the somatosensory cortex in the direction of a more normal sensory homunculus.

Figure 14.11 Mirror apparatus. (a) The view from above showing position of patient's arm intact (left) and amputated (right), (b) The view to one side showing something of the patient's perspective. Note the mirror image of intact left arm, appearing to be an intact right arm.

Within the secondary somatosensory cortex (Figure 9.19, p. 239), there is a form of mirror neuron (Ramachandran and Brang, 2009). These are activated either when (i) a person is touched or (ii) (s)he watches another individual being touched. Ramachandran and Brang studied individuals with an amputated arm and the experience of a phantom arm. When they watched the arm of another individual being touched, they felt a localized sensation in their phantom arm corresponding to the precise stimulus applied to the other individual. At the time of writing, the potential of this observation for the relief of pain has yet to be found. However, it is tantalizing that one patient reported that watching his wife massage her hand lowered the phantom pain that he felt.

The following section looks at other effects that also challenge any simple view of pain.

Section summary

1 Neuropathic pain arises within the nervous system.

2 In fibromyalgia, there is pain without tissue damage.

3 Tissue damage at one body region can trigger pain that is referred to a different region, termed 'referred pain'.

4 Pain associated with a missing body part is known as phantom pain.

5 Phantom pain provides further evidence that pain is the product of an active process organized by the brain.

Test your knowledge

14.9 With regard to Figure 14.8 suppose that there is tissue damage at the internal organ and that this is felt as coming from the skin. What would be the expected effect of, in addition to this, activity in the nociceptive neuron that projects from the skin?

Answer on page 382

Cognitive and social factors: theory and therapy

This section considers a cognitive approach to pain and links it to social factors. In these terms, therapies that address such things as goals, expectancies, attitudes and attention are given a rationale.

Cognitive interventions and basic understanding of pain

Cognitive interventions for pain tend to focus upon how patients interpret their pain in terms of its implications (Weisenberg, 1994). Therapeutic techniques used include relaxation, trying to divert attention and the forming of positive images. Therapists attempt to teach patients to see themselves as active agents who have some control, i.e. self-efficacy, rather than being hopeless and helpless victims. One theoretical rationale for the efficacy of such interventions is the gate theory, where cognitive factors influence the descending pathway. Indeed, the perception of self-efficacy in the face of pain is associated with triggering both opioid and non-opioid analgesia (Bandura *et al.*, 1987).Therapies give insights into the bases of pain.

Distraction

Presenting a 'distracting cognitive task' that draws on attention reduces the perceived intensity of pain. Bantick *et al.* (2002) applied a painful thermal stimulus to participants' left hands and, by fMRI, monitored brain activation in regions of the pain neuromatrix. The distraction by cognitive task was compared with a less demanding ('neutral') task.

Increased activation was recorded in the orbitofrontal cortex under the distraction condition. The authors suggest that this inhibits the pain neuromatrix. Distraction during a painful stimulus is associated with activation of the PAG (Tracey *et al.*, 2002). Distraction is a cognitive process, which engages forebrain processes (Figure 14.5). Via 'Cognitive modulation', this excites the PAG (part of the 'Midbrain/brain stem'), which then activates the 'Spinal descending pathway' and blocks the nociceptive messages. Hence, less afferent input from nociceptors gets to the brain. In addition, there appears to be a direct inhibition of activity in the pain neuromatrix.

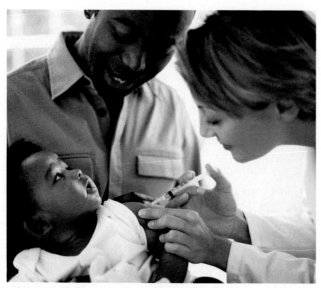

What might be going on in such situations apart from the arrival of a chemical in the body?

Source: Ian Hooton/Science Photo Library

Catastrophizing

Evidence suggests that the psychological process of 'catastrophizing' makes pain worse (Craig, 1994). This consists of focusing intense negative evaluation on the pain, rumination (mental 'chewing-over') and a perception of helplessness and hopelessness. Associated with this psychological state, there is increased activation of parts of pain neuromatrix involved with attentional and emotional processing, e.g. the anterior cingulate cortex (Gracely *et al.*, 2004). In pain, it seems that a role of regions of prefrontal cortex is to assess the controllability of the situation (Salomons *et al.*, 2007). Descending pathways then recruit lower brain regions, e.g. insula and PAG, in modulating pain. Such control appears to be deficient in patients who catastrophize their pain (Seminowicz and Davis, 2006).

Placebo effects

Introduction

The term 'placebo effect' applies to several areas of experience (Chapter 10), including pain (Beecher, 1955). In the case of pain, a placebo is an intervention (by substance or other procedure) that appears to have no *intrinsic* capacity to lower pain but, because of its context, has an analgesic capacity. For example, an injection *procedure* itself (even in the absence of a known analgesic substance) can trigger an analgesic ('placebo') effect. This capacity is demonstrated when injection of a chemically inert substance subsequently lowers pain.

In part, the effect can be the outcome of classical conditioning (Zubieta and Stohler, 2009). Suppose that there

is a history of an injection (e.g. of morphine) causing pain relief. Hence, by association, the syringe and the context of the injection can acquire some pain-relieving capacity, i.e. an association between the procedure (conditional stimulus), the drug (unconditional stimulus) and the pain relief (unconditional response). However, conditioning is not the whole explanation of the placebo effect (Stewart-Williams and Podd, 2004). It does not always require a history of associations. Thus, if a person is simply told that pain-relief is to be expected, there can be some tendency for it to be experienced.

Less well known than the placebo effect, is the symmetrical effect, the **nocebo effect**: an aversive state induced by the expectation of something aversive (Benedetti and Amanzio, 1997). An *increase* in pain can result from a contextual factor that has been associated with an increase in pain.

Examples of the placebo effect

Perhaps the best-known examples of the placebo effect concern inert chemicals. In order of increasing placebo efficacy, there is (i) a tablet, (ii) intramuscular injection (e.g. mild saline) and (iii) intravenous injection of the same substance (Wall, 1993).

There exists a surgical placebo (Cobb *et al.*, 1959). For instance, for patients suffering from angina pectoris, an inadequate supply of blood to the cardiac muscle causes pain. Most patients in one study were seriously disabled by their condition and unable to work. An operation consisted of tying arteries that run near to the heart. The rationale was that the disturbance of blood flow would stimulate sprouting of some new blood vessels through the heart muscle. Many patients were happy with the outcome. However, investigators were unable to find any sprouting of new vessels. This prompted a **double-blind study** (i.e. one in which neither patient nor therapist knows into which group a patient has been allocated) into the possibility that the benefit reflected a placebo effect.

For a control group, surgery was done only to the extent that the arteries were temporarily exposed. This gave the patient the impression that the full operation had been performed, whereas no tying of arteries was made. A serious ethical problem arises here: in the interests of research, some patients had to be told lies. This would probably mean that a similar study could not be performed these days. For both experimental and control groups there was a significant reduction in pain.

Placebo effects and the brain

In terms of an integrative biological psychology, a biological basis of the placebo must exist. Otherwise, we have inescapable mystery. Indeed, in fMRI studies, regions of the pain neuromatrix (Figure 14.6), such as the anterior

A personal angle

Patrick Wall's experience

The personal experience of the placebo effect by the eminent London pain researcher, Patrick Wall (one of the authors of 'gate theory'), is revealing. Wall (1993, p. 192) writes:

> When doctors who are not involved in a therapy under trial learn that it turns out to be a placebo, they howl with laughter. When you are the subject in a trial and discover that you have reacted to a placebo, as I have, you feel a fool. When you are the proponent or inventor of a therapy, whether based on contemporary rationale or old-fashioned faith, you are resentful of the need for placebo testing. If the test reveals a substantial placebo component in the response, diversions are created to eliminate consideration of the placebo effect.

cingulate cortex (ACC), insula and thalamus, exhibit lower activity following a placebo treatment (Petrovic *et al.*, 2002; Wager *et al.*, 2004).

The ACC has subdivisions that exhibit different properties: activity of the caudal region is associated with pain as such, whereas the rostral region is excited by opioids. This suggests that the rostral region could be a site of anti-nociception that opposes the caudal region (Petrovic, 2010). The placebo condition is associated with activation of the rostral region, as is the case with hypnotic suggestion.

Increased activity in regions of the orbitofrontal cortex (OFC) is observed during analgesia triggered by a placebo (Zubieta and Stohler, 2009). In humans, the OFC is a region associated with the formation of goals and expectations. The placebo seems to be an example of such cognitive processing. The OFC has connections with the ACC and with the brain stem and it appears to be associated with pain reduction based on cognitive processing (Petrovic, 2010).

The role of opioids in the placebo effect was established by the observation that, under some conditions, the effect is abolished by prior injection of the opioid antagonist naloxone (Levine *et al.*, 1978). If you like more detail, specifically the μ-opioid type of receptor is involved (Zubieta and Stohler, 2009). In the placebo effect, dopamine and opioids are activated in various brain regions (e.g. nucleus accumbens), corresponding to the *expectation* of beneficial effects. Comparing different people, high placebo responsiveness is associated with high activation of these neurochemicals. Opioid

receptors are found in regions of the pain neuromatrix which are reduced in activation corresponding to the placebo effect, e.g. the ACC and the insula (Petrovic, 2010). By contrast, the nocebo effect is based upon inhibition of activity in these same neurochemical systems (Scott *et al.*, 2008). The involvement of dopamine in the nucleus accumbens in pain relief by placebo suggests that this system underlies the expectation of reward (a similar message comes from Chapters 10, 11 and 15).

A pain shared?

'I feel your suffering.'

'My heart aches for you.'

'Your pain is shared with us all.'

These are expressions not just of sympathy but of **empathy**, which refers to a capacity for a person to put themselves in another's place and to experience something of what it is like. Theorists suggest that, for empathy, the observation of the emotional state of another (e.g. pain) triggers features of this same state in the brain of the observer. Brain neuroimaging permits researchers to put this to the test. They give a glimpse of what regions of the brain are doing when someone professes empathy for the pain of another (Singer *et al.*, 2004). Using an fMRI technique, women's brains were examined while their male partners were subject to painful stimulation to the hand.

Observing the partner in pain triggered parts of the brain of the observer that are normally triggered by painful stimuli, the pain neuromatrix. However, not all of the neuromatrix was triggered. Rather, only those parts

Figure 14.12 Relationship between empathy rating of individuals and the associated activation of the ACC.

Source: From Singer *et al.* (2004 Fig. 4A p.1161) Reprinted with permission from AAAS.

associated with the quality of *affect*, e.g. anterior cingulate cortex, were excited. Somatosensory cortex was not activated in empathy, again suggesting a role of this region in sensory and discriminative aspects of nociception, rather than affective aspects. Interestingly, as Figure 14.12 shows, there is a positive correlation between the score on an empathy scale and the degree of excitation of the ACC in response to the pain of the partner. (We can only imagine the breakfast table conversation that this study later triggered among the participants and the degree of marital empathy that was produced!)

What could be the functional significance of empathy? We are a social species and we have adapted to a life of bonding with others. To share the emotion of someone close to us would tend to move us into action in response to their pain. For this, we only need to trigger the affective parts of the pain neuromatrix rather than the sensory-discriminative parts. Indeed, we need to be able to discriminate pain in another person from pain that is endogenous to us (i.e. based on our own tissue damage). If too much of the pain neuromatrix were activated, we might mistake the source of pain. The sensory side of another's suffering is detected through our eyes and ears, etc., which labels it as primarily theirs in its origin.

Section summary

1 Cognition (e.g. catastrophizing) has an influence on pain.

2 A placebo is an intervention (e.g. substance or procedure) that can lower pain as a result of conditioning or a belief as to its efficacy.

3 The placebo effect has a biological basis in inhibiting parts of the pain neuromatrix.

4 A biological basis of empathy consists of the activation of regions of the observer's pain neuromatrix.

☞ Test your knowledge

14.10 Of the regions shown in Figure 14.6, which appear to be activated and which not activated during the experience of empathy for a pain sufferer?

Answer on page 382

Bringing things together

Pain is enigmatic and its study reveals anomalies. Pain is often overwhelming in its attention-grabbing capacity and the potency with which it can take control of consciousness and behaviour. Yet, it can sometimes be reduced by diverted and focused attention, as in competitive sport, or even by nothing more than taking a sugar pill in expectation of relief. We now understand pain better in terms of the contribution of types of neurons, routes of information transmission to and from the brain and brain mechanisms. Some factors can be defined at the neural level, e.g. (i) the properties of peripheral neurons, i.e. small- and large-diameter neurons and (ii) connections that neurons make within the spinal cord.

A pain neuromatrix of interacting brain regions forms the biological basis of pain but does not respond in a one-to-one fashion to nociceptive stimuli. Rather, such input is only one contributory factor to the neuromatrix. Such things as motivation, attention, mood, expectations and memories also play a part in determining pain. These involve (i) a gate mechanism at the spinal level and (ii) some active participation of the brain in pain and anti-nociception. Involvement of regions of prefrontal cortex in pain can be interpreted in terms of their general role in the control of emotion, expectation and decision-making.

The placebo effect can be better understood now in terms of its biological roots. Insights into the processes underlying the effect (e.g. expectation) reinforce our basic understanding of pain. For example, parts of the pain neuromatrix are affected by placebo treatments. Taking a biopsychosocial perspective, such observations offer the possibility of explaining a range of phenomena within a single integrative framework.

Viewing pain from a functional perspective also gives useful insights that can be linked to the neural processes. The evolution of an anti-nociceptive system in addition to the nociceptive systems raises issues on the adaptive value of such joint control. The observation that the anti-nociceptive system is recruited at times when it would be maladaptive to react to tissue damage, as in focused fight or flight, gives an indicator of function. Such considerations could provide a functional context in which to view the clinical role of distraction and positive expectation in bringing pain relief.

 See the video coverage for this chapter which shows how psychology can help people who are in pain.

Summary of Chapter 14

1 A nociceptive system underlies pain, whereas activity within an anti-nociceptive system lowers pain.

2 Pain has adaptive value in protecting animals from tissue damage and keeping them out of harm until recovery. At times it could be adaptive to inhibit pain and this seems to be the reason for the evolutionary appearance of an anti-nociceptive system.

3 Nociceptive neurons detect tissue damage and this leads normally to the sensation of pain. However, pain is not simply a one-to-one reflection of their activity.

4 As a metaphor, the spinal cord is the location of a 'gate'. As the gate opens, so nociceptive information passes, on its way to the brain. When the gate is closed information does not pass further.

5 It is possible to identify brain regions that have distinct roles in the discriminative and affective aspects of pain.

6 The role of different analgesics (pain-reducing substances) can be understood in terms of their actions at various sites in the nociceptive system.

7 Referred pain and phantom limb pain are two phenomena that challenge any simple interpretation of pain.

8 The placebo effect and pain triggered by witnessing another person in pain point to the complex cognitive processing that also forms part of the causation of pain.

Further reading

Pain is viewed in a psychological and philosophical context in Aydede (2006). For a biopsychosocial perspective on pain, see Gatchel *et al.* (2007). For the work of the pioneers of gate theory, see Melzack and Wall (2008) and Wall (2002). For hypnosis and its relation to gate theory, see Chaves and Dworkin (1997). Cognitive therapy and pain is described by Thorn (2004). For the placebo effect, see Petrovic (2010). For neuropathic pain, see Bennett (2010). For chronic pain, see Dickman and Simpson (2008). For phantom effects, see Ramachandran and Blakeslee (1998).

Answers

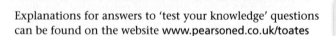

Explanations for answers to 'test your knowledge' questions can be found on the website www.pearsoned.co.uk/toates

14.1 An antagonist to the nociceptive system; an agonist to the anti-nociceptive system.

14.2 Freezing is adaptive, since by remaining motionless an animal tends to avoid detection. If it were to respond to tissue damage by, for example, licking a wound this would act counter to the effect.

14.3 An increase in pain.

14.4 The large-diameter neuron and the two neurons labelled 'Descending pathways'.

14.5 (i) The inhibitory neurochemical and (ii) enkephalin

14.6 Functional neuroimaging would be expected to show increased activity in brain regions forming the pain neuromatrix.

14.7 High; low

14.8 (ii) Lignocaine

14.9 Increased pain felt as coming from the skin.

14.10 Activated anterior cingulate cortex (and possibly interoceptive cortex); Area 3a not activated.

Visit www.pearsoned.co.uk/toates
for a range of resources to support study.
Test yourself with multiple choice questions and access a bank of over 100 videos that will bring the topics to life.

Chapter 15
Motivation

Learning outcomes for Chapter 15

After studying this chapter, you should be able to:

1 Explain the meaning of the term 'motivation' and describe the role it plays in the control of behaviour. Compare and contrast some types of motivation.

2 Describe the properties associated with motivation and its link to behaviour. In so doing, demonstrate an understanding of the terms 'appetitive', 'consummatory', 'reward' and 'incentive'.

3 Identify some neural processes underlying motivation, while linking these to specific and general factors that are involved in the translation between motivation and action.

4 Describe how both behavioural and intrinsic physiological processes contribute to the regulation of body temperature and thereby exemplify a link between homeostasis, motivation and behaviour. In this context, distinguish between negative feedback and feedforward.

5 Identify the neurohormonal processes underlying parental and affiliative behaviours. Link their operation to the functional type of explanation.

6 Describe the contribution of biological, learning, cognitive and social factors to aggressive motivation and behaviour, so as to demonstrate their interaction. In this context, apply the term 'dynamic interaction' to the links between biological factors and the social environment.

7 Describe what is meant by the expression 'exploratory behaviour'. Link this to its underlying neural bases and functional significance.

Scene-setting questions

1 Do we always like the most that which we want the most? If not, why not?
2 Is human violence inevitable? Is fighting an instinct that we can't 'bottle-up'? Is aggression reinforcing?
3 What triggers attachment?
4 Is love an addiction?
5 Why are curiosity and novelty-seeking such powerful factors in human behaviour? What makes some people sensation-seekers?

What triggers attachment? Explore the video on the website accompanying this book at www.pearsoned.co.uk/toates

What motivation underlies such behaviour? How can we best describe it?

Source: © Digital Vision.

Introduction

Consider what motivates your friends. Typically, Parminder might be nursing a broken heart after having been abandoned by Tony. She normally has a workaholic devotion to studying psychology, directed to the goal of becoming a clinical psychologist, but she is now seriously disrupted. Parminder is *motivated* to regain the bond of affection – her dominant goal. The student group is sympathetic but urges Parminder to let go: 'He was no good for you. You were never happy.'

Tom is simply motivated to seek women for what he can get out of them, not having an emotional commitment in the world. Tom is always described by the student group as their 'textbook extrovert and sensation-seeker'.

Svetlana can't go for long without a cigarette, whereas Nigel likes to gamble. Friends nag Svetlana about her smoking and she tries to quit but without success. Nigel never wins at gambling and his friends can't see why he keeps at it. By contrast, Margaret has found God and spends time in meditation and Bible reading.

Tom, forever the cynic, suggests that this is her 'opium', just like Svetlana's cigarettes. Margaret counters with the argument that every rewarding activity is bound to have a biological basis in the activity of the brain. However, this in no way undermines her beliefs.

Harry, a connoisseur of exotic foods, is feeling sorry for himself, after having eaten what was then a delicious meal but being taken ill afterwards. The mere thought of the exotic food is painful – his motivation towards it has been lost – and now, at best, he can consider only 'regular' Western food. Normally, another of his favourite pursuits is exploring the countryside but that has had to be put on hold for a day or two. Sean complains endlessly about university food and is told that, if he were hungry enough, he would be happy to eat it. Ho can never make up his mind about things. He is constantly torn between different activities.

The author's brief venture into popular fiction might, or might not (!), reflect your social circle but should illustrate a few points:

1 Motivation gives direction, intensity and goals to behaviour and is associated with a focus of attention. Parminder cannot ignore Tony to focus on psychology.

2 There can be conflict between motivations. Svetlana wants to quit smoking but finds cigarettes irresistible. Parminder accepts what her friends say but cannot let go of Tony. Ho's indecision implies competition between motivations.

3 Motivation has something to do with the search for pleasure, more or less obvious in different people. Tom appears to be motivated by a simple hedonism. Harry's motivation towards food is guided by the pleasurable or aversive consequences of tasting it.

4 Parminder illustrates that some motivation is based on powerful social attachments and trying to restore them once lost. However, the strength of her motivation is not a reflection of the level of pleasure that Tony brought to her. There appears then to be no simple equation between motivation and pleasure.

5 Some motivations relate rather clearly to basic biological processes, none more so than in Tom's case. However, Parminder's behaviour also makes sense biologically. Maintaining social bonds and resisting their break-up is of importance in survival and rearing children. Harry's exploration of the countryside provides stimulation to the senses. In our evolutionary roots, it would seem advantageous to know our environment. Other motivations reflect processes that were not involved in our early evolution. Cigarettes and casinos were not around then, but they are able to hijack basic processes of motivation and reward.

6 Motivation depends upon external and internal events. Foods vary in their attractiveness but if Sean were hungry enough, he might feel better about university food.

7 Motivation depends in part upon the consequences of past actions. We expect to find understandable consequences of actions that serve either to sustain or to deter them. Harry's aversion to exotic cuisine makes sense. We can't understand why Nigel carries on gambling. We might expect to be able to identify something that Margaret 'gets out' of her spiritual devotion, such as inner tranquility as based in opioid activation.

8 Some motivations relate to immediate rewarding consequences. Svetlana's cigarette delivers nicotine to her brain within a few seconds of puffing it. She is being asked to counter this pull with thoughts of possible aversive consequences that could be years into the future. Similarly, Parminder's goal of becoming a clinical psychologist will take years to realize.

Clearly, in what motivates people, there can be enormous variation among individuals. The richness and variety of human motivation are unique. Sometimes motivations blend in subtle ways, as in taking a meal for its nutrient value and for social contact. However, for some basic insight, we will need to focus on just a few motivations that are common across species – to regulate body temperature, seek social contact, feed, drink, mate and explore, etc. Building on these foundations, we can start to understand the special features of human motivation.

So, let us turn to some principles of motivation that are more applicable across species. There are several aspects to the term 'motivation' (Toates, 1986). It refers to the *variability* of behaviour: people tend to be motivated to seek food when they need nutrients but food becomes less attractive after ingesting a large amount. When we are hot, a cold temperature motivates approach but, when we are cold, it motivates avoidance. Similarly, people's reaction to a sexual stimulus varies as a function of their level of sexual motivation, as embodied in regions of the brain that are sensitized by sex hormones.

Some forms of motivation help to maintain the homeostasis of the body in a rather obvious way, e.g. motivations associated with temperature, food and water. The principle of homeostasis has several closely related aspects (Chapter 1):

1 Survival is possible only if certain parameters of the body such as its water level and temperature are maintained within limits.

2 Behavioural and intrinsic physiological action is taken, which maintains the parameters within these limits.

3 Deviation of a parameter from its normal value tends to cause physiological and behavioural corrective action, the latter being associated with motivation.

The motivation for social attachment is about maintaining contact with a 'special other': partner, parent or child. Loss of contact promotes the motivation to regain contact, a kind of 'social homeostasis'. Sexual motivation appears not to be directly concerned with homeostasis. Exploration is about information, i.e. motivation is directed to gaining sensory stimulation.

In terms of passing on genes, consider an animal in the wild. It needs to avoid harm, e.g. being eaten or suffering tissue injury. It needs to obtain food, water and shelter, to sleep, to explore, to defend against extremes of temperature, to mate and in some cases invest effort in raising young. Some species migrate or hibernate. To do these things, the animal needs to (a) detect information in the environment (presence of food, mate, etc.) and (b) monitor internal conditions (levels of nutrients, hormones, etc.). Regions of the brain involved with motivation produce action on the basis of a *combination* of these sources of information. Some behaviour is of the *approach* kind (termed 'appetitive'), in which increasing stimulation is of adaptive value, e.g. getting to food or a mate. Other behaviour is of the *avoidance* or *escape* kind, to prevent or minimize contact with aversive events (Glickman and Schiff, 1967).

In the wild, time is often at a premium and behaviour involves benefits and costs (Chapter 2). Given conflicting requirements, motivations compete for expression, e.g. to mate or eat. Animals appear to perform computations and arrive at decisions. For example, an animal might be dehydrated, a cost in terms of the risk to body fluids. There is the motivation to search for water, the finding of which could be very beneficial. However, the water hole might be distant and, at the time in question, a location of predators, so it could pay to wait.

Some tasks demand urgent action, whereas others can be delayed, which implies inhibition on lower-priority activities. In rats, hunger suppresses social play (Vanderschuren *et al.*, 1997). Fear inhibits a range of motivations such as that underlying play (Panksepp, 1998). From functional considerations, a time of danger is not a time for play. Chapter 2 discussed the jungle fowl, whose weight falls while she incubates eggs. Prioritization is given to incubation; the motivation to incubate inhibits the tendency to feed.

In the next two sections, we look at some common features of motivation, its expression in behaviour and some processes associated with this. Then, subsequent sections will look at some examples of particular motivations, considering common features and differences between them.

Section summary

1 Motivation refers to brain processes that take internal and external factors into consideration. They give direction and intensity to behaviour and underlie its variability.

2 There can be competition between motivations for expression in behaviour.

3 Some motivations are linked to maintaining the homeostasis of the body.

☞ Test your knowledge

15.1 Which of the following are linked to maintaining an optimal condition within the tissues of the body ('homeostasis')? Feeding, drinking, temperature regulation, sex, exploration.

Answer on page 408   WEB

Properties of motivation

Introduction

Motivation is associated with *flexibility* of behaviour, in that a given motivation can be expressed in a variety of different ways. For example, feeding motivation is revealed in the behaviour of a rat that opens a sack, presses a lever in a Skinner box or negotiates a maze to get food. The consequence of gaining food changes its future behaviour, e.g. to make lever-pressing more likely in the future. This is an example of the developmental/learning explanation (Chapter 1).

In humans, there seems an endless variety of ways in which motivation can gain expression in behaviour – think what Parminder might try next to win back Tony. In the expression of motivation in behaviour, learning plays a crucial role. We learn how to act to achieve our goals. So, among other things, this section will introduce the role of learning in the link between motivation and behaviour.

Appetitive and consummatory phases

Two phases of the control of behaviour are identified: 'appetitive' and 'consummatory' (McDougall, 1923).

The **appetitive phase** refers to the means necessary to get to an 'end-situation', e.g. running a maze to get to a sexual partner. The term **consummatory phase** refers to what the animal actually does in the end-situation, e.g. mating or eating. In non-humans, the flexibility of the appetitive phase generally contrasts with the species-typical inflexible pattern of the consummatory phase (e.g. lordosis in female rats; Chapter 3) (Epstein, 1982). Similarly, wide individual differences are evident in the appetitive phase of gaining food but the consummatory phase is usually more stereotyped.

Reward and incentive

Reward

The term **reward** is used to describe something with which the animal acts to maintain contact, e.g. a cool drink when thirsty (White, 1989). It relates to the consummatory phase and it describes a CNS consequence of sensory contact with something that is ranked as positive. The reward value of a stimulus can be assessed by, for example, the length of time an animal spends in contact with it. In human subjective terms, reward describes the degree of liking for something. As the opposite of reward, 'aversion' refers to something from which the animal withdraws and subsequently avoids. In humans, it is reflected in such terms as displeasure, pain and disgust.

Suppose that a hungry animal is first held in the white arm of a T-maze that contains food (Figure 15.1(a)). In future when given the choice, the animal typically prefers spending time in the white arm even if it is empty (parts (b) and (c)), as measured by the relative length of time spent there. A **conditioned place preference (CPP)** has been established and the food is said to be rewarding (White, 1989). By observing an animal's preference, a CPP test shows a common property shared by different rewards, e.g. food, drugs, a sexually attractive conspecific (Everitt, 1990; Harris *et al.*, 2005) and the opportunity to engage in social play with a conspecific (Vanderschuren *et al.*, 1997).

Incentive

The term **incentive** is used to describe an animal's attraction towards rewards. If you wonder why we need two terms, reward and incentive, please be patient. Incentive relates to the appetitive phase and conveys the sense of an animal being 'pulled' to the reward. Rewarding things such as food, water, drugs and sexual contact come to form incentives.

Classical conditioning between external stimuli and incentives plays a vital role in motivation. By their pairing with primary incentives, neutral stimuli become **conditional incentives** and they then exert

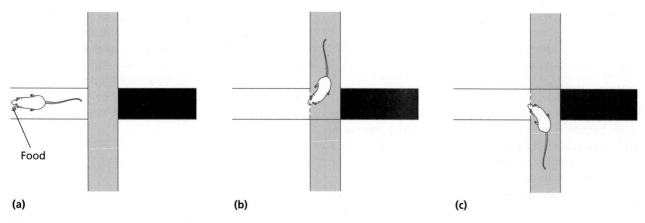

(a) **(b)** **(c)**

Figure 15.1 Conditioned place preference: (a) conditioning phase, (b) and (c) testing phase.

an influence on behaviour. For example, by its pairing with food, the white arm in Figure 15.1 has become a conditional incentive. For another example, feeding can be aroused in 'satiated' animals by a cue that has been paired with food delivery when the animal was hungry (Weingarten, 1984). The cue becomes a conditional incentive. Sexual arousal can be increased by cues that were earlier associated with mating (Domjan, 1994). A cue paired with injection of an intravenous drug in a Skinner box can revive lever-pressing for the drug following extinction (Stewart *et al.*, 1984). Conditional cues associated with shock can trigger aggression in the presence of a conspecific (Berkowitz, 1993).

Under some conditions, a given object might lose reward value but still maintain incentive value. Thus, animals occasionally are attracted to food that they do not eat (Dickinson and Balleine, 1992). Conversely, following certain brain lesions, food can trigger ingestion when it is placed in the mouth, i.e. it is rewarding, but an animal fails to be attracted towards it even following deprivation (Berridge and Valenstein, 1991), i.e. it has lost incentive value.

Hedonic ('affective') states

Introduction

In humans, associated with each positive ('appetitive') motivation there is a factor of positive affect ('pleasure'). To what extent a common system underlies the pleasures of the consummatory phase, e.g. eating and sex, is unclear (Panksepp, 1998). There might be a common neural process (e.g. in the septal area or the amygdala) and distinctions between types of reward might arise from differences in sensory channels activated.

Human experience

To humans, ingestion of food is hedonically good, bad or indifferent (Cabanac, 1971). A combination of external and internal factors, e.g. the intrinsic properties of the food and the body's level of nutrients, determines hedonic reactivity. Figure 15.2 shows a result for temperature that makes a similar point (Cabanac, 1998). For low ('hypothermic') core body temperatures, warmth at the skin is pleasant, whereas cold is pleasant when the core of the body is high ('hyperthermic'). That the pleasure or displeasure of a local skin temperature is a function of internal temperature (e.g. cold is pleasurable in hyperthermia) is termed **alliesthesia** (Cabanac, 1998). This all makes sense in terms of homeostasis and biological adaptation: e.g. when the body is hypothermic, it is advantageous to approach warm environments.

Figure 15.2 Pleasantness ratings of a temperature stimulus as a function of three different body temperatures.
Source: Cabanac (1979).

Whether we should extrapolate affect to non-humans is a matter of scientific taste but the lay public has no hesitation in doing so. An experiment relevant to this issue is described next.

Taste reactivity test

Do non-human species experience affect? We can speculate based on behaviour, an example being shown in the **taste reactivity test** (Berridge *et al.*, 1981) (Figure 15.3). A cannula is implanted so that small quantities of liquid nutrient are applied to the rat's tongue. Behaviour is observed from below in a mirror and recorded by a video camera. A lexicon of reactions, positive and negative, is constructed (Figure 15.4).

The test provides a measure of motivation as related to consummatory behaviour. Some substances (e.g. saccharine) trigger acceptance whereas others (e.g. quinine) trigger rejection. Concentrated sodium chloride solution triggers rejection when the animal is in sodium balance but, following sodium depletion, it is accepted. This indicates the influence of physiological state on motivation and clearly relates to homeostasis. After an otherwise desirable substance has been paired with gastrointestinal illness (Chapter 11), the same substance triggers rejection. A memory of the past contact modulates the reactivity to the incentive.

Very young children, even newborns, also exhibit characteristic facial reactions when coming into contact with substances, indicative of affect (Steiner, 1979) (Figure 15.5).

We now turn to consider some of the neural bases of the processes described in this section.

Ingestion sequence

Aversion sequence

Figure 15.4 Sample reactions. Top row: acceptance, i.e. ingestive reactions – rhythmic mouth movements, protrusions of the tongue, etc.; bottom row: rejection, i.e. aversive reactions – chin rubs, paw wipes, etc.
Source: Berridge *et al.* (1981, Fig. 1, p. 366).

Figure 15.3 The taste reactivity test.
Source: Grill and Berridge (1985, Fig. 3, p. 13).

Figure 15.5 Human baby feeding.
Source: © Michael Keller/CORBIS.

Section summary

1   Such things as food, water and sexual contact are rewards, i.e. an animal acts to maintain contact with them.

2   Motivation is revealed in behaviour in the appetitive and consummatory phases.

3   The term 'incentive' refers to the capacity of rewards to attract.

4   Cues paired with incentives acquire motivational value by classical conditioning. They become 'conditional incentives'.

5   Motivation arises from a combination of external ('incentives') and internal (e.g. nutrient level) signals.

6   Affective ('hedonic') experiences depend upon internal physiology in a way that makes adaptive sense.

 ## Test your knowledge

15.2 Complete the following: 'Pressing a lever in a Skinner box, is an example of the ___ phase of behaviour whereas eating the food is an example of the ___ phase'.

15.3 A tone is paired with the presentation of a drug a number of times. Subsequently, a rat presses a lever in a Skinner box to earn the tone on its own. In the terminology of conditioning, what adjective before 'incentive' qualifies the description of the tone?

15.4 A particular nutrient solution triggers positive ingestive reactions in rats. Other than over-eating, what would shift the reactions in a negative direction?

Answers on page 408

The neuroscience of motivation

Introduction

We now look at some brain mechanisms that underlie motivation, with an emphasis on those that link motivation to action. We ask two closely related questions: are there general *principles* of neural organization underlying motivation that can be applied across different motivations? Can we go further and find any common neural processes that serve different motivations?

From a 'design' point of view, we might argue along the following lines. Parameters of the body such as temperature and water level require specialized and dedicated neural processes. These monitor just one such quality and, when it departs from optimum, they play a role in a specific motivation. However, in the appetitive phase, no matter what the incentive is, the problem posed seems to be rather similar when comparing different motivations. The most potent incentive needs to form the focus of attention, engage behaviour by linking to motor control and offer competition over any other candidates for control.

Similarly, in the consummatory phase, there could be at least some common processes underlying rewarding effects, e.g. the reward of the taste of food and that of sexual contact. We might expect to find less in the way of common processes underlying the motor side of the consummatory phase – after all, mating is rather different from feeding! Consider first the role of incentives in the appetitive phase.

Dopamine, incentives and approach behaviour

The mesolimbic dopaminergic pathway

Psychologists postulate a *general* 'incentive system' or 'seeking system', which serves any *specific* motivation that gains access to it (Blackburn *et al.*, 1992). The biological basis of the 'incentive system' involves a dopaminergic pathway, the **mesolimbic dopamine pathway**, part of which starts in the ventral tegmental area (VTA) and terminates in the nucleus accumbens (N.acc.), a region of the ventral striatum (Everitt and Robbins, 1992) (Chapter 10). See Figures 10.19 (p. 271) and 15.6. When this pathway is activated by a particular incentive, the animal tends to approach the incentive. So, dopamine (DA) activation increases the power of incentives to engage behaviour.

The dopaminergic activity of the ventral striatum (which includes the N.acc.) was studied in a group of patients suffering from Parkinson's disease (de la Fuente-Fernández *et al.*, 2002) (Chapter 10). In their case, the reward was considered to be the clinical benefit following a placebo treatment. The *expectation* of receiving reward was associated with dopaminergic activation in the region of the N.acc. as measured by a PET scan.

Consider Figure 15.7. The N.acc. appears to serve as interface, in which information on motivational significance is (i) computed and (ii) transmitted towards processes ('Motor control') at or near the basal ganglia, which organize behaviour (Chapter 10; Mogenson,

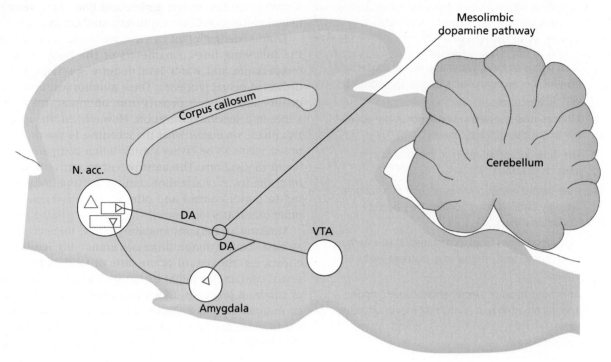

Figure 15.6 The mesolimbic dopamine (DA) pathway in the rat brain.
Source: after Bardo (1998, Fig. 1, p. 57).

1984). The N.acc. receives information from a number of other brain regions, e.g. the cortex, amygdala and hippocampus.

DA activation draws attention to the object triggering the burst and turns it into something like a 'motivational magnet', such that behaviour is directed towards it and is sustained (Leyton, 2010). The magnet would correspond to something that is, say, drug-, food- or sex-related. However, it might also correspond to a location of safety in the case of an aversive situation, i.e. 'somewhere better than here'. Dopaminergic activation ceases in cases where the animal gives up in the face of adversity (Leyton, 2010). DA could play a role in the appraisal that behaviour is serving to bring goals nearer to realization. In humans, there is a tendency for temporary DA depletion to lead to apathy, which would be consistent with such an interpretation. DA might contribute to the pleasure of goal accomplishment, without being implicated in that associated with the consummatory phase, as in eating per se.

Alternatively DA could be involved indirectly in affective states. If it is needed to motivate movement towards goals, then a low DA level might mean that few goals are ever reached. Hence there is not the positive affect that would normally derive from goal attainment. Some results found with the use of reserpine, for treating high blood pressure, are in accordance with this interpretation. A kind of 'pseudo-depression' was triggered, characterized by (Leyton, 2010, p. 231), not as sadness but as: 'sedation, decreased energy, and occasionally, decreased motivation to interact with the environment'.

We focus now on the amygdala.

The amygdala and incentive learning

The amygdala is involved in learning about the conditional significance of positive events, such as those related to food and sexual partners (Everitt, 1990; Wang *et al.*, 2005) as well as negative events (Chapter 12). That

Figure 15.7 Role of the nucleus accumbens.

is, the amygdala has a role in attributing motivational value to otherwise neutral stimuli following their pairing with rewarding or aversive events. Acting via the amygdala, these (now 'conditional') stimuli are able to engage behaviour. The lateral and basal nuclei of the amygdala are involved in attributing conditional incentive value to such things as the lever in the Skinner box associated with food reward (Wang *et al.*, 2005). This contributes to making lever-pressing the goal of behaviour. The amygdala projects to the N.acc., which is the next link in the chain leading to the motor output that underlies approach behaviour (Figure 15.7).

Drug addicts show an exaggerated response of the amygdala to drug-related cues (Bechara, 2005). This includes the reward of money, a capacity which might well depend upon an association with the purchase of drugs.

For another example, in the conditioned place preference task, a rat associates one arm of a T-maze (e.g. the white arm) with reward (e.g. mate or a drug infusion) and prefers spending time there. Following lesions to the lateral amygdala, rats show motivational indifference towards the arms (McDonald and White, 1993; White and McDonald, 1993).

Focusing specifically on the basolateral amygdala (Chapter 12), projections from here go to the nucleus accumbens (Figure 15.7; Everitt and Robbins, 1992). This link mediates the effect of conditional stimuli and damage to it disrupts their capacity to engage behaviour. However, it does not disrupt consummatory behaviour.

The functional significance of a process by which conditional stimuli gain control of behaviour is clear: based upon past experience, it leads the animal to incentives and keeps it going at a goal-directed task even in the absence of the primary reward.

Wanting and liking

Basics of the distinction

DA is implicated in the motivational role of incentives and in forming conditional incentives. Is it also involved in the reward process, e.g. the hedonics of taste? DA depletion reduces food intake but is this just because food fails to form an incentive to attract the rat? It might be that the taste of food loses its rewarding impact.

The taste reactivity test (see earlier) allows researchers to separate possible effects of DA depletion. Suppose that DA mediates the reward of something, in human terms it underlies pleasure. It would follow that when DA is depleted, food loses its hedonic impact. Berridge and Valenstein (1991) performed the taste reactivity test, expecting that the reaction to food in the mouth

would be shifted in a negative direction. This was not the case; DA-depleted rats reacted to food in the same way as did controls.

This research suggested that the *incentive value* of food (its 'incentive salience') depends upon DA, i.e. its capacity to attract attention and 'pull' the animal towards it. When DA is depleted, the appetitive ('wanting') phase is disrupted. However, if the animal receives food in the mouth, the food's hedonic impact ('liking') is not diminished. The role of DA has been described as focusing: the strength of one particular incentive is amplified in the face of competing possibilities for action which are inhibited (Mogenson *et al.*, 1993).

Of course, if not DA, then another neurochemical underlies the reward value, e.g. that of food in the mouth or sexual contact (Robinson and Berridge, 1993). Evidence suggests that activity by the brain's opioid systems is the biological basis of several, if not all, types of reward (Ågmo and Berenfeld, 1990; Panksepp *et al.*, 2002a). In a taste reactivity test, injecting opioid agonists makes the reaction to food more positive (Rideout and Parker, 1996). The injection of opiate drugs acts as a very potent reward. Loss of opioid systems lowers the reward of social contact (Moles *et al.*, 2004).

The incentive system employing dopamine and the reward system employing opioids show close interaction (Depue and Morrone-Strupinsky, 2005). On a psychological level, we tend to want what we like but there is not a perfect correlation between wanting and liking (Robinson and Berridge, 1993).

A genetic modification

Suppose that researchers create a hyper-dopaminergic state. What would Berridge and associates predict? That animals would show a heightened attraction to incentives ('wanting') but that the taste reactivity ('liking') would not alter. So how do they create this state? After its release and occupation of receptors, dopamine is taken back into the cell from which it is released, i.e. 'reuptake'. Peciña *et al.* (2003) created a strain of mutant mice using the technique of 'gene knockdown'. Specifically, the dopamine transporter gene was knocked-down, so that very little dopamine was transported back into the cell from which it was released. Hence, there is an elevation of dopamine at the receptors on the postsynaptic membrane.

For food reward, the mutant mice showed quicker learning, a decreased length of time to run a maze and fewer distractions, compared with controls. This pointed to increased wanting. However, there was no difference in reaction to the taste of the reward, pointing to liking's insensitivity to dopamine levels.

Individual differences in human personality

Humans differ in how they are influenced by rewards, e.g. by the relative weight of immediate reward ('instant gratification') versus delayed reward. Do differences in the activity of reward regions of the brain link to differences in personality?

Using fMRI, Cohen *et al.* (2005) investigated the possible link between differences in activation of regions of the brain associated with the reward of money and differences in extraversion. Figure 15.8(a) shows the activation of three such regions by money reward: the orbitofrontal cortex (Figure 5.32, p. 129), the N.acc. (Figure 5.30, p. 127) and the amygdala. Figure 15.8(b) shows differences in activation of two of these structures and the participants' scores on extroversion. A positive correlation is evident. This could give leads that enable links to be established between brain structures and individual differences in sensitivity to reward. Note also that the structures most sensitive to reward are influenced by dopamine. A challenge comes in trying to associate the individual differences revealed in Figure 15.8(b) to differences in alleles coding for dopamine receptors.

The next section turns to the 'mechanics' of the consummatory phase.

The mechanics of consummatory behaviour

The consummatory phase of rat behaviour, in eating and mating, is somewhat stereotyped. This implies tightly organized controls of the motor output. Much of the organization of consummatory behaviour such as feeding, mating and attack is done at brain stem sites (Chapter 10; Berntson and Micco, 1976). The neural

(a)   **(b)**

Figure 15.8 Linking activation of reward regions of the brain and personality differences: (a) three regions affected by reward and (b) link between activation (vertical axis) and extroversion score (horizontal axis). Increasing score on horizontal axis = increasing extroversion. Lower part activations for two participants, whose extroversion scores are indicated.

Source: Cohen *et al.* (2005, Fig. 2, p. 854 and Fig. 3, p. 856). Figures by courtesy of Dr Michael Cohen.

processes that underlie organized patterns of neuromuscular control ('prescriptions') are located in these regions.

So, what is the link between motivation and consummatory behaviour? The hypothalamus contains distinct nuclei (Chapter 5), sensitive to particular chemicals in the fluid that bathes them, e.g. glucose for feeding or testosterone for sexual behaviour. These nuclei exert a tendency towards a particular consummatory behaviour by favouring activation of the lower-level neural circuits that organize it. For example, in functional terms, feeding reflexes are potentiated at times of nutrient need (Berntson and Micco, 1976). Neural systems in, among other regions, the striatum integrate individual acts such as licking, chewing and swallowing to form functionally coherent sequences (Aldridge and Berridge, 1998).

A consideration of the appetitive and consummatory phases is central to the topic described next.

Electrical stimulation of the brain

Introduction

Psychologists observe the behaviour of animals with electrodes implanted in their brains, through which electric current is delivered. This procedure is known as 'electrical stimulation of the brain' (ESB). There are two variations on this theme: the animal or the experimenter triggers the delivery of electric current. This section looks at each.

Intracranial self-stimulation

One of the best-known results in psychology is that of Olds and Milner (1954). Electrodes are implanted into the brain of rats with the tip in one of a number of different regions, e.g. the lateral hypothalamus (LH). They are taught to press a lever to deliver electric shocks to the region: electrical self-stimulation of the brain or **intracranial self-stimulation** (ICSS). The vigour with which rats engage in ICSS suggested that they were tapping into a 'pleasure centre' and this term rapidly acquired popularity. It seemed as if they were simulating some of the conditions of, say, feeding or orgasm but bypassing the sensory processes that would normally mediate it.

Dopaminergic systems are involved in ICSS. Loss of DA is followed by a fall in ICSS. Thus, DA came to be described as a pleasure neurotransmitter and a loss of DA as 'anhedonia' (Wise, 1982). However, as just noted, we now have reason to believe that DA is not mediating pleasure but rather is involved in incentive approach ('wanting'). So, maybe rats are not triggering pleasure centres but 'incentive centres'.

For ICSS in the lateral hypothalamus, Panksepp (1998, p. 145) notes:

The outward behaviour of the animal commonly appears as if it is trying to get something behind the lever. In other words, an invigorated exploratory attitude is sustained throughout. This is not the type of behaviour one sees when animals are either pressing levers to obtain conventional rewards or when they are actually engaged in *consuming* them.

Electrically induced behaviour

If the experimenter (rather than the rat) controls the current, a rat can be induced to engage in behaviour such as going over to food and eating. This is termed **electrically induced behaviour** (EIB). Typically, if the same electrode that supports ICSS (e.g. in the lateral hypothalamus) is stimulated under the experimenter's control, the animal engages in behaviour such as sniffing and exploration. If food is present, it will eat (Valenstein, 1969).

Stimulation elicits various behaviours, according to the location of the electrode and other factors such as availability of incentives (Robbins and Everitt, 1999).

The next four sections look at some specific behaviours associated with motivation: temperature regulation, social attachment, aggression and exploration. These illustrate the general principles described so far in this chapter.

☞ **Test your knowledge**

15.5 Consider the rat shown in Figure 15.1. Which stimulus has become a conditional incentive that is capable of triggering activity in the mesolimbic dopaminergic system?

Answer on page 408   ⬤WEB➤

Section summary

1 There is an incentive system, a principal biological basis of which is the mesolimbic dopamine pathway.

2 The mesolimbic dopamine pathway starts in the ventral tegmental area (VTA) and projects to the nucleus accumbens (N.acc.).

3 Loss of dopamine from the mesolimbic dopamine pathway causes a loss of appetitive ('incentive') motivation.

4 There are specific motivational inputs to the mesolimbic dopamine pathway from other brain regions, such as the amygdala and hippocampus.

5 There is a distinction between wanting and liking and manipulations can affect one and not the other. Wanting is mediated by dopamine whereas liking appears not to be.

6 Some consummatory behaviour is organized at the brain stem and coordinated by higher brain regions, e.g. cortex and striatum.

Temperature regulation

Introduction

According to their body temperature, animals are motivated to seek warmth or cold, an example of homeostasis. Correspondingly, sources of either warmth or cold act as rewards (Figure 15.2). Life is possible only if body temperature remains within a range, the magnitude of which depends upon the species. For mammals and birds, the range is narrow.

Body temperature is said to be regulated by means of comparison with a set-point (Chapter 10) of temperature (Cabanac, 1998). The term 'set-point' describes the temperature set ('defended') by the system. Deviations from the set-point trigger actions that bring the regulated variable back to the set-point (Cabanac and Russek, 1982). The set-point shows some fluctuation over the 24 hours of day–night. However, at any time, it is defended against disturbances.

The body temperature of humans exemplifies well that deviations from the normal (set-point) level can exert a powerful influence on internal physiology, motivation and behaviour. For fish, reptiles and amphibians, although the range of tolerance is wider, there are still optimal temperatures for maximizing efficiency (Blumberg and Sokoloff, 1998).

In lay terms, animals are warm-blooded (birds and mammals) or cold-blooded (amphibians, reptiles and fish). However, body temperature of a so-called cold-blooded animal can sometimes be as warm as that of a warm-blooded one, e.g. a snake basking in the sun. The distinction refers not so much to actual body temperature but to (a) the range of temperatures compatible with life and (b) the extent to which an animal is at the mercy of the environment. A reptile can survive a wider range of body temperatures than can a mammal. The reptile's body temperature depends upon the environment to a greater extent than that of a warm-blooded

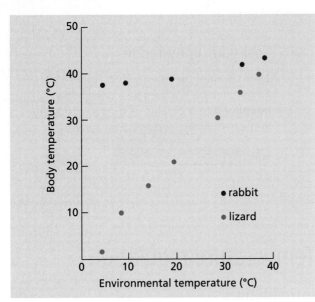

Figure 15.9 Body temperature and environmental temperature for a rabbit (blue dots) and a lizard (red dots).

animal. The body temperature of a mammal or bird tends to remain near to constant. Figure 15.9 compares body temperatures of a rabbit and a lizard when exposed to different environmental temperatures.

Regulation and control

Introduction

Actively holding body temperature near constant exemplifies regulation and homeostasis (Chapter 2). Actions that serve regulation are termed *control* actions (Cabanac and Russek, 1982). For example, sweating and panting are controlled, whereas body temperature is regulated. Similarly, drinking and urination are said to be controlled, whereas body-fluid level is regulated. For survival, it is biologically imperative that body temperature is defended, whereas it is adaptive for sweating and panting to fluctuate *in the service of* body temperature.

Two means of control

Two kinds of control are exerted to regulate body temperature: intrinsic physiological and behavioural (Blumberg and Sokoloff, 1998). Intrinsic control involves effectors of the ANS (Chapter 3) such as sweating and changing the diameter of blood vessels near the skin to facilitate heat exchange. Shivering is an intrinsic control similar to autonomic actions but involves skeletal muscle. Behavioural and autonomic controls serve the same end, are complementary and there can be a trade-off between them. When temperature regulation cannot be achieved by behaviour, more of the burden is carried by autonomic processes (Cabanac, 1998).

Autonomic processes are costly and there is an adaptive value in behavioural control relieving them of long-term exertion.

Examples of behavioural control

Behavioural control consists of certain species-typical reflexes and performing whole-body motivated actions. Whole-body actions involve (i) changing body position relative to the present environment, (ii) moving to a new environment or (iii) remaining in the same location and producing action to change it, e.g. building a nest, huddling with other animals or pressing a lever in a Skinner box for heat (Carlisle, 1966). In humans, such behaviour is associated with affect (Figure 15.2).

Among different species, behavioural control is more widely found than is intrinsic control. All species so far tested show selection of a temperature environment. Fish select an appropriate water temperature and can be trained in an operant task to gain access to it (Satinoff, 1983). There is a richness of means by which humans regulate body temperature, e.g. to light fires or seek shelter. We can also anticipate future needs by taking pre-emptive action ('feedforward'), e.g. putting on extra clothes on hearing the weather forecast. All these criteria point to the existence of motivation.

Neural processes

Neural characteristics

There are neurons the activity of which depends strongly upon body temperature. They are found in the hypothalamus and other sites in the CNS and in the periphery (Bligh, 1972; Satinoff, 1983). There are so-called 'warm neurons', where frequency of producing action potentials increases with temperature. What are termed 'cold neurons' have the opposite characteristic: as temperature falls, their frequency of generation of action potentials increases (Figure 15.10).

Temperature-sensitive neurons at the core and periphery play a role in temperature regulation. If core temperature shifts from its optimal value, autonomic and behavioural control is triggered. However, threats to body temperature usually arise first from outside the body, e.g. sudden cold winds, rather than from within it. Outside disturbances do not immediately affect core temperature (and the neurons there) since the core is shielded. However, if action is not taken, core temperature will subsequently be affected, so it is crucial that temperature detected at the periphery can trigger action.

The role of peripheral temperature-sensitive neurons in behavioural and autonomic control represents feedforward (Chapter 10). By reacting immediately to

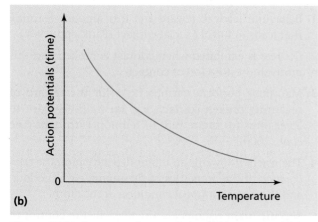

Figure 15.10 Response characteristics of (a) warm and (b) cold neurons in terms of action potentials per unit of time.

peripheral temperature, the animal can often avoid ('pre-empt') central shifts of temperature.

The preoptic area of the hypothalamus (Figure 5.31, p. 128) has attracted attention as a brain region where the motivational signal from temperature is computed (Gordon and Heath, 1986). Local heating or cooling at this site is an effective trigger for a thermoregulatory response. It is here that injections of neurotransmitters are particularly effective in altering temperature regulation.

A simple model

Figure 15.11 suggests how temperature-sensitive neurons at the core and periphery *might* interact in the control of behaviour and in changing the reward value of external temperatures. Neuron$_1$ is a 'warm neuron' in the brain (e.g. preoptic area of the hypothalamus), i.e. its activity increases with core body temperature. When it is active, it excites neuron$_3$, which motivates the animal to seek a cold environment and thereby lower body temperature. A cold environmental temperature is a reward and, to humans, is affectively positive. Neuron$_1$ is also excited by signals derived from warm neurons at the periphery (indicated as 'Warm').

Neuron$_2$ is a 'cold neuron' in the hypothalamus. Its activity increases with decreases in core body temperature. Its activity, via neuron$_4$, motivates the animal to increase body temperature. Contact with warm environments becomes rewarding. Cold neurons in the periphery excite neuron$_2$ (indicated as 'Cold'). Note inhibitory links between the 'warm control pathway' and the 'cold control pathway'.

Figure 15.12 illustrates the zones of control to each side of a thermo-neutral range and the corresponding neural bases of control. Within the thermo-neutral range, the animal is not motivated to perform temperature-related activities.

This section has looked at an example of the link between homeostasis, motivation and behaviour, which serves the inner environment. The following considers an example of social behaviour.

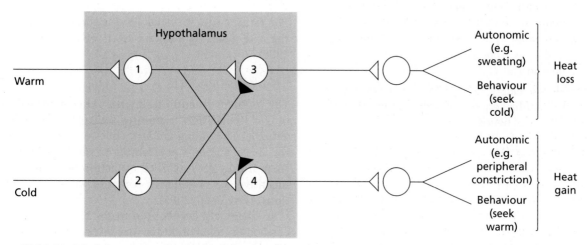

Figure 15.11 Model of the neurons involved in behavioural temperature regulation. △, excitation; ▲, inhibition.
Source: after an illustration by Albert Miller in Heller *et al.* (1978).

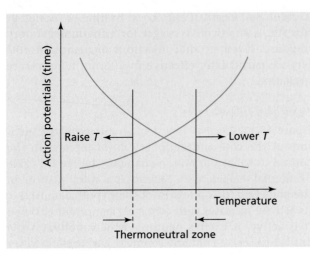

Figure 15.12 Activity of temperature-dependent neurons and the associated behavioural actions.

Section summary

1 Body temperature is regulated by control of autonomic processes and the influence of motivation on behaviour.

2 When set-point and actual body temperature get out of alignment by a significant amount, physiological and behavioural control is triggered to restore normality.

3 Temperature-sensitive neurons at the CNS and periphery play a role in temperature regulation.

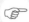 ## Test your knowledge

15.6 In Figure 15.11, suppose that the animal is in a thermoneutral environment. What would be the behavioural effect of injecting an agonist to the neurotransmitter employed in the link from the neuron marked 'Warm' to neuron$_1$?

15.7 In Figure 15.11, detection of extreme cold at the periphery has what effect on the activity of neuron$_3$?

 Answers on page 408

Social behaviour

Introduction

This section looks at two motivations and the associated behaviour: **nurturant behaviour** (parental behaviour) and **social attachment**, i.e. bonding (Chapter 12). In some species, such as humans, the two motivations overlap. That is to say, a social attachment, between an infant and mother, develops at the same time as the mother performs nurturant behaviour, e.g. suckling (Panksepp, 1998).

Nurturant behaviour and social attachment reveal several features of motivation:

1 Behaviour leads to reward and this supports learning that leads to further social contact (Panksepp, 1998).

2 Distress is exhibited when contact is broken and this motivates restoration of contact.

3 Mammals perform various tasks for the reward of regaining broken contact, e.g. rat mothers learn to lever-press for the reward of reunion with pups (Lee *et al.*, 2000).

4 The reaction towards an infant depends upon the *combination* of the properties of the infant, e.g. its odour, and the neurohormonal condition of the mother.

5 Specific brain regions are involved in the control of maternal behaviour and attachment. These regions show properties similar to those underlying certain other emotions and motivations, such as pain and sex.

We consider first nurturant (mainly maternal) behaviour and then attachment, bearing in mind that there can be considerable overlap between them.

Nurturance

The term 'nurturant behaviour' is employed to describe the care given by a parent to its offspring (Panksepp, 1998).

Motivational basis

The mother's reaction to infants varies with her physiological condition, a pointer towards a motivational variable. The young are attractive to a nursing mother rat. For example, she attempts to regain contact with them if they get lost. Such attraction to an appropriate incentive is a property in common with other motivations (Ferris *et al.*, 2005).

In mammals, events prior to the birth put the mother's body into a condition that increases the chances of nurturant behaviour following birth. Pups normally trigger avoidance or attack in female rats. However, if the female is in the appropriate neurohormonal state, she shows attraction, approach and nurturance. Prior to birth and influenced by the neurohormonal condition, rat mothers build a nest. Following birth, pups that are displaced from the nest are returned by the mother. In this neurohormonal state, environmental cues that are associated with pups attract the mother. In a place preference test shortly after giving birth, rat mothers show a preference for a location that had been associated earlier with pups. This is even when tested against a location associated with cocaine injection (Mattson *et al.*, 2003). By 16 days after giving birth, preference switches to the cocaine-associated side. Such a change in response exemplifies a central motivational change (Lee *et al.*, 2000).

Neurobiology

A nursing mother rat's approach behaviour to her pups involves the mesolimbic DA system (Ferris *et al.*, 2005). If the system is disrupted, so is maternal behaviour. Human mothers show activation in this area when confronted by the challenge of an infant cry (Lorberbaum *et al.*, 2002). The amygdala exerts a role in the attraction of a nurturant female rat to a location associated with pups.

The mother's motivational change in reaction to pups involves a cocktail of neurohormonal changes, most prominent being changes in activity of estrogens, oxytocin, prolactin and opioids (Rosenblatt, 1992). For example, injections of oxytocin into the brain increase the tendency that she will exhibit nurturant behaviour.

Figure 15.13 shows some of the brain circuitry underlying maternal behaviour in the rat. Neuronal circuits that are based in the preoptic area of the hypothalamus (POA) and the ventral bed nucleus of the stria terminalis (VBN) constitute what Panksepp (1998) terms a 'central integrator'. Information on pups and related cues ('sensory inputs') is conveyed to the central integrator, where it acquires motivational value. The neurons in these sites are a location of a high density of receptors to the neurochemicals involved in maternal behaviour. Occupation of these receptors triggers maternally positive motivational changes. Lesions to these areas are particularly disruptive of maternal behaviour (Lee *et al.*, 2000). Outputs from the integrator are projected to various brain regions concerned with organizing maternal behaviour ('behavioural output').

Towards the end of pregnancy and in the first few days following giving birth, there is an increase in oxytocin activity in the brain, involving an increase in density of oxytocin receptors at the central integrator. The periaqueductal grey (PAG) is also a region rich in receptors for oxytocin. Oestrogen acts on neurons in the region corresponding to the central integrator. These effects increase the tendency to exhibit nurturant behaviour. After the young appear, the rewarding effects of social contact are closely associated with the activity of opioids and oxytocin (Nelson and Panksepp, 1996).

Social attachment and isolation

Introduction

Following the early experience of nurturance (e.g. suckling), dedicated systems of emotion and motivation within the brains of certain species of mammals and birds maintain social attachment with selected conspecifics (Panksepp, 1994). These are exemplified by those between a caretaker (usually a parent) and the growing young, between siblings or between monogamous sexual partners. The term 'social attachment' refers to the tendency of individuals of certain species to keep proximity to another and to show distress when it is lost. Lorenz (1981) studied this process in birds, i.e. the tendency for the newly hatched to follow the mother (Chapter 6). To what extent the circuitry shown in Figure 15.13 can be generalized to cover attachment remains to be seen.

Motivational basis

It appears that a dedicated motivational process with its own form of reward underlies the formation and expression of social attachment (Bowlby, 1973; Panksepp, 1998). Babies deprived of social contact fail to thrive normally, even though their needs for warmth and nutrition, etc. might well be accommodated.

Figure 15.13 Neural processes underlying maternal behaviour in the rat. VTA = ventral tegmental area, a brain region closely connected with the attraction of incentives. PAG = periaqueductal grey, a region involved in emotional processing. S = septal area, a reward-related area. POA = preoptic area. VBN = ventral bed nucleus of the stria terminalis.
Source: Panksepp (1998, Fig. 13.4, p. 254).

Disruption of attachment

An index of a negative emotion, 'distress', is given by distress vocalization (DV): the crying that the young of all mammalian species (and some non-mammalian) exhibit on enforced separation from a caregiver (Herman and Panksepp, 1978). Consider an infant rat that gets isolated. Its vocalizations alert the mother to the pup's state and location and they facilitate retrieval and return to the nest.

The neurobiology of attachment and its breaking

The trajectory of the neural system underlying distress starts at the brain stem in structures common to all mammals and birds (Panksepp, 1994). It appears that this system overlaps with pain. In humans, the subjective feeling of social distress is commonly described in terms of pain (Eisenberger and Lieberman, 2004). In guinea pigs, electrical stimulation of the preoptic area, periacqueductal grey area and amygdala elicit DVs (Panksepp *et al.*, 1988).

A number of endogenous neurochemicals are implicated in the emotional processing underlying attachment and distress at its breaking, e.g. opioids, prolactin and endorphins. Panksepp *et al.* (1988) suggest that DVs are an index of the activity of an emotion circuit that involves opioids. Opioids and oxytocin inhibit the emotion associated with breaking social attachment (Panksepp *et al.*, 1988). Figure 15.14 shows the role of opiates in suppressing distress vocalization in 6–8-week-old puppies and Figure 15.15 shows the effect of oxytocin and prolactin in chicks.

For a range of social species, injections of opiates reduce social contact (less 'gregariousness'). Opioid antagonists increase gregariousness (Panksepp, 1998). Injection of the opioid agonist morphine to either mother or infant rhesus monkeys causes a decrease in the amount of clinging between mother and infant. Conversely, the opioid antagonist naltrexone increases it (Kalin *et al.*, 1995). When a monkey is groomed by another, there is an increase in levels of ß-endorphin (Keverne *et al.*, 1989).

Mutant mice that lack the gene coding for μ-opioid receptors do not exhibit attachment (Moles *et al.*, 2004). They are able to discriminate, for example, odours associated with the mother, so they are not deficient in sensory discrimination. Rather, they do not show a *preference* for such odour. The deficiency is related to motivation and reward. This suggests that opioids are employed in the neural systems that mediate social reward. Neither do such mice exhibit distress on removal from the mother. Again, this suggests that separation distress is based upon opioids.

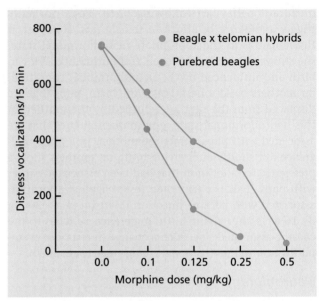

Figure 15.14 The effect of morphine (an opiate having opioid agonist properties) injections on the distress vocalizations produced by puppies following separation. *Source:* adapted from Panksepp *et al.* (1978, Fig. 2, p. 612).

Figure 15.15 The effect of prolactin and oxytocin on distress vocalizations in 5–6-day-old chicks isolated from the flock. *Source:* adapted from Panksepp (1996, Fig. 1, p. 50).

There is a role of oxytocin in the formation of the attachment that an infant rat shows to its mother. Nelson and Panksepp (1996) speculate that physical contact with the mother triggers oxytocin release, which forms part of the basis of the social reward. Olfactory stimuli associated with the mother acquire conditional incentive value for pups in that they are preferentially approached. This preference formation is abolished by oxytocin antagonists.

We now turn to a rather different example of motivation, that underlying aggression.

Section summary

1 Mammals exhibit nurturant behaviour to offspring, e.g. maternal behaviour.

2 Attachments ('bonds') are formed between parents and offspring and between reproductive partners. Animals are motivated to maintain these bonds.

3 Young animals exhibit distress vocalizations when separated from caregivers.

4 Identifiable biochemicals such as opioids and oxytocin play a role in parental and attachment behaviour and the distress of separation.

 ## Test your knowledge

15.8 How would you relate the terms 'opioid' and 'opiate'? In so doing, demonstrate the use of the term 'agonist'.

 Answer on page 408

Aggression

Introduction

For certain species, we can classify aggression into types (Siegel and Victoroff, 2009). In the case of predators, such as cats, one division is between that associated with affect ('rage') (e.g. against an attacking animal) and that directed towards a prey, termed **predatory aggression**. Our prime concern is with 'affective aggression', and the term 'aggression' will mean this unless otherwise stated. The distinction can be applied to humans. Affective aggression (but not predatory aggression) is associated with activation of the sympathetic branch of the ANS.

Aggression is a form of threatening and destructive behaviour, having a particular emotional and motivational basis. The trigger most usually arises from events in the external world and their interpretation, taking the form of challenges (McAndrew, 2009). Aggressive behaviour acts to eliminate the challenge and restore the status quo. Berkowitz (1993, p. 11) defines aggression in humans as: 'some kind of *behaviour*, either physical or symbolic, *that is carried out with the intention to harm someone'*. Such a definition is problematic when considering non-human species where behaviour itself has to be used as the index.

Aggression depends upon a combination of external and internal events: environmental, hormonal and learning factors (Panksepp, 1998). In humans, the underlying emotion is often described as 'anger' or 'rage'.

A distinction can be drawn between human aggression that is premeditated and that which is impulsive (Best *et al.*, 2002). In premeditated aggression, there is planning and reflection involving conscious intentions. By contrast, impulsive aggression appears to be triggered immediately by an environmental event, with little or no prior conscious reflection. However, it is probably wrong to see a neat dichotomy here. Presumably, a history of having minor expressions of premeditated aggression will increase the chances of impulsive aggression.

The various causes of aggression

Expectations that are violated are a primary trigger for aggression, e.g. withholding expected reward (Ulrich and Favell, 1970). However, certain trigger stimuli appear to cause aggression by their intrinsic properties. In rats, electric shock triggers attack of a nearby inanimate object (Pear *et al.*, 1972).

Learning

Learning influences aggression. For example, a history of winning fights increases the tendency to future aggression. In humans (Leyens and Fraczek, 1986) and rats (Ulrich and Favell, 1970), a cue paired with shock acquires a conditional capacity to stimulate aggression.

Is there a consequence of aggression that increases the tendency to repeat the behaviour in the longer term? Squirrel monkeys can be taught an operant task rewarded by an inanimate object that is attacked (Azrin *et al.*, 1965). Termination of shock after onset of aggression strengthened the tendency to aggression. A question to be pursued shortly is, if aggression is reinforcing, is it positively or negatively reinforcing?

The state in which aggression is reinforcing appears to be one of aversion (cf. Ulrich and Favell, 1970). An environment associated with such aggression might even acquire some conditional incentive value for the animal. From PET studies in humans, there is evidence that revenge for a perceived injustice has appetitive and positive affective qualities (de Quervain *et al.*, 2004; Knutson, 2004). The desire for punishment and the opportunity to inflict it caused activation within the caudate nucleus.

Hormonal factors

Basics

Widely across species, testosterone tends to increase aggression, there being just a few exceptions (Dabbs, 2000; A. Siegel, 2005). In a range of vertebrate species, including humans, the level of aggression correlates positively with the amount of testosterone in the blood (McAndrew, 2009).

Testosterone has organizational and activational effects on aggression (Chapter 6; Berkowitz, 1993). In non-humans, especially rodents, exposure to testosterone during development plays a role in organizing neural processes that come to form the motivational basis of adult aggression. There is an increased responsiveness to testosterone and thereby an increased tendency to aggression when the animal is adult (Brain, 1979). How far this might be generalized to humans remains unclear.

In most species, males tend to be more aggressive than females. This is usually attributed to males' relatively high level of testosterone (McAndrew, 2009).

In men, there is a positive relationship between (i) aggression and anti-social behaviour and (ii) levels of testosterone (Bernhardt, 1997). Testosterone level correlates with the tendency to gain dominance, and aggression is one way of achieving this. Competitive sport is another (Campbell *et al.*, 1997). However, socioeconomic status is an important variable. The correlation between testosterone level and antisocial behaviour holds for males of low rather than high socioeconomic status (Bernhardt, 1997).

Cognitive changes

Testosterone acts on the brain to alter the processing of threat-related information. In humans, testosterone injection increases subjective feelings of hostility (Dabbs *et al.*, 2002). A high testosterone level is associated with a selective bias to attend to angry faces (van Honk *et al.*, 1999). An injection of testosterone followed by presentation of an angry face causes an increase in heart-rate (Figure 15.16). There is no effect of testosterone on the reaction to neutral or happy faces. The authors propose a motivational interpretation that (p. 241) testosterone creates an 'enhanced willingness to fight or defend status in face-to-face challenges'.

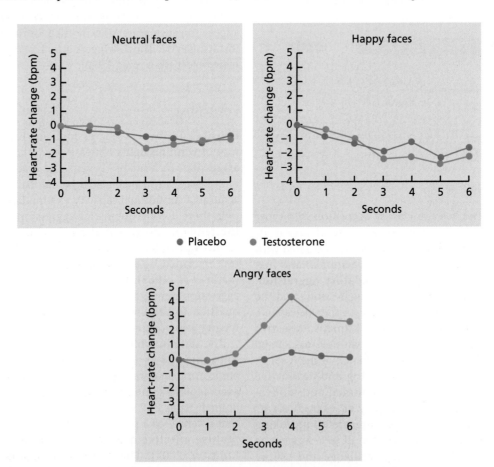

Figure 15.16 Heart-rate changes triggered by faces in testosterone or placebo-injected participants.
Source: van Honk *et al.* (2001, Fig. 1, p. 240).

Evolutionary psychology

Making sense of aggression

Much aggression in humans is triggered by threats and challenges to status and resources, as well as in situations of competition amongst males for females (McAndrew, 2009). Testosterone sensitizes brain processes that link these external factors to reactions including aggressive behaviour. Evolutionary psychology (EP) suggests that the aggressive reaction makes sense in terms of our evolutionary past in that the more assertive male would have been at an advantage. Reputations could have been established on the basis of willingness to react to challenges with ritualized, if not full, aggression. It makes adaptive sense for testosterone to increase in level in situations of threat, particularly if there is a history of winning. Of course, locked into a complex socio-cognitive web of interactions in today's industrialized society a tendency to aggression could well be very much of a mixed blessing. EP does not present a pretty picture of our ancestors and it should not be forgotten that there are also brain processes underlying altruism and cooperation. I cringe somewhat on describing this part of EP but it seems to make sense.

Dominance and aggression

Mazur and Booth (1998) distinguish aggression and dominance. They regard *antisocial behaviour* (e.g. rebelliousness) in humans as an attempt by individuals in subordinate roles to assert dominance. This does not need to be by violence, though it can be. Mazur and Booth suggest that, in men, testosterone is associated with the tendency to exert dominance, through a variety of means.

Young American males forming part of an urban street 'honour culture' of maintaining status and respect, while showing hyper-responsivity to insults, tend to exhibit high testosterone levels. This suggests that the hormone biases towards holding status. Within the USA, southerners display more of an honour culture and a higher testosterone response to a challenge than do northerners (Cohen, 1998).

Dynamic interaction

The relationship between testosterone and behaviour is a 'two-way street' (Mazur and Booth, 1998). Testosterone increases aggression. Typically, winning at fights or competitions increases the level of testosterone, whereas defeat lowers it (Campbell *et al.*, 1997; Rose *et al.*, 1975). Explicit aggression, as defined earlier,

is not necessarily shown.

In humans, a dynamic process can lead to long-term behavioural 'stability', in which cause and effect become indistinguishable (Archer, 1994). Early experiences and modelling can bias a male towards a competitive and aggressive style. An initially high testosterone level would strengthen this. Winning fights, whether physical or verbal, and exposure to violent role models could elevate testosterone level, to reinforce and maintain the strategy. (Discussions tend to be dominated by consideration of the male but females also produce testosterone and can behave aggressively; Snowdon, 1998.)

There is some malleability in hormone–environment interaction. High-testosterone men can get into a vicious circle, characterized by a downward social spiral. However, with slightly changed circumstances, and more skilled exploitation of dominance, they might ascend socially. Cohen (1998, p. 368) suggests: 'testosterone may facilitate successful boardroom maneuvering as much as successful barroom brawling'.

Neural mechanisms

Aggression is determined by interactions between particular brain regions. Manipulations of some regions with drugs and lesioning have more effect than others. Regions underlying aggression, e.g. amygdala, are sensitized by testosterone (van Honk *et al.*, 2010).

Non-humans

Lesioning and stimulation of the brain are employed to study the neural bases of fear and aggression (Kling, 1986; Moyer, 1986). There are particular neural circuits, which elicit a tendency to aggression when stimulated in the presence of a suitable target. Neurons involved in controlling aggression project from areas of sensory detection of the triggering events, through the amygdala to the *medial* hypothalamus and then to the PAG (Siegel and Victoroff, 2009). Descending signals activate the motor acts of aggressive behaviour, which are organized in part at brain stem sites. In cats, by contrast to the role of the medial hypothalamus in controlling rage-related aggression, the *lateral* hypothalamus has a prime role in predatory aggression.

Animals of various species learn to terminate stimulation of regions of hypothalamus associated with affective aggression ('rage'), suggesting negative reinforcement (A. Siegel, 2005). This is unlike neighbouring regions associated with predatory attack.

Neural bases of human aggression

Humans with implanted electrodes in their brains (e.g. amygdala) sometimes report feeling anger when the current is turned on but are able to inhibit aggression (Moyer, 1986).

Aggression can sometimes be provoked by tumours of the brain (Moyer, 1986), e.g. in the anterior hypothalamus, amygdala or septum. In some cases, removal of the tumour corrects the aggression. Aggression is not expressed as simply a particular response, suggesting a motivational interpretation. For example, a motorist might drive his car aggressively as well as commit acts of direct violence.

A personal angle

Ms X.

King (1961), in Pittsburgh, PA, studied a patient with an electrode tip implanted in her amygdala. When a current of 4 mA stimulated the brain, no effect was observed. On increasing this to 5 mA, she verbalized signs of anger and her fear of attacking the experimenter. She did not report pain. The fact that Ms X. reported anger and made aggressive remarks suggests that the electrode targeted an emotional/motivational neural system, rather than a motor system.

Mechanisms of restraint

There are personal costs and social sanctions associated with aggression, so it is likely that society is spared much violence because of restraint (inhibition) processes. There could be an inhibition of aggressive motivation *per se* or of its expression (Spoont, 1992; van Honk *et al.*, 2010).

Raine *et al.* (1997) performed a PET study (Chapter 5) on a sample of murderers who had pleaded 'not guilty by reason of insanity'. Lower glucose metabolism in several brain regions was found, as compared with controls, suggesting that these regions might normally be involved in restraining aggression. The regions included those that underlie control based upon working memory (e.g. prefrontal cortex) and the coming together of different sources of information (e.g. the corpus callosum). It would be expected that working memory would normally play a role in exerting restraint based upon anticipated (e.g. punishing) outcomes.

Following damage to the orbital/medial prefrontal cortex, there can be an increased tendency to impulsive violence (Best *et al.*, 2002). From this, Best *et al.* were led to study patients suffering from 'intermittent explosive disorder', who exhibit a chronic tendency to violence that is out of proportion to the triggers. In the sample studied, there was no evidence of prior brain damage but nonetheless patients performed relatively badly on tests designed specifically to reveal prefrontal processing (Chapter 20). Best *et al.* speculate that there is a deficiency in inhibitory projections that run from the prefrontal cortex to the amygdala. In addition, patients revealed a cognitive bias towards interpreting anger and disgust in human faces, as compared with controls.

A personal angle

Charles Whitman

In 1966, Charles Whitman killed his mother and wife, then climbed a tower at the University of Texas in Austin and took shots at students on the campus below, hitting 44 and killing 14 people (Mark and Ervin, 1970; Valenstein, 1973). His diary reveals that he had earlier experienced 'forced thoughts', in which he imagined and carefully planned the tower scenario. A postmortem showed a cancerous tumour in the amygdala. To many, the implication is that the lesion in Whitman's brain precluded normal functioning and triggered abnormal patterns of activity: hyperactivity in emotional circuits biasing towards aggression. This might be the case, though, of course, he is a sample of only one. Viewed in combination with his diary, it suggests that the tumour did not cause a sudden impulsive act. Rather, there was a long-term tendency to favour certain planned violent options.

Neurotransmitters

Acetylcholine

Acetylcholine tends to facilitate aggression (Siegel and Victoroff, 2009). Regions of hypothalamus can be identified, which, when electrically stimulated, trigger aggression. Microinjections of cholinergic agonists there also tend to trigger aggression. Application of cholinergic antagonists tends to inhibit aggression.

Catecholamines

Some evidence points to increased activity in noradrenergic and dopaminergic pathways being implicated in aggression (Haller *et al.*, 1998; Siegel and Victoroff, 2009). For humans, dopaminergic and noradrenalin (NA) activity in the brain tend to correlate positively with impulsive aggression (Coccaro, 1989; Eichelman, 1988). Drugs used in the control of impulsive aggression in humans include those having DA or NA antagonist effects, sometimes combined with a serotonin agonist effect (Coccaro, 1989).

There are reports that stimulating CNS NA release in rats leads to heightened aggression and chemically lesioning of NA reduces aggression. However, the picture is less clear than for acetylcholine. This could be because different NA receptor subtypes have different effects on aggression (A. Siegel, 2005). It is also unclear as to the extent that any effects of catecholamines are specific to aggression or are general effects common across motivations and behaviours.

Serotonin

As a rather reliable effect found across species, a negative correlation exists between (a) brain serotonin (5-HT) level and (b) the tendency to aggression (Pihl and LeMarquand, 1998; A. Siegel, 2005).

For humans, abnormally low levels of serotonin are associated with impulsive ('irritable') aggression, rather than premeditated violence (Coccaro, 1989). Aggression appears to be only one form of impulsive behaviour among others that are influenced by low levels of serotonin (Coscina, 1997). This suggests under-reactivity of a serotonin-mediated **behavioural inhibition system** (Depue and Spoont, 1986). Activity within this system acts to restrain aggression, among other impulsive behaviours. Serotonin serves a role in the inhibition of behaviour by cues that herald threat and so its reduction would remove a source of inhibition on aggression (Pihl and LeMarquand, 1998).

Bernhardt suggests that a low serotonin level can accentuate negative affect, which biases to aggression (Berkowitz, 1993).

At what locations in the nervous system does serotonin exert its effects? There are ascending serotonergic pathways that terminate in regions known to be involved in aggression, such as the amygdala (Spoont, 1992). Presumably, normal levels of serotonergic transmission at such regions restrain aggression.

Alcohol and aggression

The consumption of alcohol in large amounts by humans is associated with aggression (Pihl and LeMarquand, 1998). There are various sites of action of alcohol in the CNS at which it increases the risk of aggression. Alcohol (a) increases dopaminergic activity, which promotes forward engagement with a range of incentives, (b) encourages the breaking of boundaries, e.g. interpersonal, (c) directly sensitizes aggression and (d) lowers restraint.

If anxiety inhibits aggression, the lifting of this by alcohol will weaken a natural brake. Alcohol disrupts cognitive functioning, with a particular targeting of working memory (Chapter 11). Working memory allows the representation of anticipated future scenarios and their utilization in the control of current behaviour. Impairment of working memory might bias the weight of control, to favour physically present stimuli and weaken cognitive representations of future negative consequences of aggression.

Genes and environment

Suppose two individuals in a species differ in the tendency to aggression. Is this because of genetic or environmental differences, or both (Fuller, 1986)? In humans and other species, there is evidence that genetically determined differences exist between individuals in their tendency to aggression (Bowman, 1997; McAndrew, 2009). Such genetic differences would mediate their effects via differences in such things as brain structures and levels of hormones and neurotransmitters.

As Fuller (1986, p. 206) notes: 'The most extensive selection for differences in animal emotionality was carried out by individuals who had never taken a course in genetics nor heard of Darwin . . . '. For hundreds of years, humans have developed animals' behavioural traits (e.g. aggression in dogs) by selective breeding.

The next section, exploration, completes the discussion of the four examples of motivations.

Section summary

1 Aggression is triggered by certain unconditional and conditional stimuli, as well as the interpretation of events in terms of challenge.

2 In humans, a distinction is drawn between premeditated and impulsive aggression.

3 Testosterone promotes aggression, sometimes as a by-product of dominance-seeking.

4 Electrical stimulation of particular regions of the brain can trigger aggression.

5 Low serotonin levels bias towards aggression.

6 Differences in aggressiveness between individuals depend in part upon genetic differences.

Test your knowledge

15.9 Complete the following sentence: 'Testosterone has both _____ and activational effects on aggression'.

15.10 The combination of angry face and testosterone triggers increased activity in which branch of the autonomic nervous system (Figure 15.16)?

15.11 A region of the hypothalamus that is associated with aggression has been identified and an electrode implanted there. Suppose that a rat learns to press a lever in a Skinner box to terminate electrical stimulation of this region. What term would be used to qualify the description 'reinforcing'?

 Answers on page 408   WEB

Exploration

Introduction

Exploration of their environment is widely seen in different species (Welker, 1961). By this means, animals acquire information, e.g. that object X is situated at location Y (Menzel, 1978). Similarly, play enables the animal to learn and test possibilities for future action. The acquisition of information that involves investigation by whole-body approach to objects is termed **exploratory behaviour**.

From a functional perspective, exploration allows an updated representation of the environment that can be exploited for such things as locating food and escape routes. Regular exploration of even a familiar environment presumably confirms the *status quo* ('checking').

Species differences

Which sense organs are employed for exploration depends on the relative refinement of the species' sensory channels (Welker, 1961). The sensory channel favoured tends to correspond to an enlarged cortical representation of sensory processing in that channel (Chapter 5). In rats, exploration involves whiskering and sniffing (O'Keefe and Nadel, 1978). In the grey squirrel, visual features are the strongest trigger, whereas in the mole the tactile sense provides the principal

input. The notion of 'advanced species' is somewhat suspect in these egalitarian times. However, it is difficult to find an acceptable alternative. Exploration tends to be higher in 'advanced species', with more cerebral cortex (Glickman and Sroges, 1966; Figure 15.17).

Rats and monkeys raised in an enriched environment show a greater attraction to novelty and more manipulation of objects than those raised in a dull environment (Renner and Rosenzweig, 1986). This might have something to do with differences in dopamine levels.

The bases of exploration

Motivational basis

Exploration is especially triggered when the actual environment differs from stored representations in memory ('expectations') of this same environment (Bardo *et al.*, 1996). Although moderate disparities elicit approach and exploration, large disparities can trigger fear and

In a natural environment, could curiosity serve a useful function?

Source: Getty Images/Photographer's Choice.

Figure 15.17 Comparison of different animals in terms of exploration.

Source: Glickman and Sroges (1966, Fig. 1, p. 161).

avoidance. The reward of a novel object can reinforce lever-pressing in a Skinner box. In a place preference test, rats develop a preference for the arm of a T-maze that is associated with the opportunity to explore a novel object contained therein (Bevins and Bardo, 1999). Hence, novelty has incentive and reward properties similar to such rewards as food and sex.

In anxiety, exploration is reduced and rats favour contact with familiar regions of an environment. Hence, exploration is a measure of the efficacy of drugs designed to counteract anxiety (Chapter 12). For example, in an elevated maze, anxiolytics (anti-anxiety drugs) increase exploratory tendencies (Ramos and Mormède, 1998).

Cognitive mapping

O'Keefe and Nadel (1978) proposed that exploration helps to form a 'cognitive map' in the animal's brain – a representation of the environment (Chapter 11). Changes in the environment then revise this map. Exploration is not triggered by particular stimuli per se but by a comparison between stimuli and this internal representation. Novelty is not something 'out there' to be detected but the outcome of this comparison. A new object introduced into a familiar space prompts attention and exploration until it is represented in a revised cognitive map. Objects removed are erased from the representation. Exploration of an initially novel object is intense at first but then declines with exposure, presumably corresponding to the object becoming represented in the cognitive map.

Given a choice between arms leading to a goal, rats show **spontaneous alternation**: they tend to choose a different arm from that chosen last time (Montgomery, 1952). They tend to alternate the choice of arm (e.g.

black versus white, irrespective of side) rather than the mechanical act involved in negotiating the maze. This implies (i) a memory of the choice and (ii) selection based upon relative novelty. Alternation seems to be a variety of exploration.

The neuroscience of exploration

The neural embodiment of the motivation underlying exploration doubtless consists of numerous interacting brain regions. This section focuses on the two regions about which we have most insight. Information on novelty is extracted in such brain regions as the hippocampus (Alvarez and Alvarez, 2008), and links are then made with the mesolimbic dopamine pathway, where approach to particular objects is organized.

The mesolimbic dopaminergic pathway

The mesolimbic dopamine system and the notion of a seeking system form a focus of research in exploration and novelty-seeking (Bardo *et al.*, 1996; Besheer *et al.*, 1999). Activation of this system is associated with exploration: it appears that, under its influence, external objects become attractive as the incentives for exploration. When moving from a familiar compartment to a novel compartment there is activation of DA observed at the N.acc. The activity of single neurons of the N.acc. correlates with exploratory behaviour (Henriksen and Giacchino, 1993). Differences in exploration between strains of rat can be linked to intrinsic differences in the reactivity of this dopaminergic system (Depue and Collins, 1999).

In rats, microinjections of a DA antagonist into the N.acc. block increased activity normally seen in a novel environment, though there is no reduction in the activity in a familiar environment (Hooks and Kalivas, 1995). A DA D1 receptor antagonist blocks the attribution of incentive value to an arm associated with a novel object (Besheer *et al.*, 1999).

Role of the hippocampus

O'Keefe and Nadel (1978) attribute a role to the hippocampus in forming a cognitive map. Spontaneous alternation is a useful measure of exploration and gives an understanding of the role of this structure. Hippocampally lesioned rats tend not to show spontaneous alternation. Spontaneous alternation is only shown after 28 days of age in rats, whereas in the more precocial guinea pig it is seen in the first week of life (Altman *et al.*, 1973). This suggests that, in the infant rat, either there is an inability to hold the relevant information or, if the information is held, it is not utilized in exploration. In the rat, the hippocampus is relatively immature at birth and develops in the postnatal period, which might account for the delayed appearance of spontaneous alternation.

It appears that the hippocampus modulates other brain regions that organize exploration. It is assumed that it exerts an influence on the N.acc. such that novel objects trigger approach associated with exploration (Mogenson, 1984). Hippocampal damage does not abolish exploration (Clark *et al.*, 2005). However, the normal reduction ('habituation') of exploration as objects lose their novelty is less evident. This suggests that the loss of the hippocampus is associated with a failure of the objects to become familiar.

Sensation seeking and personality differences

A certain level of novelty seeking, especially in younger adults, could be adaptive in encouraging the seeking of new environments with the possibility of encountering new sources of food and mates (Douglas *et al.*, 2003). The observation that DA is involved in exploration led to the suggestion that human sensation-seeking might be understood in terms of DA activity (Bardo *et al.*, 1996).

Could differences in sensation-seeking between individuals be explicable by differences in the reactivity of their dopaminergic neurotransmission? There exists a known genetic contribution to differences in the dimension extrovert–introvert. There is some suggestion that

this is mediated in part through differences in dopaminergic neural systems, though the data are controversial (Rammsayer, 2004).

Section summary

1 Exploratory behaviour establishes and updates representations of the environment.

2 Novelty triggers exploration.

Test your knowledge

15.12 A rat is observed to show a high frequency of alternation of arms in a T-maze, between the left white arm and the right black arm. After having turned left on a trial, the rat is returned to the maze. However, between trials, the colour of the arms is quickly reversed so that black is now to the left and white to the right. What effect would this be expected to have on the tendency to take the right arm?

Answer on page 408

Bringing things together

The central theme of this chapter has been the search for underlying general principles of motivation as well as features specific to each motivation. Processes and principles that are applicable across motivations include incentive, reinforcement, reward, affect and conditioning, as well as the interactive role of external and internal factors. Particular brain regions are involved in attributing motivational value to appropriate stimuli, e.g. food and social stimuli. Stimuli are compared with memories and motivation depends upon the outcome of the comparison. A role of dopamine and opioids in various motivations was noted.

Motivational processes were described as those involving a changing responsiveness to external stimuli as a function of internal events. This was exemplified in various systems:

1 The reaction to a given external temperature depends upon internal body temperature, e.g. warmth is approached when in hypothermia.

2 How a mother treats social stimuli, such as infants, depends upon her neurohormonal environment, e.g. levels of oxytocin.

3 A stimulus can trigger aggression, depending upon the interpretation of the stimulus, learned associations and levels of testosterone.

4 A given object can trigger exploration or not depending upon its value of novelty/familiarity, as computed by the CNS.

Figure 15.18(a) represents general features of motivation and appetitive behaviour, determined by external

(a)

(b)

Figure 15.18 (a) Some general features of a motivational system and (b) dual role of motivation.

and internal factors. The incentive contributes to motivation and, in turn, motivation directs behaviour to maximize contact with the incentive (Bindra, 1978). Conditional stimuli (CSs) also play a role. For example, stimuli paired with presentation of food acquire a conditional strength to trigger feeding motivation. Sexual motivation is increased by stimuli that were paired in the past with sexual activity. Figure 15.18(a) shows incentives compared with memories of past contact and motivation influenced by the outcome. For example, in taste-aversion learning the animal tends to avoid the particular food in future (Chapter 11; Garcia, 1989). Factors such as fear can inhibit a motivation such as feeding, as represented by the arrow 'Inhibit'.

Figure 15.18(b) shows motivation to be involved in both flexible and more species-typical behaviour.

See the video coverage for this chapter which shows the roots of motivation.

Summary of Chapter 15

1 The term 'motivation' refers to a type of process that underlies the control of behaviour. Motivation gives behaviour direction, goals and varying responsiveness. The control of behaviour involves selection among motivations that compete for expression.

2 Certain stimuli such as food, water and sexual contact are 'rewards' and, in humans, contact with them is associated with pleasure. The expression 'incentive' defines the capacity of rewards to attract.

3 There are brain regions that are specific to particular motivations and also some general processes that serve a range of motivations.

4 Body temperature is regulated by the control exerted over behaviour and internal physiology. Deviations from an optimal body temperature motivate behaviour that tends to return temperature to its optimal value.

5 In mammals, basic and dedicated processes of motivation and reward underlie nurturant (e.g. maternal) behaviour and attachment (bonding).

6 Aggression is behaviour that inflicts damage on another and is usually a response to challenges. Testosterone increases the tendency to show aggression.

7 Exploration is behaviour that maintains variety in the flow of sensory input and assimilates information on the environment.

Further reading

For general introductions, which set the biology of motivation and emotion into a broader context of psychology, see Beck (2004) and Reeve (2008). For the neuroscience of motivation, Berridge (2004). For behavioural temperature regulation, see Hart (1988). For parental behaviour, see Numan and Insel (2003) and Kinsley and Lambert (2006). For aggression, see A. Siegel (2005) and Archer (2009).

Answers

Explanations for answers to 'test your knowledge' questions can be found on the website www.pearsoned.co.uk/toates

15.1   Feeding, drinking, temperature regulation
15.2   Appetitive; consummatory
15.3   Conditional
15.4   Taste-aversion conditioning
15.5   The white arm
15.6   A tendency to seek a cold environment
15.7   It reduces the activity of $neuron_3$
15.8   An opioid is a natural neurochemical. An opiate is something taken from outside that has similar properties to its endogenous equivalent. Opiates such as morphine are agonists at opioid receptors in the body.
15.9   Organizational
15.10   Sympathetic
15.11   Negatively
15.12   It would lower it

Visit www.pearsoned.co.uk/toates
for a range of resources to support study.
Test yourself with multiple choice questions and access a bank of over 100 videos that will bring the topics to life.

Chapter 16
Feeding and drinking

Learning outcomes for Chapter 16

After studying this chapter, you should be able to:

1 Demonstrate where the principles of homeostasis, regulation and negative feedback can be applied to understanding feeding and drinking. However, show also how behaviour can sometimes depart from the simple predictions arising from such processes.

2 Describe what happens to nutrients after they enter the body, in terms of their conversion, storage and utilization.

3 Identify some of the nutrient forms and sites in the body that are involved in the control of feeding. Describe the kind of process that links nutrients to signals that are involved in the control of feeding.

4 Describe the contribution of sensory and learning factors to the control of feeding. In so doing, explain how their contribution can only be understood in the context of internal events and the consequences of ingestion.

5 Describe what is meant by the term 'satiety' and the factors that contribute to it.

6 Identify some of the principal brain regions involved in the control of feeding and present the evidence that implicates them.

7 Describe some instances of when the control of feeding 'goes wrong'. Discuss the extent to which an understanding of basic principles of feeding control can illuminate how things go wrong and the role of therapeutic interventions.

8 Describe the physiology of body fluids and sodium and link these to the controls of water and sodium intake.

Scene-setting questions

1 What makes us hungry and what terminates this sensation?

2 If feeding evolved to serve regulation, how can it be associated with such problems as anorexia nervosa and obesity? Why do we often eat in the absence of any 'need'?

3 What kind of sociocultural factors also play a role in determining the tendency to eat or not? 🔵 WEB

4 Could pregnancy sickness serve an adaptive function connected with food intake?

5 Why does salt make us thirsty?

What kind of sociocultural factors also play a role in determining the tendency to eat or not? Explore the video on the website accompanying this book at **www.pearsoned.co.uk/toates**

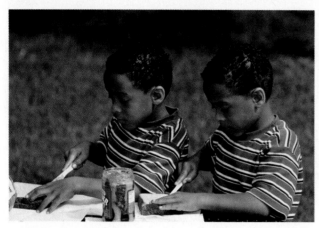

Several factors play a role in wanting and liking foods. What are they and how do they interact?

Source: TopFoto/Rachel Epstein/Image Works.

Introduction

Cast your mind back over your experience of feeding and drinking and reflect on what determines this behaviour. Consider the following:

1 Perhaps you have experienced putting on excess weight – if not, doubtless a friend has. Because of attractive foods rich in sugar and fat that are on offer, delicatessens and supermarkets are places for caution.

2 Some likes and dislikes might have arisen from *associations* with particular foods. If you ate something only under pressure, you might not now be able to face it. If a food was associated with illness, you might not have been able to eat it again.

3 You might have craved particular foods at particular times in your life.

4 You have surely declined more food on the grounds of feeling full, only to recover your appetite with the next course.

5 If you ate a particular food for lunch, you might want something different for your evening meal, even though you like very much the lunchtime food.

6 Perhaps you have skipped a meal and yet not felt particularly hungry. You might even have been surprised to be reminded that you were so occupied that you missed a regular meal.

7 Particular foods have links to particular times of eating. You might love a curry for lunch but not be attracted to it for breakfast.

8 When stressed, you might seek foods such as chocolate as a form of comfort.

Such examples illustrate a number of features of the control of feeding:

1 Although feeding motivation is sensitive to the level of nutrients in the body, there is not a tight one-to-one dependence. Excess body fat is sometimes associated with only a limited inhibition on further intake. In stimulating feeding, there is a powerful role played by attractive foods, in spite of taking in excessive amounts. Conversely, missing a meal is not necessarily associated with a greatly increased hunger.

2 A history of recent food intake influences current intake. For example, variety plays a role in food intake. Appetite can be revived by a new food.

3 Cultural factors play a role in determining what attracts us and when. For some, curry does not 'go with' breakfast.

4 Cravings are directed to particular foods, pointing to a high degree of specificity.

5 Associations that we have with a particular food can play an important role in how attractive it is.

6 Foods are eaten for various reasons, such as to relieve distress. Such intake is not tied to a deficit of nutrients.

This chapter considers how the *combination* of internal factors (e.g. nutrient levels) and external factors (e.g. food and associated conditional stimuli) determine feeding and drinking. We will discuss first the internal and then the external factor, considering how they interact in determining behaviour.

From a functional perspective, survival requires that tissues throughout the body are supplied with nutrients and water. The terms 'homeostasis' and 'regulation' refer to the tendency of the parameters of the body, such a nutrient and water levels, to remain within bounds. With respect to Figure 16.1 and 'Physiological regulation', deficits tend to trigger 'Behavioural control', i.e. feeding or drinking. Reciprocally, ingested substances affect 'Physiological regulation'.

Consider the regulation associated with feeding. For example, food deprivation is a trigger to hunger and significant food intake subsequently induces **satiety**. The

Figure 16.1 Regulation and control. Physiological regulation occurs as a result of behavioural control (feeding, drinking) and physiological control (e.g. over rate of production of urine, insulin secretion).

term satiety describes the loss, or reduction, of appetite as a result of ingestion. After a period of deprivation and weight loss, body weight recovers when feeding is restored. Conversely, force-feeding an animal causes weight gain but normal weight is regained when feeding returns to normal. Regulation ('homeostasis') is achieved in part through 'negative feedback'. A negative feedback system is one in which deviations from an optimal situation tend to trigger action that brings things back to optimal, e.g. prior deprivation of food triggers food seeking and feeding. However, it is clear that any such regulation ('negative feedback') is only one feature of the control of food intake, as evidenced by the current epidemic of obesity.

Sometimes feeding is not in response to a current energy deficit, for example, eating at a particular optimum time of day when food is most readily available. However, much of this can still be understood in terms of regulation and optimizing survival chances (Strubbe and Woods, 2004). Under abnormal conditions (such as living in London!), not all feeding and drinking contribute to optimal regulation.

Among a number of controls of drinking, one is unambiguous: body-fluids are regulated. Survival depends upon their near constancy and loss triggers drinking. Regulation is generally much tighter than is the case for body nutrients. However, an animal sometimes drinks even though there is not a deficit of body-fluids (A.N. Epstein, 1990). For example, if small pellets of food are presented intermittently to a hungry rat, it drinks enormous amounts, so-called 'schedule-induced polydipsia' (Falk, 1971). Such drinking occurs *in spite of*, rather than because of, the state of body-fluids, which is one of over-hydration. The frustration of getting only small pellets might be the trigger to drinking.

Although physiological regulation is not an all-encompassing explanation of feeding and drinking, much insight has come from considering the regulatory aspect. Regulation of nutrient and fluid environments is achieved by coordination between (1) behavioural control of ingestive behaviour and (2) physiological control over the interior of the body (Figure 16.1). Only by looking at 1 and 2 simultaneously, can we fully understand what is happening. Regulation of nutrient levels involves (1) feeding and (2) changes in such internal factors as insulin secretion (Chapter 3). Regulation of body-fluids involves control over (1) drinking and (2) blood vessel diameter and urine production by means of secretion of arginine vasopressin (Chapter 3).

Closely related to notions of incentive (Chapter 15), psychologists speak of an **appetite** directed towards a substance (Bolles, 1980). A food is coded by the CNS in terms of its basic sensory properties and its **palatability**: the tendency to ingest that the substance triggers as a result of its 'liking properties'. Palatability depends upon taste, nutrient levels in the body and any earlier associations with the substance, e.g. taste-aversion learning can change palatability from positive to negative. Palatability mediates between substances and their intake: energy and nutrient states gain expression in behaviour by their influence on palatability. However, highly palatable foods can be taken even in spite of no 'need'.

The next section considers the physiology of nutrients, energy and water.

Section summary

1 Control over behaviour and internal physiology serves regulation.

2 A complex of factors determines feeding and drinking. Not all of it is explicable in terms of regulation.

3 The nervous system computes the palatability of food, based upon intrinsic properties, physiological states and learned associations.

Test your knowledge

16.1 How do the controls of drinking and urination reveal negative feedback?

16.2 Suppose that a drug is injected that counters satiety. How might this disrupt negative feedback and regulation?

Answers on page 439

Some physiology

This section gives some background to understand the regulatory bases of feeding and drinking. Further details of body-fluids will be given when the chapter focuses on drinking.

Cells, fuel and metabolism

Various cells (e.g. neurons, skin cells), which serve different roles, have features in common (Chapter 1). Each cell is surrounded by a membrane, which shows various degrees of resistance in allowing substances to cross. The inside of the cell consists largely of fluid and the membrane is bathed on the outside by fluids. Cells require energy, vitamins and amino acids for the synthesis of proteins. Ions are needed for the cell's electrical properties (Chapter 4). These are all obtained by ingestion. They move through the stomach and intestine and are transported to the cells via the body-fluids.

Digestion

Food and water enter the mouth, pass down the oesophagus and then reach the stomach. After the stomach, substances appear in the first stage of the intestine, the duodenum. In the stomach and intestine, food is broken down and chemically changed. This is termed **digestion** and it involves the 'digestive system'. The anatomical pathway from mouth to anus is the 'alimentary tract'.

The cells

Cells need, among other things, fuel that yields energy by metabolism (Chapter 5). Figure 16.2 represents a cell. Fuel and water are transported from the fluid that bathes it, extracellular fluid, to the cell's interior. Fuel is used as a source of energy to perform the functions of the cell, e.g. synthesis of proteins and transport of ions across the membrane (Chapter 4). Heat, water and carbon dioxide are produced (as products of metabolism of fuel) and released from the cell. The rate at which fuel is used by the body is termed the **metabolic rate**, which corresponds to the rate of heat production.

The conversion of ingested chemicals is complex and only a simplified explanation is given here. Consider a species such as rat or human, taking meals of carbohydrate. During digestion, foods in the form of carbohydrates are converted to glucose. Glucose is a fuel that cells use. The problem faced by a feeding system might appear to consist simply of obtaining sufficient carbohydrate to guarantee a continuous supply of glucose to each cell. Alas, life is not so simple. Although carbohydrates can meet energy needs, other dietary constituents, i.e. ions, vitamins and amino acids, are also needed. For an animal such as a rat or human, the diet needs to consist of carbohydrates, proteins and fats.

Also, there are problems of supply and storage. Animals are not equally active throughout the 24 hours. Rats are active at night and relatively inactive during the day, whereas humans tend to show the opposite activity pattern. As Figure 16.3 shows, during the night the rat eats in excess of metabolic rate (i.e. in excess of immediate need for fuel). During the day, when the rat does most sleeping, it eats less than metabolic rate. For metabolic needs in the inactive phase, it relies upon energy stored in the body earlier. Such storage is in a different chemical form from glucose, e.g. as fat, which is a more economical form than carbohydrate.

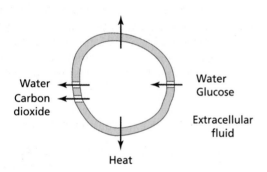

Figure 16.2 A cell.
Source: Toates (1980).

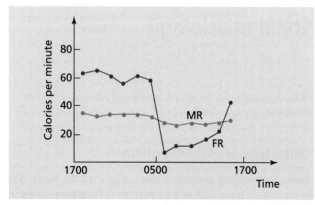

Figure 16.3 Metabolic rate (MR) and feeding rate (FR) in calories per minute (1 calorie = 4.2 joules) for a group of rats. Lights out 17.00–05.00; lights on 05.00–17.00.
Source: Le Magnen *et al.* (1973, Fig. 1).

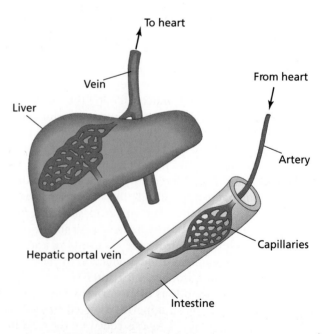

Figure 16.4 Nutrient absorption from the gut.
Source: adapted from Carlson (1977).

Absorption and the conversion of fuels

Species such as rats and humans take distinct meals with intervals between. A short time after eating, absorption of food from the alimentary tract starts: the **absorptive state** (Vander *et al.*, 1975). Nutrients are absorbed into capillaries that line the wall of the intestine and they then travel in the hepatic portal vein to the liver (Figure 16.4). At the liver, they can be dispatched immediately for use by tissues or can be chemically converted and stored. Whether stores are built up or depleted depends upon hormones (e.g. insulin) that are sensitive to energy availability.

Although not forgetting the complications, we can still focus on carbohydrates. Figure 16.5 shows the fate of glucose during the absorptive state, in the case where glucose is arriving at a rate higher than it is needed for current use as a fuel by cells. Some incoming glucose is used immediately in metabolism by cells. The remainder is chemically converted and put into storage. Storage consists of some glucose being converted to fat at the liver and then transported to deposits throughout the body, known as 'adipose tissue'. Some glucose is converted to fat at the adipose tissue. A final fraction of incoming glucose is converted to glycogen and held at the liver and muscles. Insulin is released in the absorptive state and thereby facilitates the uptake of glucose by cells.

Figure 16.6 considers where absorption of a meal is complete: the **post-absorptive state**. The fuel required by cells is now derived from intrinsic sources, i.e. the stores that were built up during earlier absorptive states.

To understand metabolic events in the post-absorptive state, physiologists distinguish between neurons and other cells. Neurons can use mainly one principal substrate of energy: glucose. Non-neural cells, by contrast, can use glucose and other substrates, e.g. those termed 'fatty acids'. In the post-absorptive state, glucose is obtained by chemical conversion of stores at adipose tissue as well as at lean tissue (i.e. muscle).

In the post-absorptive state, there is potentially a problem of availability of sufficient glucose for the nervous system. Suppose that the vast number of non-neural cells throughout the body were able to grab available glucose and thereby starve the nervous system of its one viable fuel. The brain would be in very serious trouble. What stops this from happening? Under these conditions, non-neural cells have a bias towards utilizing fatty acids and away from utilizing glucose. That is to say, there is a suppression of insulin secretion, which prevents non-neural cells from acquiring glucose. Available glucose is exploited by the nervous system. In this state, glucose is derived from other substrates (e.g. fat laid down in adipose tissue at times of abundance) (Figure 16.6). The suppression of insulin gives a bias to the breakdown of stores. This yields not only glucose but also fatty acids that are used as the energy substrate by non-neural cells.

Figures 16.5 and 16.6 provide an important lesson for the study of feeding. A term such as 'body energy store' is a convenient summary. However, there is not a single homogeneous regulated variable to which behavioural control could, even in principle, be attached. Energy is stored in various chemical substrates throughout the body and exchange between them depends upon hormones and food arriving in the body. Indeed, as will be

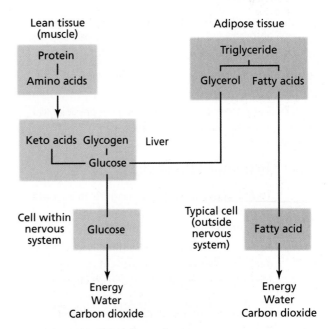

Figure 16.5 The absorptive state in the case of glucose.
Source: adapted from Vander *et al.* (1975) *Human Physiology*, Fig. 18.1, p. 603, reproduced with permission of The McGraw-Hill Companies, Inc.

Figure 16.6 The post-absorptive state.
Source: adapted from Vander *et al.* (1975) *Human Physiology*, Fig. 19.1, p. 649, reproduced with permission of The McGraw-Hill Companies, Inc.

shown, feeding depends upon multiple signals arising within the body.

Internal and external information

Anticipation is an important principle in digestion and insulin secretion (Chapter 3). In the 'cephalic phase' of digestion (that triggered via the sensory organs such as sight and sound and the brain), information about available food in the environment can influence the secretion of juices in the stomach. The advantage of such anticipation (by means of classical conditioning) is that the stomach can quickly start digestion.

A rise in blood glucose level triggers increased secretion of insulin (Chapter 3). In turn, insulin promotes the movement of glucose into cells. However, in anticipation of this, the ingestion of food, or even the sight and smell of food, releases insulin: the cephalic phase.

Having introduced some physiology, the next section looks at the control that this exerts over feeding.

Section summary

1 Cells require fuel to provide energy.

2 Fuel can be derived from carbohydrates, among other things.

3 In the absorptive state, nutrients are absorbed from the gut.

4 In the post-absorptive state, no nutrients are absorbed and fuel is derived from intrinsic sources.

5 Insulin controls glucose availability to cells.

6 Non-neural cells require insulin for glucose uptake whereas neurons do not.

7 Some control actions anticipate the physiological changes to which they relate.

 Test your knowledge

16.3 The events labelled in Figure 16.5 would be most likely to be seen in which time period of Figure 16.3? (i) 17.00–18.00, (ii) 06.00–07.00.

16.4 In Figure 16.3, at what time is metabolic need exactly matched to nutrient gain by feeding? (i) 17.00, (ii) 05.00, (iii) 06.00.

Answers on page 439

The internal cue for feeding

Introduction

What is detected in the body, where does detection occur and how does it contribute to feeding? Investigators look for the sites of the neural processes that link nutrient level to a signal underlying feeding. This section considers some possibilities.

Investigators believe that a signal derives from the level of a nutrient or something to do with its metabolism by specific cells. There now appear to be multiple systems, each sensitive to different nutrients (Berthoud, 2002). What follows is a simplified picture concentrating on the role of glucose and fats.

A glucose-based signal

Introduction

Evidence points to the brain and liver as being the sites of cells that detect glucose level or are sensitive to its metabolism (Booth, 1993a). In rats fed *ad libitum* (meaning food is freely available all the time), a small decline in blood glucose level tends to occur just prior to meals (Le Magnen, 1981). Similarly, a fall in blood glucose tends to come just before requests for meals in laboratory-based humans (Campfield, 1997). This suggests that feeding is sensitive to blood glucose level, though in itself does not prove a causal connection. A type of neuron might be sensitive to the concentration of glucose in the fluid that bathes it. In Figure 16.7, such a neuron would respond to changes in concentration with changes in frequency of action potentials.

The nature of the signal

An early idea was that, when blood glucose level fell, this was the cue to feed: the 'glucostatic theory'. In this context, **glucoreceptors** were postulated, i.e. neurons in the brain that signal the local availability of glucose or its metabolism. Figure 16.7 shows glucose receptors on the membrane. In part (a), glucose concentration is low, relatively few sites are occupied and the frequency of action potentials is low, so hunger is triggered. In part (b), glucose concentration is high, associated with a high frequency of action potentials and no hunger.

Some of the time, people with diabetes have a relatively high level of blood glucose and, if the glucostatic theory were true, they would not experience hunger. In fact, even when blood glucose is abnormally high, they still experience hunger (Smith and Epstein, 1969). Glucostatic theory cannot explain this, so a modification to it was needed.

To take up glucose, neurons in general do not require insulin. However, it was suggested that a very small

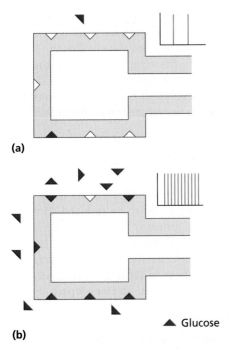

(a)

(b)

▲ Glucose

Figure 16.7 Neuron sensitive to glucose: (a) low concentration and (b) high concentration. White triangles = unoccupied glucose receptors.

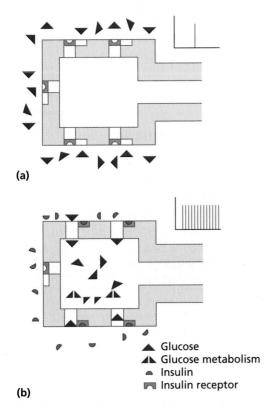

(a)

(b)

▲ Glucose
▲▲ Glucose metabolism
● Insulin
⬛ Insulin receptor

Figure 16.8 Neurons sensitive to the ability to utilize glucose for metabolism (represented by the breaking apart of glucose molecules): (a) no insulin; glucose transport across membrane blocked and (b) insulin present; receptors occupied and glucose transport facilitated.

atypical sample of neurons that are insulin-dependent is used in feeding control. Such neurons exist and there is a concentration of insulin receptors in the regions of the hypothalamus concerned with the control of feeding (Kaiyala *et al.*, 1995; Langhans and Scharrer, 1992). Figure 16.8 represents the possibility that feeding control is based on a set of neurons that are sensitive to their ability to *utilize* glucose as a fuel and that insulin is involved. Part (a) represents a lack of insulin and little glucose can be transported across the membrane. A low frequency of action potentials is generated. This would be a cue to hunger. Part (b) represents a high level of insulin and the associated transport of glucose across the membrane. There is a high rate of glucose metabolism and a high frequency of action potentials. This would be the cue not to feed.

What would this theory predict regarding people with diabetes? If glucose is unable to be transported across the membrane and to be utilized, this would trigger hunger. The fact that people with diabetes experience hunger might be explained in this way.

The substance 2-deoxy-D-glucose (2-DG) has similarities with glucose (Chapter 5) and competes with it for passage across the cell membrane (Booth, 1979). However, it is not metabolized within the cell and it prevents the metabolism of glucose. Figure 16.9 represents the injection of 2-DG (Smith and Epstein, 1969). 2-DG blocks the sites at which glucose is normally transported across the membrane. Also, the metabolism of glucose is blocked, which is represented by the locked combination of 2-DG and glucose. Since little glucose is taken into cells, its concentration in the blood is relatively high. Injection of 2-DG triggers feeding. This favours the model of Figure 16.8 rather than that of 16.7, since feeding is triggered in spite of high levels of glucose in the blood and the fluid bathing neural tissue.

Location of receptors

Nutrients are absorbed across the wall of the intestine into capillaries and then into the hepatic portal vein, and so to the liver (Figure 16.4), and then distributed throughout the body. At the liver and hypothalamus, there exist glucoreceptors: neurons sensitive to local glucose metabolism (Langhans and Scharrer, 1992). They appear to provide signals used in triggering feeding. Energy exchanges at the liver are monitored and a control signal extracted (Friedman and Stricker, 1976). Nutrients are converted from one form to another at the liver (Figures 16.5 and 16.6). The liver can derive nutrients from sources other than the alimentary tract and is in an ideal place to monitor what is leaving the gut.

When nutrient availability at the liver reaches a low level, feeding tends to be triggered (Booth, 1978). Injections of 2-DG into the hepatic portal vein are

Figure 16.9 Following the injection of 2-DG. Symbols as in Figure 16.8.

especially effective in triggering feeding (Langhans, 1996). An injection of glucose into the hepatic portal vein induces satiety, whereas the same injection made elsewhere in the circulation is less effective. Signals are carried from liver to brain as part of the vagus nerve (Chapter 3; Novin, 1993). If neural transmission along the nerve is blocked, the satiating effect of hepatic portal vein infusion is eliminated. This information is then involved in the determination of feeding. Various parts of the brain integrate such incoming sources of information to determine a feeding signal (described shortly).

Giving the liver a role in the control of feeding has an important implication (Booth and Toates, 1974; Stricker, 1990). Feeding is triggered not by an absolute deficit of energy, since there are normally large energy reserves, but by a transition in the source of energy currently being utilized. That is, in the post-absorptive state, metabolic fuel is derived from intrinsic stores rather than from the gut.

Rats are commonly exposed to a 12 hour light/12 hour dark (light–dark) environmental cycle and their activity reflects this. It appears that, depending partly upon the phase within the light–dark rhythm of activity, when the reliance upon intrinsic sources of fuel reaches a threshold, feeding is aroused.

The liver is in a strategic location to 'know' of intrinsic energy transactions (Figures 16.4–16.6). From a perspective of 'evolutionary design', it makes sense for the liver to be implicated in feeding. Although energy deficiency at the brain appears to be a cue to feed, energy availability there is normally well maintained even after an extensive fast. By contrast, the liver is affected within a few hours of fasting; it goes from being a net receiver of glucose to a net supplier. As Novin (1993, p. 20) expresses it: 'The brain is the beneficiary of this regulation, not the primary initiator'.

In principle, signals derived from the liver can convey information on general metabolic state, taking into account nutrients arriving from the gut and those converted within the liver. At times (e.g. in the inactive period of the light–dark rhythm) nutrients converted in the liver are sufficient to inhibit feeding even though no nutrients are arriving from the gut (Booth, 1978).

To summarize, the assumption is that the decision to feed is made at the brain. Therefore, neural connections that convey information from the liver to the brain, i.e. within the vagus nerve, are implicated (Langhans, 1996).

A fat-based signal

Evidence suggests that the feeding system is also sensitive to the level of fat deposits. As these increase, so feeding tendency tends to be reduced. How could the nervous system monitor these since fat deposits are located throughout the body? Specific hormones are released from fat cells and convey information to the brain. One of these is termed leptin and, as the size of fat deposits increases, so does **leptin** level (Ahima, 2005). Insulin levels also rise in proportion to the size of fat deposits.

At the brain, integration of information on nutrient state at different sites and such things as the sensory properties of food is made. The outcome is the decision to feed or not (Berthoud, 2002). A later section will look at the neural signals that are involved.

Having considered the internal factor that triggers feeding, we now look at the role of sensory factors.

Section summary

1 Detectors of nutrient/energy state ('neural transducers') are situated at the brain and liver.

2 Among others, neurons that are sensitive to their own glucose metabolism appear to be involved in feeding.

3 The decision to feed by the brain is the outcome of an integration of information, e.g. local and derived from the liver and fat stores.

4 Leptin is a hormone secreted by fat cells and which lowers the tendency to feed.

☞ Test your knowledge

16.5 Which of the following is a hormone? (i) 2-DG, (ii) leptin, (iii) insulin.

 Answer on page 439

The role of sensory factors, learning and cognition

Introduction

This section looks at the role of sensory, learning and cognitive factors in feeding. These include food and food-related stimuli, i.e. incentives, and such things as social context and time of day (Levitsky, 2005). Taste and smell are our principal concern but food-related stimuli include visual and somatosensory cues. These excite feeding at first such as to maintain ingestion but later an inhibitory effect sets in (Smith, 1996). The role of taste was summarized by Scott (1990, p. 260):

> taste is like a Janus head placed at the gateway to the city. One face is turned outward to its environment, to warn of and resist the incursion of chemical perils while recognizing and encouraging the receipt of required goods. The other looks inward to monitor the effects of admitted wares on the city's activity and to remain current with its needs.

Flavour preference

Humans and rats exhibit a preference for sweet tastes. The hedonic reaction to sweet is opioid-mediated (Rogers, 1995). From a functional perspective, why does the tongue contain receptors sensitive to sweet? In mammals, one obvious candidate is to reinforce suckling since milk tastes sweet. Ripe fruits taste sweet and thereby signal the availability of nutrients. Fruits also contain vitamins and minerals; ingestion would be positively reinforced by taste. Hedonic rating depends on a food's intrinsic properties in interaction with the physiological state of hunger/satiety (Chapter 15).

Some substances are rejected as a result of a sour or bitter taste. A memory of an experience with them is formed and they can be avoided in the future (Chapter 11). Human newborns exhibit a facial expression of rejection on tasting a sour or bitter substance (Steiner, 1979). Since a bitter sensation commonly signals poisons, we imagine that in evolutionary terms this has protected humans.

In the long term, exposure to a particular food tends to increase the liking for it. Conversely, in the short term, ingestion tends to decrease the liking (described shortly). As Logue (1991, p. 100) expresses it: 'For food preferences, familiarity does appear to breed (some) contempt, while absence makes the heart grow (somewhat) fonder.'

The role of learning

Learning plays an important role in assessing substances suitable for ingestion and determining how much to eat (Booth, 1980).

Sensory–sensory effects

Suppose that a novel taste is paired with an established, preferred taste. Following pairing, the novel taste tends to acquire properties of the established taste (Rogers, 1995). This could partly explain the following effect. Tea and coffee are intrinsically bitter and someone who tastes them for the first time tends to add sugar. However, after a number of tastings of the combination of sugar and beverage, the beverage can be perceived as tasty even without sugar. There is the problem of why the effect does not extinguish with repeated tasting of sugar-free drink.

Exteroceptive conditional stimuli

In humans and rats (Weingarten, 1984), stimuli paired with the presentation of food acquire incentive value; they can trigger intake of a food even though rats have been 'satiated' on the same food by having it ad libitum. Preschool children were given items of food to eat in a particular location and exposed to visual and auditory cues ('context') (Birch et al., 1989). Subsequently, even after having recently eaten, children were likely to be triggered to eat in a feeding-associated context compared with a non-feeding-associated context.

Sensory post-ingestive effects

Preferences and aversions are adjusted according to the consequences of ingestion, an example of learning (Booth, 1993b). The flexible parameters of the programme are determined on the basis of learning about the post-ingestive consequences of feeding. However, if these consequences alter, there remains the possibility of readjustment. For example, given a choice between arbitrary flavours added to foods, rats tend to develop a preference for the flavour associated with nutrient gain (Sclafani, 1997). Post-ingestive consequences might also involve mood-altering effects mediated by, for example, the availability of substrates used in the synthesis of different neurotransmitters (Rogers, 1995).

A substance that yields beneficial effects following ingestion, e.g. an amino acid when in a state of deficiency, tends to be positively ranked (Booth, 1993b). Preferences can be associated with taste, odour, texture or visual characteristics. The best-known relationship between ingestion and its consequences is taste-aversion learning, the Garcia effect (Chapter 11). At a neural level in studies on rats, plasticity can be identified: the palatability of a substance devalued by taste-aversion learning becomes encoded within the brain as if it were intrinsically aversive (Berridge, 1995; Scott and Giza, 1993). In rejecting the previously acceptable food, the rat acts as if the food tastes bad.

Evolutionary psychology

Pregnancy sickness

Pregnancy sickness (PS) is commonly experienced by women in the first 3 months of pregnancy. It consists of food aversions, sometimes accompanied by nausea and vomiting, and is found across cultures (Profet, 1992). Certain food-related tastes and smells, which might normally be experienced as positive, acquire an aversive value. Traditionally, PS has been viewed as pathological but might it serve some adaptive function.

Substances that are harmless to adults can prove lethal to the early developing embryo. In our early evolution as hunter-gatherers, humans probably sampled from a rich variety of plant items. Could PS prevent intake of certain substances that are potentially harmful to the vulnerable foetus? The observation that women who experience PS suffer a lower frequency of spontaneous abortions suggests that this might be so. PS appears to lower the threshold of rejection of foods that could prove toxic to the foetus.

Foods associated with PS often have a pungent smell or a bitter or highly spicy taste, which would be likely to signal possible toxins. Bland vegetables are usually well tolerated. The trigger stimuli are also ones that would probably have been present in our early evolutionary environment much the same as now. Modern industrial toxins appear not to induce PS.

Considering PS as a possible adaptation can inform the investigation of the brain mechanisms underlying it. Analysis points to the involvement of a brain stem mechanism similar, if not identical, to that involved in taste-aversion learning (Profet, 1992). Logically, in early evolution such an existing mechanism might have been co-opted by PS. It would be sensitized during early pregnancy, probably by features of the mother's hormonal environment.

Social factors and habits

In humans, the timing of the onset of meals depends on habit and social cues, such as the time of day and other people offering a meal (Langhans and Scharrer, 1992). After skipping lunch, we sometimes do not feel hungry mid-afternoon. Being with other people who are eating tends to increase the size of a meal. Another social factor facilitating intake might be imitation. Conversely, children sometimes acquire an aversion for a food by observing other children not enjoying it (Logue, 1991).

A satiated macaque monkey with food freely available will tend to start eating in response to the sight of another animal eating or simply the specific sound made (Ferrari *et al.*, 2005). This could contribute to group cohesiveness and thereby survival. The authors suggested an involvement of the mirror neuron system (Chapter 10). This might also play a role in human eating.

Cognition

The hedonic evaluation of a food depends upon its intrinsic chemical qualities and appearance, and also how it is labelled and interpreted cognitively. Thus, 'smoked-salmon ice cream' has very little hedonic appeal when labelled as ice cream but is much more acceptable when given a neutral label ('Food 386') or called 'Savoury mousse' (Yeomans *et al.*, 2008) (Figure 16.10). This suggests that strong incongruity between expectation and actual sensory stimulation can trigger a loss of positive hedonics.

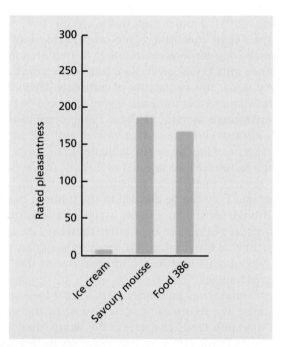

Figure 16.10 The pleasantness rating given to a food (ice cream flavoured with smoked salmon) as a function of how the food was labelled. Food 386 is an arbitrary ('neutral' label).
Source: Yeomans *et al.* (2008, Figure 2 part (A)).

Section summary

1 Taste is a determinant of food intake.

2 Within limits, the sweetness of a food increases its reward/incentive value.

3 Animals form associations between tastes and the consequences that follow ingestion.

4 Social, cognitive and time factors play a role in food intake.

 Test your knowledge

16.6 A rat comes to develop a preference for an arbitrary odour paired with a nutrient-bearing food. How would the odour be described? (i) Unconditional stimulus, (ii) conditional stimulus, (iii) innate stimulus.

 Answer on page 439   WEB

Satiety

Introduction

Satiety is the absence of hunger, when this is induced specifically by ingestion. It accounts for only one possible cause of why feeding is terminated. Other reasons include inhibition due to a competing demand, as in escaping from a predator, and loss of appetite from nausea.

In satiety, is feeding terminated by a reversal of those same events that triggered feeding? This would seem to be impossible: when a meal ends, most of what was ingested can still be in the stomach. Depending upon the size of meal and speed of taking it, relatively little might have been absorbed. Such considerations suggest that a distinct process of satiety plays a role in terminating a meal. In rats, a characteristic pattern, termed the **behavioural satiety sequence**, consists of the end of feeding and then a switch to grooming (Antin *et al.*, 1975). Its appearance in response to, say, injection of a drug designed to treat human obesity is significant for the researcher, since it suggests that, at least in rats, the drug mimics natural satiety rather than inducing distraction or nausea.

Determinants of satiety

Several factors acting in combination determine satiety (Powley and Phillips, 2004). These are (a) pre-absorptive,

e.g. oral stimulation by taste, the mechanics of chewing and swallowing, stomach stretching ('distension'), particular peptides released from the upper intestine by nutrients, and (b) post-absorptive, e.g. detection of nutrients at the liver (Meï, 1994).

The alimentary tract contains receptors for mechanical stretch and chemical contents, e.g. sugars and amino acids. Detection of nutrients in combination with detection of mass plays a role in satiety. The contribution to satiety from the stomach is conveyed neurally to the brain in the vagus nerve (Powley and Phillips, 2004). The signal from gastric factors involves some plasticity; in the light of post-ingestive consequences, the animal calibrates the gastric contribution according to the properties of the food just ingested (Deutsch, 1983).

Insulin reaching the brain plays a role in satiety (Hoebel, 1997). Since plasma insulin concentration increases as a function of body fat deposits, this would seem to provide a negative feedback effect, restraining feeding and thereby the size of the fat deposits.

Cholecystokinin (CCK)

Food in the upper gut triggers the release of 'satiety peptides', one of which is cholecystokinin (CCK) (Smith and Gibbs, 1994). CCK is also released as a neurotransmitter in the brain. In rodents, CCK that is released in the brain acts at sites involved in the control of feeding, e.g. hypothalamus, and helps to induce the behavioural satiety sequence (Antin *et al.*, 1975; Hoebel, 1997). Hence, there appears to be functional coherence in its roles as gut peptide and neurotransmitter.

Injected CCK inhibits feeding, whereas CCK antagonists increase it to above the control level (Corp *et al.*, 1997). Without further evidence, the fact that injected CCK inhibits feeding might be attributed to, say, nausea. However, the increase in food intake caused by CCK antagonists suggests a **physiological effect** of CCK on feeding (as opposed to an abnormal or pathological effect). This expression implies that the exogenous source mimics the normal role of the natural neurochemical. If a substance has one effect and its antagonist the opposite, this tends to be taken as evidence suggesting a physiological effect.

How does CCK inhibit feeding? There are receptors to CCK located at the afferent terminals of gut neurons that form part of the vagus nerve. Hence, food in the gut causes the release of CCK, which activates such neurons. CCK appears to sensitize stretch receptors in the gut (Read, 1992) and to slow gastric emptying (Blackshaw and Grundy, 1993). All such factors increase the strength of the inhibitory link from gut to brain that is triggered by food in the gut (Moran, 2000). Cutting the vagus nerve, which carries information from gut to brain, reduces or eliminates the satiety-inducing effect of CCK injections.

Sensory-specific satiety

To some extent, satiety is specific to the taste of food recently ingested, termed **sensory-specific satiety (SSS)** (Clifton *et al.*, 1987; Le Magnen, 1967). Thus, satiety depends on a memory of sensory properties along with other information (e.g. metabolic activity). External factors can only be understood in the context of the animal's history.

Figure 16.11 shows the result of an experiment on rats. To investigate the effect of variety, the amount eaten under conditions of choice is compared with when only a single diet is available. The foods A–D were of identical chemical composition, except for the addition of a different taste label to each, e.g. lemon or almond. On test day 1, rats were allowed 30 minutes with diet D, followed by 30 minutes with diet B, and so on. Variety stimulates intake, compared with when the same diet is available throughout.

Sensory-specific satiety appears to represent a special case of the broader principle of habituation (Epstein *et al.*, 2009) (Chapters 5 and 11). That is to say, the reaction to a particular food gets lower with its repeated presentation. So, the more the types of food available, the lower is the rate of habituation to any given food. However, habituation to a given food can also be reduced not only by variety in a diet but also by non-food distracters, such as watching television while eating.

Figure 16.11 The quantity of food eaten by rats in 2 hours. In phase I, they are fed four different diets, A, B, C and D, on four successive days. In phase II, either variety or no variety is allowed on alternate days.
Source: Le Magnen (1967, Fig. 13, p. 25). Used with permission.

Evolutionary psychology

Sensory-specific satiety

Sensory-specific satiety makes sense as a process for encouraging variety in the diet. Sources of food signalled by different flavours might provide different minerals, vitamins and amino acids. Also, by avoiding any one food, there is a reduced risk of accumulating particular toxins that might be associated with that food (Profet, 1992).

In our early evolutionary environment, this would have served regulation. However, in sugar-rich and variety-rich Western societies, there is the disadvantage of its contribution to obesity.

Having discussed the factors that contribute to feeding, we now turn to consider the brain mechanisms underlying feeding motivation and the behaviour of feeding.

Section summary

1 Satiety depends upon an interaction of different factors (e.g. taste, mechanics of chewing, stomach filling and CCK).

2 To some extent, satiety is specific to a recently ingested food.

☞ Test your knowledge

16.7 Is the role of CCK involving the vagus nerve (i) pre-absorptive or (ii) post-absorptive?

 Answer on page 439   WEB

Neuronal and hormonal mechanisms of eating

Introduction

This section looks at the embodiment of some of the processes underlying feeding. Considering the behavioural phenomena and physiological studies described so far, we come to an investigation of the brain alerted for processes showing the following properties:

1 In determining feeding, the brain integrates various neuronal and hormonal signals (e.g. informing on glucose levels and fat deposits) arising from various parts of the body.

2 At certain locations in the brain, information on nutrient levels is translated into signals underlying food seeking and ingestion.

3 A satiety signal arises from taste and food in the gut, among other factors.

4 Palatability is based on intrinsic properties of tasted foods and nutrient levels, among other things.

5 Learned aversions can be formed and these transform the palatability of a given substance from positive to negative.

Feeding is controlled by a *network of interacting brain regions*, including regions of the cortex, hypothalamus and brain stem (Grill and Kaplan, 1990). This idea was

introduced in simplified form in Figure 5.30 (p. 127). For example, detectors of nutrient state (e.g. glucose receptors) appear to be distributed in various brain regions. The fact that detectors exist in more than one place might contribute fail-safe ('redundancy') to the system.

Psychologists distinguish those brain processes that are engaged in, on the one hand, the appetitive phase of approaching food ('wanting') from, on the other, those engaged in liking and consuming food, such as calculating palatability (Chapter 15). Certain experimental interventions can isolate one such process rather than another. For example, manipulations of the mesolimbic dopamine pathway reveal its role in wanting. However, investigators also need to acknowledge that they are dealing with a whole interacting system of brain regions and, under natural conditions, an effect on one process might have implications for all. For example, in liking something people tend to increase their wanting for it.

Detecting nutrient state and processing the information

From periphery to brain

Figure 16.12 shows the vagus nerve, which contains the axons of neurons that project from several peripheral organs to the brain. Such axons have endings sensitive to nutrient-related events at the three organs, the liver, stomach and pancreas, and convey nutrient-related information to the brain (Clifton, 2008). Synapses are formed at the nucleus of the solitary tract (NTS) and

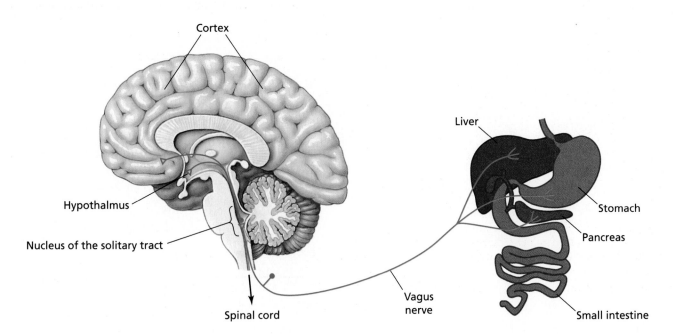

Figure 16.12 Some structures involved in the control of feeding.
Source: based upon Clifton (2008a, Fig. 5.2).

further neurons then convey the information to the hypothalamus and other brain regions.

Integrating networks

Various brain regions are involved in integrating different sources of information used in the control of feeding. For example, the NTS is informed of the nutrient levels in the body by means of neural messages, there is also a hormonal route of transmission to this structure (Berthoud *et al.*, 2006). Receptors to hormones involved in feeding and satiety, CCK and leptin, are found there. Also, information on taste arrives at the NTS (Figure 5.30, p. 127). Several nuclei of the hypothalamus serve an integrative role (Smith and Ferguson, 2008).

The brain contains an integrated 'liking' system for foods extending from the brain stem to the orbito frontal cortex (Berridge, 2009). Within this array of interconnected structures there are certain identifiable 'hedonic hotspots', sites at which neurochemical manipulations alter the liking reaction shown to tastes. For example, if agonists to opioids and cannabinoids (natural substances similar to cannabis) are injected into the nucleus accumbens (N.acc.), the liking ratings of food are enhanced. (This is distinct from the 'wanting' role also served by the N.acc.) The effects of such injected substances suggest that the natural equivalents normally play a role in liking.

Other networks integrate signals to yield 'wanting' of food. In this regard, it appears that the substance termed ghrelin acts on incentive motivation processes (Jerlhag *et al.*, 2007). In mice, microinjection of ghrelin into the ventral tegmental area triggered increased dopamine levels in the N.acc., as measured by microdialysis (Figure 16.13). Dopamine activity in this region forms an important neural basis of wanting.

A study that looked at non-food-deprived humans as they viewed food-related images also suggested a role for ghrelin in food-related incentive motivation processes (Malik *et al.*, 2008). The response of various brain regions to images that were either food-related or non-food-related (in the latter case, scenery) was measured by fMRI. By subtracting the fMRI response to the scenery from that to the food-related images, any additional effect that was due specifically to food content could be assessed. The response to food-related images, as compared to scenery images, was greater in the amygdala and left orbitofrontal cortex (OFC) only in participants treated with ghrelin. Hence, it appears that the OFC has a role in both wanting and liking foods.

Some brain areas concerned with processing visual information (e.g. pulvinar nucleus and fusiform gyrus) also showed an increase in activity in the ghrelin-treated condition. This suggests a feedback of information from regions such as the amygdala to brain regions concerned with sensory processing. There was a positive correlation between the participants' self-reports of hunger and increased activity in the amygdala and left OFC. Food-related pictures shown in the ghrelin condition (as compared to control condition) were better recalled later, indicating an effect of ghrelin on memory consolidation for food-related items.

In rats, a link between the sensory input of food in the mouth and the motor output that controls feeding is organized at the brain stem (Berridge, 1995; Grill and

Figure 16.13 Dopamine levels in the nucleus accumbens following injection of ghrelin into the ventral tegmental area. 'Vehicle' is a neutral substance acting as control.

Source: Jerlhag *et al.* (2006, Figure 2).

Figure 16.14 Modulation of brain stem circuitry by higher brain regions.

Kaplan, 1990). The mechanics of rejection based upon taste (e.g. of concentrated quinine) is also organized at this level. However, the brain stem is not a fixed pathway between oral stimulus and motor response; the relationship is modulated. Signals on energy state and satiety computed at a higher level (e.g. hypothalamus) act at the brain stem level to modulate the reaction to taste stimuli (Figure 16.14).

Brain stem controls are sufficient for the basics of the link between taste and consummatory behaviour (Grill and Kaplan, 1990). A rat with the brain stem surgically isolated from the rest of the brain, a so-called **decerebrate**, can still ingest food placed in the mouth. However, the rat will die unless it is maintained by oral or gastric infusion. The brain stem is unable to organize appetitive behaviour. Also the decerebrate cannot learn taste-aversion associations.

Two regions of special interest in investigating the neural bases of feeding are the hypothalamus and the orbitofrontal cortex, the topic of the next two sections.

The hypothalamus

Introduction

Particular nuclei of the hypothalamus contain neurons (described earlier) that are sensitive to events at their own local environment, e.g. glucose level. These nuclei are also in receipt of information on nutrient-related events occurring elsewhere, such as the liver (Blackshaw and Grundy, 1993). Such hypothalamic neurons are sensitive to inputs from the gustatory and olfactory systems (Chapter 9). This points to their role in the integration of internal and external information (Gervais, 1993).

Role of nuclei and chemical factors

The neural controls of feeding are frighteningly complex (Halford and Harrold, 2008) and Figure 16.15 shows a much-simplified version of only some of them. Its focus is the **arcuate nucleus** of the hypothalamus, which contains various groups of neurons that are involved in the control of feeding. The arcuate nucleus is a principal focus for integrating nutrient-related information. Neurons within the nucleus can be characterized by the neurochemicals that they synthesize and release. Owing to its proximity to blood vessels and cerebrospinal fluid in the brain ventricles, the arcuate nucleus is in close contact with hormonal events in the blood. In addition, it receives neural signals via the route shown in Figure 16.12.

Neurons that synthesize a substance termed neuropeptide Y (NPY) are located in the arcuate nucleus (Figure 16.15). Food deprivation increases the release of NPY.

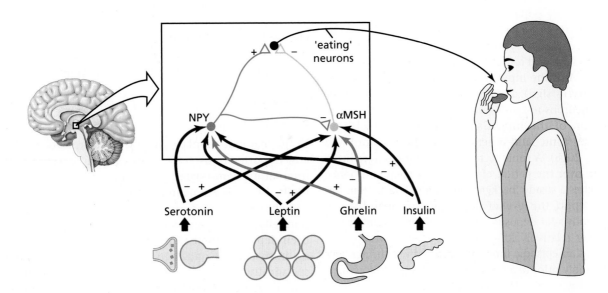

Figure 16.15 Some controls of feeding based in the arcuate nucleus and a selection of the influences on them. NPY and α-MSH are two types of neurotransmitter. See text for details.
Source: Clifton (2008a, Fig. 5.13).

Note the different hormones and neurotransmitters that have receptors on the cell bodies of NPY neurons, and thereby influence their activity. As indicated by the + sign against the arrow directed to NPY, ghrelin has an excitatory effect, whereas serotonin, leptin and insulin have inhibitory effects, as indicated by the minus signs. In turn, activation of NPY-containing neurons excites further neurons that are located in the lateral hypothalamus and thereby tends to trigger feeding. Other projections from the arcuate nucleus go to the paraventricular nucleus, which also plays a role in the control of feeding (Smith and Ferguson, 2008).

Ghrelin is a hormone released by the stomach when empty, which, when occupying receptors on NPY neurons, has the effect of stimulating appetite (Geary, 2004). Also, leptin receptors are found at a high concentration in the arcuate nucleus (Geary, 2004). Leptin, secreted from fat cells, is able to cross the blood–brain barrier and occupy receptors, thereby signalling the size of fat deposits and inhibiting feeding.

There is a concentration of insulin receptors in the arcuate nucleus. Insulin, released from the pancreas, can cross the blood–brain barrier (Chapter 5). Insulin injected into the hypothalamus *inhibits* feeding and appears to exert its effect at least in part by inhibiting the production of NPY. Caution is needed in interpreting the effects of insulin. By its action in the hypothalamus, insulin inhibits food intake and thereby indirectly limits fat storage. However, its effect in peripheral tissue is to lower blood glucose and convert such fuels into fat. The latter factor might well indirectly *stimulate* feeding by denying the brain access to glucose (Woods *et al.*, 1996).

Another key population of neurons within the arcuate nucleus employs the neurotransmitter α-MSH (Figure 16.15). As you can see, on comparing the inputs to NPY and α-MSH neurons, each + and – sign is reversed. Also the input to the 'eating' neurons is now inhibitory (– sign). In other words, the activation of α-MSH neurons restrains feeding.

Certain of the inputs shown in Figure 16.15 are classed as 'tonic' and others as 'episodic' (Halford and Harrold, 2008). A tonic factor is one that changes little, if at all, over the period of ingesting a meal and hence contributes a steady 'background' input. This is exemplified by leptin, the level of which depends upon the size of the body's fat deposits. This will change significantly only over relatively long periods of time. By contrast, ghrelin is an episodic input, the level of which increases considerably prior to a meal and falls sharply following it (Depoortere, 2009). The natural increase prior to a meal is comparable to the amount that will stimulate appetite when given experimentally, which suggests a possible role for ghrelin in the normal initiation of meals.

Within the arcuate nucleus, serotonin has a role in producing satiety (Halford *et al.*, 2005). Serotonin is also an episodic input, its level increasing as a meal is ingested and thereby it contributes to satiety (Blundell and Halford, 1998).

Lesion studies

Lesions of the lateral hypothalamus (LH) (Chapter 5) cause a cessation or reduction in feeding, termed **aphagia**. Caution is in order in interpreting lesions to the LH (Winn, 1995). In earlier studies, some reduction in feeding was due to damage to nearby neural pathways, causing a general disruption of coordinated action (Stellar, 1990). Later studies targeted more specifically the LH and revealed its role in feeding.

By contrast to the LH, damage to the ventromedial hypothalamus (VMH) causes increased food intake, termed **hyperphagia**, and obesity (Stellar, 1990). King (2006) published a paper entitled 'The rise, fall, and resurrection of the ventromedial hypothalamus in the regulation of feeding behaviour and body weight'. The meaning of the title is as follows. Lesions to the ventromedial hypothalamus (VMH) of rats are followed by an increase in food intake and massive obesity. Therefore, it was suggested that this nucleus is a satiety centre, the activity of which restrains feeding. This idea then went out of favour for several reasons. First, a general suspicion arose concerning the notions that distinct brain *centres* could have a primary responsibility for a particular behaviour. Second, researchers found that VMH lesions are immediately (i.e. prior to excessive feeding) followed by profound changes to the body's metabolism, involving the depositing of large amounts of fat. The argument was that feeding is secondary to this change in metabolism. Still later evidence led to a compromise position: both changes in metabolism and a direct reduction in satiety follow VMH lesions.

Integration of sensory and internal information

In the macaque monkey, the role of neurons of the lateral hypothalamus (LH) in integrating external and internal nutrient-related information has been studied (Rolls, 1994). These neurons respond to either the taste or sight of food or, in some cases, to both. LH neurons normally respond to food only when the animal has been deprived: their response appears to be an index of motivation. Concerning taste, they are activated specifically by nutritive solutions (e.g. glucose) on the tongue. Action potential frequency relates to nutrient concentration.

Some hypothalamic neurons appear to be part of the physical basis of sensory-specific satiety. If a monkey has been fed to satiety on a particular food, this is reflected in a lowering and then cessation of activity of certain neurons. However, if the available food is changed, corresponding to the renewed triggering of ingestion, the neurons increase in activity.

Figure 16.16 shows a simple representation of a hypothalamic 'motivation neuron', based on these considerations. This term is a summary for the role of neurons that determine motivation. A plus sign indicates an increase in motivation and a minus sign a decrease. Taste neurons detect substances in the mouth and other neurons detect food-related items via the visual pathways. This information triggers 'Memory' of past encounters with the food in question. Such memory processing of information on the food is performed at cortical and other sites and then projected to the hypothalamus. The activity of neurons conveying sensory information is independent of internal states such as energy depletion. By contrast, nutrient level and memories of previous associations with the food modulate the activity of 'motivation neurons'. For example, the phenomenon of sensory-specific satiety illustrates this role of memory; activity recovers with a change of nutrient.

Some hypothalamic neurons respond to formerly neutral stimuli that have been paired with food, e.g. the syringe delivering glucose. In the language of conditioning (Chapter 11), the taste of food is the unconditional stimulus and the response of the neuron to taste is the unconditional response. The object paired with food is the conditional stimulus and the response of the neuron to the object's presentation is the conditional response. When the object is no longer paired with food, the neurons cease firing in response to its presentation: extinction (Rolls, 1993). This embodies the process of learning about incentive cues associated with foods.

Figure 16.16 Suggested neural representation. Sensory information triggers 'Memory', which then acts to modulate activity in 'Motivation neuron'.

The orbitofrontal cortex

In primates, taste information is transmitted to the orbitofrontal cortex (Rolls, 2004). This could be one means by which motivational signals are translated into appetitive motor action, e.g. approach food.

Neuroimaging studies reveal that the orbitofrontal cortex (OFC) plays a role in encoding the reward value and the expected reward value of foods (Kringelbach, 2005). Some encoding of the subjective pleasantness of foods is carried out here. The OFC receives sensory inputs concerned with assessing food, i.e. taste, olfactory, somatosensory and visual. It seems likely that the aversion triggered when a taste departs from expectation (Figure 16.10) involves complex cognition mediated in part by the OFC.

Insights into the role of the OFC have been obtained from the study of sensory-specific satiety. Participants were fed to satiety on one food and decreases in activity of regions of OFC observed. Recovery in activity was seen with presentation of a different food. That is to say, the OFC appears to be a biological basis of the subjective hedonic value of the foods. Regions of OFC appear to integrate information on taste and odour, as well as nutrient status of the body, in yielding the overall conscious hedonic value.

Palatability and its experimental manipulation

The computation of palatability gives the signal 'ingest' or 'reject'. As represented in Figure 16.17, information is computed on the food's sensory quality and palatability.

Various manipulations allow experimenters to target the palatability computation done by the brain and thereby to estimate the role of palatability in ingestion under natural conditions. Researchers can identify some of the brain regions involved in the palatability computation. Some manipulations allow them to assess the changes in palatability that occur within a meal. Others allow researchers to examine long-term changes in the neural circuitry underlying changing palatability. This section looks at examples of each.

The role of opioids

Endogenous opioids play a role in feeding, enhancing the palatability of food (Mercer and Holder, 1997). Reciprocally, the taste of palatable foods increases endogenous opioid activity. This tends to prolong a meal (Hoebel, 1997). It seems then that endogenous opioids form part of a 'go' signal that ensures the animal keeps feeding until satiety sets in and the positive palatability rating is lost.

Injected opioid agonists increase feeding whereas antagonists decrease it. Opioid antagonists lower palatability, their impact being greater the higher the palatability. For example, the opioid antagonist naloxone decreases the intake of a 10% sucrose solution (highly palatable to rats) but not that of chow food, the standard diet of laboratory rats. Morphine injections increase palatability as indexed by facial reactions to taste (Chapter 15; Doyle *et al.*, 1993).

The injection of the opioid antagonist naltrexone affects the amount of food eaten by humans (Yeomans and Gray, 1997). See Figure 16.18. Note that the injection did not affect the hunger rating at the outset but it reduced the level of intake needed to correct hunger. This suggests that opioids do not alter the level of hunger as such but affect the palatability of the food.

In the taste reactivity test, substances are placed on the rat's tongue and palatability assessed (Chapter 15). It is a means of observing the effects of chemical manipulations. Evidence suggests that opioids naturally act on receptors at the N.acc. and thereby increase the liking of food (Peciña and Berridge, 2000). Taste information from the tongue is projected, via the nucleus of the solitary tract, to the N.acc. In rats, microinjections of morphine into the N.acc. shift the taste reactivity to food in a positive direction. It appears that a distinct region of the N.acc. mediates such liking and a different region (acting by means of dopamine) mediates wanting.

A role for GABA

There is a role of GABA in feeding. Benzodiazepine agonists potentiate GABA$_A$ neurotransmission and also potentiate food intake. They increase the positive rating of sweet tastes, pointing to an action via palatability (Richardson *et al.*, 2005) rather than through anxiety reduction. The neurons implicated in the effect appear to be located at various sites such as the brain stem and N.acc.

Taste-aversion learning

Taste-aversion learning (Chapter 11) is an example of a long-term changed reactivity to a given substance (Figure 16.17). That is to say, the previously acceptable substance becomes unacceptable as a result of

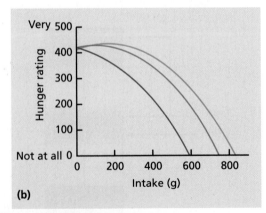

Figure 16.18 Ratings of hunger plotted against amount ingested: (a) a not highly rated pasta with cheese sauce and (b) a higher rated pasta with tomato sauce.
Source: Yeomans and Gray (1997, Fig. 1, p.18).

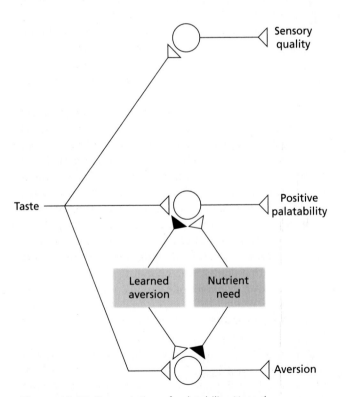

Figure 16.17 Computation of palatability. Note the excitatory contribution of nutrient need to positive palatability and the inhibitory contribution to aversion. Conversely, a learned aversion contributes an inhibitory effect on positive palatability. △, excitation; ▲, inhibition.

the nausea following ingestion. The biological basis of this is *plasticity* within the neural circuits that underlie feeding (Spray and Bernstein, 2004). In terms of Figure 16.17, we look for a biological embodiment of changes in the links from the box marked 'Learned aversion', i.e. increasing the strength of both the inhibitory and excitatory synapses.

As the neural embodiment of the acquired aversion, neural changes occur at various levels: the amygdala, hypothalamus and nucleus of the solitary tract (NTS). Taste-aversion learning transforms the activity elicited at certain regions of the NTS by the normally palatable substance saccharin to one characteristic of the bitter substance quinine. Links from the hypothalamus to the brain stem need to be intact for a rat to react to a substance as devalued following a taste-aversion experience (Berridge, 1995). This reflects hierarchical control over the brain stem.

Having looked at the bases of normal food intake, we now consider some examples of disturbances to this.

Section summary

1 Brain stem circuits assess palatability, to trigger ingestion or rejection.

2 Certain regions outside the brain stem (e.g. hypothalamus) modulate its reactivity and thereby mediate controls such as that by taste-aversion learning.

3 At the hypothalamus, information on food-related objects is integrated with signals on body nutrient state.

4 Lesions to the LH lower food intake whereas those to the VMH increase it.

5 Opioids appear to be implicated in giving foods their palatability.

☞ Test your knowledge

16.8 Concerning just the processes shown in Figure 16.15, what is suggested regarding development of agonists to treat over-eating?

 Answer on page 439   WEB ➡

Abnormalities of feeding

Introduction

Serious problems are caused by over- and under-eating, which can call for therapeutic intervention. There is potential commercial value of antagonists and agonists to neurotransmitters underlying appetite and satiety (Cooper and Higgs, 1994). A drug needs to be specific and have minimal undesirable side effects. Simply to know that it reduces appetite is not enough; it might do so by inducing sickness. To have a physiological effect of operation, it needs to exert an effect such as mimicking natural satiety.

Excessive food cravings

The term **craving** refers to a strong wanting of something and can be applied to particular foods, as in craving chocolate. It can be exhibited even in the absence of a general hunger (Pelchat *et al.*, 2004).

Craving sits uncomfortably in a section on eating disorders; who has not craved a certain food? Occasional craving is 'normal'. However, excessive craving might be considered abnormal and can be associated with binge eating, guilt and depression (Tiggemann and Kemps, 2005). Craving can involve an element of conflict, ambivalence and tension, especially when binging (Rogers and Smit, 2000). This indicates the complex cognitive and social factors that lock into the basic biology of feeding.

Cravings are more likely in certain psychological and physiological states, e.g. stress, a phase of the menstrual cycle, dieting and pregnancy. Patients suffering from depression commonly experience cravings, especially for sweets and chocolate. Those patients specifically experiencing Seasonal Affective Disorder (SAD) report that their negative mood is decreased by giving in to the craving.

Cravings might owe their existence to a memory of the combination of the intrinsic properties of the substance sought and mood-altering effects following its ingestion, such as a lowering of anxiety.

Craving could be characterized as 'excessive wanting'. Indeed, researchers are drawn to study the role of dopamine-based incentive motivational processes in trying to understand its bases (Sobik *et al.*, 2005).

Mercer and Holder (1997) propose that changes in the level of activity of opioids are part of the basis of the subjective feeling of craving. Stress induces craving for certain foods and is often associated with increases in opioid levels, as well as activation of dopaminergic systems. Mercer and Holder suggest that stress might be a mediating factor in a number of opioid-associated conditions of craving, e.g. obesity, bulimia nervosa and pregnancy. People addicted to opiates and denied access to their drug report intense cravings for sweet foods.

Rolls and McCabe (2007) used fMRI to identify brain regions that were activated differently by the sight of chocolate in 'chocolate cravers' as compared to 'non-chocolate cravers'. The ventral striatum and medial orbitofrontal cortex were more strongly activated in cravers. A wealth of other evidence also points to the role of these regions in motivation towards various incentives. In reaction to chocolate in the mouth, the primary taste cortex did not differ between cravers and non-cravers. Activity here appears to encode the sensory quality of the chocolate, whereas the ventral striatum and orbitofrontal cortex encode its incentive value.

Craving appears to be a factor linked to obesity, described next.

Obesity

In humans, **obesity** consists in having a body weight that is more than 20% higher than the ideal for the person's height (L.H. Epstein, 1990). The 'ideal' is defined by life insurance criteria.

Determinants

The stability of body-fat levels reflects equilibrium between contributory factors. One of these is that body-fat stores have some inhibitory effect on feeding (e.g. via leptin). Also, in humans, body weight is perceived in a mirror or on scales and compared against an ideal (Booth, 1980). Activity plays a crucial role in burning metabolic fuels. Alas, increased weight is often associated with lowered activity, giving rise to a vicious circle.

Given that motivation is the result of a balance of orosensory and satiety factors, it seems that in the obese this balance is achieved only at a higher level of intake. Obesity illustrates the point that feeding depends upon various factors. For example, stress and anxiety might be associated with general activation that causes salience to be attached to food-related cues (Robbins and Fray, 1980a,b). Because of its effects on peripheral tissue, excessive secretion of insulin could contribute to obesity, even though in the brain insulin tends to inhibit feeding. Another factor might be the cultural determinant of meal-time. In non-humans, a large meal tends to be followed by a large post-meal interval, whereas with humans meal-times tend to be relatively fixed. A meal may be of a size that is unjustified metabolically by the time since the last.

When obese people are compared with controls, few reliable differences are observed in feeding (Logue, 1991). However, the obese tend to be particularly externally triggered, i.e. strongly attracted by highly palatable foods (Rodin, 1980). A factor that might also play a role is the anticipatory rise in insulin secretion triggered by sweet substances appearing in the mouth or even the sight of attractive food.

Social facilitation, which is known to be a factor in increasing intake, could be a contributory factor to current high levels of obesity (Levitsky, 2005). It is possible that we are eating more frequently outside the home and in larger social groups, e.g. the business lunch or conference dinner.

Obese parents tend to have obese children. Surveys that compare identical and fraternal twins suggest a role for both genetic and environmental factors (Silventoinen and Kaprio, 2009). Multiple genes appear to be involved. Differences in metabolic rate might in part mediate the genetic effect. Pima Indians living in Arizona are especially prone to obesity, whereas those living in Mexico are not (Ravussin et al., 1994). Thus, there might be genetic bias factors towards obesity that are revealed only in certain environments, in this case the 'fast-food' culture of the United States. Of course, the onset of the epidemic of obesity has happened too rapidly to be due to genetic changes. It can be attributed to environmental change acting in association with genetic factors (some giving 'vulnerability') that have remained unchanged over this period of time (Power and Schulkin, 2009).

Watching television can increase food intake not only by encouraging inactivity but, if meals are taken

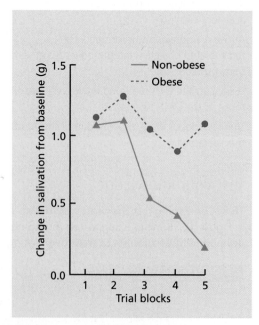

Figure 16.19 A measure of habituation (salivation) to a stimulus in obese and non-obese individuals.

Source: Epstein et al., (1996, Fig. 1 of *Psychosomatic Medicine*, 58, p.161).

while watching, this can lower habituation triggered by the food and increase intake (Epstein *et al.*, 2009). Even tested under identical conditions, obese people show slower habituation to food stimuli than do non-obese people (Figure 16.19). This raises the issue of whether a low rate of habituation characterizes children who later exhibit obesity.

Evolutionary psychology

Why obesity?

In an environment of uncertain food supply, there is value in triggering feeding when food is available and storing fuels within the body at times of abundance (VanItallie and Kissileff, 1990). Alas, in continuous abundance, this process can prove maladaptive. Also, one can speculate about the foods that are particularly attractive and which form the primary problem these days: those of high sugar and fat content. These would have been valuable in early evolution and hard to find, with much greater effort and time required in obtaining them than in sitting in a car to go to the supermarket (Power and Schulkin, 2009). Humans exhibit an attraction towards foods that have a high-energy content (Smith and Ferguson, 2008) and stress tends to increase the intake of such foods (Zellner *et al.*, 2006). Correspondingly, manufacturers and food outlets tend to present what people desire.

It is often suggested that, in our evolutionary past, energy shortage in the environment was more frequently confronted than was energy surplus. This is thought to have led to a fundamental asymmetry in controls. On the one hand, the controls of food intake and energy storage are tuned to respond strongly to food simply when it is available. The storage system of the body was 'designed' in such a way as to be 'thrifty': it is tolerant of surpluses and readily accommodates them, as is evidenced by the current epidemic of obesity. Researchers speculate that so-called 'energy-thrifty genes' played a role in surviving occasional famines (Depoortere, 2009).

On the other hand, except under relatively rare circumstances (voluntary anorexia), the system is intolerant of energy deficits. However, these circumstances invite speculation from evolutionary psychologists (discussed shortly).

Wang *et al.* (2001) measured the density of dopamine D_2 receptors in the brains of obese individuals, employing the technique of ^{11}C- raclopride (Chapter 5). Figure 16.20 shows the relationship between body mass index (BMI) a measure of obesity and levels of dopamine D_2 receptors. As obesity increases, so the level of receptors decreases. It could be that over-stimulation of the receptors by over-eating has caused them to be reduced in number, so-called 'down-regulation' (Berridge, 2009).

Therapeutic intervention

Understanding normal intake can point to therapeutic interventions for obesity. Treatments fall into three basic categories (Clifton and McLannahan, 2008).

1 Reducing the amount of food eaten by means of drugs, psychotherapeutic, behavioural or surgical techniques.

2 Lowering the percentage of ingested nutrients that are absorbed from the gut.

3 Increasing metabolic rate.

This chapter concerns primarily category (1), which includes surgery to reduce the size of the stomach, thereby massively increasing inhibitory feedback (Halmi, 1980). Reduced food intake appears to arise from a relatively strong signal from distension of the smaller stomach that remains, e.g. via increased secretion of peptides that mediate satiety (Strader and Woods, 2005). Alternatively, surgeons can try to augment negative feedback by inserting an intragastric balloon (Blackshaw and Grundy, 1993).

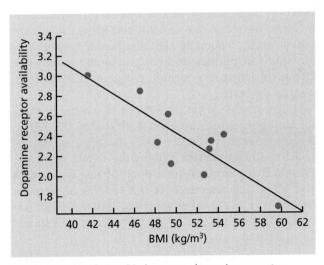

Figure 16.20 Relationship between dopamine receptor availability and body mass index (BMI) for a group of people with obesity.

Source: Wang *et al.* (2001, Fig. 2, p. 356).

Another technique is surgery for bypassing part of the intestine (Bray, 1980). This works by reducing food intake and by lowering absorption.

As behaviour therapy (L.H. Epstein, 1990), patients are taught to lower the rate of intake. This could allow more time for the secretion of satiety hormones and hence obtain stronger satiety. By restricting the availability of foods, sensory-specific satiety might be exploited.

Concerning drugs, some agonists contribute to the behavioural satiety sequence (described earlier). Hence, they appear to be mimicking satiety rather than, say, broadly disrupting all behaviour or triggering nausea (Blundell and Halford, 1998). Figure 16.15 leads logically to the consideration of neurochemicals that could be targeted by the use of agonists (to neurochemicals involved in satiety) and antagonists (to those that excite feeding).

Leptin exerts a role in satiety, so could its action be boosted? Leptin can be manufactured and is thereby potentially available as a treatment to add to the effects of endogenous leptin. Alas, if leptin is taken by mouth, it is broken down into its chemical constituents in the stomach and hence becomes unavailable to the brain. Injection of leptin into the blood avoids this problem but so far has been found to be disappointingly ineffective. Antagonists to ghrelin are another possibility that is under investigation (Depoortere, 2009).

The drug known as sibutramine (trade names Reductil and Meridia) lowers appetite and appears to do so in part by blocking the reuptake (Chapter 4) of serotonin (though it also blocks reuptake of noradrenalin). A primary role of sibutramine on feeding is mediated via boosting serotonergic activity within the arcuate nucleus (Figure 16.15). In addition, by means of its effect on noradrenergic neurotransmission, sibutramine increases metabolic rate and this also helps towards the goal of weight reduction. Alas, sibutramine is something of a blunt instrument and has potentially serious side effects by acting at serotonin receptors at other locations in the body.

It appears that a specific subtype of serotonin receptor is implicated in the control of satiety: the 5-HT$_{2C}$ receptor (Somerville et al., 2007). In mice, an agonist selective to this subtype triggers the satiety sequence. Therefore, the search is for a drug suitable for humans and which acts selectively at this subtype of receptor, leaving unaffected other subtypes. Hence, side-effects caused by the drug's action at unintended sites should be minimized.

Figure 16.15 suggests a potential role for α-MSH agonists, as well as antagonists to NPY or ghrelin, in the search for drugs to treat obesity (Clifton and McLannahan, 2008).

There are possibilities in addition to those suggested by Figure 16.15. The body contains an intrinsic ('endogenous') system similar to the action of the drug cannabis. The body produces what are termed 'cannabinoids' and has receptors for them in regions of the brain underlying appetite. People who use cannabis as a mood-altering drug report that it stimulates appetite and palatability. This raises the possibility that an endogenous equivalent plays a natural role in appetite. Hence, if an antagonist to the natural substance could be found it might lower appetite. One such antagonist is termed 'rimonabant' and it is currently under investigation (Burch et al., 2009).

Anorexia

Anorexia nervosa

The expression **anorexia** describes loss of appetite, which can arise from various causes, e.g. cancer. It is also exemplified by 'anorexia nervosa' (AN). AN can be defined as 'the relentless pursuit of thinness through self-starvation, even unto death' (Bruch, 1974, p. 4). The patient commonly has a fear of obesity and consciously pursues its avoidance (McHugh, 1990). An obsessive and perfectionist need for control appears to be universal and this gets channelled into avoidance of feeding. People with anorexia have a distorted perception of their body and tend to judge themselves as larger than they are objectively.

Anorexia is sometimes accompanied by bulimia nervosa: binges of eating followed by self-induced vomiting or taking laxatives. The nature of the typical AN patient might give some insight into its causation (McHugh, 1990), these being young women from their teenage years to their 30s.

Starvation stimulates production of endorphins, as does strenuous physical exercise and this often accompanies eating disorders (Davis and Claridge, 1998). The body might develop an 'auto-addiction' to opioids.

There are problems of disentangling cause and effect. People with anorexia tend to be abnormal in their interpretation of sensations arising from the stomach (Robinson, 1989). At times of severe starvation, the rate of gastric emptying is slowed. This could induce abnormally high satiety and thereby contribute to the condition.

The reciprocal situation to treating obesity is in treating anorexia and Figure 16.15 can similarly be used as an organizing framework. For example, the use of ghrelin agonists is under investigation (Depoortere, 2009).

Is behaviour always based on a realistic measure of the body or a distorted one?

Source: © Ariel Skelley/CORBIS.

Evolutionary psychology

Anorexia nervosa

The popular image of anorexia nervosa (AN) is as a disorder of recent times affecting young women and the result of pressure to maintain a slim body. In fact, AN has been recorded throughout history, across cultures and also affects a significant number of males (Guisinger, 2003). Could evolutionary psychology (EP) have anything to say about it?

Given that AN disrupts life and is often fatal, how could it reveal an adaptation? EP encourages lateral thinking and often suggests counter-intuitive answers. Something could have been adaptive in an early evolutionary environment but is pathological in contemporary society.

As speculation, Guisinger suggests that AN might be the outcome of a motivational process that is triggered by weight loss and that encouraged individuals to stop food-searching in a given location and move elsewhere. In our evolutionary past, the environment associated with weight loss would not have been a good one – elsewhere there might be more food available. Note that in AN, associated with refusal of food, excessive exercise is very common. A number of non-human species also show the combination of refusing food and excessive physical activity when weight falls. Consider also the natural phenomenon of 'migratory restlessness' that some species show prior to migration.

But why, in contemporary Western society, do certain humans initially let their weight fall? This could be due to social pressures.

Cancer-associated anorexia

Cancer is commonly associated with anorexia (McHugh, 1990). A number of factors appear to be implicated. The disease affects taste thresholds and distorts preferences (Grunberg, 1985) but in some cases the treatment is a factor. Cytokines, e.g. interleukin-1 and 'tumour necrosis factor', are secreted as part of the defensive response to the tumour (Chapter 13) and these have anorexic effects (Bernstein, 1996).

Taste-aversion learning plays a role in cancer-associated anorexia (Bernstein, 1996); a taste can be devalued as a result of its association with the ongoing disturbance to the body. Based upon rat models, part of the internal state that devalues the rating of food is the presence of tumour necrosis factor. In rats, the anorexic effect of a tumour, as mediated via taste-aversion learning, is reduced by cutting the vagus nerve or making lesions within the nucleus of the solitary tract. This reinforces the assumption of a role for cytokines since they mediate effects through this route (Chapter 13).

Chemotherapy can play a role in food aversion. For example, patients who eat a novel-flavoured ice cream prior to therapy can develop an aversion to its taste (Bernstein and Webster, 1985). Cancer patients commonly experience nausea and sometimes even vomiting in anticipation of receiving chemotherapy. Such nausea might then form a link with food ingested hours earlier.

The discussion now turns to drinking, where it is shown that a number of principles similar to those underlying feeding apply.

Drinking and sodium ingestion

Introduction

This section looks at drinking and the intake of sodium ('sodium' is employed as short-hand for sodium chloride: chloride ions are assumed to accompany sodium). Since sodium chloride is often located within foodstuffs, sodium appetite and ingestion would be equally at home in the feeding section. However, sodium levels are tied inextricably to body-fluid levels and there are interactions between the appetites for water and sodium.

Water and sodium ingestion are normally linked closely to regulation. Our understanding has been advanced considerably by focusing on one aspect of behaviour: the role of body fluids in controlling ingestion and thereby the role of ingestion in regulation. This focus is reflected in the present chapter.

The body-fluids

Introduction

The body of an animal such as a rat or human is about 68% water by weight. The composition of the fluid compartments, in terms of ions (e.g. sodium) and water,

is closely regulated (Ramsay and Thrasher, 1990). The behaviour involved in regulation consists in part in control over the intake of water and sodium. Water is gained by drinking, by the water content of food and from the metabolism of food. Depending on the species, there are a number of ways in which water is lost, e.g. sweat, urine, evaporation from the skin (as in rats spreading saliva) and respiration.

Gradients and equilibrium

To understand movement of water in the body, we need to reconsider concentration gradients and equilibrium (Chapter 4). Figure 16.21 shows a U-tube, with a membrane dividing it. The membrane is semipermeable, meaning that some substances can pass easily across it, whereas others encounter difficulty. On each side of the membrane, a salt solution of equal concentration is placed (part (a)). Let us relate this to body fluids and the semipermeable membrane that surrounds cells. Suppose that water can freely pass from one side of the U-tube to the other but sodium has difficulty in crossing. The system is in equilibrium.

Suppose now that some extra sodium chloride is introduced to the left side (part (b)). This disturbs the equilibrium of concentration across the membrane. Therefore, water migrates from the region of low to high sodium concentration until a new equilibrium is attained (part (c)). From this you can now understand one reason why drinking seawater makes you thirsty. The concentrated sodium chloride in the gut pulls water from the blood, dehydrating the body fluids.

Distribution of water in the body

Consider the water of the body to be divided into compartments (Figure 16.22). The largest is the cellular compartment (or 'intracellular compartment'): the total of the water in the cells. Water not in the cells is defined as the extracellular compartment, which subdivides into the plasma (the fluid part of the blood) and interstitial compartment. The term 'vascular' refers to the plasma and the cells of the blood, e.g. red blood cells. If disturbances to equilibrium arise between extracellular and cellular compartments, water will move across the membrane. We now turn to consider how the fluid compartments of Figure 16.22 relate to motivation and behaviour.

Extracting a motivational signal from the body-fluids

Introduction

Loss of body-fluids tends to trigger motivation and drinking. Ingested water corrects the loss (Fitzsimons, 1990), exemplifying negative feedback. Motivation

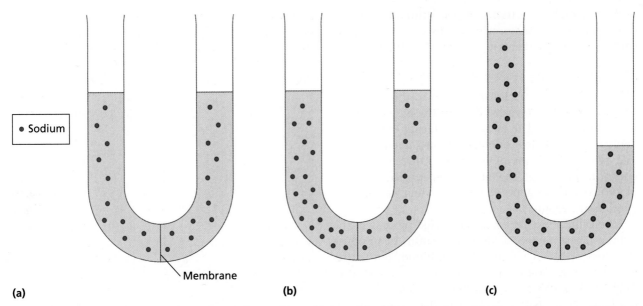

Figure 16.21 U-tube and semipermeable membrane: (a) equilibrium, (b) addition of sodium chloride and (c) new equilibrium.

increases with deficit. There is collaboration between internal physiological and behavioural controls (Figure 16.1), i.e. the kidney is also part of a similar negative feedback system (Chapter 3). For instance, injection with sodium chloride more concentrated than the blood ('hypertonic'), triggers the kidney to excrete urine concentrated in sodium chloride. This partly eliminates the disturbance. The injection also stimulates drinking, which acts in parallel to restore normality. Such control by disturbances, i.e. negative feedback, is vital but it is only part of the story.

Drinking can partly reflect habit or can be in association with meals and, in effect, anticipate loss of water (Fitzsimons, 1990), i.e. feedforward (Chapter 10), rather than negative feedback. However, we will focus on negative feedback by considering how deviations of body fluids from normal stimulate drinking.

The cellular compartment

Figure 16.23 shows what happens when some hypertonic sodium chloride solution is injected into the blood. The concentration of sodium chloride in the plasma increases, which amounts to the same thing as decreasing the concentration of water. Water moves from cellular to extracellular compartments. Cellular dehydration triggers thirst motivation and drinking. Loss is only from the cellular compartment (Figure 16.23(c)). There is expansion of extracellular volume but still drinking is triggered. This indicates that extracellular swelling does not inhibit the excitatory effect of cellular shrinkage.

The stimulus to motivation is not the overall loss of water from the cellular compartment per se. Indeed, it is difficult to see how this could be measured. Rather, a *sample* of the compartment is taken and drinking is based on this. What does this mean? When you sample food you take just a spoonful of it and taste it. You assume that the sample is representative of the whole dish. Similarly, heat-sensitive neurons in the brain are said to sample body temperature.

Figure 16.22 Distribution of water in the body.

What sample of neurons triggers drinking? A group of neurons in the brain, which constitute an **osmoreceptor**, is involved (Ramsay and Thrasher, 1990).

The extracellular stimulus

There is also an extracellular stimulus to thirst (Ramsey and Booth, 1991), revealed even in the absence of cellular dehydration. The means of inducing extracellular depletion include loss of blood, termed **haemorrhage**, and sweating. A loss of isotonic extracellular fluid (isotonic means of the same concentration as the blood) triggers an appetite for both water and sodium (Fitzsimons, 1990).

Extracellular events are also detected by cells in the kidney. These secrete a hormone, renin, in response to a loss of blood volume. In the blood, renin triggers the production of another hormone, angiotensin. Angiotensin serves a dual role: as a hormone it can cross the blood–brain barrier and act in the CNS to trigger thirst motivation and drinking, thereby reinforcing the intrinsic CNS neurotransmitter actions of angiotensin (Hoebel, 1997). Angiotensin acts throughout the body to raise blood pressure. Hence, there is functional coherence in its behavioural and physiological actions.

Water deprivation

Loss of water from either cellular or extracellular compartments triggers drinking. If both are depleted, their effects add together (Fitzsimons and Oatley, 1968). Water deprivation is associated with a loss of water from both compartments (Figure 16.24). Water is lost first from the extracellular compartment (e.g. urine, sweat) and the cells then compensate this compartment to some extent, inducing cellular dehydration.

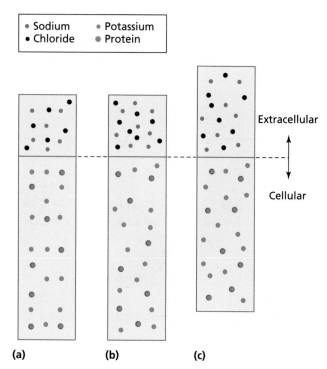

Figure 16.23 Injection of hypertonic saline into the blood: (a) prior to injection, (b) immediately following injection and (c) slightly later.

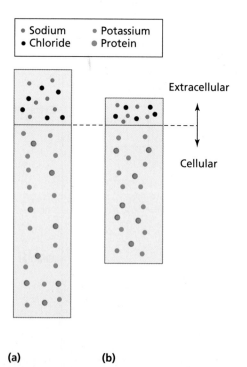

Figure 16.24 Water deprivation: (a) normal state and (b) deprived state.

A personal angle

The Black Hole of Calcutta

Human subjective reports help in understanding thirst (Fitzsimons, 1990). There is the experience of prisoners held in 'The Black Hole of Calcutta'. This expression is synonymous with being captive under hot, airless conditions and it dates from a tragic incident in Calcutta in 1758. 'Raging thirst' was described. Prisoners obtained some relief by licking their own sweat, immense pleasure being gained in capturing drops that fell from the head. This suggests that sweat was able to produce some satiety of the appetites for both water and sodium. It highlights reward obtained by oral stimulation.

Thirst satiety

From a 'design perspective', straightforward negative feedback would encounter a problem comparable to that in the feeding system. Loss of water from cellular or extracellular compartments triggers drinking. However, water that is ingested takes time to get through the stomach, intestine and into the blood. Cellular replenishment takes still longer. Yet animals drink quickly an amount that reflects the size of deficit (Ramsay and Thrasher, 1990).

By the time an animal has drunk enough to correct its deficit and terminate drinking, much of the water is still in the stomach and intestine. This implies satiety, which inhibits the excitatory tendency arising from fluid loss. In other words, there is short-term negative feedback, which, in effect, gives advance warning of the water about to arrive in the fluid compartments. Satiety derives from sites such as the mouth, stomach and liver, as well as performance of the swallowing reflex (Stricker and Sved, 2000) (Figure 16.25).

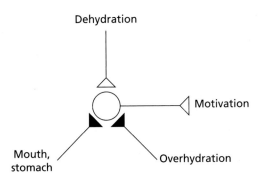

Figure 16.25 Drinking tendency as the difference between excitatory and inhibitory factors.

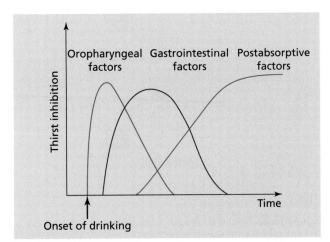

Figure 16.26 Time-course of some of the factors that contribute towards the satiety of drinking.
Source: Verbalis (1991, Fig. 19.5, p. 323).

In humans, on allowing drinking following water deprivation, thirst, as indexed by subjective reports, is reduced within 2.5–5 minutes (Verbalis, 1991). Significant correction of the loss in the cellular compartment takes about 20 minutes. Following the start of drinking, Figure 16.26 shows the time-course of the factors that contribute to satiety. Note the rise and fall in strength of (1) the oropharyangeal (mouth) factor, corresponding to detection of water by the mouth, and (2) gastrointestinal factors, corresponding to stomach filling and emptying. There is a rise in strength of the post-absorptive factor, corresponding to the absorption of water from the alimentary tract.

Normal drinking

Much of the drinking by humans and rats appears to occur for reasons other than deficits. Indeed, given an adequate supply of available fluids and a mild climate, deficits might seldom arise (Kraly, 1991). In humans, much drinking appears to be due to habit and social factors, e.g. to drink tea at break times (Rogers, 1995). This can pre-empt deficits. The quantity of fluid taken each day can vary greatly, depending on how tasty it is and its availability without exerting effort (Engell and Hirsch, 1991). Nonetheless, our focus is on drinking triggered by fluid loss, the neuroscience of which is the topic of the next section.

The neuroscience of drinking

As with feeding, the neural substrates underlying drinking appear to be distributed over brain regions (A.N. Epstein, 1990). Circuits in the brain stem organize the motor pattern of licking to gain water: these circuits are modulated by motivational influences from the forebrain. The lateral hypothalamus appears to be a site at which neural signals of body-fluid state are integrated and from which information is transmitted to the brain stem (Winn, 1995).

The cellular stimulus

Osmoreceptors are located in a region alongside the hypothalamus and the blood–brain barrier is relaxed at this site (Stricker and Sved, 2000). This permits ready interaction between the blood and these cells. Microinjections of hypertonic saline into the region, but not elsewhere, trigger drinking, which suggests that cellular dehydration at this location is the stimulus (Figure 16.27). Similarly, a control of secretion of arginine vasopressin (Chapter 3) arises from such osmoreceptors. Thereby, there is coordination between behavioural and physiological controls. In water-deprived dogs, infusion of pure water into the region where the receptors are

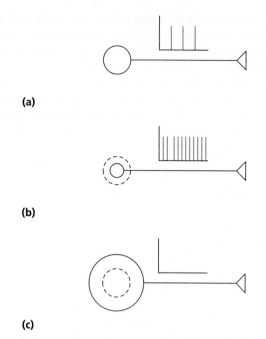

(a)

(b)

(c)

Figure 16.27 Proposed osmoreceptor: (a) equilibrium, (b) dehydration of the osmoreceptor and increased action potential frequency and (c) over-hydration and inhibition of activity.

Source: adapted from Verbalis (1990, Fig. 8, p. 444).

located inhibits drinking (Thrasher, 1991). Such small infusions do not correct dehydration in the remainder of the body's cells.

In addition to cellular detectors alongside the hypothalamus, there could be cellular detectors at other sites in the CNS or outside it, such as the alimentary tract and liver (Johnson and Thunhorst, 1997; Meï, 1993). Of course, motivation is believed to be a brain process and so a signal from peripheral detectors would be transmitted to the brain, where it would be integrated with signals from CNS detectors. The liver is located just beyond the gastrointestinal tract. Therefore, in so far as receiving ingested material, the liver could be well suited for a receptor that detects the presence of water (Haberich, 1968). A receptor could provide a short-term satiety signal, as part of an early-warning system (Novin, 1993).

The extracellular stimulus

Figure 16.28 shows a proposal for the role of detectors of extracellular fluid level. At one or more locations in the circulation, a signal on blood volume is detected, i.e. a sample is taken (labelled 'Extracellular'). This could arise from the stretch of a particular blood vessel. Humans appear to be less sensitive to such a signal than are other species, except under extreme conditions (Rolls, 1991). It seems that, under conditions of fluid balance, a signal arising from the filling of a blood vessel inhibits thirst motivation (Fitzsimons, 1991). Following

loss of extracellular volume, the signal detecting such filling diminishes in strength. This lowers the inhibition and thereby arouses thirst. Excitation is provided by a neuron that either constitutes an osmoreceptor or is triggered by one. Loss of cellular fluid ('Cellular') increases action potential frequency.

Under normal conditions, angiotensin arising from the blood and triggered by loss of body fluids is able to cross the blood–brain barrier. The barrier is relaxed at those sites where neurons sensitive to angiotensin are located (Fitzsimons, 1998). In the brain, angiotensin triggers thirst, more strongly in rats than in humans (Rolls, 1991). Angiotensin appears to act as an amplifier of the neural signal of loss of blood volume (Fitzsimons, 1990). Angiotensin also triggers sodium appetite, sodium being needed to maintain extracellular volume.

The sites where angiotensin can influence neurons are examples of circumventricular organs (Chapter 5).

(a)

(b)

Figure 16.28 Simplified model of the basis of a thirst signal. (a) Fluid balance. A 'background' level of activity arises from the osmoreceptor and the detector of stretch in a blood vessel. (b) Loss of blood (extracellular loss). The inhibitory neuron is inactive, which allows excitation of the motivation neuron.

The subfornical organ is such a site, where angiotensin-sensitive neurons are located. Signals arising there are conveyed to the hypothalamus, where they are involved in motivational processing.

Angiotensin injected into certain regions of the brain (e.g. anterior hypothalamus and preoptic area) is a potent trigger to drinking. Indeed, the efficacy of injected angiotensin represents one of the most dramatic and reliable brain–behaviour links that can be demonstrated. The effect is a motivational one; injected rats vigorously press a lever in a Skinner box for water reward (Fitzsimons, 1998).

Sodium appetite

It is easy to show a sodium appetite in rats and to relate it to regulation ('homeostasis'). In humans, within normal limits a link between sodium need and sodium appetite is less reliably revealed (Verbalis, 1990). However, a very effective control of sodium levels is exerted by the kidney, the ion being retained at times of deficiency and excreted at times of excess.

A personal angle

D.W. – The boy who craved salt

In 1940, from Baltimore, USA, a report appeared on a boy, D.W., with an excessive craving for salt (Wilkins and Richter, 1940). Owing to an abnormality with control by the kidney, he lost large amounts of salt in the urine. This created a deficit of sodium chloride in the blood, which triggered craving. At one year of age, he compulsively licked and chewed salt off various items of food. He showed pleasure when tasting pure salt. Later, the boy came to associate salt with the container in which it was kept and was agitated until he could gain access to it. The craving made sense; it fitted regulation ('homeostasis') and kept him alive. When D.W. was admitted to hospital, he was given only the standard hospital diet and, sadly, died at age $3\frac{1}{2}$ years.

In rats, loss of extracellular fluid, e.g. haemorrhage, is a stimulus to sodium appetite. Angiotensin, a mediator of thirst in response to loss of extracellular fluid, also triggers sodium appetite (Hoebel, 1997).

In humans, very early experience of sodium deficiency is associated with a high appetite for salt in later years (Leshem, 1998). This suggests that early activation of the renin–angiotensin system sensitizes sodium appetite.

Section summary

1. Loss of fluid from cellular or extracellular compartments or both triggers drinking.

2. Loss from the cellular compartment is measured by osmoreceptors in the brain.

3. Loss from the extracellular compartment is measured by detectors of blood volume.

4. Angiotensin is a powerful trigger to thirst motivation.

5. Satiety is determined by a combination of factors including stomach fullness and the oral detection of water passing the mouth.

6. In humans, much drinking reflects habit and social factors.

☞ Test your knowledge

16.10 In Figure 16.28 what effect would cellular loss of fluid have on the activity of the neuron marked 'Cellular'? (i) Increase it, (ii) decrease it.

Answer on page 439

Bringing things together

For feeding and drinking, the strength of motivation depends on the detection of physiological variables at several sites, as well as external factors such as the presence of food or water. Receptors in the brain and sites outside the CNS (e.g. liver) detect physiological variables and translate them into signals used in motivation. Multiple controls (e.g. time of day, cultural norms) are involved in triggering feeding and drinking. Negative feedback based on deficits is only one such control. Ingestive behaviour is switched off by an interaction of factors, pre-absorptive (oral and gastric) and post-absorptive, somewhat different from those that switch it on.

Insight into feeding and drinking can be gained by comparing their biological bases. Further comparisons are between these two and the bases of behavioural controls over body temperature. In each case, there is defence of a body variable and regulation ('homeostasis') applies. However, there are important differences between systems in this regard. Body temperature is tightly defended. Although the set-point varies over the course of 24 hours, at any point in time temperature normally departs little if at all from it. Body water content is also usually tightly regulated, certainly relative to nutrient levels. Just look around and see the variation in human weights and contrast this with the minute variation in body temperature between individuals.

Like heat, water cannot be stored, so excess is lost as urine. By contrast, excess calories cannot easily be lost. If nutrients are taken in excess of immediate needs, some is normally transformed and stored, e.g. as fat. The stored chemical is available for later utilization as fuel. Although there is negative feedback, food intake and consequently weight are the result of a variable balance between excitation and inhibition. It appears to be part of our 'evolutionary design' to take foods when they are available and to be triggered by sensory hedonism and variety. Alas, in present-day society with an inactive lifestyle, such a control can deliver pathological outcomes.

The proteins that form the structure of our bodies and vitamins and minerals essential for life are derived from nutrients. However, much of what we eat is simply employed as fuel and an important factor is the availability of fuels for metabolism. If intake is insufficient to maintain metabolism, the body literally burns itself. Probably a crucial factor in the evolution of controls of feeding is the ability to maintain blood glucose level so that sufficient glucose is available for the needs of the nervous system.

The body must obtain sufficient water to compensate for loss. However, constancy reflects more than simply acquiring enough water to replace losses. Maintenance of the fluid environment is crucial for optimal functioning of the body's organs. Cellular events proceed within a fluid matrix. Exchanges of ions across the cell membrane, e.g. the action potential, take place within a fluid environment. From functional considerations, it might be expected that drinking would arise unambiguously from a reduction in body fluids. This is indeed so.

 See the Video coverage for this chapter and experience the study of feeding and its disorders.

Summary of Chapter 16

1 Control exerted on (a) behaviour (feeding and drinking) and (b) physiology regulates the internal nutrient and fluid environments of the body.

2 Feeding provides the cells throughout the body with energy as well as chemicals serving particular specialized roles.

3 Feeding motivation is sensitive to levels of body glucose and fats.

4 The power of foods to trigger ingestion depends upon both their intrinsic properties and learning about the foods and the consequences of ingestion.

5 Ingested food causes satiety, which inhibits further food intake.

6 Identifiable and interacting brain regions underlie the control of feeding.

7 Although there is a range of food intake levels compatible with good health, nonetheless serious deviations to each side of this are found.

8 Body-fluids are distributed into distinct compartments. The tight regulation of these by means of the control of drinking is crucial to survival.

Further reading

For all aspects of feeding and drinking, see Stricker and Woods (2004). For motivational aspects, see Kringelbach and Berridge (2010). For obesity, see Power and Schulkin (2009).

Answers

Explanations for answers to 'test your knowledge' questions can be found on the website www.pearsoned.co.uk/toates

16.1 Loss of body water triggers thirst and, when water becomes available, drinking. An excess of water in the body triggers urination.

16.2 When sufficient food has been ingested satiety is induced and hunger switched off, thereby excessive amounts of nutrients are not ingested. This exemplifies regulation and negative feedback. A drug that disrupts satiety would cause excessive amounts to be eaten and nutrient levels to rise above their optimal level.

16.3 (i) 17.00–18.00

16.4 (ii) 05.00

16.5 (ii) Leptin and (iii) insulin

16.6 (ii) Conditional stimulus

16.7 (i) Pre-absorptive

16.8 Agonists to serotonin, leptin, insulin would be possible

16.9 (iii) A leptin agonist

16.10 (i) Increase it

Visit www.pearsoned.co.uk/toates
for a range of resources to support study.
Test yourself with multiple choice questions and access a bank of over 100 videos that will bring the topics to life.

Chapter 17
Sexual behaviour

Learning outcomes for Chapter 17

After studying this chapter, you should be able to:

1 Describe the interacting factors that underlie sexual behaviour. Summarize the role of (a) external and internal factors and (b) central and peripheral factors.

2 Describe what is meant by the term 'sex hormones' and the factors that determine their secretion.

3 Describe the insights derived from a comparative approach to the study of sexual behaviour. Give instances of similarities and differences across species and link this to their biological bases.

4 Outline some features of human sexual desire and motivation. Link this to principles of neuroscience and evolutionary psychology.

5 Describe the basic principles underlying the response of genital arousal, in terms of descending pathways, local neurons and smooth muscle. Link this to the interaction of central and peripheral factors and to how this process can fail to function optimally.

6 Describe the role of some endogenous and artificial substances in sexual desire and arousal.

7 Present a brief account of the role of biological psychology in understanding human sexual orientation.

Scene-setting questions

1 Are people aware consciously of what arouses them sexually?
2 Can certain non-sexual stimuli increase sexual motivation and, if so, by means of which brain process?
3 Are there animal models of human sexual promiscuity and fidelity?
4 Why does novelty arouse for some? Why do other people insist on only one-to-one intimacy?
5 What can neuroimaging tell us about human sexuality?
6 Is love 'blind'?
7 Is the term 'gay gene' meaningless?
8 Could there by any evolutionary significance to the expression 'a dirty mind'?

Can certain non-sexual stimuli increase sexual motivation and, if so, by means of which brain process? Explore the video on the website accompanying this book at **www.pearsoned. co.uk/toates**

How do central and peripheral factors interact in human sexual desire?

Source: Image courtesy of The Advertising Archives.

Introduction

Consider the following headlines:

- 'Top politician risked everything for one night of illicit passion – loyal wife heartbroken'.
- 'It's official now! Sex is good for your health. Over-sixties urged to keep on in there'.
- 'Emergence of a new urban group – young and happy asexual men and women'.
- 'Judge urges castration for repeat sex offenders. You are disgusting, so one chance and then you're out'.
- 'Viagra for women – the answer to loss of desire. Feminists protest – the pipe-work is not the problem'.
- 'Boffins discover the gene for adultery – bishop condemns research as giving a licence to sin'.
- 'Sobbing Hollywood star tells biographer – "When the trust went, the love went and when that happened all desire went"'.

The following represent some of the issues for biological psychology that are raised by these headlines.

1 Sex can cause people to ignore obvious dangers in answering its pull. Novelty can play a potent role for some individuals. Restraint mechanisms are often ineffective.

2 Sexual activity is said to be good for us, which points to such things as possible endorphin release by sexual behaviour and its calming effect. However, total abstinence from sexual behaviour appears to be perfectly possible for some people. Therefore, sex is different from feeding and drinking.

3 The remark about castration is surely based on the assumption that sexual motivation is powerfully influenced by sex hormones. The emotion of disgust can be triggered by sexual behaviour.

4 The claim that Viagra can solve the problem of lack of female desire assumes that a peripherally acting drug can correct what many see as a central problem. The feminist critique is that lack of appropriate and considerate sexual stimulation, poor self-image and low desire need to be addressed directly, rather than the answer being sought in the reaction of peripheral blood vessels. However, we should not ignore the role of peripheral factors.

5 The claim regarding a gene for adultery points towards the role of variety in sexual motivation. It also suggests biological determinism, in the sense that a gene could be associated directly with a feature of behaviour. Biological psychology might wish to qualify such claim of a one-to-one link.

6 The sobbing actor illustrates that complex emotions can be associated with sexual motivation and desire. To some, sexuality is intimately tied to romantic love and trust, whereas to others, such as the disgraced politician, it might be quite removed from such considerations.

This chapter discusses how events inside the body and outside interact to determine sexual motivation and behaviour.

Section summary

1 We need to distinguish the high motivation associated with sex and the lack of a life-threatening disturbance to the bodily tissues associated with sexual abstinence.

2 Variety of the partner can play a role in sexual motivation.

3 In interpreting human sexuality and its problems, we need to take care not to focus too narrowly on peripheral reactions.

☞ **Test your knowledge**

17.1 In what ways is sexual motivation (i) similar to and (ii) different from the motivations associated with feeding and drinking?

Answer on page 466

An organizing framework

Introduction

Figure 17.1 summarizes some general principles of sexual motivation, physiology and behaviour (Toates, 2009). The figure could appear daunting or 'cold'. You might wonder whether human sexuality can be captured by a series of boxes and arrows. The intention is not to reduce something complex to simply a sequence of mechanical actions. Of course, the diagram cannot capture all the factors underlying sexuality but it shows how, in part, sexuality 'works'. It can be taken apart, as follows.

Motivation and the sexual incentive

Consider first the 'object of one's desire', or, for something less romantic but more broadly applicable: the 'Incentive' for sexual motivation. Sexual motivation is excited by the 'Incentive', represented by arrow 1 from 'Incentive' to 'Sexual motivation'. For example, in humans 'Incentive' might be weighted towards visual stimuli. Also, there is evidence that both men

and women exude pheromones, which affect the person's incentive value (Hummer and McClintock, 2009; Grammer *et al.*, 2005). Of course, the incentive can also take the form of images as in erotic movies (Both *et al.*, 2005). According to the species, animals vary in the extent to which they are sexually motivated by one individual or another. Dogs show idiosyncratic choices (Beach and LeBoeuf, 1967) as do humans (as doubtless you have already observed!).

Sexual motivation is also excited by conditional stimuli (CS) that in the past have been associated with incentives (Domjan, 1994). In rats, the CS can be a light or sound that has, under the control of an experimenter, been presented at the same time that a partner has been available. In humans there are countless natural possibilities for such associations. Arrow 2, from CS to 'Sexual motivation', represents the link between CS and its effect in exciting motivation.

Various factors can inhibit sexual motivation (Ågmo *et al.*, 2004), such as fear and disgust. Therefore, arrow 3 represents inhibition ('Inhibit'). For example, in social animals, motivation depends upon the individual's place in a hierarchy (Herbert, 1995). The presence of an aggressive dominant can counteract sexual motivation.

Sexual incentives are placed into the context ('Compare') of memories of past encounters (arrow 11). In some species, mating is preferentially triggered when the potential incentive is an established mate. In other species or individuals, motivation is particularly stimulated by a change of partner.

Linking to behaviour and physiological responses

Arrow 4 represents the link between sexual motivation and sexual behaviour ('Behaviour'). The initials SNS stand for 'somatic nervous system' (SNS), the system that mediates this link. You will hardly need reminding that sexual behaviour involves the use of skeletal muscles, controlled by the SNS. Making this point is not trivial though, since, by distinction, the autonomic nervous system is also represented in the diagram. The ANS mediates internal changes at the 'Genitals', hence the initials alongside arrow 5. In humans, motivation influences vaginal congestion with blood or penile erection. Even when motivation is potentially high, inhibition (again, arrow 3) might prevent or reduce the genital reaction.

Behavioural consequences

There are 'Consequences' of behaviour (e.g. orgasm, partner's responsivity) and events at the genitals (e.g. erectile success or failure, triggering of pain) that are perceived by the individual. That is, these consequences feed back to further excite or inhibit sexual motivation

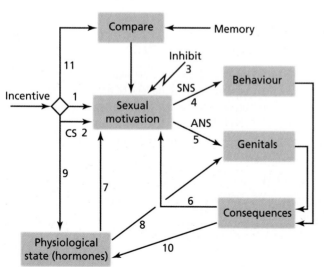

Figure 17.1 Model of sexual motivation and behaviour.

(arrow 6). The capacity of a conspecific to trigger motivation depends upon the history of past sexual contacts: a 'reinforcement' effect. This factor is, of course, particularly well known in humans. Over the longer term, in male rats, a failure to achieve penile insertion (intromission) leads to loss of interest, extinction (Everitt, 1995). In female Syrian hamsters, sexual experience sensitizes dopamine responsivity in the nucleus accumbens (Kohlert and Meisel, 1999), which might exemplify a general effect across species.

Role of hormones

Consider the box marked 'Physiological state (hormones)'. So-called sex hormones, produced at the testes, ovaries and adrenal gland, exert central (CNS) (arrow 7) and peripheral (arrow 8) effects (Bancroft, 1989). For example, testosterone sensitizes motivational processes, such that sexual stimuli trigger motivation, i.e. arrow 7 (Beach, 1947). Conversely, defeat and stress can inhibit such hormone secretion and thereby cause a reduction of interest in sexual behaviour (Rose et al., 1975). Sex hormones influence the sensitivity of the genitals (arrow 8). A sexually arousing stimulus can increase secretion of sex hormones (arrow 9), possibly contributing to positive feedback (Stewart, 1995). Sexual activity (arrow 10) might have some influence on women's menstrual cycles (Cutler and Genovese-Stone, 1998).

Special human features

Of course, human sexuality has features not shared with rats: complex cognition and emotion. For example, autonomic effects, e.g. elevated heart-rate, can be *interpreted* as sexual arousal and thereby contribute to arousal (Valins, 1970). Giving false feedback to people on an 'elevated' heart-rate can increase the attraction of a potential partner. Guilt, self-image and fantasy are

involved. By use of imagination, humans can be sexually motivated even in the absence of external cues. However, the chapter assumes that human and non-human sexuality share some features.

Human males occupy more space in the chapter than do females. This does not reflect a male chauvinist bias by the author but represents the fact that male sexuality has been more extensively researched (Bartlik et al., 1999a).

Development

Figure 17.1 represents the adult. How did this system come into being? There is a sequence of interacting developmental effects (Chapter 6). In this context, hormones play a different role from that shown in the adult system. There is early exposure of the brain to hormones, which play a role in the *formation* of 'developing motivational processes' (Figure 17.2). The direction of later sexual attraction and behaviour is influenced by various early effects including hormonal. For a social species, early interactions with conspecifics, such as playing, also influence such development (Beach, 1947). In humans, depending upon the culture, there might also be different 'role models' in the form of peers, advertising and books, etc.

The following sections look at various aspects of Figure 17.1, such as the role of hormones, conditional stimuli and the genitals. However, as well as looking at the parts, we need to consider their interdependence. We consider first hormones.

Figure 17.2 Influences on the development of sexual motivational processes.

Section summary

1 Sexual motivation arises from interaction between internal factors (e.g. hormones) and external factors (e.g. a partner and conditional stimuli).

2 There are interactions between (1) sexual motivation, a CNS process, and (2) arousal of the genitals.

3 There are some common features in the sexual behaviour of humans and non-humans. However, there are also peculiarly human factors such as guilt and self-image.

☞ Test your knowledge

17.2 In Figure 17.1, loss of motivation as a result of erectile failure would be associated with which combination of arrows?

 Answer on page 466

Control of the secretion of sex hormones

General

Hormones play a role in central motivation and peripheral (genital) processes (Figure 17.1). Some general principles are applicable to both sexes (Vander *et al.*, 1994) and we first consider these.

The term 'androgen' is a generic one used to refer to a class of hormone (Chapter 6). Androgens play a role in both male and female reproduction. The best-known androgen is testosterone. The term oestrogen is similarly a generic one used to refer to a class of hormones. Various oestrogens have some similar effects. Oestradiol, an oestrogen, is secreted by the female ovaries. Androgens and oestrogens are examples of a class of hormone termed **steroids**.

Figure 17.3 represents a sequence in the control of hormone secretion (a *hormonal axis*) that is applicable to males and females (Frohman *et al.*, 1999). This involves the hypothalamus, pituitary gland and the gonads (female ovaries and male testes). A logical starting point is the hypothalamus and the axis is termed the **hypothalamic pituitary gonadal axis**. Sexually related external stimuli excite hormone secretion in this axis. They act via pathways from, for example, olfactory detection to the hypothalamus (Larriva-Sahd *et al.*, 1993). Note the secretion of gonadotropin-releasing hormone (GnRH) from neurons in the hypothalamus.

GnRH travels only a short distance in a special blood vessel before reaching the anterior pituitary gland. Here, GnRH triggers the release of follicle-stimulating hormone (FSH) and luteinizing hormone (LH) into the general bloodstream (similar to the action of CRF, in Chapter 6).

FSH and LH circulate in the bloodsteam and exert their effects at the gonads, to cause secretion of sex hormones. Because of their effects on the gonads, FSH and LH are sometimes given the generic name **gonadotropins**. As a result of the action of FSH and LH at the gonads, androgens in the male and oestrogens in the female are secreted into the general bloodstream. They then exert various effects throughout the body, e.g. at the anterior pituitary, the hypothalamus and the reproductive tract ('produce gametes', i.e. sperm and egg cells) (Figure 17.3).

During foetal life and shortly afterwards, secretion of GnRH, FSH, LH and the sex hormones is high. This corresponds to the period of sexual differentiation (Chapter 6). It is followed by a period of inactivity on the part of GnRH and the subsequent hormones. At puberty, there is a sharp rise in activity in this axis. This reaches a stable level in human males but in females there is

oscillation in the axis corresponding to the menstrual cycle. In later years, there is a reduction in activity in the axis (Sternbach, 1998). In men and women, loss of sexual desire is a common symptom of pituitary tumours, associated in males with loss of testosterone production (Lundberg, 1992).

We now consider the features of the axis shown in Figure 17.3 that are specific to, first, the male and then the female.

The male

In men, testosterone is often taken as representative of androgens. Normally, in an adult, the neurons that secrete GnRH show bursts of action potentials at about every two hours (Bancroft, 1989). GnRH then triggers the remainder of the hormonal axis. Note both the plus and minus signs associated with the feedback effects of hormones. Represented by a minus sign, testosterone inhibits the hypothalamic neurons that secrete GnRH.

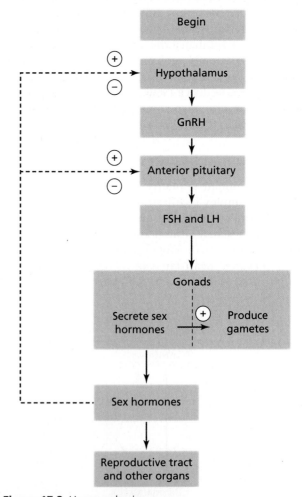

Figure 17.3 Hormonal axis.

Source: adapted from Vander *et al.* (1994) *Human Physiology*, Fig. 19-1, p. 649, reproduced with permission of The McGraw-Hill Companies, Inc.

However, acting on other regions of the hypothalamus, testosterone sensitizes neurons, as represented by the plus sign. This increases sexual motivation. In the male, there is only negative feedback at the anterior pituitary, so ignore the + sign there for the moment.

The female

The female reproductive system is characterized by its cycle of activity, the **oestrous cycle**, which, in humans, is termed the menstrual cycle (Beach, 1947). The rate of secretion of GnRH varies over the 28 day (approximately) menstrual period. There are also changes in responsiveness of the anterior pituitary to GnRH and of the ovaries to FSH and LH over the period.

At a certain time within this cycle the chances of pregnancy are greatest. These cycles are the result of interactions between the ovaries, anterior pituitary and hypothalamus. The ovaries secrete the hormones, oestrogen and progesterone. As with the male, the sequence starts with the secretion of GnRH from neurons within the hypothalamus. The feedback effect of oestrogen at the anterior pituitary and possibly also the hypothalamus is associated with minus and plus signs. This means that, at times during the monthly cycle, oestrogen excites activity and at other times it inhibits activity (Bancroft, 1989). Considering the phase represented by the + sign, such positive feedback is seen as a surge in LH preceding ovulation.

The discussion now turns to a comparative perspective on sexual behaviour and the role of hormones is described throughout.

Section summary

1 Androgens are a class of hormone that includes testosterone, whereas oestrogens are a class that includes oestradiol.

2 The hypothalamic pituitary gonadal axis starts in the hypothalamus and triggers hormonal release from the pituitary gland. Pituitary hormones then trigger release of hormones (androgens or oestrogens) at the gonads.

☞ Test your knowledge

17.3 Which hormone travels the shortest distance between release and site of action? (i) GnRH, (ii) FSH, (iii) LH.

Answer on page 466

A comparative perspective

Introduction

This section looks at general principles of sexual motivation and behaviour. The subsequent two sections concern primarily humans. Whether discussing males or females, rats or humans, some general features of Figure 17.1 will be central. For example, 'motivation' both influences, and is influenced by, peripheral events.

Stimulus factors

The stimulus of a conspecific plays a role in sexual motivation. However, the power is not simply intrinsic to the conspecific. Rather, stimuli are put into context and compared against memories of previous encounters (Figure 17.1). In this aspect, familiarity or novelty can play a role.

Pheromones

In rodents, olfaction strongly influences sexual behaviour (McCarthy and Albrecht, 1996). For most rodent species, removal of the olfactory bulbs eliminates both the motivation for, and the performance of, sexual behaviour. In humans, pheromones are detected by an olfactory organ, the vomeronasal organ (VNO) (Chapter 9) (Cutler *et al.*, 1998). The evidence on pheromones is based upon observations of a change in behaviour on being exposed to them. In humans, their efficacy is not necessarily associated with conscious awareness of their presence (Grammer *et al.*, 2005).

Conditioning

Figure 17.1 includes conditioning. Various species, e.g. the fish species the three-spine stickleback (*Gasterosteus aculeatus*), learn to associate a neutral stimulus with the presentation of an opposite-sex conspecific (Jenkins, 1997). The tendency for the male Japanese quail (*Coturnix japonica*), a bird species, to approach a female and the effectiveness of copulation are increased (e.g. a lowering of latency to copulate) by presenting a CS that has been paired with a sexually receptive female (Domjan *et al.*, 1998). Pavlovian conditioning appears to give an increase in fitness (Chapter 2), since exposure to the CS increased the amount of sperm ejaculated. It is difficult to study classical conditioning in humans under 'ecologically valid' conditions. However, if advertising and popular culture are anything to go by, a range of perfumes and other stimuli acquire incentive value by their pairing with attractive sexual stimuli.

The role of novelty

Depending upon the species, an animal, human or otherwise, that is apparently sexually satiated can sometimes be re-aroused sexually by changing the partner (Beach, 1947). This is an example of stimuli being placed in context and a role of memory of past partner(s). The phenomenon is named the **Coolidge effect**, after US President Calvin Coolidge (1872–1933).

The term 'Coolidge effect' can be used in the sense of revival from satiety by a partner change or more widely to refer to a preference for novelty. In male rats, presentation of a novel female is associated with strong activation of brain dopamine at the nucleus accumbens (Fiorino *et al.*, 1997). Species vary in the extent to which they exhibit the Coolidge effect (Dewsbury, 1981), e.g. Old-field mice, a monogamous species, do not show it (old is part of the species title not a reference to age!).

On functional grounds, the Coolidge effect relates to strategies for maximizing genetic perpetuation by increasing genetic diversity.

A personal angle

The Coolidge effect

The story, which might be apocryphal, is as follows (Dewsbury, 1981). President Coolidge (who was of Puritan background) and Mrs Coolidge were visiting a farm. They were taken on separate tours. On passing the chickens, Mrs Coolidge asked whether the rooster (i.e. male) copulates more than once per day. The answer was 'Dozens of times', to which Mrs Coolidge responded, 'Please tell that to the President'. When the President got to the pens and was told of the rooster, he asked, 'Same hen every time?' and got the reply, 'Oh no, Mr President, a different one each time'. The President then made the remark that destined him for a place in psychology, 'Tell that to Mrs Coolidge!'

A focus on the male rat

This section is primarily about rats but with an eye to extrapolation to other species. It looks at some determinants of sexual motivation and behaviour, first in males and then in females.

Appetitive and consummatory phases

There are two phases of sexual behaviour: (i) an appetitive ('preparatory') phase that brings male and female into contact and (ii) a consummatory phase, consisting of mounting and intromissions (penile thrusts) culminating in **ejaculation** (Beach and Whalen, 1959). Ejaculation is triggered by contractions of smooth muscle. Processes (i) and (ii) depend upon testosterone acting at the brain (Everitt, 1995).

The appetitive phase is associated with various measures: (i) the vigour of pursuit of a female, (ii) the preference for a location where a sexually receptive female is situated, (iii) the tendency to approach an environment where the male has been exposed to a female, i.e. a conditioned place preference (Chapter 15) and (iv) the intensity of operant behaviour rewarded with a conditional stimulus, a light (CS), that has been paired with presentation of a receptive female. Each measures the motivation towards a female but in the absence of copulatory behaviour.

In an operant task, responding for the light CS declines after castration (Everitt, 1995) and there is a loss of the preference for a place associated with a receptive female. Following replacement of testosterone, behaviour returns slowly to pre-castration levels. **Anti-androgens** are artificial substances that compete with androgens at the target sites but do not have the excitatory effects of androgens (Sitsen, 1988). They constitute antagonists to androgen. In rats, the effect of anti-androgens depends upon earlier experience. Sexual motivation is suppressed more in sexually naive than in sexually experienced animals.

Chapter 15 described a fracture line between appetitive and consummatory aspects. Lesions might disrupt one aspect but not the other. The following section looks at the evidence.

Brain structures

A number of brain structures, such as the amygdala, are implicated in sexual motivation. Neurons within these structures contain receptors for sex hormones, which sensitize the neurons.

Lesions of the basolateral region of the amygdala (Chapter 12) disrupt the capacity of a sexual stimulus to become a CS for which rats perform an operant task but do not disrupt mounting and intromission (i.e. consummatory behaviour) (Everitt *et al.*, 1989). The amygdala is involved with attaching emotional ('reward') value to CSs and its output is directed to the ventral striatum, for example, the nucleus accumbens (N.acc.). In the appetitive phase, dopamine is closely involved in the activity of the N.acc.

A region of hypothalamus (Chapter 5, Figure 5.31, p. 128), the medial preoptic area (mPOA), plays a crucial role in sexual behaviour. The mPOA is rich in receptors for testosterone and their occupation changes the characteristics of its neurons, e.g. so that they are more likely to be excited by sexual stimuli (Pfaff and Pfaffmann, 1969). The hypothalamus appears to coordinate spinal mechanisms underlying the reflexive consummatory sequence. Nuclei in the brain stem control the reflex-like acts of mounting and thrusting. By projections to the brain stem, the mPOA modulates their expression into a functionally coherent sequence.

A focus on the female rat

Appetitive and consummatory phases

A sexually motivated female exhibits appetitive behaviours towards a male. The term **proceptivity** describes this appetitive phase, i.e. the female's active approach and solicitation behaviour (e.g. running, hopping).

Corresponding to the consummatory phase, she tends to exhibit 'lordosis' (raising the rump and deflecting the tail, which facilitates intromission) in response to his tactile contact (Beach, 1947). The term **receptivity** is employed to describe the tendency to exhibit lordosis to the tactile stimulus. Motivational controls influence each of these behavioural outputs. In the wild, female rats play a role in the timing, pacing and termination of sexual contact.

Hypothalamic modulation of lordosis

Although lordosis is a response absent in most primates, it is useful as a 'model system' to study sexual behaviour. Lordosis depends upon (i) a trigger stimulus, tactile stimulation, and (ii) exposure to oestrogen and progesterone (i.e. sensitization) (Flanagan and McEwen, 1995). Loss of ovarian hormones is followed by an immediate loss of sexual behaviour (Beach, 1947).

The neurons that are sensitized by hormones are located in the hypothalamus, specifically in the ventromedial nucleus and some other nuclei (Flanagan and McEwen, 1995) and their activity has an excitatory effect on lordosis. Although, comparing species, the exact role of the hypothalamic neurons differs, neurons in the hypothalamus that are sensitive to sex hormones play a pivotal role in mating (Pfaff, 1989).

Figure 17.4 is a simplified version of the neural circuitry underlying lordosis. Tactile stimulation by the male excites somatosensory neurons (4), which transmit the information to the spinal cord. Through interneurons (5), this information is transmitted to motor neurons with cell bodies in the spinal cord (6), which activate the muscles that perform the response.

Information on the tactile stimulus ascends in the spinal cord to the brain, conveying information to neurons in the lower brain stem (7) and midbrain (8). Information descends from neurons in the hypothalamus (1), to the midbrain (2) and then to the lower brain

stem (3). From here, the message is conveyed down the spinal cord, where it has an effect on motor neurons, modulating the strength of the reflex.

When the neurons within the hypothalamus have been sensitized by oestrogen, this increases the probability that the female will show lordosis in response to the tactile stimulus. In effect, the hypothalamus allows the tactile stimulus to trigger the reflex at a time when the female is motivated and fertilization is possible.

Pair bonding

By contrast to the rat, some species form long-term **pair bonds**, which involve sharing some form of 'nest' (e.g. a burrow in the ground or a bed-sitter) and responsibility for bringing up offspring. In such species, there is a tendency towards monogamy, though this is not always an absolute. So-called 'extra-pair' mating is sometimes seen. Other species do not form pair bonds and show a more 'promiscuous' mating strategy.

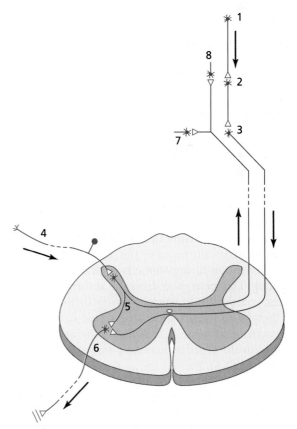

Figure 17.4 Neural circuitry underlying lordosis. (Afferent and efferent information is bilateral but for simplification only one side is shown. For convenience the spinal cord is shown as vertical, though the female would be in the horizontal position.)

Source: adapted from Pfaff (1989).

Looking at the natural lifestyle of different species has helped us to understand the neural mechanisms underlying sexual behaviour (Young and Wang, 2004). The Prairie vole (*Microtus ochrogaster*) forms pair bonds, exhibits monogamy and shares responsibility for care of offspring. Rather touchingly, fidelity is usually shown even 'beyond the grave': most who lose their mate do not acquire a new partner. By contrast, the Montane vole (*Microtus montanus*) shows neither monogamy nor shared responsibility.

A way of interpreting differences between species is in terms of variations on the 'basic design' exemplified by the rat. A focus of investigation is the motivation pathway projecting from the ventral tegmental area to the nucleus accumbens and prefrontal cortex (Chapter 15). In monogamous species, e.g. the Prairie vole, this link is selectively triggered by a *particular partner* (Young and Wang, 2004).

So how did the partner acquire this capacity and what sustains monogamy? In the Prairie vole, mating establishes the exclusive bond but sometimes just cohabitation is sufficient. Two neuropeptides are implicated: oxytocin and arginine vasopressin (AVP). Their experimental infusion promotes rapid pair bonding. In females, oxytocin is particularly effective, whereas in males AVP is most effective. In the female, infusion of antagonists to oxytocin into certain brain regions blocks the acquisition of the partner preference. This is true of the N.acc. and one of its target regions, the ventral pallidum, as well as the prefrontal cortex.

Compared with a non-monogamous species, the Prairie vole has a higher density of oxytocin receptors at the nucleus accumbens and some other regions. In these monogamous species, the targets of oxytocin correspond to brain regions involved more generally in reward. This suggests that, in evolutionary terms, these 'general' reward circuits as exemplified in the rat ('basic design') have been specifically tuned by the pair-bonding process.

The activation of dopamine is critical for pair-bond formation. Oxytocin modulates the ability of an opposite-sex conspecific to trigger activity in these regions and thereby to trigger appetitive sexual behaviour. In the female, activation of *both* dopamine and oxytocin receptors in the N.acc. is necessary for pair-bond formation (Figure 17.5). Part (a) shows the 'basic design' of a non-monogamous species such as the rat. There is a straightforward link between a DA neuron with cell body in the VTA and a neuron of the N.acc. Parts (b) and (c) show a monogamous species. In part (b), oxytocin has not yet exerted its effect. In part (c) oxytocin occupies receptors and thereby modulates activity in the pathway.

By means of gene transfer, researchers converted individuals of a promiscuous species, the Meadow vole, into animals showing pair bonding (Lim *et al.*, 2004). To do

this, the genes that code for receptors to arginine vasopressin taken from Prairie voles were injected into the brains of Meadow voles.

So what triggers the release of oxytocin? The presence of an opposite-sex conspecific does, as in cohabitation or in the first mating. That is, oxytocin mediates social recognition. So, the incentive motivation properties of dopamine activation become coupled with a particular partner signature.

Satiety

How does sexual satiety arise? Following orgasm(s)/ejaculation, satiety occurs: a feedback effect on motivation (Figure 17.1).

What lowers motivation is not a reversal of hormonal sensitization. Satiety is not caused by a fall in testosterone level. Nor in males is it caused by loss of seminal fluids as such. Rats with seminal vesicles removed still show normal motivation (Beach and Wilson, 1963).

Figure 17.5 Sequence of neurons showing possible role of oxytocin. (a) Non-monogamous species with a relatively uncomplicated link from VTA neuron to N.acc. neuron. (b) and (c) Monogamous species, showing modulation of dopaminergic link by oxytocin. In (b) dopaminergic neuron active but little DA release and (c) as for (b) but occupation of oxytocin receptors permits DA release.

Extrapolating from evidence in rats, and depending upon species and sex, orgasm/ejaculation can be quickly followed by active inhibition on sexual motivation (Rodriguez-Manzo and Fernandez-Guasti, 1994). This involves changes in serotonergic and noradrenergic neurotransmission.

GABA prolongs satiety shown post-ejaculation (Andersson and Wagner, 1995). The levels of the neurohormone oxytocin increase sharply at the time of ejaculation in human males (Murphy *et al.*, 1987) and might play some role in the inhibitory process. Oxytocinergic neurons appear to modulate ascending signals from the genitals (Murphy, 1993a). High levels of the hormone prolactin inhibit sexual behaviour and prolactin levels are elevated following orgasm, so this might contribute to satiety (Krüger *et al.*, 2005).

This section has outlined general principles of the organization of sexual motivation and behaviour. The following two sections focus on human sexuality.

Section summary

1 The Coolidge effect describes re-arousal of sexual motivation by a change of partner.

2 Acting on the brain, androgens play a role in the maintenance of sexual motivation, an activational effect.

3 Rats exhibit appetitive and consummatory phases of sexual behaviour. In females, a distinction is between proceptivity and receptivity.

4 The medial preoptic area of the hypothalamus plays a role in the organization of male rat copulatory behaviour.

5 In female rats, oestrogen-sensitive neurons in the hypothalamus provide modulation of lordosis.

6 In monogamous species, neuropeptides that are triggered by the particular partner lock into interaction with a general incentive motivation process.

7 The reduction in sexual motivation that occurs at ejaculation/orgasm appears to be the result of inhibition.

☞ Test your knowledge

17.4 In Figure 17.4, contrast the effects of activity in neurons 3 and 5, as far as activity in neuron 6 is concerned.

Answer on page 466

Human sexual desire, motivation and arousal

Introduction

With the help of Figure 17.1, this section considers such things as the role of hormones in desire (link 7). There is interdependence between desire and response: the genital response depends upon desire and, in turn, influences desire. The section after this one focuses on the genital response.

Triggers to desire

What are the features of a partner that trigger human sexual motivation/desire? Why do certain individuals attract us more than others? There are, of course, cultural variations in what is attractive such as, in some African cultures, the insertion of objects to swell the lips. There are also idiosyncratic tastes, such as being turned on by someone wearing spectacles. This has nothing to do with 'evolutionary design': wearing glasses, a recent development in evolutionary time, signals little more than relatively bad eyesight!

Brain processes

Insights derive from neuroimaging, brain stimulation and looking at the effects of brain damage. There is not yet a 'working diagram' indicating what each structure contributes to sexual motivation and behaviour but some strong pointers are available and a few are described here.

Neuroimaging

As people are sexually aroused (e.g. by viewing sexually explicit images), activity in different structures can be linked to:

1 understanding of how parts of the brain organize sexuality;

2 reports of subjective sexual feelings of desire and arousal;

3 the reactions of the genitals (a measure of the autonomic output of the brain).

Of course, sexual desire and arousal are not usually put into effect as overt behaviour, especially when participants' heads are held still in an apparatus! So, processes that underlie inhibition on sexual expression might also be identified.

In a study on men, a number of brain regions known to be involved in motivation were excited by sexual stimuli,

Evolutionary psychology

Desire

Evolutionary psychology (EP) argues that beauty is only partly 'in the eye of the beholder'. Rather, people tend to find attractive that which is most likely to help their genes to perpetuate (Little *et al.*, 2002). Thus, at the time in the menstrual cycle when there is the highest chance of becoming pregnant, women's faces and body odours are judged as most attractive to men (Roberts *et al.*, 2004; Singh and Bronstad, 2001).

There are universal standards of attraction that cut across social and cultural divides (Rhodes and Zebrowitz, 2002). Can EP identify reasons why there should be universal standards, such as favouring symmetry of the face? In principle, it could just be an arbitrary convention to which we all subscribe. By favouring certain characteristics, offspring will tend to be produced that will inherit the desirable characteristics and so will be relatively attractive to potential partners. Could there be more to it than this?

Males tend to favour youthfulness and clear skin in a woman's face. EP argues that youthfulness correlates with fertility and a clear skin correlates with health and lack of parasites. These represent unconscious influences. According to EP, women interpret information from a man's face in assessing such things as his reliability as a partner in terms of care for offspring. What is perceived as attractive in a man varies as a function of the menstrual cycle and the nature of the most likely interaction with him – as long-term partner or short-term 'fling' (Scheib, 2001).

Could it be that attractive characteristics, such as a reasonable symmetry in the face, are correlated with health and reproductive potential? Some theorists argue that symmetry is indicative of 'good genes' and a healthy development (an 'honest signal'), whereas facial asymmetry or abnormality is a signal of deviation from optimal development.

Of course, those having the money can resort to plastic surgery and thereby 'cheat': their enhanced outward phenotype is not an 'honest' signal of their genotype or internal phenotype. Critics of EP suggest that there is little evidence indicating a correlation between looks and health (see Rhodes and Zebrowitz, 2002). Even if there were, it might mean only that attractive people attract better social support.

---

e.g. the N.acc. (Redouté *et al.*, 2000). The level of activation in the right orbitofrontal cortex correlated with 'perceived sexual arousal' and genital swelling. Similarly, activation in regions of the anterior cingulate cortex (ACC) correlated positively with genital swelling. Redouté *et al.* suggested that, given the known neural connections, this reflects a causal process: ACC → autonomic output. The ACC receives input from the amygdala, a region associated with computing motivational signals.

Participants reported that, triggered by exposure to the sexually explicit images, they felt (p. 172) 'the urge to act out their sexual desire' (Redouté *et al.*, 2000). Activity in parts of the ACC correlated not only with penile swelling but also with the intensity of perceived subjective arousal. Such evidence suggested that ACC activity correlates with 'the initiation and the motivation of goal-directed behaviours' (p. 173). So what could be the biological embodiment of inhibition on action? Redouté *et al.* suggested that ACC activity might in part reflect such conflict of goals. They also note that the basal ganglia (Chapter 10) play a role in conflict resolution and the associated inhibition on unsuccessful candidates for gaining the control of behaviour. Indeed,

in their study, high activity was recorded in one such region: the head of the right caudate nucleus.

In non-human species, regions of the hypothalamus have been closely identified with sexual function (see Karama *et al.*, 2002), which suggests that it could be worth investigating in humans. There are reports of differences in the size of the preoptic nucleus of the hypothalamus (Figure 5.31, p. 128), between men and women. There is also evidence that men are more turned on instantaneously by erotic stimuli than are women (see Karama *et al.*, 2002). Could there be differences in activity in regions of the hypothalamus, when comparing men and women as they view erotic stimuli?

Using brain neuroimaging, it is possible to see whether (i) there is any correspondence with non-humans and (ii) any gender differences (Karama *et al.*, 2002). Both men and women reported sexual arousal to erotic scenes, the women less intensely than the men. Compared with viewing neutral images (non-sexual scenes), in both men and women sexual stimuli triggered activation in a number of brain regions, including the orbitofrontal cortex, the amygdala, ventral striatum, the anterior cingulate cortex and the insula. So, in general, there is a considerable overlap in the brain regions activated in the two genders. The insula is closely associated with the ANS and so might have a role in the autonomic output triggered by sexual arousal. It is also involved with bodily sensations and could form a basis of the erotic aspect of this.

In males but not females, there was a significant activation of the hypothalamus. Looking across the sample of males, their subjective arousal correlated with their level of activation of the hypothalamus. Studies indicate a positive correlation between activity of the hypothalamus and penile swelling (Redouté et al., 2000). At least with today's technology and understanding, clearer biological correlates of subjective sexual arousal can be found in men than in women (Karama et al., 2002).

One study employed images (couples engaged in sexual behaviour) that were ranked equally by men and women in the degree of arousal they triggered and their attractiveness (Hamann et al., 2004). Even so, males exhibited a higher level of activation in the amygdala and hypothalamus. If such activity is not a biological embodiment of arousal, then it is a measure of what? Hamann et al. note the greater willingness of males to react to sexual stimuli with immediate approach. So, such activity in the amygdala might reflect appetitive incentive motivation and thereby males' greater imagined intention to proceed. The signal in the hypothalamus could then reflect increased input from the amygdala as the signal proceeds en route to autonomic activation.

As just described, sexual stimuli activate a number of brain structures and thereby trigger conscious sexual desire. Might sexual stimuli still activate these structures, even when they are presented at such brief durations that they fail to reach conscious awareness? Childress et al. (2008) presented very brief (33 milliseconds) images of sexual stimuli ('target stimuli') to men followed immediately by a longer neutral stimulus (467 ms) that produced 'backward masking' of the target stimulus. As a control, brief (33 ms) neutral target stimuli were also presented followed by the long masking stimulus. The masking stimulus meant that participants consciously perceived the masking stimulus, while the target stimulus did not reach conscious awareness (see also Figure 12.3, p. 318). A considerable degree of overlap was found between structures triggered at times of conscious desire and by 'unseen' sexual stimuli.

Childress et al. suggest that there could be a clinical implication of this result (p. 4): 'The brain can strike up a prelude to passion in an instant, outside awareness, and without heavy policing from frontal regulatory regions.' The frontal regions mentioned here are those assumed to play a role in offering restraint on sexual behaviour based upon anticipated long-term negative consequences of sexual behaviour.

Researchers have employed neuroimaging to examine changes in regional cerebral blood flow (rCBF) in response to genital stimulation by the participant's partner (Holstege and Georgiadis 2004; Holstege et al., 2003). Regions of most intense activation included one containing the ventral tegmental area (VTA), a midbrain structure. The VTA area is also activated in the 'rush' associated with heroin and cocaine injection, pointing to a similar biological basis to sexual reward. Indeed, people taking these drugs often use sexual descriptions for the 'rush' of drugs. Although the participants had their eyes closed, activation was seen in the visual cortex of men, presumably reflecting use of the visual imagination.

Figure 17.6 shows the changes in activity of some structures during sexual stimulation and then orgasm (Georgiadis and Kortekaas, 2010). Note activation of the primary somatosensory cortex at a region corresponding to the representation of the genitals. Also, note activation of the cerebellum at orgasm, which implicates this region in more than motor control. The observed effect could

Figure 17.6 Changes in regional cerebral blood flow in response to genital stimulation and orgasm. Start of the shaft of arrows indicates location of neuroimage ('slice'). Scale shows reference activity (0), increased activation (7, yellow,) and decreased activity (–7, pale blue). Some regions of particular interest here are: Amy, amygdala; CbA, cerebellum; OFC, orbitofrontal cortex ; SI, primary somatosensory cortex; Thal-Mb, transition zone between thalamus and midbrain; ventr. TL, ventral temporal lobe.

Source: Georgiadis and Kortekaas (2010, Fig. 11.2, p. 185).

underlie autonomic effects. There was deactivation of the amygdala (as seen also in 'drug rushes') and ventral temporal lobe throughout. What could be the significance of this? Amygdala activation seems to cease once the person is beyond the appetitive phase of sexual searching and allocating sexual salience. In addition, the result might point to a suppression of negative emotional processing that accompanies sexual contact. Note activation of the PAG, a region associated with opioid-based analgesia (Chapter 14,). With orgasm, there was deactivation of the orbitofrontal cortex. So, it appears that increasing intensity of sexual experience corresponds to a shift of weight from cortical to subcortical activity.

Others report activation of the paraventricular nucleus of the hypothalamus (PVN) at orgasm (Komisaruk et al., 2008). PVN activity is the trigger for the release of oxytocin. Not altogether surprisingly, real and faked orgasms showed rather different patterns of brain activity.

Electrical stimulation, disruption and damage

Studies of sexual function in brain-damaged individuals lead to an inconsistent picture (Baird et al., 2007). This is true of damage to much of the temporal lobes. However, within the temporal lobes, the balance of evidence (e.g. from electrical stimulation) points to the amygdala as serving a role in attaching emotional, including sexual value, to stimuli. In humans, features of a sexual partner appear to be computed cortically, synthesized at the temporal cortex and acquire emotional significance at the amygdala (Gloor, 1986; Gorman, 1994). At the amygdala there are receptors for 'sex hormones' (Adkins-Regan et al., 1997).

Patients with epilepsy focused on the temporal lobe can experience a range of emotions triggered by epileptic discharge (Gloor, 1986). These include feelings similar to real sexual contact, related to a particular situation and in some cases resulting in orgasm. A relatively high frequency of sexual deviation is found among male temporal lobe epilepsy patients (Kolársky et al., 1967). Brain lesions present early in life might disrupt expression of normal programmes of sexual emotional labelling and produce abnormal links between perception and motivation. Changes in sexual orientation have been reported following lesions of the temporal lobe (Miller et al., 1986).

The right hemisphere appears to be more tuned to extract the emotional significance of stimuli than is the left (Chapter 12) and to be dominant for triggering desire. For people suffering a unilateral stroke, loss of sexual desire is greater if the lesion is in the right as opposed to the left hemisphere (Lundberg, 1992). In principle, this might be due, say, to depression subsequent to the stroke. However, depression is more frequently seen in damage to the left hemisphere

(Chapter 12). The cortical–amygdala links of the right brain might have more involvement in mediating information on sexuality.

Psychosurgical techniques of selectively lesioning brain structures have been employed to lower sexual motivation in people with deviant hypersexuality, one target being the ventromedial hypothalamus (Roeder et al., 1972). However, damage to the hypothalamus as part of a disease state has also been reported to lead to hypersexuality, suggesting that different hypothalamic nuclei serve antagonistic roles in sexual behaviour (Baird et al., 2007).

Restraint on emotionally coloured behaviour appears to involve the prefrontal cortex (Chapter 12). There are reports of a lifting of sexual inhibition and increased sexual expression in patients suffering from frontal damage (Miller et al., 1986), including those given frontal lobotomy for intractable emotional distress (Baird et al., 2007; Freeman, 1973). However, it is unclear whether this represents a general disinhibition of behaviour or something more specific to sexual behaviour.

The excitatory effects of the so-called 'sex hormones'

This section looks more closely at the link in Figure 17.1 that is represented by arrow 7.

Men

Extrapolating from non-humans, androgens sensitize regions of the brain that underlie sexual motivation (Everitt and Bancroft, 1991) and orgasm (Komisaruk et al., 2008). In men, androgens appear to focus interest on erotic targets and to trigger desire. Loss of androgens leads to a decline in sexual interest (Skakkebaek et al., 1981). However, an adequate level of androgens cannot compensate for deficiencies in other factors. With increasing age, most men show a slowly decreasing sexual capacity, which parallels a decrease in testosterone secretion (Bancroft, 1988). However, differences among individuals are large.

After removal of the testes (e.g. because of cancer), androgen level falls rapidly, within hours. However, the level probably does not reach zero since some androgens are produced by the adrenal gland (Bancroft, 1989). There is usually a reduction in, and then loss of, sexual motivation. This is as measured by subjective reports of the frequency with which sexual thoughts occur and the arousal associated with them. If androgens are replaced, there is a restoration of normal erotic thoughts, in frequency, content and quality (Bancroft, 1989). However, individual differences are great, with previous experience, cognitions and expectations being important (Beach, 1947).

Women

Oestrogens and androgens are involved in women's sexual behaviour (Mazenod *et al.*, 1988). Androgens are secreted from the adrenal gland (Bancroft, 1989) and ovaries (Komisaruk *et al.*, 2008). Receptors for these hormones are located in various brain regions that are involved in emotion and sexual motivation (e.g. amygdala) (Sherwin, 1991). Also, the brain contains enzymes that convert androgens to oestrogens. Boosting androgen level can increase sexual motivation (Money *et al.*, 1988), whereas anti-androgens, given to women to counter acne, reduce it. As with men, testosterone appears to exert its primary effect at cognitive and motivational processes of desire and fantasy.

If androgens play a major role, it might explain how sexual motivation can continue after menopause when oestrogen levels drop sharply. Supplementary androgen given at this time increases sensitivity of the amygdala (van Wingen *et al.*, 2010) and improves sexuality (Mazenod *et al.*, 1988).

Over the menstrual cycle, the levels of oestrogen and testosterone in the blood vary (Dabbs, 2000). Does sexual motivation vary in phase with hormones? Some found little variation (Myers and Morokoff, 1986), whereas others found a relationship to general well-being and sexual activity (Bancroft, 1989). Both variables were lowest in the week prior to menstruation and highest in the week following. Using erotic stimuli and neuroimaging, Gizewski *et al.* (2006) observed activation in brain regions associated with sexual motivation (e.g. anterior cingulate cortex and insula) mid-cycle as compared with the menstrual phase. Subjective rating of arousal correlated with the neuroimaging results. Using electromyography (Chapter 5), Mass *et al.* (2009) studied the muscles controlling the smile reaction of women. In response to erotic imagery, the smile was larger at the point in the cycle when conception chances were highest.

Of course, humans have unique insight into their biological condition and are responsive to cultural norms and taboos. Women know about their current biological state and the possibility of pregnancy, which might complicate or partly mask the effects of fluctuations in hormonal contribution on the level of sexual interest.

Compared with younger women, postmenopausal women have a lower level of androgens. However, in about half of postmenopausal women, the ovaries continue to secrete testosterone. Androgens seem to have a crucial role in female sexual motivation before and after menopause (Leiblum *et al.*, 1983).

Hormone replacement therapy offers the hope of compensating for the loss of hormones at menopause or following removal of the ovaries from premenopausal

women but is not without complications (Cutler and Genovese-Stone, 1998). Some studies have shown increased sexual enjoyment following this procedure, e.g. a heightened libido (Mazenod *et al.*, 1988). Following surgical removal of the ovaries, women experience a sharp drop in testosterone levels (Simon *et al.*, 2005). This appears to be implicated in low sexual desire, while supplementary hormones delivered by means of a skin patch can help to revive activation of brain regions underlying motivation to erotic stimulation, as well restore desire and satisfaction (Archer *et al.*, 2006).

Evolutionary psychology

A pheromonal social link?

In a controlled study, women's sexual desire and fantasy were found to be increased by exposure to the odours of other women who happened to be breastfeeding (Spencer *et al.*, 2004). What might EP say about it? In a social species, the presence of a breastfeeding woman might be indicative of an availability of nutrients and therefore a good time for mating.

Sexual desire and love

People vary in the extent to which sexual desire is associated with romantic love for one individual. So how does romantic love interact with sexual desire? Romantic attachment appears to have a different biological basis from that of sexual desire, the former sharing more in common with caregiver–infant attachment (Bartels and Zeki, 2004). People sometimes show romantic 'crushes' in the absence of sexual desire, so it seems that two somewhat distinct systems merge in the case of romance with sexual desire (Diamond, 2004). In evolutionary terms, it could be that a system underlying bonding between infant and caregiver was adapted ('co-opted') to serve monogamy.

The Prairie and Montane voles (see earlier in the present chapter) might each serve as a suitable role model for a different section of the human population! Could the Prairie vole be a model for human pair-bond formation? Young and Wang (2004) acknowledge that it would be premature to claim this. However, plasma oxytocin levels (the neurochemical involved in pair-bond formation) are elevated at the time of orgasm in women, whereas sexual arousal elevates plasma AVP levels in men.

Evolutionary psychology

Don't forget phylogeny

Chapter 1 introduced functional and evolutionary (phylogenetic) explanations. To remind you of phylogeny, the vampire bat is special in that it is a blood-sucker, a line of evolution not evident in its near relatives. The phylogenetic explanation relates to such questions as:

1   When in evolution did a particular characteristic of a species first appear?

2   Which species exhibit the characteristic?

Can evolutionary links be formed between the species that show the characteristic (if there is more than one such species)? Evolutionary psychology has predominantly concerned itself with functional explanations at the expense of evolutionary/phylogenetic explanations (Panksepp *et al.*, 2002b), and this is reflected in the present text.

Human sexuality raises questions of phylogeny concerning when its features first appeared in evolution. How did their appearance relate to the problems that they solved (Eastwick, 2009; Fraley *et al.*, 2005)? Are they features unique to humans or did they also appear in our near relatives? Take, for example, human sexual desire and attraction. Sexual attraction is also evident in our nearest ape relatives and it seems most likely that we inherited this characteristic from the evolutionary ancestors that we share with these relatives. It is surely very old in terms of evolution, probably as old as sexual reproduction itself. Similarly, the hormonal contribution to sexual motivation and reproduction is something that appears to go back far in evolution.

By contrast, life-long attachment ('pair-bonding'), as a feature associated with sexual behaviour, is not something shared with our nearest ape relatives. It appears also in a number of other species, e.g. most species of bird (Maestripieri and Roney, 2006). Given its *independent* appearance in evolution, pair-bonding in birds and humans would be said to be analogous rather than homologous (Chapter 5, p. 131).

So what were the pressures for pair-bonding in humans? One possibility is the following. Humans are a very altricial species (Chapter 6), meaning that they require a long time to reach maturity. An increasing pressure to be 'brainy' is associated with increasing time in development to reach maturity of the brain. The demands of child-rearing meant that this could only be achieved by increasing male investment in the relationship (Eastwick, 2009; Fraley *et al.*, 2005). Hence the system of infant–parent attachment was co-opted for mother–father attachment. Indeed, in pair-bonding species, males tend to make a relatively large investment in rearing offspring.

Maestripieri and Roney (2006) note that humans and other pair-bonding species show some common features associated with bonding, such as distress at breaking a bond. This makes it unlikely that human pair-bonding is a socially determined 'product of modern culture' (p. 125).

Within evolution, a phylogenetically old feature can prove somewhat counter-productive alongside a newly emergent feature. When this occurs, rather than discarding the old feature, evolution tinkers with what is there already. Additional new 'inventions' can emerge and improve the fit between phylogenetically old and new processes.

To exemplify this, it might be assumed that high levels of testosterone were adaptive prior to the emergence phylogenetically of pair-bonding. They might be adaptive also for individuals in the 'pair-bonding design' up to the time of establishing a pair bond. However, after this, Eastwick (2009) suggests that the harmony of the pair bond might be disrupted by excessive levels of testosterone, which could take the parties off into copulations outside the pair bond. He cites evidence that the formation of pair bonds is associated with a lowering of testosterone levels in human males, suggesting inhibition.

Another feature of human sexuality, which appears to be largely, if not exclusively, species-specific, is our capacity to manage and restrain sexual attraction in the service of long-term competing goals. This might become particularly valuable in pair-bonding, when demands of infants often need to dominate, and is described as 'self-control' (Eastwick, 2009). It would seem to require the emergence in evolution of brain circuitry underlying goals and inhibition based on *representations* of future events (processing which calls heavily on the prefrontal cortex), as well as language and culture.

In women, orgasm, or a series of them, is usually followed by satiety. This corresponds to a loss of physiological signs of arousal, e.g. heart-rate comes down to a normal level as does genital vasocongestion. In general, a woman's capacity for multiple orgasms is larger than that of men (Darling *et al.*, 1991). This suggests that inhibition takes effect more slowly in women though, of course, any loss of the genital reaction has a less obvious impact. It appears that neural circuits in the brain organize orgasm with associated outflows to the genitals and to hedonic circuitry. Vivid orgasmic imagery can occur even in the absence of a spinally mediated reaction, as in the dreams of patients with paraplegia. How much the link via the vagus nerve is involved is an interesting question.

What is the function of female orgasm? First, the muscular reaction might assist the movement of sperm and thereby increase the chances of fertilization. Second, the emotional aspect, coloured by intense pleasure, encourages further sexual behaviour.

A personal angle

Orgasmic dreams

M.M., a 32-year-old woman from Baltimore, fell and broke her spine (Money, 1960). She was paralyzed from the waist down. M.M. exhibited immense perseverance and was able to care for a 6-year-old son from her wheelchair. M.M. had erotic dreams and reported (p. 378): 'in my dreams I have always reached a climax and that's more than has actually happened to me since I've been like this'. There might have been an intact source of feedback from the genitals that excluded the spine (e.g. in the vagus nerve) or the intrinsic organization of the brain might on its own have provided the biological basis of the experience.

Avoiding dichotomies

It is apparent from Figure 17.7 that a dichotomy of whether genital arousal is *either* reflexive *or* psychogenic is misleading (Sachs, 1995). The process has reflex-like and psychogenic aspects, which interact.

Activity in neurons 6 and 7 depend in large part upon cognitive factors. On the excitatory side (6), these would be such things as the attractiveness of the partner, feedback on behaviour and use of the imagination.

On the descending inhibitory side (7), there might be anxiety aroused by guilt or the perception of failure. For example, if the male perceives erectile failure, this can trigger a vicious circle that removes the parasympathetic activity and triggers sympathetic activity.

Problems with the sexual response

Erectile dysfunction

The term **erectile dysfunction** (**ED**) refers to a failure to maintain an erection. Among sexual disorders in males, ED is the most common (Bancroft, 1989). There is a comparable condition in women, a failure of engorgement of the vaginal area. ED can reflect a lack of interest in the partner. It can follow damage to the neurons underlying the erectile process, in the brain, spinal cord or peripheral nerves. Another cause is the side effects of certain antidepressants, which have an anticholinergic effect that opposes vasodilation (Ellison, 1998).

Suppose that there is an inadequate excitatory activity in the descending pathway, represented by neuron 6 of Figure 17.7. This might be due to neural damage. However, the neurons might be intact but there could be a problem in producing the appropriate excitation in the brain. This is often referred to as a 'psychological' or 'psychogenic' cause. There might be excessive sympathetic activity associated with, say, anxiety, which exerts a descending inhibition on the erectile process (Krane *et al.*, 1989).

The cause of ED can be associated with the hydraulics of the circulation. Anything which impairs the blood supply to the penis will be dysfunctional. For example, there can be local blocking of blood vessels, caused by fatty deposits (Bancroft, 1989).

In explaining ED, we sometimes see a dichotomy. ED is said to reflect *either* an **organic cause**, that is to say, a recognized physiological problem (e.g. blocked arteries), *or* a **psychogenic cause**, i.e. defined, by exclusion, as something that does not have such an identifiable basis (e.g. depression or marital conflict). However, this dichotomy can be misleading (Sachs, 1995). In some cases, the *initial* cause could reflect either source but, once the problem has appeared, it is likely that interacting factors will be involved.

Spinal cord damage

Damage to the spinal cord can interrupt ascending and descending messages between brain and genitals and disrupt sexual function. There is a loss of sensation from the body corresponding to that part below the level of the break, as well as loss of top-down ('psychological') influence on erection. However, some erectile capacity might remain as a result of intact reflex pathways, e.g.

$1 \rightarrow 2 \rightarrow 3 \rightarrow 4 \rightarrow 5$ in Figure 17.7. Indeed, some men with a total break of the spinal cord can exhibit erection (Money, 1960).

A personal angle

A paraplegic patient

In Baltimore, A.S, a 23-year-old male, had suffered a spinal break (Money, 1960). A.S. had been mistakenly shot by a policeman, was paralyzed and lacking sensation from below the waist. He remained stoic, without resentment and was uninhibited in discussing sexual matters. Asked about changes in erectile patterns, A.S. replied (p. 375):

> Well the biggest thing, you don't control it, no more. It controls itself. At times you may be sitting down and playing cards or something and you won't have women or sex or nothing on your mind, and all of a sudden it rises on you. And then at times you can be – at times that you want it, it won't harden up on you for nothing.

On the occasions that A.S. was able to secure an erection it was by tactile stimulation of the penis. A.S. was able to have intercourse, noting that during this (p. 375):

> All the time it's going on up in your head you're figuring on what you could do if you could still have the movements of your hips and discharge and all like that, instead of feeling nothing happens.

Section summary

1 Swelling of local blood vessels causes penile and clitoral erection and vaginal arousal.

2 Small arteries that supply blood to the genitals are normally constricted. Sexual excitement is associated with relaxation of smooth muscle in the walls of vessels and thereby dilation.

3 A combination of local (i.e. genital) and central events determines the activity of the neurons that innervate the smooth muscles of the genitals.

4 Activity of sympathetic and parasympathetic nervous systems determines the contraction and relaxation of the smooth muscle.

5 Erectile dysfunction can be caused by local and central factors in interaction.

6 A condition in females that is analogous to erectile dysfunction is a failure of the genitals to attain engorgement.

 Test your knowledge

17.6 In Figure 17.7, which neuron(s) is/are autonomic preganglionic neurons?

17.7 With respect to Figure 17.7, consider an effect described in the text in the section 'Physiology of the female response – Genital arousal'. Oestrogen would be expected to affect activity of which neuron? (i) 1, (ii) 4, (iii) 5.

Answers on page 466

Chemical interventions and sexual behaviour

Introduction

The use of an **aphrodisiac**, a substance intended to increase sexual desire and performance, can be dated back some 3000-4000 years in Hindu culture (Shamloul, 2010). Drugs can target sexual performance by improving the levels of engorgement at the genitals. Although a distinction between desire and performance is valid in terms of target, for reasons evident in Figure 17.1 targeting either could have consequences at both.

Chemicals that target dopamine

Dopamine (DA) has a role in sexual motivation and behaviour (Krüger *et al.*, 2005) though there is not agreement on its exact role (Paredes and Ågmo, 2004). In erectile dysfunction, DA agonists, such as apomorphine, improve sexual functioning by facilitating the brain's signals to erection (Hagemann *et al.*, 2003). There can be hypersexuality and even sexual addiction following use of L-dopa (a precursor of DA) and agonists at dopamine receptors (Chapters 10 and 18; Kim *et al.*, 2008; see also Sitsen, 1988). Some DA reuptake blockers increase sexual desire in women (Bartlik *et al.*, 1999a). Evidence points to a role of dopamine in orgasm, acting as a neuromodulator of the effect of sensory stimulation. DA-enhancing drugs are said to intensify the pleasure of orgasm (Komisaruk *et al.*, 2010). Thus, the view that DA affects the wanting phase of behaviour without the liking phase (Robinson and Berridge, 1993) needs some qualification. The result here suggests a role for DA in *liking* sex, as well as *wanting* sex. Antagonists at dopamine D2 and D4 receptors interfere with orgasm.

Chemicals that target serotonin

In men and women, a side effect of certain selective serotonin reuptake inhibitors (SSRIs), e.g. clomipramine, is sometimes that of blocking ejaculation/orgasm (Komisaruk *et al.*, 2008) and a reduction in desire. However, by the same token, such drugs can also alleviate premature ejaculation. Enhancing serotonergic activity in rats reduces measures of sexual motivation (Ågmo *et al.*, 2004). Such evidence suggests an inhibitory role of serotonin in the control of sexual behaviour.

Alcohol

Men and women report that alcohol increases sexual desire and pleasure (Van Thiel *et al.*, 1988). Investigators gave participants doses of alcohol and their reactions to an erotic film were measured. For males, reactions were increased heart-rate and arousal, the latter indexed by self-report (Rosen, 1991). At low doses, a slight increase in penile swelling was observed but, conforming to the popular image, larger doses had an inhibitory effect. Males sometimes exhibited a lower engorgement but still reported that they believed alcohol to be increasing engorgement. Parallels with the effect of alcohol on actual and imagined driving skills come to mind.

A personal angle

Shakespeare's insight

If ever there were a good observer of behaviour, it was surely Shakespeare, insight into the sexual response being no exception. In *Macbeth* (Act Two, Scene Three), the effect of alcohol is described:

Lechery, sir, it provokes, and unprovokes; it provokes the desire, but it takes away the performance. Therefore much drink may be said to be an equivocator with lechery; it makes him, and it mars him . . .

Women were asked for subjective reports of arousal and their vaginal state was measured objectively. Blood flow to the genitals decreased as a function of increasing quantities of alcohol. However, levels of alcohol and subjective arousal increased together.

Short-term and long-term effects of drugs

Drugs have short- and long-term effects, which might act in the same direction or be different. There are two detrimental effects of alcohol (ethanol) on erectile capacity. First, as just noted, a short-term negative (but reversible) effect is seen. In alcoholics, there is a more serious long-term deterioration, which is seen even during abstinent periods. This loss might be attributed in part to reduced levels of testosterone, the production of which is inhibited by alcohol (Van Thiel *et al.*, 1988). Also, alcohol can damage central and peripheral neurons involved in erection.

Ethanol exerts inhibitory effects at several locations on the hypothalamic pituitary gonadal axis (Figure 17.3), e.g. hypothalamus and pituitary. It also decreases the density of gonadotropin (i.e. LH and FSH) receptors at the testes.

The immediate effect of drugs such as cannabis can be to heighten desire, arousal and enjoyment. A significant percentage of those using cannabis and cocaine do so for this purpose (Buffum *et al.*, 1988). However, these drugs and nicotine lower the production of testosterone. Hence, the long-term effect of taking them in large amounts can be to lower erectile capacity. Given the tendency to observe immediate rather than delayed effects, users might well emphasize sexually stimulating effects.

Viagra

Viagra and similar drugs treat erectile dysfunction. Viagra enhances the action of nitric oxide (NO) at the penis. In Figure 17.7, imagine stimuli acting through neurons 2 and/or 6 and then 3, 4 and 5 to trigger the release of NO, which, via a further chemical process, induces smooth muscle relaxation (Goldstein *et al.*, 1998). Viagra does not trigger muscle relaxation in the absence of sexual excitation and so spontaneous erection is not seen. Viagra is also effective in heightening sexual feelings in women (Bartlik *et al.*, 1999b).

Section summary

1 The chemical content of alcohol and beliefs on its efficacy influence the sexual response.

2 Large amounts of alcohol can have a detrimental effect on erection. Alcohol lowers testosterone secretion and can damage neurons.

3 Various drugs are associated with a short-term positive effect on sexual arousal and enjoyment but might have a long-term detrimental effect on performance.

4 Viagra enhances the effects of nitric oxide on smooth muscle relaxation.

☞ Test your knowledge

17.8 With regard to Figure 17.7, an agonist acting at which neural junctions would serve as a possible treatment for erectile dysfunction?

Answer on page 466   WEB

Sexual orientation

Introduction

In general, comparing homosexual and heterosexual men, no significant differences in testosterone levels have been established. Evidence is mixed on hormonal differences between homosexual and heterosexual women, some studies reporting higher levels of testosterone in homosexual women (Gladue, 1988). Even if hormonal differences were to appear, we could not necessarily conclude a direction of causality (hormone) → (orientation), since lifestyle differences might cause the hormonal change. There might be differences in sensitivity of neural tissue to circulating hormone or there might be early developmental differences in organization of neural structures.

Neural structure

Evidence on differences in certain brain regions has been obtained at autopsy (Figure 17.8). Homosexual and heterosexual men appear to differ in the structure of the third interstitial nucleus of the anterior hypothalamus

(LeVay, 1991). This area is smaller in women than in men and is smaller in homosexual males than in heterosexuals. Differences that correlate with brain structure have emerged in studying lesbian and heterosexual women, though they have been less well researched (Gladue, 1994).

According to one study, the suprachiasmatic nucleus of the hypothalamus (SCN) (Figure 5.31, p. 128) is 1.7 times larger in homosexual than in heterosexual men (Swaab and Hofman, 1990). No difference in SCN is found between males and females. Swaab and Hofman suggest that it is unlikely that homosexual behaviour could cause such an increase in cell number. Rather, early development is more likely to be implicated.

Figure 17.8 Brain differences between homosexual and heterosexual males. SCN, suprachiasmatic nucleus; INAH-3, third interstitial nucleus of the anterior hypothalamus.

Source: Martini *et al.* (2000, Fig. 15-13a, p. 395) (top) Copyright © 2000, 1997 by Frederic H. Martini, Inc. and Michael J. Timmons. Reprinted by permission of Pearson Education, Inc.; Baum (1999, Fig. 47.11) (bottom).

Differences between homosexual and heterosexual males in the midsagittal area of the anterior commissure (AC), which conveys information between the two hemispheres, have been reported (Allen and Gorski, 1992). The AC is not directly involved in sexual behaviour. Homosexual men were found to have an AC area 18% larger than heterosexual women and 34% larger than heterosexual men. Most of the homosexual sample had died of AIDS. As Allen and Gorski note, AIDS-associated neuropathology normally manifests as atrophy of the nervous system.

Allen and Gorski suggest that a single brain structure is unlikely to underlie sexual orientation. Rather, a number of different structures and global differences in information processing are more likely to be implicated.

A proposal for a gene

Introduction

In the early 1990s, the expression 'gay gene' appeared. What could be meant by this? We should not ask, 'which is the most important: genes or environment?' (Chapter 2). Whether an individual is homosexual, heterosexual, bisexual or uninterested in sex inevitably depends upon genes and environment acting in complex ways (Pillard and Weinrich, 1986). Also, we should not dichotomize into neat categories of homosexual or heterosexual and we need to recognize overlap. The orientation shown in the domain of fantasy needs to be considered as well as that of overt behaviour (Gladue, 1988). The genetic contribution could involve multiple genes (Hyde, 2005a).

So, how could we frame the question to fit with a scientific understanding? We might ask whether differences between individuals in terms of sexual orientation are determined in part by genetic differences. In other words, could a gene interacting with the environment give a bias towards homosexuality?

Some studies look at the correlation in sexual orientation between twins, comparing identical and fraternal twins. The correlation towards either homosexuality or heterosexuality is higher in identical than fraternal twins (Gladue, 1994; Hyde, 2005a). However, since the correlation is not perfect in identical twins, such studies suggest a role for environmental factors.

The route of influence

The identification of a genetic factor does not show how it is translated into behaviour (Chapter 6). In principle, it might act by, say, physical appearance, with certain looks being more attractive to potential homosexual, rather than heterosexual, mates. However, genetically mediated differences might act at the level of motivation. There could be differences in sexual differentiation of the brain comparing homosexuals and heterosexuals (Gladue, 1994). Genetic differences might act at the level of the biological process or bias the way that the developing child is treated.

LeVay (1991) concludes that the evidence points to there being a genetic bias towards sexual orientation. If it acts at a motivational level, what might this gene be coding for? The consistent distinction between homosexual and heterosexual males is one of the *object of desire* rather than a specific behaviour (Gorman, 1994).

Function

It might appear that a 'gay gene' would be at a strong disadvantage in terms of genetic perpetuation since by definition it would tend to bias towards sex that is genetically unproductive (Chapter 2).

Evolutionary psychology

How could the gene be favoured?

Theorists speculate that homosexual males might be unusually good helpers within a family and thereby increase the fitness of close relatives, with whom they have genetic similarity. Hence the genes are favoured indirectly. Evidence within Western societies that compares homosexual and heterosexual males does not support this. However, a study in Samoa, where there is a closer family structure than in the West, does support it (Vasey and VanderLaan, 2010). In Samoa, homosexual males take the character of 'super uncles' to nieces and nephews. It could be that Western societies, given the nature of the dispersal of families, are not conducive to showing this effect, rather as they are not conducive to showing the adaptive value of a 'super taste' for sugars and fats! As an additional factor, Camperio-Ciani *et al.* (2004) found that female relatives of homosexual males had a higher reproductive success than relatives of heterosexual males. The same allele that favours homosexuality in males could confer a biological advantage when present in females. This argument is destined to run and run!

Section summary

1   Comparing homosexual and heterosexual males, differences have been found in hypothalamic nuclei and in the area of the anterior commissure.

2   Some evidence suggests genetically determined differences underlying sexual orientation mediated via brain structure but other interpretations cannot be ruled out.

 ### Test your knowledge

17.9 Why do we need to be cautious about assuming that differences in brain structure necessarily are caused by differences in genes?

 Answer on page 466

Sexual disgust

This section describes disgust triggered in a sexual context. This takes forms ranging from physical disgust, triggered by, say, a bad odour, which inhibits sexual attraction, to disgust caused by morally unacceptable behaviour. To understand sexual disgust, it is necessary first to look more broadly at disgust.

The causal explanation

Stimuli, the triggering of disgust and types of reaction

Some basic stimuli for disgust are characterized by a bad odour, e.g. food that has 'gone off' and vomit. Visual characteristics, e.g. ulcers and wounds, can also be stimuli. Such stimuli signal the presence of disease-causing agents, termed pathogens (Chapter 13), e.g. viruses and bacteria.

On the output side of disgust, there are both stereotyped and flexible reactions. The stereotyped facial expression of disgust is produced universally and can be recognized across cultures (Ekman *et al.*, 1969). Disgust is characterized by nausea, which motivates flexible escape from the source of disgust and its future avoidance. Across cultures, specific cues trigger disgust rapidly and automatically, with little 'higher' cognitive mediation (Oaten *et al.*, 2009). In the language of evolutionary psychology, the emotion of disgust shows some features of a *module* (though some of the behaviour triggered can

exhibit flexibility). In keeping with this interpretation, rationality can easily be overridden: e.g. even a sterilized drinking utensil can trigger rejection if the person is told that it was earlier associated with contamination (Rozin *et al.*, 2000).

While having features of an automatic module, disgust is open to influences apparently from outside the module. Based upon contextual factors, there is altered sensitivity of the power of raw stimuli to trigger disgust (Oaten *et al.*, 2009). For example, stimuli to disgust are more potent when they emanate from strangers rather than oneself or kin. As someone reported in a survey, 'other people's dirt is dirtier than my own' (cited by Oaten *et al.*, 2009, p. 310). This makes functional sense; strangers are more likely to be a source of pathogens not already encountered by the self or kin.

Women are more sensitive to disgust than are men and are better able to recognize its expression in others, which relates to certain contextual factors. For example, early pregnancy is associated with heightened sensitivity to disgust triggers. At this time, the growing foetus is particularly vulnerable to pathogens.

Although disgust is triggered powerfully and automatically, there are circumstances in which it can either be suppressed or, at least, its influence overridden (Oaten *et al.*, 2009). Times of starvation are sometimes associated with the ingestion of foods that would otherwise trigger disgust. This suggests a form of cost–benefit analysis where, under certain conditions, overcoming disgust has tended to contribute to genetic perpetuation. Heightened sexual arousal is often associated with overcoming latent inhibitions. Rather obviously, an aversion to body-fluids such as saliva can be very much context-dependent.

Disgust in humans can be triggered not just by particular stimuli such as an odour but also by situations in which an assessment of disgust involves some sophisticated cognitive processing, discussed next.

Moral disgust

Some expressions employed to convey moral disapproval ('moral disgust') relate to those denoting physical disgust, e.g. 'disgusting morals', 'dirty mind' and 'moral filth', not to forget 'dirty dealing'. We can speculate that such moral censure has served a policing function by kin, as protection against, for example, the disease-triggering potential of unrestrained sexual behaviour. Although the triggers to moral censure differ somewhat across cultures, the underlying principle of a link with disgust appears to be broadly applicable (Oaten *et al.*, 2009).

Are there more than superficial similarities between moral and physical disgust? Is a similar conscious emotion triggered by both? Several sources of evidence can be brought to bear here. The notion of *cleansing* one's sins by physical washing has an important place in all the world's great religions: Judaism, Islam, Christianity and Hindu.

Zhong and Liljenquist (2006) investigated whether recalling an unethical event from the past primed cleansing-related cognitions and behaviour. Participants were asked to recall a past episode in their lives associated with either ethical or unethical behaviour. They were then asked to perform a word-completion task. Participants in the group who recalled unethical behaviour tended to complete, for example, the word fragment W_ _H to form the word WASH, rather than, say, WISH. As reward for participation, there was an increased tendency to select a cleaning instrument (pack of antiseptic wipes) in the unethical condition, as compared with the ethical condition. We cannot be certain that moral disgust was triggered in the guilt condition but it is quite possible (Oaten et al., 2009).

A personal angle

Shakespeare's insight

Zhong and Liljenquist termed the phenomenon that they studied the 'Macbeth effect', as illustrated in Shakespeare's play Macbeth (Act 5, Scene 1). This relates to the extensive hand-washing of Lady Macbeth, done in an attempt to cleanse herself of sin.

Darwin suggested that the facial expression of disgust derives from the functional value that it served in minimizing oral intake of harmful substances (Chapman et al., 2009). The same signal could be exploited to convey moral disgust. So, is there a similarity in the facial expressions of disgust at physical stimuli and moral transgressions? Chapman et al. recorded the electrical activity of the muscles that control the movements of the face. They found a similar reaction of the facial muscles to (i) a disgusting taste, (ii) a non-taste related physical stimulus (picture of a wound) and (iii) a moral transgression (an unfair financial transaction). Next time that someone describes a moral transgression as leaving a 'bad taste in the mouth', you might think that this is more than just a colourful metaphor.

Brain mechanisms

Insight into the brain mechanisms underlying disgust comes from two primary sources: (i) deficiencies in disgust associated with brain damage and (ii) neuroimaging while participants are exposed to disgust-eliciting situations. In an 'ideal world', those regions that change their activity when people are exposed to disgust-eliciting situations would correspond exactly to those that are found to be damaged in disrupted disgust.

Much (but not all) evidence suggests that the insula (Figure 12.12, p. 331) plays a central role in disgust (Fitzgerald et al., 2004). This region is excited by aversive tastes, which would link with the idea that, in an evolutionary sense (discussed shortly), disgust was initially triggered by bad tastes (Calder et al., 2000). In addition, the insula receives information in multiple sensory modalities. There are reports that the insula is excited by both happy and disgusting triggers (Chen et al., 2009). So, the insula might not constitute a disgust-specific brain region but rather might be a site of general emotional processing (Schaich Borg et al., 2008). Different subregions of the insula might code for different emotions or it might be that different circuits throughout the whole structure code for different emotions.

There appears to be some overlap in the regions of brain that are activated by physical stimuli to disgust and triggers to moral disgust, suggesting some common basis (Moll et al., 2005). For example, an fMRI study found that medial and lateral parts of the orbitofrontal cortex were excited by both classes of trigger. There also appear to be regions of non-overlap in what is excited by these two types of disgust, indicative of separable types of processing (Schaich Borg et al., 2008). For example, regions of the anterior cingulate cortex were excited by moral transgressions but not by physical stimuli to disgust. Under the general heading of 'moral disgust', there was even some observable difference in brain activation between the conditions of incest-triggered disgust and non-sexual moral disgust.

The developmental/learning explanation

Consider the universality of facial reactions to disgust, as well as the imperative of not missing sources of danger. An intuitive guess might be that human infants come into the world 'preformed' with a module that reacts immediately to certain stimuli with a stereotyped disgust reaction. Indeed, by comparison, newborns exhibit rejection reactions to bitter and sour tastes.

Surprisingly, such preformed immediacy of the disgust reaction appears not to be the case (Oaten et al., 2009; Rozin et al., 2000). This seems to illustrate that even behavioural processes that take the form of modules have a developmental history that depends to some extent upon experience. As part of evolutionary inheritance, the infant's nervous system might be strongly biased ('prepared') to learn disgust to particular classes of stimuli (Rozin et al., 2000). That is to say, infants are strongly prepared to learn to imitate their parents' reaction to disgusting stimuli. Presumably, this involves mirror neurons (Chapter 10).

Such imitation would allow a limited degree of cultural relativity based on learning. That is to say a fixed output from disgust detection coexists with some flexibility in terms what elicits such disgust (Rozin *et al.*, 2000). There are certain cultural differences in triggers to disgust. For example, rigid caste systems prescribe certain unfortunates as untouchable. Within an industrial society, we could speculate that the body odours that trigger disgust in the 21st century might have been perceived as relatively benign to most of our ancestors! Also new diseases emerge (e.g. sexually transmitted ones) and do not always advertise themselves by unique external signs, thus allowing cultural transmission of information.

The functional explanation

In contrast to depression (Chapter 2), the functional advantage of a disgust system in terms of survival and thereby genetic perpetuation is surely beyond dispute. Disgust exemplifies where the functional explanation and evolutionary psychology can provide a unifying framework for understanding (Oaten *et al.*, 2009). Disgust puts a distance (physical or psychological) between the person and the triggering event and it signals disapproval to others.

Evolutionary psychology

Broadening the basic processes

Rozin *et al.* (2000) argue that disgust emerged first as a defence against ingestion of harmful foods. They suggest that the facial gesture of disgust serves to minimize contact with the food and that nausea, the hallmark of disgust, is linked to ingested foods.

In triggering disgust, evolutionary logic suggests that an individual can err in one of two ways (Oaten *et al.*, 2009):

1 False alarms. Disgust is triggered in the absence of an actual threat.
2 False safety. Disgust is not triggered in the presence of a threat.

Evolutionary logic suggests that the cost of getting it wrong in the first case is likely to be less than in the second (where it can prove fatal) and hence we might expect an excess of false alarms. This is suggested by the tendency to form irrational disgust reactions. For example, sadly, HIV/AIDS can trigger disgust and social distancing by others, out of proportion to the actual risk of contamination. This might be linked to the sexual connotation of the infection.

Whatever its evolutionary origins, it is clear that the triggers to disgust are now much broader than stimuli that can be defined simply by their physical properties. The role of cognition becomes evident. Consider disgust triggered by sexual stimuli. Women show increased sensitivity to such disgust, compared with men, as might be expected from functional considerations since the costs can be so much greater (Tybur *et al.*, 2009).

Sexual disgust is only in part based upon physical triggers as in pathogen avoidance. Rather, sexual disgust can be triggered by unwanted and unattractive sexual advances and intrusions or sexual contact with a close relative. Such disgust would logically have served to avoid actions where the *reproductive* consequences might well have been costly in terms of fitness (Tybur *et al.*, 2009). A degree of information extraction and contextualization of this information is exemplified by avoidance of *sexual* contact with a sibling (incest avoidance), where the sibling has no intrinsic disgust-triggering qualities.

Evolutionary psychology suggests some interesting developmental questions (Tybur *et al.*, 2009). For example, assessments of a potential mating partner would present a challenge for fitness at a later age than does detection of pathogens. Therefore, one might expect the capacity for sexual disgust to mature somewhat later.

Consider the argument that moral disgust gained access to the brain processes that evolved to serve physical disgust (Rozin *et al.*, 2000). This would exemplify what is termed a 'pre-adaptation' (sometimes described as an 'exaptation'): existing processes are recruited ('co-opted') to serve an additional function. The authors draw a comparison with the teeth and tongue, which facilitate spoken language but evolved originally in the service of feeding. On moral disgust, they state (p. 650): 'A mechanism for avoiding harm to the body became a mechanism for avoiding harm to the soul'.

Moral disgust is presumably a purely human attribute. Theories of moral reasoning have traditionally emphasized its rational, cognitive and conscious quality, with the basis of moral decisions being open to introspection (Chapman *et al.*, 2009). However, as Chapman *et al.* note, this would seem to underestimate the extent to which emotions that are rooted in the evolutionary past play a crucial role.

A capacity for moral disgust and reliable signalling of it would appear to be a necessary prerequisite for social coherence in human society. There are enormous implications for society in a failure of an individual to have the capacity for moral disgust (Moll *et al.*, 2005). However, disgust seems to play a role in so many problems of human society, such as social exclusion, stigmatization, prejudice and discrimination (Tybur *et al.*, 2009). Recognizing its evolutionary roots might even help to solve the problems arising from it.

Getting out of the adaptive range

Disgust can get out of an optimal range by either being over-reactive or under-reactive. In Chapter 2, it was noted that chronic depression might be a contemporary exaggeration of a reaction that, in smaller doses, has served an adaptive function in evolution. A similar example of things going wrong could be linked to the notion of preparedness to exhibit disgust. It is interesting to speculate that moral disgust 'gone wild' might play a role in obsessive hand-washing (Phillips *et al.*, 2000). Conversely, deficiencies of disgust might well be at the basis of some sexual offences and so better understanding of the biological bases could bring therapeutic insights (Schaich Borg *et al.*, 2008).

Section summary

1 In its evolutionary roots, disgust probably evolved to avoid pathogens that result from eating contaminated food.

2 Sexual disgust probably evolved from a food-related disgust and served to restrain sexual behaviour at unsuitable and dangerous times and subsequently to permit moral censure of certain sexual behaviour.

Test your knowledge

17.10 Evolutionary psychologists sometimes suggest that such emotions as fear and disgust are like fire-alarm systems. How does the notion of 'fail-safe' apply in each case?

Answer on page 466

Bringing things together

The chapter has emphasized a dual approach: looking for features of sexual behaviour that can, with caution, be generalized across species and seeing these in the context of specifically human aspects. Features of Figure 17.1 have a broad application but there are special human aspects such as knowledge about pregnancy, guilt, moral disgust and imagination.

The importance of a *circle of causes* emerges in human sexuality (Figures 17.1 and 17.7; Bancroft, 1989). Desire and arousal can be understood in these terms. Sexual dysfunction might be understood as breaking the circle at a point between the central factors and the genital response. It might be possible to localize the initial dysfunction to a particular point in the circle. However, there can be subsequent effects at various points on the circle. A local abnormality might be corrected locally but leave lasting effects throughout the circle. For example, vaginal discomfort might be corrected by hormonal treatment. However, it might leave a lasting negative memory that cannot so easily be reversed. Similarly, the occasional erectile dysfunction might trigger anxiety that introduces positive feedback.

 See the video coverage for this chapter for how psychologists bring different types of explanation to the study of sexual behaviour.

Summary of Chapter 17

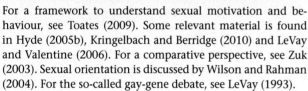

1 Interdependent factors are involved in sexual motivation and behaviour, e.g. stimuli from a partner, conditional associations, hormones, memories and reactions by the genitals. Factors such as anxiety can exert an inhibitory effect.

2 Under the initial control of events in the brain, sex hormones are released into the bloodstream and exert effects throughout the body, including the brain.

3 A study of non-human species reveals some basic principles, which can (with due caution) be generalized across species.

4 Understanding human sexual desire requires knowledge of species-specific biological and cultural determinants.

5 The blood flow to the genitals is determined by both central and local factors. In turn, there is feedback arising at the genitals and projecting to the brain.

6 An array of different neurochemicals is involved in sexual motivation and the sexual response.

7 The study of sexual orientation requires subtlety and points to caution in assertion of a 'gene for' a particular characteristic.

Further reading

For a framework to understand sexual motivation and behaviour, see Toates (2009). Some relevant material is found in Hyde (2005b), Kringelbach and Berridge (2010) and LeVay and Valentine (2006). For a comparative perspective, see Zuk (2003). Sexual orientation is discussed by Wilson and Rahman (2004). For the so-called gay-gene debate, see LeVay (1993).

Answers

Explanations for answers to 'test your knowledge' questions can be found on the website www.pearsoned.co.uk/toates

17.1 (i) Sex is similar to feeding and drinking in the sense that it is highly motivating and depends upon a combination of external and internal factors. The strength of motivation rises and falls with internal and external factors. (ii) Sex is different in that there is no life-threatening physiological disturbance associated with its abstinence.

17.2 5, 6.

17.3 (i) GnRH

17.4 Neuron 5 triggers activity in neuron 6, whereas neuron 3 only modulates the sensitivity of the process.

17.5 (ii) The adrenal gland

17.6 4

17.7 (i) 1

17.8 All except 7 → 3

17.9 As a general principle, brain structures emerge from a process of dynamic interactions between genes and environment, as summarized in Figure 6.2 (p. 154). Hence differences might arise from different environments, e.g. social.

17.10 In each case, the cost of not reacting to true danger is greater than occasionally reacting to a false alarm.

Visit www.pearsoned.co.uk/toates for a range of resources to support study.
Test yourself with multiple choice questions and access a bank of over 100 videos that will bring the topics to life.

Chapter 18
Drugs and addiction

Learning outcomes for Chapter 18

After studying this chapter, you should be able to:

1 Discuss some of the problems in trying to define the terms 'drug' and 'addiction', while relating this to an understanding of the brain and the social context.

2 Explain some of the processes that are thought to underlie the craving, seeking and taking of drugs in humans, while discussing animal models of these phenomena.

3 Describe the effects of some addictive and non-addictive drugs on the brain and explain what this tells us about the bases of addiction. Discuss addiction to non-chemical activities, noting similarities and differences with drug-based addictions.

4 Critically discuss models that have been advanced to explain addiction.

Scene-setting questions

1 Why do people keep on taking drugs – to escape from reality or because the body comes to need them?

2 Does the effect of a drug depend on social context and expectations?

3 Is love like being addicted to a drug? Can sex be addictive?

4 Can you get addicted to the Internet?

5 Which is more addictive, heroin or nicotine?

6 What effect does ecstasy have? What is an LSD trip like?

7 Why can't people 'just say no' to drugs?

8 What is the range of possible addictions?

What is the range of possible addictions? Explore the video on the website accompanying this book at **www.pearsoned.co.uk/toates**

Why are warnings so often ineffective in countering drug-taking?

Source: Image courtesy of The Advertising Archives.

Introduction

When have you noticed 'drugs and addiction' discussed in the media? What was the context and what did these terms mean? The following reflects some typical items in the news.

'Agony of pop-star on entering rehabilitation – one more drink could be the last'.

'Police find drugs in football star's penthouse love-nest'.

'Yuppie weekend cocaine users are warned by police that they are not above the law'.

'Popular family vicar's life ruined by secret Internet sex addiction'.

By contrast, here are two imaginary headlines that you probably have never encountered but which reveal as much as those above.

'One-man drug-crazed crime-wave fuelled by need for mushrooms'.

'Housing estate ruled by fear of ecstasy gangs'.

These examples illustrate a number of points:

1 The criteria used to define the term 'drug' are as much legal, social and moral as they are psychological or biological. When you read about the footballer's 'drugs', you surely thought of heroin, cocaine or cannabis rather than tobacco or alcohol. The common expression 'drugs and alcohol' suggests that alcohol is not a drug. Yet it shows clear features in common with 'drugs', such as powerful mind-altering effects and a potential for addiction.

2 Some substances that are taken for their psychological effects are addictive whereas others are not. Some are normally discussed in the context of the social problems that they produce, associated with addiction. Are all drugs addictive? Certainly some, such as heroin, can be and they make the headlines. Nicotine is addictive but is perfectly legal and only rarely associated with crime, except smuggling.

3 Can you be addicted to something that is not a chemical? Since gambling and Internet sex can take control of a person's life and lead to ruin, we might include them under this heading. The challenge is to find features of addiction that are common across chemically related and non-chemically related activities.

4 Lots of people take ecstasy and magic mushrooms for their strong mind-altering effects. In the swinging 1960s, LSD was popular. Reports of addiction are extremely rare. So, there can be mind-altering drugs that have little or no addictive potential.

5 Some addictive substances are associated with serious crime and social disruption, whereas others are not. For some individuals, casual 'social use' of drugs is possible, whereas, for others, this switches to addiction. However, addiction is not intrinsic to the substance but is a complex property of the chemical and social context. Most of us drink socially but rather few become alcoholic. Some people manage to use 'hard drugs' only occasionally, e.g. the weekend (yuppie) cocaine user. What conditions tip only some individuals into addiction?

6 One feature that seems to cover all addiction is the notion of *conflict*. The pop-singer highlights the conflict involved with the addictive use of alcohol. A person can have conscious intentions to resist but finds him/herself pulled in the opposite direction. Someone engages in an activity to excess even though it brings serious problems, such as loss of job, home, family and health. The person might acknowledge this and wish to resist.

7 Certain drugs are associated with an aversive effect when they are no longer taken, termed **withdrawal**, the symptoms being **withdrawal symptoms**. The pop-singer was suffering from the pain of withdrawal.

The word 'drug' covers many substances taken, on the one hand, to counter and avoid disease, depressed mood or pain and, on the other, for a 'euphoric high' or spiritual enlightenment. This chapter is concerned with a group of **psychoactive drugs** taken to alter mood and cognition. It looks at their effects on the CNS and behaviour and the reasons people take them. Mood-altering drugs are not a heterogeneous class. They have different effects and people differ in their motivation to take them. However, there are some common features in the effects of a number of drugs (e.g. heroin, alcohol, caffeine, nicotine).

In each case, the drug can come to exert a strong motivational pull on the user, even though he or she acknowledges harmful effects. Drugs such as heroin, cocaine, alcohol and nicotine are taken for their rapid mood-altering properties. The enormous strength of motivation associated with taking some, e.g. heroin, is shown by the fact that people pay large sums and risk disease, loss of family, violence and death to obtain them.

Insight into drug-taking comes from at least three sources:

1 Behaviour of various species.

2 Subjective reports by humans.

3 Looking at the brains of humans and non-humans.

Biologically orientated research is directed to the neural basis of drug action, i.e. linking neurobiology to behavioural and experiential evidence. This involves trying to identify brain systems that have the following properties:

1 Their activity reflects motivation, is affected by conditional stimuli and is changed by the arrival of a drug.

2 The brain systems change with the development of drug-taking, e.g. a switch to addictive use.

3 Links between these regions and both sensory input and motor output can be identified.

4 They can be related to conventional motivation, such as feeding and sex.

Although, to understand drug effects, the drug's chemical properties are crucial, they cannot alone explain drug-taking behaviour (Peele, 1985). Environmental and personality factors are also involved. So, biological insight needs to interface with an understanding of social determinants. Explanations should be compatible with the vastly different levels of drug-taking that appear when comparing individuals or cultures or a given individual over the 'ups-and-downs' of life (Alexander, 2008; Peele and Alexander, 1985).

Humans provide subjective insight into the affective and cognitive events associated with seeking and taking drugs and withdrawal. Investigators relate these to psychological theory, but urge caution in the interpretation of subjective evidence. Verbal reports give unique insight into mood and the thoughts that occupy consciousness but, as discussed later, they might not always provide an infallible guide to the causes of behaviour (Robinson and Berridge, 1993).

Of course, evolution did not produce special processes dedicated to drug-taking. Drug-taking is best understood in a context of adaptive behaviour, such as sex, feeding and exploration, with which it shares properties. Drugs motivate in a way that has similarities with conventional rewards, e.g. pressing levers to obtain the reward of either food or injections of heroin intravenously (Chapter 15). Drugs exploit ('hijack') conventional motivational processes (e.g. mesolimbic dopamine system).

The following section looks at some characteristics of drug-taking.

Section summary

1 A number of psychoactive substances strongly attract people, associated with the risk of addiction.

2 Other psychoactive substances have a low addiction potential.

3 Some activities that are not associated with taking chemicals into the body also have the potential to develop addiction.

4 Addiction is characterized by compulsion even in the face of serious harm done by the activity.

 Test your knowledge

18.1 Which of the following has a low addiction potential? (i) Nicotine, (ii) heroin, (iii) LSD.

Answer on page 490

Characteristics of drug-taking

The motivation to take drugs is a complex function of the chemical properties of the drug as well as environmental factors, such as the location, the presence of other individuals and cues associated with drug-taking (Alexander, 2008). Motivation depends also upon a range of cognitive and emotional factors such as self-image and mood. Non-humans can provide models of features of drug-taking but they need to be considered in terms of some peculiarly human features.

The link to natural neurochemicals

By interacting with receptors on neurons, psychoactive drugs have psychological effects. Some drugs, such as the opiates, are chemically very similar to substances that the body produces naturally ('opioids'). These natural substances play a role in emotions, as in social bonding and distress calls (Chapters 12 and 15) and the inhibition of pain (Chapter 14). The body also contains its own source of cannabis-like chemicals (Chapter 14). This suggests that externally obtained chemicals influence those motivational and emotional processes that employ the natural equivalent. An understanding of the role of the natural chemicals (e.g. in social bonding) could provide valuable insight into why people are motivated to supplement them from outside, e.g. to reduce loneliness or alienation. The natural chemicals are evolutionarily old and this encourages the search for general principles applicable across species.

Withdrawal effects

Observable symptoms

In both humans and rats, if taking a drug such as heroin or alcohol is discontinued, observable withdrawal symptoms can occur (Wise, 1988). In humans, for opiates, these include aversive bodily signs, such as cramps, convulsions, sweating and a 'flu-like' condition (Koob, 1999). Rats shake their bodies (termed 'wet-dog shakes'), similar to a dog after it has got wet. Such withdrawal symptoms become paired with environmental cues and there can be 'conditional withdrawal symptoms', triggered by conditional stimuli paired with earlier withdrawal (Wikler, 1965). Withdrawal symptoms can also be triggered under normal conditions by injecting an opioid antagonist such as naloxone. Presumably this is due to blocking an endogenous opioid system and hence tilting the affect process in a negative direction.

An animal model of withdrawal from cocaine exists (Mutschler and Miczek, 1998): rats in withdrawal have elevated startle reflexes and a higher rate of ultrasonic vocalizations, both indices of negative affect (Chapter 12). In a **discrimination test** researchers can, in effect, ask the rat what the state feels like. For example, it can be rewarded with food for turning to the left when in drug withdrawal but to the right when not in withdrawal. Other states can be induced to see whether they are perceived as similar to withdrawal. Rats generalize between cocaine withdrawal and the state induced by the anxiogenic (anxiety-inducing) drug pentylenetetrazol (PTZ), i.e. they are perceived as similar.

Withdrawal symptoms are different according to the drug in question but what they all share is negative affect (Baker *et al.*, 2004).

Unobserved signs

Psychologists cannot decide whether positive or negative affect is the most important for explaining the compulsive feature of drug-taking. It might well be naive to try to divide causes too neatly. However, negative affect is not necessarily always associated with observable signs of withdrawal (Baker *et al.*, 2004). On being without a drug, e.g. cocaine, there can be an aversive state reported without external signs of withdrawal (Koob, 1999). Agony can be a private thing. In rats and humans, withdrawal signs are partly dependent upon social context (Alexander *et al.*, 1985).

In any actions that are motivated to obtain drugs, the principles of conditioning are central, as described in the next two sections.

Classical conditioning

Classical conditioning plays an important role in various stages of drug-taking (Figure 18.1).

Motivational effects

Classical conditioning increases the motivation associated with drug-seeking and taking (Stewart *et al.*, 1984) (Figure 18.1(a)). Let us assume that drugs are unconditional stimuli that elicit unconditional effects on the body. If neutral stimuli in the environment are repeatedly paired with drug-taking, they become conditional stimuli (CSs). For example, a syringe is a neutral stimulus prior to its being used to inject drugs. After this, it takes on new motivational properties: the sight of a syringe can evoke wanting a drug. Similarly, an open packet of cigarettes and lighter are CSs associated with nicotine (Thewissen *et al.*, 2005). The term 'needle freak'

What is the role of context in drug-seeking and the effects of drugs?

Source: Janine Wiedel Photolibrary/Alamy.

refs to the ability of people addicted to heroin to experience something similar to the effect of a drug simply by going through the rituals of injection of a neutral substance.

By classical conditioning, a location associated with a drug can acquire incentive motivational properties (Chapter 15). For example, a rat prefers the side of a T-maze in which it received an injection of drug, a conditioned place preference (Bozarth, 1987). Given that classical conditioning underlies drug seeking and craving, it is logical to suppose that extinction procedures ('exposure') should be a therapeutic tool in combating drug-taking. Alas, exposure to drug-related cues in the absence of the drug has disappointing results (Marissen et al., 2005).

Homeostatic reactions

Apart from psychoactive effects, drugs have other effects on the body. For example, heroin has effects on respiration. These are a disturbance to homeostasis and they trigger physiological counter-measures by the body. In this context, the drug is the unconditional stimulus (UCS) that triggers physiological compensation (UCR). Such counter-measures also occur within the person's

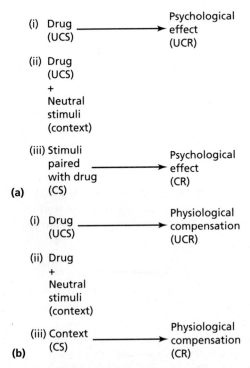

Figure 18.1 Conditioning of drug effects: (a) the motivational role, (b) role in compensation. (i) The unconditional role of a UCS triggering a UCR, (ii) pairing of drug-taking (UCS) with neutral stimuli and (iii) neutral stimuli become conditional stimuli (CS) having a capacity of their own (CR).

normal environment, which contains cues that can be conditioned, e.g. a particular room, friends and the sight of the syringe. Such conditional cues in the environment (CS) come to trigger some compensation (CR). See Figure 18.1(b).

Suppose that a person has a history of taking a drug in a particular context. Then, on one occasion, the drug is taken in a novel environment, not containing the familiar CSs. In the absence of the CR component of compensation, the counter-reaction would be expected to be weaker. Addicted people suffering or dying from an overdose commonly do so when injecting in an unfamiliar environment (Siegel, 1984). In fact, in purely chemical terms, the size of their dose might not appear excessive. However, in the absence of conditional counter-measures, the dose is, in effect, larger.

Instrumental conditioning

Introduction

In terms of instrumental conditioning, questions on drug-taking are framed around principles of reward and aversion, positive and negative reinforcement. Placed in an operant situation, animals can be persuaded to take drugs such as heroin by infusion through a cannula (Stewart et al., 1984). It appears that different brain regions mediate the positive reinforcement (e.g. gain of pleasure) and negative reinforcement (e.g. loss of pain) aspects of drug-taking (Bechara et al., 1998; Wise, 1988).

Negative reinforcement

Animals can be motivated to seek drugs because of a reduction that they cause in an aversive condition. Even though explicit physiological signs of withdrawal might not be evident, there can still be a CNS state of negative affect, the reduction of which by taking the drug constitutes negative reinforcement (Baker et al., 2004). One might be able to infer an aversive state only from an animal's avoidance of external stimuli associated with being in the state. Soon after exposure to opiates, rats show avoidance of cues associated with their absence even though there are no observable physiological signs of withdrawal. Cocaine and amphetamine are not associated with aversive signs outside the nervous system but can be negatively reinforcing in alleviating a 'psychological distress syndrome' (see Robinson and Berridge, 1993).

The periaqueductal grey (Chapter 5) appears to be the site of negative reinforcement (Wise, 1988). Drugs that target receptors in this region seem to lower an aversive effect.

Animals seem to behave so as to maintain the level of natural opioids within limits. Isolated rats take more drugs than socially housed rats (Alexander *et al.*, 1985; Wolffgramm and Heyne, 1991). In laboratory rats, there may be something equivalent to a permanent withdrawal effect as a result of chronic low levels of endogenous opioids. This offers parallels with the suggestion that humans take drugs as self-medication for social alienation or other forms of psychological distress (Markou *et al.*, 1998). A negative mental state can be associated with cognitions about self-image and worthlessness (Peele, 1985). Cocaine use in humans tends to increase at times of perceived negative self-image (Singer, 1993).

Positive reinforcement

The *positive effect* of drugs refers to reward that can be induced even in the absence of a negative state. Its physical base is associated with the dopamine (DA) pathways ascending from the ventral tegmental area (Chapter 15) (Wise, 1988). In these terms, drugs form positive incentives to be pursued like sex or food (Robinson and Berridge, 1993; Stewart *et al.*, 1984). Activity at certain nuclei would tend to be rewarding in that it would move the animal to seek and 'consume' drugs. Rats can learn an operant task for drug reward, e.g. for microinjections into selected brain regions, even in the absence of any indices of withdrawal (Stewart *et al.*, 1984). Similarly, it seems that removal of withdrawal symptoms cannot explain how humans first move in a direction of addiction. People addicted to heroin commonly crave drugs when in the presence of drug-related cues.

In both humans and rats, presentation of small amounts of drug or cues associated with it triggers drug-seeking (Shaham and Stewart, 1995). For example, suppose a rat has learned an operant for intravenous drug reward but this has been extinguished by omission of drug. A small portion of drug is then injected 'free'. This is a cue to trigger re-arousal of the operant task. An arbitrary cue that had been paired with drug-delivery can maintain drug-seeking even in the absence of drug (Falk, 1994).

The factors of (i) reward and positive reinforcement and (ii) aversion and negative reinforcement cannot always be distinguished. A consensus view appears to be that, in a given individual, both types of process play a part in drug-taking with the relative weight shifting with circumstances (Bechara *et al.*, 1998; Koob, 1999; Wise, 1988).

Craving

As an example of subjective evidence, the term 'craving' (Chapter 16) describes an urge to take a drug and mental occupation with obtaining it (Franken, 2003; Markou *et al.*, 1993). Craving is associated with limbic system activation (Chapter 12; Childress *et al.*, 1999). Similarly, humans also report cravings for particular foods (Kassel and Shiffman, 1992). As a subjective state made available by verbal report, craving is a peculiarly human phenomenon. However, features of human craving can be modelled by non-humans (Chapter 15), e.g. lever-pressing by rats on extinction conditions in a task previously reinforced with drug. In humans, a lowering of the intensity of cocaine craving is caused by the agent desmethylimipramine. In rats, this also lowers responding in extinction, i.e. they tend to stop lever-pressing sooner (Fuchs *et al.*, 1998).

Defining addiction

Addiction refers to a person's abandonment to a pursuit, involving the neglect of other things and compromising the quality of life. After discontinuation of the addictive activity for short or long periods, there is a tendency to return to it ('relapse') (Peele and Degrandpre, 1998). There are a number of criteria that are employed to justify the term 'addiction' but not universal agreement on how many of these need to be present.

Link with withdrawal

To some experts, withdrawal symptoms offer a possible objective index of addiction (discussed by Wise, 1987). Their *presence* is certainly a useful pointer. However, some people described as addicted do not show physiological signs of withdrawal. It was once argued that cocaine is not addictive since there is not a pattern of associated ('extraneural') physiological withdrawal symptoms. However, this now seems an irrational criterion given the craving associated with the drug and its social and crime-related implications (Stolerman and Jarvis, 1995; Volkow *et al.*, 1997).

Curing withdrawal symptoms often has only a minimal effect in treating addiction (Wise, 1988). Subjective withdrawal symptoms do not correlate well with physiological signs of withdrawal (Henningfield *et al.*, 1987; Peele, 1985).

Other indices and criteria

Addiction is associated with **tolerance**, meaning that increasing amounts of drug need to be taken to obtain a given effect.

These days, 'addiction' is often used in non-chemical contexts, e.g. 'love addiction'. The broad usage points to important common features between drug and non-drug objects (Koob, 1999). However, it also raises a dilemma. If everything from praying and watching football to intravenous heroin use has the potential to be 'addictive', the word might appear to be devalued.

Alternatively, are there qualitatively different types of addiction? One way round this is to employ 'addiction' only where there are elements of danger, conflict and disruption to life involved.

A contemporary view is that all addictions have physical aspects and psychological aspects, as two sides of the same coin. That is to say, the psychological aspects are rooted in the brain. Thus, drugs and non-drug-related addictive behaviour would represent two different routes to tap a similar or identical underlying process. The motivation to take drugs might, like love, be based upon positive incentive motivational properties with the possibility of aversive effects of loss and abstinence.

Contextual factors

Contextual factors are important in drug-taking. For example, in humans, substances such as nicotine and caffeine presumably owe their high intake as much to their legality, relatively low cost, ready availability and compatibility with performing other tasks as to any intrinsic chemical properties.

This section looks at two examples of contextual factors.

The social dimension

A rat or non-human primate pressing a lever in a Skinner box might seem to exemplify the pure addictive potential of a drug, uncomplicated by cognition, social interaction and culture. However, experiments in which animals have worked for a drug at a very high rate (i) make the drug readily available by intravenous infusion

Rats housed in a rich physical and social context. Why are researchers interested in the effect of environmental enrichment on the tendency to drug-taking?

Source: courtesy of Bruce Alexander.

for minimal effort, (ii) have not allowed alternative sources of reward and (iii) involve a highly restrained physical context (Peele and Degrandpre, 1998). If availability is made more difficult, intake is lower.

Alexander *et al.* (1985) measured the oral intake of morphine solution by rats in a large social environment. Intake was only one-eighth that of isolated rats. Alexander and Hadaway (1982, p. 371) remark: 'The restrictive, isolated conditions of standard laboratory housing may be inherently stressful to mobile, social animals like rats and monkeys, and their self-administration of heroin could simply provide relief'. The presence of alternative sources of reward (e.g. social) offers effective competition to drug-taking in rats and humans (Peele, 1985).

In humans and non-humans, Peele and Degrandpre (1998) see a consistent pattern: cocaine has an addictive potential that is a function of both the chemical and the social context. Many humans can be described as 'occasional users', showing controlled use, e.g. monthly. Considerations of family and professional life are taken into account and restrain intake. Most American servicemen who employed opiates in Vietnam did not take this habit back to the United States with them at the end of the war (Robins *et al.*, 1975). Patients who self-administer narcotics for pain relief do not normally crave drugs when outside the clinical context (Chapter 14).

The dimension of control

The effects of a drug depend in part upon the nature of the *control* that the user is able to exert, which seems to be important for the addictive potential.

A rat pressing a lever in a Skinner box for drug reward is performing a particular behaviour, within a particular environment, under its own control. Effects of drugs taken under the animal's own control and their withdrawal effects are stronger than those experienced by a passive paired ('yoked') control receiving the same drug (MacRae and Siegel, 1997).

In humans, taking a drug involves performance of a procedure, a mechanical act or 'ritual', in a context of environmental and social cues. Changing the ability to control a situation can change the effect of the drug. If drugs are administered outside the control of the individual, they are perceived as being not so hedonically potent (Alexander and Hadaway, 1982). The particular route of administration can be important to some users (Peele, 1985). Control is qualified by history, context and goal.

Section summary

1 Some psychoactive drugs such as the opiates are very similar to natural neurochemicals.

2 Classical conditioning plays a role in drug-seeking and the effects of drugs.

3 Cessation of drug-taking can be associated with objective measures of withdrawal. Negative affect also follows.

4 The reinforcement for drug-taking appears to be both positive and negative.

5 Human craving can be modelled by animals placed on extinction conditions.

6 Context plays a crucial role in drug-seeking.

 Test your knowledge

18.2 Consider the phenomenon termed 'needle freak' and suppose that an addict is given a neutral substance, thinking that it is heroin. Using the terminology of classical conditioning, how would you describe (i) the injection and (ii) the effect of the injection?

Answer on page 490

Drugs and drug-taking

This section looks at some of the activities that are related to drugs and addiction. It considers addictive drugs and also some drugs with little addictive potential.

Amphetamine and cocaine

The motivational potency of amphetamine and cocaine appears to depend mainly upon their ability to increase levels of dopamine (DA) at synapses (Pierce and Kalivas, 1997; Wang and McGinty, 1999). Cocaine blocks DA reuptake (Chapter 4). Amphetamine both blocks reuptake and triggers the release of DA into the synapse (Grace, 2001; Wise, 1988).

Amphetamine

In rats, microinjections of amphetamine into the nucleus accumbens (N.acc.) are rewarding in designs employing place preference and self-infusion by lever-pressing (Bardo, 1998) (Figure 18.2).

Human amphetamine users report increased attention and energy and changes in cognition (Ellinwood, 1967, 1968; Klee and Morris, 1997). An improvement in self-image is one of the first effects. Ordinary events take a heightened significance and the universe appears to 'make sense'. The drug gives novelty to an otherwise dull world, suggesting that it taps into an exploration process. Objects can (Ellinwood, 1968, p. 48): 'stimulate curiosity and a search for new categories and significance, or attempts to expand, change and distort the categories or unknown object for mutual reconciliation'. Users sometimes engage in mechanical manipulation of objects, e.g. repeated assembly and taking apart (Ellinwood and Kilbey, 1975). In distorting cognition, amphetamine has features in common with the hallucinogens (see later). On the negative side, humans can experience paranoia-inducing cognitive changes in their interpretation of the world.

Cocaine

See Figure 18.3. The N.acc. might be involved in cocaine reward (Maldonado *et al.*, 1993). However, evidence suggests that the primary site of action is outside the N.acc. For example, a conditioned place preference test is relatively insensitive to manipulation of the level of dopamine in the N.acc. (Baker *et al.*, 1996). Based on microinjection studies and conditioned place preference tests, a site of cocaine's action appears to be the DA projections to the prefrontal cortex (Bardo, 1998). However, its effect on behaviour seems to depend on connections from this region to the N.acc. (a glutamate-mediated link is shown). Why there is a difference in target neurons between amphetamine and cocaine is not clear.

In intravenous self-administration, DA antagonists sometimes increase the intake of cocaine and amphetamine, i.e. compensation occurs (Bardo, 1998). DA antagonists block a conditioned place preference. For humans, the power of cocaine to induce euphoria is reduced when DA receptors are blocked (Gunne *et al.*, 1972; Jönsson *et al.*, 1971).

Figures 18.4 and 18.5 show the level of cocaine in the brain following its injection intravenously. By comparison, the level of another substance, methylphenidate (also termed 'Ritalin'), is also shown. Like cocaine, this blocks reuptake of dopamine but it is less addictive. The subjective feeling of 'high' is also shown. In each case, you can see a sharp rise and fall of the 'high'. However, note that methylphenidate is broken down more slowly than cocaine. This suggests that cocaine's addictive potency is linked to the sharp onset and offset ('rise and fall') of its biological effect.

Try examining the diagram to see why bouts of cocaine taking, some 30 minutes or so apart, sometimes occur. You should see that by 30 minutes, there is a

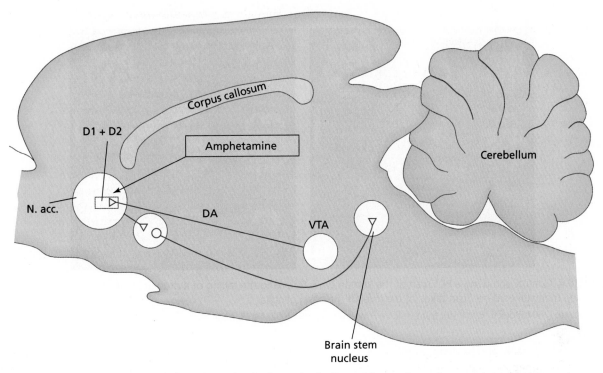

Figure 18.2 Suggested reward site of amphetamine in the rat brain. D_1 and D_2 are dopamine receptor subtypes.
Source: adapted from Bardo (1998, Fig. 1, p. 57).

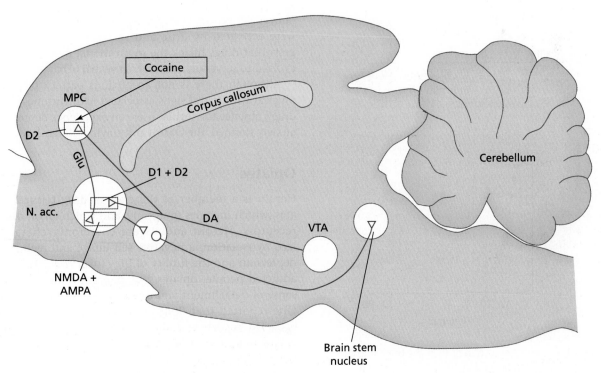

Figure 18.3 Suggested reward pathways of cocaine in the rat brain. Glu, glutamate; MPC, medial prefrontal cortex; NMDA, glutamate *N*-methyl-D-aspartate receptors.
Source: Bardo (1998, Fig. 2, p. 58).

Figure 18.4 Comparison using a PET scan of the human brain following the taking of a drug: (a) labelled cocaine and (b) labelled methylphenidate. Scan taken at the level of the basal ganglia.

Source: Toates (2004, Book 6, Fig. 1.13), from Volkow, Fowler and Wang (2002, Fig. 1, page 356).

(a)

(b)

Figure 18.5 The presence of a drug in the brain and the subjective 'high' experienced by the user: (a) cocaine, (b) methylphenidate.

Source: Toates (2004, Book 6, Fig. 1.14), after Volkow, Fowler and Wang (2002, Fig. 2, page 357).

significant fall in receptor occupation. Hence more drug could give more occupation and an upswing in the 'high'.

Chapter 17 described a study on backward masking and the use of very brief sexual stimuli (Childress *et al.*, 2008). Now it is time to add that the researchers also employed drug-related stimuli and the participants under study were cocaine users. A similar set of brain regions (amygdala, ventral striatum and the orbitofrontal cortex) were activated by drug and sexual stimuli. This suggests that drugs hijack the motivational machinery that evolved to serve such activities as sexual behaviour.

Although there is not an obvious pattern of physiological withdrawal signs associated with cocaine, in the drug's absence the regular user can experience depression, anxiety (termed 'the crash') and craving (Koob, 1999).

Opiates

Heroin is a member of the class of drug termed opiates, which includes morphine, and which target opioid receptors. Heroin addicts are commonly characterized by isolation, a negative self-image and feelings of depression and the futility of life (Tokar *et al.*, 1975). To addicted people, opiates give happiness, an increased sense of detachment and a reduced sense of awareness. One reported that 'heroin does something for a sick ego'. The reports of addicted people suggest that drugs create a euphoria that is tied to altered perceptions of self and the world.

Opiates have both rewarding and aversion-removing effects. Figure 18.6 shows some brain sites of opiate reward. Among other sites, it appears that opiates either

A personal angle

Sigmund Freud

Early in his career, Freud's interest was attracted to cocaine (Clark, 1980). Dr Theodor Aschenbrandt had experimented on cocaine's effects on weary Bavarian soldiers, whose motivation and attention were revived. Freud tried the drug and reported: 'A few minutes after taking the cocaine one suddenly feels light and exhilarated' and he wrote to his wife in 1884: 'In my last severe depression I took coca again and a small dose lifted me to the heights in a wonderful fashion. I am just now busy collecting the literature for a song of praise to this magical substance' (Clark, 1980, p. 59).

Freud was criticized for his liberal attitudes but responded that he had never advocated injection, merely ingestion. That Freud did not develop an addiction to cocaine in spite of taking it for 10 years (Sulloway, 1979) exemplifies that addiction depends on the interaction of the drug with the whole person and environment. However, Freud was wrong to assume that he could harmlessly wean an addicted friend off morphine with the help of cocaine. One might expect cross-sensitization and indeed the friend became a cocaine addict (Gay, 1988).

excite neurons that form excitatory synapses upon DA neurons in the ventral tegmental area (VTA) or they inhibit neurons that inhibit DA neurons (Wise, 1988). In rats, minute local injections of opiates into the VTA are rewarding, an effect that is reduced or eliminated when the DA system is blocked (Wise and Bozarth, 1987). Also, microinjections of opiates in the N.acc. are rewarding (Bardo, 1998).

Evidence suggests that the rewarding effect of opiates is sufficient to motivate opiate intake (Wise, 1988). In rats, the first injection has some rewarding effect, when by definition there can be no withdrawal effect, at least as defined in terms of exogenous drug. Thus, if a naive rat is exposed to a particular environment during which it experiences a single morphine injection, it will subsequently show a preference for being in

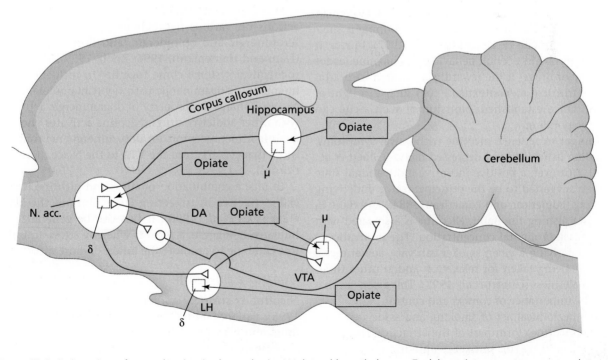

Figure 18.6 Opiate sites of reward action in the rat brain. LH, lateral hypothalamus; δ, delta opiate receptor; μ, mu opiate receptor.

Source: Bardo (1998, Fig. 3, p. 59).

that environment (Wise and Bozarth, 1987). However, we cannot ignore the suggestion that laboratory rats are permanently in a state similar to mild drug-withdrawal.

The periaqueductal grey (PAG) (Chapter 12) appears to be a principal site of aversion alleviation by opiates (Wise, 1988). Dependent rats, but not non-dependent ones, learn to press for infusion into the PAG (Wise and Bozarth, 1987). If specifically this region is first targeted with opiates and then an opiate antagonist is given, withdrawal symptoms are seen.

There are various bodily manifestations of opiate withdrawal, e.g. rats exhibit 'wet-dog shakes'. Also opiates might exert an aversion-alleviation effect outside the CNS, by, for example, removing gastrointestinal cramps (Wise, 1988).

Nicotine

Of all addictive substances, nicotine would probably rank worldwide as that causing the most harm to its users (Pomerleau and Pomerleau, 1984). However, it was only in the mid-1990s that its addictive potential was fully recognized. By comparison with opiates and cocaine, the subjective effects of cigarettes are more subtle, diffuse and hard to define.

Motivational mechanisms

Compared with opiates and cocaine, it is relatively difficult to establish nicotine as a reinforcer in an operant situation in non-humans (Donny *et al.*, 1998; Stolerman and Jarvis, 1995). Place preference conditioning is similarly more difficult (Rose and Corrigal, 1997). In rats, it is easier to obtain operant behaviour for nicotine (as for a variety of drugs) if the reward is associated with arbitrary extrinsic (i.e. 'contextual') cues such as a light or sound. Once established, omission of such a cue can lower responding.

Humans experience nicotine withdrawal symptoms, including irritability and depressed mood (Gilbert *et al.*, 1997). However, a positive incentive-motivational state is often suggested to be the principal factor underlying smoking (Pomerleau and Pomerleau, 1984), especially in first establishing the habit. Nicotine is associated with an increase in mental concentration. The motivational basis underlying a given smoker can vary, sometimes a cigarette being taken for relaxation and at other times to gain alertness (Gilbert *et al.*, 1997). This again emphasizes the importance of context and control.

The mechanical act of smoking and associated taste (e.g. of nicotine) form part of the attraction (Rose and Corrigal, 1997). For smokers, smoking-related cues are particularly strong in their ability to capture attention and increase the motivation to smoke (Hogarth *et al.*, 2003). When trying to quit, this points to the importance of avoiding smoking-related contexts, as is the case with other addictive drugs. The potent reinforcement potential in humans might, in addition to cross-species processes, depend upon the mechanical act of smoking (e.g. holding and puffing) and species-specific effects on cognitive processing.

The act of lighting is repeated regularly, specific to smoking and is stereotyped. It often tends to be a social activity and it might be expected that, when one smoker lights-up, this will trigger mirror neurons in another's brain (Iacoboni, 2008). Craving might owe something to such social facilitation. Indeed, some evidence suggests that in smokers, as compared with non-smokers, the mirror neuron system is relatively sensitive (Pineda and Oberman, 2006).

Neurochemistry

After inhaling, nicotine is taken into the blood and appears in the brain very rapidly. Within as little as seven seconds of puffing, 25% of inhaled nicotine has already crossed the blood–brain barrier (Pomerleau and Pomerleau, 1984). Nicotine leaves the brain rapidly after the cigarette has been smoked. These dynamics provide optimal conditions to associate the neurochemical changes with the sight of the cigarette, the action of smoking and the environmental context (i.e. classical conditioning). To make matters worse, nicotine is a special drug in combining universal availability and legality with a capacity to facilitate work!

Nicotine's motivational effects seem to depend upon actions on various neurochemicals, e.g. cholinergic, serotonergic and opioidergic, and hormonal systems (Dani and Heinemann, 1996; Koob, 1999). These neurochemical systems come together in influencing the mesolimbic dopaminergic pathway (Chiamulera, 2005). Nicotine shares the property of dopaminergic activation with other addictive drugs. Nicotine activates cholinergic (nicotinic) receptors on dopaminergic neurons, e.g. those that project from the VTA to the N.acc. (Rose and Corrigal, 1997).

In rats, a combination of stress and nicotine is especially effective in triggering DA activity in the N.acc. (Takahashi *et al.*, 1998). If this can be generalized to humans, it suggests a process whereby stress and nicotine combine to promote the intake of more nicotine.

Addictive potential

Nicotine is strongly addictive (Stolerman and Jarvis, 1995). Patients under treatment for addiction to hard drugs and who also smoked cigarettes ranked cigarettes as being more difficult to give up than the drug that was the target of treatment (Kozlowski *et al.*, 1989).

In Britain, the average male smoker smokes 17 cigarettes each day and the average female smoker 14 per day. Light smokers are rare. Craving is a common phenomenon in the absence of a cigarette and smokers generally rate their chances of giving up as low.

Alcohol

Acting on various neurotransmitters, alcohol has effects such as to lower anxiety, by which it can mediate negative reinforcement, and to induce mild euphoria (Chick and Erickson, 1996; Koob, 1999). Alcohol triggers activity in the body's natural opioid system, which might, in turn, promote craving for more (Mercer and Holder, 1997). Craving can be particularly exacerbated within certain external contexts (e.g. being in a bar) or internal contexts (e.g. stress or depression). The alcohol withdrawal effect has similarities with that of opiates and might also involve the PAG (Wise, 1988). Opiate agonists tend to increase alcohol consumption and antagonists tend to decrease it (Davidson and Amit, 1997). Wand *et al.* (1998) suggest that differences between individuals in tendency to alcoholism are mediated via different levels of endogenous opioid activity. Those prone to alcoholism appear to have an intrinsically low level of opioid activity.

Alcohol normally has relatively little reinforcement value to rats. However, strains of alcohol-preferring rats can be selectively bred (McBride and Li, 1998).

Marijuana

Marijuana has been used for more than 4000 years for therapeutic (Chapter 14) and recreational reasons (Stahl, 1998). The psychoactive ingredient of marijuana is delta-9-tetrahydrocannabinol (THC). The brain manufactures its own supply of a marijuana-like substance, termed anandamide, and contains cannabinoid (CB) receptors. A subtype, the CB1 receptor, is believed to mediate the rewarding effects of cannabinoid substances. Marijuana appears to act by boosting mesolimbic DA transmission and altering serotonergic neurotransmission (Gessa *et al.*, 1998).

Can marijuana become addictive? Certainly there are people for whom its use is described as 'problematic' and the term 'cannabis dependence' has entered the clinical literature (Le Strat *et al.*, 2009). To address the issue of addiction, researchers compare features of marijuana use with that of 'hard drugs'. Deprived of marijuana, heavy users crave the drug. Exposure to cues linked to marijuana use triggers activation in brain areas linked to addiction, such as the nucleus accumbens (Filbey *et al.*, 2009). The degree of activation correlates with the extent of problems experienced.

Withdrawal symptoms associated with discontinuation of supply are sometimes experienced, consisting of anger and irritability, etc. (Haughey *et al.*, 2008). That they are not more serious might be linked to the fact that there is not such a sharp onset–offset profile of effect as with other drugs; after appearing in the blood, cannabinoids are stored in body fats and then slowly released (Stahl, 1998) (which explains why some people take harder drugs, since their time-frame of detection is shorter). If there is receptor adaptation during the acute phase, the 'endogenous' source of drug from body fat might cushion the system against withdrawal effects for the time that it takes the receptor state to recover. Marijuana illustrates the earlier point about context-dependency of drug effects. People high in anxiety can find that this is increased by the drug (Szuster *et al.*, 1988).

Caffeine

Regular users of relatively large amounts of caffeine (in the form of tea or coffee) report a withdrawal effect (e.g. headaches, sleepiness, irritability) when intake ceases (Griffiths and Woodson, 1988). A double-blind placebo-controlled study demonstrated that the effects are due to loss of the caffeine content of the beverage per se (Phillips-Bute and Lane, 1998). Caffeine does not reliably cause hedonic feelings in humans. Rather, it often induces anxiety. The fact that it is the world's most widely used psychoactive drug points to the inadequacy of hedonic explanations of drug-taking and suggests that wanting relates in no simple way to liking (Chapter 15).

How does caffeine act? There are receptors in the brain to the natural substance adenosine. Occupation by adenosine inhibits the activity of the neurons bearing these receptors. Dopaminergic neurons are among those having this type of receptor on their surface. Caffeine is similar to adenosine but, by occupying its receptors, caffeine prevents the action of adenosine. Hence, a source of inhibition on neurons involved in wanting and reward is lowered.

Dopaminergic drugs

So-called 'impulse control disorders', such as excessive buying, gambling and inappropriate sexual behaviour, sometimes emerge in Parkinson's disease patients as a result of dopaminergic medication (Chapter 10; Lim *et al.*, 2008). Medication is designed to boost the level of dopaminergic activity in the affected brain region, so as to bring movement control nearer to normal. However, this inadvertently gives an over-dose of dopamine to the *intact* dopaminergic system involved with motivation (the mesolimbic dopaminergic pathway, introduced in Chapter 15). Some patients exhibit what is termed 'dopamine dysregulation syndrome' (DDS). This is a form of addiction to dopaminergic drugs, taking them in excess of what is optimal for the control of motor disorder. Such evidence lends support to the role of dopaminergic activation in addiction. It appears that drugs which give a steady long-acting boost to DA transmission provide less risk of addiction than those which trigger bursts of activation (Lawrence *et al.*, 2003). This would fit an understanding of the role of dopamine in motivation.

In terms of dopaminergic neurotransmission triggered by L-dopa in the ventral striatum, a study compared Parkinson's patients who showed DDS with those who did not (Evans *et al.*, 2006). It employed neuroimaging with positron emission tomography (PET) and ^{11}C-raclopride (RAC) (Chapter 5). Images were compared under the conditions when the patients were on and off L-dopa treatment.

Figure 18.7 compares Parkinson's patients who did not exhibit DDS (controls) with those who did exhibit it (DDS). The diagram might confuse you as much as it did me when I first saw it (through no fault of the authors). Note that the vertical axis shows the percentage *reduction* in RAC binding potential. RAC and dopamine released are in competition for occupation of receptors. So, the higher the vertical value, the less the occupation by the extraneous substance and the greater is the occupation of receptors by dopamine. Within the putamen, there is no difference between the two groups. The putamen is concerned with motor control (Chapter 10). By contrast, in the ventral striatum, a region concerned with

motivation (which includes the N.acc.), the DDS group showed a significantly higher reduction in RAC binding potential than did the control group. This points to a significantly higher occupation of receptors by dopamine in the ventral striatum in the DDS group. Figure 18.8 shows the localization in the brain, the ventral striatum, where there are significant differences between groups.

Are the effects of dopaminergic neurotransmission more closely associated with 'wanting' or 'liking' (Chapter 15)? In this case, wanting was for the dopaminergic drug L-dopa. Figure 18.9(a) shows a positive correlation between the reduction in RAC binding potential (i.e. increased occupation of ventral striatum with dopamine) and the individual's ranking of the degree of wanting. By contrast, there was a negative correlation between RAC binding potential and liking of the drug (Figure 18.9(b)).

Hallucinogens

The term **hallucinogen** refers to a class of drug for which the primary action is to change sensory perception (Aghajanian, 1994; Delgado and Moreno, 1998). It includes lysergic acid diethylamide (LSD), mescaline (from a type of cactus) and psilocybin (from a type of mushroom) and their effect in altering cognition is termed 'psychedelic' (Stahl, 1996). The person taking such a 'trip' might feel a sense of union with the universe or with God. Disorientation and panic are termed a 'bad trip', a state that can be characterized by paranoia and delusions.

It is difficult if not impossible to teach animals an operant task for hallucinogens and they have a low addictive potential in humans (Griffiths *et al.*, 1979). One special case is that monkeys in sensory isolation sometimes learn an operant task for them (Siegel and Jarvick, 1980). Monkeys exhibit orientation, tracking and startle responses, as if the drug is simulating external sensory stimulation. This might have features in common with animals kept in monotonous conditions working for a change in sensory stimulation (Chapter 15).

A common property of the substances just named is that their hallucinogenic potency is proportional to their ability to inhibit serotonergic neurons by acting at serotonin (5-HT$_2$) receptors (Aghajanian, 1994). In turn, the serotonin effect mediates changes at the locus coeruleus, which has broad noradrenergic projections throughout the brain.

Activity within the locus coeruleus appears to alter processing such that target neurons have a lower level of spontaneous activity and higher response to sensory stimulation. This seems to be the basis of distorted (e.g. heightened) perception and cognition induced by psychedelic drugs.

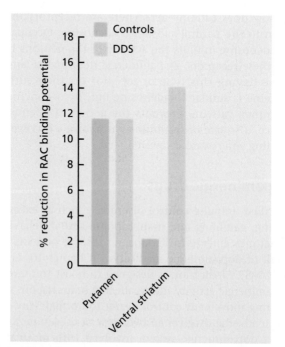

Figure 18.7 The percentage reduction in ^{11}C-raclopride (RAC) binding following administration of L-dopa, comparing two brain regions, the putamen and the ventral striatum.
Source: Evans *et al.* (2006) *Annals of Neurology*, 59, Fig. 1, p. 854.

Figure 18.8 Sagittal (top), coronal (centre) and transaxial (lower) images showing in yellow/orange region of significant differences between groups.

Source: Evans *et al.* (2006) *Annals of Neurology*, 59, Fig. 2, p. 854.

A personal angle

The doors of perception

In *The Doors of Perception*, the English writer and philosopher Aldous Huxley gives a vivid account of his experiments with mescaline. On the perception of an ordinary shelf of books, he writes (Huxley, 1972, p. 13): 'Like the flowers, they glowed, when I looked at them, with brighter colours, a profounder significance. Red books, like rubies; emerald books; books bound in white jade . . .'.

Not just perception but also priorities change, in that the mescaline user (p. 18): 'finds most of the causes for which, at ordinary times, he was prepared to act and suffer, profoundly uninteresting' and mescaline took Huxley from (p. 27): 'the world of selves, of time, of moral judgements and utilitarian considerations . . .'.

Huxley suggested that the mescaline experience was similar to one small aspect of the cognition of people with schizophrenia (Chapter 22). Huxley died on 22 November 1963 (the same day as John F. Kennedy), from cancer; his last moments being spent under the influence of LSD injected by his wife (Huxley, 1969).

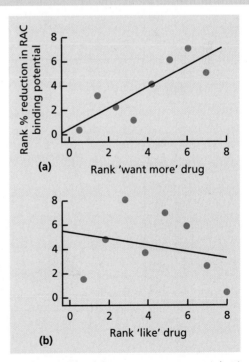

Figure 18.9 Correlations between percentage reduction in RAC binding potential and (a) wanting more drug and (b) liking the drug.

Source: Evans *et al.* (2006) *Annals of Neurology*, 59, Fig. 3, p. 855.

Ecstasy

Ecstasy, chemical name 3,4-methylenedioxymetham-phetamine (MDMA), became a popular recreational drug in the late 1980s (Steele *et al.*, 1994). It promotes the release and blocks reuptake of serotonin and dopamine, which mediates psychedelic effects. It is often taken at large social gatherings termed 'raves'. Ecstasy's effects include elevated mood, sensual awareness and a sense of 'awareness with others' (Stahl, 1996). On the negative side, there are reports of increased anxiety, panic attacks and psychosis (Steele *et al.*, 1994), as well as memory impairments and damage to the nervous system (Roberts *et al.*, 2009).

Similarities and differences among drug-related activities

In spite of diverse effects, a subgroup of psychoactive drugs activate some common neural systems. Activation of dopamine (e.g. at the N.acc.) appears to be a common factor in those that are addictive, e.g. amphetamine, cocaine, nicotine, morphine and alcohol (Everitt *et al.*, 2001). Non-addictive drugs, e.g. hallucinogens, have a primary site of action elsewhere in the brain.

In humans, there are similarities in the subjective effects of opiates, amphetamines and cocaine. A former cocaine addict can be at risk from relapse by an occasional use of heroin and the heroin addict is at risk from cocaine. In rats, an extinguished heroin habit can be reinstated by a 'free' priming delivery of cocaine and vice versa. This provides some rationale for the demand for total abstention from all drugs that is commonly made on rehabilitation programmes. Wise (1988,

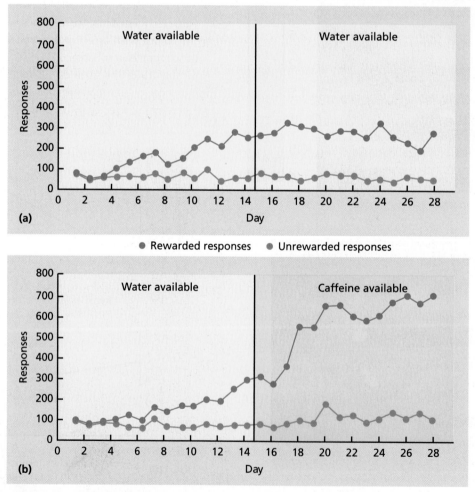

Figure 18.10 Responses rewarded with intravenous nicotine when (a) plain water is available and (b) when caffeine solution is available at day 14. The response was poking the nose into a hole (active). As a control, another hole was present into which a response did not trigger nicotine infusion (passive).

Source: Toates (2004, Figure 1.17), after Shoaib *et al.* (1999, Fig. 3).

p. 125) notes that nicotine and alcohol can activate DA neurons in the VTA:

> The possibility that nicotine, alcohol, and even caffeine may activate the same neural circuitry suggests other drug stimuli that may put an ex-addict at risk. Of these, smoking represents a potential stimulant to relapse that may be widely underestimated.

In people with a history of cocaine-taking, nicotine accentuates craving in the presence of cocaine-related cues (Reid *et al.*, 1998). Even caffeine might not be harmless in this regard. Evidence suggests that it can increase the tendency to take nicotine (Bernstein *et al.*, 2002). There is a possible rat model of this. Figure 18.10 shows the number of responses for intravenous nicotine by rats having available either plain water or water with caffeine added.

So much for this subgroup of drugs, which have the potential for addiction; let us now consider some non-drug-related activities that have similar properties.

Section summary

1 Amphetamine and cocaine increase levels of synaptic dopamine.

2 Opiates target opioid receptors and interact with dopaminergic neurotransmission. They have reward and aversion-alleviation effects.

3 Nicotine is rapidly absorbed into the bloodstream, enters the brain and affects a number of neurochemical activities, e.g. dopamine.

4 If operant behaviour for self-infusion of nicotine is associated with an arbitrary external cue, it is easier to produce.

5 Alcohol interacts with endogenous opioids.

6 People with Parkinson's disease and being treated with drugs that boost dopamine can develop an addiction to them.

7 Drugs such as LSD, termed hallucinogens, target serotonin.

☞ Test your knowledge

18.3 In the experiment shown in Figure 18.10, why have two holes and record nose-pokes in both (one connected to nicotine delivery and the other having no consequence)?

Answer on page 490

Non-drug-related activities

Introduction

Popular language refers to a number of non-chemical-related activities as being similar to drug-taking, including having the potential to become addictive. Does biological psychology offer any insights that would give a basis to such a description? As an example, playing video games can be highly engaging for some individuals. This activity is associated with activation of brain dopamine in the striatum (Koepp *et al.*, 1998).

Internet addiction

Adapting addiction to the 21st century, Griffiths (1999) identified Internet addiction, according to the core components of addiction. These are (i) salience, domination of thought processes by the target activity, (ii) a modification of mood when engaged in the activity, (iii) tolerance, increasing amounts of activity are required to achieve the same effect, (iv) withdrawal symptoms (mood lowering), (v) conflict, e.g. within the individual and with others over time and money spent, as well as disruption to life, and (vi) relapse.

All of the criteria listed can apply to any kind of Internet activity. However, specifically using the

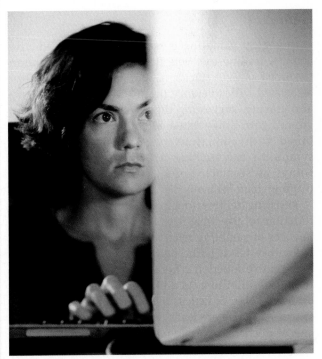

Some activities that do not involve drug-taking nonetheless show addictive properties. Could there be any underlying similarities?

Source: Luca DiCecco/Alamy.

Internet to obtain sexual excitement can combine all of these features with social disapproval or in some cases strong legal sanctions against the activity (in the case of searching for under-age images). This use of the Internet is a well-recognized problem.

Sexual addiction

The term 'sexual addiction' refers to an element of conflict, in addition to excessive sexual activity (Goodman, 2008). Often sexual addiction arises at times of particular stress (Schneider and Weiss, 2001) – stress is known to exacerbate chemical addictions too. Addictive sexual behaviour could then be reinforced by anxiety reduction (Leiblum and Rosen, 2000, p. 471).

A treatment for sex addiction is the use of selective serotonin reuptake inhibitors (SSRIs) (Coleman, 2005). There are also reports of success in using the opioid antagonist naltrexone, thereby blocking the pleasure of engaging in the addictive activity (Bostwick and Bucci, 2008). Such treatments suggest the need for an integrative psychobiological approach to its understanding.

Sometimes addictions coexist. For example, the sex addict often has simultaneously an addiction to alcohol or illicit drugs. Cross-sensitization between activities might be expected on the basis of common underlying dopaminergic bases.

Gambling

Pathological gambling is recognized as an addictive activity, leading to severe financial difficulties and in the worst cases to suicide (Goudriaan *et al.*, 2004). It is associated with tolerance (need to increase the 'dose') and craving, suggesting the value of seeing common ground with drug-related addictions. It is often combined with addictions to chemicals. Withdrawal symptoms can include irritability and even such things as stomach upset, sweating and trembling (Cunningham-Williams *et al.*, 2009).

Resisting temptation involves exerting executive function to give weight to long-term negative consequences of gambling relative to its immediate pull. In laboratory tasks, pathological gamblers show deficits in executive function. This amounts to a deficiency in response inhibition. As a likely biological basis, some evidence points to deficits in functioning of the prefrontal cortex. There are leads pointing to possible genetic and neurochemical (e.g. dopamine) differences, comparing pathological gamblers and controls.

Having presented the evidence on chemical and non-chemical addictions, the discussion now uses this information for a more detailed look at explanations of drug-taking and addictive activities.

Section summary

1 Certain non-drug-related activities exhibit properties similar to those associated with drugs.

2 Some non-drug-related activities have the potential to become addictive.

Test your knowledge

18.4 When compulsive sexual behaviour is reinforced by anxiety reduction, what adjective qualifies such reinforcement?

Answer on page 490

Trying to explain addiction

This section looks at some theories that attempt to give a broad explanation of drug-taking and addiction. Although the explanations sometimes seem to be in competition, the section will point to where their features can be reconciled.

Two orientations

In the context of opiate drugs, Alexander and Hadaway (1982) proposed a distinction between two explanatory frameworks: the **exposure orientation** and the **adaptive orientation**. According to the exposure orientation, addiction arises simply from exposure to drugs. Drugs irreversibly change the body so that, beyond a threshold, the individual wants and 'needs' more. However, according to the adaptive orientation, drugs are a support, chemotherapy for the mind, which allows the individual to function better at times of psychological need. Some people need such support ('a crutch'). The newly recognized non-chemical addictions such as to sex or the Internet appear also to provide a similar and temporary emotional support. You may feel that each perspective contains elements of the truth, possibly with the value of each differing between individuals and circumstances within an individual.

Affective states

Introduction

Taking drugs such as alcohol, heroin and cocaine has affective ('hedonic') consequences. It is therefore tempting to assume that the strength of motivation to take a drug correlates closely with the subjective euphoria obtained. Although an overall positive correlation exists, there is no simple equivalence (Robinson and Berridge, 1993), exemplified by Figure 18.9. With repeated drug use, subjectively reported hedonism can decline, whereas craving increases. In some cases, the first encounters with drugs (opiates, alcohol and nicotine) are unpleasant rather than euphoric and yet people are still moved to repeat the experience (Wise and Bozarth, 1987). Paranoia can result from amphetamine use but the habit persists (Ellinwood, 1967).

So, although affect plays an important role, it cannot fully explain addiction. Let us turn first to what might be explained by its role.

A model

Figure 18.11 represents positive and negative affective states with mutual inhibition, indicated by negative signs (Solomon and Corbit, 1974). A neutral affective state is the result of a balance between the two. These states depend in part upon stimuli, cognitions and goals, etc. Affect is closely related to cognition, e.g. negative affect biases towards experiencing negative thoughts and interpretations and triggering memories of negative events (Baker *et al.*, 2004). Negative cognition (e.g. from personal failure) tends to excite negative affect.

Given an appropriate social context, after entering the body drugs appear to tilt the balance temporarily in a positive direction. Thus, over a middle range, the distinction between gaining a positive effect and reducing a negative one becomes somewhat academic.

It appears that the normal balance giving life a slightly positive affect (if you are lucky!) is maintained by, among other things, a background level of endogenous opioid activity within the CNS (Skoubis *et al.*, 2005). See Figure 18.12(a). Opioid antagonists block the positive effect of natural opioids and thereby move the balance in a negative direction. This triggers or amplifies signs of social distress (Chapter 12). See Figure 18.12(b). Excessive stimulation in a positive direction by, say, opiate drugs (Figure 18.12(c)) would be followed by some neural adaptation of the system (Christie *et al.*, 1997). Adaptation would tend to tilt net affect in a negative direction by such means as loss of opioid receptors

(Figure 18.12(d)). Injection of an opioid antagonist would then shift it still further in a negative direction (Wise, 1988). It appears that an aversive state can arise either as a withdrawal reaction to the absence of the drug or from stress, depression, anxiety and, in addition in humans, personal life crises (Baker *et al.*, 2004; Singer, 1993). Drugs (and possibly some non-drug-based activities) then bring temporary relief.

Negative affect can be (but is not necessarily) associated with physiological signs of withdrawal outside the nervous system (Christie *et al.*, 1997; Koob, 1999). If drugs are readily available, their intake can be motivated by positive incentive processes. After they become unavailable, accompanied in some cases by explicit withdrawal, the control might shift to avoidance of negative affect (Baker *et al.*, 2004).

Automatic and controlled intake

As with other types of behaviour, that associated with drugs reflects processes organized at different levels of the CNS. These range from the controlled conscious choice to seek a drug for its anticipated beneficial effects to automatic responding to drug-related cues (Tiffany,

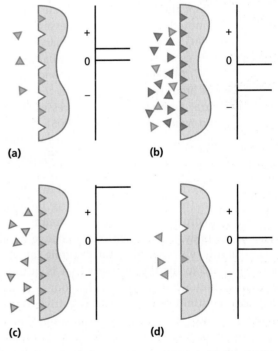

△ Opioid ▲ Opioid–antagonist △ Opiate drug

Figure 18.12 Suggested role of opioids, opioid antagonists and opiates and the associated level of affect. Neural events (left) and level of contribution to affect (graph to right). (a) Basal level in drug-free condition, (b) immediately after injection of opioid antagonist, (c) immediately after injection of opiate drug and (d) period after opiate drug has left the body.

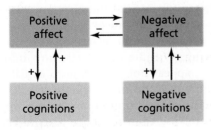

Figure 18.11 Model of affective states.

1990). Presumably, any instance of drug-seeking reflects a balance between these factors. It appears that drug-seeking starts in a conscious ('intentional') mode and then switches to a more automatic mode with experience. The addicted person becomes increasingly at the mercy of the pull of drug-related stimuli in the environment (Everitt *et al.*, 2001).

There is a rat model of this shift of weight (Vanderschuren and Everitt, 2004). Normally, activities such as feeding are inhibited by cues that signal aversive events. Lever-pressing in a Skinner box drops when such a cue is presented. Rats working for cocaine also exhibit such inhibition *early in their experience*. However, after extensive exposure, they cease to react to such cues and go on lever-pressing regardless. This might model the human addict's indifference to warning signs. Even after extensive exposure, not all rats switch to a compulsive pattern of use in which they are indifferent to such aversive cues (Deroche-Gamonet *et al.*, 2004). This points to individual differences, presumably in the sensitivity of dopaminergic pathways. Such differences might also be present between humans.

An addicted human is in a dilemma: a part of the mind seems to be offering restraint but another part, which mediates the compulsive pull, seems stronger. Which parts of the brain underlie these different tendencies? As noted, subcortical processes such as the N.acc. and PAG appear to be the primary bases of drug-seeking. It is especially the ventromedial prefrontal cortex (VMPFC) that mediates restraint and opposes the pull of lower brain regions. Activity in the VMPFC acts as the neural embodiment of processes termed 'self-directed' and 'willpower' (Bechara, 2005). With the help of this region, representations of harmful future consequences are retrieved as part of working memory and exploited in restraint. Individual differences in susceptibility to addiction could be embodied in different balances between mechanisms underlying impulsive reactivity (e.g. to drug-related cues) and restraint.

Once in the body, a drug itself might change weight between such levels. Consider, for example, alcohol. This would tend to lift the restraint that is normally offered on certain alcohol-related behaviour (e.g. seeking yet another drink) by higher-level cognitive controls (Chapter 15). Also drugs such as cocaine can damage the prefrontal cortex. This could thereby chronically weaken the role of restraint on drug-taking (or possibly any associated non-drug-based addictive activity).

Incentive sensitization theory

Introduction

A highly influential theory of drug-addiction with broad application across addictive substances is the **incentive sensitization theory** (Robinson and Berridge, 1993). It is based on three features of addiction: (i) craving, (ii) that craving and drug-taking can be reinstated long after drug use has ceased and (iii) 'as drugs come to be "wanted" more-and-more, they often come to be liked less-and-less' (p. 249). A rationale for the theory is summed up in a question posed by Ellinwood and Escalante (1970, p. 189): 'A puzzling, yet central, question in the study of the amphetamine psychosis is why individuals who are experiencing acute terror and other unpleasant effects continue to use amphetamines in large doses.'

Wanting and liking

Liking and wanting sometimes appear to increase in parallel (Willner *et al.*, 2005) but there is a paradox that drugs such as heroin can be liked less and less as they are sought more and more.

Some might explain the dissociation between wanting and liking by means of a switch from positive to negative reinforcement. Robinson and Berridge do not deny that this may capture part of the truth but suggest it is not the defining feature of the paradox, since wanting outlasts any withdrawal symptoms. Rather they argue that, with repeated use of drugs, there is sensitization of the neural system of wanting, which becomes uncoupled from liking. Only the wanting mechanism is sensitized. This causes a pathological focus of perception, attention and motivation upon drug-related stimuli and thoughts. The change in neural sensitivity is long-lasting and can be permanent, which renders addicts vulnerable to relapse even after years of abstinence. According to the theory, the mesolimbic DA system is the neural system that underlies the attribution of incentive value, termed **incentive salience**, and that is sensitized by drugs (Chapter 15). Of course, an explanation is needed as to why non-drug-related addictive activities can sometimes show similar properties to drug-related ones (Goodman, 2008). Presumably, dopaminergic activation must be intrinsically self-strengthening with repeated activation.

A lowering of DA activity is associated with a lowering of drug craving and a lowering of the strength with which drug-related cues capture attention (Leyton, 2010). However, it is not associated with a lowering of the pleasure derived from such drugs as nicotine, alcohol, amphetamine and cocaine (Leyton, 2010). Figure 18.13 shows this for the case of cocaine.

Further evidence on incentive sensitization includes the following. Withdrawal effects, unconditional or conditional, appear not to be able to explain relapse. Addicts commonly do not attribute relapse to withdrawal. Incentive sensitization can explain why addicts sometimes relapse to drug-taking years after quitting and even in the absence of negative affect (Robinson and Berridge, 2008).

Craving is often highest immediately after taking the drug, when presumably any aversive state has been partly if not wholly eliminated and withdrawal has not yet started. This provides a rationale for the advice of maintaining total abstinence. In rats, drug infusion into the brain can prime and reinstate drug-taking. Robinson and Berridge do not deny that increasing hedonism can result from drug use but merely that it alone cannot explain addiction (cf. Peele and Alexander, 1985). Nicotine is highly addictive and yet one imagines that few smokers would associate its use with unrestrained euphoria (see also earlier account of caffeine).

According to the theory, incentive salience and pleasure are not entirely separate processes. Indeed, applied to conventional motivational systems, it would be a maladaptive design feature if they were. Incentive salience is normally maintained in part by the pleasure that follows engagement with the incentive (Figure 18.14). For example, foods that evoke a positive affective rating are normally sought. However, in drug-taking some dissociation between wanting and liking is introduced. Increased sensitization is experienced subjectively as craving for drugs.

The environmental factor

The expression of incentive sensitization in behaviour is a function of the environment that has been associated with drug-taking (Robinson and Berridge, 2008). Drugs do not unconditionally sensitize a craving process divorced from the context in which the drug was taken. Hence, a drug-user might manifest the elevated craving and wanting associated with incentive sensitization only when in a drug-related environment. Incentive sensitization means that the amount of DA released in response to a given stimulus (taking a drug or an environmental cue paired in the past with drug-taking) increases (Robinson and Berridge, 2008). As noted, patients taking narcotics to counter pain do not usually crave drugs outside the clinical context (Chapter 14). Thus, particular cognitions, goals and strategies are part of the sensitization process.

Stress

Stress contributes to taking drugs. Since the drug takes away the sharp edge of stress, by implication, this seems to be a process of negative reinforcement. In addition, stress appears to increase the incentive salience attributed to drug-related stimuli. Both addictive drugs and stress sensitize DA activity (Robinson and Berridge, 1993). Stress-related sensitization of dopaminergic neurotransmission appears to act through CRF and corticosteroids (Goodman, 2008) (Chapter 13).

Therapy

As therapy, the theory gives a rationale for extinction procedures, i.e. repeated exposure to drug-related cues under guidance. However, clinically based extinction programmes might not generalize to the multitude of drug-related stimuli of the street. As noted earlier, results have been disappointing. DA antagonists would be a blunt instrument, reducing all of life's attractions. Perhaps the only effective treatment would be a chemical to undo sensitization, but there is no immediate prospect of that (Robinson and Berridge, 1993).

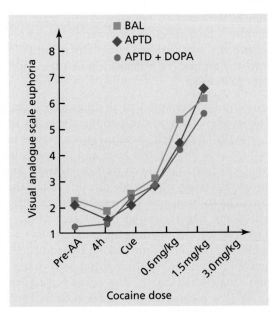

Figure 18.13 The effect of dose of cocaine on euphoria, as measured on a visual analogue scale. BAL = control condition, APTD = dopamine depletion by means of APTD; APTD + DOPA = combination of APTD plus L-dopa.
Source: Leyton (2010, Fig. 13.5, p. 229).

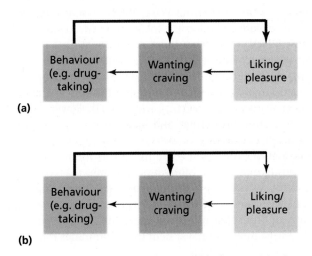

Figure 18.14 Situation (a) before and (b) after sensitization. States of positive affect ('hedonism') increase incentive salience. However, with experience, wanting/craving increases but liking/pleasure sometimes decreases.
Source: Toates (1998b, Fig. 2.25, p. 55).

A challenge to be met

It would be surprising if everything fitted neatly to a given theory. One result which appears to sit uncomfortably alongside incentive sensitization theory is that cocaine addiction is associated with a reduction in the number of DA D_2 receptors in the striatum (the region containing the N.acc.) (see Robinson and Berridge, 2008). Intuitively, one might have expected an increased number. Similarly, Chapter 16 (Figure 16.20, p. 429) showed a negative correlation between the degree of obesity and the number of D_2 receptors. This leads some to suggest that increased drug-taking or eating represents an attempt to compensate for this reduction. Can this effect be accommodated within incentive sensitization theory?

DA activation might be sufficiently intense to cause 'down-regulation' of DA receptors (loss of a number of DA receptors as a result of the impact of the transmitter). Yet still the release rate of DA might be so high that there is a net increase in DA activity over the course of addiction. There is some evidence that D_2 receptors can exist in more than one form, showing either high or low affinity for DA (Robinson and Berridge, 2008). Drug sensitization appears to cause (i) an increase in density of the high-affinity type, associated with (ii) a decrease in density of the low-affinity type. It might be that the effect of (i) far outweighs any effect of (ii).

Integration

This section will put the incentive-sensitization theory into a broader context.

A change of weight

Bechara *et al.* (1998) and Wise (1988) present models in which opiate addiction is explained by two distinct processes. First, there is an incentive motivational process. However, according to this model, once addiction develops, the weighting can change such that motivation is based largely on a second and distinct process: avoidance of aversive effects of withdrawal. Fewer 'highs' are reported and larger and larger doses are required to sustain avoidance of aversion. Craving can be based upon either process. According to this model, the role of positive incentive motivation becomes masked when control shifts to the aversion avoidance system. Suppose that withdrawal effects are alleviated, e.g. by prescription of the substitute drug methadone. The positive incentive motivational system then dominates intake.

The role of the insula

Having been largely ignored historically, the insular cortex ('insula') (Chapter 12) is now attracting interest in the study of drug addiction (Naqvi and Bechara, 2009). It might provide an integrative link for theories of drug-taking. Brain imaging has shown this structure to be activated during the experience of conscious drug urges. So, is its activity part of the causal sequence leading to drug-taking? Naqvi *et al.* (2007) compared smokers who had suffered damage to the insula or to other brain structures. Those with damage to the insula showed a disruption to their addiction in the sense that quitting was relatively easy. One reported (p. 534) that his 'body forgot the urge to smoke'. A study in rats pointed to a similar involvement of the insula: its temporary inactivation by injection of the local anaesthetic lidocaine temporarily abolished a conditioned place preference for drug administration (Contreras *et al.*, 2007).

The insula is involved in a number of functions concerned with the internal state of the body. For example, the insula receives visceral sensations from the organs such as the gut, the oesophagus and the heart. Information from the internal organs is processed and, reciprocally, output from the insula influences these organs. The insula also receives information on touch, taste and temperature. According to a contemporary understanding, the insula is the biological basis of the conscious experience of the body (Naqvi and Bechara, 2009).

Based on an understanding of the insula and its interconnections with other brain structures, Naqvi and Bechara propose a model that can integrate incentive models and withdrawal models. They suggest (p. 60):

> internal factors associated with deprivation states (such as withdrawal) are viewed as a 'gate' that determines how effective the incentive input is in exciting the motivational circuits that 'pull' and 'steer' the animal (or human) towards the appropriate goal object.

Naqvi and Bechara note that all drugs have characteristic immediate effects on the 'peripheral regions' of the body, in addition to their chemical effects on the brain. Snorted cocaine has a bitter taste and increases blood pressure and heart-rate. Each puff of cigarette smoke affects the respiratory tract, while nicotine affects the circulation. The influence on the respiratory tract triggers the insula and is perceived as pleasurable. Hence, the ritual of drug use (e.g. lighting up, puffing) plays a vital role in the motivation of drug-seeking and addiction.

The insula could integrate internal body states and external drug-related events. The insula projects to the N.acc. By this means, bodily states such as those of withdrawal could increase the wanting of drugs. The sight of another individual performing the act of injection or lighting could similarly increase wanting via the insula and N.acc.

Evolutionary considerations

So far, we have looked at the causal processes underlying drug-taking but it is useful to reconsider evolutionary aspects (Chapter 2). By directly acting on the brain, drugs have psychoactive effects. This is in contrast to, say, food or sex. In such conventional systems, rewarding effects are first mediated via sensory systems and subsequently activate the brain. Thus, drugs appear to short-circuit part of the system that underlies interaction with conventional incentives and to tap directly into reward systems.

Evolutionary psychology

A false signal

From an evolutionary perspective, taking addictive drugs can be understood by their ability to stimulate and overwhelm processes of natural reward that underlie conventional interactions, e.g. to approach food (Nesse and Berridge, 1997). As Nesse and Berridge note (p. 64): 'Drugs of abuse create a signal in the brain that indicates, falsely, the arrival of a huge fitness benefit'. (They use fitness here in the ethological sense: an increase in reproductive potential.)

Section summary

1 The exposure and adaptive orientations can each explain some features of drug-taking.

2 The incentive sensitization theory distinguishes between wanting and liking.

3 There is evidence that the insula has a role in addictive activities.

Test your knowledge

18.5 With reference to Figure 18.12, suppose that the same quantity of opiate drug as represented in part (c) were to be injected under the conditions of part (d). Which of the following would be the expected outcome in terms of affect? (i) A level the same as part (c), (ii) the same as before, i.e. as shown in part (d), (iii) somewhere between the situations shown in parts (c) and (d).

Answer on page 490

Bringing things together

To return to the contrast between the exposure orientation and the adaptive orientation, much evidence favours the latter. As a general principle, people seem to take drugs as part of a 'problem-solving exercise', to improve their cognitive and affective states. This may be in desperation, in a state of existential angst or as part of spiritual enlightenment. Both chemical and non-chemical-based activities can be recruited to such ends.

Rat models tend to support the adaptive orientation. The amount of drug that a rat takes is heavily dependent upon social context and other available rewards. The fact that nicotine is such a potent reinforcer for humans and relatively weak for rats might be explained in terms of the kinds of peculiarly human problems that it helps to solve, e.g. vigilance and promoting social interaction. However, somewhat in favour of the exposure orientation, it seems that the drug-related solution to a problem is more probable as a result of exposure, as suggested by the incentive sensitization theory. Also,

the move from controlled to automatic processes underlying intake highlights that exposure and repetition increase the tendency to take a drug.

Drug-taking appears to be motivated by positive and negative affect. A number of features are common with conventional motivations (e.g. craving and the role of classical conditioning) and non-chemical-related behaviours can take on addictive features. Drugs such as nicotine and heroin tap into conventional incentive motivational processes involving dopamine and opioids and appear to sensitize them. Such processes are clearly of adaptive value in a conventional context. For example, fitness maximization requires us to be pulled towards mates and sources of food at times of energy deficiency. Pavlovian conditioning between neutral cues and biological incentives is clearly adaptive and a conscious mind might adaptively be occupied by thoughts of biological incentives. However, this adaptive principle can break down when encountering a drug that taps

The function of sleep and its link to causation

What is the function of sleep? The answer might involve a combination of various theories, especially since sleep is not a uniform state but is composed of different types (Roffwarg *et al.*, 1966). Broadly, theories on function can be grouped into three categories, as below.

Homeostasis: a restorative function

Introduction

Homeostatic theory is closest to common sense: sleep keeps an important body parameter within safe limits. It is supported by the observation that sleep deprivation increases the pressure to sleep, lowers the latency of sleep onset and increases the length of subsequent sleep (Benington, 2000). The fact that animals (e.g. rats) die from extended sleep deprivation (Rechtschaffen, 1998) suggests a homeostatic function.

Candidate processes

Sleep could serve the homeostatic function of restoration following 'the "wear and tear" of wakefulness' (Horne, 1988, p. 25). More specifically, it might 'restore the natural balance among the neural centres' (Guyton, 1991, p. 661) or serve a restorative function within the immune system (Hobson, 1999). Sleep loss impairs information processing by the CNS. Reimund (1994, p. 231) suggests that sleep: 'maintains the integrity of neural tissue – a consequence of the energetically sensitive and demanding nature of neural tissue'.

Suppose that, during waking, a biochemical (e.g. a product of metabolism) increases in concentration in the body. Sleep might reduce or eliminate this chemical (Cravatt *et al.*, 1995). Alternatively, a biochemical might be depleted during waking. With the exception of the nervous system, the body apparently does not require sleep for repair (Horne, 1988). General bodily repair can occur during relaxed wakefulness. For example, sleep appears to serve no better than sleepless rest to correct muscular fatigue. The brain is the organ that shows the most marked change between sleep and relaxed wakefulness and that benefits most from sleep (Hobson, 1988).

Although evidence suggests a restorative function, its exact nature remains elusive (Horne, 1988). There is a list of substances that *might* constitute what is regulated by sleep (Rechtschaffen, 1998). Function could relate to several candidates. One possiblity is orexin (hypocretin), a neurotransmitter produced by orexinergic neurons in the brain (Mieda and Sakurai, 2009; Vassalli and Dijk, 2009). Their cell bodies are in the hypothalamus and their axons project widely in the brain.

Linking function and causation

If the function is that sleep serves to restore a substance ('X') to an optimal level, there might be a straightforward translation from this to causation (Figure 19.4). That is to say, deviation of X from its optimum might be detected and motivate sleep (Cravatt *et al.*, 1995). Restoration of equilibrium would trigger waking, i.e. homeostasis by negative feedback.

Inactivity/safety

Sleep might have evolved to keep animals inactive at particular times (Meddis, 1977). Depending upon their habitat, sensory systems, predators and prey, etc., a species is best equipped to be active in either the light or dark. For example, humans have relatively poor vision at night. Therefore, they are programmed to be inactive then, relatively safe from predators and accidents (Jouvet, 1975). By contrast, rats exploit smell and touch, not having good vision. According to this theory, they are active at night when they are least visible to predators. In terms of fitness (Chapter 2), animals sleep at those times when, in their evolution, there was relatively little *benefit* to be gained and a high *cost* of being active. Inactivity might also allow conservation of resources, e.g. energy (D.B. Cohen, 1979).

No matter what the functional explanation, on a causal level sleep involves a rhythmically varying internal cycle of 24 hours. Thus, the difference between explanations in terms of homeostasis and safety is not about the presence or absence of an internal signal. It is about the significance of this signal in the evolution of sleep, i.e. as regulated variable (homeostasis) or as timing cue (inactivity/safety hypothesis).

In principle, if sleep evolved to serve safety rather than homeostasis, it might prove possible to resist it. An anti-sleep tablet might be invented, e.g. an antagonist to neurotransmitters in neural circuits underlying sleep. Artificial lighting might then make sleep redundant and

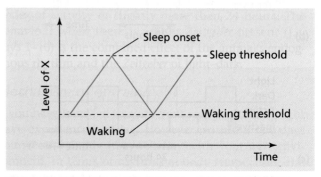

Figure 19.4 Model of sleep based on the regulation of substance X (in principle the waking and sleeping thresholds might be reversed).

we could either party or indulge the Protestant work ethic for 24 hours a day. Whether this would be desirable is another matter.

Maintaining the brain and its plasticity

Introduction

A function of sleep might be to help to maintain the functional stability and plasticity of the neural systems of the brain (Benington and Frank, 2003; Moruzzi, 1966). Such plasticity could involve the production of new neurons or changes in the connections between existing neurons. The effects of use and disuse in development of neural systems were discussed in Chapter 6. Seen in such terms, sleep might provide a process for selectively strengthening certain synapses and eliminating others, depending upon whether they are part of a functioning circuit (Jouvet, 1975). This could apply to early development or to the adult, or both. Development is a time of change in the brain and young animals exhibit much sleep (see later).

Some brain regions show little change in activity during sleep and waking (Horne, 1988). Their role is largely preprogrammed and routine. So, if the function of sleep is to facilitate plasticity, it seems as if these regions have, putting it metaphorically, no need to sleep. For example, the part of the brain stem concerned with respiration might be expected to be of this kind. Its activity is consistent over time and, of course, respiration can hardly be switched off to allow maintenance. By contrast, the cerebral cortex is commonly exposed to novel unpredictable situations and it seems to 'need to switch off-line and sleep'.

Stability of serotonergic systems

In rats, sleep deprivation disrupts serotonergic neurotransmission. More specifically, the disruption is to that mediated by one subtype of serotonin receptor: the 5-HT_{1A} subtype (Roman *et al.*, 2005). Roman *et al.* note the damaging effects of sleep deprivation on mental health, such as increasing the risk of depression. Disruption to serotonergic neurotransmission by loss of sleep might mediate such effects.

Generation of new neurons

Some regions of the brain preserve the ability to generate new cells even in the adult (Chapter 6). The hippocampus is the most studied region in this regard. Sleep deprivation seriously impairs the capacity of the CNS to generate new neurons in such regions (Guzman-Marin *et al.*, 2005). This suggests that a function of sleep is to permit the plasticity associated with the production of new neurons. By now, you might feel that you should decline your next late-night party invitation.

Learning and memory

A form of plasticity that has attracted attention in sleep research is that associated with learning and memory (Chapter 11). Those changes between neurons that embody learning and memory appear to be influenced by sleep.

Memory consolidation is thought to occur by strengthening synaptic connections in the brain with use. Sleep could allow refreshment of established, but seldom used, memories by simulating their activation (Kavanau, 1998). New experiences might be best assimilated into memory during sleep, when the organism is not actively producing behaviour (D.B. Cohen, 1979). This could be described by analogy with a library: presumably, cataloguing could be best done at times when the library is shut ('sleeping').

Some argue that consolidation of memory is harmed by sleep deprivation (Benington and Frank, 2003). Animal experiments reveal that a period of learning or exposure to environmental enrichment is followed by increased sleep. Some patterns of neural activation seen in sleep correspond to the patterns observed during an immediately prior learning experience (Hobson and Pace-Schott, 2002). Sleep seems to involve reactivation ('action-replay') of recently acquired memory and thereby to facilitate retention (Axmacher *et al.*, 2009). If a cue associated with a prior learning test is presented during (but without disturbing sleep), recall is improved for items associated with the cue, indicating a specific process of consolidation during sleep (Rudoy *et al.*, 2009).

A problem in contemporary society is an apparent increase in shallow sleep (van der Werf *et al.*, 2009). The causes include ageing, stress and noise. To study a possible consequence of this, the sleep of participants who normally showed healthy sleeping patterns was disturbed in such a way as to produce the typical brain pattern of shallow sleep. They were set a memory task, to view novel visual images and later to recall them. The manipulation of sleep produced a decrement in performance. Shallow sleep was associated with a decreased activation of parts of the hippocampus relative to normal sleep. No disruption was found on an implicit memory task. Van der Werf *et al.* concluded that deep sleep puts the hippocampus into an optimal condition for encoding novel information. It was suggested that activity pattern of the cortex could produce optimal changes in the synapses of the hippocampus.

A combined function

An explanation of the function of sleep might involve a combination of the three factors introduced above, as follows (cf. Rechtschaffen, 1998). Sleep tends to be programmed at times when, in evolutionary history, there was a net benefit to be inactive. Irrespective of whether pressure for sleep to evolve also came from homeostatic imbalance, benefits for the body might be earned by sleep. Inactivity would allow bodily resources to be conserved. During sleep, fine-tuning of neurons might occur, involving synthesis of components. The brain might be 're-programmed', i.e. exhibit plasticity.

The notion of core sleep and optional sleep

Horne (1988) proposed that neuronal repair normally occurs in the first few hours of sleep and the necessary sleep was termed **core sleep**. So, repair seems to require less time than that which we normally spend in sleep. The remainder of sleep might simply be a means of keeping us inactive, termed 'optional sleep'. Such a dual-process function might be mapped onto a dual process model of causal mechanisms. Optional sleep would be programmed by a motivational process that has an intrinsic 24-hour rhythm at its base. By contrast, the pressure for core sleep would come not from time within the intrinsic 24-hour rhythm but from the length of time since the last sleep.

Such a dual-factor theory is represented in simplified form in Figure 19.5. Part (a) shows the homeostatic ('core') factor. As the time since the last sleep increases, so the tendency to sleep increases. Part (b) shows the cyclic factor. The small peak in sleep tendency in the mid-afternoon is not shown. This coincides with the time of siesta of some cultures. Mid-afternoon can be problematic for drivers trying to stay awake (Horne and Reyner, 1995). Figure 19.5(c) indicates that the tendency to sleep depends upon a combination of factors shown in parts (a) and (b). The tendency does not increase monotonically as a function of deprivation (Figure 19.5(c)). For example, someone would feel less sleepy at time B than at time A even though they have been deprived for longer at B.

We shall return to homeostasis, considering the possibility that its regulation not only explains part of the function of sleep but also one of the causal factors.

Comparing species

Animals live in different habitats with different evolutionary pressures. Sleep occurs in most species, including all mammals (Horne, 1988), which might point to a homeostatic function. However, the relative importance of the three possible functions attributed to sleep might vary with species. Therefore, it is useful to compare species' sleeping patterns and look at development within a species. As discussed later, brain development, involving the formation of new neural structures, might pose its demands for sleep.

The natural habitat of some species of dolphin is such that sleep would appear to put their *immediate* safety at

risk (Mukhametov, 1984). Yet they show brief periods of sleep, suggesting that these are necessary for homeostasis or re-programming or both. The Indus dolphin lives in muddy waters, which are liable to serious turbulence. It is blind and, to navigate, it relies upon a very effective sonar system. Permanent alertness might seem to be imperative but, amazingly, the Indus dolphin sleeps. This consists of naps, each of a few seconds' duration, taken many times a day. Presumably, they constitute core sleep.

Researchers studied the electrical activity of the brains of two species of dolphin, the bottlenose dolphin and porpoise (Mukhametov, 1984). Each half-brain takes it in turns to sleep, hemispheres being shifted every two hours! The total time spent in sleep is about 12 hours.

Figure 19.5 Simplified representation of the strength of tendency to sleep: (a) a function of time since the last sleep, (b) a function of the intrinsic 24-hour rhythm and (c) a combination of (a) and (b). (Note that in reality the factors combine in a more complex way than indicated in part (c).)
Source: adapted from Dijk (1997, pp. 10–13).

The shift between hemispheres enables vigilance to be maintained at all times, albeit that offered by only an awake half-brain. This suggests that a role (e.g. neuronal repair) is performed in each hemisphere as it sleeps.

Effects of sleep deprivation

Enforced sleep deprivation is a controversial procedure but, as long ago as 1894, it was carried out on animals (Bentivoglio and Grassi-Zucconi, 1997). Brain damage appears to be the result. In humans, there are reports of death by sleep deprivation as punishment and torture. More benignly, people occasionally volunteer to deprive themselves of sleep.

A personal angle

Randy Gardner

There are a few heroes of sleep research, one being a 17-year-old from California, Randy Gardner. He lasted 264 hours without sleep, i.e. almost 11 days (Gulevich *et al.*, 1966). Randy's 'voluntary' deprivation was 'enforced' by a team who worked in shifts to keep him awake. His attempt was done under medical supervision and researchers thereby found a person to study. Neither during nor after deprivation, could doctors find reason for serious concern about Randy's health. Starting at day 4, Randy experienced lapses of memory. Visual perception was altered in the form of the world taking on illusory properties, 'waking dreams'. At 262 hours of wakefulness, he was given a psychiatric interview. He was coherent and no loss of contact with reality was found. In spite of these disturbances, Randy held on to reality throughout and did not show seriously disturbed ('psychotic') behaviour. Randy went to bed at the end of 11 days but slept for only 14–15 hours.

What are we to conclude regarding Randy Gardner? With a sample of one, caution is needed. However, the tentative conclusions correspond to those for other sleep-deprived people: that psychological function is disrupted but it is hard to find obvious disruption outside the CNS (Horne, 1988). Horne suggests that a number of factors were crucial to Randy's success: (i) his motivation, (ii) the support of his friends and (iii) having an activity, as an alternative to sleep. Though finding disruption is difficult, a common assumption is that physiological homeostasis is impaired by prolonged deprivation, such that death can be hastened (Hobson, 1999).

Section summary

1 There are three principal explanations of the function of sleep: it (a) serves a restorative (homeostatic) function, (b) keeps us inactive and (c) allows plasticity and repair of the brain.

2 Sleep appears to facilitate plasticity in the form of (re)structuring parts of the brain. The theory that it is involved in learning and memory is controversial.

3 Developing nervous systems involve much structuring, which might explain large amounts of sleep early in life.

4 Sleep might serve a combination of the functions described.

5 One theory postulates a dual function: core sleep is needed for effective neural, and thereby psychological, functioning. Optional sleep might serve simply to keep us immobile.

6 The wide presence of sleep across species suggests a homeostatic and/or restructuring function.

☞ Test your knowledge

19.4 Complete the following: 'The universal presence of sleep across species and individuals suggests that, in functional terms, any _____ of sleep are outweighed by its _____'.

19.5 If sleep facilitates brain plasticity, what form could this take?

Answers on page 513   WEB

The motivation to sleep

So far, the chapter has described sleep as a brain state; the animal is either asleep or awake. Of course, animals do not simply pass instantly from the brain state of waking to that of sleep. Rather, sleep–waking has motivational characteristics. Depending upon the species, an animal might need to find a suitable sleeping location and be persuaded to retire there by the onset of sleepiness. A number of species invest time and effort in finding, building and defending sleeping sites (Hobson, 1988).

A given motivation varies in strength and there is usually competition among motivations for expression in behaviour. Being sleepy can powerfully motivate us to seek a suitable shelter. In so doing, sleep can compete very effectively with other candidates for expression in behaviour. Pain competes with sleep, as many know to their cost. Also, strong competition arises from simply having something 'on your mind'.

At times, prolonged sleep seems to be an adaptive behavioural strategy. For example, animals recovering from a bacterial or viral infection often show long periods of sleep and this makes adaptive sense in aiding recovery (Hart, 1988). Under these conditions, we can envisage a tendency to sleep being dominant in any competition with, say, a tendency to get up to feed.

At other times, we might have a suitable sleeping site and a strong motivation but custom can force us to try, with limited success, to inhibit sleep tendencies. (Try looking around during the lectures at an academic conference, after lunch.) The amount of time spent sleeping also seems to increase when there is little else to do. This appears to apply equally to some non-humans. For example, when restricted to the house and fed adequately, domestic cats and dogs pass large amounts of time in sleep.

The period of sleep shows some flexibility in that its duration can be extended or shortened according to prevailing circumstances. In terms of the dichotomy between core sleep and optional sleep, it would seem logical that the optional phase offers such flexibility. Anecdotal evidence suggests that, if a task is made particularly demanding or interesting, this can increase its competitive strength relative to sleep. For example, soldiers in war have been forced to show extended periods of vigilance and hence suffer sleep deprivation. However, the notion of core sleep would be expected to offer serious limits to flexibility. Apparently, during the Second World War, a number of British pilots were killed after falling asleep in flight (Horne, 1988).

Section summary

1 Sleep is associated with motivation that directs behaviour towards a sleeping site.

2 Sleep shows competition for expression with other activities.

 ## Test your knowledge

19.6 Complete the following: 'Homeostatic theories predict an increase in motivation to sleep with increased sleep _____'.

Answer on page 513   WEB

Characterizing sleep

There are distinct types of sleep (Rechtschaffen, 1998). This section looks at these and considers an investigative tool: electroencephalography (EEG), i.e. recording the brain's electrical activity by electrodes attached to the scalp (Chapter 5).

Types of sleep

Sleep and waking vary in their quality and depth. Apart from electroencephalography, another indicator that allows characterization of different types of sleep is that of the movements of the eyes (Hobson, 1999). By this characteristic, in combination with EEG differences, a distinction in types of sleep is evident.

At stages during sleep, the eyes rotate in their sockets, known as 'rapid eye movements'. By this measure, sleep can be divided into two types: **rapid eye movement sleep (REM sleep)**, when such movements occur, and **non-rapid eye movement sleep ('non-REM sleep' or 'NREM sleep')**, when they do not (Aserinsky and Kleitman, 1955). A night's sleep is characterized by alternation between REM and NREM phases, a typical night for an adult volunteer being shown in Figure 19.6.

Bouts of REM sleep, normally lasting 5–30 minutes, occur during the night at about every 60–90 minutes. The first bout is usually at some 80–100 minutes after the start of sleep. For Randy Gardner, the REM periods during the first night of sleep following deprivation were over three times the amount normally shown. This suggests a compensation process. Apart from the presence or absence of eye movements and the EEG, sleep can be classified by reports from the sleeper after being woken, e.g. whether he or she was dreaming.

Figure 19.7 shows an electroencephalogram of a human brain during stages of waking and sleep. Figure 19.8 helps you to interpret it. In Figure 19.7, stages of alertness, relaxation and sleep are represented by a sequence of recordings from top to bottom. At the top

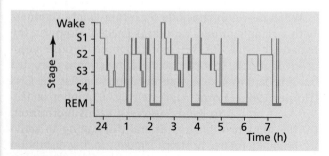

Figure 19.6 Stages of waking and sleep. S1–S4 indicate stages of non-REM sleep.

Source: Carskadon and Dement (1994, Fig. 2-7, p. 20).

Awake with eyes open (beta)

Awake with eyes closed (alpha)

Non-REM sleep
Stage 1

Sleep
spindle
Stages 2/3

Stage 4 (slow-wave sleep)

REM sleep

50μV
1 sec

Figure 19.7 Stages of waking and sleep as characterized by an electroencephalogram.

Source: Purves *et al.* (1997, Fig. 26.1, p. 498).

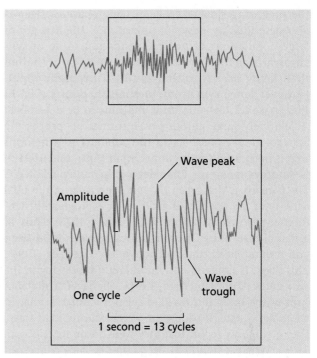

Amplitude

Wave peak

One cycle

Wave trough

1 second = 13 cycles

Figure 19.8 A closer look at part of an EEG recording.

Source: Hobson (1988, p. 14). Copyright © 1989 J. Allan Hobson, Md.

is the electrical activity termed **beta activity**, associated with alert waking. It is of a relatively low amplitude and high frequency. Drowsiness is associated with a decrease in frequency and an increase in amplitude of the signal, characterized as **alpha activity** (an alpha wave). In Figures 19.6 and 19.7, note the stages of non-REM sleep (1–4) through which the person passes first; there are a number of irregularities but, as a general trend, amplitude of the waves increases and their frequency decreases. As the person passes through stages 1 to 4, the threshold for waking becomes higher (Carskadon and Dement, 1994).

In evolutionary terms, non-REM sleep appears to be the precursor of REM sleep (Kavanau, 1994); REM sleep relates to the evolution of the cortex. Reptiles appear not to exhibit REM sleep and in birds it is a relatively small percentage of total sleep time. With a sophisticated cortex, mammals show a relatively large percentage of REM sleep. However, there is no simple relationship between the extent of REM sleep and a species' cognitive capacities (D.B. Cohen, 1979). Thus, the opossum shows more REM sleep than a human (Jouvet, 1975). We now look more closely at these two categories of sleep.

Non-REM sleep

During non-REM sleep, there is a lowering of metabolism. The sympathetic nervous system is slightly less active than in quiet waking and the parasympathetic system is activated (Hobson, 1988, 1999), thereby biasing towards conservation of resources. Arterial pressure, respiratory rate, heart-rate and metabolic rate are reduced.

In non-REM sleep, there is some inhibition of sensory information at the level of the thalamus (Coenen, 1995). For example, even if the optic nerve is active, this can fail to excite the corresponding LGN neurons in the thalamus (Chapter 8). Cognitive/mental activity appears to be minimal in this phase (Carskadon and Dement, 1994), which is sometimes termed 'dreamless sleep'. However, dreams do occasionally occur during non-REM sleep.

Because of the low frequency of the waveform, stage 4 of non-REM sleep is termed **slow-wave sleep** ('synchronized sleep') (Figure 19.7). The activity of a large number of neurons is synchronized, thereby giving a relatively large electrical signal. The brain's oxygen consumption falls by up to 45%. Core sleep corresponds to periods of both slow-wave sleep and REM sleep (Horne, 1988).

REM sleep

Characteristics

REM sleep is characterized by a relatively low amplitude of EEG signal, in distinction to the large amplitude of the preceding slow-wave sleep. This phase of sleep is also described as 'desynchronized', i.e. the activity of large populations of neurons tends not to be in synchrony. Individual neurons fire independently rather than being driven collectively by a rhythmic input. However, some synchrony presumably occurs even in this phase for low-amplitude rhythms to be detectable. A relatively large amount of information processing appears to take place across the population of neurons that is freed from the rhythmic input (Antrobus, 1991).

Another name for REM sleep is 'paradoxical sleep'. The paradox is that, even though sleep is deep, the total activity of the brain is as great as, or even greater than, in attentive waking (Figure 19.7) (Jouvet, 1975). Thus, at a neural level there are similarities between REM sleep and waking, both states of 'activation' (Steriade, 1994). This suggests similarities in information processing in the two states (Llinás and Paré, 1991). The level of metabolism of the brain during REM sleep is similar to that in the waking state. If people are woken during REM sleep, they commonly report that they were dreaming (Hobson, 1999). Whereas non-REM sleep appears to be concerned with physiological homeostasis, REM sleep appears to serve a psychological function (D.B. Cohen, 1979).

During REM sleep, in contrast to the cortex, the hippocampus shows synchronized waves of activity termed **theta waves** (Siegel, 1994).

Motor systems

During REM sleep, the motor cortex is excited (Jouvet, 1975). Why then do we normally not aimlessly move arms and legs? Inhibition is exerted on motor neurons, which opposes excitatory effects and prevents movement. Although most muscles are inhibited, those that determine the rotation of the eyes function normally, as revealed in rapid eye movements.

Broader implications

During REM sleep, people can process information on salient stimuli, which can become incorporated into the story-line of a dream (Rechtschaffen *et al.*, 1966). What could appear to be a paradox is that, during this state, the evoked potential (Chapter 5) in response to sensory stimulation can be as high as during waking even though the person is not woken by the stimulus (Llinás and Paré, 1991). The thalamic–cortical projections that convey sensory information are working much as in waking (Steriade, 1994). So why isn't sleep interrupted?

If we feel that the brain should be quiet during sleep and any abnormal signal will wake it up, we are thinking of a passive brain which merely reacts to events. The evidence of sleep is that the brain is normally highly active. Sensory input *modulates* rather than *instigates* brain activity (Llinás and Paré, 1991).

Having defined some properties of sleep, we now consider the brain mechanisms that control sleep.

Section summary

1   Sleep can be divided into phases, according to the pattern of the EEG and other criteria.

2   The rapid eye movement phase (REM sleep) is associated with desynchronized electrical activity of the brain.

3   By exclusion, the other phase of sleep is defined as non-rapid eye movement sleep (non-REM sleep).

4   One type of non-REM sleep, 'slow-wave sleep' (synchronized sleep), is characterized by synchronization of the activity of relatively many neurons.

Test your knowledge

19.7 The motor neurons controlling which skeletal muscles are not inhibited during paradoxical sleep?

19.8 Complete the following: 'Stage 4 of non-REM sleep is characterized by a relatively _____ frequency and _____ amplitude of signal'.

 Answers on page 513

Brain mechanisms

Introduction

Which brain processes determine waking–sleep and are there regions that have a particular responsibility? A number of interacting brain regions form the basis of sleep waking.

A search for sleep mechanisms is guided by theory, patterns of neural activity and behavioural phenomena. For example, sleep is not a passive state that occurs when neurons fatigue (Aserinsky and Kleitman, 1955). Animals are motivated to find a suitable sleep site. They do not normally fall into inactivity and unconsciousness, like losing the picture when the power supply to a TV set is drastically reduced. Sleep can be induced by electrical stimulation at brain sites (e.g. midbrain), which is compatible with its being an active state (Hobson, 1988).

Are there particular neurotransmitters or hormones associated with particular brain regions, the level of which shows an association with times of sleep? Can investigators identify brain regions where the circadian rhythm that underlies sleep is generated?

Transitions between states of waking–sleep, as seen in the thalamus and cortex and other linked structures such as the amygdala, appear to be determined in large part by projections from the brain stem (Llinás and Paré, 1991). These projections spread extensively and appear to modulate brain states, discussed next.

Brain stem mechanisms and their projections

The ascending reticular activating system

A system orginating in the reticular formation of the brain stem is termed the ascending reticular activating system (ARAS) (Moruzzi and Magoun, 1949). See Chapter 5, Figures 5.15 and 5.16, pp. 115–116.

Sensory information is transmitted to the brain along the spinal cord and in the cranial nerves. These are sometimes termed the classical sensory pathways, e.g. visual, tactile and nociceptive pathways. Collaterals of the axons in the classical pathways project to the ARAS. By this means, sensory information in the classical pathways increases the activity of the ARAS (Jouvet, 1975; see Figure 5.16). In turn, by its projections throughout the brain (e.g. to the thalamus) the ARAS triggers waking. For example, electrical stimulation of the ARAS triggers waking and EEG signs of arousal (Jouvet, 1975). Lesions to the ARAS can disrupt the cycle of sleep–waking.

The ARAS is non-specific in that sensory information in a number of channels project to it. Researchers have been able to specify details of brain stem nuclei that have an activational role and, in addition, other nuclei, which, by their activity oppose waking and promote sleep. This forms one of the biological bases of the assertion that sleep is an active process.

Identifying nuclei

Looking at the ARAS and other regions, researchers have identified specific parts of the brain stem containing distinct groups of neurons that play *integrative* roles in waking and sleep (Hobson, 1999). Ascending projections of these neurons broadcast information widely to other brain regions (e.g. cortex, thalamus and hypothalamus). Activity in ascending pathways sets higher brain regions into states along the dimension of sleep–waking (Steriade, 1994). The integrative nature of certain regions of brain stem in sleep–waking is indicated by the fact that their excitation has several functionally related effects at different sites in the CNS.

Apart from inducing the characteristic sleep–waking pattern by means of ascending projections, descending pathways from the brain stem inhibit skeletal muscles, hence preventing motor activity (Hobson, 1999). Thus, there can be activation of motor regions of the brain without behaviour. Hobson suggests that this might play a role in the widespread appearance of imagined movement in dreams.

Sleep is not determined by brain stem nuclei acting in isolation. Having something important 'on our mind' can prevent us from falling asleep. This effect would seem to be mediated by connections from the cortex to lower brain regions (Hobson, 1988).

A number of different groups of brain stem neurons have different roles in sleep, as follows.

Noradrenergic systems

Noradrenergic (NA) neurons from the locus coeruleus project widely, e.g. to the cortex (Chapter 5; Chapman, 1995). See Figure 13.8, p. 353. Wakefulness is in part determined by increased activity of these neurons, and REM sleep by their decreased activity (Hobson and Stickgold, 1994). They are almost silent during REM sleep. Neurons carrying information from the body on threatening stimuli (e.g. tissue damage) make projections to the locus coeruleus. These serve to trigger waking and alertness (Chapman, 1995).

Serotonergic systems

Serotonergic neurons with cell bodies in brain stem nuclei termed the raphe nuclei play a role in waking–sleep (Jouvet, 1975). Their activity appears to act like the NA neurons to promote waking (Sutton *et al.*, 1992). Blocking serotonin synthesis leads to insomnia. Waking corresponds to a dominance of the NA and serotonergic neurons. Corresponding to the shift from waking to non-REM sleep, there is a decline in activity of NA and serotonergic neurons, accompanied by increased activity of cholinergic neurons (Hobson, 1999).

Cholinergic systems

Cholinergic neurons with cell bodies in the pons region of the brain stem and elsewhere are involved in sleep–waking (Figure 19.9) (Hobson, 1996). Some exhibit a high activity at times of REM sleep (Hobson and Stickgold, 1994), which suggests that normally they play a role in programming REM sleep. When electrically stimulated, they trigger a change in the EEG from synchronized to desynchronized. Injecting a cholinergic agonist into the pons triggers signs of REM sleep (Hobson, 1999).

During REM sleep, there is activation of the lateral geniculate nucleus (LGN) by cholinergic signals (Jouvet, 1975). A neural circuit from the pons (P) to the LGN (G)

Figure 19.9 Role of ACh neurons in pons.
Source: adapted from Carlson (1994, p. 289). Reprinted by permission of the Pearson Education, Inc.

and then to the occipital cortex (O) is usually abbreviated as the **PGO system** (see Figure 5.21, p. 120, for the latter part of this system). This same neural system is responsible for the eye movements that designate the REM state.

In parallel with triggering activity in the PGO system, there is modulation of sensory inputs. The combination of this and inhibition upon motor output during REM sleep means that the brain is 'off-line', i.e. relatively functionally isolated and under intrinsic control (Hobson, 1999). PGO signals also form an input to the amygdala (Chapter 12), which could account for the emotional tone of dreams (Hobson, 1999).

A reciprocal interaction model

Based upon the brain stem nuclei just described, Hobson and McCarley (see Hobson, 1988) proposed a **reciprocal interaction model** of sleep. It was designed to show how transitions between REM and non-REM sleep occur. The model was based on mutual inhibition between, on the one hand, cholinergic neurons (ACh) and, on the other, serotonergic and noradrenergic (NA) neurons (Figure 19.10). When the cholinergic system dominates, REM sleep is programmed, whereas domination of noradrenergic and serotonergic systems inhibits REM sleep. Reciprocal inhibition enables decisive swings between REM and non-REM sleep (Pace-Schott and Hobson, 2002). The neurons shown to the left of Figure 19.10 appear to employ GABA and to provide an input that switches ('flip-flop') dominance between [ACh] and [NA/serotonin] (Rosenwasser, 2009).

This model is relevant to the issue of whether REM sleep is necessary for memory consolidation (discussed earlier). People taking the class of antidepressant termed MAO inhibitors give a bias towards noradrenergic/serotonergic control and hence have reduced REM sleep.

However, there is no evidence that they have impaired capacity for learning and memory (J.M. Siegel, 2005).

The hypothalamus

Basics

Various interacting nuclei of the hypothalamus have a role in producing sleep and waking (Mistlberger, 2005). For example, activity by the anterior hypothalamus promotes sleep, whereas activity of the posterior hypothalamus promotes waking. There appears to be a 'push-pull', or 'flip-flop', reciprocal antagonism between the neural systems within these regions. Hence, transitions between waking and sleeping tend to be decisive, with the brain being in either one state or the other.

Rhythm generation

A characteristic of sleep–waking is its 24-hour rhythm. Certain hypothalamic and brain stem nuclei (just described) exert rhythmic effects upon a broad expanse

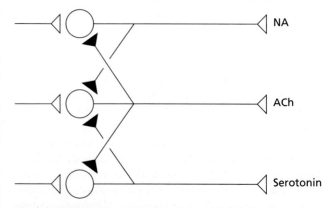

Figure 19.10 Reciprocal interaction model of sleep.
Source: Reprinted with permission from SLACK Incorporated: Sutton, J.P. *et al.*, Modelling states of waking and sleeping, *Psychiatric Annals*, 1992.1, 137–143.

of other brain regions as the basis of sleep–waking. But what determines the rhythm of these controls? A nucleus of the hypothalamus, the suprachiasmatic nucleus (SCN) (see Chapter 5, Figure 5.31, p. 128), plays a principal role, as 'master clock', in generating the circadian rhythm (Pace-Schott and Hobson, 2002). There are links from this master clock to brain regions that underlie sleep and arousal: other hypothalamic and brain stem nuclei (Mistlberger, 2005).

Although the SCN rhythm is endogenous, its phase is influenced by *Zeitgebers*. How do *Zeitgebers* influence the rhythm? One route is as follows. Pathways from the retina to the SCN (Chapter 8, Figure 8.17, p. 207) convey information on the light–dark cycle of the external world (Harrington *et al.*, 1994). By means of this information, the SCN entrains the internal rhythm to the light–dark cycles of the external world. A lesion of the SCN disrupts the circadian rhythm of sleep (Mistlberger, 2005).

Figure 19.5 suggested two factors underlying sleep, a cyclical and a non-cyclical one. Lesions to the SCN leave the non-cyclical contribution somewhat undisturbed. A tendency to sleep still arises as a function of time since the last sleep and roughly the same amounts of REM and non-REM sleep occur as in intact animals (Mistlberger, 2005). The lesion disrupts the circadian factor and sleep phases occur at random throughout the 24 hours.

Even isolated individual neurons of the SCN show a strong circadian rhythm in their activity and metabolism, indicating that 'rhythmicity' is an intrinsic property of them (Moore, 1999). In early development, such neurons show rhythms even before they form synapses with other neurons. Presumably, the rhythmicity of the individual neurons contributes to rhythmicity of the collection of neurons within the SCN.

The SCN pacemaker triggers a circadian cycle of release of the hormone melatonin from the pineal gland (Figure 5.11, p. 113; Arendt, 1997). Some evidence suggests that this hormone plays a role in the coordination of the effects of pacemaker neurons of the SCN.

A sleep factor?

To return to an earlier discussion, is it possible to identify a natural **sleep factor** ('Factor S'), e.g. in the CNS (Garcia-Garcia *et al.*, 2009)? Is there a substance that increases in level during sleep deprivation and that, if injected into the body, induces sleep? Cerebrospinal fluid taken from the brain of a sleepy animal tends to induce sleep in a recipient (Pappenheimer, 1983). Using goats, researchers extracted a substance ('Factor S') from the fluid in the ventricles of the brain (Chapter 5, Figure 5.26, p. 125). Injection of Factor S into other animals triggered sleep. It is also possible to extract Factor S from human urine. Human Factor S causes increases in sleep when injected into rabbits.

The halves of a dolphin's brain show independence in their times of sleep, as do estimated REM cycles of human mother and foetus (D.B. Cohen, 1979). This suggests that any principal sleep factor is intrinsic to the CNS, rather than being a general circulatory factor.

A personal angle

Siamese twins

Lenard and Schulte (1972), in Göttingen, Germany, observed the sleep–waking patterns of a pair of female Siamese twins (with common circulation), joined at the head. Independent EEG records point to independent brains. The authors reported: 'From their behaviour and their reactions towards the environment they appeared to be completely different personalities'.

In comparing the twins by EEG recording, they exhibited sleep and waking, as well as REM and non-REM phases of sleep, at completely separate times. The authors suggest that this case and others, in which there is extensive connections between the circulations, argue against a factor in the blood as being a trigger for sleep–waking. Unfortunately, at age 21 days, the twins died under anaesthesia before they were able to receive an operation designed to separate them.

Recent evidence points to adenosine as being a sleep factor (Bjorness and Greene, 2009). It serves as a neuromodulator, acting in a functionally coordinated way at different brain sites. Caffeine, found in coffee and tea, is an antagonist to adenosine and counters sleep. During extensive waking, adenosine accumulates in the brain. Adenosine attaches to receptors and thereby changes patterns of neural activity. The assumption is that the affected neurons form part of the neural basis of sleep. Microinjection of adenosine into the preoptic nucleus of the hypothalamus, as well as certain brain stem regions known to be implicated in sleep, triggers sleep. As implied by Figure 19.5, there must be a site of integration between any such homeostatic sleep factor and the circadian influence. Specific nuclei in the hypothalamus are thought to play this role.

There are also other candidates that appear to contribute to sleep. Oscillations in the cerebrospinal fluid level of the cytokine interleukin-1 (IL-1), are synchronized with sleep–waking cycles, peak values being at the start of sleep or during sleep (Krueger *et al.*, 1998). Apart from any intrinsic role within the brain as a neurochemical, IL-1 is produced in the body following infections and a response by the immune system. Activated IL-1 appears to promote sleep at times when it is adaptive for the animal to remain immobile, e.g. following infection.

So much for the adult system of sleep–waking; we now turn to development.

Section summary

1 The axons of cholinergic, noradrenergic and serotonergic neurons with cell bodies in the brain stem project to the cortex and other regions and modulate activity corresponding to the basis of sleep–waking.

2 The suprachiasmatic nucleus is the site of a circadian rhythm generator.

3 The tendency to sleep can be influenced by outside factors, such as the level of light serving as a *Zeitgeber*. The suprachiasmatic nucleus mediates the influence of such outside factors.

4 Research is directed to identifying a so-called 'sleep factor', adenosine being a prime candidate.

 Test your knowledge

19.9 Acting via the retina, *Zeitgebers* influence activity at the suprachiasmatic nucleus, to bring the circadian rhythm into phase with the external light–dark cycle. What is the term used to describe this process?

19.10 How is the relationship of caffeine to adenosine described?

 Answers on page 513   WEB

Development

Sleep occupies a varying fraction of the 24-hour period at different ages. A study of the development of sleep might give insights into its function and underlying mechanisms.

Humans

A circadian rhythm appears to function at birth but does not make connection with the control of sleep until the child is about 6–12 weeks of age (Ferber, 1994). At age 6, the average human spends about 600 minutes a night sleeping (Horne, 1988). By age 30, they are spending about 420 minutes. The longer sleep in children correlates with brain development, and might be explained in terms of it.

Changes with age are seen not only in the total amount of sleep but also in its components. The maximum amount of REM sleep (15 or more hours per 24 hours) is observed in the foetus at 6 months of age (Hobson, 1988). There is a high rate of brain development at this age (Chapter 6). These observations suggest that sleep is necessary for structuring (or restructuring) CNS circuits (Vassalli and Dijk, 2009).

Foetuses exhibit considerable muscular activity in REM sleep. This could be a practice effect as connections within the motor regions of the brain are structured. The existence of activity in the PGO system in REM sleep suggests a form of surrogate 'visual' stimulation that could be used for neural structuring within the visual system (Roffwarg *et al.*, 1966). In such terms, sleep would reflect endogenous stimulation in the absence of exogenous stimulation.

Comparing individuals and species

The newborn of various species, including most mammals and chicks, show a high percentage of REM sleep at around birth or hatching (Kavanau, 1994). In the newborn human, about one half of sleep is REM sleep. For a baby born 2 months prematurely it is 80%.

Not all species exhibit a high percentage of REM sleep immediately following birth. So-called 'precocial' species (e.g. the guinea pig and antelope) do not (Jouvet-Mounier *et al.*, 1969). This term refers to species that get up and go soon after birth or hatching, as opposed to a relatively helpless ('altricial') species such as humans. Precocial species emerge into the world already equipped with relatively advanced brains and physical abilities for movement. For REM sleep, a precocial species (guinea pig) is compared with two altricial species (cat and rat) in Figure 19.11. For the altricial species, there is a sharp decline in percentage of REM sleep with age.

The ontogenetic hypothesis

The observation of a large percentage of REM sleep in newborns led to the **ontogenetic hypothesis** of REM sleep (Horne, 1988), which suggests that its function is to do with development of the brain. As age increases, neural development declines in parallel with the decline in REM sleep. According to this hypothesis, REM sleep is a means of providing the brain with the stimulation needed for development.

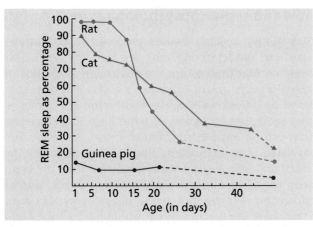

Figure 19.11 REM sleep as a percentage of total sleep for rat, cat and guinea pig.

Source: Jouvet-Mounier *et al.* (1969, Fig. 21, p. 236).

The hypothesis might also explain why the percentage decline in REM sleep following birth is much less in precocial species. Presumably, development largely takes place before birth, when REM sleep would provide 'surrogate stimulation' of the brain. Following birth, stimulation necessary for remaining neural development might derive from sensory input from the world. In adulthood, REM sleep might provide a minimal stimulation to maintain the working efficiency of the brain.

Section summary

1. The newborn or newly hatched of many (altricial) species show a high percentage of REM sleep relative to adults.

2. The newborn of precocial species do not show this high percentage of REM sleep.

3. According to the ontogenetic hypothesis, REM sleep is connected with brain development.

☞ Test your knowledge

19.11 Consider again the reciprocal interaction model, described in the last section. The type of sleep shown by the rat immediately following birth suggests that it is controlled by a domination of which neurochemical system?

 Answer on page 513   WEB ➡

Dreaming

Basic principles

A person woken during non-REM sleep will occasionally report dreaming. However, REM sleep is the phase that is primarily associated with dreaming (McCarley, 1995). The function of REM sleep might be that important information processing related to the meaningful dream content can take place. However, there are good arguments against this. For example, dream content typically bears little resemblance to the kind of cognitive tasks that engaged the dreamer in the days prior to the dream (J.M. Siegel, 2005). It is difficult to see that the foetus could have much to dream about during its 15 hours of REM sleep per 24 hours. REM sleep in early development might represent a 'test-run' of the information processing circuits that will be used later.

Dreams normally appear to arise from activity within the visual system (McCarley, 1995), with some individuals dreaming in colour. The material of dreams is primarily visual and involves movement (Hobson, 1988). In REM sleep, blood flow is relatively high in cortical areas associated with visual processing but relatively low in frontal regions concerned with planning and organization (Madsen *et al.*, 1991). Rational planning and coherence seem to be absent in dreams with their often chaotic organization, as one is 'carried along through time by circumstances that crop up in an unpredictable way' (Melges, 1982, p. 4; Carlson, 1994). In dreams 'the temporal structure of past, present, and future is often condensed and interchanged' (Madsen *et al.*, p. 506). Over certain episodes, there is at least some coherence between, on the one hand, dream content and, on the other, emotional and autonomic processing (Roffwarg *et al.*, 1966). An exciting content is associated with bodily signs of activation. Erotic dreams are associated with bodily sexual arousal (Hobson, 1988).

During the dreaming phase, the brain has relatively little noradrenalin (norepinephrine) available. This might explain why we are so bad at recalling dreams, since increasing NA availability increases recall.

Who dreams?

It seems that dreaming in those born blind or who lost sight when they were very young does not correspond to 'seeing' (Hobson, 1989). They appear to tap into auditory or tactile processing when they dream. People born blind do not perform rapid eye movements during sleep periods that would be classified as REM sleep by the criterion of EEG recording. However, people who, later in life, suffer blindness do show rapid eye movements. The content of dreams commonly involves the theme of movement and the motor cortex is activated during REM sleep (McCarley, 1995).

Do only humans dream? This raises philosophical issues since we do not know that non-humans have subjective awareness. The essence of dreaming is its subjective nature. As far as objective indices are concerned, rapid eye movements, among other bodily responses, are shown during sleep by most species of mammal (Hobson, 1988). Dog owners sometimes report signs of agitation in their animals during sleep.

Function

What is the function of dreams, if any? A library analogy might help: dreaming could represent 're-cataloguing' the events acquired during the day, involving removal of some information. Indeed, some argue that there is meaningful cognition corresponding to dreams. Times of trauma might correspond to when emotionally significant material needs to be processed (Davis, 1985) and this could produce the material of nightmares.

Some authors see here a creative aspect to dreams (D.B. Cohen, 1979). Noting that their frequency increases at times of stress, Panksepp (1998, p. 128) suggests that dreams provide: 'an endless variety of ideas, especially when life is stressful and we need to entertain new alternatives'. However, it could be that dreaming has no such function and might simply be an inevitable by-product of brain activity, an 'epiphenomenon'. The bizarre nature of dreams with their sudden and irrational changes of story-line might equally suggest that they represent the product of a process that has little meaning. A model that might be able to account for this aspect of dreams is described next.

Do dreams relate to real-life problems in need of a solution?

Source: John Anster Fitzgerald/Private Collection/Bridgeman Art Library.

Towards a neuropsychological model

R. McCarley and J.A. Hobson proposed an **activation–synthesis model** of dreaming (see Hobson, 1988). This suggests that dreams are the subjective awareness of neural events in, for example, the visual system triggered by influences from the brain stem. The dream is, in a sense, the best guess or hypothesis of a story-line that can be imposed on neural events, i.e. a synthesis based upon activation. The fact that primarily the visual and motor systems are stimulated from the brain stem might explain the visual and movement content of dreams. Presumably, if the olfactory system were stimulated, the dream content would have a strong representation from smell.

A personal angle

Heresy in sleep research

In response to the reciprocal interaction model, Hobson (1996, p. 471) writes:

> By challenging the reigning Freudian theory of psychoanalysis, these heretical articles elicited more letters to the editor than the *American Journal of Psychiatry* had ever received before. Naturally and understandably, most of the letters attacked us as insensitive materialists and unenlightened Philistines. We proposed, for example, that dream amnesia could be ascribed to aminergic [refers to the ascending pathways of catecholamines] demodulation of the forebrain (rather than Freudian repression) . . .

Unlike the psychoanalytic model, the activation–synthesis model does not involve disguises or codes. The psychoanalytic interpretation has difficulty with the explicitly sexual, terrifying and disgusting content of dreams (Hobson, 1988). If these represent merely a censored version, the mind boggles in trying to imagine what the unconscious content might be like! However, Hobson does not dismiss all psychoanalytic interpretation and retains (p. 166):

> the emphasis of psychoanalysis upon the power of dreams to reveal deep aspects of ourselves, but without recourse to the concept of disguise and censorship or to the now famous Freudian symbols. My tendency, then, is to ascribe the nonsense to brain–mind dysfunction and the sense to its compensatory effort to create order out of chaos.

That order is a function of our own personal view of the world, our current preoccupations, our remote memories, our feelings, and our beliefs.

The dreams that occur in REM sleep might be similar to certain psychopathological states or LSD-induced states (Panksepp, 1998). Specifically, this is suggested by their qualities of hallucination and delusion, confabulation and irrational transitions of logic and creative novel combinations of ideas.

Section summary

1 During REM sleep, dreams frequently occur.

2 A possible analogy is that dreams are like recataloguing a library.

3 A model of dreams is based on neuromodulation of areas of the brain by neurons with cell bodies at the brain stem.

 Test your knowledge

19.12 The brain state associated with dreaming is normally dominated by control from which neurochemical system?

Answer on page 513   WEB

Issues of health

Introduction

Estimates suggest that up to 40 million Americans have chronic problems of disturbed sleep (Edelman, 1994). In terms of a need for sleep, some experts quote the figure of 7 to 8 hours per 24. People who sleep less than 4 hours or more than 9 hours per night have an increased mortality from stroke, coronary artery disease and cancer (Chokroverty, 1994).

A circadian pattern, consisting of two distinct periods of sleep and waking, tends to be the norm for young people. By old age, the two-state circadian pattern is less evident. It is often replaced by frequent night-time waking and daytime naps.

There are a number of sleep disorders (e.g. excessive daytime sleepiness, insomnia, night terrors and sleep walking) that either can be treated or which one would like to treat. Insomnia is an example of this.

Insomnia and managing sleep

The phenomenon

The term **insomnia** describes a subjective feeling of inadequate sleep (Zorick, 1994). Insomniacs seem to overrate the extent to which they lose sleep. There is disparity between subjective report and an EEG measure (Mendelson, 1990). Insomniacs are poor at estimating how much time it takes them to fall asleep; they tend to overestimate by a factor of 3 (Walsh *et al.*, 1994). Similarly, the effects of sleeping pills, although often only modest, are perceived to be much greater in terms of increased length of sleep.

Insomniacs commonly attribute poor work performance, irritability, fatigue and mood disturbances to the disorder. They suffer from a relatively high frequency of other medical (e.g. heart attacks) and psychological problems (Walsh *et al.*, 1994), though, of course, separating cause and effect poses great difficulty. Insomniacs also have a relatively high frequency of traffic accidents.

Causes

There are various causes of insomnia, including stress, disruption of a social bond, excess alcohol, pain, disturbance to the circadian rhythm with shift-working and psychiatric disorders (Zorick, 1994). Insomnia can be a cause of insomnia, e.g. worry about the consequences of insomnia can promote it (Watts *et al.*, 1995).

Treatment

The search for chemical treatments is guided by the rationale of finding agonists to sleep-promoting neurochemicals (e.g. adenosine) tailored to the receptor subtypes involved. Antagonists to neurochemicals involved in waking are another target.

In terms of environmental interventions, light should be kept out of the bedroom. Coffee, alcohol and nicotine should be avoided, particularly near to sleep time (Zarcone, 1994). Sleep appears to be subject to Pavlovian conditioning (Hobson, 1988). Animals sleep best in a place where they have slept in the past. Associations between the bedroom and activities that are connected with being awake should be minimized (Stepanski, 1994). Reading or watching television in bed might be a bad idea.

Some daytime napping is often inevitable in elderly people. However, too much can impair night-time sleep (Horne, 1992). The elimination of the ingredients of sleeping pills from the body is relatively slow in the elderly. This can increase daytime sleepiness. Not surprisingly, insomniacs tend to take daytime naps more frequently than controls. Horne recommends that, for young and middle-aged insomniacs, such naps should be avoided. Naps tend to reduce tiredness and thereby reduce the capacity to fall asleep at night. They lower the strength of control that the circadian rhythm exerts over sleep (Zorick, 1994). For drivers, the afternoon period is one of a relatively high risk of accidents and sleepiness might contribute to this (Horne and Reyner, 1995). Journeys might usefully be broken for a nap at such times.

Sleep, affect and emotion

The relationship between (i) sleep and (ii) affect/emotions is important (Walker and van der Helm, 2009) since:

1 there is overlap between brain processes that are involved in the control of sleep and emotions;

2 disturbances of sleep are seen in almost all disorders of emotion.

According to the phase of sleep (REM or NREM), various brain regions show increased or decreased activity. Some of these, e.g. amygdala and anterior cingulate cortex, are concerned with emotion.

Sleep deprivation, either prior to or following a learning task, disrupts memory formation. The excitability of neurons in the hippocampus is reduced by deprivation of REM sleep such that encoding into memory is impaired. Sleep prior to learning seems necessary to maintain the condition of neurons that are involved with encoding information into memory (Walker and van der Helm, 2009).

Figure 19.12 shows the effect of prior sleep deprivation on memory formation in humans. The effect is most marked when it concerns forming memories of positive and neutral emotional stimuli, whereas there is not a significant effect on negative stimuli. The bias in favour of encoding negative information might have considerable relevance to sleep-deprivation associated with disorders of mood and affect.

Sleep deprivation is associated with emotional disturbance, including subjective irritability. It is possible to identify some of the likely biological bases of this. Figure 19.13 shows the result of an fMRI investigation into the reaction of the 'emotional brain' to emotionally aversive pictures (Walker and van der Helm, 2009). Sleep-deprived participants are compared with controls. Amygdala activation is 60% greater in those who were sleep-deprived. Sleep-deprivation impairs the strength of the functional link from the medial prefrontal cortex to the amygdala, reducing a source of restraint on the amygdala. This has been observed in a number of emotional disorders that are associated with abnormalities of sleep. In depression, sleep disturbance is a diagnostic criterion. This raises the issue of whether, in such cases, the direction of causation runs, at least in part, from sleep disturbance to emotional disturbance. That sleep which does occur in depression is characterized by an increased percentage of REM sleep.

Figure 19.12 The effect of prior sleep deprivation on the efficiency of memory formation for stimulus words of different quality: (a) for all stimulus types; (b) for different categories of stimulus types.
Source: Walker and van der Helm (2009, Fig. 3, p. 734).

Figure 19.13 The effect of sleep deprivation: (a) the effect on activity of the amygdala seen in a fMRI scan; (b) intensity and extent of amygdala activation; (c) and (d) functional connection between medial prefrontal cortex (mPFC) and amygdala, following (c) sleep and (d) sleep deprivation. (Note that enlarged representation of amygdala in (d) indicates, of course, increased activation, not swelling of the physical structure!)

Source: Walker and van der Helm (2009, Fig. 6).

Behavioural disturbances during sleep

In some disorders of non-REM sleep, e.g. sleep walking, sleep talking and night terrors, inhibition is inadequate. There are unopposed motor commands to certain sets of muscles and behaviour is thereby triggered (Keefauver and Guilleminault, 1994). During REM sleep, some people act out their dreams with overt behaviour such as hitting. This can have obvious dangers for the sufferer and their sleep partner.

A personal angle

A nightmare scenario

Schenck *et al.* (1986) working in Minneapolis, reported the case of a 72-year-old retired farmer, without any history of aggression or psychiatric disturbance. In his 'wild dreams', he would shout, hit out and kick not only his wife but also the walls and furniture. The following day his hands were sore. A CT brain scan suggested neural degeneration in the pons and cerebellum. Another patient, a 70-year-old retired farmer, tried to strangle his wife as he enacted a struggle with a bear. Behaviour indicates a failure of the inhibition of skeletal muscles, manifest in acting out the dream. In some cases, damage to the pons caused by a tumour can be identified, pointing to a deficiency in this region in the organization of descending inhibition on skeletal muscles.

Narcolepsy

The term **narcolepsy** refers to bouts of sudden sleepiness (an 'irresistible urge to sleep') experienced during the day, associated with weakness of skeletal muscles (Siegel, 2004). Narcolepsy is associated with abnormally low levels of orexin (Mieda and Sakurai, 2009). Targeting this neural system by drugs is an active research area in trying to find a cure.

Section summary

1 Insomnia is a subjective feeling of inadequate sleep.

2 It is possible to bring sleep under better control, e.g. to avoid substances that promote waking and to resist naps and 'sleep-ins'.

3 Narcolepsy involves sudden intense sleepiness during the day.

☞ Test your knowledge

19.13 Suppose that the room in which someone sleeps regularly acquires a capacity to trigger sleep. What term might be used to describe such a stimulus to sleep?

Answer on page 513

Bringing things together

Sleep is a good example of the value of considering causal, developmental, evolutionary and functional types of explanations together (Chapter 2). However, we do not know the function served by this behaviour, with which we spend a third of our lives. Evidence suggests a combination of functions: homeostatic (restorative), keeping immobile and reorganization of the brain.

Investigators have a reasonably good understanding of how neural processes contribute to sleep and waking, e.g. the role of projections from nuclei in the brain stem. The fact that periods of the most brain development are also periods of the most sleep suggests that the facilitation of reorganization of the brain ('plasticity') provides a functional reason for sleep. This fits with the observation that sleep deprivation disrupts the generation of new neurons in the hippocampus.

There is still much room for informed speculation.

 See the video coverage for this chapter which shows how psychologists study sleep.

Summary of Chapter 19

1 Sleep represents an altered state of consciousness. It is accompanied by a limited range of behaviour and characteristic patterns of brain activity.

2 Sleep is controlled in part by an internally driven rhythm, a circadian rhythm.

3 There are likely to be several functions served by sleep.

4 The parameter of sleep–waking is associated with motivation, which directs an animal towards finding a sleeping site.

5 The electrical activity of the brain points to more than one type of sleep.

6 Neural processes adjust the activity of brain processes in a cyclical fashion, corresponding to sleeping and waking, and to different types of sleep.

7 Development is associated with fundamental changes in sleep patterns.

8 Dreaming represents a subjective experience associated with identifiable patterns of activity in the brain.

9 Disorders of sleep can help us to understand the basics of sleep.

Further reading

For the thoughts of a leading researcher in the area, see Hobson (2003, 2004). For biological aspects, Monti *et al.* (2008). For rhythms, Green (2010). For the link to emotions, Cartwright (2010).

Answers

Explanations for answers to 'test your knowledge' questions can be found on the website www.pearsoned.co.uk/toates

19.1 Functional
19.2 Phase; period
19.3 *Zeitgeber*; circadian
19.4 Costs; benefits
19.5 Formation of new neurons, loss of neurons, growth of new synapses or loss of synapses.
19.6 Deprivation
19.7 Those responsible for eye movements
19.8 Low; high
19.9 Entrainment
19.10 Antagonist
19.11 Cholinergic
19.12 Acetylcholine
19.13 Conditional stimulus

Visit www.pearsoned.co.uk/toates
for a range of resources to support study.
Test yourself with multiple choice questions and access a bank of over 100 videos that will bring the topics to life.

 Interactions and animations relating to topics discussed in this chapter can be found on the website at www.pearsoned.co.uk/toates. These include:

Animation: The brain stem and sleep
Animation: The suprachiasmatic nucleus and sleep
Interaction: The main brain areas involved in circadian rhythms

Chapter 20
Cognition and action

Learning outcomes for Chapter 20

After studying this chapter, you should be able to:

1 Describe some links between cognition and action and explain what is meant by the term 'goal'.

2 Present a balanced account of modularity, linking this to how real brains work.

3 Explain why cognition and action require a process of attention. Relate this to the biological bases of attention.

4 Describe what is meant by 'hemispheric asymmetry' and the types of evidence that lead to this notion.

5 Describe the link between goal-directed action and the role of the prefrontal cortex.

6 Show where understanding of language can be enriched by an application of the four types of explanation: causal, developmental, evolutionary and functional. Link this to the brain mechanisms underlying language and what is special about language in humans.

Scene-setting questions

1 Why can't we do several things at the same time?

2 Is the mind organized as modules?

3 What happens when you 'pay attention'?

4 Is using a mobile phone while driving hazardous?

5 A 'new-age' image is that the left hemisphere is reductionist, 'Western', logical and mathematical, whereas the right is holistic, 'Eastern', creative, intuitive and artistic. Is this true?

6 In the brain, what is involved when we resist temptation? Why are some people not so good at it?

7 Why do people tend to gesture while speaking, even on the telephone?

Why do people tend to gesture while speaking, even on the telephone? Explore the video on the website accompanying this book at **www.pearsoned.co.uk/toates**

How do we manage to do more than one thing at a time?

Source: Getty Images/The Image Bank.

Introduction

The term **cognition** refers to knowledge about the world and this chapter concerns how cognition is exploited in action. Cognition can be used in action only if it can link to motor control, which is inevitably a further consideration of the chapter. Cognition and action are linked to motivation and goals (Norman and Shallice, 1986). For example, we are motivated towards social company, so we invite friends for a meal, thereby combining social and food-related goals.

Imagine you are preparing a meal, having set the 'high-level' goal of presenting the meal to guests. Moving towards this goal requires sub-goals to be met, e.g. to boil potatoes. Each goal and sub-goal is associated with memories of actions that are expected to lead to its achievement. Each sub-goal requires yet further sub-goals to be met, e.g. remove lettuce from the refrigerator, turn on the tap and finally put the lettuce in a salad dryer. Within each level of goal, there can be competition for control, as in interrupting the drying of the lettuce to switch off the boiling potatoes. So, successful behaviour involves goals, plans for achieving them, allocation of time and calling up memories of appropriate actions.

While making the meal, the telephone rings and a friend asks how to get to your home. So, your attention becomes occupied by the auditory channel, as you focus on the conversation. You balance the phone under your chin, listening, as always, with the right ear (or for some people, the left). You talk and continue the cooking. At one point, you 'automatically' stop cooking in order to make arm gestures to accompany giving directions.

In your lifetime's experience, the behaviour of picking up an egg has a strong association with the mechanics of breaking it against the edge of a dish. However, this time the goal requires the unbroken egg to be placed in a saucepan and boiled. While your attention is diverted by the conversation, the stimulus of the sight of the egg and a dish triggers the breaking reaction. This is against the interests of the goal and, as your attention returns to the sub-goal of boiling the egg, you realize what you have done.

You are strongly tempted to taste what you are making. You find this hard to resist even though you know that it will show on your waist-line some time later.

A number of features of cognition and the link to action are illustrated by this example:

1 Behaviour has a goal: a state that does not at present exist is represented by the brain/mind and action is taken to bring an actual state into alignment with it.

2 Attention is involved in allocating cognitive resources and priority among the possible controls of behaviour. Attention shifts the focus between them, according to changing circumstances.

3 Behaviour can be captured by strong stimulus–response links (e.g. egg → break), especially when attention is directed elsewhere.

4 In processing information, there could be a difference in sensory channels between the sides of the head. Is this indicative of a hemispheric difference?

5 It comes naturally to use hands to give directions, even though it cannot be of much help to your distant friend. Speech seems to be linked naturally with motor acts. This suggests that speech is not a self-contained cognitive system.

6 There can be conflict between the temptation of immediate rewards (taste of food) and delayed punishments (increased weight).

The chapter will look at goal direction, decision-making, attention, hemispheric differences and language. It starts by considering modularity: whether the brain is made up of a number of specialized processors.

Section summary

1 Actions are associated with goals.

2 Goals are associated with sub-goals.

3 Attention is allocated to different stimuli and tasks.

4 Behaviour can be captured by certain stimuli, particularly if attention wanders from the task set.

☞ ### Test your knowledge

20.1 Complete the following sentence: 'In holding a telephone to one ear, we give a selective advantage to the contralateral _____ '.

Answer on page 544

Modularity

Introduction

To what extent is information processing in the brain done by specialized *modules* that act in parallel, each dedicated to solving only a *single* type of problem, i.e. **modularity** (Fodor, 1985)? By contrast, to what extent is it done by flexible all-purpose *central processes*? Figure 20.1 shows this distinction. According to the modularity view, both encapsulated modules and general-purpose central processing exist and serve complementary roles in cognition and behaviour.

Damage to a module would be expected to disrupt just one sort of information processing, leaving the rest intact, whereas disruption to central processing would be expected to produce gross global deficits revealed in many domains.

Of course, ears and the auditory channel do a very different job from eyes and the visual channel, and, if this were all the argument is saying, it would be banal. Rather, it is claiming that processing within sensory channels *and beyond* is specialized to a high degree.

There is clearly some dedication of brain structures to particular tasks. For example, the brain mechanisms underlying the processing of colour seem to be dedicated to only this task, as do those for face recognition (Chapter 8). Some human conditions suggest modularity, since just one feature of cognition appears to be impaired, among otherwise apparently normal functioning (Karmiloff-Smith *et al.*, 1995). In autism, social cognition is deficient in the context of some normal non-social cognition. In 'Williams syndrome' (also known as Beuren's syndrome), speech and social interaction are typically normal, in the face of severe disruption to problem-solving, visuospatial integration and planning (Karmiloff-Smith *et al.*, 1995). Face recognition is normal or even better than that of controls.

Properties and function of modules

The term 'information encapsulation' refers to the property of modular processes to operate with independence from influences outside the module, e.g. central processes. Fodor (1985) argues that modular systems are hard-wired, autonomous, domain specific and innately specified. They are typified by perceptual processes, which are driven automatically by sensory input ('bottom-up') and are very fast. As another example, with the help of a rapidly reacting 'fear module', you tend to survive to see another day (Chapter 12).

Also pointing to modularity, visual illusions appear even when having accurate knowledge about the object. For example, the Muller–Lyer illusion (Figure 7.5, p. 189) occurs even though we know rationally that the lines are of equal length. The illusion is said to be the product of a module and thereby immune from the central processing that knows that the lengths are equal. We are consciously aware of only the output of modules, in this example the conscious perception that the lines are unequal. We have no insight into how we arrived at that conscious perception. By contrast, we can be aware of some intermediate steps and processing operations of central processes (Moscovitch and Umiltà, 1990). What Fodor calls 'higher' cognitive processes, e.g. thinking, are said not to show modularity and encapsulation.

Figure 20.1 Modules and central processes.

On functional significance, Moscovitch and Umiltà (1990, p. 13) suggest that modules supply central processing with information about the world '. . . quickly, efficiently, and without distortion from the beliefs, motivations, and expectations of the organism'. Such modules must be 'immune to higher-order influences'.

According to Fodor, the development of modular systems follows a fixed course as does their malfunction. By contrast, there exist 'true higher cognitive faculties' (Fodor, 1985, p. 4), central processes that are 'slow, deep, global rather than local, largely under voluntary (or, as one says, 'executive') control'. They are exemplified by thought and problem-solving. Fodor (p. 4) suggests:

> The surface plausibility of the *Modularity* picture thus lies in the idea that Nature has contrived to have it both ways, to get the best out of fast dumb systems *and* slow contemplative ones, by simply refusing to choose between them.

With experience, component modules are sometimes assembled and the assembly takes on features of a bigger module. Reading is a possible example of this. Presumably, modules devoted to speech and vision are integrated in reading (Jusczyk and Cohen, 1985). With experience, reading can take on automatic properties.

Links to the brain

In principle, the domain of a module could be identified by brain damage. This might selectively disrupt just one module, or leave one spared in the face of disruption to others (Morris, 1996a,b). For example, modular processing includes that for colours, location of sounds and faces. It appears that each of these can be impaired in isolation and each can survive even severe **dementia** (gross and general cognitive impairment) (Chapter 22).

Another feature of modules is their 'shallow output'. For example, patients with dementia can sometimes reproduce, say, speech but without insight into its semantic content. Some people with Alzheimer's disease are able to read and even correct grammatical mistakes without understanding the material.

Double dissociations (Chapter 8) are one possible feature of modules. That is, brain damage x would disrupt behaviour X, while leaving Y intact. Conversely, damage y would disrupt behaviour Y while leaving X intact. Such evidence is suggestive of modular organization.

Critiques of modularity

Critiques of modularity can stimulate our thinking. For example, there might be a double dissociation *within* the so-called central all-purpose system (Moscovitch and Umiltà, 1990). Following damage, one form of memory can be disrupted while others remain essentially intact

(Chapter 11; Gross, 1985). Double dissociations can occur between episodic and semantic memory (Temple and Richardson, 2004).

Is modularity genetically specified? Traditionally, the notions of modularity and genetic specification have been linked. However, in terms of understanding development (Chapter 6), modularity appears to arise in part from interaction with the environment. Thus, a module might be 'the *emergent product* of development, not its starting point' (Karmiloff-Smith *et al.*, 1995).

Rather than strict encapsulation, there can be interactions between so-called modules, such as visual and auditory processing (see later) (Glucksberg, 1985).

There are problems with Fodor's criteria for distinguishing modular and central systems (Moscovitch and Umiltà, 1990). For example, attention is 'central' and yet a switch of it can be both rapid and mandatory, e.g. in response to one's own name said loudly.

There is reason to blur Fodor's distinction between modules and a central system, so that a dichotomy gets replaced by a continuum (that must give you feeling of déjà vu!) (Gardner, 1985). Even central systems can exhibit features of modularity and can break down in ways that suggests modularity (as in the case of memory). Conversely, processing within modules can be subject to central top-down controls, which reduces their encapsulation (Caplan, 1985). For example, Chapter 8 described top-down factors in perception, e.g. expectancy.

The message to take with us

In the spirit of modularity, psychologists can gain insight by looking at fracture lines: brain damage can sometimes disrupt one information processing system, leaving another apparently intact. We should not make dogmatic assumptions about unitary global processes that in reality might be composed of a number of divisible subsystems (cf. Rizzolatti and Berti, 1993). In a clinical context, it might prove hazardous to assume a broad disruption of all processing and thereby to miss islands of intact functioning. However, certain cautions need to be sounded. There can sometimes be parallel ways of solving a problem, only one of which might be disrupted by a lesion (Coltheart, 1985). We need to be vigilant for ways in which features of modularity can manifest. For example, comparing *between* memories, either semantic or episodic memory can be disrupted (showing some properties of modules), with no global impairment (Temple and Richardson, 2004). However, there can also be disruption *within* each of these, e.g. semantic memory for numbers can remain intact in the face of disruption to memory for non-number information.

Given several 'ifs' and 'buts', modularity is a useful concept to hold in mind in discussing cognition and action.

Attention

Introduction

The term **attention** describes the experience that a given stimulus can be perceived with different amounts of subjective clarity at different times (Rizzolatti, 1983). That is, the power of a stimulus to engage awareness depends upon the amount of attention allocated to its processing. The present section concerns the role of attention in directing processing to particular stimuli and away from others, at a given point in time. Such attention is needed for the efficient focus on only certain stimuli, the generation of *coordinated* behaviour based on a limited sub-set of the total sensory input and, thereby, the avoidance of chaos.

Stimuli compete for access to awareness and attention biases their competitive value (Posner, 1993). Broadly speaking, the competition is not just for awareness but also for the control of action based on this. Bringing sensory events to awareness involves a high degree of selection (Desimone, 1992). For example, on looking at a crowd, in spite of many faces forming an image on the retina, we usually recognize only one or two at a time.

Attention is commonly studied in the context of vision and hearing (Driver and Spence, 1994) but it applies also to other senses, e.g. the tactile (Lloyd *et al.*,

1999). Attention is also involved with internal events. For example, we might be able to attend to mental arithmetic or, conversely, be unable to resist the intrusion into awareness of pain or unwanted thoughts (Eccleston and Crombez, 1999; Tallis, 1995).

Attentional processes are distinct from sensory and motor processes but clearly interact with them.

Top-down and bottom-up factors

A distinction can be made between two factors that determine attention (Posner, 1980). There is a 'bottom-up factor' (also termed 'involuntary' and 'passive'), as when a *stimulus* captures attention by its strength, novelty or sudden appearance. There is a 'top-down factor' (also termed 'voluntary' and 'active'). This describes the role of such things as knowledge of the situation, motivation, instructions given by an experimenter, or goals set in a search task. Though a convenient distinction, active and passive factors interact.

Types of attention

Attention can be classified as described below (Perry and Hodges, 1999). However, these are not mutually exclusive classes. Accounting for a given instance of cognitive processing might need to involve two or three such types.

Sustained attention

Sustained attention refers to the ability to hold attention over considerable periods of time ('vigilance') and to detect a signal over such periods (Broadbent, 1958), e.g. to report when a signal appears on a radar screen. At times we show high attention in a general sense ('vigilance'), whereas at other times we lack vigilance (Chapter 19). Sleepiness represents a state of the brain that can be contrasted with the ability to show high sustained attention.

Selective attention

Selective attention and its shifting refer to the capacity to focus on a limited range of information while reducing the strength of distraction. We orientate attention such that one particular stimulus is processed rather than another. For another example, even with the eyes stationary, we can be cued to expect an object at one location in space. Cueing means that preferential processing is allocated to information corresponding to this area (Aston-Jones *et al.*, 1999). Selective attention applies also to auditory information: for example, in the 'cocktail party phenomenon' (Cherry, 1966), one voice or word engages attention.

To what extent does selective attention within one sensory system interact with that of another? A focus of one modality tends to give a selective advantage to the compatible spatial field in the other modality also (Driver and Spence, 1994). This makes functional sense. Salient information detected in one modality and from one side (e.g. the sound of a potential predator) might usefully cause a focus of attention on other sensory information to that side (e.g. visual stimuli of movement).

Selective attention is served by two processes. First, consider when the eyes move to bring the image of a selected part of the world to the fovea (Chapter 8) or when the body turns to maximize the impact of a particular event. Such realignment of the body or part of it to alter sensory inflow is termed **overt orientating**. By contrast, **covert orientating** refers to the act of focusing on a particular object, location or stimulus feature *without making any movement of eyes or other body region* (Posner, 1980). For example, even with the image stationary at the centre of the retina, there are features of the image to which we can direct attention and subject to more detailed processing.

There are similarities between overt and covert orientating (Desimone, 1992) and they work as an integrated system (Rizzolatti *et al.*, 1987). A change of covert orientation (from A to B) is usually associated with a corresponding eye movement shortly afterwards, to bring B into alignment with the fovea (Wurtz *et al.*, 1982).

Divided attention

Divided attention is the ability to share attention processes and perform more than one task simultaneously (Perry and Hodges, 1999). Typically, participants perform tasks A and B separately, their performance is measured, and then they are asked to perform A and B simultaneously. The detriment in performance as compared to the scores for A and B separately is a measure of the difficulty of simultaneous performance.

The discussion now considers two experimental tests of attention.

The Stroop test

The cognitive Stroop

A classic example of selective attention and the role of top-down and bottom-up factors is the **Stroop test** (Figure 20.2). A person is asked to name the colour of ink in which words are written, the words being incompatible colour names (Stroop, 1935). Thus, the word GREEN is written in red ink and the task requires the person to respond 'red', ignoring the stimulus 'green'. This task is difficult since it requires controlled processing ('top-down') to override the automaticity ('bottom-up') of a lifetime's experience of responding 'green' to the word GREEN. Have a go at it and you will

RED	GREEN
GREEN	RED
YELLOW	BLUE
BLUE	YELLOW
RED	BLUE
YELLOW	GREEN
BLUE	RED
GREEN	YELLOW
(a)	**(b)**

Figure 20.2 The cognitive Stroop test: (a) incompatible and (b) compatible lists.

soon see. If your fellow students appear to be doing very well, check that they are not cheating by squinting and so blurring the word that it is unreadable!

The task is particularly difficult for people with damage to certain frontal regions of the brain, who exhibit increased capture of attention by the word. Hence, it can suggest where damage has arisen (Vendrell *et al.*, 1995), described shortly.

The emotional Stroop

A variation of the Stroop test is the **emotional Stroop** (see Figure 20.3). The speed of reactions to words of emotional significance and neutral words are compared in a colour-naming task. For example, in investigating disgust (Chapter 17), the reaction time for making the response 'red' to the word 'vomit' or 'rotting', written in red, is compared with the reaction time of 'red' for the neutral word 'table', written in red (Charash and McKay, 2002). The emotional Stroop arises from an attention bias towards the emotionally loaded words. For fear (Chapter 12), the emotional words might be, for example, 'terror'. For participants with strong emotional reactivity, the reaction times are lengthened when the word coincides

FEAR	PLAN
TERROR	HUMOUR
HORROR	THINKS
ANXIETY	CONSIGN
SCARED	DOUBTS
ALARM	BOARD
(a)	**(b)**

Figure 20.3 The emotional Stroop task: (a) emotional and (b) control words.

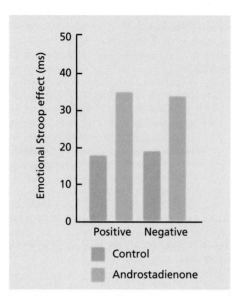

Figure 20.4 The increased latency to name colours in the case of words having an emotional meaning (positive, e.g. 'holiday', or negative, e.g. 'pathetic'), under conditions of treatment with androstadienone or control solution.

Source: Hummer and McClintock (2009) *Hormones and Behavior,* **55**, Fig. 3, p. 553.

with their particular vulnerabilities. Control participants without strong vulnerabilities do not exhibit this effect. For example, people high on disgust sensitivity and primed with a disgust-related narrative prior to the test exhibit a lengthening for disgust-related words. People

who are addicted to drugs display an emotional Stroop reaction to a word such as 'syringe'.

The task can be used to assess therapy, e.g. a heavy smoker might be expected to be disrupted by the word 'nicotine'. Effective treatments for addiction might be expected to lower the capacity of drug-related words to capture attention. The biological basis of addiction can be investigated by altering particular neurotransmitter systems with agonists or antagonists to see whether the emotional Stroop is strengthened or weakened (Munaf *et al.,* 2007).

The emotional Stroop has been used to investigate the possible role of human pheromones (Chapter 7). They are likely to exert subtle effects, unlike the more automatic effects found in other species (Hummer and McClintock, 2009). Rather than directly instigating behaviour, they are likely to *modulate* human emotion, motivation or cognition. The substance termed Δ4,16-androstadien-3-one (mercifully 'abbreviated' to androstadienone) appears to act as a human pheromone.

A cotton swab dipped in a 'carrier solution' containing androstadienone was applied to participants' upper lips. The carrier solution contained a strong odour, to mask the androstadienone and prevent conscious detection. In the control condition, participants were swabbed with only the carrier solution. Interference with naming the colours of emotionally loaded words was increased by androstadienone (Figure 20.4). It had no effect on naming colour when the words were neutral.

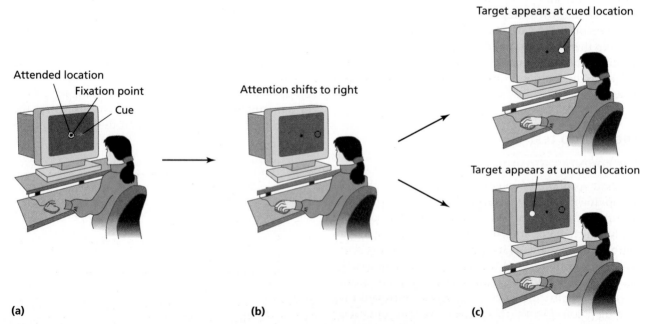

Figure 20.5 Experiment demonstrates covert orientating: (a) cue presented, (b) attention shifts and (c) target appears.
Source: Bear *et al.* (1996, Fig. 21.15, p. 603).

A test of covert orientating

Basic design

Figure 20.5 shows a demonstration of selective attention involving covert orientating. The person was first required to fixate the eyes on a central point on a screen ('Fixation point'). A cue was presented to direct the focus of attention. When the cue took the form of a plus sign appearing in the centre, this indicated an equal chance of the target being to left or right. On other trials, to see whether attention could be directed to right or left, the cue took the form of an arrow. A target, a circle, was then flashed very briefly onto the screen. The task was to detect whether this target appeared to the left, to the right, or at the fixation point. Thus, if people were able to exert selective attention towards one side, they would be expected to do better when cued correctly by the arrow.

Only trials in which no eye movements occurred were used, hence revealing the effect of purely covert shifts of attention. When the arrow pointed to the appropriate direction ('honest signal'), reaction time of detection was faster than for no cue. For the opposite direction of pointing ('dishonest signal'), it was slower. This demonstrates increased efficiency arising from exploiting the cue to focus on an appropriate area of visual space. This area was allocated priority in terms of processing information arising there.

A biological application

Figure 20.6 shows a 'dot probe' study with a biological application. Participants were instructed to focus on the cross in the centre and were then presented with images of two faces, so briefly that they did not reach conscious awareness. One face expressed emotion (happy or angry), while the other was neutral. Then a dot was presented on the screen, either to the left or right. The participant was asked to identify which side of the screen the dot appeared and to respond by pressing a button accordingly. Consider a trial in which the side of the dot corresponded to the side of the emotional face. If the emotional face engaged attention, the participant should be relatively fast in identifying the side of the dot. Conversely, reaction time would be expected to be relatively slow when the dot appeared on the opposite side to the emotional face. If androstadienone sensitizes the effect of emotion, it would be expected to enlarge the difference in reaction times. This was indeed the case for angry and happy faces. Androstadienone did not have any general effect on increasing attention.

So, the emotional Stroop and dot probe tasks point in the same direction: androstadienone alters the brain's information processing to increase the engagement of attention with emotional material.

Brain regions, controls of attention and brain damage

Introduction

This section considers what is the nature of the attentional effect and where it acts. It then looks at the brain regions that provide the sources of the attentional signals.

Chapter 19 considered the brain stem controls of sleeping and waking, which set the overall tone of the brain so that it exhibits varying degrees of alertness. Activation in the prefrontal and parietal regions of the right hemisphere is indicative of sustained attention in any sensory channel (Sarter et al., 2001). The vigilance decrement over time is mirrored in reduced levels of activation there.

The focus of this section is upon selective attention.

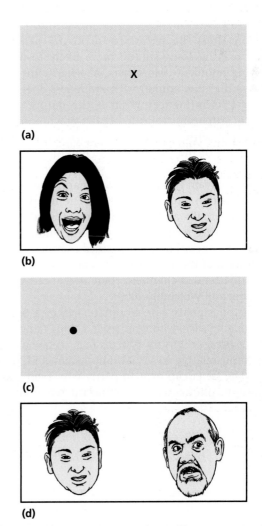

Figure 20.6 The experiment performed by Hummer and McClintock (2009): (a) target, (b) happy and neutral faces, (c) dot probe, (d) neutral and angry faces.
Source: after Hummer and McClintock (2009).

What is happening in the brain when we focus attention?

Source: Ethno Images, Inc./Alamy.

Nature of influence

Attention alters the sensitivity of neural pathways, thereby making some stimuli more likely to capture processing resources than others. At what point in the pathways that link stimuli with awareness does attention exert its influence? What is the nature of this influence? Attention seems to act top-down upon various stages in sensory pathways. In vision, these range from regions of the thalamus (e.g. pulvinar), through the primary visual cortex, to later stages of processing in the ventral stream (Chapter 8) (Saalmann and Kastner, 2009; Shomstein and Yantis, 2004). The nature of the influence is usually assumed to be one of 'modulation', alas a confusing term given the use of 'module' just described. It suggests that, in attended channels, there is amplification of the activity that would otherwise occur and, in unattended channels, there is reduced activity (Kanwisher and Wojciulik, 2000).

Attention signals can modulate *within* a sensory system (e.g. in vision, to emphasize colour rather than shape) or *between* sensory systems (e.g. to favour auditory stimuli relative to visual (Shomstein and Yantis, 2004)). The latter can explain partly why even hands-free mobile phones can be a hazard when driving (Strayer *et al.*, 2003).

Covert selective attention within the visual system

Moran and Desimone (1985) and Luck *et al.* (1997) projected images onto the retina of monkeys and measured the responses of neurons at various locations in the visual system. They examined the ventral stream, i.e. primary visual cortex → prestriate area → inferior temporal cortex (Chapter 8). Monkeys were trained to fixate

A personal angle

S.B.

In Germany, S.B., a former student of engineering, suffered strokes at age 22 years and again one year later (Engelien *et al.*, 2000). These severely damaged his auditory cortex on both sides, such that S.B. was not usually aware consciously of sounds. PET studies revealed that S.B.'s auditory cortex was normally only very slightly triggered by sounds. The remainder of the auditory system appeared to function normally. Researchers found that S.B. was consciously aware of sounds only when his selective and undivided attention was paid to the auditory channel. For example, he could voluntarily focus on this channel, as in trying to hear the sound of the door-bell at a time when visitors were expected. S.B. exemplifies the role of the top-down factor in attention.

their eyes upon a spot on a screen throughout the test and the receptive field of a particular neuron in the inferior temporal (IT) cortex was mapped in terms of area on the screen. IT neurons have large receptive fields and are triggered by complex patterns. With eyes still fixed, the animal was trained to shift covert orientation to one of two locations within the receptive field as directed by a cue (Figure 20.7).

In the first part of the experiment, single stimuli were employed. An IT neuron that was sensitive to a red stimulus but insensitive to a green stimulus within its receptive field was found. (Other IT neurons would be sensitive to green and insensitive to red.) Compare parts (a) and (b), where single stimuli are used. In the second part of the experiment, red and green stimuli were presented together and attention was cued to the location of each stimulus in turn. Compare parts (c) and (d), where the identical two stimuli are present but the site of cueing changes. When attention was drawn to the location of the red stimulus, activity in the IT neuron was high. When it was drawn to the location of the green stimulus, activity in the neuron was low. This was in spite of the fact that the otherwise effective red stimulus was still present (compare (d) with (a) and (c)).

Comparing (c) and (d), since the eyes did not move and the same red and green stimuli were present in both cases, stimulation at the retina was the same. However, the effect of the red stimulus depended upon the target of covert orientation. In other words, attention modulated the activity of neurons according to its locus.

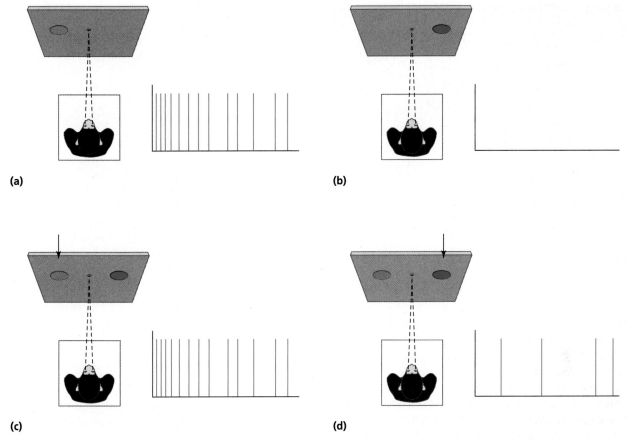

Figure 20.7 Selective attention and the response of an IT neuron with animal's eyes fixated at the central spot. Responses to (a) red stimulus alone (note activity), (b) green stimulus alone (note absence of activity), (c) and (d) to both stimuli with attention cued to (c) red and (d) green.

What is the source of the attentional signals directed to *particular features* of sensory input? A network of brain regions controls such attention, distinct from, though interacting with, sensory and motor systems (Desimone, 1992; Karnath *et al.*, 2002; Posner and Petersen, 1990). The 'fronto-parietal system' is embodied in interacting neural circuits that involve parts of the frontal and parietal lobes (Kanwisher and Wojciulik, 2000). It is the source of modulatory attention signals that are transmitted to other regions. We will look next at the role of some of the brain regions.

Prefrontal cortex

Forming the so-called 'anterior attention system', the prefrontal cortex (PFC) plays a top-down role in the three forms of attention (D'Esposito *et al.*, 1995; Sarter *et al.*, 2001). Regarding divided attention, the investigators looked at performance on two separate tasks that each predominantly activated posterior brain regions. Performing either task on its own was not associated with PFC activation. When people performed both tasks simultaneously, the dorsolateral PFC was activated. D'Esposito

et al. suggest that a role of the dorsolateral PFC is to allocate and coordinate the limited resource of attention. Damage to this area has a particularly disruptive effect in performing the Stroop test (Vendrell *et al.*, 1995).

The parietal lobe

A 'posterior attention system' (PAS) is located within the posterior parietal lobe of each hemisphere (Posner and Petersen, 1990). The PAS modulates the sensitivity of certain neural systems that perform cognitive processing. When a person switches attention from one location to another (a top-down influence), there is activation of the posterior parietal lobe (Posner, 1993). It appears that the PAS is involved in covert switches of attention from one location to another.

The anterior cingulate cortex

The Stroop task has been employed to study which brain regions have responsibility for resolution of the conflict that is the tasks' defining feature (Bush *et al.*, 2000). The anterior cingulate cortex (ACC) (Figure 20.8) has subdivisions, one of which is implicated in

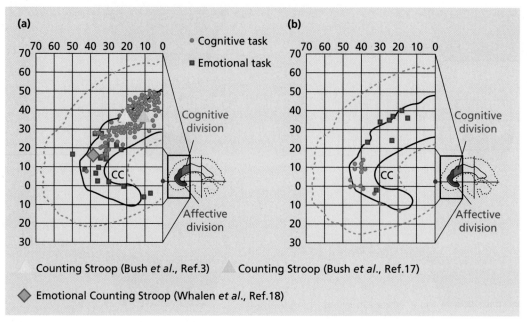

Figure 20.8 A meta-analysis of the areas of (a) activation and (b) deactivation of the ACC. Yellow/orange triangles: two cognitive Stroop tasks; blue diamond: emotional Stroop task. (CC = Corpus callosum)

Source: Bush *et al.* (2000) *Trends in Cognitive Sciences,* **4**(6), Fig. 2, p. 217.

cognitive Stroop tasks and the other in affective/emotional Stroop tasks.

A double dissociation is apparent (Figure 20.8): affective/emotional tasks tend to excite a region at the front of the ACC (affective division) and inhibit a region just behind this (cognitive division). Conversely, cognitive tasks tend to inhibit the region at the front and excite that just behind it. The cognitive division is implicated in sensory and/or response selection (e.g. divided attention tasks) and has connections to brain regions such as the lateral prefrontal cortex and the premotor area. The affective division has connections to such structures as the orbitofrontal cortex and the amygdala (Chapter 12).

Figure 20.8 shows a meta-analysis of the regions of activation and deactivation of the ACC (the term meta-analysis refers to an analysis that draws its information from several studies).

The neglect syndrome

Certain sites of brain damage are followed by a **neglect syndrome** (also termed 'sensory neglect' or 'spatial neglect'), and this provides insight into brain mechanisms of attention (Posner, 1993). Stimuli that would normally undergo processing in the hemisphere contralateral to the lesion are processed abnormally. For example, they are associated with an unusually long reaction time or there is no awareness of them. In severe cases, half the visual world including half the patient's own body appears not to exist to them (Halligan and

Marshall, 1993). The neglect syndrome highlights a normal capacity to divide attention along a spatial dimension (Farah *et al.,* 1993). Neglect is more common with damage to the right hemisphere than the left (Posner, 1993). This suggests that the basis of the control of attention in both hemispheres is located within the right hemisphere.

Traditionally, in humans damage to the posterior parietal cortex is thought to be the cause of the cortical contribution to neglect, though some associate it more closely with regions of temporal cortex (Karnath *et al.,* 2001). Damage to regions of basal ganglia and thalamus is also followed by sensory neglect (Karnath *et al.,* 2002).

So far we have briefly mentioned a hemispheric difference. We now look in more detail at hemispheric specialization.

Section summary

1 Attention refers to systems that modulate access to awareness.

2 A passive switch of attention is in response to external events, whereas an active change is due to a top-down factor.

3 Investigators distinguish sustained attention, selective attention and divided attention.

Hemispheric asymmetry

Introduction

The term **lateralization** (Kosslyn *et al.*, 1999) refers to an asymmetry, whereby one side of the brain takes a disproportionate role in a type of information processing. It appears to be especially evident in humans (Trevarthen, 1984). We normally show little evidence of asymmetry in everyday life (except the preferential use of one hand), since the brain works as an integrated whole. Special tests are needed to reveal it.

In right-handed people, the basis of language tends to be lateralized in the left hemisphere (discussed later). The right hemisphere typically is specialized for perception of visual patterns, e.g. faces, and global or holistic organization, including emotionally loaded information. The left hemisphere is better at analytic cognition (Tucker and Williamson, 1984).

Some evidence for functional asymmetry derives from deficits shown by patients suffering disease or brain damage. However, apart from general difficulties of interpretation of brain damage (Chapter 5), plasticity of the brain means that compensation can sometimes mask the failure of a damaged region.

4 Overt orienting serves selective attention by a realignment of the body (or part of it) to alter sensory inflow.

5 Covert orienting refers to an intrinsic change in the focus of attention without moving the body or part of it.

6 The activity of neurons in sensory processing pathways reflects the role of attentional factors.

7 A neglect syndrome refers to a failure of part of the sensory space to enter awareness.

☞ Test your knowledge

20.3 Complete the following statement, which relates to Figure 20.7(c) and (d): 'Cueing of attention to the ___ corresponding to the green light lowers activity in the cell indicated'.

Answer on page 544   WEB

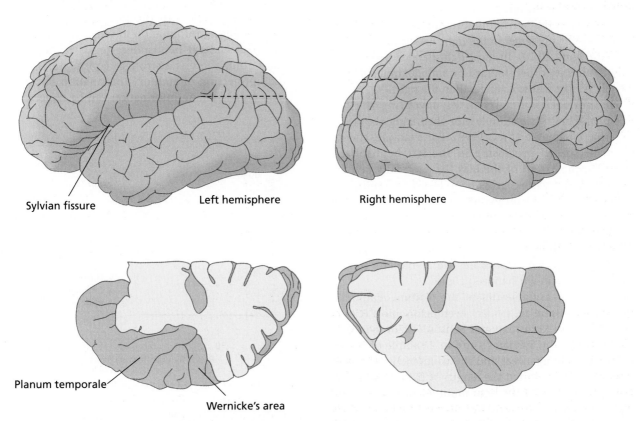

Figure 20.9 Comparison of left and right hemispheres, showing larger planum temporale of left.
Source: Geschwind (1979, p. 165). Courtesy of Carol Donner.

Left hemisphere   Right hemisphere

Sylvian fissure

Figure 20.10 The angle that the Sylvian fissure forms with the horizontal.
Source: Kosslyn *et al.* (1999, Fig. 58.4, p. 1526).

Anatomical differences

In humans, differences in the anatomy of the hemispheres appear to be related to differences in function (Kosslyn *et al.*, 1999). A region termed the planum temporale (PT) is generally larger in the left hemisphere than in the right (Figure 20.9) (Geschwind and Levitsky, 1968) and for most people speech is based in regions of the left hemisphere that include the PT. In right-handed people, the angle that the Sylvian fissure forms with the horizontal is generally larger in the right hemisphere than in the left (Figure 20.10). In most right-handed people, but only a minority of left-handed or ambidextrous people, the left Sylvian fissure is longer than the right.

The normal asymmetry in PT, favouring the left side of the brain is a stimulus for theorizing about the PT's role (Shapleske *et al.*, 1999). For example, the PT performs speech processing in the left hemisphere. However, the extent of the bias that normally favours the left in fact varies across people and in a minority of cases it is either non-existent or there is even a bias in favour of the right hemisphere. Such individual differences are the trigger to try to correlate the extent of hemispheric differences in brain anatomy with behavioural differences. For example, the asymmetry in size tends to be less in left-handed people.

In humans, asymmetries in the planum temporale and Sylvian fissure are evident even before birth (Chi *et al.*, 1977). Yeni-Komshian and Benson (1976) looked at the length of the Sylvian fissure in a sample of brains of humans, chimpanzees and rhesus monkeys. For each individual, they plotted the length of fissure of the left brain against that of the right brain (Figure 20.11). The left fissure was longer in 84% of the humans, 80% of the chimpanzees and 44% of the rhesus monkeys. A particularly strong deviation from equality in humans is evident.

Asymmetry extends to prehistory. Neanderthals lived during a period of some 30 000 to 230 000 years ago (Stringer and Gamble, 1993). Evidence suggests that they showed hemispheric asymmetry (LeMay, 1976).

Differential targeting

Differences between hemispheres can be revealed by presenting information to the left or the right. For example, presenting information to only one ear means that the contralateral hemisphere tends to be at an advantage since there is a stronger contralateral than ipsilateral projection of auditory information (Chapter 9). In the visual system, information can be targeted to

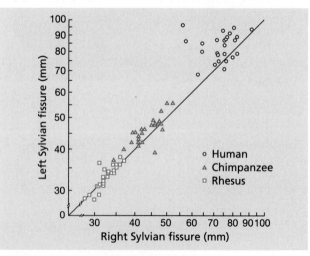

Figure 20.11 The length of the Sylvian fissure of the left half of the brain against that of the right for each individual. Sloping line represents equality.

Source: from Yeni-Komshian and Benson (1976, Fig. 1, p. 388). Reprinted with permission from AAAS.

An asymmetrical 'French' Neanderthal

The remains of a Neanderthal male were found in 1908 in a cave at La Chapelle-aux-Saints in south-west France (Boule and Anthony, 1911). From mouldings made of the skull, the form of the underlying brain tissue could be estimated. The left hemisphere appeared slightly different from the right in a way similar to modern humans.

one or other hemisphere (Chapter 8), though with an intact corpus callosum it becomes available to both.

Visual tasks

Even for people with intact inter-hemispheric communication, information can be directed to one hemisphere (Kosslyn *et al.*, 1999). Suppose that such information is of a kind normally processed predominantly in one hemisphere. If it is directed to the hemisphere not normally employed, it must either be processed by different means from normal or cross inter-hemispheric connections to be processed in the usual way. Crossing the hemispheres takes some 15 ms. Either way, slowing of reaction and degradation of processing might appear.

Consider the three word forms, GOAT, *goat* and goat. In meaning, they are of course the same, but in specific form they are different. People were asked whether such words are the same or different, being asked to respond by a criterion of either semantics or specific form. In applying different criteria, different input–output processors are, by definition, involved. By projecting sensory information to one or other hemisphere, e.g. by a 'divided visual field presentation' (Chapter 8), it is possible to detect differences in the way in which the hemispheres process information. There is evidence for parallel processing with a superiority of the left hemisphere in identifying meaning (e.g. GOAT is the same as goat) and for the right hemisphere in extracting form information (e.g. it is different) (Geffen *et al.*, 1972).

Selective brain damage

By neuroimaging (Chapter 5), patients with a region of brain damage can be studied and compared with controls. It can be useful to be reminded of the need for caution in interpreting brain lesions.

Global and local processing

There appears to be a distribution of responsibility between hemispheres for the analysis of a visual scene based upon its content (Robertson *et al.*, 1988). There are various ways of trying to capture the basis of the distinction, e.g. in terms of global and local levels.

Which way is the triangle of Figure 20.12(a) pointing? Most people see it pointing to the left (i.e. 270° from the vertical in a clockwise direction) but, in principle, it might equally point either at 30° or 150° from the vertical. Consider the same triangle embedded in the pattern of part (b); people now tend to see it pointing at 30° from the vertical. The solution depends upon whether local or global processing is employed. Responding at a local level is faster when an image is briefly projected in the right visual field (left hemisphere) and it is faster at a global level when projected to the left visual field (right hemisphere) (Robertson and Delis, 1986).

Robertson and Delis studied patients who had suffered unilateral brain damage through a stroke or had had a tumour removed. Patients had intact visual fields and normal visual acuity. They were briefly presented with an image of a triangle and asked to state the direction in which it was pointing. The triangle was embedded within a configuration of other stimuli forming a straight line, similar to Figure 20.12(b). Patients could respond either according to the orientation of the line ('aligned' condition) or according to one of the other two possible orientations of the triangle, i.e. when taken out of context ('single' condition). They were told that there was no right answer and should report only the way that the triangle appeared to be. Patients with damage to the left hemisphere had a stronger tendency to perceive the triangle according to context than did controls. Patients with damage to the right hemisphere showed a weaker tendency.

You first met Figure 20.13 in Chapter 8 (Figure 8.34, p. 221). On a global ('coarse-grained') level it is a letter S but, on a local ('fine-grained') level, it is a series of Ls. Humans with damage to the temporal–parietal region were presented briefly with such a stimulus. Damage to the right hemisphere had a more disruptive effect upon global processing whereas damage to the left hemisphere tended to disrupt local processing (Robertson *et*

(a) **(b)**

Figure 20.12 Triangle (a) alone and (b) embedded into larger pattern.

Source: Robertson and Delis (1986, Fig. 1).

Figure 20.13 Visual stimulus.

Source: Frith and Dolan (1997, Figure 4, p.1224).

al., 1988). Robertson and Delis (1986) suggest that their results support the proposal that local and global processing are performed by parallel processes. These are, at least during early stages, independent.

Such results are important to a discussion in psychology – is local processing done first and then the global picture extracted from this or is there a coarse analysis of the whole picture and then fine-grained analysis performed (Robertson *et al.*, 1988)? Rather than either of these, there appears to be parallel processing of global and local features. This could offer an advantage in speed of processing.

The emergence of this hemispheric difference might relate to the specialization of the left hemisphere for development of reading skills (Kosslyn, 1988).

Split-brain patients

People with a cut in the axons linking the two hemispheres, so-called 'split-brain patients' (Chapter 8), provide valuable evidence on hemispheric differences (Sperry, 1974). A surgical cut of the corpus callosum and anterior commissure to control epileptic seizures prevents communication between hemispheres. Thus, split-brain patients offer the advantage that information can be targeted to one hemisphere, in the absence of communication with the other through the corpus callosum. Patients reveal the possibilities for information processing by the isolated system. By projecting sensory information to one or other hemisphere, the mode of processing by this hemisphere can be studied in what is as near to controlled within-participant conditions as might be hoped for. The patient's history and temperament, etc., are 'controlled' in this within-participant design.

The damage is under surgical control and targets 'only' a defined and observable population of axons (Kosslyn *et al.*, 1999). Cell bodies are spared, hence avoiding the complications of interpretation and spread of effect that damage there would entail. However, conclusions need some qualifications:

1 Behaviour is normally the product of interaction between hemispheres (Sperry, 1974). The performance of a hemisphere in isolation might be deceptive regarding its role prior to surgery, when in interaction with the opposite hemisphere. There might be reorganization of processing systems following surgery (particularly if the patient is young), so that the performance of a hemisphere is changed.

2 The operation is a last resort after years of suffering and failed medication (Kosslyn *et al.*, 1999). These patients cannot be assumed to be like controls in other regards.

3 Split-brain patients would not normally act in such a way that information is projected solely to one hemisphere.

In general, the left hemisphere is superior in the perception of words presented visually and the right hemisphere is superior in non-language-related visuospatial tasks (Trevarthen, 1984).

Sperry (1974, p. 11) reports: 'The mute, minor hemisphere, by contrast seems to be carried along much as a passive, silent passenger who leaves the driving of behaviour mainly to the left hemisphere'. Sperry reports that the right hemisphere shows a specialization for holistic ('*Gestalt*') cognition, e.g. perceiving spatial relationships.

Creativity

Evidence suggests that the left hemisphere is specialized for fine-grained and reductionist processing whereas the right's role is global, holistic and large scale. Does this support the popular assumption that the left is rational, logical and scientific, whereas the right is intuitive and creative? Similarly, the Eastern world is seen to be holistic and the Western rational and logical.

It is simplistic to argue that science is not creative while art is not rational (Hines, 1991). If the dichotomy were true, it suggests a double dissociation: left hemisphere damage should disrupt rational processes but not artistic, whereas right hemisphere damage should have the opposite effect. In general, there is no evidence to suggest such a neat dichotomy (Alajouanine, 1948). Visual creative skills are indeed often undisturbed after left hemisphere damage. However, creative writing is typically disrupted by left hemisphere damage (Gardner, 1982).

Creativity appears to depend upon several component skills, e.g. high motivation and a capacity for extensive prior organizing of information, the bases presumably having a wide distribution throughout the brain. Creativity appears to be a complex amalgam of detail and holistic form. The left hemisphere might well have more responsibility for the former and the right for the latter but is detail any less creative than overall form? Only through cooperation between these component processes does creativity emerge.

Section summary

1 One side of the brain is favoured in performing a particular type of information processing. This asymmetry is termed 'lateralization'.

2 The left hemisphere is normally favoured for the processing of language.

3 The left hemisphere shows an advantage for local processing and the right shows this for global processing.

 Test your knowledge

20.4 Complete the following sentence, which relates to the study of hemispheric differences: 'To link most readily visual and language-based cognition, visual stimuli need to be presented in the ___ visual field'.

Answer on page 544

Goal-directed behaviour

Introduction

For something to become the goal of action, it needs to attract attention and thereby dominate processing capacity (Duncan, 1993). Irrelevant external stimuli need to be ignored or resisted. The goal can suddenly change, implying a switch of attention from one feature of the environment to another. Thus, the material here meshes naturally with that on attention.

Goals, sub-goals and action

As noted earlier, there is a hierarchy of control, consisting of high-level goals (e.g. make a meal) and sub-goals that serve the high-level goal (e.g. boil eggs). There is competition for expression at different levels, e.g. to wash lettuce or interrupt this to switch off boiling potatoes. Behaviour can be 'ambushed' by powerful stimuli, even though the behaviour that they trigger is at odds with the overall goal (Reason, 1984).

Humans have the capacity to think things out 'offline'. We could plan a meal while sitting on the train going home. We can run simulations and test outcomes. This has features in common with the logical ordering and sequencing involved in really making the meal.

A psychological model

Goal-directed tasks are said to be under the control of a central executive system (CES) (similar to a 'supervisory attentional system') (SAS) (Norman and Shallice, 1986). The CES selects memories and holds them 'online' (Chapter 11), even in the face of competing goals. Behaviour adjusts to changing circumstances to meet the goal. If behaviour is assessed to be failing, it can be replaced by a different behaviour directed to the same goal. Investigators associate the CES with the prefrontal cortex, a principal focus of this section.

The prefrontal cortex

Figures 5.32 (p. 129) and 5.38 (p. 135) show the prefrontal cortex and some of its divisions.

Introduction to role of the PFC

In hierarchical terms, Fuster (1999) describes the PFC as: '. . . "motor" cortex of the highest order in that it supports the cognitive functions that co-ordinate the execution of the most elaborate and novel actions of the organism'.

The PFC plays a role in holding a memory in an *active* state (Chapter 11), so that it can be utilized in action and in inhibition of competing tendencies (Dehaene and Changeux, 1989; Fuster, 1997). However, this process is vulnerable to interference, e.g. capture by salient stimuli. The PFC guides memory searches, directs thought processes, plans action and resists capture. Patients with PFC damage are often deficient in these regards. Thus, the PFC forms a biological basis for the control of the sequencing of complex and often creative behaviour, e.g. speech, as well as 'pure cognition', such as reasoning that can ultimately lead to action (Waltz *et al.*, 1999).

Goal-directed action is based on the temporal integration of component behaviours. For example, speech usually (!) depends on the responses of another person. The PFC embodies plans of the kind 'if event y occurs and situation M prevails, do A, but if event z occurs do B'. This involves information on the memory of recent events, computation based upon this, holding representations of motor action and inhibiting incompatible behaviour (Fuster, 1999). In some cases, the logic represented is of the kind 'if event (x) then wait time T and perform X'.

In ontogeny and phylogeny, PFC is among the last brain regions to develop (Fuster, 1999). In ontogeny, it is one of the last regions to undergo myelination (Chapter 6), associated with the emergence of more complex goal-directed behaviour.

Rolls (2004) and colleagues investigated the role of the orbitofrontal region of the PFC (Figure 5.32,

p. 129) in goal-directed activity in non-human primates. Certain neurons in the orbitofrontal region encode the value of rewards, information exploited in decision-making. For example, a high activity of particular neurons encodes the high reward value of the taste of a palatable food when in need of nutrients.

Prefrontal lobe connections

The PFC has rich interconnection with other brain regions (Fuster, 1997, 1999), mediating its role as a coordinator of action. There are reciprocal links with other regions of cortex, the brain stem, hypothalamus, amygdala, hippocampus and thalamus. Signals from the brain stem and hypothalamus convey information to the PFC on the body's internal environment. This can be used in decision-making, e.g. to seek food. Information exchanged with other cortical regions appears to be used in high-level sensory-motor integration (Chapter 10), e.g. messages to primary motor cortex reflect goals that need to trigger movement. There are projections from PFC to the nucleus accumbens (Deutch *et al.*, 1993), forming a link to motivated activities. Connections from the PFC to the basal ganglia also implicate a role of the PFC in action control.

Damage to the PFC

Monkeys with PFC lesions have difficulty with tasks that involve bridging a delay between presentation of the stimulus cue and the associated reaction (Jacobsen, 1936). This points to a failure to retain information on-line over the delay. Bianchi (1922, p. 186) found that lesioned animals lack coherence and focus.

Humans with PFC damage exhibit failures in holding a memory in an active state (working memory) and resisting interference to goal-directed behaviour (Fuster, 1997). Damage to the dorsolateral PFC is associated with a lack of motivation and spontaneity (Fuster, 1999). Behaviour is described as being routine and in the here-and-now, without planning and perspective. Patients with PFC damage, especially of the orbitofrontal region, tend to exhibit one or more of the following: (i) an abnormally high distractibility, (ii) hyperactivity and (iii) problems with the inhibition of impulsivity. Luria *et al.* (1964) noted the failure of feedback to correct errors.

Patients are deficient on tasks that involve changing behaviour in the light of changing outcomes of action. For example, they do badly at the Wisconsin card sorting task (Chapter 6). They are said to be socially disabled, lacking social judgement and deficient in taking into account the effect of their behaviour on others (Cummings and Miller, 2007). The disruption following PFC damage represents a: 'defect in the way behaviour is controlled by the match between what is to be,

and what has been achieved' (Duncan, 1986, p. 281). Patients typically disengage from a task before it is completed but without this failure motivating completion. Human frontal patients can often articulate verbally what is the nature of the task and acknowledge their failure to achieve the goal but be unable to utilize this information in correcting future behaviour.

Irrelevant factors intrude, as in the capture of behaviour by extraneous stimuli and the failure to recruit task-relevant information in the completion of a task (Duncan, 1986). Patients have difficulty resisting the action of reaching out and grasping nearby attractive objects (Lhermitte, 1983). A patient on being asked to draw a square was 'captured' by a conversation going on nearby and incorporated features of it into the drawing (Luria, 1966). Behaviour appears to lose its active nature, being more a passive reaction to stimuli.

Monitoring brain events

Suppose that a task requires a subject to wait time T between stimulus presentation and performing a response. In monkeys, increases in electrical activity over time T can be recorded from neurons in the dorsolateral region of the PFC and appear to encode the plan for motor action ('preparatory set') to be put on-line after T elapses (Fuster, 1999). Apart from such 'set-cells', other neurons, located in the dorsolateral PFC, play a role in encoding events ('memory cells') used in the formulation of plans. Such neurons play a role in encoding working memory (Chapter 11). They are activated for so long as the task requires the utilization of the memory. In such terms, the CES would be responsible for activation of such memories.

A personal angle

Wilder Penfield and his sister

Tragic circumstances provided the pioneering Canadian neurosurgeon, Wilder Penfield, with a unique opportunity to study the effects of frontal lobe disruption on behaviour. His sister suffered from a tumour of the prefrontal region, which he removed when she was aged 43. During the six-hour operation in Montreal, she talked to the surgeons. Tissue to within a centimetre of the prefrontal gyrus (Chapter 5) was removed. Following the operation, Penfield observed a disruption in her capacity to plan, a 'loss of power of initiative' (Penfield and Evans, 1935).

Social behaviour

The PFC patient often has problems with social behaviour, as exemplified by Phineas Gage (Chapter 12). Baddeley *et al.* (1997, p. 192) observe: 'it is possible that skilful social behaviour inherently involves a dual-task component requiring the simultaneous maintenance of one's own interests and concerns at the same time as paying due attention to the concerns of those around'.

The failure of PFC patients to inhibit socially inappropriate behaviour (e.g. temper tantrums) is particularly associated with damage to the orbitofrontal region (Fuster, 1997). The patient has problems utilizing memories that could provide information on scripts of possible future social interaction and thereby lacks social skills (Grafman, 1989). Undue weight is given to current situations and powerful physically present stimuli.

Decision-making and the somatic marker hypothesis

According to the 'somatic marker hypothesis' (Damasio, 1996), decision-making is normally guided by a kind of rerun of basic emotions (Chapter 12). For example, a fear-evoking stimulus ('primary inducer') triggers a basic emotion. Memories of such events or simply imagining them ('secondary inducers') triggers something of a copy of the basic emotion, mediated via the ventromedial region of the prefrontal cortex (corresponding approximately to what others term 'orbitofrontal cortex'). Triggering negative emotion by the prospect of a future negative outcome tends to deter an unwise action and contribute to rational decision-making.

Patients with damage to the ventromedial region of the prefrontal cortex (VM PFC) exhibit serious deficits in decision-making even though they have no general loss of intelligence (Bechara, 2004). They have problems with planning.

The **Iowa gambling task** is employed to assess decision-making (it is named after the university location of Damasio, Bechara and colleagues, and sometimes termed the 'Bechara gambling task' but, with modesty, not by Bechara himself!). Participants are asked to gamble and, to do so, to make a series of choices from any one of four decks of cards. Two of these decks (A and B) deliver a high immediate gain early in the game but a particularly high loss later, and are characterized as 'disadvantageous decks'. The two other decks (C and D) yield a small immediate gain but also only a very small future loss, an 'advantageous deck'. The relative gain and loss of each deck is known to the experimenter but not to the participant.

Figure 20.14 shows the result for patients with damage to the VM PFC, compared with controls with no brain damage ('normal controls') and controls with damage to the occipital or temporal cortex ('brain-damaged controls'). As can be seen, controls learn by experience. They give due weight to the long-term negative outcome of choice A or B. VM PFC patients do not show this and exhibit 'myopia for the future'.

This failure to take long-term negative consequences into account appears to model the patients' failure in their social lives. Bechara *et al.* made a physiological measure, an index of autonomic arousal, during the task: the skin conductance response (SCR). Both VM PFC patients and controls showed a SCR response on picking a card and being told the outcome: good or bad (Figure 20.15). However, a striking difference came in the moment just prior to selection, particularly from the risky piles A and B. This suggests that decision-making is normally guided by an emotional signal and this is deficient in VM PFC patients.

Bechara *et al.* compared unilateral and bilateral VM PFC damage. Damage to the right VM PFC has a particularly disruptive effect (Figure 20.16), which suggests that it is usually more strongly involved in such decision-making based on anticipation of negative outcomes.

It could be that control populations vary naturally in the extent to which somatic markers mediated via the VM PFC exert an influence. Imagine yourself wondering whether to take that second portion of pizza. The prospect of immediate reward is pulling you in the here-and-now. With luck, the prospect of future weight gain will evoke a negative emotion, a 'somatic marker',

Figure 20.14 Relative choice of advantageous and disadvantageous cards over the sessions of trials.
Source: Bechara (2004, Fig. 2, p. 32).

Figure 20.15 Results of skin-conductance response for normal controls and VM PFC patients, under conditions of reward and punishment, as well as anticipation.
Source: Bechara (2004, Fig. 3, p. 32).

which will deter you. The point of this balance appears to vary among people such that, for example, people with obesity or drug addiction are less sensitive than controls to future negative consequences. They tend to do badly at the Iowa gambling task (Davis *et al.*, 2004).

Although poor performance on the Iowa gambling task is sometimes treated as almost synonymous with damage to the VM PFC, caution is in order. People with damage to other regions of the PFC also exhibit profound deficiencies on the task. For example, dorsolateral PFC damage also has this effect (MacPherson *et al.*, 2009). Disruption to the use of working memory is a possible reason.

Figure 20.16 Results of the net advantageous choices over trials for normal controls, unilateral left VM PFC damage, unilateral right PFC damage and bilateral damage.
Source: Bechara (2004, Fig. 4, p. 33).

Section summary

1   The notion of behaviour being goal-directed involves:

    (a) a hierarchy of goals and sub-goals;

    (b) a tendency for behaviour to persist until the goal is met;

    (c) competition between goals;

    (d) inhibition of inappropriate behaviour.

2   Goal-directed behaviour can be 'ambushed' by strong stimuli.

3   Psychologists suggest that there is a 'central executive system', serving a coordination role.

4   The prefrontal cortex is involved in planning and executing sequences of goal-directed action.

5   Damage to the prefrontal cortex disrupts the capacity to exert coherent action.

6   Somatic markers play a role in decision-making.

Language

Introduction

This section describes language and considers speaking, listening, reading and writing. It discusses brain structures that underlie language and the evolution of language. Across species, something corresponding to a 'language' allows the transmission of information. In humans, the content of language can take an apparently infinite variety of forms and is unique in its abstractness. Components of information (words) are combined in unique ways to convey information on any aspect of experience or imagination. Spoken language is composed of individual sounds termed **phonemes**.

The listener's understanding of spoken language involves processes similar to those of vision (Chapter 8). Invariance is involved: a word needs to be interpreted to mean the same in spite of diverse pronunciations. Conversely, the same pronunciation might need to be interpreted differently according to context, e.g. 'pen' as a writing instrument or something to restrain cattle.

Evolutionary and functional perspectives

Introduction

Language is universal in human societies, which suggests an evolutionary advantage (Liberman, 1995). It is easy to appreciate its value to hunting and gathering, in terms of conveying intentions and contributing to coordinated action (Pinker and Bloom, 1990). Also, information can be transmitted from generation to generation, circumventing the need to learn by direct experience of hazardous things, such as dangerous animals and floods.

One view is that language evolved from gestures made with the hands and face (see Richards, 1987). It can hardly be coincidence that we tend to accompany words with hand gestures. There are functional advantages of spoken as opposed to gestural language, e.g. that it frees the hands for other uses and can still be employed when the listener is out of sight (Lieberman, 1991).

Psychologists describe reading and writing as 'culturally engineered' (Caplan *et al.*, 1999); genetics and development do not produce an organism with a natural tendency to acquire them. Explicit education is needed. These skills have appeared rather late in evolution and it seems that we do not have the comparable dedicated sensory-motor pathways as we have for speaking and understanding speech. However, we use ('co-opt') brain regions dedicated to vision and spoken language, pointing to something like modularity emerging with development in a particular culture.

Comparative issues

Non-humans also communicate information, e.g. warning signals on sighting a predator, and of course communal hunting (as in wolves) requires coordination. Some non-human languages even involve symbolic representations. For example, by means of dances, bees communicate information on the location of food sites (Caplan *et al.*, 1999). Non-human primates convey signals on intentions and thereby sometimes employ deceit ('telling lies').

The essence of human language, defined by Bear *et al.* (1996, p. 579) is: 'a remarkably complex, flexible, and powerful *system* for communication that involves the creative use of words according to the rules of a systematic grammar'.

How do we explain the association between speech and manual gestures?
Source: Corbis/Patrick Robert.

Opinion differs on whether human language is best considered qualitatively different from the communication of other species or different only in degree (Caplan *et al.*, 1999). Are there evolutionary precursors evident in non-linguistic skills of non-humans, or is it an evolutionary 'shot-in-the dark' peculiar to humans (Pinker and Bloom, 1990)? To consider this topic requires integration between evolutionary theory and understanding of neural mechanisms (Greenfield, 1991), discussed shortly.

One is reluctant to assert dogmatically that no non-human equivalent of human language exists but this seems likely to be so. Whether non-humans can be taught a symbolic language is controversial. For example, chimpanzees use stereotyped vocal expressions in a limited range of situations and these can be mapped in stimulus–response terms. There are instances of combinations of symbols being employed but the evidence of an abstract skill of creative symbol manipulation and expression is not compelling. That is not to deny the richness of problem solving in non-humans. However, nothing compares with the seemingly infinite variety of messages that humans exchange.

Brain mechanisms – classical studies

Introduction

Speech involves a neural system that extends from the inner ear to the motor mechanisms underlying control of speaking. Some extraction of speech sounds and their accentuation occurs at the cochlea and subsequent levels within the auditory pathway (Chapter 9; Honjo, 1999). As with other motor skills, language appears to exhibit some capacity for automatization, implying parallel pathways triggered under different circumstances (Whitaker, 1983).

Patients with brain damage, resulting from trauma, as in accidents, or stroke, or a result of brain surgery, provide insight into the neural bases of language (Lenneberg, 1967). Disruption, or loss, of language ability is termed **aphasia**. Patients appear not to have literally 'lost' language, as in being returned to a pre-linguistic state; rather, they have problems with language. Aphasia is commonly associated with some disruption of writing, termed **agraphia**, and reading, termed **alexia**.

Broca and Wernicke

Disruption to speech follows damage to a region of the frontal lobe of the left hemisphere (Broca, 1861). Comparable damage to the right hemisphere is not associated with aphasia in most cases (Geschwind, 1972; Marie and Foix, 1917). Subsequently, this region of the left frontal lobe came to be known as **Broca's area** (pronounced roughly as in the English 'broker's') (Figure

20.17). Exactly what constitutes the boundaries of Broca's area is open to discussion (Greenfield, 1991) and there are sub-areas within it. However, as a first approximation for relating structure and function, Broca's area serves as a landmark.

Wernicke (1874) found another region of the left hemisphere where accidental damage also disrupted speech, and this became known as **Wernicke's area** (pronounced roughly as Vehr-knee-ker's). The planum temporale, discussed earlier in this chapter, corresponds to a large part of Wernicke's area. Figure 20.17 shows Wernicke's area in the context of Broca's area, the auditory cortex and the angular gyrus. Exactly what constitutes Wernicke's area is also open to discussion; there are individual differences in the exact site of the processing attributed to it (Honjo, 1999).

Characterizing aphasias

Although damage to either Broca's or Wernicke's area disrupts speech, there tends to be a difference in the nature of the disruption (Lenneberg, 1967). What follows is the 'textbook' distinction, though individual differences are large and there is often an overlap of symptoms. Usually any lesion that disturbs language affects both production and comprehension to some extent.

In **Broca's aphasia** (sometimes called 'motor aphasia', 'expressive aphasia' or 'non-fluent aphasia'), the problem is principally with the organization of speech *production* (Damasio and Geschwind, 1984). Speech becomes slow, laboured, without its usual rhythms and with the endings of words omitted (Geschwind, 1972). Patients sometimes have difficulty finding the right word and in constructing grammatically correct

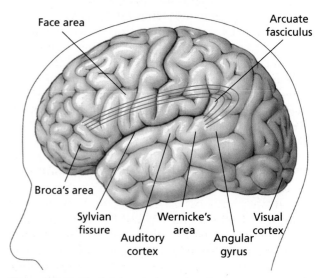

Figure 20.17 The left hemisphere showing areas concerned with language.

Source: Geschwind (1972, p. 78). Courtesy of Donald Garber.

(a)

(b)

Figure 20.18 The brain of Mr Leborgne (a) whole brain, (b) close up of affected region of cortex.
Source: Dronkers *et al.* (2007, Fig. 3, p. 1436 part A and B).

A personal angle

Paul Broca and Mr Leborgne

A patient, Mr Leborgne, in the hospital at Bicêtre, France, had lost his speech, except for single syllables (Broca, 1861). He responded simply with 'tan, tan' to each question and made gestures. Thereby, he acquired the name Tan. He was aware of his situation and showed normal intelligence. As the extent of the lesion spread, he came to lose the use of his right arm and could gesticulate only with his left arm and hand. Mr Leborgne died on 17 April 1861, aged 51 years. Autopsy revealed damage to the left frontal lobe. From this observation, the affected area controlling speech acquired the name 'Broca's area'. Mr Leborgne

reminds us that a lesion in motor regions of the left brain affects motor control on the right of the body.

Broca refused to dissect the brain of Mr Leborgne and preserved it intact (Figure 20.18), along with that of a similar patient Mr Lelong. Years later, their brains were subject to an MRI study (Dronkers *et al.*, 2007), which revealed that there was not just cortical damage but also subcortical damage on the left side but an intact right hemisphere. The investigators reported (p.1441): 'Fortunately Broca had great foresight in preserving these historic brains and in some ways, Leborgne and Lelong can speak to us more eloquently now than they could over 140 years ago.'

sentences (Geschwind, 1979). They often have particular difficulty with 'function words', those for which the role is defined by context, e.g. 'if' and 'but'. They are not completely free of problems with comprehension, which appear particularly in more difficult sentences.

Broca's area has links with the region of motor cortex that controls motor aspects of speech, e.g. muscles of the face ('face area'). However, Broca's aphasia is not synonymous with paralysis of the muscles involved in speech (Geschwind, 1972) and the term 'motor' in describing aphasia needs qualification. A patient might be able to sing a melody using such muscles. Patients can utter certain words, e.g. familiar nouns such as chair, relatively easily.

Broca's area should not be viewed in isolation. Rather, disruption of speech appears to depend on breaking subcortical neural connections between Broca's area and anterior regions of the frontal cortex (Lieberman, 1991). Liberman (1995, p. 568) describes the prefrontal cortex as 'at once our "think tank" and fine motor control sequencer'. Language appears to exemplify the role of this structure in terms of the control of action.

As a first approximation, in **Wernicke's aphasia** (sometimes termed 'receptive aphasia' or 'fluent aphasia'), understanding written and spoken language is disrupted but speech is relatively fluent (Damasio and Geschwind, 1984). Function words can be expressed as well as words denoting content. Speech can sound normal. Only on analysis of content is abnormality detected (Geschwind, 1972). Speech often fails to convey a rational meaning. The location of Wernicke's area next to the auditory cortex (Figure 20.17) suggests that it is where word meanings are associated with word sounds. It appears to represent the site of a higher order of analysis comparable to later stages of the ventral stream in visual processing (Chapter 8). Wernicke's area is linked to Broca's area by a bundle of neurons termed the 'arcuate fasciculus', a route of information transfer (Figure 20.17).

The Wernicke–Geschwind model

Geschwind (1972, 1979) developed a model of language processing based upon the ideas of Wernicke: the **Wernicke–Geschwind model**. It shows connections between the brain regions involved (Figure 20.19). The model draws attention to disruption that can arise from disconnecting components of the system. Although an over-simplification, it summarizes important features of how language works and has served well to stimulate research, organize thinking and give a framework for clinical practice.

In the model, the role of Broca's and Wernicke's areas is roughly as just described. Note the link from Broca's area to the area of the motor cortex that controls the face. Figure 20.19(a) represents repeating aloud words spoken by another person. Information is processed at the auditory cortex ('Primary auditory area'), which passes information to Wernicke's area. This information is linked to a word representation at Wernicke's area, which then transmits information on the word representation to Broca's area. At Broca's area, information on the word calls up an articulation programme for uttering it, which is then transmitted to the motor cortex

where the muscular response of speech is instigated. In Wernicke's aphasia, Broca's area is not sent appropriate information to generate rational speech.

Part (b) represents the sequence involved in repeating aloud a word presented visually. Information on words, extracted by the 'primary visual area', is conveyed to Wernicke's area and enters the same pathway as that involved in auditory processing. The visual information might tap into the same representations of words as are triggered by sounds. The model can account for Broca and Wernicke aphasias and also for some additional phenomena.

Damage to tissue lying between Broca's and Wernicke's areas causes 'conduction aphasia' (Damasio and Geschwind, 1984). As predicted by the model, a problem arises in repeating words, since this involves transferring auditory information to the motor system of speech.

Brain mechanisms: later insights

Beyond the Wernicke–Geschwind model

Later insights have shown levels of complexity that are not captured by the Wernicke–Geschwind model. There is not simply a one-way flow of information. Impairment of Broca's area can disturb language perception as well as production (Geschwind and Iacoboni, 2007). Broca's area is activated even in trying to think of a word without pronouncing it (Hinke *et al.*, 1993). This points to similarities in the organization of thought and overt action. Broca's and Wernicke's areas are no longer understood as playing homogeneous or monolithic roles in language (Poeppel and Hickok, 2004). Rather there are subdivisions of each, serving different roles.

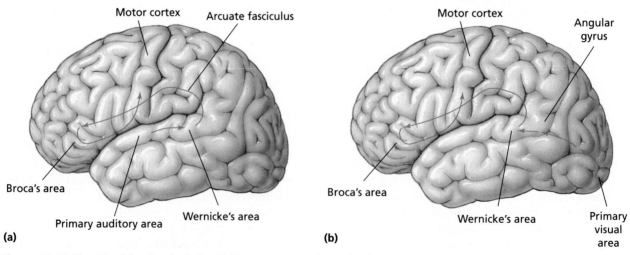

Figure 20.19 The Wernicke–Geschwind model in representing the tasks of repeating in speech (a) a spoken word and (b) a written word.

Source: Geschwind (1979, p. 163). Courtesy of Carol Donner.

The Wernicke–Geschwind model assumes a channelling of information in auditory and visual codes into a common auditory processing system. For reading, it suggests an obligatory translation of visual information into an auditory code. Under some conditions, such a flow of information between visual and auditory processing occurs but it appears not to be the only route of information transfer (Coltheart, 1985; Henderson, 1986). In some cases, reading can survive intact from damage to Wernicke's area that severely disrupts speech, which suggests a route that bypasses speech mechanisms.

The Wernicke–Geschwind model was a stimulus to Petersen *et al.* (1988), who used a PET study to investigate changes in cerebral blood flow accompanying processing of words. People were presented with words and, over trials, processing demands were changed. Different levels of complexity were required of the participants. The logic was that, as the level of complexity increased, additional brain regions would be activated. Activation at one level was subtracted from the immediately higher level. In this way, an estimate was made of additional processing needed at each increasing task demand. Words were either presented visually or by sound.

At the first level, the word was simply presented, either visually or spoken. This enabled just the lowest level of pure sensory processing to be measured (in principle, at least!). To calculate this in the case of visual presentation, visual fixation upon a target word was compared with fixation without word presentation. This comparison gave a measure of visual processing demands triggered by a word (termed 'sensory' condition).

At the second level of task demand, people were asked to speak aloud the word. This was to enable regions concerned with output coding and motor control to be identified ('output' condition). At the third level, people were asked to find a use for the word, e.g. if 'cake' were the word, a person might find 'eat'. This level allowed brain regions associated with semantics to be identified ('association' condition).

Figure 20.20 shows regions of *additional* activation seen with each new level of task demand. Note the distinct non-overlapping regions of sensory cortical activation for visual (e.g. areas 1 and 2) and auditory (e.g. areas 7 and 8) stimuli. Responses of the visual cortex to words (1 and 2) are similar to responses to non-word visual cues. Activation of areas of occipital cortex

Figure 20.20 Lateral (top) and medial (bottom) views of regions of activation under different conditions for each hemisphere.

Source: Reprinted by permission from Macmillan Publishers Ltd: Positron emission tomographic studies of the cortical anatomy of single-word processing. *Nature*, 331, Fig. 1, p. 586 (Petersen, S.E. *et al.* 1988), copyright 1988.

outside primary visual cortex (3, 4 and 5) is peculiar to words and could represent areas concerned with processing visual word forms. Damage to such areas can lead to alexia, a disruption to reading words not associated with other language disruption (Damasio and Damasio, 1983). Areas of motor cortex involved in producing output overlap between visual (e.g. 12) and auditory (e.g. 18) presentations. Note the prefrontal areas involved in the association task for visual and auditory presentations (e.g. 26 and 29).

These results are not in accordance with the serial processing of the Wernicke–Geschwind model, where access to semantic information whether visually or auditorily triggered is via a phonological code (a sound-based code). No activation near to Wernicke's area or the angular gyrus was seen in response to visual stimuli (Figure 20.20). Visual and auditory information appeared to take parallel routes to the output side.

A more comprehensive explanatory model would need also to accommodate the following observation. According to the site of lesion, patients can be selectively disrupted in understanding *either* spoken *or* written words. (Under some conditions, visual information on words is encoded phonologically.) Still further features that would need to be incorporated into an explanatory account would include a reference to the importance of subcortical pathways, e.g. thalamus and basal ganglia (Chapter 10), involved in language.

Split-brain patients

Evidence from split-brain patients (Chapter 8) confirms that the left hemisphere is normally dominant for speech (Sperry, 1969). When information on an object is presented visually in a way that triggers processing by the left hemisphere, the person is normally able to identify verbally what it is. When visual information arrives at the right hemisphere, verbal identification is often not possible since the cut corpus callosum means that visual information cannot connect with the language apparatus. Similarly, if the right hand feels an object out of sight, the patient can name it but not if the left hand feels it. However, the right hemisphere has some language abilities. Split-brain patients can react on the basis of some simple visual language cues such as the written word of a common noun projected to the right hemisphere.

Disrupting normal processing

Various techniques for producing what is termed a **functional lesion** have brought insight into the bases of language (Boatman, 2004; Penfield and Rasmussen, 1968). Unlike conventional lesions, which involve permanent damage (e.g. cutting pathways), functional lesions involve only a temporary inactivation of part of the brain. The techniques are used for patients about to undergo brain surgery.

In **electrocortical mapping**, an electrical current is generated for a period of 5–10 s. The current passes between two electrodes located at the surface of the cortex, so just a local portion of the grey matter is targeted. This disrupts processing by the targeted region, thereby producing a functional lesion for the duration of stimulation. Any deficits in language processing can be correlated with the site of the functional lesion. For example, disruption of a very circumscribed region of temporal lobe of the left hemisphere (specifically within the superior temporal gyrus) disrupted the discrimination of syllables (Figure 20.21). This region was adjacent to the primary auditory cortex (Boatman, 2004).

At certain sites in the left hemisphere, stimulation disrupts the capacity to name objects (Ojemann, 1990) (Figure 20.22). For bilingual people, the site of disruption of naming a given object can be different for the two languages. Wide individual differences were found in the sites at which naming was disrupted.

Electrocortical mapping is a means of creating functional lesions at local sites *within* a hemisphere. The next technique to be described enables comparison *between* hemispheres.

In the **Wada technique**, a fast-acting anaesthetic is injected into the carotid artery supplying blood to one hemisphere (Milner, 1974). The duration of action of the anaesthetic is 5–10 minutes (Boatman, 2004). On the side contralateral to the injection, the limbs quickly become immobile and there is a loss of sensation. When the injection is made to the side dominant for speech, there is disruption of speech. The technique confirms that the left hemisphere is normally dominant. Where there is early damage to the left hemisphere, speech tends to be more often controlled by the right hemisphere. The technique reveals right hemispheric dominance in only a very small percentage of the population (Boatman, 2004).

Streaming

Evidence suggests a basic distinction between streams of processing of auditory information that is comparable to the distinction between ventral stream and dorsal stream of vision (Chapter 8) (Hickok and Poeppel, 2004). There appears to be a common route until the superior temporal gyrus is reached at which point there is a streaming. Rather as with vision, a dorsal stream is involved in action (in this case, speech production), whereas a ventral stream is concerned with speech perception and attribution of meaning.

The dorsal stream is strongly lateralized to the left hemisphere, whereas the ventral stream appears to be less strongly lateralized. Thus, damage to the left temporal cortex does not invariably disrupt speech comprehension. Results in split-brain patients, as well as those undergoing the Wada test with anaesthetic targeted to the left hemisphere, also point to the retention of speech comprehension ability by the right hemisphere.

A comparative approach to the brain mechanisms

Could there be some common features between brain regions underlying language and other forms of information processing (Ullman, 2004)? Given that evolution is a tinkerer building upon pre-existing structures, we might expect some common principles of organization. For example, in vision, there is an interaction between cortical regions and subcortical structures (Chapter 8). So, we might expect that any features unique to language and humans will coexist with processes and brain regions common to other forms of cognition and other species. There is a rich source of comparative data.

It appears that the production of language, as with other motor skills, depends upon interactions between cortical structures, the basal ganglia and cerebellum. Developmental language impairments can occasionally be associated with other motor impairments (e.g. shown on a task that calls for rapid finger tapping). These tasks relate to procedural memory and evidence points to disruption to the basal ganglia and cerebellum as being involved.

Development, learning and plasticity

Basics

On learning to speak, the infant is influenced primarily by hearing spoken sounds. This implies the formation of links between systems underlying sensory speech codes and the motor system responsible for speech production (Hickok and Poeppel, 2004). The auditory–speech link arising in early development remains intact in the adult.

A famous dispute

One of psychology's best-known controversies, that between Skinner (1957) and Chomsky (1959), concerns the acquisition of language. Skinner suggested that learning a language is much like learning anything else, i.e. dependent upon an environment of reinforcers.

By contrast, Chomsky suggested that a dedicated, specialist and genetically determined brain structure organizes language, i.e. a module, an adaptation peculiar to humans. Metaphorically, this structure is 'just waiting' for even a minimal exposure to a language and it springs into action. From the start, there is implicit ('advance') knowledge of a grammar common to all languages. In this view, modularity is such that language requires little influence from other cognitive systems for its inevitable development (see Abbeduto and Boudreau, 2004). Modularity is also suggested by cases of spared language ability in the presence of retarded development in other cognitive domains.

So, is language learning, as Skinner suggested, just like learning any other skill? Alternatively, is it, as Chomsky argued, based upon a genetically determined speech module? You might be experiencing echoes from an earlier dichotomy on genes versus environment, which has been largely laid to rest with the understanding of contemporary psychology.

A compromise position

Subsequent insights point to a compromise, with both a genetic tendency and environmental stimulation playing roles. That is, there exists some tendency towards language acquisition particularly based in the

Figure 20.21 Location of brain region that is associated with a deficit in auditory discrimination (black line). Grey lines are regions stimulated without effect on auditory discrimination.
Source: Boatman (2004, Figure 1, p. 51).

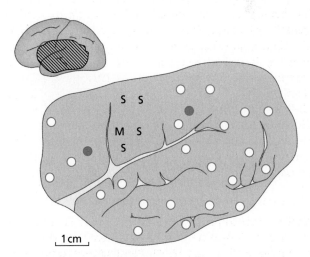

Figure 20.22 Sites of stimulation and locations at which naming was significantly disrupted for a 24-year-old female patient. Shaded area in small figure is shown enlarged in larger figure.
Source: Ojemann (1990, Fig. 1).

left hemisphere, given a normal exposure to a spoken language. Humans are said to be *prepared* to learn a language, expressed in speech (Caplan *et al.*, 1999). Given the structure of the brain and vocal apparatus and the presence of a linguistic culture, sensory-motor pathways develop such that the emergence of spoken language is a near certainty (Liberman, 1995).

There is a distinct developmental time-course of language acquisition up to the age of 7 years (Trout, 2001). If access to a language is denied during this period, subsequent acquisition is more laboured and production is not so effortless. Johnson (1997, p. 142) suggests that: 'small variations on the basic architecture of the cortex may be sufficient to "attract" language processing to some regions during normal functional brain development'.

Evidence on early damage to brain regions is crucial to the issue of dedicated regions. Although Broca associated speech with the left hemisphere, he was aware that in some cases of early damage to the left, the right can take over responsibility (Smith and Sugar, 1975). For the young brain, there is some 'equipotentiality', i.e. early damage to the left hemisphere has little effect on subsequent language acquisition, which is equally well handled by the right. Adults suffering comparable damage experience serious disruption. However, even in children, there appear to be subtle disorders of language following left hemisphere damage (Vargha-Khadem *et al.*, 1994). This suggests some initial bias towards language acquisition by the left hemisphere but again points to the need to qualify the notion of dedicated modules. Beyond the phase of early neural development and plasticity, structures become more fixed and committed (Lenneberg, 1967).

Are brain areas that are normally used for sound and language understanding triggered by, say, visual input in deaf people? In the absence of normal input, they might be captured by other channels. Looking at temporal lobe areas normally associated with auditory/speech processing, Neville (1991) found event-related potentials (Chapter 5) to visual stimuli to be greater in deaf people than in those with hearing.

Brain damage and adult plasticity

The recovery of people who have suffered a stroke affecting speech provides insights into the plasticity underlying language. When damage to the language regions of the left hemisphere is relatively small, intact regions of that hemisphere tend to take over responsibility or even damaged areas can sometimes be 'reactivated'. When the damage is more extensive, greater weight tends to shift to the right hemisphere (Crosson *et al.*, 2007). It is assumed that recovery corresponds to new neural connections being formed.

Therapeutic techniques also provide information on the conditions that facilitate plasticity. For example, Crosson *et al.* devised a task in which patients were asked to name pictures, accompanied by a pointing gesture by the *left* hand. The rationale of pointing was to engage *right* hemisphere processes at the time demands were being placed on speech production.

Using neuroimaging, Schlaug *et al.* (2009) studied stroke patients with Broca's aphasia, where the arcuate fasciculus of the left hemisphere was largely destroyed. Patients received what is known as 'melodic intonation therapy' (MIT). MIT's invention was triggered by the observation that patients are often able to sing a familiar song even though they are unable to speak the same words. Singing more strongly engages the right hemisphere than the left. Simple exercises were started by asking the patients to sing expressions in the hope that spoken words could 'piggyback' onto the same words expressed in the form of singing. The patients' expressions were paced by asking them to tap with the left hand.

Schlaug *et al.* note the normally close association between speaking and hand gestures. The tapping could serve to trigger latent processes in the right hemisphere that correspond to the left hemisphere process of coordination between speaking and hand gestures. In addition, by feedforward and feedback of sound and touch it could provide a timing signal. The arcuate fasciculus of the right hemisphere is usually relatively undeveloped. Successful therapy was associated with enlargement of the number of fibres forming the arcuate fasciculus.

Another technique is that of repetitive transcranial magnetic stimulation (rTMS) (Martin *et al.*, 2009). Strong localized magnetic fields applied to the cortex permit non-invasive stimulation of regions underlying language. The volume of brain stimulated is about 1 cm³. Depending upon the frequency of stimulation, rTMS can either facilitate or inhibit the activity of the targeted region. Low frequency stimulation inhibits the

A personal angle

A successful executive

In 1953, Smith and Sugar, in Ann Arbor, Michigan and Chicago, removed the left hemisphere of a boy aged 5½ years to counter epileptic seizures. He exhibited normal language, verbal and non-verbal reasoning at age 26 years. He was a successful executive and simultaneously pursued a university degree in sociology. Since the entire cortex on the left side was removed, it is to the right hemisphere that we need to look for the site of the function. Both parents were right-handed.

cortical region, whereas high frequency stimulation increases its excitability.

Counter-intuitively, evidence suggests that the plasticity that underlies greater involvement of the right hemisphere in speech can sometimes actually impair recovery. This is because it can inhibit recovery of the more effective processes of the left hemisphere (Martin *et al.*, 2009).

Sign language

Is the organization of language described here specific to vocal expression? Insight can be gained by studying those who employ a visual system of gestures, termed 'sign language', e.g. in the absence of a speech facility and/or to speak to deaf people (Poizner *et al.*, 1990). Information conveyed by hands and face can be as grammatically structured, semantically rich and subtle as the spoken word. In deaf people, sign language activates some cortical areas normally triggered by the spoken word in controls with hearing (Nishimura *et al.*, 1999).

Poizner *et al.* studied sign language in patients with damage to the right hemisphere. Sign language showed minimal disruption. Conversely, in patients with left hemispheric damage, disruption was serious for sign language but minimal for non-language-based visuospatial cognition (though this is controversial; Greenfield, 1991).

The Wada test and PET scans also point to a left hemispheric specialization for sign language, leading to the conclusion that this hemisphere specializes for language irrespective of its mode of perception and expression (Poizner *et al.*, 1990). That is to say, sound is not a necessary input to obtain such left hemisphere specialization.

Patients with disrupted sign language typically retain the ability of non-language-based manual mime, e.g. the gesture of smelling a flower. This suggests different neural bases for language and non-language-based gesture and that the left hemisphere is specialized for symbolic expression (Nishimura *et al.*, 1999).

Language and object manipulation

Both language and assembling objects with the hands involve hierarchical control of sequential action (Greenfield, 1991). For example, children as young as 20 months spear food objects with a fork, dip the combination of food-on-fork into sauce and then bring it to the mouth. Similarly, language has a hierarchical structure: phonemes combine to form words, words form sentences and sentences are subordinate to the goal of conveying meaning. Greenfield suggests that the skills of language and object combination involve parallel development in terms of ontogeny and phylogeny.

Figure 20.23 shows an example of hierarchical development of language with age. The words 'more' and 'grapejuice' form a sub-assembly.

Do the skills of language and object combination represent distinct cognitive modules with distinct neural bases? If so, in adapting the language of evolution (Chapter 5), there is an 'analogy' between them. Alternatively, both might be based on the same neural system, and we would speak of 'homology'. It is surely no coincidence that the favoured hand for fine-grained object manipulation is the right, with control primarily in the left hemisphere along with speech (Lieberman, 1991). Both involve hierarchical control of sequencing.

Brain damage could give us some pointers. For example, are people with Broca's aphasia also disrupted in other hierarchical tasks? Grossman (1980) found a subgroup who were unable to produce hierarchically organized speech. Rather, they emitted a series of agrammatical single word utterances and had difficulty in forming a hierarchical structure in a visuo-mechanical copying task.

Greenfield suggests that Broca's area consists of two subregions, which derive from common precursor tissue (Figure 20.24). Broca's area might start life as tissue that is undifferentiated (Chapter 6) with regard to the potential modality. Modality-specific development then occurs. Region 1 develops a speciality for manual object manipulation and region 2 becomes specialized as a grammar circuit for speech. In Figure 20.24, note the input from anterior regions of frontal cortex. These develop with maturation of prefrontal cortex and mediate planning and sequencing.

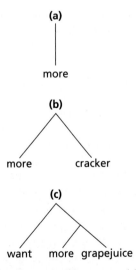

(a)

more

(b)

more   cracker

(c)

want   more grapejuice

Figure 20.23 Development of language: (a) one word utterance, (b) combination of words and (c) hierarchical organization in which 'more' and 'grapejuice' are combined at a lower level than the combination with 'want'.
Source: Greenfield (1991, p. 533).

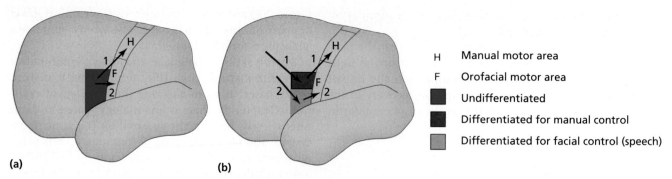

Figure 20.24 Suggested subdivisions of Broca's area (marked blue). (a) Early in development, the system is relatively undifferentiated. However, there is a bias towards links between Broca's area and motor cortex responsible for manual control (H) (link 1) and orofacial motor control, involved in speech (F) (link 2). (b) Later in development. Boundary lines associated with Broca's area are now shown, indicating delineation of the area and a clear division of responsibility within the area. Also shown to appear at this stage (arrows coming from the left) are inputs from prefrontal cortex.
Source: Greenfield (1991, Fig. 11, p. 543).

Imitation and mirror neurons

A region of premotor cortex (termed F5) of the monkey's brain is homologous to Broca's area in the human brain (Rizzolatti and Arbib, 1998; Iacoboni, 2008). In the left hemisphere of humans, Broca's area is richly endowed with mirror neurons (Chapter 10).

Heiser *et al.* (2003) investigated a non-linguistic imitation task, while Broca's area was temporarily inactivated. Repetitive transcranial magnetic stimulation (rTMS) inactivates a targeted brain region, creating a kind of reversible ('virtual') lesion. The effect of inactivation of Broca's area in the left hemisphere was compared with that of a comparable region of the right hemisphere. On both sides, imitation of the finger movements of an actor was disrupted more than was non-imitative responding.

When people perceive speech, there is activation within regions of the premotor cortex involved with speech production (Wilson *et al.*, 2004). Damage to the left prefrontal cortex can disrupt speech perception. Repetitive transcranial magnetic stimulation applied to the premotor cortex of the left hemisphere temporarily disrupts speech perception (Meister *et al.*, 2007). These phenomena point to the perception of speech being closely tied to its production and suggest the involvement of mirror neurons. Meister *et al.* (p. 1692) argue: 'that the hearer might perceive speech by simulating the articulatory gestures of the speaker'.

Listening to expressions such as 'biting the peach' activates regions of premotor cortex in the left hemisphere concerned with controlling the mouth, whereas the expression 'pressing the piano pedal' triggers regions concerned with controlling the feet (Aziz-Zadeh *et al.*, 2006). Even metaphorical reference to action by the body excites the appropriately located representation of action, as in 'biting off more than you can chew'.

Section summary

1 Spoken language is universal. This suggests the possibility of a genetically based tendency towards its acquisition.

2 Reading and writing are not universal and usually involve extensive education.

3 Among other areas, Broca's and Wernicke's are involved in processing of language.

4 The nature of aphasia depends upon the brain region damaged.

5 In the absence of a spoken language, brain regions that would normally underlie this ability can be taken over by other processing, e.g. that mediating sign language.

6 Neural mechanisms underlying speech might differentiate from precursor neural tissue having a potential to be involved in other hierarchically organized action.

7 Speech could have built upon a system of hand gestures and mirroring.

☞ Test your knowledge

20.7 When the brain has developed, the regions marked H and F in Figure 20.24 will come to be located where in terms of (i) anatomical description and (ii) a functional description of the region named in (i).

20.8 Complete the following: 'The arcuate fasciculus consists of the ___ of neurons, linking Wernicke's and Broca's areas'.

Answers on page 544

Evolutionary psychology

Mirroring and speech

Psychologists speculate on the evolutionary origins of human language: upon what did it build and when and how did it emerge? Insight requires understanding of brain mechanisms and the principles of evolution.

One suggestion is that language built upon an evolutionarily old system of vocalization, shared with numerous other species: that underlying non-linguistic vocal responses, e.g. yelling and alarm calls. Rizzolatti and Sinigaglia (2008) reject this, since the brain mechanisms underlying such vocalization are largely subcortical and distinct from those forming the basis of language. They argue (p. 158): 'Would it really be feasible to maintain that in the course of primate evolution the vocal system bounced from the lower regions into the lateral surface of the cortex?'

Human language could have evolved from the system of mirror neurons (Chapter 10) that forms the basis of manual and facial gestures (Corballis, 2010; Rizzolatti and Sinigaglia, 2008). Rizzolatti and Arbib (1998) suggest that, before speech appeared, the location corresponding to Broca's area was equipped with neural systems for recognizing the actions of others and for producing actions with the hands and face. This would facilitate rudimentary communication involving gestures, culminating, over evolutionary time, in the emergence of spoken language. Of course, a facility for mirroring actions is only useful if it can be used flexibly, including being withheld from expression when circumstances call for this. Hence, a capacity for inhibition of mirroring-based action is also part of the 'design'.

Standing on two legs rather than four would have freed the hands for gestures. Hand gestures are able to represent such things as speed, location, size and shape of an object. Accompanying, voluntary facial gestures could have conveyed information on emotional connotations. Facial gestures could have been the evolutionary link to voiced language using lips and tongue. In a range of species, the production of sounds is based within the left hemisphere and so sound production could have got linked to the mirroring system.

Various bits of evidence lead to the conclusion that manual gestures and speech (a) have a common origin and (b) this involves the mirror neuron system:

1 Mirror neurons are activated by observing gestures as well as performing them. This could underlie the reciprocity of language between sender and receiver.
2 In the frontal cortex of monkeys, mirror neurons are found in an area that is homologous to Broca's area in humans.
3 Broca's area is involved in both spoken and sign language output.
4 We normally accompany speech with gesturing, even on the telephone.
5 Hand gestures normally accompany babbling in very young children and, in development, hand gestures appear prior to speech.
6 Watching someone speaking activates speech-related areas of the left hemisphere.

Rizzolatti and Arbib speculate as follows. Suppose that a gesture of wide opening of the arms indicated the notion of 'large', whereas a narrow opening of the fingers indicated 'small'. Suppose that gestures were accompanied by distinct sounds. Here could be the emergence of a rudimentary vocabulary.

So how rapidly did speech appear in evolution? Was it is sudden emergence? Corballis suggests a gradual emergence in association with manual gestures, wherein speech took a progressively increasing role. He suggests that the human ability for 'time-travel' was another factor that played a role in the evolution of language. By spoken words, we can relate to the future or past (e.g. by use of tenses) or even purely fictional worlds. A capacity for mental time-travel would surely have conferred an advantage within a social group in terms of conveying information on remote events and might well have evolved in parallel with language.

The sequence of events appearing within individual development (ontogeny) is often similar to its appearance in evolution (phylogeny). Gestures and language seem to exemplify this: children exhibit hand gestures prior to spoken words (Iacoboni, 2008).

Bringing things together

Aspects of cognition and action can be related, as exemplified by language. Language provides a good example of a function that shows some degree of modularity, e.g. in its survival in Williams syndrome. However, it does not depend on a unique encapsulated brain module. Rather, certain cortical architecture lends itself to capture as a result of exposure to a language culture. Thereby, certain properties of modularity develop with experience. Comprehension and production of language involve the focusing of attention on particular aspects of incoming information. Language illustrates principles of goal-direction and hierarchy, involving inhibition on inappropriate associations. Hemispheric differences underlying the control of language are well established.

See the video coverage for this chapter and exerience something of the controversy surrounding the study of language.

Summary of Chapter 20

1 Actions are associated with goals and, to achieve these, various amounts of attention are allocated to associated stimuli and tasks.

2 The notion of modularity in cognition has proven to be a valuable stimulus to thinking but needs careful qualification.

3 The capacity of a stimulus or cognition to occupy awareness is not constant. Rather, it is modulated by attention.

4 There is a difference between the hemispheres in terms of the information processing that they carry out.

5 The prefrontal cortex has a principal role in setting goals and adjusting behaviour to meet them.

6 Certain brain structures give a bias towards the acquisition of language but there is developmental plasticity and environmental stimulation is crucial.

Further reading

For most of the material in this chapter, see Gazzaniga (2010) and Ward (2009). For the prefrontal cortex, Fuster (2010). For the orbitofrontal cortex, Zald and Rauch (2006).

Answers

Explanations for answers to 'test your knowledge' questions can found on the website www.pearsoned.co.uk/toates

20.1 Hemisphere
20.2 Behaviour; intact; behaviour; intact (instead of behaviour, cognition is another possibility)

20.3 Area (or, of course, location or region)
20.4 Right
20.5 Myelination
20.6 Immediate; anticipation
20.7 (i) precentral gyrus; (ii) motor homunculus
20.8 Axons

Visit www.pearsoned.co.uk/toates
for a range of resources to support study.
Test yourself with multiple choice questions and access a bank of over 100 videos that will bring the topics to life.

Interactions and animations relating to topics discussed in this chapter can be found on the website at www.pearsoned.co.uk/toates. These include:

Animation: The function of the two cerebral hemispheres
Interaction: The hemispheric localization of language function in right and left handers
Animation: Wernicke–Geschwind model
Interaction: The location of the main areas involved in language comprehension and production
Interaction: Can you spot the difference between Broca's and Wernicke's aphasia?

Chapter 21
Brains, minds and consciousness

Learning outcomes for Chapter 21

After studying this chapter, you should be able to:

1 Explain why biological psychologists study consciousness and what is meant by subjective and objective perspectives.

2 Compare and contrast information processing done with conscious awareness and that done unconsciously. Thereby, define the special features of conscious processing.

3 Explain what is meant by 'neural correlates of consciousness'. Identify some neural correlates and describe the evidence that implicates the brain regions. Discuss whether we can infer a causal brain–consciousness link.

4 Describe the evidence and speculation that is involved in a comparative approach to consciousness, applying evolutionary and functional explanations.

5 Discuss the philosophical issue of how consciousness links to the physical brain.

Scene-setting questions

1 Why is the relationship between mind and brain sometimes termed the 'mind–brain problem'? Could it be described as the 'consciousness–brain problem'?

2 Does conscious insight give a good account of the causes of behaviour?

3 Do non-humans experience consciousness?

4 Is there a 'ghost in the machine' – something immaterial?

5 Is the conscious mind united or divisible?

6 Can a computer be conscious?

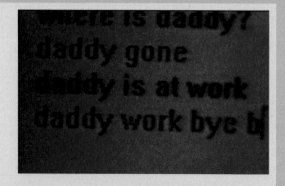

Can a computer be conscious? Explore the video on the website accompanying this book at www.pearsoned.co.uk/toates

What is it like to be a bat?
Source: PhotoDisc, Inc.

Introduction

What is stimulating your sensory systems now? The smell of coffee or the sound of a CD? Take a glance around. What is happening in your visual world as you look up from *Biological Psychology?* You probably answered in terms of conscious awareness. However, there are also stimuli impinging of which you normally have little conscious awareness. The tightness of a shoe or the pressure of your weight on the chair can be brought into conscious awareness, even though it is unlikely that they were there just before starting this chapter. However, they were providing information to the CNS.

You probably thought about external stimuli but your internal organs are also providing the CNS with information, e.g. concerning the contraction of your stomach. If you are lucky, much of this does not reach conscious awareness.

Now try reflecting on your past, on episodes of special personal experience. These will occupy your conscious mind even though they are of events no longer present, and some will be tinged with emotion. Now speculate on plans for the future. Conscious thought opens up possibilities that take us beyond the present.

Suppose that you hear a telephone number and search for a pen to write it down. While doing so, you repeat the number to yourself aloud or silently. The number engages your conscious processing as you repeat it. So, the content of **consciousness** can have something to do with the maintenance of sensory activity over time.

Consciousness appears to have certain characteristics: a capacity to self-reflect upon existence, to recall experiences from the past ('episodic memories'), to hold information in the mind's eye and to manipulate it, to run mental simulations of future possible scenarios and to feel the heat of emotion. Consciousness appears to be associated with the feeling of being a free agent, able to act voluntarily or refrain from acting. I am also conscious of being conscious.

People employ a theory of mind of others (Chapter 6), which often means a theory of their conscious awareness. We associate consciousness with free-will, personal agency and responsibility. We judge others by what we suppose to be the content of their conscious awareness, involving their intentionality. Such considerations are important to how we view ourselves as humans, with social, ethical and religious connotations.

Consciousness has been mentioned at several points in the book and the present chapter will return to these topics and introduce some new material. The focus now is consciousness in its own right, viewed in the context of brains and minds. For example, Chapter 1 described identity theory, which attempts to link brain and mind, and we can illuminate this using biological evidence.

Consciousness is a feature of the **mind**, one having certain peculiar properties not possessed by all aspects of 'mind'. Much of the mind functions unconsciously. Consciousness means (Searle, 1993, p. 61): 'subjective states of sentience or awareness'. There is a 'raw feel' of experience associated with consciousness and this aspect is sometimes termed **phenomenal consciousness**. It is difficult to capture 'phenomenal consciousness' in words; the best I can do is 'what it feels like to be conscious'.

Of course, consciousness cannot be observed objectively and publicly. However, to each conscious being, their own phenomenal consciousness surely seems to be especially vivid and obvious. It is perhaps the feature of existence about which we are most familiar and expert. Yet philosophers and psychologists agonize over even how to construct the right questions to gain deep insight (Nagel, 1974).

Biological psychology has a role at the interface between the objective and the subjective. This is between (i) an account of the brain in terms of neurons and synapses, etc., and (ii) reports of conscious awareness. Such terms as 'seeing', 'believing', 'feeling' and 'fearing' normally all imply phenomenal consciousness. Biological psychology tries to identify which patterns of neural activity and which brain regions are consistently associated with each such conscious state (Dehaene and Naccache, 2001). It asks – what characterizes such brain states, as distinct from those not associated with conscious awareness?

The core symptom of depression (Chapter 2), as experienced by patients, is a negative subjective conscious state. However, depression can equally be characterized in terms of the activity of neurons and hormones, etc. Similarly, for pain (Chapter 14), the conscious report is, of course, central to any diagnosis. The conscious report of craving for drugs (Chapter 18) tells a corresponding story.

The 1990s saw a mushrooming of articles and books on consciousness, which argued that its study should be at the heart of psychology (e.g. Baars, 1997). Some proclaimed it as the last and most important scientific challenge. Some pioneering authors on consciousness are biological psychologists (Gray, 1995; Panksepp, 1998; Pribram, 1986; Rozin, 1976; Weiskrantz, 1997). In theorizing about consciousness, psychological concepts, e.g. the 'self', appear alongside definable biological events such as blood flows to brain regions and dopamine levels. This makes the study of consciousness a rather unconventional science.

Questions raised in the present chapter include the following.

In terms of brain processes:

1 What is the relationship between activity of the brain and conscious experience?

2 What kind of information processing, involving which brain regions, is associated with consciousness, as distinct from unconscious processes?

3 Can a study of consciousness be reduced to a study of the physical brain?

4 What is the effect of brain damage on conscious experience?

5 Can a study of the brains of different species illuminate consciousness?

In terms of function:

1 Do conscious processes confer an advantage in fitness (Chapter 2)?

2 Do they come at a cost?

3 Does the lifestyle of certain species suggest the existence of, and functional advantage of, consciousness?

First we look at consciousness in the context of information processing.

Section summary

1 Consciousness is a subjective feature of our existence with which we are well acquainted.

2 An aspect of the study of consciousness consists of trying to relate phenomenal consciousness to activity of the brain.

 ## Test your knowledge

21.1 Why is it wrong to equate consciousness with the mind?

Answer on page 562

Conscious and unconscious information processing

Introduction

Cognition and behaviour are mediated by a combination of conscious and unconscious processes (Bargh and Chartrand, 1999). Only a very limited subset of information processing is available to conscious inspection (Gray, 1995). For example, people have no conscious insight into the stages of sensory processing, as in size constancy. People simply have access to the *products* of processing in the form of a conscious perception (Chapters 7–9). Similarly, people normally have no insight into motor programming underlying their behaviour, e.g. a choice of which muscle is activated. Even with controlled processing (Chapter 10), people have conscious insight into only (i) intended actions, which then automatically recruit the appropriate motor apparatus, and (ii) the consequences of actions.

This section looks at the distinction between conscious and unconscious processes and asks what are their characteristics?

The basics of conscious processing and experience

The contents of consciousness are described by the term **qualia** (Searle, 1993), e.g. the conscious perception of the colour red or, a moment later, the smell of coffee. Of course, qualia depend upon such things as activity by sensory receptors and neurons of the brain. However, the term 'qualia' conveys the subjective conscious aspect that requires a description over and above such objective data.

Conscious experiences are structured; although they are influenced by sensory data, patterns are constructed based upon this and categories are imposed. For example, Chapter 8 noted the intolerance that conscious processing shows towards ambiguity. The face–vase (Figure 7.2, p. 187) is seen as *either* two faces *or* a vase but not both at once. Figure 21.1 is usually seen as a face, even though no actual face looks like this (Searle, 1993).

Conscious states are associated with moods, e.g. elation, depression or joy.

Conscious contents ('qualia') that are generated in the absence of corresponding external stimuli appear to have features in common with what is generated by actual external events (Kosslyn, 1988). Objective evidence gives this a biological basis. For example, the fusiform face area (Chapter 8) is triggered by an image of a face and by simply imagining a face (O'Craven and Kanwisher, 2000). Inner 'speech' contains mistakes ('slips') rather like external speech (Baars, 1993). Simulation of action in the imagination has similarities to real action (Chapter 10). Simulation of a careful movement is slow, corresponding to the speed of the real movement.

Figure 21.1 Face
Source: Searle (1993, Fig. 1, p. 66).

The cognitive unconscious

Paradoxically, placing scientific attention on consciousness reveals how much of the control of cognition and behaviour is performed by processes to which people do *not* have conscious access (Bargh and Chartrand, 1999). The processing of stimulus information can proceed to a surprising extent without engaging conscious awareness. Not only raw stimulus features but also semantic associations can be triggered at a preconscious level (Velmans, 1991).

The so-called 'cognitive unconscious' involves the simultaneous parallel processing of several streams of information. Belief in its existence is based on various observations, some within biological psychology (Kihlstrom, 1993). For example, consider activity in the amygdala, a region associated with emotion (Chapter 12). Activity can be triggered by the very brief presentation of an image of a face expressing fear, even though this image does not reach conscious awareness (Morris *et al.*, 1999). Similarly, consider the priming of word completion in amnesic patients with temporal lobe damage (Chapter 11). Such patients cannot consciously recall the word but provide evidence of its processing at an unconscious level. For example, presenting a word, e.g. ELASTIC, in a way that it is not consciously registered means that subsequently the cue ELA..... is more likely to be completed as ELASTIC than as, say, ELATED.

The link between conscious and unconscious processing

Introduction

Various features of cognition and behaviour point to the special role that conscious processing plays, as distinct from unconscious processing. Figure 21.2 shows the link between these types of processing. A range of unconscious processes provide information to conscious processing and in turn are influenced by conscious processing. Conscious processing selects from the information provided and exploits unconscious processing in the production of behaviour.

Perception

Conscious processing interprets the actions of specialized unconscious processing (Gazzaniga, 1993). For example, consider the ambiguous face–vase figure (Chapter 7). Processors of the visual system present both possible interpretations to conscious processing, which selects alternately *either* two faces *or* a vase as the content of awareness.

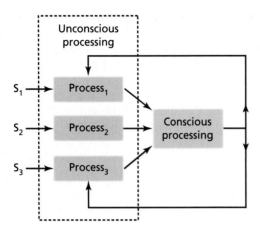

Figure 21.2 Unconscious and conscious processes.

Whether one uses the language of modules and central processors (Chapter 20) or automatic versus controlled processing (Chapter 10), the point is much the same. An array of unconscious parallel operations extract information and process it, while only a fraction of this gains access to conscious awareness (Kihlstrom, 1993). So, the contents of conscious awareness are focused and limited (Baars, 1993).

Conscious processing is specialized to handle information at times of uncertainty, i.e. when things do not run according to plan. For example, in anxiety ('something on the mind') there is repeated intrusion of anxiety-related cognition into other sequences of conscious thought (Gray, 1995). Such prioritizing can be awful – e.g. when you can't get an unwanted thought out of your mind – but it is not difficult to see that it has served an adaptive role.

Goal-setting

The spontaneous setting of goals ('having intentions') (Dehaene and Naccache, 2001) and pursuit of them by various routes are processes that are accessible to consciousness. Such conscious goals are implemented by processes lower in the hierarchy, to which people do not have conscious access. People consciously monitor progress towards the goal. Goal-setting is associated with a central executive system, which is involved in allocating processing resources to task demands (Block, 1991).

Conscious processing instigates action where routines ('habits') are not available or helps to resist routines and temptation (Norman and Shallice, 1986; Schrödinger, 1958). For example, consider the Stroop test (Chapter 20). We set the conscious goal of reporting ink colour, though there is interference from word meaning. Conscious processing is involved in the attempt to override the response of reporting word meaning, in the interests of ink colour.

If consciousness is engaged when things do not go according to plan, this implies feedback on the state of the world, which is compared with intentions (Baars, 1997). When these coincide we 'tick over' on automatic control. However, significant disparity is brought to conscious awareness for specialized processing. This can result in novel action to solve the present problem and formation of new memories for future reference.

Creativity

Conscious processing has a role in intuitive and creative operations that cannot (at least, as yet!) be modelled by computer (Penrose, 1990). Within consciousness we are able to associate weird ideas and images, and thereby arrive at novel creative combinations. However, even creative inspiration sometimes appears to pop into consciousness from nowhere, presumably after extensive unconscious processing (Baars, 1997; Velmans, 1991). This suggests a time sequence of information processing: conscious → unconscious → conscious, pointing to downwards and upwards flows of information (Figure 21.2).

The self and theories of mind

Consciousness is involved in predicting the moves of others. This involves information on their conscious intentions (Klein, 1991). Whether we are psychologists, preachers, traffic wardens, tax inspectors, con artists or whatever, we tend to explain the behaviour of others in terms of their preceding behaviour and (inferred) mental states, a 'theory of mind'. We form representations

A personal angle

A neuroscientist's unconscious processing

The neuroscientist, Nobel prize-winner and theorist of brain-mind relations, Sir John Eccles, described the role of unconscious processing in yielding creative solutions (Eccles, 1989, p. 233). You might take inspiration from him:

When I am searching for a good new idea, I fill up my mind with the knowledge of the problem and my critical evaluation of the attempted solutions of that problem. Then I await the outcome of the mental tension so created. Maybe I take a walk, as Einstein often did, or I listen to music . . . I don't struggle with my mind under tension, but hope that a good creative idea will burst forth, and often it does.

('models') of the mental states of others, involving their affective states and intentions, and we extrapolate to their most likely behaviour.

Barlow (1990) notes that neuroscience's insights play little role in how we treat other people but our 'folk theories' of the minds of others play a profound role. Even though they sometimes fail, people's models of the mind appear to have utility in predicting behaviour.

Section summary

1 Conscious processing imposes order on cognition and behaviour and is associated with moods.

2 Consciousness provides a means for simulating conditions in the absence of sensory input.

3 The cognitive unconscious, a system of rapid parallel processing, provides information to consciousness.

4 Various roles are attributed to consciousness in generating adaptive and coherent sequences of cognition and behaviour.

5 Modelling the self and the mind of others is attributed to advanced (e.g. human) conscious cognition.

 Test your knowledge

21.2 Complete the missing words in the following: 'For the ambiguous face–vase figure, sensory systems provide ___ possible interpretations and conscious perception ___ between these interpretations'.

Answer on page 562   WEB

Neuroscience perspectives

Introduction

What kind of neural activity is necessary and sufficient for conscious experience? Which brain regions and neurochemicals are implicated? We shall discuss the **neural correlates of consciousness** (Dehaene and Naccache, 2001), i.e. those patterns of neural activity that are associated particularly with conscious processing. The link here between biology and psychology is a two-way street. Psychological data and theory can provide

clues in the search for neural processes (Crick, 1994). For example, a privileged route to reaching conscious awareness is given to novel information. So, Gray (1995) asked, where is novelty detected by the brain?

Linking psychology and biology

This section looks at a range of phenomena related to consciousness that arise within psychology. It considers what they show about the conscious–unconscious distinction and what they suggest regarding the link to neural processes.

Representing information

Evidence suggests that conscious processing is needed to maintain stimulus information in an *active* state following termination of the stimulus (Dehaene and Naccache, 2001). In the absence of conscious processing, much stimulus information will normally be lost. An 'active state' means that patterns of activity in particular circuits of neurons are triggered by the stimulus and encode its presence after the stimulus is no longer present. Working memory and its anatomical basis in regions such as the prefrontal cortex are important parts of this.

The notion that conscious processes represent events even in their physical absence is relevant to patients with Charles Bonnet syndrome, named after the French-Swiss philosopher. These people experience spontaneous hallucinations, the occurrence of which is accompanied by increased activity in the ventral stream of visual processing (ffytche *et al.*, 1998). Activity is somewhat specific to the nature of the hallucination, being particularly evident in regions processing colour when the hallucination is in colour and in the fusiform face area when the hallucination is of faces.

The controlled-automatic dimension

Activity in brain regions changes as a task moves from controlled ('conscious') processing to unconscious ('automatic') control (Chapter 10). Hence, certain regions are identified as having a special role in conscious processing. For example, with automaticity, a lowering of activation is seen in the prefrontal cortex and anterior cingulate cortex but reactivation occurs there if the routine fails.

Attention

Conscious awareness is linked to attention (Chapter 20), which points to the modulation of sensory information by such structures as the prefrontal cortex, brain stem, parietal cortex and thalamus. A stimulus needs to gain attention in order to appear within conscious processing and there is competition between stimuli for this resource (Dehaene and Naccache, 2001). Using Crick's (1994) metaphor, there is a 'spotlight of attention' that brings into conscious awareness only a small fraction of the available information, e.g. a subset of the information extracted by the sense organs. In the neglect syndrome, a stimulus might be undetectable at one location in sensory space as a result of the presence of a stimulus at another. However, the neglected stimulus can be detected if presented on its own.

Speed of switches within conscious processing

The contents of consciousness can change very quickly as in the switches of the face–vase figure. This directs the search to the comparable dynamics of switches in the underlying neural activity. Such switches in patterns of neural activity have been identified (Chapter 8).

Complexity is not enough

You are a highly sophisticated mathematician! You might not have realized this and find my claim bizarre. The reason that you might not know this is that the sophistication does not necessarily reach conscious awareness. It resides in parts of the brain associated with unconscious processing. Consider the formidable unconscious computation that is involved in the motor skills of walking upright or even having an amateurish shot at playing tennis. So, complexity of processing on its own is insufficient for an association with consciousness. Thus, highly complex parallel processing that proceeds automatically does not trigger awareness, e.g. the computations predicting the limbs' optimal location in tennis.

The cerebellum is specialized for some of the parallel computation involved in automatic and unconscious features of cognition and behavioural control (Figure 21.2). The cerebellum is usually involved little, if at all, in discussions of consciousness (Penrose, 1990), in spite of having more neurons than any other brain region. The tasks that it performs would probably defy any but the most sophisticated mathematician if they were to be made explicit in numbers. We simply could not perform them consciously. Yet, consider being asked to solve a relatively trivial but normally rare problem, such as 'What is 13 times 3 minus 4?' Most of us need to bring conscious awareness to solving it since we lack automatic routines for doing so (Dehaene and Naccache, 2001).

Sleep–waking

The brain alternates between states of consciousness in sleep–waking (Chapter 19). Changes in level of awareness are programmed by the ascending neural processes and these structures are important in understanding consciousness (Coenen, 1998). REM sleep, involving dreaming, has features in common with conscious awareness and might be considered a special 'altered state of consciousness'. Ascending cholinergic projections to the thalamus and cortex appear to play a crucial role in consciousness, including that of the REM phase of sleep. Their disruption can profoundly change conscious experience (Perry et al., 1999). Changes of conscious awareness with anaesthetics are associated with changes of cholinergic transmission.

Having looked at the general principles of linking the brain and consciousness, we now look more closely at brain structures.

Identifying brain regions

General points

Activity in the brain stem and thalamus seems to be necessary for consciousness (Penfield, 1966). Damage to these regions can destroy the capacity for most behaviour, whether consciously or unconsciously mediated (Gray, 1995). Parts of the brain stem that control respiration are clearly vital to conscious experience but they are probably no more vital to it than they are to unconscious cognition or to spinal reflexes. By comparison, activity of the heart is also necessary. The quest is to locate brain regions that have a special contribution to *conscious* processes (Libet, 1993b).

In spite of many investigators' emphasis on sophisticated cortical structures, Panksepp (1998) argues persuasively that subcortical emotional systems provide a fundamental ingredient to consciousness (Chapter 12). These systems set the emotional tone of the brain and are reflected in moods.

Cortical–subcortical interaction

Some believe that an important basis of conscious experience lies in the neural activity associated with interactions between the cortex and thalamus (Crick, 1994). There appear to be both direct and indirect links, involving patterns of reverberation in neuronal activity throughout the circuits (Figure 21.3).

As shown, the thalamus is a gateway for access of sensory input to the cortex (Baars, 1993). For example, there are reciprocal circuits linking the lateral geniculate nucleus (LGN) and the visual cortex. Particular activity within a subset of thalamic neurons, as in the LGN, might be able to sustain awareness on a visual input. Activity of such a circuit is believed to underlie the 'conscious-like' cognition of dreaming in REM sleep (Chapter 19).

Figure 21.3(b) shows a suggested role of the hippocampus and some other structures in forming a loop involving the cortex. In this model, the hippocampus detects disparity between actual states of the world and expected states. When disparity is detected, there is a biasing of the content of consciousness so as to process the associated sensory information. Conscious awareness corresponds to the information that gains access to such loops. Novel input readily gains access. However, we should not simply see the hippocampus as the seat of conscious awareness; its damage does not destroy consciousness (Chapter 11), though it distorts its contents (see commentaries to Gray, 1995).

As a general point, loops of neural connections must have special features for consciousness to emerge from them. There are neural loops in the CNS that are associated with processing that is inaccessible to conscious awareness, e.g. motor control via the cerebellum and basal ganglia (Gray, 1995).

Changes in brain activity

We speak of the neural *correlates* of consciousness, as in the face–vase illusion, but correlation does not prove causation. Do particular changes in neural activity *cause* changes in conscious perception? In some cases, when specific brain damage occurs, aspects of conscious perception are lost (described shortly). Also, investigators can manipulate brain events and observe what happens

to conscious awareness (Dehaene and Naccache, 2001). Reversible changes in brain activity can be triggered and the effects noted. An example of this is the temporary inactivation of the brain regions that process visual motion, which abolishes the conscious perception of movement (Beckers and Zeki, 1995). Patients undergoing brain surgery have received electrical stimulation, described next.

Penfield's study

The pattern of temporal lobe activation preceding an epileptic attack is accompanied by complex visual sensations, pointing to a correlation (Penfield and Rasmussen, 1968). Artificial electrical stimulation of the visual cortex evokes subjective visual sensations, which suggests that electrical activity of the cortex is a basis of consciousness (Newsome and Salzman, 1993). Penfield (1966) found that specific episodic sensations were triggered by stimulation through cortical electrodes (Chapter 11).

Libet's study

Libet *et al.* (1991) found that a low intensity of brain stimulation had to last a minimum time T before a signal reached conscious awareness. At the same intensity, if stimulation lasted for less than T, it would trigger only non-conscious processing. The experiment was carried out on patients being treated for intractable pain. Electrodes had been implanted in the ventrobasal thalamus, whereby researchers were able to stimulate the system normally involved in tactile detection and involving the somatosensory cortex (Chapter 9).

Neuroimaging of brain structure and activity

Neuroimaging acts as a 'microscope' to probe neural correlates of consciousness. Links can thereby be made with consciousness as a form of 'arena' for cognitive processing, as revealed by the individual's own report. The notion of mind-reading comes a little closer with the development of neuroimaging techniques. This section gives a few examples.

Interoception

An awareness of one's own body is central to conscious awareness, sometimes involving awareness of the heartbeat (Craig, 2009). Anterior regions of the insula and the anterior cingulate cortex receive neural projections of information from the body. Neuroimaging allows researchers to identify subjective awareness of the body with activity in these regions. Seeing one's own image in a mirror also activates the insula. It is activated in

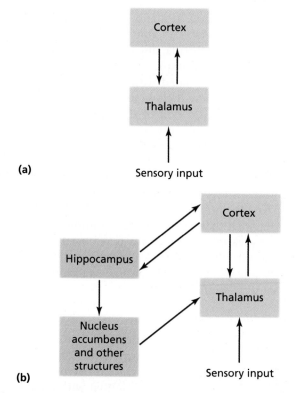

Figure 21.3 Reverberatory circuits between the thalamus and cortex: (a) direct, described by Crick (1994) and (b) involving the hippocampus, described by Gray (1995).

states of emotion. Self-awareness and euphoria are grossly exaggerated in some cases of epilepsy, described as 'ecstatic epileptic seizures' and evidence suggests hyper-activity in the anterior insula as its biological basis (Picard and Craig, 2009).

Memory

Chadwick *et al.* (2010) performed an fMRI investigation focused on the hippocampus and its regions. Would measuring activation of the hippocampus enable researchers to distinguish which episodic memory a participant is recalling in consciousness? A frame of reference was first provided by observing three different activity patterns when three target visual stimuli (x, y, z) were presented. Would recall of the memory of x be associated with activity pattern *X* in region X, whereas recall of memory y would be associated with activity pattern *Y* in region Y, and *Z* with Z? This was indeed the case in that researchers could distinguish the activity patterns and these corresponded to the answers given by participants concerning which memory they were holding in conscious awareness at that particular time.

Self-directed messages

People tend to reward or hurt themselves with self-directed and non-vocal messages that reassure or criticize the self (Longe *et al.*, 2010). Such messages are important in understanding self-esteem and depression. The insula tends to be activated by self-reassurance but not by self-criticism. Self-criticism tends to activate regions of prefrontal cortex.

Vegetative and minimally conscious states

Neuroimaging has allowed investigators to communicate with a small percentage of patients in 'vegetative' or 'minimally conscious states' (Monti *et al.*, 2010). Where there is no overt behaviour that can be stimulated, investigators can still ask patients to make so-called 'willful modulation' of their brain activity. The technique relies on the observation that, in control participants, imagining different scenarios is associated with different patterns of brain activity. Swinging a tennis racket in the imagination activates the supplementary motor area, whereas to imagine the navigation of a familiar town, activates a region of cortex surrounding the hippocampus (the parahippocampal gyrus). In response to a question (e.g. 'is your father's name Thomas?'), patients were asked to signal a 'yes' response by imagining one scene and a 'no' response by imagining the other. Shifts in the fMRI activity between these target brain regions were then used as a measure of the response, which could be compared with information provided by a relative. The procedure seems to have vital clinical, ethical and legal implications. For

example, a patient might be asked 'are you in pain?' and 'did this procedure lower your pain?' As Ropper (2010, p. 648) notes: 'it will now be difficult for physicians to tell families confidently that their unresponsive loved ones are "not in there somewhere".'

Amnesic patients (with temporal lobe damage) are deficient in showing 'Pavlovian trace conditioning' (in this, CS and UCS are separated by a period of time) (Chapter 11). The capacity to show such conditioning correlates with the extent to which the person consciously realizes the nature of the CS–UCS relationship. How would people in vegetative or minimally conscious states perform (Bekinschtein *et al.*, 2009)? Some degree of learning was shown and this correlated with measures of brain function derived from neuroimaging. The extent of learning predicted recovery months later. By contrast, control participants with experimentally controlled unconsciousness induced by an anesthetic showed no conditioning. Bekinschtein *et al.* speculate as to whether training on such tasks might aid recovery of consciousness.

Effects of specific brain damage
General

A way of gaining insight is to look at (i) how the action of particular neural processes relates to the nature and content of consciousness and (ii) how abnormality of such processes relates to abnormal consciousness (an example is schizophrenia, discussed in the next chapter) (Gray, 1995). For example, profound changes to consciousness are associated with loss of dopamine (DA) (Sacks, 1982). These include loss of will, emptiness of consciousness, distortion of time and hallucinations. For another example, the neglect syndrome (Chapter 20) can be associated with damage to the parietal cortex (Umiltà and Zorzi, 1995).

Although studies point to a crucial role of the cortex in consciousness (just described), somewhat paradoxically, based upon surgical experience, Penfield (1966, p. 234) reported that 'Consciousness continues, regardless of what area of cerebral cortex is removed'. It appears that specific areas of cortex are involved with triggering specific aspects of conscious awareness related to particular sensory events.

Disrupted memory

Chapter 11 described dissociations between explicit and implicit memories. Can you remember Claparède's pin experiment? There was dissociation between implicit and explicit memory. We assume that with a failure of episodic memory, H.M. (Chapter 11) suffered from a seriously disordered consciousness in terms of its potential for information processing.

Disrupted visual processing

Damage to the ventral stream of cortical processing disrupts conscious visual perception but leaves intact the patient's ability to perform rapid unconscious visually guided action (Chapter 8). This was exemplified by Dee Fletcher. Another dissociation in vision that tells a similar story, is as follows.

It used to be believed that in humans a lesion in the visual cortex caused total blindness in the corresponding region of the visual field. The effect would be comparable to that of a lesion in the retina, i.e. total blindness in an affected region. However, patients can retain a certain visual capacity corresponding to the affected area, termed 'blindsight' (Weiskrantz, 1976) (Chapter 1).

A personal angle

Blindsight in 'D.B.'

D.B. was born in 1940 in a market town in England (Weiskrantz, 1976). When aged 14, D.B. reported headaches on the right side of his head. These were usually preceded by the appearance of a phantom flashing light. In his 20s, D.B. noticed a blank region in the left visual field. A tumour in the the primary visual cortex (V1) was identified. In 1973, the diseased tissue was surgically removed and this greatly improved his well-being. He was largely free of headaches and phantom flashes of light. However, most of D.B.'s left visual field was blind.

D.B.'s ophthalmic surgeon observed that D.B. retained a capacity to locate objects more accurately than at chance level, in what was apparently a blind left visual field. For example, by his own account, D.B. was not able to see an outstretched hand but nonetheless would reach for it with some accuracy. D.B. was able to point to objects, while denying that he could see them. He could even discriminate a pattern of stripes from a uniform grey. There was a separation between D.B.'s ability and his conscious awareness of it.

Where is the unconscious processing taking place in blindsight? Neurons that pass from the lateral geniculate nucleus to cortical regions other than the primary visual cortex (Fries, 1981) could play a role. The route involving the superior colliculus (subcortical system) (Figures 8.17, p. 207, and 8.24, p. 212), and projecting to the dorsal stream, is another possibility.

To generalize from D.B., control humans might be expected under some conditions to detect events and behave on the basis of them without having conscious awareness of doing so. Traditionally, human sensory and perceptual systems have been studied on the basis of people's reports of what they perceive, this being fundamental to clinical assessment. However, D.B. serves as a warning that such reports might need careful qualification. As Weiskrantz (1976, p. 118) notes: 'an 'unexpected' revelation of a capacity may occur when one uses an unusual method of testing for it'.

So, based on a comparison with blindsight patients, what does conscious perception bring that is distinct from unconscious processing? For visual stimulation in the 'blind' region, these patients can *react to* particular triggers automatically. For example, at better than chance, they can respond to the question, 'Was that vertical or horizontal?' They can *react* by shaking the experimenter's outstretched hand, a highly probable stimulus-response connection. However, they cannot *act* – they are unable to instigate novel actions based on the visual information extracted in the 'blind' region (Weiskrantz, 1997). So, here is a feature of normal conscious processing that is highlighted by its absence. Furthermore, controls can report conscious mental states based on visual stimulation whereas, by definition, blindsight patients have nothing to report regarding visual stimulation of the blind part of the field (Dehaene and Naccache, 2001).

Inter-hemispheric communication

Surprising to any view on consciousness is the observation that if one hemisphere is anaesthetized, as in the Wada technique (Chapter 20), patients retain consciousness (discussed by Kinsbourne, 1993).

What is the result of splitting the cerebral hemispheres by cutting the corpus callosum (Sperry, 1974)? Is consciousness split in two, as if there are two conscious minds associated with one brain?

If information is targeted to each hemisphere in turn, separate cognitive processing can be triggered in each hemisphere (Sperry, 1974). These cognitions can be in conflict with each other as far as coherent behaviour is concerned. This strongly suggests that the necessary cognition underlying consciousness can be truly split. Whether phenomenal consciousness itself is split remains a tricky philosophical question. Lacking access to the dominant left hemispheric speech system, the right hemisphere of split-brain patients is often described as 'minor' or 'silent' (Sperry, 1974). Does the right hemisphere have, in any sense, a conscious mental life of its own? Is it simply acting on 'autopilot' control in the absence of awareness? Without having the

A personal angle

A potential martyr for psychology

William McDougall, one of the founders of British psychology, believed in the unitary nature of consciousness, unconditional upon a unified brain. Sir Cyril Burt (a co-founder) remembers McDougall:

> saying more than once that he had tried to bargain with Sherrington . . . that if ever he should be smitten with an incurable disease, Sherrington should cut through his corpus callosum. 'If the physiologists are right' – and by physiologists I suppose he meant Sherrington himself – 'the result should be a split personality'. 'If I am right', he said, 'my consciousness will remain a unitary consciousness'. And he seemed to regard that as the most convincing proof of the existence of something like a soul.
>
> (Quoted from Zangwill, 1974, p. 265.)

operation, we do not know 'what it is like to be a split-brain patient'.

Differential targeting of information to different hemispheres is, of course, an artificial procedure. In a situation of 'normal' processing, it would possibly have been of some comfort to McDougall to know that cutting the corpus callosum can have little effect on processing, e.g. verbal IQ remains intact (Gazzaniga, 1993). In split-brain patients, it sometimes appears that the unified conscious experience arises from the dominant left hemisphere imposing an interpretation upon behaviour that is elicited from either disconnected hemisphere.

Could two conscious entities associated with one brain enter into a dialogue with each other, commenting upon their consciousnesses? In split-brain patients, MacKay (1987) found independence in terms of simultaneous and different sensory evaluations. There were also distinct modes of motor control between the two hemispheres. However, he found no evidence to suggest two distinct forms of consciousness. Indeed, in response to some subtle probing, one patient responded, 'Are you guys trying to make two people out of me?'

The binding problem

The unity of conscious experience involves the integration of components of information. The problem of how this is achieved is sometimes termed the **binding problem** (Searle, 1993). For example, there is integration of the smell and sight of a rose to give a unified perception. So, are different patterns of neuronal activity, representing the colour and smell, *in some way* bound together? Does everything come together at one point, sometimes described as a 'theatre' of consciousness? Some argue that, in reality, there is no convergence of neural inputs to one site (Dennett, 1993). They suggest that no brain area derives input from every sensory source. Information processing remains parallel, e.g. as in the visual streams (Chapter 8).

This debate will doubtless run and run, as will the topic of the next section!

Section summary

1. Activity within circuits linking the cortex and thalamus appears to form a basis of conscious awareness.

2. Under certain conditions, electrical brain stimulation of less than time T can be associated with unconscious processing. Extending the duration to beyond T gains access to conscious awareness.

3. Neuroimaging can give insights into cognitive processing in people with apparently minimal states of consciousness.

4. In blindsight, people can respond to visual stimuli without consciously perceiving them.

5. Cognitive processing that provides a basis for consciousness appears to be split with a cut of the corpus callosum. Whether consciousness is divisible remains a topic of philosophical speculation.

6. How the combination of components of awareness yields a unified awareness is termed the binding problem.

☞ Test your knowledge

21.3 Complete the following sentence: 'Blindsight is associated with damage to a brain region termed the ___. The vision that remains in the affected area of visual field is associated with a subcortical route via the ___'.

Answer on page 562

Functional and comparative issues

This section will describe the close links between speculation on function and evolutionary emergence. It exemplifies insights to be gained from comparing different species.

Function

Consciousness appears to be an evolutionary development that builds on unconscious cognitive processing (Rozin, 1976). Its function seems to be one of exerting control over unconscious processes. This may be necessary once brains reach a certain complexity, so that there can be coordination and coherence in behaviour and cognition. Thereby flexibility can be achieved and processing that was originally encapsulated within a range of single parallel processes can be integrated and exploited as part of a coherent strategy.

Consciousness must presumably serve some adaptive function for it to have emerged in evolution. Suppose that consciousness requires specific brain mechanisms for its support, or, at least, it requires development of existing structures. Their appearance in evolution might have come at a considerable cost. Human brains are large and energy-demanding, and the size of head needed to contain them creates problems for mother and child at birth.

The severe disability of amnesic patients points to an advantage of conscious processing (Weiskrantz, 1997). Similarly, as noted earlier, a blindsight patient will not normally *instigate* action based upon the blind visual field.

Dennett (1993) suggests a possible evolutionary scenario. Having evolved language for social communication, our ancestors found an advantage in talking out loud to themselves. This could trigger memories and serve as a 'holding device' for keeping a memory active, necessitating working memory (Chapter 11). An evolutionary refinement of this was sub-vocal speech, one feature of consciousness.

Comparative issues

Introduction

At what stage in evolution consciousness appears is a matter of debate (Reber, 1992). The roles that consciousness is thought to serve, e.g. goal-setting and coordinated action, seem to be needed widely across species. Therefore, consciousness might not be a recent arrival (MacKay, 1991). Psychologists need to distinguish between necessary background conditions and specific conditions for consciousness to exist. For example, consciousness presumably builds on processes involved in wakefulness, since these provide a necessary condition for the experience and, of course, exist very widely across species (Chapter 19; Coenen, 1998).

What is it like ...?

It is often asked whether dogs, or fish or even amoeba are conscious. One way of expressing this is: what is it *like to be* a certain species? Nagel (1974) asked 'What is it like to be a bat?' He speculated on the basis of the bat's sensory apparatus, e.g. possession of sonar guidance and nociceptive neurons, but concluded that it is impossible to know what it is like, without being a bat! Lacking language, a bat most likely has a limited range of conscious content compared with us. Presumably, it cannot entertain the conscious cognition of, for example, fear of old age, since this requires a symbolic language. However, a bat might experience affective conscious states, such as those associated with tissue damage or mating. The neural mechanisms that support these show broad generality across mammalian species (Chapter 12; Panksepp, 1998). Why was the bat chosen, when the subject might equally have been, say, the spider or chimpanzee? Dennett (1993) speculates that few would want to attribute consciousness to the former and few would deny it to the latter, so the bat is a more challenging choice for speculation.

Despite the impressive cognitive skills of a number of non-human species, especially among the primates, their behaviour suggests a limited range of conscious processing, confined largely to present events (Donald, 1991).

Brain structure

Gray (1993) asked, 'Does a species have the brain structure assumed to underlie conscious experience?' His argument is based on abnormal consciousness of schizophrenia (next chapter) and is attributed to abnormal interactions between structures such as the cortex and hippocampus. On this basis, rats are candidates, in terms of meeting a necessary condition, and amoebas are not. However, consciousness might also emerge in evolution by some other mechanism. By analogy, vision in insects and vertebrates is based on rather different processes (Gray, 1995).

Monkeys with damage to the visual cortex exhibit blindsight. By means of an operant task, monkeys are, in effect, asked the question, did you see that light? When information is projected to the affected region, they report that they did not see any stimulus but nonetheless react appropriately on the basis of its presence (Cowey and Stoerig, 1995; Weiskrantz, 1997).

Memory

The capacity to recall episodes of personal experience would seem to be a crucial feature of human conscious experience. Do other species show evidence of episodic memory? Some bird species do (Chapters 1, 5 and 11), which might reflect a necessary component for the experience (Griffiths *et al.*, 1999).

A self-concept

It might be useful to distinguish between consciousness in the sense of (a) some form of sentience and a possession of goal-setting processes and (b) *self*-consciousness involving complex representations of the mental state of self and others. The latter might be an evolutionary development of the former, apparent only in species with a sophisticated social cognition, such as us.

Do different species have a 'self-concept'? Gallup (1977) observed the behaviour of monkeys and apes in front of mirrors. Under anaesthetic, Gallup placed red marks on some animals at a location out of sight by their direct vision, e.g. on the forehead. On recovery and after inspection in the mirror, in some cases, the animals repeatedly touched the area marked. This suggested that they identified it as part of their own body (a 'theory of self'). In both human infants and those non-human primate species that exhibit the effect, it appears at a certain developmental stage (de Veer and van den Bos, 1999).

The issue of animal consciousness is more than one of intellectual curiosity. An input to the animal welfare debate and thereby agricultural policy derives from such theorizing (Wiepkema, 1987).

Section summary

1 Consciousness appears to be an evolutionary development of unconscious processing.

2 We can ask, 'What is it like to be . . .?' This can be illuminated by knowledge of the species' sensory systems and brain processes.

3 In comparing species, we might need to distinguish some form of sentience from *self*-consciousness involving representation of the mental state of self and others.

☞ Test your knowledge

21.4 Complete the following: 'For consciousness to have evolved, it is assumed that the ___ outweighed the ___'.

 Answer on page 562   WEB

Some philosophical considerations

Introduction

This section briefly considers what biological psychology can learn from philosophical discussion and how it might contribute.

Consciousness and the mind–body problem

Basics

Why do philosophers use the expression mind–body *problem*? The aim of science is to reduce the diversity of nature to a few fundamental principles (Nagel, 1993). The problem comes in the conceptual difficulty of fitting the mind–body relation to such principles.

It is not that we lack data; we have a rich source of information from first-hand experience. For example, a person can report when an ambiguous figure changes in its conscious interpretation, as in the face–vase figure, etc. (Chapter 7). This can be correlated with changes in activation of brain regions. Rather, we lack a conceptual framework in which to interpret why such brain activity is associated with *phenomenal* consciousness. This is the **hard problem** of consciousness (Chalmers, 1996).

So, instead of the 'mind–body problem', we might describe it as the 'brain–consciousness problem' (Gray, 1993). In principle, there is no insurmountable problem in explaining how the aspect of mind that consists of unconscious cognition can arise from the brain. A computer analogy gives good insight. As Nagel writes (p. 2): 'The facts of consciousness are facts about how things are *for* some conscious subject, whereas physical facts are facts about how things are, full stop'. Consciousness is essentially a 'first-person' phenomenon and cannot be understood in such terms from another's perspective (Searle, 1993). Thus, Searle suggests it is not meaningful to ask whether a computer is conscious.

Nagel sees the task of psychology as to be relating such 'how things are *to*' (italics added) to 'how things are', the latter being defined by brain processes. Although the presence of particular neural mechanisms is a prior condition for certain conscious experiences, we cannot infer the existence of the experiences based on those mechanisms. For example, certain minimal conditions need to be met at the retinal level for the experience of colour but these mechanisms only predict a capacity to discriminate wavelength (Chapter 8), not the phenomenal consciousness ('raw feel' or 'qualia') of colour.

Chapter 1 noted that identity theory is accepted by most biological psychologists. However, this is not the only theory on mind–brain. Another is as follows.

Dualism

Some philosophers, most notably René Descartes, have argued that the domains of mind and brain are fundamentally different, such that one could exist without the other. In this view, the conscious mind might even take leave of the physical brain and wander off on its own or it might survive the death of the physical body. Such a view is termed **dualism**, since it involves a fundamental duality between a physical and a mental domain (Crick, 1994; Eccles, 1989).

Even if one believes in such duality then, at the least, it is necessary to postulate that an interaction normally exists between the mental and physical domains. Ideas arising in the mental domain can only be translated into action with the help of muscles, so a mind → body link is needed. Conversely, it is clear that events in the physical body influence mental life (i.e. body → mind). For example, a rotting tooth is very much in the world of the physical and yet its manifestations can become all too evident to your conscious mind.

These days, dualism is not favoured in biological psychology.

Emergent properties

Implying an 'emergent property' (Chapter 1), Searle (1993) argues (p. 64): 'just as one cannot reach into a glass of water and pick out a molecule and say 'this one is wet', so one cannot point to a single synapse or neuron in the brain and say 'this one is thinking about my grandmother' '. However, Gray (1987b) points out a weakness in such analogies: based upon the properties of the constituent molecules, the liquidity of water can be predicted. There is nothing about neurons or their assemblies that predicts subjective awareness.

When we consider the qualities of consciousness such as intentionality and goal-setting, to most of us it becomes no clearer. Thus, we can build goal-seeking into a room temperature control system employing a thermostat (e.g. hold temperature at 18 °C) but most of us would not suppose that we have thereby built consciousness into it. The experiment with the face–vase illusion can give us confidence in the generality of similar conscious experiences across individuals but does not help to explain how it arises. All we might be able to do is, given that we know of the existence of conscious experience, to predict qualities of its content, as in the frequency of switches in conscious perception (Libet, 1993a).

The astonishing hypothesis

Francis Crick's work entitled *The Astonishing Hypothesis: The Scientific Search for the Soul* is a neuroscience perspective on consciousness and an assault on dualism (Crick, 1994). In words much cited, Crick defines the astonishing hypothesis as (p. 3):

that 'You', your joys and your sorrows, your memories and your ambitions, your sense of personal identity and free will, are in fact no more than the behaviour of a vast assembly of nerve cells and their associated molecules.

The term 'no more than' is, as elsewhere, open to some ambiguity and controversy. Clearly, complex properties emerge from such an assembly of pure physical matter and Crick does not deny this. He denies that there is a consciousness or soul that can have an existence *distinct from the physical body*.

Free-will

Introduction

Personal attitudes to mind–brain tend to be associated with corresponding attitudes to that of free-will and determinism (Zohar, 1990). For example, a denial of the special significance of consciousness tends to be associated with a parallel dismissal of free-will (e.g. Skinner, 1971, 1984), whereas consciousness tends to be emphasized by those putting their faith in free-will (Rogers, 1959). Traditionally, the approach of biological psychology holds to a belief that, at least in principle, events are determined in ways that are open to public observation and prediction (Chapter 1). For example, the behaviour of both saints and sinners is often rather predictable (Sutherland, 1975) but need that imply that they act without free-will?

An elusive problem

The notion of free-will is elusive, even though many have the feeling that they possess it. It is very difficult to state clearly what we mean by it. We risk falling for the homunculus fallacy, of inventing a little ('free') person and putting him/her in the head (Chapter 7; see Bargh and Chartrand, 1999). Although few could doubt that our behaviour is largely determined by genes and environment, the notion of free-will seems to suggest (i) an element of indeterminacy that stands outside such deterministic processes and (ii) the process is open to scrutiny only to the person concerned. That is, a person could always have acted otherwise.

The issue is commonly framed in terms of a dichotomy between free-will and determinism. However, it might be more fruitful to see genes and environment setting a framework for, and limits on, the exercise of free-will (Stevens, 1990; cf. Bargh and Chartrand, 1999). For example, if deterministic genetic and environmental factors exert a bias towards, say, drug addiction, it might take greater exertion of this mysterious inner factor of free-will to stay off drugs (Zohar, 1990).

The law treats the guilty as free agents responsible for their own behaviour. Is there anything biological psychology could contribute to this issue?

Source: James andrew/Alamy.

An input from neuroscience

Even having to live with dilemmas ('conundrums'), can neuroscience give some help? It probably cannot give any answers that would allow you to win your case, for or against free-will, in the student bar or debating society. However, it can give a framework for approaching the debate – bits of circumstantial evidence that might tentatively be brought out for one or other viewpoint.

The capacity to represent the self and the consequences of one's actions and to utilize these in the control of behaviour would seem to be a necessary condition for free-will (Frith, 1996). Such representations appear to involve the prefrontal cortex, in actions based upon anticipated future costs and benefits. Phineas Gage (Chapter 1) might exemplify a person who lost some social and moral responsibility following damage to his prefrontal cortex. Brain damage tends to be a mitigating factor in moral responsibility (Chapter 1), especially if it disrupts the capacity to link decision-making and action (MacKay, 1974). PET and fMRI scans might permit a refinement of this notion, which seems analogous to a computer hardware fault. One might perform PET scans of people's brains and correlate activity with their reports

of the conscious feeling of making free decisions, as opposed to acting in response to external triggers. In the absence of any such fault, abnormal behaviour might be analogous to a computer software abnormality.

Reacting on the basis of conscious goals, rather than by automatic processing based upon stimulus input, might seem to be one criterion of being free. Resisting temptation by means of a conscious goal would be a good example. These seem to move us near to the notion of 'will' but the 'free' remains problematic. Consider the capacity to generate future scenarios in conscious awareness but not to put them into action. This might be sufficient to give us the perception of free-will (Crick, 1994).

Much of the activity of the ANS (Chapter 3) appears to be 'involuntary', whereas much of the control of the skeletal muscles appears to be 'voluntary' (Baars, 1997). You might like to consider whether any of this provides insight into hard determinism.

An experimental approach

Can we bring the issue of free-will into the laboratory? Libet (1993b) did this and worked on the basis that a self-paced voluntary act is normally accompanied by a readiness potential (Chapter 10). This potential, which is recorded from the scalp, is observed some 800 ms or so before the movement (Chapter 5).

The readiness potential appears to begin some 350 ms before a conscious intention to act arises. Following the logic of this paradigm, one is consciously aware of the 'decision' to act only after the programming of the act has already been instigated

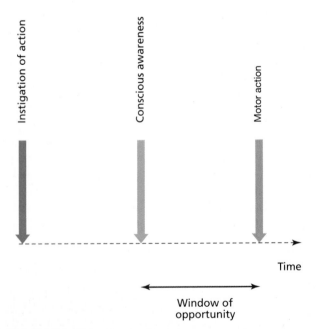

Figure 21.4 Components of action.

unconsciously. The somewhat counterintuitive conclusion is that we know what we have 'chosen' to do only after we have already decided unconsciously to do it! This alarms many people since it seems to reduce us to mere automatons, slaves to the environment and unconscious forces. So what is the role of consciousness in voluntary acts?

Normally we have a feeling of free-will surrounding much of our day-to-day integrated long-term planning and execution of action. However, Libet suggests that conscious processes do not play a role in the *instigation* of a voluntary motor act. There is a 'window of opportunity' between the conscious awareness of a decision to act and its execution (Figure 21.4). Within this time, consciousness can veto the decision and block it. Thus, a somewhat constrained role for consciously mediated free-will might be suggested – it has been expressed as we don't have 'free-will' but we have 'free-won't'. How good this experimental paradigm is as a representation of conscious choice in real life is a matter of debate. However, based on evidence such as Libet's, some argue that such free-will is an illusion (Wegner, 2003).

Frankly, what we mean by 'free' remains a philosophical problem that biological psychology can do little to illuminate. Sorry!

Section summary

1 The 'mind–body' problem is one of how mind and body relate, i.e. how does phenomenal consciousness relate to the physical brain?

2 Consciousness is often described as an emergent property of the brain.

3 It is unclear how phenomenal consciousness emerges from matter.

4 Crick's 'astonishing hypothesis' suggested that we are nothing but an assembly of such biological components as neurons.

5 Circumstantial evidence can be gathered to illuminate the issue of free-will and determinism but no conclusive case yet made.

☞ Test your knowledge

21.5 Why does the hard problem present itself to a follower of identity theory?

Answer on page 562   🔊 WEB

Bringing things together

The chapter has shown where we can approach consciousness from the perspective of biological psychology. Causal, evolutionary and functional explanations each have a role to play. The study of consciousness is based upon (i) objective evidence from studying the brain, (ii) subjective reports of phenomenal consciousness and (iii) trying to form links between (i) and (ii) by the use of metaphor and analogy (e.g. 'binding', 'searchlight', 'theatre' and 'executive').

Consciousness has a curious Janus-head nature. Pointing one way, and relatively non-controversially, 'consciousness' describes a class of information processing. This distinguishes it from instances of information processing to which we do not have conscious access. In principle, there is relatively little difficulty in describing the nature of at least some of the information processing that is associated with consciousness (Oatley, 1988). Although there are problems, they are relatively 'easy problems'. Sophisticated computer models related to neural structures might seem to be the way to gain insight here.

As shown in various chapters, biological psychology is making considerable progress in identifying the neural correlates of consciousness and also showing evidence of causal links from neural activity to conscious events. There is equally little difficulty in answering the question, what is consciousness for?

It appears that there are no special brain regions that are exclusively associated with conscious processing, though some appear to be exclusively associated with unconscious processing. Certain brain regions and their processing might operate at either unconscious or conscious levels, depending upon the activity within them. For example, it was noted that stimulation for a time period below T might not reach awareness, whereas that of duration above T becomes conscious. The same processes that are involved in visual perception in response to a stimulus are activated when the person simply imagines the same stimulus.

With the Janus-head pointing in the other direction, the personal and phenomenological aspects of consciousness remain elusive, the 'hard problem'. It has a holistic and idiosyncratic feel that seems to defy scientific analysis. The nature of the hard problem of consciousness can be summed up as, why does some processing have this peculiar state of existential awareness and subjective affect associated with it?

Summary of Chapter 21

1 The study of consciousness involves trying to relate objective data (brain events and behaviour) and subjective data (conscious experience).

2 Much information processing occurs outside conscious awareness. Processing that is accompanied by conscious awareness gives overall coherence and co-ordination to cognition and behaviour.

3 Psychologists identify certain types of information processing and particular brain regions as having a role in consciousness.

4 Speculations on the function of consciousness and its emergence in evolution are closely linked.

5 Biological psychology is central to the issue of how the conscious mind relates to the physical brain.

See the video coverage for this chapter and be challenged on what is the essence of consciousness and how it relates to brains. WEB

Further reading

For a clear introduction, see Carter (2010). Jeffrey Gray, a distinguished biological psychologist, tackled consciousness (Gray, 2004). Velmans and Schneider (2006) give an excellent perspective from various eminent researchers and theorists. Wegner (2003) gives a controversial perspective on free will. For 'personal angle' accounts of links with emotion, see Panksepp (1998) and Damasio (1999). Libet (2005) presents an account of his life's work in this area. Personally, I like Velmans (2000) for clear statements of the problem of consciousness. For the neuroscience of consciousness, see Gazzaniga *et al.* (2008).

Answers

Explanations for answers to 'test your knowledge' questions can found on the website **www.pearsoned.co.uk/toates**

21.1 Because in doing so, one ignores the unconscious aspect of 'mind'.
21.2 Two; alternates/switches
21.3 Visual cortex; superior colliculus
21.4 Benefits; costs
21.5 Because, unlike dualism, identity theory suggests that consciousness is a property of the brain, identical with brain states.

Visit www.pearsoned.co.uk/toates WEB
for a range of resources to support study.
Test yourself with multiple choice questions and access a bank of over 100 videos that will bring the topics to life.

Chapter 22
When things go wrong

Learning outcomes for Chapter 22

After studying this chapter, you should be able to:

1 Discuss critically some issues that are raised, in the study of brain, mind and behaviour, by the expression 'going wrong'. Relate biological events to conscious awareness.

2 Describe why a comprehensive understanding of dementia requires investigation at cellular, whole-brain and psychological levels.

3 Explain why it is imperative to consider both causal and developmental explanations in trying to understand schizophrenia. Link disordered cognition and conscious awareness to disordered brain processing.

4 Describe what is 'obsessive-compulsive disorder' and some of its biological bases.

5 Present the evidence that attention deficit hyperactivity disorder represents a conflict between controls of behaviour.

Scene-setting questions

1 Does a psychological disturbance imply a brain disturbance?

2 How can disease disturb the contents of conscious awareness?

3 What is it like to live with Alzheimer's disease? What is lost and what is spared?

4 What is it like to experience schizophrenia?

5 What is the scientific meaning of 'obsession'? How can obsessive-compulsive disorder drive us to act against our rational insight?

6 Is attention deficit disorder a biological abnormality or social labelling? Is this a logical dichotomy?

What is it like to live with Alzheimer's disease? What is lost and what is spared? Explore the video on the website accompanying this book at www.pearsoned.co.uk/toates

Howard Hughes was a talented, fearless and creative test pilot, engineer and film producer. How could he have fallen ill with a condition in which the rational mind is dominated by irrational fear?

Source: © Bettmann/CORBIS.

Introduction

How do psychologists decide when things have gone wrong in brain, behaviour and conscious experience? Classifications and explanations can be controversial, with dichotomies of the form 'biological versus social'. The theme of the present book is that such dichotomies are misleading. Thus, social causes of psychological distress are mediated via the brain. Reciprocally, biological causes of distress affect our social cognitions and interactions.

'Going wrong' might be defined as a *deviation from normal*, i.e. in contrast to what occurs in most of the population. However, this is problematic. The brains/minds of Einstein and Mozart doubtless differed greatly from normal but we would not thereby attribute mental illness to them. Conversely, if most of the population became depressed, this would suggest that the problem has somehow solved itself!

Another possible, but imperfect, criterion is in terms of function: things have gone wrong when the person has a greatly reduced reproductive capacity, as in clinical depression. This state is associated with neurohormonal imbalances that can harm the structure of the brain and cause withdrawal from social contact.

Perhaps least controversially, things can go wrong by the criterion of mental distress. They can also go wrong for society, in that a person might be a danger or nuisance to others. No single criterion of things going wrong offers a gold standard, and in practice psychologists usually adopt a composite of all three. By each criterion, biological psychology assumes a key role in understanding abnormality and in devising treatments.

You might have had experience of things becoming upset in your psychological life or you have observed this in others. Try to reflect on this, in terms of deviation from what is desired in both conscious mental life and behaviour. For another example, you might have experienced intense negative emotions as in fear or the breaking of a romantic relationship. These are not abnormal in terms of how frequently they occur, since many people have experienced at least one such event. However, they are deviations from what is desired. Your conscious mind would have been inescapably focused on the negative event, and you might have noted deviations from normal in behaviour and activities controlled by your autonomic nervous system. Your functioning might have been disrupted.

Have you been troubled by intrusive thoughts that enter your head and refuse to go away? For example, it could be that you have been unduly worried as to whether you locked the front door or switched off the gas. This might have led you to check more than usual.

Did you ever feel apathy, lack of volition, e.g. in response to psychological overload or after exposure to an infectious illness? Can you recall how it felt?

In such cases, a deviation of mental processing from what is desired can dominate mental life and behaviour, with luck only temporarily. Reflecting on these experiences can give you at least some insight into serious psychological distress.

Have you ever woken from a nightmare, relieved to have gained your voluntary, rational and sequential pattern of conscious thoughts and contact with reality? Reflecting on this, can you recall what it felt like to be the victim of seemingly random thoughts, with only the most tenuous and irrational associations between them? This might give some glimpse into the kind of mental disturbance where contact with reality is lost.

You have surely reacted impulsively in a situation in order to gain immediate benefit, when, on reflection, restraint would have better served your long-term interests. For example, you might have rubbed eyes made sore by hay fever in the certain knowledge that this will bring immediate relief but be followed by greater discomfort.

This might give some insight into conditions in which impulsivity comes to dominate behaviour.

Taking examples of when things go wrong, this chapter will consider the links between cognition (including that evident in conscious awareness), behaviour and biology. Patients' reports are usually in terms of distressing conscious experiences, beliefs, persuasions and emotions but treatments are often pharmacological. The chapter reflects a crucially important question: how does psychology bridge the gap between these areas of description, so that integrative explanations can be provided (Kapur, 2003)?

We will look at four examples of things going wrong: dementia, schizophrenia, obsessive-compulsive disorder and attention deficit hyperactivity disorder.

Section summary

1 Biological psychologists attempt to link abnormality of underlying biology to when things go wrong in cognition, conscious experience and behaviour.

2 An important criterion of things going wrong is human suffering. Others include reduction in functional ability and, more problematically, deviation from the most common experience.

 Test your knowledge

22.1 What is a problem inherent in using abnormality as a criterion of things going wrong?

 Answer on page 586

Dementia

Introduction

The term 'dementia' (Chapter 20) describes a 'cognitive impairment in multiple spheres' (Brandt and Rich, 1995, p. 243). An impairment of memory is necessary for the diagnosis of dementia, though in some cases there might be more a failure of attention than memory as such (Richards, 1996). Broadly, dementia can arise from various causes, e.g. stroke or hardening of the arteries of the brain. This section describes dementia

A personal angle

Alois Alzheimer and Auguste D.

Alois Alzheimer was born in Marktbreit, Germany, in 1864. In 1906, he described a form of dementia, termed Alzheimer's disease by his colleague, Kraepelin (Maurer *et al.*, 1997). Alzheimer's observations were of a 51-year-old woman, Auguste D., who showed impaired memory and comprehension. In 1995, Alzheimer's file on Auguste D. was discovered with an entry for 26 November 1901:

> She sits on the bed with a helpless expression. What is your name? *Auguste.* Last name? *Auguste.* What is your husband's name? *Auguste, I think.* Your husband? *Ah, my husband.* She looks as if she didn't understand the question.

Auguste D. died in 1906. From the autopsy, Alzheimer identified abnormalities in the cellular structure of her cerebral cortex, consisting of the loss of intact cells and the accumulation of pathological material. Alzheimer's observations represent an important identification of a biological basis of cognitive change.

arising from degenerative brain disease, the most common being **Alzheimer's disease (AD)**.

The AD patient normally deteriorates slowly (Morris, 1996a), starting with slight impairments in episodic memory (personal autobiographic events) and the ability to find words. Names that were previously familiar are often forgotten and objects misplaced. As disease advances, there can be deficits in attention, language, reasoning and spatial memory (Brandt and Rich, 1995), as well as disturbances to emotion and perception (including hallucinations). On a more optimistic note, education, an active mind and rich experience seem to help prevention of dementia (Ott *et al.*, 1995).

AD is characterized by patterns of specific cognitive decline rather than a 'global impairment' and cognitive changes are linked to malfunction of particular biological structures (Morris and Becker, 2004). Brain regions can be linked to their normal contribution to cognition and, in AD, to disruption of this contribution. Researchers can relate cognitive decline to changes in cerebral blood flow and EEG patterns. Fine-grained changes in the cellular structure of the nervous system can be linked to gross structural changes in brain regions and cognition.

A personal angle

Iris Murdoch

The Oxford academic Iris Murdoch suffered from Alzheimer's disease, a description being written by her husband, the Oxford academic, John Bayley.

Iris Murdoch provided researchers with an ideal opportunity for a natural ('ecologically viable') 'within-subject' observation. By objective analysis, they compared her early writing style with the writing done when there was reason to believe that early signs of AD were present (Garrard *et al.*, 2005). A reduction in the complexity of the language used in the final novel was noted. Reviews labelled it as disappointing in comparison to earlier works.

The researchers suggest that Iris Murdoch exemplifies a subtle cognitive decline that can be present years before overt symptoms appear.

What might the creative work of the famous novelist Iris Murdoch tell us about Alzheimer's disease?

Source: © Julian Calder/CORBIS.

The cognitive deficit

Memory

An early failure of episodic memory is a feature of AD. After this, there tends to be dysfunction of semantic memory. For example, the AD patient might respond 'hippopotamus' or more broadly 'animal' on being shown a picture of a rhinoceros.

In some respects, AD resembles the amnesic syndrome. In both cases, performance can be normal in tasks that involve procedural memory, such as sensory-motor skills (Brandt and Rich, 1995). However, AD patients can show certain selective deficits of memory (e.g. spatial memory) not shown in the amnesic syndrome.

Knowledge of the self (e.g. what kind of person am I?) can be preserved in AD, in the face of the broader loss of episodic and semantic memories (Klein *et al.*, 2002b).

Attention and executive control

AD patients show deficits in attention (Francis *et al.*, 1999). Some researchers characterize the disorder as a lack of awareness (Perry *et al.*, 1999), including that of the impairment itself. Patients often have difficulty shifting attention, e.g. between local and global processing (Perry and Hodges, 1999). Problems with divided attention are seen when AD patients are exposed to a conversation between two or more people and are asked to identify 'who said what?'

The central executive often shows signs of malfunction, since AD patients have difficulty in allocating processing capacity within working memory, holding a given cognition in focus and inhibiting inappropriate responses (Baddeley *et al.*, 1991).

Psychiatric symptoms

AD patients sometimes exhibit 'psychiatric symptoms' (Lopez and Becker, 2004). These include psychotic symptoms, such as hallucinations and delusions, as well as disruptive behaviour, e.g. aggression. Apathy is commonly seen (Morris and Hannesdottir, 2004).

Fracture lines

Access to the meaning of words can be impaired, while their correct grammatical use is retained (Chertkow and Bub, 1990). A group of AD patients were able to distinguish objects from non-objects as well as were controls. However, they were impaired in the ability to attach a name to the objects.

For some AD patients, perception of individual items and appreciation of their semantic significance are intact only if the items appear in a simple context. Other items disrupt perception of target items (Saffran *et al.*, 1990). This is demonstrated by the 'tablecloth experiment'. People are asked to close their eyes, an item is placed on the table and they are then asked to open their eyes and 'pick up the thing on the table'. Patterns on the tablecloth make the task more difficult.

Changes in gross brain structure and activity

Introduction

AD is somewhat selective to regions of brain and types of cell within regions (Damasio *et al.*, 1990). Gross changes in various structures are noted. The gyri become thin whereas the ventricles and sulci (Chapter 5) are enlarged (Figure 22.1). Most atrophy is in temporal lobe structures, e.g. hippocampus and entorhinal cortex (a region of cortex in contact with the hippocampus). There is a marked reduction in cerebral blood flow and glucose metabolism in the temporal lobe, indicative of loss of neurons or lower activity in remaining neurons or both (Morris, 1996c). A spread of pathology from the temporal lobes to parietal and frontal lobes can be associated with a disruption of attention, in addition to an initial impairment of memory (Perry and Hodges, 1999).

Linking structure and function

There is a correspondence between brain regions that exhibit hypo-metabolism (as revealed during PET scans) and the loss of faculties normally associated with these structures (Morris, 1996a). Degeneration of pathways linking particular structures can be linked to the normal

Figure 22.1 Sections through human brains. Left: Alzheimer's patient; right: control brain
Source: Alfred Pasieka/Science Photo Library

interdependence between these structures as the basis of features of cognition.

The entorhinal cortex is a channel of communication between other cortical structures and the hippocampus. Degeneration of the hippocampus and the closely associated cortex occurs early in the disorder and underlies the early disruption of episodic memory (Morris and Becker, 2004). As measured by MRI, reductions in hippocampal volume and deficits in episodic memory can serve as a warning ('preclinical') sign of a risk of AD before the full symptoms appear. They are predictive (a 'diagnostic marker'), albeit not perfectly, of a transition from 'mild cognitive impairment' to full AD (Frisoni *et al.*, 2010). Brain atrophy correlates with disruption at a cellular level.

Degeneration of the temporal and parietal cortex is associated with disruption of language and semantic memory. Low levels of metabolism ('hypo-metabolism') of the parietal lobe correspond to a disruption of attention (Parasuraman, 2004). Conversely, sparing of the motor cortex from pathology is correlated with a preservation of motor skills (Damasio *et al.*, 1990). Motor skills are also associated with the basal ganglia and cerebellum among other regions (Chapter 10) and these areas are preserved in AD.

A gradient of pathology can sometimes be seen, extending from the so-called higher-order cortical areas, where more abstract computation is performed (Chapter 8), to primary sensory areas, e.g. visual cortex, where little pathology is seen.

Connections between cortical regions, assumed to be essential for executive function, are disrupted (Perry and Hodges, 1999). Although loss of executive function points to frontal damage, some reports suggest that frontal regions are affected later and often less severely than other areas (Morris, 1996c). Executive function requires the capacities to call upon memories located in the temporal cortex. So, loss of executive function might be caused by affected regions outside the frontal region. Psychotic symptoms are particularly associated with disruption to regions of prefrontal cortex and anterior regions of temporal cortex (Lopez and Becker, 2004).

In some cases, cerebral asymmetry (Chapter 20) in reduced metabolism can be linked to aspects of cognitive decline. For example, visuospatial decline is associated with right hemispheric hypo-metabolism, whereas verbal deficits are associated with left hemisphere hypo-metabolism (Morris, 1996b,c).

Occasionally, on performing a cognitive task, AD patients show a more widespread activation of cortical structures than controls. This suggests that failures can sometimes trigger recruitment of processing capacity elsewhere. Disruption of the corpus callosum interferes with inter-hemispheric communication (Morris, 2004).

A genetic factor

AD is not 'genetically determined', unlike Huntington's disease (Chapter 2). However, a number of genes appear to exert a tendency towards its appearance. As one such, an allele of the *ApoE* gene, termed the ε4 allele, has been identified (Reitz and Mayeux, 2009). Changes in cognition in individuals with this genotype can be observed, even in the absence of dementia (possible 'preclinical signs'). People aged 50–65 years and with the allele but not showing dementia tend to have reduced metabolism in various cortical regions (Reiman *et al.*, 1996) and some mild failures of episodic memory (Bondi *et al.*, 1999). These are possible warning signs for AD.

Cellular changes

At a cellular level, the first stage of AD can be characterized as the 'cell sickness stage' (Small, 2005). Neurons start to show malfunction in terms of reduced activity. In the second phase, the 'histological stage', an accumulation of pathological material is observed (described shortly). The final stage, the 'cell death stage', consists of the loss of neurons, seen as gross changes in brain volume (Figure 22.1). Detection of the cell sickness stage, associated with mild cognitive impairment, could perhaps offer most hope for therapeutic intervention. PET and fMRI neuroimaging can detect the lowered metabolic activity characterizing this stage.

A feature of AD is the presence in the brain of abnormal tissue, termed 'neurofibrillary tangles' and 'senile plaques' ('neuritic plaques') (Damasio *et al.*, 1990). A neurofibrillary tangle is initially found within neurons, where it disrupts neural communication. It later comes to represent the remains of a once-functioning neuron that has degenerated. Senile plaques are extracellular pathological material that arises from the degeneration of cells. Postmortem staining of brain tissue reveals the presence of such material.

Senile plaques contain ß-amyloid protein (Morris, 1996c). This accumulates during the illness (McDonald and Overmier, 1998). The fact that injections of ß-amyloid protein into rats cause neuronal degeneration and impairment of memory suggests a causal role in AD, though there are some doubts on this (Neve and Robakis, 1998).

Recent research has established a serious complication to the simple picture: these cellular measures of pathology can also be found in the brains of elderly people *without* cognitive signs of dementia (Fotuhi *et al.*, 2009). People *with* AD frequently show additional signs of pathology, such as damage to blood vessels in the brain.

A diagnosis based on behavioural and cognitive tests is provisional until autopsy, when biological changes can be investigated.

Neurotransmitter changes

Abnormalities in various neurotransmitters are seen in AD (Monti and Contestabile, 2009). The disorder probably reflects disturbed interactions between neurochemical pathways. However, a principal focus of investigation is a deficiency in cholinergic transmission.

Cholinergic transmission

Acetylcholine (ACh) has a role in attention, learning and memory (Francis *et al.*, 1999). Most ACh derives from the terminals of neurons which project to the cortex from subcortical sites.

Alzheimer's patients show deficits of the enzyme choline acetyltransferase (ChAT), which is responsible for the synthesis of ACh. Hence, depletion of ACh and failures of cholinergic transmission occur in the cerebral cortex and are thought to form an important basis of AD (Parasuraman, 2004). This is termed the **cholinergic hypothesis** of AD. Disruption of cholinergic transmission is seen early in the disease and its magnitude correlates with the degree of cognitive impairment.

A causal link from ACh disruption to cognitive impairment is suggested by the observation that, in controls, temporary blocking of cholinergic transmission (e.g. with antagonists) produces similar symptoms of memory impairment (Curran and Kopelman, 1996). A possible animal model of such features consists of making lesions that damage the ascending cholinergic pathways (Robbins *et al.*, 1997). Some of the resultant cognitive deficits appear to reflect disrupted attention.

Therapy consists of trying to increase cholinergic transmission. This can occur by administration of substances that boost ACh synthesis, block the breakdown of ACh at the synapse, act as agonists to ACh or boost its release (Monti and Contestabile, 2009) (Figure 22.2). Such drugs can offer some limited hope of delaying the advance of AD.

Suppose that an intervention boosts cholinergic transmission. Unless this is targeted, the effect will be a general one. Cholinergic systems other than the target neurons are likely to exhibit exaggerated function. For instance, brain regions unaffected by AD, e.g. brain stem and thalamus (Richards, 1996) and the ANS, employ ACh. Gastrointestinal tract discomfort is a common side-effect of drugs that target ACh (Francis *et al.*, 1999). Sceptics suggest that in some cases chemical therapy is analogous to trying to solve the problems of a country with a petrol shortage by flying over it in helicopters and pouring petrol over it (Baddeley, 1997).

Not all evidence suggests that the deficit in cholinergic transmission is primary (Damasio *et al.*, 1990). Although patients tend to show cholinergic deficiencies, some have normal levels of cholinergic activity, indexed

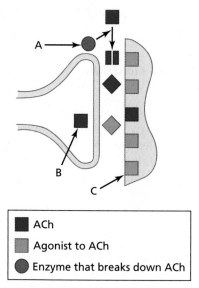

Key:
- ■ ACh
- ▦ Agonist to ACh
- ● Enzyme that breaks down ACh

Figure 22.2 Some targets for ACh-related drugs in treating AD. A, inhibit enzyme that breaks down ACh; B, boost synthesis of ACh; C, inject agonist to ACh.

by, for example, ChAT levels. Conversely, other disorders that do not involve dementia are associated with an ACh deficiency.

Glutamatergic transmission

A theory proposed as an addition to the cholinergic hypothesis is the glutamatergic hypothesis. Glutamate is a principal excitatory amino acid (EAA) neurotransmitter within the brain (van Wageningen *et al.*, 2010). A major target of cholinergic neurons appears to be EAA neurons (Francis *et al.*, 1999). Loss of EAA neurotransmission might be exacerbated by loss of ACh input. Glutamatergic neurons convey information between cortical regions and from the cortex to other regions, e.g. to the thalamus and basal ganglia (Francis *et al.*, 1993). There is extensive use of glutamatergic neurons in the input and output pathways of the hippocampus. Evidence suggests that such pathways degenerate at an early stage of AD.

Protective factors

Surprisingly, some individuals have considerable damage to neural systems indicative of AD but show little or no cognitive decline (Erten-Lyons *et al.*, 2009). A larger brain and, in particular, a larger hippocampus were associated with such retained cognitive function.

Given that individuals vary greatly in how they are affected by a degree of neurodegeneration, naturally there is great interest in how to explain this and how to find potential protective factors (Petrosini *et al.*, 2009).

An explanatory concept is that of 'reserve', i.e. aspects of brain structure and function can be potentially available to compensate for pathological changes. Reserve might in part depend upon earlier experience, such as a high educational level, as well as physical activity. Education appears not to prevent AD but can offer some protection against the severity of its symptoms. A brain with high reserve has the capacity to show compensatory plasticity in the face of neural damage.

Good diet, exercise and cognitive enrichment might result in a higher density of neural connections in the brain, with potential redundancy of neural circuitry (Fotuhi *et al.*, 2009). This could offer alternative routes of information processing when cellular disruption occurs. Obviously it is a large leap to go from human education to the study of non-humans. However, could there be an animal model of 'reserve' that would demonstrate sensitivity to early environmental factors such as enrichment and novelty (Petrosini *et al.*, 2009)? In rats, features of cortical neuronal structure (e.g. growth of dendrites, number of synaptic vesicles) are enhanced by environmental complexity. Such enrichment improves cognition and the capacity to compensate for experimentally induced neurodegeneration.

To end, AD remains a very distressing condition for many families and it is an imperative to find a cure for it.

Section summary

1 Alzheimer's disease is a dementia associated with progressive degeneration of the brain.

2 An early feature is a failure of episodic memory.

3 Loss of semantic memory and disruption of attention, language, reasoning and spatial ability typically follow.

4 The defining feature of AD is biological, the presence of amyloid-containing plaques and neurofibrillary tangles.

5 Neurochemical disturbances, e.g. to acetylcholine and glutamate, are seen.

☞ Test your knowledge

22.2 How might cholinergic neurotransmission be boosted?

Answer on page 586

Schizophrenia

Introduction

Consider the following accounts made by people with schizophrenia:

'... I avoided going out because people on the street could read my thoughts. My mind was transparent ... I complained of hearing voices telling me to do different things, which I felt compelled to do ... I felt everyone was against me, even the nurses and doctors ...' (22-year-old man, Joe, cited by Birchwood and Jackson, 2001).

'... I announced to my aged father, who was in bed, Satan in the form of the Loch Ness Monster was going to land on the lawn and do it for us if we both remained together in the house. By this time, I heard the voice pretty constantly ... the voice continued for four months' (26-year-old man, Errol, cited by Birchwood and Jackson, 2001).

The condition **schizophrenia** covers a range of sub-conditions, having features in common. In the popular imagination, schizophrenia is taken to mean 'two people in one head'. This is misleading, since there is the one unitary individual, albeit a disturbed one. In 1911, Bleuler described schizophrenia as 'the 'splitting' of the differing psychic functions' within one individual (Bleuler, 1950, p. 8), characterized by 'a specific type of alteration of thinking, feeling, and relation to the external world' (p. 9). The split is typically between cognition and emotion, e.g. inappropriate emotional reactions to events.

Core symptoms include (a) hallucinations, often auditory (e.g. 'hearing' absent voices that make utterances of a personal nature), (b) **delusions** and (c) thought disorder, e.g. as manifest in incomprehensible speech (Frith, 1987). Delusions are beliefs that are at odds with cultural norms, e.g. (i) that actions are controlled by an outside agency, (ii) that messages for the sufferer are being inserted into TV broadcasts or (iii) that the sufferer is Napoleon.

The patient's ability to 'recognize reality' is impaired (Birchwood and Jackson, 2001). Of course, many people hold views that are at odds with cultural norms but we would not say that such eccentrics have serious mental illness. For people with schizophrenia, abnormal consciousness and behaviour are experienced as distressing and they can sometimes be a danger to themselves or others. Typically, there can be 'emotional blunting', loss of volition (apathy) and a withdrawal from contact with the outside world.

The age of onset of the illness is most usually in the mid to late 20s. For some, there is just one episode of schizophrenia but for most there are repeated episodes or the condition becomes chronic (Birchwood and Jackson, 2001).

Describing and classifying schizophrenic behaviour

Schizophrenia is classified as a **psychosis**, in that there is a break with reality. Signs and symptoms of schizophrenia are classified into positive and negative and most patients exhibit both (Frith, 1992; van Os and Kapur, 2009). The positive group is defined by what is *present* relative to controls, e.g. delusions, thought disorder, hallucinations and repetitive stereotyped behaviour. The negative group is defined by *absence*, e.g. deficiencies of motivation, social interaction, energy, fluency of speech and normal signs of affect. However, this distinction is not entirely clear-cut (Frith, 1987). For example, does thought disorder exemplify the presence of abnormal cognition or the absence of normal cognition? Another classification is into experiential ('inner world') symptoms and observable signs. Experiential symptoms include delusions and hallucinations. Observable signs include social withdrawal and abnormalities of speech.

Kraepelin (1919, p. 21) observed: 'We almost always meet in the train of thought of the patients indications of stereotypy, of the persistence of single ideas'. It seems there is a deficiency in the ability to perform temporal ordering and balancing of cognition and stimulus information. He wrote (p. 25):

the patients are not in a position to accomplish that mental grouping of ideas which is requisite for their survey and comparison, their subordination among one another and for the discovery of contradictions. In this respect they resemble dreamers . . .

Bleuler (1950, p. 16) described the guidance of normal thought and behaviour by a goal, involving exclusion of irrelevant thoughts. By contrast, he gave (p. 26) the example of a schizophrenic patient who, on being asked to name members of her family, responded with 'father, son' followed by 'and the Holy Ghost'. This is not an arbitrary association (Chapman and Chapman, 1973); it might be quite appropriate in a theological context. However, *in the context* of the utterance, it was an intrusion into the rational sequence of thoughts/words.

Overcoming the tendency to react to stimuli having well-established associations, presents difficulty for people with schizophrenia. Sensory strength ('salience') tends to dominate over meaning ('semantic relevance'). For example, in being asked to generate lists of bird names and producing 'swan', the patient is then likely to give 'lake' rather than, say, 'duck' (Frith, 1992). Cognitive processing is captured by the association 'swan-lake'.

There are deficiencies in using a theory of mind (intention) of the other. Hence, metaphor is missed in the interests of literal meaning. Kalat (2004) offers the example that, on being told 'When the cat is away the mice will play', the person with schizophrenia tends to take this as a literal account of animal behaviour, rather than a metaphor for human action.

Whereas people with schizophrenia can perform normally on relatively straightforward motor tasks, difficulties emerge with increasing task complexity (Schmolling, 1983). This points to a disturbance to central integrative control. For negative signs, Frith (1992) suggests that deficiencies of action, social interaction and speech exemplify a defect of *self-instigated* behaviour. Typically, a patient responds to questions but will not enlarge upon the straightforward answer.

At a psychological (i.e. cognitive) level, how do we explain what has gone wrong? The next section addresses this.

Psychological explanations

This section looks at several psychological explanations for what goes wrong in schizophrenia. Each captures a different feature and so they are not in competition. Later sections link the psychological phenomena to their biological bases.

Immediacy hypothesis

Salzinger (1971) proposed the **immediacy hypothesis**: schizophrenic behaviour is (p. 601) 'more often controlled by stimuli which are immediate in their spatial and temporal environment . . . '. For example, in speaking, people with schizophrenia come under the control of words that they have just uttered rather than being able to suppress their influence on the basis of having just uttered them. Hence they tend to repeat these same words.

Goal-directed action, whether in external behaviour or thinking, requires central executive control. This accentuates some intrinsically weak but contextually salient ideas and associations to bring them into expression. It inhibits those that are physically salient but semantically inappropriate to current intentions. This is impaired in schizophrenia.

Regularity and novelty

Hemsley (1996, p. 143) notes that stored information:

> normally interacts with the encoding, comprehension, and/or retrieval of new information by guiding attention, expectancies, interpretation, and memory search. Schizophrenia, therefore, is viewed as a disturbance in the moment by moment integration of stored material with current sensory input.

Stimuli that are experienced as familiar by controls tend to be treated as novel by people with schizophrenia, i.e. they are deficient in exploiting 'redundancy'. A move from controlled to automatic processing (Chapter 10) exemplifies the normal exploitation of stored regularity, by which information processing demands are minimized and this is deficient in schizophrenia (Serper *et al.*, 1990).

Metarepresentation

Frith (1992) suggests that schizophrenia involves a failure of a **metarepresentation** of the self (which underlies normal self-awareness). Not only do we have goals and intentions but *we are aware* that *we* are having them. We form mental representations of ourselves in relation to our intentions and their achievement or otherwise. Such a theory is needed to assess the intentions of others, for example, in distinguishing pretence from serious intent. The intentions of others are likely to be misinterpreted since people with schizophrenia show deficiencies in interpreting the emotions of others (Wong and Van Tol, 2003). This appears relevant to delusions of persecution.

Action control

Closely connected to the notion of disrupted metarepresentation, Frith (1992) argued that schizophrenia is a disturbance to the instigation of action; patients feel that they do not control their own actions. Rather, an external agent 'pulls the strings'.

As positive symptoms, thoughts are perceived as being inserted into the head from outside. In auditory hallucinations, the voice might be recognized as being the person's own but is nonetheless felt as alien. Whether behaviour or a private thought, the person perceives something *unwilled* to be happening.

A personal angle

External agency

Mellor (1970, p. 18), in Manchester, England, reports a conversation with a female patient, a 29-year-old shorthand typist:

> When I reach my hand for the comb it is my hand and arm which move, and my fingers pick up the pen, but I don't control them . . . . I sit there watching them move, and they are quite independent, what they do is nothing to do with me . . . . I am just a puppet who is manipulated by cosmic strings. When the strings are pulled my body moves and I cannot prevent it.

Comparing theories

These theories have a common feature: schizophrenic behaviour reveals a breakdown of cognition as used in rational thought processing, the control of behaviour and social interaction. There is a move away from sequential control by appropriate internal representations and towards determination by external stimuli and irrelevant internally produced cognition. There is a fault in the processing of 'what leads to what' and 'what causes what'.

Having considered psychological aspects of schizophrenia, we can now link these to biology.

Disrupted brain regions

Introduction

Insight can be obtained from examining the brains of people with schizophrenia and comparing with individuals not suffering from schizophrenia but who exhibit some similar symptoms, e.g. from trauma and tumours (Weinberger, 1987). This occurs most frequently when damage affects subcortical brain regions, e.g. those of the limbic system. In non-schizophrenic patients, unusual electrical activity particularly in the temporal cortex, amygdala and hippocampus is associated with hallucinations and perceptual distortions.

Concerning the negative symptoms, e.g. social withdrawal and loss of motivation, these are most commonly associated with lesions of the frontal lobe, especially the dorsolateral prefrontal cortex (Weinberger, 1987).

Researchers report lower than normal sizes both of the overall brain of patients with schizophrenia and of various brain regions, as well as under-activity in such regions. However, there are also counter-examples of normal overall volumes of whole brains and regions, so these are trends rather than absolutely reliable indicators (Wong and Van Tol, 2003).

Evidence from ventricle size

Enlarged ventricle size in patients was important in directing researchers and psychiatrists to the biological bases of schizophrenia (Bullmore and Fletcher, 2003). However, enlarged ventricles are rather a non-specific biological index, not peculiar to schizophrenia. Indeed, there appears to be no unique index (by analogy with crime fiction, no 'smoking gun') of this condition.

The hippocampus

Patients with schizophrenia typically show a reduction in the size of the hippocampus that cannot be accounted for by overall shrinkage of the brain (Nelson *et al.*, 1998). Schmajuk and Tyberg (1991) note a relationship between schizophrenia and pregnancy or birth complications (PBC). A combination of PBC and a genetic predisposition to hippocampal vulnerability might bias towards the condition. Hippocampal damage could result from anoxia (lack of oxygen) or a viral infection. The hippocampus has connections to the mesolimbic dopamine system (described shortly), which might mediate its role in schizophrenia.

The hippocampus appears to be overactive in schizophrenia. This leads some to propose deep brain stimulation of this structure at a frequency that would inhibit neural activity, as a potential form of therapy (Mikell *et al.*, 2009).

The cortex

Neuroimaging studies permit insights into structural and functional differences between control brains and those of people with schizophrenia. Grey matter reductions in a number of cortical areas have been observed (Glahn *et al.*, 2008). Occasionally schizophrenia appears in childhood. With the help of MRI scanning, such cases offer an opportunity to study brain development and compare this with development in unaffected individuals (Thompson *et al.*, 2001). Figure 22.3 compares the loss of grey matter observed in two such populations over a five-year period. The accelerated loss in affected individuals is evident in a range of cortical regions: frontal, temporal and parietal.

Another neuroimaging study asked, what is the biological basis of hallucinations ('hearing voices')? McGuire and Shah (1993) performed a PET scan on the brains of schizophrenic patients at the time when they were experiencing auditory hallucinations and when they had recovered from hallucinations. Increased blood flow was seen particularly in Broca's area (which underlies the production of speech), when auditory hallucinations were experienced.

Figure 22.4 shows a result of a PET scan of a patient who experienced both auditory and visual hallucinations (Silbersweig *et al.*, 1995). He was requested to relax, with eyes closed and to press a button when the hallucination occurred. Although the primary visual and auditory cortices were not activated, later stages of processing that normally derive information from these channels were activated. The result points to common features between hallucinations and actual sensory experience in terms of their biological bases. Note the lack of activation in the prefrontal cortex, which might also be significant in terms of the lack of volition concerning the experiences. Unlike in the study by McGuire and Shah, Broca's area was not activated.

People with schizophrenia often show a 'hypofrontal' pattern, e.g. low frontal blood flow (measured by rCBF) when performing certain cognitive tasks (Berman and

Figure 22.3 Average rate of grey matter loss over a 5-year period in (a) controls and (b) adolescents suffering from schizophrenia.

Source: Thompson et al. (2001, Fig. 1a, p. 11651).

Weinberger, 1991; Wong and Van Tol, 2003), e.g. the Wisconsin card sorting test (Chapter 6). This task exemplifies the use of context: participants need to sort cards according to a rule that they extract from observing their earlier choices and from the experimenter's feedback. Although patients with PFC damage exhibit some similarities with schizophrenic patients, there are also differences and so this could only be a part of the problem with schizophrenia (Fuster, 1999). Theorists speculate that, in schizophrenia, abnormalities arise in cortical–subcortical pathways of which the PFC forms a part.

Deficiencies in working memory, planning and executive function suggest abnormality of the dorsolateral prefrontal cortex (DLPFC) (Abi-Dargham, 2004). As just noted, there is overlap in the symptoms of schizophrenia and frontal lobe damage, specifically damage to the DLPFC, e.g. low motivation, social withdrawal,

Figure 22.4 Brain activity during the experience of hallucinations as studied by PET.

Source: Reprinted by permission from Macmillan Publishers Ltd: A functional neuroanatomy of hallucinations in schizophrenia, *Nature*, 378, Fig. 2a, p. 178 (Silbersweig, D. A. *et al.* 1995), copyright 1995.

unchanging facial expressions and impaired judgment (Frith, 1992). In both disorders, there are problems with the use of working memory.

The medial prefrontal cortex (MPFC) shows abnormalities in schizophrenia (Wong and Van Tol, 2003). Projections from this region play a role in modulating subcortical dopamine levels. The MPFC and hippocampus are implicated in schizophrenia and they not only both influence subcortical dopamine levels but are interconnected.

Patients have difficulty with attributing affective (e.g. reward) value to predictive cues, a process associated with the orbitofrontal part of the PFC (Gold *et al.*, 2008).

We now turn to a principal neurochemical pathway that is implicated in schizophrenia. Thereby, we can link the structures just described with the neurochemistry of the neurons involved.

The dopamine hypothesis

Evidence suggests that deviations from normal in multiple neurochemical systems are implicated in schizophrenia (Buchanan *et al.*, 2007). However, dopamine (DA) has formed the principal focus for investigators, though the assumption of its centrality has not gone unchallenged (Moncrieff, 2009). The **dopamine hypothesis** proposes that a biological basis of schizophrenia consists of an abnormality within DA neurotransmission (Carlsson, 1998; Carlsson and Carlsson, 1991). Consider the efficacy of **neuroleptic drugs**, such as chlorpromazine, in treating schizophrenia (Lipska *et al.*, 1999). These reduce DA transmission. Conversely, drugs that enhance DA transmission, e.g. amphetamine and L-dopa, can make the condition worse.

A role of dopamine in the control of behaviour is to attribute 'motivational salience' to events (Kapur, 2003). Normally, a neutral stimulus acquires such salience *only by virtue of repeated pairing* with an unconditional stimulus. The neutral stimulus becomes a conditional stimulus able to attract attention and, in the case of reward-associated events, act as a 'magnet' for behaviour. Conversely, a stimulus paired with an aversive UCS would acquire a fear-evoking capacity. This process appears aberrant in schizophrenia, which can be characterized as (i) inappropriate dopamine activity and therefore (ii) correspondingly inappropriate salience ('importance') being attached to events.

Suppose that, in schizophrenia, dopamine is activated in a similar way regardless of the sensory event or cognition. Thereby, inappropriate salience would act in two 'mirror image' ways. Events that would be described as neutral ('redundant') by controls can attract relatively high salience (Kapur, 2003), which could contribute to the positive symptoms. For example, innocuous events might appear threatening. Internally generated cognitions might also attract undue salience, thereby contributing to hallucinations and delusions. Conversely, objectively significant events fail to attract sufficient salience. Negative symptoms of schizophrenia, e.g. apathy and social withdrawal, could arise as a result of attaching inappropriately low salience to what would, to controls, be motivationally potent events (Roiser *et al.*, 2009; Ziauddeen and Murray, 2010).

The reports of patients commonly lend support to this notion, e.g. 'I felt that there was some overwhelming significance in this' (Kapur, 2003, p. 15). The 'understanding and narrative' in the conscious minds of patients might arise from attempts to make sense of events having inappropriate salience (van Os and Kapur, 2009). Van Os (2009) suggests replacing the term 'schizophrenia' with 'salience syndrome', which would locate the disorder on a continuum with normal attribution of salience to items in the world.

Studies of schizophrenic brains do not suggest an overall increase in DA activity (Davis *et al.*, 1991). Rather, subcortical DA *over-activity* appears to coexist with prefrontal cortical DA *under-activity* (Buchanan *et al.*, 2007; Weinberger, 1987). Under-activity could give rise to the negative symptoms such as apathy. Such observations have led to the dopamine hypothesis being refined. Neuroleptics exert a beneficial effect at subcortical D_2 receptors. However, their action at DA D_2 receptors in the prefrontal cortex might also bring therapeutic value (Winterer and Weinberger, 2004). Reduced cortical D_2 activity might, in effect, increase the relative activity at cortical D_1 receptors. D_1 receptors appear to be under-stimulated, which is implicated in failures of working memory in schizophrenia (Abi-Dargham, 2004).

So-called 'animal models' of features of schizophrenia also point to abnormalities of DA transmission in particular brain regions.

Animal models of features of schizophrenia

As a disturbance to thinking and the will, schizophrenia might appear to be a peculiarly human disorder. Doubtless some features cannot be captured by animal models. However, a number of experimental procedures used on non-humans produce results resembling schizophrenia (Ellenbroek and Cools, 1990).

Amphetamine-induced effects

In humans, amphetamine (which stimulates DA transmission) can exacerbate the symptoms of schizophrenia and induce symptoms in people without schizophrenia (Kokkinidis and Anisman, 1980). Users report its effect as being to produce 'an acute sense of novelty and curiosity' (Ellinwood, 1967, p. 278) and they experience auditory and visual hallucinations.

In non-humans, behaviour that resembles schizophrenia is triggered by amphetamine (Chapter 18). This includes stereotyped repetitive behaviour, the idiosyncratic focus of attention on a seemingly arbitrary object ('abnormal salience') and self-grooming of particular body parts (Ellenbroek and Cools, 1990).

Amphetamine-injected monkeys exhibit persistence, cognitive inflexibility and reduced social interaction. The frantic grooming of a particular bit of skin (analogous to skin-picking by human users) suggests triggering by hallucinatory bugs (Nielsen *et al.*, 1983). Such monkeys show eye-tracking, grabbing into the air and attacking, as if targeted to non-existent objects, which might capture features of psychotic hallucinations (Nielsen *et al.*, 1983; Schlemmer and Davis, 1983).

People with schizophrenia tend to persist with directing behaviour to a stimulus even though it is no longer associated with reward (Ridley and Baker, 1983). Similarly, amphetamine appears to amplify the capacity of particular stimuli to trigger behaviour in situations where controls can inhibit such tendencies (Frith, 1992). This behaviour might have features in common with the maintenance of psychotic delusional beliefs and persistence of cognitive set (cf. Shakow, 1963).

Prepulse inhibition

Schizophrenic patients exhibit a problem of overload when stimuli appear in rapid succession (Geyer *et al.*, 1990). They suffer fragmentation of cognition and action in a situation that would, to controls, represent a coherent and manageable sequence of events. A possible animal model of this is as follows.

On presenting a loud sound or air-puff, animals, including humans, exhibit a 'startle response' (Chapter 12). Let us use 'S2' to refer to a stimulus that triggers this response. 'S1' describes a weaker stimulus that does not trigger startle. The response to S2 alone can be compared with that shown to S2 presented in association with S1. If a stimulus (S2) that normally triggers startle is preceded by a weak stimulus (S1) given 60–120 ms before S2, controls show inhibition of the startle response (Geyer *et al.*, 1990). Since S1 is of inadequate strength to trigger the startle response itself, the effect of S2 can be clearly compared under the two conditions (Figure 22.5). The influence of S1 on the response to S2 is termed **prepulse inhibition (PPI)** and is deficient in people with schizophrenia, i.e. they show a relatively large response to S2. Figure 22.6 shows the deficiency, as measured by eyelid movements.

Rats injected with the DA agonist apomorphine show a reduction in the strength of prepulse inhibition (Geyer *et al.*, 1990). Micro-injections into the nucleus accumbens but not other brain regions disrupt prepulse inhibition. Geyer *et al.* relate this to the observation of

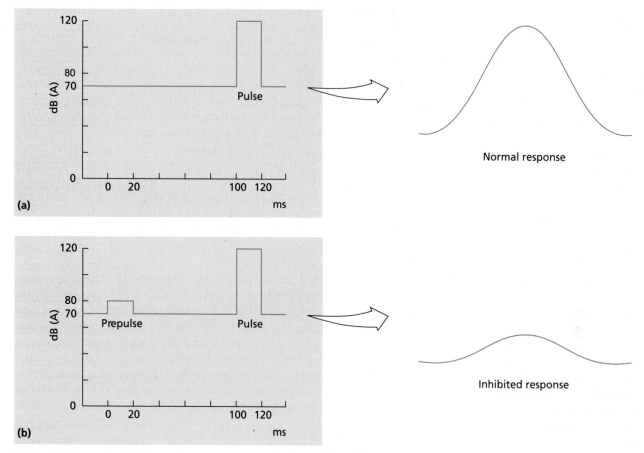

Figure 22.5 Prepulse inhibition: (a) response to a pulse alone (S2) and (b) response to the same pulse (S2) when a 'prepulse' (S1) is given.
Source: Geyer et al. (1990, p. 486).

mesolimbic DA over-activity in schizophrenia and suggest that the disruption of prepulse inhibition might capture features of the human condition.

Latent inhibition

Normally, after exposure to repetitive stimuli that signal nothing of significance, the stimuli fail to engage conscious processing. As noted, schizophrenic patients tend to pay attention to stimuli that are ignored by controls. For example, a repeated anonymous car horn heard from a distance could be interpreted as a personal message.

The term **latent inhibition** refers to the effect of pre-exposure to a stimulus on retarding the subsequent capacity of the stimulus to form predictive associations (Solomon and Staton, 1982; Young *et al.*, 1993). Suppose a group of rats are given pairings of tone and shock and then the capacity of the tone to elicit fear is tested (Figure 22.7). Group 1 rats are subject to such conditioning and exhibit fear to the tone. Group 2 rats are treated in the same way, except that a prior phase of exposure to the tone alone is given. Such prior exposure reduces

the subsequent capacity of the tone to trigger fear. It seems that, in the phase of prior exposure, the rats learn that the tone signals nothing of importance; it is 'redundant'. This makes it more difficult to learn later that the tone predicts shock. Group 3 rats are treated like group 2 but in the phase of prior exposure to the tone they are injected with amphetamine. Note that this disrupts the effect of the prior exposure, moving group 3 in the direction of group 1, an effect obtained also in humans (Solomon *et al.*, 1981).

Gray *et al.* (1991) describe this as 'over-attention' to what is classified as a redundant stimulus by controls. In rats, the effect of microinjections of amphetamine on latent inhibition is specific to the nucleus accumbens (Solomon and Staton, 1982). Excess DA in the prior-exposure phase is subsequently associated with attending to the tone. Schizophrenic patients tested in the acute phase of the illness fail to show latent inhibition, i.e. they exhibit over-attention to redundant stimuli. They act something like amphetamine-injected subjects (Group 3).

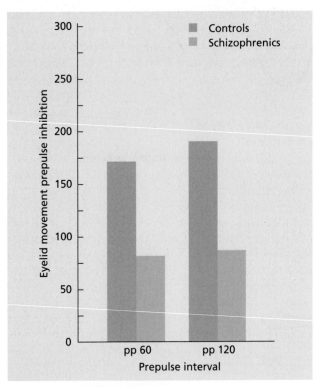

Figure 22.6 The magnitude of prepulse inhibition in controls and patients with schizophrenia. The graph shows not the response as such but the *difference* between the response to pulse alone and the response to pulse when accompanied by the prepulse. pp = prepulse interval in ms.

Source: Geyer *et al.* (1990, Fig. 2, p. 487).

Rats with hippocampal lesions

Rats with hippocampal lesions exhibit features in common with schizophrenic patients (Schmajuk and Tyberg, 1991). Hippocampal lesions disrupt the capacity to utilize contextual information. Similarly, people with schizophrenia have difficulty with utilizing context. Lesioned rats perform straightforward stimulus–response tasks with little problem but have difficulty with utilizing cognitive information in over-coming habits (Hirsh, 1974). Schizophrenic patients exhibit similar difficulties (Gold *et al.*, 2008). Prepulse inhibition is disrupted in rats with hippocampal lesions (Miller *et al.*, 2010) and there are indications of a similar effect in people with schizophrenia (Patterson *et al.*, 2008)

Common features

Are there common features in these models? Amphetamine boosts levels of DA, suggesting the involvement of a hyper-dopaminergic state in schizophrenia. The disruption of prepulse inhibition and latent inhibition by amphetamine appear to involve an over-reactivity to stimuli, a shift in the weighting of control away from cognitions (e.g. memories of past events) and to current sensory information processed out of context. These phenomena appear to fit Hemsley's argument on schizophrenia being a failure to contextualize sensory information (earlier). Abnormalities of neurotransmission in certain brain regions seem to give an abnormal weight to information that would be treated as redundant by controls. Hippocampal lesions disrupt contextual processing and prepulse inhibition.

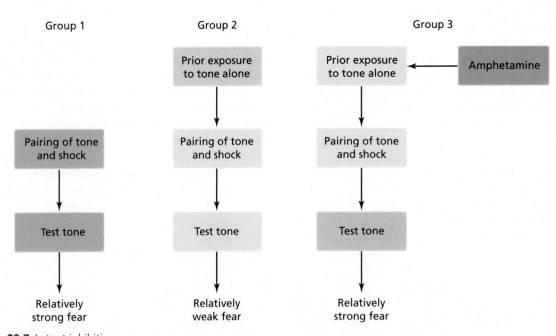

Figure 22.7 Latent inhibition.

We need now to ask when and how the disorder appears and to look at genetic, evolutionary and developmental factors.

Development, evolution, genes and environment

Multiple genetic and environmental factors appear to exert a bias towards abnormalities in neural development that underlie schizophrenia (van Os and Kapur, 2009). Any theory of interactive genetic–environmental development must mesh with the assumption that disturbed behaviour and mental processes reflect abnormality in the brain.

The role of genes

Twin studies suggest a genetic factor in schizophrenia (Gottesman and Moldin, 1998; Lenzenweger and Dworkin, 1998). There is a higher concordance (Chapter 6) of schizophrenia when comparing monozygotic (genetically identical) twins, than dizygotic ('fraternal' or 'non-identical') twins. If one half of the pair of monozygotic twins is affected, it is likely that the other half is also. However, the concordance of monozygotic twins is far from perfect, pointing to the role of environmental factors.

Evidence arises from close relatives of people with schizophrenia, who as yet show no signs of the disorder and consider themselves to be well (Fletcher, 2004). They tend to show certain mild cognitive abnormalities, as well as abnormal patterns of brain activity in those regions associated with schizophrenia. This again suggests a genetic contribution.

Understanding genes and schizophrenia is probably like understanding the role of genes in height or IQ (Chapter 2). Rather than a single gene, several appear to act jointly in their contribution to schizophrenia, although a focus of interest is upon an allele of the gene coding for the dopamine D2 receptor (Bertolino and Blasi, 2009). The genetic influence is probably not all-or-none but lies on a continuum throughout the whole population, and presents varying degrees of **liability** to the disorder.

With a strong liability, environmental factors would then be more likely to trigger it (Claridge, 1990). The environmental factor could be complications during the birth or later stress. How might interacting genetic and environmental factors be manifest? One possibility is in the disruption of dopamine neurotransmission, just discussed.

Developmental abnormalities

The age at which schizophrenia appears is most commonly in the 20s and 30s (Frith, 1992). Prior to this, certain relatively mild cognitive, emotional and motor abnormalities are commonly evident in those going on to manifest the disorder. They exhibit some lack of a sense of 'agency'. These indicators point to a long-term developmental course to what is later revealed more explicitly and unambiguously (Birchwood and Jackson, 2001). What could be the biological basis of such development?

Weinberger (1987) suggests that an abnormality in the development of the nervous system starting at the foetal stage is manifest in relatively mild abnormalities of cognition and behaviour in childhood. A possible specific biological basis is abnormal development of the hippocampus (Antonova and Kumari, 2010). Later, with further brain development, the trajectory of this same abnormality underlies the full expression of the disorder. There appears to be a relatively high incidence of trauma during pregnancy in those babies who subsequently develop schizophrenia. For example, after epidemics of influenza, there is an increased frequency of births of infants who develop schizophrenia (Sham et al., 1992). Another factor suggesting a developmental trajectory leading to the full-blown disorder is that the maturation of the dorsolateral prefrontal cortex only occurs in early adulthood. This structure is closely associated with schizophrenia (Weinberger, 1987).

Role of stress

What could trigger the initial signs of schizophrenia and why should symptoms return after years of being free of them? There are probably many factors but one possibility is psychosocial stress (Antonova and Kumari, 2010). In individuals with a tendency to schizophrenia, stressors such as those of disturbed family dynamics might be sufficient to trigger the symptoms or their reappearance. This is termed the **vulnerability model** (Zubin and Spring, 1977). It suggests that, the stronger the tendency, the milder the stress that is sufficient to reach the threshold of triggering the disorder. Of course, the experience of schizophrenia itself would be expected to constitute a stressor, with the risk of a vicious circle. Stressful events commonly occur in the lives of people prior to the onset of the disorder (Bebbington et al., 1993).

Stress causes the release of DA (Gray et al., 1991). Also, corticosteroids are triggered by stressors; they accentuate DA activity and are commonly at elevated levels in schizophrenia (Walker et al., 1998). Such elevation could be toxic to the hippocampus (Antonova and Kumari, 2010).

Evolutionary explanations

Schizophrenia exerts a terrible cost on sufferers and inflicts disruption on families. In functional terms, the fitness value of the sufferer is relatively low (Avila et al., 2001). Given that the evidence points to a genetic involvement, you might wonder why evolution has not selected out the alleles that are responsible.

Evolutionary psychology

Costs and benefits?

Suppose that, under some conditions, the particular alleles tend to confer an *advantage* on their possessors. However, under other conditions these same alleles can lead to schizophrenia. For example, it could be that possessing the alleles but without the experience of stressors in early development is advantageous, whereas with stressors it becomes disadvantageous. Life is invariably a trade-off between costs and benefits, and this could be one example.

Is there any evidence that the alleles underlying schizophrenia might under some conditions be advantageous? There are tantalizing suggestions, e.g. some similarities between artistically creative individuals and people with schizophrenia (Andreasen, 2005; Nettle and Clegg, 2006). These two groups tend to occur together in families. Finding novel creative solutions to problems of survival could surely have been an advantage in evolution. Furthermore, such individuals tend to be attractive to the opposite sex (Nettle and Clegg, 2006), the functional advantage of which seems clear!

Biological or social? A false dichotomy

Schizophrenia used to attract radical critiques of the 'medical model' (Barney, 1994), e.g. the 'anti-psychiatry' of the 1960s and 1970s (Laing, 1960; Szasz, 1971). Some suggested that there is no biological basis to schizophrenia; rather it is simply a way of reacting to an impossible social context. Simplistic social–biological dichotomies have now been shown to be seriously inadequate. However, we need to recognize (i) the role of stress in exacerbating the symptoms (Wright and Woodruff, 1995) and (ii) that genes are only suggested as bias factors. Recognizing a genetic factor does not undermine the importance of environmental determinants in the womb and later.

For an analogy, consider that high blood pressure lies on a continuum from low through normal to high. High blood pressure increases the chances of stroke and heart failure, etc. but it does not mean that they will inevitably follow. High blood pressure is 'biological', even though it is continuous with normal pressure (Claridge, 1990; van Os and Kapur, 2009).

The incidence of schizophrenia is higher in disadvantaged social groups, such as low-income immigrant families (Cooper, 2005; van Os and Kapur, 2009). Part of

this can be accounted for by 'social drift', i.e. a history of schizophrenia tends to cause social decline. However, not all can be explained in this way. Being brought up in a decaying inner-city area is a risk factor. Why socioeconomic disadvantage gives a bias to this condition is as yet unknown and is a topic of investigation. Stress would seem a probable candidate. Recognition of the socioeconomic factor and sharing the motivation to improve people's lives in no way undermines the importance of considering biological (e.g. genetic) factors.

Section summary

1 Signs and symptoms of schizophrenia can be divided into positive and negative.

2 Positive signs include delusions, thought disorder, hallucinations and a tendency to stereotyped behaviour. Negative signs include deficiencies of motivation and social interaction.

3 Schizophrenic behaviour exhibits a tendency towards control by physically present stimuli and away from control by representations and context.

4 A disturbance to dopaminergic neurotransmission appears to be a fundamental feature of the disorder. This manifests as aberrant incentive salience.

5 Injection of amphetamine mimics some symptoms of the disorder.

6 Disruption of inhibition of the startle reflex and latent inhibition are features of the condition and can be demonstrated in 'animal models'.

7 The neural abnormality underlying schizophrenia appears to emerge during the course of development.

8 Accounts in terms of biology *versus* social context are inherently misleading.

 Test your knowledge

22.3 What is it about the processing of a neutral stimulus that is disrupted by amphetamine injections?

22.4 For schizophrenia, what can be said about the concordance of identical twins, both in absolute terms and relative to fraternal twins?

Answers on page 586

Obsessive-compulsive disorder

Introduction

Consider the following accounts by people with **obsessive-compulsive disorder (OCD)**.

'... an irresistible intrusion of a disagreeable image, which you always wished away, but could not dismiss, an incessant persecution of a troublesome thought ...' *Samuel Johnson, 18th century English writer and philosopher.*

'... I found myself touching particular objects that were near me, and to which my fingers seemed to be attracted by an irresistible impulse ... what impelled me to these actions was the desire to prevent my mother's death ...' *George Borrow, 19th century English author and explorer.*

'... I heard the woman who sat next to me telling this other woman that she had just come back from the children's hospital where she had visited her grandson who had leukaemia. I immediately left; I registered in a hotel and washed for three days'. *Judy, an American OCD patient, reported by Dr Edna Foa.*

'I'm still thinking about the bad impression I must have made on the former colleague I met in the supermarket ...' *Herr Z., a German patient, in response to his psychiatrist's question, 'What are you thinking now?', posed 4 hours into a 9 hour session of brain surgery to treat OCD.*

Each consists of the repetitive intrusion into consciousness of an unwanted thought (Toates and Coschug-Toates, 2002). This usually frightens, shames or disgusts, and engages processing resources that would, for the sufferer, be better engaged with other cognition. The intrusion sounds an alarm and the brain is brought into a defensive ('security') mode (Szechtman and Woody, 2004).

The thought is associated with a compulsion: action that attempts to solve the problem. Examples include washing hands in response to the obsession of contamination, checking in response to the fear that a door is not locked or touching something to prevent a death. The obsession sometimes triggers a 'cognitive compulsion' rather than overt behaviour, i.e. a counter thought or extensive thinking ('rumination') that has the goal of solving the problem.

Certain common contents of obsessions are found across cultures and relate to adaptive considerations of security. However, in OCD, they are an irrational exaggeration of what is adaptive. For example, within limits, washing is adaptive, whereas washing hands for hours in detergent until they are bleeding is unambiguously pathological. Similarly, within limits, protecting the family and checking are surely of adaptive value. At times of scarcity, limited hoarding makes sense.

Defining and trying to explain OCD

People with OCD have insight: they realize that the intrusions arise internally rather than from an outside agency. They usually acknowledge irrationality and excessiveness. For example, 'knowledge' that the door is locked is inadequate to resist the 'habit-like' pressure to keep checking. In other words, there is competition between systems of processing within the brain (Szechtman and Woody, 2004).

A personal angle

OCD and Hollywood

The film producer and aviation pioneer Howard Hughes was obsessed with fear of contamination. He was depicted by Leonardo DiCaprio in the film *The Aviator*. DiCaprio was so keen to give an accurate portrayal that he was coached by the OCD expert Jeffrey Schwartz, author of *Brain Lock*. The actor also observed an OCD patient going about his rituals. DiCaprio had experienced mild 'obsessional quirks' when a child, such as not stepping on the cracks of the pavement, and these reappeared during shooting. As a result of the film, he developed a keen interest in the disorder and gave his highly valued support to OCD charity work.

Brain processes

Introduction

In OCD, there are indications of malfunction in the brain: a reduction in volume of the orbitofrontal cortex and abnormal activity within neural networks involving the prefrontal (e.g. orbitofrontal) cortex, striatum and thalamus (Menzies *et al.*, 2008). Also, damage to the striatum can trigger OCD. Functional neuroimaging reveals abnormalities of regional cerebral blood flow (rCBF) and glucose metabolism in the caudate nucleus of the basal ganglia and the orbitofrontal cortex (OFC) during baseline conditions (Chamberlain *et al.*, 2005). Figure 22.8 shows a PET scan of the brain of an OCD sufferer and a control. High levels of activity in the OFC could reflect conscious efforts to resolve the problem posed by the obsessions. However, other evidence points to underactivity in such brain regions during inhibitory tasks, suggesting a possible basis for how unwanted intrusions can occur (Page *et al.*, 2009). Evidence also suggests abnormalities in other brain regions outside the orbitofrontal–striatum–thalamus complex that is usually associated with OCD. For example, high activation of the cerebellum, a region associated with attention and planning, is observed (Menzies *et al.*, 2008).

It is possible to provoke the symptoms of OCD by presentation of individually specific trigger stimuli and observe brain activity. The caudate nucleus and OFC exhibit particular increases relative to baseline. When therapeutic techniques are successful, levels of activity in such regions appear to normalize (Menzies *et al.*, 2008).

Do patterns of abnormal activity form a causal basis of OCD or might they be a consequence of it, e.g. an effect of medicine? The discovery of an endophenotype for OCD, something reflecting genetic inheritance and evident also in relatives unaffected by OCD, would suggest (brain activity) → (disorder) causation and help the search for candidate genes. Using structural neuroimaging, reduced grey matter volume in the OFC was identified as an endophenotype (Menzies *et al.*, 2007).

(a)

(b)

Figure 22.8 PET scans of control and OCD brain, indicating (a) high activity level of OFC in OCD patient. Horizontal 'slice' of the brain and (b) coronal slice at location of caudate nucleus. rCd = right caudate nucleus (pre- and post-treatment).
Source: courtesy of Jeffrey Schwartz.

This is associated with abnormalities in the generation of inhibition in people with OCD and their near relatives.

Habit formation

Habit formation is an adaptive feature of behaviour (Chapter 10). Routine activities go onto a kind of 'autopilot control', mediated by the basal ganglia. Thereby, people do not normally need to devote conscious processing resources to them. Graybiel (1997) suggests that, in OCD, this malfunctions. Conscious awareness is alerted as the habit becomes excessive, yet the resources normally made available by conscious processing are inadequate to resist. Failures of inhibition in OCD (Chamberlain *et al.*, 2005) lead investigators to suppose that there is a failure of the orbitofrontal cortex to make appropriate inhibitory modulation of basal ganglia activity underlying the excessive habits.

The basal ganglia are involved in the control of movement and also in cognition (Graybiel, 1997). They have a role in producing motor habits and appear also to generate 'cognitive habits', adaptive routines of processing information. In OCD, this process gets out of control, with the triggered cognition being repeatedly brought into conscious awareness.

Treatments

Some treatments of OCD are psychological, e.g. cognitive therapy. Others are biological, e.g. drugs. Whichever is used, the evidence suggests that successful therapy corresponds to parallel corrections of abnormalities of brain events and mental events.

Psychological treatments

Psychological treatment often consists of encouraging the patient to confront the content of the obsession under the therapist's support. For example, someone with a fear of contamination would be encouraged to reduce slowly the amount of time spent hand-washing and to experience the consequences. The rationale is that the OCD will be undermined by learning that nothing bad happens.

The technique of **brain lock** is based on the patient's acceptance that there are abnormal patterns of brain activity (Figure 22.8) (Schwartz, 1996). The patient is encouraged to entertain a healing 'counter thought' of the kind 'it is not me – rather, it is simply my brain that has got stuck'. Therapeutic benefit corresponds to some normalization of the results of neuroimaging, which the patient can inspect.

Pharmacological treatment

The favoured pharmacological treatment for OCD is selective serotonin reuptake inhibitors (SSRIs) (Marazziti and Consoli, 2010). These boost levels of serotonin at the synapse. There are reports that successful SSRI therapy is associated with normalization of activity in the orbito-frontal cortex (i.e. decreased activity), probably mediated via changes in ascending serotonergic neural pathways.

Electrical stimulation

Where other treatments fail, *deep brain stimulation* (DBS) (Chapter 10) has been used (Bear *et al.*, 2010), targets include the caudate nucleus and nucleus accumbens. The rationale is that such regions are part of pathways between cortical and subcortical structures. Hence, stimulating one electrically is likely to alter the flow of information in the circuits implicated in the cycling of unwanted information in OCD. The current might cause, in effect, a lesion by blocking the normal traffic of action potentials. It might trigger inhibitory circuits.

Surgical lesions

As a last resort, some patients have received surgical lesioning of part of the brain (Mashour *et al.*, 2005). A possible rationale is the over-activity exhibited in certain links between the prefrontal cortex and basal ganglia. These appear to correspond to endless loops of unwanted information cycling therein. One target of lesions has been the anterior cingulate cortex. The dilemma is whether the risk of surgical complications (Bear *et al.*, 2010) and serious consequences of the operation, such as a tendency to anti-social behaviour, outweighs the benefits (Bejerot, 2003).

Link with other disorders

Sufferers from OCD have a relatively high probability of also suffering from other disorders, e.g. Tourette's syndrome, which consists of unwanted repetitive movements such as tics (Chamberlain *et al.*, 2005). This suggests a common genetic tendency to OCD and such disorders. It also focuses attention on a possible common basis of each abnormality in the basal ganglia, which might give rise to repetitive automatic reactions of different kinds. In OCD, there is also a very high risk of depression. Antidepressants are the favoured medication for OCD, which suggests a possible common feature in the causation of depression and OCD.

Animal models

Since the *conscious experience* of obsessive thought and the link with compulsion is a defining feature of OCD, there are limits on how far a non-human species can provide a model. However, behaviour taken to excess and lacking an appropriate degree of adaptive goal-direction might capture features (Boulougouris

et al., 2009). Possible animal models consist of excessive and repetitive behaviour, as in hair-pulling in cats and excessive grooming in mice and protracted avoidance behaviour triggered by a cue predictive of shock even after the link with shock has been broken. Operant behaviour that becomes excessive and disconnected from reward is another possibility (Joel and Avisar, 2001). It is reduced by SSRIs but not by the drug diazepam, which lowers anxiety. This corresponds to the effects of these drugs on OCD.

The following section considers another disorder that has some overlap with OCD (Chamberlain *et al.*, 2005) and also exhibits pointers to a failure of inhibitory processes.

Section summary

1 OCD consists of the repetitive intrusion into consciousness of unwanted thoughts.

2 Obsessions trigger behavioural or cognitive compulsions, which represent a fruitless attempt to counter the obsession.

3 OCD is associated with abnormal activity of the orbitofrontal cortex and caudate nucleus.

 Test your knowledge

22.5 What is the immediate biological effect of drugs termed SSRIs?

Answer on page 586

Attention deficit hyperactivity disorder

Introduction

The condition termed **attention deficit hyperactivity disorder (ADHD)** consists of three primary symptoms: (i) problems with attention, (ii) hyperactivity and (iii) impulsiveness (Barkley, 1997). Some individuals show a predominance of inattention, while others show a predominance of hyperactivity/impulsiveness. Some exhibit a combination of these (Levy and Hay, 2001). Inattention is associated with a relatively high distractibility. Children with ADHD have problems with executive function and the use of working memory (Douglas, 2005). ADHD is associated with poor school performance and later employment and social problems. At the start of the 20th century, there were reports of a condition termed 'failure of moral control' (Still, 1902), which appears to be very similar to today's ADHD.

The study of language could yield insights into ADHD (Barkley, 1997). Human language is a means of communication and also of reflection. The person formulates plans and runs mental simulations of them. There can be a delay between the receipt of information and a response (if any) made on the basis of it. During such a delay, speech can be used as an internal means of communication. Self-directed speech is thought to underlie the developing child's capacity to anticipate consequences of actions and to bridge gaps between events with, for example, restraint (Sagvolden et al., 2005). This capacity appears to be deficient in children with ADHD, who are said to be poor at self-monitoring and self-regulation (Douglas, 2005).

Should ADHD be seen as a distinct condition, i.e. identifiable pathology with observable biological roots? Current researchers are inclined to view it as representing an extreme location on a continuum that encompasses the entire population (Levy and Hay, 2001).

Characterizing the underlying dysfunction

General features

The child with ADHD is more strongly determined by physically present stimuli and immediate reinforcement, relative to such internally represented determinants as hindsight and forethought (Barkley, 1997). So, ADHD appears to be a deficiency in the top-down exertion of processing resources, e.g. attention (Borchgrevink, 1989) and the ability to restrain behaviour, relative to controls. This might suggest that there is a single over-arching restraint process that is deficient and which potentially allows the identification of a single defining biological basis of ADHD.

On comparing individuals, closer examination tentatively suggests, rather than a deficit in a single over-arching process, deficits arise in one or more somewhat independent psychological processes (Castellanos et al., 2006; Sonuga-Barke et al., 2010). That is, comparing individuals, different pathways to ADHD exist, which might none the less lead to the same clinical outcome (Sonuga-Barke and Halperin, 2010). Sonuga-Barke et al. (2010) identify three capacities that can be deficient:

1 Inhibition of responding.

2 Coping with a delay imposed between behaving and a reward appearing, so-called 'delay aversion'.

3 Timing of events in the world.

Capacity (1) is measured by various tests (Rhodes et al., 2005), one of which is the so-called 'stop-signal task'. Participants are asked to repeat a strong ('pre-potent') motor response, e.g. tapping, each time that a 'go' signal is given. However, they are instructed to withhold responding on those occasions when the 'go' signal is accompanied by a stop signal.

Concerning capacity (2), as a general principle, delayed reinforcers are less effective than immediate reinforcers, i.e. there exists a 'delay of reinforcement gradient'. In ADHD, there appears to be a steeper than normal gradient: an abnormality in the capacity of delayed consequences to control behaviour (Sagvolden et al., 2005). Under experimental conditions, children with ADHD also show impaired extinction compared with controls. That is to say, when the reinforcer is omitted, they continue to respond for longer. Under natural conditions, this could be manifest in the child's failure to prune maladaptive responses from the behavioural repertoire.

Although deficiencies of capacity (2) might also appear to reflect a failure to inhibit (specifically to inhibit the tendency to respond before the delay has elapsed), evidence suggests a distinction in processes 1 and 2. Some children with ADHD are deficient on the stop–go task but are not delay averse and vice versa (Sonuga-Barke, 2005). For a given individual, ADHD might arise from deficits in any or all of these factors.

Deficiencies in capacity (3) could disrupt tasks where a delay is needed between gaining information and acting on the basis of it.

It is not difficult to appreciate that distinct difficulties in processes 1, 2 or 3 could contribute to an overall 'generic' difficulty in executive control. Such control requires giving appropriate weight to the anticipation of delayed rewarding consequences in the face of competition, timing when to act and inhibition of inappropriate candidates for control.

Valuable evidence on these capacities and their deficiency in ADHD would be to find distinct brain processes underlying them (described later).

The brain and ADHD

Brain structure and function – general principles

Brain volume and overall grey matter volume in all four lobes of the brain are lower in children with ADHD than in age-matched controls (Batty et al., 2010). However, the effect tends to be most marked in a region of pre-frontal cortex, the inferior frontal region, which forms a focus of research interest.

Employing fMRI and a task requiring inhibition of responding, Vaidya et al. (1998) found abnormalities of function in the frontal cortex and striatum of ADHD children. Rubia *et al.* (1999) observed lower activity in the frontal lobes in people with ADHD aged 12–18 years than in controls. They suggested that this fits with the notions of delayed maturation of the frontal lobes in children with ADHD and impaired inhibitory control.

The role of the prefrontal cortex (PFC)

The PFC can represent temporal sequences of events and utilize past events and projections to future events in the goal-directed control of cognition and behaviour. It is required for complex novel behaviour, e.g. involving delays between instigating events and response performance. This delay needs to be protected from interference by extraneous events.

The use of working memory in planning and goal-direction of cognition and behaviour involves the PFC, which plays a pivotal role in functional ('executive') coordination (Chapters 5 and 6). It does this in interaction with other (cortical and subcortical brain regions). Relevant information is held in memory 'on-line' and 'top-down' control exerted, even in the face of potential distraction (Robbins and Arnsten, 2009). This involves allocation of attention and modulation (e.g. inhibition) of certain processes (Arnsten, 2009). Following exposure to the 'to-be-remembered' stimulus, information on it is held 'on-line' in its absence. Thereby, gaps in time are bridged. The PFC appears to compute information on meaning. In this way, it is able to direct attention and action to intrinsically weak events, since by being contextualized they take meaning (Arnsten, 2009). For example, a book singularly lacking any intrinsic virtue or excitement value (I hope not this one!) might be useful for an essay.

Structural and functional evidence suggests defective functioning of the PFC in children with ADHD (Arnsten and Li, 2005), similar to patients with damage to the PFC. A particular region, the inferior part of the PFC in the right hemisphere, has a special interest in the study of ADHD. It is activated at times of stopping in a stop-signal action and tends to be underactive in ADHD, though it is not simply involved in inhibition (Hampshire *et al.*, 2010).

Catecholamines (dopamine and noradrenalin) play a crucial role in the functioning of the PFC by altering sensitivity of ('modulating') the neural processes located there (Robbins and Arnsten, 2009). Successful treatments for ADHD target catecholamines, which suggests deficiencies in their activity in the disorder (Arnsten and Li, 2005). Low doses of dopamine D1 agonists improve the function of the PFC in terms of working memory. The biological basis of the effect of agonists there is to enhance the maintenance of firing of PFC neurons that encode memory. Similarly, boosting NA activity by low doses of agonists improves PFC function, the effect being mediated at specific receptors: α-2a-adrenergic receptors. Blocking of these receptors disrupts working memory and increases impulsivity.

Chamberlain *et al.* (2009) used fMRI and a start-stop task to study the drug atomoxetine. It boosted catecholamine levels in the cortex, activated the right inferior PFC and improved inhibitory control.

The role of the cerebellum

There is some evidence of abnormalities in the cerebellum of people with ADHD (Cubillo and Rubia, 2010) and this could underlie difficulties with timing as well as with motor control.

Animal models

There are two possible animal models of ADHD: (i) non-human species treated in such a way as to trigger features in common with ADHD and (ii) the 'natural' behaviour of particular inbred strains of animal.

In rats, damage to the core region of the nucleus accumbens results in hyperactivity, suggesting a model of an aspect of ADHD (model (i)). They also show something much like 'impulsivity' and 'delay aversion', in that they prefer a small sub-standard reward over a delayed higher quality reward (Cardinal *et al.*, 2001). Such findings fit the hypothesis that ADHD reflects a deficit in the signaling of reward ('reward prediction', as described in Chapter 11) by activation of dopamine, as triggered normally by cues predictive of reward (Tripp and Wickens, 2009). It could also model delayed extinction in ADHD, corresponding to a deficiency in signaling 'no reward'.

With regard to model (ii), there is the rat strain termed the 'spontaneously hypertensive rat' (SHR). They show a number of features of behaviour similar to children with ADHD. For example, when trained in an instrumental situation but with reward no longer available ('extinction conditions'), such animals have difficulty in inhibiting responding (Sagvolden, 2000).

The term 'cognitive impulsiveness' describes a feature of ADHD and it means deficits in planning ahead. Consider the following possible animal model (Sagvolden, 2000). A rat is exposed to two levers. In order to earn reward, it is required to press lever 1 a number of times and then press lever 2. In other words, lever 2 is more closely associated in time with reward than is lever 1. Compared with control rats, it is very difficult to train SHR rats to perform more than six or seven presses of lever 1 before switching to lever 2.

It is not just behaviour that shows similarities: dopamine deficiencies have been found in the SHR strain, modelling a feature of the biology of ADHD.

Cognitive deficits shown by the SHR strain can to some extent be remedied by rearing in an enriched environment (Pamplona *et al.*, 2009). Pamplona *et al.* suggest that this might be mediated by greater plasticity of neuronal connections in such regions as the PFC and speculate that there could be implications for ADHD.

Drug treatments

A standard treatment for ADHD, methylphenidate ('Ritalin') increases levels of dopamine and noradrenalin at synapses by blocking their reuptake sites. It has often been regarded as a paradox that 'Ritalin', described as a **stimulant**, should be a treatment for ADHD. After all, surely stimulants *stimulate* behaviour rather than facilitating restraint.

If we may extrapolate from a rat model, the paradox might be resolved (Berridge *et al.*, 2006). It is *subcortical* dopamine that is thought to be implicated in the hyperactivity seen in ADHD (Arnsten and Li, 2005). Low doses of Ritalin might selectively target *PFC* catecholamine action (and improve performance of working memory tasks), rather than subcortical dopamine action. The latter site is implicated in any stimulant effect but this is only seen at higher doses of such stimulants. Ritalin could also selectively favour reward-signalling by dopamine (Tripp and Wickens, 2009).

Suppose that the cause of the deficiency of PFC function in ADHD is a PFC that is smaller than normal and/ or an abnormally low number of functioning and catecholamine-sensitive neurons located there. Even so, given that there is some functioning population of such neurons, there is logic as to why boosting catecholamine activity could be therapeutic (Arnsten and Li, 2005).

Although up to a point low doses of catecholamine-stimulating agents improve PFC function, increasing the dose beyond a certain level leads to a disruptive effect (Arnsten and Li, 2005). Similarly, stress can increase catecholamine activity in the PFC to where there is a disruptive effect on working memory tasks.

Genes, environment and development

Genes

ADHD tends to run in families (Faraone and Biederman, 1998). Parents of ADHD children have a relatively high probability of exhibiting it. As is also the case for schizophrenia (see earlier), twin studies point to a genetic heritability. ADHD appears to be a so-called 'multi-factorial disorder', meaning that multiple genes and environmental factors play a role in causation (Rutter, 2001). ADHD is associated with several interacting genes, each contributing only a small effect

(Sonuga-Barke *et al.*, 2008). To be more precise, it appears that certain genes have *alleles* (Chapter 2) that are associated with ADHD.

To better understand the genetic contribution, comparisons can be made between (i) children with ADHD, (ii) siblings who do not themselves exhibit ADHD and (iii) unrelated children not showing ADHD (Sonuga-Barke *et al.*, 2010). Children with ADHD and specific domains of deficit can be compared with siblings in terms of their particular deficit. For example, timing deficits can be investigated. Siblings tend to lie somewhere between the child with ADHD and controls. Hence, the deficit as manifest by the sibling could act as an endophenotype for the condition.

Candidate genes involved in dopaminergic function and implicated in ADHD have been identified. One candidate is the genes that code for the structures (the 'transporter') involved in the reuptake of dopamine from the synaptic cleft into the presynaptic neuron (Waldman and Rhee, 2002). Abnormality here seems to be reflected in a higher than normal clearance of dopamine from the synaptic cleft (Castellanos and Swanson, 2002).

It is possible that genes bias towards seeking particular environments, which in themselves help to trigger ADHD. For example, they could, from generation to generation, lead their possessors to environments that encourage sensation-seeking.

Environment

ADHD in children tends to be associated with their mother suffering pregnancy and delivery complications (PDCs) (Sprich-Buckminster *et al.*, 1993). PDCs are frequently associated with hypoxia (low availability of oxygen) at birth which could have a damaging effect upon neural tissue. The prefrontal cortex could be particularly vulnerable (Sullivan and Brake, 2003). Children with ADHD typically have low birth weights (Sagvolden *et al.*, 2005). ADHD families tend to be troubled by psychosocial adversity, conflict and negative communication (Faraone and Biederman, 1998). There are difficulties here in disentangling cause and effect, and distinguishing causation and correlation. In principle, there might be the same genetic predisposition to both ADHD and social conflict.

ADHD is not purely a Western disease, a product of a particular technological lifestyle, but is represented in various cultures throughout the world (Faraone *et al.*, 2003). However, cultural differences, as in different styles of parenting, might contribute to its frequency. Our culture places a high premium upon education and remaining focused on abstract problems. This could create a context in which impulsivity is problematic. One can imagine other contexts such as hunting, where different demands are posed.

Development

Children with ADHD show delayed maturation of the cortex, this being particularly so in the prefrontal region, which, also from other evidence (earlier), is implicated in the condition (Shaw *et al.*, 2007).

Evidence suggests that ADHD emerges in the course of development and dynamic gene–environment interactions are a route to identifying how such emergence occurs (Sonuga-Barke and Halperin, 2010). ADHD appears to arise during development from *certain* genotypes acting in combination only with *certain* social environments ('G × E interaction') (Sonuga-Barke *et al.*, 2008). Other social environments might moderate the effect of such genes.

It was noted earlier that, when individuals with ADHD are compared, deficiencies in different processes appear to be implicated in arriving at the same clinical condition. This has focused investigators attention on finding different developmental pathways by which these deficiencies arise (Sonuga-Barke and Halperin, 2010).

Training programmes designed to enhance executive function (e.g. computer-based or involving parents and giving reinforcement) at an age when the brain is still 'plastic' have therapeutic potential (Klingberg *et al.*, 2005). Given different pathways for ADHD, an intervention (e.g. drug or behavioural) designed to target a developmental pathway in one individual might be inappropriate for another.

Section summary

1 ADHD consists of three primary symptoms: (a) poor sustained attention, (b) hyperactivity and (c) impulsiveness.

2 ADHD is often associated with a failure of response inhibition, which implicates a deficiency in control by a region of the frontal lobes.

3 The process of reinforcement can be abnormal in ADHD, reflecting delay aversion.

4 A timing deficiency is evident in some people with ADHD.

5 Multiple genes appear to be implicated in ADHD, each contributing a slight effect.

6 A tendency to ADHD could arise from a combination of particular genes and a particular social environment.

 ### Test your knowledge

22.6 What is it about the spontaneously hypertensive rat under extinction conditions that suggests that it is a suitable animal model of ADHD?

Answer on page 586

Bringing things together

This chapter has looked at four disorders, which illustrate different aspects of a biological perspective, where understanding behavioural and cognitive disorder can be gained by considering events within the brain. We also looked at the developmental/learning explanation of how things go wrong.

Alzheimer's disease illustrates a disorder for which there is an abnormality at a cellular level: looked at under a microscope, the brain tissue of patients often shows differences from controls. People with schizophrenia show certain biological markers such as enlarged ventricular size, though there is not such a clear cellular index as in AD. OCD was used to illustrate a condition in which people with this can have great insight as to its causation. ADHD illustrated a disorder of behavioural control. In each case, distinct biological bases were described.

There are some similarities between schizophrenia and ADHD. Schizophrenic patients and children with ADHD (Barkley, 1997) have great difficulty with the Stroop task and there is the suggestion that in both cases there are problems with the prefrontal lobes in exerting control.

Schizophrenia and ADHD have been the target of arguments on the role of biology versus the environment. If the logic developed in this book is correct, the term 'versus' is singularly inappropriate, since only by considering the dynamic interaction can we understand the disorder.

 See the video coverage for this chapter to get a patient's perspective on what it is like to experience mental suffering.

Summary of Chapter 22

1 Biological psychologists link (a) abnormal cognition and behaviour to (b) abnormality of biological processes.

2 Alzheimer's disease is a breakdown of cognitive processes, which is associated with pathology at the levels of cellular structure and gross brain anatomy.

3 Schizophrenia is an example of a psychosis, a class of disorder in which contact with reality is problematic. Neural abnormalities appear to arise during development.

4 In OCD, contact with reality is preserved. Evidence reveals links between the cognitive abnormality of obsessive thoughts and biological abnormality.

5 Attention deficit hyperactivity disorder can be characterized by abnormalities of attention, reinforcement and response inhibition. Animal models capture some of its features.

Further reading

For Alzheimer's disease, see Maccioni and Perry (2009). For schizophrenia, see Lieberman *et al.* (2006) and Mueser and Jeste (2008). For OCD, see Schwartz (1996) and Toates and Coschug-Toates (2002). For ADHD, see Banaschewski *et al.* (2009) and Nigg (2009).

Answers

Explanations for answers to 'test your knowledge' questions can be found on the website www.pearsoned.co.uk/toates

22.1 You would tend to include deviations in such desirable features as creativity but would exclude such things as depression once a majority of a population suffered from them.

22.2 Agonists that occupy ACh receptors, boosting synthesis of ACh, lowering the enzymatic breakdown of ACh.

22.3 Amphetamine injections tend to disrupt the learning that a neutral stimulus signals nothing of significance, i.e. it is redundant.

22.4 The concordance of identical twins is higher than that of fraternal twins but is not 100%.

22.5 To block the reuptake of serotonin and hence to increase synaptic levels of this neurotransmitter and increase occupation of postsynaptic receptors.

22.6 It persists with responding for a relatively long time in extinction.

Visit www.pearsoned.co.uk/toates
for a range of resources to support study.
Test yourself with multiple choice questions and access a bank of over 100 videos that will bring the topics to life.

 Interactions and animations relating to topics discussed in this chapter can be found on the website at www.pearsoned.co.uk/toates. These include:

Animation: The time lag of antidepressant drug therapy
Animation: How traditional antipsychotic drugs work
Interaction: The Carlsson–Lindqvist model of how chlorpromazine works

Glossary

A

ablation Surgical removal of part of the brain, a form of lesioning (Chapter 5).

absorptive state The state after eating, during which absorption of food from the alimentary tract occurs (Chapter 16).

accommodation The changes in curvature of the lens as the distance of an object changes. These serve to keep the object in focus (Chapter 8).

across-fibre pattern coding The language in which taste information is encoded, involving a comparison between signals carried by different neurons (Chapter 9).

action Behaviour that is not obviously triggered as a reaction, in the case of humans, 'voluntarily' (Chapter 2). Movement defined in relation to what is achieved rather than its precise form, e.g. hitting a nail with a hammer (Chapter 10).

action potential A sudden spike of electrical activity in a neuron. Action potentials form the language of the nervous system (Chapter 3).

activational effect A reversible change in sensitivity or activity as a result of hormone (Chapter 6).

activation-synthesis model A model of dreaming, which suggests that dreams are the subjective awareness of neural events in, for example, the visual system triggered by influences from the brain stem (Chapter 19).

acuity The ability of a sensory system to resolve fine detail (Chapter 8).

adaptation (a) A characteristic that has been selected because it fits an animal to its environment (Chapter 2). (b) Decrease in activity in a sensory neuron over the period of application of a stimulus (Chapter 7).

adaptive Something that evolved because it served a function that helped to promote the survival of the genes of the animal showing that specific characteristic (Chapter 1).

adaptive orientation The view that drugs are a support that allows the individual to function better at times of psychological need (Chapter 18).

adrenal cortex The outer layer of the adrenal gland, the source of corticosteroids (Chapter 13).

adrenal medulla The inner region of the adrenal gland. The source of catecholamines secreted as hormones (Chapter 13).

affect A quality along a dimension of pleasure–displeasure associated with conscious awareness. One might extrapolate that some non-human species have a similar experience (Chapter 2).

affective neuroscience A school of thought which suggests that there are systems of emotion and affect that have crucially important common characteristics across different mammalian species (Chapter 12).

afferent neuron A neuron that conveys information towards a given site (Chapter 3).

after-image The effect of a visual stimulus, still perceived after it has been extinguished (Chapter 8).

agonist A substance that occupies receptors and has a similar effect to the natural chemical that would normally occupy them (Chapter 4).

agraphia Disruption of writing ability (Chapter 20).

alexia Disruption of reading ability (Chapter 20).

allele A variant of a gene (Chapter 2).

alliesthesia The change in hedonic reaction to a given stimulus as a function of changing internal state (Chapter 15).

alpha activity (an alpha wave) A phase of EEG activity associated with drowsiness (Chapter 19).

alpha motor neuron Type of motor neuron that innervates extrafusal muscle fibres (Chapter 10).

altricial An animal born dependent upon parental help (Chapter 6).

Alzheimer's disease (AD) A type of dementia with characteristic biological indices in terms of brain cellular structure (Chapter 22).

amnesia An inability to learn new declarative information or to retrieve such information that has been acquired. Associated with pathology (Chapter 11).

amnesic syndrome An apparent failure to assimilate new episodic and semantic information following damage to the medial temporal lobe involving the hippocampus (Chapter 11).

analgesia The process of reducing pain (Chapter 14).

analgesic A substance, the effect of which is to reduce pain, e.g. morphine (Chapter 14).

analogy (a) A system that can be compared with another and exhibits some common features (Chapter 1) and (b) a term that refers to the independent emergence of a characteristic in evolution. Common evolutionary pressures gave rise to the same characteristic (Chapter 5).

androgen A class of hormone that induces the reproductive system to take the male form. Testosterone is one of this class (Chapter 6).

animal model The use of an animal example to capture features of a human system (Chapter 1).

anorexia Literally, loss of appetite. More objectively, a reduction in food intake (Chapter 16).

A-not-B test A test in which a participant must select a target (A) under which an object has been seen to be recently placed, even though there has been extensive prior experience of selecting target B (Chapter 6).

antagonist A substance that occupies receptors but does not exert any effect on the second cell, thereby blocking the natural neurotransmitter action (Chapter 4).

antagonist muscles Skeletal muscles that exert contraction acting in opposite directions (Chapter 10).

anterograde amnesia A failure to remember events experienced after trauma (Chapter 11).

anti-androgen An artificial substance that competes with androgens at their target sites but does not have the excitatory effects of androgens (Chapter 17).

anti-nociception An intrinsic process that is triggered under certain conditions and that blocks the transmission of nociceptive information (Chapter 14).

anxiogenics A class of drug that increases anxiety (Chapter 12).

anxiolytics A class of drug that lowers anxiety, e.g. benzodiazepine (Chapter 12).

aphagia Cessation or reduction in feeding observed over a considerable period of time, e.g. as a result of a brain lesion (Chapter 16).

aphasia Disruption or loss of language ability (Chapter 20).

aphrodisiac Chemical that increases sexual desire (Chapter 17).

appetite A measure of the tendency to gain access to a substance and ingest it, by virtue of its taste properties (Chapter 16).

appetitive phase A phase of behaviour leading up to contact with biologically appropriate objects such as a mate (Chapter 15).

arcuate nucleus A nucleus of the hypothalamus, which forms a principal focus for integrating nutrient-related information (Chapter 16).

aromatization The process of converting androgens to oestradiol (Chapter 6).

arousal A state recorded from the brain indicating concentration and focus (Chapter 13).

as if loop Activity that is intrinsic to the CNS and is based upon a memory of how 'gut feelings feel' (Chapter 12).

ascending reticular activating system (or just 'reticular activating system', abb. ARAS) A system of ascending projections from the brain stem that modulate the brain's responsivity to external stimuli. Adjusts dimension of sleep–arousal (Chapter 5).

associative learning Learning in which the experimenter arranges a contingency between two events (or nature presents a similar contingency). Classical and instrumental learning are two types of associative learning (Chapter 11).

atherosclerosis (or arteriosclerosis) Gathering of fatty substances on the walls of arteries (Chapter 13).

attention A process that gives weight to some sensory input relative to other inputs (Chapter 20).

attention deficit hyperactivity disorder (ADHD) A disorder characterized by poor sustained attention, hyperactivity and impulsiveness (Chapter 22).

auditory cortex The region of cortex at which auditory information arrives and where the cortical processing of it first occurs (Chapter 5).

autism A condition in which there are deficiencies in the area of social communication and behaviour and failures in the use of the imagination in solving social problems (Chapter 6).

automatic processing That which is unconscious and effortless (Chapter 10).

autonomic ganglion (pl: autonomic ganglia) A structure that houses the cell bodies of neurons of the autonomic nervous system, lying between CNS and effectors (Chapter 3).

autonomic nervous system (ANS) That part of the nervous system that exerts action on the internal environment (Chapter 3).

axon The long process that forms part of a neuron and along which action potentials are transmitted in serving the neuron's role in communication (Chapter 3).

B

basal ganglia A group of subcortical nuclei that are involved in the control of movement among other things (Chapter 10).

behavioural inhibition system A system that serves to restrain impulsive reactions (Chapter 15).

behavioural satiety sequence A characteristic sequence observed in rats following the termination of feeding as a result of having ingested sufficient food. Grooming forms part of the sequence (Chapter 16).

belonging Being part of a stable community and having a harmonious lifestyle, social context and way of reacting (Chapter 13).

benefit A positive contribution to fitness associated with a particular behaviour (Chapter 2).

beta activity A phase of EEG activity associated with alert waking (Chapter 19).

beta-blocker A type of drug that blocks sympathetic neurotransmission at the cardiac muscle and hence restrains heart-rate (Chapter 12).

binding problem The problem of how distinct streams of information come together to form a unified conscious perception (Chapter 21).

binocular rivalry A situation of competition in perception that arises from the presentation of different images to the two eyes (Chapter 8).

biological clock An intrinsic timing process having features in common with a manufactured clock. It underlies the circadian rhythm (Chapter 19).

biopsychosocial perspective A way of looking at psychological disorder which sees biological, psychological and social contributions as all being equally important and being interactive (Chapter 2).

blindsight The capacity to react appropriately to visual stimuli about which the person has no conscious awareness (Chapter 1).

blood–brain barrier A barrier between the brain's neurons and blood vessels (Chapter 5).

bottom-up (or 'data-driven') The contribution to perception or behaviour deriving from stimuli physically present (Chapter 7).

brain Rostral part of the central nervous system (Chapter 1).

brain lock A technique used in the treatment of obsessive compulsive disorder, which involves the patient's attribution of the problem to dysfunction of their brain (Chapter 22).

Broca's aphasia Aphasia that arises from damage to Broca's area. It is particularly associated with difficulty in expressing language (Chapter 20).

Broca's area An area of the human left frontal cortex concerned with speech production (Chapter 20).

C

catecholamine A subgroup of monoamines, consisting of dopamine, adrenalin and noradrenalin (Chapter 3).

causal explanation Explanation in terms of one event causing something to happen a moment later (sometimes called 'proximate causation') (Chapter 1).

cell The very small building blocks of the body (e.g. neurons). The body contains many billions of cells (Chapter 1).

cell body The part of the cell that houses the genetic material of the cell (Chapter 3).

central executive A suggested process which supervises the subsystems of working memory (Chapter 11).

central nervous system (CNS) The brain and spinal cord (Chapter 3).

central pattern generator (CPG) A motor programme that generates oscillations and is organized at the brain stem and spinal cord (Chapter 10).

centre–surround A form of organization of receptive field (e.g. at the retina) in which stimulation of a centre region exerts an opposite effect to that of the surround (Chapter 8).

cephalic phase In the case described in this book, the release of a hormone triggered by external sensory information arriving at the brain (Chapter 3).

cerebral cortex A telencephalic structure, the outer layer of the brain, made up of folds and ridges (Chapter 5).

cerebrospinal fluid (CSF) Fluid derived as a filtration from the fluid component of the blood. It fills the brain's ventricles and the central canal that runs throughout the spinal cord (Chapter 5).

chemoattraction Attraction of part of a growing cell towards chemical cues in its environment (Chapter 6).

chemoreceptor A type of receptor that is sensitive to the presence of chemicals. Chemoreceptors are the first stage of the taste and smell systems (Chapter 9).

cholinergic hypothesis A hypothesis to account for Alzheimer's disease, in terms of the loss of cholinergic function (Chapter 22).

chromosome Structure at which genes are located. With the exception of gametes, the human nucleus contains 46 chromosomes (Chapter 2).

circadian rhythm A rhythm that (a) has a period of approximately 24 hours and (b) is generated internally (Chapter 19).

circumventricular organs Specialized collections of neurons not protected by the blood–brain barrier and which serve to detect chemicals within the blood (Chapter 5).

classical conditioning A type of conditioning in which a neutral stimulus is paired with an unconditional stimulus. Also termed 'Pavlovian conditioning' (Chapter 11).

closed programme Programme underlying development which results in an animal that reacts in a certain situation in a rather fixed species-typical way (Chapter 6).

cognition Knowledge about the world (Chapter 20).

cognitive map A cognitive representation of the environment (Chapter 11).

command neuron For certain systems, a neuron in the brain that plays a high-level role in coordinated hierarchical control (Chapter 3).

comparative approach An approach to explanation that is based on the comparison of the behaviour of different species, often with the aim of explaining human behaviour (Chapter 1).

complete androgen insensitivity syndrome (CAIS) A condition in which genetic males produce normal levels of testosterone but have a dysfunction in the gene coding for the androgen receptor (Chapter 6).

computerized tomography (CT) A technique of structural imaging for forming 3-dimensional images (Chapter 5).

concentration gradient A gradient for a specific chemical arising from an uneven distribution. The gradient tends to break down the uneven division (Chapter 4).

concept-driven The contribution to perception from concepts, e.g. memories, expectations (Chapter 7).

concordance The extent to which twins correlate in something, such as height or IQ score (Chapter 6).

conditional incentive Something (e.g. a sound) that owes its incentive value to a process of pairing with an incentive such as food (Chapter 15).

conditional response (CR) The response produced by a conditional stimulus (Chapter 11).

conditional stimulus (CS) A stimulus that owes its capacity to a history of association with an unconditional stimulus, e.g. the bell in a salivary conditioning experiment (Chapter 11).

conditioned emotional response An emotional reaction to a conditional stimulus that has been paired with a traumatic event (Chapter 12).

conditioned place preference (CPP) A preference for a location based upon an earlier experience there, such as drug infusion (Chapter 15).

cone A type of sensory receptor, located at the retina (Chapter 8).

congenital adrenal hyperplasia (CAH) The condition in which some girls are exposed to high levels of testosterone prior to birth and show some masculinization of the genitals and a tendency to engage in male-typical play (Chapter 6).

consciousness A phenomenon associated with a sub-set of cognitive processing skills and with awareness and feelings (Chapter 21).

consolidation The process of strengthening a memory after its acquisition (Chapter 11).

constancy The perception of constant features of a given object, in spite of differences in the image that it forms at the retina, e.g. perception of a constant size even as distance varies (Chapter 8).

consummatory phase The phase of behaviour involving direct interaction with a biologically relevant object, e.g. the act of eating food (Chapter 15).

contingency The relationship that exists between two events, i.e. given one the other will occur (Chapter 11).

contralateral The opposite side of the brain to the region under consideration (Chapter 5).

controllability The capacity to exert control over a stressor, e.g. to terminate a loud sound by pressing a lever (Chapter 13).

controlled processing That which is conscious, effortful and planned (Chapter 10).

convergence The pooling of the output of a number of light receptors, so as to feed, via bipolar cells, onto a single ganglion cell (Chapter 8).

Coolidge effect Revival of sexual motivation by means of novelty of the partner (Chapter 17).

coping strategy A strategy to put into effect when exposed to a stressor that helps to make the situation less aversive (Chapter 13).

core sleep The amount of sleep that is needed to serve restorative functions, e.g. neuronal repair (Chapter 19).

corollary discharge A signal equal and parallel to that sent to the muscles and which is used in the computation of perception. Also termed 'efference copy' (Chapter 10).

coronary heart disease (CHD) A disorder of the vessels that supply blood to the heart, mainly atherosclerosis within the coronary arteries (Chapter 13).

corticospinal tract (or pathway) A tract running from the motor cortex to local levels of spinal cord. Neurons of the tract synapse either at or near to motor neurons. Sometimes termed pyramidal system (Chapter 10).

cost A negative contribution to fitness associated with a particular behaviour (Chapter 2).

covert orientating Intrinsic focusing of processing on part of the sensory information without bodily movement (Chapter 20).

cranial nerve Nerve linking the brain and periphery not by the spinal cord (Chapter 3).

craving An urge for something, e.g. drug, such that conscious awareness is occupied by thoughts of the missing thing (Chapter 16).

cytokine Chemical released from activated cell of the immune system (Chapter 13).

D

Dale's principle The principle that any given neuron synthesizes and releases only one type of neurotransmitter. It is now known to be only partly true (Chapter 4).

data-driven (or 'bottom-up') The contribution to perception or behaviour deriving from stimuli that are physically present (Chapter 7).

decerebrate A subject with the brain stem surgically isolated from the rest of the brain (Chapter 16).

declarative memory A form of memory involved in knowing something, e.g. a fact about the world. It can be articulated verbally (Chapter 11).

deep brain stimulation (DBS) A form of treatment in which an electrode is implanted surgically and then electric current is passed through the electrode's tip. A treatment for OCD (Chapter 10).

delusion A belief of a kind that is at odds with cultural norms (Chapter 22).

dementia A cognitive impairment involving memory and attention (Chapter 20).

denervation Loss of a neural input to a structure (Chapter 6).

depolarization A move of membrane potential towards zero, away from the polarized value (Chapter 4).

dermatome A region of body associated with the innervation of a particular spinal nerve (Chapter 3).

design A metaphor employed to understand the principles of evolution, suggesting that it is as if living beings were designed for life in their environment (Chapter 2).

determinism The notion that for every event there can in principle be identified a cause (Chapter 1).

determinist One who believes in a lawfulness of behaviour (Chapter 1).

developmental/learning explanation A type of explanation of behaviour that is based upon events over substantial portions of time, such as hours or days. It embraces both development and learning (Chapter 1).

differentiation The formation of different cells from more similar precursor cells (Chapter 6).

digestion The chemical breakdown of food in the alimentary tract (Chapter 16).

discrimination test A test in which, in order to earn a reward, a rat must discriminate its bodily state as being one of, e.g., hunger or withdrawal from cocaine. Choice in the test and earning of reward is based on such discrimination (Chapter 18).

discriminative touch A system with receptors covering the skin surface, which performs fine-grained resolution of tactile stimuli at the skin. It is involved in the recognition of the location, shape, size and texture of mechanical objects that contact the skin (Chapter 9).

dishabituation A particular example of sensitization as an increase in strength of a response that had previously been habituated (Chapter 11).

display rules The social rules and conventions that govern the expression of behaviour (e.g. emotional reactions) in public (Chapter 12).

distress vocalization (DV) The crying that the young exhibit on enforced separation from a caregiver (Chapter 12).

dizygotic twins (or 'fraternal twins', abb. DZ) Each member of a pair of DZs derives from a separate zygote and so they are not genetically identical (Chapter 6).

dopamine hypothesis A hypothesis to account for schizophrenia, in terms of disrupted dopamine function (Chapter 22).

dorsal Towards the back or top of the head (Chapter 3).

dorsal root ganglion Structure that contains the cell bodies of sensory neurons (Chapter 3).

dorsal stream A stream of visual information leading to the parietal cortex, and which organizes action (Chapter 8).

double-blind study A study in which neither the participant nor the person with whom they are in contact (normally scientist or therapist) knows to which group (experimental or control) each participant has been allocated (Chapter 14).

double dissociation Damage at a brain region (x) impairs an aspect of behaviour (X) but leaves Y intact, whereas damage to another brain region (y) disrupts another behaviour (Y) but leaves X intact (Chapter 8).

down-regulation The process by which there is a loss of receptors at a postsynaptic membrane as a result of high levels of stimulation by neurotransmitter (Chapter 4).

dualism The philosophical suggestion that there exists a distinction between two separate domains: physical and mental (Chapter 21).

E

effector Muscle or gland (Chapter 3).

efferent neuron Neuron that carries information away from a given structure (Chapter 3).

ejaculation Expulsion of seminal fluids from penis (Chapter 17).

electrically induced behaviour (EIB) Behaviour triggered by electrical current applied through an implanted electrode, where the timing of the application of current is controlled by the experimenter (Chapter 15).

electrical synapse A synapse where there is direct electrical contact between the presynaptic neuron and the postsynaptic neuron (Chapter 4).

electrocortical mapping A technique that involves generating an electrical current for a period of some 5–10 seconds. The current passes between two electrodes located at the surface of the cortex and disruptions to behaviour are noted (Chapter 20).

electroencephalography (EEG) The study of the brain's activity by electrodes that are attached to the surface of the head. The record is termed an electroencephalogram (also abbreviated EEG) (Chapter 5).

electromyogram (EMG) A recording of the electrical activity of skeletal muscles, e.g. taken by surface electrodes (Chapter 5).

electron microscopy A technique for obtaining a very high magnification of a sample of tissue so that its details can be resolved (Chapter 5).

embryo (at times also termed 'fetus') The animal at the start of life, e.g. in the uterus (Chapter 6).

emergent property The notion that, at each level of increasing complexity, new properties emerge. These are not evident at the lower level (Chapter 1).

emotional Stroop A version of the Stroop test in which words of an emotional character are written in colour and the task is to name the colour (Chapter 20).

empathy A capacity for a person to put themselves in another's place and to experience something of what it is like (Chapter 14).

encephalization The degree to which brain size exceeds what might be expected on the basis of body weight (Chapter 5).

endocrine system The system consisting of the hormones of the body and their receptors at target organs (Chapter 3).

endophenotype A marker for a condition, e.g. something like depression that has arisen in the past or has a tendency to arise in the future. It might be observed in relatives not showing a condition (Chapter 2).

engram The durable physical embodiment of memory (Chapter 11).

enteric nervous system (ENS) Network of neurons in the wall of the gut (Chapter 3).

enzyme A chemical that alters the speed of a chemical reaction (Chapter 2).

episodic memory A memory of a particular episode of personal experience (Chapter 11).

erectile dysfunction (ED) Failure to maintain an erection (Chapter 17).

ethology A branch of zoology concerned with the study of behaviour (Chapter 1).

event-related potential (ERP) (or 'evoked potential', abb. ERP) The change in electrical activity in the brain triggered by a stimulus, as recorded at the scalp (Chapter 5).

evolution The theory that animals emerge from a simpler form of life by a gradual series of changes over long periods of time (Chapter 1).

evolutionary explanation A type of explanation which is in terms of events in the evolutionary history of the animal under consideration (Chapter 1).

evolutionary psychology A school of psychology concerned to explain behaviour in functional terms appropriate to the early evolutionary environment (Chapter 2).

explicit memory A term that means much the same as declarative memory. We can be verbally explicit about the content (Chapter 11).

exploratory behaviour Behaviour that serves to increase the information available to an animal by means of investigation and orientation of sense organs (Chapter 15).

exposure orientation The view that addiction arises simply from a certain level of exposure to drugs (Chapter 18).

extension Movement of a limb in which the angle is increased (Chapter 10).

exteroceptive A term to describe those senses, such as vision, that convey information to the brain concerning the external environment (Chapter 7).

extracellular fluid The fluid that is not in the cells and is made up of the interstitial fluid and the plasma (Chapter 4).

extrafusal muscle fibre Fibres of skeletal muscle the function of which is the exertion of force (Chapter 10).

extrapyramidal pathways Pathways of motor control that start in the brain stem (hence contrast to the pyramidal tract that starts in the cortex) (Chapter 10).

eye-blink reflex Reflex reaction of the eyelid to noxious stimulus such as an air-puff (Chapter 11).

F

feature detection The extraction of information on particular features of sensory events such as their location in space (Chapter 9).

feedforward Action taken, not in response to a departure of a regulated variable from a set-point, but in anticipation of a deviation that might arise (Chapter 10).

feminization The process of forming the typical female structures (Chapter 6).

fitness The potential of an animal to pass on its genes (Chapter 2).

flavour The sensation triggered by food that is a product of the combination of taste and olfactory stimulation (Chapter 9).

flexion Movement of a limb in which the angle is decreased (Chapter 10).

fovea A small depression at the centre of the retina specialized to resolve fine detail (Chapter 8).

frequency coding Information carried by the frequency of action potentials (Chapter 7).

frontal lobe syndrome A syndrome that follows damage to the prefrontal cortex (Chapter 5).

functional explanation Explanation in terms of how something has contributed to reproductive success during evolutionary history (Chapter 1).

functional lesion Local disruption to a site of neural tissue in a way that is reversible (Chapter 20).

functional magnetic resonance imaging (fMRI) A form of magnetic resonance imaging that detects activity patterns of different regions of the brain and forms images of them (Chapter 5).

functional neuroimaging A technique for looking at the brain in action, i.e. which parts of the brain are relatively active or inactive at given times (Chapter 5).

functional specialization Beyond the primary visual cortex, distinct cortical regions analyze particular qualities of the visual image, such as form, colour or motion (Chapter 8).

G

gamete Collective term for sperm and egg cells (Chapter 2).

ganglion (pl: 'ganglia') A group of the cell bodies of neurons in the peripheral nervous system (Chapter 3).

gate theory The theory of Melzack and Wall, which suggests that nociceptive information is gated at sites within the spinal cord (Chapter 14).

gender identity Acquisition of the concept 'I am a girl' or 'I am a boy' (Chapter 6).

gene The unit of inheritance of information from one generation to another by means of reproduction (Chapter 1).

gene expression The switching on of genes, triggering the manufacture of proteins (Chapter 6).

genotype The collection of all the genes within an individual. Each cell contains an identical set of genes, constituting the genotype (Chapter 2).

gestation The period from fertilization to birth or hatching (Chapter 6).

gland Site at which hormones are secreted (Chapter 3).

glial cell A type of cell found in the nervous system but distinct from neurons. It serves a supportive role (Chapter 4).

glucoreceptor A neuron the activity of which depends upon its availability of glucose or the metabolism of glucose (Chapter 16).

Golgi stain The result of a technique of staining (Golgi staining), which reveals whole cells (Chapter 5).

gonadotropin A generic term for FSH and LH (Chapter 17).

gonads The male testes and female ovaries. Adjective is gonadal (Chapter 6).

grandmother cell A hypothetical cell at the core of the theory that we have a specific neuron for the perception of each object, e.g. we would have a neuron specific to a particular grandmother (Chapter 8).

growth cone The swollen ending of an extending axon or dendrite, with fine extensions termed 'filopodia' (Chapter 6).

H

habituation A form of non-associative learning in which there is a decline in the response to a stimulus that is presented repeatedly but with no significant consequence (Chapter 11).

haemorrhage Loss of blood (Chapter 16).

hair cell A type of cell in which deformation causes electrical changes that are the start of the process of detection. Hair cells are found in the ear (Chapter 9).

hallucinogen A class of drug, the primary action of which is to change sensory perception (Chapter 18).

hard problem The problem of how physical matter can give rise to phenomenal consciousness (Chapter 21).

hard-wired A description for synaptic connections and neuronal systems that exhibit little flexibility and often show consistency from one animal to another within a species (Chapter 2).

Hebb synapse When memory consolidation occurs, structural changes are assumed to take place at one or more synapses. Such modified synapses are termed 'Hebb synapses' (Chapter 11).

hedonic Having a quality of positive affect or pleasure (Chapter 2).

heritability The degree to which differences in a characteristic are due to genetic differences (Chapter 2).

hierarchical control Control in which higher levels of the CNS (more rostral) control lower (more caudal) levels (Chapter 3).

homeostasis The principle that physiological events are maintained nearly constant and that action is taken to defend this (Chapter 1).

homology Comparing two species, a term that refers to a common evolutionary origin of something (i.e. a common precursor at an earlier stage of evolution) (Chapter 5).

homunculus fallacy The fallacy of explaining perception or behaviour by explicitly or implicitly involving a person in the head doing the controlling (Chapter 7).

hormone Chemical messenger secreted into the blood at one location and carried in the blood to another location(s) where it exerts effects (Chapter 1).

Huntington's disease (or 'Huntington's chorea') Disorder characterized by involuntary movements of the body, personality changes and forgetfulness (Chapter 2).

hyperalgesia An increase in pain (e.g. caused by the injection of a chemical) (Chapter 14).

hyperphagia Excessive intake of food over a considerable period of time, e.g. as a result of a brain lesion (Chapter 16).

hyperpolarization A move of membrane potential to a more negative value than the resting potential (Chapter 4).

hypothalamic pituitary gonadal axis A causal sequence of events running from (1) activity in the hypothalamus (secretion of gonadotropin-releasing hormone) to (2) the secretion of pituitary hormones and (3) their effect at the gonads in triggering hormonal release (Chapter 17).

I

identity theory A theory that suggests that for every mental event there is a corresponding brain event (Chapter 1).

illusion A distortion of perception relative to an objective measure of sensory information (Chapter 7).

immediacy hypothesis A hypothesis to account for schizophrenia, in terms of a heightened sensitivity to physically present stimuli as opposed to representations (Chapter 22).

immune system A system involving specialist cells that serves to defend the body against invasion (e.g. from viruses and bacteria) and against cancerous cells (Chapter 1).

implicit memory Another term for non-declarative memory (Chapter 11).

imprinting The process whereby the behaviour of newly hatched chicks of some species is fixed by a single early experience. For example, the chick follows the first moving object that it sees (Chapter 6).

incentive A stimulus, e.g. food or a mate, which plays a role in producing motivation and attraction (Chapter 15).

incentive salience The value of an incentive as measured by its capacity to attract (in terms of attention and movement) (Chapter 18).

incentive sensitization theory A theory that drugs such as opiates increase the salience of stimuli related to drug-taking, e.g. the sight of the needle. This leads to craving (Chapter 18).

induction The influence of a group of cells on the development of a neighbouring cell (Chapter 6).

inflow theory The theory that the perception of movement is based in part upon feedback from the muscles (Chapter 10).

inhibitory neuron A neuron, the activity of which has the effect of lowering the activity in a postsynaptic neuron (Chapter 3).

insomnia A subjective feeling of inadequate sleep (Chapter 19).

instrumental conditioning A form of associative learning in which an outcome (e.g. getting food) depends upon behaviour (e.g. turning left in a maze) (Chapter 11).

interneuron A neuron that is neither sensory nor motor (Chapter 3).

intracellular fluid The fluid that is inside cells (Chapter 4).

intracranial self-stimulation (ICSS) Electrical stimulation of the brain through an implanted electrode that is contingent on a response (e.g. lever-pressing) by the subject (Chapter 15).

intrafusal muscle fibres Fibres that intermingle with extrafusal fibres and serve the function of detecting muscle stretch (Chapter 10).

invariance That which is unchanging about sensory information with regard to its source. Perceptual systems can extract this, based upon changing sensory input from the source (Chapter 7).

invertebrate Those species of animal that do not have a backbone (Chapter 5).

involuntary reaction Something triggered by external stimulus and avoiding conscious decision-making (Chapter 10).

ion Electrically active particle (Chapter 4).

Iowa gambling task A task in which the relative weights of gains and losses associated with choices can be adjusted to test participants' choices. Also known as the Bechara gambling task (Chapter 20).

ipsilateral The same side of the brain as the region under consideration (Chapter 5).

irritable bowel syndrome (IBS) A disorder of the gut consisting of inappropriate contraction, triggered by both local events at the gut and central stress-related factors (Chapter 13).

K

Klüver–Bucy syndrome A syndrome that follows ablation of parts of the limbic system in monkeys (Chapter 12).

Korsakoff's syndrome A subgroup of the amnesic syndrome, normally due to vitamin deficiency associated with excessive alcohol intake (Chapter 11).

L

labelled-line coding A system of coding in which a particular neuron would be sensitive to, and transmit information on, a particular quality such as sweetness or salt (Chapter 9).

labelled-line principle Differences in encoding information can be in terms of the particular nerves that carry the information (Chapter 7).

latent inhibition The effect of pre-exposure to a stimulus on retarding the subsequent capacity of the stimulus to form predictive associations. In the pre-exposure phase, it appears that the stimulus is labelled as redundant (Chapter 22).

lateral inhibition Inhibition across the sensory surface from one location to another (e.g. light at one retinal location inhibits the effect of light at another) (Chapter 8).

lateralization Asymmetry in which one side of the brain takes a disproportionate role in a particular aspect of processing, e.g. language tends to be handled mainly by the left hemisphere (Chapter 20).

learned helplessness Based on exposure to unavoidable trauma, the acquisition of a cognition of powerlessness and inability to influence events (Chapter 13).

learning A process or procedure by which, in the light of experience, an animal either (a) changes behaviour or (b) acquires the potential for future change (Chapter 11).

leptin A hormone released from fat stores and which plays a role in satiety (Chapter 16).

lesion Disruption of part of the brain, either deliberate or accidental. The procedure is called lesioning (Chapter 5).

leucocyte Mobile cell that forms part of the immune system (Chapter 13).

liability The notion that there exists a tendency to suffer from a disorder such as schizophrenia that could reflect a genetic influence (Chapter 22).

limbic system A collection of brain structures, e.g. amygdala, the activity of which is assumed to underlie emotion (Chapter 12).

lock and key principle The principle that (1) the neurotransmitter is like a key that fits only one lock: the receptor (Chapter 4) and (2) that a particular odour attaches to a particular receptor (Chapter 9).

long-term memory (LTM) A memory held over long periods of time. The potential storage capacity is unlimited (Chapter 11).

long-term potentiation (LTP) A change in the reactivity of a postsynaptic neuron that lasts for hours or even days, following brief activity in a presynaptic neuron (Chapter 11).

lordosis In female rats, a stereotyped reflexive body arching organized largely at a spinal and midbrain level and shown when she is sexually receptive (Chapter 3).

lymphocyte One class of leucocyte (Chapter 13).

M

magnetic resonance imaging (MRI) A technique for revealing structural details of the brain. A version termed 'functional magnetic resonance imaging' (fMRI) detects changes in oxygen consumption (Chapter 5).

magno system A system of communication in which a magno ganglion cell communicates with a magno LGN cell and thereby segregated information is projected to the cortex (Chapter 8).

malleability The property of certain neural processes that they are able to compensate for disturbances (Chapter 6).

masculinization The formation of typical male structures under the influence of androgen (Chapter 6).

maturation Changes that occur in the nervous system corresponding to development, e.g. formation of myelin (Chapter 6).

membrane potential Electrical voltage across a cell (magnitude normally −60 to −70 mV) (Chapter 4).

memory A change in the nervous system that underlies learning and its recall (Chapter 11).

mesolimbic dopamine pathway A pathway of dopaminergic neurons, which starts in the ventral tegmental area (VTA) and terminates in, among other places, the nucleus accumbens (N.acc.) (Chapter 15).

metabolic rate The rate at which fuel is used by the body, which corresponds to the rate of heat production (Chapter 16).

metabolism Chemical conversion of a substance within the body. For example, the term is used with reference to the obtaining of energy from chemicals (Chapter 3).

metabolite The breakdown product of the metabolism of a chemical (Chapter 4).

metarepresentation A representation of a representation (Chapter 22).

microelectrode An electrode with a very fine tip, capable of recording from single neurons. The technique of making recordings from a single neuron is termed 'single-unit recording' (Chapter 5).

mind As used here, it refers to the information processing systems of the human brain, some of which are open to conscious introspection but most of which are unconscious (Chapter 21).

mirror neuron A type of neuron that is active when an animal performs a particular motor action or watches another animal do so (Chapter 10).

modality segregation A segregation of information arising from different types of sensory receptor, e.g. between touch and temperature, as this information is projected to the brain and processed therein (Chapter 9).

modularity The notion that the brain is composed of a number of modules each dedicated to a particular task (Chapter 20).

module Largely self-contained unit of processing which is able to handle only one type of information. Evolutionary psychology postulates their existence. An influential theory of Fodor is based on the suggestion that the brain contains a number of such units (Chapter 2).

monoamine Class of neurochemical including dopamine, adrenalin, noradrenalin (known, respectively, as 'epinephrine' and 'norepinephrine' in the American literature), and serotonin (also termed 5-HT) (Chapter 3).

monozygotic twins (or 'identical twins', abb. MZ) MZs derive from a single zygote and are genetically identical (Chapter 6).

motivation A process underlying the control of behaviour and giving it strength and direction (Chapter 2).

motor homunculus A bizarre figure drawn alongside the motor cortex, defined by the areas of the body over which control is exerted by neurons in corresponding regions of motor cortex (Chapter 5).

motor imagery The simulation of movement in the imagination, in the absence of actually moving (Chapter 10).

motor neuron A neuron that carries information to a muscle, causing contraction (Chapter 3).

motor unit A motor neuron and the muscle fibres that it innervates (Chapter 10).

muscle fibre The constituent cells of muscle (Chapter 10).

muscle spindle Combination of muscle fibre, motor neuron and sensory neuron (Chapter 10).

mutation A change in the genes contributed to reproduction by one partner, with respect to the precursor genes. The altered phenotype that results from this change in genotype is termed a 'mutant' (Chapter 2).

myelin Part of specialized glial cell forming an insulating coating around an axon. Such an axon is said to be myelinated (Chapter 4).

N

narcolepsy Bouts of sudden sleepiness experienced during the day, associated with weakness of skeletal muscles (Chapter 19).

natural selection The selection of characteristics on the basis of their viability in the environment. A means by which evolution occurs (Chapter 2).

nature The contribution to behaviour that arises from what is given, normally a reference to the genetic contribution at fertilization (Chapter 1).

negative feedback A system in which deviations from an optimal state tend to cause action that returns the state to its optimal value (Chapter 1).

neglect syndrome A consequence of damage to the posterior parietal lobe involving neglect of part of the sensory input, e.g. denying that a part of the sensory world of touch or vision exists (Chapter 20).

nerve A bundle of axons in the peripheral nervous system, physically located alongside each other and extending over the same distance (Chapter 3).

nerve growth factor (NGF) A specific neurotrophic factor (Chapter 6).

nervous system The brain, spinal cord and peripheral nerves (Chapter 1).

neural correlates of consciousness Those patterns of neural activity that are associated particularly with conscious processing (Chapter 21).

neurogenesis The formation of new neurons from general ('precursor') cells (Chapter 6).

neurohormone A chemical having features of both a hormone and a neurotransmitter. They are released from neurons and travel in the blood (Chapter 3).

neuroimaging A technique of viewing a structure or structure/activity of the brain by means of forming images of it, such as PET or MRI (Chapter 5).

neuroleptic drug A type of drug used in the treatment of schizophrenia, which acts by blocking dopamine receptors (Chapter 22).

neuromodulation The action of modulating the activity of neurons by means of a neuromodulator (Chapter 3).

neuromodulator A chemical messenger having a relatively diffuse modulatory effect. Compared with neurotransmission, there can be a relatively large distance within the CNS from the site of release to that of action (Chapter 3).

neuromuscular junction Special type of synapse that links a neuron and a muscle cell (Chapter 4).

neuron A type of cell within the nervous system, which is specialized at transmitting and processing information (Chapter 1).

neuropathic pain Pain that arises intrinsically as a result of damage to, or malfunction within, the nervous system (Chapter 14).

neuropeptides A group of chemical messengers, which includes natural opioids. (Chapter 12).

neurotransmitter A substance that communicates one-to-one between a neuron and either another neuron or a muscle cell. It acts at a synapse. Also known simply as 'transmitter' (Chapter 3).

neurotrophic factor (or 'chemotrophic factor') A life-giving chemical secreted by target cells and taken into cells with which they make contact (Chapter 6).

neutral stimulus (NS) A stimulus having no particular effect, other than orientation of sense organs (Chapter 11).

Nissl stain The result of a technique of staining (Nissl staining), which reveals cell bodies (Chapter 5).

nocebo effect An aversive state induced by the expectation of something aversive (Chapter 14).

nociception The detection of tissue damage (Chapter 14).

nociceptive neuron A neuron the tip of which is sensitive to tissue damage, thereby instigating action potentials (Chapter 3).

nociceptive system The system involved with detecting tissue damage and taking action to minimize this (Chapter 14).

nociceptor The tip of specialized neurons, nociceptive neurons, which detect noxious stimulation (Chapter 14).

node of Ranvier The exposed portion of an axon between myelin sheaths (Chapter 4).

non-corticospinal tracts Tracts of descending motor control that start in the brain stem (in contrast to corticospinal tracts) (Chapter 10).

non-declarative memory A form of memory that the person cannot articulate by conscious recall, e.g. how to ride a bicycle (Chapter 11).

non-rapid eye movement sleep ('non-REM sleep' or 'NREM sleep') Generic term for those phases of sleep during which rapid eye movements are not observed (Chapter 19).

nuclei Plural of nucleus (Chapter 3).

nucleus (a) The structure that contains the genetic material of the cell (Chapter 2). (b) A group of cell bodies of neurons in the brain (Chapter 3).

nurturant behaviour Behaviour that describes the care given by a parent to its offspring (Chapter 15).

nurture The contribution to behaviour that arises from the environment (Chapter 1).

O

obesity Excessive weight. In humans, it consists in having a body weight that is more than 20% higher than the ideal for the person's height (Chapter 16).

object permanence task A task in which a child observes an object being hidden behind a screen. At a stage of development, the child acts on the basis that the object still exists (Chapter 6).

obsessive-compulsive disorder (OCD) A condition characterized by intrusive thoughts and often associated compulsive rituals (Chapter 22).

oestrogens A generic term for a class of hormones produced by the female ovaries and involved in sexual behaviour (Chapter 3).

oestrous cycle A cycle of hormonal secretion in females, which underlies reproduction and sexual motivation (Chapter 17).

ontogenetic hypothesis A hypothesis to explain the amount of REM sleep shown by the newborn of different species. It proposes that REM sleep serves a developmental function in the brain (Chapter 19).

ontogeny The history of the development and growth of the individual. Sometimes compared and contrasted with phylogeny (Chapter 1).

open programme A programme underlying development which involves flexibility as a function of different environmental events (Chapter 6).

operant conditioning The type of instrumental learning in which the animal paces itself, normally demonstrated with a Skinner box (Chapter 11).

opiate An artificial form of chemical that has very similar properties to the opioids that the body produces naturally (Chapter 12).

opioid A class of natural chemical that has similar properties to morphine and heroin, and which modulates behaviour, e.g. to reduce reactions to tissue damage (Chapter 12).

opponent-process coding Coding in which one sensory quality, e.g. green light, excites a neuron, whereas another, e.g. red light, inhibits it (Chapter 8).

optic ataxia The result of damage typically to the superior region of the posterior parietal cortex, part of the dorsal stream. Patients have difficulty with visually guided actions (Chapter 8).

organic cause Something for which a disturbance in the physiology of the body can be identified (Chapter 17).

organizational effect A change in the structure that occurs during development as a result of hormones (Chapter 6).

osmoreceptor A neuron or group of neurons the activity of which is sensitive to their swelling as a result of their fluid content. They are assumed to provide a signal for thirst and its satiety (Chapter 16).

outflow theory The theory that the perception of movement is based in part on the command to move the muscles (Chapter 10).

overt orientating A change in position of the body or part of it to alter sensory inflow (Chapter 20).

P

pain neuromatrix The collection of interacting brain regions that forms the biological basis of pain (Chapter 14).

pair bond A bond formed between monogamous sexual partners (Chapter 17).

palatability The reaction to a substance, which depends upon taste, deficit and any earlier associations with the substance (Chapter 16).

parallel processing The situation where information arising from a given source is processed by two or more streams acting in parallel, e.g. in the visual system (Chapter 8).

parasympathetic branch ('system' or 'division') A branch of the autonomic nervous system. It is generally excited at times of passivity (e.g. relaxation) (Chapter 3).

parvo system A system of communication in which a parvo ganglion cell communicates with a parvo LGN cell and thereby segregated information is projected to the cortex (Chapter 8).

passive avoidance A contingency arranged such that an animal can avoid an aversive outcome by refraining from performing a behaviour, such as stepping down from a platform (Chapter 11).

pathogen Threat to the body that is within its boundary, e.g. bacteria (Chapter 13).

perception The conscious awareness of events in the world associated with sensation through sensory systems (Chapter 8).

period The time that it takes a rhythm to complete one cycle (Chapter 19).

peripheral nervous system That part of the nervous system that is not in the brain or spinal cord (Chapter 3).

PGO system A neural circuit that projects from the pons (P) to the LGN (G) and then to the occipital cortex (O) and which plays a role in sleep (Chapter 19).

phantom pain The perception of pain in a bodily location that no longer exists (Chapter 14).

phenomenal consciousness Impossible to capture the term in words but something like 'what it feels like to be conscious' (Chapter 21).

phenotype The biological form or behaviour which exists at any point in time: the form that appears as a result of the genotype exerting an effect within the environment (in distinction to genotype, which is simply the genetic contribution) (Chapter 2).

phenylketonuria A mental disorder associated with a metabolic imbalance and caused by a mutation in a single gene (Chapter 2).

pheromone An airborne chemical that plays a role in communication between animals of the same species (with reference to mating) (Chapter 7).

phoneme The individual sounds that make up a language (Chapter 20).

phylogeny The history of development of species. Sometimes compared and contrasted with ontogeny (Chapter 1).

physiological effect The effect of a chemical intervention that seems to mimic a natural effect (Chapter 16).

physiology The science involved in the study of how the body works, involving such things as the circulation and nervous system, etc. (Chapter 1).

pituitary adrenocortical system (or pituitary adrenocortical axis) The sequence of hormone actions: CRF → ACTH → corticosteroids (Chapter 13).

place code A code in which different frequencies of sound are represented in terms of different locations in the nervous system, e.g. at the basilar membrane (Chapter 9).

placebo effect An otherwise neutral process that has a pain reduction effect based on belief as to its efficacy and/or learning (Chapter 10).

plasticity The capacity of nervous systems and behaviour to exhibit change, e.g. in the light of experience (Chapter 3).

population coding Information encoded by means of which of a population of neurons is activated (Chapter 7).

positive reinforcement A strengthening procedure by which a behaviour is more likely to be repeated in the future as a result of its positive consequences on past occasions (Chapter 11).

positron emission tomography (PET) A measure of metabolism and blood flow in different regions of the brain (Chapter 5).

post-absorptive state The state when absorption of food is complete and the body relies on intrinsic sources of energy (Chapter 16).

postsynaptic neuron A neuron that is influenced by activity in a presynaptic neuron. At a chemical synapse, it has receptors for the neurochemical released (Chapter 3).

postsynaptic potential The change in membrane potential at a site in a postsynaptic neuron caused by the arrival of an action potential at the terminal of a presynaptic neuron (Chapter 4).

post-traumatic stress disorder (PTSD) A type of stress reaction triggered by traumatic experience and involving regular activation of memories relating to the incident, nightmares and high sympathetic arousal (Chapter 13).

precocial An animal born in a condition relatively competent for independent existence (Chapter 6).

predatory aggression Aggression that a predator directs towards its prey (Chapter 15).

predictability The capacity to predict events, e.g. the arrival of a stressor such as shock based on prior cues such as a light (Chapter 13).

prefrontal cortex The anterior part of the cortex of the frontal lobes (i.e. excluding regions directly concerned with motor control such as the motor cortex) (Chapter 5).

prepulse inhibition (PPI) The inhibition of the response to a stimulus S2 by presenting a weak stimulus S1 just prior to S2 (Chapter 22).

presynaptic neuron A neuron that instigates activity in a postsynaptic neuron. At a chemical synapse, it releases neurotransmitter (Chapter 3).

primary visual cortex The region of occipital lobe at which visual information arrives. It is known as the 'striate cortex', 'V1' and 'area 17' (Chapter 8).

primate The group of species made up of monkeys, chimpanzees, gorillas and humans, among others (Chapter 1).

priming A beneficial effect of prior exposure on subsequent recall (Chapter 11).

principle of localization Discrete parts of the nervous system are concerned with discrete roles (Chapter 5).

procedural memory A memory that takes the form of a procedure, i.e. how to do something (Chapter 11).

proceptivity Active approach and solicitation behaviour by a female (Chapter 17).

programmed cell death (PCD) Systematic death of large numbers of cells, in a way that has functional significance for the establishment of an effective nervous system (Chapter 6).

proprioception The system that involves detection of the contraction of skeletal muscles and transmission of this information to the CNS (Chapter 10).

prosopagnosia A defect in face recognition (following brain damage) (Chapter 6).

protein Large chemical structures that are constituents of our bodies (Chapter 1).

protein synthesis The building of proteins, fundamental constituents of the body (Chapter 11).

psychoactive drug A type of drug that exerts a psychological effect (Chapter 18).

psychogenic cause Something not having an identifiable initial trigger in the body's physiology and assumed to represent a psychological cause (normally with reference to a disturbance) (Chapter 17).

psychopharmacology The science involved with the effects of drugs on the nervous system and thereby behaviour (Chapter 3).

psychosis A kind of disruption to mental activity in which there is a break with reality (Chapter 22).

pyramidal system See pyramidal tract and corticospinal tract (Chapter 10).

pyramidal tract Pathway of axons that make up the corticospinal tract (Chapter 10).

Q

qualia States of conscious awareness expressed in terms of content (Chapter 21).

R

rapid eye movement sleep (REM sleep) A phase of sleep characterized by the appearance of rapid jerks of the eyes in their sockets and a signature EEG pattern (Chapter 19).

reaction Behaviour triggered by an external event, as in the case of a reflex (Chapter 2).

readiness potential A change in electrical activity seen at the SMA, some 800 ms before the muscular activity starts (Chapter 10).

receptive field The area of sensory surface, stimulation of which changes the activity of the neuron in question (with regard to location and size at the sensory surface) (Chapter 7).

receptivity The willingness of a female animal to accept the male's sexual approach, involving the performance of a mating posture (Chapter 17).

receptor (a) Structures at a cell that are occupied by natural chemicals, which then affect the functioning of the cell. (b) The tip of a sensory neuron that is sensitive to a physical event (not to be confused with a receptor molecule) (Chapter 3).

receptor cells (or 'receptors') Cells that are sensitive to physical events, e.g. light receptors in the eye (Chapter 5).

reciprocal inhibition A control process in which an increase of excitation of a flexor muscle is accompanied by a decreased excitation of the antagonist extensor and vice versa (Chapter 10).

reciprocal interaction model A model of the neural basis of sleep in which there is mutual inhibition between (1) cholinergic neurons and (2) serotonergic and noradrenergic neurons (Chapter 19).

reductionism A process of trying to explain events at one level (e.g. behaviour) by looking at a lower level (e.g. the interactions between neurons and hormones) (Chapter 1).

referred pain Pain felt to be associated not with a site of actual tissue damage but 'referred to' another site (Chapter 14).

reflex A relatively stereotyped response to a given stimulus (Chapter 2).

refractory period Period of time that must elapse following an action potential before a given section of axon can be stimulated again to produce another (Chapter 4).

regional cerebral blood flow (rCBF) The blood flow to a particular region of the brain (Chapter 5).

regulatory behaviour Behaviour that regulates the internal environment, e.g. drinking in response to dehydration (Chapter 2).

reinforcement (a) Defined as a procedure that changes behaviour, e.g. if a hungry rat turns left at a choice point in a maze and receives food, the food is said to reinforce the left turn (Chapter 2). (b) At a theoretical level, a process of strengthening S–R links (Chapter 11).

replication The process of producing new cells from the division of precursor cells. The process is intrinsic to a given individual (Chapter 2).

reproduction The process of forming a fertilized egg cell from a sperm cell joining with an egg cell (Chapter 2).

resting potential The membrane potential of a neuron when it is not conducting an action potential (normally about –60 to –70 mV) (Chapter 4).

retina A layer at the back of the eye where light-sensitive cells are situated (Chapter 8).

retrieval Gaining access to stored information, activating a memory (Chapter 11).

retrograde amnesia A failure to recall events experienced before the trauma (Chapter 11).

reuptake The process by which neuro-transmitter is taken back into the neuron from which it was released (Chapter 4).

reuptake inhibitor A drug that blocks the reuptake of neurotransmitter from the neuron that released it (Chapter 4).

reward An outcome of behaviour, the experience of which motivates further contact with the given object and to which animals are motivated to regain contact (Chapter 15).

rod A type of sensory receptor, located at the retina (Chapter 8).

S

saccadic eye movement Rapid movements of the eyes in their sockets that serve to keep the fovea in alignment with the object of attention (Chapter 8).

satiety The loss, or inhibition, of appetite following ingestion as a result of a sufficiency of intake (Chapter 16).

schizophrenia A form of psychosis having a developmental origin and characterized by symptoms such as hallucinations (Chapter 22).

second messenger A chemical that is released within a neuron as a result of the occupation of receptors by neurotransmitter and which serves a communication role (Chapter 4).

selfish gene The notion that the actions of a gene are such as to code for its own success, even at a cost to others, hence the metaphor 'selfish' (Chapter 2).

semantic memory A memory for facts, e.g. 'Paris is in France' (Chapter 11).

sensitive period (sometimes termed a 'critical period') A period (usually with regard to development) during which a process is sensitive to a change, e.g. as triggered by a hormone (Chapter 6).

sensitivity A measure of the ability to detect the presence or absence of even weak stimuli (Chapter 8).

sensitization A term to describe a system that responds more strongly even to innocuous stimuli, after a noxious stimulus has been applied (Chapter 11).

sensory homunculus A bizarre-looking person located alongside the somatosensory cortex, defined by regions of cortex associated with corresponding regions of the sensory surface of the body (Chapter 5).

sensory neuron A neuron that detects information on events in the external world or inside the body (Chapter 3).

sensory receptor Cell or part of cell that detects physical events and links this to a change in membrane potential (Chapter 7).

sensory-specific satiety (SSS) Satiety that is specific to a particular, recently ingested, food (Chapter 16).

sensory system A system that detects physical events, conveys information about them to the brain and does some processing of information (Chapter 7).

sensory threshold Minimum level of stimulation that can be detected (Chapter 7).

set-point The value at which a negative feedback system tends to maintain a regulated variable. Deviations of the variable from the set-point tend to be self-eliminating (Chapter 10).

sex chromosomes The 23rd pair of chromosomes, which differ between males and females. Females have an XX combination and males an XY combination (Chapter 2).

sexual development Development of sex organs and neural systems underlying sexual behaviour, as well as secondary sexual characteristics such as the male voice breaking (Chapter 6).

sexual differentiation Formation of either a typical female or typical male reproductive system (e.g. genitals, breasts, brain mechanisms of motivation) from an undifferentiated precursor structure (Chapter 6).

sexually dimorphic nucleus (SDN) A nucleus of the preoptic area of the hypothalamus, which is the target of androgens and larger in males than females (Chapter 6).

short-term memory (STM) A memory of limited capacity and concerning recently acquired information (sometimes termed 'primary memory') (Chapter 11).

side effect Effect of a drug that is unintended in its prescription (Chapter 4).

size constancy A phenomenon in which a given object tends to trigger a constant perception, in spite of variation in the image that it produces at the retina as a function of change in distance (Chapter 8).

skeletal muscles Muscles through which action is exerted on the external world (Chapter 3).

Skinner box An apparatus in which an animal effects change, such as pressing a lever or pecking a key and thereby earns a reward, such as a pellet of food (Chapter 1).

sleep factor A suggested natural chemical that arises in the body and which triggers sleep (Chapter 19).

slow-wave sleep ('synchronized sleep') A stage of non-REM sleep characterized by a low-frequency signal measured by EEG (Chapter 19).

smooth muscle Muscle through which the autonomic nervous system exerts action on the internal environment, e.g. changing the diameter of blood vessels (Chapter 3).

social attachment The attachment that exists between a parent and offspring or between monogamous sexual partners (Chapter 15).

social constructivism (or 'social constructionism') A school of thought within psychology that suggests that much of our mental life and behaviour is to be understood in terms of the constructs that a society places upon these events (Chapter 12).

sodium–potassium pump Pump that expels Na$^+$ from cells and pulls in K$^+$ (Chapter 4).

soft-wired A description for neuronal systems and connections that exhibit plasticity, e.g. as a result of experience (Chapter 3).

somatic-marker hypothesis The hypothesis that emotions are labelled in the CNS in terms of their physiological associations outside the CNS. Thus, a frame of reference for fear might be, among other things, an accelerated heart-rate. The brain then

models these effects and can create something of them even in the absence of the peripheral effect (Chapter 12).

somatic nervous system That part of the nervous system that effects action on the external world (Chapter 3).

somatosensory cortex The region of cortex at which tactile information arrives and where the cortical processing of it first occurs (Chapter 5).

somatosensory neuron A type of neuron the tip of which is sensitive to tactile stimuli. The tips are located across the surface of the skin (Chapter 9).

somatosensory system The system involving the detection and processing of information on touch (Chapter 9).

spatial summation The addition of the effects at a postsynaptic neuron that arise from inputs to this neuron occurring at different locations (Chapter 4).

species-typical behaviour (STB) A type of behaviour exhibited by most, if not all, members of a particular species (Chapter 2).

spinal cord Column of neurons within the backbone (Chapter 1).

spinal nerve A nerve formed by the convergence of neurons transmitting afferent and efferent information between the CNS and the periphery (Chapter 3).

spinal reflex A reflex organized at the level of the spinal cord (Chapter 3).

spinothalamic tract (STT) A pathway in the spinal cord, which carries, among other things, ascending nociceptive information (Chapter 14).

split-brain A brain in which communication between hemispheres is restricted, or eliminated, by cutting the corpus callosum (Chapter 8).

spontaneous alternation The tendency of a rat to alternate its choices of arm taken in a T-maze (Chapter 15).

staining A histological technique whereby neurons are labelled chemically to aid their identification (Chapter 5).

startle reflex A reaction of, among other things, flinching and defensive adjustment when exposed to particular, e.g. intense, stimuli (Chapter 12).

stereotypy A repetitive behaviour with no obvious goal or end-point, such as head-shaking (Chapter 2).

steroid A class of hormone that includes androgens and oestrogens (Chapter 17).

stimulant A class of drug that boosts noradrenergic and dopaminergic neurotransmission and is used in the treatment of ADHD (Chapter 22).

stimulus–response association (S–R) Learning that involves forming an association between a particular stimulus and a particular response (Chapter 11).

stimulus–stimulus association An association that an animal learns of the form that one stimulus leads to another stimulus (Chapter 11).

strain A subdivision within a species (Chapter 2).

stress A state of lengthy disturbance to homeostasis, deriving from physiological or cognitive triggers. A protracted inability to resolve an underlying problem (Chapter 13).

stressor Something that triggers stress, such as infection, noise or social conflict (Chapter 13).

stretch receptor Tip of a sensory neuron that is sensitive to stretch in associated muscle (Chapter 10).

stretch reflex A reflex that counters disturbances to the set position of a limb (Chapter 10).

stroke Disruption of brain function caused by blocking an artery in the brain or rupture of a blood vessel (Chapter 5).

Stroop test A test in which a person is asked to name the colour of ink in which words are written, the words being incompatible colour names (Chapter 20).

structural neuroimaging A technique for looking at the structure ('anatomy') of the brain in terms of sizes and locations of different regions, etc. (Chapter 5).

subcortical pathway A pathway by which sensory information is transmitted other than via the cortex (Chapter 8).

sympathetic branch ('system' or 'division') A branch of the autonomic nervous system. It is generally excited at times of activity (Chapter 3).

synapse The region where one neuron communicates with another cell, normally by chemical means (Chapter 3).

synaptic cleft The gap between the membrane of the presynaptic and postsynaptic cells (Chapter 4).

synaptic delay The time taken for information to pass across a synapse, i.e. between arrival of an action potential and the start of electrical events in the postsynaptic cell (Chapter 3).

T

taste reactivity test A test in which samples of solutions are placed on the tongue of rats and the rat's affective reactions monitored by video (Chapter 15).

taste-aversion learning (or the 'Garcia effect') Devaluation of a particular taste as a result of it being followed by gastrointestinal upset (Chapter 1).

T cell Neuron that transmits nociceptive information from local regions of spinal cord to the brain. They are excited by nociceptive neurons which form synapses on them within the spinal cord (Chapter 14).

temporal summation The addition of postsynaptic potentials that arise as a result of a sequence of events in a presynaptic neuron (Chapter 4).

testosterone A hormone secreted in males and females and involved in sexual motivation and aggression (Chapter 3).

theory of mind The cognitive representation within one animal of the state of mind of another, e.g. regarding the other's emotion and intention (Chapter 5).

theory of mind mechanism A proposed mechanism, which is thought to serve to extract information on the intentions and desires of others (Chapter 6).

theta wave Synchronized waves of activity shown by the hippocampus during REM sleep and at other times (Chapter 19).

threshold The level of depolarization at which an action potential is triggered (Chapter 4). The point at which a sensory event starts to influence detection (Chapter 7).

tolerance A situation of drug use, where increasing amounts of drug need to be taken to obtain a given effect. Can also be applied to some non-drug-related activities such as gambling (Chapter 18).

tonotopic representation A representation in which different locations at the basilar membrane are represented by different locations at the auditory cortex. Thus, different frequencies of sound correspond to different cortical locations (Chapter 9).

top-down A mode of influence from higher levels of the nervous system to lower, e.g. from perception to sensory analysis (Chapter 7).

topographical map A representation in which adjacent regions of sensory surface (e.g. retina) are associated with adjacent neurons in the brain (e.g. visual cortex) (Chapter 8).

tract (or 'pathway') A number of axons within the CNS transmitting information along the same route (Chapter 3).

transcutaneous electrical nerve stimulation (TENS) A technique that involves applying weak electrical stimulation at the skin and thereby reducing pain (Chapter 14).

transduction Translation from physical events (e.g. a chemical on the tongue) to an electrical signal, a change in membrane potential of neurons (Chapter 7).

two-point threshold The distance between two points used as tactile stimuli at the skin at which the person can discriminate that there are two points rather than one point present. The smaller the distance, the higher is the tactile acuity at that point (Chapter 9).

Type A behaviour Behaviour consisting of being under excessive time-pressure, aggressively competitive, over-ambitious and easily aroused to hostility (Chapter 13).

Type B behaviour Relaxed behaviour, without undue hostility and competitiveness (Chapter 13).

U

ulcer A type of damage (lesion), in this case to the gut, caused by both local factors, e.g. bacterial infection, and central stress-related factors (Chapter 13).

unconditional reflex A reflex the formation of which does not require conditioning, e.g. in dogs, the reflex underlying the production of salivation to food in the mouth (Chapter 11).

unconditional response (UCR) A response that does not depend upon a history of conditioning, e.g. salivation to food in the mouth (Chapter 11).

unconditional stimulus (UCS) A stimulus that has a capacity to elicit a response without a prior history of conditioning, e.g. food can unconditionally elicit salivation in hungry dogs (Chapter 11).

up-regulation The process by which there is an increased density of receptors at a postsynaptic membrane as a result of abnormally low levels of stimulation by neurotransmitter (Chapter 4).

utilization behaviour Behaviour shown by patients with damage to the prefrontal cortex, in which they reach out to a familiar object and grab it even though this would otherwise have been considered 'inappropriate behaviour' (Chapter 10).

V

ventral Towards the belly or lower part of the brain (Chapter 3).

ventral stream A stream of visual information leading to the temporal cortex and associated with conscious perception (Chapter 8).

ventricles Large spaces in the brain that are filled with cerebrospinal fluid (Chapter 5).

vertebrate Those species of animal that have a backbone (Chapter 5).

vestibular apparatus A mechanism in the inner ear, which provides the sensory input to the vestibular system. The apparatus detects changes in the position of the head and transmits information on this to the brain along a cranial nerve (Chapter 9).

vestibular system The system that underlies balance based upon information arising in the vestibular apparatus (Chapter 9).

vestibulo-ocular reflex Compensatory movement of the eyes, accompanying head movement, so that the image tends to be stabilized on the retina (Chapter 10).

viscera The internal organs of the body, e.g. stomach and intestine. The associated adjective is 'visceral' (Chapter 3).

visual agnosia A condition in which there is an inability to recognize objects by the use of vision (Chapter 8).

visual cortex The region of cortex at which visual information arrives and where the cortical processing of it first occurs (Chapter 5).

voluntary action Behaviour that requires conscious decision-making and is said to have a purpose, which we can consciously reflect upon and articulate (Chapter 10).

voluntary behaviour Human behaviour that is associated with a conscious goal or intention (Chapter 2).

vomeronasal system A distinct olfactory system, with receptors in the nose, and which is responsible for the detection of pheromones (Chapter 9).

vulnerability model A model which suggests that stress contributes to the vulnerability of a person to suffer from schizophrenia (Chapter 22).

W

Wada technique A technique in which a fast-acting anaesthetic is injected into the carotid artery supplying blood to one hemisphere. Changes in cognition and behaviour are then observed (Chapter 20).

wavelength The distance between any two corresponding points on a cycle (Chapter 7).

Wernicke's aphasia Aphasia that is associated with damage to Wernicke's area. It is particularly associated with understanding language (Chapter 20).

Wernicke's area An area of the human temporal cortex concerned with the interpretation of language (Chapter 20).

Wernicke–Geschwind model A model of language involving interactions between a number of brain regions (Chapter 20).

wind-up The phenomenon of increased sensitivity of synapses in the nociceptive pathway (Chapter 14).

win–shift A situation where, having obtained reward at one location, an animal needs to move elsewhere to obtain another reward (Chapter 11).

win–stay A situation in which, having obtained reward at one location, an animal needs to revisit that location to obtain further reward (Chapter 11).

Wisconsin card-sorting test A task in which people need to sort cards according to a criterion of either their colour or form. The criterion changes at the request of the experimenter (Chapter 6).

withdrawal An aversive state triggered by the termination of drug intake (Chapter 18).

withdrawal symptoms Aversive bodily and psychological events triggered by the absence of a drug in dependent individuals (Chapter 18).

working memory A broad and multi-aspect memory class. In addition to a temporary store of information, it also performs manipulation of stored information (Chapter 11).

Z

Zeitgeber An extrinsic factor that sets the timing of a circadian rhythm (Chapter 19).

References

A

Abbeduto, L. and Boudreau, D. (2004) Theoretical influences on research on language development and intervention in individuals with mental retardation. *Mental Retardation and Developmental Disabilities Research Reviews,* **10**, 184–192.

Abi-Dargham, A. (2004) Do we still believe in the dopamine hypothesis? New data bring new evidence. *International Journal of Neuropsychopharmacology,* **7** (Suppl. 1), S1–S5.

Adamec, R. (1997) Transmitter systems involved in neural plasticity underlying increased anxiety and defense – implications for understanding anxiety following traumatic stress. *Neuroscience and Biobehavioral Reviews,* **21**, 755–765.

Ader, R. and Cohen, N. (1985) CNS–immune system interactions: conditioning phenomena. *Behavioral and Brain Sciences,* **8**, 379–394.

Adkins-Regan, E. (2004) *Hormones and Animal Social Behavior,* Princeton University Press, Princeton.

Adkins-Regan, E., Mansukhani,V., Thompson, R. and Yang, S. (1997) Organizational actions of sex hormones on sexual partner preference. *Brain Research Bulletin,* **44**, 497–502.

Adolphs, R. (2003) Cognitive neuroscience of human social behaviour. *Nature Reviews Neuroscience,* **4**, 165–178.

Adolphs, R. (2009) The social brain: neural basis of social knowledge. *Annual Review of Psychology,* **60**, 693–716.

Adolphs, R., Tranel, D. and Damasio, A.R. (1998) The human amygdala in social judgement. *Nature,* **393**, 470–474.

Adolphs, R., Damasio, H., Tranel, D., Cooper, G. and Damasio, A.R. (2000) A role for somatosensory cortices in the visual recognition of emotion as revealed by three-dimensional lesion mapping. *The Journal of Neuroscience,* **20**, 2683–2690.

Aggleton, J.P. and Mishkin, M. (1986) The amygdala: sensory gateway to the emotions. In *Emotion – Theory, Research and Experience. Volume 3: Biological Foundations of Emotion* (eds R. Plutchik and H. Kellerman), Academic Press, Orlando, pp. 281–299.

Aghajanian, G.K. (1994) Serotonin and the action of LSD in the brain. *Psychiatric Annals,* **24**, 137–141.

Aglioti, S., DeSouza, J.F.X. and Goodale, M.A. (1995) Size–contrast illusions deceive the eye but not the hand. *Current Biology,* **5**, 679–685.

Ågmo, A. and Berenfeld, R. (1990) Reinforcing properties of ejaculation in the male rat: role of opioids and dopamine. *Behavioral Neuroscience,* **104**, 177–182.

Ågmo, A., Turi, A.L., Ellingsen, E. and Kaspersen, H. (2004) Preclinical models of sexual desire: conceptual and behavioural analyses. *Pharmacology, Biochemistry and Behavior,* **78**, 379–404.

Agosti, C., Borroni, B., Akkawi, N.M., De Maria, G. and Padovani, A. (2008) Transient global amnesia and brain lesions: new hints into clinical criteria. *European Journal of Neurology,* **15**, 981–984.

Ahima, R.S. (2005) Central actions of adipocyte hormones. *Trends in Endocrinology and Metabolism,* **16**, 307–313.

Aiello, L.C. and Wheeler, P. (1995) The expensive-tissue hypothesis. *Current Anthropology,* **36**, 199–221.

Ainslie, G. (1975) Specious reward: a behavioral theory of impulsiveness and impulse control. *Psychological Bulletin,* **82**, 463–496.

Aitkin, L.M., Irvine, D.R.F. and Webster, W.R. (1984) Central neural mechanisms of hearing. In *Handbook of Physiology.* Section 1: *The Nervous System,* Vol. III, Part 2 (ed. I. Darian-Smith), American Physiological Society, Bethesda, pp. 675–738.

Akil, H., Campeau, S., Cullinan, W.E., Lechan, R.M., Toni, R., Watson, S.J. and Moore, R.Y. (1999) Neuroendocrine systems 1: overview – thyroid and adrenal axes. In *Fundamental Neuroscience* (eds M.J. Zigmond, F.E. Bloom, J.L. Roberts and L.A Squire), Academic Press, San Diego, pp. 1127–1150.

Alajouanine, T. (1948) Aphasia and artistic realization. *Brain,* **71**, 17–241.

Alaoui-Ismaïli, O., Robin, O., Rada, H., Dittmar, A. and Vernet-Maury, E. (1997) Basic emotions evoked by odorants: comparison between autonomic responses and self evaluation. *Physiology and Behavior,* **62**, 713–720.

Aldridge, J.W. and Berridge, K.C. (1998) Coding of serial order by neostriatal neurons: a 'natural action' approach to movement sequence. *Journal of Neuroscience,* **18**, 2777–2787.

Alexander, B. (2008) *The Globalization of Addiction: A Study in the Poverty of the Spirit,* Oxford University Press, Oxford.

Alexander, B.K. and Hadaway, P.F. (1982) Opiate addiction: the case for an adaptive orientation. *Psychological Bulletin,* **92**, 367–381.

Alexander, B.K., Peele, S., Hadaway, P.F., Morse, S.J., Brodsky, A. and Beyerstein, B.L. (1985) Adult, infant, and animal addiction. In *The Meaning of Addiction* (ed. S. Peele), Lexington Books, Lexington, pp. 73–96.

Allan, R. and Scheidt, S. (1996a) *Heart and Mind. The Practice of Cardiac Psychology,* American Psychological Association, Washington.

Allan, R. and Scheidt, S. (1996b) Empirical basis for cardiac psychology. *In Heart and Mind. The Practice of Cardiac Psychology* (eds R. Allan and S. Scheidt), American Psychological Association, Washington, pp. 63–123.

Allen, L.S. and Gorski, R.A. (1992) Sexual orientation and the size of the anterior commissure in the human brain. *Proceedings of the National Academy of Sciences, USA,* **89**, 7199–7202.

Allen, N.B. and Badcock, P.B.T. (2003) The social risk hypothesis of depressed mood: evolutionary, psychosocial, and neurobiological perspectives. *Psychological Bulletin,* **129**, 887–913.

Altman, J. (1962) Are new neurons formed in the brains of adult mammals? *Science*, **135**, 1127–1128.

Altman, J., Brunner, R.L. and Bayer, S.A. (1973) The hippocampus and behavioural maturation. *Behavioural Biology*, **8**, 557–596.

Alvarez, E.O. and Alvarez, P.A. (2008) Motivated exploratory behaviour in the rat: the role of hippocampus and the histaminergic neurotransmission. *Behavioural Brain Research*, **186**, 118–125.

Amaral, D.G. and Sinnamon, H.M. (1977) The locus coeruleus: neurobiology of a central noradrenergic nucleus. *Progress in Neurobiology*, **9**, 147–196.

Anderson, J.R. (2000) *Learning and Memory: An Integrated Approach,* 2nd edition, Wiley, New York.

Andersson, K-E. and Wagner, G. (1995) Physiology of penile erection. *Physiological Reviews*, **75**, 191–236.

Andrade, J. (2002) *Working Memory in Perspective*, Psychology Press, Hove.

Andreasen, N.C. (2005) *The Creating Brain: The Neuroscience of Genius*, Dana Press, New York.

Andreassi, J.L. (2007) *Psychophysiology: Human Behaviour and Physiological Response*, Lawrence Erlbaum, Mahwah.

Andrews, P.W. and Thomson, J.A. (2009) The bright side of being blue: depression as an adaptation for analyzing complex problems. *Psychological Review*, 116, 620–654.

Andrews, T.J., Schluppeck, D., Homfray, D., Matthews, P. and Blakemore, C. (2002) Activity in the fusiform gyrus predicts conscious perception of Rubin's vase–face illusion. *NeuroImage*, **17**, 890–901.

Anisman, H., Zaharia, M.D., Meaney, M.J. and Merali, Z. (1998) Do early-life events permanently alter behavioral and hormonal responses to stressors? *International Journal of Developmental Neuroscience*, **16**, 149–164.

Antin, J., Gibbs, J., Holt, J., Young, R.C. and Smith, G.P. (1975) Cholecystokinin elicits the complete behavioral sequence of satiety in rats. *Journal of Comparative and Physiological Psychology*, **89**, 784–790.

Antonova, E. and Kumari, V. (2010) Where will insights into hippocampal activity in schizophrenia lead us? *Expert Review of Neurotherapeutics*, **10**, 1–4.

Antrobus, J. (1991) Dreaming: cognitive processes during cortical activation and high afferent thresholds. *Psychological Review*, **98**, 96–121.

Archer, J. (1979) *Animals under Stress*, Edward Arnold, London.

Archer, J. (1994) Testosterone and aggression. *Journal of Offender Rehabilitation*, **21**, 3–25.

Archer, J. (1996) Sex differences in social behavior. *American Psychologist*, **51**, 909–917.

Archer, J. (2009) Does sexual selection explain human sex differences in aggression? *Behavioral and Brain Sciences*, **32**, 249–311.

Archer, J.S., Love-Geffen, T.E., Herbst-Damm, K.L., Swinney, D.A. and Chang, J.R. (2006) Effects of estradiol versus estradiol and testosterone on brain-activation patterns in postmenopausal women. *Menopause*, **13**, 528–537.

Arendt, J. (1997) Melatonin. In *Sleep Science: Integrating Basic Research and Clinical Practice*. Monographs in Clinical Neuroscience, Vol. 15 (ed. W.J. Schwartz), Karger, Basle, pp. 196–228.

Arnow, B.A., Desmond, J.E., Banner, L.L., Glover, G.H., Solomon, A., Polan, M.L., Lue, T.F. and Atlas, S.W. (2002) Brain activation and sexual arousal in healthy, heterosexual males. *Brain*, **125**, 1014–1023.

Arnsten, A.F.T. (2009) Toward a new understanding of attention-deficit hyperactivity disorder pathophysiology: An important role for prefrontal cortex dysfunction. *CNS Drugs*, **23** Suppl. 1, 33–41.

Arnsten, A.F.T. and Li, B-M. (2005) Neurobiology of executive functions: catecholamine influences on prefrontal cortical functions. *Biological psychiatry*, **57**, 1377–1384.

Aserinsky, E. and Kleitman, N. (1955) Two types of ocular motility occurring in sleep. *Journal of Applied Physiology*, **8**, 1–10.

Aston-Jones, G.S., Desimone, R., Driver, J., Luck, S.J. and Posner, M.I. (1999) Attention. In *Fundamental Neuroscience* (eds M.J. Zigmond, F.E. Bloom, S.C. Landis, J.L. Roberts and L.R. Squire), Academic Press, San Diego, pp. 1385–1409.

Avila, M., Thaker, G., and Adami, H. (2001) Genetic epidemiology and schizophrenia: a study of reproductive fitness. *Schizophrenia Research*, **47**, 233–241.

Axmacher, N., Draguhn, A., Elger, C.E. and Fell, J. (2009) Memory processes during sleep: beyond the standard consolidation theory. *Cellular and Molecular Life Sciences*, **66**, 2285–2297.

Aydede, M. (2006) *Pain: New Essays on its Nature and the Methodology of its Study*. MIT Press, Cambridge.

Aziz-Zadeh, L., Wilson, S.M., Rizzolatti, G. and Iacoboni, M. (2006) Congruent embodied representations for visually presented actions and linguistic phrases describing actions. *Current Biology*, **16**, 1818–1823.

Azrin, N.H., Hutchinson, R.R. and McLaughlin, R. (1965) The opportunity for aggression as an operant reinforcer during aversive stimulation. *Journal of the Experimental Analysis of Behavior,* **8**, 171–180.

B

Baars, B.J. (1993) How does a serial, integrated and very limited stream of consciousness emerge from a nervous system that is mostly unconscious, distributed, parallel and of enormous capacity? In *Experimental and Theoretical Studies of Consciousness* (eds G.R. Bock and J. Marsh), Wiley, Chichester, pp. 282–303.

Baars, B.J. (1997) *In the Theatre of Consciousness*, Oxford University Press, New York.

Baddeley, A. (1994) Working memory: the interface between memory and cognition. *In Memory Systems 1994* (eds D.L. Schacter and E. Tulving), MIT Press, Cambridge, pp. 351–637.

Baddeley, A. (1997) *Human Memory – Theory and Practice*, Psychology Press, Hove.

Baddeley, A.D. and Hitch, G. (1974) Working memory. In *The Psychology of Learning and Motivation*, Vol. 8 (ed. G.H. Bower), Academic Press, New York, pp. 47–89.

Baddeley, A.D., Bressi, S., Della Sala, S., Logie, R. and Spinnler, H. (1991) The decline of working memory in Alzheimer's disease. *Brain*, **114**, 2521–2542.

Baddeley, A., Della Sala, S., Papagno, C. and Spinnler, H. (1997) Dual-task performance in dysexecutive and nondysexecutive patients with a frontal lesion. *Neuropsychology*, **11**, 187–194.

Baird, A.D., Wilson, S.J., Bladin, P.F., Saling, M.M. and Reutens, D.C. (2007) Neurological control of human sexual behaviour: insights from lesion studies. *Journal of Neurology, Neurosurgery and Psychiatry*, **78**, 1042–1049.

Baizer, J.S., Ungerleider, L.G. and Desimone, R. (1991) Organization of visual inputs to the inferior temporal and posterior parietal cortex in macaques. *Journal of Neuroscience*, **11**, 168–190.

Baker, D.A., Khroyan, T.V., O'Dell, L.E., Fuchs, R.A. and Neisewander, J.L. (1996) Differential effects of intra-accumbens sulpiride on cocaine-induced locomotion and conditioned place preference. *Journal of Pharmacology and Experimental Therapeutics*, **279**, 392–401.

Baker, T.B., Piper, M.E., McCarthy, D.E., Majeskie, M.R. and Fiore, M.C. (2004) Addiction motivation reformulated: an affective processing model of negative reinforcement. *Psychological Review*, **111**, 33–51.

Balleine, B.W. and Dickinson, A. (1998) Goal-directed instrumental action: contingency and incentive learning and their cortical substrates. *Neuropharmacology*, **37**, 407–419.

Ballieux, R.E. and Heijnen, C.J. (1987) Brain and immune system: a one-way conversation or a genuine dialogue? In *Progress in Brain Research*, Vol. 72 (eds E.R. de Kloet, V.M. Wiegant and D. de Wied), Elsevier Science, Amsterdam, pp. 71–77.

Balu, D.T. and Lucki, I. (2009) Adult hippocampal neurogenesis: regulation, functional implications, and contribution to disease pathology. *Neuroscience and Biobehavioral Reviews*, **33**, 232–252.

Banaschewski, T., Coghill, D., Danckaerts, M., Döpfner, M., Rohde, L., Sergeant, J.A., Sonuga-Barke, E.J.S., Taylor, E. and Zuddas, A. (2009) *Attention-deficit Hyperactivity Disorder and Hyperkinetic Disorder*, Oxford University Press, Oxford.

Bancroft, J. (1988) Reproductive hormones and male sexual function. In *Handbook of Sexology*. Vol. 6: *The Pharmacology and Endocrinology of Sexual Function* (ed. J.M.A. Sitsen), Elsevier Science Publishers, Amsterdam, pp. 297–315.

Bancroft, J. (1989) *Human Sexuality and its Problems*, Churchill Livingstone, Edinburgh.

Bandler, R. and Shipley, M.T. (1994) Columnar organization in the midbrain periaqueductal gray: modules for emotional expression? *Trends in Neurosciences*, **17**, 379–389.

Bandura, A., O'Leary, A., Taylor, C.B., Gauthier, J. and Gossard, D. (1987) Perceived self-efficacy and pain control: opioid and nonopioid mechanisms. *Journal of Personality and Social Psychology*, **53**, 563–571.

Bantick, S.J., Wise, R.G., Ploghaus, A., Clare, S., Smith, S.M. and Tracey, I. (2002) Imaging how attention modulates pain in humans using functional MRI. *Brain*, **125**, 310–319.

Bao, A.M., Meynen, G. and Swaab, D.F. (2008) The stress system in depression and neurodegeneration: focus on the human hypothalamus. *Brain Research Reviews,* **57**, 531–553.

Barden, N., Reul, J.M.H.M. and Holsboer, F. (1995) Do anti-depressants stabilize mood through actions on the hypothalamic–pituitary–adrenocortical system? *Trends in Neurosciences*, **18**, 6–11.

Bardo, M.T. (1998) Neuropharmacological mechanisms of drug reward: beyond dopamine in the nucleus accumbens. *Critical Reviews in Neurobiology*, **12**, 37–67.

Bardo, M.T., Donohew, R.L. and Harrington, N.G. (1996) Psychobiology of novelty seeking and drug seeking behavior. *Behavioural Brain Research*, **77**, 23–43.

Bargh, J.A. and Chartrand, T.L. (1999) The unbearable automaticity of being. *American Psychologist*, **54**, 462–479.

Bargh, J.A. and Tota, M.E. (1988) Context-dependent automatic processing in depression: accessibility of negative constructs with regard to self but not others. *Journal of Personality and Social Psychology*, **54**, 925–939.

Barkley, R.A. (1997) Behavioural inhibition, sustained attention, and executive functions: constructing a unified theory of ADHD. *Psychological Bulletin*, **121**, 65–94.

Barkley, R.A. (2005) *ADHD and the Nature of Self-control*, Guilford Press, New York.

Barkow, J.H., Cosmides, L. and Tooby, J. (1992) *The Adapted Mind: Evolutionary Psychology and the Generation of Culture*, Oxford University Press, New York.

Barlow, H. (1990) The mechanical mind. *Annual Review of Neurosciences*, **13**, 15–24.

Barlow, H. (1995) The neuron doctrine in perception. In *The Cognitive Neurosciences* (ed. M.S. Gazzaniga), MIT Press, Cambridge, pp. 415–435.

Barney, K. (1994) Limitations of the critique of the medical model. *Journal of Mind and Behavior*, **15**, 19–34.

Baron-Cohen, S. (1999) The cognitive neuroscience of autism: evolutionary approaches. In *The New Cognitive Neurosciences* (ed. M.S. Gazzaniga), MIT Press, Cambridge, pp. 1249–1257.

Barot, S.K., Kyono, Y., Clark, E.W. and Bernstein, I.L. (2008) Visualizing stimulus convergence in amygdala neurons during associative learning. *Proceedings of the National Academy of Sciences*, **105**, 20959–20963.

Bartels, A. and Zeki, S. (2000) The neural basis of romantic love. *NeuroReport*, **11**, 3829–3834.

Bartels, A. and Zeki, S. (2004) The neural correlates of maternal and romantic love. *NeuroImage*, **21**, 1155–1166.

Bartlik, B., Kaplan, P., Kaminetsky, J., Roentsch, G. and Goldberg, J. (1999a) Medications with the potential to enhance sexual responsivity in women. *Psychiatric Annals*, **29**, 46–52.

Bartlik, B., Legere, R. and Andersson, L. (1999b) The combined use of sex therapy and testosterone replacement therapy for women. *Psychiatric Annals*, **29**, 27–33.

Bartoshuk, L.M. and Beauchamp, G.K. (1994) Chemical senses. In *Annual Review of Psychology*, Vol. 45 (eds L.W. Porter and M.R. Rosenzweig), Annual Reviews Inc., Palo Alto, pp. 419–449.

Bastian, A.J., Mugnaini, E. and Thach, W.T. (1999) Cerebellum. In *Fundamental Neuroscience* (eds M.J. Zigmond, F.E. Bloom, S.C. Landis, J.L. Roberts and L.R. Squire), Academic Press, San Diego, pp. 973–992.

Batchelor, S., Thompson, E.O. and Miller, L.A. (2008) Retrograde memory after unilateral stroke. *Cortex*, **44**, 170–178.

Bateson, P. (1979) How do sensitive periods arise and what are they for? *Animal Behaviour*, **27**, 470–486.

Batty, M.J., Liddle, E.B., Pitiot, A., Toro, R., Groom, M.J., Scerif, G., Liotti, M., Liddle, P.F., Paus, T. and Hollis, C. (2010) Cortical gray matter in attention-deficit/hyperactivity disorder: a structural magnetic resonance imaging study. *Journal of the American Academy of Child and Adolescent Psychiatry*, **49**, 229–238.

Bauer, R.M. (1982) Visual hypoemotionality as a symptom of visual-limbic disconnection in man. *Archives of Neurology*, **39**, 702–708.

Bauer, R.M. and Verfaellie, M. (1992) Memory dissociations: a cognitive psychophysiology perspective. In *Neuropsychology of Memory* (eds L.R. Squire and N. Butters), Guilford Press, New York, pp. 58–71.

Baum, M.J. (1999) Psychosexual development. In *Fundamental Neuroscience* (eds M.J. Zigmond, F.E. Bloom, S.C. Landis and L.R. Squire), Academic Press, San Diego, pp. 1229–1244.

Baxter, D.W. and Olszewski, J. (1960) Congenital universal insensitivity to pain. *Brain*, **83**, 381–393.

Baxter, J.D. and Rousseau, G.G. (1979) Glucocorticoid hormone action: an overview. In *Glucocorticoid Hormone Action* (eds J.D.

Baxter and G.G. Rousseau), Springer-Verlag, Berlin, pp. 1–24.

Beach, F.A. (1947) A review of physiological and psychological studies of sexual behavior in mammals. *Physiological Reviews*, **27**, 240–307.

Beach, F.A. (1975) Behavioral endocrinology: an emerging discipline. *American Scientist*, **63**, 178–187.

Beach, F.A. and LeBoeuf, B.J. (1967) Coital behaviour in dogs. I. Preferential mating in the bitch. *Animal Behaviour*, **15**, 546–558.

Beach, F.A. and Whalen, R.E. (1959) Effects of ejaculation on sexual behavior in the male rat. *Journal of Comparative and Physiological Psychology*, **52**, 249–254.

Beach, F.A. and Wilson, J.R. (1963) Mating behavior in male rats after removal of the seminal vesicles. *Proceedings of the National Academy of Sciences USA*, **49**, 624–626.

Bear, M.F., Connors, B.W. and Paradiso, M.A. (1996) *Neuroscience: Exploring the Brain*, Williams and Wilkins, Baltimore.

Bear, M.F., Connors, B.W. and Paradiso, M.A. (2006) *Neuroscience: Exploring the Brain*, 3rd edition, Lippincott Williams and Wilkins, Baltimore.

Bear, R.E., Fitzgerald, P., Rosenfeld, J.V. and Bittar, R.G. (2010) Neurosurgery for obsessive-compulsive disorder: contemporary approaches. *Journal of Clinical Neuroscience*, **17**, 1–5.

Bebbington, P., Wilkins, S., Jones, P., Foerster, A., Murray, R., Toone, B. and Lewis, S. (1993) Life events and psychosis: initial results from the Camberwell Collaborative Psychosis Study. *British Journal of Psychiatry*, **162**, 72–79.

Bechara, A. (2004) The role of emotion in decision-making: evidence from neurological patients with orbitofrontal damage. *Brain and Cognition*, **55**, 30–40.

Bechara, A. (2005) Decision making, impulse control and loss of willpower to resist drugs: a neurocognitive perspective. *Nature Neuroscience*, **8**, 1458–1463.

Bechara, A., Tranel, D., Damasio, H., Adolphs, R., Rockland, C. and Damasio, A.R. (1995) Double dissociation of conditioning and declarative knowledge relative to the amygdala and hippocampus in humans. *Science*, **269**, 1115–1118.

Bechara, A., Nader, K. and van der Kooy, D. (1998) A two-separate-motivational-systems hypothesis of opioid addiction. *Pharmacology, Biochemistry and Behavior*, **59**, 1–17.

Beck, A.T. (1967) *Depression – Clinical, Experimental, and Theoretical Aspects*, Staples Press, London.

Beck, R.C. (2004) *Motivation: Theories and Principles*, Pearson Education, Upper Saddle River.

Becker, J.B., Breedlove, S.M. and Crews, D. (1992) *Behavioral Endocrinology*, MIT Press, Cambridge.

Beckers, G. and Zeki, S. (1995) The consequences of inactivating areas V1 and V5 on visual motion perception. *Brain*, **118**, 49–60.

Beecher, H.K. (1955) The powerful placebo. *Journal of the American Medical Association*, **159**, 1602–1606.

Bejerot, S. (2003) Psychosurgery for obsessive-compulsive disorder – concerns remain. *Acta Psychiatrica Scandinavica*, **107**, 241–243.

Bekinschtein, T.A., Shalom, D.E., Forcato, C., Herrera, M., Coleman, M.R., Manes, F.F. and Sigman, M. (2009) Classical conditioning in the vegetative and minimally conscious state. *Nature Neuroscience*, **12**, 1343–1351.

Benedetti, F. and Amanzio, M. (1997) The neurobiology of placebo analgesia: from endogenous opioids to cholecystokinin. *Progress in Neurobiology*, **51**, 109–125.

Benington, J.H. (2000) Sleep homeostasis and the function of sleep. *Sleep*, **23**, 959–966.

Benington, J.H. and Frank, M.G. (2003) Cellular and molecular connections between sleep and synaptic plasticity. *Progress in Neurobiology*, **69**, 71–101.

Benington, J.H. and Heller, H.C. (1995) Restoration of brain energy metabolism as the function of sleep. *Progress in Neurobiology*, **45**, 347–360.

Bennett, E.L. (1976) Cerebral effects of differential experience and training. In *Neural Mechanisms of Learning and Memory* (eds M.R. Rosenzweig and E.L. Bennett), MIT Press, Cambridge, pp. 279–287.

Bennett, M. (2010) *Neuropathic Pain*. Oxford University Press, Oxford.

Benson, J.B (1990) The significance and development of crawling in human infancy. In *Advances in Motor Development Research*, Vol. 3 (eds J.E. Clark and J.H. Humphrey), AMS Press, New York, pp. 91–142.

Bentivoglio, M. and Grassi-Zucconi, G. (1997) The pioneering experimental studies on sleep deprivation. *Sleep*, **20**, 570–576.

Berenbaum, S.A. (1999) Effects of early androgens on sex-typed activities and interests in adolescents with congenital adrenal hyperplasia. *Hormones and Behavior*, **35**, 102–110.

Berkowitz, L. (1993) *Aggression – Its Causes, Consequences and Control*, McGraw-Hill, New York.

Berman, K.F. and Weinberger, D.R. (1991) Functional localization in the brain in schizophrenia. In *Review of Psychiatry*, Vol. 10 (eds A. Tasman and S.M. Goldfinger), American Psychiatric Press, Washington, pp. 24–59.

Bernhardt, P.C. (1997) Influences of serotonin and testosterone in aggression and dominance: convergence with social psychology. *Current Directions in Psychological Science*, **6**, 44–48.

Berns, G.S. and Sejnowski, T.J. (1998) A computational model of how the basal ganglia produce sequences. *Journal of Cognitive Neuroscience*, **10**, 108–121.

Bernstein, G.A., Carroll, M.E., Thuras, P.D., Cosgrove, K.P. and Roth, M.E. (2002) Caffeine dependence in teenagers. *Drug and Alcohol Dependence*, **66**, 1–6.

Bernstein, I.L. (1996) Neural mediation of food aversions and anorexia induced by tumour necrosis factor and tumours. *Neuroscience and Biobehavioral Reviews*, **20**, 177–181.

Bernstein, I.L. and Webster, M.M. (1985) Learned food aversions: a consequence of cancer chemotherapy. In *Cancer, Nutrition, and Eating Behavior: A Biobehavioral Perspective* (eds T.G. Burish, S.M. Levy and B.E. Meyerowitz), Lawrence Erlbaum, Hillsdale, pp. 103–116.

Berntson, G.G. and Micco, D.J. (1976) Organization of brainstem behavioral systems. *Brain Research Bulletin*, **1**, 471–483.

Berridge, C.W., Devilbiss, D.M., Andrzejewski, M.E., Arnsten, A.F.T., Kelley, A.E., Schmeichel, B., Hamilton, C. and Spencer, R.C. (2006) Methylphenidate preferentially increases catecholamine neurotransmission within the prefrontal cortex at low doses that enhance cognitive function. *Biological Psychiatry*, **60**, 1111–1120.

Berridge, K.C. (1995) Food reward: brain substrates of wanting and liking. *Neuroscience and Biobehavioral Reviews*, **20**, 1–25.

Berridge, K.C. (2004) Motivation concepts in behavioral neuroscience. *Physiology and Behavior*, **81**, 179–209.

Berridge, K.C. (2009) 'Liking' and 'wanting' food rewards: brain substrates and roles in eating disorders. *Physiology and Behavior*, **97**, 537–550.

Berridge, K.C. and Valenstein, E.S. (1991) What psychological process mediates feeding evoked by electrical stimulation of the lateral hypothalamus? *Behavioral Neuroscience*, **105**, 3–14.

Berridge, K.C., Grill, H.J. and Norgren, R. (1981) Relation of consummatory responses and preabsorptive insulin release to palatability and learned taste aversions. *Journal of Comparative and Physiological Psychology*, **95**, 363–382.

Berthoud, H-R. (2002) Multiple neural systems controlling food intake and body weight. *Neuroscience and Biobehavioral Reviews*, **26**, 393–428.

Berthoud, H-R., Sutton, G.M., Townsend, R.L., Patterson, L.M. and Zheng, H. (2006) Brainstem mechanisms integrating gut-derived satiety signals and descending forebrain information in the control of meal size. *Physiology and Behavior*, **89**, 517–524.

Berthoz, A. (1996) Neural basis of decision in perception and in the control of movement. In *Neurobiology of Decision-making* (eds A.R. Damasio, H. Damasio and Y. Christen), Springer, Berlin, pp. 83–100.

Bertolino, A. and Blasi, G. (2009) The genetics of schizophrenia. *Neuroscience*, **164**, 288–299.

Besheer, J., Jensen, H.C. and Bevins, R.A. (1999) Dopamine antagonism in a novel-object recognition and a novel-object place conditioning preparation with rats. *Behavioural Brain Research*, **103**, 35–44.

Best, M., Williams, J.M. and Coccaro, E.F. (2002) Evidence for a dysfunctional prefrontal circuit in patients with an impulsive aggressive disorder. *Proceedings of the National Academy of Sciences USA*, **99**, 8448–8453.

Bevins, R.A. and Bardo, M.T. (1999) Conditioned increase in place preference by access to novel objects: antagonism by MK-801. *Behavioural Brain Research*, **99**, 53–60.

Bianchi, L. (1922) *The Mechanism of the Brain and the Function of the Frontal Lobes*, Livingstone, Edinburgh.

Billings, J.H., Scherwitz, L.W., Sullivan, R., Sparler, S. and Ornish, D.M. (1996) The lifestyle heart trial: comprehensive treatment and group support therapy. In *Heart and Mind. The Practice of Cardiac Psychology* (eds R. Allan and S. Scheidt), American Psychological Association, Washington, pp. 233–253.

Bindra, D. (1978) How adaptive behaviour is produced: a perceptual–motivational alternative to response-reinforcement. *Behavioral and Brain Sciences*, **1**, 41–91.

Birch, L.L., McPhee, L., Sullivan, S. and Johnson, S. (1989) Conditioned meal initiation in young children. *Appetite*, **13**, 105–113.

Birchwood, M. and Jackson, C. (2001) *Schizophrenia*. Psychology Press, Hove.

Bjorklund, A. and Cenci-Nilsson, A. (2010) *Recent Advances in Parkinson's Disease: Basic Research*. Elsevier, New York.

Bjorness, T.E. and Greene, R.W. (2009) Adenosine and sleep. *Current Neuropharmacology*, **7**, 238–245.

Blackburn, J.R. and Pfaus, J.G. (1988) Is motivation really modulation? A comment on Wise. *Psychobiology*, **16**, 303–304.

Blackburn, J.R., Pfaus, J.G. and Phillips, A.G. (1992) Dopamine functions in appetitive and defensive behaviours. *Progress in Neurobiology*, **39**, 247–279.

Blackmore, S. (2005) *Conversations on Consciousness: Interviews with Twenty Minds*, Oxford University Press, Oxford.

Blackshaw, L.A. and Grundy, D. (1993) Gastrointestinal mechanoreception in the control of ingestion. In *Neurophysiology of Ingestion* (ed. D.A. Booth), Pergamon Press, Oxford, pp. 57–77.

Blake, R. and Logothetis, N.K. (2002) Visual competition. *Nature Reviews Neuroscience*, **3**, 13–23.

Blakemore, C. (1973) Environmental constraints on development in the visual system. In *Constraints on Learning* (eds R.A. Hinde and J. Stevenson-Hinde), Academic Press, London, pp. 51–73.

Blakemore, S-J. and Frith, U. (2005) *The Learning Brain: Lessons for Education*, Blackwell Publishing, Oxford.

Bleuler, E. (1950) *Dementia Praecox or the Group of Schizophrenias*, International Universities Press, New York.

Bligh, J. (1972) Neuronal models of mammalian temperature regulation. In *Essays on Temperature Regulation* (eds J. Bligh and R. Moore), North-Holland, Amsterdam, pp. 105–120.

Bliss, T.V.P. and Lømo, T. (1973) Long-lasting potentiation of synaptic transmission in the dentate area of the anaesthetized rabbit following stimulation of the perforent path. *Journal of Physiology*, **232**, 331–356.

Block, N. (1991) Evidence against epiphenomenonalism. *Behavioral and Brain Sciences*, **14**, 670–672.

Blumberg, M.S. and Sokoloff, G. (1998) Thermoregulatory competence and behavioral expression in the young of altricial species – revisited. *Developmental Psychobiology*, **33**, 107–123.

Blundell, J.E. and Halford, J.C.G. (1998) Serotonin and appetite regulation: implications for the pharmacological treatment of obesity. *CNS Drugs*, **9**, 473–495.

Boatman, D. (2004) Cortical bases of speech perception: evidence from functional lesion studies. *Cognition*, **92**, 47–65.

Bocanegra, B.R. and Zeelenberg, R. (2009) Emotion improves and impairs early vision. *Psychological Science*, **20**, 707–713.

Bohus, B. and de Kloet, E.R. (1981) Adrenal steroids and extinction behaviour: antagonism by progesterone, deoxycorticosterone and dexamethesone of a specific effect of corticosterone. *Life Sciences*, **28**, 433–440.

Bohus, B. and Koolhaas, J.M. (1993) Stress and the cardiovascular system: central and peripheral physiological mechanisms. In *Stress – From Synapse to Syndrome* (eds S.C. Stanford and P. Salmon), Academic Press, London, pp. 75–117.

Bolles, R.C. (1970) Species-specific defense reactions and avoidance learning. *Psychological Review*, **77**, 32–48.

Bolles, R.C. (1980) Historical note on the term 'appetite'. *Appetite*, **1**, 3–6.

Bolles, R.C. and Fanselow, M.S. (1980) A perceptual–defensive–recuperative model of fear and pain. *Behavioral and Brain Sciences*, **3**, 291–323.

Bolton, D. and Hill, J. (1996) *Mind, Meaning, and Mental Disorder – The Nature of Causal Explanation in Psychology and Psychiatry*, Oxford University Press, Oxford.

Bondi, M.W., Salmon, D.P., Galasko, D., Thomas, R.G. and Thal, L.J. (1999) Neuropsychological function and apolipoprotein E genotype in the preclinical detection of Alzheimer's disease. *Psychology and Aging*, **14**, 295–303.

Bonner, J.T. (1958) *The Evolution of Development*, Cambridge University Press, Cambridge.

Booth, D.A. (1978) *Hunger Models: Computable Theory of Feeding Control*, Academic Press, London.

Booth, D.A. (1979) Metabolism and the control of feeding in man and animals. In *Chemical Influences on Behaviour* (eds K. Brown and S.J. Cooper), Academic Press, London, pp. 79–134.

Booth, D.A. (1980) Acquired behaviour controlling energy intake and output. In *Obesity* (ed. A.J. Stunkard), W.B. Saunders, Philadelphia, pp. 101–143.

Booth, D.A. (1993a) *Neurophysiology of Ingestion,* Pergamon Press, Oxford.

Booth, D.A. (1993b) A framework for neurophysiological studies of ingestion. In *Neurophysiology of Ingestion* (ed. D.A. Booth), Pergamon Press, Oxford, pp. 1–17.

Booth, D.A. and Toates, F.M. (1974) A physiological control theory of food intake in the rat. *Bulletin of the Psychonomic Society,* **3**, 442–444.

Borchgrevink, H.M. (1989) Cerebral processes underlying neuropsychological and neuromotor impairment in children with ADD/MBD. In *Attention Deficit Disorder: Clinical and Basic Research* (eds T. Sagvolden and T. Archer), Lawrence Erlbaum, Hillsdale, pp. 105–130.

Bostwick, J.M. and Bucci, J.A. (2008) Internet sex addiction treated with naltrexone. *Mayo Clinic Proceedings,* **83**, 226–230.

Both, S., van Boxtel, G., Stekelenburg, J., Everaerd, W. and Laan, E. (2005) Modulation of spinal reflexes by sexual films of increasing intensity. *Psychophysiology,* **42**, 726–731.

Boule, M. and Anthony, R. (1911) L'encéphale de l'homme fossile de la Chapelle-aux-Saints. *L'Anthropologie,* **22**, 129–196.

Boulougouris, V., Chamberlain, S.R. and Robbins, T.W. (2009) Cross-species models of OCD spectrum disorders. *Psychiatry Research,* **170**, 15–21.

Boussaoud, D., di Pellegrino, G. and Wise, S.P. (1996) Frontal lobe mechanisms subserving vision-for-action versus vision-for-perception. *Behavioural Brain Research,* **72**, 1–15.

Bovard, E.W. (1985) Brain mechanisms in effects of social support on viability. In *Perspectives in Behavioral Medicine,* Vol. 2 (ed. R.B. Williams), Academic Press, Orlando, pp. 103–129.

Bower, G.H. (1992) How might emotions affect learning? In *The Handbook of Emotion and Memory – Research and Theory* (ed. S-A. Christianson), Lawrence Erlbaum, Hillsdale, pp. 3–31.

Bowers, J.S. (2009) On the biological plausibility of grandmother cells: implications for neural network theories in psychology and neuroscience. *Psychological Review,* **116**, 220–251.

Bowlby, J. (1973) *Attachment and Loss,* Vol. II, *Separation,* Hogarth Press, London.

Bowmaker, J.K. and Dartnall, H.J.A. (1980) Visual pigments or rods and cones in a human retina. *Journal of Physiology,* **298**, 501–511.

Bowman, M.L. (1997) Brain impairment in impulsive violence. In *Impulsivity – Theory,*

Assessment, and Treatment (eds C.D. Webster and M.A. Jackson), Guilford Press, New York, pp. 116–141.

Boyke, J., Driemeyer, J., Gaser, C., Büchel, C. and May. A. (2008) Training-induced brain structure changes in the elderly. *The Journal of Neuroscience,* **28**, 7031–7035.

Bozarth, M.A. (1987) *Methods of Assessing the Reinforcing Properties of Abused Drugs,* Springer-Verlag, New York.

Bracke, P.E. and Thoresen, C.E. (1996) Reducing Type A behavior patterns: a structured-group approach. In *Heart and Mind. The Practice of Cardiac Psychology* (eds R. Allan, and S. Scheidt), American Psychological Association, Washington, pp. 255–290.

Brady, J. (1979) *Biological Clocks,* Edward Arnold, London.

Brain, P.F. (1979) Effects of the hormones of the pituitary–gonadal axis on behaviour. In *Chemical Influences on Behaviour* (eds K. Brown and S.J. Cooper), Academic Press, London, pp. 255–329.

Brandt, J. and Rich, J.B. (1995) Memory disorders in the dementias. In *Handbook of Memory Disorders* (eds A.D. Baddeley, B.A. Wilson and F.N. Watts), Wiley, Chichester, pp. 243–270.

Bray, G.A. (1980) Jejunoileal bypass, jaw wiring, and vagotomy for massive obesity. In *Obesity* (ed. A.J. Stunkard), W.B. Saunders, Philadelphia, pp. 369–387.

Breier, A., Kelsoe, J.R., Kirwin, P.D., Beller, S.A., Wolkowitz, O.M. and Pickar, D. (1988) Early parental loss and development of adult psychopathology. *Archives of General Psychiatry,* **45**, 987–993.

Bremner, J.D. (1999) Does stress damage the brain? *Biological Psychiatry,* **45**, 797–805.

Bremner, J.D. (2005) *Brain Imaging Handbook,* W.W Norton, New York.

Brennan, P.A. and Keverne, E.B. (2004) Something in the air? New insights into mammalian pheromones. *Current Biology,* **14**, R81–R89.

Broadbent, D.E. (1958) *Perception and Communication,* Pergamon Press, Oxford.

Broca, M. (1861) Perte de la parole, ramollissement chronique et destruction partielle du lobe antérieur gauche du cerveau. *Bulletin de la Société Anthropologie,* **2**, 235–238.

Bromm, B. (1995) Consciousness, pain and cortical activity. In *Pain and the Brain: From Nociception to Cognition* (Advances in Pain Research and Therapy, Vol. 22) (eds B. Bromm and J.E. Desmedt), Raven Press, New York, pp. 35–59.

Bronson, G.W. (1982) Structure, status, and characteristics of the nervous system at birth. In *Psychobiology of the Human Newborn* (ed. P. Stratton), Wiley, Chichester, pp. 99–118.

Brown, A.S., van Os, J., Driessens, C., Hoek, H.W. and Susser, E.S. (2000) Further evidence of relation between prenatal famine and major affective disorder. *American Journal of Psychiatry,* **157**, 190–195.

Brown, M., Keynes, R. and Lumsden, A. (2001) *The Developing Brain,* Oxford University Press, Oxford.

Brown, M.C. (1999) Audition. In *Fundamental Neuroscience* (eds M.J. Zigmond, F.E. Bloom, S.C. Landis, J.L. Roberts and L.R. Squire), Academic Press, San Diego, pp. 791–820.

Bruce, C., Desimone, R. and Gross, C.G. (1981) Visual properties of neurons in a polysensory area in superior temporal sulcus in the macaque. *Journal of Neurophysiology,* **46**, 369–384.

Bruch, H. (1974) *Eating Disorders,* Routledge and Kegan Paul, London.

Bruer, J.T. (1998) Brain and child development: time for some critical thinking. *Public Health Reports,* **113**, 388–397.

Buchanan, R.W., Freedman, R., Javitt, D.C., Abi-Dargham, A., Lieberman, J.A. (2007) Recent advances in the development of novel pharmacological agents for the treatment of cognitive impairments in schizophrenia. *Schizophrenia Bulletin,* **33**, 1120–1130.

Buffum, J., Moser, C. and Smith, D. (1988) Street drugs and sexual function. In *Handbook of Sexology.* Vol. 6: *The Pharmacology and Endocrinology of Sexual Function* (ed. J.M.A. Sitsen), Elsevier Science Publishers, Amsterdam, pp. 462–477.

Buller, D.J. (2005) *Adapting Minds: Evolutionary Psychology and the Persistent Quest for Human Nature,* MIT Press, Cambridge.

Bullier, J. (2004) Communications between cortical areas of the visual system. In *The Visual Neurosciences* (Vol. 1) (eds L.M. Chalupa and J.S. Werner), MIT Press, Cambridge, pp. 522–540.

Bullmore, E. and Fletcher, P. (2003) The eye's mind: brain mapping and psychiatry. *British Journal of Psychiatry,* **182**, 381–384.

Burch, J., McKenna, C., Palmer, S., Norman, G., Glanville, J., Sculpher, M. and Woolcott, N. (2009) Rimoabant for the treatment of overweight and obese people. *Health Technology Assessment,* **13**, 13–22.

Burell, G. (1996) Group psychotherapy in project new life: treatment of coronary-prone behaviors for patients who have had coronary artery bypass graft surgery. In *Heart and Mind. The Practice of Cardiac Psychology* (eds R. Allan and S. Scheidt), American Psychological Association, Washington, pp. 291–310.

Burgdorf, J. and Panksepp, J. (2006) The neurobiology of positive emotions. *Neuroscience and Biobehavioral Reviews*, **30**, 173–187.

Burton, H. and Sinclair, R. (1996) Somatosensory cortex and tactile perceptions. In *Pain and Touch* (ed. L. Kruger), Academic Press, San Diego, pp. 105–177.

Bush, G., Luu, P. and Posner, M.I. (2000) Cognitive and emotional influences in anterior cingulate cortex. *Trends in Cognitive Sciences*, **4**, 215–222.

Buss, D.M. (2008) *Evolutionary Psychology: The New Science of the Mind*. Pearson Education.

Buss, D.M., Haselton, M.G., Shackelford, T.K., Bleske, A.L. and Wakefield, J.C. (1998) Adaptations, exaptations, and spandrels. *American Psychologist*, **53**, 533–548.

Buss, D.M., Larsen, R.J. and Westen, D. (1996) Sex differences in jealousy: not gone, not forgotten, and not explained by alternative hypotheses. *Psychological Science*, **7**, 373–375.

Buss, D.M., Larsen, R.J., Westen, D. and Semmelroth, J. (1992) Sex differences in jealousy: evolution, physiology and psychology. *Psychological Science*, **3**, 251–255.

Butler, A.B. and Hodos, W. (2005) *Comparative Vertebrate Neuroanatomy: Evolution and Adaptation*, 2nd edition, Wiley, New York.

Butters, N. and Cermak, L.S. (1986) A case study of the forgetting of autobiographical knowledge: implications for the study of retrograde amnesia. In *Autobiographical Memory* (ed. D.C. Rubin), Cambridge University Press, Cambridge, pp. 253–272.

C

Cabanac, M. (1971) Physiological role of pleasure. *Science*, **173**, 1103–1107.

Cabanac, M. (1979) Sensory pleasure. *Quarterly Review of Biology*, **54**, 1–29.

Cabanac, M. (1992) Pleasure: the common currency. *Journal of Theoretical Biology*, **155**, 173–200.

Cabanac, M. (1998), Thermiatrics and behavior. In *Physiology and Pathophysiology of Temperature Regulation* (ed. C.M. Blatteis), World Scientific Publications, Singapore, pp. 107–125.

Cabanac, M. and Russek, M. (1982) *Régulation et Controle en Biologie*, Les Presses de l'Université Laval, Quebec.

Cacioppo, J.T. and Berntson, G.G. (1992) Social psychological contributions to the decade of the brain. *American Psychologist*, **47**, 1019–1028.

Cacioppo, J.T., Uchino, B.N., Crites, S.L., Snydersmith, M.A., Smith, G., Berntson, G.G. and Lang, P.J. (1992) Relationship between facial expressiveness and sympathetic activation in emotion: a critical review, with emphasis on modeling underlying mechanisms and individual differences. *Journal of Personality and Social Psychology*, **62**, 110–128.

Cahill, L., Haier, R.J., Fallon, J., Alkire, M.T., Tang, C., Keator, D., Wu, J. and McGaugh, J.L. (1996) Amygdala activity at encoding correlated with long-term, free recall of emotional information. *Proceedings of the National Academy of Sciences USA*, **93**, 8016–8021.

Cairns, R.B. (1979) *Social Development*, W.H. Freeman, San Francisco.

Calder, A.J., Keane, J., Manes, F., Antoun, N. and Young, A.W. (2000) Impaired recognition and experience of disgust following brain injury. *Nature Neuroscience*, **3**, 1077–1078.

Campbell, A., Muncer, S. and Odber, J. (1997) Aggression and testosterone: testing a bio-social model. *Aggressive Behavior*, **23**, 229–238.

Campbell, C.M. and Edwards, R.R. (2009) Mind–body interactions in pain: the neurophysiology of anxious and catastrophic pain-related thoughts. *Translational Research*, **153**, 97–101.

Camperio-Ciani, A., Corna, F. and Capiluppi, C. (2004) Evidence for maternally inherited factors favouring male homosexuality and promoting female fecundity. *Proceedings of the Royal Society of London B*, **271**, 2217–2221.

Campfield, L.A. (1997) Metabolic and hormonal controls of food intake: highlights of the last 25 years – 1972–1997. *Appetite*, **29**, 135–152.

Cannon, W.B. (1927) The James–Lange theory of emotions: a critical examination and an alternative theory. *American Journal of Psychology*, **39**, 106–124.

Caplan, D. (1985) A neo-Cartesian alternative. *Behavioral and Brain Sciences*, **8**, 6–7.

Caplan, D., Carr, T., Gould, J. and Martin, R. (1999) Language and communication. In *Fundamental Neuroscience* (eds M.J. Zigmond, F.E. Bloom, S.C. Landis, J.L. Roberts and L.R. Squire), Academic Press, San Diego, pp. 1487–1519.

Cardinal, R.N., Pennicott, D.R., Sugathapala, C.L., Robbins, T.W. and Everitt, B.J. (2001) Impulsive choice induced in rats by lesions of the nucleus accumbens core. *Science*, **292**, 2499–2501.

Carlisle, H.J. (1966) Heat intake and hypothalamic temperature during behavioral temperature regulation. *Journal of Comparative and Physiological Psychology*, **61**, 388–397.

Carlson, N.R. (1977) *Physiology of Behavior*, 1st edition, Allyn and Bacon, Boston.

Carlson, N.R. (1994) *Physiology of Behavior*, 5th edition, Allyn and Bacon, Boston.

Carlson, N.R. (1998) *Physiology of Behavior*, 6th edition, Allyn and Bacon, Boston.

Carlson, N.R. (2003) *Physiology of Behavior*, 8th edition, Allyn and Bacon, Boston.

Carlson, N.R. (2009) *Physiology of Behaviour*, 10th edition, Allyn and Bacon, Boston.

Carlsson, A. (1988) The current status of the dopamine hypothesis of schizophrenia. *Neuropsychopharmacology*, **1**, 179–203.

Carlsson, A. (2002) Treatment of Parkinson's with L-DOPA. The early discovery phase, and a comment on current problems. *Journal of Neural Transmission*, **109**, 777–787.

Carlsson, A. and Carlsson, M. (1991) A faulty negative feedback control underlies the schizophrenic syndrome? *Behavioral and Brain Sciences*, **14**, 20–21.

Carlsson, K., Petersson, K.M., Lundqvist, D., Karlsson, A., Ingvar, M. and Öhman, A. (2004) Fear and the amygdala: manipulation of awareness generates differential cerebral responses to phobic and fear-relevant (but nonfeared) stimuli. *Emotion*, **4**, 340–353.

Carpenter, A.F., Georgopoulos, A.P. and Pellizzer, G. (1999) Motor control encoding of serial order in a context-recall task. *Science*, **283**, 1752–1757.

Carr, L., Iacoboni, M., Dubeau, M-C., Mazziotta, J.C. and Lenzi, G.L. (2003) Neural mechanisms of empathy in humans: a relay from neural systems for imitation to limbic areas. *Proceedings of the National Academy of Sciences*, **100**, 5497–5502.

Carraher, R.G. and Thurston, J.B. (1966) *Optical Illusions and the Visual Arts*, Reinhold Publishing Corporation, New York

Carskadon, M.A. and Dement, W.C. (1994) Normal human sleep: an overview. In *Principles and Practice of Sleep Medicine* (eds M.H. Kryger, T. Roth and W.C. Dement), Saunders, Philadelphia, pp. 16–25.

Carter, R. (2010) *Exploring Consciousness,* University of California Press, Berkeley.

Cartwright, R. (2010) *The Twenty-four Hour Mind,* Oxford University Press, New York.

Carver, C.S. and Harmon-Jones, E. (2009) Anger is an approach-related affect: Evidence and implications. *Psychological Bulletin,* **135,** 183–204.

Carver, C.S. and Scheier, M.F. (1990) Origin and functions of positive and negative affect: a control-process view. *Psychological Review,* **97,** 19–35.

Castanon, N. and Mormède, P. (1994) Psychobiogenetics: adapted tools for the study of the coupling between behavioral and neuroendocrine traits of emotional reactivity. *Psychoneuroendocrinology,* **19,** 257–282.

Castellanos, F.X. and Swanson, J. (2002) Biological underpinnings of ADHD. In *Hyperactivity and Attention Disorders of Childhood,* 2nd edition (ed. S. Sandberg), Cambridge University Press, Cambridge, pp. 336–366.

Castellanos, F.X., Sonuga-Barke, E.J.S., Milham, M.P. and Tannock, R. (2006) Characterizing cognition in ADHD: beyond executive dysfunction. *Trends in Cognitive Sciences,* **10,** 117–123.

Chadwick, M.J., Hassabis, D., Weiskopf, N. and Maguire, E.A. (2010) Decoding individual episodic memory traces in the human hippocampus. *Current Biology,* **20,** 1–4.

Chalmers, D.J. (1996) *The Conscious Mind: In Search of a Fundamental Theory,* Oxford University Press, New York.

Chamberlain, S.R., Blackwell, A.D., Fineberg, N.A., Robbins, T.W. and Sahakian, B.J. (2005) The neuropsychology of obsessive compulsive disorder: the importance of failures in cognitive and behavioral inhibition as candidate endophenotypic markers. *Neuroscience and Biobehavioral Reviews,* **29,** 399–419.

Chamberlain, S.R., Hampshire, A., Müller, U., Rubia, K., del Campo, N., Craig, K., Regenthal, R., Suckling, J., Roiser, J.P., Grant, J.E., Bullmore, E.T., Robbins, T.W. and Sahakian, B.J. (2009) Atomoxetine modulates right inferior frontal activation during inhibitory control: a pharmacological functional magnetic resonance imaging study. *Biological Psychiatry,* **65,** 550–555.

Champagne, F.A. and Mashoodh, R. (2009) Genes in context: gene–environment interplay and the origins of individual differences in behavior. *Current Directions in Psychological Science,* **18,** 127–131.

Chapman, C.R. (1995) The affective dimension of pain: a model. In *Pain and the Brain: From Nociception to Cognition* (Advances in Pain Research and Therapy, Vol. 22) (eds B. Bromm and J.E. Desmedt), Raven Press, New York, pp. 283–301.

Chapman, H.A., Kim, D.A., Susskind, J.M. and Anderson, A.K. (2009) In bad taste: evidence for the oral origins of moral disgust. *Science,* **323,** 1222–1226.

Chapman, L.J. and Chapman, J.P. (1973) *Disordered Thought in Schizophrenia,* Appleton-Century-Croft, New York.

Charash, M. and McKay, D. (2002) Attention bias for disgust. *Anxiety Disorders,* **16,** 529–541.

Charney, D.S., Deutch, A.Y., Southwick, S.M. and Krystal, J.H. (1995) Neural circuits and mechanisms of post-traumatic stress disorder. In *Neurobiological and Clinical Consequences of Stress. From Normal Adaptation to Post-traumatic Stress Disorder* (eds M.J. Friedman, D.S. Charney and A.Y. Deutch), Lippincott-Raven, Philadelphia, pp. 271–287.

Chaves, J.F. and Dworkin, S.F. (1997) Hypnotic control of pain: historical perspectives and future prospects. *International Journal of Clinical and Experimental Hypnosis,* **XLV,** 356–376.

Chen, Y-H., Dammers, J., Boers, F., Leiberg, S., Edgar, J.C., Roberts, T.P.L. and Mathiak, K. (2009) The temporal dynamics of insula activity to disgust and happy facial expressions: a magnetoencephalography study. *Neuroimage,* **47,** 1921–1928.

Cherry, C. (1966) *On Human Communication: A Review, a Survey and a Criticism,* MIT Press, Cambridge.

Chertkow, H. and Bub, D. (1990) Semantic memory loss in Alzheimer-type dementia. In *Modular Deficits in Alzheimer-type Dementia* (ed. M.F. Schwartz), MIT Press, Cambridge, pp. 207–244.

Chi, J.G., Dooling, E.C. and Gilles, F.H. (1977) Left–right asymmetries of the temporal speech areas of the human fetus. *Archives of Neurology,* **34,** 346–348.

Chiamulera, C. (2005) Cue reactivity in nicotine and tobacco dependence: a 'multiple-action' model of nicotine as a primary reinforcement and as an enhancer of the effects of smoking-associated stimuli. *Brain Research Reviews,* **48,** 74–97.

Chick, J. and Erickson, C.K. (1996) Conference summary: consensus conference on alcohol dependence and the role of pharmacotherapy in its treatment. *Alcoholism: Clinical and Experimental Research,* **20,** 391–402.

Childress, A.R., Mozley, P.D., McElgin, W., Fitzgerald, J., Reivich, M. and O'Brien, C.P. (1999) Limbic activation during cue-induced cocaine craving. *American Journal of Psychiatry,* **156,** 11–18.

Childress, A.R., Ehrman, R.N., Wang, Z., Li, Y., Sciortino, N., Hakun, J., Jens, W., Suh, J., Listerud, J., Marquez, K., Franklin, T., Langleben, D., Detre, J. and O'Brien, C.P. (2008) Prelude to passion: limbic activation by 'unseen' drug and sexual cues. *PLoS One,* 3, e1506. doi:10.1371/journal.pone.0001506.

Chokroverty, S. (1994) *Sleep Disorders Medicine: Basic Science, Technical Considerations and Clinical Aspects,* Butterworth-Heinemann, Boston.

Chomsky, N. (1959) Review of 'Verbal Behaviour' by B.F. Skinner. *Language,* **35,** 26–58.

Chorpita, B.F. and Barlow, D.H. (1998) The development of anxiety: the role of control in the early environment. *Psychological Bulletin,* **124,** 3–21.

Christie, M.J., Williams, J.T., Osborne, P.G. and Bellchambers, C.E. (1997) Where is the locus in opioid withdrawal? *Trends in Pharmacological Sciences,* **18,** 134–140.

Chugani, H.T. (1994) Development of regional brain metabolism in relation to behaviour and plasticity. In *Human Behavior and the Developing Brain* (eds G. Dawson and K.W. Fischer), Guilford Press, New York, pp. 153–175.

Chugani, H.T., Behen, M.E., Muzik, O., Juhász, C., Nagy, F. and Chugani, D.C. (2001) Local brain functional activity following early deprivation: a study of post institutionalized Romanian orphans. *Neuroimage,* **14,** 1290–1301.

Chwalisz, K., Diener, E. and Gallagher, D. (1988) Autonomic arousal feedback and emotional experience: evidence from the spinal cord injured. *Journal of Personality and Social Psychology,* **54,** 820–828.

Claparède, M.E. (1911) Récognition et Moïté. *Archives de Psychologie,* **11,** 79–80.

Claridge, G. (1990) Can a disease model of schizophrenia survive? In *Reconstructing Schizophrenia* (ed. R.P. Bentall), Routledge, London, pp. 157–183.

Clark, B.J., Hines, D.J., Hamilton, D.A. and Whishaw, I.Q. (2005) Movements of exploration intact in rats with hippocampal lesions. *Behavioural Brain Research,* **163,** 91–99.

Clark, R.E. and Squire, L.R. (1998) Classical conditioning and brain systems: the role of awareness. *Science,* **280,** 77–81.

Clark, R.W. (1980) *Freud – The Man and the Cause*, Random House, New York.

Clayton, N.S. and Dickinson, A. (1998) Episodic-like memory during cache recovery by scrub jays. *Nature*, **395**, 272–274.

Clifton, P. (2008) Brain and behaviour. In *Challenging Obesity* (eds H. McLannahan and P. Clifton), Oxford University Press, Oxford, pp. 93–116.

Clifton, P. and McLannahan, H. (2008) Treating obesity: drugs and surgery. In *Challenging Obesity* (eds H. McLannahan and P. Clifton), Oxford University Press, Oxford, pp. 187–210.

Clifton, P.G., Burton, M.J. and Sharp, C. (1987) Rapid loss of stimulus-specific satiety after consumption of a second food. *Appetite*, **9**, 149–156.

Clow, A. and Hucklebridge, F. (2002) *International Review of Neurobiology. 52. The Neurobiology of the Immune System*. Academic Press, New York.

Cobb, L.A., Thomas, G.I., Dillard, D.H., Merendino, K.A. and Bruce, R.A. (1959) An evaluation of internal-mammary-artery ligation by a double-blind technique. *New England Journal of Medicine*, **260**, 1115–1118.

Coccaro, E.F. (1989) Central serotonin and impulsive aggression. *British Journal of Psychiatry*, **155** (suppl. 8), 52–62.

Coenen, A.M.L. (1995) Neuronal activities underlying the electroencephalogram and evoked potentials of sleeping and waking: implications for information processing. *Neuroscience and Biobehavioral Reviews*, **19**, 447–463

Coenen, A.M.L. (1998) Neuronal phenomena associated with vigilance and consciousness: from cellular mechanisms to electroencephalographic patterns. *Consciousness and Cognition, 7*, 42–53.

Cohen, D. (1979) *J.B. Watson – The Founder of Behaviourism*, Routledge and Kegan Paul, London.

Cohen, D. (1998) Shaping, channeling, and distributing testosterone in social systems. *Behavioral and Brain Sciences*, **21**, 367–368.

Cohen, D.B. (1979) *Sleep and Dreaming: Origins, Nature and Functions*, Pergamon Press, Oxford.

Cohen, G. (1990) Memory. In *Introduction to Psychology*, Vol. 2 (ed. I. Roth), Lawrence Erlbaum, Hove, pp. 570–621.

Cohen, M.X., Young, J., Baek, J-M., Kessler, C. and Ranganath, C. (2005) Individual differences in extraversion and dopamine genetics predict neural reward responses. *Cognitive Brain Research*, **25**, 851–861.

Cohen, S. (1996) Psychological stress, immunity, and upper respiratory infections. *Current Directions in Psychological Science, 5*, 86–90.

Colcombe, S.J., Erickson, K.I., Scalf, P.E., Kim, J.S., Prakash, R., McAuley, E., Elavsky, S., Marquez, D.X., Hu, L. and Kramer, A.F. (2006) Aerobic exercise training increases brain volume in aging humans. *Journal of Gerontology: Medical Sciences*, **61A**, 1166–1170.

Cole, J. (1991) *Pride and a Daily Marathon*, Duckworth, London.

Coleman, E. (2005) Neuroanatomical and neurotransmitter dysfunction and compulsive sexual behavior. In *Biological Substrates of Human Sexuality* (ed. J.S. Hyde), American Psychological Association, Washington, pp. 147–169

Collingridge, G. (1997) Mind the gap. *Medical Research Council News,* No. 74, pp. 24–27.

Coltheart, M. (1985) Cognitive neuropsychology and the study of reading. In *Attention and Performance XI* (eds M.I. Posner and O.S.M. Marin), Lawrence Erlbaum, Hillsdale, pp. 3–37.

Conrad, C.D. (2008) Chronic stress-induced hippocampal vulnerability: the glucocorticoid vulnerability hypothesis. *Reviews in the Neurosciences*, **19**, 395–411.

Contreras, M., Ceric, F. and Torrealba, F. (2007) Inactivation of the interoceptive insula disrupts drug craving and malaise induced by lithium. *Science*, **318**, 655–658.

Cooper, B. (2005) Immigration and schizophrenia: the social causation hypothesis revisited. *British Journal of Psychiatry*, **186**, 361–363.

Cooper, C.L. and Dewe, P. (2004) *Stress: A Brief History*, Blackwell Publishing, Oxford.

Cooper, S.J. and Higgs, S. (1994) Neural processing related to feeding in primates. In *Appetite – Neural and Behavioural Bases* (eds C.R. Legg and D. Booth), Oxford University Press, Oxford, pp. 212–242.

Coover, G.D., Ursin, H. and Levine, S. (1973) Plasma-corticosterone levels during active-avoidance learning in rats. *Journal of Comparative and Physiological Psychology*, **82**, 170–174.

Corballis, M.C. (2010) Mirror neurons and the evolution of language. *Brain and Language*, **112**, 25–35.

Coren, S., Ward, L.M. and Enns, J.T. (1994) *Sensation and Perception*, Harcourt Brace, Fort Worth.

Corkin, S. (1968) Acquisition of motor skill after bilateral temporal-lobe excision. *Neuropsychologia*, **6**, 255–265.

Corkin, S. (2002) What's new with the amnesic patient H.M.? *Nature Reviews Neuroscience*, **3**, 153–160.

Corkin, S., Amaral, D.G., González, R.G., Johnson, K.A. and Hyman, B.T. (1997) H.M.'s medial temporal lobe lesion: findings from magnetic resonance imaging. *Journal of Neuroscience*, **17**, 3964–3979.

Corp, E.S., Curcio, M., Gibbs, J. and Smith, G.P. (1997) The effect of centrally administered CCK-receptor antagonists on food intake in rats. *Physiology and Behavior,* **61**, 823–827.

Coscina, D.V. (1997) The biopsychology of impulsivity: focus on brain serotonin. In *Impulsivity – Theory, Assessment, and Treatment* (eds C.D. Webster and M.A. Jackson), Guilford Press, New York, pp. 95–115.

Coté, L. and Crutcher, M.D. (1991) The basal ganglia. In *Principles of Neural Science* (eds E.R. Kandel, J.H. Schwartz and T.M. Jessell), Appleton and Lange, Norwalk, pp. 647–659.

Courchesne, E. and Allen, G. (1997) Prediction and preparation, fundamental functions of the cerebellum. *Learning and Memory*, **4**, 1–35.

Cowey, A. and Stoerig, P. (1995) Blindsight in monkeys. *Nature*, **373**, 247–249.

Craig, A.D. (2003) Pain mechanisms: labelled lines versus convergence in central processing. *Annual Review of Neuroscience*, **26**, 1–30.

Craig, A.D. (2004) Human feelings: why are some more aware than others? *Trends in Cognitive Sciences*, **8**, 239–241.

Craig, A.D. (2009) How do you feel – now? The anterior insula and human awareness. *Nature Reviews Neuroscience*, **10**, 59–70.

Craig, K.D. (1994) Emotional aspects of pain. In *Textbook of Pain* (eds P.D. Wall and R. Melzack), Churchill Livingstone, Edinburgh, pp. 261–274.

Craig, K.D. (1995) From nociception to pain: the role of emotion. In *Pain and the Brain: From Nociception to Cognition* (Advances in Pain Research and Therapy, Vol. 22) (eds B. Bromm and J.E. Desmedt), Raven Press, New York, pp. 303–317.

Cravatt, B.F., Prospero-Garcia, O., Siuzdak, G., Gilula, N.B., Henriksen, S.J., Boger, D.L. and Lerner, R.A. (1995) Chemical characterization of a family of brain lipids that induce sleep. *Science*, **268**, 1506–1509.

Crick, F. (1994) *The Astonishing Hypothesis: The Scientific Search for the Soul*, Simon and Schuster, London.

Critchley, H.D., Wiens, S., Rotshtein, P., Öhman, A. and Dolan, R.J. (2004) Neural systems supporting interoceptive awareness. *Nature Neuroscience*, **7**, 189–195.

Crosson, B., McGregor, K., Gopinath, K.S., Conway, T.W., Benjamin, M., Chang, Y-L., Moore, A.B., Raymer, A.M., Briggs, R.W., Sherod, M.G., Wierenga, C.E. and White, K.D. (2007) Functional MRI of language in aphasia: a review of the literature and the methodological challenges. *Neuropsychology Review*, **17**, 157–177.

Cubillo, A. and Rubia, K. (2010) Structural and functional brain imaging in adult attention-deficit/hyperactivity disorder. *Expert Review of Neurotherapeutics*, **10**, 603–620.

Cullinan, W.E., Herman, J.P., Helmreich, D.L. and Watson, S.J. (1995) A neuroanatomy of stress. In *Neurobiological and Clinical Consequences of Stress. From Normal Adaptation to Post-traumatic Stress Disorder* (eds M.J. Friedman, D.S. Charney and A.Y. Deutch), Lippincott-Raven, Philadelphia, pp. 3–26.

Cummings, J.L. and Miller, B.L. (2007) Conceptual and clinical aspects of the frontal lobes. In *The Human Frontal Lobes: Functions and Disorders* 2nd edition (eds. B.L. Miller and J.L. Cummings), The Guilford Press, New York, pp.12–21.

Cunningham-Williams, R.M., Gattis, M.N., Dore, P.M., Shi, P. and Spitznagel, E.L. (2009) Towards DSM-V: considering other withdrawal-like symptoms of pathological gambling disorder. *International Journal of Methods in Psychiatric Research*, **18**, 13–22

Curran, H.V. and Kopelman, M.D. (1996) The cognitive psychopharmacology of Alzheimer's disease. In *The Cognitive Neuropsychology of Alzheimer-type Dementia* (ed. R.G. Morris), Oxford University Press, Oxford, pp. 255–277.

Curtis, A.L. and Valentino, R.J. (1994) Corticotropin-releasing factor neurotransmission in locus coeruleus: a possible site of antidepressant action. *Brain Research Bulletin*, **35**, 581–587.

Cutler, W.B. and Genovese-Stone, E. (1998) Wellness in women after 40 years of age: the role of sex hormones and pheromones. *Disease-a-Month*, **44**, 423–546.

Cutler, W.B., Freidman, E. and McCoy, N.L. (1998) Pheromonal influences on sociosexual behavior in men. *Archives of Sexual Behaviour*, **27**, 1–13.

D

Dabbs, J.M. (2000) *Heroes, Rogues and Lovers*, McGraw-Hill, New York.

Dabbs, J.M., Karpas, A.E., Dyomina, N., Juechter, J. and Roberts, A. (2002) Experimental raising or lowering of testosterone level affects mood in normal men and women. *Social Behavior and Personality*, **30**, 795–806.

Damasio, A.R. (1996) *Descartes' Error*, Papermac, London.

Damasio, A.R. (1999) *The Feeling of What Happens: Body and Emotion in the Making of Consciousness*, Harcourt Brace, New York.

Damasio, A.R. and Damasio, H. (1983) The anatomic basis of pure alexia. *Neurology*, **33**, 1573–1583.

Damasio, A.R. and Geschwind, N. (1984) The neural basis of language. *Annual Review of Neuroscience* (eds W.M. Cowan, E.M. Shooter, C.F. Stevens and R.F. Thompson), Annual Reviews Inc., Palo Alto, pp. 127–147.

Damasio, A.R., Van Hoesen, G.W. and Hyman, B.T. (1990) Reflections on the selectivity of neuropathological changes in Alzheimer's disease. In *Modular Deficits in Alzheimer-type Dementia* (ed. M.F. Schwartz), MIT Press, Cambridge, pp. 83–100.

Damasio, H., Grabowski, T., Frank, R., Galaburda, A.M. and Damasio, A.R. (1994) The return of Phineas Gage: clues about the brain from the skull of a famous patient. *Science*, **264**, 5162, 1102–1105.

Dampney, R. (1990) The subretrofacial nucleus: its pivotal role in cardiovascular regulation. *News in Physiological Sciences*, **5**, 63–67.

Dampney, R.A.L. (1994) Functional organization of central pathways regulating the cardiovascular system. *Physiological Reviews*, **74**, 323–364.

Dancause, N., Barbay, S., Frost, S.B., Plautz, E.J., Chen, D., Zoubina, E.V., Stowe, A.M. and Nudo, R.J. (2005) Extensive cortical rewiring after brain injury. *The Journal of Neuroscience*, **25**, 10167–10179.

Dani, J.A. and Heinemann, S. (1996) Molecular and cellular aspects of nicotine abuse. *Neuron*, **16**, 905–908.

Dantzer, R. (1986) Behavioural, physiological and functional aspects of stereotyped behaviour: a review and a reinterpretation. *Journal of Animal Science*, **62**, 1776–1786.

Darian-Smith, I. (1984) The sense of touch: performance and peripheral neural processes. In *Handbook of Physiology*. Section 1: *The Nervous System*, Vol. III, Part 2 (ed. I. Darian-Smith), American Physiological Society, Bethesda, pp. 739–788.

Darling, C.A., Davidson, J.K. and Jennings, D.A. (1991) The female sexual response revisited: understanding the multiorgasmic experience in women. *Archives of Sexual Behavior*, **20**, 527–540.

Darwin, C. (1872/1934) *The Expression of the Emotions in Man and Animals*, Watts and Co., London.

Darwin, C. (1874/1974) *The Descent of Man and Selection in Relation to Sex*, Rand, McNally and Co., Chicago.

Davidson, D. and Amit, Z. (1997) Effect of ethanol drinking and naltrexone on subsequent drinking in rats. *Alcohol*, **14**, 581–584.

Davidson, R.J. (1984) Hemispheric asymmetry and emotion. In *Approaches to Emotion* (eds K.R. Scherer and P. Ekman), Lawrence Erlbaum, Hillsdale, pp. 39–57.

Davidson, R.J. (2003) Affective neuroscience and psychophysiology: toward a synthesis. *Psychophysiology*, **40**, 655–665.

Davidson, R.J., Pizzagalli, D., Nitschke J.B. and Putnam, K. (2002) Depression: perspectives from affective neuroscience. *Annual Review of Psychology*, **53**, 545–574.

Davidson, R.J., Scherer, K.R. and Goldsmith, H.H. (2009) *Handbook of Affective Sciences*, Oxford University Press, New York.

Davis, B.D. (1985) Sleep and the maintenance of memory. *Perspectives in Biology and Medicine*, **28**, 457–464.

Davis, C. and Claridge, G. (1998) The eating disorders as addiction: a psychobiological perspective. *Addictive Behaviors*, **23**, 463–475.

Davis, C., Levitan, R.D., Muglia, P., Bewell, C. and Kennedy, J.L. (2004) Decision-making deficits and overeating: a risk model for obesity. *Obesity Research*, **12**, 929–935.

Davis, K.L., Kahn, R.S., Ko, G. and Davidson, M. (1991) Dopamine in schizophrenia: a review and reconceptualization. *American Journal of Psychiatry*, **148**, 1474–1486.

Davis, L.L., Suris, A., Lambert, M.T., Heimberg, C. and Petty, F. (1997) Post-traumatic stress disorder and serotonin: new directions for research and treatment. *Journal of Psychiatry and Neuroscience*, **22**, 318–326.

Davis, M. (1992) Analysis of aversive memories using the fear-potentiated startle paradigm. In *Neuropsychology of Memory* (eds L.R. Squire and N. Butters), Guilford Press, New York, pp. 470–484.

Dawkins, M.S. (2007) *Observing Animal Behaviour: Design and Analysis of Quantitative Data,* Oxford University Press, Oxford.

Dawkins, R. (1976) *The Selfish Gene,* Oxford University Press, Oxford.

Dawson, G. (1994) Development of emotional expression and emotion regulation in infancy – contributions of the frontal lobe. In *Human Behavior and the Developing Brain* (eds G. Dawson and K.W. Fischer), Guilford Press, New York, pp. 346–379.

de Araujo, I.E.T., Kringelbach, M.L., Rolls, E.T. and Hobden, P. (2003) Representation of umami taste in the human brain. *Journal of Neurophysiology,* **90,** 313–319.

de Groat, W.C. and Booth, A.M. (1993) Neural control of penile erection. In *Nervous Control of the Urogenital System* (ed. C.A. Maggi), Harwood Academic, Chur, pp. 467–524.

de la Fuente-Fernández, R., Phillips, A.G., Zamburlini, M., Sossi, V., Calne, D.B., Ruth, T.J. and Stoessl, A.J. (2002) Dopamine release in human ventral striatum and expectation of reward. *Behavioural Brain Research,* **136,** 359–363.

de Lanerolle, N.C. and Lang, F.F. (1988) Functional neural pathways for vocalization in the domestic cat. In *The Physiological Control of Mammalian Vocalization* (ed. J.P. Newman), Plenum Press, New York, pp. 21–41.

de Lange, F.P., Koers, A., Kalkman, J.S., Bleijenberg, G., Hagoort, P., van der Meer, J.W.M. and Toni, I. (2008) Increase in prefrontal cortical volume following cognitive behavioural therapy in patients with chronic fatigue syndrome. *Brain,* **131,** 2172–2180.

de Quervain, D.J-F., Fischbacher, U., Treyer, V., Schellhammer, M., Schnyder, U., Buck, A. and Fehr, E. (2004) The neural basis of altruistic punishment. *Science,* **305,** 1254–1258.

De Valois, R.L. and De Valois, K.K. (1980) Spatial vision. *Annual Review of Psychology,* **31,** 309–341.

de Veer, M.W. and van den Bos, R. (1999) A critical review of methodology and interpretation of mirror self-recognition research in nonhuman primates. *Animal Behaviour,* **58,** 459–468.

DeCasper, A.J. and Fifer, W.P. (1980) Of human bonding: newborns prefer their mothers' voices. *Science,* **208,** 1174–1176.

Decety, J. and Michel, F. (1989) Comparative analysis of actual and mental movement times in two graphic tasks. *Brain and Cognition,* **11,** 87–97.

Decety, J., Jeannerod, M. and Prablanc, C. (1989) The timing of mentally represented actions. *Behavioural Brain Research,* **34,** 35–42.

Decety, J., Sjöholm, H., Ryding, E., Stenberg, G. and Ingvar, D.H. (1990) The cerebellum participates in mental activity: tomographic measurements of regional cerebral blood flow. *Brain Research,* **535,** 313–317.

Decety, J., Jeannerod, M., Germain, M. and Pastene, J. (1991) Vegetative response during imagined movement is proportional to mental effort. *Behavioural Brain Research,* **42,** 1–5.

Decety, J., Jeannerod, M., Durozard, D. and Baverel, G. (1993) Central activation of autonomic effectors during mental simulation of motor actions. *Journal of Physiology,* **461,** 549–563.

de Charms, R.C., Maeda, F., Glover, G.H., Ludlow, D., Pauly, J.M., Soneji, D., Gabrieli, J.D.E. and Mackey, S.C. (2005) Control over brain activation and pain learned by using real-time functional MRI. *Proceedings of the National Academy of Sciences,* **102,** 18626–18631.

DeFelipe, J. (2006) Brain plasticity and mental processes: Cajal again. *Nature Reviews Neuroscience,* **7,** 811–817.

Dehaene, S. and Changeux, J-P. (1989) A simple model of prefrontal cortex function in delayed-response tasks. *Journal of Cognitive Neuroscience,* **1,** 244–261.

Dehaene, S. and Naccache, L. (2001) Towards a cognitive neuroscience of consciousness: basic evidence and a workspace framework. *Cognition,* **79,** 1–37.

Delgado, P.L. and Moreno, F.A. (1998) Hallucinogens, serotonin and obsessive-compulsive disorder. *Journal of Psychoactive Drugs,* **30,** 359–366.

Dement, W.C. (1994) History of sleep physiology and medicine. In *Principles and Practice of Sleep Medicine* (eds M.H. Kryger, T. Roth and W.C. Dement), Saunders, Philadelphia, pp. 3–15.

Dennett, D.C. (1993) *Consciousness Explained,* Penguin, Harmondsworth.

Depoortere, I. (2009) Targeting the ghrelin receptor to regulate food intake. *Regulatory Peptides,* **156,** 13–23.

Depue, R.A. and Collins, P.F. (1999) Neurobiology of the structure of personality: dopamine, facilitation of incentive motivation, and extraversion. *Behavioral and Brain Sciences,* **22,** 491–569.

Depue, R.A. and Morrone-Strupinsky, J.V. (2005) A neurobehavioral model of affiliative bonding: implications for conceptualizing a human trait of affiliation. *Behavioral and Brain Sciences,* **28,** 313–395.

Depue, R.A. and Spoont, M.R. (1986) Conceptualizing a serotonin trait – a basic dimension of constraint. *Annals of the New York Academy of Sciences,* **487,** 47–62.

Derbyshire, S.W.G., Whalley, M.G. and Oakley, D.A. (2009) Fibromyalgia pain and its modulation by hypnotic and non-hypnotic suggestion: an fMRI analysis. *European Journal of Pain,* **13,** 542–550.

Deroche-Gamonet, V., Belin, D. and Piazza, P.V. (2004) Evidence for addiction-like behavior in the rat. *Science,* **305,** 1014–1017.

Deschenes, M., Veinante, P. and Zhang, Z-W. (1998) The organization of corticothalamic projections: reciprocity versus parity. *Brain Research Reviews,* **28,** 286–308.

Desimone, R. (1992) Neural circuits for visual attention in the primate brain. In *Neural Networks for Vision and Image Processing* (eds G.A. Carpenter and S. Grossberg), MIT Press, Cambridge, pp. 343–364.

D'Esposito, M., Detre, J.A., Alsop, D.C., Shin, R.K., Atlas, S. and Grossman, M. (1995) The neural basis of the central executive system of working memory. *Nature,* **378,** 279–281.

DeSteno, D.A. and Salovey, P. (1996) Evolutionary origins of sex differences in jealousy? Questioning the 'fitness' of the model. *Psychological Science,* **7,** 367–372.

Deutch, A.Y. and Roth, R.H. (1999) Neurotransmitters. In *Fundamental Neuroscience* (eds M.J. Zigmond, F.E. Bloom, S.C. Landis, J.L. Roberts and L.R. Squire), Academic Press, San Diego, pp. 193–234.

Deutch, A.Y., Bourdelais, A.J. and Zahm, D.S. (1993) The nucleus accumbens core and shell: accumbal compartments and their functional attributes. In *Limbic Motor Circuits and Neuropsychiatry* (eds P.W. Kalivas and C.D. Barnes), CRC Press, Boca Raton, pp. 45–88.

Deutsch, J.A. (1983) Dietary control and the stomach. *Progress in Neurobiology,* **20,** 313–332.

Dewsbury, D.A. (1981) Effects of novelty on copulatory behavior: the Coolidge effect and related phenomena. *Psychological Bulletin,* **89,** 464–482.

Di Pellegrino, G., Fadiga, L., Fogassi, L., Gallese, V. and Rizzolatti, G. (1992) Understanding motor events: a neurophysiological study. *Experimental Brain Research*, **91**, 176–180.

Diamond, A. (1996) Evidence for the importance of dopamine for prefrontal cortex functions early in life. *Philosophical Transactions of the Royal Society of London B*, **351**, 1483–1494.

Diamond, A., Ciaramitaro, V., Donner, E., Kjali, S. and Robinson, M.B. (1994a) An animal model of early-treated PKU. *Journal of Neuroscience*, **14**, 3072–3082.

Diamond, A., Werker, J.F. and Lalonde, C. (1994b) Toward understanding commonalities in the development of object search, detour navigation, categorization, and speech perception. In *Human Behavior and the Developing Brain* (eds G. Dawson and K.W. Fischer), Guilford Press, New York, pp. 380–426.

Diamond, L.M. (2004) Emerging perspectives on distinctions between romantic love and sexual desire. *Current Directions in Psychological Science*, **13**, 116–119.

Dickerson, J.W.T. (1981) Nutrition, brain growth and development. In *Maturation and Development: Biological and Psychological Perspectives* (eds K.J. Connolly and H.F.R. Prechtl), William Heinemann Medical Books, London, pp. 110–130.

Dickinson, A. and Balleine, B. (1992) Actions and responses: the dual psychology of behaviour. In *Problems in the Philosophy and Psychology of Spatial Representation* (eds N. Eilan, R.A. McCarthy and M.W. Brewer), Blackwell, Oxford, pp. 277–293.

Dickman, A. and Simpson, K.H. (2008) *Chronic Pain*. Oxford University Press, Oxford.

Dienstbier, R.A. (1989) Arousal and physiological toughness: implications for mental and physical health. *Psychological Review*, **96**, 84–100.

Dijk, D-J. (1997) Physiology of sleep homeostasis and its circadian regulation. In *Sleep Science: Integrating Basic Research and Clinical Practice*. Monographs in Clinical Neuroscience, Vol. 15 (ed. W.J. Schwartz), Karger, Basle, pp. 10–33.

Dimberg, U., Thunberg, M. and Elmehed, K. (2000) Unconscious facial reactions to emotional facial expressions. *Psychological Science*, **11**, 86–89.

Dismukes, R.K. (1979) New concepts of molecular communication among neurons. *Behavioral and Brain Sciences*, **2**, 409–448.

Dobbing, J. (1976) Vulnerable periods in brain growth and somatic growth. In *The Biology of Human Fetal Growth* (eds D.F. Roberts and A.M. Thomson), Taylor and Francis, London, pp. 137–147.

Dodd, J. and Castellucci, V.F. (1991) Smell and taste: the chemical senses. In *Principles of Neural Science* (eds E.R. Kandel, J.H. Schwartz and T.M. Jessell), Appleton and Lange, Norwalk, pp. 512–529.

Dolan, R.J., Fink, G.R., Rolls, E., Booth, M., Holmes, A., Frackowiak, R.S.J. and Friston, K.J. (1997) How the brain learns to see objects and faces in an impoverished context. *Nature*, **389**, 596–599.

Dominey, P., Decety, J., Broussolle, E., Chazot, G. and Jeannerod, M. (1995) Motor imagery of a lateralized sequential task is asymmetrically slowed in hemi-Parkinson's patients. *Neuropsychologia*, **33**, 727–741.

Domjan, M. (1994) Formulation of a behavior system for sexual conditioning. *Psychonomic Bulletin and Review*, **1**, 421–428.

Domjan, M., Blesbois, E. and Williams, J. (1998) The adaptive significance of sexual conditioning: Pavlovian control of sperm release. *Psychological Science*, **9**, 411–415.

Donald, M. (1991) *Origins of the Modern Mind: Three Stages in the Evolution of Culture and Cognition*, Harvard University Press, Cambridge.

Donny, E.C., Caggiula, A.R., Mielke, M.M., Jacobs, K.S., Rose, C. and Sved, A.F. (1998) Acquisition of nicotine self-administration in rats: the effects of dose, feeding schedule and drug contingency. *Psychopharmacology*, **136**, 83–90.

Doran, M. and Gadian, D.G. (1992) Magnetic resonance imaging and spectroscopy of the brain. In *Quantitative Methods in Neuroanatomy* (ed. M. Stewart), Wiley, Chichester, pp. 163–179.

Douglas, L.A., Varlinskaya, E.I. and Spear, L.P. (2003) Novel-object place conditioning in adolescent and adult male and female rats: effects of social isolation. *Physiology and Behavior*, **80**, 317–325.

Douglas, V. (2005) Cognitive deficits in children with attention deficit hyperactivity disorder: a long-term follow-up. *Canadian Psychology*, **46**, 23–31.

Doyle, T.G., Berridge, K.C. and Gosnell, B.A. (1993) Morphine enhances hedonic taste palatability in rats. *Pharmacology Biochemistry and Behavior*, **46**, 745–749.

Drevets, W.C. (2001) Neuroimaging and neuropathological studies of depression: implications for the cognitive-emotional features of mood disorders. *Current Opinion in Neurobiology*, **11**, 240–249.

Drevets, W.C., Price, J.L., Simpson, J.R., Todd, R.D., Reich, T., Vannier, M. and Raiche, M.E. (1997) Subgenual prefrontal cortex abnormalities in mood disorders. *Nature*, **386**, 824–827.

Driver, J. and Spence, C.J. (1994) Spatial synergies between auditory and visual attention. In *Attention and Performance XV* (eds C. Umiltà and M. Moscovitch), MIT Press, Cambridge, pp. 311–332.

Dronkers, N.F., Plaisant, O., Iba-Zizen, M.T. and Cabanis, E.A. (2007) Paul Broca's historic cases: high resolution MR imaging of the brains of Leborgne and Lelong. *Brain*, **130**, 1432–1441.

Dudai, Y. (2002) *Memory from A to Z: Keywords, Concepts and Beyond*, Oxford University Press, Oxford.

Duhamel, J-R., Colby, C.L. and Goldberg, M.E. (1992) The updating of the representation of visual space in parietal cortex by intended eye movements. *Science*, **255**, 90–92.

Dunbar, R.I.M. (2009) Darwin and the ghost of Phineas Gage: neuro-evolution and the social brain. *Cortex*, **45**, 1119–1125.

Duncan, J. (1986) Disorganization of behaviour after frontal lobe damage. *Cognitive Neuropsychology*, **3**, 271–290.

Duncan, J. (1993) Selection of input and goal in the control of behaviour. In *Attention: Selection, Awareness, and Control – A Tribute to Donald Broadbent* (eds A. Baddeley and L. Weiskrantz), Clarendon Press, Oxford, pp. 53–71.

Dunn, A.J. and Berridge, C.W. (1990) Physiological and behavioral responses to corticotropin-releasing factor administration: is CRF a mediator of anxiety or stress responses? *Brain Research Reviews*, **15**, 71–100.

Dutton, D.G. and Aron, A.P. (1974) Some evidence for heightened sexual attraction under conditions of high anxiety. *Journal of Personality and Social Psychology*, **30**, 510–517.

E

Eastwick, P.W. (2009) Beyond the Pleistocene: using phylogeny and constraint to inform the evolutionary psychology of human mating. *Psychological Bulletin*, **135**, 794–821.

Eccles, J.C. (1989) *Evolution of the Brain: Creation of the Self*, Routledge, London.

Eccleston, C. and Crombez, G. (1999) Pain demands attention: a cognitive–affective model of the interruptive function of pain. *Psychological Bulletin*, **125**, 356–366.

Edelman, G.M. (1987) *Neural Darwinism*, Oxford University Press, Oxford.

Edelman, N.H. (1994) Foreword. In *Sleep Disorders Medicine: Basic Science, Technical Considerations and Clinical Aspects* (ed. S. Chokroverty), Butterworth-Heinemann, Boston, pp. 219–239.

Edelman, S. and Kidman, A.D. (1997) Mind and cancer: is there a relationship? – A review of evidence. *Australian Psychologist*, **32**, 1–7.

Ehrlichman, H. and Bastone, L. (1992) Olfaction and emotion. In *Science of Olfaction* (eds M.J. Serby and K.L. Chobar), Springer-Verlag, New York, pp. 410–438.

Ehrlichman, H., Kuhl, S.B., Zhu, J. and Warrenburg, S. (1997) Startle reflex modulation by pleasant and unpleasant odors in a between-subjects design. *Psychophysiology*, **34**, 726–729.

Eibl-Eibesfeldt, I. (2007) *Human Ethology*. Aldine Transaction, Piscataway.

Eichelman, B. (1988) Toward a rational pharmacotherapy for aggressive and violent behavior. *Hospital and Community Psychiatry*, **39**, 31–39.

Eichenbaum, H. (1994) The hippocampal system and declarative memory in humans and animals: experimental analysis and historical origins. In *Memory Systems 1994* (eds D.L. Schacter and E. Tulving), MIT Press, Cambridge, pp. 147–201.

Eichenbaum, H. and Cohen, N.J. (2001) *From Conditioning to Conscious Recollection*, Oxford University Press, New York.

Eisenberger, N.I., Lieberman, M.D. and Williams, K.D. (2003) Does rejection hurt? An fMRI study of social exclusion. *Science*, **302**, 290–292.

Ekman, P. (1984) Expression and the nature of emotion. In *Approaches to Emotion* (eds K.R. Scherer and P. Ekman), Lawrence Erlbaum, Hillsdale, pp. 319–343.

Ekman, P. (1992) Facial expressions of emotion: new findings, new questions. *Psychological Science*, **3**, 34–38.

Ekman, P., Sorenson, E.R. and Friesen, W.V. (1969) Pan-cultural elements in facial displays of emotion. *Science*, **164**, 86–88.

Ekman, P., Levenson, R.W. and Friesen, W.V. (1983) Autonomic nervous system activity distinguishes among emotions. *Science*, **221**, 1208–1210.

Elbert, T., Pantev, C., Wienbruch, C., Rockstroh, B. and Taub, E. (1995) Increased cortical representation of the fingers of the left hand in string players. *Science*, **270**, 305–307.

Ellenbroek, B.A. and Cools, A.R. (1990) Animal models with construct validity for schizophrenia. *Behavioural Pharmacology*, **1**, 469–490.

Ellinwood, E.H. (1967) Amphetamine psychosis: I. Description of the individuals and process. *Journal of Nervous and Mental Disease*, **144**, 273–283.

Ellinwood, E.H. (1968) Amphetamine psychosis: II. Theoretical implications. *International Journal of Neuropsychiatry*, **4**, 45–54.

Ellinwood, E.H. and Escalante, O. (1970) Chronic amphetamine effect on the olfactory forebrain. *Biological Psychiatry*, **2**, 189–203.

Ellinwood, E.H. and Kilbey, M.M. (1975) Amphetamine stereotypy: the influence of environmental factors and prepotent behavioral patterns on its topography and development. *Biological Psychiatry*, **10**, 3–16.

Elliott, B., Joyce, E. and Shorvon, S. (2009) Delusions, illusions and hallucinations in epilepsy: 1. Elementary phenomena. *Epilepsy Research*, **85**, 162–171.

Ellison, J.M. (1998) Antidepressant-induced sexual dysfunction: review, classification, and suggestions for treatment. *Harvard Review of Psychiatry*, **6**, 177–189.

Elman, J.L., Bates, E.A., Johnson, M.H., Karmiloff-Smith, A., Parisi, D. and Plunkett, K. (1996) *Rethinking Innateness. A Connectionist Perspective on Development*, MIT Press, Cambridge.

Emerson, E. and Howard, D. (1992) Schedule-induced stereotypy. *Research in Developmental Disabilities*, **13**, 335–361.

Engel, G.L. (1977) The need for a new medical model: a challenge for biomedicine. *Science*, **196**, 129–136.

Engelien, A., Huber, W., Silbersweig, D., Stern, E., Frith, C.D., Döring, W., Thron, A. and Frackowiak, R.S.J. (2000) The neural correlates of 'deaf-hearing' in man. *Brain*, **123**, 532–545.

Engell, D. and Hirsch, E. (1991) Environmental and sensory modulation of fluid intake in humans. In *Thirst: Physiological and Psychological Aspects* (eds D.J. Ramsey and D. Booth), Springer-Verlag, London, pp. 382–390.

Epstein, A.N. (1982) Instinct and motivation as explanations for complex behavior. In *The Physiological Mechanisms of Motivation* (ed. D.W. Pfaff), Springer, New York, pp. 25–58.

Epstein, A.N. (1990) Prospectus: thirst and salt appetite. In *Handbook of Behavioral Neurobiology*, Vol. 10, *Neurobiology of Food and Fluid Intake* (ed. E.M. Stricker), Plenum Press, New York, pp. 489–512.

Epstein, L.H. (1990) Behavioural treatment of obesity. In *Handbook of Behavioral Neurobiology*, Vol. 10, *Neurobiology of Food and Fluid Intake* (ed. E.M. Stricker), Plenum Press, New York, pp. 61–73.

Epstein, L.H., Paluch, R. and Coleman, K.J. (1996) Differences in salivation to repeated food cues in obese and nonobese women. *Psychosomatic Medicine*, **58**, 160–164.

Epstein, L.H., Temple, J.L., Roemmich, J.N. and Bouton, M.E. (2009) Habituation as a determinant of human food intake. *Psychological Review*, **116**, 384–407.

Erikson, K., Drevets, W. and Schulkin, J. (2003) Glucocorticoid regulation of diverse cognitive functions in normal and pathological emotional states. *Neuroscience and Biobehavioral Reviews*, **27**, 233–246.

Erickson, K.I., Prakash, R.S., Voss, M.W., Chaddock, L., Hu, L., Morris, K.S., White, S.M., Wójcicki, T.R., McAuley, E. and Kramer, A.F. (2009) Aerobic fitness is associated with hippocampal volume in elderly humans. *Hippocampus*, **19**, 1030–1039.

Eriksson, P.S., Perfilieva, E., Björk-Eriksson, T., Alborn, A-M., Nordborg, C., Peterson, D.A. and Gage, F.H. (1998) Neurogenesis in the adult human hippocampus. *Nature Medicine*, **4**, 1313–1317.

Erten-Lyons, D., Woltjer, R.L., Dodge, H., Nixon, R., Vorobik, R., Calvert, J.F., Leahy, M., Montine, T. and Kaye, J. (2009) Factors associated with resistance to dementia despite high Alzheimer disease pathology. *Neurology*, **72**, 354–360.

Ervin, F.R. and Martin, J. (1986) Neurophysiological bases of the primary emotions. In *Emotion – Theory, Research and Experience*. Vol. 3, *Biological Foundations of Emotion* (eds R. Plutchik and H. Kellerman), Academic Press, Orlando, pp. 145–170.

Evans, A.H., Pavese, N., Lawrence, A.D., Tai, Y.F., Appel, S., Doder, M., Brooks, D.J., Lees, A.J. and Piccini, P. (2006) Compulsive drug use linked to sensitized ventral striatal dopamine transmission. *Annals of Neurology*, **59**, 852–858.

Evans, P., Clow, A. and Hucklebridge, F. (1997) Stress and the immune system. *The Psychologist*, **10**, 303–307.

Evans, P., Hucklebridge, F. and Clow, A. (2000) *Mind, Immunity and Health: The Science of Psychoneuroimmunology*, Free Association Books, London.

Evarts, E.V. (1984) Hierarchies and emergent features in motor control. In *Dynamic Aspects of Neocortical Function* (eds G.M. Edelman, W.E. Gall and W.M. Cowan), Wiley, New York, pp. 557–579.

Evarts, E.V., Shinoda, Y. and Wise, S.P. (1984) *Neurophysiological Approaches to Higher Brain Functions*, Wiley, New York.

Everitt, B.J. (1990) Sexual motivation: a neural and behavioural analysis of the mechanisms underlying appetitive and copulatory responses of male rats. *Neuroscience and Biobehavioral Reviews*, **14**, 217–232.

Everitt, B.J. (1995) Neuroendocrine mechanisms underlying appetitive and consummatory elements of masculine sexual behaviour. In *The Pharmacology of Sexual Function and Dysfunction* (ed. J. Bancroft), Excerpta Medica, Amsterdam, pp. 15–35.

Everitt, B.J. and Bancroft, J. (1991) Of rats and men: the comparative approach to male sexuality. In *Annual Review of Sex Research*, 2 (ed. J. Bancroft), Society for the Scientific Study of Sex, Allentown, pp. 77–117.

Everitt, B.J. and Robbins, T.W. (1992) Amygdala–ventral striatal interactions and reward-related processes. In *The Amygdala: Neurobiological Aspects of Emotion, Memory, and Mental Dysfunction* (ed. J.P. Aggleton), Wiley, New York, pp. 401–429.

Everitt, B.J., Cador, M. and Robbins, T.W. (1989) Interactions between the amygdala and ventral striatum in stimulus–reward associations: studies using a second-order schedule of sexual reinforcement. *Neuroscience*, **30**, 63–75.

Everitt, B.J., Dickinson, A. and Robbins, T.W. (2001) The neuropsychological basis of addictive behaviour. *Brain Research Reviews*, **36**, 129–138.

Eysenck, H.J. (1985) *Decline and Fall of the Freudian Empire*, Penguin, Harmondsworth.

Eysenck, M. (1998) Perception and attention. In *Psychology: An Integrated Approach* (ed. M. Eysenck), Addison Wesley Longman, Harlow, pp. 138–166.

F

Falk, J.L. (1971) The nature and determinants of adjunctive behavior. *Physiology and Behavior*, **6**, 577–588.

Falk, J.L. (1994) The discriminative stimulus and its reputation: role in the instigation of drug abuse. *Experimental and Clinical Psychopharmacology*, **2**, 43–52.

Farah, M.J., Wallace, M.A. and Vecera, S.P. (1993) 'What' and 'where' in visual attention: evidence from the neglect syndrome. In *Unilateral Neglect: Clinical and Experimental Studies* (eds I.H. Robertson and J.C. Marshall), Lawrence Erlbaum, Hove, pp. 123–137.

Farah, M., Humphreys, G.W. and Rodman, H.R. (1999) Object and face recognition. In *Fundamental Neuroscience* (eds M.J. Zigmond, F.E. Bloom, S.C. Landis, J.L. Roberts and L.R. Squire), Academic Press, San Diego, pp. 1339–1361.

Faraone, S.V. and Biederman, J. (1998) Neurobiology of attention-deficit hyperactivity disorder. *Biological Psychiatry*, **44**, 951–958.

Faraone, S.V., Sergeant, J., Gillberg, C. and Biederman, J. (2003) The worldwide prevalence of ADHD: is it an American condition? *World Psychiatry*, **2**, 104–113.

Fasano, A., Elia, A.E., Soleti, F., Guidubaldi, A. and Bentivoglio, A.R. (2006) Punding and computer addiction in Parkinson's disease. *Movement Disorders*, **21**, 1217–1275.

Feltz, D.L. and Landers, D.M. (1983) The effects of mental practice on motor skill learning and performance: a meta-analysis. *Journal of Sport Psychology*, **5**, 25–57.

Fenwick, P. (1993) Discussion. In *Experimental and Theoretical Studies of Consciousness* (eds G.R. Bock and J. Marsh), Wiley, Chichester, pp. 118–119.

Ferber, R. (1994) Sleep disorders of childhood. In *Sleep Disorders Medicine: Basic Science, Technical Considerations and Clinical Aspects* (ed. S. Chokroverty), Butterworth-Heinemann, Boston, pp. 417–428.

Ferrari, P.F., Maiolini, C., Addessi, E., Fogassi, L. and Visalberghi, E. (2005) The observation and hearing of eating actions activates motor programs related to eating in macaque monkeys. *Behavioural Brain Research*, **161**, 95–101.

Ferris, C.F., Kulkarni, P., Sullivan, J.M., Harder, J.A., Messenger, T.L. and Febo, M. (2005) Pup suckling is more rewarding than cocaine: evidence from functional magnetic resonance imaging and three-dimensional computational analysis. *Journal of Neuroscience*, **25**, 149–156.

Ferster, D. (2004) Assembly of receptive fields in primary visual cortex. In *The Visual Neurosciences* (Vol. 1) (eds L.M. Chalupa and J.S. Werner), MIT Press, Cambridge, pp. 695–703.

ffytche, D.H., Howard, R.J., Brammer, M.J., David, A., Woodruff, P. and Williams, S. (1998) The anatomy of conscious vision: an fMRI study of visual hallucinations. *Nature Neuroscience*, **1**, 738–742.

Fields, H.L. and Basbaum, A.I. (1994) Central nervous system mechanisms of pain modulation. In *Textbook of Pain* (eds P.D. Wall and R. Melzack), Churchill Livingstone, Edinburgh, pp. 243–275.

Fields, R.D. (2004) The other half of the brain. *Scientific American*, **290**(4), 54–61.

Fifer, W.P. and Moon, C. (1988) Auditory experience in the fetus. In *Behavior of the Fetus* (eds W.P. Smotherman and S.R. Robinson), Telford Press, Caldwell, pp. 175–188.

Filbey, F.M., Schacht, J.P., Myers, U.S., Chavez, R.S. and Hutchison, K.E. (2009) Marijuana craving in the brain. *Proceedings of the National Academy of Sciences USA*, **106**, 13016–13021.

Filshie, J. and Morrison, P.J. (1988) Acupuncture for chronic pain: a review. *Palliative Care*, **2**, 1–14.

Fink, G.R., Halligan, P.W., Marshall, J.C., Frith, C.D., Frackowiak, R.S.J. and Dolan, R.J. (1996) Where in the brain does visual attention select the forest and the trees? *Nature*, **382**, 626–628.

Finlay, B.L. and Darlington, R.B. (1995) Linked regularities in the development and evolution of mammalian brains. *Science*, **268**, 1578–1584.

Fiorino, D.F., Coury, A. and Phillips, A.G. (1997) Dynamic changes in nucleus accumbens dopamine efflux during the Coolidge effect in male rats. *Journal of Neuroscience*, **17**, 4849–4855.

Fischer, K.W. and Rose, S.P. (1994) Dynamic development of coordination of components in brain and behaviour – a framework for theory and research. In *Human Behavior and the Developing Brain* (eds G. Dawson and K.W. Fischer), Guilford Press, New York, pp. 3–66.

Fitch, R.H. and Denenberg, V.H. (1998) A role for ovarian hormones in sexual differentiation of the brain. *Behavioral and Brain Sciences*, **21**, 311–352.

Fitzgerald, D.A., Posse, S., Moore, G.J., Tancer, M.E., Nathan, P.J. and Phan, K.L. (2004) Neural correlates of internally-generated disgust via autobiographical recall: a functional magnetic resonance imaging investigation. *Neuroscience Letters*, **370**, 91–96.

Fitzsimons, J.T. (1990) Thirst and sodium appetite. In *Handbook of Behavioral Neurobiology*, Vol. 10, *Neurobiology of Food and Fluid Intake* (ed. E.M. Stricker), Plenum Press, New York, pp. 23–44.

Fitzsimons, J.T. (1991) Evolution of physiological and behavioural mechanisms in vertebrate body fluid homeostasis. In *Thirst: Physiological and Psychological Aspects* (eds D.J. Ramsey and D. Booth), Springer-Verlag, London, pp. 3–22.

Fitzsimons, J.T. (1998) Angiotensin, thirst, and sodium appetite. *Physiological Reviews*, **78**, 583–686.

Fitzsimons, J.T. and Oatley, K. (1968) Additivity of stimuli for drinking in rats. *Journal of Comparative and Physiological Psychology*, **66**, 450–455.

Flanagan, L.M. and McEwen, B.S. (1995) Ovarian steroid interactions with hypothalamic oxytocin circuits involved in reproductive behaviour. In *Neurobiological Effects of Sex Steroid Hormones* (eds P.E. Micevych and R.P. Hammer), Cambridge University Press, Cambridge, pp. 117–142.

Fletcher, P.C. (2004) Functional neuroimaging of schizophrenia: from a genetic predisposition to the emergence of symptoms. *Brain*, **127**, 457–459.

Flint, J., Greenspan, R.J. and Kendler, K.S. (2010) *How Genes Influence Behavior*. Oxford University Press, New York.

Floeter, M.K. (1999a) Muscle, motor neurons, and motor neuron pools. In *Fundamental Neuroscience* (eds M.J. Zigmond, F.E. Bloom, S.C. Landis, J.L. Roberts and L.R. Squire), Academic Press, San Diego, pp. 863–887.

Floeter, M.K. (1999b) Spinal motor control, reflexes, and locomotion. In *Fundamental Neuroscience* (eds M.J. Zigmond, F.E. Bloom, S.C. Landis, J.L. Roberts and L.R. Squire), Academic Press, San Diego, pp. 889–912.

Flor, H. and Diers, M. (2009) Sensorimotor training and cortical reorganization. *Neuro-Rehabilitation*, **25**, 19–27.

Flor, H., Denke, C., Schaefer, M. and Grüsser, S. (2001) Effect of sensory discrimination training on cortical reorganization and phantom limb pain. *The Lancet*, **357**, 1763–1764.

Flor, H., Knost, B. and Birbaumer, N. (2002) The role of operant conditioning in chronic pain: an experimental investigation. *Pain*, **95**, 111–118.

Flor, H., Nikolajsen, L. and Jensen, T.S. (2006) Phantom limb pain: a case of maladaptive CNS plasticity? *Nature Reviews Neuroscience*, **7**, 873–881.

Fodor, J.A. (1985) Precis of *The Modularity of Mind*. *Behavioral and Brain Sciences*, **8**, 1–42.

Foster, J.K. and Jelicic, M. (1999) *Memory: Systems, Process, or Function*, Oxford University Press, Oxford.

Fotuhi, M., Hachinski, V. and Whitehouse, P.J. (2009) Changing perspectives regarding late-life dementia. *Nature Reviews Neurology*, **5**, 649–658.

Fowles, D.C. (1982) Heart rate as an index of anxiety: failure of a hypothesis. In *Perspectives in Cardiovascular Psychophysiology* (eds J.T. Cacioppo and R.E. Petty), Guilford Press, New York, pp. 93–123.

Fraley, R.C., Brumbaugh, C.C. and Marks, M.J. (2005) The evolution and function of adult attachment: a comparative and phylogenetic analysis. *Journal of Personality and Social Psychology*, **89**, 731–746.

Francis, P.T., Sims, N.R., Procter, A.W. and Bowen, D.M. (1993) Cortical pyramidal neurone loss may cause glutamatergic hypoactivity and cognitive impairment in Alzheimer's disease: investigative and therapeutic perspectives. *Journal of Neurochemistry*, **60**, 1589–1604.

Francis, P.T., Palmer, A.M., Snape, M. and Wilcock, G.K. (1999) The cholinergic hypothesis of Alzheimer's disease: a review of progress. *Journal of Neurology, Neurosurgery, and Psychiatry*, **66**, 137–147.

Franken, I.H.A. (2003) Drug craving and addiction: integrating psychological and neuropsychopharmacological approaches. *Progress in Neuro-Psychopharmacology and Biological Psychiatry*, **27**, 563–579.

Freeman, W. (1973) Sexual behaviour and fertility after frontal lobotomy. *Biological Psychiatry*, **6**, 97–104.

Freud, S. (1967) *New Introductory Lectures on Psychoanalysis*, Hogarth Press, London.

Friedlander, Y., Kark, J.D. and Stein, Y. (1987) Religious observance and plasma lipids and lipoproteins among 17-year-old Jewish residents of Jerusalem. *Preventive Medicine*, **16**, 70–79.

Friedman, M. (1996) *Type A Behavior: Its Diagnosis and Treatment*, Plenum Press, New York.

Friedman, M. and Rosenman, R.H. (1959) Association of specific overt behavior pattern with blood and cardiovascular findings. *Journal of American Medical Association*, **169**, 1286–1296.

Friedman, M.I. and Stricker, E.M. (1976) The physiological psychology of hunger: a physiological perspective. *Psychological Review*, **83**, 409–431.

Fries, W. (1981) The projection from the lateral geniculate nucleus to the prestriate cortex of the macaque monkey. *Proceedings of the Royal Society of London B*, **213**, 73–80.

Frisoni, G.B., Fox, N.C., Jack, C.R., Scheltens, P. and Thompson, P.M. (2010) The clinical use of structural MRI in Alzheimer disease. *Nature Reviews Neurology*, **6**, 67–76.

Frith, C. (1987) The positive and negative symptoms of schizophrenia reflect impairments in the perception and initiation of action. *Psychological Medicine*, **17**, 631–648.

Frith, C. (1996) Brain mechanisms for 'having a theory of mind'. *Journal of Psychopharmacology*, **10**, 9–15.

Frith, C. and Dolan, R.J. (1997) Brain mechanisms associated with top-down processes in perception. *Philosophical Transactions of the Royal Society of London B*, **352**, 1221–1230.

Frith, C.D. (1992) *The Cognitive Neuropsychology of Schizophrenia*, Lawrence Erlbaum, Hove.

Frohman, L., Cameron, J. and Wise, P. (1999) Neuroendocrine systems II: Growth, reproduction, and lactation. In *Fundamental Neuroscience* (eds M.J. Zigmond, F.E. Bloom, S.C. Landis, J.L. Roberts and L.R. Squire), Academic Press, San Diego, pp. 1151–1187.

Fuchs, R.A., Tran-Nguyen, L.T.L., Specio, S.E., Groff, R.S. and Neisewander, J.L. (1998) Predictive validity of the extinction/reinstatement model of drug craving. *Psychopharmacology*, **135**, 151–160.

Fuller, J.L. (1986) Genetics and emotions. In *Emotion – Theory, Research and Experience*, Vol. 3, *Biological Foundations of Emotion* (eds R. Plutchik and H. Kellerman), Academic Press, Orlando, pp. 199–216.

Fuster, J.M. (1997) *The Prefrontal Cortex – Anatomy, Physiology and Neuropsychology of the Frontal Lobe*, Raven Press, New York.

Fuster, J.M. (1999) Synopsis of function and dysfunction of the frontal lobe. *Acta Psychiatrica Scandinavica*, **99** (Suppl. 395), 51–57.

Fuster, J.M. (2008) *The Prefrontal Cortex*. Academic Press, New York.

G

Gallese, V. (2006) Intentional attunement: a neurophysiological perspective on social cognition and its disruption in autism. *Brain Research*, **1079**, 15–24.

Gallistel, C.R. (1980) *The Organization of Action – A New Synthesis*, Lawrence Erlbaum, Hillsdale.

Gallo, L.C. and Matthews, K.A. (2003) Understanding the association between socioeconomic status and physical health. *Psychological Bulletin*, **129**, 10–51.

Gallup, G.G. (1977) Self-recognition in primates. *American Psychologist*, **32**, 329–338.

Gandevia, S.C., Killian, K., McKenzie, D.K., Crawford, M., Allen, G.M., Gorman, R.B. and Hales, J.P. (1993) Respiratory sensations, cardiovascular control, kinesthesia and transcranial stimulation during paralysis in humans. *Journal of Physiology*, **470**, 85–107.

Ganzel, B.L., Morris, P.A. and Wetherington, E. (2010) Allostasis and the human brain: Integrating models of stress from the social and life sciences. *Psychological Review*, **117**, 134–174.

Gao, J-H., Parsons, L.M., Bower, J.M., Xiong, J., Li, J. and Fox, P.T. (1996) Cerebellum implicated in sensory acquisition and discrimination rather than motor control. *Science*, **272**, 545–547.

Garcia, J. (1989) Food for Tolman: cognition and cathexis in concert. In *Aversion, Avoidance and Anxiety – Perspectives on Aversively Motivated Behavior* (eds T. Archer and L-G. Nilsson), Lawrence Erlbaum, Hillsdale, pp. 45–85.

Garcia-Garcia, F., Acosta-Pena, E., Venebra-Munoz, A. and Murillo-Rodriguez, E. (2009) Sleep-inducing factors. *CNS and Neurological Disorders – Drug Targets*, **8**, 235–244.

Garcia-Reboll, L., Mulhall, J.P. and Goldstein, I. (1997) Drugs for the treatment of impotence. *Drugs and Aging*, **11**, 140–151.

Gardner, H. (1982) *Art, Mind, and Brain: A Cognitive Approach to Creativity*, Basic Books, New York.

Gardner, H. (1985) The centrality of modules. *Behavioral and Brain Sciences*, **8**, 12–14.

Garrard, P., Maloney, L.M., Hodges, J.R. and Patterson, K. (2005) The effects of very early Alzheimer's disease on the characteristics of writing by a renowned author. *Brain*, **128**, 250–260.

Gatchel, R.J., Peng, Y.B., Peters, M.L., Fuchs, P.N. and Turk, D.C. (2007) The biopsychosocial approach to chronic pain: scientific advances and future directions. *Psychological Bulletin*, **133**, 581–624.

Gay, P. (1988) *Freud – A Life for our Time*, J.M. Dent, London.

Gazzaley, A. and D'Esposito, M. (2007) Unifying prefrontal cortex function: executive control, neural networks, and top-down modulation. In *The Human Frontal Lobes: Functions and Disorders,* 2nd edition (eds B.L. Miller and J.L. Cummings), The Guilford Press, New York, pp.187–206.

Gazzaniga, M.S. (1993) Brain mechanisms and conscious experience. In *Experimental and Theoretical Studies of Consciousness* (eds G.R. Bock and J. Marsh), Wiley, Chichester, pp. 247–262.

Gazzaniga, M.S. (2009) *The Cognitive Neurosciences*, 4th edition, MIT Press, Cambridge.

Gazzaniga, M.S., Ivry, R.B. and Mangun, G.R. (2008) *Cognitive Neuroscience: The Biology of the Mind*, W.W Norton, New York.

Geary, N. (2004) Endocrine controls of eating: CCK, leptin, and ghrelin. *Physiology and Behavior*, **81**, 719–733.

Geffen, G., Bradshaw, J.L. and Nettleton, N.C. (1972) Hemispheric asymmetry: verbal and spatial encoding of visual stimuli. *Journal of Experimental Psychology,* **95**, 25–31.

Georgiadis, J.R. and Kortekaas, R. (2010) The sweetest taboo: functional neurobiology of human sexuality in relation to pleasure. In *Pleasures of the Brain* (eds. M.L. Kringelbach and K.C. Berridge) Oxford University Press, Oxford, pp.178–201.

Gervais, R. (1993) Olfactory processing controlling food and fluid intake. In *Neurophysiology of Ingestion* (ed. D.A. Booth), Pergamon Press, Oxford, pp. 119–135.

Geschwind, D.H. and Iacoboni, M. (2007) Structural and functional asymmetries of the human frontal lobes. In *The Human Frontal Lobes: Functions and Disorders* 2nd edition. (eds B.L. Miller and J.L. Cummings), The Guilford Press, New York, pp. 68–91.

Geschwind, N. (1972) Language and the brain. *Scientific American*, **226**, No. 4, 76–83.

Geschwind, N. (1979) Specializations of the human brain. *Scientific American*, **241**, No. 3, 158–168.

Geschwind, N. and Levitsky, W. (1968) Human brain: left–right asymmetries in temporal speech region. *Science*, **161**, 186–187.

Gessa, G., Melis, M., Muntoni, A. and Diana, M. (1998) Cannabinoids activate mesolimbic dopamine neurons by an action on cannabinoid CB_1 receptors. *European Journal of Pharmacology*, **341**, 39–44.

Geyer, M.A., Swerdlow, N.R., Mansbach, R.S. and Braff, D.L. (1990) Startle response models of sensorimotor gating and habituation deficits in schizophrenia. *Brain Research Bulletin*, **25**, 485–498.

Ghez, C. (1991a) Voluntary movement. In *Principles of Neural Science* (eds E.R. Kandel, J.H. Schwartz and T.M. Jessell), Appleton and Lange, Norwalk, pp. 609–625.

Ghez, C. (1991b) The cerebellum. In *Principles of Neural Science* (eds E.R. Kandel, J.H. Schwartz and T.M. Jessell), Appleton and Lange, Norwalk, pp. 626–646.

Gianaros, P.J. and Sheu, L.K. (2009) A review of neuroimaging studies of stressor-evoked blood pressure reactivity: emerging evidence for a brain–body pathway to coronary heart disease risk. *NeuroImage*, **47**, 922–936.

Gilbert, D.G., McClerlon, F.J. and Gilbert, B.O. (1997) The psychology of the smoker. In *The Tobacco Epidemic* (eds C.T. Bollinger and K.O. Fagerström), Karger, Basle, pp. 132–150.

Gilbert, P. (1998) Evolutionary psychopathology: why isn't the mind designed better than it is? *British Journal of Medical Psychology*, **71**, 353–373.

Gilbert, P. and Allan, S. (1998) The role of defeat and entrapment (arrested flight) in depression: an exploration of an evolutionary view. *Psychological Medicine*, **28**, 585–598.

Gizewski, E.R., Krause, E., Karama, S., Baars, A., Senf, W. and Forsting, M. (2006) There are differences in cerebral activation between females in distinct menstrual phases during viewing of erotic stimuli: a fMRI study. *Experimental Brain Research*, **174**, 101–108.

Gladue, B.A. (1988) Hormones in relationship to homosexual/bisexual/heterosexual gender orientation. In *Handbook of Sexology*, Vol. 6, *The Pharmacology and Endocrinology of Sexual Function* (ed. J.M.A. Sitsen), Elsevier Science, Amsterdam, pp. 388–409.

Gladue, B.A. (1994) The biopsychology of sexual orientation. *Current Directions in Psychological Science*, **3**, 150–154.

Glahn, D.C., Laird, A.R., Ellison-Wright, I., Thelen, S.M., Robinson. J.L., Lancaster, J.L., Bullmore, E. and Fox, P.T. (2008) Meta-analysis of gray matter anomalies in schizophrenia: application of anatomic likelihood estimation and network analysis. *Biological Psychiatry*, **64**, 774–781.

Glickman, S.E. and Schiff, B.B. (1967) A biological theory of reinforcement. *Psychological Review*, **74**, 81–109.

Glickman, S.E. and Sroges, R.W. (1966) Curiosity in zoo animals. *Behaviour*, **26**, 151–188.

Gloor, P. (1986) Role of the human limbic system in perception, memory, and affect: lessons from temporal lobe epilepsy. In *The Limbic System: Functional Organization and Clinical Disorders* (eds B.K. Doane and K.E. Livingstone), Raven Press, New York, pp. 159–169.

Glover, S. (2004) Separate visual representations in the planning and control of action. *Behavioral and Brain Sciences*, **27**, 3–78.

Glucksberg, S. (1985) Modularity: contextual interactions and the tractability of nonmodular systems. *Behavioral and Brain Sciences*, **8**, 14–15.

Glue, P., Nutt, D. and Coupland, N. (1993) Stress and psychiatric disorder: reconciling social and biological approaches. In *Stress – From Synapse to Syndrome* (eds S.C. Stanford and P. Salmon), Academic Press, London, pp. 53–73.

Gold, J.M., Waltz, J. A., Prentice K.J., Morris, S,E., and Heerey, E.A. (2008) Reward processing in schizophrenia: a deficit in the representation of value. *Schizophrenia Bulletin*, **34**, 835–847.

Goldberg, J.M. and Fernández, C. (1984) The vestibular system. In *Handbook of Physiology. Section 1: The Nervous System*, Vol. III, Part 2 (ed. I. Darian-Smith), American Physiological Society, Bethesda, pp. 977–1022.

Goldman-Rakic, P.S. (1987) Circuitry of primate prefrontal cortex and regulation of behavior by representational memory. In *Handbook of Physiology. Section 1: The Nervous System*, Vol. V. *Higher Functions of the Brain*, Part 1 (eds V.B. Mountcastle, F. Plum and S.R. Geiger), American Physiological Society, Bethesda, pp. 373–417.

Goldman-Rakic, P.S. (1995) Toward a circuit model of working memory and the guidance of voluntary motor action. In *Models of Information Processing in the Basal Ganglia* (eds J.C. Houk, J.L. Davis and D.G. Beiser), MIT Press, Cambridge, pp. 131–148.

Goldstein, I., Lue, T., Padma-Nathan, H., Rosen, R.C., Steers, W.D. and Wickler, P.A. (1998) Oral sildenafil in the treatment of erectile dysfunction. *New England Journal of Medicine*, **338**, 1397–1404.

Goodale, M.A. and Humphrey, G.K. (1998) The objects of action and perception. *Cognition*, **67**, 181–207.

Goodale, M.A. and Milner, A.D. (2004) *Sight Unseen: An Exploration of Conscious and Unconscious Vision*, Oxford University Press, Oxford.

Goodale, M.A., Milner, A.D., Jakobsen, L.S. and Carey, D.P. (1991) A neurological dissociation between perceiving objects and grasping them. *Nature*, **349**, 154–156.

Goodman, A. (2008) Neurobiology of addiction: an integrative review. *Biochemical Pharmacology*, **75**, 266–322.

Gordon, C.J. and Heath, J.E. (1986) Integration and central processing in temperature regulation. *Annual Review of Physiology*, **48**, 595–612.

Gordon, J. (1991) Spinal mechanisms of motor coordination. In *Principles of Neural Science* (eds E.R. Kandel, J.H. Schwartz and T.M. Jessell), Appleton and Lange, Norwalk, pp. 581–595.

Gordon, J. and Ghez, C. (1991) Muscle receptors and spinal reflexes: the stretch reflex. In *Principles of Neural Science* (eds E.R. Kandel, J.H. Schwartz and T.M. Jessell), Appleton and Lange, Norwalk, pp. 564–580.

Gorman, M.R. (1994) Male homosexual desire: neurological investigations and scientific bias. *Perspectives in Biology and Medicine*, **38**, 61–81.

Goswami, U. (2008) *Cognitive Development: The Learning Brain*. Psychology Press, Hove.

Gottesman, I.I. and Moldin, S.O. (1998) Genotypes, genes, genesis, and pathogenesis in schizophrenia. In *Origins and Development of Schizophrenia* (eds M.F. Lenzenweger and R.H. Dworkin), American Psychological Association, Washington, pp. 5–26.

Gottlieb, G. (1973) *Behavioral Embryology: I. Studies on the Development of Behavior and the Nervous System*, Academic Press, New York.

Gottlieb, G. (1997) A systems view of psychobiological development. In *The Lifespan Development of Individuals: Behavioral, Neurobiological, and Psychosocial Perspectives. A Synthesis* (ed. D. Magnusson), Cambridge University Press, New York, pp. 76–103.

Gottlieb, G. (1998) Normally occurring environmental and behavioral influences on gene activity: from central dogma to probabilistic epigenesis. *Psychological Review*, **105**, 792–802.

Goudriaan, A.E., Oosterlaan, J., de Beurs, E. and van den Brink, W. (2004) Pathological gambling: a comprehensive review of

biobehavioural findings. *Neuroscience and Biobehavioral Reviews*, **28**, 123–141.

Gould, E., Woolley, C.S. and McEwen, B.S. (1991) The hippocampal formation: morphological changes induced by thyroid, gonadal and adrenal hormones. *Psychoneuroendocrinology*, **16**, 67–84.

Gould, E., Reeves, A.J., Graziano, M.S.A. and Gross, C.G. (1999) Neurogenesis in the neocortex of adult primates. *Science*, **286**, 548–552.

Gould, S.J. and Vrba, E.S. (1982) Exaptation – a missing term in the science of form. *Paleobiology*, **8**, 4–15.

Grace, A.A. (2001) Psychostimulant actions on dopamine and limbic system function: relevance to the pathophysiology and treatment of ADHD. In *Stimulant Drugs and ADHD: Basic and Clinical Neuroscience* (eds M.V. Solanto, A.F.T. Arnsten and F.X. Castellanos), Oxford University Press, Oxford, pp. 134–157.

Gracely, R.H., Geisser, M.E., Giesecke, T., Grant, M.A.B., Petzke, F., Williams, D.A. and Clauw, D.J. (2004) Pain catastrophising and neural responses to pain among persons with fibromyalgia. *Brain*, **127**, 835–843.

Grafman, J. (1989) Plans, actions, and mental sets: managerial knowledge units in the frontal lobes. In *Integrating Theory and Practice in Clinical Neuropsychology* (ed. E. Perecman), Lawrence Erlbaum, Hillsdale, pp. 93–138.

Grafton, S.T., Woods, R.P. and Tyszka, M. (1994) Functional imaging of procedural motor learning: relating cerebral blood flow with individual subject performance. *Human Brain Mapping*, **1**, 221–234.

Grammer, K., Fink, B. and Neave, N. (2005) Human pheromones and sexual attraction. *European Journal of Obstetrics and Gynecology and Reproductive Biology*, **118**, 135–142.

Grant, N., Hamer, M. and Steptoe, A. (2009) Social isolation and stress-related cardiovascular, lipid, and cortisol responses. *Annals of Behavioral Medicine*, **37**, 29–37.

Grant, V.J. (1994a) Sex of infant differences in mother–infant interaction: a reinterpretation of past findings. *Developmental Review*, **14**, 1–26.

Grant, V.J. (1994b) Maternal dominance and the conception of sons. *British Journal of Medical Psychology*, **67**, 343–351.

Graven-Nielsen, T., Kendall, S.A., Henriksson, K.G., Bengtson, M., Sørenson, J., Johnson, A., Gerdle, B. and Arendt-Nielson, L. (2000) Ketamine reduces muscle pain, temporal summation, and referred pain in fibromyalgia patients. *Pain*, **85**, 483–491.

Gray, J. (2004) *Consciousness: Creeping up on the Hard Problem*, Oxford University Press, Oxford.

Gray, J.A. (1987a) *The Psychology of Fear and Stress*, Cambridge University Press, Cambridge.

Gray, J.A. (1987b) The mind–brain identity as a scientific hypothesis: a second look. In *Mindwaves: Thoughts on Intelligence, Identity and Consciousness* (eds C. Blakemore and S. Greenfield), Basil Blackwell, Oxford, pp. 461–483.

Gray, J.A. (1993) Consciousness, schizophrenia and scientific theory. In *Experimental and Theoretical Studies of Consciousness* (eds G.R. Bock and J. Marsh), Wiley, Chichester, pp. 263–281.

Gray, J.A. (1995) The contents of consciousness: a neuropsychological conjecture. *Behavioral and Brain Sciences*, **18**, 659–722.

Gray, J.A., Feldon, J., Rawlins, J.N.P., Hemsley, D.R. and Smith, A.D. (1991) The neuropsychology of schizophrenia. *Behavioral and Brain Sciences*, **14**, 1–84.

Graybiel, A.M. (1997) The basal ganglia and cognitive pattern generators. *Schizophrenia Bulletin*, **23**, 459–469.

Graybiel, A.M., Aosaki, T., Flaherty, A.W. and Kimura, M. (1994) The basal ganglia and adaptive motor control. *Science*, **265**, 1826–1831.

Green, D.M. and Wier, C.C. (1984) Auditory perception. In *Handbook of Physiology. Section 1: The Nervous System*, Vol. III, Part 2 (ed. I. Darian-Smith), American Physiological Society, Bethesda, pp. 557–594.

Green, S. (2010) *Biological Rhythms, Sleep and Hypnosis*. Palgrave Macmillan, Basingstoke.

Greenberg, M.S. (1992) Olfactory hallucinations. In *Science of Olfaction* (eds M.J. Serby and K.L. Chobor), Springer-Verlag, New York, pp. 467–499.

Greene, J. (1990) Perception. In *Introduction to Psychology*, Vol. 2 (ed. I. Roth), Lawrence Erlbaum, Hove, pp. 475–527.

Greenfield, P.M. (1991) Language, tools and brain: the ontogeny and phylogeny of hierarchically organized sequential behaviour. *Behavioral and Brain Sciences*, **14**, 531–595.

Greenough, W.T. (1976) Enduring brain effects of differential experience and training. In *Neural Mechanisms of Learning and Memory* (eds M.R. Rosenzweig and E.L. Bennett), MIT Press, Cambridge, pp. 255–278.

Greenspan, J.D. and Bolanowski, S.J. (1996) The psychophysics of tactile perception and its peripheral basis. In *Pain and Touch* (ed. L. Kruger), Academic Press, San Diego, pp. 25–103.

Gregory, R.L. (1997) *Eye and Brain*, Oxford University Press, Oxford.

Gregory, R.L. (1998) *Eye and Brain: The Psychology of Seeing*, Oxford University Press, Oxford.

Gregory R.L. (2009) *Seeing through Illusions: Making Sense of the Senses*. Oxford University Press, Oxford.

Griffiths, D., Dickinson, A. and Clayton, N. (1999) Episodic memory: what can animals remember about their past? *Trends in Cognitive Sciences*, **3**, 74–80.

Griffiths, M. (1999) Internet addiction: fact or fiction? *The Psychologist*, **12**, 246–250.

Griffiths, P.E. (1997) *What Emotions Really Are*, University of Chicago Press, Chicago.

Griffiths, R.R and Woodson, P.P. (1988) Caffeine physical dependence: a review of human and laboratory animal studies. *Psychopharmacology*, **94**, 437–451.

Griffiths, R.R., Brady, J.V. and Bradford, L.D. (1979) Predicting the abuse liability of drugs with animal drug self-administration procedures: psychomotor stimulants and hallucinogens. In *Advances in Behavioral Pharmacology*, Vol. 2 (eds T. Thompson and P.B. Dews), Academic Press, New York, pp. 163–208.

Grill, H.J. and Berridge, K.C. (1985) Taste reactivity as a measure of the neural plasticity of palatability. In *Progress in Psychobiology and Physiological Psychology*, Vol. 11 (eds J.M. Sprague and A.N. Epstein), Academic Press, Orlando, pp. 1–61.

Grill, H.J. and Kaplan, J.M. (1990) Caudal brainstem participates in the distributed neural control of feeding. In *Handbook of Behavioral Neurobiology*, Vol. 10 *Neurobiology of Food and Fluid Intake* (ed. E.M. Stricker), Plenum Press, New York, pp. 125–149.

Grobstein, P. (1988) On beyond neuronal specificity: problems in going from cells to networks and from networks to behaviour. In *Advances in Neural and Behavioral Development*, Vol. 3 (ed. P.G. Shinkman), Ablex Publishing, Norwood, pp. 1–58.

Gross, C.G. (1985) On Gall's reputation and some recent 'new phrenology'. *Behavioral and Brain Sciences*, **8**, 16–18.

Gross, C.G. (2000) Neurogenesis in the adult brain: death of a dogma. *Nature Reviews Neuroscience*, **1**, 67–73.

Gross, C.G. (2009) Three before their time: neuroscientists whose ideas were ignored by their contemporaries. *Experimental Brain Research*, **192**, 321–334.

Gross, C.G., Rodman, H.R., Gochin, P.M. and Colombo, M.W. (1993) Inferior temporal cortex as a pattern recognition device. In *Computational Learning and Cognition* (ed. E.B. Baum), Society for Industrial and Applied Mathematics, Philadelphia, pp. 44–73.

Grossman, M. (1980) A central processor for hierarchically structured material: evidence from Broca's aphasia. *Neuropsychologia*, **18**, 299–308.

Groves, P.M. and Thompson, R.F. (1970) Habituation: a dual process theory. *Psychological Review*, **77**, 419–450.

Grunberg, N.E. (1985) Specific taste preferences: an alternative explanation for eating changes in cancer patients. In *Cancer, Nutrition, and Eating Behavior: A Biobehavioral Perspective* (eds T.G. Burish, S.M. Levy and B.E. Meyerowitz), Lawrence Erlbaum, Hillsdale, pp. 43–61.

Guisinger, S. (2003) Adapted to flee famine: adding an evolutionary perspective on anorexia nervosa. *Psychological Review*, **110**, 745–761.

Gulevich, G., Dement, W. and Johnson, L. (1966) Psychiatric and EEG observations on a case of prolonged (264 hours) wakefulness. *Archives of General Psychiatry*, **15**, 29–35.

Gunne, L.M., Änggård, E. and Jönsson, L.E. (1972) Clinical trials with amphetamine-blocking drugs. *Psychiatria, Neurologia and Neurochirurgia*, **75**, 225–226.

Guyton, A.C. (1991) *Textbook of Medical Physiology*, W.B. Saunders, Philadelphia.

Guzman-Marin, R., Suntsova, N., Methippara, M., Greiffenstein, R., Szymusiak, R. and McGinty, D. (2005) Sleep deprivation suppresses neurogenesis in the adult hippocampus of rats. *European Journal of Neuroscience*, **22**, 2111–2116.

H

Haberich, F.J. (1968) Osmoreception in the portal circulation. *Federation Proceedings*, **27**, 1137–1141.

Hagemann, G.H., Berding, G., Bergh, S., Sleep, D.J., Knapp, W.H., Jonas, U. and Stief,

C.G. (2003) Effects of visual sexual stimuli and apomorphine SL on cerebral activity in men with erectile dysfunction. *European Urology*, **43**, 412–420.

Halford, J.C.G. and Harrold, J.A. (2008) Neuropharmacology of human appetite expression. *Developmental Disabilities Research Reviews*, **14**, 158–164.

Halford, J.C.G., Harrold, J.A., Lawton, C.L. and Blundell, J.E. (2005) Serotonin (5-HT) drugs: effects on appetite expression and use for the treatment of obesity. *Current Drug Targets*, **6**, 201–213.

Hall, M. and Halliday, T. (1998) *Behaviour and Evolution*, Springer, Berlin.

Haller, J., Makara, G.B. and Kruk, M.R. (1998) Catecholaminergic involvement in the control of aggression: hormones, the peripheral sympathetic, and central noradrenergic systems. *Neuroscience and Biobehavioral Reviews*, **22**, 85–97.

Halliday, T. (1998) *The Senses and Communication*, Springer, Berlin.

Halligan, P.W. and Marshall, J.C. (1993) The history and clinical presentation of neglect. In *Unilateral Neglect: Clinical and Experimental Studies* (eds I.H. Robertson and J.C. Marshall), Lawrence Erlbaum, Hove, pp. 3–25.

Halmi, K. (1980) Gastric bypass for massive obesity. In *Obesity* (ed. A.J. Stunkard), W.B. Saunders, Philadelphia, pp. 388–394.

Hamann, S., Herman, R.A., Nolan, C.L. and Wallen, K. (2004) Men and women differ in amygdala response to visual sexual stimuli. *Nature Neuroscience*, **7**, 411–416.

Hamburger, V. (1963) Some aspects of the embryology of behaviour. *Quarterly Review of Biology*, **38**, 342–365.

Hampshire, A., Chamberlain, S.R., Monti, M.M., Duncan, J. and Owen, A.M. (2010) The role of the right inferior frontal gyrus: inhibition and attentional control. *Neuroimage*, **50**, 1313–1319.

Hanin, I., Fisher, A. and Cacabelos, R. (2005) *Recent Progress in Alzheimer's and Parkinson's Diseases*, Taylor and Francis, London.

Harlow, H.F. and Harlow, M.K. (1962) Social deprivation in monkeys. *Scientific American*, **207**, No. 5, 136–146.

Harrington, M.E., Rusak, B. and Mistlberger, R.E. (1994) Anatomy and physiology of the mammalian circadian system. In *Principles and Practice of Sleep Medicine* (eds M.H. Kryger, T. Roth and W.C. Dement), Saunders, Philadelphia, pp. 286–300.

Harris, A.J. (1999) Cortical origin of pathological pain. *Lancet*, **354**, 1464–1466.

Harris, C.R. and Christenfeld, N. (1996) Gender, jealousy, and reason. *Psychological Science*, **7**, 364–366.

Harris, G.C., Wimmer, M. and Aston-Jones, G. (2005) A role for lateral hypothalamic orexin neurons in reward seeking. *Nature*, **437**, 556–559.

Harris, J.A. (1996) Descending antinociceptive mechanisms in the brainstem: their role in the animal's defensive system. *Journal of Physiology (Paris)*, **90**, 15–25.

Harris, R.E., Sundgren, P.C., Pang, Y., Hsu, M., Petrou, M., Kim, S-H., McLean, S.A., Gracely, R.H. and Clauw, D.J. (2008) Dynamic levels of glutamate within the insula are associated with improvements in multiple pain domains in fibromyalgia. *Arthritis and Rheumatology*, **58**, 903–907.

Harris, R.E., Sundgren, P.C., Craig, A.D., Kirshenbaum, E., Sen, A., Napadow, V. and Clauw, D.J. (2009) Elevated insular glutamate in fibromyalgia is associated with experimental pain. *Arthritis and Rheumatism*, **60**, 3146–3152.

Harris, W.A. and Hartenstein, V. (1999) Cellular determination. In *Fundamental Neuroscience* (eds M.J. Zigmond, F.E. Bloom, S.C. Landis, J.L. Roberts and L.R. Squire), Academic Press, San Diego, pp. 481–517.

Hart, B.L. (1988) Biological basis of the behavior of sick animals. *Neuroscience and Biobehavioral Reviews*, **12**, 123–137.

Harvey, P.H. and Krebs, J.R. (1990) Comparing brains. *Science*, **249**, 140–146.

Haughey, H.M., Marshall, E., Schacht, J.P., Louis, A. and Hutchison, K.E. (2008) Marijuana withdrawal and craving: influence of the cannabinoid receptor1 (CNR1) and fatty acid amide hydrolase (FAAH) genes. *Addiction*, **103**, 1676–1686.

Healy, S. and Guilford, T. (1990) Olfactory-bulb size and nocturnality in birds. *Evolution*, **44**, 339–346.

Heath, R.G. (1986) The neural substrate for emotion. In *Emotion – Theory, Research and Experience*, Vol. 3, *Biological Foundations of Emotion* (eds R. Plutchik and H. Kellerman), Academic Press, Orlando, pp. 3–35.

Hebb, D.O. (1949) *The Organization of Behavior*, Wiley, New York.

Heilman, K.M. and Bowers, D. (1990) Neuropsychological studies of emotional changes induced by right and left hemispheric lesions. In *Psychological and Biological Approaches to Emotion* (eds N.L. Stein, B. Leventhal and T. Trabasso), Lawrence Erlbaum, Hillsdale, pp. 97–113.

Heiser, M., Iacoboni, M., Maeda, F., Marcus, J. and Mazziotta, J.C. (2003) The essential role of Broca's area in imitation. *European Journal of Neuroscience*, **17**, 1123–1128.

Helfert, R.H., Snead, C.R. and Altschuler, R.A. (1991) The ascending auditory pathways. In *Neurobiology of Hearing: The Central Auditory System* (eds R.A. Altschuler, R.P. Bobbin, B.M. Clopton and D.W. Hoffman), Raven Press, New York, pp. 1–26.

Heller, H.C., Crawshaw, L.I. and Hammel, H.T. (1978) The thermostat of vertebrate animals. *Scientific American*, **239**, 88–96.

Heller, W. (1990) The neuropsychology of emotion: developmental patterns and implications for psychopathology. In *Psychological and Biological Approaches to Emotion* (eds N.L. Stein, B. Leventhal and T. Trabasso), Lawrence Erlbaum, Hillsdale, pp. 167–211.

Hemsley, D.R. (1996) Schizophrenia – a cognitive model and its implications for psychological intervention. *Behavior Modification*, **20**, 139–169.

Henderson, V.W. (1986) Anatomy of posterior pathways in reading: a reassessment. *Brain and Language*, **29**, 119–133.

Hendry, S.H.C., Hsiao, S.S. and Bushnell, M.C. (1999) Somatic sensation. In *Fundamental Neuroscience* (eds M.J. Zigmond, F.E. Bloom, S.C. Landis, J.L. Roberts and L.R. Squire), Academic Press, San Diego, pp. 761–789.

Hennenlotter, A., Schroeder, U., Erhard, P., Castrop, F., Haslinger, B., Stoecker, D., Lange, K.W. and Ceballos-Baumann, A.O. (2005) A common neural basis for receptive and expressive communication of pleasant facial affect. *NeuroImage*, **26**, 581–591.

Henningfield, J.E., Johnson, R.E. and Jasinski, D.I. (1987) Clinical procedures for the assessment of abuse potential. In *Methods of Assessing the Reinforcing Properties of Abused Drugs* (ed. M.A. Bozarth) Springer-Verlag, New York.

Henriksen, S.J. and Giacchino, J. (1993) Functional characteristics of nucleus accumbens neurons: evidence obtained from *in vivo* electrophysiological recordings. In *Limbic Motor Circuits and Neuropsychiatry* (eds P.W. Kalivas and C.D. Barnes), CRC Press, Boca Raton, pp. 101–124.

Henry, J.P. (1982) The relation of social to biological processes in disease. *Social Science and Medicine*, **16**, 369–380.

Henry, J.P. (1986) Neuroendocrine patterns of emotional response. In *Emotion – Theory, Research and Experience*, Vol. 3, *Biological Foundations of Emotion* (eds R. Plutchik and H. Kellerman), Academic Press, Orlando, pp. 37–60.

Herbert, J. (1995) Neuropeptides, stress and sexuality: towards a new psychopharmacology. In *The Pharmacology of Sexual Function and Dysfunction* (ed. J. Bancroft), Excerpta Medica, Amsterdam, pp. 77–96.

Herman, B.H. and Panksepp, J. (1978) Effects of morphine and naloxone on separation distress and approach attachment: evidence for opiate mediation of social affect. *Pharmacology Biochemistry and Behavior*, **9**, 213–220.

Herz, R.S. (1997) Emotion experienced during encoding enhances odor retrieval cue effectiveness. *American Journal of Psychology*, **110**, 489–505.

Hess, W.R. (1981) *Biological Order and Brain Organization: Selected Works of W.R. Hess* (ed. K. Akert), Springer-Verlag, Berlin.

Hickok, G. and Poeppel, D. (2004) Dorsal and ventral streams: a framework for understanding aspects of the functional anatomy of language. *Cognition*, **92**, 67–99.

Hilton, S.M. (1979) The defense reaction as a paradigm for cardiovascular control. In *Integrative Functions of the Autonomic Nervous System* (eds C.McC. Brooks, K. Koizumi and A. Sato), University of Tokyo Press/Elsevier, Amsterdam, pp. 443–449.

Hines, M., Ahmed, S.F. and Hughes, I.A. (2003) Psychological outcomes and gender-related development in complete androgen insensitivity syndrome. *Archives of Sexual Behavior*, **32**, 93–101.

Hines, T. (1991) The myth of right hemisphere creativity. *Journal of Creative Behavior*, **25**, 223–226.

Hinke, R.M., Hu, X., Stillman, A.E., Kim, S-G., Merkle, H., Salmi, R. and Ugurbil, K. (1993) Functional magnetic resonance imaging of Broca's area during internal speech. *Neuro Report*, **4**, 675–678.

Hinkelmann, K., Moritz, S., Botzenhardt, J., Riedesel, K., Wiedemann, K., Kellner, M. and Otte, C. (2009) Cognitive impairment in major depression: association with salivary cortisol. *Biological Psychiatry*, **66**, 879–885.

Hirsh, R. (1974) The hippocampus and contextual retrieval of information from memory: a theory. *Behavioral Biology*, **12**, 421–444.

Hobson, J.A. (1988) *The Dreaming Brain*, Basic Books, New York.

Hobson, J.A. (1990) Activation, input source, and modulation: a neurocognitive model of the state of the brain–mind. In *Sleep and Cognition* (eds R.R. Bootzin, J.F. Kihlstrom and D.L. Schacter), American Psychological Association, Washington, pp. 25–40.

Hobson, J.A. (1996) Dreams and the brain. In *Neuroscience: Exploring the Brain* (eds M.F. Bear, B.W. Connors and M.A. Paradiso), Williams and Wilkins, Baltimore, p. 471.

Hobson, J.A. (1999) Sleep and dreaming. In *Fundamental Neuroscience* (eds M.J. Zigmond, F.E. Bloom, S.C. Landis, J.L. Roberts and L.R. Squire), Academic Press, San Diego, pp. 1207–1227.

Hobson, J.A. (2003) *Dreaming: An Introduction to the Science of Sleep*, Oxford University Press, Oxford.

Hobson, J.A. (2004) *13 Dreams Freud Never Had: A New Mind Science*, Pi Press, New York.

Hobson, J.A. and Pace-Schott, E.F. (2002) The cognitive neuroscience of sleep: neuronal systems, consciousness and learning. *Nature Reviews Neuroscience*, **3**, 679–693.

Hobson, J.A. and Stickgold, R. (1994) Dreaming a neurocognitive approach. *Consciousness and Cognition*, **3**, 1–15.

Hoebel, B.G. (1997) Neuroscience and appetitive behavior research: 25 years. *Appetite*, **29**, 119–133.

Hofer, M.A. (1988) On the nature and function of prenatal behavior. In *Behavior of the Fetus* (eds W.P. Smotherman and S.R. Robinson), Telford Press, Caldwell, pp. 3–18.

Hogan, J.A. (1980) Homeostasis and behaviour. In *Analysis of Motivational Processes* (eds F.M. Toates and T.R. Halliday), Academic Press, London, pp. 3–21.

Hogarth, L., Dickinson, A. and Duka, T. (2003) Discriminative stimuli that control instrumental tobacco-seeking by human smokers also command selective attention. *Psychopharmacology*, **168**, 435–445.

Hollis, K.L. (1997) Contemporary research on Pavlovian conditioning. *American Psychologist*, **52**, 956–965.

Holmes, G. (1939) The cerebellum of man. *Brain*, **62**, 1–30.

Holsboer, F. and Barden, N. (1996) Antidepressants and hypothalamic–pituitary–adrenocortical regulation. *Endocrine Reviews*, **17**, 187–205.

Holstege, G. and Georgiadis, J.R. (2004) Brain activation during orgasm is basically the same in men and women. *Hormones and Behavior*, **46**, 132.

Holstege, G., Georgiadis, J.R., Paans, A.M.J., Meiners, L.C., van der Graaf, F.H.C.E. and Reinders, A.A.T. (2003) Brain activation during human male ejaculation. *Journal of Neuroscience*, **23**, 9185–9193.

Hommet, C., Sauerwein, H.C., De Toffol, B., and Lassonde, M. (2005) Idiopathic epileptic syndromes and cognition. *Neuroscience and Biobehavioral Reviews*, **30**, 85–96.

Honjo, I. (1999) *Language Viewed from the Brain*, Karger, Basle.

Hooks, M.S. and Kalivas, P.W. (1995) The role of mesoaccumbens-pallidal circuitry in novelty-induced behavioural activation. *Neuroscience*, **64**, 587–597.

Hoon, P.W., Wincze, J.P. and Hoon, E.F. (1976) Physiological assessment of sexual arousal in women. *Psychophysiology*, **13**, 196–204.

Horne, J. (1988) *Why We Sleep*, Oxford University Press, Oxford.

Horne, J. (1992) Insomnia, *The Psychologist*, May, 216–218.

Horne, J.A. and Reyner, L.A. (1995) Sleep related vehicle accidents. *British Medical Journal*, **310**, 565–567.

Hosokawa, T., Rusakov, D.A., Bliss, T.V.P. and Fine, A. (1995) Repeated confocal imaging of individual dendritic spines in the living hippocampal slice: evidence for changes in length and orientation associated with chemically induced LTP. *Journal of Neuroscience*, **15**, 5560–5573.

Hsiao, S.S., O'Shaughnessy, D.M. and Johnson, K.O. (1993) Effects of selective attention on spatial form processing in monkey primary and secondary somatosensory cortex. *Journal of Neurophysiology*, **70**, 444–447.

Hsiao, S.S., Johnson, K.O., Twombly, A. and DiCarlo, J. (1996) Form processing and attention effects in the somatosensory system. In *Somesthesis and the Neurobiology of the Somatosensory Cortex* (eds O. Franzén, R. Johansson and L. Terenius), Birkhäuser Verlag, Basle, pp. 229–247.

Hubel, D.H. (1982) Exploration of the primary visual cortex, 1955–78. *Nature*, **299**, 515–524.

Hubel, D.H. and Wiesel, T.N. (1959) Receptive fields of single neurons in the cat's striate cortex. *Journal of Physiology (London)*, **148**, 574–591.

Hubel, D.H. and Wiesel, T.N. (1965) Binocular interaction in striate cortex of kittens reared with artificial squint. *Journal of Neurophysiology*, **28**, 1041–1059.

Hudspeth, A.J. and Konishi, M. (2000) Auditory neuroscience: development, transduction, and integration, *Proceedings of the National Academy of Sciences*, **97**, 11690–11691.

Hummer, T.A. and McClintock, M.K. (2009) Putative human pheromone androstadienone attunes the mind specifically to emotional information. *Hormones and Behavior*, **55**, 548–559.

Humphreys, G.W., Riddoch, M.J. and Price, C.J. (1997) Top-down processes in object identification: evidence from experimental psychology, neuropsychology and functional anatomy. *Philosophical Transactions of the Royal Society of London B*, **352**, 1275–1282.

Huttenlocher, P.R. (1994) Synaptogenesis in human cerebral cortex. In *Human Behavior and the Developing Brain* (eds G. Dawson and K.W. Fischer), Guilford Press, New York, pp. 137–152.

Huxley, A. (1972) *The Doors of Perception and Heaven and Hell*, Chatto and Windus, London.

Huxley, L.A. (1969) *This Timeless Moment: A Personal View of Aldous Huxley*, Chatto and Windus, London.

Hyde, J.S. (2005a) The genetics of sexual orientation. In *Biological Substrates of Human Sexuality* (ed. J.S. Hyde), American Psychological Association, Washington, pp. 9–20.

Hyde, J.S. (2005b) *Biological Substrates of Human Sexuality*, American Psychological Association, Washington.

Hyde, K.L., Samson, F., Evans, A.C. and Mottron, L. (2010) Neuroanatomical differences in brain areas implicated in perceptual and other core features of autism revealed by cortical thickness analysis and voxel-based morphology. *Human Brain Mapping*, **31**, 556–566.

I

Iacoboni, M. (2008) *Mirroring People*, Farrar, Straus and Giroux, New York.

Insel, T., Miller, L., Gelhard, R. and Hill, J. (1988) Rat pup ultrasonic isolation calls and the benzodiazepine receptor. In *The Physiological Control of Mammalian Vocalization* (ed. J.D. Newman), Plenum Press, New York, pp. 331–342.

Ito, M. (1984) *The Cerebellum and Neural Control*, Raven Press, New York.

Iversen, S.D. and Iversen, L.L. (2007) Dopamine: 50 years in perspective. *Trends in Neurosciences*, **30**, 188–193.

J

Jacob, F. (1977) Evolution and tinkering. *Science*, **196**, 1161–1166.

Jacobs, K.M., Mark, G.P. and Scott, T.R. (1988) Taste responses in the nucleus tractus solitarius of sodium-deprived rats. *Journal of Physiology*, **406**, 393–410.

Jacobsen, C.F. (1936) Studies of cerebral function in primates. *Comparative Psychology Monographs*, **13**, 1–68.

Jacobsen, E. (1931) Electrical measurements of neuromuscular states during mental activities. V. Variation of specific muscles contracting during imagination. *American Journal of Physiology*, **96**, 115–121.

Jahanshahi, M. and Frith, C.D. (1998) Willed action and its impairments. *Cognitive Neuropsychology*, **15**, 483–533.

Jahanshahi, M., Jenkins, I.H., Brown, R.G., Marsden, C.D., Passingham, R.E. and Brooks, D.J. (1995) Self-initiated versus externally triggered movements I. An investigation using measurement of regional cerebral blood flow with PET and movement-related potentials in normal and Parkinson's disease subjects. *Brain*, **118**, 913–933.

James, W. (1890/1950) *The Principles of Psychology*, Vol. 2, Dover Publications, New York.

Jarrard, L.E. (1993) On the role of the hippocampus in learning and memory in the rat. *Behavioral and Neural Biology*, **60**, 9–26.

Jeannerod, M. (1997) *The Cognitive Neuroscience of Action*, Blackwell, Oxford.

Jenkins, I.H., Brooks, D.J., Nixon, P.D., Frackowiak, R.S.J. and Passingham, R.E. (1994) Motor sequence learning. A study with positron emission tomography. *Journal of Neuroscience*, **14**, 3775–3790.

Jenkins, J. (1997) Pavlovian conditioning of sexual behavior in male three-spine stickleback (*Gasterosteus aculeatus*). *Behaviour*, **41**, 133–137.

Jerison, H.J. (1976) Principles of the evolution of the brain and behaviour. In *Evolution, Brain, and Behavior: Persistent Problems* (eds R.B. Masterton, W. Hodos and H. Jerison), Lawrence Erlbaum, Hillsdale, pp. 23–45.

Jerison, H.J. (1991a) *Brain Size and the Evolution of Mind*, American Museum of Natural History, New York.

Jerison, H.J. (1991b) Fossil brains and the evolution of the neocortex. In *The Neocortex: Ontogeny and Phylogeny* (eds B.L. Finlay, G. Innocenti and H. Scheich), Plenum, New York, pp. 5–19.

Jerlhag, E., Egecioglu, E., Dickson, S.L., Douhan, A., Svensson, L. and Engel, J.A. (2007) Ghrelin administration into tegmental areas stimulates locomotor activity and increases extracellular concentration of dopamine in the nucleus accumbens. *Addiction Biology*, **12**, 6–16.

Jessell, T.M. and Kelly, D.D. (1991) Pain and analgesia. In *Principles of Neural Science* (eds E.R. Kandel, J.H. Schwartz and T.M. Jessell), Appleton and Lange, East Norwalk, pp. 385–399.

Joel, D. and Avisar, A. (2001) Excessive lever pressing following post-training signal attenuation in rats: a possible animal model of obsessive compulsive disorder. *Behavioural Brain Research*, **123**, 77–87.

Johnson, A.K. and Thunhorst, R.L. (1997) The neuroendocrinology of thirst and salt appetite: visceral sensory signals and mechanisms of central integration. *Frontiers in Neuroendocrinology*, **18**, 292–353.

Johnson, M.H. (1997) *Developmental Cognitive Neuroscience – An Introduction*, Blackwell, Oxford.

Johnson, M.K. and Chalfonte, B.L. (1994) Binding complex memories: the role of reactivation and hippocampus. In *Memory Systems 1994* (eds D.L. Schacter and E. Tulving), MIT Press, Cambridge, pp. 311–350.

Johnson, M.K. and Multhaup, K.S. (1992) Emotion and MEM. In *The Handbook of Emotion and Memory – Research and Theory* (ed. S-A. Christianson), Lawrence Erlbaum, Hillsdale, pp. 33–66.

Jones, E.G. and Friedman, D.P. (1982) Projection pattern of functional components of thalamic ventrobasal complex on monkey somatosensory cortex. *Journal of Neurophysiology*, **48**, 521–544.

Jönsson, L-E., Änggård, E. and Gunne, L.-M. (1971) Blockade of intravenous amphetamine euphoria in man. *Clinical Pharmacology and Therapeutics*, **12**, 889–896.

Jordan, D. (1990) Autonomic changes in affective behaviour. In *Central Regulation of Autonomic Functions* (eds A.D. Loewy and K.M. Spyer), Oxford University Press, New York, pp. 349–366.

Jouvet, M. (1975) The function of dreaming: a neurophysiologist's point of view. In *Handbook of Psychobiology* (eds M.S. Gazzaniga and C. Blakemore), Academic Press, New York, pp. 499–527.

Jouvet-Mounier, D., Astic, L. and Lacote, D. (1969) Ontogenesis of the states of sleep in rat, cat, and guinea pig during the first postnatal month. *Developmental Psychobiology*, **2**, 216–239.

Jung, C.G. (1963) *Memories, Dreams, Reflections,* Collins and Routledge and Kegan Paul, London.

Jusczyk, P.W. and Cohen, A. (1985) What constitutes a module? *Behavioral and Brain Sciences*, **8**, 20–21.

K

Kaas, J.H. (1996) The somatosensory cortex. In *Somesthesis and the Neurobiology of the Somatosensory Cortex* (eds O. Franzén, R. Johansson and L. Terenius), Birkhäuser Verlag, Basle, pp. 163–171.

Kaiyala, K.J., Woods, S.C. and Schwartz, M.W. (1995) New model for the regulation of energy balance and adiposity by the central nervous system. *American Journal of Clinical Nutrition*, **62** (suppl.), 1123S–1134S.

Kalat, J.W. (1998) *Biological Psychology*, 6th edition, Brooks/Cole, Pacific Grove.

Kalat, J.W. (2004) *Biological Psychology,* 8th edition, Brooks/Cole, Pacific Grove.

Kalin, N.H., Shelton, S.E. and Lynn, D.E. (1995) Opiate systems in mother and infant primates coordinate intimate contact during reunion. *Psychoneuroendocrinology*, **20**, 735–742.

Kandel, E.R. (1976) *Cellular Basis of Behavior: An Introduction to Behavioral Neurobiology,* W.H. Freeman, San Francisco.

Kandel, E.R. (1991) Cellular mechanisms of learning and the biological basis of individuality. In *Principles of Neural Science* (eds E.R. Kandel, J.H. Schwartz and T.M. Jessell), Appleton and Lange, Norwalk, pp. 1009–1031.

Kandel, E.R. and Jessell, T.M. (1991) Touch. In *Principles of Neural Science* (eds E.R. Kandel, J.H. Schwartz and T.M. Jessell), Appleton and Lange, Norwalk, pp. 367–384.

Kanwisher, N. and Wojciulik, E. (2000) Visual attention: insights from brain imaging. *Nature Reviews Neuroscience*, **1**, 91–100.

Kaplan, E. (2004) The M, P, and K pathways of the primate visual system. In *The Visual Neurosciences* (Vol. 1) (eds L.M. Chalupa and J.S. Werner), MIT Press, Cambridge, pp. 481–493.

Kapur, S. (2003) Psychosis as a state of aberrant salience: a framework linking biology, phenomenology, and pharmacology in schizophrenia. *American Journal of Psychiatry*, **160**, 13–23.

Kar, B.R., Rao, S.L. and Chandramouli, B.A. (2008) Cognitive development of children with chronic protein energy malnutrition. *Behavioral and Brain Functions*, **4**, 31.

Karama, S., Lecours, A.R., Leroux, J-M., Bourgouin, P., Beaudoin, G., Joubert, S. and Beauregard, M. (2002) Areas of brain activation in males and females during viewing of erotic film excerpts. *Human Brain Mapping*, **16**, 1–13.

Karmiloff-Smith, A., Klima, E., Bellugi, U., Grant, J. and Baron-Cohen, S. (1995) Is there a social module? Language, face processing, and theory of mind in individuals with Williams syndrome. *Journal of Cognitive Neuroscience*, **7**, 196–208.

Karnath, H-O., Ferber, S. and Himmelbach, M. (2001) Spatial awareness is a function of the temporal not the posterior parietal lobe. *Nature*, **411**, 950–953.

Karnath, H-O., Himmelbach, M. and Rorden, C. (2002) The subcortical anatomy of human spatial neglect: putamen, caudate nucleus and pulvinar. *Brain*, **125**, 350–360.

Kassel, J.D. and Shiffman, S. (1992) What can hunger teach us about drug craving? A comparative analysis of the two constructs. *Advances in Behaviour Research and Therapy*, **14**, 141–167.

Kavanau, J.L. (1994) Sleep and dynamic stabilization of neural circuitry: a review and synthesis. *Behavioural Brain Research*, **63**, 111–126.

Kavanau, J.L. (1998) Vertebrates that never sleep: implications for sleep's basic function. *Brain Research Bulletin*, **46**, 269–279.

Keefauver, S.P. and Guilleminault, C. (1994) Sleep terrors and sleep walking. In *Principles and Practice of Sleep Medicine* (eds M.H. Kryger, T. Roth and W.C. Dement), Saunders, Philadelphia, pp. 567–573.

Keefe, F.J., Abernethy, A.P. and Campbell, L.C. (2005) Psychological approaches to understanding and treating disease-related pain. *Annual Review of Psychology*, **56**, 601–630.

Keller, P.A., McCluskey, A., Morgan, J. and O'Connor, S.M. (2006) The role of the HPA axis in psychiatric disorders and CRF antagonists as potential treatments. *Archiv der Pharmazie*, **339**, 346–355.

Kellerman, H. (1987) *The Nightmare*, Columbia University Press, New York.

Keltner, D. and Buswell, B.N. (1997) Embarrassment: its distinct form and appeasement functions. *Psychological Bulletin*, **122**, 250–270.

Kenshalo, D.R. and Douglass, D.K. (1995) The role of cerebral cortex in the experience of pain. In *Pain and the Brain: From Nociception to Cognition* (Advances in Pain Research and Therapy, Vol. 22) (eds B. Bromm and J.E. Desmedt), Raven Press, New York, pp. 21–34.

Keverne, E.B., Martensz, N.D. and Tuite, B. (1989) Beta-endorphin concentrations in cerebrospinal fluid of monkeys are influenced by grooming relationships. *Psychoneuroendocrinology*, **14**, 155–161.

Kiecolt-Glaser, J.K., Page, G.G., Marucha, P.T., MacCallum, R.C. and Glaser, R. (1998) Psychological influences on surgical recovery: perspectives from psychoneuroimmunology. *American Psychologist,* **53**, 1209–1218.

Kihlstrom, J.F. (1993) The psychological unconscious and the self. In *Experimental and Theoretical Studies of Consciousness* (eds G.R. Bock and J. Marsh), Wiley, Chichester, pp. 147–167.

Kim, J.J. and Diamond, D.M. (2002) The stressed hippocampus, synaptic plasticity and lost memories. *Nature Reviews Neuroscience*, **3**, 453–462.

Kim, Y.Y., Park, H.Y., Kim, J.M., and Kim, K.W. (2008) Pathological hypersexuality induced by dopamine replacement therapy in a patient with progressive supranuclear palsy. *The Journal of Neuropsychiatry and Clinical Neurosciences*, **20**, 496–497.

King, B.M. (2006) The rise, fall, and resurrection of the ventromedial hypothalamus in the regulation of feeding behaviour and body weight. *Physiology and Behavior*, **87**, 221–244.

King, H.E. (1961) Psychological effects of excitation in the limbic system. In *Electrical Stimulation of the Brain* (ed. D.E. Sheer), University of Texas Press, Austin, pp. 477–486.

Kinsbourne, M. (1993) Integrated cortical field model of consciousness. *The Experimental and Theoretical Studies of Consciousness* (CIBA Foundation Symposium 174) (eds R. Bock and J. Marsh), Wiley, Chichester, pp. 43–60.

Kinsley, C.H. and Lambert, K.G. (2006) The maternal brain. *Scientific American*, **294**(1), 72–79.

Klee, H. and Morris, J. (1997) Amphetamine misuse: the effects of social context on injection related risk behaviour. *Addiction Research*, **4**, 329–342.

Klein, R. (1991) Is consciousness information processing? *Behavioral and Brain Sciences*, **14**, 683.

Klein, S.B., Cosmides, L., Tooby, J. and Chance, S. (2002a) Decisions and the evolution of memory: multiple systems, multiple functions. *Psychological Review*, **109**, 306–329.

Klein, S.B., Rozendal, K. and Cosmides, L. (2002b) A social-cognitive neuroscience analysis of the self. *Social Cognition*, **20**, 105–135.

Kleschevnikov, A.M., Belichenko, P.V., Villar, A.J., Epstein, C.J., Malenka, R.C. and Mobley, W.C. (2004) Hippocampal long-term potentiation suppressed by increased inhibition in Ts65Dn mouse, a genetic model of Down syndrome. *Journal of Neuroscience*, **24**, 8153–8160.

Kling, A.S. (1986) The anatomy of aggression and affiliation. In *Emotion – Theory, Research and Experience*, Vol. 3, *Biological Foundations of Emotion* (eds R. Plutchik and H. Kellerman), Academic Press, Orlando, pp. 237–264.

Klingberg, T., Fernell, E., Olesen, P.J., Johnson, M., Gustafsson, P., Dahlström, K., Gillberg, C.G., Forssberg, H. and Westerberg, H. (2005) Computerized training of working memory in children with ADHD – a randomized, controlled trial. *Journal of the American Academy of Child and Adolescent Psychiatry*, **44**, 177–186.

Klüver, H. and Bucy, P.C. (1939) Preliminary analysis of functions of the temporal lobes in monkeys. *Archives of Neurology and Psychiatry*, **42**, 979–1000.

Knibestol, M. and Vallbo, A. (1980) Intensity of sensation related to activity of slowly adapting mechanoreceptive units in the human hand, *Journal of Physiology* (London), **300**, 251–267.

Knutson, B. (2004) Sweet revenge? *Science*, **305**, 1246–1247.

Koepp, M.J., Gunn, R.N., Lawrence, A.D., Cunningham, V.J., Dagher, T., Jones, T., Brooks, D.J., Bench, C.J. and Grasby, P.M. (1998) Evidence for striatal dopamine release during a video game. *Nature*, **393**, 266–268.

Kohler, E., Keysers, C., Umiltà, M.A., Fogassi, L., Gallese, V. and Rizzolatti, G. (2002) Hearing sounds, understanding actions: action representation in mirror neurons. *Science*, **297**, 846–848.

Kohlert, J.G. and Meisel, R.L. (1999) Sexual experience sensitizes mating-related nucleus accumbens dopamine responses of female Syrian hamsters. *Behavioural Brain Research*, **99**, 45–52.

Kokkinidis, L. and Anisman, H. (1980) Amphetamine models of paranoid schizophrenia: an overview and elaboration of animal experimentation. *Psychological Bulletin*, **88**, 551–597.

Kolársky, A., Freund, K., Machek, J. and Polák, O. (1967) Male sexual deviation. *Archives of General Psychiatry*, **17**, 735–743.

Kolb, B., Forgie, M., Gibb, R., Gorny, G. and Rowntree, S. (1998) Age, experience and the changing brain. *Neuroscience and Biobehavioral Reviews*, **22**, 143–159.

Komisaruk, B.R. and Whipple, B. (2005) Brain activity imaging during sexual response in women with spinal cord injury. In *Biological Substrates of Human Sexuality* (ed. J.S. Hyde), American Psychological Association, Washington, pp. 109–145.

Komisaruk, B.R., Beyer, C. and Whipple, B. (2008) Orgasm. *The Psychologist*, **21**, 100–103.

Komisaruk, B.R., Whipple, B. and Beyer, C. (2010) Sexual pleasure. In *Pleasures of the Brain.* eds M.L. Kringelbach and K.C. Berridge) Oxford University Press, Oxford, pp.169–177.

Koob, G.F. (1999) Drug reward addiction. In *Fundamental Neuroscience* (eds M.J. Zigmond, F.E. Bloom, S.C. Landis, J.L. Roberts and L.R. Squire), Academic Press, San Diego, pp. 1261–1279.

Koob, G.F. and Le Moal, M. (2006) *Neurobiology of Addiction*, Elsevier, Amsterdam.

Korsakoff, S. (1889) Étude médico-psychologique sur une forme des maladies de la mémoire. *Revue Philosophique*, **28**, 501–530.

Kosfeld, M., Heinrichs, M., Zak, P.J., Fischbacher, U. and Fehr, E. (2005) Oxytocin increases trust in humans. *Nature*, **435**, 673–676.

Kosslyn, S.M. (1988) Aspects of a cognitive neuroscience of mental imagery. *Science*, **240**, 1621–1626.

Kosslyn, S.M., Gazzaniga, M.S., Galaburda, A.M. and Rabin, C. (1999) Hemispheric specialization. In *Fundamental Neuroscience* (eds M.J. Zigmond, F.E. Bloom, S.C. Landis, J.L. Roberts and L.R. Squire), Academic Press, San Diego, pp. 1521–1542.

Kozlowski, L.T., Wilkinson, A., Skinner, W., Kent, C., Franklin, T. and Pope, M. (1989) Comparing tobacco cigarette dependence with other drug dependencies. *Journal of the American Medical Association*, **261**, 898–901.

Kraepelin, E. (1919) *Dementia Praecox and Paraphrenia*, Livingstone, Edinburgh.

Kraly, F.S. (1991) Effects of eating on drinking. In *Thirst: Physiological and Psychological Aspects* (eds D.J. Ramsey and D. Booth), Springer-Verlag, London, pp. 297–312.

Krane, R.J., Goldstein, I. and Saenz de Tejada, I. (1989) Impotence. *New England Journal of Medicine*, **321**, 1648–1659.

Krebs, J.R. (2009) The gourmet ape: evolution and human food preferences. *American Journal of Clinical Nutrition*, **90**, 707S–711S.

Kringelbach, M.L. (2005) The human orbitofrontal cortex: Linking reward to hedonic experience. *Nature Reviews Neuroscience*, **6**, 691–702.

Kringelbach, M.L. and Berridge, K.C. (2010) *Pleasures of the Brain.* Oxford University Press, Oxford.

Kringelbach, M.L., Jenkinson, N., Owen, S.L.F. and Aziz, T.Z. (2007) Translational principles of deep brain stimulation. *Nature Reviews Neuroscience*, **8**, 623–635.

Krolak-Salmon, P., Hénaff, M-A., Vighetto, A., Bauchet, F., Bertrand, O., Mauguière, F. and Isnard, J. (2006) Experiencing and detecting happiness in humans: the role of the supplementary motor area. *Annals of Neurology*, **59**, 196–199.

Kronenberg, G., van Elst, L.T., Regen, F., Deuschle, M., Heuser, I. and Colla, M. (2009) Reduced amygdala volume in newly admitted psychiatric in-patients with uniploar major depression. *Journal of Psychiatric Research*, **43**, 1112–1117.

Kropotov, J.D. and Etlinger, S.C. (1999) Selection of actions in the basal ganglia–thalamocortical circuits: review and model. *International Journal of Psychophysiology*, **31**, 197–217.

Krueger, J.M., Fang, J., Hansen, M.K., Zhang, J. and Obál, F. (1998) Humoral regulation of sleep. *News in Physiological Sciences*, **13**, 189–194.

Krüger, T.H.C., Hartmann, U. and Schedlowski, M. (2005) Prolactinergic and dopaminergic mechanisms underlying sexual arousal and orgasm in humans. *World Journal of Urology*, **23**, 130–138.

Krupa, D.J., Thompson, J.K. and Thompson, R.F. (1993) Localization of a memory trace in the mammalian brain. *Science*, **260**, 989–991.

Kucharska-Pietura, K., Phillips, M.L., Gernand, W. and David, A.S. (2003) Perception of emotions from faces and voices following unilateral brain damage. *Neuropsychologia*, **41**, 1082–1090.

Kuffler, S.W. (1953) Discharge patterns and functional organization of mammalian retina. *Journal of Neurophysiology*, **16**, 37–68.

Kuffler, S.W. and Nicholls, J.G. (1976) *From Neuron to Brain*, Sinauer Associates, Sunderland.

Kurihara, K. and Kashiwayanagi, M. (2000) Physiological studies on umami taste. *Journal of Nutrition*, **130**, 931S–934S.

L

Lacquaniti, F., Grasso, R. and Zago, M. (1999) Motor patterns in walking. *News in Physiological Sciences*, **14**, 168–174.

Laing, R.D. (1960) *The Divided Self*, Tavistock Publications, London.

Lal, S.K.L., Henderson, R.J., Carter, N., Bath, A., Hart, M.G., Langeluddecke, P. and Hunyor, S.N. (1998) Effect of feedback signal and psychological characteristics on blood pressure self-manipulation capability. *Psychophysiology*, **35**, 405–412.

Lang, P.J., Bradley, M.M. and Cuthbert, B.N. (1990) Emotion, attention and the startle reflex. *Psychological Review*, **97**, 377–395.

Langhans, W. (1996) Role of the liver in the metabolic control of eating: what we know and what we do not know. *Neuroscience and Biobehavioral Reviews*, **20**, 145–153.

Langhans, W. and Scharrer, E. (1992) Metabolic control of eating. *World Review of Nutrition and Diatetics*, **70**, 1–67.

Larriva-Sahd, J., Rondán, A., Orozco-Estévez, H. and Sánchez-Robles, M.R. (1993) Evidence of a direct projection of the vomeronasal organ to the medial preoptic nucleus and hypothalamus. *Neuroscience Letters*, **163**, 45–49.

Larson, C.R., Ortega, J.D. and DeRosier, E.A. (1988) Studies on the relation of the midbrain periaqueductal gray, the larynx and vocalization in awake monkeys. In *The Physiological Control of Mammalian Vocalization* (ed. J.D. Newman), Plenum Press, New York, pp. 43–65.

Larson, S.J. (2002) Behavioral and motivational effects of immune-system activation. *Journal of General Psychology*, **129**, 401–414.

Laudenslager, M.L., Ryan, S.M., Drugan, R.C., Hyson, R.L. and Maier, S.F. (1983) Coping and immunosuppression: inescapable but not escapable shock suppresses lymphocyte proliferation. *Science*, **221**, 568–570.

Lawrence, A.D., Evans. A.H., Lees, A.J. (2003) Compulsive use of dopamine replacement therapy in Parkinson's disease: reward systems gone awry? *The Lancet Neurology*, **2**, 595–604.

Lazarus, R.S. (1984) On the primacy of cognition. *American Psychologist*, **39**, 124–129

Le Doux, J. (1998) *The Emotional Brain*, Weidenfeld and Nicolson, London.

Le Doux, J.E. (1989) Cognitive–emotional interactions in the brain. *Cognition and Emotion*, **3**, 267–289.

Le Doux, J.E. (1991) Emotion and the limbic system concept. *Concepts in Neuroscience*, **2**, 169–199.

Le Doux, J.E. (1992) Emotion as memory: anatomical systems underlying indelible neural traces. In *The Handbook of Emotion and Memory – Research and Theory* (ed. S-A. Christianson), Lawrence Erlbaum, Hillsdale, pp. 269–288.

Le Doux, J.E. (1994) Emotion, memory and the brain. *Scientific American*, **270**, 32–39.

Le Magnen, J. (1967) Habits and food intake. In *Handbook of Physiology, Section 6, Alimentary Canal*, Vol. 1, American Physiological Society, Washington, pp. 11–30.

Le Magnen, J. (1981) The metabolic basis of dual periodicity of feeding in rats. *Behavioral and Brain Sciences*, **4**, 561–607.

Le Magnen, J., Devos, M., Gaudillière, J-P., Louis-Sylvestre, J. and Tallon, S. (1973) Role of a lipostatic mechanism in regulation by feeding of energy balance in rats. *Journal of Comparative and Physiological Psychology*, **84**, 1–23.

Le Strat, Y., Ramoz, N., Horwood, J., Fallissard, B., Hassler, C., Romo, L., Choquet, M., Fergusson, D. and Gorwood, P. (2009) First positive reactions to cannabis constitute a priority risk factor for cannabis dependence. *Addiction*, **104**, 1710–1717.

Lee, A., Clancy, S. and Fleming, A.S. (2000) Mother rats bar-press for pups: effects of lesions of the mpoa and limbic sites on maternal behavior and operant responding for pup-reinforcement. *Behavioral Brain Research*, **108**, 215–231.

Lehrner, J., Marwinski, G., Lehr, S., Johren, P. and Deecke, L. (2005) Ambient odors of orange and lavender reduce anxiety and improve mood in a dental office. *Physiology and Behavior*, **86**, 92–95.

Leiblum, S., Bachmann, G., Kemmann, E., Colburn, D. and Swartzman, L. (1983) Vagi-

nal atrophy in the postmenopausal woman. *Journal of the American Medical Association*, **249**, 2195–2198.

Leiblum, S.R. and Rosen, R.C. (2000) *Principles and Practice of Sex Therapy*, Guilford Press, New York.

LeMay, M. (1976) Morphological cerebral asymmetries of modern man, fossil man, and nonhuman primate. *Annals of the New York Academy of Sciences*, **280**, 349–366.

Lenard, H.G. and Schulte, F.J. (1972) Polygraphic sleep study in craniopagus twins. (Where is the sleep transmitter?) *Journal of Neurology, Neurosurgery, and Psychiatry*, **35**, 756–762.

Lenneberg, E.H. (1967) *Biological Foundations of Language*, Wiley, New York.

Lenzenweger, M.F. and Dworkin, R.H. (1998) *Origins and Development of Schizophrenia*. American Psychological Association, Washington.

Leopold, D.A., Maier, A. and Logothetis, N.K. (2003) Measuring subjective visual perception in the nonhuman primate. *Journal of Consciousness Studies*, **10**, 115–130.

Leshem, M. (1998) Salt preference in adolescence is predicted by common prenatal and infantile mineralofluid loss. *Physiology and Behavior*, **63**, 699–704.

Leslie, A.M. (1999) 'Theory of mind' as a mechanism of selective attention. In *The New Cognitive Neurosciences* (ed. M.S. Gazzaniga), MIT Press, Cambridge, pp. 1235–1247.

Leslie, K.R., Johnson-Frey, S.H. and Grafton, S.T. (2004) Functional imaging of face and hand imitation: towards a motor theory of empathy. *NeuroImage*, **21**, 601–607.

LeVay, S. (1991) A difference in hypothalamic structure between heterosexual and homosexual men. *Science*, **253**, 1034–1037.

LeVay, S. (1993) *The Sexual Brain*, MIT Press, Cambridge.

LeVay, S. and Valentine, S.M. (2006) *Human Sexuality*. Sinauer Associates, Sunderland, MA.

Levenstein, S. (1998) Stress and peptic ulcer: life beyond *helicobacter*. *British Medical Journal*, **316**, 538–541.

Levine, J.D., Gordon, N.C. and Fields, H.L. (1978) The mechanism of placebo analgesia. *The Lancet*, **2**, 654–657.

Levitsky, D.A. (2005) The non-regulation of food intake in humans: hope for reversing the epidemic of obesity. *Physiology and Behavior*, **86**, 623–632.

Levy, F. and Hay, D.A. (2001) *Attention, Genes and ADHD,* Brunner-Routledge, Hove.

Lewis, D.J. (1979) Psychobiology of active and inactive memory. *Psychological Bulletin,* **86,** 1054–1083.

Lewis, M., Haviland-Jones, J.M. and Barrett, L.F. (2008) *Handbook of Emotions,* Guilford Press, New York.

Lewis, S.J.G. and Barker, R.A. (2010) A pathophysiological model of freezing of gait in Parkinson's disease. *Parkinsonism and Related Disorders,* **15,** 333–338.

Leyens, J-P. and Fraczek, A. (1986) Aggression as an interpersonal phenomenon. In *The Social Dimension. European Developments in Social Psychology,* Vol. 1 (ed. H. Tajfel), Cambridge University Press, Cambridge, pp. 184–203.

Leyton, M. (2010) The neurobiology of desire: dopamine and the regulation of mood and motivational states in humans. In *Pleasures of the Brain* (eds M.L. Kringelbach and K.C. Berridge), Oxford University Press, New York, pp. 222–243.

Lhermitte, F. (1983) 'Utilization behaviour' and its relation to lesions of the frontal lobes. *Brain,* **106,** 237–255.

Liberman, A.M. (1995) The relation of speech to reading and writing. In *Speech and Reading: A Comparative Approach* (eds B. de Gelder and J. Morais), Taylor and Francis, Hove, pp. 17–31.

Libet, B. (1993a) Discussion. In *Experimental and Theoretical Studies of Consciousness* (eds G.R. Bock and J. Marsh), Wiley, Chichester, p. 35.

Libet, B. (1993b) The neural time factor in conscious and unconscious events. In *Experimental and Theoretical Studies of Consciousness* (eds G.R. Bock and J. Marsh), Wiley, Chichester, pp. 123–146.

Libet, B. (2005) *Mind Time: The Temporal Factor in Consciousness,* Harvard University Press, Cambridge.

Libet, B., Pearl, D.K., Morledge, D.E., Gleason, C.A., Hosobuchi, Y. and Barbaro, N.M. (1991) Control of the transition from sensory detection to sensory awareness in man by the duration of a thalamic stimulus. *Brain,* **114,** 1731–1757.

Lichtman, J.W., Burden, S.J., Culican, S.M. and Wong, R.O.L. (1999) Synapse formation and elimination. In *Fundamental Neuroscience* (eds M.J. Zigmond, F.E. Bloom, S.C. Landis, J.L. Roberts and L.R. Squire), Academic Press, San Diego, pp. 547–580.

Lidstone, S.C., de la Fuente-Fernandez, R. and Stoessl, A.J. (2005) The placebo response as a reward mechanism. *Seminars in Pain Medicine,* **3,** 37–42.

Lieberman, J.A., Stroup, T.S. and Perkins, D.O. (2006) *The American Psychiatric Publishing Textbook of Schizophrenia,* American Psychiatric Press, Inc., Arlington.

Lieberman, P. (1991) Speech and brain evolution. *Behavioral and Brain Sciences,* **14,** 566–568.

Lim, M.M., Wang, Z., Olazábal, D.E., Ren, X., Terwilliger, E.F. and Young, L.J. (2004) Enhanced partner preference in a promiscuous species by manipulating the expression of a single gene. *Nature,* **429,** 754–757.

Lim, S-Y., Evans, A.H., and Miyasaki, J.M. (2008) Impulse control and related disorders in Parkinson's disease. *Annals of the New York Academy of Sciences,* **1142,** 85–107.

Lipina, S.J. and Colombo, J.A. (2009) *Poverty and Brain Development During Childhood: An Approach from Cognitive Psychology and Neuroscience,* American Psychological Association, Washington.

Lipska, B.K., Khaing, Z.Z. and Weinberger, D.R. (1999) Neonatal hippocampal damage in the rat: a heuristic model of schizophrenia. *Psychiatric Annals,* **29,** 157–160.

Lisander, B. (1979) Somato-autonomic reactions and their higher control. In *Integrative Functions of the Autonomic Nervous System* (eds C.M. Brooks, K. Koizumi and A. Sato), University of Tokyo Press/Elsevier, Amsterdam, pp. 385–395.

Lisberger, S.G. (1988) The neural basis for learning of simple motor skills. *Science,* **242,** 728–735.

Lissauer, H. (1988) A case of visual agnosia with a contribution to theory. *Cognitive Neuropsychology,* **5,** 157–192.

Little, A.C., Penton-Voak, I.S., Burt, D.M. and Perrett, D.I. (2002) In *Facial Attractiveness: Evolutionary, Cognitive, and Social Perspectives* (eds G. Rhodes, and L.A. Zebrowitz), Ablex, Westpoint, pp. 59–90.

Liu, D., Diorio, J., Tannenbaum, B., Caldji, C., Francis, D., Freedman, A., Sharma, S., Pearson, D., Plotsky, P.M. and Meaney, M.J. (1997) Maternal care, hippocampal glucocorticoid receptors, and hypothalamic–pituitary–adrenal responses to stress. *Science,* **277,** 1659–1662.

Liu, T. (2009) Acupuncture: what underlies needle administration? *Evidence-Based Complementary and Alternative Medicine,* **6,** 185–193.

Livingstone, M. and Hubel, D. (1988) Segregation of form, colour, movement, and depth: anatomy, physiology, and perception. *Science,* **240,** 740–749.

Livingstone, M. and Hubel, D. (1995) Through the eyes of monkeys and men. In *The Artful Eye* (eds R. Gregory, J. Harris, P. Heard and D. Rose), Oxford University Press, Oxford, pp. 52–65.

Llinás, R.R. and Paré, D. (1991) Of dreaming and wakefulness. *Neuroscience,* **44,** 521–535.

Lloyd, D.M., Bolanowski, S.J., Howard, L. and McGlone, F. (1999) Mechanisms of attention in touch. *Somatosensory and Motor Research,* **16,** 3–10.

Loewy, A.D. (1990) Anatomy of the autonomic nervous system: an overview. In *Central Regulation of Autonomic Functions* (eds A.D. Loewy and K.M. Spyer), Oxford University Press, New York, pp. 3–16.

Logue, A.W. (1991) *The Psychology of Eating and Drinking.* W.H. Freeman, New York.

Lombardo, M.V., Chakrabarti, B., Bullmore, E.T., Sadek, S.A., Pasco, G., Wheelwright, S.J., Suckling, J., MRC AIMS Consortium and Baron-Cohen, S. (2010) Atypical neural self-representation in autism. *Brain,* **133,** 611–624.

Longe, O., Maratos, F.A., Gilbert, P., Evans, G., Volker, F., Rockliff, H. and Rippon, G. (2010) Having a word with yourself: Neural correlates of self-criticism and self-reassurance. *NeuroImage,* **49,** 1849–1856.

Lopez, O.L. and Becker, J.T. (2004) The natural history of Alzheimer's disease. In *Cognitive Neuropsychology of Alzheimer's Disease,* 2nd edition (eds R.G. Morris and J.T. Becker), Oxford University Press, Oxford, pp. 47–61.

Lorberbaum, J.P., Newman, J.D., Horwitz, A.R., Dubno, J.R., Lydiard, R.B., Hamner, M.B., Bohning, D.E. and George, M.S. (2002) A potential role for thalamocingulate circuitry in human maternal behaviour. *Biological Psychiatry,* **51,** 431–445.

Lorenz, K.Z. (1981) *The Foundations of Ethology,* Springer-Verlag, New York.

Lozano, A.M. and Kalia, S.K. (2005) New movements in Parkinson's disease. *Scientific American,* **293**(1), 68–75.

Luck, S.J., Chelazzi, L., Hillyard, S.A. and Desimone, R. (1997) Neural mechanisms of spatial selective attention in areas V1, V2, and V4 of Macaque visual cortex. *Journal of Neurophysiology,* **77,** 24–42.

Lundberg, P.O. (1992) Sexual dysfunction in patients with neurological disorders. *Annual Review of Sex Research*, **3**, 121–150.

Luria, A.R. (1966) *Higher Cortical Function in Man*, Tavistock Press, London.

Luria, A.R. (1973) *The Working Brain: An Introduction to Neuropsychology*, Penguin Books, Harmondsworth.

Luria, A.R. and Homskaya, E.D. (1964) Disturbance in the regulative role of speech with frontal lobe lesions. In *The Frontal Granular Cortex and Behavior* (eds J.M. Warren and K. Akert), McGraw-Hill, New York, pp. 353–371.

Luria, A.R., Pribram, K.H. and Homskaya, E.D. (1964) An experimental analysis of the behavioral disturbance produced by a left frontal arachnoidal endothelioma (meningioma). *Neuropsychologia*, **2**, 257–280.

Lustig, C., Shah, P., Seidler, R., Reuter-Lorenz, P.A. (2009) Aging, training, and the brain: a review and future directions. *Neuropsychology Review*, **19**, 504–522.

M

Maccioni, R.B. and Perry, G. (2009) *Current Hypotheses and Research Milestones in Alzheimer's Disease*, Springer, New York.

MacKay, D. (1987) Divided brains – divided minds? In *Mindwaves: Thoughts on Intelligence, Identity and Consciousness* (eds C. Blakemore and S. Greenfield), Basil Blackwell, Oxford, pp. 5–16.

MacKay, D.M. (1966) Cerebral organization and the conscious control of action. In *Brain and Conscious Experience* (ed. J.C. Eccles), Springer-Verlag, Berlin, pp. 422–445.

MacKay, D.M. (1974) *The Clockwork Image*, Inter-Varsity Press, London.

MacKay, W.A. (1991) Consciousness is king of the neuronal processors. *Behavioral and Brain Sciences*, **14**, 687–688.

Mackintosh, N. (1974) *The Psychology of Animal Learning*, Academic Press, London.

MacLean, P.D. (1958) Contrasting functions of limbic and neocortical systems of the brain and their relevance to psychophysiological aspects of medicine. *American Journal of Medicine*, **25**, 611–626.

Macmillan, M.B. (1986) A wonderful journey through skull and brains: the travels of Mr. Gage's tamping iron. *Brain and Cognition*, **5**, 67–107.

MacPherson, S.E., Phillips, L.H., Della Sala, S. and Cantagallo, A. (2009) Iowa gambling task impairment is not specific to ventromedial prefrontal lesions. *The Clinical Neuropsychologist*, **23**, 510–522.

MacRae, J.R. and Siegel, S. (1997) The role of self-administration in morphine withdrawal in rats. *Psychobiology*, **25**, 77–82.

Madsen, P.L., Holm, S., Vorstrup, S., Friberg, L., Lassen, N.A. and Wildschiødtz, G. (1991) Human regional cerebral blood flow during rapid-eye-movement sleep. *Journal of Cerebral Blood Flow and Metabolism*, **11**, 502–507.

Maestripieri, D. and Roney, J.R. (2006) Evolutionary developmental psychology: Contributions from comparative research with nonhuman primates. *Developmental Review*, **26**, 120–137.

Maguire, E.A., Gadian, D.G., Johnsrude, I.S., Good, C.D., Ashburner, J., Frackowiak, R.S.J. and Frith, C.D. (2000) Navigation-related structural change in the hippocampi of taxi drivers. *Proceedings of the National Academy of Sciences*, **97**, 4398–4403.

Maier, S.F. and Watkins, L.R. (1998) Cytokines for psychologists: implications of bidirectional immune-to-brain communication for understanding behavior, mood, and cognition. *Psychological Review*, **105**, 83–107.

Maier, S.F., Watkins, L.R. and Fleshner, M. (1994) Psychoneuro-immunology. *American Psychologist*, **49**, 1004–1017.

Maldonado, R., Robledo, P., Chover, A.J., Caine, S.B. and Koob, G.F. (1993) D1 dopamine receptors in the nucleus accumbens modulate cocaine self-administration in the rat. *Pharmacology, Biochemistry and Behavior*, **45**, 239–242.

Malik, S., McGlone, F., Bedrossian, D. and Dagher, A. (2008) Ghrelin modulates brain activity in areas that control appetitive behavior. *Cell Metabolism*, **7**, 400–409.

Marie, P. and Foix, C. (1917) Les aphasies de Guerre. *Revue Neurologique*, **1**, 53–87.

Marissen, M.A.E., Franken, I.H.A., Blanken, P., van den Brink, W. and Hendriks, V.M. (2005) Cue exposure therapy for opiate dependent clients, *Journal of Substance Use*, **10**, 97–105.

Mark, V.H. and Ervin, F.R. (1970) *Violence and the Brain*, Harper and Row, New York.

Markou, A., Weiss, F., Gold, L.H., Caine, B., Schulteis, G. and Koob, G.F. (1993) Animal models of drug craving. *Psychopharmacology*, **112**, 163–182.

Markou, A., Kosten, T.R. and Koob, G.F. (1998) Neurobiological similarities in depression and drug dependence: a self-medication hypothesis. *Neuropsychopharmacology*, **18**, 135–174.

Markowitsch, H.J. (1995) Anatomical basis of memory disorders. In *The Cognitive Neurosciences* (ed. M.S. Gazzaniga), MIT Press, Cambridge, pp. 765–779.

Marmot, M.G. and Syme, S.L. (1976) Acculturation and coronary heart disease in Japanese-Americans. *American Journal of Epidemiology*, **104**, 225–247.

Marr, D. (1969) A theory of cerebellar cortex. *Journal of Physiology*, **202**, 437–470.

Marazziti, D. and Consoli, G. (2010) Treatment strategies for obsessive compulsive disorder. *Expert Opinion on Pharmacotherapy*, **11**, 331–343.

Marsden, C.D. (1984) Which motor disorder in Parkinson's disease indicates the true motor function of the basal ganglia? *CIBA Foundation Symposium*, **107**, 225–241.

Marsden, C.D. (1987) What do the basal ganglia tell premotor cortical areas? *CIBA Foundation Symposium*, **132**, 282–300.

Marsden, C.D., Rothwell, J.C. and Day, B.L. (1984) The use of peripheral feedback in the control of movement. *Trends in Neurosciences*, **7**, 253–257.

Marshall, B.J. (1995) *Helicobacter pylori* in peptic ulcer: have Koch's postulates been fulfilled? *Annals of Medicine*, **27**, 565–568.

Martin, G.N. (1996) Olfactory remediation: current evidence and possible applications. *Social Science and Medicine*, **43**, 63–70.

Martin, J.H. (1991) Coding and processing of sensory information. In *Principles of Neural Science* (eds E.R. Kandel, J.H. Schwartz and T.M. Jessell), Prentice Hall, Englewood Cliffs, pp. 329–340.

Martin, J.H. (1996) *Neuroanatomy: Text and Atlas*, Prentice Hall, London.

Martin, J.H. and Jessell, T.M. (1991) Anatomy of the somatic sensory system. In *Principles of Neural Science* (eds E.R. Kandel, J.H. Schwartz and T.M. Jessell), Appleton and Lange, Norwalk, pp. 353–366.

Martin, P.I., Naeser, M.A., Ho, M., Treglia, E., Kaplan, E., Baker, E.H. and Pascual-Leone, A. (2009) *Current Neurology and Neuroscience Reports*, **9**, 451–458.

Martin, P.R. (1998) Colour processing in the primate retina: recent progress. *Journal of Physiology*, **513**, 631–638.

Martin, S.J., Grimwood, P.D. and Morris, R.G.M. (2000) Synaptic plasticity and memory: an evaluation of the hypothesis. *Annual Review of Neuroscience*, **23**, 649–711.

Martini, F.H., Timmons, M.J. and McKinley, M.P. (2000) *Human Anatomy*, Prentice Hall, Upper Saddle River.

Martini, F.H., Timmons, M.J. and Tallitsch, R.B. (2008) *Human Anatomy*, 6th edition, Benjamin Cummings (Pearson), Upper Saddle River.

Mashour, G.A., Walker, E.E. and Martuza, R.L. (2005) Psychosurgery: past, present, and future. *Brain Research Reviews*, **48**, 409–419.

Mason, G.J. (1991) Stereotypies: a critical review. *Animal Behaviour*, **41**, 1015–1037.

Mason, P. (1999) Central mechanisms of pain modulation. *Current Opinion in Neurobiology*, **9**, 436–441.

Mass, R., Hölldorfer, M., Moll, B., Bauer, R. and Wolf, K. (2009) Why we haven't died out yet: changes in women's mimic reactions to visual erotic stimuli during their menstrual cycles. *Hormones and Behavior*, **55**, 267–271.

Mattson, B.J., Williams, S.E., Rosenblatt, J.S. and Morrell, J.I. (2003) Preferences for cocaine- or pup-associated chambers differentiates otherwise behaviorally identical postpartum maternal rats. *Psychopharmacology*, **167**, 1–8.

Maurer, K., Volk, S. and Gerbaldo, H. (1997) Auguste D and Alzheimer's disease. *The Lancet*, **349**, 1546–1549.

May, A. (2008) Chronic pain may change the structure of the brain. *Pain*, **137**, 7–15.

Mayr, E. (1974) Behavior programs and evolutionary strategies. *American Scientist*, **62**, 650–659.

Mazenod, B., Pugeat, M. and Forest, M.G. (1988) Hormones, sexual function and erotic behaviour in women. In *Handbook of Sexology*, Vol. 6, *The Pharmacology and Endocrinology of Sexual Function* (ed. J.M.A. Sitsen), Elsevier Science, Amsterdam, pp. 316–351.

Mazur, A. and Booth, A. (1998) Testosterone and dominance in men. *Behavioral and Brain Sciences*, **21**, 353–397.

McAndrew, F.T. (2009) The interacting roles of testosterone and challenges to status in human male aggression. *Aggression and Violent Behavior*, **14**, 330–335.

McBride, W.J. and Li, T-K. (1998) Animal models of alcoholism: neurobiology of high alcohol-drinking behaviour in rodents. *Critical Reviews in Neurobiology*, **12**, 339–369.

McBurney, D.H. (1984) Taste and olfaction: sensory discrimination. In *Handbook of Physiology. Section 1: The Nervous System*, Vol. III, Part 2 (ed. I. Darian-Smith), American Physiological Society, Bethesda, pp. 1067–1086.

McCabe, C., Cowen, P.J. and Harmer, C.J. (2009) Neural representation of reward in recovered depressed patients. *Psychopharmacology*, **205**, 667–677.

McCarley, R.W. (1995) Sleep, dreams and states of consciousness. In *Neuroscience in Medicine* (ed. P.M. Conn), J.B. Lippincott, Philadelphia, pp. 537–553.

McCarthy, M.M. and Albrecht, E.D. (1996) Steroid regulation of sexual behaviour. *Trends in Endocrinology and Metabolism*, **7**, 324–327.

McCartney, K. and Phillips, D. (2008) *Blackwell Handbook of Early Childhood Development*, WileyBlackwell, Hoboken.

McCaughey, S.A. and Scott, T.R. (1998) The taste of sodium. *Neuroscience and Biobehavioral Reviews*, **22**, 663–676.

McClintock, M.K. (1971) Menstrual synchrony and suppression. *Nature*, **229**, 244–245

McClintock, M.K. (1984) Estrous synchrony: modulation of ovarian cycle length by female pheromones. *Physiology and Behavior*, **32**, 701–705.

McDonald, M.P. and Overmier, J.B. (1998) Present imperfect: a critical review of animal models of the mnemonic impairments in Alzheimer's disease. *Neuroscience and Biobehavioral Reviews*, **22**, 99–120.

McDonald, R.J. and White, N.M. (1993) A triple dissociation of memory systems: hippocampus, amygdala and dorsal striatum. *Behavioral Neuroscience*, **107**, 3–22.

McDonnell, P.M. and Corkum, V.L. (1991) The role of reflexes in the patterning of limb movements in the first six months of life. In *The Development of Timing Control and Temporal Organization of Coordinated Action* (eds J. Fagard and P.H. Wolff), North-Holland, Amsterdam, pp. 151–173.

McDougall, W. (1923) *An Outline of Psychology*, Methuen, London.

McEwen, B.S. (2004) *The End of Stress as We Know It*, Joseph Henry Press, Washington.

McEwen, B.S., De Kloet, E.R. and Rostene, W. (1986) Adrenal steroid receptors and actions in the nervous system. *Physiological Reviews*, **66**, 1121–1188.

McGaugh, J.L. (1992) Affect, neuromodulatory systems and memory storage. In *The Handbook of Emotion and Memory – Research and Theory* (ed. S-A. Christianson), Lawrence Erlbaum, Hillsdale, pp. 245–268.

McGaugh, J.L. (2004) The amygdala modulates the consolidation of memories of emotionally arousing experiences. In *Annual Review of Neuroscience*, **27** (eds S.E. Hyman, T.M. Jessell, C.J. Shatz and C.F. Stevens), Annual Reviews, Palo Alto, pp. 1–28.

McGuffin, P. and Katz, R. (1993) Genes, adversity and depression. In *Nature, Nurture and Psychology* (eds R. Plomin and G.E. McClearn), American Psychological Association, Washington, pp. 217–230.

McGuire, P.K. and Shah, G.M.S. (1993) Increased blood flow in Broca's area during auditory hallucinations in schizophrenia. *Lancet*, **342**, 703–706.

McHugh, P.R. (1990) Clinical issues in food ingestion and body weight maintenance. In *Handbook of Behavioral Neurobiology*, Vol. 10, *Neurobiology of Food and Fluid Intake* (ed. E.M. Stricker), Plenum Press, New York, pp. 531–547.

McIntyre, C.C., Savasta, M., Kerkerian-LeGoff, L. and Vitek, J.L. (2004) Uncovering the mechanism(s) of action of deep brain stimulation: activation, inhibition, or both. *Clinical Neurophysiology*, **115**, 1239–1248.

McKee, D.P. and Quigley, E.M.M. (1993) Intestinal motility in irritable bowel syndrome: is IBS a motility disorder? Part 2. Motility of the small bowel, esophagus, stomach, and gall-bladder. *Digestive Diseases and Sciences*, **38**, 1773–1782.

McMurray, G.A. (1950) Experimental study of a case of insensitivity to pain. *Archives of Neurology and Psychiatry*, **64**, 650–667.

McRae, C., Cherin, E., Yamazaki, G., Diem, G., Vo, A.H., Russell, D., Ellgring, H., Fahn, S., Greene, P., Dillon, S., Winfield, H., Bjugstad, K.B. and Freed, C.R. (2010) Effects of perceived treatment on quality of life and medical outcomes in a double-blind placebo surgery trial. *Archives of General Psychiatry*, **61**, 412–420.

Meaney, M.J., Diorio, J., Francis, D., Widdowson, J., LaPlante, P., Caldji, C., Sharma, S., Seckl, J.R. and Plotsky, P.M. (1996) Early environmental regulation of forebrain glucocorticoid receptor gene expression: implications for adrenocortical responses to stress. *Developmental Neuroscience*, **18**, 49–72.

Meddis, R. (1977) *The Sleep Instinct*, Routledge and Kegan Paul, London.

Meeter, M. and Murre, J.M.J. (2004) Consolidation of long-term memory: evidence and alternatives. *Psychological Bulletin*, **130**, 843–857.

Meï, N. (1993) Gastrointestinal chemoreception and its behavioural role. In *Neurophysiology of Ingestion* (ed. D.A. Booth), Pergamon Press, Oxford, pp. 47–56.

Meï, N. (1994) Role of digestive afferents in food intake regulation. In *Appetite: Neural and Behavioural Bases* (eds C.R. Legg and D. Booth), Oxford University Press, Oxford, pp. 86–97.

Meissner, W. (2009) The role of acupuncture and transcutaneous-electrical nerve stimulation for postoperative pain control. *Current Opinion in Anaesthesiology*, **22**, 623–626.

Meister, I.G., Wilson, S.M., Deblieck, C., Wu, A.D. and Iacoboni, M. (2007) The essential role of premotor cortex in speech perception. *Current Biology*, **17**, 1692–1696.

Melges, F.T. (1982) *Time and the Inner Future: A Temporal Approach to Psychiatric Disorders*, Wiley, New York.

Mellerio, J. (1966) Ocular refraction at low illuminations. *Vision Research*, **6**, 217–237.

Mellor, C.S. (1970) First rank symptoms of schizophrenia. *British Journal of Psychiatry*, **117**, 15–23.

Meltzoff, A.N. and Moore, M.K. (1977) Imitation of facial and manual gestures by human neonates. *Science*, **198**, 75–78.

Melzack, R. (1988) The tragedy of needless pain: a call for social action. In *Proceedings of the Vth World Congress on Pain* (eds R. Dubner, G.F. Gubner and M.R. Bond), Elsevier Science Publishers, Amsterdam, pp. 1–11.

Melzack, R. (1989) Phantom limbs, the self and the brain (The D.O. Hebb Memorial Lecture). *Canadian Psychology*, **30**, 1–16.

Melzack, R. (1993) Pain: past, present and future. *Canadian Journal of Experimental Psychology*, **47**, 615–629.

Melzack, R. and Scott, T.H. (1957) The effects of early experience on the response to pain. *Journal of Comparative and Physiological Psychology*, **50**, 155–161.

Melzack, R. and Wall, P.D. (1965) Pain mechanisms: a new theory. *Science*, **150**, 971–979.

Melzack, R. and Wall, P. (2008) *The Challenge of Pain*, Penguin Books, Harmondsworth.

Melzack, R. and Wall, P. (1996) *The Challenge of Pain*, Penguin Books, Harmondsworth.

Mendelson, W.B. (1990) Insomnia: the patient and the pill. In *Sleep and Cognition* (eds R.R. Bootzin, J.F. Kihlstrom and D.L. Schacter), American Psychological Association, Washington, pp. 139–147.

Menzel, E. (1978) Cognitive mapping in chimpanzees. In *Cognitive Processes in Animal Behavior* (eds S.H. Hulse, H. Fowler and W.K. Honig), Lawrence Erlbaum, Hillsdale, pp. 375–422.

Menzies, L., Achard, S., Chamberlain, S.R., Fineberg, N., Chen, C-H., del Campo, N., Sahakian, B.J., Robbins, T.W. and Bullmore, E. (2007) Neurocognitive endophenotypes of obsessive-compulsive disorder. *Brain*, **130**, 3223–3236.

Menzies, L., Chamberlain, S.R., Laird, A.R., Thelen, S.M., Sahakian, B.J. and Bullmore, E.T. (2008) Integrating evidence from neuroimaging and neuropsychological studies of obsessive-compulsive disorder: the orbito-fronto-striatal model revisited. *Neuroscience and Biobehavioral Reviews*, **32**, 525–549.

Mercer, M.E. and Holder, M.D. (1997) Food cravings, endogenous opioid peptides and food intake: a review. *Appetite*, **29**, 325–352.

Merigan, W.H. and Maunsell, J.H.R. (1993) How parallel are the primate visual pathways? *Annual Review of Neuroscience*, **16**, 369–402.

Merzenich, M.M., Kaas, J.H., Wall, J.T., Sur, M., Nelson, R.J. and Felleman, D.J. (1983) Progression of change following median nerve section in the cortical representation of the hand in areas 3b and 1 in adult owl and squirrel monkeys. *Neuroscience*, **10**, 639–665.

Merzenich, M.M., Wang, X., Xerri, C. and Nudo, R. (1996) Functional plasticity of cortical representations of the hand. In *Somesthesis and the Neurobiology of the Somatosensory Cortex* (eds O. Franzén, R. Johansson and L. Terenius), Birkäuser Verlag, Basle, pp. 249–269.

Meyer, E.A. and Gebhart, G.F (1994) Basic and clinical aspects of visceral hyperalgesia. *Gastroenterology*, **107**, 271–293.

Michel, G.F. and Moore, C.L. (1995) *Developmental Psychobiology: An Interdisciplinary Science*, MIT Press, Cambridge.

Mieda, M. and Sakurai, T. (2009) Integrative physiology of orexins and orexin receptors. *CNS and Neurological Disorders – Drug Targets*, **8**, 281–295.

Mikell, C.B., McKhann, G.M., Segal, S., McGovern, R.A., Wallenstein, M.B. and Moore, H. (2009) The hippocampus and nucleus accumbens as potential therapeutic targets for neurosurgical intervention in schizophrenia. *Stereotactic and Functional Neurosurgery*, **87**, 256–265.

Miller, B. (2007) The human frontal lobes: an introduction. In *The Human Frontal Lobes: Functions and Disorders,* 2nd edition (eds B.L. Miller and J.L. Cummings), Guilford Press, New York, pp. 3–21.

Miller, B.L. and Cummings, J.L. (2007) *The Human Frontal Lobe: Function and Disorders*, 2nd edition, Guildford Press, New York.

Miller, B.L., Cummings, J.L., McIntyre, H., Ebers, G. and Grods, M. (1986) Hypersexuality or altered sexual preference following brain injury. *Journal of Neurology, Neurosurgery and Psychiatry*, **49**, 867–873.

Miller, E.J., Saint Marie, L.R., Breier, M.R. and Swerdlow, N.R. (2010) Pathways from the ventral hippocampus and caudal amygdala to forebrain regions that regulate sensorimotor gating in the rat. *Neuroscience*, **165**, 601–611.

Miller, R.E., Caul, W.F. and Mirsky, I.A. (1967) Communication of affects between feral and socially isolated monkeys. *Journal of Personality and Social Psychology*, **7**, 231–239.

Milner, B. (1964) Some effects of frontal lobectomy in man. In *The Frontal Granular Cortex and Behavior* (eds J.M. Warren and K. Akert), McGraw-Hill, New York, pp. 313–334.

Milner, B. (1966) Amnesia following operation on the temporal lobes. In *Amnesia* (eds C.W.M. Whitty and O.L. Zangwill), Butterworths, London, pp. 109–133.

Milner, B. (1971) Interhemispheric differences in the localization of psychological processes in man. *British Medical Bulletin*, **27**, 272–277.

Milner, B. (1974) Hemispheric specialization: scope and limits. In *The Neurosciences. Third Study Program* (eds F.O. Schmitt and F.G. Worden), MIT Press, Cambridge, pp. 75–89.

Milner, M. and Goodale, M. (2006) *The Visual Brain in Action,* 2nd edition, Oxford University Press, Oxford.

Mineka, S. and Öhman, A. (2002) Phobias and preparedness: the selective, automatic, and encapsulated nature of fear. *Biological Psychiatry*, **52**, 927–937.

Mink, J.W. (1999) Basal ganglia. In *Fundamental Neuroscience* (eds M.J. Zigmond, F.E. Bloom, S.C. Landis, J.L. Roberts and L.R. Squire), Academic Press, San Diego, pp. 951–972.

Mishkin, M. (1982) A memory system in the monkey. *Philosophical Transactions of the Royal Society B*, **298**, 85–95.

Mishkin, M., Ungerleider, L.G. and Macko, K.A. (1983) Object vision and spatial vision: two cortical pathways. *Trends in Neurosciences*, **6**, 414–417.

Mistlberger, R.E. (2005) Circadian regulation of sleep in mammals: role of the suprachiasmatic nucleus. *Brain Research Reviews*, **49**, 429–454.

Mistlberger, R.E. and Rusak, B. (1994) Circadian rhythms in mammals: formal properties and environmental influences. In *Principles and Practice of Sleep Medicine*, 2nd edition (eds M.H. Kryger, T. Roth and W.C. Dement), W.B. Saunders, Philadelphia, pp. 277–285.

Mistlberger, R.E. and Rusak, B. (2005) Circadian rhythms in mammals: formal properties and environmental influences. In *Principles and Practice of Sleep Medicine*, 4th edition (eds M.H. Kryger, T. Roth and W.C. Dement), Saunders, Philadelphia, pp. 321–334.

Mistlberger, R.E. and Skene, D.J. (2004) Social influences on mammalian circadian rhythms: animal and human studies. *Biological Reviews*, **79**, 533–556.

Mitchell, A.J. (1998) The role of corticotropin releasing factor in depressive illness: a critical review. *Neuroscience and Biobehavioral Reviews*, **22**, 635–651.

Moberg, G.P. (1985) Biological response to stress: key to assessment of animal well-being. In *Animal Stress* (ed. G.P. Moberg), American Physiological Society, Bethesda, pp. 27–49.

Moberg, G.P. and Mench, J.A. (2000) *The Biology of Animal Stress*, CAB International, Wallingford.

Modolo, J. and Beuter, A. (2009) Linking brain dynamics, neural mechanisms, and deep brain stimulation in Parkinson's disease. *Medical Engineering and Physics*, **31**, 615–623.

Mogenson, G.J. (1984) Limbic–motor interaction – with emphasis on initiation of exploratory and goal directed locomotion. In *Modulation of Sensorimotor Activity During Alteration in Behavioral States* (ed. R. Bandler), A.R. Liss, New York, pp. 121–137.

Mogenson, G.J., Brudzynski, S.M., Wu, M., Yang, C.R. and Yim, C.C.Y. (1993) From motivation to action: a review of dopaminergic regulation of limbic → nucleus accumbens → ventral pallidum → pedunculopontine nucleus circuitries involved in limbic–motor integration. In *Limbic Motor Circuits and Neuropsychiatry* (eds P.W. Kalivas and C.D. Barnes), CRC Press, Boca Raton, pp. 193–236.

Moles, A., Kieffer, B.L. and D'Amato, F.R. (2004) Deficit in attachment behavior in mice lacking the μ-opioid receptor gene. *Science*, **304**, 1983–1986.

Moll, J., de Oliveira-Souza, R., Moll, F.T., Ignácio, F.A., Bramati, I.E., Caparelli-Dáquer, E.M. and Eslinger, P.J. (2005) The moral affiliations of disgust: A functional MRI study. *Cognitive and Behavioural Neurology*, **18**, 68–78.

Moncrieff, J. (2009) A critique of the dopamine hypothesis of schizophrenia and psychosis. *Harvard Review of Psychiatry*, **17**, 214–225.

Money, J. (1960) Phantom orgasm in the dreams of paraplegic men and women. *Archives of General Psychiatry*, **3**, 373–382.

Money, J., Leal, J. and Gonzalez-Heydrich, J. (1988) Aphrodisiology: history, folklore and efficacy. In *Handbook of Sexology*, Vol. 6, *The Pharmacology and Endocrinology of Sexual Function* (ed. J.M.A. Sitsen), Elsevier Science, Amsterdam, pp. 499–515.

Monti, B. and Contestabile, A. (2009) Memory-enhancing drugs: a molecular perspective. *Mini-Reviews in Medicinal Chemistry*, **9**, 769–781.

Monti, J., Pandi-Perumal, S.R. and Sinton, C.M. (2008) *Neurochemistry of Sleep and Wakefulness*, Cambridge University Press, Cambridge.

Monti, M.M., Vanhaudenhuyse, A., Coleman, M.R., Boly, M., Pickard, J.D., Tshibanda, L., Owen, A.M. and Laureys, S. (2010) Willful modulation of brain activity in disorders of consciousness. *The New England Journal of Medicine*, **362**, 579–589.

Montgomery, K.C. (1952) A test of two explanations of spontaneous alternation. *Journal of Comparative and Physiological Psychology*, **45**, 287–293.

Monti-Bloch, L., Jennings-White, C., Dolberg, D.S. and Berliner, D.L. (1994) The human vomeronasal system. *Psychoneuroendocrinology*, **19**, 673–686.

Moore, R.Y. (1999) Circadian timing. In *Fundamental Neuroscience* (eds M.J. Zigmond, F.E. Bloom, S.C. Landis, J.L. Roberts and L.R. Squire), Academic Press, San Diego, pp. 1189–1206.

Moore-Ede, M.C., Sulzman, F.M. and Fuller, C.A. (1982) *The Clocks that Time Us*, Harvard University Press, Cambridge.

Mora, F., Segovia, G. and del Arco, A. (2007) Aging, plasticity and environmental enrichment: structural changes and neurotransmitter dynamics in several areas of the brain. *Brain Research Reviews*, **55**, 78–88.

Moran, J. and Desimone, R. (1985) Selective attention gates visual processing in the extrastriate cortex. *Science*, **229**, 782–784.

Moran, T.H. (2000) Cholecystokinin and satiety: current perspectives. *Nutrition*, **16**, 858–865.

Morris, J.A., Jordan, C.L. and Breedlove, S.M. (2004) Sexual differentiation of the vertebrate nervous system. *Nature Neuroscience*, **7**, 1034–1039.

Morris, J.S., Öhman, A. and Dolan, R.J. (1998) Conscious and unconscious emotional learning in the human amygdala. *Nature*, **393**, 467–470.

Morris, J.S., Öhman, A. and Dolan, R.J. (1999) A subcortical pathway to the right amygdala mediating 'unseen' fear. *Proceedings of the National Academy of Sciences USA*, **96**, 1680–1685.

Morris, R.G. (1996a) *The Cognitive Neuropsychology of Alzheimer-type Dementia*, Oxford University Press, Oxford.

Morris, R.G. (1996b) A cognitive neuropsychology of Alzheimer-type dementia. In *The Cognitive Neuropsychology of Alzheimer-type Dementia* (ed. R.G. Morris), Oxford University Press, Oxford, pp. 3–10.

Morris, R.G. (1996c) Neurobiological correlates of cognitive dysfunction. In *The Cognitive Neuropsychology of Alzheimer-type Dementia* (ed. R.G. Morris), Oxford University Press, Oxford, pp. 223–254.

Morris, R.G. (2004) Neurobiological abnormalities in Alzheimer's disease: structural, genetic, and functional correlates of cognitive dysfunction. In *Cognitive Neuropsychology of Alzheimer's Disease*, 2nd edition (eds R.G. Morris and J.T. Becker), Oxford University Press, Oxford, pp. 299–319.

Morris, R.G. and Becker, J.T. (2004) *Cognitive Neuropsychology of Alzheimer's Disease*, 2nd edition, Oxford University Press, Oxford.

Morris, R.G. and Hannesdottir, K. (2004) Loss of 'awareness' in Alzheimer's disease. In *Cognitive Neuropsychology of Alzheimer's Disease*, 2nd edition (eds R.G. Morris and J.T. Becker), Oxford University Press, Oxford, pp. 275–296.

Morris, R.G.M. (1981) Spatial localization does not require the presence of local cues. *Learning and Motivation*, **12**, 239–260.

Moruzzi, G. (1966) The functional significance of sleep with particular regard to the brain mechanisms underlying consciousness. In *Brain and Conscious Experience* (ed. J.C. Eccles), Springer-Verlag, Berlin, pp. 345–388.

Moruzzi, G. and Magoun, H.W. (1949) Brain stem reticular formation and activation of the EEG. *Electroencephalography and Clinical Neurophysiology,* **1**, 455–473.

Moscovitch, M. (1994) Memory and working with memory: evaluation of a component process model and comparisons with other models. In *Memory Systems 1994* (eds D.L. Schacter and E. Tulving), MIT Press, Cambridge, pp. 269–310.

Moscovitch, M. and Umiltà, C. (1990) Modularity and neuropsychology: modules and central processes in attention and memory. In *Modular Deficits in Alzheimer-type Dementia* (ed. M.F. Schwartz), MIT Press, Cambridge, pp. 1–60.

Moseley, G.L. (2003) A pain neuromatrix approach to patients with chronic pain. *Manual Therapy,* **8**, 130–140.

Mountcastle, V.B. (1984) Central nervous mechanisms in mechanoreceptive sensibility. In *Handbook of Physiology, Section 1: The Nervous System,* Vol. III, Part 2 (ed. I. Darian-Smith), American Physiological Society, Bethesda, pp. 789–878.

Mouras, H. (2007) Central role of somatosensory processes in sexual arousal as identified by Neuroimaging techniques. *Behavioral and Brain Sciences,* **30**, 217.

Moyer, K.E. (1986) Biological bases of aggressive behaviour. In *Emotion – Theory, Research and Experience,* Vol. 3, *Biological Foundations of Emotion* (eds R. Plutchik and H. Kellerman), Academic Press, Orlando, pp. 219–236.

Mueser, K.T. and Jeste, D.V. (2008) *Clinical Handbook of Schizophrenia,* Guilford Press, New York.

Mukhametov, L.M. (1984) Sleep in marine mammals. In *Sleep Mechanisms* (eds A. Borbély and J-L. Valatx), Springer-Verlag, Berlin, pp. 227–238.

Munafó, M.R., Mannie, Z.N., Cowen, P.J., Harmer, C.J. and McTavish, S.B. (2007) Effects of acute tyrosine depletion on subjective craving and selective processing of smoking-related cues in abstinent cigarette smokers. *Journal of Psychopharmacology,* **21**, 805–814.

Munakata, Y., Casey, B.J. and Diamond, A. (2004) Developmental cognitive neuroscience: progress and potential. *Trends in Cognitive Sciences,* **8**, 122–128.

Murotani, T., Ishizuka, T., Nakazawa, H., Wang, X., Mori, K., Sasaki, K., Ishida, T. and Yamatodani, A. (2010) Possible involvement of histamine, dopamine, and noradrenalin in the periaqueductal gray in electroacupuncture pain relief. *Brain Research,* **1306**, 62–68.

Murphy, M. (1993a) The neuroanatomy and neurophysiology of erection. In *Impotence: An Integrated Approach to Clinical Practice* (eds A. Gregoire and J.P. Pryor), Churchill Livingstone, Edinburgh, pp. 29–48.

Murphy, M. (1993b) The pharmacology of erection and erectile dysfunction. In *Impotence: An Integrated Approach to Clinical Practice* (eds A. Gregoire and J.P. Pryor), Churchill Livingstone, Edinburgh, pp. 55–77.

Murphy, M.R., Seckl, J.R., Burton, S., Checkley, S.A. and Lightman, S.L. (1987) Changes in oxytocin and vasopressin secretion during sexual activity in men. *Journal of Clinical Endocrinology and Metabolism,* **65**, 738–741.

Musselman, D.L., Evans, D.L. and Nemeroff, C.B. (1998) The relationship of depression to cardiovascular disease. *Archives of General Psychiatry,* **55**, 580–592.

Mutschler, N.H. and Miczek, K.A. (1998) Withdrawal from IV cocaine 'binges' in rats: ultrasonic distress calls and startle. *Psychopharmacology,* **135**, 161–168.

Myers, L.S. and Morokoff, P.J. (1986) Physiological and subjective sexual arousal in pre- and postmenopausal women and postmenopausal women taking replacement therapy. *Psychophysiology,* **23**, 283–292.

Myers, R., Spinks, T.J., Luthra, S.K. and Brooks, D.J. (1992) Positron-emission tomography. In *Quantitative Methods in Neuroanatomy* (ed. M. Stewart), Wiley, Chichester, pp. 117–161.

N

Nader, K. (2003) Memory traces unbound. *Trends in Neurosciences,* **26**, 65–72.

Nagel, T. (1974) What is it like to be a bat? *Philosophical Review,* **83**, 435–451.

Nagel, T. (1993) What is the mind–body problem? In *Experimental and Theoretical Studies of Consciousness* (eds G.R. Bock and J. Marsh), Wiley, Chichester, pp. 1–13.

Naqvi, N.H. and Bechara, A. (2009) The hidden island of addiction: the insula. *Trends in Neurosciences,* **32**, 56–66.

Naqvi, N.H., Rudrauf, D., Damasio, H. and Bechara, A. (2007) Damage to the insula disrupts addiction to cigarette smoking. *Science,* **315**, 531–534.

Nelson, E. and Panksepp, J. (1996) Oxytocin mediates acquisition of maternally associated odor preferences in preweanling rat pups. *Behavioral Neuroscience,* **110**, 583–592.

Nelson, M.D., Saykin, A.J., Flashman, L.A. and Riordan, H.J. (1998) Hippocampal volume reduction in schizophrenia as assessed by magnetic resonance imaging. A meta-analytic study. *Archives of General Psychiatry,* **55**, 433–440.

Nesse, R. (2009) Explaining depression: neuroscience is not enough, evolution is essential. In *Understanding Depression: A Translational Approach* (eds C.M. Pariante, R.M. Nesse, D. Nutt and L. Wolpert), Oxford University Press, Oxford, pp. 17–35.

Nesse, R.M. (2005) An evolutionary framework for understanding grief. In *Spousal Bereavement in Late Life* (eds. D. Carr, R.M. Nesse and C.B. Wortman), Springer Publishing, New York, pp. 195–225.

Nesse, R.M. and Berridge, K.C. (1997) Psychoactive drug use in evolutionary perspective. *Science,* **278**, 63–66.

Nettle, D. (2004) Evolutionary origins of depression: a review and reformulation. *Journal of Affective Disorders,* **81**, 91–102.

Nettle, D. and Clegg, H. (2006) Schizotypy, creativity and mating success in humans. *Proceedings of the Royal Society B Biological Sciences,* **273**, 611–615.

Neve, R.L. and Robakis, N.K. (1998) Alzheimer's disease: a re-examination of the amyloid hypothesis. *Trends in Neurosciences,* **21**, 15–19.

Neville, H.J. (1991) Neurobiology of cognitive and language processing: effects of early experience. In *Brain Maturation and Cognitive Development: Comparative and Cross-cultural Perspectives* (eds K.R. Gibson and A.C. Petersen), Aldine de Gruyter, New York, pp. 355–380.

Newsome, W.T. and Salzman, C.D. (1993) The neuronal basis of motion perception. In *Experimental and Theoretical Studies of Consciousness* (eds G.R. Bock and J. Marsh), Wiley, Chichester, pp. 217–246.

Nielsen, E., Eison, M., Lyon, M. and Iversen, S. (1983) Hallucinatory behaviors in primates produced by around-the-clock amphetamine treatment for several days via implanted capsules. In *Ethopharmacology: Primate Models of Neuropsychiatric Disorders* (ed. K. Miczek), Alan Liss, New York, pp. 79–100.

Nielsen, J.M. (1958) *Memory and Amnesia*, San Lucus Press, Los Angeles.

Nigg, J.T. (2009) *What Causes ADHD?* Guilford Press, New York.

Nilsson, M., Perfilieva, E., Johansson, U., Orwar, O. and Eriksson, P.S. (1999) Enriched environment increases neurogenesis in the adult rat dentate gyrus and improves spatial memory. *Journal of Neurobiology*, **39**, 569–578.

Nishimura, H., Hashikawa, K., Doi, K., Iwaki, T., Watanabe, Y., Kusuoka, H., Nishimura, T. and Kubo, T. (1999) Sign language 'heard' in the auditory cortex. *Nature*, **397**, 116.

Nolte, J. (2008) *The Human Brain: An Introduction to its Functional Anatomy*, 6th edition, Mosby, St. Louis.

Norgren, R. (1984) Central neural mechanisms of taste. In *Handbook of Physiology. Section 1: The Nervous System,* Vol. III, Part 2 (ed. I. Darian-Smith), American Physiological Society, Bethesda, pp. 1097–1128.

Norman, D.A. and Shallice, T. (1986) Attention to action – willed and automatic control of behaviour. In *Consciousness and Self-regulation: Advances in Research and Theory*, Vol. 4 (eds R.J. Davidson, G.E. Schwartz and D. Shapiro), Plenum Press, New York, pp. 1–18.

Norman, J. (2002) Two visual systems and two theories of perception: an attempt to reconcile the constructivist and ecological approaches. *Behavioral and Brain Sciences*, **25**, 73–96.

Northcutt, R.G. and Kaas, J.H. (1995) The emergence and evolution of mammalian neocortex. *Trends in Neuroscience*, **18**, 373–379.

Nottebohm, F. (2002) Neuronal replacement in adult brain. *Brain Research Bulletin*, **57**, 737–749.

Novin, D. (1993) Regulatory control of food and water intake and metabolism by the liver. In *Neurophysiology of Ingestion* (ed. D.A. Booth), Pergamon Press, Oxford, pp. 19–32.

Nowakowski, R.S. and Hayes, N.L. (1999) CNS development: an overview. *Development and Psychopathology*, **11**, 395–417.

Numan, M. and Insel, T.R. (2003) *The Neurobiology of Parental Behavior*, Springer-Verlag, New York.

O

O'Craven, K.M. and Kanwisher, N. (2000) Mental imagery of faces and places activates corresponding stimulus-specific brain regions. *Journal of Cognitive Neuroscience*, **12**, 1013–1023.

O'Keefe, J. and Dostrovsky, J. (1971) The hippocampus as a spatial map. Preliminary evidence from unit activity in the freely moving rat. *Brain Research*, **34**, 171–175.

O'Keefe, J. and Nadel, L. (1978) *The Hippocampus as a Cognitive Map*, Clarendon Press, Oxford.

O'Leary, A. (1990) Stress, emotion and human immune function. *Psychological Bulletin*, **108**, 363–382.

Oaten, M., Stevenson, R.J. and Case, T.I. (2009) Disgust as a disease-avoidance mechanism. *Psychological Bulletin*, **135**, 303–321.

Oatley, K. (1988) On changing one's mind: a possible function of consciousness. In *Consciousness in Contemporary Science* (eds A.J. Marcel and E. Bisiach), Clarendon Press, Oxford, pp. 369–389.

Oatley, K. and Jenkins, J.M. (1996) *Understanding Emotions*, 1st edition, Blackwell Publishers, Oxford.

Oatley, K., Keltner, D. and Jenkins, J. (2006) *Understanding Emotions*, 2nd edition, Blackwell Publishers, Oxford.

Öhman, A. (1986) Face the beast and fear the face: animal and social fears as prototypes for evolutionary analyses of emotion. *Psychophysiology*, **23**, 123–145.

Öhman, A. (2005) The role of the amygdala in human fear: automatic detection of threat. *Psychoneuroendocrinology*, **30**, 953–958.

Öhman, A. and Mineka, S. (2001) Fears, phobias, and preparedness: toward an evolved module of fear and fear learning. *Psychological Review*, **108**, 483–522.

Öhman, A. and Mineka, S. (2003) The malicious serpent: snakes as a prototypical stimulus for an evolved module of fear. *Current Directions in Psychological Science*, **12**, 5–9.

Ojemann, G.A. (1990) Organization of language cortex derived from investigations during neurosurgery. *Seminars in the Neurosciences*, **2**, 297–305.

Olds, J. and Milner, P. (1954) Positive reinforcement produced by electrical stimulation of septal area and other regions of rat brain. *Journal of Comparative and Physiological Psychology*, **47**, 419–427.

Olton, D.S., Becker, J.T. and Handelmann, G.E. (1979) Hippocampus, space and memory. *Behavioral and Brain Sciences*, **2**, 313–365.

Oppenheim, R.W. (1999) Programmed cell death. In *Fundamental Neuroscience* (eds M.J. Zigmond, F.E. Bloom, S.C. Landris, J.L. Roberts and L.R. Squire), Academic Press, San Diego, pp. 581–609.

Orford, J. (2001) *Excessive Appetites: A Psychological View of Addictions*, Wiley, Chichester.

Orr, S.P., Lasko, N.B., Shalev, A.Y. and Pitman, R.K. (1995) Physiological responses to loud tones in Vietnam veterans with posttraumatic stress disorder. *Journal of Abnormal Psychology*, **104**, 75–82.

Oscar-Berman, M., Kirkley, S.M., Gansler, D.A. and Couture, A. (2004) Comparisons of Korsakoff and non-Korsakoff alcoholics on neuropsychological tests of prefrontal brain imaging. *Alcoholism: Clinical and Experimental Research*, **28**, 667–675.

Oshiro, Y., Quevedo, A.S., McHaffie, J.G., Kraft, R.A. and Coghill, R.C. (2009) Brain mechanisms supporting discrimination of sensory features of pain: a new model. *Journal of Neuroscience*, **29**, 14924–14931.

Oswald, I., Taylor, A.M. and Treisman, M. (1960) Discriminative responses to stimulation during human sleep. *Brain*, **83**, 440–453.

Ott, A., Breteler, M.M.B., van Harskamp, F., Claus, J.J., van der Cammen, T.J.M., Grobbe, D.E. and Hofman, A. (1995) Prevalence of Alzheimer's disease and vascular dementia: association with education. The Rotterdam study. *British Medical Journal*, **310**, 970–973.

Ottesen, B., Wagner, G. and Fahrenkrug, J. (1988) Peptidergic innervation of the sexual organs. In *Handbook of Sexology*, Vol. 6: *The Pharmacology and Endocrinology of Sexual Function* (ed. J.M.A. Sitsen), Elsevier Science, Amsterdam, pp. 66–97.

Overmier, J.B. and Murison, R. (1997) Animal models reveal the 'psych' in the psychosomatics of peptic ulcers. *Current Directions in Psychological Science*, **6**, 180–184.

P

Pace-Schott, E.F. and Hobson, J.A. (2002) The neurobiology of sleep: genetics, cellular physiology and subcortical networks. *Nature Reviews Neuroscience*, **3**, 591–604.

Packard, M.G., Hirsh, R. and White, N.M. (1989) Differential effects of fornix and caudate nucleus lesions on two radial maze tasks: evidence for multiple memory systems. *Journal of Neuroscience, ***9**, 1465–1472.

Page, L.A., Rubia, K., Deeley, Q., Daly, E., Toal, F., Mataix-Cols, D., Giampietro, V., Schmitz,

N. and Murphy, D.G.M. (2009) A functional magnetic resonance imaging study of inhibitory control in obsessive-compulsive disorder. *Psychiatry Research: Neuroimaging*, **174**, 202–209.

Pallis, C.A. (1955) Impaired identification of faces and places with agnosia for colours. *Journal of Neurology, Neurosurgery and Psychiatry*, **18**, 218–224.

Pallmeyer, T.P., Blanchard, E.B. and Kolb, L.C. (1986) The psychophysiology of combat-induced post-traumatic stress disorder in Vietnam veterans. *Behaviour Research and Therapy*, **24,** 645–652.

Pamplona, F.A., Pandolfo, P., Savoldi, R., Prediger, R.D.S. and Takahashi, R.N. (2009) Environmental enrichment improves cognitive deficits in spontaneously hypertensive rats (SHR): relevance for attention deficit/hyperactivity disorder (ADHD). *Progress in Neuro-Psychopharmacology and Biological Psychiatry*, **33**, 1153–1160.

Panksepp, J. (1982) Toward a general psychobiological theory of emotions. *Behavioral and Brain Sciences*, **5**, 407–467.

Panksepp, J. (1986) The neural substrate for emotion. In *Emotion – Theory, Research and Experience,* Vol. 3, *Biological Foundations of Emotion* (eds R. Plutchik and H. Kellerman), Academic Press, Orlando, pp. 91–124.

Panksepp, J. (1994) Affective neuroscience: a paradigm to study the animate circuits for human emotions. In *Emotion: Interdisciplinary Perspectives* (eds R.D. Kavanaugh, B. Zimmerberg and S. Fein), Lawrence Erlbaum, Mahwah, pp. 29–60.

Panksepp, J. (1996) Affective neuroscience: a paradigm to study the animate circuits for human emotions. In *Emotions: Interdisciplinary Perspectives* (eds R.D. Kavanaugh, B. Zimmerberg and S. Fein), Lawrence Erlbaum, Mahwah, pp. 29–60.

Panksepp, J. (1998) *Affective Neuroscience*, Oxford University Press, New York.

Panksepp, J., Herman, B., Conner, R., Bishop, P. and Scott, J.P. (1978) The biology of social attachments: opiates alleviate separation distress. *Biological Psychiatry*, **9**, 213–220.

Panksepp, J., Normansell, L., Herman, B., Bishop, P. and Crepeau, L. (1988) Neural and neurochemical control of the separation distress call. In *The Physiological Control of Mammalian Vocalization* (ed. J.D. Newman), Plenum Press, New York, pp. 263–299.

Panksepp, J., Knutson, B. and Burgdorf, J. (2002a) The role of brain emotional systems in addictions: a neuro-evolutionary perspective and new 'self-report' animal model. *Addiction*, **97**, 459–469.

Panksepp, J., Moskal, J.R., Panksepp, J.B. and Kroes, R.A. (2002b) Comparative approaches in evolutionary psychology: molecular neuroscience meets the mind. *Neuroendocrinology Letters*, **23**, Special Issue suppl. 4, 105–115.

Papanicolaou, A.C. (1998) *Fundamentals of Functional Brain Imaging: A Guide to the Methods and their Applications to Psychology and Behavioral Neuroscience*, Swets and Zeitlinger, Lisse.

Pappenheimer, J.R. (1983) Induction of sleep by muramyl peptides. *Journal of Physiology*, **336**, 1–11.

Parasuraman, R. (2004) Attentional functioning in Alzheimer's disease. In *Cognitive Neuropsychology of Alzheimer's Disease*, 2nd edition (eds R.G. Morris and J.T. Becker), Oxford University Press, Oxford, pp. 81–102.

Paredes, R.G. and Ågmo, A. (2004) Has dopamine a physiological role in the control of sexual behavior? A critical review of the evidence. *Progress in Neurobiology*, **73**, 179–226.

Patterson, J.V., Hetrick, W.P., Boutros, N.N., Jin, Y., Sandman, C., Stern, H., Potkin, S. and Bunney, W.E. (2008) P50 sensory gating ratios in schizophrenics and controls: a review and data analysis. *Psychiatry Research*, **158**, 226–247.

Pause, B.M., Adolph, D., Prehn-Kristensen, A. and Ferstl, R. (2009) Startle response potentiation to chemosensory anxiety signals in socially anxious individuals. *International Journal of Psychophysiology*, **74**, 88–92.

Pavlov, I.P. (1935/1955) *Selected Works*, Foreign Languages Publishing House, Moscow.

Pear, J.J., Moody, J.E. and Persinger, M.A. (1972) Lever attacking by rats during free-operant avoidance. *Journal of the Experimental Analysis of Behavior*, **18**, 517–523.

Peciña, S. and Berridge, K.C. (2000) Opioid site in nucleus accumbens shell mediates eating and hedonic 'liking' for food: map based on microinjection Fos plumes. *Brain Research*, **863**, 71–86.

Peciña, S., Cagniard, B., Berridge, K.C., Aldridge J.W. and Zhuang, X. (2003) Hyperdopaminergic mutant mice have higher 'wanting' but not 'liking' for sweet rewards. *Journal of Neuroscience*, **23**, 9395–9402.

Peele, S. (1985) *The Meaning of Addiction*, Lexington Books, Lexington.

Peele, S. and Alexander, B.K. (1985) Theories of addiction. In *The Meaning of Addiction* (ed. S. Peele), Lexington Books, Lexington, pp. 47–72.

Peele, S. and Degrandpre, R.J. (1998) Cocaine and the concept of addiction: environmental factors in drug compulsions. *Addiction Research*, **6**, 235–263.

Pelchat, M.L., Johnson, A., Chan, R., Valdez, J. and Ragland, J.D. (2004) Images of desire: food-craving activation during fMRI. *Neuro Image*, **23**, 1486–1493.

Penfield, W. (1966) Speech, perception and the cortex. In *Brain and Conscious Experience* (ed. J.C. Eccles), Springer-Verlag, Berlin, pp. 217–237.

Penfield, W. and Evans, J. (1935) The frontal lobe in man: a clinical study of maximum removals. *Brain*, **58**, 115–133.

Penfield, W. and Rasmussen, T. (1968) *The Cerebral Cortex of Man*, Hafner Publishing, New York.

Penrose, R. (1987) Minds, machines and mathematics. In *Mindwaves: Thoughts on Intelligence, Identity and Consciousness* (eds C. Blakemore and S. Greenfield), Basil Blackwell, Oxford, pp. 259–276.

Penrose, R. (1990) Précis of *The Emperor's New Mind: Concerning Computers, Minds, and The Laws of Physics*. *Behavioral and Brain Sciences*, **13**, 643–705.

Pereira, A.C., Huddleston, D.E., Brickman, A.M., Sosunov, A.A., Hen, R., McKhann, G.M., Sloan, R., Gage, F.H., Brown, T.R. and Small, S.A. (2007) An *in vivo* correlate of exercise-induced neurogenesis in the adult dentate gyrus. *Proceedings of the National Academy of Sciences*, **104**, 5638–5643.

Peres, M.F.P., Zukerman, E., Senne Soares, C.A., Alonso, E.O., Santos, B.F.C. and Faulhaber, M.H. (2004) Cerebrospinal fluid glutamate levels in chronic migrane. *Cephalalgia*, **24**, 735–739.

Perrett, D.I., Burt, D.M., Penton-Voak, I.S., Lee, K.J., Rowland, D.A. and Edwards, R. (1999) Symmetry and human facial attractiveness. *Evolution and Human Behavior*, **20**, 295–307.

Perry, E., Walker, M., Grace, J. and Perry, R. (1999) Acetylcholine in mind: a neurotransmitter correlate of consciousness? *Trends in Neurosciences*, **22**, 273–280.

Perry, R.J. and Hodges, J.R. (1999) Attention and executive deficits in Alzheimer's disease. *Brain*, **122**, 383–404.

Petersen, S.E., Fox, P.T., Posner, M.I., Mintun, M. and Raichle, M.E. (1988) Positron emission tomographic studies of the cortical anatomy of single-word processing. *Nature*, **331**, 585–589.

Petri, H.L. and Mishkin, M. (1994) Behaviorism, cognitivism and the neuropsychology of memory. *American Scientist*, **82**, 30–37.

Petrides, M. (1994) Frontal lobes and working memory: evidence from investigations of the effects of cortical excisions in nonhuman primates. In *Handbook of Neuropsychology*, Vol. 9 (eds F. Boller and J. Grafman), Elsevier, Amsterdam, pp. 59–82.

Petrosini, L., De Bartolo, P., Foti, F., Gelfo, F., Cutuli, D., Leggio, M.G. and Mandolesi, L. (2009) On whether the environmental enrichment may provide cognitive and brain reserves. *Brain Research Reviews*, **61**, 221–239.

Petrovic, P. (2010) Placebo analgesia and the brain. In *Pleasures of the Brain* (eds M.L. Kringelbach and K.C. Berridge), Oxford University Press, Oxford, pp. 287–301.

Petrovic, P., Kalso, E., Petersson, K.M. and Ingvar, M. (2002) Placebo and opioid analgesia – imaging a shared neuronal network. *Science*, **295**, 1737–1740.

Pfaff, D.W. (1989) Features of a hormone-driven defined neural circuit for a mammalian behavior. *Annals of the New York Academy of Sciences*, **563**, 131–147.

Pfaff, D.W. and Pfaffmann, C. (1969) Olfactory and hormonal influences on the basal forebrain of the male rat. *Brain Research*, **15**, 137–156.

Pfaff, D.W., Phillips, M.I. and Rubin, R.T. (2004) *Principles of Hormone Behavior Relations*, Elsevier Academic Press, Amsterdam.

Pfaff, D.W., Martin, E.M. and Ribeiro, A.C. (2007) Relations between mechanisms of CNS arousal and mechanisms of stress. *Stress*, **10**, 316–325.

Phan, K.L., Wager, T., Taylor, S.F. and Liberzon, I. (2002) Functional neuroanatomy of emotion: A meta-analysis of emotion activation studies in PET and fMRI. *NeuroImage*, **16**, 331–348.

Phelps, J.A., Davis, J.O. and Schartz, K.M. (1997) Nature, nurture, and twin research strategies. *Current Directions in Psychological Science*, **6**, 117–121.

Phillips, M.L., Marks, I.M., Senior, C., Lythgoe, D., O'Dwyer, A-M., Meehan, O., Williams, S.C.R., Brammer, M.J., Bullmore, E.T. and McGuire, P.K. (2000) A differential neural response in obsessive-compulsive disorder patients with washing compared with checking symptoms to disgust. *Psychological Medicine*, **30**, 1037–1050.

Phillips, M.L., Drevets, W.C., Rauch, S.L. and Lane, R. (2003) Neurobiology of emotion perception I: The neural basis of normal emotion perception. *Biological Psychiatry*, **54**, 504–514.

Phillips-Bute, B.G. and Lane, J.D. (1998) Caffeine withdrawal symptoms following brief caffeine deprivation. *Physiology and Behavior*, **63**, 35–39.

Phoenix, C.H., Goy, R.W., Gerall, A.A. and Young, W.C. (1959) Organizing action of prenatally administered testosterone propionate on the tissues mediating mating behavior in the female guinea pig. *Endocrinology*, **65**, 369–382.

Piaget, J. (1954) *The Child's Construction of Reality*, Routledge and Kegan Paul, London.

Picard, F. and Craig, A.D. (2009) Ecstatic epileptic seizures: a potential window on the neural basis for human self-awareness. *Epilepsy and Behaviour*, **16**, 539–546.

Pierce, R.C. and Kalivas, P.W. (1997) A circuitry model of the expression of behavioral sensitization to amphetamine-like psychostimulants. *Brain Research Reviews*, **25**, 192–216.

Pierrot-Deseilligny, E. and Burke, D. (2005) *The Circuitry of the Human Spinal Cord: Its Role in Motor Control and Movement Disorders*, Cambridge University Press, Cambridge.

Pihl, R.O. and LeMarquand, D. (1998) Serotonin and aggression and the alcohol–aggression relationship. *Alcohol and Alcoholism*, **33**, 55–65.

Pillard, R.C. and Weinrich, J.D. (1986) Evidence of familial nature of male homosexuality. *Archives of General Psychiatry*, **43**, 808–812.

Pineda, J.O.A. and Oberman, L.M. (2006) What goads cigarette smokers to smoke? Neural adaptation and the mirror neuron system. *Brain Research*, **1121**, 128–135.

Pinker, S. and Bloom, P. (1990) Natural language and natural selection. *Behavioral and Brain Sciences*, **13**, 707–784.

Pitman, R.K., Orr, S.P. and Shalev, A.Y. (1993) Once bitten, twice shy: beyond the conditioning model of PTSD. *Biological Psychiatry*, **33**, 145–146.

Plomin, R. (1989) Environment and genes. *American Psychologist*, **44**, 105–111

Plomin, R. and Rutter, M. (1998) Child development, molecular genetics, and what to do with genes once they are found. *Child Development*, **69**, 1223–1242.

Plomin, R., DeFries, J.C., McClearn, G.E. and Rutter, M. (1997) *Behavioral Genetics*, W.H. Freeman, New York.

Ploog, D. (1986) Biological foundations of the vocal expressions of emotions. In *Emotion – Theory, Research and Experience*, Vol. 3 *Biological Foundations of Emotion* (eds R. Plutchik and H. Kellerman), Academic Press, Orlando, pp. 173–197.

Plutchik, R. (1980) *Emotion: A Psychoevolutionary Synthesis*, Harper and Row, New York.

Poeppel, D. and Hickok, G. (2004) Towards a new functional anatomy of language. *Cognition*, **92**, 1–12.

Pohl, W. (1973) Dissociation of spatial discrimination deficits following frontal and parietal lesions in monkeys. *Journal of Comparative and Physiological Psychology*, **82**, 227–239.

Poizner, H., Bellugi, U. and Klima, E.S. (1990) Biological foundations of language: clues from sign language. *Annual Review of Neurosciences*, **13**, 283–307.

Polosa, C., Mannard, A. and Laskey, W. (1979) Tonic activity of the autonomic nervous system: functions, properties, origins. In *Integrative Functions of the Autonomic Nervous System* (eds C.M. Brooks, K. Koizumi and A. Sato), University of Tokyo Press/Elsevier, Amsterdam, pp. 342–354.

Pomeranz, B., Wall, P.D. and Weber, W.V. (1968) Cord cells responding to fine myelinated afferents from viscera, muscle and skin. *Journal of Physiology*, **199**, 511–532.

Pomerleau, O.F. and Pomerleau, C.S. (1984) Neuroregulators and the reinforcement of smoking: towards a biobehavioral explanation. *Neuroscience and Biobehavioral Reviews*, **8**, 503–513.

Popper, K. and Eccles, J.C. (1977) *The Self and Its Brain*, Springer International, Berlin.

Posner, M.I. (1980) Orienting of attention. *Quarterly Journal of Experimental Psychology*, **32**, 3–25.

Posner, M.I. (1993) Interaction of arousal and selection in the posterior attention network. In *Attention: Selection, Awareness, and Control – A Tribute to Donald Broadbent* (eds A. Baddeley and L. Weiskrantz), Clarendon Press, Oxford, pp. 390–405.

Posner, M.I. and Petersen, S.E. (1990) The attention system of the human brain. *Annual Review of Neurosciences*, **13**, 25–42.

Post, S.G. (2007) *Altruism and Health: Perspectives from Empirical Research*, Oxford University Press, New York.

Povinelli, D.J. and Preuss, T.M. (1995) Theory of mind: evolutionary history of a cognitive specialization. *Trends in Neurosciences*, **18**, 418–424.

Power, M.L. and Schulkin, J. (2009) *The Evolution of Obesity*, Johns Hopkins University Press, Baltimore.

Powley, T.L. (1999) Central control of autonomic functions. In *Fundamental Neuroscience* (eds M.J. Zigmond, F.E. Bloom, S.C. Landis, J.L. Roberts and L.R. Squire), Academic Press, San Diego, pp. 1027–1050.

Powley, T.L. and Phillips, R.J. (2004) Gastric satiation is volumetric, intestinal satiation is nutritive. *Physiology and Behavior*, **82**, 69–74.

Prechtl, H.F.R. (1981) The study of neural development as a perspective of clinical problems. In *Maturation and Development: Biological and Psychological Perspectives* (eds K.J. Connolly and H.F.R. Prechtl), William Heinemann Medical Books, London, pp. 198–215.

Prechtl, H.F.R. (1982) Assessment methods for the newborn infant, a critical evaluation. In *Psychobiology of the Human Newborn* (ed. P. Stratton), Wiley, Chichester, pp. 21–52.

Prescott, T.J., Redgrave, P. and Gurney, K. (1999) Layered control architectures in robots and vertebrates. *Adaptive Behavior*, **7**, 99–127.

Preuss, T.M. and Kaas, J.H. (1999) Human brain evolution. In *Fundamental Neuroscience* (eds M.J. Zigmond, F.E. Bloom, S.C. Landis, J.L. Roberts and L.R. Squire), Academic Press, San Diego, pp. 1283–1311.

Pribram, K.H. (1986) The cognitive revolution and mind/brain issues. *American Psychologist*, **41**, 507–520.

Price, J., Sloman, L., Gardner, R., Gilbert, P. and Rohde, P. (1994) The social competition hypothesis of depression. *British Journal of Psychiatry*, **164**, 309–315.

Profet (1992) Pregnancy sickness as adaptation: a deterrent to maternal ingestion of teratogens. In *The Adapted Mind: Evolutionary Psychology and the Generation of Culture* (eds J.H. Barkow, L. Cosmides and J. Tooby), Oxford University Press, Oxford, pp. 327–365.

Provine, R.R. (1988) On the uniqueness of embryos and the difference it makes. In *Behavior of the Fetus* (eds W.P. Smotherman and S.R. Robinson), Telford Press, Caldwell, pp. 35–46.

Purves, D. (1994) *Neural Activity and the Growth of the Brain*, Cambridge University Press, Cambridge.

Purves, D. and Lichtman, J.W. (1985) *Principles of Neural Development*, Sinauer Associates, Sunderland.

Purves, D., Augustine, G.J., Fitzpatrick, D., Katz, L.C., LaMantia, A-S. and McNamara, J.O. (1997) *Neuroscience,* Sinauer Associates, Sunderland.

R

Rabagliati, A. (1883) Book review: E. Swedenborg *The Brain, considered Anatomically, Physiologically and Philosophically*. *Brain*, **6**, 404–413.

Råberg, L., Grahn, M., Hasselquist, D. and Svensson, E. (1998) On the adaptive significance of stress-induced immunosuppression. *Proceedings of the Royal Society of London B*, **265**, 1637–1641.

Rahn, E.J. and Hohmann, A.G. (2009) Cannabinoids as pharmacotherapies for neuropathic pain: from the bench to the bedside. *Neurotherapeutics*, **6**, 713–737.

Raichle, M.E., Fiez, J.A., Videen, T.O., MacLeod, A-M.K., Pardo, J.V., Fox, P.T. and Petersen, S.E. (1994) Practice-related changes in human brain functional anatomy during nonmotor learning. *Cerebral Cortex*, **4**, 8–26.

Raine, A., Buchsbaum, M. and LaCasse, L. (1997) Brain abnormalities in murderers indicated by positron emission tomography. *Biological Psychiatry*, **42**, 495–508.

Rainville, P., Duncan, G.H., Price, D.D., Carrier, B. and Bushnell, M.C. (1997) Pain affect encoded in human anterior cingulate but not somatosensory cortex. *Science*, **277**, 968–971.

Rakic, P. (1971) Guidance of neurons migrating to the fetal monkey neocortex. *Brain Research*, **33**, 471–476.

Ramachandran, V.S. and Altschuler, E.L. (2009) The use of visual feedback, in particular mirror visual feedback, in restoring brain function. *Brain*, **132**, 1693–1710.

Ramachandran, V.S. and Blakeslee, S. (1998) *Phantoms in the Brain: Human Nature and the Architecture of the Mind*. Fourth Estate, London.

Ramachandran, V.S. and Brang, D. (2009) Sensations evoked in patients with amputation from watching an individual whose corresponding intact limb is being touched. *Archives of Neurology*, **66**, 1281–1284.

Rammsayer, T.H. (2004) Extraversion and the dopamine hypothesis. In *On the Psychobiology of Personality* (ed. R.M. Stelmack), Elsevier, Oxford, pp. 411–430.

Ramos, A. and Mormède, P. (1998) Stress and emotionality: a multidimensional and genetic approach. *Neuroscience and Biobehavioral Reviews*, **22**, 33–57.

Ramsay, D.J. and Booth, D. (1991) *Thirst: Physiological and Psychological Aspects*, Springer-Verlag, London.

Ramsay, D.J. and Thrasher, T.N. (1990) Thirst and water balance. In *Handbook of Behavioral Neurobiology*, Vol. 10, *Neurobiology of Food and Fluid Intake* (ed. E.M. Stricker), Plenum Press, New York, pp. 353–386.

Ramstrom, M. (1910) Emanuel Swedenborg as an anatomist. *The British Medical Journal*, **2598**, 1153–1155.

Randolph, M. and Semmes, J. (1974) Behavioral consequences of elective subtotal ablations in the postcentral gyrus of *Macaca mulatta*. *Brain Research*, **70**, 55–70.

Rankin, K.P. (2007) Social cognition in frontal injury. In *The Human Frontal Lobes: Functions and Disorders,* 2nd edition (eds B.L. Miller and J.L. Cummings), Guilford Press, New York, pp. 345–360.

Raper, J.A. and Tessier-Lavigne, M. (1999) Growth cones and axon pathfinding. In *Fundamental Neuroscience* (eds M.J. Zigmond, F.E. Bloom, S.C. Landis, J.L. Roberts and L.R. Squire), Academic Press, San Diego, pp. 519–546.

Ratcliffe, J.M., Fenton, M.B. and Galef, B.G. (2003) An exception to the rule: common vampire bats do not learn taste aversions. *Animal Behaviour*, **65**, 385–389.

Ravussin, E., Valencia, M.E., Esparza, J., Bennett, P.H. and Schulz, L.O. (1994) Effects of a traditional lifestyle on obesity in Pima Indians. *Diabetes Care*, **17**, 1067–1074.

Read, N.W. (1992) Role of gastrointestinal factors in hunger and satiety in man. *Proceedings of the Nutrition Society*, **51**, 7–11.

Reason, J. (1984) Lapses of attention in everyday life. In *Varieties of Attention* (eds R. Parasuraman and D.R. Davies), Academic Press, Orlando, pp. 515–549.

Reber, A.S. (1992) The cognitive unconscious: an evolutionary perspective. *Consciousness and Cognition*, **1**, 93–133.

Rechtschaffen, A. (1998) Current perspectives on the function of sleep. *Perspectives in Biology and Medicine*, **41**, 359–390.

Rechtschaffen, A., Hauri, P. and Zeitlin, M. (1966) Auditory awakening threshold in REM and NREM sleep stages. *Perceptual and Motor Skills*, **22**, 927–942.

Redgrave, P. and Dean, P. (1991) Does the PAG learn about emergencies from the superior colliculus? In *The Midbrain Periaqueductal Gray Matter – Functional, Anatomical, and Neurochemical Organization* (eds A. Depaulis and R. Bandler), Plenum Press, New York, pp. 199–209.

Redgrave, P., Prescott, T.J. and Gurney, K. (1999) The basal ganglia: a vertebrate solution to the selection problem? *Neuroscience*, **89**, 1009–1023.

Redouté, J., Stoléru, S., Grégoire, M-C., Costes, N., Cinotti, L., Lavenne, F., Le Bars, D., Forest, M.G. and Pujol, J-F. (2000) Brain processing of visual sexual stimuli in human males. *Human Brain Mapping*, **11**, 162–177.

Reeve, J.M. (2008) *Understanding Motivation and Emotion*. 5th edition, Wiley, New York.

Reeves, A.G. and Plum, F. (1969) Hyperphagia, rage, and dementia accompanying a ventromedial hypothalamic neoplasm. *Archives of Neurology*, **20**, 616–624.

Reid, M.S., Mickalian, J.D., Delucchi, K.L., Hall, S.M. and Berger, S.P. (1998) An acute dose of nicotine enhances cue-induced cocaine craving. *Drug and Alcohol Dependence*, **49**, 95–104.

Reid, R.C. (1999) Vision. In *Fundamental Neuroscience* (eds M.J. Zigmond, F.E. Bloom, S.C. Landis, J.L. Roberts and L.R. Squire), Academic Press, San Diego, pp. 821–851.

Reiman, E.M., Caselli, R.J., Yun, L.S., Chen, K., Bandy, D., Minoshima, S., Thibodeau, S.N. and Osborne, D. (1996) Preclinical evidence of Alzheimer's disease in persons homozygous for the ε4 allele for apolipoprotein E. *New England Journal of Medicine*, **334**, 752–758.

Reimund, E. (1994) The free radical flux theory of sleep. *Medical Hypotheses*, **43**, 231–233.

Reiner, A., Medina, L. and Veenman, C.L. (1998) Structural and functional evolution of the basal ganglia in vertebrates. *Brain Research Reviews*, **28**, 235–285.

Reinisch, J.M. and Sanders, S.A. (1992) Prenatal hormonal contributions to sex differences in human personality development. In *Handbook of Behavioral Neurobiology*, Vol. 11, *Sexual Differentiation* (eds A.A. Gerall, H. Moltz and I.L. Ward), Plenum Press, New York, pp. 221–243.

Reisenzein, R. (1983) The Schachter theory of emotion: two decades on. *Psychological Bulletin*, **94**, 239–264.

Reitz, C. and Mayeux, R. (2009) Use of genetic variation as biomarkers for alzheimer's disease. *Annals of the New York Academy of Sciences*, **1180**, 75–96.

Rendeiro, C., Spencer, J.P.E., Vauzour, D., Butler, L.T., Ellis, J.A. and Williams, C.M. (2009) The impact of flavonoids on spatial memory in rodents: from behaviour to underlying hippocampal mechanisms. *Genes and Nutrition*, **4**, 251–270.

Renner, M.J. and Rosenzweig, M.R. (1986) Object interactions in juvenile rats (*Rattus norvegicus*): effects of different experiential histories. *Journal of Comparative Psychology*, **100**, 229–236.

Rhodes, G. and Zebrowitz, L.A. (2002) *Facial Attractiveness: Evolutionary, Cognitive, and Social Perspectives,* Ablex, Westpoint.

Rhodes, S.M., Coghill, D.R. and Matthews, K. (2005) Neuropsychological functioning in stimulant-naïve boys with hyperkinetic disorder. *Psychological Medicine*, **35**, 1109–1120.

Ribot, T.H. (1885) *Diseases of Memory*, Kegan Paul, Trench and Co., London.

Richards, G. (1987) *Human Evolution*, Routledge and Kegan Paul, London.

Richards, M. (1996) Neurobiological treatment of Alzheimer's disease. In *The Cognitive Neuropsychology of Alzheimer-type Dementia* (ed. R.G. Morris), Oxford University Press, Oxford, pp. 327–342.

Richardson, D.K. Reynolds, S.M., Cooper, S.J. and Berridge, K.C. (2005) Endogenous opioids are necessary for benzodiazepine palatability enhancement: naltrexone blocks diazepam-induced increase of sucrose 'liking'. *Pharmacology, Biochemistry and Behavior*, **81**(3), 657–663.

Richardson, L.K., Frueh, B.C. and Acierno, R. (2010) Prevalence estimates of combat-related post-traumatic stress disorder: critical review. *Australian and New Zealand Journal of Psychiatry*, **44**, 4–19.

Richerson, P.J. (2006) *Not by Genes Alone: How Culture Transformed Human Evolution*. Chicago University Press, Chicago.

Rideout, H.J. and Parker, L.A. (1996) Morphine enhancement of sucrose palatability: analysis by the taste reactivity test. *Pharmacology Biochemistry and Behavior*, **53**, 731–734.

Ridley, R.M. and Baker, H.F. (1983) Is there a relationship between social isolation, cognitive inflexibility, and behavioral stereotypy? An analysis of the effects of amphetamine in the marmoset. In *Ethopharmacology: Primate Models of Neuropsychiatric Disorders* (ed. K.A. Miczek), Alan R. Liss, New York, pp. 101–135.

Rivier, C. (1991) Neuroendocrine mechanisms of anterior pituitary regulation in the rat exposed to stress. In *Stress – Neurobiology and Neuroendocrinology* (eds M.R. Brown, G.F. Koob and C. Rivier), Marcel Dekker, New York, pp. 119–136.

Rizzo, T.A., Metzger, B.E., Dooley, S.L. and Cho, N.H. (1997) Early malnutrition and child neurobehavioral development: insights from the study of children of diabetic mothers. *Child Development, **68**, 26–38.

Rizzolatti, G. (1983) Mechanisms of selective attention in mammals. In *Advances in Vertebrate Neuroethology* (eds J-P. Ewert, R.R. Capranica and D.J. Ingle), Plenum Press, New York, pp. 261–297.

Rizzolatti, G. and Arbib, M.A. (1998) Language within our grasp. *Trends in Neurosciences*, **21**, 188–194.

Rizzolatti, G. and Berti, A. (1993) Neural mechanisms of spatial neglect. In *Unilateral Neglect: Clinical and Experimental Studies* (eds I.H. Robertson and J.C. Marshall), Lawrence Erlbaum, Hove, pp. 87–105.

Rizzolatti, G. and Craighero, L. (2004) The mirror-neuron system. In *Annual Review of Neuroscience*, Vol. 27 (eds S. E. Hyman, T.M. Jessell, C.J. Shatz and C.F. Stevens), Annual Reviews, Palo Alto, pp. 169–172.

Rizzolatti, G. and Sinigaglia, C. (2008) *Mirrors in the Brain – How Our Minds Share Actions and Emotions*. Oxford University Press, Oxford.

Rizzolatti, G., Riggio, L., Dascola, I. and Umiltà, C. (1987) Reorienting attention across the horizontal and vertical meridians: evidence in favour of a premotor theory of attention. *Neuropsychologia*, **25**, 31–40.

Robbins, T.W. and Arnsten, A.F.T. (2009) The neuropsychopharmacology of fronto-executive function: monoaminergic modulation. *Annual Review of Neuroscience*, **32**, 267–287.

Robbins, T.W. and Everitt, B.J. (1992) Functions of dopamine in the dorsal and ventral striatum. *Seminars in the Neurosciences*, **4**, 119–127.

Robbins, T.W. and Everitt, B.J. (1999) Motivation and reward. In *Fundamental Neuroscience* (eds M.J. Zigmond, F.E. Bloom, S.C. Landis, J.L. Roberts and L.R. Squire), Academic Press, San Diego, pp. 1245–1260.

Robbins, T.W. and Fray, P.J. (1980a) Stress-induced eating: fact, fiction or misunderstanding? *Appetite*, **1**, 103–133.

Robbins, T.W. and Fray, P.J. (1980b) Stress-induced eating; reply to Bolles, Rowland and Marques, and Herman and Polivy. *Appetite*, **1**, 231–239.

Robbins, T.W., McAlonan, G., Muir, J.L. and Everitt, B.J. (1997) Cognitive enhancers in theory and practice: studies of the cholinergic hypothesis of cognitive deficits in Alzheimer's disease. *Behavioural Brain Research*, **83**, 15–23.

Robbins, T.W., Everitt, B. and Nutt, D. (2010) *The Neurobiology of Addiction*, Oxford University Press, Oxford.

Roberts, G.M.P., Nestor, L. and Garavan, H. (2009) Learning and memory deficits in ecstasy users and their neural correlates during a face-learning task. *Brain Research*, **1292**, 71–81.

Roberts, S.C., Havlicek, J., Flegr, J., Hruskova, M., Little, A.C., Jones, B.C., Perrett, D.I. and Petrie, M. (2004) Female facial attractiveness increases during the fertile phase of the menstrual cycle. *Proceedings of the Royal Society of London B* (Suppl.), **271**, S270–S272.

Roberts, W.C. (1996) Coronary atherosclerosis: description, manifestations, and prevention. In *Heart and Mind. The Practice of Cardiac Psychology* (eds R. Allan and S. Scheidt), American Psychological Association, Washington, pp. 147–177.

Robertson, L.C. and Delis, D.C. (1986) 'Part–whole' processing in unilateral brain-damaged patients: dysfunction of hierarchical organization. *Neuropsychologia*, **24**, 363–370.

Robertson, L.C., Lamb, M.R. and Knight, R.T. (1988) Effects of lesions of temporal–parietal junction on perceptual and attentional processing in humans. *Journal of Neuroscience*, **8**, 3757–3769.

Robins, L.N., Helzer, J.E. and Davis, D.H. (1975) Narcotic use in Southeast Asia and afterward. *Archives of General Psychiatry*, **32**, 955–961.

Robinson, M.J., Edwards, S.E., Iyengar, S., Bymaster, F., Clark, M. and Katon, W. (2009) Depression and pain. *Frontiers in Bioscience*, **14**, 5031–5051.

Robinson, P.H. (1989) Gastric function in eating disorders. *Annals of the New York Academy of Sciences*, **575**, 456–465.

Robinson, R.G. and Price, T.R. (1982) Post-stroke depressive disorders: a follow-up study of 103 patients. *Stroke*, **13**, 635–641.

Robinson, S.R. and Smotherman, W.P. (1988) Chance and chunks in the ontogeny of fetal behavior. In *Behavior of the Fetus* (eds W.P. Smotherman and S.R. Robinson), Telford Press, Caldwell, pp. 95–115.

Robinson, T.E. and Berridge, K.C. (1993) The neural basis of drug craving: an incentive-sensitization theory of addiction. *Brain Research Reviews*, **18**, 247–291.

Robinson, T.E. and Berridge, K.C. (2008) The incentive sensitization theory of addiction: some current issues. *Philosophical Transactions of the Royal Society B*, **363**, 3137–3146.

Rodgers, R.J. and Randall, J.I. (1987) On the mechanisms and adaptive significance of intrinsic analgesia systems. *Reviews in the Neurosciences*, **1**, 185–200.

Rodin, J. (1980) The externality theory today. In *Obesity* (ed. A.J. Stunkard), W.B. Saunders, Philadelphia, pp. 226–239.

Rodriguez-Manzo, G. and Fernandez-Guasti, A. (1994) Reversal of sexual exhaustion by serotonergic and noradrenergic agents. *Behavioural Brain Research,* **62**, 127–134.

Rodriguez-Raecke, R., Niemeier, A., Ihle, K., Ruether, W. and May, A. (2009) Brain gray matter decrease in chronic pain is the consequence and not the cause of pain. *The Journal of Neuroscience*, **29**, 13746–13750.

Roeder, F., Orthner, H., and Müller, D. (1972) The stereotaxic treatment of pedophilic homosexuality and other sexual deviations. In *Psychosurgery* (eds E. Hitchcock, L. Laitinen and K. Vaernet), C.C. Thomas, Springfield, pp. 87–111

Roffwarg, H.P., Muzio, J.N. and Dement, W.C. (1966) Ontogenetic development of the human sleep–dream cycle. *Science*, **152**, 604–619.

Rogers, C.R. (1959) A theory of therapy, personality, and interpersonal relationships, as developed in the client-centered framework. In *Psychology: A Study of a Science*, Vol. 3 (ed. S. Koch), McGraw-Hill, New York, pp. 184–256.

Rogers, P.J. (1995) Food, mood and appetite. *Nutrition Research Reviews*, **8**, 243–269.

Rogers, P.J. and Smit, H.J. (2000) Food craving and food 'addiction': a critical review of the evidence from a biopsychosocial perspective. *Pharmacology Biochemistry and Behavior*, **66**, 3–14.

Roiser, J.P., Stephan, K.E., den Ouden, H.E.M., Barnes, T.R.E., Friston, K.J. and Joyce, E.M. (2009) Do patients with schizophrenia exhibit aberrant salience? *Psychological Medicine*, **39**, 199–209.

Roland, P.E. and Friberg, L. (1985) Localization of cortical areas activated by thinking. *Journal of Neurophysiology*, **53**, 1219–1243.

Rolls, B.J. (1991) Physiological determinants of fluid intake in humans. In *Thirst: Physiological and Psychological Aspects* (eds D.J. Ramsey and D. Booth), Springer-Verlag, London, pp. 391–399.

Rolls, E.T. (1993) The neural control of feeding in primates. In *Neurophysiology of Ingestion* (ed. D.A. Booth), Pergamon Press, Oxford, pp. 137–169.

Rolls, E.T. (1994) Neural processing related to feeding in primates. In *Appetite – Neural and Behavioural Bases* (eds C.R. Legg and D. Booth), Oxford University Press, Oxford, pp. 11–53.

Rolls, E.T. (2004) The functions of the orbito-frontal cortex. *Brain and Cognition*, **55**, 11–29.

Rolls, E.T. (2005) *Emotion Explained,* Oxford University Press, Oxford.

Rolls, E.T. and McCabe, C. (2007) Enhanced affective brain representations of chocolate in cravers vs. non-cravers. *European Journal of Neuroscience*, **26**, 1067–1076.

Roman, V., Walstra, I., Luiten, P.G.M. and Meerlo, P. (2005) Too little sleep gradually desensitizes the serotonin 1A receptor system. *Sleep*, **28**, 1505–1510.

Ropper, A.H. (2010) *Cogito ergo sum* by MRI. *The New England Journal of Medicine*, **362**, 648–649.

Rose, J.E. and Corrigal, W.A. (1997) Nicotine self-administration in animals and humans: similarities and differences. *Psychopharmacology*, **130**, 28–40.

Rose, J.E., Hind, J.E., Anderson, D.J. and Brugge, J.F. (1971) Some effects of stimulus intensity on response of auditory nerve fibres in the squirrel monkey. *Journal of Neurophysiology,* **34**, 685–699.

Rose, R.M., Bernstein, I.S. and Gordon, T.P. (1975) Consequences of social conflict on plasma testosterone levels in rhesus monkeys. *Psychosomatic Medicine*, **37**, 50–61.

Rose, S. (1992) *The Making of Memory*, Bantam, London.

Rosen, J.B. and Schulkin, J. (1998) From normal fear to pathological anxiety. *Psychological Review*, **105**, 325–350.

Rosen, R.C. (1991) Alcohol and drug effects on sexual response: human experimental and clinical studies. In *Annual Review of Sex Research*, **2** (ed. J. Bancroft), Society for the Scientific Study of Sex, Allentown, pp. 119–179.

Rosenblatt, J.S. (1992) Hormone-behavior relations in the regulation of parental behavior. In *Behavioral Endocrinology* (eds J.B. Becker, S.M. Breedlove and D. Crews), MIT Press, Cambridge, pp. 219–259.

Rosenblueth, A., Wiener, N. and Bigelow, J. (1968) Behavior, purpose and teleology. In *Modern Systems Research for the Behavioral Scientist* (ed. W. Buckley), Aldine, Chicago, pp. 221–225.

Rosenwasser, A.M. (2009) Functional neuroanatomy of sleep and circadian rhythms. *Brain Research Reviews*, **61**, 281–306.

Rosenzweig, M.R., Leiman, A.L. and Breedlove, S.M. (1996) *Biological Psychology*, 1st edition, Sinauer Associates, Sunderland.

Rothwell, J. (1994) *Control of Human Voluntary Movement*, Chapman and Hall, London.

Rouby, C., Schaal, B., Dubois, D., Gervais, R. and Holley, A. (2005) *Olfaction, Taste and Cognition*, Cambridge University Press, Cambridge.

Rozin, P. (1976) The evolution of intelligence and access to the cognitive unconscious. In *Progress in Psychobiology and Physiological Psychology* (eds J.M. Sprague and A.N. Epstein), Academic Press, New York, pp. 245–280.

Rozin, P., Haidt, J. and McCauley (2000) Disgust. In *Handbook of Emotions*, 2nd edition (eds M. Lewis and J.M. Haviland-Jones), Guilford Press, New York, pp. 637–653.

Rozin, P.N. and Schulkin, J. (1990) Food selection. In *Handbook of Behavioral Neurobiology*, Vol. 10, *Neurobiology of Food and Fluid Intake* (ed. E.M. Stricker), Plenum Press, New York, pp. 297–328.

Rubens, A.B. and Benson, D.F. (1971) Associative visual agnosia. *Archives of Neurology*, **24**, 305–316.

Rubia, K., Overmeyer, S., Taylor, E., Brammer, M., Williams, S.C.R., Simmons, A. and Bullmore, E.T. (1999) Hypofrontality in attention deficit hyperactivity disorder during higher-order motor control: a study with functional MRI. *American Journal of Psychiatry*, **156**, 891–896.

Rudoy, J.D., Voss, J.L., Westerberg, C.E. and Paller, K.A. (2009) Strengthening individual memories by reactivating them during sleep. *Science*, **326**, 1079.

Rule, R.R., Shimamura, A.P. and Knight, R.T. (2002) Orbitofrontal cortex and dynamic filtering of emotional stimuli. *Cognitive, Affective and Behavioral Neuroscience*, **2**, 264–270.

Rumelhart, D.E. and Norman, D.A. (1989) Introduction. In *Parallel Models of Associative Memory* (eds G.E. Hinton and J.A. Anderson), Lawrence Erlbaum, Hillsdale, pp. 15–21.

Rutter, M. (2001) Child psychiatry in the era following sequencing the genome. In *Attention, Genes and ADHD* (eds F. Levy and D.A. Hay), Brunner-Routledge, Hove, pp. 225–248.

S

Saalmann, Y.B. and Kastner, S. (2009) Gain control in the visual thalamus during perception and cognition. *Current Opinion in Neurobiology*, **19**, 408–414.

Sachs, B.D. (1995) Placing erection in context: the reflexogenic–psychogenic dichotomy reconsidered. *Neuroscience and Biobehavioral Reviews*, **19**, 211–224.

Sackeim, H.A., Greenberg, M.S., Weiman, A.L., Gur, R.C., Hungerbuhler, J.P. and Geschwind, N. (1982) Hemispheric asymmetry in the expression of positive and negative emotions: neurological evidence. *Archives of Neurology*, **39**, 210–218.

Sacks, O. (1982) *Awakenings*, Pan Books, London.

Saffran, E.M., Fitzpatrick-DeSalme, E.J. and Coslett, H.B. (1990) Visual disturbances in dementia. In *Modular Deficits in Alzheimer-type Dementia* (ed. M.F. Schwartz), MIT Press, Cambridge, pp. 297–328.

Sagvolden, T. (2000) Behavioral validation of the spontaneously hypertensive rat (SHR) as an animal model of attention-deficit/ hyperactivity disorder (AD/HD). *Neuroscience and Biobehavioral Reviews*, **24**, 31–39.

Sagvolden, T., Johansen, E.B., Aase, H. and Russell, V.A. (2005) A dynamic developmental theory of attention-deficit/hyperactivity disorder (ADHD) predominantly hyperactive/ impulsive and combined subtypes. *Behavioral and Brain Sciences*, **28**, 397–468.

Sakakibara, M., Takeuchi, S. and Hayano, J. (1994) Effect of relaxation training on cardiac parasympathetic tone. *Psychophysiology*, **31**, 223–228.

Salamy, A. (1978) Commissural transmission: maturational changes in humans. *Science*, **200**, 1409–1411.

Salkovskis, P.M. (1985) Obsessional-compulsive problems: a cognitive–behavioural analysis. *Behavior Research and Therapy*, **23**, 571–583.

Salomons, T.V., Johnstone, T., Backonja, M-M., Shackman, A.J. and Davidson, R.J. (2007) Individual differences in the effects of perceived controllability on pain perception: critical role of the prefrontal cortex. *Journal of Cognitive Neuroscience*, **19**, 993–1003.

Salzinger, K. (1971) An hypothesis about schizophrenic behavior. *American Journal of Psychotherapy*, **25**, 601–614.

Sanes, J.N. and Evarts, E.V. (1985) Psychomotor performance in Parkinson's disease. In *Clinical Neurophysiology in Parkinsonism* (eds P.J. Delwaide and A. Agnoli), Elsevier, Amsterdam, pp. 117–132.

Sano, K., Mayanagi, Y., Sekino, H., Ogashiwa, M. and Ishijima, B. (1970) Results of stimulation and destruction of the posterior hypothalamus in man. *Journal of Neurosurgery*, **33**, 689–707.

Sapolsky, R. (2005) Sick of poverty. *Scientific American*, **293**(6), 92–99.

Sapolsky, R., Rivier, C., Yamamoto, G., Plotsky, P. and Vale, W. (1987) Interleukin-1 stimulates the secretion of hypothalamic corticotropin-releasing factor. *Science*, **238**, 522–524.

Sapolsky, R.M. (1990a) Adrenocortical function, social rank, and personality among wild baboons. *Biological Psychiatry*, **28**, 862–878.

Sapolsky, R.M. (1990b) Stress in the wild. *Scientific American*, **262**, No. 1, 106–113.

Sapolsky, R.M. (1992) Neuroendocrinology of the stress response. In *Behavioral Endocrinology* (eds J.B. Becker, S.M. Breedlove and D. Crews), MIT Press, Cambridge, pp. 287–324.

Sapolsky, R.M. (1997) The importance of the well-groomed child. *Science*, **277**, 1620–1621.

Sapolsky, R.M. (2004) *Why Zebras don't get Ulcers*, St Martin's Press, New York.

Sarter, M., Givens, B. and Bruno, J.P. (2001) The cognitive neuroscience of sustained attention: where top-down meets bottom-up. *Brain Research Reviews*, **35**, 146–160.

Satinoff, E. (1983) A reevaluation of the concept of the homeostatic organization of temperature regulation. In *Handbook of Behavioral Neurobiology*, Vol. 6: *Motivation* (eds E. Satinoff and P. Teitelbaum), Plenum Press, New York.

Schachter, S. and Singer, J.E. (1962) Cognitive, social and physiological determinants of emotional state. *Psychological Review*, **69**, 379–399.

Schacter, D.L. (1997) False recognition and the brain. *Current Directions in Psychological Science*, **6**, 65–69.

Schacter, D.L. and Tulving, E. (1994a) *Memory Systems 1994*, MIT Press, Cambridge.

Schacter, D.L. and Tulving, E. (1994b) What are the memory systems of 1994? In *Memory Systems 1994* (eds D.L. Schacter and E. Tulving), MIT Press, Cambridge, pp. 1–38.

Schacter, S. (1975) Cognition and peripheralist–centralist controversies in motivation and emotion. In *Handbook of Psychobiology* (eds M.S. Gazzaniga and C. Blakemore), Academic Press, New York, pp. 529–564.

Schaich Borg, J.S., Lieberman, D. and Kiehl, K.A. (2008) Infection, incest, and iniquity: Investigating the neural correlates of disgust and morality. *Journal of Cognitive Neuroscience*, **20**, 1529–1546.

Schanberg, S.M. and Field, T.M. (1987) Sensory deprivation stress and supplemental stimulation in the rat pup and preterm human neonate. *Child Development*, **58**, 1431–1447.

Scheib, J.E. (2001) Context-specific mate choice criteria: women's trade-offs in the contexts of long-term and extra-pair mateships. *Personal Relationships*, **8**, 371–389.

Scheidt, S. (1996) A whirlwind tour of cardiology for the mental health professional. In *Heart and Mind. The Practice of Cardiac Psychology* (eds R. Allan and S. Scheidt), American Psychological Association, Washington, pp. 15–62.

Schenck, C.H., Bundlie, S.R., Ettinger, M.G. and Mahowald, M.W. (1986) Chronic behavioral disorders of human REM sleep: a new category of parasomnia. *Sleep*, **9**, 293–308.

Schieber, M.H. (1999) Voluntary descending control. In *Fundamental Neuroscience* (eds M.J. Zigmond, F.E. Bloom, S.C. Landis, J.L. Roberts and L.R. Squire), Academic Press, San Diego, pp. 931–949.

Schlaug, G., Marchina, S. and Norton, A. (2009) Evidence of plasticity in white-matter tracts of patients with chronic Broca's aphasia undergoing intense intonation-based speech therapy. *Annals of the New York Academy of Sciences*, **1169**, 385–394.

Schlemmer, R.F. and Davis, J.M. (1983) A comparison of three psychotomimetic-induced models of psychosis in nonhuman primate social colonies. In *Ethopharmacology: Primate Models of Neuropsychiatric Disorders* (ed. K.A. Miczek), Alan R. Liss, New York, pp. 33–78.

Schmajuk, N.A. and Tyberg, M. (1991) The hippocampal-lesion model of schizophrenia. In *Neuromethods*, Vol. 18, *Animal Models in Psychiatry I* (eds A. Boulton, G. Baker and M. Martin-Iverson), Humana Press, Totowa, pp. 67–102.

Schmidt, R.A. and Lee, T.D. (2005) *Motor Control and Learning*, Human Kinetics Europe Ltd, Leeds.

Schmolling, P. (1983) A systems model of schizophrenic dysfunction. *Behavioral Science*, **28**, 253–267.

Schneider, J. and Weiss, R. (2001) *Cybersex Exposed: Simple Fantasy or Obsession?*, Hazelden, Center City.

Schneider, W. and Shiffrin, R.M. (1977) Controlled and automatic human information processing: I. Detection, search and attention. *Psychological Review*, **84**, 1–66.

Schrödinger, E. (1958) *Mind and Matter*, Cambridge, Cambridge University Press.

Schulkin, J. (1994) Melancholic depression and the hormones of adversity: a role for the amygdala. *Current Directions in Psychological Science*, **3**, 41–44.

Schulte, F.J. (1974) The neurological development of the neonate. In *Scientific Foundations of Paediatrics* (eds J.A. Davis and J. Dobbing), William Heinemann, London, pp. 587–615.

Schultz, W., Apicella, P., Romo, R. and Scarnati, E. (1995) Context-dependent activity in primate striatum reflecting past and future behavioural events. In *Models of Information Processing in the Basal Ganglia* (eds J.C. Houk, J.L. Davis and D.G. Beiser), MIT Press, Cambridge, pp. 11–28.

Schultz, W., Dayan, P. and Montague, P.R. (1997) A neural substrate of prediction and reward. *Science*, **275**, 1593–1599.

Schwartz, J.M. (1996) *Brain Lock*, HarperCollins, New York.

Sclafani, A. (1997) Learned controls of ingestive behaviour. *Appetite*, **29**, 153–158.

Scott, D.J., Stohler, C.S., Egnatuk, C.M., Wang, H., Koeppe, R.A. and Zubieta, J-K. (2008) Placebo and nocebo effects are defined by opposite opioid and dopaminergic responses. *Archives of General Psychiatry*, **65**, 220–231.

Scott, T.R. (1990) Gustatory control of food selection. In *Handbook of Behavioral Neurobiology*, Vol. 10, *Neurobiology of Food and Fluid Intake* (ed. E.M. Stricker), Plenum Press, New York, pp. 243–263.

Scott, T.R. and Giza, B.K. (1993) Gustatory control of ingestion. In *Neurophysiology of Ingestion* (ed. D.A. Booth), Pergamon Press, Oxford, pp. 99–117.

Scoville, W.B. and Milner, B. (1957) Loss of recent memory after bilateral hippocampal lesions. *Journal of Neurology, Neurosurgery and Psychiatry*, **20**, 11–21.

Searle, J.R. (1993) The problem of consciousness. In *Experimental and Theoretical Studies of Consciousness* (eds G.R. Bock and J. Marsh), Wiley, Chichester, pp. 61–80.

Seeman, T.E. and Robbins, R.J. (1994) Aging and hypothalamic–pituitary–adrenal response to challenge in humans. *Endocrine Reviews*, **15**, 233–260.

Segerstrom, S.C. and Sephton, S.E. (2010) Optimistic expectancies and cell-mediated immunity: the role of positive affect. *Psychological Science*, **21**, 448–455.

Seifert, F. and Maihöfner, C. (2009) Central mechanisms of experimental and chronic neuropathic pain: findings from functional imaging studies. *Cellular and Molecular Life Sciences*, **66**, 375–390.

Seitz, R.J. and Roland, P.E. (1992) Learning of sequential finger movements in man: a combined kinematic and positron emission tomography (PET) study. *European Journal of Neuroscience*, **4**, 154–165.

Seligman, M. (1975) *Helplessness*, W.H. Freeman, San Francisco.

Seligman, M.E.P. and Hager, J.L. (1972) *Biological Boundaries of Learning*, Appleton-Century-Crofts, New York.

Selye, H. (1973) The evolution of the stress concept. *American Scientist*, **61**, 692–699.

Seminowicz, D.A. and Davis, K.D. (2006) Cortical responses to pain in healthy individuals depends on pain catastrophising. *Pain*, **120**, 297–306.

Serper, M.R., Bergman, R.L. and Harvey, P.D. (1990) Medication may be required for the development of automatic information processing in schizophrenia. *Psychiatry Research*, **32**, 281–288.

Shaham, Y. and Stewart, J. (1995) Stress reinstates heroin-seeking in drug-free animals: an effect mimicking heroin, not withdrawal. *Psychopharmacology*, **119**, 334–341.

Shakow, D. (1963) Psychological deficit in schizophrenia. *Behavioral Science*, **8**, 275–305.

Shallice, T. (1981) Phonological agraphia and the lexical route in writing. *Brain*, **104**, 413–429.

Shallice, T. and Jackson, M. (1988) Lissauer on agnosia. *Cognitive Neuropsychology*, **5**, 153–156.

Sham, P.C., O'Callaghan, E., Takei, N., Murray, G.K., Hare, E.H. and Murray, R.M. (1992) Schizophrenia following pre-natal exposure to influenza epidemics between 1939 and 1960. *British Journal of Psychiatry*, **160**, 461–466.

Shamloul, R. (2010) Natural aphrodisiacs. *Journal of Sexual Medicine*, **7**, 39–49.

Shankle, W.R., Landing, B.H., Rafii, M.S., Schiano, A., Chen, J.M. and Hara, J. (1998) Evidence for a postnatal doubling of neuron number in the developing human cerebral cortex between 15 months and 6 years. *Journal of Theoretical Biology*, **191**, 115–140.

Shapleske, J., Rossell, S.L., Woodruff, P.W.R. and David, A.S. (1999) The planum temporale: a systematic, quantitative review of its structural, functional and clinical significance. *Brain Research Reviews*, **29**, 26–49.

Sharpless, S. and Jasper, H. (1956) Habituation of the arousal reaction. *Brain*, **79**, 655–680.

Shaw, P., Eckstrand, K., Sharp, W., Blumenthal, J., Lerch, J.P., Greenstein, D., Clasen, L., Evans, A., Giedd, J. and Rapoport, J.L. (2007) Attention-deficit/hyperactivity disorder is characterized by a delay in cortical maturation. *Proceedings of the National Academy of Sciences U. S. A.*, **104**, 19649–19654.

Shaw, W.A. (1940) The relation of muscular action potentials to imaginal weight lifting. *Archives of Psychology*, **35**, 5–50.

Sherry, D.F. (1992) Memory, the hippocampus, and natural selection: studies of food-storing birds. In *Neuropsychology of Memory* (eds L.R. Squire and N. Butters), Guilford Press, New York, pp. 521–532.

Sherry, D.F. and Schacter, D.L. (1987) The evolution of multiple memory systems. *Psychological Review*, **94**, 439–454.

Sherry, D.F., Vaccarino, A.L., Buckenham, K. and Herz, R.S. (1989) The hippocampal complex of food-storing birds. *Brain Behavior and Evolution*, **34**, 308–317.

Sherwin, B.B. (1991) The psychoendocrinology of aging and female sexuality. In *Annual Review of Sex Research, 2* (ed. J. Bancroft), Society for the Scientific Study of Sex, Allentown, pp. 181–198.

Shoaib, M., Swanner, L.C., Yasar, S. and Goldberg, S.R. (1999) Chronic caffeine exposure potentiates nicotine self-administration in rats. *Psychopharmacology*, **142**, 327–333.

Shomstein, S. and Yantis, S. (2004) Control of attention shifts between vision and audition in human cortex. *Journal of Neuroscience*, **24**, 10702–10706.

Siebert, M., Markowitsch, H.J. and Bartel, P. (2003) Amygdala, affect and cognition: evidence from 10 patients with Urbach–Wiethe disease. *Brain*, **126**, 2627–2637.

Siegel, A. (2005) *The Neurobiology of Aggression and Rage*, CRC Press, Boca Raton.

Siegel, A. and Victoroff, J. (2009) Understanding human aggression: new insights from neuroscience. *International Journal of Law and Psychiatry*, **32**, 209–215.

Siegel, J.M. (1994) Brainstem mechanisms generating REM sleep. In *Principles and Practice of Sleep Medicine* (eds M.H. Kryger, T. Roth and W.C. Dement), Saunders, Philadelphia, pp. 125–144.

Siegel, J.M. (2004) Hypocretin (orexin): role in normal behavior and neuropathology. *Annual Review of Psychology*, **55**, 125–148.

Siegel, J.M. (2005) The incredible, shrinking sleep-learning connection. *Behavioral and Brain Sciences*, **28**, 82–83.

Siegel, R.K. and Jarvik, M.E. (1980) DMT self-administration by monkeys in isolation. *Bulletin of the Psychonomic Society*, **16**, 117–120.

Siegel, S. (1984) Pavlovian conditioning and heroin overdose: reports by overdose victims. *Bulletin of the Psychonomic Society*, **22**, 428–430.

Siffre, M. (1965) *Beyond Time*, Chatto and Windus, London.

Silbersweig, D.A., Stern, E., Frith, C., Cahill, C., Holmes, A., Grootoonk, S., Seaward, J., McKenna, P., Chua, S.E., Schnorr, L., Jones, T. and Frackowiak, R.S.J. (1995) A functional neuroanatomy of hallucinations in schizophrenia. *Nature*, **378**, 176–179.

Silventoinen, K. and Kaprio, J. (2009) Genetics of tracking of body mass index from birth to late middle age: evidence from twin and family studies. *Obesity Facts*, **2**, 196–202.

Simon, J., Braunstein, G., Nachtigall, L., Utian, W., Katz, M., Miller, S., Waldbaum, A., Bouchard, C., Derzko, C., Buch, A., Rodenberg, C., Lucas, J. and Davis, S. (2005) Testosterone patch increases sexual activity and desire in surgically menopausal women with hypoactive sexual desire disorder. *The Journal of Clinical Endocrinology and Metabolism*, **90**, 5226–5233.

Singer, J.L. (1993) Experimental studies of ongoing conscious experience. In *Experimental and Theoretical Studies of Consciousness* (eds G.R. Bock and J. Marsh), Wiley, Chichester, pp. 100–122.

Singer, T., Seymour, B., O'Doherty, J., Kaube, H., Dolan, R.J. and Frith, C.D. (2004) Empathy for pain involves the affective but not sensory components of pain. *Science*, **303**, 1157–1162.

Singh, D. and Bronstad, P.M. (2001) Female body odour is a potential cue to ovulation.

Proceedings of the Royal Society of London B, **268**, 797–801.

Sitsen, J.M.A. (1988) Prescription drugs and sexual function. In *Handbook of Sexology*, Vol. 6, *The Pharmacology and Endocrinology of Sexual Function* (ed. J.M.A. Sitsen), Elsevier Science Publishers, Amsterdam, pp. 425–461.

Skakkebaek, N.E., Bancroft, J., Davidson, D.W. and Warner, P. (1981) Androgen replacement with oral testosterone undecanoate in hypogonadal men: a double blind controlled study. *Clinical Endocrinology*, **14**, 49–61.

Skinner, B.F. (1957) *Verbal Behavior*, Appleton-Century-Crofts, New York.

Skinner, B.F. (1966) *The Behavior of Organisms*, Appleton-Century-Crofts, New York.

Skinner, B.F. (1971) *Beyond Freedom and Dignity*, Penguin, Harmondsworth.

Skinner, B.F. (1979) *The Shaping of a Behaviorist*, Alfred A. Knopf, New York.

Skinner, B.F. (1983) *A Matter of Consequences*, Alfred A. Knopf, New York.

Skinner, B.F. (1984) Behaviorism at fifty. *Behavioral and Brain Sciences*, **7**, 615–667.

Skoubis, P.D., Lam, H.A., Shoblock, J., Narayanan, S. and Maidment, N.T. (2005) Endogenous enkephalins, not endorphins, modulate basal hedonic state in mice. *European Journal of Neuroscience*, **21**, 1379–1384.

Small, D.M. and Prescott, J. (2005) Odor/taste integration and the perception of flavor. *Experimental Brain Research*, **166**, 345–357.

Small, S.A. (2005) Alzheimer disease, in living colour. *Nature Neuroscience*, **8**, 404–405.

Smith, A. and Sugar, O. (1975) Development of above normal language and intelligence 21 years after left hemispherectomy. *Neurology*, **25**, 813–818.

Smith, C. (2009) *Biology of Sensory Systems*, Wiley-Blackwell, Hoboken.

Smith, D.V. and Duncan, H.J. (1992) Primary olfactory disorders: anosmia, hyposmia and dysosmia. In *Science of Olfaction* (eds M.J. Serby and K.L. Chobor), Springer-Verlag, New York, pp. 439–466.

Smith, G.P. (1996) The direct and indirect controls of meal size. *Neuroscience and Biobehavioral Reviews*, **20**, 41–46.

Smith, G.P. and Epstein, A.N. (1969) Increased feeding in response to decreased glucose utilization in the rat and monkey. *American Journal of Physiology*, **217**, 1083–1087.

Smith, G.P. and Gibbs, J. (1994) Satiating effect of cholecystokinin. *Annals of the New York Academy of Sciences*, **713**, 236–240.

Smith, P.M. and Ferguson, A.V. (2008) Neurophysiology of hunger and satiety. *Developmental Disabilities Research Reviews*, **14**, 96–104.

Smith, W.S. and Fetz, E.E. (1987) Noninvasive brain imaging and the study of higher brain function in humans. In *Higher Brain Functions: Recent Explorations of the Brain's Emergent Properties* (ed. S.P. Wise), Wiley, New York, pp. 311–346.

Snowdon, C.T. (1998) The nurture of nature: social, developmental and environmental controls of aggression. *Behavioral and Brain Sciences*, **21**, 384–385.

Sobik, L., Hutchison, K. and Craighead, L. (2005) Cue-elicited craving for food: a fresh approach to the study of binge eating. *Appetite*, **44**, 253–261.

Solomon, P.R. and Staton, D.M. (1982) Differential effects of microinjections of d-amphetamine into the nucleus accumbens or the caudate putamen on the rats' ability to ignore an irrelevant stimulus. *Biological Psychiatry*, **17**, 743–756.

Solomon, P.R., Crider, A., Winkelman, J.W., Turi, A., Kamer, R.M. and Kaplan, L.J. (1981) Disrupted latent inhibition in the rat with chronic amphetamine or haloperidol-induced supersensitivity: relationship to schizophrenic attention disorder. *Biological Psychiatry*, **16**, 519–537.

Solomon, R.L. and Corbit, J.D. (1974) The opponent-process theory of motivation. I. *Psychological Review*, **81**, 119–145.

Somerville, E.M., Horwood, J.M., Lee, M.D., Kennett, G.A. and Clifton, P.G. (2007) 5-HT$_{2C}$ receptor activation inhibits appetitive and consummatory components of feeding and increases brain c-*fos* immunoreactivity in mice. *European Journal of Neuroscience*, **25**, 3115–3124.

Sonuga-Barke, E.J.S. (2005) Causal models of attention-deficit/hyperactivity disorder: from common simple deficits to multiple developmental pathways. *Biological Psychiatry*, **57**, 1231–1238.

Sonuga-Barke, E.J.S. and Halperin, J.M. (2010) Developmental phenotypes and causal pathways in attention deficit/hyperactivity disorder: potential targets for early intervention. *The Journal of Child Psychology and Psychiatry*, **51**, 368–389.

Sonuga-Barke, E., Bitsakou, P. and Thompson, M. (2010) Beyond the dual pathway model: evidence for the dissociation of timing, inhibitory, and delay-related impairments in attention-deficit/hyperactivity disorder. *Journal of the American Academy of Child and Adolescent Psychiatry*, **49**, 345–355.

Sonuga-Barke, E.J.S., Lasky-Su, J., Neale, B.M., Oades, R., Chen, W., Franke, B., Buitelaar, J., Banaschewski, T., Ebstein, R., Gill, M., Anney, R., Miranda, A., Mulas, F., Roeyers, H., Rothenberger, A., Sergeant, J., Steinhausen, H.C., Thompson, M., Asherson, P. and Faraone, S.V. (2008) Does parental expressed emotion moderate genetic effects in ADHD? An exploration using a genome wide association scan. *American Journal of Medical Genetics*, Part B, **147B**, 1359–1368.

Sorg, B.A. and Kalivas, P.W. (1995) Stress and neuronal sensitization. In *Neurobiological and Clinical Consequences of Stress. From Normal Adaptation to Post-traumatic Stress Disorder* (eds M.J. Friedman, D.S. Charney and A.Y. Deutch), Lippincott-Raven, Philadelphia, pp. 83–102.

Southwick, C.H. (1968) Effect of maternal environment on aggressive behavior of inbred mice. *Communications in Behavioral Biology*, Part A, **1**, 129–132.

Spangler, K.M. and Warr, W.B. (1991) The descending auditory system. In *Neurobiology of Hearing: The Central Auditory System* (eds R.A. Altschuler, R.P. Bobbin, B.M. Clopton and D.W. Hoffman), Raven Press, New York, pp. 27–46.

Spencer, N.A., McClintock, M.K., Sellergren, S.A., Bullivant, S., Jacob, S. and Mennella, J.A. (2004) Social chemosignals from breastfeeding women increase sexual motivation. *Hormones and Behavior*, **46**, 362–370.

Sperry, R.W. (1969) Hemisphere deconnection and unity in conscious awareness. *American Psychologist*, **23**, 723–733.

Sperry, R.W. (1970) Perception in the absence of the neocortical commissures, *Perception and its Disorders*, Res. Publ. A.R.N.M.D. **48**, 123–138.

Sperry, R.W. (1974) Lateral specialization in the surgically separated hemispheres. In *The Neurosciences. Third Study Program* (eds F.O. Schmitt and F.G. Worden), MIT Press, Cambridge, pp. 5–19.

Spillmann, L. (2009) Phenomenology and neurophysiological correlations: two approaches to perception research. *Vision Research*, **49**, 1507–1521.

Spoont, M.R. (1992) Modulatory role of serotonin in neural information processing: implications for human psychopathology. *Psychological Bulletin*, **112**, 330–350.

Spray, K.J. and Bernstein, I.L. (2004) Afferent and efferent connections of the parvicellular subdivision of iNTS: defining a circuit involved in taste aversion learning. *Behavioural Brain Research*, **154**, 85–97.

Sprich-Buckminster, S., Biederman, J., Milberger, S., Faraone, S.V. and Lehman, B.K. (1993) Are perinatal complications relevant to the manifestation of ADD? Issues of comorbidity and familiality. *Journal of American Academy of Child and Adolescent Psychiatry*, **32**, 1032–1037.

Spruijt, B.M., Van Hooff, J.A.R.A.M. and Gispen, W.H. (1992) Ethology and neurobiology of grooming behaviour. *Physiological Reviews*, **72**, 825–852.

Squire, L.R. (1994) Declarative and non-declarative memory: multiple brain systems supporting learning and memory. In *Memory Systems 1994* (eds D.L. Schacter and E. Tulving), MIT Press, Cambridge, pp. 203–231.

Squire, L.R. (2009) The legacy of patient H.M. for neuroscience. *Neuron*, **61**, 6–9.

Squire, L.R. and Zola-Morgan, S. (1991) The medial temporal lobe memory system. *Science*, **253**, 1380–1386.

Squire, L.R., Bloom, F.E., Spitzer, N.C., du Lac, C., Ghosh, A. and Berg, D. (2008) *Fundamental Neuroscience*, Academic Press, New York.

Stahl, S.M. (1996) *Essential Psychopharmacology*, Cambridge University Press, Cambridge.

Stahl, S.M. (1997) Estrogen makes the brain a sex organ. *Journal of Clinical Psychiatry*, **58**, 421–422.

Stahl, S.M. (1998) Getting stoned without inhaling: anandamide is the brain's natural marijuana. *Journal of Clinical Psychiatry*, **59**, 566–567.

Stam, R., Akkermans, L.M.A. and Wiegant, V.M. (1997) Trauma and the gut: interactions between stressful experience and intestinal function. *Gut*, **40**, 704–709.

Stebbins, G.L. (1969) *The Basis of Progressive Evolution*, University of North Carolina Press, Chapel Hill.

Steele, T.D., McCann, U.D. and Ricaurte, G.A. (1994) 3,4-Methylenedioxymethamphetamine (MDMA, 'Ecstasy'): pharmacology and toxicology in animals and humans. *Addiction*, **89**, 539–551.

Stein, M., Miller, A.H. and Trestman, R.L. (1991) Depression, the immune system, and health and illness. *Archives of General Psychiatry*, **48**, 171–177.

Stein, N.L. and Jewett, J.L. (1986) A conceptual analysis of the meaning of negative emotions: implications for a theory of development. In *Measuring Emotions in Infants and Children*, Vol. II (eds C.E. Izard and P.B. Read), Cambridge University Press, Cambridge, pp. 238–267.

Stein, Z., Susser, M., Saenger, G. and Marolla, F. (1972) Nutrition and mental performance. *Science*, **178**, 708–713.

Steiner, J.E. (1979) Human facial expressions in response to taste and smell stimulation. *Advances in Child Development and Behavior*, **13**, 257–295.

Stellar, E. (1990) Brain and behaviour. In *Handbook of Behavioral Neurobiology*, Vol. 10, *Neurobiology of Food and Fluid Intake* (ed. E.M. Stricker), Plenum Press, New York, pp. 3–22.

Stepanski, E.J. (1994) Behavioral therapy for insomnia. In *Principles and Practice of Sleep Medicine* (eds M.H. Kryger, T. Roth and W.C. Dement), Saunders, Philadelphia, pp. 535–541.

Stephan, K.M., Fink, G.R., Passingham, R.E., Silbersweig, D., Ceballos-Baumann, A.O., Frith, C.D. and Frackowiak, R.S.J. (1995) Functional anatomy of the mental representation of upper extremity movements in healthy subjects. *Journal of Neurophysiology*, **73**, 373–386.

Steptoe, A. (1993) Stress and the cardiovascular system: a psychosocial perspective. In *Stress – From Synapse to Syndrome* (eds S.C. Stanford and P. Salmon), Academic Press, London, pp. 119–141.

Steptoe, A., Dockray, S. and Wardle, J. (2009) Positive affect and psychobiological processes relevant to health. *Journal of Personality*, **77**, 1747–1775.

Steriade, M. (1994) Brain electrical activity and sensory processing during waking and sleep states. In *Principles and Practice of Sleep Medicine* (eds M.H. Kryger, T. Roth and W.C. Dement), Saunders, Philadelphia, pp. 105–124.

Stern, J.M. (1997) Offspring-induced nurturance: animal–human parallels. *Developmental Psychobiology*, **31**, 19–37.

Stern, K. and McClintock, M.K. (1998) Regulation of ovulation by human pheromones. *Nature*, **392**, 177–179.

Sternbach, H. (1998) Age-associated testosterone decline in men: clinical issues for psychiatry. *American Journal of Psychiatry*, **155**, 1310–1318.

Stevens, R. (1990) Humanistic psychology. In *Introduction to Psychology*, Vol. 1 (ed. I. Roth), Lawrence Erlbaum, Hove, pp. 419–469.

Stevenson, R.J. (2010) An initial evaluation of the functions of human olfaction. *Chemical Senses*, **35**, 3–20.

Stewart, J. (1995) How does incentive motivational theory apply to sexual behaviour? In *The Pharmacology of Sexual Function and Dysfunction* (ed. J. Bancroft), Excerpta Medica, Amsterdam, pp. 3–14.

Stewart, J., de Wit, H. and Eikelboom, R. (1984) Role of unconditioned and conditioned drug effects in the self-administration of opiates and stimulants. *Psychological Review*, **91**, 251–268.

Stewart-Williams, S. and Podd, J. (2004) The placebo effect: dissolving the expectancy versus conditioning debate. *Psychological Bulletin*, **130**, 324–340.

Still, G.F. (1902) Some abnormal psychical conditions in children. *The Lancet*, April 12th, 1008–1012.

Stocchi, F. (1998) Dopamine agonists in Parkinson's disease. *CNS Drugs*, **10**, 159–170.

Stolerman, I.P. and Jarvis, M.J. (1995) The scientific case that nicotine is addictive. *Psychopharmacology*, **117**, 2–10.

Strader, A.D. and Woods, S.C. (2005) Gastrointestinal hormones and food intake. *Gastroenterology*, **128**, 175–191.

Stratton, G.M. (1897) Vision without inversion of the retinal image. *Psychological Review*, **4**, 341–360.

Strayer, D.L., Drews, F.A. and Johnston, W.A. (2003) Cell phone-induced failures of visual attention during simulated driving. *Journal of Experimental Psychology, Applied*, **9**, 23–32.

Stricker, E.M. (1990) Homeostatic origins of ingestive behaviour. In *Handbook of Behavioral Neurobiology*, Vol. 10, *Neurobiology of Food and Fluid Intake* (ed. E.M. Stricker), Plenum Press, New York, pp. 45–60.

Stricker, E.M. and Sved, A.F. (2000) Thirst. *Nutrition*, **16**, 821–826.

Stricker, E.M. and Woods, S. (2004) *Neurobiology of Food and Fluid Intake* (Handbook of Behavioral Neurobiology 14), 2nd edition, Springer, New York.

Stringer, C. and Gamble, C. (1993) *In Search of the Neanderthals*, Thames and Hudson, New York.

Stroop, J.R. (1935) Studies of interference in serial verbal reactions. *Journal of Experimental Psychology*, **18**, 643–662.

Strubbe, J.H. and Woods, S.C. (2004) The timing of meals. *Psychological Review*, **111**, 128–141.

Sufka, K. and Turner, D. (2005) An evolutionary account of chronic pain: integrating the natural method of evolutionary psychology. *Philosophical Psychology*, **18**, 243–257.

Sullivan, E.V. and Marsh, L. (2003) Hippocampal volume deficits in alcoholic Korsakoff's syndrome. *Neurology*, **61**, 1716–1719.

Sullivan, R.M. and Brake, W.G. (2003) What the rodent prefrontal cortex can teach us about attention-deficit/hyperactivity disorder: the critical role of early developmental events on prefrontal function. *Behavioural Brain Research*, **146**, 43–55.

Sulloway, F.J. (1979) *Freud – Biologist of the Mind,* Burnett Books, London.

Suslow, T., Konrad, C., Kugel, H., Rumstadt, D., Zwitserlood, P., Schöning, S., Ohrmann, P., Bauer, J., Pyka, M., Kersting, A., Arolt, V., Heindel, W. and Dannlowski, U. (2010) Automatic mood-congruent amygdala responses to masked facial expressions in major depression. *Biological Psychiatry*, **67**, 155–160.

Sutanto, W. and de Kloet, E.R. (1993) The role of GABA in the regulation of the stress response. In *Stress – From Synapse to Syndrome* (eds S.C. Stanford and P. Salmon), Academic Press, London, pp. 333–354.

Sutherland, N.S. (1975) Is the brain a physical system? In *Explanation in the Behavioural Sciences* (eds R. Borger and F. Cioffi), Cambridge University Press, Cambridge, pp. 97–138.

Sutherland, S. (1976) *Breakdown: A Personal Crisis and a Medical Dilemma*, Weidenfeld and Nicolson, London.

Sutton, J.P., Mamelak, A.N. and Hobson, J.A. (1992) Modelling states of waking and sleeping. *Psychiatric Annals*, **22**, 137–143.

Swaab, D.F. and Hofman, M.A. (1990) An enlarged suprachiasmatic nucleus in homosexual men. *Brain Research*, **537**, 141–148.

Szasz, T.S. (1971) *The Manufacture of Madness*, Routledge and Kegan Paul, London.

Szechtman, H. and Woody, E. (2004) Obsessive-compulsive disorder as a disturbance of security motivation. *Psychological Review*, **111**, 111–127.

Szuster, R.R., Pontius, E.B. and Campos, P.E. (1988) Marijuana sensitivity and panic attack. *Journal of Clinical Psychiatry*, **49**, 427–429.

T

Taché, Y. and Brunnhuber, S. (2008) From Hans Selye's discovery of biological stress to the identification of corticotrophin-releasing factor signaling pathways. *Annals of the New York Academy of Sciences,* **1148**, 29–41.

Takahashi, H., Takada, Y., Nagai, N., Urano, T. and Takada, A. (1998) Effects of nicotine and footshock stress on dopamine release in the striatum and nucleus accumbens. *Brain Research Bulletin,* **45**, 157–162.

Takatsu, H., Owada, K., Abe, K., Nakano, M. and Urano, S. (2009) Effect of vitamin E on learning and memory deficit in aged rats. *Journal of Nutritional Science and Vitaminology,* **55**, 389–393.

Tallis, F. (1995) *Obsessive Compulsive Disorder,* Wiley, Chichester.

Tanei, T., Kajita, Y., Kaneoke, Y., Takebayashi, S., Nakatsubo, D. and Wakabayashi, T. (2009) Staged bilateral deep brain stimulation of the subthalamic nucleus for the treatment of Parkinson's disease. *Acta Neurochirurgica,* **151**, 589–594.

Tanji, J. and Kurata, K. (1985) Contrasting neuronal activity in supplementary and precentral motor cortex of monkeys. I. Responses to instructions determining motor responses to forthcoming signals of different modalities. *Journal of Neurophysiology,* **53**, 129–141.

Taylor, S.E., Kemeny, M.E., Reed, G.M., Bower, J.E. and Gruenewald, T.L. (2000) Psychological resources, positive illusions, and health. *American Psychologist,* **55**, 99–109.

Teicher, M.H., Dumont, N.L., Ito, Y., Vaituzis, C., Giedd, J.N. and Andersen, S.L. (2004) Childhood neglect is associated with reduced corpus callosum area. *Biological Psychiatry,* **56**, 80–85.

Teitelbaum, P. (1977) Levels of integration of the operant. In *Handbook of Operant Behavior* (eds W.K. Honig and J.E.R. Staddon), Prentice Hall, Englewood Cliffs, pp. 7–27.

Temple, C.M. and Richardson, P. (2004) Developmental amnesia: a new pattern of dissociation with intact episodic memory. *Neuropsychologia,* **42**, 764–781.

Terzian, H. (1964) Behavioural and EEG effects of intracarotid sodium amytal injection. *Acta Neurochirurgica,* **12**, 230–240.

Teutsch, S., Herken, W., Bingel, U., Schoell, E. and May, A. (2008) Changes in brain gray matter due to repetitive painful stimulation. *NeuroImage,* **42**, 845–849.

Thach, W.T. (1998) What is the role of the cerebellum in motor learning and cognition? *Trends in Cognitive Sciences,* **2**, 331–337.

Thach, W.T., Goodkin, H.P. and Keating, J.G. (1992) The cerebellum and the adaptive coordination of movement. *Annual Review of Neuroscience,* **15**, 403–442.

Thewissen, R., van den Hout, M., Havermans, R.C. and Jansen, A. (2005) Context-dependency of cue-elicited urge to smoke. *Addiction,* **100**, 387–396.

Thompson, P.M., Vidal, C., Giedd, J.N., Gochman, P., Blumenthal, J., Nicolson, R., Toga, A.W. and Rapoport, J.L. (2001) Mapping adolescent brain change reveals dynamic wave of accelerated gray matter loss in very early-onset schizophrenia. *Proceedings of the National Academy of Sciences USA,* **98**, 11650–11655.

Thompson, R.F. (1990) Neural mechanisms of classical conditioning in mammals. *Philosophical Transactions of the Royal Society of London B,* **329**, 161–170.

Thorn, B.E. (2004) *Cognitive Therapy for Chronic Pain,* Guilford Press, New York.

Thornhill, N.W. (1991) An evolutionary analysis of rules regulating human inbreeding and marriage. *Behavioral and Brain Sciences,* **14**, 247–293.

Thrasher, T.N. (1991) Volume receptors and the stimulation of water intake. In *Thirst: Physiological and Psychological Aspects* (eds D.J. Ramsey and D. Booth), Springer-Verlag, London, pp. 93–109.

Tiffany, S.L. (1990) A cognitive model of drug urges and drug-use behaviour: role of automatic and nonautomatic processes, *Psychological Review,* **97**, 147–168.

Tiggemann, M. and Kemps, E. (2005) The phenomenology of food cravings: the role of mental imagery. *Appetite,* **45**, 305–313.

Tinbergen, N. (1963) On aims and methods of ethology. *Zeitschrift für Tierpsychologie,* **20**, 410–433.

Toates, F. (1980) *Animal Behaviour – A Systems Approach,* Wiley, Chicester.

Toates, F. (1986) *Motivational Systems,* Cambridge University Press, Cambridge.

Toates, F. (1990) Biological perspectives. In *Introduction to Psychology,* Vol. 1 (ed. I. Roth), Lawrence Erlbaum, Hove, pp. 191–249.

Toates, F. (1992) *Control of Behaviour,* The Open University, Milton Keynes.

Toates, F. (1995) *Stress – Conceptual and Biological Aspects,* Wiley, Chichester.

Toates, F. (1997a) The control of movement. In *Growing and Responding* (SK220, Book 2) (ed. M. Stewart), The Open University, Milton Keynes, pp. 109–154.

Toates, F. (1997b) Pain. In *The Human Condition* (SK220, Book 4) (ed. F.M. Toates), The Open University, Milton Keynes, pp. 66–93.

Toates, F. (1997c) Human sexuality. In *The Human Condition* (SK220, Book 4) (ed. F. Toates), The Open University, Milton Keynes, pp. 43–65.

Toates, F. (1998a) The interaction of cognitive and stimulus–response processes in the control of behaviour. *Neuroscience and Biobehavioral Reviews,* **22**, 59–83.

Toates, F. (1998b) The biological bases of behaviour. In *Psychology – An Integrated Approach* (ed. M. Eysenck), Addison Wesley Longman, Harlow, pp. 23–67.

Toates, F. (1998c) Sensory systems. In *Psychology – An Integrated Approach* (ed. M. Eysenck), Addison Wesley Longman, Harlow, pp. 100–137.

Toates, F. (2004) Introduction to brains, mind and consciousness. In *From Cells to Consciousness.* Book 1 of Course SD226 *Biological Psychology: Exploring the Brain,* The Open University, Milton Keynes.

Toates, F. (2007) *Pain,* Oxford University Press, Oxford.

Toates, F. (2009) An integrative theoretical framework for understanding sexual motivation, arousal and behaviour. *Journal of Sex Research,* **46**, 168–193.

Toates, F. and Coschug-Toates, O. (2002) *Obsessive Compulsive Disorder,* Class Publishing, London.

Tobet, S.A. and Fox, T.O. (1992) Sex differences in neuronal morphology influenced hormonally throughout life. In *Handbook of Behavioral Neurobiology,* Vol. 11, *Sexual Differentiation* (eds A.A. Gerall, H. Moltz and I.L. Ward), Plenum Press, New York, pp. 41–83.

Tokar, J.T., Brunse, A.J., Stefflre, V.J., Sodergren, J.A. and Napior, D.A. (1975) Determining what heroin means to heroin addicts. *Diseases of the Nervous System,* **36**, 77–81.

Tolman, E.C. (1932) *Purposive Behavior in Animals and Men,* The Century Co., New York.

Tooby, J. and Cosmides, L. (1990) The past explains the present. *Ethology and Sociobiology,* **11**, 375–424.

Tracey, I., Ploghaus, A., Gati, J.S., Clare, S., Smith, S., Menon, R.S. and Matthews, P.M. (2002) Imaging attentional modulation of pain in the periaqueductal gray in humans. *The Journal of Neuroscience*, **22**, 2748–2752.

Tranel, D., Damasio, A.R. and Damasio, H. (1988) Intact recognition of facial expression, gender, and age in patients with impaired recognition of face identity. *Neurology*, **38**, 690–696.

Trevarthen, C. (1984) Hemispheric specialization. In *Handbook of Physiology. Section 1: The Nervous System*, Vol. III, Part 2 (ed. I. Darian-Smith), American Physiological Society, Bethesda, pp. 1129–1190.

Tricomi, E., Balleine, B.W. and O'Doherty, J.P. (2009) A specific role for posterior dorsolateral striatum in human habit learning. *European Journal of Neuroscience*, **29**, 2225–2232.

Tripp, G. and Wickens, J.R. (2009) Neurobiology of ADHD. *Neuropharmacology*, **57**, 579–589.

Tronick, E.Z. (1989) Emotions and emotional communication in infants. *American Psychologist*, **44**, 112–119.

Trout, J.D. (2001) The biological basis of speech: what to infer from talking to the animals. *Psychological Review*, **108**, 523–549.

Tryon, R.C. (1940) X.III. Genetic differences in maze-learning ability in rats. *Yearbook for the National Society for the Study of Education*, **39**, 111–119.

Tsuchitani, C. and Johnson, D.H. (1991) Binaural cues and signal processing in the superior olivary complex. In *Neurobiology of Hearing: The Central Auditory System* (eds R.A. Altschuler, R.P. Bobbin, B.M. Clopton and D.W. Hoffman), Raven Press, New York, pp. 163–194.

Tucker, D.M. and Frederick, S.L. (1989) Emotion and brain lateralization. In *Handbook of Social Psychophysiology* (eds H. Wagner and A. Manstead), Wiley, Chichester, pp. 27–70.

Tucker, D.M. and Williamson, P.A. (1984) Asymmetric neural control systems in human self-regulation. *Psychological Review*, **91**, 185–215.

Tucker, D.M., Vannatta, K. and Rothlind, J. (1990) Arousal and activation systems and primitive adaptive controls on cognitive priming. In *Psychological and Biological Approaches to Emotion* (eds N.L. Stein, B. Leventhal and T. Trabasso), Lawrence Erlbaum, Hillsdale, pp. 145–166.

Tulving, E. (1972) Episodic and semantic memory. In *Organization of Memory* (ed. E.

Tulving and W. Donaldson), Academic Press, New York, pp. 381–403.

Tulving, E. (1985a) How many memory systems are there? *American Psychologist*, **40**, 385–398.

Tulving, E. (1985b) Memory and consciousness. *Canadian Psychology*, **26**, 1–12.

Tulving, E. (1995) Introduction. In *The Cognitive Neurosciences* (ed. M.S. Gazzaniga), MIT Press, Cambridge, pp. 751–753.

Tulving, E. (1999) Study of memory: processes and systems. In *Memory: Systems, Process, or Function* (eds J.K. Foster and M. Jelicic), Oxford University Press, Oxford, pp. 11–30.

Tybur, J.M., Lieberman, D. and Griskevicius, V. (2009) Microbes, mating, and morality: Individual differences in three functional domains of disgust. *Journal of Personality and Social Psychology*, **97**, 103–122.

U

Ullman, M.T. (2004) Contributions of memory circuits to language: the declarative/procedural model. *Cognition*, **92**, 231–270.

Ulrich, R.E. and Favell, J.E. (1970) Human aggression. In *Behavior Modification in Clinical Psychology* (eds C. Neuringer and J.L. Michael), Appleton-Century-Crofts, New York, pp. 105–132.

Umiltà, C. and Zorzi, M. (1995) Consciousness does not seem to be linked to a single neural mechanism. *Behavioral and Brain Sciences*, **18**, 701–702.

Ungerleider, L.G. and Mishkin, M. (1982) Two cortical visual systems. In *Analysis of Visual Behavior* (eds D.J. Ingle, M.A. Goodale and R.J.W. Mansfield), MIT Press, Cambridge, pp. 549–586.

Uno, H., Tarara, R., Else, J.G., Suleman, M.A. and Sapolsky, R.M. (1989) Hippocampal damage associated with prolonged and fatal stress in primates. *Journal of Neuroscience*, **9**, 1705–1711.

Ur, E., White, P.D. and Grossman, A. (1992) Hypothesis: cytokines may be activated to cause depressive illness and chronic fatigue syndrome. *European Archives of Psychiatry and Clinical Neuroscience*, **241**, 317–322.

Ursin, H. and Olff, M. (1993) The stress response. In *Stress – From Synapse to Syndrome* (eds S.C. Stanford and P. Salmon), Academic Press, London, pp. 3–22.

V

Vahle-Hinz, C. Brüggemann, J. and Kniffki, K-D. (1995) Thalamic processing of visceral pain. In *Pain and the Brain: From Nociception to Cognition* (Advances in Pain Research and Therapy, Vol. 22) (eds B. Bromm and J.E. Desmedt), Raven Press, New York, pp. 125–141.

Vaidya, C.J., Austin, G., Kirkorian, G., Ridlehuber, H.W., Desmond, J.E., Glover, G.H. and Gabrieli, J.D.E. (1998) Selective effects of methylphenidate in attention deficit hyperactivity disorder: a functional magnetic resonance study. *Proceedings of the National Academy of Sciences USA*, **95**, 14494–14499.

Valenstein, E.S. (1969) Behavior elicited by hypothalamic stimulation – a prepotency hypothesis. *Brain Behavior and Evolution*, **2**, 295–316.

Valenstein, E.S. (1973) *Brain Control – A Critical Examination of Brain Stimulation and Psychosurgery*, Wiley, New York.

Valins, S. (1970) The perception and labelling of bodily changes as determinants of emotional behavior. In *Physiological Correlates of Emotion* (ed. P. Black), Academic Press, New York, pp. 229–243.

Vallbo, A.B. (1995) Single-afferent neurons and somatic sensation in humans. In *The Cognitive Neurosciences* (ed. M.S. Gazzaniga), MIT Press, Cambridge, pp. 237–252.

Van der Loos, H. and Woolsey, T.A. (1973) Somatosensory cortex: structural alterations following early injury to sense organs. *Science*, **179**, 395–397.

van der Werf, Y.D., Altena, E., Schoonheim, M.M., Sanz-Arigita, E.J., Vis, J.C., de Rijke, W. and van Someren, E.J. (2009) Sleep benefits subsequent hippocampal functioning. *Nature Neuroscience*, **12**, 122–123.

van Dijken, H.H., de Goeij, D.C.E., Sutanto, W., Mos, J., de Kloet, E.R. and Tilders, F.J.H. (1993) Short inescapable stress produces long-lasting changes in the brain–pituitary–adrenal axis of adult male rats. *Neuroendocrinology*, **58**, 57–64.

van Honk, J., Tuiten, A., van den Hout, M., Koppeschaar, H., Thijssen, J., de Haan, E. and Verbaten, R. (1998) Baseline salivary cortisol levels and preconscious selective attention for threat. A pilot study. *Psychoneuroendocrinology*, **23**, 741–747.

van Honk, J., Tuiten, A., Verbaten, R., van den Hout, M., Koppeschaar, H., Thijssen, J. and de Haan, E. (1999) Correlations among salivary testosterone, mood, and selective attention to threat in humans. *Hormones and Behavior,* **36**, 17–24.

van Honk, J., Tuiten, A., Hermans, E., Putman, P., Koppeschaar, H., Thijssen, J., Verbaten, R. and van Doornen, L. (2001) A single administration of testosterone induces cardiac accelerative responses to angry faces in healthy young women. *Behavioral Neuroscience*, **115**, 238–242.

van Honk, J., Harmon-Jones, E., Morgan, B.E. and Schutter, D.J.L.G. (2010) Socially explosive minds: the triple imbalance hypothesis of reactive aggression. *Journal of Personality*, **78**, 67–94.

van Os, J. (2009) 'Salience syndrome' replaces 'schizophrenia' in DSM-V and ICD-11: Psychiatry's evidence-based entry into the 21st century? *Acta Psychiatrica Scandinavica*, **120**, 363–372.

van Os, J. and Kapur, S. (2009) Schizophrenia. *The Lancet*, **374**, 635–645.

Van Thiel, D.H., Gavaler, J.S. and Tarter, R.E. (1988) The effects of alcohol on sexual behaviour and function. In *Handbook of Sexology*, Vol. 6, *The Pharmacology and Endocrinology of Sexual Function* (ed. J.M.A. Sitsen), Elsevier Science Publishers, Amsterdam, pp. 478–498.

van Wageningen, H., Jørgensen, H.A., Specht, K. and Hugdahl, K. (2010) A [1]H-MR spectroscopy study of changes in glutamate and glutamine (Glx) concentrations in frontal spectra after administration of memantine. *Cerebral Cortex*, **20**, 798–803.

van Wingen, G., Mattern, C. Verkes, R.J., Buitelaar, J. and Fernández, G. (2010) Testosterone reduces amygdala–orbitofrontal cortex coupling. *Psychoneuroendocrinology*, **35**, 105–113.

Vander, A.J., Sherman, J.H. and Luciano, D.S (1975) *Human Physiology*, McGraw-Hill, New York.

Vander, A.J., Sherman, J.H. and Luciano, D.S. (1994) *Human Physiology,* McGraw-Hill, New York.

Vanderschuren, L.J.M.J. and Everitt, B.J. (2004) Drug seeking becomes compulsive after prolonged cocaine self-administration. *Science,* **305**, 1017–1019.

Vanderschuren, L.J.M.J., Niesink, R.J.M. and Van Ree, J.M. (1997) The neurobiology of social play behavior in rats. *Neuroscience and Biobehavioral Reviews*, **21**, 309–326.

Vane, J.R. (1960) *CIBA Foundation Symposium on Adrenergic Mechanisms*, J. and A. Churchill, London.

VanItallie, T.B. and Kissileff, H.R. (1990) Human obesity – a problem in body energy economics. In *Handbook of Behavioral Neurobiology*, Vol. 10, *Neurobiology of Food and Fluid Intake* (ed. E.M. Stricker), Plenum Press, New York, pp. 207–240.

Vargha-Khadem, F., Isaacs, E. and Muter, V. (1994) A review of cognitive outcome after unilateral lesions sustained during childhood. *Journal of Child Neurology*, **9** (Suppl.), 2S67–2S73.

Vasey, P.L. and VanderLaan, D.P. (2010) An adaptive cognitive dissociation between willingness to help kin and nonkin in Samoan fa'afafine. *Psychological Science*, **21**, 292–297.

Vassalli, A. and Dijk, D-J. (2009) Sleep function: current questions and new approaches. *European Journal of Neuroscience*, **29**, 1830–1841.

Velmans, M. (1991) Is human information processing conscious? *Behavioral and Brain Sciences*, **14**, 651–726.

Velmans, M. (2000) *Understanding Consciousness*, Taylor and Francis, London.

Velmans, M. and Schneider, S. (2006) *The Blackwell Companion to Consciousness*. WileyBlackwell, Hoboken.

Vendrell, P., Junqué, C., Pujol, J., Angeles Jurado, M., Molet, J. and Grafman, J. (1995) The role of prefrontal regions in the Stroop task. *Neuropsychologia*, **33**, 341–352.

Venneri, A., Brazzelli, M. and Della Sala, S. (1998) Transient global amnesia by mild head injury. *Brain Injury*, **12**, 605–612.

Verbalis, J.G. (1990) Clinical aspects of body fluid homeostasis in humans. In *Handbook of Behavioral Neurobiology*, Vol. 10, *Neurobiology of Food and Fluid Intake* (ed. E.M. Stricker), Plenum Press, New York, pp. 421–462.

Verbalis, J.G. (1991) Inhibitory controls of drinking: satiation of thirst. In *Thirst: Physiological and Psychological Aspects* (eds D.J. Ramsey and D. Booth), Springer-Verlag, London, pp. 313–334.

Verney, E.B. (1947) The anti-diuretic hormone and the factors which determine its release. *Proceedings of the Royal Society of London B*, **135**, 25–106.

Verrey, Dr (1888) Hémiachromtopsic droite absolue – conservation partielle de la perception lumineuse et des formes. Ancien kyste hémorrhagique de la partie inférieure du lobe occipital gauche. *Archives d'Ophtalmologie*, **8**, 289–301.

Vessie, P.R. (1932) On the transmission of Huntington's chorea for 300 years – The Bures family group. *Journal of Nervous and Mental Disease*, **76**, 553–573.

Viamontes, C.T. (2009) The sickness response: an adaptive brain-body reaction to medical illness. *Psychiatric Annals*, **39**, 985–996.

Vingerhoets, J.J.M. (1985) The role of the parasympathetic division of the autonomic nervous system in stress and the emotions. *International Journal of Psychosomatics*, **32**, 28–33.

Volkow, N.D., Wang, G.-J., Fowler, J.S., Logan, J., Gatley, S.J., Hitzemann, R., Chen, A.D., Dewey, S.L. and Pappas, N. (1997) Decreased striatal dopaminergic responsiveness in detoxified cocaine-dependent subjects. *Nature*, **386**, 830–833.

Volkow, N.D., Fowler, J.S. and Wang, J-W. (2002) Role of dopamine in drug reinforcement and addiction in humans: results from imaging studies. *Behavioural Pharmacology*, **13**, 355–366

von Békésy, G. (1960) *Experiments in Hearing*, McGraw-Hill, New York.

von der Heydt, R. (1995) Form analysis in visual cortex. In *The Cognitive Neurosciences* (ed. M.S. Gazzaniga), MIT Press, Cambridge, pp. 365–382.

von der Heydt, R. and Peterhans, E. (1989) Mechanisms of contour perception in monkey visual cortex. I. Lines of pattern discontinuity. *Journal of Neuroscience*, **9**, 1731–1748.

von Holst, D. (1986) Vegetative and somatic components of tree shrews' behaviour. *Journal of the Autonomic Nervous System*, Suppl. 657–670.

von Holst, E. and Mittlestaedt, H. (1950) Das Reafferenzprinzip. *Naturwissenschaften*, **37**, 464–476. English translation in Gallistel, C.R. (1980) *The Organization of Action: A New Synthesis*, Lawrence Erlbaum, Hillsdale, pp. 176–209.

W

Waddington, C.H. (1936) *How Animals Develop*, W.W. Norton, New York.

Waddington, C.H. (1975) *The Evolution of an Evolutionist*, Edinburgh University Press, Edinburgh.

Wager, T.D., Rilling, J.K., Smith, E.E., Sokolik, A., Casey, K.L., Davidson, R.J., Kosslyn, S.M., Rose, R.M. and Cohen, J.D. (2004) Placebo-induced changes in fMRI in the anticipation and experience of pain. *Science*, **303**, 1162–1167.

Wagner, G. and Sjöstrand, N.O. (1988) Autonomic pharmacology and sexual function. In *Handbook of Sexology*, Vol. 6, *The Pharmacology and Endocrinology of Sexual Function* (ed. J.M.A. Sitsen), Elsevier Science Publishers, Amsterdam, pp. 32–43.

Waldman, I.D. and Rhee, S.H. (2002) Behavioural and molecular genetic studies. In *Hyperactivity and Attention Disorders of Childhood* 2nd edition (ed. S. Sandberg), Cambridge University Press, Cambridge, pp. 290–335.

Walker, E.F., Baum, K.M. and Diforio, D. (1998) Developmental changes in the behavioral expression of vulnerability for schizophrenia. In *Origins and Development of Schizophrenia* (eds M.F. Lenzenweger and R.H. Dworkin), American Psychological Association, Washington, pp. 469–491.

Walker, M.P. and van der Helm, E. (2009) Overnight therapy? The role of sleep in emotional brain processing. *Psychological Bulletin*, **135**, 731–748.

Wall, P.D. (1993) Pain and the placebo response. In *Experimental and Theoretical Studies of Consciousness* (eds G.R. Bock and J. Marsh), Wiley, Chichester, pp. 187–216.

Wall, P.D. (2002) *Pain: The Science of Suffering*, Columbia University Press, New York.

Wall, P.D. and Egger, M.D. (1971) Formation of new connections in adult rat brains after partial deafferentation. *Nature*, **232**, 542–545.

Walsh, J.K., Hartman, P.G. and Kowall, J.P. (1994) Insomnia. In *Sleep Disorders Medicine: Basic Science, Technical Considerations and Clinical Aspects* (ed. S. Chokroverty), Butterworth-Heinemann, Boston, pp. 219–239.

Waltz, J.A., Knowlton, B.J., Holyoak, K.J., Boone, K.B., Mishkin, F.S., de Menezes Santos, M., Thomas, C.R. and Miller, B.L. (1999) A system for relational reasoning in human prefrontal cortex. *Psychological Science*, **10**, 119–125.

Wand, G.S., Mangold, D., El Deiry, S., McCaul, M.E. and Hoover, D. (1998) Family history of alcoholism and hypothalamic opioidergic activity. *Archives of General Psychiatry*, **55**, 1114–1119.

Wang, G-J., Volkow, N.D., Logan, J., Pappas, N.R., Wong, C.T., Zhu, W., Netusil, N. and Fowler, J.S. (2001) Brain dopamine and obesity. *The Lancet*, **357**, 354–357.

Wang, J.Q. and McGinty, J.F. (1999) Glutamate–dopamine interactions mediate the effects of psychostimulant drugs. *Addiction Biology*, **4**, 141–150.

Wang, S-H., Ostlund, S.B., Nader, K. and Balleine, B.W. (2005) Consolidation and reconsolidation of incentive learning in the amygdala. *Journal of Neuroscience*, **25**, 830–835.

Wang, Z., Neylan, T.C., Mueller, S.G., Lenoci, M., Truran, D., Marmar, C.R., Weiner, M.W. and Shuff, N. (2010) Magnetic resonance imaging of hippocampal subfields in post-traumatic stress disorder. *Archives of General Psychiatry*, **67**, 296–303.

Ward, J. (2010) *The Student's Guide to Cognitive Neuroscience*, Psychology Press, Hove.

Warr, W.B., Guinan, J.J. and White, J.S. (1986) Organization of the efferent fibers: the lateral and medial olivocochlear systems. In *Neurobiology of Hearing: The Cochlea* (eds R.A. Altschuler, D.W. Hoffman and R.P. Bobbin), Raven Press, New York, pp. 333–348.

Warren, J. (2007) *Head Trip: Adventures on the Wheel of Consciousness*. OneWorld Publications, Oxford.

Warrington, E.K. and Weiskrantz, L. (1970) Amnesic syndrome: consolidation or retrieval? *Nature*, **228**, 628–630.

Watson, P.J. and Andrews, P.W. (2002) Toward a revised evolutionary adaptationist analysis of depression: the social navigation hypothesis. *Journal of Affective Disorders*, **72**, 1–14.

Watts, F.N., East, M.P. and Coyle, K. (1995) Insomniacs' perceived lack of control over sleep. *Psychology and Health*, **10**, 81–95.

Waugh, C.E., Wager, T.D., Fredrickson, B.L., Noll, D.C., Taylor, S.F. (2008) The neural correlates of trait resilience when anticipating and recovering from threat. *Social Cognitive and Affective Neuroscience*, **8**, 322–332.

Weaver, D.F. (2010) *Consciousness*, Wiley-Blackwell, Hoboken.

Wegner, D.M. (2003) *The Illusion of Conscious Will*, MIT Press, Cambridge.

Weinberger, D.R. (1987) Implications of normal brain development for the pathogenesis of schizophrenia. *Archives of General Psychiatry*, **44**, 660–669.

Weinberger, N.M. (1993) Learning-induced changes of auditory receptive fields. *Current Opinion in Neurobiology*, **3**, 570–577.

Weiner, H. (1996) Use of animal models in peptic ulcer disease. *Psychosomatic Medicine*, **58**, 524–545.

Weingarten, H.P. (1984) Meal initiation controlled by learned cues: basic behavioral properties. *Appetite*, **5**, 147–158.

Weinstein, A., Wilson, S., Bailey, J., Myles, J. and Nutt, D. (1997) Imagery of craving in opiate addicts undergoing detoxification. *Drug and Alcohol Dependence*, **48**, 25–31.

Weinstein, S. (1968) Intensive and extensive aspects of tactile sensitivity as a function of body part, sex and laterality. In *The Skin Senses* (ed. D.R. Kenshalo), C.C. Thomas, Springfield, pp. 195–222.

Weisenberg, M. (1994) Cognitive aspects of pain. In *Textbook of Pain* (eds P.D. Wall and R. Melzack), Churchill Livingstone, Edinburgh, pp. 275–289.

Weiskrantz, L. (1976) *Blindsight – A Case Study and Implications*, Clarendon Press, Oxford.

Weiskrantz, L. (1982) Comparative aspects of studies of amnesia. *Philosophical Transactions of the Royal Society B*, **298**, 97–109.

Weiskrantz, L. (1997) *Consciousness Lost and Found*, Oxford University Press, Oxford.

Weiskrantz, L. and Saunders, R.C. (1984) Impairments of visual object transforms in monkeys. *Brain*, **107**, 1033–1072.

Weiskrantz, L. and Warrington, E.K. (1979) Conditioning in amnesic patients. *Neuropsychologia*, **17**, 187–194.

Weiss, J.M. (1971) Effects of coping behaviour in different warning signal conditions on stress pathology in rats. *Journal of Comparative and Physiological Psychology*, **77**, 1–13.

Weiss, J.M. (1972) Psychological factors in stress and disease. *Scientific American*, **226**, No. 6, 104–113.

Weiss, J.M., Pohorecky, L.A., Salman, S. and Gruenthal, M. (1976) Attenuation of gastric lesions by psychological aspects of aggression in rats. *Journal of Comparative and Physiological Psychology*, **90**, 252–259.

Welge-Lussen, A. (2009) Ageing, neurodegeneration, and olfactory and gustatory loss. *B-ENT*, **5** (suppl. 13), 129–132.

Welker, W.I. (1961) An analysis of exploratory and play behavior in animals. In *Functions of Varied Experience* (eds D.W. Fiske and S.R. Maddi), Dorsey Press, Homewood, pp. 175–226.

Weller, A. (1998) Communication through body odour. *Nature*, **392**, 126–127.

Wernicke, C. (1874) *Der Aphasische Symptomenkomplex*, Cohn und Weigert, Breslau.

West, R. (2006) *Theory of Addiction*, Wiley-Blackwell, Hoboken.

Whatson, T. and Sterling, V. (1998) *Development and Flexibility*, Springer (The Open University), Berlin.

Whipple, B. and Komisaruk, B.R. (1999) Beyond the G spot: recent research on female sexuality. *Psychiatric Annals*, **29**, 34–37.

Whitaker, H.A. (1983) Towards a brain model of automatization: a short essay. In *Memory and Control of Action* (ed. R.A. Magill), North-Holland, Amsterdam, pp. 199–214.

White, N.M. (1989) Reward or reinforcement: what's the difference? *Neuroscience and Biobehavioral Reviews*, **13**, 181–186.

White, N.M. and McDonald, R.J. (1993) Acquisition of a spatial conditioned place preference is impaired by amygdala lesions and improved by fornix lesions. *Behavioural Brain Research*, **55**, 269–281.

Wicker, B., Keysers, C., Plailly, J., Royet, J-P., Gallese, V. and Rizzolatti, G. (2003) Both of us disgusted in my insula: the common neural basis of seeing and feeling disgust. *Neuron*, **40**, 655–664.

Wiepkema, P.R. (1987) Behavioural aspects of stress. In *Biology of Stress in Farm Animals: An Integrative Approach* (eds P.R. Wiepkema and P.W.M. Van Adrichem), Martinus Nijhoff, Dordrecht.

Wijeyekoon, R. and Barker, R.A. (2009) Cell replacement therapy for Parkinson's disease. *Biochimica et Biophysica Acta*, **1792**, 688–702.

Wikler, A. (1965) Conditioning factors in opiate addiction and relapse. In *Narcotics* (eds D.I. Wilner and G.G. Kassanbaum), McGraw-Hill, New York, pp. 399–414.

Wilgus, J. and Wilgus, B. (2009) Face to face with Phineas Gage. *Journal of the History of the Neurosciences*, **18**, 340–345.

Wilkins, L. and Richter, C.P. (1940) A great craving for salt by a child with cortico-adrenal insufficiency. *Journal of the American Medical Association*, **114**, 866–868.

Williams, C.L., Villar, R.G., Peterson, J.M. and Burks, T.F. (1988) Stress-induced changes in intestinal transit in the rat: a model for irritable bowel syndrome. *Gastroenterology*, **94**, 611–621.

Williams, R. (1989) *The Trusting Heart*, Times Books, New York.

Willingham, D.B. (1998) A neuropsychological theory of motor skill learning. *Psychological Review*, **105**, 558–584.

Willner, P. (1993) Animal models of stress: an overview. In *Stress – From Synapse to Syndrome* (eds S.C. Stanford and P. Salmon), Academic Press, London, pp. 145–165.

Willner, P., James, D. and Morgan, M. (2005) Excessive alcohol consumption and dependence are associated with parallel increases in subjective ratings of both 'wanting' and 'liking'. *Addiction*, **100**, 1487–1495.

Wilson, D.S. and Csikszentmihalyi, M. (2007) Health and the ecology of altruism. In *Altruism and Health: Perspectives from Empirical Research* (ed. S.G. Post), Oxford University Press, New York, pp. 314–331.

Wilson, G. and Rahman, Q. (2004) *Born Gay?: The Psychobiology of Sex Orientation*, Peter Owen, London.

Wilson, S.M., Saygun, A.P., Sereno, M.I. and Iacoboni, M. (2004) Listening to speech activates motor areas involved in speech production. *Nature Neuroscience*, **7**, 701–702.

Windmann, S. and Krüger, T. (1998) Subconscious detection of threat as reflected by an enhanced response bias. *Consciousness and Cognition*, **7**, 603–633.

Winkielman, P., Berridge, K.C. and Wilbarger, J.L. (2005) Unconscious affective reactions to masked happy versus angry faces influence consumption behavior and judgments of value. *Personality and Social Psychology Bulletin*, **31**, 121–135.

Winn, P. (1995) The lateral hypothalamus and motivated behaviour: an old syndrome reassessed and a new perspective gained. *Current Directions in Psychological Science*, **4**, 182–187.

Winterer, G. and Weinberger, D.R. (2004) Genes, dopamine and cortical signal-to-noise ratio in schizophrenia. *Trends in Neuroscience*, **27**, 683–689.

Wise, R.A. (1982) Neuroleptics and operant behaviour: the anhedonia hypothesis. *Behavioral and Brain Sciences*, **5**, 39–87.

Wise, R.A. (1987) Sensorimotor modulation and the variable action pattern (VAP): toward a noncircular definition of drive and motivation. *Psychobiology*, **15**, 7–20.

Wise, R.A. (1988) The neurobiology of craving: implications for the understanding and treatment of addiction. *Journal of Abnormal Psychology*, **97**, 118–132.

Wise, R.A. and Bozarth, M.A. (1987) A psychomotor stimulant theory of addiction. *Psychological Review*, **94**, 469–492.

Wise, S.P. (1984) The nonprimary motor cortex and its role in the cerebral control of movement. In *Dynamic Aspects of Neocortical Function* (eds G.M. Edelman, W.E. Gall and W.M. Cowan), Wiley, New York, pp. 525–555.

Wolffgramm, J. and Heyne, A. (1991) Social behavior, dominance, and social deprivation of rats determine drug choice. *Pharmacology Biochemistry and Behavior*, **38**, 389–399.

Wong, A.H.C. and Van Tol, H.H.M. (2003) Schizophrenia: from phenomenology to neurobiology. *Neuroscience and Biobehavioral Reviews*, **27**, 269–306.

Wood, J.D. (1979) Neurophysiology of the enteric nervous system. In *Integrative Functions of the Autonomic Nervous System* (eds C.M. Brooks, K. Koizumi and A. Sato), University of Tokyo Press/Elsevier, Amsterdam, pp. 177–193.

Woodruff-Pak, D.S. (1999) New directions for a classical paradigm: human eyeblink conditioning. *Psychological Science*, **10**, 1–3.

Woodruff-Pak, D.S., Vogel, R.W., Ewers, M., Coffrey, J., Boyko, O.B. and Lemieux, S.K. (2001) MRI-assessed volume of cerebellum correlates with associative learning. *Neurobiology of Learning and Memory*, **76**, 342–357.

Woods, S.C. and Stricker, E.M. (1999) Food intake and metabolism. In *Fundamental Neuroscience* (eds M.J. Zigmond, F.E. Bloom, S.C. Landis, J.L. Roberts and L.R. Squire), Academic Press, San Diego, pp. 1091–1109.

Woods, S.C., Chaverz, M., Park, C.R., Reidy, C., Kaiyala, K., Richardson, R.D., Figlewicz, D.P., Schwartz, M.W., Porte, D. Jr and Seeley, R.J. (1996) The evolution of insulin as a metabolic signal influencing behaviour via the brain. *Neuroscience and Behavioral Reviews*, **20**, 139–144.

Woolsey, T.A. and Wann, J.R. (1976) Areal changes in mouse cortical barrels following vibrissal damage at different postnatal ages. *Journal of Comparative Neurology*, **170**, 53–66.

Workman, L. and Reader, W. (2008) *Evolutionary Psychology: An Introduction*, 2nd edition, Cambridge University Press, Cambridge.

Wright, I. and Woodruff, P. (1995) Aetiology of schizophrenia – a review of theories and their clinical and therapeutic implications. *CNS Drugs*, **3**, 126–144.

Würbel, H., Freire, R. and Nicol, C.J. (1998) Prevention of stereotypic wire-gnawing in laboratory mice: effects on behaviour and implications for stereotypy as a coping response. *Behavioural Processes*, **42**, 61–72.

Wurtz, R.H., Goldberg, M.E. and Robinson, D.L. (1982) Brain mechanisms of visual attention. *Scientific American*, **246**, No. 6, 100–107.

X

Xerri, C., Stern, J.M. and Merzenich, M.M. (1994) Alterations of the cortical representation of the rat ventrum induced by nursing behavior. *Journal of Neuroscience*, **14**, 1710–1721.

Y

Yamamoto, T. (2007) Brain regions responsible for the expression of conditioned taste aversion in rats. *Chemical Senses*, **32**, 105–109.

Yates, B.J. and Stocker, S.D. (1998) Integration of somatic and visceral inputs by the brainstem. *Experimental Brain Research*, **119**, 269–275.

Yehuda, R., Giller, E.L., Levengood, R.A., Southwick, S.M. and Siever, L.J. (1995) Hypothalamic–pituitary–adrenal functioning in post-traumatic stress disorder. In *Neurobiological and Clinical Consequences of Stress. From Normal Adaptation to Post-traumatic Stress Disorder* (eds M.J. Friedman, D.S. Charney and A.Y. Deutch), Lippincott-Raven, Philadelphia, pp. 351–365.

Yeni-Komshian, G.H. and Benson, D.A. (1976) Anatomical study of cerebral asymmetry in the temporal lobe of humans, chimpanzees, and rhesus monkeys. *Science*, **192**, 387–389.

Yeomans, M.R. and Gray, R.W. (1997) Effects of naltrexone on food intake and changes in subjective appetite during eating: evidence for opioid involvement in the appetizer effect. *Physiology and Behavior*, **62**, 15–21.

Yeomans, M.R., Chambers, L., Blumenthal, H. and Blake, A. (2008) The role of expectancy in sensory and hedonic evaluation: the case of smoked salmon ice-cream. *Food Quality and Preference*, **19**, 565–573.

Yin, H.H., Knowlton, B.J. and Balleine, B.W. (2004) Lesions of dorsolateral striatum preserve outcome expectancy but disrupt habit formation in instrumental learning. *European Journal of Neuroscience*, **19**, 181–189.

Young, A.M.J., Joseph, M.H. and Gray, J.A. (1993) Latent inhibition of conditioned dopamine release in rat nucleus accumbens. *Neuroscience*, **54**, 5–9.

Young, L.J. and Wang, Z. (2004) The neurobiology of pair bonding. *Nature Neuroscience*, **7**, 1048–1054.

Z

Zajonc, R.B. (1980) Feeling and thinking – preferences need no inferences. *American Psychologist*, **35**, 151–175.

Zald, D. and Rauch, S. (2006) *The Orbitofrontal Cortex*, Oxford University Press, Oxford.

Zangwill, O.L. (1974) Consciousness and the cerebral hemispheres. In *Hemisphere Function in the Human Brain* (eds S.J. Dimond and J.G. Beaumont), Elek Science, London, pp. 264–278.

Zarcone, V.P. (1994) Sleep hygiene. In *Principles and Practice of Sleep Medicine* (eds M.H. Kryger, T. Roth and W.C. Dement), Saunders, Philadelphia, pp. 542–546.

Zeki, S. (1993) *A Vision of the Brain*, Blackwell, Oxford.

Zellner, D.A., Loaiza, S., Gonzalez, Z., Pita, J., Morales, J., Pecora, D. and Wolf, A. (2006) Food selection changes under stress. *Physiology and Behavior*, **87**, 789–793.

Zhong, C-B. and Liljenquist, K. (2006) Washing away your sins: threatened morality and physical cleansing. *Science*, **313**, 1451–1452.

Zhou, Q., Filllingim, R.B., Riley, J.L., Malarkey, W.B. and Verne, G.N. (2010) Central and peripheral hypersensitivity in the irritable bowel syndrome. *Pain*, **148**, 454–461.

Ziauddeen, H. and Murray, G.K. (2010) The relevance of reward pathways for schizophrenia. *Current Opinion in Psychiatry*, **23**, 91–96.

Zigmond, M.J., Finlay, J.M. and Sved, A.F. (1995) Neurochemical studies of central noradrenergic responses to acute and chronic stress. In *Neurobiological and Clinical Consequences of Stress. From Normal Adaptation to Post-traumatic Stress Disorder* (eds M.J. Friedman, D.S. Charney and A.Y. Deutch), Lippincott-Raven, Philadelphia, pp. 45–60.

Zihl, J., von Cramon, D. and Mai, N. (1983) Selective disturbance of movement vision after bilateral brain damage. *Brain*, **106**, 313–340.

Zohar, D. (1990) *The Quantum Self*, Flamingo, London.

Zorick, F. (1994) Overview of insomnia. In *Principles and Practice of Sleep Medicine* (eds M.H. Kryger, T. Roth and W.C. Dement), Saunders, Philadelphia, pp. 483–485.

Zubieta, J-K. and Stohler, C.S. (2009) Neurobiological mechanisms of placebo responses. *Annals of the New York Academy of Sciences*, **1156**, 198–210.

Zubin, J. and Spring, B. (1977) Vulnerability – a new view of schizophrenia. *Journal of Abnormal Psychology*, **86**, 103–126.

Zuk, M. (2003) *Sexual Selections: What We Can and Can't Learn from Animals*, University of California Press, Berkeley.

Index

Note: page references in *italics* refer to Figures

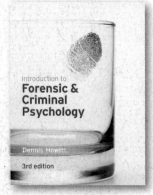